TEACHER'S ANNOTATED EDITION

MACMILLAN
Biology

Joan G. Creager
Paul G. Jantzen
James L. Mariner

Program Components for *Macmillan Biology*
Student Text
Teacher's Annotated Edition
Laboratory Manual with Study Skills Handbook
Teacher's Annotated Edition of Laboratory Manual
Testing Masters

Macmillan Publishing Co., Inc.
New York
Collier Macmillan Publishers
London

An authorship team that combines strong scientific backgrounds with practical classroom experience.

JOAN G. CREAGER is presently editor of the *American Biology Teacher* and Professor of Science at Marymount College of Virginia. She was formerly Staff Biologist and Coordinator of the Education Division of the American Institute of Biological Sciences. Dr. Creager has contributed articles to a variety of scientific publications and has presented numerous workshops at conventions of the National Association of Biology Teachers.

PAUL G. JANTZEN has been a biology and chemistry teacher at Hillsboro High School, Hillsboro, Kansas, for over twenty years. He is an active member of the Kansas Association of Biology Teachers and is editor of their newsletter. Mr. Jantzen is on the review panel of the *American Biology Teacher* and has written frequently for that publication and for the *Kansas School Naturalist*.

JAMES L. MARINER has taught high school biology for twenty years both in Fountain Valley School, Colorado Springs, Colorado, and as a member of the Peace Corps in Ghana, West Africa. He is a member of the Board of Directors of the National Association of Biology Teachers. Mr. Mariner is also the author of several books for high school students on the topics of ecology, genetics, and reproduction.

Printed in the United States of America
Teacher's Annotated Edition: ISBN 0-02-277430-0

MACMILLAN
Biology

Macmillan Biology provides a comprehensive introduction to biology for a broad range of high-school students. Readable, beautifully illustrated, and clearly organized, *Macmillan Biology* promotes student's awareness of the diversity of life by carefully analyzing organisms from the simple to the complex.

- **Comprehensive, accurate content reflects the very latest biological advances**

- **Consistent emphasis on six basic biological concepts provides an underlying structure that helps students retain information and understand relationships**

- **Comparison sections, in which external characteristics and internal systems are compared across organisms, reinforce the major ideas about each organism**

- **Functional illustrations, closely correlated with the text, provide motivation and promote comprehension**

- **Readable text that highlights new terms and main ideas helps students master content**

- **Clearly stated objectives alert students to important concepts and provide the foundation for a comprehensive testing program**

- **Emphasis on current issues, practical applications, and careers makes biology relevant for today's student**

Macmillan Biology is organized into nine units and thirty-five chapters. Each chapter is subdivided into several manageable sections, each with its own objectives and questions. The consistent chapter organization is easy to follow and promotes maximum student learning.

CHAPTER INTRODUCTION
- Basic Concepts
- Motivating Questions

CHAPTER SECTION
- Objectives
- Comprehensive Development
- Questions

MODEL OF DNA MOLECULE

CHAPTER 10

GENES AND CHROMOSOMES

Mendel's principles answered a number of long-standing questions on the nature of heredity. Answering one set of questions often raises a variety of others. A close look at many organisms reveals that inheritance is often not as simple as Mendel's principles might seem to suggest. To be sure, garden peas are either tall or short. Their seeds are either green or yellow. Most plants, as well as animals, do not conform to such simple limitations. Instead, there seems to be a great diversity among every kind of plant or animal. By making careful observations and measurements, you discover that there is a great variety among living things.

The concept of unity and diversity among living things is one of the most basic concepts in biology. In the study of heredity, it can be viewed on at least two levels. First, there is considerable variety among all members of one kind of organism. For example, humans come in all sizes, shapes, and colors. Nevertheless, they represent only a single kind of organism.

At the second level, there are different kinds of living things. This represents diversity on a grand scale. Yet, the basic activities of life lend a unity that cannot be denied.

Two other basic concepts of biology are woven into the study of heredity. One of these is *change through time*. Many forces are at work to alter the appearance and activities of living things. Some of these forces produce changes that affect future generations. The other concept is that there is a fundamental *continuity of life*. Despite the fact that offspring are not exactly like their parents, they are very similar.

Most of the application of Mendel's principles has come from genetic research during the last 50 to 75 years. This chapter will provide knowledge to answer these questions:
- How can there be such variety in eye color and blood type?
- Why do some traits such as blonde hair and blue eyes often seem to occur together?
- Why do males often seem to have certain traits or characteristics such as color blindness while females rarely do?

Chapter Introductions
designed to stimulate student interest

Clarifies relationship of chapter to previous learnings

Stresses real-life phenomena related to chapter

Highlights basic concepts which will provide structure for new material

Presents thought-provoking questions to be answered in chapter

1 MECHANISMS OF CHANGE

The Species Concept

A species is a group of organisms that have the ability to interbreed. They are isolated from other such groups in a reproductive sense. This means that the members of a group recognized as a species may breed among themselves. However, they cannot breed outside that group. Furthermore, it means that the members of a species share a common gene pool. For example, all dogs are members of the same species (*Canis familiaris*). To be sure, there is great variety in size, color, and other features. Even so, two quite different dogs can still contribute to a future generation.

Biologists may recognize a number of different kinds of hawks as different species. There are Cooper's hawks, red-tailed hawks, Swainson's hawks, and many more. Many of these look more alike than many dogs. (See Fig. 14-1.) Why should these be given different species names? The reason is that breeding does not normally occur between the recognized groups. Thus, we see that a group can have a lot of obvious variety and still be a single species. Likewise, we see that several different species can be very similar.

There are problems, however, with this definition for a species. In the first place, it may happen that interbreeding sometimes does take place between recognized species. This is taken as evidence of a high degree of relatedness between the two groups. Sometimes, closely related groups may interbreed. If so, the offspring dies or is sterile. The line separating the two species in this case remains intact. At times, an offspring is normal and it survives to reproduce. In this case the line separating the two species becomes blurred.

OBJECTIVES FOR SECTION 1

A. Define the following terms in your own words: *species, isolating mechanism, preadaptation, divergence, speciation.*

B. Discuss the reasons why the term species is such a problem to biologists.

C. Compare and contrast the three types of selection.

D. Describe the various isolating mechanisms.

14-1. (left) red-tailed hawk, (right) Cooper's Hawk.

...ple of a ...4-6.) The ...Mules are ...y remain ...es cannot ...osomes ...s cannot ...stmating ...g or the

Mechanisms Of Change 247

QUESTIONS FOR SECTION 1

1. Define and give examples of the following terms: species, isolating mechanism, preadaptation, divergence, speciation.
2. Distinguish between divergence and adaptation.
3. Describe how divergence can lead to speciation.
4. Give an example of a single species with a high degree of diversity. Give an example of several species that are very similar, without many obvious differences.
5. Describe two reasons that the term species is such a problem to biologists.
6. Distinguish between the three types of selection using examples. Under what kinds of conditions would each operate?
7. What are the two main types of isolating mechanisms?
8. What are the differences between the four kinds of premating factors that serve to isolate populations from each other.
9. Describe how isolating mechanisms can lead to reproductive isolation and divergence.

Chapter Sections
self-contained and designed for easy lesson planning

Section Objectives serve as guides to important concepts and vocabulary

Important Vocabulary is listed in the section objectives and highlighted where defined in the text

Functional Illustrations and Photographs are referred to directly in the text and positioned for ease of use

Section Questions test mastery of objectives

Each chapter contains a Chapter Investigation that allows students of varying abilities to experience successful scientific investigations. Each investigation contains illustrations and three questions of increasing complexity. These pages are located between the first and second section of each chapter.

Chapter Investigations

develop skills of scientific investigation while reinforcing chapter concepts

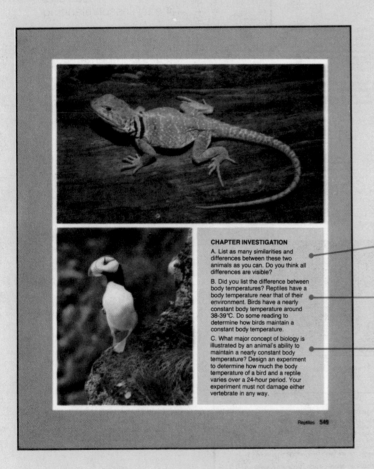

CHAPTER INVESTIGATION

A. List as many similarities and differences between these two animals as you can. Do you think all differences are visible?

B. Did you list the difference between body temperatures? Reptiles have a body temperature near that of their environment. Birds have a nearly constant body temperature around 38-39°C. Do some reading to determine how birds maintain a constant body temperature.

C. What major concept of biology is illustrated by an animal's ability to maintain a nearly constant body temperature? Design an experiment to determine how much the body temperature of a bird and a reptile varies over a 24-hour period. Your experiment must not damage either vertebrate in any way.

Reptiles 549

Type A Questions can be answered by studying the illustrations

Type B Questions can be answered by analyzing the text

Type C Questions require library research or laboratory experimentation

At the end of each chapter is a Chapter Review and Chapter Test. The Chapter Review contains a summary of the chapter, questions which extend the chapter concepts, and a vocabulary review. The Chapter Test contains twenty-five test items to facilitate scoring on a percentile basis.

CHAPTER REVIEW

First seen in primitive worms, bilateral symmetry is continued in annelids, molluscs, and larval echinoderms. Also continued are the three embryonic cell layers. A split appears in the mesoderms of all three. This develops into a coelom. It provides space for circulatory organs. The coelom also allows for independent movement of body wall and food tube.

The link between the *structure of an organ and its function* is illustrated by gills, radulas, nephridia, and the heart.

The three phyla illustrate *unity within diversity*. The annelids all display internal and external segmentation. But various annelids have tentacles, suckers, or a reduced head. Most molluscs have unsegmented, soft bodies with a shell. But wide variations exist within the group. The echinoderms share a spiny epidermis, radial symmetry, a water vascular system, and bilateral larvae. Yet their shapes vary from spheres, to stars, disks, and cylinders. These *similarities and differences* are used to classify them according to ancestral relationships.

Many of the forms in these phyla are sluggish. Also, they have methods of reproduction that insure *continuity of the species* even when they are scattered. These methods include hermaphroditism, some care of the fertilized eggs, and the regeneration of lost parts. Dispersal is performed by swimming larvae.

As the animals become larger and leave the sea, the means to maintain *homeostasis* become more complex. Improvements in circulatory and nervous systems make these changes possible. Many of the forms in these phyla *interact with their surroundings* in ways that touch human life.

Using the Concepts

1. Refer to the pollution problems of Great South Bay off the south shore of Long Island, New York. Which industry should have the right to use the bay: duck raisers, clam fishermen, or oyster farmers? How does one decide?
2. The largest vertebrate and the largest invertebrate live in the ocean. Why might this be true?
3. The study of trace elements in ancient clam shells suggested a deficiency of certain elements in the soil. How do you suggest restoring those elements naturally?

Unanswered Question

4. Why does learning ability seem to be so closely related to body symmetry?

Career Activities

5. Find out how cultured pearls are produced.

VOCABULARY REVIEW

1 coelom	intestine	mantle cavity	hemocyanin
clitellum	peristalsis	gills	kidney
trochophore larvae	capillaries	radula	nacre
sperm receptacles	hemoglobin	bivalves	3 endoskeleton
pharynx	nephridium	atrium	tube feet
crop	2 visceral mass	ventricle	skin gills
gizzard	mantle	blood sinus	

CHAPTER 25 TEST

Copy the number of each test item and place your answer to the right.

486

PART 1 Multiple Choice: Select the letter of the phrase that best completes each of the following.

1. The walls of small blood vessels through which blood exchanges materials with surrounding fluids are   a. mesenteries   b. receptacles   c. capillaries   d. blood sinuses.
2. The red pigment which increases the ability of an earthworm's blood to carry oxygen is   a. hemoglobin   b. hemocyanin   c. prostmium   d. nacre.
3. Earthworms digest proteins, fats, and carbohydrates using enzymes secreted by the   a. pharynx   b. crop   c. gizzard   d. intestine.
4. The receiving chambers of a clam's heart are the   a. atria   b. ventricles   c. blood sinuses   d. mantle cavity.
5. Of the three phyla studied in this chapter, the one least capable of learning is   a. Annelids   b. Molluscs   c. Echinoderms   d. Polychaetes.
6. The coelom is an important development in animals because it provides space for a true   a. circulatory system   b. respiratory system   c. digestive system   d. reproductive system.
7. An animal that can insert its stomach between the two valves of a clam and digest it is the   a. sea cucumber   b. crinoid   c. sea urchin   d. starfish.
8. The starfish preys on and is preyed upon by   a. clams   b. oysters   c. coral   d. leeches.
9. Earthworms are hermaphroditic but practice   a. fertilization in water   b. larval parasitism   c. larval development in clam gills   d. cross fertilization.
10. Pearls form as a response to   a. peristalsis   b. filter feeding   c. fright   d. irritation.

PART 2 Matching: Match the letter of the term in Column I with its description in Column II.

COLUMN I
a. clitellum   e. gizzard   i. nephridium
b. coelom   f. hormones   j. peristalsis
c. endoskeleton   g. mantle
d. gills   h. nacre

COLUMN II

11. A mesoderm-lined, fluid-filled cavity that allows free motion of body wall and the food tube
12. A saddle-like swelling on earthworms that secretes a cocoon
13. A muscular ogran that grinds food
14. A muscular action that pushes food through the food tube
15. A long tube that directs fluid with wastes from the coelom to the outside of an earthworm
16. Organs that allow gas exchanges between blood and air or water
17. The products of endocrine glands
18. Mother of pearl
19. The limy plates imbedded in the outer flesh of starfish
20. The fleshy outer body wall that secretes the shell in molluscs

PART 3 Completion: Complete the following.

21. A circulatory system in which the blood is continuously confined in muscular tubes is said to be ____.
22. Irregular cavities within tissues through which the blood of molluscs flows are called ____.
23. The near destruction of both oyster and clam industries in Long Island Sound resulted from ____.
24. The pair of organs which removes organic wastes from body fluids in clams are ____.
25. Of the phyla described in this chapter, the one with the most highly developed nervous system is Phylum ____.

Chapter Reviews
summarize major ideas presented in the chapter

Summary relates all new material to the relevant basic concepts

Using the Concepts — practical applications stressing current concerns

Unanswered Questions — unresolved biological issues

Career Activities — career-related questions and projects

Important vocabulary introduced in the chapter is listed by section

Chapter Tests
assess student mastery of objectives

10 Multiple-Choice Questions

10 Matching Items

5 Sentence Completions

Macmillan Biology is organized phylogenetically. Units 5, 6, 7, and 8 present a comprehensive analysis of microorganisms, plants, invertebrates, and vertebrates. The last section in each of these units compares the simpler organisms with the more complex.

TABLE 29-1   SUMMARY OF ANIMAL CHARACTERISTICS

SYSTEMS	Invertebrates	General Vertebrates	Bony Fishes	Amphibians
BODY PLAN AND EXTERNAL CHARACTERISTICS	different for each phylum	head, trunk, and tail; four appendages	no neck; fins and protective scales	legs with simple feet, thin moist scale-free skin
REPRODUCTIVE SYSTEM AND DEVELOPMENT	asexual or sexual, some with larvae	sexual, fertilization external or internal; go through cleavage, blastula stages	external fertilization; eggs unattended in water	external fertilization; metamorphosis
DIGESTIVE SYSTEM	none to simple tube	modified tube with accessory glands	pyloric caeca	tongue traps prey in some
CIRCULATORY SYSTEM	none to open or closed system	closed with single heart	heart has two chambers	heart has three chambers
RESPIRATORY SYSTEM	none, gills, or spiracles	moist membrane for gas exchange	blood becomes oxygenated in gills	gas exchange takes place in skin and simple lungs
EXCRETORY SYSTEM	none, flame cells or nephridia	kidneys with tubes to carry urine out of body	simple kidneys	
NERVOUS SYSTEM	none to simple brain	brain, spinal cord, nerves	medulla, optic lobes prominent	some increase
SENSE ORGANS	none to simple	simple to well developed senses	simple senses	
MUSCULAR AND SKELETAL SYSTEMS	no skeleton or exoskeleton; muscle variable	endoskeleton with muscles attached	adapted for swimming	
ENDOCRINE SYSTEM	none to highly specialized in arthropods	isolated cells produce hormones	simple system	

578 CHAPTER 29 • The Mammals

Comparison Sections
summarize and reinforce the major ideas about each organism

External characteristics and internal systems are compared across organisms

All comparisons are executed in three forms:
   written form
   chart form
   pictorial form

The pictorial comparisons have been provided by George Kelvin, a leading scientific illustrator whose works appear frequently in *Scientific American*.

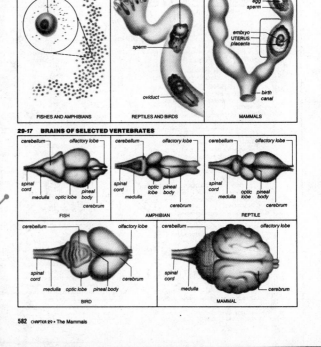

29-15   REPRODUCTION IN SELECTED VERTEBRATES

FISHES AND AMPHIBIANS

REPTILES AND BIRDS

MAMMALS

29-17   BRAINS OF SELECTED VERTEBRATES

FISH

AMPHIBIAN

REPTILE

BIRD

MAMMAL

582 CHAPTER 29 • The Mammals

MACMILLAN
Biology

MACMILLAN Biology

Joan G. Creager
Paul G. Jantzen
James L. Mariner

Macmillan Publishing Co., Inc. • New York
Collier Macmillan Publishers • London

Joan G. Creager
Editor of *The American Biology Teacher*
Reston, Virginia

Paul G. Jantzen
Science Department
Hillsboro High School
Hillsboro, Kansas

James L. Mariner
Science Department Chairperson
Fountain Valley School
Colorado Springs, Colorado

Acknowledgements: Cover and Title Page Credit: Brown Pelican copyright © Calvin Larsen/PHOTO RESEARCHERS, INC. 1977; Unit Openers: 1, © John Moss/PHOTO RESEARCHERS, INC.; 2, © Hugh Spencer of National Audubon Society/PHOTO RESEARCHERS, INC.; 3, © Wolfgang Bayer/BRUCE COLEMAN, INC.; 4, © SHOSTAL ASSOCIATES, INC.; 5, © Lawrence Lowry/ PHOTO RESEARCHERS, INC.; 6, © David Muench; 7, © John Running/ STOCK, BOSTON; 8, © Jeff Smith/PHOTO RESEARCHERS, INC.; 9, © Foster/THE IMAGE BANK. Figures 35-14 and 35-15 are from the book A CHILD IS BORN by Lennart Nilsson. English Translation Copyright © 1966, 1977 by Dell Publishing Co., Inc. Originally published in Swedish under the title ETT BARN BLIR TILL by Albert Bonniers Forlag. Copyright © 1965 by Albert Bonniers Folag, Stockholm. Revised edition copyright © 1976 by Lennart Nilsson, Mirjam Furuhjelm, Axel Ingleman-Sundberg, Cales Wirson. Used by permission of DELACORTE PRESS/SEYMOUR LAWRENCE. (Continued on page 751.)

Macmillan Publishing Co., Inc.
866 Third Avenue
New York, New York 10022
Collier Macmillan Canada, Ltd.

Printed in the United States of America

Pupil Edition: ISBN 0-02-277420-3

0123456789   9 8 7 6 5 4 3 2 1

TABLE
OF CONTENTS

UNIT 1 THE WORLD OF LIVING THINGS

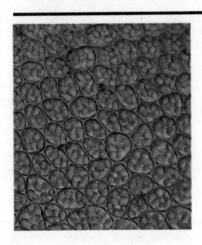

UNIT 2 UNITY OF ALL LIVING THINGS

UNIT 3 CONTINUITY OF LIFE

UNIT 4 HISTORY OF LIFE

UNIT 5 VIRUSES, MONERA, PROTISTA, AND FUNGI

UNIT 6 PLANTS

UNIT 7 ANIMALS: INVERTEBRATES

UNIT 8 ANIMALS: VERTEBRATES

UNIT 9 HUMAN BODY SYSTEMS

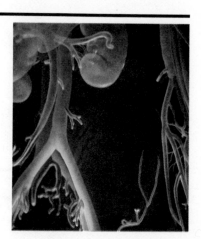

Acknowledgements

The authors and editors would like to express their appreciation to the following consultants who made suggestions in the development stage of the program.

Dr. Donald Alsum
Associate Professor, Biology
  Department
Saint Mary's College
Winona, Minnesota

Dr. John E. Hendrix
Associate Professor
Department of Botany and Plant
  Pathology
Colorado State University

Dr. A. Harry Brenowitz
Professor, Biology Department
Adelphi University

Dr. Donald Humphreys
Professor of Science and Education
Temple University
College of Education

Dr. Albert F. Eble
Professor of Biology
Trenton State College

Dr. Richard Kowles
Chairperson, Biology Department
Saint Mary's College
Winona, Minnesota

Dr. Thomas P. Evans
Chairperson, Department of
  Science Education
Oregon State University

Dr. Arthur Livermore
Program Head of Office of Science
  Education
American Association for the
  Advancement of Science

Dr. Walter Farmer
Department of Teacher Education
State University of New York
  at Albany

Dr. David Ost
Chairperson, Biology Department
California State College, Bakersfield

Miss Ann Elizabeth Fullerton, North Shore High School, Glen Head, New York, helped us by reviewing the entire manuscript. We are extremely grateful for her help.

The following classroom teachers and supervisors reviewed parts of the manuscript. We appreciate their comments: **Mr. Donald Buell,** Framingham North High School, Framingham, Massachusetts; **Mr. Don Cooper,** Morrow Junior High School, Morrow, Georgia; **Ms. Doris Countee,** Lee High School, Houston, Texas; **Mrs. Barbara Evans,** B.C. High School, Cayce, South Carolina; **Ms. Mary N. Long,** L.B. Johnson High School, Austin, Texas; **Mr. Paul E. Peknik, Jr.,** Science and Math Coordinator, Belltown School, Stamford, Connecticut; **Miss Joyce L. Smith,** Midlothian High School, Midlothian, Virginia; **Mr. William Talbott,** Education Specialist, Baltimore City School District, Baltimore, Maryland; **Mr. Truman O. Terrell,** Richland Senior High School, Fort Worth, Texas.

PROLOGUE

WHAT IS BIOLOGY? Biology *is the science of life.* Life is a dynamic process. All living things are constantly changing — using energy, growing, reproducing, and responding to the environment. Students of biology have been fascinated by its study throughout history. Our success as a life form has been dependent upon our understanding of a number of biological principles.

WHY STUDY BIOLOGY? For biologists, the study of life is interesting and exciting for its own sake. They are challenged by the problems of understanding how living things stay alive. How do bees find food? What makes flowers bloom? Why do children look like their parents? They are challenged by the problems of how living things interact with their environment. How do plants and animals survive the cold of winter? How do green plants capture energy from the sun? Is there life on other planets?

In addition to being interesting for its own sake, biology can be applied to many other areas. In agriculture, the knowledge of biology has been used to improve food crops. In dealing with environmental problems biological information helps us to understand how natural processes occur. From this understanding we are better able to deal with pollution and its dangers. The study of animals and their activities helps us to protect endangered species. In medicine, biology helps us to understand how the normal human body works. In turn, we are better able to prevent or control some of the things that go wrong from time to time such as the control of infectious disorders.

Biology is detailed subject matter. Biologists have collected so many facts about living things, and there are millions of living things. Some way of putting all of these facts together is needed if we are to make sense of things.

BASIC CONCEPTS OF BIOLOGY Careful study of the characteristics of living things has revealed at least six major unifying themes in biology. These basic concepts will serve as the focal point of this book. Let us begin with a brief description of each concept.

1. *Unity and Diversity* We are still very young when we become aware of a huge variety of life forms. In spite of this variety, or diversity, there is a basic unity of pattern of living things. For example, all dogs are similar in that they can interbreed and have

the same basic body plan. Yet, if we look at each breed, they can be very different.

Different kinds of animals such as a horse and a zebra are quite similar in many ways, but each has characteristics not found in the other. Their characteristics, in turn, are very different from those of a lizard or a sparrow.

2. *Interaction of Living Things and the Environment* Each living thing, or organism, is adapted to the conditions of its environment. Evidence of this adaptation is how successful each is meeting the demands for survival. Living things affect and are affected by their environment. For example, the number of wolves in an area helps control the rabbit population. On the other hand, the temperature of their surroundings causes changes in the thickness of the animals' fur.

3. *Complementarity of Structure and Function* The qualities of the parts of an organism and their arrangement complement, or are related to, the functions of that part or organ. Consider how your elbow joint differs from the joint attaching your arm to your shoulder. These are different structures with different functions. In different organisms the same structure can be used differently based on its structure. The beaks of birds are an example. A woodpecker uses its beak differently from a robin.

4. *Continuity of Life* Elm trees produce elm trees. Dogs give birth to dogs. Humans give birth to humans. Each generation is much like its parent generation. This is what is meant by continuity. Here too, is an expression of unity in the living world. Life is thus seen as a continuing process, being passed from one generation to the next.

5. *Homeostasis* This concept refers to the preservation of life in the face of change. Organisms are constantly being acted upon by their environments. Indeed, even their internal environments change as they carry on life's activities. Living things respond to these changes by activities that tend to restore the delicate balance of the life condition. Room temperature changes do not affect your body temperature because your body makes adjustments. Your houseplant does not die if you skip just one watering. Thus, homeostasis is a dynamic condition of living things.

6. *Change Through Time* Many biologists believe living organisms are not the same as they were in the past. They point to evidence such as materials in rocks left in ages past by living organisms. By comparing these materials and forms to living organisms they can identify differences. That changes take place is seldom disputed. How they occur, and how they can effect other changes are questions that have not been answered. Several theories have been proposed, but none have been proved.

One theory of how changes take place is evolution. In this program where evolution is discussed, the concept of evolution is presented as theory, not fact.

Study Aids

Basic Concepts The six basic concepts discussed above are used throughout the text to provide structure. In the introduction of each chapter the relevant concepts are mentioned. The summary ties these concepts to the ideas learned in the chapter. The basic concepts stand out in *italic type.*

Chapter Sections Each chapter is divided into numbered and titled sections, each with its own objectives and questions. Use the objectives as guides to the most important points in the sections. The questions test your mastery of objectives.

Biology contains many words with which you may not be familiar. The most important terms are listed in *italic type* in the objectives. These terms are then defined in the section in ***boldface italic*** to make them easy to find. These terms are also defined in the glossary. Some words may be hard to pronounce. They are phonetically respelled in parentheses. The syllable that is emphasized is in *italic type.* Use the pronunciation key on page 714 as a guide.

Chapter Investigation In each chapter there is a special page called Chapter Investigation. Each uses the information in the text in new ways. Chapter Investigations consist of illustrations and three different types of questions. Type A questions can be answered by studying the illustration. Type B questions require some reading to answer them. Type C questions may require work outside of the text in the library or in the laboratory.

Chapter Review The materials at the end of the chapter will help you to review and apply the material introduced in the chapter. The summary relates the new material to the basic concepts. The vocabulary list provides new words by section, and the questions give you an opportunity to make use of the new concepts.

Chapter Test The chapter concludes with a test which will help you evaluate your recall of the material in the chapter.

THE WORLD OF LIVING THINGS

Living things are not surrounded by empty space. They are surrounded by other living things and nonliving things with which they interact. This unit describes the characteristics of these organisms and the features of the physical world in which they make their home. It suggests that all organisms have similar needs which are met in a variety of ways.

The stage is set by the description of conditions needed for life and the variety of places where life is found. We then examine the many ways living things affect one another and trace the path of energy from the sun through living things. Finally, how human activities affect the natural world is explained.

FLAMINGOS

THE ENVIRONMENT

One characteristic of living things, or organisms, is that they respond to changes around them. *These surroundings are known as their* **environment.**

In a dramatic production, the actors and actresses perform on a stage. That stage is equipped with special scenery, furniture, backdrops, and lighting. Like a stage, Earth has a variety of environments, but all exist within definite limits. Living things perform their acts on or near the surface of Earth.

The basic concepts in this chapter include: *unity within the diversity of living things,* and *interactions within the environment.*

Saying that there are several million kinds of living things suggests that each kind differs from the others in some way. *The term* **diversity** *refers to those differences.* In spite of the diversity among organisms, they all have certain ways in which they are the same. In the prologue you read about some of the characteristics of living things. Kangaroo rats, penguins, starfish, earthworms, cacti, and algae differ from each other in appearance. Yet, all of them have features common only to living things. *These features reflect what we refer to as the* **unity of living things.**

Living organisms affect their environment. In turn, they are affected by changes in their environment. Interactions in biological and physical systems usually take in or give off energy.

Because living things are always interacting with the objects and conditions around them, their environment is important. We will examine several factors in their environment that are important to organisms.

- What conditions on our planet permit life to exist here?
- What happens to organisms if they get too hot or too cold?
- How does Earth's atmosphere determine the clothes you wear and the scheduling of your activities?
- How do the sun's rays determine the kinds of plants and animals that live in your area?

MARSHALL ISLAND

1 CONDITIONS THAT MAKE LIFE POSSIBLE

Life on the Moon?

When Astronaut Neil Armstrong took humankind's first step on the moon in July 1969, he received a harsh welcome. (See Fig. 1-1.) With little or no atmosphere, there could be no breathing, no screening of the sun's radiation, and no transmission of sound. This barren landscape consisted of a light gray desert without plants, animals, or even pools of water. The temperature on the lighted side of the moon was 122°C, hot enough to make blood boil. That on the dark side was a chilling −173°C. To avoid both extremes Armstrong landed near the edge of the lighted side and wore a space suit. The suit contained a portion of Earth's more friendly environment and protected him from temperature extremes.

The moon's silent, barren landscape is without air, food, or water. Yet it is mild compared to that of most of the planets in our solar system. What makes Earth's surface more hospitable to life?

Earth's Advantages

The advantages that Earth's surface provides for living things include (1) a protective atmosphere, (2) a moderate temperature, and (3) important chemical substances. Let us consider each of these further.

PROTECTIVE ATMOSPHERE   Earth attracts an atmosphere because of its mass. **Mass** *is a measure of a body's tendency to resist changes in its motion.* The greater a body's mass, the greater the force needed to get it started, change its speed, or stop it. Mass also determines the amount of gravitational attraction between objects. Objects are matter. **Matter** *is anything that has mass and takes up space.* Earth's mass is 81 times that of the moon. For this reason, it attracts particles of matter with greater force than the moon does. It has an atmosphere and the moon does not. (See Fig. 1-2 on page 4.)

Having an atmosphere protects Earth's inhabitants from harmful radiations and meteorite showers. Much of the sun's harmful ultraviolet radiation is absorbed by the ozone layer of our atmosphere. (Ozone is a special form of oxygen gas.) Yet the atmosphere allows the penetration of those portions of the sun's energy on which all life depends. **Energy** *is the ability to produce motion in an object.*

MODERATE TEMPERATURE   Living things are made of tiny units called *cells.* The protein of living cells is sensitive to temperature extremes. You have seen the protein of egg white change when it is boiled or fried. That change cannot be reversed. At high tempera-

OBJECTIVES FOR SECTION 1

A. Describe each of the three advantages that Earth provides for living things.

B. Demonstrate how the Earth's day-night cycle affects plants and animals.

1-1. *What features of the moon make it difficult for life to exist?*

A fast freeze may cause ice crystals to form in cells and damage cell parts.

tures proteins are permanently damaged. At low temperatures the water surrounding the cells may freeze. As a result, water leaves the cells and they are left dry. Such drying is particularly damaging to proteins. Much of Earth's surface has temperatures between such extremes. The moon's temperature varies between 122°C and −173°C. Earth's temperature ranges only between 58°C and −88°C.

Another reason that temperature is important to life is its effect on water. Organisms are composed largely of liquid water. It is in water that most chemical reactions of organisms occur. Planets near the sun have surface temperatures above water's boiling point. Those farther from the sun are too cold to keep water from freezing. In addition to those effects on proteins and water, low temperatures cause important reactions to occur too slowly to sustain life.

CHEMICAL SUBSTANCES   The third factor that makes life possible on Earth is the density-layering of its surface. **Density** *refers to the amount of mass of a substance in a given space.* In a mixture of liquids, the denser liquids tend to sink; the less dense ones float. For example, oil floats on water. In general, density-layering tended to concentrate at Earth's surface many materials important to living things. These include materials that contain oxygen, hydrogen, nitrogen, carbon, and phosphorus. The lightest substances, such as hydrogen and helium gases, escaped into space.

The Changing Environment

1-2. Compare the features of the moon with the earth's. The earth's atmosphere helps to make earth livable.

DAY-NIGHT CYCLE   Our environment is constantly changing. Each evening, you experience the movement of your area from direct exposure to sunlight into Earth's shadow. The activity cycles of many

1-3. Birds are affected by the seasons. In fall and spring they migrate. In spring they raise their young.

plants and animals are related to this day-night cycle. For robins, mockingbirds, and cardinals, increased light intensity appears to be the trigger that begins their morning song. Darkness begins the food searching activity of raccoons and opossums. The length of the night determines when some plants flower.

SEASONAL CYCLE   Earth's annual revolution around the sun results in the seasonal cycle. In some areas these seasonal cycles bring dramatic changes. For plants, the temperature affects food production and reproductive activity. These in turn determine the time and amount of food available to animals. Many kinds of birds spend their long northern summer days eating seeds and insects and raising their young. (See Fig. 1-3.) But before snow and ice return they migrate to warmer areas.

QUESTIONS FOR SECTION 1

1. List three advantages Earth provides for living things that the moon does not provide.
2. How do atmosphere and temperature affect living things?
3. In what specific ways would your activities be affected if you lived on the moon with a different light-dark cycle?

Answers to Questions for Section 1

A. 1. Protective atmosphere, moderate temperature, important substances.
B. 2. Atmosphere blocks harmful radiation but allows essential radiation to pass through. Extremes of high and low temperature damage proteins, and freeze or boil water that must be liquid in cells; very low temperatures slow life-sustaining reactions.
*3. Answers will vary.

CHAPTER INVESTIGATION

A. What differences do you see in the kinds of organisms in these four scenes?

B. What are some ways that the pictured organisms are suited to their environment?

C. For what specific reasons do you suppose each pictured organism might or might not survive in either of the other environments pictured?

With a microscope, observe small organisms in various environments in your area. Answer questions A–C about your organisms.

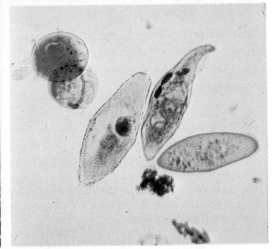

② DIVISIONS IN THE BIOSPHERE

The environment we have described reaches from Earth's core beneath us to the sun out in space. But life is known to exist only in a 19-kilometer thick layer at Earth's surface. ***Earth's life-supporting layer of air, soil, and water is known as the* biosphere.** Within the biosphere are over a million kinds of animals. Also, nearly a half million kinds of plants are known. In addition there are probably several million kinds of organisms not yet classified or even seen by biologists.

These organisms are far from being evenly distributed. They are grouped according to medium, altitude, climate, and geology. Medium means air, water, and soil. Altitude includes shallow ponds, ocean depths, and mountain tops. Geology includes the kind of terrain such as fertile or rocky areas. Let us examine the characteristics of some of the major divisions of the biosphere. (See Fig. 1-4.)

OBJECTIVES FOR SECTION 2

C. Define the terms *biosphere, biome, humus, deciduous trees, desert.*

D. Distinguish between marine, freshwater, and estuary environments.

E. Describe how the climate affects the kinds of plants and animals that exist in various biomes.

1-4. Major divisions of the biosphere.

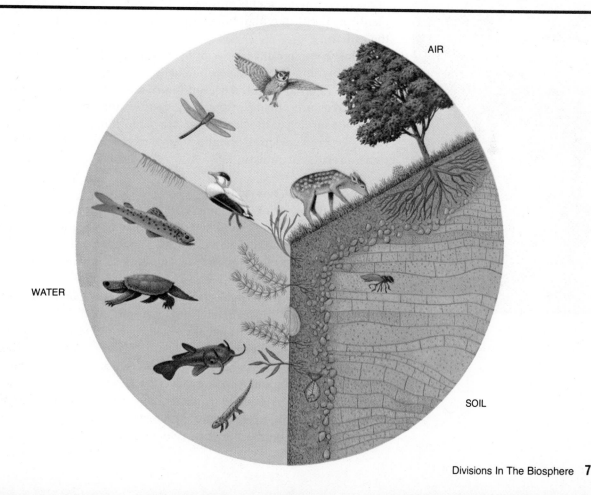

AIR

WATER

SOIL

Marine Environments

The ocean covers almost 70 percent of Earth's biosphere and descends nearly 11 kilometers to its depth. In it occur a variety of environments. It supports organisms ranging in size from microscopic organisms to the 30-meter blue whale, the largest animal that ever lived. Also, it includes the giant kelp, an alga which may be as long as the whale.

The shallow bottom contains many organisms. Included are the sea anemones, clams, starfish, and crabs. At or near the surface are the jellyfishes, Portuguese-men-of-war, tuna, sea horses, and many other fishes. Deeper down are the giant squids and the sperm whales. (See Fig. 1-5.) On the deeper bottom exist certain sponges, sea lilies, and sea cucumbers.

Organisms that are adapted to life in the sea can tolerate a high concentration of salts, but freshwater organisms cannot. *An estuary (es chōo er ē) is a partly enclosed portion of the sea which is fed by a freshwater stream.* (See Fig. 1-6.) It is a mixture of marine and freshwater. A relatively small number of kinds of organisms exist in such an environment. However, their food supply is generally plentiful. Very often high tides carry a fresh supply of nutrients into the estuary.

Most commercial varieties of oysters and crabs live in estuaries. River-spawning fish like salmon usually spend time in estuaries before they migrate from the sea up the rivers to lay eggs. Such protected areas are nurseries for many deep-water fish whose young could not survive in the harsh open sea. Thus it is important that estuaries be protected from pollution. Also, rivers leading to them must remain relatively undisturbed.

Freshwater Environments

When rains fall or snow melts on land areas, some of the water moves into the ground. Some soil water is used by plants. But much of it reappears on the surface as springs. Spring water rejoins surface water flowing directly from rain or snow melt. Streams of flowing water join together to form rivers. These rivers finally enter a lake or sea. *Water running in streams or standing in lakes, ponds, marshes, and swamps is called* freshwater. It is not salty.

A beginning stream is usually small, narrow, fast flowing, and contains abundant oxygen. Many organisms are adapted to these conditions. Some insects become permanently attached to stones or logs. Furthermore, some worms have flattened bodies that stick to stones underwater. These organisms have streamlined bodies that offer little resistance to water flow. Downstream, the slope and speed of current tend to decrease and the river widens. This causes a change

1-5. A variety of organisms live in marine environments.

in the types of organisms present. Catfish and carp cruise through bottom waters. Also, several kinds of algae can be found here.

In lakes and ponds, one finds frog tadpoles, snails, clams, muskrats and worms. Sunfish and bass are more likely found distributed throughout the water. Visible and microscopic algae are also widespread. On the surface of quiet pools one sees whirling beetles and water striders. Organisms such as alligators are more likely to live in the swamp.

Soil Environments

The thin top surface of our land areas provides the minerals used in the building of the bodies of land organisms. For this reason our lives depend on the soil. Part of the soil is the mineral material resulting from the breakdown of rock. Mixed with these mineral particles is humus. **Humus *is the partially decomposed remains of plants, animals, and animal wastes.*** Humus greatly increases the soil's ability to hold water and minerals. A balance of minerals, humus, water, air, and organisms make up the top soil.

1-6. *(left) Tidal estuary and organisms which can live there. (top right) Seahorse. (bottom right) Sea perch, mussels, and anemone.*

Answers to questions for Section 2

7. Deciduous forest: 4 seasons; variable rainfall; animals hibernate. Grasslands: extreme temp.; 25-75 cm rain/yr.; grasses dominant. Chaparral: rainy winters; shrubs dominate; few animals. Desert: cold nights, hot days; scant rainfall; plants adapted to store water.

*8. Answers will vary.

9. No. Soil is infertile; humus does not form; and roots of trees absorb the minerals.

1-7. A millipede lives in the soil. They and thousands of bacteria, algae, and fungi are part of the soil.

Organisms of the soil include microscopic organisms and fungi which decompose plant and animal remains. Algae and other microscopic organisms exist near the surface. Worms, millipedes, and larger burrowing animals stir up the soil and are themselves part of it. (See Fig. 1-7.)

Land Environments

Land environments are divided according to the major plant communities that are maintained by the climate. Such major divisions of the biosphere are called **biomes** *(bī ōmz). See Figure 1-8 for a map of the major biomes.*

TROPICAL RAIN FOREST　Tropical rain forests occur near the equator. Daily rainfall is heavy. Average monthly temperatures are high and are almost constant. Such conditions support a great variety of

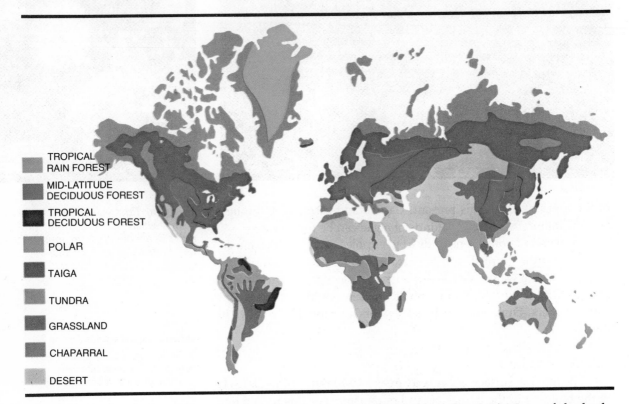

- TROPICAL RAIN FOREST
- MID-LATITUDE DECIDUOUS FOREST
- TROPICAL DECIDUOUS FOREST
- POLAR
- TAIGA
- TUNDRA
- GRASSLAND
- CHAPARRAL
- DESERT

1-8. Map of the world's biomes.

animals and plants in this biome. (See Fig. 1-9.) Many of the backboned animals are those that can fly or climb trees. These include birds, lizards, snakes, and monkeys. Also, there are many large insects in this biome. These include moths, beetles, and ants. Most kinds of plants are trees up to 50 meters tall. In this biome trees branch only near the top. Thus, the forest floor is too shaded for most

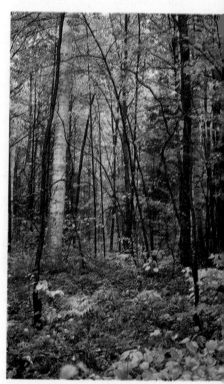

1-9. *In a tropical rain forest most trees are tall and branch only near the top. Thus the forest floor is too dark for most other plants.*

The sequence of biome descriptions is from the equator to the poles — toward less radiant energy.

plants to grow there. Moisture and heat result in such rapid decay that humus is almost non-existent. If minerals were not quickly absorbed by plant roots, they would seep down below root level. Most nutrients of the rain forest remain bound up in plant tissue. Thus the soils are left infertile. This is why clearing and farming a rain forest fails

TROPICAL DECIDUOUS FOREST   Most tropical areas experience wet and dry seasons. **Deciduous** (di *sij* o͞o əs) **trees and shrubs** *are those that lose their leaves during the dry season.* These plants form the tropical deciduous forest biome. The canopy formed by overhead branches and leaves is less dense than that of the rain forest. Therefore, it allows the development of a dense jungle of undergrowth.

MID-LATITUDE DECIDUOUS FOREST   Mid-latitude deciduous forests experience four distinct seasons. (See Fig. 1-10.) Thus plants and animals must survive temperature variations, some droughts, and snow. The dominant plants are broad-leaved trees. These include the birches of the northern and mountainous regions. Also found within this biome are the oak, hickory, walnut, birch, and maple trees. These trees shed their leaves before winter begins. This activity is important since roots cannot easily absorb water from cold soil. Thus, losing leaves prevents water loss. The loss of leaves has other effects on this biome. Cold temperatures and wind are more severe. Moreover, there is less food available. These changes create a dormant period during the winter months. Animal life is scarce on the forest floor. Long winter sleeps, or hibernation, are common among animals. Rainfall varies through the seasons and averages 100 centimeters per year. Animals of these forests include the beaver, whitetailed deer, squirrels, raccoons, and foxes. These forests also contain many songbirds, snakes, frogs, and mice.

1-10. *Seasons are about to change in this mid-latitude deciduous forest.*

Deciduous forest, grasslands, chaparral, and deserts may all occur at mid-latitudes. They differ in amount of rainfall.

1-11. In a mid-latitude grassland low rainfall and fires inhibit the growth of forest. Fertile soil makes it good farmland.

1-12. A chaparral is a shrubland which usually has dry summers.

1-13. A mid-latitude desert receives air that has lost its moisture over the tropics or on the windward side of a mountain range.

GRASSLANDS Areas receiving only 25 to 75 centimeters of rainfall per year cannot support forests. Among other places, these biomes are the grasslands, or prairies, of the United States and Canada. Here the winters are cold and the summers are hot and dry. (See Fig. 1-11.) Humus is plentiful and the soil is fertile. Much of the naturally occurring grasses have been replaced with vast fields of wheat and corn. Grassland animals include burrowing mammals such as prairie dogs and ground squirrels. Before being overhunted, hoofed-grazing mammals such as the bison and elk were plentiful. Common birds include meadowlarks and quail which nest on the ground.

CHAPARRAL In the *chaparral* (shap ə ral) or shrublands, most of the 50-75 cm of rainfall occurs in the winter. This biome is found in parts of Europe, southern Australia, and in areas of California. (See Fig. 1-12.) Leaves of plants in these areas have waxy coatings. This helps prevent evaporation of water. Typical plants of the chaparral include oak and sycamore trees as well as holly and poison ivy. Rabbits, coyotes, and rattlesnakes are only a few of the animals that are found here.

DESERT *Areas receiving 25 centimeters or less of rainfall per year are* **deserts.** They are found all over the world. Deserts make up more than one-third of the Earth's land surface. There are two types of deserts, cold and warm. Cold deserts, as in Nevada, have cold winters and hot summers. Warm deserts, as in Arizona and Africa, have hot temperatures year round. In both types, there are cold nights to accompany the hot days.

In these biomes there is no regular pattern of rainfall. Many months, or even years, may go by with hardly any rain. At times a heavy rainfall may occur. However, this water evaporates very fast. It also tends to run off the dry barren land. Shortly after a rainfall, there is much activity in these biomes. Both plants and animals attempt to capture and use as much water as possible. Organisms living in desert biomes must be able to adapt to this unreliable supply of rain. (See Fig. 1-13.) Some desert plants such as the cacti are adapted to store water in thick stems. Others avoid water loss by having small, narrow leaves. Mesquite bushes have long roots. These extend as much as 30 meters into the ground to obtain water. Many animals such as rodents, lizards, and snakes reduce water loss by burrowing into the ground. Also, they search for food only during the cooler nights.

THE TAIGA BIOME In the taiga (tī gə) cone-bearing, or coniferous trees are common, especially spruce and firs. (See Fig. 1-14.) The growing season is shorter than that in mid-latitudes. The winters are colder and bring more snow. Many cone-bearing evergreen trees bear needle-like leaves. They easily shed snow and withstand hard frosts. They do not lose water as easily as broad leaves do. Taiga soils are shallow and porous. There are many lakes and ponds in this biome. Organisms called fungi decompose needles fallen from the trees. The fungi absorb most of the nutrients of decomposition and leave the soil infertile. Because of low temperatures the fungi work slowly, thus needles often accumulate under the trees. The taiga of North America is inhabited by a variety of birds including jays, warblers, and nuthatches. Shrews, jumping mice, elk, and the larger moose also make their homes here.

THE TUNDRA BIOME   Most of the tundra exists primarily in the northern hemisphere. The climate is too harsh to allow even coniferous trees to exist. (See Fig. 1-15.) Plant life consists mostly of grasses, lichens, mosses, and a few small willows and birches. During the short summer, there is so little heat that the frozen soil beneath the surface never thaws. Thus, lack of drainage causes melting snow to collect in ponds and marshes. Most organisms either migrate south or are inactive in winter. Most plants live over the winter as inactive roots. They grow and reproduce above ground quickly during the short summer. Animals of the tundra include caribou, lemmings, snowy owls, arctic foxes, mosquitoes, and deerflies. Plovers, horned larks, and sandpipers are migratory birds which nest in the tundra. They take advantage of the long summer days for feeding their young. Because decomposition and plant growth are slow, tundra areas require a long recovery time from destruction.

THE POLAR REGIONS   Antarctica is a cold desert. Though mostly covered with ice more than 1,000 meters thick, it receives little or no rainfall and little snow. The air is too cold to hold much water vapor. Winter temperatures remain at about −60°C. Summer temperatures rise above freezing only in coastal areas. Plants and animals are rare indeed. (See Fig. 1-16.) Penguins, a few migratory birds, and several

1-14. In the taiga most trees have needle-like leaves. How are such leaves an advantage in cold, snowy winters?

1-15. Snowy owls in the tundra. The tundra climate is too cold for even coniferous trees to survive.

1-16. In polar regions summer temperatures rise above freezing only along the sea coast.

Divisions In The Biosphere   13

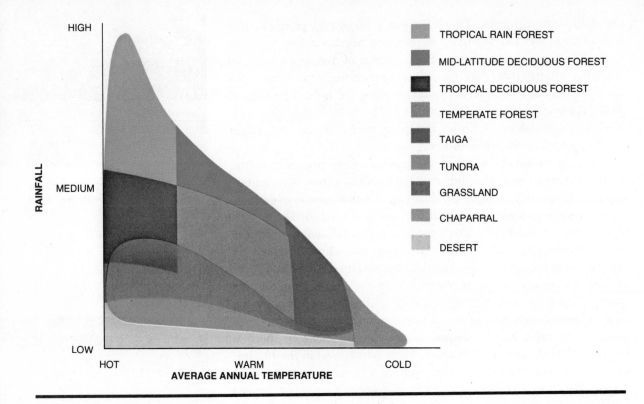

RAINFALL — HIGH / MEDIUM / LOW

AVERAGE ANNUAL TEMPERATURE — HOT / WARM / COLD

TROPICAL RAIN FOREST

MID-LATITUDE DECIDUOUS FOREST

TROPICAL DECIDUOUS FOREST

TEMPERATE FOREST

TAIGA

TUNDRA

GRASSLAND

CHAPARRAL

DESERT

1-17. Relationships between temperature, rainfall, and type of biome.

Answers to questions for Section 2

C. **1.** See glossary or boldface type in section.

  * **2.** No. Conditions required for life may vary.

D. **3.** Marine: high salt content, ocean water. Freshwater: low salt content. Estuary: mixture or marine and freshwater in a partially enclosed portion of sea fed by fresh water.

  * **4.** Less competition, and varied environments.

  5. Animals have streamlined bodies and high metabolic rates.

E. **6.** See pages 10-14. Compare temperature range, rainfall, seasons, latitude, plant life, soil, and animal life.

kinds of insects are seen there. A few flowering plants, lichens, and mosses have been found some distance from the South Pole. The Arctic, in the Northern Hemisphere, is less harsh. But even there winters are too cold and dry for trees to grow.

Some relationships between temperature, rainfall, and type of biome are shown in Figure 1-17.

QUESTIONS FOR SECTION 2

1. Define biosphere, biome, humus, deciduous trees, desert.
2. Within the 19-km thick biosphere, do you think organisms are evenly distributed in altitude? Give reasons.
3. In what ways do marine, freshwater, and estuary environments differ?
4. What might be some advantages for organisms living in the ocean rather than in freshwater or on land?
5. What special features would you expect to find in organisms living in a fast moving stream?
6. Briefly describe one tropical, one mid-latitude, the taiga, tundra, and polar biome and explain how each differs from the one before.
7. Briefly describe the mid-latitude biomes and explain how they differ.
8. Give an example from your area of how climate determines the dominant plant life, and how that determines the dominant animal life.
9. Would tropical rain forests be well suited for agriculture? Why?
(See page 9 for other answers.)

3 CYCLES IN NATURE

Natural cycles refer to the repeated circulation of substances. These occur through a series of interactions between organisms and storage forms. The substances that make up the bodies of living things are limited in quantity. When organisms die their bodies decay. The products of decay become part of the soil, air, ocean, or rocks. They are available to form the bodies of the next generation of organisms.

The Water Cycle

Without water, life as we know it cannot exist. Most of Earth's creatures live in the waters of its oceans, lakes, streams, swamps, and marshes. Water makes up 60-96 percent of the weight of living things. Most chemical reactions of importance to living things take place in, or involve, water.

Water is by far the most abundant single substance in the biosphere. Yet its short supply on land areas determines the vegetation of whole biomes. Water is the limiting factor in what farms and industries can produce.

OBJECTIVES FOR SECTION 3
F. Organize the various pathways of water into a word diagram illustrating a cycle.
G. Organize the various pathways of phosphorus into a word diagram illustrating the phosphorus cycle.
H. Describe how unity within diversity, interactions in the environment, and the natural cycles are illustrated in this chapter.

1-18. Water cycle.

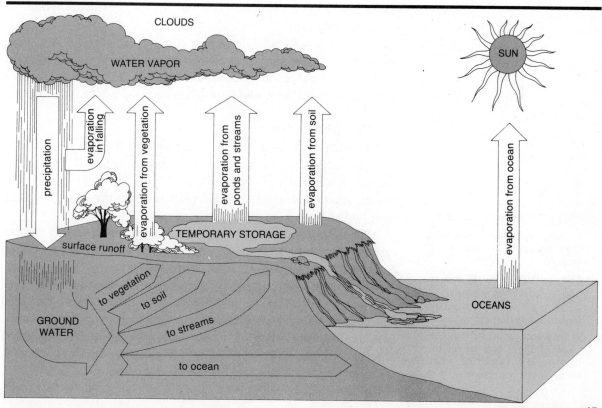

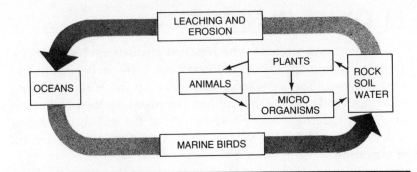

1-19. The phosphorus cycle.

An estimated 97 percent of Earth's water is in its oceans. Yet many human societies depend on the water of rivers and lakes. Rooted plants depend on the water held in small spaces between soil particles. Without the continual resupplying of these small amounts of water, life on the land would be impossible. Rivers, lakes, and underground water are supplied by rain or snow. This comes from condensing water vapor in the air. (See Fig. 1-18.) A portion of this vapor forms by evaporation of water from land, lakes, rivers, and the surface of plants. But most of it comes from the ocean's surface. The circulating atmosphere holds only about 0.03 percent of Earth's water. But it is only in this form that water is carried from the great ocean reservoir to the land. Without it, our continents would be barren deserts.

Most atmospheric water vapor comes from the sea. However, most rain falls on the land. This is balanced by the run-off water carried by rivers back to the sea. *This movement of water from ocean to atmosphere, to land, and back to ocean is called the* **water cycle.**

The Phosphorus Cycle

Another cycle essential to organisms is that of phosphorus. Phosphorus is a mineral found in shells, bones, and teeth. It is part of the substance that transmits inherited traits from parents to their young. Also, organisms use phosphorus in energy changes inside their bodies.

Phosphorus is in short supply. Soils that receive heavy rainfall easily lose phosphorus. The low phosphorus content of the open ocean is the main reason that few things live there.

The phosphorus used by organisms was stored in the form of phosphate millions of years ago. As phosphate dissolves in rain water, it is washed onto valley soils or through rivers to the ocean. Land plants absorb the phosphate. Later, these plants are eaten by animals. Dead bodies and wastes decay. Finally, their phosphate is taken up by plant roots to continue the cycle. (See Fig. 1-19.)

Answers to Questions for Section 3.

* 5. Heavy rainfall would wash away the phosphorus and corn couldn't grow.

H. 6. Within the diversity, all share the need for energy and materials, moderate temperature, protection from harmful radiation, etc.

7. The materials that make up the bodies of living things is in limited supply, so substances must be freed for successive generations.

Phosphate does not dissolve easily in water. For that reason, some that washes into the ocean settles to the bottom. The remainder may be absorbed by marine algae. The phosphate-rich algae in turn may be eaten by fish. Sea birds eating the fish return some of the phosphates to the land in their waste droppings. Great deposits of such droppings, called *guano* (*gwä nō*), occur off the coast of Peru. They are an important source of fertilizer.

Water and phosphorus are only two examples of the many kinds of matter that are cycled at or near the surface of Planet Earth.

QUESTIONS FOR SECTION 3

1. Briefly sketch a word diagram of the water cycle.
2. Why is the water vapor in the atmosphere so important?
3. Why, in many areas of the United States, are water supplies running low?
4. Sketch a word diagram illustrating the phosphorus cycle.
5. What might happen to phosphate in a rain forest converted to a corn field?
6. Explain the meaning of unity within the diversity of living things.
7. Discuss the importance of recycling in living things.

(See page 16 for other answers.)

Answers to Questions for Section 3

F. 1. water vapor condenses rain in atmosphere ⟶ & snow
evaporates / falls
land & bodies of water

*2. Only through condensing of atmospheric water vapor into rain and snow can water in rivers, lakes, and the ground be resupplied from the ocean reservoir.

*3. Answers will vary.

G. 4. phosphate — dissolves — rivers
in ground   in rainwater
droppings   oceans
birds   eaten by   taken up by
fish   eaten by   algae

CHAPTER REVIEW

Within the diversity of living things all have certain characteristics in common. These features illustrate *the unity within the diversity of living things.*

Life requires a source of energy, the presence of needed materials, a moderate temperature, and protection from harmful radiations and meteorites. These conditions exist within a narrow layer at Earth's surface.

Within the biosphere there is an uneven distribution of heat energy and moisture. These factors cause wide differences in climate and changes in weather within each biome. Because of great differences in the biosphere and the variations among living things, organisms are not equally fit for a specific environment. Thus living things are distributed unevenly in the biosphere.

The materials that make up the bodies of living things are limited in amount. When an organism dies, its materials are recycled. Recycling frees substances for the next generations of organisms. This recycling illustrates the *interactions of organisms with the environment.*

Using the Concepts

1. Describe a life-support system that would allow you to survive in space.
2. What are some of the problems involved in using the ocean as a food source?

VOCABULARY REVIEW

1. environment
   diversity
   natural cycles
   mass
   density

2. biosphere
   estuary
   biome
   humus
   deciduous forest
   desert

3. water cycle
   phosphorus cycle
   guano

CHAPTER 1 TEST

Copy the number of each test item and place your answer to the right.

PART 1   Multiple Choice: Select the letter of the phrase that best completes each of the following.

c **1.** Earth's atmosphere protects living things by absorbing radiation in the form of **a.** light **b.** infrared **c.** ultraviolet **d.** X rays.

b **2.** Many of the materials important to living things are concentrated near Earth's surface because of their **a.** high density **b.** low density **c.** heat holding ability **d.** temperature.

a **3.** Earth's temperature varies between **a.** 58° and −88°C **b.** 122° and −173°C **c.** 30° and 0°C **d.** 0° and 100°C.

d **4.** Temperature is important to living things because it affects **a.** proteins **b.** water **c.** the rate of chemical reactions **d.** all of these.

c **5.** The cycles forest animals are least affected by are **a.** day-night **b.** seasonal **c.** tidal **d.** reproductive.

b **6.** The part of soil which greatly increases its ability to hold water and minerals is **a.** rock **b.** humus **c.** air **d.** living things.

b **7.** Most rain or snow that falls on the land condenses as water vapor that originated from **a.** rivers and lakes **b.** oceans **c.** underground water **d.** plants.

b **8.** Phosphorus is returned from the seas to the land through slow geologic processes and **a.** rain and snow **b.** bird droppings **c.** the water cycle **d.** ocean currents.

c **9.** What we commonly refer to as jungle is the **a.** chaparral **b.** tropical rain forest **c.** tropical deciduous forest **d.** mid-latitude deciduous forest.

a **10.** The differences in living things are called **a.** diversity **b.** unity **c.** interaction **d.** cycling.

PART 2   Matching: Match the letter of the term in Column I with its description in Column II.

COLUMN I

a. biosphere
b. biome
c. estuary
d. deciduous forest
e. tropical rain forest
f. grassland
g. guano
h. humus
i. desert
j. density

COLUMN II

c **11.** A partially enclosed portion of the sea which is fed by a freshwater stream

i **12.** Areas receiving 25 centimeters or less of rainfall a year

a **13.** Earth's life-supporting layer of air, soil, and water

g **14.** Phosphorus-rich deposits of bird droppings

e **15.** A biome in which most nutrients are bound up in plant tissue resulting in infertile soil with little humus

f **16.** A biome in which fertile soil contains much humus

h **17.** Partially decomposed plant and animal tissue or wastes

j **18.** The amount of mass in a given volume of a substance

b **19.** Any major plant community maintained by a certain climate

d **20.** A biome of trees that lose their leaves during dry or cold seasons

PART 3   Completion: Complete the following.

21. Three advantages that Earth's surface provides for living things are ____.

22. Mass is a measure of ____.

23. One example of an interaction in the environment is ____.

24. Three characteristics adapting organisms for life in fast-flowing streams are ____.

25. Middle latitude biomes listed in order of decreasing rainfall are ____.

Chapter 1 Test Answers

21. protective atmosphere, moderate temperature, and important chemical substances

22. a body's tendency to resist changes in its motion.

23. water cycle or seasonal cycles and the day-night cycle on plants and animals

24. Some organisms: permanent attachment to objects, streamlined bodies, flattened bodies

25. deciduous forest, chaparral, grasslands, taiga, tundra

CHAPTER 2

INTERRELATION - SHIPS IN THE ENVIRONMENT

If Earth with its oceans, land areas, and atmosphere is the stage, the plants, animals, and microscopic organisms that inhabit the planet are the actors. In Chapter 1 we set the stage. In this chapter we will observe various events. These are woven together to form the exciting drama taking place on that great stage, Planet Earth. Figure 2-1 portrays part of that stage and its cast of actors. The ways these events are woven together form interrelationships in the environment.

We can study interrelationships by focusing on some basic concepts. These include: *structure-function relationships*, and *interactions of organisms with their environment*.

Consider the basic concept that is the relationship existing between a structure and its function. For example, a flesh-eating hawk has a hooked beak and a seed-eating cardinal has a short, stout beak. Animals spend much of their time getting food which is their source of energy. Plants use the energy from light to make food. The human population makes use of both the plants' and animals' ability to convert energy into usable forms. How living things get energy is influenced by the structure-function relationship.

The increase in human population will increase the stress on Earth's limited resources, especially its natural communities. But human beings are subject to the same forces that control the lives of all organisms. The understanding of these forces may be necessary for our survival.

In this chapter we will investigate many ways in which living things affect each other:

- What value to the community are organisms of decay?
- How do termites get energy from wood?
- Why does crowding cause some problems to get worse?
- What happens if a farmer or gardener abandons a field?

TADPOLES IN A POND

◘ NUTRITIONAL RELATIONSHIPS AMONG ORGANISMS

OBJECTIVES FOR SECTION 1

A. Define *nutrition* and the terms that describe nutritional relationships.

B. Give five examples of special adaptations in each predator organism and prey organism.

C. Draw and describe a *food chain* and a *food web*.

Obtain examples of local producers and primary and secondary consumers from students or supply them for study.

2-1. Deer are common at the edge of meadows and mountain forests. What might be reasons for lack of vegetation in these areas?

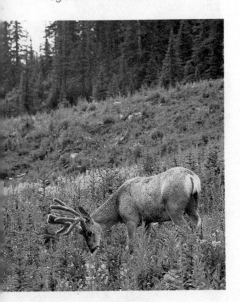

Cells and Nutrition

The basic unit of structure and function of organisms is the **cell**. The simplest organisms are unicellular. Each is composed of a single cell. Most plants, fungi, and animals are multicellular, composed of many cells. An adult human being is composed of about 60 million million (6×10^{13}) cells. About 100 different kinds are present like red cells of the blood, nerve cells, and muscle cells.

It is the functions of individual cells that determine the needs of the entire organism. One of these functions is nutrition. **Nutrition** *is taking in and using organic food for energy, growth, or repair of living things.* Organic substances are compounds that contain carbon. Compounds result when simple substances called elements combine chemically. Originally found mainly in organisms, compounds containing the element carbon were called organic compounds. Only the simplest carbon compounds, such as carbon dioxide, are not considered to be organic. These and cell substances without carbon are said to be inorganic.

Nutrition may be either autotrophic or heterotrophic. **Autotrophic nutrition** *refers to the making and use of organic compounds from inorganic substances in the environment.* For example, green plants are autotrophic. **Heterotrophic nutrition** *is the use of already-made organic compounds.* All animals are heterotrophic.

Since all organisms require organic food, nutrition is involved in some of the best known interrelationships among organisms. Even small children know that cows eat grass or hay. Some birds eat insects. And cats eat birds. Food provides energy and substances. Organisms use these to grow, replace parts, and to carry out all of their activities.

Producers and Consumers

A deer eating green plants represents a consumer-producer relationship. (See Fig. 2-1.) *Because the clover plant is autotrophic and able to produce its own food, it is a* **producer**. A green pigment, chlorophyll, in a plant's leaves absorbs energy from sunlight. The energy plus water and carbon dioxide are converted into an organic substance, carbohydrate, and oxygen gas. *This complex food-making process using light energy is* **photosynthesis** (fō tə *sin* thə sis). It will be discussed in Chapter 7. Carbohydrates can be changed into other substances that the plant uses. The oxygen gas is released into the atmosphere. Both plants and animals use oxygen to get energy from food.

The rabbit is heterotrophic and depends on food made by plants. When the rabbit eats the plant the rabbit is a consumer. **Consumers** *are organisms that eat other living things or their remains. Animals that eat only plants are primary consumers or* **herbivores** (*hur* bə vôrs).

The rabbit, in turn, may be eaten by a coyote. In this case, the coyote is a *secondary consumer* because it eats the primary consumer. *Any animal that eats mostly other animals is a* **carnivore** (*kär* nə vôr). *Any organism that devours another organism is called a* **predator**. *The organisms eaten by predators are the* **prey**.

Special Adaptations in Predators and their Prey

The obtaining of food is important in the lives of animals. This has resulted in special adaptations in various predators. **Adaptations** *are features which help any organism survive in its environment.* (See Table 2-1.)

Think of predators in your area and describe the special adaptations that fit them for capturing their prey.

While predators are adapted to capture and kill, their prey are adapted for escape. The ptarmigan with its mottled brown plumage in summer and its white plumage in winter blends in with its surroundings. (See Fig. 2-2.) The scent gland of the skunk is an effective defense mechanism. Certain plants have protective spines, unpleasant odors, or a bitter taste. The tasty viceroy butterfly looks much like the bitter-tasting monarch butterfly. (See Fig. 2-3.) The squid often escapes its predators by releasing an underwater "smoke screen." Then it propels itself away unseen.

TABLE 2-1 ADAPTATIONS OF SOME PREDATORS

Predator	Adaptation
Cheetah	speed
Great Horned Owl	silent flight
Black Widow Spider	poison
Eel	electric shock
Bobcat	teeth and claws
Woodpecker	beak and barbed tongue
Web-spinning Spider	trap building

2-2. *In late winter ptarmigans molt and change color from white to mottled brown.*

2-3. Monarch butterfly, above; viceroy butterfly, below.

2-4. Bacteria and fungi are saprophytes. They cause leaves to decay on the forest floor. Materials from the leaves are recycled into the soil and air. These materials can then be used again by green plants.

Some animals cooperate with others of their kind to protect themselves from predators. As a honeybee stings an intruder it releases a substance. Its odor attracts other bees of the colony who join the attack. These organisms all show specific features of structure, color, or behavior. These equip them for escaping their predators. Because of the protective adaptations in their prey, most carnivorous predators work hard for their kills. For this reason many predators kill no more than what they can eat.

Both predators and their prey play important roles in nature. The prey provide food for their predators. Predators often limit the number of their prey. The surviving prey then usually can get enough food. Hence, the best adapted prey are able to produce the next generation. In this manner coyotes prevent an overpopulation of rabbits. The remaining rabbits have enough food to grow and have healthy young.

Other Nutritional Relationships

Similar to the predator-prey relationship is the parasite-host relationship. A tick attaches itself to a dog's ear and sucks blood. A tapeworm absorbs nourishment from inside the dog's intestine. *A parasite is an organism that lives on or in the body of another organism, the host, from which it receives nourishment.* The host receives no benefit. It is damaged to some degree but the relationship is usually not fatal. If it were, the parasite would have to find a new host or die.

While predators catch their prey alive, some carnivores find dead animals to eat. A vulture may eat the remains of a dead sheep. A dung beetle depends on feces for food. *Animals that feed on dead organisms or the wastes of organisms and digest them in their intestines are scavengers.*

Other organisms like the common bread mold produce substances which convert the starch of bread into sugar. The dissolved sugar is then absorbed by the mold. A mushroom in a similar way digests the wood of a dead tree. *Organisms which secure their food by absorbing it from decaying organic matter are saprophytes* (sap rə fīts). This group of organisms includes most fungi and bacteria. (See Fig. 2-4.)

Scavengers, saprophytes, and a host of insects, worms, millipedes, and pillbugs need both energy and minerals. They obtain these by breaking down the bodies of dead organisms and wastes. *All consumers that derive nourishment by decomposing dead organisms and wastes are decomposers.* No one kind can produce complete decay. Therefore, a variety of decomposers is necessary to finish the task.

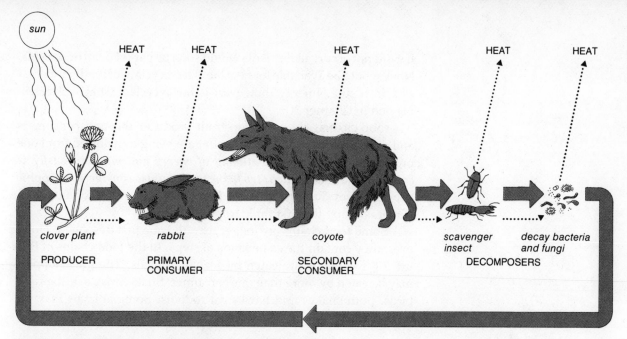

2-5. The paths of energy (--→) and matter (→) through a food chain. Energy runs a one way course. Matter is recycled. If it were not recycled, all matter would be tied up in dead organisms. In each step some energy escapes as heat.

Pathways of Energy and Matter in Food Chains

The paths of energy and matter in the relationships described above are summarized in Figure 2-5. Energy from the sun was stored in the food produced in the plant. The plant was consumed by the rabbit. The rabbit was consumed by the coyote. When the coyote dies, its body is decomposed by a variety of insects, worms, fungi, and bacteria. The substances in the coyote's body are released. These are made available for reuse. Decomposition is extremely important.

2-6. Food chains are interconnected to form complex food webs.

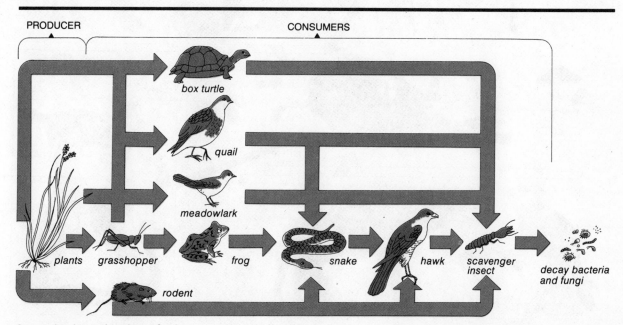

Arrange local organisms into a food chain or web.

If it did not occur, all nutrients would soon be part of dead organisms. None would be available for new life. The recycling of matter is necessary in nature. Energy, however, is not recycled. That will be explained in Chapter 3.

FOOD CHAINS At each step from producer through consumers and decomposers, energy and matter are being transferred from one organism to another. *A pathway of energy and matter transfer is called a* **food chain.** *Each step in the food chain is considered a* **trophic** (*trō* fik) **level.** Producers, primary consumers, and secondary consumers occupy the first three trophic levels.

Some food chains are longer than the one just described. However, they contain the same kinds of steps. In the food chains of Figure 2-6 the plants are eaten by several animals. The grasshoppers may be eaten by more than one consumer. Snakes may eat frogs and birds. Both snakes and hawks eat rodents. Some animals may eat both primary and secondary consumers. *Some are* **omnivores,** *that is*

2-7. A food web.

A classroom activity that illustrates the web of life is described in the teachers' guide.

2-8. A snake seizes a frog. The frog has eaten a dragonfly which has devoured a butterfly which took nectar from a flower. Which link in the food chain is the snake?

they eat both plant and animal tissue. Box turtles, quail, and people are omnivores.

FOOD WEBS   Because most animals eat and are eaten by a variety of organisms, various food chains are usually interconnected. *The pattern of interconnected food chains is called a* **food web.** Where there are many kinds of organisms, food webs may be complex. (See Fig. 2-7.) An advantage to a complex food web is its several possible routes. If a drought or disease reduces frog populations, quail, meadowlarks, and box turtles continue to eat grasshoppers. Without frogs, snakes can still eat rodents. Natural communities having a large variety of organisms are often less likely to be severely disturbed by changes like the one described. In a simple food chain, if one link is missing, the chain breaks. Only a few kinds of organisms survive the low temperatures of the arctic. The plants are eaten by lemmings. Lemmings are eaten by the arctic fox and the snowy owl. A shortage of either plants or lemmings seriously disrupts the food chain.

QUESTIONS FOR SECTION 1

1. Define and give an example of: interrelationship, producer, consumer, decomposer.
2. Describe predator-prey and parasite-host relationships.
3. Are decomposers also consumers?
4. Look up the meaning of the prefixes hetero- and auto-. Apply those meanings to the terms heterotrophic and autotrophic.
5. Give one special adaptation each of hawks, rattlesnakes, and tigers that adapt them as predators.
6. Give one special adaptation each of cactus, grasshopper, and deer that adapt them to escape their predators.
7. Name several predators from your area and not mentioned in this chapter. What adaptations do they have for capturing prey?
8. Repeat for prey organisms in your community.
9. Draw a food chain or web of the following organisms: honeysuckle flower, robin, butterfly, flea, cat, microorganisms.
10. On what group of organisms do all members of a food chain depend?

Answers to Questions for Section 1

A. 1. Interrelationship: the way events are woven together in the environment; example: how various organisms get and use energy from the environment and one another. Producer: organism able to produce own food; example: clover. Consumer: organism that eats other living things; example: rabbit. Decomposer: consumer that gets food by decomposing dead organisms or wastes; example: fungus.

2. A predator is an organism that devours another organism, the prey. A parasite lives on or in the body of another organism, the host, from which it gets food.

3. Yes. (See answer to 1. above.)

*4. Hetero-: other. Auto-: self. Heterotrophic: using food made by another organism. Autotrophic: makes food for itself.

B. *5. Hawks: beak rattlesnakes: poison fangs; tigers: claws.

*6. Cactus: spines; grasshopper: jumping legs; deer: running ability.

*7. Answers will vary.

*8. Answers will vary.

C. 9. honeysuckle flower→butterfly →robin→cat→flea→micro-organism.

10. Green plants.

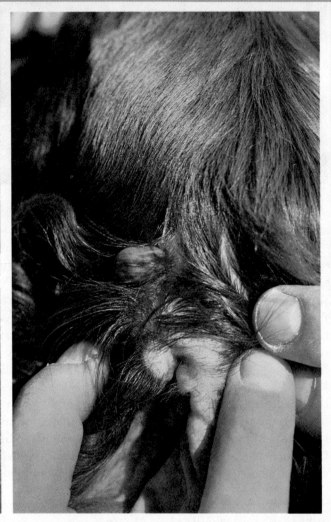

CHAPTER INVESTIGATION

A. What kind of relationship exists between the tick and the dog?

B. How does the tick's survival depend on the dog? What does the dog gain from the relationship?

C. Search the library for information about the tick's life history. How can a tick live for several months, or even years, without a meal? As a tick pierces the dog's skin, the tick's dissolving saliva speeds up the penetration of its mouthparts. How may this saliva occasionally be dangerous to humans?

☑ OTHER INTERSPECIES RELATIONSHIPS

The species concept is discussed further in Chapter 14.

The relationships we have described so far are those between different kinds of organisms. *The term that refers to a particular kind of organism is* **species** (both singular and plural). Later you will learn a more nearly complete definition of species. There are relationships between various species of organisms other than the nutritional ones we have discussed.

Negative Interactions Among Organisms

In the food web just studied not only frogs but other organisms fed on grasshoppers. In the same manner the plants in a garden or forest compete for water, light, and soil nutrients. *Interactions in which two organisms limit another's supply of food, space, nutrients, water, or light are known as* **competition**.

Generally competition is most severe between species with similar needs. Meadowlarks and cotton rats may compete for nesting space, but not for food. Meadowlarks and cowbirds may compete for food. But their nesting habits differ. Lark sparrows probably provide the meadowlarks with the most competition. They share both nesting and eating habits.

In competition, each of the interacting organisms is a possible threat to the others. An example of another type of competition is that between a mold and some kinds of microscopic organisms. The mold *Penicillium notatum* produces a substance. It prevents the growth of these organisms. For this reason penicillin is commonly used to control some kinds of infections. Black walnut trees produce a compound. It inhibits the growth of some nearby plants. In this type of interaction one species thrives as it inhibits the other.

Positive Interactions Among Organisms

COMMENSALISM Competition and the production of growth-inhibiting substances are negative interactions. There are also interactions that benefit one of the reacting species. It does not harm the other. A bluebird occupies a hollow tree limb abandoned by a woodpecker. A remora attaches itself to a shark and consumes scraps of the shark's prey. (See Fig. 2-9.) *A relationship in which one species is benefited but the other is not affected is called* **commensalism** (kə men sə liz əm).

MUTUALISM *When both species benefit in a relationship it is called* **mutualism** (mū choo ə liz əm). An example of mutualism is that of termites and the wood-digesting microorganisms in their in-

2-9. *A remora attaches itself to a shark and consumes scraps left over from the shark's meals.*

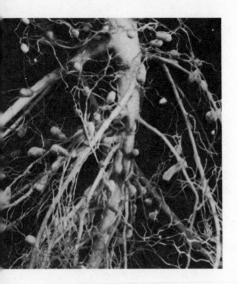

2-10. The nodules on the roots of this legume plant form in response to the invasion by nitrogen-fixing bacteria. What do these bacteria do for the plant? What does the plant do for the bacteria?

testines. When the microorganisms are removed from their digestive tract, the termites starve to death. They are unable to digest the wood they eat. The termites' digestive tract provides a steady supply of food for the microorganisms. The microorganisms digest food for the termites. At the same time, they meet their own needs in the process.

LEGUMES   There is one further important example of mutualism. This is the relationship between certain soil microorganisms and many kinds of plants including legumes. Legumes are plants of the pea family. Examples are beans and peas. Both kinds of organisms can live independently. However, both benefit from living together. This relationship exists since green plants cannot use nitrogen directly from the atmosphere. Legumes contain certain microorganisms in the nodules on their roots. (See Fig. 2-10.) In these nodules the microorganisms carry on a function of importance to the food chain. They convert nitrogen from the air into a form the plant can use. In turn, the legume supplies the microorganisms with nutrients.

THE COMMUNITY   In any sizeable area of the biosphere there are likely to be a number of relationships. These include producer-consumer, predator-prey, and parasite-host relationships. Also, there will be scavengers and saprophytes, the clean-up crew. In addition, there will likely be competition, commensalism, and mutualism. There is interaction among the organisms within each of these events. *A group of interacting organisms form a* **biotic community.** We may speak of a pond community to include all of the organisms living in a pond. We can study a forest community, or the community in a rotting log. The term *biotic* means that a community makes up the living part of the environment.

Answers to Questions for Section 2.

D. 1. Species: a particular kind of organism; examples: meadowlark, cotton rat, cowbird. Biotic community: a group of interacting organisms; examples: pond, forest, rotting log.

E. 2. Competition, (1) in which two individuals or species limit one another's supplies; example: meadowlark and lark sparrow compete for nesting space and food; (2) in which one species thrives as it inhibits the other; example: *Penicillium notatum* inhibits growth of microorganisms.

*3. Answers will vary.

*4. Answers will vary.

F. 5. Commensalism, in which one species benefits but other not affected; example: remora and shark mutualism, in which both benefit; example: termites and wood-digesting micro-organisms.

*6. Mutualism. Each benefits.

QUESTIONS FOR SECTION 2

1. Define and give three examples each of species and biotic communities.
2. Describe and give an example of each of two kinds of negative interactions among organisms.
3. Name two species in your area that compete with each other.
4. Devise an experiment to determine whether a common plant in your area produces a substance that keeps other plants from growing.
5. Describe and give an example of each of two kinds of positive interaction among organisms.
6. Is the relationship between a cow and a farmer or a dog and its owner competition, commensalism, or mutualism? Explain.

3 RELATIONSHIPS WITHIN A SPECIES

Populations

All of the relationships in a community are between individuals of different species. Many important interactions also occur between members of the same species. Consider courtship, mating, and nesting behavior of various animals. For example, two rams fight for the same ewe. In another case, a pecking order is established in a flock of chickens or in a human neighborhood.

Each of these interactions occurs with individuals of the same species. *Any group of interacting, interbreeding, individuals of one kind of organism is a* **population.** Two examples of a population are all the bass in a lake and all the people in a city. We can study a population by observing how it changes over a period of time. An easy population to observe in the classroom is yeast cells. A few yeast cells are added to a solution containing all they need. Each day a sample can be removed. At this point the number of cells are counted. From this, the population density can be estimated. **Population density** *is the number of a particular kind of organism in a limited area.* Data from such an exercise done by a high school biology class are graphed in Figure 2-11. Why is there such a rapid population increase at first? Why doesn't it continue?

Population Trends

Population trends have been studied for some time. As early as 1755 Benjamin Franklin noticed that populations of organisms tend to grow rapidly. In 1798 Thomas Malthus, an English clergyman, noted that a "population, when unchecked, increases in a geometric ratio." **Geometric population growth** *is one that each year, or each generation, increases by a constant percentage of the population.* For example, a population that increases 100% each year is doubling each year. Beginning with 100 organisms, in three years we would have 100×2^3 = 800 or $(100 \times 2 \times 2 \times 2)$.

Population Control Factors

Let us return to our yeast population. In the beginning they have all the nutrients, oxygen, and water they need. They are held at a proper temperature. They are not poisoned by wastes. They are not destroyed or inhibited by predators or parasites. Therefore, their reproductive rate (natality) is high. For the same reasons the death rate (mortality) is low. Under such ideal conditions, the new population grows rapidly. For a while, it will follow the geometric growth pattern suggested by Malthus.

OBJECTIVES FOR SECTION 3

G. Define each of the following: *population, population density, carrying capacity, home range, territory, geometric population growth.*

H. Describe ideal conditions for a small new population, and factors that affect growth of a population.

I. List four density-dependent factors and four density-independent factors that determine population growth.

J. Explain how crowding is prevented among animals of a species and among plants of a species.

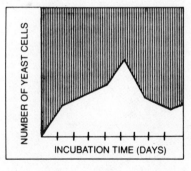

2-11. *The growth of a yeast population. Can you explain the changes in yeast population density?*

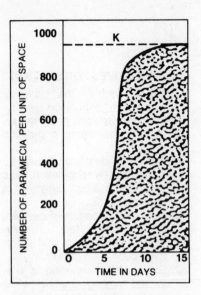

2-12. *The S-shaped growth curve of a Paramecium population being fed a constant amount of bacteria each day. The population increased geometrically for about 10 days. It then leveled out as density neared the carrying capacity, K.*

In time, however, food and oxygen supplies are reduced. Wastes accumulate. Parasites may enter and multiply. Even though the population has increased, the space has not. For these reasons, the rate of population growth levels off. The rate varies for a time, and then the population dies out.

The yeast cells were in a closed system that allowed no migration. However, in most natural communities, migration can occur. For example, individual turtles may leave a woodlot or emigrate. Others may enter from elsewhere or immigrate.

Graphing a young population in an ideal habitat often gives an S-shaped curve. A small *Paramecium* population was fed daily with a constant supply of bacteria. Figure 2-12 shows that the population grew geometrically at first. Finally, it leveled off. The population had reached the environment's carrying capacity. **Carrying capacity** *is the number of individuals of a species that a particular environment can support indefinitely.*

DENSITY-DEPENDENT FACTORS In a natural community additional factors that may limit a population become important. As the density of a population of mice increases, the rate at which the mice reproduce usually drops. When a population of mice is dense, predators find them easier to catch. Diseases spread more quickly. Parasites transfer more easily. Thus, the death rate increases. Some of the mice may emigrate. As food supplies are depleted, members of the population may kill and eat each other. In these ways, population densities tend to be regulated. The more dense the population the greater the effect of these factors. *Population control factors that have a greater effect as population density increases are known as* **density-dependent factors.** The factors of reproductive rate, predation, disease, parasitism, death rate, and migration are density-dependent factors.

DENSITY-INDEPENDENT FACTORS Other population-limiting factors are not influenced by population density. Among these are certain physical conditions. Some of these are temperature, rainfall patterns, and humidity. A hard freeze will kill all ragweeds in a field whether there are only two or 200. *Population-limiting factors that are not influenced by population density are called* **density-independent factors.**

Competition Within a Species

One of the interrelationships observed in both populations and communities is competition. Competition is most severe between organisms with similar needs. Thus, the meadowlark's keenest competitor is another meadowlark. All meadowlarks require the same needs for food, nesting sites, and mates.

Plants of the same species are competitors also. Ragweeds growing in the same field have similar needs for water and minerals. They all have about the same length of roots through which they fulfill these needs.

One solution to this severe competition between individuals of a species is to spread them out in space. Robins gather in flocks during the winter. But they separate into different territories before the breeding season. These territories are identified by songs and other behavioral displays. Male sunfish defend their "nesting" areas in the shallows of a pond. They display colorful fins and dart toward intruders of the same species. *The area to which an individual or small group of animals confines its activities is called a* **home range.** *If the area is actively defended, it is called a* **territory.** Distributing individuals or pairs into territories prevents overcrowding and reduces competition. Reducing competition and confining activities to a limited area conserves energy. Food resources for the species are thus gathered from a larger area.

Some animals and plants achieve isolation by chemical means. For example, the giant ragweed releases a substance into the soil water which inhibits the growth of other nearby plants. In high concentrations, the substance may also inhibit the growth of the plant's own seedlings. The substance builds up in the soil during drought. Thus, it prevents high population density where water supply is limited. When rainfall increases, the inhibiting substance is diluted and becomes less effective.

These are but a few of the interactions between members of a species. All of the interactions that we have studied show the complex nature of interrelationships in a natural community.

QUESTIONS FOR SECTION 3

1. Define population, population density, carrying capacity, home range, and territory.
2. Continue the two series for a total of 10 steps: 2, 4, 6, 8, 10 . . . 2, 4, 8, 16, 32 . . . Which illustrates a geometric increase?
3. Why might it be important to know what Earth's carrying capacity for human beings might be?
4. Describe ideal conditions for human population growth. List reasons for the less-than-ideal conditions we experience.
5. List four density-dependent factors that determine population growth.
6. List four density-independent factors that determine population growth.
7. Explain how crowding is avoided among a population of animals.
8. Explain how crowding is avoided among some populations of plants.
9. Why do many hooved grazing animals live in herds if spreading out would make more food available to each individual?

Answers to Questions for Section 3

G. 1. Population: group of interacting, interbreeding individuals of one kind of organism in a limited area. Carrying capacity: number of individuals of a species that a particular environment can support indefinitely. Home range: area to which an individual or small group of animals confines its activities. Territory: home range that is actively defended.

*2. The second, which is completed thus: 64, 128, 256, 512, 1024. The first is completed thus: 12, 14, 16, 18, 20.

*3. Answers will vary.

H. *4. Answers will vary.

I. 5. Reproductive rate, predation, disease, migration.

6. Temperature, rainfall patterns, humidity.

J. 7. By spreading of individuals out in space, thus reducing competition and conserving energy.

8. By chemical means, such as the release of substance into soil water that inhibits growth of nearby plants.

*9. Answers will vary.

4 BIOLOGICAL-PHYSICAL INTERRELATIONSHIPS

Abiotic Factors

All the organisms of a natural community interact with each other. Also, they interact with their nonliving, or abiotic, environment. **Ecology** *is the study of how living things relate to each other and to their nonliving environment.*

We have already seen how populations of organisms may be affected by various weather conditions. A water lily would have as much difficulty in a desert as a cactus would have in a pond. There are many abiotic factors in the environment that affect living things. Some of these are the climate, the fertility of the soil, and water.

Furthermore, the physical environment of organisms can be changed by the activities of these organisms. Your breathing affects the composition of the air that surrounds you. In addition, plant, animal, and microbial activity affect the soil.

ECOSYSTEMS   All of the interactions we have discussed occur in an ecosystem. *An* **ecosystem** *is a combination of a biotic community and the nonliving environment with which it interacts.* An ecosystem may be all the contents of a field, a cave, a forest, a pond, or an aquarium. (See Fig. 2-13.) An ecosystem is a useful unit in which to study energy flow and matter cycles.

The Carbon Cycle

Green plants use the sun's radiant energy to make food. To do this the green plant uses several elements and inorganic compounds. The recycling of these substances through the food chain is illustrated with matter cycle diagrams. (See Fig. 2-14.)

Carbon makes up about 18% by weight of living substances. This carbon comes from the atmosphere which is about 0.03% carbon dioxide. Green plants take in carbon dioxide from the air. It combines with hydrogen to produce carbohydrates. These carbohydrates can be converted into other nutrients such as fats and proteins. The carbohydrates, fats, and proteins make up the cells of the plant body.

When herbivores consume plants, those carbon-containing substances are converted into substances needed to make the cells of that animal. At each step of the food chain — producers, consumers, decomposers — some of these substances are used to release energy. This occurs through the process of respiration. The energy from food is released by producers, consumers, and decomposers to return carbon dioxide to the atmosphere. Here it is available once again to green plants. Hence we say that the carbon has been recycled. When water

2-13. A pond ecosystem. How does an ecosystem differ from a community?

organisms use food as fuel they release carbon dioxide into the water, where it is used by water plants and algae. Photosynthesis in plants and the respiration of plants and animals complement each other.

CARBON RESERVOIRS   Excess carbon dioxide in the atmosphere is absorbed by the oceans. As its concentration increases in the oceans, more of it is converted into limestone. The limestone settles out of the oceans as rock. In addition, skeletons and shells of sea animals settle to the bottom of the ocean when they die. Thus, the great stores of carbon are the atmosphere, the oceans, and the rock deposited at the ocean bottom. Carbon is also stored in the form of coal and oil. As these fuels are burned, carbon dioxide is returned to the atmosphere. Volcanic activity also returns carbon to the atmosphere.

CLOSED CYCLE   The movement of carbon is basically a closed cycle. It passes from atmosphere or ocean through the producer-consumer-decomposer chain. Also, as the amount of carbon dioxide in the atmosphere decreases, more is returned to it from the sea.

Such delicate balances are common in the biosphere. The carbon dioxide content of the atmosphere has increased during the last 20 years. This is due largely to the burning of fuels and the removal of plants through the clearing of forests. What this increase means to us will be discussed in Chapter 4.

2-14. *The carbon cycle.*

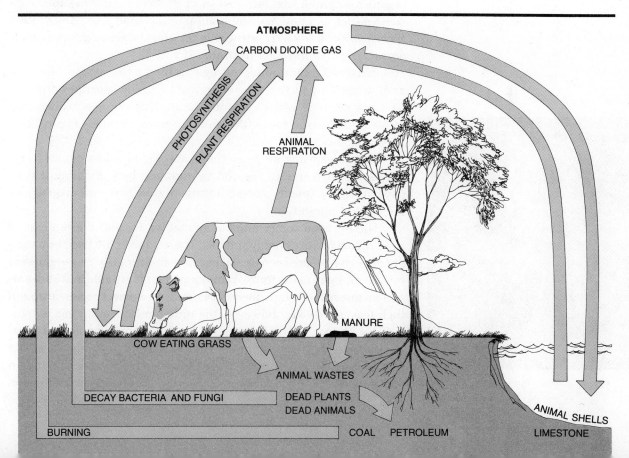

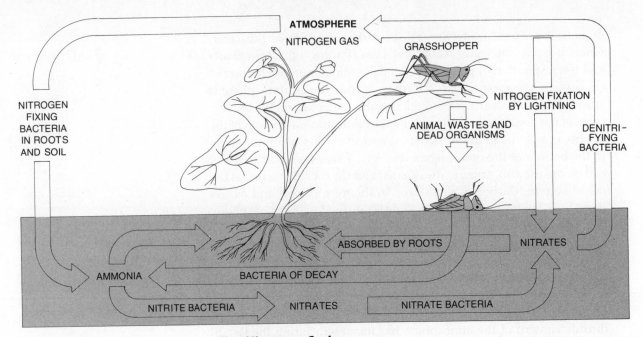

ATMOSPHERE
NITROGEN GAS

GRASSHOPPER

NITROGEN FIXATION
BY LIGHTNING

NITROGEN
FIXING
BACTERIA
IN ROOTS
AND SOIL

ANIMAL WASTES AND
DEAD ORGANISMS

DENITRI-
FYING
BACTERIA

ABSORBED BY ROOTS

NITRATES

AMMONIA

BACTERIA OF DECAY

NITRITE BACTERIA

NITRATES

NITRATE BACTERIA

2-15. *The nitrogen cycle.*

The Nitrogen Cycle

Nitrogen is another element that is important to all living things. It makes up about 79% of the atmosphere. While it is plentiful, most organisms cannot use nitrogen until it is converted to other substances such as ammonia, ammonium nitrate, and urea. *Any process that chemically converts nitrogen in the atmosphere to chemical compounds is called* **nitrogen fixation.**

In natural communities, nitrogen is fixed two ways, by lightning and by microorganisms. The energy of lightning separates nitrogen so it can combine with oxygen in the air. The nitrogen oxides thus formed are dissolved in the rain to form nitrates. Figure 2-15 illustrates the cycle.

Microorganisms such as those associated with legumes and others that live free in the soil fix nitrogen by combining it with oxygen. Thus, plants absorb nitrogen from the soil, usually in the form of nitrates.

The nitrogen compounds in animal wastes and the proteins of dead organisms are energy sources. These sources are used by a variety of decomposers such as soil bacteria and fungi. These organisms release nitrogen in the form of ammonia. Plants are able to absorb ammonia directly through their roots and, in some species, through their leaves. Usually, however, the nitrogen from ammonia is combined with oxygen. This is caused by other organisms called nitrifying bacteria. *The formation of nitrates by bacteria is called* **nitrification.** Another group of bacteria changes nitrates to nitrogen and returns it to the atmosphere. These denitrifying bacteria live in

2-16. *Lichens on rock.*

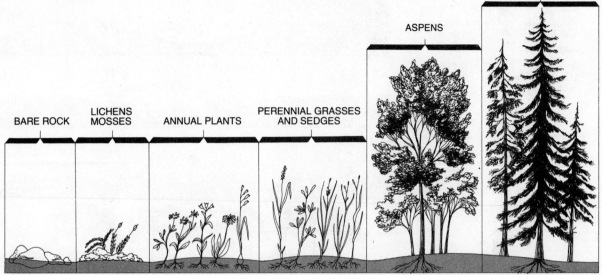

BARE ROCK   LICHENS MOSSES   ANNUAL PLANTS   PERENNIAL GRASSES AND SEDGES   ASPENS   SPRUCE-FIR FOREST

soils that are low in oxygen. They use nitrates as an oxygen source. Denitrification is common in soils that have their air spaces filled with water for long periods of time. Such soils have low fertility.

2-17. *In the taiga biome, succession usually proceeds to the climax stage, the spruce-fir forest. This climax is determined by climate and geology.*

Ecologic Succession

Plant and animal communities are not permanent. The taiga biome reaches from Maine across Canada and Alaska. It is characterized by spruce-fir forests. But occasional areas of exposed rock interrupt the forests. The bare rock may harbor lichens. These organisms produce food and then decay. (See Fig. 2-16.) The carbon dioxide lichens release dissolves in rainwater, forming an acid. The action of the acid dissolves rock. The freezing and thawing of water in the cracks of the rock gradually breaks them apart. These rock bits and the decay of dying lichens produce enough soil to support mosses. The mosses crowd out the lichens and prepare the way for short-lived seed plants. Eventually longer-lived plants are able to grow. In time, aspens that thrive in sunlight appear. In the shade of the aspens, the seedlings of spruce and fir appear. They grow tall and produce too much shade for the aspens. These spruce and fir finally replace them. *The series of progressive changes in plant and animal communities in an area is called* **ecological succession.** Study this example of succession in Figure 2-17.

Figure 2-18 is an example of succession that takes place when a pond fills in. The erosion of soil from the surrounding watershed supports the development of meadow vegetation. This change finally leads to the spruce-fir forest.

Non-legumes capable of forming mutualistic relationships which fix nitrogen include many trees and shrubs.

Abandoned, infertile fields follow certain stages of succession as they slowly return to the final climax stage characteristic of the area. Ask students for photos of local areas they have taken over the years. Arrange them chronologically for study.

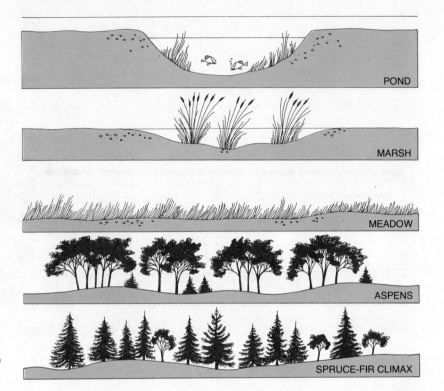

POND

MARSH

MEADOW

ASPENS

SPRUCE-FIR CLIMAX

2-18. *Many small lakes and ponds are temporary disturbances in an ecosystem. They fill in and proceed toward their climax stage.*

BIOSPHERE
BIOMES
ECOSYSTEMS
COMMUNITY PLUS NONLIVING ENVIRONMENT
COMMUNITIES
POPULATIONS
INDIVIDUALS
ORGAN SYSTEMS
ORGANS
TISSUES
CELLS
ORGANELLES
MOLECULES

2-19. *Living things can be organized in various ways. Each level of organization is based on the one below it.*

As succession proceeds, one population of plants can change the environment. This change makes it unfavorable for itself and more favorable for another species. Usually the changes produced result in more than the replacement of one population. These changes involve replacement of the whole community of plants and animals. The spruce-fir forest supports a different group of animals and microorganisms than the meadow did.

The final stage of ecological succession seems to be determined by the climate and geology of the area. Fires, overgrazing, farming, lumbering, droughts, and floods interrupt the process of succession. They return it temporarily to an earlier stage of succession.

Habitats and Niches

As we observe an ecosystem, we see that organisms are not distributed uniformly. Redwings nest in the cattails at the edge of the pond. Meadowlarks nest out in the prairie grasses. The great blue heron incubates her eggs high in a sycamore tree. A beaver munches on willow twigs in the water. Each of these organisms lives in a particular place. *Where an organism lives is its* **habitat.**

As important as an organism's habitat is its **niche** (*nich*) –*the role it plays in the ecosystem.* Its niche includes the organism's position in the food chain and whether it is active during the day or night. It also includes how it behaves, how it changes its environment, with whom and how it interacts.

QUESTIONS FOR SECTION 4

1. Define ecosystem.
2. Define and give two examples of ecologic succession.
3. Explain each step in the carbon cycle diagram.
4. Explain each step in the nitrogen cycle diagram.
5. What human activities during the last two centuries may be affecting the carbon cycle? How? The nitrogen cycle? Explain.
6. Define habitat and niche.
7. How do the terms habitat and niche differ?
8. What are the relationships between an organism's niche and its habitat?
9. For an ecosystem you are familiar with, explain the relationships among individual populations and communities.

Answers to Questions for Section 4

K. 1. Combination of a biotic community and the nonliving environment with which it interacts.

2. Series of progressive changes in plant and animal communities in an area. lichens → moss → seed plants → aspens → spruce forest; pond → meadow → forest.

L. 3. See pages 32-33. Release of CO_2 into atmosphere and decay. Capture of CO_2 by plants, and solution in water. Storage of CO_2 in plants and cycle is repeated.

(See page 36 for other answers.)

CHAPTER REVIEW

Living things relate to each other and to their nonliving environment in many ways. These *relationships* often involve energy interactions. Autotrophic organisms store energy in the foods they make. Heterotrophic organisms get their energy from foods made by the autotrophs. Food chains trace matter and energy through producers, consumers, and decomposers. They illustrate the cycling of matter and the flow and use of energy.

The *relationship between structures and their functions* are clearly seen in the adaptations of predators to capture their prey. Their prey are likewise adapted for escape.

Using the Concepts

1. Devise an experiment that would show whether or not shade tolerance (or nutrient requirements) is a factor involved in succession in a specific community.

Unanswered Question

2. It is estimated that 99.9 percent of all species of organisms that have ever existed are now extinct. Should we be concerned about extinctions? Explain.

Career Activities

3. Determine which business and agencies in your area employ ecologists. Contact the ecologists and ask them about training requirements, professional opportunities, and satisfaction with their vocation.
4. Of what advantage might a knowledge of ecology have for a physician, legislator, farmer, rancher, detective, city engineer, homemaker, and gardener?

VOCABULARY REVIEW

ecology	predator	food chain	legume	4 ecosystem
interrelationships	prey	trophic level	biotic community	respiration
1 autotrophic	adaptations	omnivores	3 population	nitrogen fixation
heterotrophic	parasite	food web	population density	nitrification
producer	host	2 species	geometric growth	ecologic succession
consumer	scavenger	competition	carrying capacity	habitat
herbivores	saprophyte	commensalism	home range	niche
carnivores	decomposer	mutualism	territory	

CHAPTER 2 TEST

Copy the number of each test item and place your answer to the right.

PART 1 Multiple Choice: Select the letter of the phrase that best completes each of the following.

c 1. The chemistry of organic compounds is based on the element **a.** oxygen **b.** hydrogen **c.** carbon **d.** nitrogen.

d 2. Meadowlarks are primary consumers. They live in grasslands. These facts identify the meadowlarks' **a.** habitat and niche **b.** trophic level and habitat **c.** niche and trophic level **d.** niche and habitat.

d 3. Animals such as vultures or dung beetles which feed on dead organisms or body wastes are **a.** saprophytes **b.** predators **c.** parasites **d.** scavengers.

c 4. Organisms which absorb food from decaying organic matter are **a.** hosts **b.** parasites **c.** saprophytes **d.** scavengers.

d 5. In order to release nutrients from dead organisms, a community must have producers, consumers, and **a.** parasites **b.** herbivores **c.** carnivores **d.** decomposers.

c 6. A correct way to represent population density of oak trees would be **a.** 10 trees **b.** 10 oak trees **c.** 10 oak trees/hectare **d.** 10/hectare.

c 7. A food web is more likely to survive the loss of one link if it is **a.** long **b.** short **c.** complex **d.** simple.

b 8. A group of interacting organisms form a/an **a.** ecosystem **b.** biotic community **c.** population **d.** biome.

a 9. The interaction of organisms and their nonliving environment is a/an **a.** ecosystem **b.** biotic community **c.** population **d.** home range.

c 10. The series of changes by which bare rock becomes a forest or an abandoned field becomes a prairie is ecologic **a.** mutualism **b.** commensalism **c.** succession **d.** recycling.

PART 2 Matching: Match the letter of the term in Column I with its description in Column II.

COLUMN I

a. ecology   **e.** food web   **i.** predation
b. nutrition   **f.** mutualism   **j.** competition
c. autotrophic **g.** commensalism
d. heterotrophic **h.** parasitism

COLUMN II

f 11. A relationship between two kinds of organisms in which both benefit from the association

a 12. The study of how living things relate to each other and to their nonliving environment

d 13. The type of nutrition in consumers

j 14. A relationship between two kinds of organisms, or two organisms of the same kind, in which both have about the same needs

b 15. The taking in and using of organic food for energy, growth, and replacing of cells

i 16. A relationship between two kinds of organisms in which one benefits by killing and eating the other

e 17. A term that describes the complex nutritional relationships within a community

h 18. A relationship between two kinds of organisms in which one benefits at the expense of the other but often without killing it

c 19. The nutrition in green plants

g 20. A relationship between two kinds of organisms in which one benefits but the other is apparently unaffected

PART 3 Completion: Complete the following.

21. An example of the relation between structure and function is ____.

22. Four population control factors that affect larger proportions of individuals as population density increases are ____.

23. Three population control factors unaffected by population density are ____.

24. List the next two numbers in the geometric growth sequence: 1000, 1500, 2250 . . . ____.

25. Before atmospheric nitrogen can be used by plants, it must first be ____.

Chapter 2 Test Answers

21. answers will vary
22. reproductive rate, predation, disease, parasitism.
23. temperature, rainfall patterns, humidity.
24. 3375, 5062.5
25. converted to other substances by nitrogen fixation.

CHAPTER 3

ENERGY IN THE ENVIRONMENT

Among the interrelationships discussed in Chapter 2 were those related to food-getting. We saw that all organisms require food as a source of energy. We saw that energy from the sun is passed through a chain of organisms ending with decomposers. It is time to take another step in our understanding of energy in the biosphere.

When an automobile runs out of gasoline, its engine stops. An engine needs a continuous supply of energy to keep going. In a similar way, living organisms need a continuous supply of energy to stay alive. Ecosystems need a continuous supply of energy to function. *Interaction of organisms and their environment* is the major concept you will find in this chapter.

The use of scientific methods of investigation is also given special attention. You now know enough about organisms to use scientific methods to find out more. Scientific methods are really logical ways of thinking. They include gathering observations, organizing them, and searching for order in them. Curiosity and logical reasoning are helpful in the study of biology. They are also useful tools in all other areas of life.

From your study of energy and scientific methods you may be able to answer questions like:

- Is it possible to recycle energy?
- Why doesn't Earth get hotter as it keeps absorbing energy from the sun?
- How do biologists measure the energy content of living things?
- How efficient is modern agriculture?
- Why is hamburger more expensive than potatoes?
- What is a good hypothesis?
- How do scientists learn new things?

THE SUN, SOURCE OF OUR ENERGY

1 SCIENTIFIC INVESTIGATION

How Do We Learn About Energy?

Let us use the study of energy in organisms to see how scientific methods work. Biology is more than a collection of facts. Equally important is its role in seeking new knowledge. Biologists are always making new observations. Without this seeking there would be no body of knowledge. Though scientists use many designs, the method shown in Figure 3-1 is in common use.

Asking a Good Question

Heat energy is often given off by living organisms. Which life processes release heat? Do germinating (sprouting) seeds release heat? If so, how much heat is released? Asking good questions is not always easy. Scientists must learn to ask the kinds of questions that can be answered by observation.

Making Observations

Scientists first must clearly state the question or define the problem. Next, they make careful observations. You may have noticed that as seeds germinate, part of the seed gets smaller. Perhaps stored food is being used to supply nutrients and energy to the growing plants. If so, perhaps some heat energy is released. To gather evidence, we can place moist pea seeds and a thermometer in a vacuum bottle.

Developing an Hypothesis

We observe that the moist pea seeds usually germinate. Also, we observe that the temperature around them increases. We find the same thing happens if we repeat the experiment several times. If these observations convince us that germinating seeds release heat energy, we are using inductive reasoning. **Inductive reasoning** *is the development of a general statement based on a collection of observations.* Inductive reasoning leads to the formation of an hypothesis (hī *poth ə sis*). *An* **hypothesis** *is a temporary explanation.* For example, we might hypothesize that germinating seeds release energy. We use this hypothesis to predict the results of similar experiments. The hypothesis must be stated in such a way that it can be tested. Our hypothesis regarding the seeds might be that moist seeds will give off heat as food in the seeds is used for the development of the plant.

Designing an Experiment

To test an hypothesis one designs controlled laboratory or field observations. A prediction is made on the basis of the hypothesis. For

OBJECTIVES FOR SECTION 1

A. Define and give examples of *inductive reasoning, hypothesis, deductive reasoning, control treatment, experimental treatment*.

B. Design an experiment to test an hypothesis.

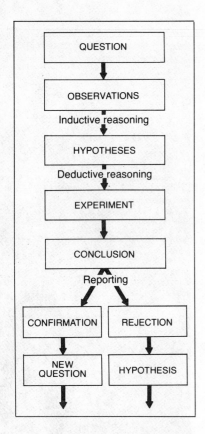

3-1. A summary of the research method showing points at which inductive and deductive reasoning are made. Reporting is needed so that other investigators can review work and build on it.

this, deductive reasoning is used. Earlier, we said that inductive reasoning proceeds from many observations to a general statement. **Deductive reasoning** *proceeds from the general statement to a specific case.* For example:

General statement: Moist seeds will give off heat as food in the seeds is used for the development of the plant.

Specific case: Moist pea seeds will increase the temperature in a vacuum bottle.

A successful prediction based on that general statement would support the hypothesis. The hypothesis, however, will never be proven. After a hundred successful predictions the next might be unsuccessful. Each unsuccessful prediction would weaken one's confidence in the hypothesis. For example, we may find a kind of seed that when moistened failed to give off heat.

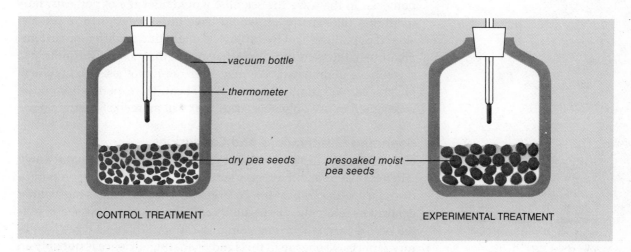

vacuum bottle

thermometer

dry pea seeds

presoaked moist pea seeds

CONTROL TREATMENT

EXPERIMENTAL TREATMENT

Many experiments consist of at least two treatments. All important conditions in the two treatments are kept identical with a single exception. In our example we might set up two vacuum bottles, each with a thermometer. (See Fig. 3-2.) The set-up with moist pea seeds would be experimental. The one with dry pea seeds would be considered the control set-up. *The* **control treatment** *provides the basis of comparison for the experimental treatment. The* **experimental treatment** *differs from the control in only one way*. It is the moisture in our example. The two treatments may produce different results. The differences must be due to the variable condition. It cannot be due to any differences in seeds, bottles, or thermometers.

3-2. In a controlled experiment there may be two or more set-ups. The set-ups may be identical with a single exception. The exception is the experimental factor. In this example the experimental factor is moisture. What is the purpose of the control treatment?

Observing and Recording the Data

A good question, a good hypothesis, and a well-designed experiment are not enough. The results of the experiment must be accurately observed and recorded. In our example, the temperature in both bottles should be taken at the start of the experiment. The readings should be accurately recorded to the nearest tenth of a degree. Furthermore, the temperature should be observed every hour until the end of the experiment.

Drawing Conclusions

If a good hypothesis is tested with a good experiment, the results may clearly support or reject the hypothesis. The bottle with the moist pea seeds may be several degrees warmer than the one with the dry seeds. Our observations support our hypothesis. In that case we might wish to do the same experiment with seeds of beans, lettuce, tomatoes, cotton, corn, and other plants.

The results of an experiment could also clearly disprove the hypothesis. In that case the scientist would alter the hypothesis. Furthermore, the experiment would have to be redesigned to test the altered hypothesis. For example, one might find no difference in temperature in the two bottles. We may notice that none of the moist pea seeds have germinated. We may alter the hypothesis to: only new moist seeds will germinate and give off heat. The experiment could be redesigned to use only new seeds that will more likely germinate.

Reporting Observations and Conclusions

A scientific discovery adds to the understanding of nature only when it is shared with other scientists. When one scientist reports a discovery, others repeat the experiment. These scientists must either confirm or refute the observations and conclusions. This sharing often occurs through written communication. When we write laboratory reports we engage in this kind of sharing. Science is not only an individual effort. It is the product of the work of a community of scientists. If an hypothesis continues to generate successful predictions it may be promoted to the status of a theory. *A **theory** is an hypothesis that is supported by many observations*.

QUESTIONS FOR SECTION 1

1. Define and give examples of inductive reasoning, hypothesis, deductive reasoning, control treatment, experimental treatment.
2. How would you develop an hypothesis from the observation that mosquitoes bite some people more than others?
3. Design an experiment that tests this hypothesis: color does not influence the choice of flowers visited by bees.
4. Make a prediction on the basis of the hypothesis in question 3.

Answers to Questions for Section 1.
A. 1. Inductive reasoning: development of a general statement based on a collection of observations. Example: observations about germinating seeds convince us that seeds release energy. Hypothesis: a temporary explanation. Example: that germinating seeds release energy. Deductive reasoning: proceeds from the general statement to a specific case. Example: prediction that moist seeds give off heat as they germinate. Control treatment: provides the basis of comparison of the experimental treatment. Example: a set-up of seeds in two identical vacuum bottles but with moist seeds in one and dry in the other, the control. Experimental treatment: one that varies from the control in only one way. Example: the moisture in above example is only variable.
  *2. Answers will vary.
B. 3. Answers will vary.
  *4. Answers will vary.

CHAPTER INVESTIGATION

After a peanut flower blooms, the petals wither. The base of the flower turns downward and pushes into the ground. There the top swells and develops into a fruit with enclosed seeds, the peanut. Peanut seeds are about 50% peanut oil, 25% protein, 20% carbohydrate and 5% cellulose.

Observe these pictures.

A. How do you know that a peanut seed contains energy?

B. Where does a peanut seed's energy originate?

C. Is energy more concentrated or less concentrated in a peanut's seed than in its stem and leaves? Convert the question into an hypothesis. Devise an experiment to test it.

2 ENERGY AND LIFE

Life is Orderly

A library is an organized collection of books. Such a collection does not just happen. It requires effort. Even after the books are organized, effort is required to keep the books in proper order. In the same way, life requires a high degree of organization. Energy is required to maintain that state of organization. Why is this so?

In all cases observed in nature, there is a tendency for processes to proceed toward a state of disorder. Continuous input of energy is required to maintain order. This is true for every organism. It must also be true for groups of organisms such as human societies, natural ecosystems, and the entire biosphere.

Energy and Matter

Now we will examine the role of energy in our environment. However, first we need to understand more about what energy is and how it interacts with matter. We have defined matter as anything that has mass and volume. You remember that mass is a measure of a body's resistance to changes in motion. **Volume** *refers to the amount of space a substance occupies.* All solids, liquids, and gases are composed of matter. Matter is composed of tiny particles called molecules.

OBJECTIVES FOR SECTION 2

C. Define and give examples of *matter, molecules, energy, transduction, potential energy, kinetic energy, heat.*
D. Explain why life requires energy.
E. State and give an illustration of energy transduction.
F. Explain why energy is not recycled.

3-3. Energy appears in many forms.

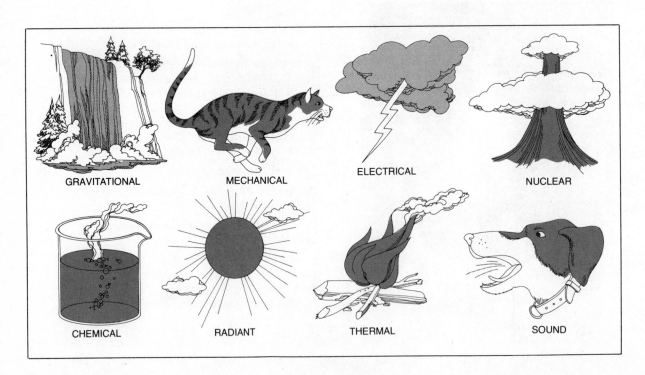

GRAVITATIONAL   MECHANICAL   ELECTRICAL   NUCLEAR

CHEMICAL   RADIANT   THERMAL   SOUND

Unlike matter, energy cannot be seen. We can only observe its effects. Energy is the ability to produce motion in an object. Gravitational energy has the ability to move a stream of water down a hill. The mechanical energy of a muscle moves your arm. Radiant energy, such as light, moves electrons in certain substances such as green leaves. Thermal energy (heat) is the energy of molecules in motion. (See Fig. 3-3.)

Energy not only appears in different forms. It can be transformed from one kind into another. *This conversion of energy from one form to another is called energy* **transduction.** (See Fig. 3-4.) Most forms of energy can be changed to heat energy.

Potential and Kinetic Energy

There are many forms of energy. Each form may exist as either potential or kinetic energy. *Energy that is inactive or stored in any form is described as* **potential energy.** *The energy of motion is* **kinetic energy.** A boulder perched at the rim of a canyon possesses potential energy. (See Fig. 3-5.) As it falls into the canyon its potential energy is converted into kinetic energy. The chemical energy in food is potential energy. As organisms use food the potential energy is converted into kinetic energy. This energy makes possible all the activities of living things.

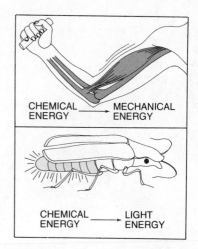

CHEMICAL ENERGY → MECHANICAL ENERGY

CHEMICAL ENERGY → LIGHT ENERGY

3-4. Energy can be transduced from one form to another.

3-5. The potential energy of the rock is converted to kinetic energy as it moves down the hill. What kind of energy does the rock have at the foot of the hill?

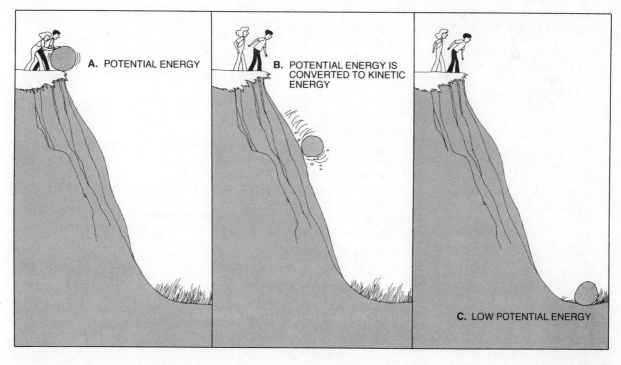

A. POTENTIAL ENERGY

B. POTENTIAL ENERGY IS CONVERTED TO KINETIC ENERGY

C. LOW POTENTIAL ENERGY

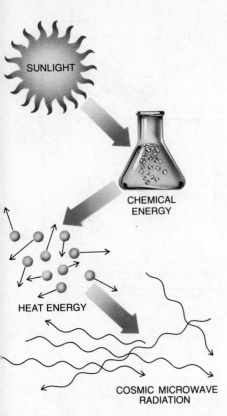

SUNLIGHT

CHEMICAL ENERGY

HEAT ENERGY

COSMIC MICROWAVE RADIATION

3-6. Energy flows freely down the "energy hill" like water flows downstream. It is possible to move water and energy upstream. The process requires energy and some energy is converted to heat energy. Try carrying a bucket of water up a hill. Is heat energy generated?

Answers to Questions for Section 2.

C. 1. Matter: anything that has mass and volume. Examples: water, oxygen, sugar. Molecules: tiny particles of which matter is composed. Examples: molecules of water, oxygen, sugar. Energy: the ability to produce motion in an object. Example: gravitational energy, heat energy. Potential energy: inactive or stored in any form. Example: chemical energy in food. Kinetic energy: energy of motion. Example: energy of life activities.

Energy is Conserved

Most forms of energy are interchangeable. However, when changes occur, energy is neither gained nor lost. This statement applies to all physical, chemical, and biological systems. A boulder that has fallen half way into the canyon has lost half its potential energy. However, it has gained as much kinetic energy. Just prior to its landing all of the boulder's potential energy will have become kinetic. When it lands all the kinetic energy will appear in different forms. Some will appear as sound energy. If the boulder strikes another rock, energy may appear as light in the sparks formed. Furthermore, some energy will have been converted into the work done to crush the underbrush or compress the soil. The boulder's potential energy can be restored. This can be done if an equal amount of energy is applied to the boulder to return it to its original position.

From Order to Chaos

Energy is vital to an understanding of life. Energy can be transferred from one substance to another. Also, it can be changed from one form to another. Because of these activities less of the total energy is usable in further changes. None has vanished! But it has become less organized, less concentrated, and is less useful to organisms. Energy given off as heat is no longer available for other uses.

In living things, all energy is eventually transformed into heat energy. **Heat** *is the energy of the continuous random motion of molecules.* While sunlight is highly organized energy, heat is disordered energy. Energy always flows freely in such direction that it becomes less organized. (See Fig. 3-6.) It cannot be used by green plants to make food like light energy can. Therefore, energy takes a one-way path through the biosphere. It is not cycled as matter is.

QUESTIONS FOR SECTION 2

1. Define and give examples of matter, molecules, energy, transduction, potential energy, kinetic energy, heat.
2. Explain why life requires energy.
3. Think of an example which illustrates the tendency of processes to proceed toward a state of disorder.
4. What is energy transduction? Give an illustration.
5. Explain why energy is not recycled.

(See page 47 for other answers.)

3 STORING ENERGY IN GREEN PLANTS

How Sunlight is Distributed

Only a small part of the sun's energy reaches Planet Earth. But it is this energy that sustains all living systems in the biosphere. It supplies energy for rabbits, jellyfish, spring rains, and the student reading this book.

Of the solar radiation reaching Earth's surface, less than five percent is used by green plants in photosynthesis. Yet this small amount of energy annually produces the 175 billion tons of dry organic matter used by living things. In photosynthesis, solar energy converts water and carbon dioxide into carbohydrates and oxygen. The carbohydrates may be converted into other plant substances or used as energy sources.

The display of electromagnetic radiations arranged in order of wave length is called the **electromagnetic spectrum.** About half of the sun's radiation is in the visible region of the electromagnetic spectrum. Figure 3-7 on page 48 shows the range of electromagnetic radiations from the long radio waves to the very short gamma rays. The energies of the spectrum are arranged in order of decreasing wavelength. As wavelengths decrease, energy increases. It is the ultraviolet, higher energy, portion that causes sunburn and stimulates suntanning. The longer, lower energy, infrared radiations are sometimes described as heat waves. They can be generated by the vibrating particles of warm objects.

Measuring Energy and Plant Productivity

To understand the role of energy in the biosphere, biologists need to measure the energy content of living materials. All energy is sooner or later changed into heat. Therefore, it is convenient to use heat units to measure energy. The basic unit of heat and all energy is the calorie (cal). *The* **calorie** *is defined as the amount of heat energy required to warm one gram (g) of water one Celsius degree (C°).* One thousand calories are equal to one kilocalorie (kcal). The kilocalorie is sometimes called a Calorie. It is the unit weight watchers count.

To determine the potential chemical energy in plant materials they are first dried. The water content does not contribute to total energy content. The dried plants are burned. The heat from the burning plants heats a known mass of water. Let's say that 10 g of burning plant material warms 1000 g of water from 15.0°C to 58.0°C. This temperature change of 43.0C° requires 43,000 calories or 43 kcal of heat energy. Thus each gram of plant material contained 4.3 kcal.

OBJECTIVES FOR SECTION 3

G. Define *electromagnetic spectrum, calorie, kilocalorie, net productivity, limiting factor, energy subsidy, cultural energy.*

H. Determine the net productivity of a vegetated area.

I. Describe the distribution of the sun's energy.

J. Explain reasons for the different net productivities of different land biomes and water environments.

K. Compare and explain the difference in energy efficiencies of primitive and modern agriculture.

Answers to Questions to Section 2

D. 2. Without energy, nothing could move, and without movement, life would be impossible.

E. *3. Answers will vary.

4. Transduction: conversion of energy from one form to another. Example: in muscles, chemical energy to mechanical energy.

F. 5. Because energy, when changing form (transduction) or being transferred, tends to become less organized, concentrated, or useful to organisms; and when given off as heat, energy is no longer available for other uses.

The amount of energy produced =

$$\frac{(1000g \text{ water}) (58°C - 15°C) (1 \text{ cal}/gC°)}{10 \text{ g tissue}}$$

= 43000 cal/ g tissue.

$$\frac{43000 \text{ cal}}{\text{g tissue}} \times \frac{1 \text{ kcal}}{1000 \text{ cal}} = \frac{4.3 \text{ kcal}}{\text{g tissue}}.$$

SUN

HIGH ENERGY   LOW ENERGY

SHORT
WAVELENGTH   LONG
WAVELENGTH

| GAMMA RAYS | X RAYS | ULTRAVIOLET | VISIBLE | NEAR INFRARED | FAR INFRARED | RADIO WAVES |

major
portion of
the sun's
energy that
reaches
Earth

heat energy
flowing
back into
space

*3-7. The range of electromagnetic
radiation.*

This is part of the procedure used to measure energy storage in an ecosystem. The plant material produced by one square meter (m^2) of land is collected after a given time of growth. We know that each gram of dried material yields about 4.3 kcal of energy. From it we can calculate *the amount of energy produced by each square meter of land known as* **net productivity.**

Of course, the plants themselves have used energy in their own life processes. So net productivity refers to the amount of energy stored in addition to that used by the plant. This stored energy is available for use as food by other organisms in the ecosystem.

Comparing Net Productivities

Table 3-1 lists the net plant production for a number of ecosystems. These are estimates of world averages. Wide variations exist. Notice that the average productivity of land ecosystems is about five times that of the total ocean. In fact the open oceans are little better in productivity than are deserts. However, waters of shallow seas have both the nutrients and light required for high productivity.

Suppose all except one of an organism's needs are met with abundance. *The scarce item that limits the survival and productivity of the organism is known as the* **limiting factor.** A limiting factor in the open oceans is often the lack of phosphate or nitrate. A limiting factor may also refer to a single pollutant whose overabundance limits growth. All of these factors tend to reduce the net productivity of an ecosystem.

Agricultural Productivity

Agricultural productivity is of great interest in this time of increasing human population. In agricultural ecosystems desired plants are given special care. Energy for this care supplements the solar energy used directly in photosynthesis. *The energy supplied in addition to solar radiation in crop production is known as an* **energy subsidy.** *Energy subsidies supplied by humans, their animals, or their machines, are known as* **cultural energy.**

In primitive societies human labor supplied the cultural energy. More developed societies have used oxen, buffalo, or horses to ease human labor. Table 3-2 illustrates how modern agriculture depends on massive inputs of cultural energy. Energy, and much of the raw materials for fertilizers and pesticides originate in coal, petroleum, and natural gas. Thus, in a sense, high-yield agriculture borrows from the productivity of ecosystems of the past.

Table 3-2 shows that modern agriculture returns about three calories of corn for each calorie of cultural energy invested. Much additional energy is used to process, package, transport, refrigerate, and

TABLE 3-1 ESTIMATED AVERAGE PLANT PRODUCTION

Biome or ecosystem type	Average annual rate of net plant production in kcal/m²/yr
Tropical rain forest	9,000
Mid-latitude deciduous forest	5,850
Taiga (coniferous forest)	3,600
Agricultural land	2,925
Lake and stream	1,126
Tundra	630
Desert and semi-desert	315
Average total land	3,285
Algal beds and reefs	10,750
Estuaries	6,450
Continental shelf	1,575
Open ocean	563
Average total ocean	700
Average total Earth	1,440

TABLE 3-2 CORN PRODUCTION

Input	1945	1970
Labor	3.1 kcal/m²	1.2
Machinery	44.5	103.8
Gasoline	134.3	196.9
Nitrogen	14.5	232.5
Phosphorus	2.6	11.7
Potassium	1.3	16.8
Seeds for planting	8.4	15.6
Irrigation	4.7	8.4
Insecticides	0.0	2.7
Herbicides	0.0	2.7
Drying	2.5	29.7
Electricity	7.9	76.6
Transportation	4.9	17.3
Total input	228.7	715.9
Corn yield (output)	846.9	2,017.5
Kcal return/input kcal	3.7	2.8

cook foods. An estimated total of 10 calories of cultural energy is required to bring one calorie of energy to your plate. Technology produces convenience and high yields per labor-hour. However, it does so at the expense of energy efficiency.

Table 3-1. *Calculations from data from Whittaker, R.H., Communities and Ecosystems. New York: Macmillan Publishing Company, 1975.*

Table 3-2. *This cultural energy is in addition to the photosynthetic input of 8,150 kcal/m². It is calculated from data by Pimentel, David, et. al., 1973. Food production and the energy crisis. Science 182:445.*

QUESTIONS FOR SECTION 3

1. Define electromagnetic spectrum, calorie, kilocalorie, net productivity, limiting factor, energy subsidy, cultural energy.
2. When tides or rivers bring nutrients into an estuary, productivity is increased. Relate this to the terms net productivity, limiting factor, energy subsidy, and cultural energy.
3. Describe how to determine the net productivity of plants in an area.
4. List the kinds of radiation included in sunlight.
5. What are some basic reasons for the differences in net productivity among various biomes and for various water environments?
6. What appear to be the limiting factors that control productivity on land biomes?
7. Compare and explain the difference in energy efficiencies of primitive and modern agriculture.

Answers to Questions for Section 3.

G. 1. See glossary or note them in boldface in section.

H. *2. The estuary may have lacked nutrients now provided by the increasing net productivity, due to the energy subsidy of nutrients from cultural energy, e.g., agriculture.

3. Plants produced by one square meter of land are collected, dried, and burned. The caloric content measured is the net productivity.

I. 4. Gamma rays, X rays, ultraviolet, visible light, near infrared, infrared, radio waves.

J. 5. Lack of phosphate or nitrate in open ocean, and pollutants.
  *6. Answers will vary.
K. *7. Answers will vary.

4 ENERGY FLOW IN THE ECOSYSTEM

Animal Productivity

We said that to measure productivity, plants are dried and weighed. From this mass one calculates the amount of stored energy they contain. The same method can be used to determine energy values in other steps of the food chain. Animal material usually yields 5.0 to 5.5 kcal/gram of dry mass. Using values appropriate to the kinds of organisms, biologists can convert from mass to energy units.

Pyramid of Energy

To understand the flow of energy in ecosystems a thorough study was made of the food chains in Silver Springs, Florida. The net productivity of each trophic level was calculated.

Figure 3-8 illustrates a significant decrease in productivity from producer to tertiary consumer. *This characteristic pattern of food chains is called a* **pyramid of energy.**

Why is the productivity of each level less than that of the one before? There are several reasons. First, not all of the food of one level is actually eaten by the next level. At Silver Springs, of the total plant material available, less than half was actually eaten by herbivores. The rest decayed or was carried downstream. In many ecosystems less than 10 percent of available material is eaten. Also, some that is available is not edible. These include tree trunks and poisonous plants. Among carnivores, bones, and shells may be left behind.

3-8. *Net productivities of each of four levels in the food chains of Silver Springs, Florida. Figures are in kcal produced by an area of a square meter in a year. Why is each higher level smaller than the one before it?*

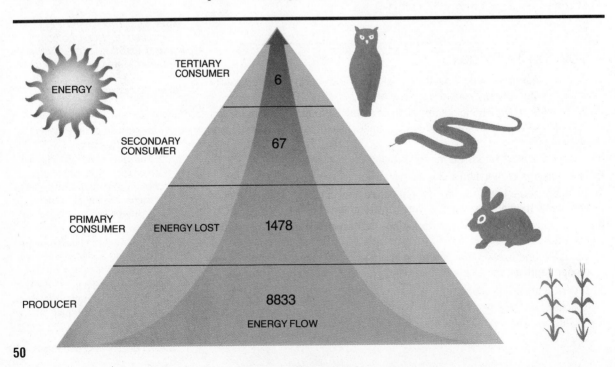

ENERGY

TERTIARY CONSUMER   6

SECONDARY CONSUMER   67

PRIMARY CONSUMER   ENERGY LOST   1478

PRODUCER   8833

ENERGY FLOW

Second, not all the food eaten is useful to the animal that eats it. Food does not always contain nutrients in the proper proportions. For example, nitrogen may be a limiting factor in diet. An organism may waste large quantities of energy-rich foods in order to get enough nitrogen. Caterpillars absorb only half of the plant tissue eaten. The rest is passed on as waste.

A third source of energy loss is metabolism (mi *tab* ə liz əm). **Metabolism *is the sum of all the chemical reactions involved in life's activities.*** Much energy is spent in the normal activities of life. These include maintenance and repair of body tissues. In caterpillars, for example, about two-thirds of the absorbed food provides energy. In herbivores, energy is used to locate, eat, and digest suitable vegetation. Carnivores may spend huge amounts of energy to capture and overpower their prey.

In agriculture, all three energy losses can be reduced. Farmers feed their livestock the quantity of food needed for desired growth and weight gain. Nutrients are supplied in needed proportions. Hence, energy needed by the animal to locate food is reduced. Unnecessary activity is limited by confining cattle, hogs, and poultry in pens. Furthermore, hogs and poultry are kept warm. Of course, these energy savings require inputs of cultural energy. (See Fig. 3-9.)

During metabolism, energy is being transformed through a series of changes. At each step the energy becomes less ordered. More is converted into heat. Yet it is through these energy changes that organisms obtain energy needed to survive. The portion converted into

3-9. *Hogs gathered in pens.*

3-10. *No transfer of energy from one trophic level to another is 100%. Undigested material at each trophic level is acted upon by decomposers.*

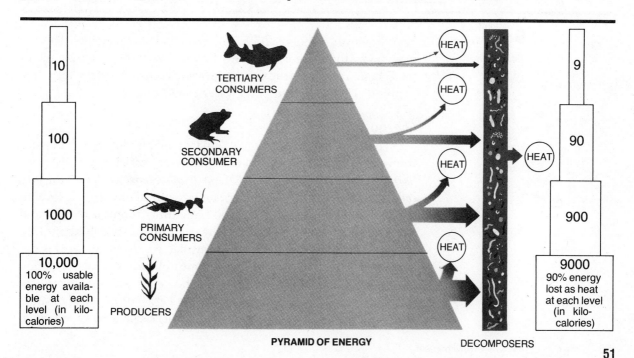

10	9
100	90
1000	900
10,000 100% usable energy available at each level (in kilocalories)	9000 90% energy lost as heat at each level (in kilocalories)

TERTIARY CONSUMERS

SECONDARY CONSUMER

PRIMARY CONSUMERS

PRODUCERS

HEAT

PYRAMID OF ENERGY

DECOMPOSERS

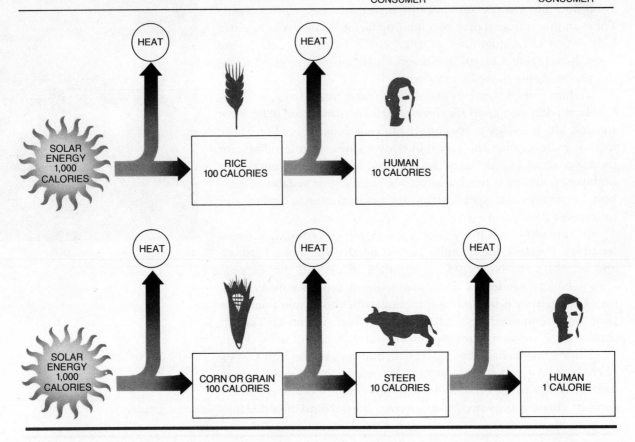

| ENERGY | PRODUCER | PRIMARY CONSUMER | SECONDARY CONSUMER |

HEAT

HEAT

SOLAR ENERGY 1,000 CALORIES

RICE 100 CALORIES

HUMAN 10 CALORIES

HEAT

HEAT

HEAT

SOLAR ENERGY 1,000 CALORIES

CORN OR GRAIN 100 CALORIES

STEER 10 CALORIES

HUMAN 1 CALORIE

3-11. For every calorie a human eating grain-fed meat obtains from the atmosphere, a human eating grain obtains ten calories.

heat, however, is not useful to the next level of consumers. This explains why there are usually only four or five levels in a pyramid or food chain. It explains the small number of carnivores at the top of the pyramid. The prairie supports fewer coyotes than rabbits.

Energy Efficiency

There are various ways to calculate efficiency of energy transfer from one level to the next. In our discussion, **efficiency** *is the comparison of the net productivity of one trophic level to that of the preceding trophic level.* No transfer of energy from one trophic level to another is 100%. At Silver Springs, comparing trophic levels one and two we get an efficiency of 17%. However, in forests only about 10% of the energy entering the plants is available to herbivores. This decreased efficiency is due to the volumes of indigestible vegetation such as wood and fibers. This material, however, provides energy for the decomposer chain of organisms. (See Fig. 3-10.) Animal tissue is more digestible than plant tissue. However, carnivores spend much energy seeking and capturing their prey. As a rule of thumb, we use 10 percent as the very rough average efficiency from one trophic level to the next. In other words, in each transfer 90% of the energy is lost as heat to the environment. (Refer to Fig. 3-10 on page 51.)

Whatever the variations in efficiency, this rough average of 10 percent is of great importance. It means that a certain amount of plant material can support a plant-eating human population 10 times as large as one that eats herbivores. It explains why people of densely populated, poor countries are more likely to eat grain than meat. Each calorie derived from beef represents 10 calories of grain. Each person that exists mostly on corn-fed beef extracts as much energy from the biosphere as 10 grain-fed people do. (See Fig. 3-11.)

These figures are not necessarily an argument against raising livestock. Many of the world's cattle are not grain fed. They graze on rangeland which should not be cultivated. Low rainfall, seasonal droughts, severe soil erosion, or shallow soils may make the land most useful to humankind as grassland. Cattle can live on a grass diet. People cannot. The cattle do us a favor by converting grass into meat which we can digest.

The Last Dance

The top carnivores are not captured alive. But they finally die and they, too, are eaten. They, and other dead organisms and their wastes, still contain usable energy. So the extraction of energy continues on through the decomposer chain. The giant molecules built with the sun's energy finally break apart. They release their stored energy to earthworms, bacteria, and fungi. The nutrients are released back into the soil and the water to be used again by producers. The energy, by contrast, is not cycled but is lost as heat. So the ordered energy generated by our nearest star becomes the disordered dance of molecules radiating their nearly-spent energy out into space.

QUESTIONS FOR SECTION 4

1. Define pyramid of energy, metabolism, efficiency.
2. Explain the reduced net productivity at each level of the energy pyramid.
3. How might knowledge of the energy pyramid be used in trying to solve the problem of world hunger?
4. Why can an area support more plant eaters than meat eaters?
5. As the world population increases what changes do you predict in human diets? Why?
6. Summarize what happens to energy from the time it leaves the sun until it leaves Earth as heat.
7. How do cave-dwelling organisms survive without light? These include salamanders, fish, worms, insects, and spiders.

Answers to Questions for Section 4.

L. 1. Pyramid of energy: a pattern of food chains showing a significant decrease in productivity from producer to tertiary consumer. Metabolism: the sum of all the chemical reactions involved in life's activities. Efficiency: the comparison of the net productivity of one trophic level to that of the preceding trophic level.

M. 2. In each transfer to another trophic level, 90% of the energy is lost as heat.

N. *3. If people were to eat more plant foods and fewer animal foods, there would be greater energy efficiency.

4. The food of plant eaters is lower on the energy pyramid than that of the meat eaters.

*5. People will eat more foods on lower trophic levels, to enable the biosphere to support more people per square meter of land.

O. *6. Most of the sun's energy dissipates as heat; the rest reaches earth as various forms of radiation. Photosynthesis captures some of this and stores it as chemical energy in plants. These may be eaten by primary, then secondary and tertiary consumers. Both the producers and consumers release some energy as heat, as they carry on life processes, as do the decomposers. All the heat is reradiated into the atmosphere.

*7. Answers will vary.

Much of the information we have learned about our world has been gathered by the logical thought processes known as scientific methods. They involve asking the right questions, making observations, developing hypotheses, conducting experiments, analyzing data, reporting observations and conclusions, repeating the experiments, and developing theories.

Life is highly organized. Maintaining organization requires continuous input of energy. Energy can be changed from one kind to another. It can also be transferred from one organism to another. Such conversions are always less than 100 percent efficient.

Energy interactions are essential to life. The energy that sustains living systems originates as highly ordered sunlight. A tiny fraction of it passes through photosynthetic plants and a series of other organisms. All is finally reradiated into space in less organized, degraded form.

Net productivity is a measure of the quantity of energy stored in organic matter of a group of organisms. Agricultural societies have devised ways to increase net productivity by adding cultural energy. This may be human labor, work done by animals, or fuels.

Efficiency in energy conversion from one level in the food chain to the next varies widely but averages about 10 percent. The reduced net productivity from one level to the next produces the pyramid of energy. It explains why land can support larger vegetarian populations than meat-eating populations.

Because energy is continually degraded as it passes through the biosphere, it follows a one-way path. It is not recycled. All of these activities of life are dependent upon the *interaction of organisms with their environment.*

Using the Concepts

1. What fraction of the cultural energy expended by farmers is due to human labor — in the rain forest of New Guinea? — in a corn field of Illinois in 1945? — in a corn field of Illinois in 1970?

2. Each 10 calories of cultural energy invested by a primitive New Guinea farmer yields 150 calories of food. The same investment on a modern farm yields 30 calories of unprocessed corn. How can less than five percent of the U.S. population (the farmers) produce enough food for all the rest of us?

VOCABULARY REVIEW

🔟 inductive reasoning	volume	heat	energy subsidy
hypothesis	molecules	🔟 electromagnetic spectrum	cultural energy
deductive reasoning	energy	calorie	🔟 pyramid of energy
control treatment	transduction	kilocalorie	metabolism
experimental treatment	potential energy	net productivity	efficiency
🔟 matter	kinetic energy	limiting factor	

21. questioning, observing, hypothesizing, recording data, drawing conclusions.

Copy the number of each test item and place your answer to the right.

PART 1   Multiple Choice:
Select the letter of the phrase that best completes each of the following.

d 1. Living things need energy because natural processes tend toward a state of   **a.** orderliness   **b.** high energy   **c.** high potential   **d.** disorder.

d 2. An example of kinetic energy is   **a.** chemical energy in food   **b.** a wound up watch spring   **c.** a boulder on the rim of a cliff   **d.** heat.

d 3. Energy enters ecosystems as highly organized light energy. It leaves as disordered energy in the form of   **a.** food   **b.** electrical energy   **c.** chemical energy   **d.** heat.

a 4. The sum of all chemical reactions involved in life's activities is   **a.** metabolism   **b.** energy subsidy   **c.** transduction   **d.** pyramid of energy.

b 5. The rough average efficiency of energy transfer from one step of the food chain to the next is   **a.** 5%   **b.** 10%   **c.** 20%   **d.** 50%.

b 6. The flow of energy through an ecosystem differs from that of minerals by   **a.** having a storage pool   **b.** not being cycled   **c.** involving no decomposers   **d.** being entirely above ground.

b 7. Twenty grams of plant tissue are dried and burned. They increase the temperature of 1000 grams of water from 7°C to 93°C. The kilocalories of heat energy produced by each gram of plant is   **a.** 1.72   **b.** 4.3   **c.** 1720   **d.** 4300.

a 8. People of densely-populated poor countries eat more grain than meat because   **a.** a certain amount of plant material can support a population 10 times as large as one that eats herbivores   **b.** plant tissue is more digestible than animal tissue   **c.** growing plants is more efficient than raising livestock   **d.** most people do not like meat.

d 9. Farmers reduce energy losses by   **a.** confining livestock to pens   **b.** supplying nutrients in needed quantities   **c.** providing food to animals in convenient places   **d.** all of the above.

a 10. For each calorie of food produced by primitive farmers, modern farmers invest cultural energy that is   **a.** larger in amount   **b.** smaller in amount   **c.** the same amount   **d.** more at planting time than at harvest time.

CHAPTER 3 TEST

PART 2   Matching:
Match the letter of the term in Column I with its description in Column II.

COLUMN I

a. inductive reasoning
b. deductive reasoning
c. hypothesis
d. control group
e. experimental group
f. energy efficiency
g. transduction
h. limiting factor
i. net productivity
j. cultural energy

Answers

22. continuous random motion of molecules.

23. needed to warm 1 g of water 1 C°.

24. energy supplied in addition to solar radiation in crop production.

COLUMN II

c 11. A possible explanation for poor plant growth is that the soil it is in lacks iron

e 12. To test whether plants need iron to grow, plants were rooted in soil lacking iron

d 13. A second group of plants were rooted in the same soil conditions except that iron was added

a 14. A study of 110 nests of barn swallows revealed that swallows lay more eggs in sunny seasons than in cold, wet ones

b 15. Knowing the above, a biologist predicted fewer eggs would be laid by local swallows during cold, wet seasons

h 16. Scarcity of this item threatens the survival or productivity of organisms

f 17. Comparison of the net productivity of one trophic level with the preceding level.

j 18. Labor supplied by humans, animals, and machines in crop production

g 19. The conversion of energy from one form to another

i 20. The amount of potential energy produced and the energy used by an organism

PART 3   Completion:
Complete the following.

21. List the steps in the scientific method as described in this chapter: ____.

22. Heat is the energy of the ____.

23. The calorie is the amount of heat that ____.

24. Energy subsidy is ____.

25. The productivity in each level of a food chain is less than that of the preceding level for the following three reasons _not all the food of one level is eaten by next; not all eaten food is useful; metabolism—much energy is spent in normal activities of life.

CHAPTER 4

BALANCES AND IMBALANCES

Chapter 1 described the biosphere as the great stage on which living things act out their lives. Chapter 2 pointed out a few of the many relationships that exist between various kinds of living things. Also mentioned were the relaionships between living things and their physical surroundings. Chapter 3 stressed that living things need a continuous supply of energy just to keep alive. Scientific methods of investigation were also studied.

In this chapter, we will emphasize a single basic concept: *the interaction of organism and environment.* We will consider several ways in which human activities have disturbed some of the interrelationships in the biosphere.

Some of the questions you will consider are:

- For what reasons has the human population increased?
- How have human populations increased food supply?
- How can farmers prevent the loss of soil and water?
- Why is pollution a more serious problem now than it was in the past?
- Why are some plants and animals in danger of becoming extinct?

ALGAE BLOOM

1 THE HUMAN POPULATION GROWS IN KNOWLEDGE AND NUMBERS

The human organism has had a greater effect on the biosphere than any other creature in recorded history. The human brain has given us the power to alter the environment in many ways. Now, in increasing numbers, we are applying our powers to an ever-greater area of Earth's surface. Even the oceans, ice caps, and upper atmosphere cannot escape the human presence.

Hunting and Gathering

Early human populations were directly dependent upon the natural ecosystem for food, clothing, and shelter. Because of their intelligence, tools and social organization, they were effective predators. Their populations, like their plant and animal prey, were dependent upon the amount and distribution of rainfall. Their populations were probably small because they required about 500 hectares to support each person.

Hunter-gatherers were mostly wanderers. Some returned each year to sites with abundant plant or animal foods in given seasons. In some instances a favorable combination of resources encouraged a more permanent settlement. Village living and increased hunting skills tended to increase the human population.

Agriculture

Stationary settlements allowed additional activities not possible with constant moving. One can imagine the seeds of wild grains being left with food scraps at a garbage dump. The garbage-enriched soil stimulated their growth. Those plants which failed to release seeds could easily be harvested at convenient times. Those seeds were the basis of the next crop. Similarly the more tame of the animals might have been chosen from wild herds. By centuries of such selection early villagers domesticated a variety of plants and animals. Domestication is really a case of mutualism. Humankind and its domestic plants and animals became dependent on each other for survival. *The raising and care of plants and animals that are used for food and clothing is called* agriculture. Agriculture made possible the support of a person on only 10 hectares of land.

Village life and agriculture influenced human culture in several ways. They encouraged division of labor. A few people could produce food for everyone. Others were free to become tool makers, builders, traders, or even poets. Agriculture also contributed to the

OBJECTIVES FOR SECTION 1

A. Identify features of the lifestyle of the hunter-gatherer society that make it different from the agricultural society.
B. Describe early agricultural societies. Explain how they resulted in an increase in the human population.
C. Explain how the scientific-industrial revolution and health revolution encouraged an increase in the human population.

A favorable combination of resources includes rich coastal areas, a variety of game animals available through the year, or plentiful wild grains.

Dogs were domesticated 13,000 years ago followed by goats, sheep, and cattle. Plant cultivation was practiced 7,000 years ago or earlier.

Answers to Questions for Section 1

C. 5. The result of scientific discoveries and inventions of the last 200 years, greatly reducing the amount of human energy needed to produce food.
6. The germ theory of disease and improvements in nutrition, hygiene, and medical care have led to control of much disease and reduced infant mortality.

4-1. Using agriculture people became managers of ecosystems.

4-2. The scientific-industrial revolution brought another increase in farm productivity. Each farmer could farm more land.

Answers to Questions for Section 1

A. **1.** The people were wandering predators, taking food, clothing, shelter directly from the natural ecosystem; sometimes returning to sites seasonally from which they hunted; rarely, settled in villages.

*2. No, because the population is too large, by far.

3. Grain plants that failed to release their seeds afforded convenient collection and selection; and the more tame animals were selected from wild herds for domestication. Re-selection through many generations led to useful varieties.

B. ***4.** Agricultural societies expend much more cultural energy in growing food, so that land yields much more per hectare.

population explosion. Children were more useful on a farm than in a hunter-gatherer society. Having children to inherit the property and care for the elderly seemed to become more important. Farming required knowledge of the seasons and long-term planning.

The hunter-gatherer was dependent on natural ecosystems. With agriculture humankind became manager of ecosystems. (See Fig. 4-1.)

The Scientific-Industrial Revolution

Scientific discoveries and inventions resulted in the industrial revolution beginning about 1760. It continues today. One person and a machine or a computer may have a greater impact on our environment today than Earth's entire human population did several thousand years ago. As a result the industrial revolution produced another increase in human population. (See Fig. 4-2.) Today human energy provides less than one percent of the total energy applied to the raising of corn.

The Health Revolution

The age of discovery that introduced the industrial revolution also brought in the health revolution. Primitive people were no doubt hosts for many kinds of bacteria and other parasites. Populations became more concentrated. Hence, disease became an important factor in population control. From this, the germ theory of disease was developed. This led to the knowledge and control of many diseases that had long plagued humankind. The inventions of vaccination and

TABLE 4-1 POPULATION ESTIMATES FOR CONTINENTS AND AREAS

Area	Population (millions)	Growth rate (%)	Birth rate (per 1000)	Death rate (per 1000)	Number of US meals per person per day
Africa	455.0	2.8	46	19	1.3
Asia	2,547.0	2.3	35	12	1.2
North America	247.9	0.9	15	9	3.6
Latin America	351.7	2.7	37	9	1.7
Europe	480.3	0.5	15	11	3.2
More developed countries	1,161.9	0.8	16	10	3.3
Less developed countries	3,203.4	2.4	37	13	1.2
World	4,365.3	2.0	32	12	1.8

asceptic surgery saved lives. Furthermore, the discovery of antibiotics and other drugs have nearly conquered infectious diseases. Improvements in nutrition, hygiene, and medical care have reduced infant deaths. All of these measures have reduced disease as a population control device.

Because our birth rate has not decreased, the human population has increased dramatically. Figure 4-3 illustrates world population growth through history. Table 4-1 shows that this increase is usually highest in those countries that can least afford it. They already have a greater population than they can support.

In 1978 the world population was estimated at about 4.2 billion. The birth rate was 29 per 1000 population. The death rate stood at 12 per thousand. The birth rate has grown to 43 per 1000 population. You may live to see the world population double in your lifetime.

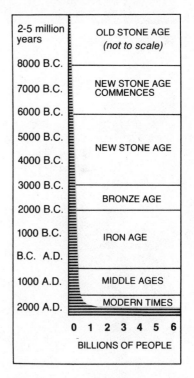

4-3. *Human population reached one billion about 1800 A.D. By 1975 it had reached four billion. By the year 2000 another two billion may be added.*

QUESTIONS FOR SECTION 1

1. Describe the lifestyle of the hunter-gatherer society.
2. Could our ecosystems survive if all people today were hunter-gatherers?
3. Describe how varieties of plants and animals useful to humans might have been developed.
4. How can agricultural societies support a person on only 10 hectares when hunter-gatherer tribes require 500 hectares per person?
5. What is the scientific-industrial revolution? Explain how it encouraged an increase in the human population.
6. What is the health revolution? Explain how it encouraged an increase in the human population.

(See pages 57 and 58 for other answers.)

CHAPTER INVESTIGATION

A. These are descendants of European rabbits that were introduced into Australia in 1859. Rabbits usually get both food and water from plants. Why are these rabbits drinking from a pool?

B. The dozen pairs of European rabbits had in six years multiplied to 30,000. By 1953 one billion rabbits were grazing lands that would have supported another 100 million sheep. How do you explain this population explosion?

C. Suggest some methods of controlling these rabbits without damaging the eco-system. Then search the library for a control method introduced in 1950. Evaluate its success.

2 THE NEED FOR RESOURCES GROWS

Food

Each person in a human population needs basic resources. These are food, water, and space. Thus as a population grows the total need for these resources grows too. In 1798 Thomas Malthus predicted that human numbers would eventually overtake food production. Could this prediction come true in our lifetime?

Worldwide, food supplies have generally been adequate. But they are distributed unevenly. While millions of people overeat, many others die of starvation or malnutrition. Starvation is due to a simple lack of enough food. Malnutrition results from a diet that lacks one or a few elements. Malnutrition may be more important than starvation in contributing to deaths from poor diets. Food productivity is often expressed in energy units. However, we need to know that food must provide for growth and repair, too. For example, protein deficiencies before the age of two years can cause mental damage. This damage cannot be remedied by later corrective dietary measures.

Ways of Increasing Food Productivity

Food productivity has been increasing in both developed countries and developing countries. But the increase has been largely balanced by the population increases in the poor nations.

BREEDING Historically, agriculture has increased food productivity in several ways. It has concentrated on a few kinds of plants and animals and developed their edible parts through selection and breeding. Out of 80,000 species of edible plants, only about 50 are cultivated on a large scale. Eleven plant species provide about 80 percent of the human food supply. Out of several hundred edible species of animals, the top three (pigs, cattle, chickens) contribute 17 times as much meat as the next four combined. (See Fig. 4-4.) Our food supply now depends on very few species. Thus, the failure of one of them could result in mass starvation.

MONOCULTURING Also contributing to the increased productivity of agriculture has been the monoculture of crops. In natural communities, there is usually a mixture of many kinds of plants. However, in monoculture a plot of land is devoted to the growth of a single plant species. Cultural energy is spent to prevent natural ecologic succession. The resources of soil, water, and light are all channeled into the desired crop. Production is increased by human labor and machines. (See Fig. 4-5 on page 62.)

OBJECTIVES FOR SECTION 2
D. List three ways that agriculture has increased food productivity. Give five possible solutions to the food shortage.
E. Contrast the effects on soil of high rainfall, and human activity.
F. List human uses of water and the possible methods of meeting increased demands for it.

4-4. Farmers have concentrated on a relatively few species of animals for food.

4-5. *In monoculture, cultural energy is used to channel all resources into the desired crop. Here pineapple is being grown.*

4-6. *The oceans provide about 10 percent of the protein consumed by human populations.*

But crops grown in monoculture are more convenient for insects and fungi too. With a plentiful food supply the insects and fungi build up their populations. For this reason monocultures require the input of more cultural energy. This input helps to control insect or disease damage. Some organic farmers and gardeners claim that planting several different vegetable crops in a plot reduces insect damage. More time is required for insects to find the next prey plant after one has been devoured. Planting different crops in successive years also reduces insect damage.

THE GREEN REVOLUTION   In the 1960's, an effort to increase food production in underdeveloped countries was organized. The plan was to develop high-yielding varieties of wheat, rice, and corn. They would be designed to respond to fertilizers and irrigation. Impressive yields resulted, especially with wheat and rice. *The increased crop production through the use of high-yield varieties, fertilizers, irrigation, and pesticides was given the name, "Green Revolution."*

As in the other agricultural revolutions, yields were increased. But each time the increase involved higher energy input. Only the wealthy farmers can buy the equipment and supplies required to adopt the new technology. Whether the green revolution will eventually help the poor farmer in underdeveloped countries is doubtful. Supporters of the green revolution admit that it only buys a little more time in which to feed the world.

THE OCEANS   Another possible source of food is the oceans. They now provide about 10 percent of the protein consumed by the human population. Productivity measurements indicate that we may already be harvesting the oceans at their upper limits. (See Fig. 4-6.)

A problem exists with harvesting the ocean at a lower level in the food chain. That is, many of the harvestable organisms are small and scattered widely. Gathering them requires much cultural energy.

OTHER SOLUTIONS   There are other solutions to the threat of a food shortage. Historically, as human populations increase in wealth they consume more animal products such as meat, milk, and eggs. Even grains and legumes which can be eaten by human beings are fed to cattle, hogs, and chickens. Table 4-2 shows that the Chinese convert about 22 percent of their grain into livestock. In the United States more than 90 percent of the grain is converted into livestock. Eliminating that grain-to-livestock step would provide food for larger populations.

Retaining animals in the food chain may have some merit. This comes from their ability to transform products of little or no human value into nutritious human food.

About 10 percent of Earth's cultivated lands are producing cotton, tobacco, rubber, coffee, tea, and jute. If survival demanded it, these fields could be converted to food production.

Of the world's 3.2 billion hectares of potentially cultivatable land, about half is under cultivation. But much uncultivated land is infertile or would require irrigation. It is only in areas where fertilizers and water are available that they may hold some promise. Moreover, many tracts of land are more productive if kept in grass or trees.

About 10 percent of Earth's cultivatable land requires irrigation to raise even a single crop. More intensive culturing can increase production on already-cultivated land. In some tropical areas up to three crops can be harvested each year.

But all of these measures must be considered temporary if the human population continues to grow. Earth's carrying capacity would finally be reached. Human numbers will be controlled either by our decision or by the natural forces that control populations. (See Fig. 4-7.)

TABLE 4-2 GRAIN USE IN CHINA AND THE UNITED STATES

Grain used for adequate human diet	
China	205 kg/yr
U.S.	920 kg/yr
Eaten as grain	
China	160 kg/yr
U.S.	68 kg/yr
Grain fed to livestock used for meat	
China	45 kg/yr
U.S.	852 kg/yr

4-7. *Human numbers could expand beyond Earth's carrying capacity.*

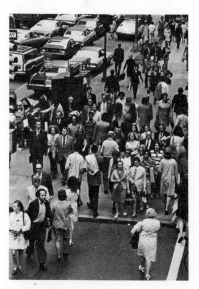

Archeologic evidence in an Italian lake bottom showed that 2-3 cm of land surface were eroded away every 1000 years before human activity began. After human arrival erosion increased to about 20 cm/1000 yrs.

4-8. *Terraces reduce erosion and make better use of water.*

Soil

PRODUCTIVITY OF SOIL   Land covers about one-third of Earth's surface. But its total productivity is three times that of the oceans. Thus the soil in which most land plants grow plays an important role in the biosphere. It is from the soil that most plants receive water and soil minerals.

Soils subject to high rainfall tend to have their minerals washed down to the water table. These soils become acid or sour, and infertile. A rainfall of only 50 cm carries minerals down to plant root depth. From here the minerals are returned to the surface by plants. This movement of minerals keeps fertility high and acidity low. In deserts, water evaporates from the surface. This condition leaves the soil so alkaline or bitter, and salty that most crops cannot grow.

Soils are formed slowly, depending on the slow release of materials from parent rock. At the same time they are continuously wearing, washing, and blowing away. As soon as a continent pushes up out of the sea, erosion proceeds to wear it down.

CULTIVATING THE SOIL   In general, erosion is rare in Europe and Asia. Farmers there understand that they must preserve soil and put back into it what they take out. Terracing has been practiced for centuries. **Terraces** *are the banks of soil built across the slope of a hill.* They cause water to run slowly across the main slope instead of rapidly down the steep hillside. This reduces erosion. Terraces also increase the amount of water absorbed by the soil and made available to plants. (See Fig. 4-8.)

In newer countries, people have tended to move on when soils became eroded or infertile. Thousands of years will be required to build up the top soil ruined by poor farming practices in the Eastern United States. In portions of the American Great Plains much of the thick layer of soil was eroded away during 100 years of agriculture. By 1924, the phosphate content of the prairie was reduced by 36 percent. But since 1935 the U.S. Soil Conservation Service has encouraged farmers to build terraces and practice contour farming. In addition, strip cropping and gully control were also encouraged. These practices conserve both soil and water. **Contour farming** *makes use of furrows or trenches across the slope of a hill.* These furrows are really small terraces. Terraces and contour furrows generally guide water to a grassed waterway. Grass prevents the formation of gullies. *In strip* **cropping** *strips of land planted with crops that need cultivation are alternated with strips of crops whose roots hold the soil.* Strips of corn or cotton are alternated with wheat or alfalfa. (See Fig. 4-9.)

In the plains wind erosion may be more of a problem than water erosion. Furrows across the direction of winds help control soil loss. Rows of trees help break the force of winds.

4-9. *Contour farming and strip cropping reduce soil erosion. Run-off water is directed to a grassed waterway.*

Water

Water is often a limiting factor in ecosystems. During the water cycle most evaporation occurs from the surface of seas. The slope of the land's surface promotes more precipitation over the land. As the water flows back toward the oceans it is used in various ways. Among other uses, water irrigates crops, generates electric power, and carries away wastes.

About 10 percent of the water that falls as rain or snow enters the ground. From here it penetrates to the water table. *The* **water table** *is the level below which the ground is saturated with water.* This water

(5) Limit population growth: if not done by human choice, nature will eventually take over as it does with other populations.
*3. Answers will vary. Students may mention: Use contour plowing, use terracing, plant a variety of crops in alternating rows (strip cropping), plant different crops in successive seasons (crop rotation), return organic wastes to the soil as fertilizer, avoid killing the natural enemies of insect pests.
*4. Yes, if carefully planned to provide all the essential amino acids; but it is easier to include some animal foods in a diet that is only primarily vegetarian.
E. 5. High: carries minerals down to water table, leaving soil acid and infertile. Moderate: carries minerals to plant roots, resulting in low acidity and high fertility. Low: water evaporates from surface leaving soil too alkaline and salty for crops to grow.
6. In the U.S., the quantity of soil has been greatly decreased, as has its phosphorus content. This has occurred to lesser extent in Europe and Asia, where erosion-preventing practices are common.
7. Terracing, contour farming, strip cropping, and furrows.

F. 8. To irrigate crops, generate electric power, and carry away wastes.
9. Removal of salts from sea water, reclamation of waste water, and transporting water from distant locations. They are all expensive.

Lowering of the water table means that water is being removed faster than it is being replenished by rain and melting snow.

usually flows toward streams, lakes, or oceans. It is to tap this ground water that humans have dug wells. However, in recent years excessive pumping of water from irrigation wells has resulted in lowering of the water table.

There are several possible methods of meeting an increasing demand for water. They include the removal of salts from sea water and the reclamation of wastewater. Yet another way is to transport water from distant locations. All of these methods are expensive. It seems certain that plentiful free water is a thing of the past.

Other Resources

We have discussed the resources of food, soil, and water. Moreover, we have examined their close ties to human survival. One could as well mention forests, grasslands, wildlife, space, and various minerals. Like nature, humankind will have to learn to recycle minerals. Many mineral sources are being used up as human populations and technology grow.

An example of the struggle for control of natural resources is found in the western states. The lands vary from forested mountains and valleys to grasslands and dry deserts. Much of the land is used for lumbering, grazing, mining, and housing. In addition, these lands are the source of many activities, such as camping, hunting, fishing, and skiing. The conflicting interests of these industries and ecologists will become intense. This will be a bigger problem as the human population grows and pushes into the ranges of these wild areas. It is possible that in the United States our forests could become a memory. That is all that remains of the forested hills of China and the cedars of Lebanon. (See Fig. 4-10.)

4-10. Forests require careful management to prevent their destruction.

QUESTIONS FOR SECTION 2

1. Describe and evaluate each of the three ways that agriculture has increased food productivity.
2. Evaluate five possible solutions to the food shortage.
3. You are asked to aid in agricultural development in a developing country. What advice would you give to a farmer not wealthy enough to afford fertilizer, irrigation, pesticides, and the equipment to apply them?
4. Can a vegetarian diet provide all needed nutrients?
5. What are the effects on the soil of high, moderate, and low amounts of rainfall?
6. Describe the effects of human activity on soil quantity and quality.
7. What are four methods of preventing soil loss by water, and by wind.
8. Describe or list human uses of the water that falls on the land and flows back toward the ocean.
9. Describe three possible methods of meeting increased demands for water and a problem they share.

(See answers on pages 64 and 65.)

3 POLLUTION ACCUMULATES

As human populations grow, their natural wastes increase. As technology develops, new substances or forms of energy appear. *Any substance or energy in such quantity that it degrades the environment is* **pollution.**

Household Wastes

A camper throws the non-edible parts of a fish into the river. They are eaten or decomposed by water organisms. Indeed, the river quickly recovers. But if the garbage of several million city dwellers is dumped into the river, the river is at once overwhelmed. Add to that human wastes, dish water, and a hundred new substances that nature is not able to decompose. As you can see, the river becomes a flowing cesspool. (See Fig. 4-11.) About 10 percent of the sewage collected in the United States passes into rivers, streams, or the ocean untreated. Fortunately, most cities treat their sewage before it is released.

Most sewage systems remove up to 90 percent of the organic components of sewage. But they fail to remove the inorganic ions such as nitrate and phosphate. Phosphate was an important ingredient of detergents manufactured in the 1960's. Phosphates and nitrates are often limiting factors in water ecosystems. If they are suddenly available, a population explosion of algae may result. *Such a population increase in algae that occurs when the water suddenly becomes enriched with phosphate and/or nitrate is known as an* **algal bloom.** After a period of explosive growth, the algae of lower layers are shaded out by layers above. They die and decay. As they decay much of the dissolved oxygen is used up by the decomposers. Hence, the fish population suffocates and dies. (See Fig. 4-12.)

To remove phosphate, nitrate, and many other ions from sewage is very difficult. A technique being researched to remove these substances involves the use of soil with its plant roots and microorganisms.

Agricultural Wastes

Wastes of range-fed cattle are widely scattered. However, grainfed hogs or cattle are concentrated in feedlots. Hence, more manure is produced than can be used in nearby fields. Until recent requirements for pre-treatment were set up, rain run-off from feedlots went directly into streams and rivers. This led to numerous fish-kills. But feedlot wastes present an even greater hazard. Most of the salt fed to feedlot animals ends up in their wastes. This salt will eventually inhibit plant growth.

4-11. Human populations produce more wastes than rivers can digest.

4-12. As lower layers of algae are shaded out they provide food for decomposers. The decomposers use up oxygen in the water.

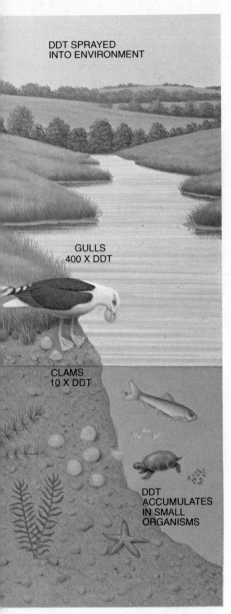

DDT SPRAYED
INTO ENVIRONMENT

GULLS
400 X DDT

CLAMS
10 X DDT

DDT
ACCUMULATES
IN SMALL
ORGANISMS

4-13. DDT increases in concentration as it moves up a food chain. DDT interferes with reproduction.

Recently farmers have turned to synthetic fertilizers. Little organic matter is returned to the soil from crops like corn. So inorganic fertilizers show obviously improved yields. To realize a high yield many farmers have over-fertilized. Because of this, excess nitrate runs off into rivers or seeps down to the water table. Increases in infant deaths have been linked to these contaminated water supplies.

Pesticide Residues

In 1963, DDT had in many areas nearly eliminated the mosquito that transmits the malarial parasite. But in 1972 the use of DDT in the United States was forbidden. It had been learned that, in addition to killing insects, DDT was damaging other species like earthworms, fish, and robins. It was present in the tissues of many organisms including human beings.

DDT is resistant to decay and tends to be stored in fatty tissue rather than excreted by animals. Furthermore, the concentration of DDT is often highest in those organisms highest in the food chain. For example, when a marsh is sprayed to control mosquitoes, traces of DDT accumulate in small aquatic organisms. As those are eaten by clams, DDT accumulates in the clam's fatty tissue. DDT concentrations in clams have been measured to be 10 times higher than in the organisms on which they feed. Gulls feeding on clams have had more than 40 times the concentration of DDT present in clams. This is 400 times the concentration in smaller organisms. *This process of concentration from one step in the food chain to the next is known as biological magnification.* (See Fig. 4-13.) Because of biological magnification the carnivores at the top of longer food chains have the highest concentration of DDT. Pelicans, falcons, and eagles are among those affected. Because of DDT they form thin egg shells. This results in the death of the developing chicks.

Industrial Pollution

The use of city sewage as fertilizer creates a serious problem. It is likely to contain certain harmful chemicals that could accumulate in the soil. Furthermore, industrial chemicals may also be dumped into lakes and streams. One such group of chemicals is the mercury compounds used in many industries. These compounds can be converted into the dangerous methyl mercury by microorganisms in the bottom of lakes, as well as by fish and mammals. Humans may then take in fatal doses through the fish they eat.

Within the last 200 years the burning of petroleum and coal has also added large quantities of pollutants to Earth's atmosphere. Of special interest are compounds of sulfur and nitrogen. These are converted into strong acids when dissolved in the moisture of the air.

These acids then fall to the ground in rain and snow. They have a variety of harmful effects on plant and animal life. Other common industrial wastes that have caused concern are lead, asbestos, and the polychlorinated biphenols (PCBs).

Thermal Pollution

Thermal pollution refers to the addition of waste heat to either the air or water. The most common source is electrical generating plants powered by nuclear reactors or by burning gas, oil, or coal. Usually water is taken in to cool the generators and then returned to a lake or stream. (See Fig. 4-14.) Ecologists have expressed concern over the biological effects of the increase in water temperature. As water temperature increases, the body processes of certain animals speed up. That increases their need for oxygen. However, as the temperature of water increases less oxygen can dissolve in it. A food chain can be disrupted if a temperature change alters the ability of a predator fish to capture its prey. At the same time, the ability of the prey to escape also affects the food chain. Altered reproduction and maturity rates are other possible effects.

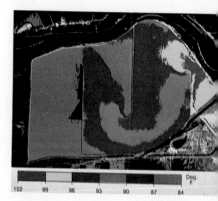

4-14. Water used to cool generators is passed through a cooling pond before flowing into natural streams. Note color code for various water temperatures.

Radioactive Wastes and Fallout

If nuclear reactors and nuclear weapons increase in numbers, the problem of disposing of radioactive wastes will continue to grow. These wastes will be radioactive for millions of years. (See Fig. 4-15.) That is, they will continue to emit radiations harmful to living organisms and their unborn offspring. Some such wastes have been dumped into the sea. However, that action was banned by international agreement. To overcome this, abandoned salt mines have been considered as depositories of radioactive wastes.

The use or testing of nuclear weapons introduces radioactive materials into the atmosphere. They return to Earth as fallout and may be inhaled by organisms or deposited on plants. When eaten or inhaled by organisms, radioactive fallout may cause cancer.

Air Pollution

Until 1950 most air pollution came from burning coal. Today most air pollution is released from the engines of cars. These pollutants are responsible for many eye irritations and serious damage to plant life. Calculations show that a non-smoker in a large city suffers lung damage from air pollution. This damage may be equivalent to that of a rural dweller who smokes a pack of cigarettes per day.

The effects of smog are magnified by certain atmospheric conditions. Occasionally the air near the ground is cooler than a warm layer above it. The warm air acts as a lid and prevents the cool air from ris-

4-15. Wastes generated by nuclear reactors will be radioactive for millions of years.

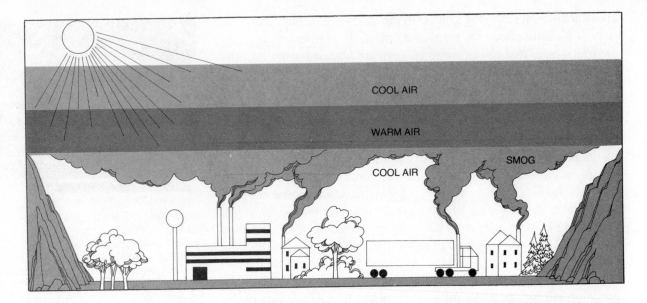

COOL AIR

WARM AIR

COOL AIR

SMOG

4-16. *A temperature inversion may trap polluted air overnight or for several days.*

ing. Such a temperature inversion may trap the air pollutants of a city through the night. Sometimes the inversion lasts for several days and causes serious illness and death. Chimneys tall enough to penetrate the trap reduce ground-level concentrations of pollutants. But they discharge their pollutants higher in the air. This allows them to be carried farther away to other communities. (See Fig. 4-16.)

Industries are installing devices to reduce the quantity of pollutants they discharge into the air. Auto manufacturers now are required to install anti-pollution devices on all new automobiles.

Answers to Questions for Section 3 (Note: All questions in section 3 relate to Objectives G. and H. together.)

G. **1.** Algal bloom: increase in algae
& that occurs when a water ecosystem
H. is suddenly enriched with phosphate or nitrate, as a result of sewage.

2. Rain run-off carries wastes from feedlots into river, killing fish; salt in the wastes also inhibits plant growth.

3. Contamination of water by excess nitrate from fertilizer has been linked to infant deaths.

4. DDT, e.g., becomes concentrated in tissues of carnivores at tops of food chains, with harmful effects.

5. Toxic mercury compounds dumped in water enter the food chain in the water.

6. Sulfur and nitrogen compounds released into the air by industry form strong acids with water, and fall as rain that harms organisms.

QUESTIONS FOR SECTION 3

1. Describe the algal bloom and its cause.
2. Describe the problems of feedlots in terms of waste accumulation and rain runoff.
3. What is a danger in the use of synthetic fertilizers?
4. How can pesticides damage natural ecosystems by what they kill and by biological magnification?
5. Give one example of dangerous industrial pollution.
6. Describe the formation and danger of acid rain.
7. Describe ecologists' concerns about thermal pollution.
8. What is the problem of storing radioactive wastes?
9. Describe the effects of automobile wastes on living things.
10. Describe a temperature inversion and its dangers.
11. Describe the various ways that are used to handle body and household wastes.
12. Antipollution devices on automobiles reduce fuel efficiency. How can one decide whether such devices should be required on cars?

(See more answers on page 71, and 73.)

4 NATURAL ECOSYSTEMS ARE THREATENED

The increasing size of the human population and its technology is having increasing effects on the natural ecosystems. Many human activities interrupt or threaten the balance of ecosystems.

Habitat Destruction

Some species have been severely threatened by reduction of their home range. Many species occupy habitats desired by human beings. The marshes of the prairie states were the original nesting areas of the whooping crane. As marshes were drained and put under cultivation the crane was pushed to near extinction.

Plant species are also being threatened through habitat destruction. In Hawaii, for example, 266 plants have become extinct.

Removal of Predators

Human beings have suggested the extermination of predators for two reasons. One is their threat to human life. The other is their removal as competitors for food. While a 300-kg grizzly bear may be a fearsome sight, only a few have ever killed or hurt people. It is true that some wild predators do kill game and domestic livestock. Farmers and hunters have sometimes suggested exterminating these competing predators. In Kansas, massive coyote roundups have been organized during the same year that great numbers of jack rabbits were damaging wheat plants. You can see why this occurred since jack rabbits were an important part of the coyote diet.

Introduction of Foreign Species

Before Earth's continents drifted to their present positions, the single land mass allowed plant and animal migrations. However, continental separation plus mountain and glacial barriers limited the interaction of various species. In recent centuries the introduction of plants and animals to new areas has occurred on a scale never before possible.

What happens when an organism is introduced into new areas? If the ecosystem has all its niches filled, severe competition usually results. Sometimes the results are surprising.

Let's examine the introduction of the gypsy moth to the United States. A French astronomer working in Massachusetts was trying to cross-breed several silk moths. He hoped to develop a disease-resistant strain useful to the French silk industry. One of his species was the gypsy moth, known in Europe for its destruction of shade

OBJECTIVES FOR SECTION 4

I. Describe the roles of habitat destruction, removal of natural predators, introduction of foreign species, and human hunters in threatening the survival of natural populations.

J. Give reasons for using pesticides and their dangers.

K. Describe how human activities can affect the oceans, a river-sea system, and separate marine ecosystems.

L. Suggest a reason for concern over the increased rate of extinction of plants and animals.

The ax, chain saw, tractor, and bulldozer have often been more threatening to wildlife than are hunters and their guns.

Further examples of introduced species include European rabbits and the prickly pear cactus in Australia, and the English sparrow in Philadelphia.

Answers to Questions for Section 3

7. Thermal pollution warms the bodies of animals living in water and thus increases their demand for oxygen. Warmer water holds less oxygen in solution. Food chains are disrupted, and reproductive rates are altered. Solution: Find ways to convert the waste heat to useful heat.

8. They continue to emit deadly radiation for thousands of years.

9. Lung damage and eye irritation to humans; serious damage to plant life.

trees. In 1869 some of these insects accidentally escaped. Twenty years later the swarm of caterpillars, the larval stage of the moth, was so large that "the sound of their feeding could plainly be heard." The moth had no natural predator in the United States, so there was nothing to control its numbers. Thousands of trees were defoliated and killed in several northeastern states. (See Fig. 4-17.)

Also, during the last century, a fungus disease nearly destroyed the wine industry in France. The fungus had been imported on grape twigs shipped from America.

Another example of a foreign induced species developed when Europeans invaded North America. Native Americans were greeted with newly imported disease organisms. Smallpox, brought to the New World by Cortes, eventually killed an estimated 3.5 million Indians. Later an immunity would be built up against it. However, smallpox contributed to the collapse of the Aztec and Inca civilizations.

4-17. Gypsy moth larva. Gypsy moths were released in the U.S. accidentally. They had no natural predators. As a result the moths multiplied rapidly and destroyed thousands of trees.

Gnus have been killed to make fly swatters with their tails. Elephants have been hunted to make wastebaskets out of their feet.

4-18. The great auk became extinct by 1850. Once extinct an organism is gone forever.

Human Hunters

The oceans surrounding the barren Antarctica are teeming with life. Organisms here include the largest animal that ever lived — the blue whale. But its population has dropped from about 200,000 individuals in 1900 to an estimated 6,000. Some marine biologists believe the blue whale is destined for extinction. Since no one owns the open seas, individual whalers continue to operate for immediate economic gain. Regretfully, they do not consider the long-range ecologic good.

Human hunters have already brought on the extinction of the great auk (1844), the bison as a wild animal (about 1900), the passenger pigeon (1914), and the heath hen (1933). (See Fig. 4-18.) Nearing extinction are many of the big game animals of Africa, the whooping crane, the Indian tiger, and many others.

Pesticides

Mature, natural ecosystems generally support a wide variety of organisms whose activities are interrelated. Modern agriculture is based on simplified systems, often on a single species. Such monocultures show two tendencies of human importance. Unattended monocultures tend to follow succession, returning to the normal climax stage with a variety of organisms. Cultural energy is applied to keep this from happening. This may include cultivation or application of chemical herbicides to eliminate weedy invaders.

Monocultures also favor an increase in the number of herbivorous predators. The presence of a concentrated food supply is a convenient target for grasshoppers or other insects. Chemical insecticides have been developed to combat those insects.

One problem with synthetic chemical insecticides is that they are not specific. They destroy not only the target species but predator insects as well. This means that those insects that naturally control the pest are destroyed, too. Although the insecticide may cause a rapid decrease in the pest population, resistant individuals soon replace the original population. This happens much later in predator populations. So the natural enemies are less able to control the pest than they were before the spraying occurred.

Other organisms of the ecosystem are also affected. Honeybees killed by insecticides no longer pollinate crops. Wild mammals and livestock may be affected. Fish are especially sensitive to these insecticides. Many insecticides are poisonous to humans as well. Yet, it is with the help of insecticides that productivity has increased at least temporarily.

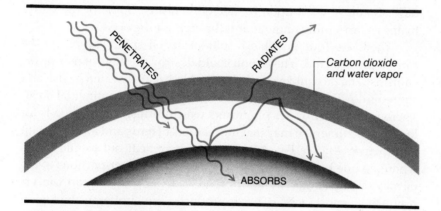

4-19. Radiation from Earth to space is of longer wavelength than that coming from the sun. It does not penetrate the layer of carbon dioxide and water vapor. Thus as carbon dioxide increases in the atmosphere, more heat is trapped near Earth's surface.

Earth as a Greenhouse

Materials that human beings dump into the atmosphere can affect the weather. Pollutant particles can act as centers around which water vapor can condense. This action hastens rainfall. Moreover, human activities may alter the global climate. Increasing the quantity of carbon dioxide in the air can affect the Earth's temperature.

On a hot summer day a car with closed windows stores much heat. The windows allow sunlight in. The car's interior absorbs the energy. The heat is trapped. Greenhouses do the same thing. So does Earth's atmosphere. Carbon dioxide does not absorb the shortwave solar radiation entering the atmosphere. But it does absorb the longer-wave heat radiated from Earth. Thus carbon dioxide causes a warming of the atmosphere. In a day when the burning of fossil fuels powers civilization, we are increasing the carbon dioxide content of our atmosphere. As a result, could we be raising Earth's average temperature? (See Fig. 4-19.)

Answers to Questions for Section 3

10. When the air near the ground is cooler than a warm layer above it, the warm air may act as a lid and prevent the cool air from rising: this is a temperature inversion. Its danger is that it may trap the air pollutants from a city, sometimes for several days, causing serious illness and death.

11. Dumping into rivers, streams, or the ocean, sometimes with pre-treatment, sometimes "raw".

*12. Answers will vary, but should include a weighing of the costs and benefits of both fuel efficiency and clean air.

4-20. *Duck being cleansed after being covered with oil from spill.*

Earth's atmosphere was warming slowly from 1840 to 1960. It has cooled a bit since then. If our recent cooling trend continues, the polar ice sheets could enlarge and sea levels could drop. However, if Earth warms up, sea levels could rise and some coastal cities would be flooded.

Oil on the Waters

Flowing water has always seemed a good place to dump wastes. But our rivers eventually empty into the oceans. Pollutants dumped into inland rivers are now found far out at sea.

The largest source of ocean pollution is oil. Crude oil consists of a mixture of thousands of different chemical substances. Most of them are less dense than water and float on the sea. Some are dense enough to sink to the bottom where they can affect the lives of bottom dwelling organisms. A part of the crude oil evaporates within a few days. Some is acted upon by microorganisms. Some of the oil remains as tarry lumps now found throughout the ocean.

There are four possible results of an oil spill. The oil can be carried toward land. This action could destroy the eggs of marine organisms. The oil could also kill the creatures usually eaten by fish and shore birds. The oil may float over the protective continental shelf. There it may destroy sea organisms which furnish protein foods for human consumers. It may mat the feathers of birds and interfere with their activities. (See Fig. 4-20.) The oil may float out to mid-ocean where no one knows the effects. Some of the denser portions of the oil may sink and enter the marine food web. Some of these are cancer-producing substances. These products can undergo biological magnification and finally form part of the human diet.

Endangered Species

Increasingly hostile conditions threaten the existence of many of the world's wild creatures. Attempts to improve the quality of human life have at the same time endangered all life. Between the years 1 and 1650 A.D. about 10 kinds of mammals and 10 species of birds became extinct. This is a rate for each of one per 165 years. Between 1650 and 1850 bird and mammal extinction occurred at a combined rate of one species per five years. From 1900 to 1950 the extinction rate averaged one every 8 months. World-wide, eight percent of the mammals and 10 percent of all species of birds and flowering plants are on the endangered list.

People are beginning to recognize that there is a problem. They are studying which species of plants and animals are endangered. The knowledge will help people take definite action to protect and save our endangered species of plants and animals.

Answers to Questions for Section 4.

J. 3. By favoring an increase in the number of herbivorous predators that require insecticides, and need to eliminate weeds with herbicides.

*4. Answers will vary.

K. 5. By adding carbon dioxide to the atmosphere we may be warming it significantly.

6. Oil spills can destroy many sea and shore organisms that provide food for humans. They may also cause entrance of cancer-causing chemical into the marine food web that eventually also affects humans.

7. An environment so hostile to wildlife may also be damaging to humans.

L. *8. Yes. Besides the loss to humankind of the aesthetic and purely scientific value of species, there is always the danger that the balance of life will be upset in ways that have far-reaching harmful effects if a species becomes extinct.

QUESTIONS FOR SECTION 4

1. Describe separate cases in which habitat destruction, removal of natural predators, introduction of foreign species, and human hunters have caused serious problems in certain ecosystems.
2. Describe how natural predators of insects and the non-target species are affected by insecticides.
3. Tell how monoculturing has led to the use of herbicides and insecticides.
4. Should people be allowed to use any pesticide in any quantity they wish? Explain.
5. How may humans be affecting climate?
6. Describe how humans are affecting the oceans.
7. What is a general reason for the concern over the increasing rate of extinctions of plants and animals?
8. Should we care if some species become extinct? Explain.

(See more answers on page 74.)

Answers to Questions for Section 4

1. 1. Habitat destruction: draining marshes threatened whooping crane with extinction. Removal of predators: coyote roundups coincided with great damage to wheat by jackrabbits. Introduction of foreign species: defoliation of trees by gypsy moth. Human hunters: caused extinction of passenger pigeon in 1914.

2. Insecticides are not specific. Resistant individuals occur later in predators than in target species. Net result is natural enemies are less effective.

CHAPTER REVIEW

Technology and the increasing human population have placed large demands on food and other resources. Pollution accumulates as more humans manufacture, use, and discharge products into the environment. These wastes threaten the existence of our natural ecosystems. Each of these factors interfere with the natural balance in ecosystems. The concept of *interaction of organism and environment* shows how natural balance has been disturbed. It also illustrates how it has been restored.

Will an environment that is hostile to wildlife be fit for human habitation? This unit gave you a broad look at the biosphere and various interrelationships in it. In the next unit you will take a more detailed look at how organisms function and the similarities they share with each other.

Using the Concepts

1. Study an endangered species and explain what interrelationships put it on the endangered list.
2. How should decisions regarding the use and abuse of the oceans be made?

3. The Federal government owns about 50 percent of the land in western states. What are the advantages and disadvantages of government ownership of these lands?

Unanswered Question

4. Some believe that human beings will continue to abuse our biosphere until it can no longer support us. Which organisms might replace us as dominant creatures?

Career Activities

5. From this list of vocational areas determine the training, specific work, and future demand for those that interest you most: farmer, truck gardener, horticulturalist, stockman, commercial fisherman, range specialist, forest service, department of agriculture, soil conservation, ecologist, game biologist, water resources, environmental protection, sewage engineer, land use planner, anthropologist.

VOCABULARY REVIEW

1 agriculture
2 Green Revolution

terracing
contour farming

strip cropping
water table

3 algal bloom
biological magnification

CHAPTER 4 TEST

Copy the number of each test item and place your answer to the right.

PART 1 Multiple Choice: Select the letter of the phrase that best completes each of the following.

c 1. The health revolution increased population growth mainly by **a.** increased food production **b.** increased birth rate **c.** reduced death rate **d.** increased migration.

b 2. The agricultural method that most stimulates growth of pest and disease organisms is **a.** strip cropping **b.** monoculturing **c.** the Green Revolution **d.** contour farming.

b 3. A problem with the Green Revolution is that it **a.** increases insect and disease activity **b.** is expensive **c.** does not increase crop production **d.** benefits mostly poor farmers.

c 4. A certain plot of ground can provide food for more people if they eat **a.** meat **b.** eggs **c.** grain **d.** milk.

c 5. Name the product of coal and petroleum burning which may cause an increase in Earth's average temperature. **a.** heat **b.** water vapor **c.** carbon dioxide **d.** smoke.

a 6. The largest source of ocean pollution is **a.** oil **b.** fertilizer **c.** human wastes **d.** human garbage.

c 7. Insecticides kill **a.** only "pest" insects **b.** only "beneficial" insects **c.** insects and other organisms **d.** the host plants.

d 8. An important danger of nuclear weapons and reactors is that their radiations can produce **a.** heart attacks **b.** cancer **c.** genetic damage **d.** both b and c.

d 9. Large quantities of sewage or manure in a body of water can cause a severe drop in **a.** temperature **b.** fertility **c.** carbon dioxide concentration **d.** oxygen concentration.

c 10. Habitat destruction has been increased by **a.** extermination of predators **b.** introduction of foreign species **c.** growth of human population **d.** all of these.

PART 2 Matching: Match the letter of the term in Column I with its description in Column II.

COLUMN I
a. agriculture
b. terracing
c. contour farming
d. strip cropping
e. Green Revolution
f. monoculture of crops
g. biological magnification
h. pollution
i. eutrophication
j. temperature inversion

COLUMN II

a 11. Raising and caring for plants and animals used for food and clothing

f 12. Devoting a plot of land to the growth of a single plant species

d 13. Alternating rows of cultivated crops with crops whose roots hold the soil

b 14. Farming on banks of soil built across the slope of a hill

c 15. Planting in trenches or furrows across the slope of a hill

e 16. Increasing crop production by using high yield varieties adapted to fertilizers, irrigation, and pesticides

i 17. Increased productivity in a body of water due to nutrient enrichment

g 18. The increased concentration of a substance in each step of a food chain

j 19. A condition in which a layer of warm air traps a layer of cool air beneath and keeps polluted air from escaping

h 20. Any substance that degrades the environment

PART 3 Completion: Complete the following.

21. Five important natural resouces in addition to food, soil, and water are ____.

22. Seven factors that are threatening natural ecosystems are ____.

23. Three possible future sources of water are ____.

24. Soils subject to high rainfall tend to become _acid_ & infertile.

25. Over-nitrate fertilization of farm land has resulted in _increased crop production_.

Chapter 4 Test Answers

21. forests, grasslands, wildlife, space, minerals.
22. growth of human population, habitat destruction, removal of predators, introduction of foreign species, pesticides, pollutant particles, oil spills.
23. salt water, waste water, and transportation of water.

UNITY OF ALL LIVING THINGS

From the study of diversity of living things in Unit 1, we now focus on how these organisms are similar. Through observation and study, scientists have discovered that living things are made of cells. The study of the cell and its functions is basic biology. In this unit we will study chemical make up of cells, their parts and functions. Having established the cell model we will then consider how energy from the sun is used by green plants. Finally, we examine how animals get energy from plants.

MOSS CELLS WITH CHLOROPLASTS

CHAPTER 5

CHEMISTRY OF LIVING THINGS

In your study of the environment, you have learned some things about water, oxygen, and carbon dioxide. These simple chemicals play an important part in life functions. Furthermore, these chemicals are used over and over again by living organisms. Thus, you already know some chemistry of living things.

We can begin to understand the unity of living things by looking at how they are alike chemically. In fact, *the chemical structures of all living things are quite similar.* Knowing what things are made of will help us to understand how they are alike at more complex levels. If we were to understand the structure of buildings, we might begin by studying building materials. In the same manner, if we want to understand living things, we can start by studying their chemical building materials. Likewise, knowing how chemical building blocks are used in living things will help us to understand better how living things function.

Many of the chemical functions in living things are involved in the process of metabolism. *Metabolism includes the breakdown of food for energy and the making of all of the chemical substances found in all living organisms.*

Because the chemical level of structure is the most basic level in living things, we need to study that level first. We will then be able to relate chemical structure to cellular structure and chemical function to cellular function. As you study these relationships you will also learn

- Why you need water
- What the difference is between saturated and unsaturated fats
- Why you need a variety of foods to stay healthy.

LABORATORY APPARATUS

1 BUILDING BLOCKS OF MATTER AND HOW THEY COMBINE

Matter

Matter *is anything that has mass or substance and occupies space.* Look around you. Look at yourself. Everything you can see is matter. Some things you cannot see, such as the air you breathe, are matter. Even your own body and that of every other living thing is matter.

Scientists have studied matter and learned that it is composed of *elements.* They have also found that elements are made up of *atoms.* Atoms of different elements combine with each other and form different kinds of matter called *compounds.* For example, the elements of oxygen and hydrogen combine chemically and form the compound, water.

We can think of living things as highly organized forms of matter. Atoms of the four elements, *oxygen, carbon, hydrogen,* and *nitrogen* make up most of the matter in living things. Table 5-1 lists these and other elements found in living things.

OBJECTIVES FOR SECTION 1

A. Define the terms, *matter* and *element*, and explain how they are related.

B. Describe the structure of an *atom* in terms of *protons*, *neutrons*, and *electrons*.

C. Distinguish between *ionic* and *covalent bonds*.

D. Define the terms, *ion*, *molecule*, and *compound*.

TABLE 5–1 ELEMENTS FOUND IN LIVING ORGANISMS.

Element	Symbol	Approximate percent of human body weight
Oxygen	O	65
Carbon	C	18
Hydrogen	H	10
Nitrogen	N	3
Calcium	Ca	1.5
Phosphorous	P	1
Potassium	K	less
Sulfur	S	than
Sodium	Na	one
Chlorine	Cl	per-
Magnesium	Mg	cent
Iron	Fe	
Manganese	Mn	
Iodine	I	only
Silicon	Si	a
Fluorine	F	trace
Copper	Cu	amount
Zinc	Zn	

Answers to Questions for Section 1.

4. The electrons move around the nucleus at various energy levels, with no more than 2 electrons at the level nearest the nucleus and not more than 8 electrons at the outermost level.

C. 5. See Figure 5-4 for covalent bond. See Figure 5-6 for ionic bond.

*6. If one or two outer electrons the atom is likely to form an ionic bond; if four, a covalent bond.

7. Water: H_2O; carbon dioxide: CO_2.

D. 8. Ion: charged particle formed with an atom loses or gains one or more electrons. Molecule: the smallest unit of a substance that can exist by itself. Compound: a substance that contains two or more elements combined in definite proportions.

*9. $H_2O + CO_2 \rightarrow H_2CO_3$

PARTICLE	MASS NUMBER	CHARGE
P⁺ proton	large	positive
N⁰ neutron	large	neutral
e⁻ electron	very small	negative

5-1. *Types of particles in an atom.*

You might want to use magnets to show how charged particles behave.

The term, energy levels, is used here instead of orbits because electron energy is the important point. Also the term better reflects the current views about electrons in a simple way.

5-2. *The atomic structure of a hydrogen atom.*

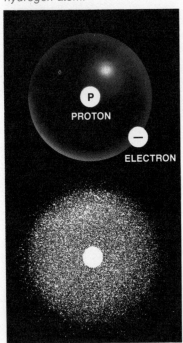

What is the Structure of an Atom?

The basic unit of any element is an **atom.** Inside atoms are smaller particles called *protons, electrons,* and *neutrons*. (See Fig. 5-1.) Properties of these particles contribute to the structure and function of chemicals in living things. Two of these properties are mass and electrical charge.

Protons are positively charged, electrons are negatively charged, and neutrons have no charge. You may already know that opposite charges attract each other. Furthermore, atoms are neutral because they contain the same numbers of electrons and protons. Protons and neutrons have about the same mass. Both are much heavier than electrons, almost 2000 times heavier. They are located in the center or nucleus of the atom and account for most of the mass of the atom.

All atoms of the same element have the same number of protons. Hydrogen is the simplest of all atoms. (See Fig. 5-2.) Usually it has one proton, one electron, and no neutrons. The electron moves around the nucleus containing the proton so rapidly that it forms what chemists call an *electron cloud.* Larger and more complex atoms have more protons and neutrons in the nucleus and more electrons in the electron cloud. Figure 5-3 shows the number and arrangements of particles in the atoms of a few elements. These diagrams are models to help us understand what we cannot see. They are related to atoms like floor plans are related to houses.

Some electrons move around in a distinct pattern fairly near the nucleus of the atom. Other electrons move at a greater distance from the nucleus. Of course, atoms are too small to be seen even with the best microscopes. Even so, chemists found that atoms generally have a maximum number of electrons that can occupy each energy level. These energy levels are represented by circles around the nucleus of the atom. (See Fig. 5-3.) Notice that the energy level closest to the nucleus contains no more than two electrons. The energy levels farthest from the nucleus contain no more than eight electrons in the atoms in the diagram.

What you have learned about the structures of atoms is based on many careful observations made by scientists using special laboratory equipment. From these observations the scientists inferred how the particles in atoms must be arranged.

Molecules and Compounds

Now that we have an idea of the structure of atoms, we can consider how they combine. *The smallest unit of a substance that can exist by itself is called a* **molecule.** For example, a molecule of oxygen gas contains two atoms of oxygen. We can write that as O_2, where the symbol, O, stands for oxygen and 2 indicates that there are two atoms of oxygen present. Hydrogen and nitrogen gases also each contain two atoms per molecule. A molecule of hydrogen gas is written H_2. The symbol for nitrogen is N. How would you write a molecule of nitrogen gas?

A **compound** *is a substance that contains two or more elements combined in definite proportion.* Water, H_2O, and carbon dioxide, CO_2, are compounds. The basic unit of a compound is one molecule of that compound. Two atoms of hydrogen and one atom of oxygen combine and form a molecule of water. Ten molecules of water would be written 10 H_2O.

How Are Atoms Held Together?

The outer electrons of an atom are involved in holding atoms together. A chemical bond forms between the outer electrons of the atoms. Let us see how two atoms of hydrogen combine with one atom of oxygen and form water. The outer electrons of one atom sometimes are attracted to the nucleus of another atom. Remember the electrons are negatively charged and the protons in the nucleus are positively charged. Refer back to Figure 5-3. Notice the outer energy level of an oxygen atom contains six electrons, but needs eight to become stable. Two electrons are needed to fill the energy level of oxygen. The hydrogen atom contains only one electron. It needs one

5-3. In these models P represents protons, N neutrons, and dots electrons.

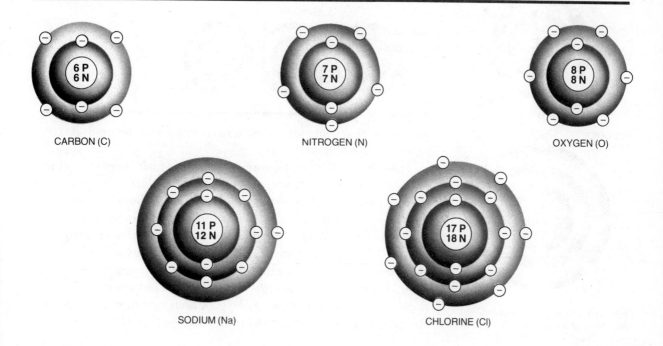

CARBON (C)

NITROGEN (N)

OXYGEN (O)

SODIUM (Na)

CHLORINE (Cl)

5-4. *Atoms of hydrogen and oxygen share electrons and form the covalent bonds of a water molecule.*

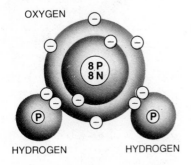

OXYGEN

8 P
8 N

HYDROGEN   HYDROGEN

We have provided examples of chemist's shorthand for elements, compounds, and chemical reactions to help students understand concepts. We would not expect that they memorize the short-hand.

SODIUM
ION (Na⁺)

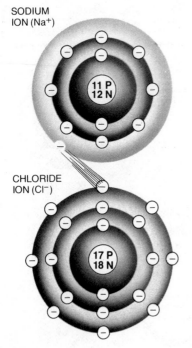

11 P
12 N

CHLORIDE
ION (Cl⁻)

17 P
18 N

5-6. *Atoms that carry positive or negative charges are called ions.*

more electron to fill its electron energy level. Figure 5-4 shows how the atoms share electrons and how the energy levels are filled. *When two atoms share a pair of electrons a* **covalent bond** *is formed.*

Carbon atoms regularly form covalent bonds. Each carbon atom has four outer electrons. These electrons of carbon are shared with electrons of other atoms. Figure 5-5 shows the covalent bonds in a molecule of the gas methane. The methane molecule has four covalent bonds. These four bonds represent the sharing of four pairs of electrons. Each dash shows a pair of electrons that form a covalent bond. The dashes show how methane is held together without showing all of the electrons. Carbon dioxide is also held together by covalent bonds. In this case each oxygen atom shares two electrons with two of the electrons of carbon. *A covalent bond formed between*

5 – 5 COVALENT BONDS

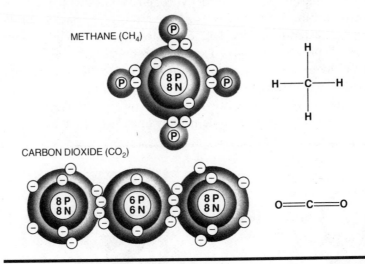

METHANE (CH_4)

8 P
8 N

CARBON DIOXIDE (CO_2)

8 P
8 N

6 P
6 N

8 P
8 N

two atoms that share four electrons is called a **double bond.** It is represented by a double dash.

Instead of sharing electrons, some atoms form bonds by gaining or losing electrons. *When an atom gains or loses an electron, a charged particle, or* **ion,** *is formed.* Atoms like sodium have only one outer electron. This electron is easily attracted to the positive nucleus of another atom. When a sodium atom loses an electron it becomes a positively charged sodium ion. Atoms like chlorine have seven outer electrons. They tend to gain an electron and complete the energy level. When chlorine accepts or gains an electron it becomes a negative ion. The outer energy level of both ions now contain eight electrons but the ions have electrical charges. (See Fig. 5-6.)

82 CHAPTER 5 • Chemistry Of Living Things

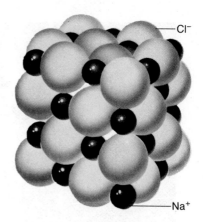

An **ionic bond** *is a bond formed by the transfer of electrons from one atom to another.* Some atoms have only one or two electrons in their outer shell. These electrons are easily attracted to other atoms. Atoms which contain six or seven electrons in their outer shell tend to attract the electrons from other atoms. This giving and taking of electrons completes the number of electrons (8) in the outer shells of each atom. Some examples are sodium chloride, Na^+Cl^-, and potassium iodide, K^+I^-.

Chemical Reactions

Chemical reactions involve the breaking and forming of chemical bonds. Energy changes always occur in chemical reactions. Chemical reactions in living things often involve the storage or release of energy. Your body makes use of the food you eat by chemically releasing energy stored in that food. The energy was stored in the food by the plants and animals you eat.

Much of the use we will make of chemistry in our study of biology will involve chemical reactions. So it will be worthwhile for us to learn to use the chemist's shorthand for representing chemical reactions. This shorthand uses *letter symbols* for elements and *formulas* for compounds. It uses subscripts to show how many atoms of each element are present if more than one is present. For example:

$$C \quad + \quad O_2 \longrightarrow CO_2$$

| 1 atom | 1 molecule | 1 molecule of |
| of carbon | of oxygen | carbon dioxide |

The plus sign means combines with and the arrow means yields.

$$2Na \quad + \quad Cl_2 \longrightarrow 2Na^+Cl^-$$

| 2 atoms | 1 molecule | 2 sodium chloride |
| of sodium | of chlorine | |

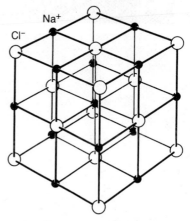

5-7. *The positively charged sodium ions are attracted to the negatively charged chloride ions. The resulting structure is a sodium chloride crystal.*

QUESTIONS FOR SECTION 1

1. Define the terms matter and element.
2. How could you demonstrate that air is composed of matter?
3. Make a diagram to show the arrangement of protons, neutrons, and electrons in carbon.
4. Describe the arrangement of electrons around the nucleus of an atom.
5. Draw a diagram of two atoms held together by a covalent bond; an ionic bond.
6. What kind of bond (ionic or covalent) would an atom be likely to form if it had one or two outer electrons? If it had four outer electrons?
7. Use chemical symbols to write the formulas for water and carbon dioxide.
8. What is an ion; a molecule; a compound?
9. Write an equation to show that water and carbon dioxide combine to form carbonic acid, H_2CO_3.

(See page 79 for more answers.)

Answers to Questions for Section 1

A. **1.** Matter: anything that has mass and occupies space. Element: substance that is made up of just one kind of atom.

   *2. Weigh a deflated balloon, fill the balloon with air, then weigh again. The increase in weight will indicate that the air has mass, and the increase in size that the air occupies space.

B. **3.** See Figure 5-3.

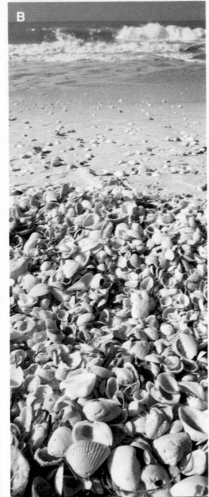

CHAPTER INVESTIGATION

A. What do all of the pictures have in common? What would happen to all of the living things if that substance were taken away?

B. What are the properties of water that make it so important to the survival of living things?

C. How might the plants and animals in each of these environments use water differently? How do you think the water might get to the top of the tree in (C) or to the leaves in (B)? What would happen to the person in (D) if the water came from the ocean? How do you know the water you drink is safe? Design an experiment to demonstrate that water is important to life. (With your instructor's permission carry out the experiment.)

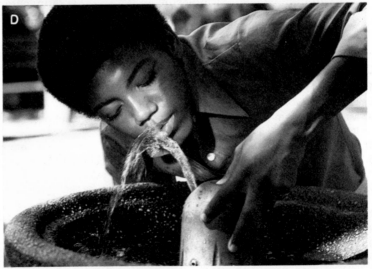

☑ SIMPLE CHEMICALS OF LIFE

Water—What Is Its Importance to Living Things?

In Unit I you learned that many things live in water and that even those that live on land need water to survive. You could live only a few days without water and an even shorter time in a hot dry place.

Water accounts for a large part of the total weight of living things. (See Table 5-2.) In general, chemical reactions in living things take place in water. How organisms function depends to a large extent on the properties of water. Let us consider some of those properties.

Water holds a lot of heat. It can absorb heat from the environment when the air is hot. It can release heat as the air cools. Water helps to reduce the variation in temperatures in the environment. For example, the air cools rapidly at night in the desert but cools slowly at night near the ocean. The high water content of the bodies of many living things helps to keep their body temperatures from changing rapidly.

As water cools it becomes most dense at 4°C and decreases in density as it freezes. **(Density *is a measure of the mass per unit volume.)*** This property is important to the survival of things that live in bodies of water such as lakes and rivers. As shown in Figure 5-8, when water on the surface cools to 4°C it falls below the surface. As the temperature of water drops below 4°C, it rises to the surface and freezes. Therefore, ice first forms on the top of the water. Deeper water fails to freeze. This allows living things to avoid being frozen and trapped in the ice. The salts and other substances in ocean water keep it from freezing, except at very cold temperatures.

OBJECTIVES FOR SECTION 2

E. List some properties of water and describe how it is important to living things.

F. List some properties of *solutions*, *colloids*, and *suspensions* and describe how each is important in biology.

G. Define the terms, *acid* and *base*.

H. Explain why carbon is important to living things.

TABLE 5.2 WATER AS A PERCENT OF BODY WEIGHT.

Organism	Percent
Steers ready for market	55
Adult's human body	60
Body of a newborn baby	75
Jellyfish	96
Peas	70
Carrots	88
Watermelon	93

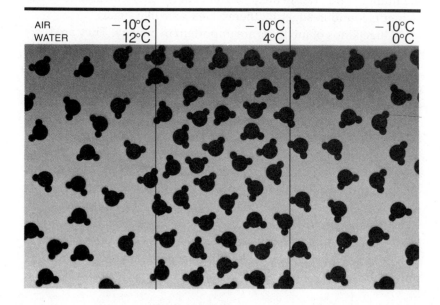

| AIR | −10°C | −10°C | −10°C |
| WATER | 12°C | 4°C | 0°C |

5-8. Ice is less dense than liquid water.

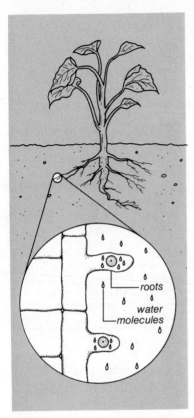

5-9. *Water transports ions of substances into the bodies of living things.*

Other properties of water are important to living things. Water is a good solvent, for instance, water dissolves salt. It is the medium in which salt is dissolved. Because water is a good solvent, it can transport substances through the bodies of living things. For example, your blood contains a lot of water and carries many different dissolved substances. Water is transparent, and its molecules stick together. Because water is transparent it allows light to reach plants that live below its surface so they can make food. Because water molecules stick together it has a high surface tension. This property allows water molecules to creep up through the soil and reach the roots of plants or spread over surfaces and keep them moist. (See Fig. 5-9.) As we shall see in later chapters, many surfaces such as the inside of the mouth, nose, and lungs must be kept moist to function properly.

Solutions, Colloids, and Suspensions: Different Kinds of Mixtures

In our study of the building blocks of matter, we have considered atoms, molecules, and compounds. We have been concerned with chemical changes. Here we will consider mixtures. Mixtures differ from compounds in several ways. First, no chemical change is involved in making a mixture. Second, the amounts of the two or more substances in a mixture can vary. This is unlike a compound where a specific ratio of atoms of each of the elements must be present. Finally, each of the substances in a mixture contributes to the properties of the mixture. For example, in a mixture of equal amounts of sugar and salt, you would be able to taste both the sugar and the salt. In contrast the sweet taste of a compound such as table sugar is due to the number and arrangement of atoms in the molecule. None of the elements found in sugar by themselves taste like sugar.

Three kinds of mixtures are important in biology. They are *solutions, colloids,* and *suspensions* (See Fig. 5-10.)

A **solution** *consists of a mixture of two or more substances in which the molecules of the substances are evenly distributed.* One substance is the *solvent*, the medium in which the other is dissolved. The dissolved substance is the *solute*. Solutions may have more than one solute and also may have more than one solvent. Most solutions in living things contain water as the solvent. Many different solutes are found in these solutions. They include solids such as the sugar, glucose, and gases such as oxygen and carbon dioxide, and many different kinds of ions.

Suspensions *are formed from particles larger than ions or molecules.* If we drop a handful of soil into a glass of water and stir it around, the water will look muddy. After standing for a period of time, the water will look clear again. The soil particles form a sus-

A.

B.

C.

pension while they are spread through the water. A suspension lasts only until the force of gravity causes the particles to fall to the bottom of the container.

Colloids *are formed from particles too large to form true solutions and too small to form suspensions.* Gelatin is an example of a colloid. *Protoplasm*, the substance of living things, is also a colloid. The ability of a colloid to change back and forth from liquid to semisolid is important in the functioning of living things. This change is like the change in gelatin when it sets and then melts.

Solutions, and other mixtures, can vary in concentration. *The* **concentration** *of a solution is the amount of solute dissolved in a certain amount of solvent.* For example, you could prepare a salt solution with such a low concentration of salt that you could not taste it. Or you could use such a high concentration of salt that no more would dissolve in the amount of water used. You can see the effects of different concentrations by mixing grape juice and water in varying proportions. (See Fig. 5-11.)

5-10. ***A.*** *A solution is clear.* ***B.*** *A colloid is usually cloudy.* ***C.*** *A suspension is cloudy.*

Though traditionally protoplasm has been called a colloid, recent research indicates that this is not precisely true. Many minute discrete structures (microtubules and microfilaments described in Chapter 6) are now known to contribute to the internal movements and changes in shapes of cells—and to the apparent colloidal properties of protoplasm. Yet these structures are not colloidal particles.

5-11. *The color becomes more intense as the concentration of the grape juice increases.*

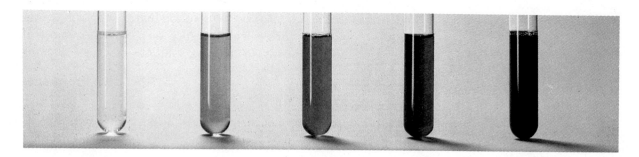

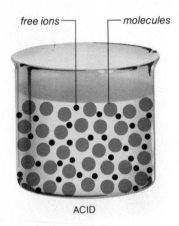

free ions ——   —— molecules

ACID

WATER

BASE

5-12. *Acids and bases form many more ions than water.*

Acids and Bases

You are already familiar with some acids and bases. Vinegar, lemon juice, and most other fruit juices are acidic. The sour or tart taste of these foods is due to the acids they contain. Household ammonia and lye (sodium hydroxide) are examples of bases that you may have used. Pure water is neutral.

Most living things exist in an environment that is near neutral. The environment is neither very acidic nor very basic. The internal environment of living things is also maintained very near neutral. Changes in the concentration of acids or bases have important effects on living things. So we need to know something about acids and bases to help us to understand the effects of changes in their concentrations.

One of the properties of acids and bases is that they form ions which separate when they are dissolved in water. The equations below show the ions in the water solutions of HCl, and the base, NaOH.

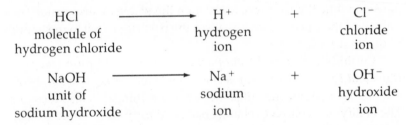

$$HCl \longrightarrow H^+ \quad + \quad Cl^-$$

molecule of   hydrogen   chloride
hydrogen chloride   ion   ion

$$NaOH \longrightarrow Na^+ \quad + \quad OH^-$$

unit of   sodium   hydroxide
sodium hydroxide   ion   ion

Note that in these reactions the acid formed hydrogen ions (H^+) and the base formed hydroxide ions (OH^-). Solutions that have an excess of H^+ ions are acidic. Solutions that have an excess of OH^- ions are basic. Solutions that have the same number of H^+ and OH^- are neutral.

Pure water is neutral. It forms ions as shown below:

$$H_2O \longrightarrow H^+ \quad + \quad OH^-$$

molecule of   hydrogen   hydroxide
water   ion   ion

Notice that when water forms ions it forms the same number of hydrogen and hydroxide ions. Any solution that has the same number of H^+ and OH^- ions is neutral. Also only a small number of water molecules form ions. In contrast, solutions of acids and bases contain many ions. (See Fig. 5-12.)

The pH Scale

It is helpful to be able to express how acidic or how basic a solution is. The pH scale does this. (See Fig. 5-13.) It ranges from 0 to 14

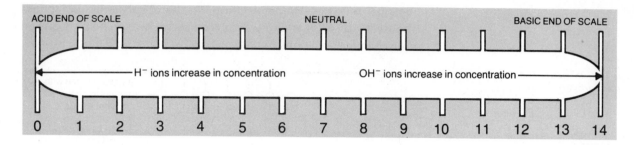

ACID END OF SCALE	NEUTRAL	BASIC END OF SCALE

← H⁻ ions increase in concentration   OH⁻ ions increase in concentration →

0 1 2 3 4 5 6 7 8 9 10 11 12 13 14

5-13. *The pH scale measures the H⁺ ion concentration in solutions.*

with 7 being neutral. A solution with a pH below 7 is acid. Above 7, a solution is basic. The lower the number is, the more strongly acidic the solution. Each unit on the scale represents a tenfold change in concentration. For example, compared to a solution of pH 3, a solution of pH 2 is ten times as acidic. A solution of pH 1 is one hundred times as acidic as one of pH 3. Above 7, the higher the number, the more basic the solution.

Carbon and Other Elements Important to Living Things

We have already noted that the bodies of many living things are about 70% water. Almost all of the remaining 30% consists of chemical compounds that contain carbon. Only a little more than 1% of the weight of most living things consists of substances other than water or carbon compounds. These substances are mostly minerals. (See Fig. 5-14.)

Among the elements, carbon is special. It can form rings and chains. (See Fig. 5-15.) It can, with other elements, form many different compounds important to life. The atoms of these molecules are held together by covalent bonds. In plants and animals the elements hydrogen, oxygen, and nitrogen are bonded to carbon in a great many ways and form a large number of compounds. Some of these compounds also contain sulfur and phosphorus.

The minerals found in living organisms are generally present in very small quantities. (See Table 5-1.) However, animals with bony skeletons have fairly large amounts of the minerals, calcium and

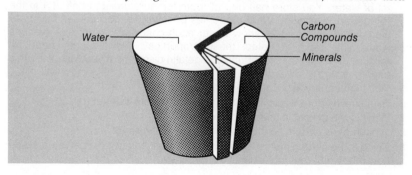

Water
Carbon Compounds
Minerals

5-14. *Proportions of substances in living things.*

phosphorus. These minerals form the hard substance of bones. Almost all other minerals are involved in some way in helping one or more chemical reactions to take place.

5-15. *In molecules, carbon atoms can form chains or rings.*

A carbon chain with dashes to show covalent bonds.

How the carbon chain begins to form a ring.

One way atoms of hydrogen and oxygen can be added to the carbon chain. The molecule is a fatty acid.

One way atoms of hydrogen and oxygen can be added to the carbon chain. The molecule is glucose.

Answers to Questions for Section 2

E. 1. Holds a lot of heat; helps to reduce variation in temperature in the environment; is most dense at 4° C, and decreases in density as it freezes; is a good solvent, is transparent; and has a high surface tension.

2. Water accounts for a large part of the bodies of living things and their environment.

F. 3. Solution: mixture of two or more substances in which the molecules of the substances are evenly distributed. Colloid: formed from particles too large to form true solutions and too small to form suspensions. Suspension: formed from particles larger than ions or molecules.

*4. Room temperature: the sand would settle out, a property of a suspension; some — but not all — of the sugar would dissolve, a property of a solution. (There isn't enough solvent present to dissolve all the sugar.) The gelatin would form a colloid in its liquid phase.

Refrigerator: the sand would all settle out, as before: a property of a suspension; some, but less than before, of the sugar would remain dissolved, a property of a solution (most solutes decrease in solubility with a decrease in temperature); the gelatin would be in the semi-solid phase of a colloid.

G. 5. Acid: The hydrogen ion. Base: the hydroxide ion.

6. Pure water contains equal numbers of hydrogen ions and hydroxide ions.

7. It expresses how acidic or basic a solution is.

QUESTIONS FOR SECTION 2

1. List at least five properties of water.
2. Why are the properties of water important to living things?
3. Define the terms solution, colloid, and suspension.
4. Suppose you have a mixture of 1 g gelatin, 10 g sugar, and 10 g sand in 30 ml of water. You store half of it at room temperature and half of it in the refrigerator overnight. What properties of solutions, colloids, and suspensions would the mixture show under each condition? What observations would you make to detect these properties? (Note: Gently heat the mixture of gelatin and water until the gelatin dissolves if you wish to try this experiment.)
5. What ion causes a solution to be an acid, a base?
6. Explain why pure water is neither acidic nor basic, but neutral.
7. What is the pH scale used to express?
8. What makes carbon so important to living organisms?
9. Using three carbon atoms, six hydrogen atoms, and two oxygen atoms, see how many different molecules you can draw.

(See more answers on page 91.)

3 COMPLEX CHEMICALS OF LIFE

Classes of Complex Chemicals

We have already noted that carbon atoms form chains and rings and that hydrogen, oxygen, and nitrogen are bonded to the carbon atoms. These properties make possible an almost unlimited number of compounds that contain carbon. Many of these compounds are very important in the structure and function of living things. We will study four classes of these compounds. They are *carbohydrates*, (kär bō *hi* drāts) *fats, proteins*, and *nucleic* (noō *klē* ik) *acids*. We will consider the general structure of each class of compound and see how each is related to the function of living things.

What are Carbohydrates and How Do They Function?

No matter what you ate at your last meal, you must have eaten some carbohydrates. Potatoes, rice, all kinds of breads and cereals, even fruits and vegetables contain carbohydrates. *The main function of carbohydrates in living things is to provide a source of energy.* Plants make their own carbohydrates. Animals get their carbohydrates from eating plants. Why do the foods listed above all come from plants?

The carbohydrate compound found in nearly all living things is *glucose*. The atoms in a molecule of glucose are held together by covalent bonds. As we discussed earlier, energy is stored in chemical bonds. Each of the dashes in the structural formula for glucose represents a chemical bond in which some energy is stored. (See Fig. 5-16.)

OBJECTIVES FOR SECTION 3

I. Describe the properties of *carbohydrates* and tell how they function.
J. Describe the properties of *fats* and tell how they function.
K. Describe the properties of *proteins* and tell how they function.
L. Describe the properties of *nucleic acids* and tell how they function.
M. Summarize some ways the chemical structures found in living things are related to their functions.

Answers to Questions for Section 2.

H. 8. With other elements, carbon forms many different compounds important to life; next to water, these compounds make up nearly all the substances of which living things are made.

*9. Students' drawings will vary. Some possible ones (not all represent compounds that actually exist).

Where structural formulas are given, they are intended to help students visualize those complex molecules. We would not expect the students to memorize them.

GLUCOSE

The perspective of the mole-cule of glucose

5-16. *Two ways to represent the structure of glucose.*

5-17. Water is released in dehydration synthesis. Water is added to a substance in hydrolysis.

GLUCOSE

GLUCOSE

ENZYMES

DEHYDRATION SYNTHESIS
(−H_2O)

HYDROLYSIS
(+H_2O)

+H_2O

MALTOSE

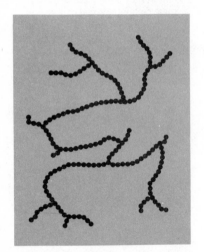

5-18. The branched chains of glucose molecules in starch.

SACCHARIDES   Glucose is one of many simple sugars or *monosaccharides*. (män ō *sak* ə rīd) Two monosaccharides can be joined together to produce a *disaccharide*. (dī *sak* uh rīd) Two glucose units linked together form one molecule of the disaccharide *maltose*. (See Fig. 5-17.) When two glucose molecules combine and form maltose, one molecule of water is released. This kind of reaction is called *dehydration synthesis*.

There are many other disaccharides. You are most familiar with table sugar or *sucrose*. Sucrose is a disaccharide composed of glucose and another monosaccharide called fructose.

Many glucose units linked together form a *polysaccharide*. (päl i *sak* ə rīd). Living things contain three main kinds of polysaccharides. They are *starch, cellulose,* (*sel* yə lōs) and *glycogen* (*gli* k ə jən). (See Fig. 5-18.) You are familiar with starch as the white part of a potato and with cellulose as the stringy part of celery. Cellulose often forms part of the structure of a plant. Furthermore, glycogen is found only in animals.

In general, living things use their ability to form polysaccharides as a way to store energy. They can chemically remove glucose units one at a time to supply energy as it is needed. When a glucose molecule is released, a molecule of water is used in the reaction. The water molecule is broken into H and OH. This kind of reaction is called *hydrolysis* (hī drol ə sis) because water is lysed or broken. It is the opposite of dehydration synthesis. (Refer back to Fig. 5-17.)

What are Fats and How Do They Function?

Compared to carbohydrates, fats are a more efficient way of storing energy. The body of animals cannot store any other form of food in such large amounts. Some fats also form part of the structure of cells, as we shall see in the next chapter.

Foods such as butter, oleomargarine, and salad oil, are composed primarily of fat. Other foods such as milk, meat, and fried foods contain some fat.

FATS   A fat molecule consists of one molecule of glycerol and three molecules of fatty acids. (See Fig. 5-19.) Notice that each fatty acid has a long chain of carbon atoms. (See Fig. 5-20.) It also has lots of hydrogen atoms and only a few oxygen atoms associated with the carbon atoms in the chain. As a general rule, molecules with large amounts of hydrogen bonded to the carbon release more energy when burned than those that contain large amounts of oxygen. When a fat is burned it releases a lot of energy. It makes a good fuel. This makes sense if we consider what happens when fuels are burned. Burning requires the addition of oxygen. Substances that already contain oxygen release less energy when burned. A certain amount of fatty acid provides more energy than the same amount of carbohydrate.

Ask interested students to review current literature about the effects of saturated and unsaturated fats on the human body.

5-19.   *The formation of a fat.*

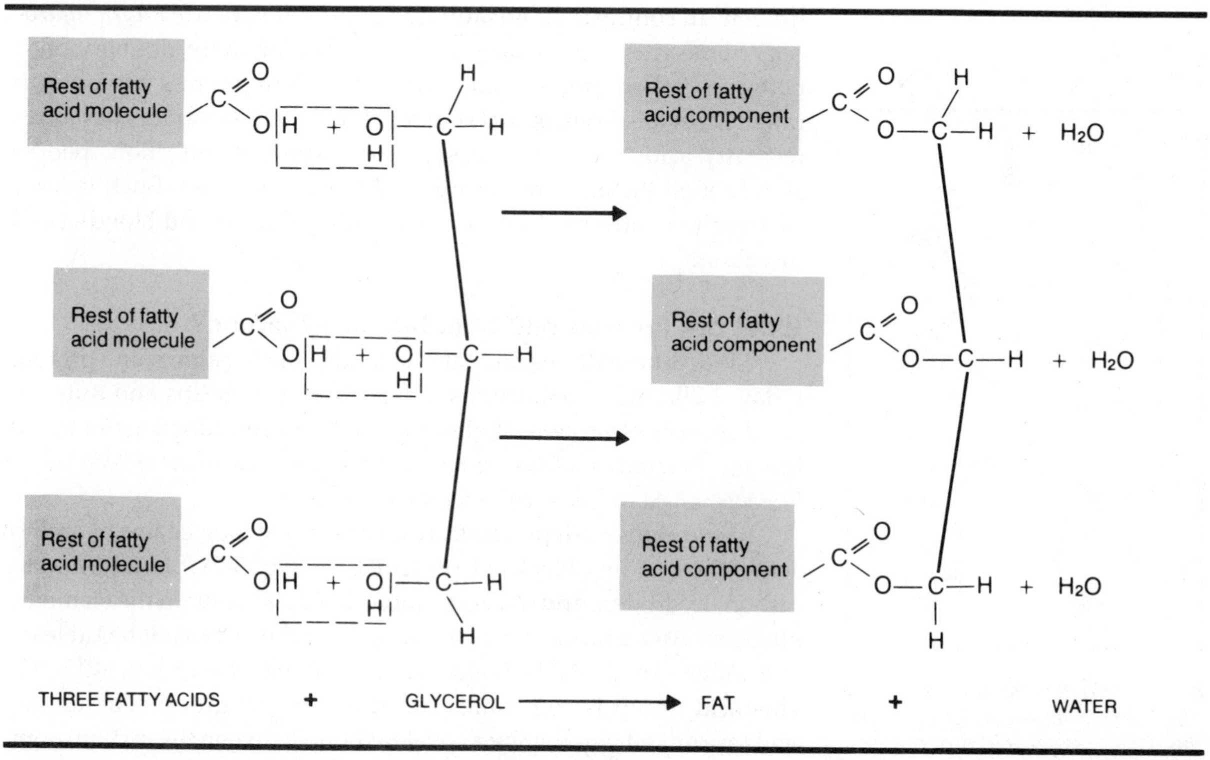

THREE FATTY ACIDS   +   GLYCEROL ⟶ FAT   +   WATER

STEARIC ACID (A SATURATED FATTY ACID)

LINOLENIC ACID (AN UNSATURATED FATTY ACID)

FATTY ACIDS   The fatty acid part of a simple fat can be saturated or unsaturated. (See Fig. 5-20.) *A **saturated** fat is one in which each carbon atom in the fatty acid chain (except the end carbon atoms) is bonded to two hydrogen atoms.* The acid chains are *saturated* with hydrogen. In contrast, *an **unsaturated** fat is not saturated with hydrogen.* Somewhere in its fatty acids are one or more double bonds between carbon atoms. Many fats from plant sources are unsaturated. Most fats from animal sources contain large amounts of saturated fatty acids. As we shall see in our study of nutrition, people should limit the amount of saturated fats in their diet. Such fats are thought to contribute to the development of heart and blood vessel diseases.

What are Proteins and How Do They Function?

Like carbohydrates and fats, you have likely eaten some protein today. Milk, meat, poultry, fish, eggs, and even beans and nuts are good sources of protein. Proteins serve two main functions in living things. *Structural proteins are needed for growth and repair of body parts. Proteins, called enzymes, control chemical reactions.*

AMINO ACIDS   All proteins are composed of long chains of amino acids, the building blocks of protein. (See Fig. 5-21.) In addition to carbon, hydrogen, and oxygen, amino acids also contain the element, nitrogen. An amino acid gets its name from the fact that it has at least one amino group, $-NH_2$. It also has at least one acid group, $-COOH$. This acid group is sometimes called a carboxyl group. The amino acids are linked together by a covalent bond between the carbon atom

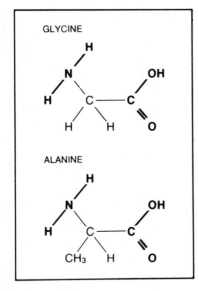

GLYCINE

ALANINE

5-21. *Two simple amino acids. The -NH₂ is an amino group, and the -COOH is an acid group.*

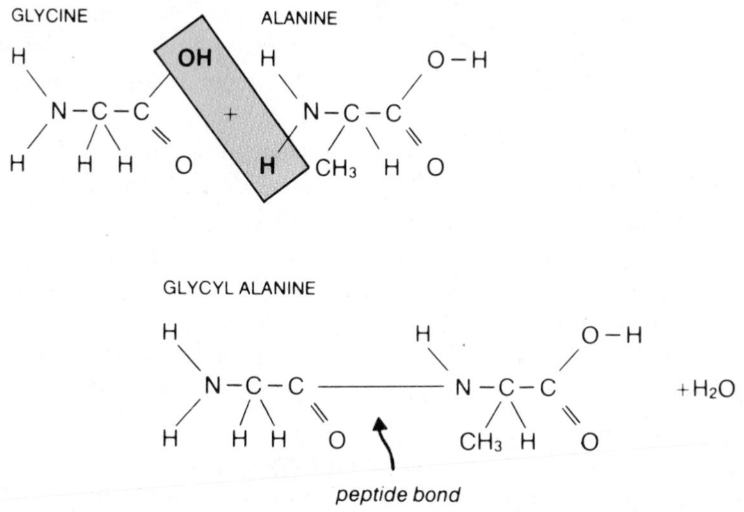

of the acid group of one amino acid and a nitrogen atom of the amino group of another amino acid. This bond is called a *peptide bond*. (See Fig. 5-22.) *A short chain of amino acids held together by peptide bonds is called a* **peptide.** A *protein* contains several hundred amino acid units bonded by peptide bonds.

PROTEINS   Each kind of protein is composed of a specific sequence of amino acids. Thousands of different proteins can be made from the twenty kinds of amino acids commonly found in living things. This is a little like using an alphabet of twenty letters to write words several hundred letters long. Changing one letter in one of these long words would make it a different word. So changing one amino acid in a protein makes it a different protein.

Proteins are affected by changes in temperature and pH. You know that when you cook an egg, the clear part around the yolk becomes solid and turns white. Eggwhite is made up of protein. What you see when you cook an egg is the effect of heat on protein. Changing the pH by putting a few drops of acid or base on an egg would also cause the clear part to turn white and solid. Conditions inside living things are maintained in a narrow range of temperatures and near neutral pH. Failure to maintain these conditions could damage proteins.

What Are Nucleic Acids and How Do They Function?

You eat nucleic acids in almost every food. Nucleic acids are found in all cells, especially in the nucleus or control center of the cells. (We will study more about cells in the next chapter.) Each of the

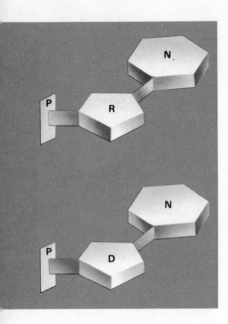

5-23. *The structure of a nucleotide. P = phosphate, R = ribose, D = deoxyribose, N = nitrogenous base.*

Answers to Questions for Section 3.

L. 8. DNA transmits information from parent to offspring so the offspring look like their parents. RNA carries information from the DNA and controls how proteins are made.

*9. Similarities: basic unit in both is a nucleotide, consisting of a molecule each of phosphoric acid, a 5-carbon sugar, and a nitrogenous base. The bases A (adenine), G (guanine) and C (cytosine) present in both. Differences: sugar in RNA is ribose, and in DNA is deoxyribose. DNA contains the additional base thymine (T) and RNA the additional base uracil (U). RNA consists of a single strand of nucleotides, while DNA consists of two strands of nucleotides, coiled in a spiral.

10. Base, sugar, phosphate.

two types of nucleic acids serves a particular function in living things. *Deoxyribonucleic* (dē ok si rī bō noo̅ *klē* ik) *acid or DNA transmits information from parent to offspring so the offspring look like their parents. Ribonucleic* (rī bō noo̅ *klē* ik) *acid or RNA carries information from the DNA and controls how proteins are made.*

The story of the discovery of the structure of DNA in the early 1950s is an intriguing one, full of the suspense and drama of a who-done-it. This story has been told by one of the co-discoverers, James Watson, in a book, *The Double Helix.* Watson, along with Francis Crick and Maurice Wilkins, was awarded the Nobel Prize in Medicine and Physiology in 1962 for helping to decipher the DNA code.

NUCLEOTIDES The basic unit of both DNA and RNA is a nucleotide. A *nucleotide* (noo̅ *klē* ə tīd) consists of one molecule each of *phosphoric acid,* a *five-carbon sugar,* and a compound called a *nitrogenous* (nī *troj* ə nəs) *base.* It is called a nitrogenous base because it contains nitrogen and has a basic pH. All of the sugar molecules in RNA are *ribose* and all of the sugar molecules in DNA are *deoxyribose.* Deoxyribose has one less oxygen atom than ribose. Three of the bases are found in both DNA and RNA. We will use letters to stand for them: *A* for *adenine* (*ad* ən ēn), *G* for *guanine* (*gwä* nēn), and *C* for *cytosine* (*si* tō sēn). In addition, DNA contains the base, *thymine* (*thi* mēn) *(T),* and RNA contains the base, *uracil* (*yoo̅r* ə sil) *(U).* Careful analysis revealed that there was always a constant 1:1 ratio between adenine (A) and thymine (T). A similar ratio always existed between guanine (G) and cytosine (C). No particular ratio, however, seemed to exist between any other pairs of bases. See Figure 5-23 for the general structure of nucleotides. As we shall see in Chapter 8, the ability of DNA and RNA to transmit information lies in the arrangement of these bases.

Another important difference exists between DNA and RNA besides the kind of sugar each contains. RNA molecules consist of a single strand of nucleotides. On the other hand, DNA molecules consist of two strands of nucleotides coiled so they resemble a spiral staircase (See Fig. 5-24.) The phosphoric acid and sugar units are like the banisters on the staircase and the bases are like the steps. The two strands are held together by weak chemical bonds between bases in each of the strands. These bonds always form between A in one strand and T in the other or between C in one strand and G in the other. A given nucleic acid can be of almost any length. However, there are only four different nucleotides in a strand of DNA. These must therefore be repeated along the entire length of the ladder. This repetition was found to be in no apparent order at first. However, it did suggest an answer to the operation of DNA.

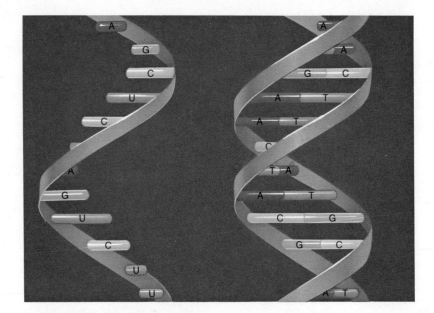

5-24. *Part of m-RNA molecule (left); part of DNA molecule (right). The phosphates and sugars are part of the strands and only the nitrogenous bases are shown.*

QUESTIONS FOR SECTION 3

1. What is the main building block of carbohydrates?
2. What are the functions of carbohydrates in living things?
3. What are the two building blocks of fats?
4. Why are fat molecules good for storing energy?
5. How is an unsaturated fat different from a saturated fat?
6. What are two functions of protein?
7. What effect would changing the sequence of amino acids have on a protein?
8. What are the functions of DNA, RNA?
9. Make a list of the similarities and differences between DNA and RNA.
10. What are the building blocks in nucleic acids?

(See more answers on page 96.)

Answers to Questions for Section 3

I. 1. Glucose.

2. To provide energy for the activities of life, and a means of storing that energy.

J. 3. Glycerol and fatty acids.

4. They have many hydrogen atoms and few oxygen atoms, compared to carbohydrates. Compounds with more hydrogen-carbon bonds release more energy when burned.

5. A saturated fat is one in which each carbon atom in the fatty acid chain (except at the ends) is bonded to two hydrogen atoms. In an unsaturated fat, the acid chains are not saturated: one or more double bonds are in the chain, so that some carbon atoms are bonded to just one hydrogen atom.

K. 6. Growth and repair of body parts, and — as enzymes — control of chemical reactions in organisms.

7. It would change it into a different protein.

CHAPTER REVIEW

Structure and function are related chemically. For example, the functions of water in living things are closely related to the chemical structure of water. Likewise, the large amounts of hydrogen in carbohydrates and even larger amounts in fats make these molecules useful for energy storage. The arrangement of amino acids in proteins determines the function of each protein, so structure is again related to function. Finally, the arrangement of nucleotides in DNA and RNA determines the kind of information they carry. These molecules can alter the information in them. Even small molecules and ions affect the function of living things. Variations in the concentration of acids and bases can affect the way other chemicals react. *At all levels from ions to complex molecules the structure of the chemical components plays an important role in how a living thing functions.*

Career Activities

1. Biochemists have helped to make available such things as antibiotics, fertilizers, pesticides, and tranquilizers. Each of these substances can benefit living things. Each can be misused to harm living things. Discuss some of the benefits and possible harmful effects of each of these substances.

VOCABULARY REVIEW

1 matter
element
atom
proton
neutron
electron
ionic bond
covalent bond

ion
molecule
compound

2 solution
colloid
suspension
acid
base

pH

3 carbohydrate
monosaccharide
disaccharide
polysaccharide
lipid
saturated fat
unsaturated fat

protein
amino acid
peptide
peptide bond
enzyme
nucleic acid
nucleotide

CHAPTER 5 TEST

Copy the number of each test item and place your answer to the right.

PART 1   Multiple Choice: Select the letter of the phrase that best completes each of the following.

b   1. The breakdown of food and the making of chemical substances is called   **a.** chemistry
b. metabolism   **c.** hydrolysis   **d.** synthesis.

c   2. The electrons of an atom move around its nucleus and form   **a.** a colloid   **b.** an acid or base
c. an electron cloud   **d.** a compound.

d   3. Two atoms sharing a pair of electrons form
a. a suspension   **b.** a solution   **c.** an ionic bond   **d.** a covalent bond.

a   4. An atom that has gained or lost electrons is called
a. an ion   **b.** a molecule   **c.** a compound
d. an acid.

b   5. A mixture in which the solvent and the solute are evenly distributed is called a   **a.** compound
b. solution   **c.** colloid   **d.** suspension.

b   6. A substance that releases H⁺ when dissolved in water is   **a.** a colloid   **b.** an acid   **c.** a base   **d.** an element.

a   7. An element that forms chains or rings and combines with other elements is   **a.** carbon
b. hydrogen   **c.** nitrogen   **d.** oxygen.

d   8. A mixture that contains large particles which settle (in time) is called a   **a.** molecule   **b.** solution
c. colloid   **d.** suspension.

b   9. The substances that store the most energy in the body are   **a.** carbohydrates   **b.** fats
c. proteins   **d.** nucleic acids.

c   10. The substances that make up the structure of the body and control chemical reactions are
a. carbohydrates   **b.** fats   **c.** proteins
d. nucleic acids.

PART 2   Matching: Match the letter of the term in Column I with its description in Column II.

COLUMN I

a. proton
b. glucose
c. DNA
d. electron
e. enzyme
f. atom
g. sucrose
h. glycerol
i. neutron
j. element

Answers

24. peptide bonds
25. the structures of the chemical components are important in how a living thing functions.

COLUMN II

j   11. Any one of many kinds of matter
i   12. An uncharged particle
c   13. An important nucleic acid
a   14. A positively-charged particle
f   15. The basic unit of matter
g   16. A disaccharide molecule
e   17. A protein which acts as a catalyst
h   18. One part of a fat molecule
d   19. A negatively-charged particle
b   20. A monosaccharide or simple sugar

PART 3   Completion: Complete the following.

21. Ice forms on top of water because water at 4°C has its greatest ___density___

22. Water helps to regulate temperature because of its ability to hold ___heat___

23. The two information molecules in living things are ____ DNA/RNA

24. Amino acids are held together in proteins by ____.

25. State the major idea in this chapter ____.

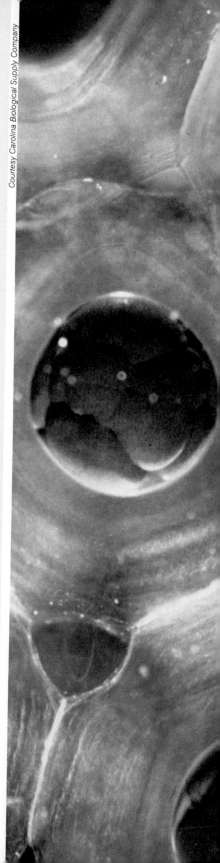

Courtesy Carolina Biological Supply Company

CHAPTER 6

THE CELL

We began our study of biology at the level of living things in their environments. After getting a view of this "big picture" we moved to the most basic level to study the chemical structure of living things. In this chapter we will see how chemical structures are organized to form cells.

Have you ever seen a cell? Most are too small to be seen without a microscope. But the yolk of an egg is really one giant cell. We use the word cell to describe a small unit or compartment such as a cell in a battery, a cell in a prison, or a cell in an organism. *The cell is the basic unit of structure and function in living things.*

Structure and function are related at all levels of organization within living things. At the chemical level, the structure of molecules is related to their function. At the cellular level, the structure of cell parts is related to their function. Furthermore, the various parts of cells work together. Their functions are regulated so that nearly constant conditions are maintained within cells. *This concept of homeostasis extends to all of the cells and thus to the whole organism.*

The study of cells will help you to understand better some things you observe every day. Hunger and thirst are signals that the organs and cells of the body need materials to maintain themselves, to develop and grow, and to perform their other functions. In your study of cells you will learn:

- Why lettuce wilts
- Why too much fertilizer can "burn" a lawn
- How leaves change color in the fall.

You will also begin to see how scientists make observations and attempt to explain them.

FROG'S EGGS

☐ THE CELL THEORY

Development of the Cell Theory

As you learned in Chapter 3, when scientists observe an event they often try to find out how it happened. They make an hypothesis. As the scientists make more observations they check to see if the hypothesis explains each new observation. As more and more information is found that is explained by the hypothesis, it is promoted to the rank of a *theory*. **A theory** *offers an explanation for a large number of observations.* The cell theory is an example.

The cell theory has undergone the kind of development described above. Like many other scientific theories, the cell theory could not evolve until the proper tool was developed. In this case, the tool was the microscope. Figure 6-1 shows several different kinds of microscopes. Cells are generally too small to be seen with the unaided eye, so a microscope is needed to study them.

Imagine what it might have been like to have lived three centuries ago and to have had one of the earliest kind of microscope to use. What would you have studied? You might have chosen something simple at first just as Robert Hooke did in 1665, when he studied thin

6-1. **A.** *Robert Hooke's microscope.* **B.** *Light microscope magnifies about 100 X.* **C.** *Electron microscope magnifies about 200,000 X.* **D.** *Scanning electron microscope magnifies about 50,000 X.*

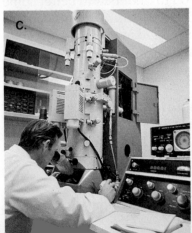

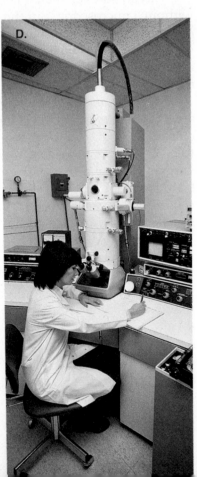

slices of bark from the cork oak tree. Figure 6-2 shows what he saw. How would you have described it? Hooke called the spaces cells. He was the first person to use the term cell to describe material from a living organism. We now know that bark consists of dead cells. Therefore, Hooke was seeing cell walls and hollow spaces inside them where living cells had once been.

By 1838, nearly two centuries later, microscopes had been greatly improved. Many different samples of living things had been observed also. In that year, M.J. Schleiden, a German botanist, reported that all plants were made of cells. In the following year, zoologist Theodor Schwann reported that animals too were organized in the form of cells. He proposed a cellular basis for all life. Two decades later, Rudolf Virchow, a pathologist, added the hypothesis that all cells come only from preexisting cells. By the end of the nineteenth century these ideas were put together and became the cell theory. *The cell theory states that all living things are composed of cells and that all cells arise from other living cells.* This theory emphasizes the basic sameness of all living things. In addition, it brings a unity to the study of many different kinds of organisms.

Generally, the cell theory is workable because it explains many observations. Yet, the discovery of viruses caused biologists to revise their thinking slightly. As we shall see, viruses do not have the same structure as cells. However, they are capable of reproducing themselves. This observation is a good example of how scientists must continually revise their theories in the light of new evidence.

The Cell as the Basic Unit of Living Things

As the microscope was improved, techniques for staining cells with different colored dyes were developed. Simple staining techniques showed that cells generally have a boundary, now called the *cell membrane.* These techniques also showed that cells generally contain a dark-staining *nucleus.* Lighter staining particles are seen scattered throughout the remainder of the cell, the *cytoplasm* (sī tə plaz əm). Details of these structures were unknown until the development of the electron microscope in the 1930's.

Today two basic kinds of cells are known. They are the procaryotes (prō *ker* ē ōt) and eucaryotes (yü *ker* ē ōt). The procaryotes are simple cells with no nucleus. Bacteria and blue-green algae consist of these cells, as we will see later. All other cells are eucaryotic.

In studying cells, we must keep in mind that cells are three-dimensional objects like spheres and cubes. When we look through a microscope or at a photograph taken through a microscope we usually see a flat surface. By focusing up and down on an object we can observe optical "slices." From these we can see that the object has

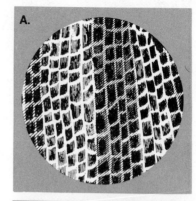

A.

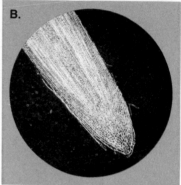

B.

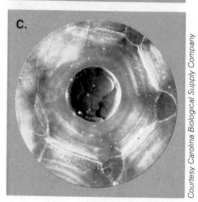

C.

Courtesy Carolina Biological Supply Company

6-2. *A. These cork cells look very much like what Hooke might have seen. B. Schleiden may have seen a root tip like this one. C. Schwann studied frog's eggs like these.*

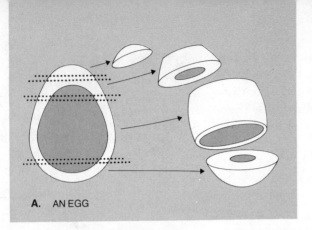

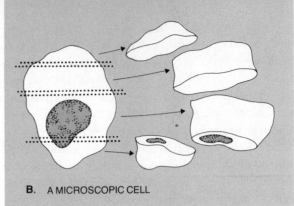

A. AN EGG

B. A MICROSCOPIC CELL

6-3. *A. Different amounts of yolk are seen in slices of an egg.* ***B.*** *Different amounts of nucleus are seen as one focuses up and down on a cell.*

depth. We can construct in our mind a picture of a three-dimensional cell. This is a lot like trying to reconstruct a hard-boiled egg after it has been sliced. (See Fig. 6-3.)

A Typical Animal Cell

Cells are so varied in the details of their structure that it is difficult to select a typical cell. Even so, look at the picture of a cell from the inside of a human cheek in Figure 6-4. It has many of the properties of an animal cell. You may be able to observe them in your school laboratory. Notice that this cell has a *nucleus*, a *nucleolus* (n$\overline{oo}$ *kl*e ə ləs), and fairly clear *cytoplasm* with some granules in it. Furthermore, there is a boundary formed by the *cell membrane*. These cells that line the inside of your mouth are flatter than many other cells. You may even see some that are rolled up. They are constantly being lost and replaced so that the inside of your mouth is always protected by many layers of healthy cells. These cells contain many tiny structures that are too small to be seen with a light microscope.

A Typical Plant Cell

The plant cell shown in Figure 6-5 is from *Elodea*, a simple plant often used in aquariums. With a light microscope you can see a *cell*

6-4. *A. These cells are from the inner lining of a human cheek.* ***B.*** *Model of a typical animal cell.*

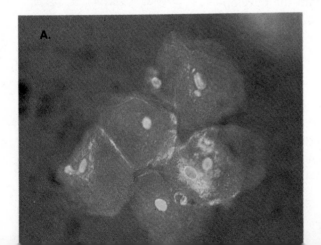

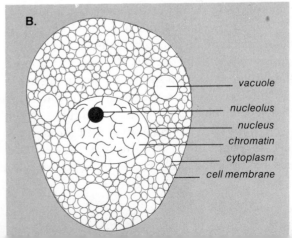

vacuole

nucleolus

nucleus

chromatin

cytoplasm

cell membrane

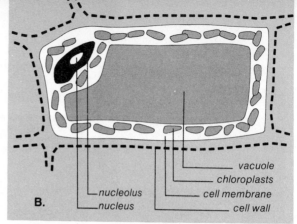

vacuole
chloroplasts
cell membrane
cell wall

nucleolus
nucleus

B.

A.

wall, a *nucleus*, a *nucleolus*, a large central *vacuole* (vak ū ōl), and many *chloroplasts* (klôr ə plasts). The cell wall forms a rigid support for the inner contents of the cell. Plant cells also have a *cell membrane*. It is usually pressed up against the cell wall and not visible with a light microscope. The large central vacuole contains fluid or *cell sap*. If you have a chance to observe some of these cells in the laboratory, you will see the many chloroplasts moving around the vacuole. The green color of the chloroplasts is due to *chlorophyll* (klôr ə fil) and not to any stain that was used.

The movement of the chloroplasts and other small structures in the cytoplasm of Elodea cells is called *cytoplasmic streaming*. This constant churning around of the internal contents of a cell is observable evidence of the fact that movement takes place inside cells.

Comparison of Plant and Animal Cells

All of the structures we saw in the animal cell are also present in plant cells. In addition, plant cells also have cell walls and chloroplasts. Moreover, plant cells generally have one very large vacuole. In contrast, animal cells often have many small vacuoles. These differences may seem to indicate that plant and animal cells are not much alike at all. However, as you study the structure of cells as seen with an electron microscope, it will become evident that all cells have many important characteristics in common. Later you will learn about some cells that do not fit in either the plant or animal category.

6-5. *A. Elodea showing the organelles you will be able to see under your microscope.* **B.** *Model of a typical plant cell.*

Answers to Questions for Section 1.

A. **1.** That all living things are composed of cells and that all cells arise from other living cells.

   2. After the invention of the microscope, the essential tool, Hooke identified "cells" in cork. Next, Schleiden stated all plants were made of cells, followed by Schwann who said all animals and all forms of life were made of cells. Virchow proposed that cells come only from pre-existing cells. By the end of the 19th Century, all those hypotheses were united in the cell theory.

B. **3.** Cell membrane, nucleus, nucleolus, cytoplasm, vacuole (for all cells); chloroplasts, vacuole, cell wall (for plant cells).

   *****4.** The chromosomes.

C. **5.** Cell membrane, nucleus, nucleolus, cytoplasm, vacuoles.

   *****6.** If the cells contained a cell wall and large vacuoles, they would be plant, not animal.

QUESTIONS FOR SECTION 1
1. What is the cell theory?
2. Describe the major events that led to the cell theory.
3. List the structures in a typical cell that can be seen with a light microscope.
4. What particular structures are located in the nucleus?
5. What structures are found in all cells?
6. If you were given some cells, how would you determine whether they were plant or animal?

9:00 AM **3:00 PM** **9:00 PM**

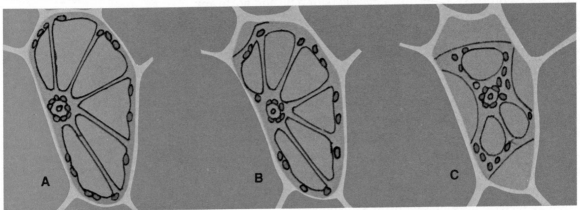

A

B

C

CHAPTER INVESTIGATION

The owner of this plant carelessly watered it with salt water. The photos show what happened after 6 and 12 hours. The drawings below the photos show how the cells were affected.

A. Describe what happened to the plant and to the cells.

B. Explain why you think these things happened.

C. Restate your explanation in the form of a hypothesis. Using a different experiment than that shown above, design a way to test your hypothesis. If possible, carry out your experiment.

2 ORGANELLES, THE LITTLE ORGANS OF THE CELL

The Discovery of Organelles

In the two decades following the invention of the electron microscope, biologists discovered that the internal structure of cells was much more complex than it had appeared with the light microscope. They identified many small particles which they called *organelles* (ôr gə *nelz*), or little organs. Most of their observations were limited to describing the location and structure of these organelles. During the same time biochemists were also studying cells. They ground the cells into small particles and studied the chemical functions of the particles. In the 1950's the biologists and the biochemists were excited to discover that both had been studying some of the same particles. What the biologists had learned about structure and location of organelles could be combined with what the biochemists had learned about their function.

Since then techniques have continued to improve. The scanning electron microscope is now used to obtain three-dimensional views of the surface of organelles. A special rapid freezing technique, the freeze-fracture technique, is used to break organelles apart so their internal structure can be studied.

With this background on how scientists have observed cells, we are now ready to look at some of their findings. We will consider first the structure of the cell membrane. Then we will examine the characteristics of the organelles that have membranes.

The Cell Membrane

The boundary of the living portion of a cell is called the **cell membrane** *or* **plasma membrane.** This boundary separates the contents of the cell from the surrounding environment. The membrane regulates the passage of materials into and out of the cell. It also receives and transmits information from the outside environment to the inside of the cell. Thus, the cell membrane helps to maintain a relatively stable internal environment within the cell.

Much research has gone into determining membrane structure. The Singer *fluid mosaic model* is now accepted by most biologists as the structure of cell membranes. (See Fig. 6-6.) According to this model the membrane has two layers of lipid molecules. Each molecule has one end that is water soluble and another end that is lipid soluble. The fats we studied in Chapter 5 are examples of a lipid.

Knowing how lipid molecules behave will help us to understand how cell membranes function. The water soluble ends of the molecules face the surfaces of the membrane. One end faces toward the

Ask students why "organelle" is a good name for these structures. Interested students might report in more detail on one of the organelles discussed here.

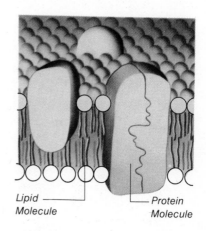

Lipid Molecule — Protein Molecule

6-6. *Fluid mosaic model of a cell membrane.*

A. NUCLEUS AND NUCLEOLUS

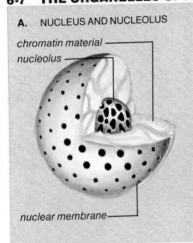

chromatin material

nucleolus

nuclear membrane

B. MITOCHONDRIA

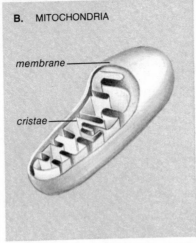

membrane

cristae

C. LYSOSOME

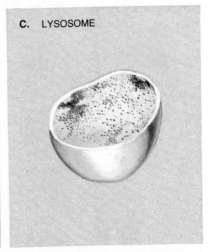

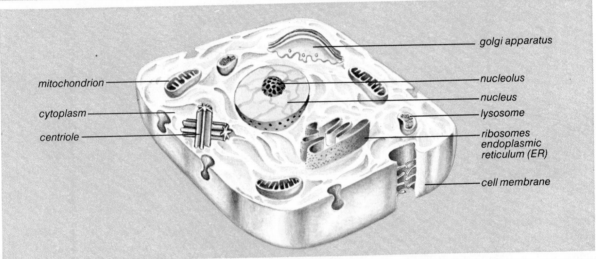

golgi apparatus

mitochondrion

nucleolus

nucleus

cytoplasm

lysosome

centriole

ribosomes
endoplasmic
reticulum (ER)

cell membrane

**D. ENDOPLASMIC RETICULUM
WITH RIBOSOMES**

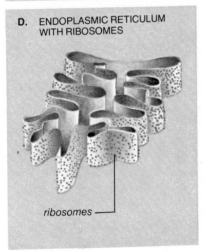

ribosomes

E. GOLGI APPARATUS

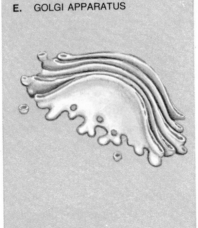

F.

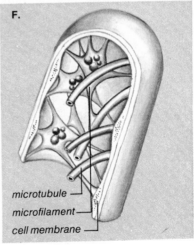

microtubule

microfilament

cell membrane

outside of the cell while the other end faces inward. The lipid soluble ends of the molecules are next to each other in the middle of the membrane. Protein molecules are imbedded at intervals along the membrane. However, some protein molecules protrude from both surfaces. Most membranes are about 60 percent protein and 40 percent lipid. The relationship of the structure of the membrane to the control of materials entering the cell will be discussed later in this chapter.

Other Organelles of an Animal Cell

The arrangement of organelles in a typical animal cell is shown in Figure 6-7. Of these organelles, five are bounded by membranes. They are the *endoplasmic reticulum* (en ́də *plaz* mik ri *tik* yə ləm), *ribosomes* (rī bə sōmz), *Golgi* (gôl jē) *apparatus, lysosomes* (lī sə sōmz), and *mitochondria* (mīt ə *kän* drē ə).

6-8. *The endoplasmic reticulum (ER) forms a network of channels within the cytoplasm of the cell.*

ENDOPLASMIC RETICULUM   The **endoplasmic reticulum (ER)** *is a system of interconnected membranes that extends throughout the cell.* It is the assembly line of the cell. The ER also provides surfaces for chemical reactions. It also consists of tubules for the transport and storage of molecules made by the cell. In some places the endoplasmic reticulum is rough and in other places it is smooth. Smooth ER is the site of the synthesis of lipids. Rough ER is so named because of the presence of ribosomes. It is found in cells making large amounts of protein. (See Fig. 6-8.)

RIBOSOMES   **Ribosomes** *are the sites at which protein synthesis takes place.* The more proteins a cell is making, the greater the number of ribosomes it has. Proteins such as digestive enzymes are synthesized on ribosomes that are attached to the ER. These proteins enter the tubules of the ER and are eventually transported to the cell membrane. Some of these proteins are used to form part of the cell membrane. Others are transported out of the cell to other parts of the organism. In contrast, ribosomes that are free in the cytoplasm make proteins that will be used within the cell.

GOLGI APPARATUS   The **Golgi apparatus** *is the warehouse of the cell.* It consists of flat, membranous sacs stacked one on top of the other. The Golgi apparatus receives protein molecules from the tubules of the ER. Sometimes it adds carbohydrate to the protein. Other times the Golgi apparatus removes a short chain of amino acids from the protein. These changes often convert the protein into a form the cells can use. Finally, the Golgi apparatus packs these proteins into membranes and sends them to the cell's surface. The Golgi apparatus is very large in cells that produce large amounts of secretions. (See Fig. 6-9.) These cells include liver cells that produce bile to digest foods and mucous cells that produce mucus for lubrication.

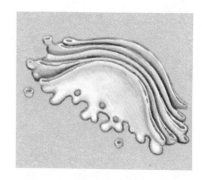

6-9. *An enlargement of the Golgi apparatus to show vacuoles and flat, membranous sacs.*

6-10. *The size and shape of lyso-somes change with the stage of their activity.*

6-11. *Mitochondrion. A cutaway diagram shows the double-layered membranous wall.*

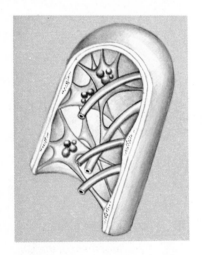

6-12. *Microtubules and micro-filaments.*

LYSOSOMES **Lysosomes** *are the cell's self-destruct organelles.* They are small membranous sacs filled with destructive enzymes. Lysosomes vary in size and number and are found only in animal cells. However, plant cells are now thought to have a similar organelle. Somehow the enzymes are stored in an inactive form but can be activated by the presence of a foreign particle. When a cell surrounds a large particle, it becomes engulfed in a membrane-enclosed sac, a vacuole. When this occurs, lysosomes surround the enclosed particle. Finally, the lysosomes release their energy into the vacuole and destroy the foreign particle.

Lysosomes also release enzymes when a cell dies. These enzymes digest the remains of the dead cell. Some biologists believe that as cells get older the lysosomes become leaky and release enzymes. The pain of arthritis and gout may be related to the escape of these enzymes. The reason why the enzymes do not destroy the membranes of the lysosomes that contain them is still an unanswered question in biology.

MITOCHONDRIA Most cells contain as many as 10,000 mitochondria. **Mitochondria** *are the powerhouses of the cell.* They are small rod-shaped organelles that have a smooth outer membrane and an extensively-folded inner membrane. These folds are known as *cristae.* On the surfaces of the inner membrane are the enzymes that produce energy for the cell. This energy is stored in a molecule called **a**denosine **t**riphosphate (ə *den* ə sen trī *fäs* fat), or **ATP.** ATP is energy currency of cells and it will be discussed in the next two chapters.

MICROTUBULES AND MICROFILAMENTS In addition to the organelles that have membranes around them, there are thread-like organelles, the *microtubules* and the *microfilaments.* **Microtubules** *form the skeleton of cells.* They extend out from the cell center ending near the cell surface. Microtubules consist of fibers made of protein. All cells that can divide have microtubules that are involved in the division process. Some cells have *cilia* or *flagella* that project from the surface of the cell. (See Fig. 6-14.) They aid in moving the whole cell or in moving materials along the cell surface. Cilia and flagella have bundles of microtubules inside them.

Microfilaments *are involved in movements within the cytoplasm* They consist of thin strands of protein and can change state from liquid to gel and back to liquid. As the filaments change state, the cytoplasm of cells, like an ameba, creeps along a surface. Bundles of microfilaments are usually lined up lengthwise near the moving edge of the cell. As the cell changes directions, the microfilaments also change direction. In addition to this, they can form projections that help the cell adhere to surfaces.

The Nucleus — Control Center of the Cell

Because of its large size, the nucleus was the first organelle to be recognized. It is now known to be surrounded by a double layer of membrane, the *nuclear envelope*. This envelope is continuous with the ER. The nuclear envelope has large pores through which materials can pass between the nucleus and the cytoplasm. In most cells the nuclear envelope disappears during cell division. The largest body inside the nucleus is the nucleolus. It contains a large amount of RNA and is the site of assembly of the ribosomes. In addition, the chromosomes are found inside the nucleus. They consist of protein and DNA. Each cell normally has a specific number of chromosomes. Human cells have 23 pairs or 46 chromosomes. The DNA of each chromosome is arranged in a particular sequence of nucleotides. Segments of DNA called *genes* contain the hereditary information necessary for the development of the organism. More will be said in later chapters about how chromosomes transmit information and control cell function.

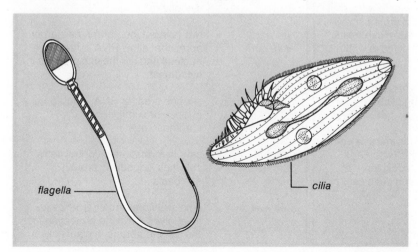

6-13. *Nucleus and nucleolus.*

Organelles of a Typical Plant Cell

Plant cells generally contain the same organelles as animal cells. In addition, they usually have *plastids* (*plas* tə dz), a large central *vacuole,* and a *cell wall.* (See Fig. 6-15 on page 110.)

PLASTIDS Plastids *are involved in the capture and storage of energy from the sun.* They are somewhat similar in structure to the mitochondria in that they have a smooth outer membrane and a complex, folded inner membrane. Plastids are of three types, of which chloroplasts are the most common. They contain a green chemical, chlorophyll. Chlorophyll is capable of capturing energy from the sun and other light sources. This energy is used to produce carbohy-

flagella ——

—— cilia

6-14. *Flagella or cilia aid some cells in moving.*

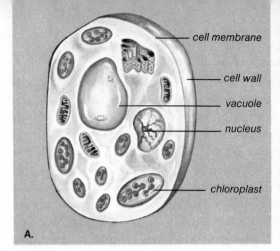

cell membrane

cell wall

vacuole

nucleus

chloroplast

A.

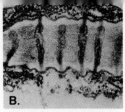

B.

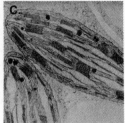

C.

6-15. *A. The organelles of a plant cell. B. Cell wall X 10,000. C. Chloroplast X 10,000.*

TABLE 6-1.   RELATIONSHIPS OF STRUCTURE AND FUNCTION IN ORGANELLES

Organelle	Relationship of structure and function	Organelle	Relationship of structure and function
Cell membrane	fluid mosaic model has pores through which small molecules and ions pass; has lipid layer through which lipid soluble substances pass; proteins are involved in active transport and information transmission; ability of membrane to form and release vesicles also regulates movement	Mitochondrion	outer membrane allows entry of molecules to be used for energy; inner membrane folded so it provides large surface for enzyme reactions to produce ATP
Endoplasmic reticulum	membrane serves many of the above functions within the cytoplasm; tubules and sac within ER provide means of transport within cell	Chloroplast	membranes contain enzymes that can use energy captured by chlorophyll to make carbohydrates
		Microtubule	proteins provide structure for cilia and flagella
Ribosome	composed of RNA; works with other RNAs in synthesis of protein; provides surface for protein synthesis either on rough ER or loose within the cytoplasm	Microfilaments	proteins provide structure within cytoplasm, ability to change from sol to fluid allows for movement within cytoplasm
		Nuclear envelope	two-layered membrane has large pores that allow RNA to leave the nucleus and synthesize proteins in cytoplasm
Golgi apparatus	membrane forms large sacs for storage and packing of cell's secretions	Nucleolus	storage area for RNA, located in close proximity to chromosomes
Lysosome	membrane surrounds inactive enzymes that can be activated and released to digest foods, foreign substances, and even dead cells	Chromosomes	carry information to control cell's activities, especially protein synthesis
		Cell wall	rigid structure formed from cellulose, gives form and protection to the cell membrane in plant cells

drates. Another plastid, the colorless *leucoplast* (lü kə plast), serves as a storage area for the starch, and at times, proteins. A variety of other plastids called *chromoplasts* (krō mō plasts) contain other colored chemicals.

All of the brilliant colors displayed by plants are due to the presence of colored substances in plastids. Some plastids contain more than one pigment. A few plastids, like those in the white potato, contain no colored pigments, only starch. Tomatoes, before they ripen, have a mixture of chlorophyll and other pigments. The chlorophyll breaks down and allows the orange, yellow, and red pigments to become visible during the ripening process. The colorful display of autumn leaves also involves the breakdown of chlorophyll to allow the other pigments to be seen.

VACUOLES   **Vacuoles *are membrane-surrounded sacs that are prominent in plant cells.*** Small vacuoles are also found in some animal cells. Mature plant cells contain a single large central vacuole filled with water and some salts. Young plant cells have many small vacuoles. These vacuoles play an important part in the transport of water in many plants.

CELL WALL   **The cell wall *is the rigid outer boundary of a plant cell that lies outside the cell membrane.*** Only plant cells have cell walls. These walls are made up of several layers of cellulose that form a rigid but porous supporting structure for the cell. Pectin, a carbohydrate substance, holds plant cells together. Pectins are compounds that make jellies jell. Wood is the cell walls of plant cells.

Information about the relationships between the structure and function of cell organelles is summarized in Table 6-1.

QUESTIONS FOR SECTION 2

1. Describe the structure of a cell membrane.
2. List the structures you can see in a picture taken through an electron microscope that you could not see with a light microscope.
3. How would changing the size of pores in a cell membrane alter its function?
4. What effect on the function of a cell would occur if one of the following organelles were missing?
   a. mitochondria   d. nucleus
   b. ribosomes   e. lysosomes
   c. chloroplasts   f. microfilaments
5. How is the structure of each of the following organelles suited to its function:
   a. cell wall   d. ribosome
   b. mitochondria   e. chlorplast
   c. endoplasmic reticulum f. cell membrane
6. Make a list of all of the relationships between structure and function that you can think of.

Answers to Questions for Section 2.

D. 1. It is made up of two layers of lipid molecules, each with one water soluble end and one lipid soluble end; and protein molecules at intervals throughout.

2. Endoplasmic reticulum, ribosomes, Golgi apparatus, lysosomes, mitochondria, microtubules and microfilaments.

*3. Answers will vary.

E. 4. Impairment of: a. energy and storage and production; b. protein synthesis; c. carbohydrate production; d. assembly of ribosomes and division of the cell; e. enzyme activity; f. cytoplasmic movement.

*5. a. Layers of cellulose form rigid but porous structure that supports cell. b. Folded inner surfaces provide large area for energy production. c. Structure provides surfaces for chemical reaction and tubules for transport and storage of molecules made. d. Ribosomes attached to the ER produce proteins both for the cell membrane and use by other cells. Free ribosomes produce proteins that are used within the cell. e. Inner folder membrane provides large surface area for chemical reactions. f. Lipid molecules have both water soluble and lipid soluble ends, with the former facing outward and the latter inward, thus facilitating passage of both type of materials through the membrane.

*6. Answers will vary.

❸ THE FUNCTIONS OF CELL MEMBRANES

Movement of Substances Across Membranes

Cell membranes perform two kinds of functions. First, they regulate the movement of substances into and out of the cell. Second, they also receive information from the cell's environment and transmit it to the nucleus or another organelle. The way membranes function is closely related to the properties of the lipids and protein that form the structure of the membrane.

Diffusion

Diffusion (di fū zhən) *is the movement of ions and small molecules from an area of high concentration to an area of lower concentration.* It is the simplest process by which substances cross the membrane. When you smell food cooking its aroma reaches you by diffusion. As food molecules are heated they move faster. Some diffuse out of the cooking pan (their area of high concentration). They move through the air in all directions (to areas of lower concentration). Diffusion can also take place through a liquid as when you dissolve sugar in a beverage. (See Fig. 6-16.)

Fats dissolve in the lipid layer of the cell membrane and diffuse through it to enter the cell. Other ions and molecules that move by diffusion are first dissolved in water. When a watery solution reaches a cell membrane, it can diffuse through pores in the membrane. These pores are now thought to be the result of the movements of the large protein molecules that make up the cell membrane. Substances may move into or out of cells by diffusion, depending on where their concentration is the greatest. Diffusion is a passive process. The cell expends no energy for diffusion to occur. Some molecules are too large to cross the cell membrane by diffusion. These molecules are carried into the cell by the protein molecules of the cell membrane.

OBJECTIVES FOR SECTION 3

F. Use the following terms to describe how materials cross cell membranes: *diffusion*, *osmosis*, *active transport*, *phagocytosis*, and *pinocytosis*.

G. Describe how cell membranes receive information.

H. Define homeostasis. Explain how the structure and function of cell membranes contribute to maintaining homeostasis.

I. Summarize the processes that go on in a cell that justify calling it the basic unit of living structure.

6-16. Diffusion of dye in a beaker of water.

One of the effects of smog illustrates the process of diffusion. A form of oxygen called *ozone* (ō zōn) (O_3) is found in some polluted air. It diffuses into plant cells and destroys chlorophyll. Thus, it impairs the plant's ability to collect energy. Some of Southern California's plant life has been destroyed by this process.

Osmosis

Osmosis (oz mō sis) *is the diffusion of water through a selectively permeable membrane.* In a selectively permeable membrane, some things can pass through the pores while others cannot. (Permeable means allowing to pass through.) The cell membrane is selectively permeable in that it allows water to pass through freely but prevents many larger molecules from doing so. In osmosis, water moves from an area of high concentration to an area of lower concentration. The pressure put on the cell membrane as a result of this movement of water is known as *osmotic* (oz mät ik) *pressure*. (See Fig. 6-17.)

Water molecules move across the membrane in both directions regardless of the osmotic pressure. However, they move in greater numbers from *their* area of high concentration to *their* area of lower concentration. When the concentration of water molecules relative to solute is equal on both sides of the membrane the environment is said to be *isotonic* to the cell. ("Iso" means same.)

When the concentration of dissolved particles outside the cell is greater than inside, the fluid outside the cell is said to be *hypertonic*. ("Hyper" means excessive.) In this situation the net movement of water is out of the cell.

When the concentration of dissolved particles outside the cell is less than inside, the fluid is said to be *hypotonic*. ("Hypo" means low or under.) The net movement of water is into the cell. Notice that the terms, isotonic, hypertonic, and hypotonic, always refer to the condition outside the cell compared to that inside the cell itself. The effects of different osmotic environments on cells are shown in Figure 6-18.

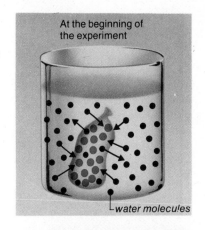

At the beginning of the experiment

water molecules

Same beaker several hours later

sugar molecules

6-17. *Through osmosis, a large amount of water has entered the bag, causing it to increase in volume.*

6-18. *Osmosis affects plant and animal cells differently.*

Emphasize that water molecules are always moving in both directions across the membrane. More water molecules move from the dilute solution to the concentrated solution than move in the opposite direction. The net movement is in the direction that tends to equalize the concentration.

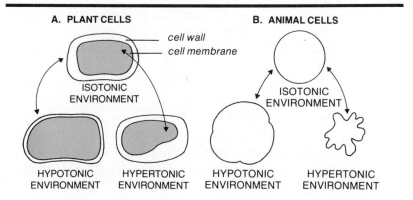

A. PLANT CELLS

cell wall
cell membrane

ISOTONIC ENVIRONMENT

HYPOTONIC ENVIRONMENT

HYPERTONIC ENVIRONMENT

B. ANIMAL CELLS

ISOTONIC ENVIRONMENT

HYPOTONIC ENVIRONMENT

HYPERTONIC ENVIRONMENT

The pressure created within plant cells serves to help maintain the rigidity of the plant. When plant cells lack water, they lose this pressure. At this point, the plant wilts. If an excess of fertilizer is applied to a lawn, it creates a hyperosmotic environment. In this case, water is pulled out of the plant cells. This gives the plants a dried or "burned" look.

Active Transport — How the Cell Uses Energy to Move Substances

When substances are moved from an area of low concentration to one of already higher concentration, energy is required. This energy comes from a special energy-carrying molecule, adenosine triphosphate. In addition to ATP, active transport requires an enzyme and a carrier molecule. The carrier molecule is a substance in the cell

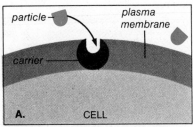
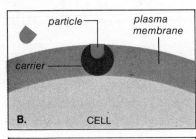
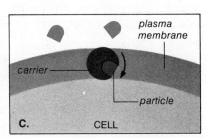
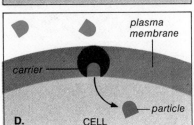
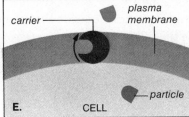
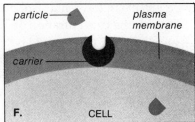

6-19. *In active transport a carrier molecule moves particles across the cell membrane. ATP is needed to complete the movement and release the particle to the inside of the cell.*

or cell membrane that can hold on to another particle. The particle to be transported is attached to the carrier molecule. It can then move across the thickness of the membrane. At the surface of the membrane, energy from ATP is used to release the particle from the carrier. The empty carrier moves back across the membrane. It then becomes available for the transport of another particle. (See Fig. 6-19.)

Movement of Larger Particles

When the cell moves large particles into or out of the cell, energy is also expended. In this process, a part of the cell membrane is involved in forming a sac or vesicle around the particles. Cells that secrete proteins or other large molecules first package these secretions in vesicles in the Golgi apparatus. The vesicles then move to the membrane and fuse with it. Their contents are then released to the exterior of the cell. In an opposite process, substances are packed in vesicles and moved into the cell. If the particle taken in by the cell is large, the process is called *phagocytosis* (fag ə sə *tō* səs). If it is dissolved or a water droplet, the process is called *pinocytosis* (pin ə sə *tō* səs). These processes are shown in Figure 6-20.

Information and Membranes

The outer surface of the cell membrane is in contact with the environment of the cell. In unicellular organisms the environment is usually the water in which the organism lives. Within this environment, the cell's membrane responds to signals such as changes in temperature and pH. In many-celled organisms, the environment of

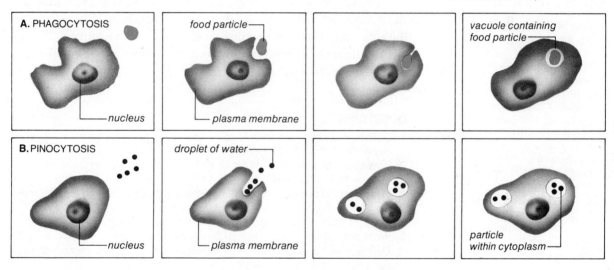

cells is the fluid that occupies the tiny spaces between them. Cells are able to communicate with one another through chemical messages. In other cases, communication occurs from close contact between cells.

One kind of chemical messenger is a hormone, such as insulin that regulates the amount of glucose entering cells. Many hormones attach to receptor sites on the surface of the membranes. The presence of the hormone molecule causes the membrane to release another chemical into the cytoplasm. This chemical is a special kind of nucleotide called cyclic adenosine monophosphate (c-AMP). It causes the cell to respond to the hormone.

Another kind of chemical messenger is a *neurotransmitter*. It is released by nerve cells. When this chemical attaches to a receptor on an-

6-20. *A. Phagocytosis. A large particle is engulfed by the cell and enclosed by the cell membrane. Digestion occurs within a vacuole. B. Pinocytosis. Small vacuoles form from the surface membrane of cells and take in dissolved particles.*

Point out to students that pinocytosis and phagocytosis differ from the type of active transport previously studied in that they move substances through cell membranes in one direction only.

other nerve cell it relays the nerve impulse. When it reaches a receptor on a muscle cell it causes the muscle to respond in a way that results in a contraction.

As you know, there are proteins on the surface of membranes. These proteins allow cells to detect the presence of cells that do not belong to the organism. The body tries to destroy microorganisms and other cells that it recognizes as not belonging to itself. This same action sometimes causes the body to reject a transplanted organ.

Finally, cells respond to the presence of other cells. When cells become crowded their membranes come in contact with each other. Normally this signal tells the cells to stop dividing. Cancer cells seem to ignore this signal.

Homeostasis

The cell membrane is very important in maintaining homeostasis. It controls the passage of substances into and out of the cell so that the contents of the cell remains much the same at all times. The cell membrane receives information from the environment. It makes use of this information to keep the inside of the cell functioning normally.

QUESTIONS FOR SECTION 3

1. Define: osmosis, diffusion, active transport, phagocytosis, pinocytosis, isosmotic, hyposmotic, hyperosmotic.
2. How does the way small particles and large particles enter cells differ?
3. How do fats enter cells?
4. How does the behavior of plant and animal cells differ in isotonic, hypotonic, and hypertonic environments?
5. To what kinds of chemicals do cell membranes respond?
6. What other kinds of information do membranes receive?
7. Define *homeostasis* and give an example of how the cell membrane functions to maintain homeostasis.
8. Of what advantage to the cell is active transport in maintaining homeostasis?

(See more answers on page 115.)

CHAPTER REVIEW

The cell is considered the basic unit of living things. All living organisms are composed of cells. Though some important differences exist between plant and animal cells, each contains the organelles to carry out the functions of the cell. *The structure of these organelles is closely related to their functions.* As we shall see in the next two chapters, most of the functions of living things take place within cells. Even in large organisms, life is maintained by activities at the cellular level. *Through the activities of cells homeostasis is maintained.*

Using the Concepts

1. Devise an experiment to show a fourth-grader the effects of diffusion.
2. How can you explain to your family why not to use too much fertilizer?

VOCABULARY REVIEW

[1] cell
cell membrane
cell sap
cell wall
chlorophyll
chloroplast
[2] chromosones
electron microscope
endoplasmic reticulum

fluid mosaic model
gene
Golgi apparatus
lysosome
microfilament
mitochondria
nuclear envelope
organelle
ribosome

cytoplasm
cytoplasmic streaming
nucleolus
nucleus
theory
vacuole
[3] active transport
ATP
diffusion

homeostasis
hypertonic
hypotonic
isotonic
osmosis
phagocytosis
pinocytosis

CHAPTER 6 TEST

Copy the number of each test item and place your answer to the right.

PART 1   Multiple Choice: Select the letter of the phrase that best completes each of the following.

d 1. All living things are composed of cells is   **a.** an observation   **b.** an assumption   **c.** an hypothesis   **d.** a theory.

a 2. Which of the following is *not* usually seen through a light microscope?   **a.** lysosomes   **b.** nucleus   **c.** cytoplasm   **d.** vacuole.

b 3. Which of the following is found only in plant cells?   **a.** cell membrane   **b.** cell wall   **c.** nucleus   **d.** cytoplasm.

d 4. The structure that regulates what enters and leaves a cell is the   **a.** mitochondrion   **b.** ribosome   **c.** Golgi apparatus   **d.** cell membrane.

c 5. Which of the following is found only in animal cells?   **a.** cell membrane   **b.** cell wall   **c.** lysosomes   **d.** nucleus.

a 6. The cell's ability to change state is due to   **a.** microfilaments   **b.** ribosomes   **c.** cilia   **d.** microtubules.

b 7. The organelles involved in protein synthesis are   **a.** mitochondria   **b.** ribosomes   **c.** lysosomes   **d.** cell walls.

c 8. The organelle that releases energy is the   **a.** chloroplast   **b.** ribosome   **c.** mitochondrion   **d.** nucleus.

c 9. A process that requires energy is   **a.** osmosis   **b.** diffusion   **c.** active transport   **d.** both a & b.

d 10. Membranes receive information from   **a.** hormones   **b.** neurotransmitters   **c.** vacuoles   **d.** both a & b.

PART 2   Matching: Match the letter of the term in Column I with its description in Column II.

COLUMN I

a. pinocytosis
b. chloroplast
c. vacuole
d. isotonic
e. Golgi apparatus

f. hypertonic
g. hypotonic
h. microtubule
i. lysosome
j. diffusion

COLUMN II

c 11. Membrane surrounded sac
a 12. Movement of small vacuoles into cells
e 13. Warehouse of the cell
j 14. Movement of substances from areas of higher to lower concentration
f 15. More dissolved substances in water outside cells than inside cells
h 16. Forms skeleton of cell
b 17. Captures light energy
i 18. Cell's self-destruct organelle
g 19. More dissolved substances in water inside cells than outside
d 20. The same concentration of dissolved substances inside and outside cells

PART 3   Completion: Complete the following.

21. The movement of materials inside an Elodea cell is called __cytoplasmic streaming__.

22. The molecule that carries energy is __ATP__.

23. The process by which cells take in large particles is __phagocytosis__

24. The maintenance of nearly constant internal conditions is __homeostasis__

25. Cells are the basic unit of living things because __the cell is the site of the functioning of each living organism__

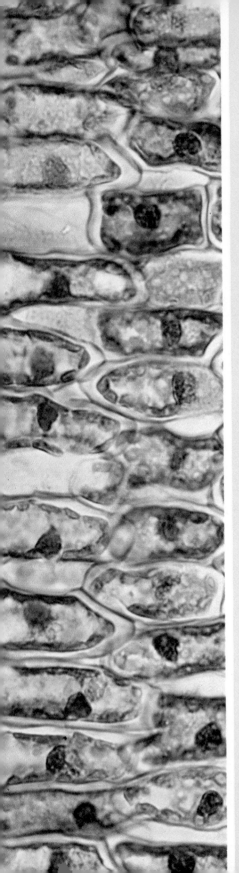

CHAPTER 7

ENERGY RELATIONSHIPS IN THE CELL

Now is the time to make use of what you know about energy relationships in the environment. Your knowledge of cells and the substances that make up living things will also be useful as you study energy relationships in cells.

Green plants capture light energy from the sun and store it in a form they and other living organisms can use. Nearly all living cells use the energy stored by green plants. The process of using energy is very similar in all cells. *The similarity in how cells use energy is an example of unity in living things.*

Metabolism includes all of the chemical reactions in living organisms. It makes it possible for cells to obtain and use energy for their many activities. Metabolism also contributes to maintaining internal balance or homeostasis. *Metabolism and homeostasis are two important concepts in this chapter.*

- How do plants capture energy?
- How do they provide food and oxygen for you and other animals?
- What do the cells in your body do with the food you eat?
- Why do your cells need oxygen to use food?
- How does metabolism that takes place in cells affect the environment?

In this chapter you will learn the answers to these and other questions about metabolism. You already know that in many cities the natural plants have been replaced by buildings and streets. What effect do you think the presence of fewer plants would have on the quality of air in a city?

CROSS SECTION OF A LEAF

1 ENZYMES AND METABOLISM

Metabolism is the sum total of all chemical reactions that take place in living things. In some of these reactions energy is stored. In others it is released. In many reactions *a*denosine *tri*phosphate or ATP is involved in the transfer of energy. ATP is like money. We can save money until we need it and we can use it for many purposes. Likewise, cells can save ATP until they need it and they can use it for many purposes. In this chapter we will be concerned with the processes of metabolism that produce ATP. In Chapter 8 we will study the many ways cells use ATP to perform their activities.

The chemical reactions of metabolism are controlled by enzymes. Without enzymes most of these reactions would occur very slowly or not at all. Let us find out more about enzymes and how they control reactions.

OBJECTIVES FOR SECTION 1
A. Define *metabolism, ATP, enzyme,* and *coenzyme.*
B. Describe the chemical and physical properties of enzymes.
C. Interpret the role of ATP in metabolism.

Properties of Enzymes

Enzymes are complex *protein* molecules made by cells. Like other protein molecules they are affected by changes in temperature and by changes in pH. Most enzymes are destroyed by high temperatures and by very acidic or very basic conditions.

ENZYMES AS CATALYSTS Enzymes are the *catalysts* of biological reactions. *A catalyst* (*kat əl əst*) *increases the rate of a reaction without being used up in it.* Thus, enzymes increase the rate of reactions in living cells. Many of the reactions that are controlled in living cells by enzymes could occur at high temperatures without enzymes. For example, sugar could be burned and caused to release carbon dioxide and water. Enzymes make it possible for a similar reaction to occur at much lower temperatures. That is, at the body temperature of living things. Enzymes are not changed in the reactions they control. Thus the same enzyme molecules can be used many times.

ACTIVATION ENERGY Many reactions require energy called *activation energy* to get them started. *Enzymes control reactions by lowering the activation energy.* To see how this works, think of a wagon sitting in a rut at the top of a hill. (See Fig. 7-1.) If the bump in front of the wagon can be removed or the wagon can be lifted over the bump, it will roll down the hill. Activation energy is like the energy needed to lift the wagon over the bump. An enzyme reduces the activation energy needed. The action of the enzyme is like removing the bump. Once the reaction has been activated it will proceed at a rapid rate.

ENZYME ACTION The names of enzymes usually end in "ase" and include the name of the substance upon which they act. For example, the enzyme sucrase acts to break down the common table sugar, sucrose.

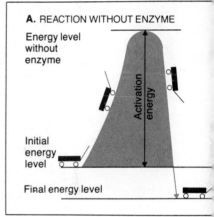

A. REACTION WITHOUT ENZYME

Energy level without enzyme

Activation energy

Initial energy level

Final energy level

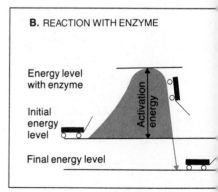

B. REACTION WITH ENZYME

Energy level with enzyme

Activation energy

Initial energy level

Final energy level

7-1. *An enzyme reduces the amount of activation energy required for a chemical reaction to take place.*

Most enzymes are very selective in their action. That is, they act on a particular substance, like sucrase acts on sucrose. One idea of how an enzyme works follows. It has a particular shape that allows only a specific kind of substance to attach to it. *The exact place the substance is attached to the enzyme is called the enzyme's* **active site.** Chemists compare this fit between the enzyme and the substance it acts on to a lock and key. (See Fig. 7-2.) A key will open only a certain lock. An enzyme will activate only a certain kind of reaction. Thus, an enzyme is said to be *specific* for a particular reaction.

7-2. *Sucrose and sucrase fit together like a lock and key.*

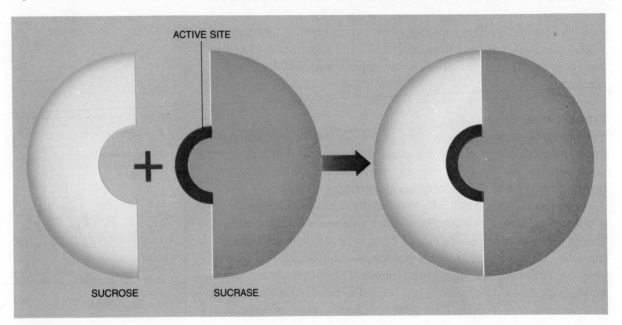

ACTIVE SITE

SUCROSE   SUCRASE

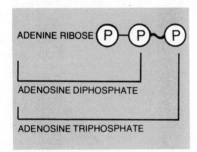

7-3. *The molecule, adenosine triphosphate (ATP), contains adenine, ribose, and three phosphate groups. The chemical bond between the last two phosphate groups contains a large amount of energy.*

Coenzymes

Many enzymes require a coenzyme to carry out a reaction. *A coenzyme is a substance that works with an enzyme.* Sometimes a coenzyme makes the enzyme and the substance upon which it acts fit together better. Vitamins and minerals often act as coenzymes. They may be used by the cell to make coenzymes. If our diet does not contain enough of these vitamins and minerals, our cells will not have enough coenzymes.

ATP and Energy

All enzyme reactions either produce or use energy. Remember, that although energy cannot be created or destroyed, it can be changed from one form to another. In living organisms energy in food is changed into a form of energy that cells can use. This energy is stored in a chemical called *ATP*. (See Fig. 7-3.)

ATP, *a*denosine *tri*phosphate, consists of adenine, ribose, and three phosphate groups. The two phosphate groups on the end of the molecule are held together by a chemical bond. It contains a very large amount of energy. We can write it like this: A-P-P~P. The wavy line represents this high energy bond. The bond between the other phosphates also contains a fairly large amount of energy. Much of the energy that is available to do the work of the cell is stored in high energy bonds. When the cell is storing energy, ATP is produced. When the cell is using energy, ATP is broken down into ADP (A-P-P) and a

7-4. *A. The release of energy from ATP. ADP and phosphate are formed. B. ADP plus energy form ATP. C. The reaction is reversible, so energy can be stored or released.*

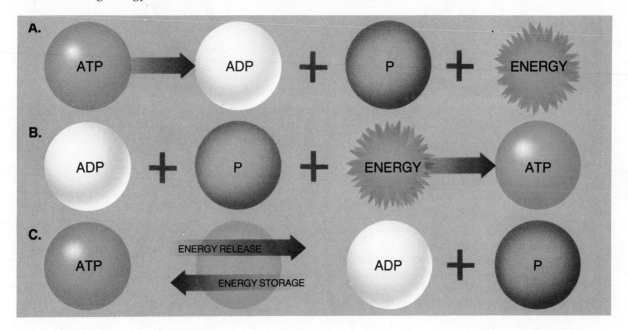

free phosphate group, P. (See Fig. 7-4.) In a normal cell ADP and free phosphate groups are available to form a supply of ATP for meeting the cell's energy needs. This energy is used for many purposes as we shall see in Chapter 8.

QUESTIONS FOR SECTION 1

1. What are enzymes and coenzymes?
2. How is ATP like money?
3. How are enzymes and ATP related to metabolism?
4. List the properties of an enzyme.
5. What happens at the active site of an enzyme?
6. What is the difference between ATP and ADP?
7. What is the main role of ATP in metabolism?
8. What is the significance of the high energy bond in ATP?

(See more answers on page 123.)

Answers to Questions for Section 1.

A. 1. Enzymes: complex protein molecules made by cells that increase the rate of a reaction without being used up in it.

2. Like money, ATP can be saved by cells until needed and then used for many purposes.

*3. ATP stores and releases energy. Enzymes control the rate of chemical reactions that are part of metabolism.

B. 4. Enzymes are proteins and catalysts. They lower the energy needed to start a reaction and are specific for particular reactions. The chemical they work on attaches to a particular active site on an enzyme.

A.

B.

C.

D.

CHAPTER INVESTIGATION

A. Describe what you see in each of the flasks above. How is each flask different from the others?

B. If you were told that the chemical that causes the color in the flasks is blue in basic solutions and yellow in acid solutions, what more could you say about the differences between the flasks? (With your instructor's help set up this experiment and observe it for a few days.)

What effect on the pH of a solution has a plant? an animal?

C. What process is taking place in flask B? What would happen if you put this flask in the dark? What process would still occur?

What process is taking place in flask C? flask D?

What interactions are occurring in this flask? How do you know? Can you use information from the other flasks to determine this?

In which flask would something stay alive for the longest time? Give reasons for your answer.

☑ CELLULAR RESPIRATION — GETTING ENERGY INTO USEABLE FORM

Living cells use food to provide energy to perform their functions. Most cells use glucose as their main energy source. Even plants that make their own food make glucose. When glucose enters a cell it is broken down by a series of chemical reactions called cellular respiration. **Cellular respiration** *is the breakdown of foods and the release of energy from them.* It takes place inside cells. Do not confuse it with the breathing in of oxygen that takes place in many animals.

In most cells cellular respiration requires oxygen and may also be called *aerobic* (ā rō bik) *respiration.* Aerobic means in the presence of oxygen. The overall process is shown in this reaction:

$$ADP + P + \underset{\text{glucose}}{C_6H_{12}O_6} + \underset{\text{oxygen}}{6O_2} \xrightarrow{\text{enzymes}}$$

$$\underset{\substack{\text{carbon} \\ \text{dioxide}}}{6CO_2} + \underset{\text{water}}{6H_2O} + \underset{\text{energy}}{ATP}$$

In some cells cellular respiration occurs without oxygen and is called *anaerobic* (ən ā rō bik) *respiration.* We will study anaerobic processes first and then aerobic processes.

Anaerobic Respiration

In most organisms glucose is the main molecule used to produce energy. The first steps in its breakdown do not require oxygen. Regardless of what happens to glucose later, it is always first broken down into two molecules of *pyruvic* (pi *ru* vik) *acid.* Pyruvic acid can then be broken down in three different ways. (See Fig. 7-5.) First, **the**

OBJECTIVES FOR SECTION 2

D. Define *cellular respiration, aerobic respiration, anaerobic respiration, fermentation,* and *glycolysis.*

E. Interpret the importance of cellular respiration to living things.

Answers to Questions for Section 1.

5. The chemical attached to the active site fits like a lock and key. The enzyme causes a change in the chemical.

*6. ATP has 3 phosphates and contains a lot of energy. When one phosphate is removed energy is released and ADP is produced.

C. 7. ATP stores and releases energy in a controlled way so that cells can obtain and use energy for their many activities.

8. The high energy bond in ATP provides a way to store energy in living things.

7-5. *Three ways that pyruvic acid can be metabolized.*

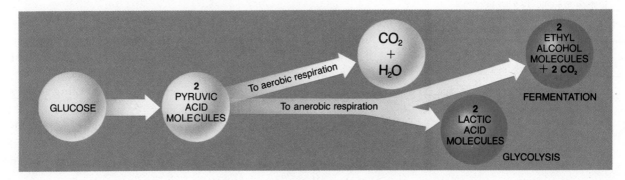

7-6. *The process of fermentation occurs in the making of bread. The production of carbon dioxide causes the dough to expand.*

formation of ethyl alcohol and carbon dioxide from pyruvic acid is the process called **fermentation**. *Second, if the pyruvic acid is used to form lactic acid the process is called* **glycolysis** (glī *kȧl ə səs).* Third, *if the pyruvic acid is combined with oxygen the process is called* **aerobic respiration.**

FERMENTATION   Many microorganisms can carry out fermentation. People make use of this ability of microorganisms in the making of wine and bread. (See Fig. 7-6.) In winemaking, the organisms produce the alcohol that is found in finished wine. In breadmaking, the organisms produce carbon dioxide which makes the bread rise. The overall process of fermentation is represented by the following reaction:

$$2ADP \ + \ 2P \ + \ \underset{\text{glucose}}{C_6H_{12}O_6} \ \xrightarrow{\text{enzymes}}$$

$$\underset{\substack{\text{ethyl} \\ \text{alcohol}}}{2C_2H_5OH} \ + \ \underset{\substack{\text{carbon} \\ \text{dioxide}}}{2CO_2} \ + \ \underset{\text{energy}}{2ATP}$$

Only a small amount of the energy that was stored in the glucose molecules is made available to the cells. Much energy remains in the alcohol molecules and hence they can be used for fuel. It is likely that the ability of microorganisms to make ethyl alcohol will be an important factor in the production of fuels to replace our dwindling supply of petroleum.

GLYCOLYSIS   Glycolysis occurs in the muscles and liver of multicellular animals. The ability of the cells of your muscles and liver to carry on glycolysis makes you able to do strenuous exercise. When

Fermentation produces only a small amount of energy because much of the hydrogen from glucose is still present in alcohol. The more hydrogen there is attached to a carbon molecule, the more energy it contains. Likewise, the more oxygen there is attached to a carbon molecule the less energy it contains. For example, methane (CH_4) contains a large amount of energy and is in fact used as a fuel; carbon dioxide (CO_2) contains very little energy. Much of what happens in cellular respiration involves decreasing the hydrogen and increasing the oxygen associated with each carbon atom.

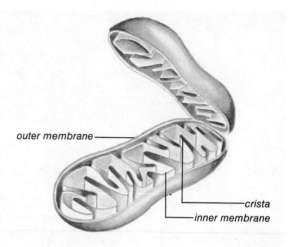

outer membrane

crista

inner membrane

you exercise rapidly the cells of your body spend the oxygen supply carried to them by your blood. However, they can continue to use glucose for a short period of time in the absence of oxygen. During this time the cells convert glucose to lactic acid. The build up of lactic acid produces the sensation of muscle fatigue. After you stop exercising, you breathe rapidly. Oxygen is delivered to your cells. The lactic acid is converted to pyruvic acid which is used in aerobic respiration. The process of glycolysis is summarized in the following reaction:

$$C_6H_{12}O_6 \longrightarrow 2C_3H_6O_3 + 2ATP$$

glucose   lactic acid   energy

7-7. *Section of a mitochondrion. Enzymes for aerobic respiration reactions are lined up on inner membranes.*

Aerobic Respiration

Aerobic respiration occurs only in the presence of oxygen. All of the cells of your body normally carry on aerobic respiration. As in anerobic respiration, one molecule of glucose is first broken down to two molecules of pyruvic acid. Then, the pyruvic acid is further broken down into a two-carbon activated acetate molecule and carbon dioxide. The activated molecule then combines with a coenzyme called coenzyme A, forming *acetyl-CoA*. It is acetyl-CoA that undergoes aerobic respiration.

KREBS CYCLE   The reactions of aerobic respiration take place in the mitochondria. Two processes are involved. One is called the *Krebs cycle* or *citric acid cycle*. A biochemist, Hans Krebs, did much of the work that led to our understanding of the cycle. The other is called *biological oxidation*. The enzymes that carry out these processes are all located

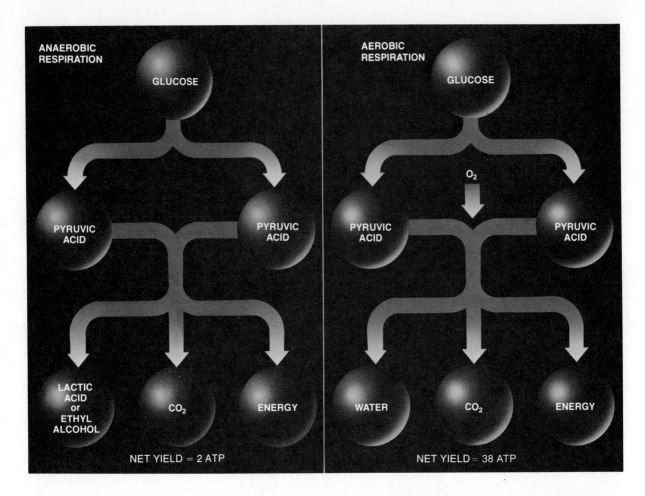

ANAEROBIC
RESPIRATION

GLUCOSE

PYRUVIC
ACID

PYRUVIC
ACID

LACTIC
ACID
or
ETHYL
ALCOHOL

CO_2

ENERGY

NET YIELD = 2 ATP

AEROBIC
RESPIRATION

GLUCOSE

O_2

PYRUVIC
ACID

PYRUVIC
ACID

WATER

CO_2

ENERGY

NET YIELD = 38 ATP

7-8. *Comparison between an-aerobic and aerobic respiration.*

on the membranes of the mitochondria. (See Fig. 7-7.) They are lined up so the product of one reaction is passed on to the enzyme that controls the next reaction.

The **Krebs cycle** *is the process in which acetyl-CoA is broken down into carbon dioxide with the release of electrons and energy.* Some energy is released directly and stored immediately in ATP. In cells the loss of electrons is usually achieved by removing hydrogen from a molecule. Each hydrogen atom separates into a hydrogen ion and electron. The electrons are transferred to the enzymes that carry out biological oxidation. **Biological oxidation** *is the process in which hydrogen is combined with oxygen forming water, and energy is released in the form of ATP.* With the formation of water, the electrons have given up all the energy they are able to. The overall significance of biological oxidation is that it allows large quantities of energy from hydrogen atoms removed from the bonds of the glucose molecules to be transferred to ATP. Energy stored in ATP is available for cells.

Significance of Cellular Respiration

Cellular respiration produces ATP from glucose. (See Fig. 7-8.) We can write a net equation for aerobic cellular respiration as follows:

$$C_6H_{12}O_6 + 6H_2O + 6O_2 + 38ADP + 38P \xrightarrow{\text{enzymes}}$$

glucose   water   oxygen

$$6CO_2 + 12H_2O + 38ATP$$

carbon   water   energy
dioxide

In the absence of oxygen only 2 ATP molecules are produced from one molecule of glucose. This occurs in glycolysis and fermentation. In aerobic respiration, a total of 38 molecules of ATP are produced from each of the molecules of glucose. These processes are summarized as follows:

fermentation:
    glucose $\longrightarrow$ pyruvic acid $\longrightarrow$ ethyl alcohol + CO_2 + 2ATP
glycolysis:
    glucose $\longrightarrow$ pyruvic acid $\longrightarrow$ lactic acid + 2ATP
aerobic respiration:
    glucose $\longrightarrow$ pyruvic acid $\longrightarrow CO_2$ + H_2O + 38ATP

Clearly, aerobic respiration produces much more energy from a molecule of glucose than anaerobic respiration. All cells release energy either aerobically or anaerobically. The most important thing about these processes is that energy is produced in a form that cells can use. Cells must have a constant supply of energy to carry out their activities. Energy is necessary for survival.

QUESTIONS FOR SECTION 2

1. Define cellular respiration.
2. What is the difference between aerobic and anaerobic respiration?
3. What is the difference between glycolysis and fermentation?
4. How are the Krebs cycle and biological oxidation related to cellular respiration?
5. Why is cellular respiration important to living things?
6. How is the amount of energy from aerobic respiration different from the energy from anaerobic respiration?
7. What would happen to a cell that could not carry out cellular respiration? Why?

Much larger amounts of energy are captured in ATP when electrons and hydrogen are transferred to oxygen. Ask students which kind of respiration makes the most efficient use of energy stored in carbohydrates.

Answers to Questions for Section 2.

D. 1. The breakdown of foods and the release of energy from them.

2. Aerobic respiration occurs only when oxygen is present; anaerobic respiration occurs in the absence of oxygen.

3. Glycolysis produces lactic acid and fermentation produces ethyl alcohol and carbon dioxide.

*4. Both occur in aerobic respiration. The Krebs cycle releases carbon dioxide, hydrogen, and energy. Biological oxidation combines the hydrogen with oxygen to release water and energy.

E. 5. Cellular respiration produces energy for the activities of the cell.

6. Aerobic respiration produces far more energy than anaerobic respiration and is thus a much more efficient process. However, anaerobic respiration allows for some energy to be produced in the absence of oxygen.

*7. It would die. Cellular respiration is essential for a cell to use energy.

3 PHOTOSYNTHESIS — CAPTURING AND STORING ENERGY

We now know that all living things carry out respiration and obtain energy from their food. But where did the energy in the food come from? To answer this question take another look at the green plants — the producers we studied earlier.

Green plants are able to make their food by photosynthesis. **Photosynthesis** (fō tə *sin* thə sis) *is the process of capturing light energy and storing it in glucose molecules.* The meaning of the word is in the word itself. Photo means light. Synthesis means putting together. The light energy from the sun is changed into chemical energy in the bonds of the glucose molecules.

Light enables leaves and flowers to grow. Furthermore, light regulates photosynthesis, on which all life depends. To understand photosynthesis, we need to start by learning something about light. We also need to learn about the parts of a plant that are involved in capturing light.

Light

Light is a kind of energy that travels in waves. The waves of light have different wavelengths and different amounts of energy. By passing ordinary white light through a prism we can see light of different wavelengths. (See Fig. 7-9.) Our eyes can detect these different wavelengths as colors. Of these waves, those with the longest wavelength and least energy are red. Those with the shortest wavelength and most energy are violet. If you were to look out the window, you might see green trees and grass, a red brick house, and a red flower. You see each of these objects as a particular color be-

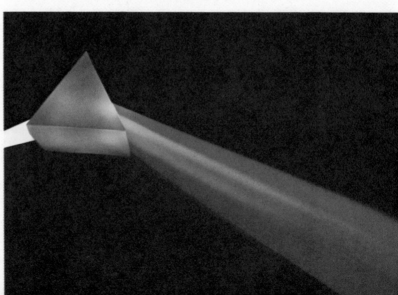

7-9. Visible light separates into different wavelengths or colors when passed through a prism.

cause the object absorbs some light waves and reflects others. The flower looks red because it absorbs all of the light waves except the ones in the red range. It reflects the red waves. Your eye detects these waves and your brain interprets them as red.

Plant Parts that Function in Photosynthesis

Green plants look green because they absorb most light waves except the green ones. A chemical called chlorophyll is present in green plants. Chlorophyll absorbs light in the violet, blue, and red wavelengths. Since it reflects green light, it appears green. Chlorophyll is found in chloroplasts. Any part of a plant that is green has chloroplasts in most of its cells. The cells of a leaf usually have 40 to 50 chloroplasts each. The cross-section of a leaf shows where these cells are located. (See Fig. 7-10.)

Overview of Photosynthesis

The absorbed wavelengths provide the plant with the energy to go through the process of photosynthesis. During photosynthesis, plants change light energy into chemical bond energy. We can write a summary reaction for photosynthesis as follows:

$$\text{light} + \underset{\substack{\text{carbon} \\ \text{dioxide}}}{6CO_2} + \underset{\text{water}}{12H_2O} \xrightarrow{\text{chlorophyll}}$$

$$\underset{\text{glucose}}{C_6H_{12}O_6} + \underset{\text{oxygen}}{6O_2} + \underset{\text{water}}{6H_2O}$$

The biochemist Melvin Calvin did much of the work that led to our understanding of photosynthesis. Indeed, the steps in the pro-

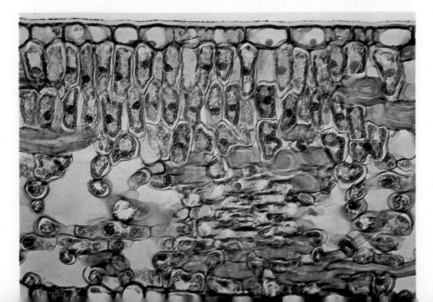

7-10. Cross section of a leaf showing epidermis on the surface and cells containing chloroplasts inside.

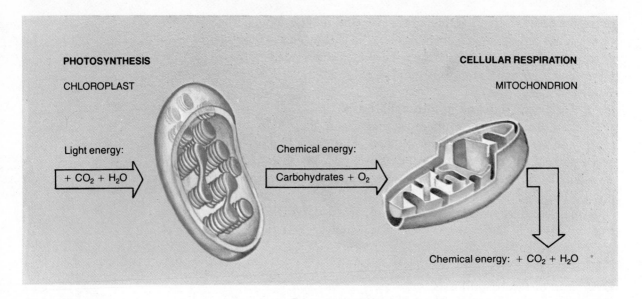

PHOTOSYNTHESIS

CHLOROPLAST

Light energy:

+ CO_2 + H_2O

CELLULAR RESPIRATION

MITOCHONDRION

Chemical energy:

Carbohydrates + O_2

Chemical energy: + CO_2 + H_2O

7-11. *Photosynthesis uses energy, CO_2 and H_2O to produce carbohydrates and O_2. Cellular respiration uses carbohydrates and O_2 to produce energy, CO_2 and H_2O.*

cess of photosynthesis are quite different from those of respiration. The products of photosynthesis, glucose and oxygen, are the essential starting materials of respiration. And the starting materials of photosynthesis, carbon dioxide and water, are the products of respiration. Thus, the process appears to be the reverse of respiration and in some general ways it is. (See Fig. 7-11.)

Photosynthesis can be separated into the *light reactions* and the *dark reactions*. This is done only to help us understand the process. The process of photosysnthesis is a continuous one. The light reactions require energy from light and occur only in the presence of light. The dark reactions do not require light. They may occur in either light or dark. some biologist call them the light-independent reactions. To take place, however, the dark reactions do require the products of light reactions.

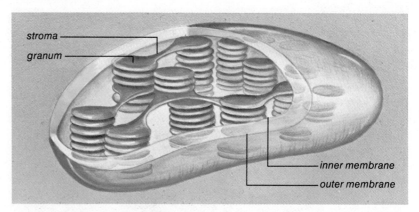

stroma

granum

inner membrane

outer membrane

7-12. *A cutaway view of a chloroplast showing stroma, granum, and the double-layered membrane.*

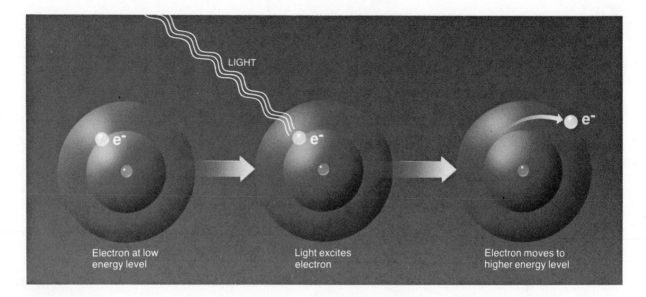

LIGHT

Electron at low
energy level

Light excites
electron

Electron moves to
higher energy level

Chloroplasts

All of the reactions of photosynthesis take place in chloroplasts. (See Fig. 7-12.) Each chloroplast is surrounded by two outer membranes. A dense protein solution, the *stroma,* lies within the inner membrane. Within the chloroplast is a complex system of membranes which form the *grana.* These can be viewed through the electron microscope as layers of flattened sacs. Chlorplasts are similar to mitochondria in many ways. The activities that occur in these structures provide energy for life. The enzymes of chloroplasts are arranged in a certain order. This enables the product of one reaction to be passed directly on to the enzyme that controls the next reaction.

The Light Reactions

Chlorophyll is the molecule that is responsible for the capture of light energy. When light strikes a molecule of chlorophyll, an electron in one of its atoms is raised to a higher energy level. (See Fig. 7-13.) This electron is said to be in an excited state. Energy from electrons in this excited state splits water molecules. Electrons pulled away from these water molecules thus provide the energy for two important processes. First, some of the energy is used to make ATP. The rest of the available energy from the electrons is later used in the dark reaction to make glucose from carbon dioxide. *Chemical energy produced from light energy is the product of the first step of photosynthesis, the light reaction.* Conversion of carbon dioxide into carbohydrates occurs in the dark reactions. Think of the light reactions as the *photo* part of photosynthesis, and the dark reactions as the *synthesis* part of photosynthesis.

7-13. *Light energy is absorbed by an electron of chlorophyll. The electron becomes energized and is raised to a higher energy level.*

7-14 A SUMMARY OF THE REACTION OF PHOTOSYNTHESIS

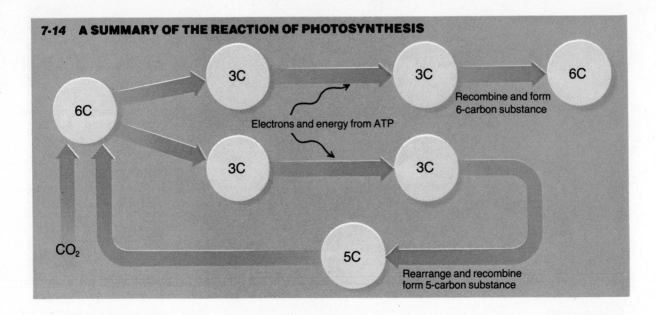

The Dark Reactions

In the dark reactions, carbon dioxide is the main starting material. (See Fig. 7-14.) It enters the leaf from the air and moves to the stroma of the chloroplasts. The electrons and ATP used in converting carbon dioxide into carbohydrate are stored there from the light reactions. In the first step in the process, carbon dioxide combines with a five-carbon sugar. A six-carbon molecule is created. The six-carbon molecule

7-15 HOW THE PROCESS OF PHOTOSYNTHESIS AND RESPIRATION FIT TOGETHER

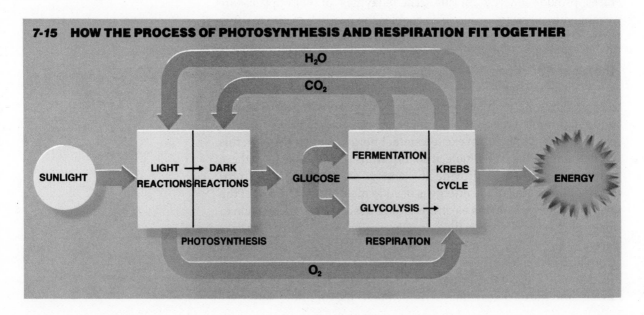

then breaks down into two three-carbon molecules. The next step is to add electrons to these molecules. Energy from ATP is used in this step and much of that energy is stored in the molecule. The new three-carbon molecules are used in two ways. Some combine to form the six-carbon sugar, glucose, or other carbohydrate molecules. Others go through a series of reactions and are rearranged and recombined to form the five-carbon sugar that was used to start the process. *The end result is the production of glucose and the replacement of the five-carbon sugar needed to keep the process going.*

Importance of Photosynthesis

The single most important source of energy for all living things is the light that is captured by photosynthesis. This process creates all of the nu-

TABLE 7-1. COMPARISON OF PHOTOSYNTHESIS AND CELLULAR RESPIRATION

Photosynthesis	Cellular Respiration
stores energy	releases energy
synthesizes foods	breaks down foods
raw materials are CO_2 and H_2O	raw materials are glucose and O_2
products are glucose and O_2	products are CO_2 and H_2O
occurs in cells that contain chlorophyll	occurs in nearly all cells (some carry out fermentation)
takes place only in the presence of light	takes place all the time in light or dark

trients that all living things, plant and animal, use for energy. The green plants that can capture light energy and convert it to chemical energy are nature's own solar energy systems. Their abilities far exceed any that have been built by humans. We depend on photosynthesis not only for our food and oxygen, but also for fibers for clothing and for lumber for construction and firewood. In addition, ornamental plants could not grow without photosynthesis. Even our fossil fuels come from past photosynthesis. *In all, photosynthesis is essential to life because it provides the energy for life in a form that organisms can use.* Photosynthesis and cellular respiration are compared in Table 7-1. The ways that photosynthesis and respiration fit together are shown in Figure 7-15.

Ask students to explain why animals cannot live without plants though plants can live without animals.

Answers to Questions for Section 3.

2. In the light reaction, electrons are activated and hydrogen and energy are produced. Energy from the light reaction is used to attach hydrogen to carbon dioxide in the dark reaction. The end product of the dark reaction is glucose, a molecule that contains much energy.

G. 3. Photosynthesis is the process by which energy from the sun is made available to living things.

H. 4. Photosynthesis captures energy. Cellular respiration provides a way for cells to use energy stored by photosynthesis. Together these processes help to maintain a balance between energy capture and energy use in living things.

5. The light reaction is called the photo reaction because it is where energy from light is captured. The dark reaction is called the synthesis reaction because it is where energy is stored and glucose molecules are made.

*6. It would die because it would have no way to get energy.

*7. They would die because they are dependent on energy stored in green plants for energy from their own cells.

Have students study Figure 7-15 and explain what would happen if any one of the substances were removed from the reactions.

Answers to Questions for Section 3.
F. 1. The process of capturing light
energy and storing it in glucose
molecules.

QUESTIONS FOR SECTION 3
1. What is photosynthesis.
2. What are the differences between the light and dark reactions?
3. What is the importance of photosysthesis for living things?
4. How are photosynthesis and cellular respiration related?
5. Why is it appropriate to refer to the light and dark reactions as the *photo* and the *synthesis* reactions?
6. What would happen if a plant received no light? Why?
7. What would happen to animals if they could not eat green plants? Why?
(See more answers on page 133.)

CHAPTER REVIEW

Light is essential to start the process of photosynthesis. Energy from light is stored in glucose. Glucose is used by living things to provide energy. The products of photosynthesis are the reactants of respiration. The products of respiration, combined with light energy, are the reactants for photosynthesis.

All living things carry on respiration or fermentation. Only green plants can carry on photosynthesis. New energy enters the system only by photosynthesis. For this reason, all living things, including the green plants, are dependent on photosynthesis.

The combination of photosynthesis and respiration accounts for a large share of the total of chemical reactions in metabolism. Unless both are occurring, living things would eventually run out of energy to carry on their activities. When metabolism is occurring in a normal way, living things can maintain homeostasis. They can make or get nutrients. They can rid themselves of wastes. The wastes of respiration are used to produce more nutrients. *Because of the way photosynthesis and respiration fit together they help living things to maintain homeostasis.*

Using the Concepts
1. Given that lead destroys enzymes, what would happen to a child that had eaten paint chips containing lead?
2. The saliva in your mouth contains an enzyme that digests starch. Design an experiment to demonstrate this.
3. Why is it desirable to have plants growing indoors?
4. Design an experiment to show that yeast cells produce carbon dioxide. Why should you *not* perform this experiment in a closed container?

Unanswered Questions
5. Many green plants live in the ocean. How might they be used to create new food sources? What might be done to get people to accept these new foods?
6. Why is it very inefficient use of resources to eat meat rather than foods from plant sources?

VOCABULARY REVIEW

1	2	3
activation energy	aerobic	chlorophyll
active site	anaerobic	chloroplast
ATP	biological oxidation	dark reaction
catalyst	fermentation	light reaction
coenzyme	gylcolysis	metabolism
enzyme	Krebs cycle	homeostasis
specificity (of enzyme)	cellular respiration	

CHAPTER 7 TEST

Copy the number of each test item and place your answer to the right.

PART 1   Multiple Choice: Select the letter of the phrase that best completes each of the following.

b   1. Living things store and use energy in the form of
     a. ADP   **b.** ATP   **c.** enzymes   **d.** coenzymes.

d   2. The process that includes all chemical reactions in living things is   **a.** aerobic respiration
     b. anaerobic respiration   **c.** photosynthesis
     d. metabolism.

c   3. Which of the following is *not* a property of enzymes?   **a.** protein   **b.** active site
     c. carbohydrate   **d.** catalyst.

a   4. Which form of respiration produces the most energy?   **a.** aerobic   **b.** anaerobic
     c. fermentation   **d.** glycolysis.

c   5. Glycolysis occurs during   **a.** intake of oxygen
     b. wine making   **c.** strenuous exercise
     d. resting.

d   6. The most important thing about respiration is that it releases   **a.** pyruvic acid   **b.** ethyl alcohol
     c. lactic acid   **d.** energy.

b   7. The chemical substance that absorbs light energy is called   **a.** chloroplast   **b.** chlorophyll
     c. chloroform   **d.** chromoplast.

a   8. Energy is captured by plants in   **a.** the light reaction   **b.** the dark reaction   **c.** the Krebs
     cycle   **d.** biological oxidation.

d   9. The end product of the dark reaction is   **a.** CO_2
     b. excited electrons   **c.** water   **d.** glucose.

b   10. The most important thing about photosynthesis is that it   **a.** captures light energy   **b.** stores energy in a form usable by living things   **c.** gives off
CO_2 **d.** uses oxygen.

PART 2   Matching: Match the letter of the term in Column I with its description in Column II.

COLUMN I

a. coenzyme   **f.** Krebs cycle
b. respiration   **g.** mitochondria
c. fermentation   **h.** photosynthesis
d. glycolysis   **i.** light reaction
e. glucose   **j.** dark reaction

COLUMN II

b   11. cellular breakdown of foods to release energy

c   12. anaerobic breakdown of glucose to CO_2 and alcohol

g   13. site of respiration

h   14. captures light energy and stores it in glucose

j   15. reaction that uses CO_2 to build carbon compounds

a   16. chemical that works with an enzyme

d   17. anaerobic breakdown of glucose to lactic acid

e   18. major source of energy for the activities of life

i   19. reaction that converts light energy to chemical energy

f   20. series of reactions that make hydrogen ions and electrons available to build ATP molecules and water

PART 3   Completion: Complete the following.

21. The way cells use energy is an example of unity in ____.

22. Photosynthesis may be summarized by the equation ____.

23. Respiration is necessary in living things because it releases ____.

24. Fermentation takes place during ____.

25. Metabolism helps to maintain homeostasis by ____.

Chapter 7 Test Answers

21. living things

22. light $+ 6CO_2 + 12H_2O \xrightarrow{\text{chlorophyll}} C_6H_{12}O_6 + 6O_2 + 6H_2O$

23. energy

24. making wine or bread

25. chemical reactions that make it possible for cells to obtain and use energy.

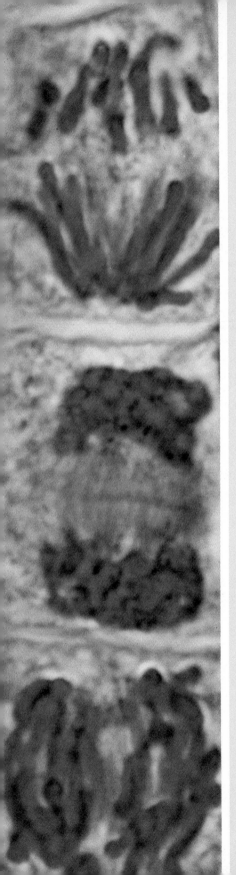

CHAPTER 8

ACTIVITIES OF LIVING CELLS

In chapters 6 and 7, we learned that cells contain many different organized bodies in the cytoplasm called organelles. We also discussed how cells release energy in the form of ATP. With these things in mind, we are now prepared to learn more about the function of some of the organelles and what cells do with their energy.

Cells use energy in many ways to carry out the activities necessary for them to stay alive. Cells respond to changes in their immediate environment. All cells are constantly taking in new substances. These substances are altered chemically in a variety of ways to build new cellular materials. Cells are capable of both growth and reproduction. In multicellular organisms, cells are joined together in ever increasing complexity to perform certain body functions. *All of these activities require energy. Together these activities help the cells to maintain homeostasis.*

In this chapter you will discover more about the ways that cells use energy to carry out their many activities. You will see how these activities take place.

- How does your body grow?
- What is cork and where does it come from?
- How are cells organized in your body?

In this chapter you will find answers to these and other questions.

CELL DIVISION—ONION

1 HOW DO CELLS USE ENERGY?

Cells Respond to their Environment

One of the ways cells use energy is to respond to stimuli in their environment. Certain cells in the nose respond to chemical stimuli. You can detect both pleasant and unpleasant odors. Special cells in the skin respond to changes in temperature and pressure. A pin prick brings about an immediate response. Cells use active transport to move things across the cell membrane. Each of these ways of responding to certain stimuli by cells requires energy.

All Living Organisms need Energy to Respond to their Environment

Some living organisms consist of a single cell. They are called *unicellular organisms.* These organisms often live in water where they react to changes. For example, some move toward light and others move away from light. A change in temperature or a change in the pH of the water may cause these organisms to move. To produce these movements, the cell needs and uses energy.

Most living organisms have a high level of complexity and consist of many cells. They are called *multicellular organisms.* These organisms are capable of many types of movement. But movement requires energy. For example, when animals run, walk, or swim, they use energy. When they eat, energy is needed to transport the food through their digestive system. Energy is also needed to cause the heart to beat and to move blood through all parts of the body. All of these movements occur in individual cells even though many cells may be affected. Energy is used to stimulate nerves to send messages which cause muscles to contract. Plants also use energy to cause movement. The cells move water up from the roots and food from the leaves to other parts of the plant.

The constant production and flow of energy within the cell is essential to its life. One way that living things use energy is shown in Figure 8-1.

Cell Metabolism

Cells need many substances to stay alive. The chemical activities of the cell provide for its growth, maintenance, and repair. Cells maintain a supply of enzymes to carry out the chemical reactions that produce energy. As we discovered, the cells of living organisms contain carbohydrates, lipids, proteins, and nucleic acids. These substances are produced by the cells themselves. Let us look first at how cells make proteins.

OBJECTIVES FOR SECTION 1

A. Explain how cells use energy in response to their environment.

B. Describe how cells make and use proteins.

C. Name some other substances that cells make and tell how they are used.

Stress the point that things people can do are the product of what their cells can do. Energy to do anything comes from chemical reactions in cells.

8-1. Stages in germination of a corn seed.

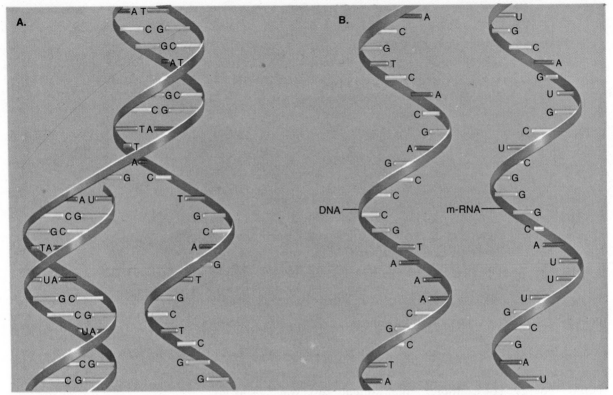

A.

B.

DNA

m-RNA

8-2. *m-RNA being made according to the information contained in DNA.*

How Cells Make Proteins (Protein Synthesis)

TRANSFER OF INFORMATION FROM DNA TO m-RNA   Inside the nucleus of a cell are the chromosomes. Chromosomes contain DNA arranged in a coiled double strand of nucleotides. The code to produce a certain protein is contained within the DNA molecule. However, proteins are produced outside the nucleus in the cytoplasm. To overcome this problem, the code within DNA must be copied and transported to the cytoplasm. When a cell gets ready to produce a protein molecule, some of the DNA separates. (See Fig. 8-2.) Nucleotides that are present in the nucleus line up along the DNA in a particular order to form a molecule of RNA. The base uracil (U) of RNA always pairs with adenine (A) of DNA. All of the other nucleotides follow the rules of base pairing. The base-pair rule insures that C-G, A-U and A-T pairs form along the length of the molecule. The molecule of RNA that is formed is called *messenger-RNA* (m-RNA).

MESSENGER RNA   Messenger-RNA separates from the DNA and moves out of the nucleus and into the cytoplasm. Here the messenger-RNA becomes associated with and appears to move across a site on a ribosome. The messenger-RNA is now ready to direct the making of a protein molecule. (See Fig. 8-4A. on page 140.) In the production of m-RNA, the nucleotides were arranged in a partic-

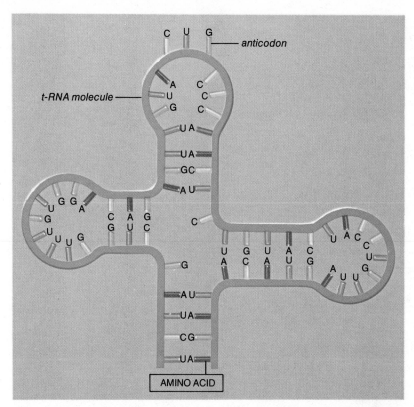

t-RNA molecule

C U G — anticodon

AMINO ACID

8-3. *This is one way a molecule of t-RNA may be folded. Base-pairing holds the folded strands together, and each amino acid attaches to a specific place. Notice also the anticodon that pairs with the codon of m-RNA.*

ular sequence. This follows the order of the nucleotides in the DNA. This is how information in the DNA is transferred to the messenger-RNA. Each group of three nucleotides in the messenger-RNA provides the information for the placement of one amino acid. *Such a group of three nucleotides on the messenger-RNA is called a* **codon**. There is one codon for each of the twenty amino acids normally found in proteins. There is more than one codon for some amino acids. A few codons even serve as punctuation marks. The amino acids and some of their codons are shown in Table 8-1.

TRANSFER RNA Another kind of RNA, transfer-RNA, is also needed in the synthesis of a protein molecule. There are many different kinds of transfer-RNA (t-RNA). Each is usually shaped like a cloverleaf. (See Fig. 8-3.) On the t-RNA, there is a specific location for the attachment on an amino acid. Each t-RNA molecule has a certain location where there are three exposed nucleotides extending out from the surface. *These three nucleotides of t-RNA are the anticodon for the amino acid which is attached to it.* The anticodons pair with particular codons of messenger-RNA. Let's examine the mechanism of protein synthesis. (See Fig. 8-4.)

BUILDING PROTEIN MOLECULES The messenger-RNA moves along the surface of the ribosome. It is believed that the ribosome helps to

TABLE 8-1. AMINO ACIDS AND THEIR CODONS

Amino Acid	Codons		
Alanine	GCU	GCC	GCA
Arginine	CGU	CGC	CGA
Asparagine	AAU	AAC	
Aspartic acid	GAU	ACG	
Cysteine	UGU	UGC	
Glutamic acid	GAA	GAG	
Glutamine	CAA	CAG	
Glycine	GUG	GGC	GGA
Histidine	CAU	CAC	
Isoleucine	AUU	AUC	
Leucine	UUA	UUG	CUU
Lysine	AAA	AAG	
Methionine	AUG		
Phenyl-alanine	UUU	UUC	
Proline	CCU	CCC	CCA
Serine	UCU	UCG	
Threonine	ACU	ACC	ACG
Tryptophan	UGG		
Tyrosine	UAU		
Valine	GUU		
Punctuation marks	UAG	UAA	UGA

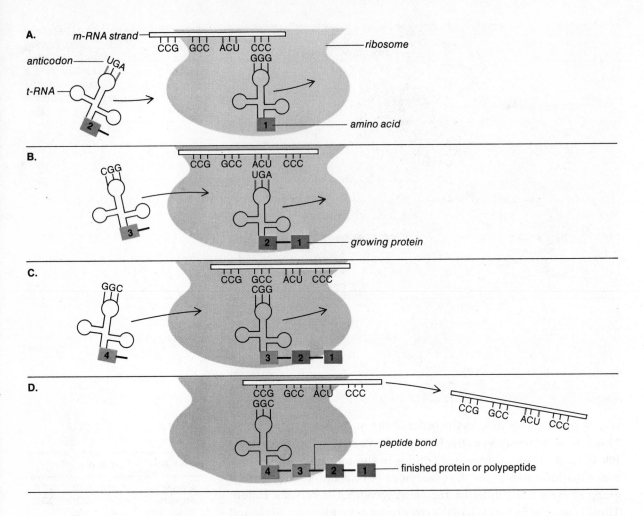

A.
m-RNA strand — ribosome
CCG GCC ACU CCC GGG
anticodon — UGA
t-RNA
2
1 — amino acid

B.
CGG
CCG GCC ACU CCC UGA
3
2 — 1 — growing protein

C.
GGC
CCG GCC ACU CCC CGG
4
3 — 2 — 1

D.
CCG GCC ACU CCC GGC
CCG GCC ACU CCC
4 — 3 — 2 — 1
peptide bond
finished protein or polypeptide

8-4. *The mechanism of protein synthesis.*

bring the t-RNA molecule into line at the correct position with m-RNA. As the first codon is exposed, a particular transfer-RNA with the correct anticodon joins with it. (See Fig. 8-4A.) This action brings the first amino acid of the protein into place. The messenger-RNA moves across the site of a ribosome and a second codon is exposed. A second transfer-RNA brings another amino acid into position. Through the action of special enzymes, a peptide bond is formed between the two amino acids and the first transfer-RNA is released. (See Fig. 8-4B.) This transfer-RNA is free to carry another molecule of its amino acid for further reactions. (See Fig. 8-4C.) This pairing continues until a codon is reached that has no matching amino acid. This marks the end of the protein molecule. The finished protein molecule is released into the cytoplasm or into the inside of the ER. The messenger-RNA is then free to direct the synthesis of another molecule of protein. (See Fig. 8-4D.)

Thus, information to produce a specific protein is transferred with great precision from DNA through messenger-RNA and transfer-RNA. The amino acids of any protein must be in correct sequence for that protein to work properly. Several enzymes along with some ATP molecules are required to carry the process of protein synthesis to completion. The RNA molecules can be used many times before they wear out. The DNA of the nucleus remains as an always available master code for the making of proteins needed by the cell. This is like keeping a master audio tape for making many copies of musical records. Years and years of painstaking work by many scientists were required to find out how this complex process works.

How Cells Use Proteins

Every cell contains hundreds of different proteins. Moreover, each kind of cell contains some proteins which are special to that cell. Proteins form the main structure of both the cell membrane and the organelles.

Proteins act as the fundamental part of an enzyme and may even serve as fuel for the release of energy. Protein molecules are needed both in the growth and eventual repair of all cell structures. When cells divide, proteins are needed to form the substance of new cells.

Cells Make Other Substances

Cells are also capable of producing lipids. In addition to proteins, cell membranes and organelles contain lipids. Lipids are important as fuels and as structural parts of cells, especially cell membranes. Fats yield considerable energy and thus are an economical form for the storage of food reserves. The seeds of plants often contain large amounts of fat. Carbohydrates are a readily available fuel to supply energy for the metabolic processes of the cell. Plants are capable of producing starch as a molecule for storing energy. Plant cells also synthesize cellulose which is used as a supporting structure in the cell wall. Furthermore, animals sometimes make the polysaccharide, glycogen. It serves for storing energy.

QUESTIONS FOR SECTION 1

1. Name some ways cells use energy to respond to their environment.
2. How is the use of energy in cells related to the production of energy in cells?
3. What is the role of the nucleus in protein synthesis?
4. What is the role of the ribosomes, messenger RNA and transfer RNA in protein synthesis?
5. Summarize the process of protein synthesis.
6. What other substances besides proteins can cells make?
7. Name three kinds of polysaccharides made by cells and tell the use of each.

Interested students may want to find out more about substances made from plants or animals that are of economic importance. These might include some kind of medicine or some manufactured substances such as paint, perfume, or even natural products such as milk.

Answers to Questions for Section 1.
A. 1. Detection of stimuli and movement of various kinds.
  *2. As cells use energy, the amount of energy stored in them decreases. More energy-carrying molecules enter the cell and are available to be used. There is a balance between the production and use of energy that helps to maintain homeostasis.
B. 3. Nucleus contains DNA that provides information for making proteins.
  4. Ribosomes serve as a site for protein synthesis. m-RNA carries information from nucleus to the ribosomes. t-RNA carries amino acids to site of snythesis.
  *5. Protein synthesis begins with the DNA serving as a template for the making of m-RNA, which moves to the ribosome and directs the formation of a particular protein molecule through the action of t-RNA. The ribosome serves as a site for protein synthesis.
C. 6. Cells make carbohydrates and lipids. When dividing or making proteins, they also make nucleic acids.
  *7. Glycogen is made by some animal cells and is used to store energy. Starch is made by some plant cells and is also used to store energy. Cellulose is made by some plant cells and is a structural part of most plants.

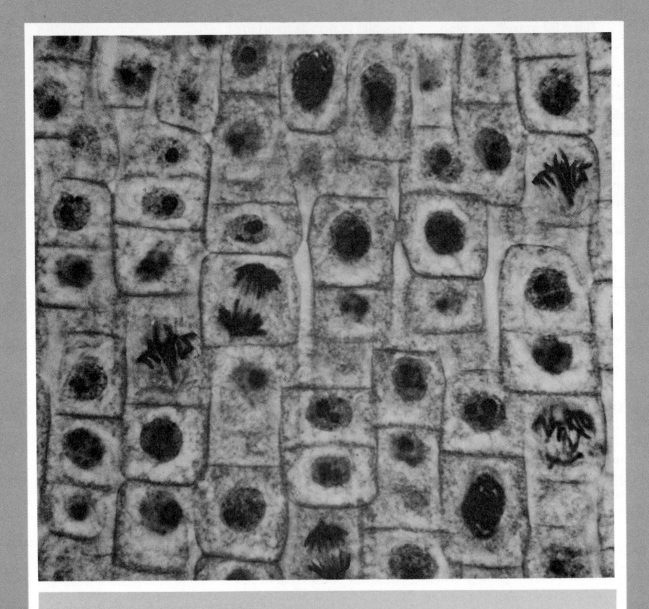

CHAPTER INVESTIGATION

A. What activity is going on in these cells? How do you know?

B. Make a series of sketches showing the steps in the process in the proper sequence.

C. Devise a way to tell about what proportion of the time needed for the whole process the cells spend in each phase of the process.

2 CELL DIVISION

Mitosis

Biologists learned about the process of cell division by observing living cells through the microscope. The most striking changes they observed were those that occurred in the nucleus. *The duplication of the nucleus in such a way that each new cell receives exactly the same number and kind of chromosomes is called* **mitosis** (mī *tō* sis). Mitosis is a continuous process with each stage merging into the next one. It may be helpful to imagine the process of mitosis as being similar to going around a circular track. (See Fig. 8-5.)

Replication of DNA During Interphase

DNA STRUCTURE   As cells grow to a certain size, they begin to undergo the process of cell division. During *interphase* (*in* ter fāz), each chromosome begins to **replicate** (*rep* lə kāt) *or make a duplicate of itself.* (See Fig. 8-6.) As you already know from Chapter 5, each chromosome contains a long molecule of DNA. Each DNA molecule consists of two complementary strands of nucleotides twisted about one another in an orderly fashion. This arrangement forms a double helix. The paired bases of the two complementary strands are held together by special chemical bonds.

NUCLEOTIDE SEQUENCE   The key to the question of DNA function is tied to the particular sequence of nucleotides. Given enough length, it would be possible to compose an infinite number of combinations of nucleotides. For example, a sequence of 1000 nucleotides provides information for the placement of over 300 amino acids. This is like a word of 1000 letters. Even though the alphabet of DNA contains only 4 different letters, A, T, C, and G, the number of ways they can be arranged in 1000 letter words is very large indeed. Scientists have estimated that a typical gene contains at least 1000 nucleotides. The nucleus of a human cell contains at least 10,000 genes. Thus the number of nucleotides exceeds ten million!

DNA REPLICATION   In the process of DNA duplication, the original nucleotide strands begin to separate, as shown in Figure 8-6. As the two halves separate, each side serves as a template or model for the building of a new complementary strand. Nucleotides and other raw materials are available in the nucleus of the cell for use in building the new strand. Each adenine nucleotide in the model attracts a thymine nucleotide. Likewise, thymine attracts adenine. Guanine attracts cytosine and cytosine attracts guanine. The sugar and phosphate molecules are also chemically bonded into their proper positions. New DNA has been formed. The process of duplication is completed.

Why is it important that new cells receive exactly the same chromosomes as the parent cell? What might happen if a cell did not get the right chromosomes?

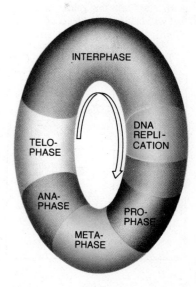

8-5. *Each time a cell divides it goes through this cycle.*

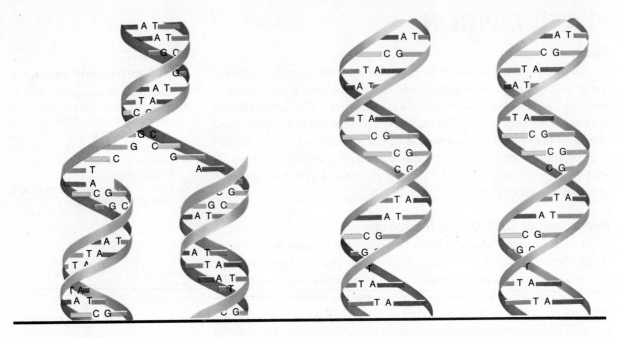

8-6. The process of DNA duplication.

Ask students to account for the existence of cells that appear to be half way between two stages of mitosis.

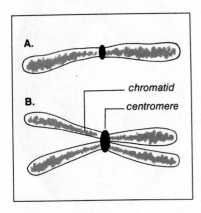

8-7. **A.** *Single-stranded chromosome before replication.* **B.** *Double-stranded chromosome after replication.*

After the replication is finished, each chromosome temporarily consists of two molecules of DNA. Both DNA molecules contain exactly the same sequence of nucleotides. Therefore, both molecules contain the same genetic information as the original one. Each chromosome has a certain area where the two molecules of DNA are held together. **This specialized region of the chromosome is called the centromere** (*sen* trə mẽr). Each part of the doubled chromosome is called a *chromatid* (*krō* mə tid). (See Fig. 8-7.)

Division of the Nucleus

Once the DNA is replicated, the nucleus is ready to divide through the process of mitosis. Even though mitosis is a continuous process, biologists have given names to the various stages of mitosis. This makes it easy to discuss the process. The stages of mitosis are *prophase* (*prō* fãz), *metaphase* (*met* ə fãz), *anaphase* (*an* ə fãz), and *telophase* (*tel* ə fãz). (See Fig. 8-8.)

In *prophase* the nuclear envelope disappears. The chromosomes shorten and thicken, so they are easy to see with a light microscope. The nucleolus, if present, breaks up into pieces. *In the cytoplasm adjacent to the nucleus in animal cells are two small dark staining, cylindrical bodies called the* **centrioles** (*sen* trẽ olz). The centrioles separate and move toward opposite sides of the cell. *Threads of protein,* the *spindle fibers,* appear between the centrioles. The spindle fibers stretch from pole to pole and form a definite structure. Plant cells do not have centrioles but they do have spindle fibers.

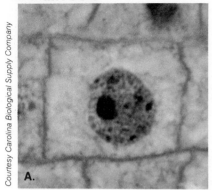

A.

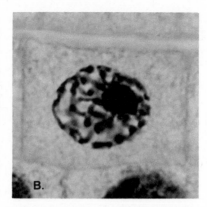

B.

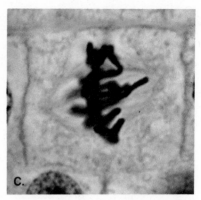

C.

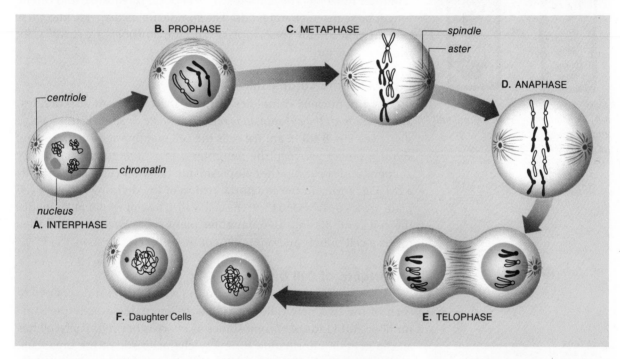

B. PROPHASE

C. METAPHASE

spindle

aster

D. ANAPHASE

centriole

chromatin

nucleus

A. INTERPHASE

F. Daughter Cells

E. TELOPHASE

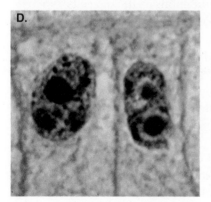

D.

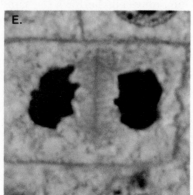

E.

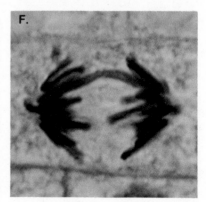

F.

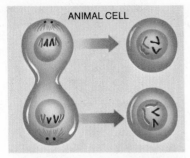
ANIMAL CELL

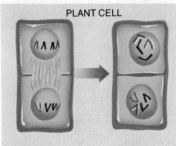
PLANT CELL

8-9. *Cytokinesis in an animal cell and a plant cell.*

Studies of human cells have shown that they have a very finite life span. Cancer cells are an exception. They can keep dividing indefinitely as long as they are provided with nutrients. Ask interested students to report in more detail on some form of cancer or some effect of aging.

In *metaphase* the chromosomes gather in the center of the cell. Each becomes attached to a spindle fiber at its centromere. During this time the chromatids form separate chromosomes.

In *anaphase* the two molecules of DNA in each chromosome separate. The chromosomes are drawn toward the poles by the spindle fibers so that one DNA molecule goes to each side of the cell. These separated DNA molecules are the chromosomes of the new cells. Remember each molecule contains all of the information that was present in the original chromosome.

In *telophase* the chromosomes have reached the opposite poles. The nucleolus reappears. The nuclear envelope forms around each daughter nucleus. The chromosomes become thread-like and can no longer be seen as separate rods. The spindle fibers disperse into small protein molecules in the cytoplasm and the centrioles are set aside for the next division.

Division of the Cytoplasm

As the nucleus completes mitosis, the cytoplasm also divides. *The division of the cytoplasm is referred to as* **cytokinesis** (sī t ō kə nē səs). (See Fig. 8-9.) In animal cells the cell membrane forms a furrow about midway between the daughter nuclei. The furrow gradually deepens and separates the cytoplasm into two new cells. In plant cells a *cell plate* forms in the equatorial region of the dividing cell. The cell plate grows outward to form the cell wall. The cell wall finally divides the cell contents into two daughter plant cells. Each new cell then forms a cell membrane on its side of the cell plate.

Importance of Cell Division

Cell division insures the precise and equal distribution of DNA to each of the two new cells. Each new cell contains exactly the same number and kinds of chromosomes as every other cell. Each cell has all the genetic information for every characteristic of the organism. Thus, new cells perform the same functions as the old cells. No matter how many times cell division occurs, the new cells are like the old ones. Therefore, genetic continuity is maintained. Furthermore, cell division provides a way for living things to grow and to repair themselves. There are many different types of cells in your body. Each of these cells grow and divide. As they do so, each passes on its own unique set of instructions for the development of the new cell.

Cancer — What Is It?

The mechanisms that control cell growth and division are not very well understood. We do not know exactly what starts it or stops it. We do know that sometimes cell division gets out of control and continues to occur again and again. *This uncontrolled cell division is cancer.* Much of the research on cancer is directed towards the molecular and biochemical reactions of normal cell growth and division.

We do not know all about the mechanisms that control normal cell growth. Still we have knowledge of some techniques that will stop the division of cancer cells. Radioactive substances and certain chemicals are known to interfere with cell division. The radioactive substances give off particles that bombard and distort the information found in the DNA of the cancer cells. (See Fig. 8-10.) Chemicals interfere with cell division in other ways such as destroying enzymes that are needed for cell division to occur. These substances do more damage to cancer cells than normal cells. This results because the cancer cells are dividing more rapidly. Surgery is used to remove cancer cells when they are located in one place. One of the problems in the treatment of cancer is that the cells often break off from the main growth or tumor. These are then spread throughout the body. *This process of cancer spreading from one place to many places in the body is called metastasis* (mi *tas* tə sis).

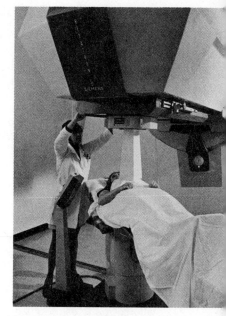

8-10. *A patient being given radiation treatment to destroy cancer cells.*

Aging and Death of Cells

Most cells grow and divide throughout the lifetime of an organism. Aging of cells may be viewed as a continuation of that process. In multicellular organisms aging occurs as the whole organism becomes less able to adapt to changes in the environment. Although the effects of aging are seen in the whole organism, the particular events often occur at the cellular level. For example, in humans the cells in the inner ear begin to become less effective in the teens. They continue to lose their ability to detect sounds gradually throughout life. Muscular strength reaches a peak at age 20 to 30 and gradually declines.

No one knows for sure what causes cells to age and die. But several theories have been proposed. They include the effects of radiation, chemical changes, and genetic changes. Radiation may damage particular cells causing them to age and die. Chemical changes may occur in proteins. For example, molecules are caused to change their shape and lose their ability to function. Some biologists believe that aging is programmed into the genes of organisms. These changes in function throughout life are controlled by the genes.

QUESTIONS FOR SECTION 2

1. How are new chromosomes produced?
2. Name the main events that occur in each stage of mitosis.
3. How is cell division important in growth and repair?
4. What is cancer?

Answers to Questions for Section 2.

D. 1. New chromosomes are produced when the double strands of DNA separate and each acts as a template for the base-pairing of new nucleotides.

E. 2. Interphase: replication of DNA; prophase: disappearance of nuclear membrane, separation of centrioles, and formation of spindle fibers; metaphase: chromosomes gather in center of cell; anaphase: movement of chromosomes to poles; telophase: formation of two nuclei and surrounding cells.

F. 3. It is only through cell division that new cells can be added for growth, or for repair by replacing cells that have died.

G. 4. Cancer is uncontrolled cell division.

3 LEVELS OF ORGANIZATION

Tissues

Answers to Questions for Section 3.
*2. Division of labor allows different cells to carry out different functions. Specialization makes it possible for the organism to become more complex and function more efficiently. It also allows the organism to increase in size. For example, organisms with transport systems can be much more complex than those that depend on diffusion for the movement of substances.

I. 3. Seed plants: meristem, epidermis, parenchyma, supporting tissue, vascular tissue. Vertebrates: epithelium, connective tissue, muscle, nerve.

*4. Many multicellulor organisms have transport systems. Plants have storage areas and photosynthetic areas. Animals have digestive systems, nervous systems, etc.

J. 5. The taking on of separate functions by different parts of the body.

K. *6. Examples include: movement of substances into and out of cells, use of energy and its replenishment, synthesis of proteins as they are needed by the cell.

Multicellular organisms have several levels of organization. (See Fig. 8-11.) The cells that make up the body of a human or any other multicellular organism are not all alike. Each cell becomes specialized to carry out certain functions. This specialization allows the cells to function more effectively. *A group of similarly specialized cells that carry out a particular function is called a* **tissue.** Each type of tissue is made up of cells that have a distinct shape, size, and arrangement. Let's see what kinds of tissues are found in the more complex multicellular organisms.

Plant Tissues

The cells of the higher plants are grouped into five main kinds of tissues. These are meristem, epidermis, parenchyma, supporting tissues, and vascular tissues. (See Fig. 8-12 on page 150.)

MERISTEM TISSUES **Meristem** (*mer* ə stem) *tissues contain cells that are capable of dividing throughout the life of the plant.* They are found wherever growth can occur in a plant. Meristem tissues form all of the other tissues of the plant. The tips of roots and stems contain meristem tissues.

EPIDERMIS Epidermis consists of sheets of cells that cover the surfaces of leaves, stems, and roots. The epidermis usually consists of a single layer of protective cells. Most of these cells secrete a fatty *cuticle* on their outer surfaces. The cuticle retards water loss.

PARENCHYMA *Parenchyma* (pə *reng* kə mə) is the packing material of the plant. It consists of loosely packed cells inside leaves, stems, and roots. The cells of parenchyma are large and thin walled.

SUPPORT TISSUES Supporting tissues consist of cells with thick, tough walls that provide mechanical support for the plant. The strings of celery stalks, the outer coverings of seeds and nuts, and the gritty texture of pears are examples of supporting tissues. The fibers that are used to produce thread, string, yarn, rope, and canvas come from these supporting tissues. Cork, a particular supporting tissue, forms the outer bark of woody plants. By the time cork cells have become bark, they are dead. But while cork cells are alive they secrete *suberin* (soo *ber* in). This is a fatty substance that makes the walls of these cells waterproof. The cork oak tree produces so much cork that it can be removed every three or four years. This type of cork is used to make bottle stoppers, life preservers, and insulation.

VASCULAR TISSUES **Vascular** (*vas* kyə lər) **tissues** *form tubes that conduct substances through the body of the plant.* They are of two main types: *xylem* (zī ləm) and *phloem* (flō əm). Xylem conducts water

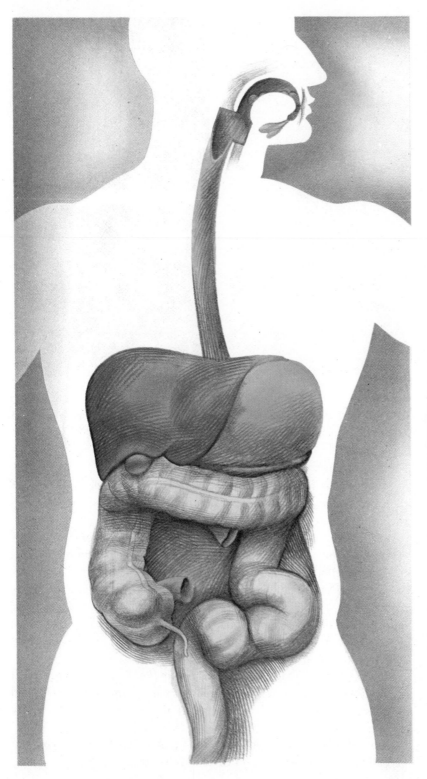

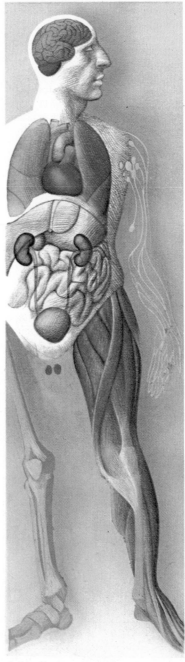

8-11. Organization is an outstanding characteristic both of body structure and of life. The human body consists of systems arranged in an orderly manner. **A.** Digestive system. **B.** Various systems making up organism.

Notice that the kinds of tissues found in plants are very different from the kinds found in animals. Also, the organization of the bodies of plants and of animals are quite different. Ask students to use what they already know about plants and animals to list some similarities and differences. You might also want to ask how plants and animals can be so different when their cells are so much alike.

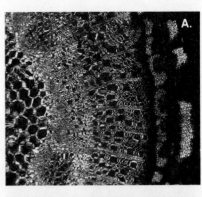

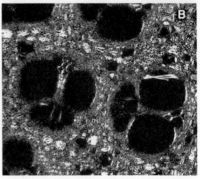

*8-12. Some types of tissue found in seed plants. **A.** The epidermis normally consists of one surface layer of flattened cells. **B.** Vascular tissues carry water and food through the plant.*

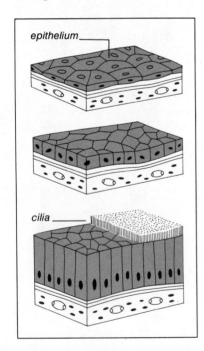

8-13. Epithelium tissue has a variety of shapes. It may have cilia on the free surface.

and dissolved minerals from roots to leaves. Phloem carries food from the leaves to other parts of the plant.

Animal Tissues

Vertebrate animals are those that have backbones. The cells of their bodies are composed of four main kinds of tissue. They are epithelial, connective, muscle, and nervous tissue.

EPITHELIAL TISSUE   **Epithelial** (ep ə *thē* lē əl) *tissue consists of layers of cells that cover outer and inner surfaces of the body.* Several types of epithelial tissues are shown in Figure 8-13.

CONNECTIVE TISSUE   **Connective tissue** *includes a number of different kinds of tissue, but most of them are involved in connecting or holding together the various parts of the body.* The cells of connective tissue are imbedded in a substance called the *matrix.* Some examples of connective tissues are shown in Figure 8-14.

MUSCLE TISSUE   **Muscle tissue** *is tissue that is able to contract.* It is divided into three categories: skeletal muscle, smooth muscle, and cardiac muscle. The characteristics of these types of muscle are shown in Figure 8-15.

NERVOUS TISSUE   **Nervous tissue** *is tissue that is able to conduct nerve impulses.* The cells are called *neurons.* (See Fig. 8-16.)

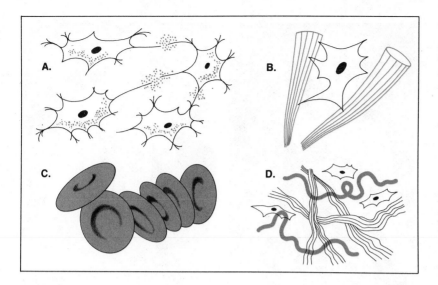

8-14. **A.** Bone cells in solid matrix. **B.** Connective tissue cell. **C.** Blood cells in fluid matrix. **D.** Loose connective tissue.

Organs

Tissues combine to form organs, the next higher level of organization. *An **organ** is a group of tissues that work together to carry out a set of functions.* For example, your stomach is an organ that contains several kinds of tissue. One type of tissue produces the secretions that digest food. A second type, muscle tissue, contracts to mix the food and push it out of the stomach. Finally, nerve tissue sends impulses that control the digestion and movement of food.

Systems

Organs combine to form systems, the highest level of organization in an organism. *A **system** is a group of organs that work together to carry out a major body function.* Your body has several systems. For example, the digestive system breaks down large food particles to molecules the cells can use. There is a system for each of the major activities of the body. The systems of the human body are shown in Figure 8-17.

Division of Labor

Any one cell does not have to carry out all of the functions of the body. The levels of structural organization in higher animals allows different parts of the body to take on different functions. *The taking on of separate functions by different parts of the body is called **division of labor**.* The activities of some body parts are under the control of one or more systems. This interrelated network of systems function together for the support of the organism. *An **organism** is an independently functioning living thing.*

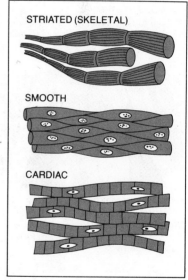

8-15. Some types of muscle tissue.

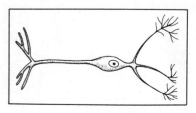

8-16. A neuron is the basic cell of nervous tissue.

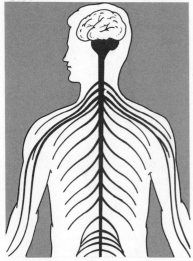

NERVOUS SYSTEM
The nervous system and sense organs receive stimuli, transport impulses, and control the organism

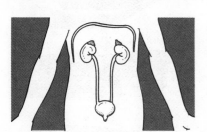

EXCRETORY AND REPRODUCTIVE SYSTEMS
The excretory system removes wastes and the reproductive system produces eggs or sperm

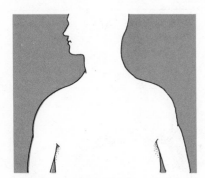

INTEGUMENTARY SYSTEM
The integumentary system covers and protects the body

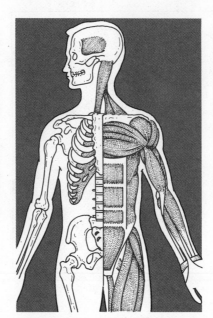

MUSCULOSKELETAL SYSTEM
The musculoskeletal system protects and provides for movement

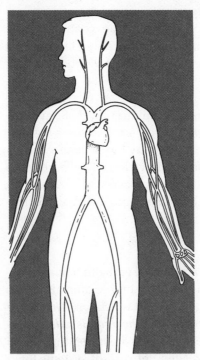

CIRCULATORY SYSTEM
The circulatory system transports substances to all cells

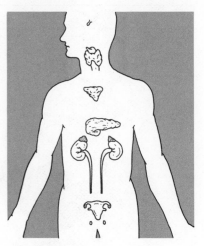

ENDOCRINE SYSTEM
The endocrine system controls the organism by producing hormones

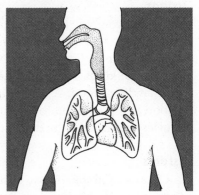

RESPIRATORY SYSTEM
The respiratory system allows for oxygen to enter body and carbon dioxide to leave

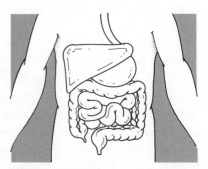

DIGESTIVE SYSTEM
The digestive system breaks food into molecules cells can use

QUESTIONS FOR SECTION 3

1. Arrange the levels of organization from simple to complex.
2. What is the significance of levels of organization in multicellular organisms?
3. What tissues are found in seed plants; animals with backbones?
4. List several ways that the function of multicellular organisms differs from that of unicellular organisms because of division of labor.
5. What is meant by the term division of labor?
6. List as many examples as you can of homeostasis in the activities of cells (include information from all of the chapters in this unit.

Answers to Questions for Section 3.

H. 1. Organelle, cell, tissue, organ, system, organism.

(See page 148 for more answers.)

CHAPTER REVIEW

How do the activities of cells maintain homeostasis? Most of the activities of living things take place at the cellular level. Thus what happens in cells determines what happens in the whole organism. For example, your digestive system breaks down food. It moves it through the food tract, absorbs nutrients, and gets rid of solid wastes. These are functions of a system. The specific activities are carried out by individual cells.

Living organisms are capable of detecting changes in and responding to their environment. In multicellular organisms messages are received by certain cells. Then they are relayed to other cells. Thus cells are stimulated to carry out activities that keep the organism alive in the changed environment. *Being able to respond to change in the environment is one way living things maintain homeostasis.*

All cells can make proteins. The DNA in the chromosomes of cells directs the making of a variety of proteins. Each is in the correct amount. For example, enzymes are proteins that are produced by individual cells. These enzymes are further used by the cell to direct the synthesis of many other substances. *Being able to make the things it needs in the right amount at the right time is another way living things maintain homeostasis.*

Cells divide to produce new cells. Each is capable of growth and repair. We have limited knowledge about how cell division is started or stopped. We do know that it is

controlled. Cell division is normally rapid in young, growing organisms. Yet it is kept under control so that most organisms stop growing when they reach adult size. Many plants continue to grow throughout life. But their rate of growth is controlled. Cell division starts at the onset of an injury and continues until the repair is complete. *Being able to control cell division is a third way organisms maintain homeostasis.*

In unicellular organisms all of the activities take place in one cell. However, in more complex, multicellular organisms, division of labor occurs. Cells are organized into tissues, organs, and systems. Their activities are controlled so the organism functions as a whole. *Being able to control the various activities of cells is yet another way living things maintain homeostasis.*

Using the Concepts

1. All living things use the same set of codons for amino acids. What do you think might be the significance of this?
2. There are more organisms in a hay infusion after several days than there were at the time the infusion was made. What happened to cause this increase?
3. Find all of the sequential processes described in this chapter and make a list of the steps in each.

VOCABULARY REVIEW

1			
Messenger RNA	replicate	centrioles	3 tissue	epithelium
codon	centromere	anaphase	meristem	muscle
transfer RNA	chromatid	cytokinesis	epidermis	organ
anticodon	prophase	cancer	parenchyma	system
2 mitosis	metaphase	metastasis	xylem	
interphase	telophase	recombinant DNA	phloem	

CHAPTER 8 TEST

Copy the number of each test item and place your answer to the right.

PART 1   Multiple Choice: Select the letter of the phrase that best completes each of the following.

d 1. Cells use energy to   **a.** grow and divide
   b. respond to their environment   **c.** make proteins   **d.** all of the above.

d 2. In the pairing of DNA and RNA nucleotides, which of these does *not* occur?   **a.** C-G
   b. A-U   **c.** A-T   **d.** T-U.

a 3. Information is carried from the nucleus by
   a. messenger RNA   **b.** transfer RNA
   c. ribosomal RNA   **d.** DNA.

d 4. In mitosis, each new cell has   **a.** the same number of chromosomes   **b.** the same kind of chromosomes   **c.** the same cytoplasm
   d. both a & b.

b 5. In the replication of DNA, the new DNA is like the old because of   **a.** the RNA template
   b. base pairing   **c.** spindle formation
   d. the centromere.

b 6. The daily activities of cells help to maintain
   a. the environment   **b.** homeostasis
   c. cell metabolism   **d.** all of the above.

c 7. The taking on of separate functions by different parts of the body is called   **a.** metastasis
   b. mitosis   **c.** division of labor
   d. homeostasis.

a 8. The three nucleotide units of m-RNA that specify which amino acids are to go into a protein are
   a. codons   **b.** clones   **c.** centromeres
   d. anticodons.

c 9. Where are proteins synthesized?   **a.** the nucleus   **b.** the cytoplasm   **c.** the ribosome
   d. the mitochondria.

a 10. Cell division is important for   **a.** growth and repair   **b.** causing diversity among cells
   c. protein synthesis   **d.** division of labor.

PART 2   Matching: Match the letter of the term in Column I with its description in Column II.

COLUMN I

a.   anaphase   **f.**   nerve
b.   interphase   **g.**   vascular
c.   metaphase   **h.**   muscle
d.   prophase   **i.**   meristem
e.   telophase   **j.**   parenchyma

COLUMN II

d 11. nuclear envelope disappears
a 12. chromosomes move to the poles of the cell
b 13. chromosomes replicate
e 14. the new cells are formed
c 15. chromosomes gather at the center of the cell
i 16. a plant tissue that is capable of dividing
j 17. the packing material of plants
g 18. the plant tissues that conduct substances through the plant
h 19. an animal tissue that can contract
f 20. an animal tissue that can conduct impulses

PART 3   Completion: Complete the following.
21. Arrange the five stages of mitosis in sequence _____.
22. List the levels of organization from organelles to organisms _____.
23. Three ways cells maintain homeostasis are _____.
24. Division of labor means that different parts of the body _____.
25. Uncontrolled cell division is _____.

Chapter 8 Test Answers

21. interphase, prophase, metaphase, anaphase, telophase
22. organelle, cell, tissue, organ, system, organism
23. responding to change in environment; making materials cells need in right amounts at right time; controlling all activities.
24. take on separate functions
25. cancer

CONTINUITY OF LIFE

Scientists have known for centuries that cats come from other cats. We know that any form of life comes only from another form like itself. In this unit we will study heredity. It is the passing on of traits from one generation to the next. Basic principles govern how this information is passed from parents to offspring. We will consider the effect of these principles upon populations of plants and animals and specifically humans.

PRIDE OF LIONS

CHAPTER 9

PRINCIPLES OF HEREDITY

Cells, as we have seen in the previous unit, are the centers for the activities of life. In one way or another, all living cells engage in these activities. They may grow, respond to their environment, respire, divide, and even move about. But not all cells are the same. Activities may vary considerably from one kind of cell to another. In fact, cells may not even look as if they share any common features.

Cellular differences are also found in many-celled organisms. For example, your body is composed of many different kinds of cells. There are skin cells, muscle cells, bone cells and blood cells, to name only a few. But the differences do not end here. You are different from your friends despite the fact that you have the same kinds of cells. Moreover, human beings are obviously different from other kinds of animals. And animals are different from plants.

What causes these differences? How can the cell be a fundamental unit of life and yet produce different kinds of organisms? *What contributes to the continuity of life*? These are some of the basic questions that will be explored in this unit. We will begin, however, with a study of the fundamental concepts of heredity. As we explore these ideas, you will also discover:

- How characteristics of plants and animals may be passed from one generation to the next generation
- How variety can exist in spite of how much organisms look alike
- What kinds of traits are inherited

PEA PLANT

1 BASIC INHERITANCE

Variety Within Limits

All dogs are different — no two are exactly alike. Nevertheless, they are still recognizable as dogs. Thus, the variety we observe in dogs has certain limits. Variety exceeding these limits causes us to recognize another kind of animal, perhaps a wolf or coyote. The same can be said for any kind of organism although we may have to look very closely to observe much variety.

Most of the physical features of organisms that we see are *inherited*. That is, these features have been transmitted from parents to offspring in some biological manner. The mechanism for this transfer was unknown until Gregor Mendel published the results of his experiments in 1865. During the 20th Century, many new discoveries have expanded our knowledge and understanding of inheritance. This knowledge, coupled with the new questions it raises, is the focus of *the science of inheritance known as* **genetics.**

The inheritance pattern for some traits is fairly simple. For others, it is very complex or even unknown. Some inherited characteristics are influenced by the environment. Others are not at all. Understanding how traits are passed from one generation to the next is important to our understanding of the nature of life.

Gregor Mendel

We do not need to understand the principles of electricity to make it work for us. In the same manner, people have used the principles of inheritance for many centuries. The domestication of many useful plants and animals would not have been possible otherwise. Cattle, sheep, horses, dogs, cats and many other animals are products of selective breeding practices over a long period of time. Food materials such as corn, rice and wheat are also the results of such practices. Even without an understanding of the principles involved, humans have been able to direct nature to their own use.

REASONS FOR SUCCESS   Early attempts to make some sense from observed patterns of inheritance had not been too rewarding. Biologists failed in their efforts because of the seemingly endless variety of inherited traits. The experiments of Father Gregor Mendel, an Austrian monk, proved to be much more successful for two main reasons.

The first reason was years of hard work. Others had been observing traits in organisms that tended to blend with each other. In fact, most traits do just that. This makes them difficult to observe in pure form. While such phenomena are understandable today, they are confusing without a knowledge of more basic principles. Mendel

OBJECTIVES FOR SECTION 1

A. Define the following terms: *dominant, recessive, hybrid, F_1 and F_2 generations, homozygous, heterozygous.*

B. State and explain Mendel's *Principles of Unit Characters* and *Dominance*.

C. Trace a Mendelian inheritance for a single trait through two generations using an appropriate diagram.

9-1. *Gregor Mendel laid the foundation for the modern principles of heredity.*

tested many characteristics before he decided upon the garden pea. It provided him with an organism that displayed seven easily-observed traits. (See Fig. 9-2.)

Furthermore, these traits were seen to exist in only two forms. For example, when observing seeds, he saw that they were either round or wrinkled. Plants were either tall or short. There were no intermediate forms in any of the seven traits. *Such traits, existing in either one of only two alternative forms, are called* **Mendelian traits.**

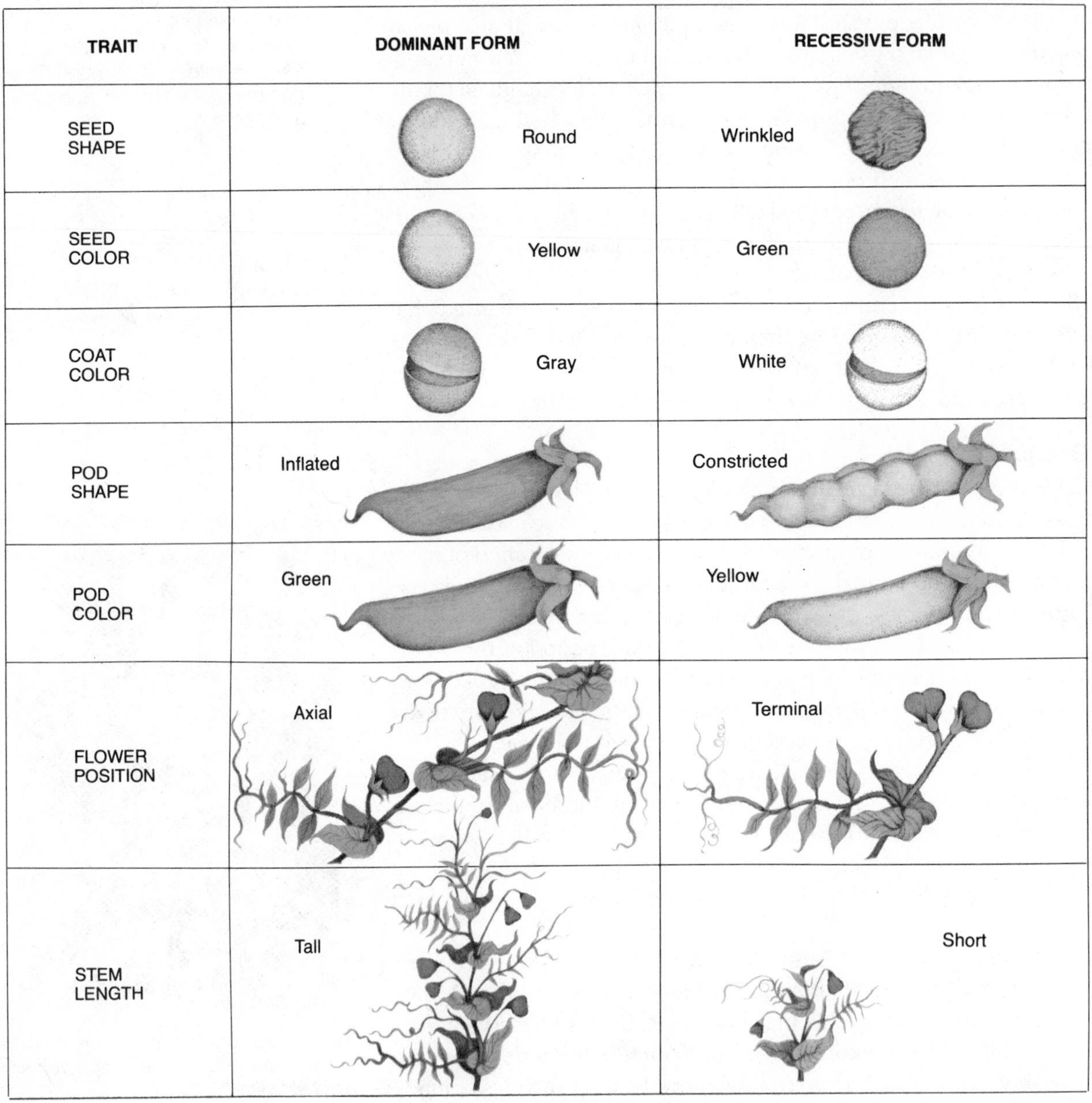

9-2. *Seven traits of garden peas studied by Mendel.*

TRAIT	DOMINANT FORM	RECESSIVE FORM
SEED SHAPE	Round	Wrinkled
SEED COLOR	Yellow	Green
COAT COLOR	Gray	White
POD SHAPE	Inflated	Constricted
POD COLOR	Green	Yellow
FLOWER POSITION	Axial	Terminal
STEM LENGTH	Tall	Short

The second reason that Mendel succeeded where others had failed was his background in mathematics as well as biology. This combination allowed him to plan experiments that were unique on three counts. First, he made a point to observe only one, and later, two traits at a time. Second, he used a large number of identical crosses or matings of plants. He pooled his results. This gave him a much larger sample than single crosses could produce. And finally,

TABLE 9-1

Results of breeding F_1 pea hybrids in Mendel's original experiments.

Trait	Number Dominant	Number Recessive	Ratio
Seed shape	5,474 round	1,850 wrinkled	2.96:1
Seed color	6,022 yellow	2,001 green	3.01:1
Seed coat color	705 grey	224 white	3.15:1
Pod shape	882 inflated	299 wrinkled	2.95:1
Pod color	428 green	152 yellow	2.82:1
Flower position	651 axial	207 terminal	3.14:1
Stem length	787 tall	277 short	2.84:1
TOTAL	14,949 Dominant	5,010 Recessive	2.98:1

he analyzed his results by counting and calculating ratios. This enabled him to observe patterns that might not be readily apparent in the results of single crosses.

LACK OF RECOGNITION   Mendel began his studies in the garden of his Austrian monastery in 1857. Over a period of seven years, he carefully cultivated nearly 20,000 plants. He kept careful records for each cross and the offspring produced. From these results emerged the principles that today form the cornerstone of modern genetics. Unfortunately, Mendel's work went unnoticed until the turn of the century. Also, leading biologists of the day did not properly understand Mendel's paper. This, along with lack of recognition, and the increasing demands of his work at the monastery, possibly prevented him from even greater discoveries in genetics.

Mendel's Experiments

Mendel's first task was to obtain plants that were pure-breeding for each of the seven traits he was observing. **Pure-breeding populations** *produce only one form of a trait over many generations.* This meant that he had to have two contrasting populations of plants for each trait. For example, one population of pea plants always produced round seeds. Another population always produced wrinkled seeds. *Crossing populations that differ in one or more traits produces* *off-spring we call* **hybrids** (*hi* brid). For instance, offspring resulting from a cross between plants with round seeds and plants that produce wrinkled seeds would be hybrids. To make sure that the parent plants were indeed pure-breeding, he had to grow several generations of each population. Only when each population produced several generations that bred true could Mendel begin his experiments.

FIRST STEP   The experiments were actually quite simple. First, he removed the pollen-producing organs from the flowers of each population. This was done to ensure that the flowers could not self-pollinate accidentally (as pea plants normally do). The pollen collected from each population was then placed on flowers of the contrasting population. (See Fig. 9-3.) For example, pollen from round-seeded plants was used to fertilize flowers from wrinkle-seeded plants. Mendel also made a number of *reciprocal crosses*. That is, he fertilized flowers of round-seeded plants with pollen from plants that produced wrinkled seeds.

9-3. A cross is made by placing the pollen from the male organs (stamen) of a flower onto the female organs (pistil) of another plant. A reciprocal cross takes place by placing pollen from plant 2 onto the female organs of plant 1.

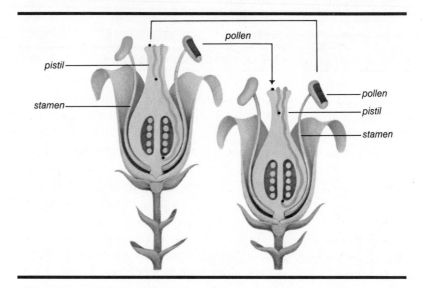

This procedure was repeated for each of the seven contrasting traits. (See Fig. 9-2 for the traits.) As you can see, although the experiment was simple in design, it was very time-consuming. A great deal of patience is often required to carry on scientific research.

The results of these crosses were most surprising. *All of the off-spring of the original crosses (usually called the* F_1 **generation**) *for each trait were identical.* Only one of the two contrasting forms for each trait appeared. In the case of the round-wrinkled cross, for instance, there were no intermediate forms. All of the F_1 generation produced round seeds. Mendel referred to the *form of the trait that appeared in the F_1 generation as the* **dominant form.**

SECOND STEP The next step in the experiment was to cross members of the F₁ generation with each other. The resulting F₂ generation held more surprises. Mendel discovered that both of the original forms for each trait appeared! Apparently, he reasoned, the factor necessary for the second form to appear was still present in the F₁ hybrids. *This hidden form in the F₁ generation is called* **recessive.** It had receded into the background for one generation, being dominated by the other form. Repeated experiments supported these results.

Analyzing the Results

Mendel then used his background in mathematics to analyze the results of his experiments. He found that in all seven traits, the F₂ generation seemed to produce three dominant plants for each recessive one. That is, the dominant and recessive forms existed in a 3:1 ratio. And this was in spite of the fact that no recessive forms had appeared in the F₁ generation at all!

At this point, Mendel's line of reasoning becomes very important. Remember that the recessive condition did not appear in the F₁ plants. But it reappeared in the F₂ plants. He concluded that members of the F₁ must have been carrying some factor for the recessive condition while expressing the dominant condition. Thus, *each plant must be carrying two factors for each trait.* This is known today as Mendel's **Principle of Unit Characters.** Each offspring, therefore, must receive one factor for each trait from each parent plant. This one factor comes from the *sex cell* or *gamete* from each parent.

If an offspring receives two dominant factors, one from each parent, it would exhibit the dominant form of the trait. Should it receive two recessive factors, the recessive form would appear. Receiving one dominant and one recessive factor, the recessive factor would be masked. The dominant trait would appear. In this case, the appearance of the offspring would be identical to the one receiving two dominant factors. Mendel's **Principle of Dominance** follows from this reasoning. *This principle states that one of the two factors for a trait can mask or overpower the other.*

MENDELISM TODAY Geneticists today have created a sort of code for explaining how this occurs. They represent Mendel's inheritance "factors" with letters of the alphabet. For Mendelian traits, the two forms of the letter, upper case *(A)* and lower case *(a)*, represent the two forms of the factor. Usually, the form is represented by the upper case first letter of the word for the dominant form of the trait. The recessive form would thus be the lower case letter of the same word. For example, the factor for the dominant seed shape would be represented by *R* for roundness. The wrinkled factor would be represented by the letter *r*.

Principle of Dominance works only for some traits. The reasons for this will be brought out in later sections.

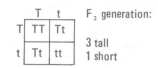

P₁ = TTxtt
F₁ = all tall hybrids

	T	t
T	TT	Tt
t	Tt	tt

F₂ generation:

3 tall
1 short

Students will need to learn how to determine ratios in genetics studies. Refer to Study Skills in Laboratory Investigations Manual.

Pure Bred Round (RR) and Pure Bred Wrinkled (rr)

PARENTS: RR x rr
GAMETES: R and r
F_1 GENERATION: Rr
hibrids with round seeds

P_1	R	R
r	Rr	Rr
r	Rr	Rr

Hybrid Round (Rr) and Hybrid Round (Rr)

PARENTS: Rr x Rr
GAMETES: R and r
F_2 GENERATION:
   1 RR
   2 Rr
   1 rr

P_2	R	r
R	RR	Rr
r	Rr	rr

F_2 generation will be in the proportion of 3 Round to 1 Wrinkled

9-4. *A monohybrid cross. The F_2 generation results from crossing members of the F_1 generation with each other.*

Answers to Questions for Section 1.

A. 1. See Glossary. In peas, round is dominant, wrinkled in recessive.

  2. See Glossary.

MENDEL'S TERMS Since each individual possesses two of these factors, pure breeding plants would be represented as *RR* or *rr*. They could only pass on one kind of factor. Today, *individuals who can pass only one kind of factor are called* **homozygous** (hō mə *zi* gəs). Members of the F_1 generation have one of each of these factors. They would be represented as *Rr* and be called *heterozygous*. **Heterozygous** (het ə rō *zi* gəs) *means that an individual possesses both the dominant and recessive forms of a factor.*

MONOHYBRID CROSS Let us use the alphabet code to follow Mendel's experiments. (See Fig. 9-4.) The initial crosses were between two homozygous groups in each case, *RR* and *rr*. The offspring would be heterozygous, *Rr*, and exhibit the dominant trait. Crossing two heterozygous F_1 plants resulted in the F_2 generation. We can see that each parent would donate either a dominant factor (*R*) or a recessive factor (*r*) to each offspring. If they each donate an *R*, the offspring will be *RR* and will be round-seeded. Offspring receiving an *r* from both parents will be *rr*, and their seeds will be wrinkled.

However, if the offspring receives an *R* from one parent and an *r* from the other, it will be heterozygous, *Rr* . Such plants will, of course, produce round seeds. Note that there are two ways for the dominant factor to be exhibited if both parents are heterozygous. The male parent could donate a dominant factor while the female donates a recessive one. Or the reverse could occur. The results, however, are the same. Thus, there are three round-seeded plants among the F_2 offspring for each plant with wrinkled seeds. The 3:1 ratio observed by Mendel has been established.

QUESTIONS FOR SECTION 1

1. Define and distinguish between dominant and recessive traits.
2. Define hybrid.
3. Define and distinguish between the F_1 and F_2 generations.
4. Define and distinguish between homozygous and heterozygous conditions.
5. What is the study of genetics?
6. What is a Mendelian trait? Give an example.
7. State the Principle of Unit Characteristics.
8. State the Principle of Dominance.
9. What is meant by the Principle of Unit Characteristics? What observations contributed to Mendel's formulation of this principle?
10. In Figure 9-5 why does one wrinkled seed appear in the F_2 generation and none in the F_1?
11. Suppose you crossed two plants which breed pure, but differently for a trait. What could you tell about the parent plants from the F_1 generation?
12. Using an appropriate diagram, illustrate the inheritance of plant height in pea plants for two generations. Tall is dominant to short.

(See page 161 for more answers.)

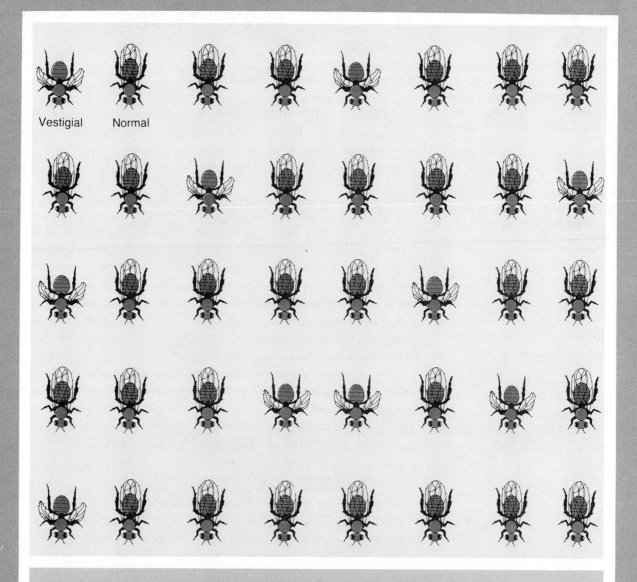

Vestigial   Normal

CHAPTER INVESTIGATION

A. How many of each wing-types have appeared in this F$_2$ generation?

B. What is the ratio of normal-winged flies to vestigial-winged flies? (refer to study skills for determining ratios.)

C. Assuming that this wing feature is Mendelian, (i) what is the genotype of the vestigial-winged flies? (ii) What genotypes are possible for the normal-winged flies? (iii) Design an experiment that would enable you to determine the actual genotype of one of the normal-winged flies.

2 APPLICATION OF MENDEL'S EXPERIMENTS

Chromosome Theory of Inheritance

Mendel's principles may be interpreted in terms of the **Chromosome Theory of Inheritance.** This theory explains that *chromosomes are responsible for the inherited characteristics of organisms, acting through their genes.* Thus, we may refer to *Mendel's inheritance factors as* **genes.** *The two alternative forms of a gene for a Mendelian trait are called* **alleles** (ə *lelz*). The alleles for a Mendelian trait would be the dominant and recessive forms. Mendel was observing the effect of the gene for seed shape in our example. This gene has two alleles. One allele produces round-seeded plants. The particular allelic combination, *RR, rr,* or *Rr,* is called the *genotype.* **The genotype is the particular combination of alleles for a trait.** The genotypic information is found in the cells of the organism. Thus, the genotype for plants with round seeds could be *RR* or *Rr.* These genotypes are called homozygous dominant or heterozygous. Plants with wrinkled seeds would have the genotype *rr.* These are referred to as being homozygous recessive.

In the F2 generation the ratio of round-seeded plants to wrinkle-seeded plants is expected to be 3:1. Remember that the three round-seeded plants can have a genotype of either *RR* or *Rr.* Therefore, in the F2 generation, the ratio is 1*RR*:2*Rr*:1*rr*. This is typical of the genotype of the F2 generation for a single Mendelian trait.

Use characteristics of Mendel's peas to distinguish between the *gene* for a trait (e.g., stem length) and its alleles (e.g., tall or short).

TABLE 9-2   *COMPARISON OF GENOTYPE AND PHENOTYPE*

Genotype	Phenotype
The pair of alleles for a trait in the cell	The appearance of a trait in an organism
Pure bred round: RR	round seed
Hybrid round: Rr	round seed
Pure bred wrinkled: rr	wrinkled seed

One other part of vocabulary is necessary at this point. The term **phenotype** *is used to denote the appearance of the organism with respect to a given trait.* When a trait is completely hereditary, the phenotype is the result of the genotype. The phenotype of *RR* and *Rr* plants would be round seeds. The phenotype for the homozygous recessive condition, *rr,* would be wrinkled seeds.

The Test Cross

Agriculture and horticulture depend upon successful breeding programs. Breeders must be able to predict what kind of offspring will be produced. But organisms that are homozygous dominant (*RR*) appear to be the same as those that are heterozygous (*Rr*). Thus, there is a need to distinguish between these two genotypes. To do this, a breeder uses a *test cross*. **Test crosses *involve the mating of an unknown genotype with a homozygous recessive phenotype (rr).*** (See Fig. 9-5.) For example, the genotype for a round-seeded plant may be either *RR* or *Rr*. To determine its actual genotype , it is crossed with one that produces wrinkled seeds. If no wrinkle-seeded plants appear in the offspring, the unknown genotype must have been *RR*. The appearance of the recessive phenotype in the offspring means that the unknown parent had to have passed on a recessive allele. Thus, it must have had the heterozygous genotype.

The offspring of the mating are then observed to see if there are any with the recessive condition. Recessive individuals indicate that the parent with the unknown genotype must have been heterozygous (*Rr*). Remember that the recessive phenotype depends upon the presence of *two* recessive alleles. One must be donated by each parent. For the recessive phenotype to appear would require that the unknown parent donate a recessive allele (*r*) to the offspring. The recessive parent, of course, always donates a recessive allele. If no recessive individuals occur in the offspring, the unknown parent can be assumed to be homozygous for the dominant condition (*RR*).

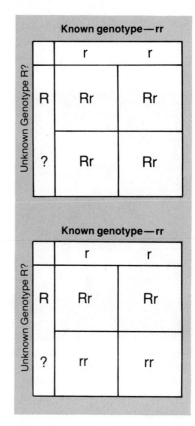

9-5. *The test cross is used to determine the genotype of an individual. Why does the presence of a recessive phenotype among the offspring prove that the parent was not pure bred?*

Probability and the Test Cross

It is important to realize that in using the test cross, we are concerned with an element of probability. Many offspring are required for a proper test. If only a few offspring occur, nothing may have been proven. For example, what if only two or three offspring were to be produced and these had the dominant phenotype? Chance might have caused a dominant allele from the unknown parent to be passed to the offspring each time. The more offspring that occur with the dominant phenotype, the surer we can be that the genotype of the unknown parent is homozygous.

It would take but a single offspring, however, to prove the heterozygous nature of the unknown parent. The genotype remains constant except for the rare genetic changes known as mutations. One individual with the recessive phenotype would be conclusive. It is difficult and impractical to use the test cross in organisms that produce few offspring. Test crosses are usually confined to plants and animals that reproduce quickly with large numbers of offspring.

Emphasize (a) why several offspring might be required to prove a parent to be heterozygous and (b) why a single dominant-appearing offspring would be sufficient.

Principle of Segregation

Remember that Mendel reasoned that each plant must carry two factors for each trait. Even so, he had also pointed out that these factors must somehow become separated during reproduction. This separation meant that the sex cells, male and female gametes, must contain only one allele for each trait. Thus, a particular gamete from a heterozygous individual (*Rr*) would contain either an *R* or an *r*. It could not contain both alleles. *The separation of factors during the formation of gametes constitutes Mendel's* **Principle of Segregation.** It is his third principle of inheritance.

The explanation for how this segregation occurs was not made until early in the 20th Century. The existence of chromosomes in the nuclei of cells had been known for a long time. In spite of this, their relationship to heredity was not suspected until 1902. Then, Walter Sutton, a graduate student at Columbia University, made an important contribution. He had observed the special activity of chromosomes during cell division (mitosis). He reasoned that this might account for the distribution of hereditary information to the daughter cells.

Sutton had also observed a special type of cell division during the production of sex cells. These divisions resulted in cells that had only one-half the number of chromosomes as the parent cell. Even in 1902, these observations were not new. However, Sutton's interpretation was new. He saw that this would provide an explanation for the segregation of alleles predicted by Mendel. Only one allele for each pair of alleles might be included in the gametes of each parent. In this way, the offspring would receive one allele for each gene from each parent.

9-6. *Walter S. Sutton pointed out that parents must pass genetic factors to their offspring by means of the gametes.*

Answers to Questions for Section 2.

D. 1. Gene: inheritance factors. Alleles: two alternative forms of a gene for a Mendelian trait. Alleles for a Mendelian trait would be the dominant and recessive forms. The gene for seed color has two alleles. One allele produces yellow, the other green.

2. Phenotype: the appearance of the organism with respect to a given trait. Genotype: a particular combination of alleles for a trait.

*3. If black is dominant over white, the result of a cross between two hybrid (Bb) black guinea pigs would show the following results:

	B	b
B	BB	Bb
b	Bb	bb

F₁ genotype: 2 homozygous black: 1 heterozygous black: 1 homozygous white. Phenotype: 3 black: 1 white

QUESTIONS FOR SECTION 2

1. Define and distinguish between gene and allele.
2. Define and distinguish between the genotype and phenotype of a trait.
3. Using black and white guinea pigs, distinguish between the terms homozygous and heterozygous in terms of the genotype and phenotype.
4. State the Chromosome Theory of Inheritance.
5. Explain how this theory is related to Mendel's principles.
6. Define test cross.
7. Describe how you would determine the genotype of a dominant-appearing individual.
8. State Mendel's Principle of Segregation.
9. Does this principle help to explain the fact that each parent passes only one allele for each gene to its offspring?

(See page 167 for more answers.)

3 EXPANSION OF MENDEL'S EXPERIMENTS

Meiosis

The cellular process that reduces the chromosome number of a cell by one-half is known as **meiosis** (mī ō sis). It occurs only in the production of the sex cells or gametes. The meiotic process takes place in a series of two cell divisions. The first division reduces the chromosome number. The second division is similar to *somatic* cell division or mitosis. **Somatic cells** *are all the cells of the body except the reproductive cells.* Great improvements in the construction and use of microscopes have aided scientists in understanding the meiotic process. Figure 9-7 illustrates the essential steps of meiosis. Follow it as you read the description.

FIRST DIVISION   Let us use a cell with four chromosomes to illustrate the meiotic process (a). These chromosomes constitute two *homologous* (hə *mol* ə gəs) pairs, one of each pair from the father and one from the mother (b). The homologous chromosomes pair with each other, shorten and thicken. Before the chromosomes become visible as distinct units, each becomes replicated. *Each pair of homologous chromosomes thus contains four strands and is called a* **tetrad** (c).

The replicated strands remain attached to each other at the *centromere*. Furthermore, chromatids within each tetrad may become entangled with each other. When this occurs, there may be an exchange of corresponding portions of chromatids (d). *This exchange of chromosome parts in order to assort genes into new combinations is called* **crossing over.** As you can see, crossing-over greatly increases variety within the genetic pool.

A spindle then forms as in mitosis and the four chromosomes become attached to the spindle near the equator of the cell (e). As meiosis continues, the paired chromosomes separate (f). Two nuclei form at each end of the initial cell. Then the cytoplasm divides (g). At this point, there are two cells. Each cell has two, non-paired, double-stranded chromosomes.

SECOND DIVISION   The second division then occurs (h, i). This division is similar to mitosis in that the strands become separated from each other (j). Each daughter cell formed from this division contains two chromosomes (k). The chromosome number of the new cells is said to be *haploid*. *A* **haploid cell** *contains one chromosome from each pair and therefore one-half the total number of the original cell.* These haploid cells then mature into male and female gametes. See differences between mitosis and meiosis in Figure 9-8.

OBJECTIVES FOR SECTION 3

H. Define the following terms: *haploid, diploid, gametes, somatic, chromatid, centromere, tetrad, fertilization.*

I. Describe the process of *meiosis* and be able to explain its application to Mendel's Laws.

J. Distinguish between somatic cells and gametes with respect to chromosome number.

Answers to Questions for Section 2.

E. 4. Chromosomes are responsible for the inherited characteristics of organisms, acting through their genes.

5. Mendel's "inheritance factors" are now called genes. These genes exist in either one of only two alternate forms, alleles. One gene for a trait, dominant, can mask or overpower the recessive form.

F. 6. Test crosses involve the mating of an unknown genotype with a homozygous recessive phenotype.

*7. The dominant characteristic could either be homozygous or heterozygous. To determine the genotype, cross the dominant form with the recessive form. Examine the offspring of the cross. If the F_1 show only the dominant form, then the dominant-appearing individual is homozygous. If the F_1 show both dominant and recessive forms of the trait, the unknown parent is heterozygous.

G. 8. Principle of Segregation: The separation of factors during the formation of gametes.

9. Yes, the sex cells then contain only one allele for each trait. A particular gamete from a heterozygous individual (Tt) would contain either a T or a t—not both.

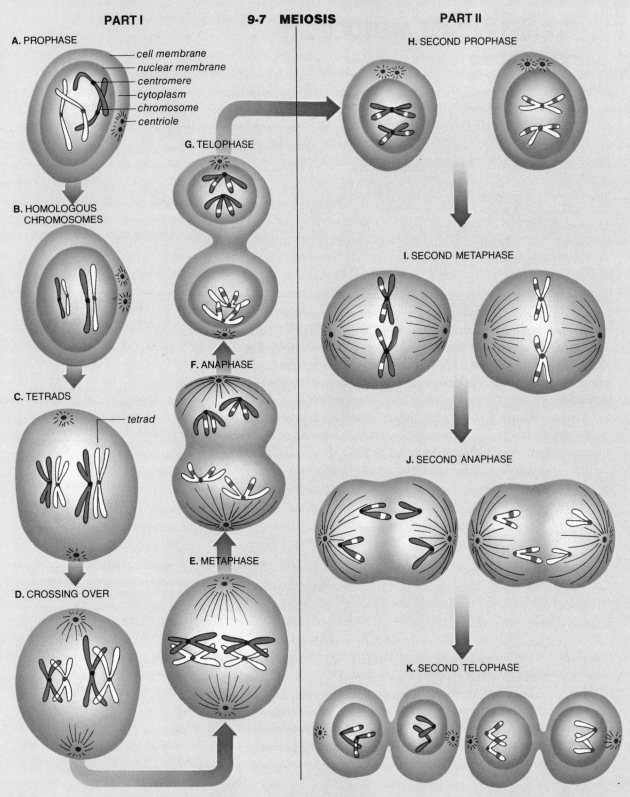

9-7 MEIOSIS

PART I

A. PROPHASE

cell membrane
nuclear membrane
centromere
cytoplasm
chromosome
centriole

B. HOMOLOGOUS CHROMOSOMES

C. TETRADS

tetrad

D. CROSSING OVER

E. METAPHASE

F. ANAPHASE

G. TELOPHASE

PART II

H. SECOND PROPHASE

I. SECOND METAPHASE

J. SECOND ANAPHASE

K. SECOND TELOPHASE

9-8 COMPARISON OF MITOSIS AND MEIOSIS

MITOSIS

INTERPHASE
Each cell has four chromosomes.

PROPHASE
Each chromosome has two parts called chromatids.

METAPHASE
Chromosomes begin to line up in the center of the cell. Spindle fibers attach to chromosomes.

ANAPHASE AND TELOPHASE
As chromosomes are pulled apart, the chromatids separate to opposite sides of the cell.

CELL DIVISION
Cell division produces two cells, each with four chromosomes.

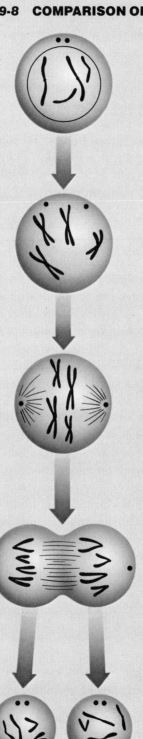

MEIOSIS

INTERPHASE
Each cell has four chromosomes.

PROPHASE
Each chromosome has two parts called chromatids. Similar chromosomes come together to form a tetrad.

FIRST METAPHASE
Tetrads line up in the center of the cell. Spindle fibers attach to chromosomes.

FIRST ANAPHASE AND TELOPHASE
Chromosomes are pulled apart to opposite sides of the cells. Chromosomes are still composed of two chromatids.

CELL DIVISION
Cell division produces two cells. Each cell has only one set of chromosomes.

SECOND METAPHASE AND TELOPHASE
Chromosomes line up in the center of the cell. Spindle fibers attach to chromosomes.

CELL DIVISION
These cells are either sperm or eggs. Cell division produces four cells. Each contains two chromosomes.

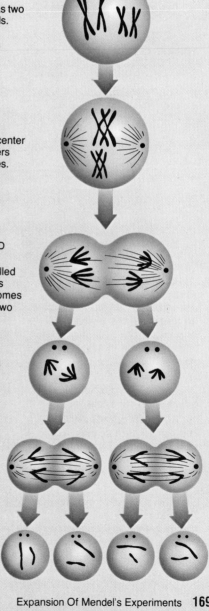

Expansion Of Mendel's Experiments **169**

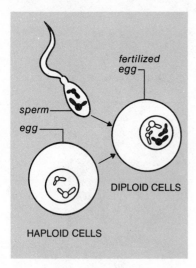

sperm

egg

fertilized egg

DIPLOID CELLS

HAPLOID CELLS

9-9. *Fertilization produces diploid cells.*

We should point out here that the process of gamete formation in the female varies from that of the male. The formation of male gametes occurs as described. Four gametes develop from each original parent cell. Male gametes are called sperm.

In the female, however, only one gamete is produced from each parent cell. The cytoplasm of each of the two cell divisions is unequal. One of the resulting cells is considerably larger than the other. The smaller cell possesses the same number of chromosomes as the larger one, but it does not undergo maturation to become a gamete. The three smaller cells that are produced are called polar bodies. The female gamete is called an ovum or egg, and is usually considerably larger than those produced by the male.

Fertilization

The process of sexual reproduction is completed with *fertilization* (See Fig. 9-9.) **Fertilization** *is the process of two gametes of the opposite sex uniting.* It restores the original chromosome number. *Since the number of chromosomes is now twice that contained in the gametes, it is referred to as the* **diploid number.** These two processes, meiosis and fertilization, constitute the two essential features of sexual reproduction. The fertilized egg now carries hereditary information from both male and female parents on homologous chromosomes.

Each species possesses a specific number of chromosomes that is characteristic for that species. This is the diploid number in most organisms. The diploid number of chromosomes is made up of a specific number of pairs of chromosomes. Each pair of these chromosomes is made up of two homolgous chromosomes. The number of pairs is the haploid number. For convenience, we often refer to the haploid number as the N chromosome number. Thus, the diploid number would be $2N$. During meiosis, the chromosome number of certain cells is reduced from $2N$ to N. Fertilization then restores the $2N$ number. The diploid, or $2N$, number for humans is 46. Human male and female gametes, therefore, would contain 23 chromosomes.

QUESTIONS FOR SECTION 3

1. Define haploid and diploid.
2. What is meiosis?
3. What is the function of meiosis?
4. Describe how meiosis contributes to an understanding of Mendel's Principle of Segregation.
5. What is the chromosome number of gametes with respect to these terms?
6. What two basic processes are the essential elements of sexual reproduction?

4 INDEPENDENT ASSORTMENT

The Dihybrid Cross

The foregoing account of Mendel's contributions would be significant by itself. But Mendel carried his experiments even further. He was satisfied that all seven traits were inherited according to the dominant-recessive pattern. Furthermore, all seemed to follow his hypothesis of segregation as well. But he wondered if there could be any pattern to the manner in which traits were inherited together. This is where a stroke of good fortune fell his way.

F₁ GENERATION   Mendel developed populations of his peas that bred pure for the dominant and recessive alleles of two traits in the same plant. Then he crossed plants that differed with regard to two pairs of alleles. For example, one might cross populations of yellow, round-seeded plants with green, wrinkle-seeded plants. This is called a **dihybrid cross** *because the cross involves two different traits.* From his earlier results, Mendel was not surprised to see that the offspring all exhibited the dominant characteristics for both traits. In our example, the F₁ generation would all be plants producing yellow, round seeds.

F₂ GENERATION   Breeding members of the F₁ among themselves introduced new variety. Four different phenotypes appeared. This variety might have appeared to be somewhat random at first, but the ratios again revealed a pattern. The four possible phenotypes appeared in a specific ratio of 9:3:3:1. That is, for each 16 offspring, on the average, nine were dominant for both traits. Three were dominant for one and recessive for the other. Three others were recessive for the first trait and dominant for the second. Only 1/16 of the offspring appeared recessive for both traits. Furthermore, only the ones that appeared recessive for both traits seemed to breed pure.

Analysis of the Dihybrid Cross

Again using seed shape and color to illustrate, we can summarize these results. Yellow, round-seeded plants were bred with green, wrinkle-seeded plants. The members of the F₁ generation would have yellow, round seeds. They exhibited the dominant characteristics. The F₂ generation would appear as follows:

9/16 with yellow, round seeds
3/16 with yellow, wrinkled seeds
3/16 with green, round seeds
1/16 with green, wrinkled seeds

Using the alphabet code for the genotypes, these results can be explained. The original parents would be represented as *YYRR* and *yyrr*. Gametes from these parents would have to contain one allele for

OBJECTIVES FOR SECTION 4

K. Define *independent assortment* and *dihybrid*.
L. Explain the results of a *dihybrid cross* including genotypes and phenotypes of the F₁ and F₂ generations.

Have students construct diagrams that will show the results of a dihybrid cross for other traits.

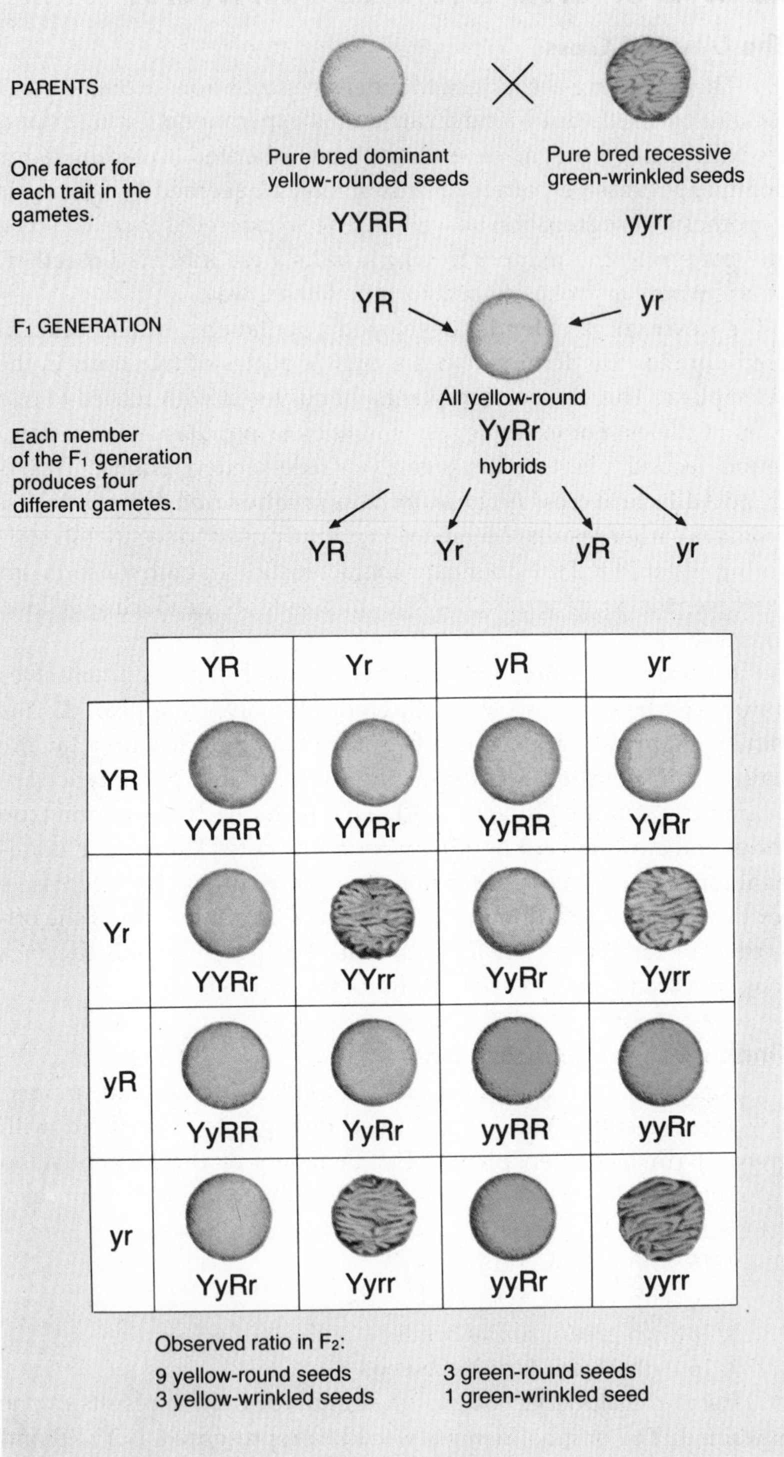
PARENTS
Pure bred dominant yellow-rounded seeds
YYRR
Pure bred recessive green-wrinkled seeds
yyrr
One factor for each trait in the gametes.
F₁ GENERATION
YR
yr
All yellow-round
YyRr
hybrids
Each member of the F₁ generation produces four different gametes.
YR
Yr
yR
yr
YR Yr yR yr
YR: YYRR YYRr YyRR YyRr
Yr: YYRr YYrr YyRr Yyrr
yR: YyRR YyRr yyRR yyRr
yr: YyRr Yyrr yyRr yyrr
Observed ratio in F₂:
9 yellow-round seeds
3 yellow-wrinkled seeds
3 green-round seeds
1 green-wrinkled seed

9-10. One of the experiments from which Mendel derived his principle of independent assortment is shown here. A plant homozygous for yellow-round (YYRR) peas is crossed with a plant having green-wrinkled (yyrr) peas. The F_1 generation are all yellow-round. In the F_2 generation the following results are seen: 9 show two dominant traits (YR), 3 each show one combination of the dominant and recessive trait (Yr and yR), and 1 shows the two recessive traits (yr). Hence, the final ratio of this dihybrid cross is 9:3:3:1.

each trait. Thus, we can represent them as *YR* and *yr*, respectively. Fertilization of these two gametes would produce the F₁ generation and a genotype of *YyRr* in the offspring.

Gamete formation in members of the F₁ would produce a variety of possibilities. In any event, one must remember that one allele for each trait must be present in each gamete. Thus, four different combinations are possible: *YR, Yr, yR,* and *yr*. Each gamete contains a factor for seed shape and one for seed color. They never have two factors for the same characteristics. Both the male and female produce similar gametes. In this case, any male gamete could unite with any female gamete. The diploid chromosome number would be restored, and each offspring would possess two alleles for each trait. Figure 9-10 shows a simple and convenient method for illustrating the make-up of the F₁ and F₂ generations.

Principle of Independent Assortment

The fact that all combinations of the possible phenotypes occur means that the genes for each trait are on separate chromosomes. The factor for seed shape and the one for seed color are not on the same chromosome. Thus, when meiosis takes place, two traits will separate or assort independently of each other. It is just as if each trait was being considered separately. In our example, the ratio of yellow to green plants in the F₂ generation is still 3:1. There is also a 3:1 ratio between the round-seeded and wrinkle-seeded plants.

Mendel saw that the two traits were always independent of each other, and this became the basis of the fourth principle of inheritance. **The Principle of Independent Assortment** *states that pairs of factors separate independently during gamete formation.* As long as different gene pairs assort independently of each other their behavior can be explained by their presence on separate chromosomes. Therefore, given the genotypes of the parents, all possible combinations of alleles occur in the gametes.

We now know that not all traits assort independently. Fortunately, Mendel selected seven traits that did. This enabled him to avoid the confusing results that would have otherwise occurred. This, in turn, enabled him to see the basic principles of heredity in operation. Armed with these principles, we can interpret the more complex processes that also take place.

QUESTIONS FOR SECTION 4

1. Define dihybrid.
2. Define independent assortment.
3. What is a dihybrid cross?

Answers to Questions for Section 4.

K. **1.** Dihybrid: the study of two traits at the same time.

2. Independent Assortment: pairs of factors separate independently during gamete formation.

L. **3.** Dihybrid Cross: a cross that involves two different traits.

CHAPTER REVIEW

The science of inheritance is genetics. Gregor Mendel is credited with being the first to demonstrate the principles of genetics. From his work with the common garden pea, Mendel demonstrated four basic principles of inheritance:

1. The Principle of Unit Characters—each individual carries two factors for each inheritable trait.
2. The Principle of Dominance — one of the two factors for a trait can dominate the other.
3. The Principle of Segregation—the two factors carried by an individual for an inherited trait must separate during gamete formation.
4. The Principle of Independent Assortment — the pair of factors for an inherited trait separate independently of other pairs of factors during gamete formation.

Although later research demonstrated exceptions to some of the principles, it also provided the explanations. These concepts remain today as the cornerstone of modern genetics.

Today, we recognize Mendel's "factors" as genes. Genes may exist in dominant and recessive forms which we call alleles. The genotype of the individual is a description of the particular combination of alleles for a trait. The individual may be homozygous if both alleles are the same. If the alleles are different, the individual is said to be heterozygous.

The phenotype of an individual is dependent upon the genotype. The presence of at least one dominant allele produces the dominant phenotype. Recessive phenotypes are possible only with two recessive alleles.

The process of meiosis is responsible for the separation of alleles during gamete formation. Meiosis reduces the chromosome number by one-half in the male and female gametes. These haploid cells contain a variety of genetic information. This is due to crossing over of the chromosomes. The full chromosome number is restored when the female gamete is fertilized. These two processes occur in sexual reproduction.

The orderly transfer of hereditary information from one generation to the next insures a continuity of life. Dogs will continue to produce dogs, and elm trees will produce elm trees. *It is the continuous shuffling and recombination of genes and their alleles which allows great variety in individuals.*

Genetic Problems

1. Assume that brown eyes are dominant to blue.
   (a) What genotype possibilities exist for a brown-eyed person?
   (b) How might you find out if you are correct in part (a) above?
   (c) What phenotypes are possible for the parents of the brown-eyed person?
2. Diagram in an appropriate manner the results of the following crosses involving Mendelian traits:
   (a) homozygous tall pea plants and homozygous short pea plants (tall being dominant).
   (b) heterozygous tall pea plants with homozygous short pea plants.
   (c) heterozygous tall pea plants with each other.
   (d) AABB x aabb (show F_1 and F_2 generations).
   (e) AAbb x aaBB (show F_1 and F_2 generations).

Using the Concepts

3. Why is a knowledge of genetics important to agriculture and horticulture?

VOCABULARY REVIEW

inheritance
genetics
Mendelian trait
reciprocal cross
hybrid
dominant
monohybrid
homozygous

heterozygous
gene
allele
genotype
phenotype
test cross
segregation
gamete

meiosis
haploid
diploid
somatic
homologous
tetrad
fertilization
dihybrid

CHAPTER 9 TEST

Copy the number of each test item and place your answer to the right. (Do not write in this book)

PART 1 Multiple Choice: Select the letter of the phrase that best completes each of the following.

b **1.** If an animal's diploid chromosome number is 16, the chromosome number in each gamete would be **a.** 4 **b.** 8 **c.** 16 **d.** 32.

a **2.** Crossing a normally-pigmented squirrel with an albino squirrel (NN x nn) would yield offspring in the F_1 generation that are **a.** all normally-pigmented **b.** all albino **c.** ½ normally-pigmented and ½ albino **d.** ¾ normally-pigmented and ¼ albino.

c **3.** Which statement describes the Chromosome Theory of Heredity? **a.** Genes are composed of chromosomes **b.** Chromosomes are composed of complex organic chemicals, DNA and protein **c.** Genes located on chromosomes determine hereditary traits **d.** Every organism must possess a pair of chromosomes.

d **4.** The two essential events in sex reproduction involve **a.** mitosis and fertilization **b.** mitosis and meiosis **c.** meiosis and ovulation **d.** meiosis and fertilization.

d **5.** The phenotype ratio found in the F_2 generation of a standard dihybrid cross would be **a.** 1:1 **b.** 3:1 **c.** 1:2:1 **d.** 9:3:3:1.

c **6.** When Mendel crossed peas with round seeds and peas with wrinkled seeds, all the offspring had round seeds. When plants grown from these seeds were crossed, 5474 plants produced round seeds and 1850 produced wrinkled seeds. Which ratio shows this result? **a.** 1:1 **b.** 2:1 **c.** 3:1 **d.** 3:2.

c **7.** If an organism has a genotype of Dd, which alleles do its gametes have? **a.** all have D **b.** all have d **c.** ½ have D and ½ have d **d.** three have D for each one that has d.

b **8.** An organism with a genotype of AaBb can produce which one of the following combinations of alleles in the gametes? **a.** A, a, B, b **b.** AB, Ab, aB, ab **c.** AA, aa, BB, bb **d.** AA, AB, Aa, Ab, BB, bb, ab, aB.

a **9.** The ratio of the offspring (9:3:3:1) is an expression of **a.** phenotype only **b.** genotype only **c.** both phenotype and genotype **d.** a mating between homozygotes.

a **10.** Sutton explained Mendel's Principle of Segregation as the two members of a pair of alleles **a.** are distributed to separate gametes **b.** may contaminate one another **c.** are assorted dependently **d.** are codominant.

PART 2 Matching: Match the description in Column II with the term it describes in Column I.

COLUMN I

  a. allele   **f.** homozygous
  b. recessive   **g.** hybrid
  c. gamete   **h.** meiosis
  d. heterozygous   **i.** Mendel
  e. homologous   **j.** test cross

COLUMN II

c **11.** Sex cell, male or female

h **12.** Nuclear division of a cell which provides new cells with ½ the number of chromosomes

e **13.** Chromosomes constituting a pair

d **14.** Cell or organism in which the two alleles for a trait are different

a **15.** Alternative form for a gene

i **16.** Father of modern genetics

f **17.** Cell or organism in which the two alleles for a trait are identical

g **18.** Offspring of mating individuals that differ in one or more traits

b **19.** Allele that is masked in the presence of one that is expressed

j **20.** Mating of homozygous recessive individual with one of unknown genotype to determine the unknown genetic make-up

PART 3 Completion: Complete the following.

21. The outward appearance of an organism with respect to a given trait is its ____ phenotype

22. The genotype ratio found in the F_2 generation of a monohybrid cross is ____. 1:2:1

23. The appearance of four phenotypes in the F_2 generation of a dihybrid cross can be explained by Mendel's Principle of ____ Independent Assortment

24. The gametes from a RrYy parent could be represented as ____. RY, Ry, rY, ry

25. To prove that an unknown genotype in a test cross is heterozygous an offspring must be ____ recessive

CHAPTER 10

GENES AND CHROMOSOMES

Mendel's principles answered a number of long-standing questions on the nature of heredity. Answering one set of questions often raises a variety of others. A close look at many organisms reveals that inheritance is often not as simple as Mendel's principles might seem to suggest. To be sure, garden peas are either tall or short. Their seeds are either green or yellow. Most plants, as well as animals, do not conform to such simple limitations. Instead, there seems to be a great diversity among every kind of plant or animal. By making careful observations and measurements, you discover that there is a great variety among living things.

The concept of unity and diversity among living things is one of the most basic concepts in biology. In the study of heredity, it can be viewed on at least two levels. First, there is considerable variety among all members of one kind of organism. For example, humans come in all sizes, shapes, and colors. Nevertheless, they represent only a single kind of organism.

At the second level, there are different kinds of living things. This represents diversity on a grand scale. Yet, the basic activities of life lend a unity that cannot be denied.

Two other basic concepts of biology are woven into the study of heredity. One of these is *change through time*. Many forces are at work to alter the appearance and activities of living things. Some of these forces produce changes that affect future generations. The other concept is that there is a fundamental *continuity of life*. Despite the fact that offspring are not exactly like their parents, they are very similar.

Most of the application of Mendel's principles has come from genetic research during the last 50 to 75 years. This chapter will provide knowledge to answer these questions:

- How can there be such variety in eye color and blood type?
- Why do some traits such as blonde hair and blue eyes often seem to occur together?
- Why do males often seem to have certain traits or characteristics such as color blindness while females rarely do?

MODEL OF DNA MOLECULE

1 DIVERSITY WITHIN THE EXISTING GENE POOL

Genetic Recombination

The simple shuffling of alleles in sexual reproduction can, by itself, produce a tremendous variety in organisms. For a single Mendelian trait with two alleles, for example, there are two phenotypes and three genotypes. Seeds may be either yellow or green. Yellow seeds may have the genotype YY or Yy and green seeds are homozygous recessive, yy. For two traits, there would be four phenotypes and nine genotypes, as in a dihybrid cross. The number of phenotypes possible for a given number of genes with two alleles can easily be calculated. The calculation is based upon the fact that there are two phenotypes possible with a single gene. Simply raise this value of two phenotypes to the power of the number of genes being considered. Hence, for three genes there are eight phenotypes ($2^3 = 8$). Table 10-1 shows a sample of such calculations.

TABLE 10-1.

A summary of the possible phenotypes and genotypes for independently-assorting genes, each with only two alleles.

No. of Genes	Possible Alleles	Possible Phenotypes	Possible Genotypes
1	2	2^1 (2)	3^1 (3)
2	4	2^2 (4)	3^2 (9)
3	6	2^3 (8)	3^3 (27)

The number of genotypes possible can also be determined for a series of Mendelian traits. First, there are three genotypes for a single trait, for example, YY, Yy, and yy. Second, this value of genotypes is raised to the power of the number of genes being considered, that is, 3. Third, the resulting number is the number of genotypes possible for these genes. There would be 27 genotype possibilities for three genes with three alleles ($3^3 = 27$).

Many genes exist on the same chromosome, of course. As a result, not all genes can assort independently. We can see that a great variety of combinations can be achieved simply by shuffling the alleles existing within a population. For example, the variety in the sizes, shapes, and colors of dogs is very great. This variety is a result of a number of different alleles for each existing gene being expressed in different combinations with other alleles. This shuffling occurs directly as a result of sexual reproduction.

OBJECTIVES FOR SECTION 1

A. Define the following terms: *gene pool, incomplete dominance, codominance, polygenic inheritance.*

B. Determine how genetic variety can be produced within the limits of the existing gene pool.

C. Calculate the number of phenotypes and genotypes possible for any number of independently-assorting genes with two alleles.

D. Explain how multiple alleles for a gene contribute to increased variability. Use the ABO blood type in humans as an example.

Answers to Questions for Section 1.

A. 1. See glossary.
2. Incomplete dominance: two alleles are both expressed in a heterozygote by being blended. Example: pink four o'clocks. Codominance: expression of two alleles in one individual at the same time. Example: human blood type, AB.

B. 3. Incomplete dominance: pink color in four o'clocks. Codominance: roan color in cattle. Multiple alleles: hair color in humans. Polygenic inheritance: height in humans.

*C. *4. For 5 genes, there are 10 possible alleles, 2^5 or 32 possible phenotypes, and 3^5 or 243 possible genotypes.

D. 5.
Phenotype	Genotype
Blood Type A	$I^A I^A$ or $I^A i$
Blood Type B	$I^B I^B$ or $I^B i$
Blood Type AB	$I^A I^B$
Blood Type O	ii

*6. Because two alleles, I^A and I^B, are codominant, and therefore expressed in phenotype.

*7. The father cannot be type AB, because the child would have received either I^A or I^B, both of which are dominant over i, and would be expressed in the phenotype.

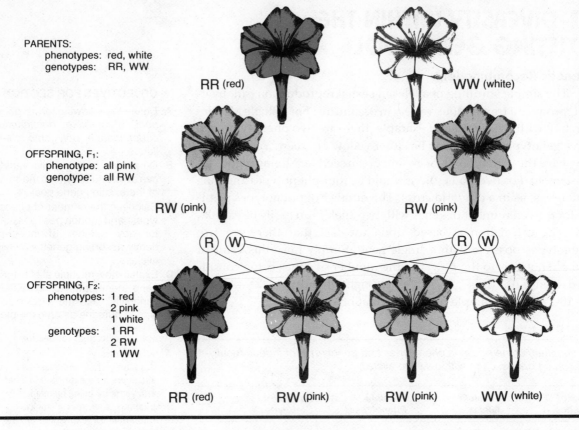

PARENTS:
    phenotypes: red, white
    genotypes: RR, WW

RR (red)   WW (white)

OFFSPRING, F₁:
    phenotype: all pink
    genotype: all RW

RW (pink)   RW (pink)

Ⓡ Ⓦ   Ⓡ Ⓦ

OFFSPRING, F₂:
    phenotypes: 1 red
                2 pink
                1 white
    genotypes: 1 RR
                2 RW
                1 WW

RR (red)   RW (pink)   RW (pink)   WW (white)

10-1. Incomplete dominance in four-o'clocks results in a blending of traits in the heterozygous offspring.

Answers to Questions for Section 1
 *8. Let Xx, Yy, and Zz represent three genes, each with two alleles. Then the following diagram would represent all the possible genotypes for the trait.

Eggs → Sperm ↓	XYZ	XYz	Xyz	xYZ	xyZ	xyz
XYZ						
XYz						
Xyz						
xYZ						
xyZ						
xyz						

THE GENE POOL   Not all individuals possess every allele that the population as a whole possesses. For example, some yellow-seeded pea plants may be homozygous dominant *(YY).* They do not possess a recessive allele *(y)* for that trait. Others in the same population may have green seeds and be homozygous recessive *(yy).* They do not have a dominant allele *(Y).* ***The sum of all the genes with their respective alleles possessed by a population at a given time is known as the gene pool.*** If mating is random within the population, that is, if its occurrence between two individuals is a chance event, then continued shuffling of allelic combinations occurs.

Incomplete Dominance

Mendel's discoveries resulted from several rather fortunate events. One of these was his choice of the garden pea as a test organism. Another researcher, working with four-o'clocks, would have had a quite different experience. Crossing homozygous dominant red and recessive white four-o'clocks does not result in dominant appearing offspring. (See Fig. 10-1.) The F₁ generation produces all pink flowers! There seems to be a blending of parent phenotypes.

Crossing members of the F₁ generation enables us to understand better the nature of the blending. The F₂ offspring produce red, pink, and white flowers. These occur in a 1:2:1 ratio, respectively. Red and white alleles together produce pink flowers. Therefore, the red and white flowers must come from plants that are homozygous for flower color. That is, they have only one kind of allele in their make-up — both red or both white. In such cases, there are no alleles that can be referred to as being dominant or recessive. Thus, with four offspring, we would indicate their respective genotypic ratio as follows: 1*RR*:2*RW*:1*WW* (1 red flower:2 pink flowers:1 white flower). The letters *R* and *W* are used here instead of *R* and *r* because the white trait is not recessive to the red trait. In fact, the red trait is incompletely dominant over the white, and the two are blended. These results indicate that only the expressions of the red and white alleles were blended. The alleles themselves were not. *This condition, in which two alleles are both expressed in a heterozygote by being blended is called* **incomplete dominance.**

Codominance

Matings between red and white shorthorn cattle produce offspring of a roan color. Roan coloration appears because there are both red and white hairs making up the coat of the offspring. (See Fig. 10-2.) The hairs themselves are not roan colored. **Codominance** *is the expression of two alleles at the same time in one individual without being blended.*

BLOOD TYPES   Another example of two alleles being expressed at the same time is that of blood type in humans. The means by which blood type is inherited was first discovered in the early 1900's. In this system, there are three different alleles of a single gene. Two of the three alleles show codominance. The third allele is recessive to the other two. The gene is identified by the letter *I.* Its alleles are usually designated as *I^A*, *I^B*, and *i,* respectively. Table 10-2 summarizes the possible allelic combinations for the production of the blood types *A, B, AB,* and *O.* Note that if the two dominant alleles occur together in an offspring, the blood type will be *AB.* Heterozygous individuals carrying the recessive allele, *i,* will be of a type indicated by the particular dominant allele present. Type *O* individuals must be homozygous for the recessive allele, *ii.*

Multiple Alleles

The mechanism of blood type inheritance in humans also illustrates the concept of multiple alleles. We have assumed thus far that genes take only two forms. They may exist as either dominant or

10-2.   *When neither allele dominates the other, both traits may be expressed. The two alleles are then said to be codominant. The offspring possess both red and white hairs. The hair color is not a result of blending.*

TABLE 10-2.

Three alleles, I^A, I^B, and i, are responsible for the phenotype of blood. Note that I^A and I^B are codominant. But ii is recessive. Thus, four phenotypes are possible.

Blood type	Genotype
A	I^AI^A, I^Ai
B	I^BI^B, I^Bi
AB	I^AI^B
O	ii

recessive alleles. It is not at all uncommon to find that many genes exist in three or more forms. That is, there may be three or more alleles for a given gene. The I^A, I^B, and i alleles that govern the inheritance of blood type is a good example. Such conditions of multiple alleles provide for more diversity than can be achieved with only two alleles.

There are a number of other traits occurring in humans that are also a result of multiple alleles. Hair color and blood type are only two of these. The gene pool normally possesses several alleles for each of these genes. As males and females marry and produce offspring, a kind of genetic roulette occurs. How a trait will be expressed depends upon which two alleles the offspring receives for each trait from the gene pool.

Polygenic Inheritance

Within the framework of the existing gene pool, variety may be further enhanced through other types of inheritance. **Polygenic** (päl i *jen* ik) **inheritance** *is two or more genes, each with its respective alleles, jointly affecting the expression of a given phenotype.* Many familiar traits are the result of polygenic inheritance. (See Fig. 10-3.) Included among these are height, intelligence, skin color, and various sexual characteristics. The more genes that operate to produce a given trait, the greater will be the phenotype variety. Most human traits are probably the result of polygenic inheritance and/or multiple alleles. It is no wonder, then, that the chances for duplicate individuals are small. The success of many organisms in their respective environments is due largely to the polygenic character of the species.

QUESTIONS FOR SECTION 1
1. Define gene pool, genetic recombination.
2. Define and differentiate between the terms incomplete dominance and co-dominance, using appropriate examples.
3. List and give an example of each way that genetic variety can occur within the limits of the gene pool.
4. Calculate the number of phenotypes and genotypes possible for five independently-assorting genes with two alleles each.
5. List the genotypes possible for the three alleles of the ABO blood type system in humans. For each, give the appropriate phenotype.
6. Explain why the I^A I^B genotype is able to produce its own characteristic phenotype.
7. If a mother's blood type is "A" and her child's type is "O", what type(s) can the father NOT be? Explain.
8. Make a diagram that might illustrate the possible genotypes of a trait inherited by three genes, each with two alleles.

10-3. Skin tone is a result of polygenic inheritance.

(See page 177 and 178 for answers.)

CHAPTER INVESTIGATION

A. The bacterial plate below was inoculated with a test bacteria. A paper disk soaked with the antibiotic penicillin was placed on the agar. Describe the growth of bacteria on the plate.

B. Why are a few bacterial colonies able to grow within the ring surrounding the antibiotic disk?

C. How might the constant use of antibiotics backfire on human medical practices?

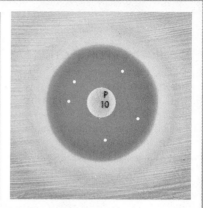

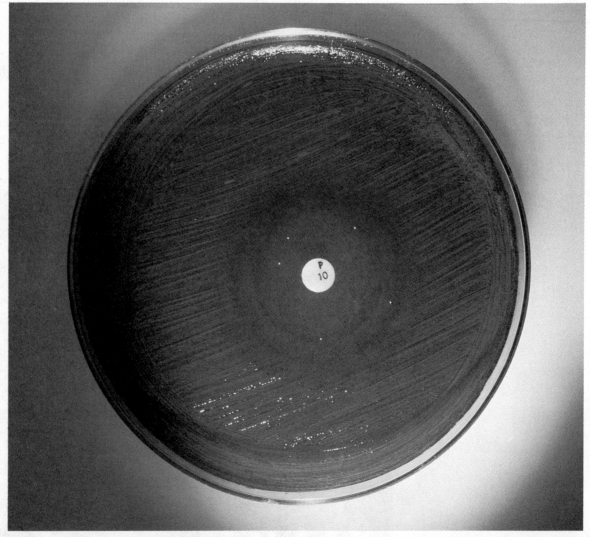

2 THE GENETIC MATERIAL

DNA Structure and Function

OBJECTIVES FOR SECTION 2

E. Define the following terms: *mutation, mutagen.*
F. Explain how DNA can dictate the structure of a protein.
G. Describe how a mutation might occur, including its cause.
H. List four usual characteristics of mutations.

In the process of mitosis and meiosis, chromosome replication is required. The end result of DNA duplication would be two identical DNA molecules where only one had been. The model for DNA duplication provides a means by which chromosome duplication can be visualized. (See Fig. 10-4.) How a cell translates genetic information into routine operations has already been discussed in Unit 2. A short summary is provided in this section to help you tie some concepts together.

One strand of DNA can dictate the sequence of nucleotides in the other strand. It also dictates the sequence in a strand of m-RNA. Thus produced, m-RNA moves out of the nucleus. In the cytoplasm of the cell, it becomes attached to ribosomes. Transfer-RNA (t-RNA) molecules in the cytoplasm are coded to pick up specific amino acids. Since pairing between nucleotides is very specific, a t-RNA can only attach to an m-RNA at a specific point. This, in turn, establishes a particular sequence in the amino acids in the formation of a specific polypeptide. Thus, we see that the DNA dictates the construction of specific molecules. These molecules are then used by cells for a variety of purposes.

10-4. DNA is an intricate, complex molecule.

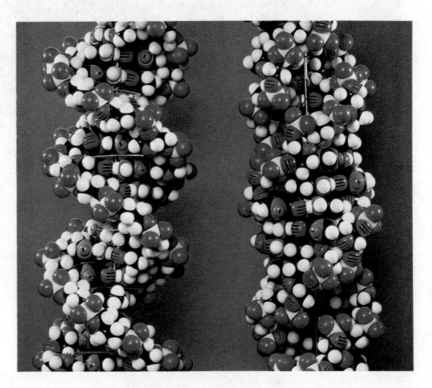

Mutations: Simple Gene Changes

We have seen that under ordinary circumstances, a DNA molecule would contain only A-T pairs and G-C pairs. Occasionally improper pairs may be allowed to form. This pairing will produce a **mutation,** *or change in the hereditary material that may result in a change in the phenotype of the offspring.* (See Fig. 10-5.) This change might occur at the moment of duplication when a given nucleotide in a sequence is altered slightly for some reason. In such an altered state, it might be caused to attract the wrong nucleotide to pair with it. Thus, when the other side of the ladder has been rebuilt, there is a minor alteration in the nucleotide sequence. The DNA molecule has not been duplicated exactly.

While the alteration may be minor, its consequences might not be. A mutation occurring in the gamete-producing tissue can be transmitted to the offspring. Many genetic disorders occur by a mutation in the genetic material. Examples are cystic fibrosis, Huntington's disease, albinism, and sickle-cell anemia.

What factor or factors might be responsible for mutations? Experiments have shown that certain kinds of radiation, including X-rays, cosmic rays, and radioactivity may cause mutation. Exposure to certain chemicals may possibly be responsible also. *Mutation causing factors are often called* **mutagens** (*myoot* ə jəns). Some genes

Emphasize that in order for a mutation to be inherited, it must occur in the genetic material of a gamete.

10-5. Irradiation of fruit flies with X rays can produce a wide variety of mutations that are hereditary.

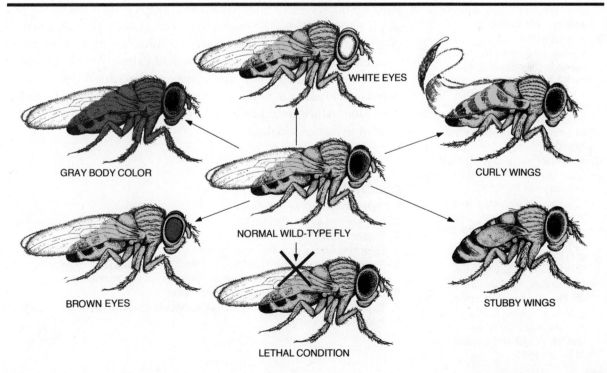

GRAY BODY COLOR

WHITE EYES

CURLY WINGS

BROWN EYES

NORMAL WILD-TYPE FLY

LETHAL CONDITION

STUBBY WINGS

Mutations tend to be rare, random, recessive, and deleterious. But they do occur, some are dominant, and some are advantageous to the organism in terms of its survival.

are apparently less stable than others. They may mutate without outside influence.

CHARACTERISTICS OF MUTATIONS Our knowledge of mutations suggests that they occur at random. Although we may be able to identify several mutagens, we cannot predict what mutations they cause. Many disorders of humans have been traced to a genetic origin. These are often caused by a single gene that has produced an abnormal allele by mutation. Researchers are presently trying to find ways to correct such genetic mistakes. One possibility might involve causing harmful alleles to "back-mutate" to the normal form. Only by getting rid of the harmful allele can a genetic disorder be truly cured.

In general, mutation rates for a given gene may vary from one in one thousand gametes to one in one million. In humans, the average seems to be that each gene will mutate once or twice in the production of 100,000 gametes. If a human has 50,000 genes per gamete, a fair estimate would be that one gamete in two will carry a mutant gene. A mutation, then, is a relatively rare event.

Another important characteristic of mutations is that they are usually recessive, such as sickle-cell anemia. Furthermore, most are harmful to the organism. A mutation such as PKU, occurring in an otherwise adapted human would work against the well-adapted status. The failure to metabolize a specific amino acid in this instance would only appear in the homozygous state. This mutation is dictated by the recessive mutated allele. It helps protect the bearer of a single harmful allele. The bearer would most likely possess a normal dominant allele. If the mutation were dominant, however, every individual possessing the new allele would exhibit the phenotype of the mutation. Such an event occurs in the dominant disorder polydactyly (päl i dak tə lē), in which the person has extra fingers or toes. Dominance would be an advantage, of course, if the mutation proved to be beneficial.

QUESTIONS FOR SECTION 2

1. Define mutation and mutagen.
2. List several kinds of mutagens.
3. Explain how DNA can dictate the structure of a protein.
4. Describe how a mutation might occur.
5. Explain how a change in the nucleotide sequence of a DNA molecule results in a change within the structure or operation of an organism.
6. List four usual characteristics of mutations.
7. Explain why the ability of the DNA molecule to duplicate itself is such an important property.

3 THE ROLE OF CHROMOSOMES

Sex-Determination: X and Y Chromosomes

We have implied that all of the traits an organism inherits are the result of particular genes and gene combinations. It has no doubt occurred to you to ask if the sex of an organism is also determined genetically. The answer is yes.

CELL KARYOTYPE   If a biologist was to make a preparation of human chromosomes on a microscope slide and then photograph them, one might observe something like the arrangement in Figure 10-6. It is evident that some of the chromosomes are larger than others. Other than that they would all look pretty much alike. The next step would be to cut out the individual chromosomes. Then arrange them by size on a piece of paper. This arrangement enables us to make a more critical analysis of the chromosomes present. Recent technology in staining techniques has made this task easier. It seems that certain stains reveal unique banding patterns in the chromosomes. This aids in the identification of homologous chromosome pairs. When completed, **the arranged preparation of chromosomes is called a**

OBJECTIVES FOR SECTION 3

I. Define the following terms: *karyotype, autosome, sex chromosome, sex-linked trait.*

J. Describe the karyotype of a normal male and female.

K. Explain how sex is determined in humans.

L. Describe the inheritance of a sex-linked trait such as hemophilia or color-blindness.

M. Explain why autosomal linkage should produce a 3:1 phenotype ratio in the F_2 generation.

10-6.   *Preparation of a karyotype.*

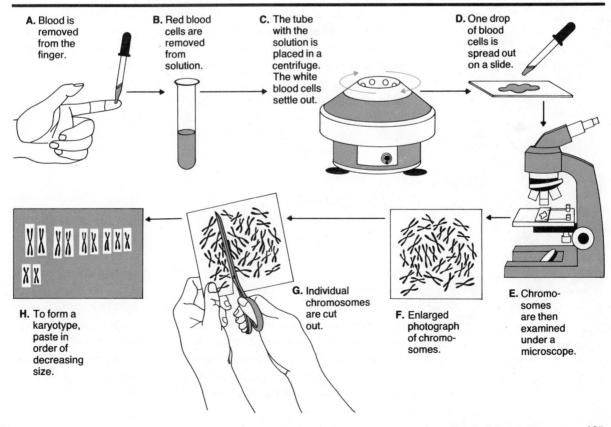

A. Blood is removed from the finger.

B. Red blood cells are removed from solution.

C. The tube with the solution is placed in a centrifuge. The white blood cells settle out.

D. One drop of blood cells is spread out on a slide.

E. Chromosomes are then examined under a microscope.

F. Enlarged photograph of chromosomes.

G. Individual chromosomes are cut out.

H. To form a karyotype, paste in order of decreasing size.

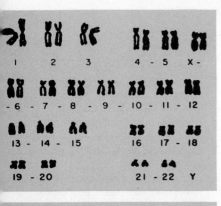

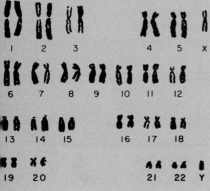

10-7. *Karyotypes of human chromosomes prepared from the process described in Figure 10-6.*

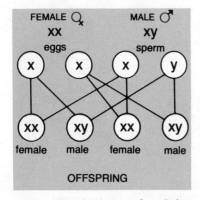

10-8. *The inheritance of sex in humans. The male parent determines the sex of the offspring. (Can you explain why?)*

karyotype (*kar* ē ə tīp). (See Fig. 10-7.) By examining karyotypes of both males and females, one striking observation emerges: in females there are 23 complete pairs while in males there are 22 pairs plus two non-paired chromosomes. In either case, the whole complement of 46 chromosomes occurs. Closer inspection reveals that the 22 pairs in the males are the same size and shape as 22 of the female pairs. Furthermore, the larger of the two unpaired chromosomes in the males is identical to both members of the 23rd pair of the female karyotype.

Biologists now recognize the **23rd "pair" of chromosomes as being the sex chromosomes.** *The other 22 pairs are referred to as* **autosomes.** The paired members of the female sex chromosomes are known as the *X* chromosomes. The larger of the two sex chromosomes in the male is also recognized as an *X* chromosome. The smaller member of the "pair" is known as the *Y* chromosome. Thus, the female karyotype would include two *X* chromosomes in the 23rd position *(XX).* The male would possess an *X* and a *Y* in the 23rd position *(XY).*

SEX DETERMINATION   During meiosis, each member of a given pair of chromosomes ends up in a different gamete. This is equally true for the sex chromosomes. Any gamete produced by a female would possess an *X* chromosome since both members of the 23rd pair are *X's.* But this would not be true in male gamete production. The separation of *X* and *Y* chromosomes results in one-half of the sperm containing an *X* chromosome. The other half would contain a *Y* chromosome. Upon fertilization, the sex of the offspring is determined by which kind of sperm fertilizes the egg. (See Fig. 10-8.) Fertilization by *an X-containing sperm would result in an XX* combination in the offspring. The result would be a female. Fertilization by *a Y-containing sperm* would result in an *XY* combination. A male would be produced by this combination.

Sex-Linked Traits

The *X* and *Y* chromosomes also carry genes for other specific traits. Since these traits are carried on the sex chromosome, certain ones have a tendency to be expressed by males. *Recessive characteristics that are carried on the X chromosome but usually expressed only in the male are called* **sex-linked traits.** For example, in humans, the traits for baldness, color-blindness, and hemophilia (hē mə *fil* ē ə), or bleeder's disease, are usually associated with males. Under certain conditions, sex-linked traits may appear in females as well.

HEMOPHILIA   One of the classic cases of the inheritance of a sex-linked trait occurred in the royal families of Europe during the 19th Century. It involved the recessive allele for hemophilia, carried on

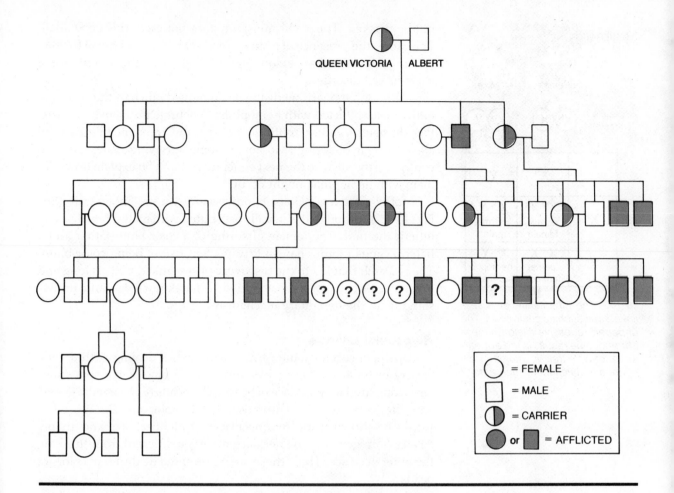

QUEEN VICTORIA | ALBERT

◐	= FEMALE
○	= FEMALE
□	= MALE
◑	= CARRIER
● or ■	= AFFLICTED

the X chromosome. **Hemophilia** *is a condition in which the blood is unable to clot following an injury*. At best, it clots only slowly. Until modern medical techniques were developed to cause blood to clot, most victims bled to death in infancy or early childhood. The trait appeared in a son and three grandsons of England's Queen Victoria. (See Fig. 10-9.) Hemophilia did not appear in her husband, Albert, nor in either of her parents. Since hemophilia is sex-linked, Queen Victoria must have been a "carrier" of the harmful recessive allele. Therefore, Queen Victoria appears to have inherited it from a mutation in her mother's genetic material.

If we assume that the allele for hemophilia is recessive and carried on the X chromosome, we can understand why a female would not be expected to express this disorder. It would be certain to be masked by the normal dominant allele on the other X chromosome. If the male receives an X containing this harmful allele, it will

10-9. *The inheritance of hemophilia by the descendants of Queen Victoria. How might this disorder have changed the course of history?*

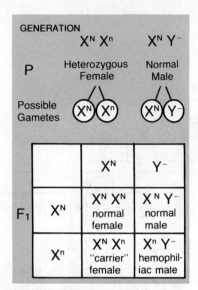

GENERATION		
P	$X^N X^n$ Heterozygous Female	$X^N Y^-$ Normal Male
Possible Gametes	X^N X^n	X^N Y^-

F_1		X^N	Y^-
	X^N	$X^N X^N$ normal female	$X^N Y^-$ normal male
	X^n	$X^N X^n$ "carrier" female	$X^n Y^-$ hemophil-iac male

10-10. The inheritance of a sex-linked trait such as hemophilia. The unpaired recessive allele on the X chromosome results in the appearance of the trait in males. How might a female inherit such a trait?

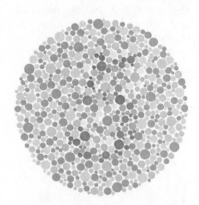

10-11. Charts such as this one are used to detect different kinds of colorblindness.

not be masked. The Y chromosome does not carry this gene at all. Therefore, the presence of a single recessive allele will cause the disorder to appear in that person. Figure 10-10 shows the inheritance of a sex-linked disorder.

Although modern medicine has removed much of the suffering of the males afflicted with hemophilia, a definite problem still exists. Female heterozygotes continue to exist and transmit this harmful allele to their offspring. Moreover, some surviving males can also contribute the allele to the next generation. Can you explain how a female with hemophilia might occur?

COLOR-BLINDNESS Color-blindness is also a sex-linked trait. (See Fig. 10-11.) Although it is usually associated with males, females may inherit the trait. The female offspring of a color-blind father and a heterozygous mother have a fifty-percent risk of being color-blind. The research that led to the discovery of sex-linked traits is long and involved. But this work has added to our knowledge and understanding of the hereditary mechanism.

Autosomal Linkage

A single chromosome carries many genes dealing with a wide variety of traits. In fact, genes and chromosomes have sometimes been compared to a necklace of beads. The beads represent the genes, and the necklace, the chromosome. Homologous chromosomes would be shown using two necklaces of identical size and shape. Alleles for a gene on one necklace might be different from those on the other necklace. Thus, these are represented by different colors of beads.

It would not be possible for genes appearing on the same chromosome to assort independently. For example, if the gene for seed color in pea plants appeared on the same chromosome as the one for seed shape, only two kinds of gametes could be formed from the heterozygotes of the F_1 generation *(YyRr)*. One chromosome might contain both dominant alleles *(YR)* while the other chromosome would contain both recessive alleles *(yr)*. During meiosis only *YR* and *yr* gametes could be formed. The F_2 generation would be limited to three genotypes *(YYRR, YyRr, and yyrr)* and two phenotypes (yellow, round-seeded plants and green, wrinkle-seeded plants). (See Fig. 10-12.) Independent assortment can occur only when the genes for different traits are on separate chromosomes.

Shortly after Sutton's theory describing the distribution of homologous chromosomes during meiosis a unique idea was put forth. It was suggested that if two different genes resided on the same chromosome, they would not assort independently. For two such traits, Mendel's results for the F_2 generation would not occur.

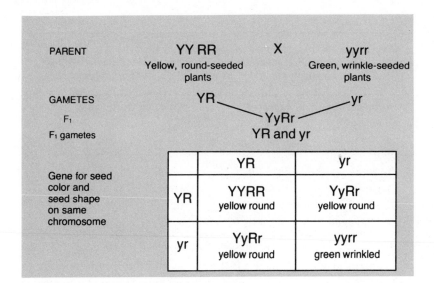

10-12. *If the genes for seed color and seed shape had been linked, the 9:3:3:1 ratio that is characteristic of independent assortment would have been impossible for Mendel to discover.*

Have students draw the diagram of another dihybrid cross in which the genes for two traits are linked; i.e., with P and E on one chromosome and p and e on the other.

Indeed, experiments using the sweet pea verified this prediction in 1905. These tests involved two Mendelian traits. One type of plant had purple flowers and elongated pollen grains. The other type was red-flowered and had round pollen grains. As expected, all members of the F₁ generation exhibited the dominant phenotype: purple flowers and elongated pollen grains.

10-13. *The inheritance of two completely linked traits produces the same genotype and phenotype ratios in the F₂ as in a monohybrid cross.*

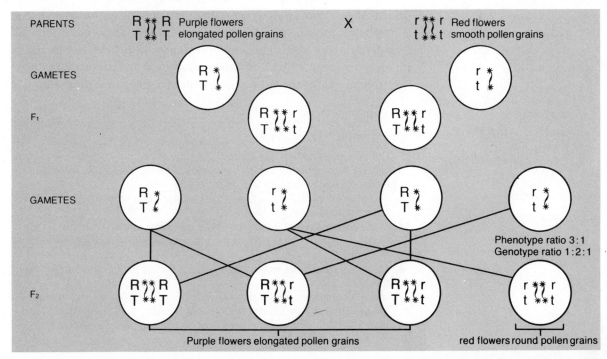

Answers to Questions for Section 3.

I. 1. Karyotype: an arranged preparation of chromosomes in regard to number, size, and shape. Sex-linked trait: a recessive trait carried on the X chromosome and usually expressed only in the male.

2. Autosome: chromosome other than those related to sex determination; sex chromosome: the X and Y chromosomes, which function in the determination of the sex of an individual. Sex-linked trait: trait carried by a gene or genes on the X chromosome; autosomal linkage: occurrence of two or more genes on a single autosome.

J. 3. The male has the XY chromosomal pair, and the female has the matching XX pair.

K. 4. Diagram as on page 186 (Fig. 10-8).

L. 5. Diagram as on page 188 (Fig. 10-10).

*6.

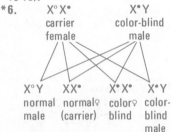

$X^\circ X^\bullet$
carrier
female

$X^\bullet Y$
color-blind
male

$X^\circ Y$
normal
male

$XX^\bullet$
normal♀
(carrier)

$X^\bullet X^\circ$
color♀
blind

$X^\bullet Y$
color-blind
male

$^\circ$ = gene for normal
$^\bullet$ = gene for colorblindness or other sex-linked trait

M. 7. Diagram as on page 189 (Fig. 10-13).

8. It can help identify chromosome defects.

TABLE 10-3.

Demonstration of linkage between flower color and shape of pollen grain in the sweet pea. Note that linkage occurs, but the offspring do not approach the 9:3:3:1 expected ratio if the genes were on different chromosomes.

Phenotype of F_2	Expected with Independent assortment	Expected with linkage	Actual
Purple-Elongate	3910 (9)	5214 (3)	4831
Purple-Round	1303 (3)	none	390
Red-Elongate	1303 (3)	none	393
Red-Elongate	435 (1)	1738 (1)	1338

LINKAGE REDUCES VARIETY   If the traits assorted independently, a typical 9:3:3:1 ratio should occur in the F_2 generation. However, if they were linked, a simple 3:1 ratio would be expected. (See Fig. 10-13.) There were notable exceptions. (See Table 10-3 on page 190.) But a definite tendency suggested linkage between flower color and pollen shape. The explanation for the exceptions will be considered in the next section. The tendency of blonde hair and blue eyes to occur together in humans can also be explained at least in part on the basis of linkage of these traits on a single chromosome.

It should now be apparent that linkage tends to reduce variety. But as the evidence above suggests, complete linkage has been found to be rare. Thus, in spite of linkage, there is still a small but significant tendency for genes to assort independently. This tendency increases variety in organisms. This almost endless diversity produces gene combinations that might be successful in a given environment.

QUESTIONS FOR SECTION 3

1. Define karyotype, sex-linked trait.
2. Differentiate between the following pairs of terms: autosome and sex chromosome, sex-linked trait and autosomal linkage.
3. Describe the difference between the karyotype of a normal male and that of a normal female.
4. Make a diagram that describes how sex is determined in humans.
5. Make a diagram that describes the inheritance of a sex-linked trait such as hemophilia.
6. Make a diagram that would explain how a female might inherit a sex-linked trait.
7. Make a diagram that explains how a 3:1 ratio would be expected in the F_2 generation if two genes are autosomally linked.
8. How might a karyotype of a person be useful in modern medicine?

4 CHROMOSOMAL VARIABILITY

Crossing Over

We found that the tendency for two traits to occur together was due to the fact that the two genes resided on the same chromosome. Such genes are said to be linked. In spite of this, there often seemed to be many cases of independent assortment. Theory and observation were not in agreement.

It was not long before careful observations of chromosomes began to supply some possible answers. Chromosomes were seen to cross over. (See Fig. 10-14.) At the points of contact, it was later shown that the two chromosomes actually broke and rejoined. The upper part of one chromosome would join with the lower member of its homologue, and *vice versa*.

Unlinking of genes appeared to occur often in a common research organism, the fruit fly. In humans, it may be seen in persons with blonde hair and dark eyes. At this point, the significance of crossing over as seen under the microscope was noted immediately by T.H. Morgan. He realized that such chromosomal activity could account for the rearrangement of certain genes. (See Fig. 10-15 on page 192.) Strong support for this idea came through a mathematical analysis of large amounts of data. The concept was simple. It was based on the distance between two genes on a given chromosome. The farther apart that two linked genes resided, the greater should be the chance that crossing over would occur at a point between them.

Students with a particular interest in genetics may wish to report to the class on the techniques of chromosome mapping.

OBJECTIVES FOR SECTION 4

N. Define the following terms: *inversion, deletion, translocation, duplication, non-disjunction, polyploidy.*

O. Explain why some degree of independent assortment may occur with autosomal linkage.

P. Explain how inversions might tend to increase the chances for crossing over to occur between linked genes.

Q. Describe how an abnormal number of chromosomes might occur in an offspring.

R. Explain why a polyploid organism would be a different species from its parent.

10-14. In crossing over, there is an exchange of chromosome segments.

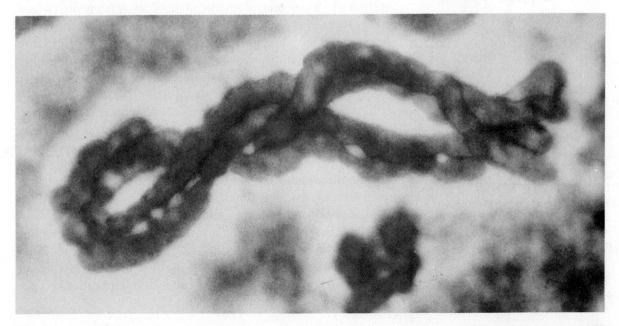

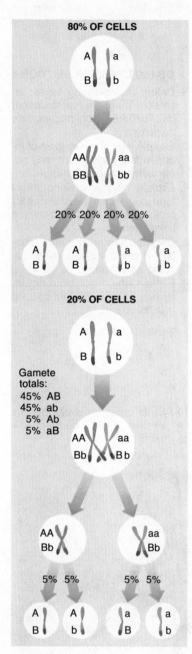

80% OF CELLS

20% 20% 20% 20%

20% OF CELLS

Gamete totals:
45% AB
45% ab
5% Ab
5% aB

5% 5%   5% 5%

10-15. *In this example, crossing over occurs in 20% of the cells. As a result, some offspring will show independent assortment.*

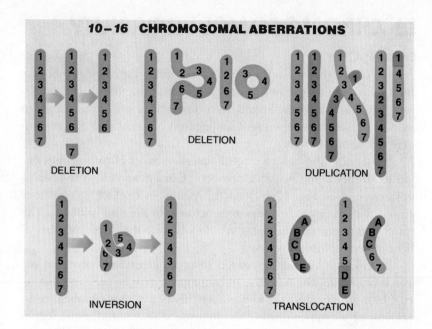

10-16 CHROMOSOMAL ABERRATIONS

DELETION

DELETION

DUPLICATION

INVERSION

TRANSLOCATION

Crossing over between genes that were close neighbors on a chromosome would be a highly unlikely event. Between others, however, it might occur frequently enough to produce independent assortment. Thus, crossing over is another way variation among members of a species is assured.

Chromosomal Aberrations

Other chromosomal phenomena have also been discovered. (See Fig. 10-16.) For example, a chromosome might become looped on itself. If the loop became broken and the ends rejoined in a reversed position, an *inversion* would occur. This could, in turn, affect the frequency with which crossing over would occur between two linked genes.

Short sections of chromosomes might also become lost as segments become broken off. This would produce *deletions*. A deletion on one chromosome might allow a recessive trait to be expressed if the dominant allele was on a deleted segment of the homologue.

If a chromosome fragment becomes attached to another non-paired chromosome, the phenomenon is known as *translocation*. Translocations do unlink some genes. They result in linkage between others. They may also undergo *duplication* of certain genes. Duplications may be harmful to the individual in which they occur. Down Syndrome, usually caused by the duplication of a whole chromosome, may also be caused by a translocation and duplication of a part of the 21st chromosome in humans.

A detailed discussion of such chromosomal mistakes is not necessary here. This brief description, however, points out the many ways that variety can be introduced into a species. Most of these aberrations are harmful to the organism, and hence to the population as a whole.

Changes in Chromosome Number

Variation in organisms can occur in still another way. If meiosis fails to occur normally, the gametes produced may have an abnormal number of chromosomes. Occasionally, a single pair of homologous chromosomes will fail to separate during meiosis. The resulting gametes will therefore possess one more or one less chromosome than the normal haploid. *The failure of chromosomes to separate during the meiotic process is called* **non-disjunction.** Gametes formed in this manner often do not survive. If one survives and is involved in fertilization, an abnormal offspring usually is produced. The results of non-disjunction in humans will be discussed in Chapter 12.

Occasionally, meiosis will not result in a reduction of chromosome number (2N →N). Gametes thus produced will be diploid (2N). Upon fertilization with a normal gamete, the offspring will contain three sets of chromosomes. These are called triploids (3N). *The increase of chromosome number by one or more whole sets of chromosomes is called* **polyploidy** (păl i ploid ē). Polyploidy is not a common phenomenon in animals. In plants, however, it plays a major role in the evolution of new species. (See Fig. 10-17.) Plants with 4N, 6N or other multiples are fairly common. Many of our cultivated garden and agricultural plants are actually polyploids.

Answers to Questions to Section 4

O. *3. See fig. 1-15 on page 192.

P. *4. See fig. 10-16 on page 192.

Q. *5.

abnormal
meiosis

R.*6. Polyploid cells arise as the result of a mistake in mitosis. The chromosomes divide, but the cell does not.

*7. If a polyploid cell further divides by mitosis, a new "individual" is produced with twice the number of chromosomes as its parents. The development of a new species will occur if this larger chromosome number is passed on successfully to the offspring.

Point out to students that non-disjunction in single chromosomes can occur with any chromosome, including the sex chromosomes. Moreover, it can occur in either of the meiotic divisions.

10-17. Many plants of horticultural and agricultural value are polyploids.

Answers to Questions for Section 4.

N. 1. Inversion: the rejoining, in a reversed position, of the ends of a looped, broken chromosome. Deletion: the loss of a short section of a chromosome. Translocation: the attachment of a chromosomal fragment to another non-paired chromosome.

2. In non-disjunction, chromosomes fail to separate during meiosis. In polyploidy, meiosis does not result in reduction of chromosome number, so that gametes are diploid and zygotes polyploid (3N or more).

QUESTIONS FOR SECTION 4

1. Define the following: inversion, deletion, translocation, duplication.
2. Differentiate between non-disjunction and polyploidy.
3. Make a diagram that explains why some degree of independent assortment may occur even though two genes may be linked.
4. Make a diagram to explain how an inversion in an autosome might increase the chances for crossing over to occur between two linked genes.
5. Make a diagram to show how an abnormal number of chromosomes might occur in the gametes when non-disjunction occurs.
6. Explain how polyploidy might be responsible for producing a new species from an existing one.
7. Explain why a polyploid organism would be a different species from its parent.

(See page 193 for more answers.)

CHAPTER REVIEW

There are a number of ways that genetic variation can occur within the limits of the existing gene pool. These include genetic recombination, the involvement of multiple alleles, incomplete dominance, and codominance. Others are polygenetic inheritance, crossing over, and various chromosomal aberrations.

Novelty in the gene pool can arise by changes in the hereditary material itself. Changes in the nucleotide sequences of a DNA molecule can produce phenotypic changes in an individual. Generally, such mutations are relatively rare, random, recessive, and harmful.

Sex determination is a result of the interaction of the X and Y chromosomes. Recessive traits occurring on the X chromosome in humans may result in sex-linked characters. These traits are usually carried by a heterozygous mother. Her sons have a 50/50 chance of showing traits.

Genes occurring together on the same chromosome are said to be linked and tend to produce phenotypes that occur together. They may become unlinked by crossing over. Other chromosomal phenomena may also increase variety in a population. These include inversion, translocation, deletion, and duplication of chromosome material.

There may also be changes in the chromosome number of an individual.

Thus, great variety exists in all organisms. Most of this variety occurs within fairly well-defined limits, and serves to maintain a certain *unity* in spite of great *diversity*. Nevertheless, within the genetic material, there is great potential for new varieties. *Change through time* has its origin in the hereditary material itself. Successful varieties survive. Unsuccessful ones will be eliminated or at least reduced in number.

Career activities

1. How might an animal breeder be important to various animal industries such as horse-racing?
2. How might a geneticist help us to know more about the effects of pollution on our health?

Using the concepts

3. Some forms of cancer are brought about by environmental factors that disrupt the normal genetic operations in certain cells. What role should the government play in controlling these factors?

VOCABULARY

1 Gene pool
multiple alleles
incomplete dominance
codominance
polygenic inheritance
2 mutation

3 mutagen
sex chromosome
autosome
karyotype
sex linked trait
linkage

4 inversion
duplication
translocation
deletion
non-disjunction
polyploidy

CHAPTER 10 TEST

Copy the number of each test item and place your answer to the right.

PART 1 Multiple Choice: Select the letter of the phrase that best completes each of the following.

d **1.** Variations within a breeding population may arise from **a.** mutations **b.** genetic recombinations **c.** chromosomal aberrations **d.** all of these.

c **2.** A mother's blood type is *B* and her child's type is *O*. Which blood type could the father *not* have? **a.** *A* **b.** *B* **c.** *AB* **d.** *O*.

c **3.** Polyploidy may occur as a result of cellular accidents during the process of **a.** mitosis **b.** protein synthesis **c.** meiosis **d.** crossing over.

b **4.** Which of the following is not considered a potential mutagen? **a.** X rays **b.** coffee **c.** radioactivity **d.** cosmic rays.

b **5.** In which of the following may the genotype of an individual be determined by observing the phenotype? **a.** in traits that are clearly either dominant or recessive **b.** in traits that are codominant **c.** in traits in which the environment has a great effect upon the genotype **d.** all of these.

b **6.** The inheritance of two X chromosomes in humans results in **a.** a male offspring **b.** a female offspring **c.** a colorblind offspring **d.** sterility.

a **7.** The occurrence of roan cattle is an example of **a.** incomplete dominance **b.** codominance **c.** the expression of a dominant allele over a recessive one **d.** a sex-linked trait.

d **8.** The inheritance of blood type in humans can be explained by **a.** simple Mendelian genetics (one pair of alleles) **b.** linked genes **c.** polygenic inheritance **d.** multiple alleles.

b **9.** Mutations are believed to be a result of **a.** alterations in the double helix configuration of DNA **b.** changes in the nucleotide sequence of DNA **c.** changes in the shape of certain nucleotides **d.** chromosomal break downs.

c **10.** Two traits that tend to appear together in many individuals are most likely **a.** mutations **b.** a result of crossing over **c.** a result of linkage **d.** dominant.

PART 2 Matching: Match the letter of the term in Column I with its description in Column II.

COLUMN I

a. sex-linked
b. crossing over
c. deletion
d. DNA
e. gene pool
f. incomplete dominance
g. karyotype
h. mutation
i. polyploidy
j. polygenic

COLUMN II

e **11.** All of the genes possessed by a given population at a given time

f **12.** Condition in which two alleles are both expressed in a heterozygote by blending

j **13.** Condition in which two or more genes interact to affect the expression of a phenotype

h **14.** A change in the hereditary material

d **15.** Substance of which the hereditary material is made

g **16.** Characteristic set of chromosomes of an individual arranged for study

a **17.** Recessive traits carried on the *X* chromosome normally expressed only in the male

b **18.** Exchange of parts between homologous chromosomes

c **19.** Failure of a chromosome or chromosome fragment to be included in a gamete

i **20.** Increase of chromosome number by a whole haploid set of chromosomes

PART 3 Completion: Complete the following.

21. Two alleles appearing on the same chromosome are said to be ____. linked

22. Normally sterile plant hybrids may become fertile by ____. polyploidy

23. Chromosomes other than those related to sex determination are referred to as ____. autosomes

24. Linkage between two genes would result in an F_2 generation with a phenotype ratio of ____. 3:1

25. The change through time of varieties of organisms has its basis in ____. hereditary material

CHAPTER 11

GENETICS AND POPULATIONS

In the first two chapters of this unit, our attention has been focused on the individual. We have presented basic information concerning inheritance in plants and animals. However, we must now turn to these questions as they relate to whole populations.

The reason for this concern is simple. Many observations tell us that the life forms we see today are not the same as those of the past. Thus, we must ask, "How do these long term changes occur?" Individuals do not exhibit such changes. They possess specific characteristics. They cannot alter these characteristics in a way that will affect future generations. But faced with the fact of change, we must try to understand how it occurs.

The diversity studied in Chapter 10 exists within rather well defined limits. New genetic features arising through mutations are random and seem to be without particular continuity. How, then, can trends occur in populations? Throughout this chapter, the three basic themes of the unit will continue to thread their ways. These are the themes of *unity and diversity, change through time,* and *continuity of life.*

Careful study of this chapter should help you to answer the following questions:

- How can the genetic character of a population be measured?
- How can we measure genetic changes in a population?
- What factors might cause inheritable trends to occur in populations?
- Why do some harmful genetic traits seem to appear more often than one might expect?

PENGUINS

◼ PROBABILITY AND POPULATIONS

Individuals and Populations

The genetic make-up of one person is set. At least with our present reason and knowledge, it cannot be changed. Potential gene combinations within the gene pool are not significant to his or her survival. Thus, it is the population, not the individual, that changes through time.

The population does possess diversity. Differences in size, color, resistance to disease, and behavior are only a few ways that members of a population differ from each other. If the population is to survive, it must reproduce at a rate high enough to produce a variety of genetic combinations. (See Fig. 11-1.) Also, if the reproductive rate is too slow, the best the gene pool has to offer may not be realized. Changes in the environment may favor certain gene combinations. Slow reproductive rates may not be enough to achieve these combinations. As a result, the survival of the population may be threatened.

Where the environment is stable for long periods of time, diversity in gene pools can become reduced. Variety is reduced as a high degree of specialization develops among members of a population. For example, the Galapagos tortoises differ from each other in only very minor ways. Their environment is one that is very stable. Such specialization may benefit a species, of course. But this is as a rule true only if there is a stable environment. On the other hand, to reduce the gene pool could be harmful if and when the environment does change. Populations might not have the genetic potential to adapt to the new conditions. For example, many animals live and reproduce within a warm, stable climate. Weather conditions may change and bring cold temperatures to the area. With this change, only those animals that still have genes to adapt to a cold environment will survive. Biologists today can see that the final fate of highly specialized species has often been extinction.

It is important to emphasize that the survival of a population in the face of a changing environment is dependent on its rate of offspring production. Populations with large numbers of offspring and short generation intervals are more likely to survive. Contrast the survival of insects over geologic time with that of the dinosaurs.

11-1. Muskrat population. The success of a species depends on the number of offspring that survive to reproduce.

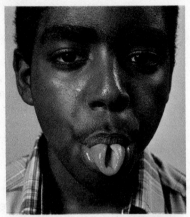

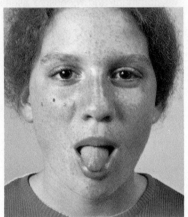

11-2. What is the genotype of persons who can roll their tongues? Of those who cannot? How do you know?

Allele Frequency

The number of times an event occurs is known as the frequency of that event. In genetics, *the frequency of an allele is how often it occurs in a population compared to how often all alleles for that gene appear.* With two equally-occurring alleles for a given gene, we could say that each has a frequency of 1/2 or 0.5. It begins to be clear, then, that some knowledge of probability will be necessary at this point. Gamblers are well versed in these principles. They try to use them to their advantage when betting. If the odds for drawing a needed card are high, they bet so. A gambler may win or lose, but a thorough knowledge of the chances cuts losses.

Let us assume that all members mating within a population do so at random. Under such conditions, the alleles for a trait will occur in the next generation in a predictable ratio. For example, consider the Mendelian trait of tongue rolling in humans. (See Fig. 11-2.) The ability to roll the tongue is dominant. Thus, there are three possible genotypes: *RR*, *Rr*, and *rr*. Let us assume that in the population, 25% of the individuals are homozygous for "rolling" *(RR)*. Another 50% are heterozygous *(Rr)*. And the remaining 25% are homozygous recessive *(rr)*, and cannot roll their tongues. This means that out of every 100 people in the population, 75 will be able to roll their tongues. Twenty-five will not be able to do so. (See Table 11-1.) In that population, 25 will possess two dominant alleles, 50 will have a dominant and a recessive allele, and 25 will have two recessive alleles.

Remember that each person has two alleles for tongue-rolling. Therefore, 100 people will possess a total of 200 alleles for the trait. Of these, half, or 100 alleles will be dominant. The other 100 will, of course, be recessive. This statement may be expressed in another way by saying that the frequency of the dominant allele is 1/2 or 0.5. The frequency of the recessive allele would also be 0.5.

TABLE 11-1.   ALLELE FREQUENCY FOR TONGUE-ROLLING

Phenotype	75% "rollers"		25% "nonrollers"
Genotype	25% RR	50% Rr	25% rr
Population of 100	25 RR	50 Rr	25 rr
Number of R alleles	50	50	0
Number of r alleles	0	50	50

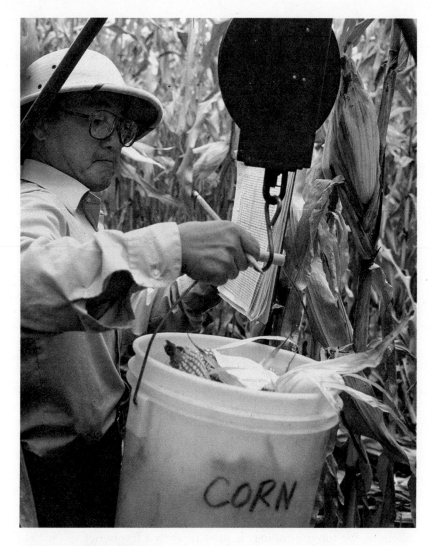

11-3. *Plant breeders are constantly searching for new varieties that are resistant to drought, insects, or diseases.*

Laws of Probability

FIRST LAW OF PROBABILITY   The frequency of the dominant allele is often expressed as p. That of the recessive allele is given as q. Since there are only two alternatives in this particular Mendelian trait, the relationship between p and q must represent the total, or 100% of the alleles. Hence, $p + q = 1$. This is an expression of the **First Law of Probability**. *It states that the sum of the probabilities (or frequencies) of occurrence for a chance event is equal to one.*

SECOND LAW OF PROBABILITY   Knowledge of allelic frequencies can be important in many fields. Animal husbandry, agriculture, and horticulture, as well as human medicine, make use of this information. (See Fig. 11-3.) Plant and animal breeders must "play the odds"

Determine the frequencies of a number of things: boys or girls in the class, dog owners on a city block, etc. Refer to the Study Skill exercise on the determination of frequency.

3. Environmental changes may favor certain gene combinations, and reproductive rates must keep pace with these changes.

*4. It reduces variety in gene pools, which is an advantage in a stable environment but a disadvantage in a changing one, because populations might lack the genetic potential to adapt.

C. 5. The sum of the frequencies of occurrence for a chance event is equal to one. If p is the frequency of the dominant allele and q the frequency of the recessive allele, $p + q = 1$.

6. The probability that two or more chance events will occur together is equal to the multiplication product of their chances for occuring separately. If p is the frequency of the allele R, and p = 0.5, then the frequency of RR = p^2 or 0.25.

*7. Law: as stated in 5. The chance that each of the 6 numbers will occur is one in six, or $\frac{1}{6}$. The sum of all six is $6 \times \frac{1}{6}$ or 1.

*8. Law: as stated in 6. For "heads" the chance is one in two, or $\frac{1}{2}$. For "6", the chance is one in six or $\frac{1}{6}$. The chance that both will occur is $\frac{1}{2} \times \frac{1}{6} = \frac{1}{12}$ or 0.083.

*9. If p = frequency of D and q = frequency of d, then D = $\frac{650}{1000}$ = 0.65 and d = 1.00 − .65 = .35, because p + q = 1 and p:q :: 650:350.

D. *10. Let p = frequency of d and q = frequency of D. Then q^2 = 0.64. Solving the equation $p^2 + 2pq + q^2 = 1.00$, p = 0.2, and q = 0.8.

*11. Given 510 tongue rollers in a population of 1000, and if p = frequency of the R allele and q = frequency of r, $p^2 + 2pq = 0.51$. 1.00 − .51 = 0.49, the frequency of the homozygous recessive. $\sqrt{.49}$ = .7, the frequency of the recessive allele. 1.00 − .7 = .3, the frequency of the dominant allele. $(.3)^2$ = .09, the frequency of the homozygous dominant. 2 (.7) (.3) = .42, the frequency of the heterozygotes. The frequencies of the three genotypes total: .49 + .09 + .42 = 1.00.

as they attempt to develop new varieties of corn, beef cattle or other products. As we shall see in Chapter 12, genetic counselors also use the knowledge gained from knowing allelic frequencies. They help their patients to predict the probabilities for certain genetic disorders in their children.

These calculations are based upon the **Second Law of Probability.** *It states that the chances for two or more events happening together are equal to the product of their chances for happening separately.* For example, if p, the frequency of the R allele, $=0.5$, then the genotype RR would be expected to occur with a frequency of $p \times p$ or p^2, or 0.25. This number conforms to the proportions observed in the original population. Homozygous recessive offspring would be expected to occur with a frequency of q^2, or 0.25 also. The heterozygous condition which can occur as Rr or rR, would be expected to be $2pq$ or 0.50.

TABLE 11-2. GENE FREQUENCY AMONG OFFSPRING

		Proportion and types of gametes in male parents	
		.5 R (p)	.5 r (q)
Proportion and types of gametes in female parents	0.5 R (p)	.25 RR (p^2)	.25 Rr (pq)
	0.5 r (q)	.25 Rr (pq)	.25 rr (q^2)

Not all Mendelian traits occur with alleles in equal proportions. This may be shown by using a population in which the dominant allele, R for tongue-rolling, is present with a frequency of 0.6. The frequency of the recessive allele, r for those not able to roll their tongues, would have to be 0.4. This is so since *the sum of the frequencies for the two alleles must equal one.* The frequencies of the three genotypes within the population would be figured as follows:

frequency of RR $= p^2$ $= (0.6)^2$ $= 0.36$
frequency of Rr $= 2pq$ $= 2(0.6)(0.4)$ $= 0.48$
frequency of rr $= q^2$ $= (0.4)^2$ $= 0.16$

$p^2 + 2pq + q^2$ $= 1.00$

Allelic Frequencies in Populations

Usually, the allelic frequencies are not known. They must be determined from population data. It is a fairly easy task to sample a population and find the frequencies for each genotype of a Mendelian trait. (See Fig. 11-4.) From this knowledge, the frequencies for the individual alleles may be determined.

Let us again use the tongue-rolling example to show how this is done. Suppose that a population is sampled for the occurrence of the trait. Suppose, further, that 840 out of 1000 people sampled showed the dominant phenotype. Thus, 160 people in the population could not roll their tongues.

The "rollers" consist of two different genotypes: *RR* and *Rr*. Furthermore, the frequencies for the *R* and *r* alleles are probably not the same. The genotype for each of the "non-rollers," however, is known. All must be homozygous for the recessive condition *(rr)*. The frequency of the recessive genotype is $\frac{160}{1000}$, or 0.16. In our probability statement we can say $q^2 = 0.16$ (see above). The frequency of the recessive allele, q, may be computed by taking the square root of q^2. The frequency of the recessive allele is 0.4 or $(q = \sqrt{q^2} = \sqrt{0.16} = 0.4)$.

Since $p + q$ must equal 1.0, from the First Law of Probability, the dominant allele must exist in a frequency of 0.6 or $(1.0 - 0.4 = 0.6)$. The frequencies of the homozygous dominant and heterozygous genotypes may now be determined, as above.

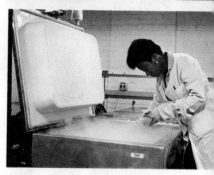

11-4. Washing, storing, and freezing of blood. Genetics can be important in planning how much blood of each type to keep on hand for emergencies.

QUESTIONS FOR SECTION 1

1. What is meant by the phrase frequency of an allele?
2. Why is a rapid reproductive rate necessary to achieve the potential of the gene pool?
3. How are the requirements for an adequate reproductive rate and the speed with which the environment changes related?
4. Describe the advantages and disadvantages of a high degree of specialization to a species.
5. State and give an example of the First Law of Probability.
6. State and give an example of the Second Law of Probability.
7. State the First Law of Probability and demonstrate its truth by using the probability for each number on a die (one of a pair of dice).
8. State the Second Law of Probability. Demonstrate its truth by determining the probability of throwing a "heads" and a "6" using a coin and a die.
9. If 650 alleles out of 1000 are dominant, calculate the frequencies of the dominant and recessive alleles in the population.
10. If 640 out of 1000 people exhibit the recessive phenotype, calculate the frequencies of the dominant and recessive alleles.
11. Calculate the frequency of the homozygous dominant, heterozygous, and homozygous recessive individuals from the following data: number of tongue-rollers in a population sample of 1000 persons = 510. (Remember that tongue-rolling is dominant.)

Answers to Questions for Section 1.

A. 1. The number of times the allele occurs in a population compared to the number of times all alleles for that gene appears.

B. 2. In order to produce a variety of genetic combinations and to realize the best the gene pool has to offer.

(See more answers on page 200.)

CHAPTER INVESTIGATION

A. What is the ratio of purple to yellow kernels?

B. Assuming these kernels represent the F_2 generation of a Mendelian cross, what are the genotypes of the two types of kernels?

C. (i) What are the frequencies of the two alleles?
    (ii) Sample a human population (e.g. your class) for a Mendelian trait and calculate the frequencies for the two alleles.

2 THE HARDY-WEINBERG PRINCIPLE

Genetic Equilibrium

Are dominant alleles more common in a population than recessive ones? Will a dominant mutation eventually cause a drop in the frequency of a recessive allele? Such questions were posed by experienced geneticists in the early part of this century. It is therefore clear to see that a beginning genetics student might also ask the same questions.

Before attempting to answer these and other questions, it would be wise to explain two terms. These terms are dominance and prevalence (or frequency). Dominance simply refers to an allele's ability to show up when present. It has nothing to do with how common or rare the allele is in a population. The prevalence of an allele has only to do with how common it is. Recessive alleles can be very prevalent. That is, they may have a high frequency. Figure 11-5 shows a recessive trait, blue eyes, which is more prevalent in Scandinavia, than the dominant dark-eye color. On the other hand, dominant alleles may be very rare and have a low frequency.

The credit for pointing out the difference between dominance and prevalence has been given to G.H. Hardy and W. Weinberg. Each working on their own explained the basic principle of population genetics that today bears their names. Simply stated, **the Hardy-Weinberg Principle** *explains that under certain conditions, the frequencies of alleles in a population will remain constant from generation to generation.* There are four conditions that must be met for the statement to be true.

Conditions Affecting the Frequencies of Alleles

FIRST CONDITION   The first condition requires a large randomly breeding population. (See Fig. 11-6.) Furthermore, reproduction

11-5. Blue eyes are recessive to dark eyes.

11-6. If mating is random in a large breeding population, and there are no mutations, migrations, or selective factors, the Hardy-Weinberg principle points out that allele frequencies will remain constant.

The Hardy-Weinberg Principle   **203**

TABLE 11-3. FREQUENCY OF A DOMINANT ALLELE

Generation	p	q
P	0.25	0.75
1	0.27	0.73
2	0.26	0.74
3	0.27	0.73
4	0.28	0.72
5	0.29	0.71
6	0.27	0.73
7	0.26	0.74
8	0.27	0.73
9	0.26	0.74
10	0.26	0.74

must lead to offspring that can themselves reproduce. There must be reproductive continuity. Several factors can affect the population's potential for reproductive continuity. These factors include mate selection, fertility, embryonic development, the number of births, and the number of individuals reaching reproductive age. Reproduction is not simply the mating of individuals. For reproduction to be random these factors must be independent of the genotypes of the individuals in the population. It should be noted that the factors that determine reproductive continuity are related to one's genotype. Therefore, complete random reproduction probably does not occur in natural populations. Non-random reproduction plays an important part in change.

SECOND CONDITION The second condition assumes that there will be *no differential migrations*. This means that *alleles exchanged between populations must be in equal proportions.* Consider the fact that a certain number of individuals may leave a population. It follows that the same proportion of the various alleles must move into the population. Allele frequencies would thus not change.

THIRD CONDITION Mutations must be in equilibrium. This means that the number of mutations in one direction ($A \rightarrow a$) must equal the number in the reverse direction ($a \rightarrow A$). The introduction of new alleles or a change in the proportion of existing alleles changes their frequencies.

FOURTH CONDITION Finally, there must be no favoring (or selecting) of certain alleles in the gene pool. If individuals with certain alleles or allelic sets are favored or prevented from breeding, the proportions of their alleles in the population changes. Thus, changes in gene frequencies is a fourth factor that contributes to change. Let us now look at the importance of each of the conditions.

Disturbing Forces

Continuous observation of populations tells us that allelic frequencies do change. Therefore, one or more of the conditions must have been broken. The Hardy-Weinberg Principle, then, leads to a list of the kinds of factors that will produce changes in allelic frequencies.

POPULATION SIZE Ideally, the contents of the gene pool are there for every potential offspring. In practice, this is often not the case. The actual breeding population is only a small part of the total. As a result, only the genetic contents of the breeding population can be given to the offspring. The breeding population may have somewhat different allele frequencies from those in the population as a whole. These differences will show up in the offspring. The frequencies of the alleles in the gene population will change.

For example, assume that we observe ten generations of a population of 200 gulls. From this population, only 30 pairs are allowed to breed each season. Those left are too young or not tough enough to compete for mates. The breeding population, then, is fairly small. Table 11-3 shows the changes in the frequencies of the dominant and recessive alleles over a period of ten generations. The breeding population consists of 30 per cent of the total population for a certain trait during this period.

Changes in the populations will occur by chance matings. To illustrate, imagine a bucket containing 250 red marbles and 750 white ones. (See Fig. 11-7.) A handful of 30 or so marbles would probably not conform to the 1:3 ratio in the bucket. In fact, the smaller the sample, the less accurate would be the final ratio.

Small breeding populations will result in sampling errors just as in the marble analogy. *The changing of allelic frequencies due to sampling errors is called* genetic drift. Sampling errors may be caused by many diverse factors. As in the example of the gulls, not all of the population may be reproducing. Once in a while, we find that fairly few males will mate with a large number of females. Horses, elk, deer, and elephant seals are examples of this breeding pattern. (See Fig. 11-8.) Natural disasters may also result in genetic drift. Such disasters could sharply alter the genetic make-up of the population that survives. A small group of organisms breaking off from a larger population and founding a colony may also result in genetic drift. The chance that the alleles these individuals have are in the same proportion as the general population is slim. In any event, population size is an important factor in changing allele frequencies.

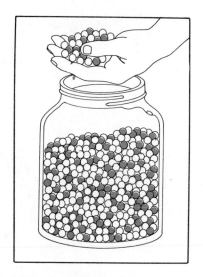

11-7. A small sample from a container with a 1:3 ratio of red to white marbles will not necessarily have the same ratio.

11-8. Genetic drift can result when single males take on a number of females during mating season as in the elephant seals shown here.

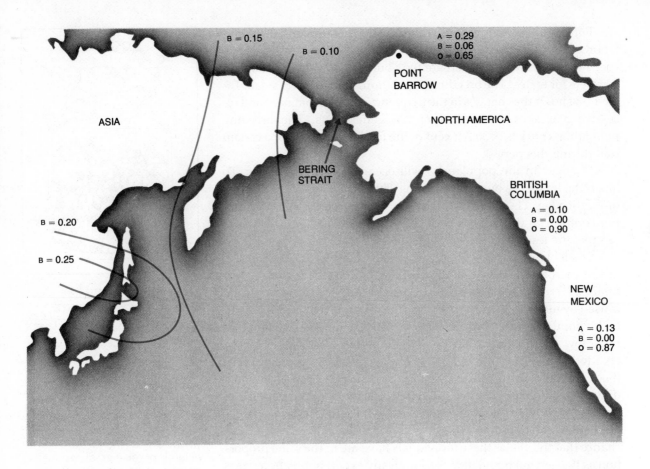

B = 0.15

B = 0.10

A = 0.29
B = 0.06
O = 0.65

POINT
BARROW

ASIA

NORTH AMERICA

BERING
STRAIT

BRITISH
COLUMBIA

A = 0.10
B = 0.00
O = 0.90

B = 0.20

B = 0.25

NEW
MEXICO

A = 0.13
B = 0.00
O = 0.87

11-9. *The first people to reach the Bering Strait may not have had the* B *allelle in their gene pool. Thus,* B *appears with decreasing frequency from Asia to North America.*

DIFFERENTIAL MIGRATION It is not uncommon to find that neighboring populations of the same species differ a great deal from each other. There are a number of reasons for these differences. One includes genetic drift. Populations, themselves, are not static. There is often some movement of members between populations. Because this movement is small, differences are kept low. However, the farther apart populations are, the less contact occurs between them. For example, the frequency of the B allele for blood type drops off sharply across the Bering Strait. (See Fig. 11-9.) In turn, genetic differences increase as distance increases.

In the event that breeding contact is set up between two differing populations, the offspring will show the genetic nature of both populations. As the offspring change, the genetic nature of the population changes. The impact of the change upon the population will depend upon three factors:

(1) the number of immigrants making reproductive contact,
(2) the number of offspring that result from each mating, and
(3) the advantage or disadvantage given to the offspring.

Thus, reproductive contact between differing populations may have a major effect on allele frequencies in both populations. Differential migration may not be a steady event. It may not occur each breeding season. In fact, it may occur only rarely. But it does occur. There are many sub-populations of song sparrows, for example. Each is slightly different from the others. There is enough genetic contact between the populations, however, to maintain a single species. In addition, there is not enough genetic contact to make the sub-populations all alike. The result is a change in the allele frequencies through the offspring. But more than that, it is an important way that species can maintain some degree of unity through continuity.

MUTATIONS   The third factor that contributes to changes in allelic frequencies is that of mutation. The effect of mutations on the offspring of individuals has already been treated in Chapter 10. However, we need to consider at least briefly their effect upon otherwise stable allelic frequencies.

We have seen that mutations are generally rare, random, recessive, and harmful. As a result, their effects upon a population might not show up at first. In fact, they might be quite small. A recessive mutation might take several generations to appear in the offspring. This is due to the fact that only homozygotes will exhibit a recessive condition. Once they appear, their harmful nature may keep a number of homozygous individuals from breeding.

But mutations do become incorporated into the gene pools. (See Fig. 11-10.) Since they are new elements to the genetic make-up of a population, their very existence is a change in the frequency of the new allele and in the one it replaced. Thus, mutations will alter allelic frequencies and show a disturbing influence.

SELECTION   The final, but by no means least disturbing factor to genetic equilibrium is that of selection. The advantage or disadvantage of certain genotypes will cause a change in the frequencies of the affected alleles. Certain genotypes may cause an individual to become more adapted to its niche. The result may be a longer life span and/or the production of more offspring. The reverse may also be true. Certain genotypes may be selected against. Many human genetic disorders greatly reduce the life expectancy of the victim. Hence, affected individuals will not live as long, and will not produce as many offspring.

It is possible that selection favoring or opposing an individual is often not complete. Let us look at three situations in which the selection is against the homozygous recessive genotype, *aa*. The recessive genotype might be cystic fibrosis or sickle-cell anemia, for example. It does not matter if these individuals die before reproducing or they simply fail to reproduce for some other reason. We will look at situa-

11-10.   *Mutations and artificial selection were used to develop Ancorn sheep that cannot jump fences.*

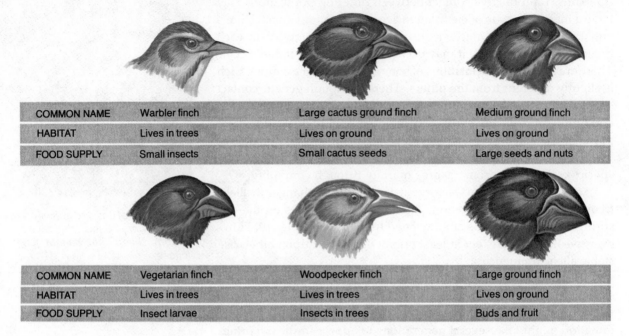

COMMON NAME	Warbler finch	Large cactus ground finch	Medium ground finch
HABITAT	Lives in trees	Lives on ground	Lives on ground
FOOD SUPPLY	Small insects	Small cactus seeds	Large seeds and nuts

COMMON NAME	Vegetarian finch	Woodpecker finch	Large ground finch
HABITAT	Lives in trees	Lives in trees	Lives on ground
FOOD SUPPLY	Insect larvae	Insects in trees	Buds and fruit

11-11. *Darwin's finches. How do the shapes of the bills relate to their use?*

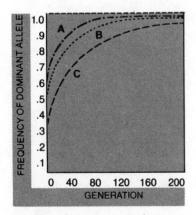

11-12. *Changes in the frequency of the dominant allele over 200 generations. The selection pressure against the recessive allele is **A.**, 100%; **B.**, 50%; **C.**, 15%. The initial frequency of the dominant allele was 0.25.*

tions in which the selection pressure against these individuals is 100%, 50%, and 15%. Each population begins with a frequency of the dominant allele being 0.25. The recessive allele would, of course, be 0.75 at the time selection is begun. (See Table 11-4.)

Figure 11-12 illustrates the effect of favoring the homozygous dominant and heterozygous individuals. In each case, the frequency of the dominant allele is increased. The rates for each case, however, differ somewhat.

Perhaps you are wondering how many generations it would take for the frequency of the recessive allele to reach zero under these selective conditions. How many generations would it take for the frequency of the dominant allele to reach 1.0? The answer is the same for all these cases. Never! Recessive alleles will always remain in the gene pool. In spite of selection against cystic fibrosis, hemophilia, and sickle-cell anemia, these recessive alleles remain with us. Remember that selection in this case was only against the homozygous recessive individuals *(aa)*. The heterozygotes also have a recessive allele. Not being selected against, heterozygotes will continue to pass recessive alleles on to future generations. Heterozygotes *(Aa)* can only rarely be distinguished from homozygous dominants *(AA)*.

Another factor helps to prevent the total loss of a recessive allele from the gene pool in spite of selection. Once in a while, nearly all genes will undergo spontaneous mutation. Often, this involves the mutation of dominant alleles to recessive forms. Thus, the impact of

TABLE 11-4. CHANGES IN ALLELE FREQUENCY

Generation	Frequency of Dominant Allele with Selection of		
	15%	50%	100%
Parent	0.25	0.25	0.25
1	.27	.34	.55
2	.29	.44	.69
3	.31	.49	.73
4	.32	.54	.77
5	.33	.57	.80
10	.40	.71	.87
20	.51	.83	.92
30	.61	.88	.92
40	.68	.89	.93
50	.71	.89	.93

mutagenic agents in the environment becomes suddenly critical. Radioactivity, asbestos, artificial food additives and other factors increase the frequency of mutations. Might this increase the frequency of harmful recessive alleles? Harmful alleles in a population make up a genetic load for that population. Of course, mutagens contribute to the genetic load in many populations, including humans. We will look at some of the implications of this aspect of genetics in the next chapter.

QUESTIONS FOR SECTION 2

1. Define the terms genetic equilibrium, differential migration, selection, genetic drift, genetic load.
2. What is genetic drift? Give an example in human populations.
3. What kinds of alleles are usually affected by genetic drift?
4. State the Hardy-Weinberg Principle.
5. What forces are necessary for the Hardy-Weinberg Principle to hold true?
6. From the previous question, explain how a violation of each condition acts to upset the genetic equilibrium of a population.
7. Explain why the frequency of the dominant allele never would reach 1.0 even under the most strict of selective environments.
8. What would be the frequency of the recessive allele at each of the points on the line of 15% selection, Figure 11-12? Explain.
9. Explain why a harmful recessive allele would not actually disappear from a population even under the most stringent of selective pressures.
10. Explain how mutagens can increase the genetic load of a population.

Answers to Questions for Section 2.

E. 1. Genetic equilibrium: constancy of frequency of alleles in a population. Differential migration: condition in which the exchange of alleles between populations is on unequal proportion. Selection: the favoring of certain alleles in a gene pool. Genetic drift: the changing of allelic frequencies due to sampling. Genetic load: the harmful alleles in a population.

2. Definition in 1. Example among humans is the drop in frequency of the B allele for blood type across the Bering Strait.

*3. Non-adaptive or "neutral".

F. 4. Under certain conditions, the frequencies of alleles in a population will remain constant from generation to generation.

5. (1) A large, randomly breeding population; (2) no differential migration, (3) equilibrium among mutations, (4) no selection of certain alleles.

6. (1) Certain alleles will be passed on in different proportions to the next generation. (2) When two differing populations interbreed, offspring show genetic nature of both, and this shows up as a population change. (3) Mutations are usually rare, random, recessive, and harmful; but they do become part of gene pools and thus alter allelic frequencies. (4) The advantage or disadvantage of certain genotypes causes changes in the frequencies of affected alleles.

*7. Heterozygotes are not removed by selection, yet they also have recessive alleles.

G. *8.
$$1.00 - .25 = .75 \quad 1.00 - .91 = .09$$
$$1.00 - .49 = .51 \quad 1.00 - .92 = .08$$
$$1.00 - .65 = .35 \quad 1.00 - .93 = .07$$
$$1.00 - .80 = .20 \quad 1.00 - .94 = .06$$
$$1.00 - .85 = .15 \quad 1.00 - .95 = .05$$
$$1.00 - .90 = .10 \quad 1.00 - .96 = .04$$

*9. For same reason in question 7.

H. 10. Mutagens produce mutations, which are generally harmful alleles.

3 MAINTAINING VARIETY

Heterozygote Superiority

OBJECTIVES FOR SECTION 3

I. Define the terms *balanced polymorphism*, *hybrid vigor*.
J. In terms of allele frequencies, predict the effect of equal selective forces upon the homozygous dominant and on the homozygous recessive individuals in a population.
K. Describe an example of balanced polymorphism in humans. Explain how a harmful allele might come to exist at more than token frequencies in such a population.
L. Explain why selective action of evironmental factors upon the human genetic constitution is such a difficult subject for study.
M. Explain the importance of genetic variety to populations living in changing environments.

It is fairly easy to see how selection can alter the frequencies of alleles. Adjustment of the frequencies takes place until an equilibrium is reached. At that point, further change is not significant, as long as the environment remains the same. Once in a while, however, we find that a certain apparently harmful allele defies this prediction. For some reason it exists in a proportion that does not seem to be in keeping with its harmful nature.

Quite often in animals, plants, and humans, the proportion of a harmful allele seems to be higher than normal. It is often difficult to determine the reason. In many cases, however, the reason has been traced to the fact that the heterozygote is somehow superior in fitness to either of the homozygotes. The harmful allele would, of course, be selected against. But for some reason, the dominant allele also seems to be unsuitable at least to some degree. On the other hand, there does seem to be a favoring of the heterozygous state. The result is an unusually high frequency of the heterozygous genotype. *The maintenance of such harmful alleles at higher than normal frequencies is known as* **balanced polymorphism** (p̈ al ē *mor* fiz əm).

In the extreme case, selection against both homozygotes is equal, and perhaps total. This would result in a population made up solely of heterozygotes. Since only heterozygotes would be breeding, half of the alleles would be dominant and half would be recessive. Thus, the frequency of both alleles would be 0.5.

This is not usually the case, however. Selection against the homozygous dominant individuals is often different from that against the recessives. The discussion of sickle-cell anemia in the next section is a case in point. The resulting frequencies would reflect a higher proportion of the less harmful alleles. However, a balance is set up that clearly shows an unexpected proportion of the recessive allele.

Balanced polymorphism is clearly shown in a situation called *hybrid vigor*. This term was first used to describe *offspring that exhibited increased "fitness."* We must understand, however, that fitness depends largely upon the viewpoint of the observer. Animal and plant breeders usually use growth rate or crop yield as a measure of fitness. Special hybrid cattle, for example, often show high growth rates. Also, hybrid forms of wheat, corn, and other crops mature faster or are more resistant to disease or drought. In natural populations, however, fitness must be measured in terms of the number of offspring that survive to produce another generation.

Emphasize that "fitness" does depend on the viewpoint of the observer. For example, the mule is more "fit" for certain tasks, but it is sterile and thus less fit from the standpoint of survival.

Balanced Polymorphism in Humans

One of the classic examples of balanced polymorphism occurs in humans. Red blood cells of normal individuals are found to be round to oval in shape, and slightly thinner in the center. (See Fig. 11-13.) In persons suffering from a disease called sickle-cell anemia, however, the blood cells take on an odd sickled shape. Sickle-cell anemia behaves as an autosomal recessive disorder. That is, it is due to a harmful allele that appears on a non-sex chromosome. Sufferers must be homozygous recessive to show the disease under normal conditions. The sickling is a result of an abnormal hemoglobin molecule. This important molecule is the main oxygen-carrying component of the blood. Its changed shape reduces its ability to carry oxygen. Furthermore, the sickled shape of the cell prevents them from passing freely through the small vessels of the body. Blood vessels become clogged and adequate circulation is thus prevented.

Until the advent of modern medical practices, victims of sickle-cell usually died in early childhood. It would appear, then, that this deadly allele would be expected to occur in very low frequencies. In certain geographical areas of the world, however, this is not the case. In fact, its frequency is fairly high — perhaps as high as 0.25 in some populations!

In 1949, researchers demonstrated a high correlation of the incidence of sickle-cell with the incidence of malaria. These high incidence areas included Africa, Greece, Sicily, and parts of the Near East. A high correlation, however, does not prove the existence of a relationship. Further study of this phenomenon was fruitful. Anthony Allison, a British physician, found that heterozygote children seemed to be more resistant to the malarial parasite than were homozygous dominant children. The heterozygotes, therefore, were more fit. This situation resulted in a very high frequency for the harmful recessive allele. Where malaria does not exist, the frequency of the harmful allele decreases. The environment plays an important role in determining gene frequencies.

A great deal remains to be learned about the role of polymorphism in humans. One possible area of its operation may be in examining the various blood types. There does not seem to be any clear advantage conferred to persons with a certain blood type. There is some evidence, however, to suggest such advantages do exist. This would mean that blood type differences between groups may indeed be the result of selective factors. For example, research shows some correlation between certain forms of ulcers and having *O*-type blood. Such studies on humans are difficult to carry out. People move around a great deal and subject themselves to changing environ-

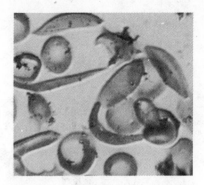

11-13. *Normal blood cells are disc shaped. Notice odd sickle cells throughout.*

Recent studies on the distribution of sickle cell anemia tend to indicate that there may be other factors than malaria involved.

Answers to Questions for Section 3.

*4. A reduction in the frequency of the recessive allele.

5. See answer to 3.

*6. Malaria does not exist in the U.S., and so does not act as a factor favoring sickle-cell.

L. 7. Because people subject themselves to changing environments.

8. It allows them to adapt to new conditions.

ments. Adequate analysis of all of the environmental factors is a very large task, and perhaps impossible. These and other relationships, however, remain to be studied thoroughly.

Answers to Questions for Section 3.

I. 1. Balanced polymorphism: the maintenance of harmful alleles at higher than normal frequencies. Hybrid vigor: offspring exhibiting increased "fitness", due to balanced polymorphism.

J. 2. A favoring of the heterozygous state.

K. *3. Sufferers from sickle-cell anemia are homozygous for the recessive allele. But individuals heterozygous for sickle-cell are more resistant to malaria than are dominant homozygotes. Thus, more heterozygotes survive to transmit sickle-cell.

(See more answers on page 211.)

QUESTIONS FOR SECTION 3

1. Define the terms balanced polymorphism, hybrid vigor.
2. What is the effect upon the frequencies of the dominant alleles when equal selective forces act upon the homozygous dominant and recessive individuals in a population?
3. Describe an example of balanced polymorphism in humans.
4. What would be the effect upon the allele frequencies if the selective forces slightly favored the homozygous dominant?
5. Describe the relationship between sickle-cell anemia and malaria.
6. Explain why the sickle-cell allele exists in lower frequencies in the United States among the descendants of people from areas where it was relatively high.
7. Explain why selective action of environmental factors upon the human genetic constitution is such a difficult subject for study.
8. Describe the advantage of genetic variety to populations living in a changing environment.

CHAPTER REVIEW

Genetic variety is important to populations living in changing environments. It allows them to adapt to the demands of the new conditions. Stable environments tend to encourage the loss of variety and increased specialization. Thus, there is a delicate balance between the unity and diversity within a species.

The First and Second Laws of Probability may be used to find the frequencies of some alleles in a population. These laws can also be used to predict genotypic frequencies in offspring. Changes in populations over a period of several generations may be observed in changing allele frequencies.

The Hardy-Weinberg Principle points out those conditions that, if met, predict genetic stability. *Deviations from these conditions lead to increased diversity and change in the population over time.* In natural populations, one or more of the conditions is nearly always vio-

lated. Thus, change over time occurs.

Opposing selection forces may result in balanced polymorphism and hence, greater diversity in a population. *The continuity of a species from one generation to the next is assured through the transmission of genetic information from parent to offspring. Various natural forces insure diversity and hence, adaptability in a species.*

Using the Concepts

1. Explain why diversified agriculture is a more sound practice than extensive monoculture.
2. Give some examples where hybrid vigor is of agricultural value.
3. How has modern medicine tended to increase the genetic load in human populations?

VOCABULARY REVIEW

1 frequency
2 genetic equilibrium
differential migration

selection
genetic drift
genetic load

Hardy-Weinberg Principle
3 balanced polymorphism
hybrid vigor

CHAPTER 11 TEST

Copy the number of each test item and place your answer to the right.

PART 1   Multiple Choice: Select the letter of the phrase that best completes each of the following.

d 1. If the frequency of the recessive allele in a population is 0.1, what is the frequency of the homozygous dominant individuals in that population?   **a.** 0.9   **b.** 0.1   **c.** 0.18   **d.** 0.81.

a 2. An allele found to be unfavorable in a given environment would disappear completely from the gene pool only if it was   **a.** dominant   **b.** recessive   **c.** a mutation   **d.** a result of polyploidy.

a 3. Balanced polymorphism generally favors the   **a.** heterozygote   **b.** homozygous recessive   **c.** homozygous dominant   **d.** dominant allele.

d 4. The actual genetic load in a population may be influenced by   **a.** the environment   **b.** mutation rates for various genes   **c.** selection   **d.** all of these.

b 5. The term first used to describe "offspring that exhibited increased fitness" was: **a.** balanced polymorphism   **b.** hybrid vigor   **c.** allele frequency   **d.** prevalence

b 6. Factors that tend to reduce or prevent gene flow between populations are called   **a.** mutagens   **b.** selectors   **c.** isolating mechanisms   **d.** population determiners.

c 7. Since one or more of the conditions of the Hardy-Weinberg Principle are violated in most natural populations, the genetic make-up   **a.** usually remains constant   **b.** is dependent upon the proportion of the two sexes   **c.** is expected to exhibit change over a period of generations   **d.** gradually takes on the dominant features as expressed through its genes.

a 8. What do mutation, genetic drift, gene flow, and selection all have in common?   **a.** all ways in which the gene pool might change   **b.** all means by which hybrids occur   **c.** all characteristics of individuals   **d.** all unique to human populations.

d 9. A recessive allele that is subject to very strong selection pressure would disappear from the population   **a.** within 100 generations   **b.** within 10 generations   **c.** within 250 generations   **d.** never.

c 10. Which one of the following genetic disorders is an example of balanced polymorphism?   **a.** diabetes   **b.** hemophilia   **c.** sickle-cell anemia   **d.** albinism.

PART 2   Matching: Match the letter of the term in Column I with its description in Column II.

COLUMN I
a. balanced polymorphism
b. sickle-cell anemia
c. differential migration
d. frequency
e. genetic drift
f. 1st Law of Probability
g. genetic load
h. Hardy-Weinberg Principle
i. random mating
j. selection

COLUMN II
f 11. The sum of the probabilities for a given chance event is equal to one

h 12. A statement that describes the conditions for genetic equilibrium

e 13. Random alteration of allelic frequency in a population due to sampling errors

c 14. Cause of alteration of allelic frequency due to population mobility

g 15. Detrimental alleles in a population

d 16. The number of times an allele occurs in a population compared to the number of times that all alleles for that gene appear

j 17. The favoring or rejecting of certain gene or allele combinations resulting in altered frequencies

a 18. Maintenance of harmful alleles in a population at unexpected frequencies

b 19. Example of balanced polymorphism in humans

i 20. One requirement for genetic equilibrium

PART 3   Completion: Complete the following.

21. Four factors that produce genetic equilibrium (unchanging allele frequencies) include ____.

22. Offspring that exhibit increased fitness have ____.

23. Sickle-cell anemia has been shown to be an hereditary disorder in humans whose frequency is related to the distribution of ____.   malaria

24. The probability that two or more chance events will occur together is equal to the multiplication product of their chances for occurring separately. This statement is known as ____.   2nd Law of Probability

25. The frequency of the dominant allele in a population of 500 individuals, 320 of whom showed the dominant phenotype, would be ____.   0.4

CHAPTER 12

HUMAN HEREDITY

The first three chapters of this unit have been devoted to basic principles of inheritance. Where possible, examples of these principles have been used as they occur in humans. Most of us are especially interested in how inheritance applies to humans. It is to this question that we now turn our full attention.

The study of other organisms, of course, has helped us in important ways. It has given us a grasp of the basic concepts of inheritance. It has helped us to appreciate several important principles of biology. *Unity and diversity* and the *continuity of life* apply as much to humans as to the rest of the living world. Studies of other organisms have also helped us to apply these principles to our advantage.

In this chapter, we will focus on a number of hereditary disorders in humans. Special attention will be given to their mode of inheritance, treatment, and prevention. Some emphasis will be placed on their costs to society and the questions such burdens raise. On a more basic level, however, you should look at the following questions:

- Why should you be concerned with hereditary disorders?
- How can you know if you are a "carrier" of a recessive disorder that you might pass on?
- What effect does modern medicine have upon the genetic load of human populations?
- Why do we often hear of some ethnic groups being more prone to certain disorders than others?

1 GENETIC DISEASE

Studying Heredity in Humans

The study of human heredity is involved. It is made difficult for several reasons. First, there is a long time between human generations. This time lag makes it hard to observe family inheritance patterns over several generations. Studying inheritance in other organisms is much easier in this regard. Fruit flies, bacteria, molds, and mice are often used in the study of genetics. We can look at many generations in a very short time period.

Second, humans have only a small number of offspring in each generation compared to other organisms. Statistical study of offspring is hampered by small numbers. Social reasons also contribute to the difficulty in studying human heredity.

In the last 25 years, a number of human disorders have been shown to be inherited. These are commonly known as genetic diseases. However, this name is somewhat inaccurate. Many of them are not strictly genetic. They often involve whole chromosomes and cannot be attributed to single genes or alleles.

Genetic disorders can be looked at as a kind of vertical disease. We often think of diseases as being horizontal. That is, when they are contagious, they are passed from one person to another within a population. But genetic disorders are passed on from parent to child, not to members of the same generation.

The Size of the Problem

Disorders that are present at birth are called congenital defects. Not all of these, however, are hereditary. Many are caused by outside factors such as infection, drugs, or radiation. In the United States alone, some 250,000 babies, or nearly 5% of all live births, are born each year with some form of birth defect. As many as 80% of these are at least or partly a result of flawed hereditary factors.

A birth defect could be defined as any change from the "normal." This might include such simple problems as birthmarks or nearsightedness. For our purposes, however, we will use the term in a more selective manner. We will include only those problems that seriously affect the way of life for the affected person.

Each of us "carry" a certain number of *deleterious* (del ə *tir* ē əs), or *harmful* alleles. As a rule, these are masked by normal, dominant alleles. The average U.S. couple runs about a 3% risk of having a genetically defective child. The risk becomes somewhat greater in certain high-risk groups. Nearly 2,000 heritable disorders are presently known. Another 75 to 100 are being added every year.

12-1. *It is estimated that each of us carries between three and ten harmful alleles. Most people are normal, however, because these alleles are usually recessive.*

12-2. *Every ethnic group has a higher frequency of certain hereditary disorders than do other groups.*

High Risk Groups

A **high-risk group** *is one whose risk for a specific disorder is higher than average.* Some of these may be grouped on the basis of parental age or ethnic origin.

Why are some groups more prone to certain disorders than others? The answer depends upon the group. Couples over the age of 35 tend to be at greater risk for having children with chromosomal disorders. This has been credited to a breakdown in the meiotic process as age increases. The mother's age has been considered more important in this regard. However, there is growing evidence that the age of the father may also be significant.

Many disorders are associated with certain ethnic groups. This is only to say that certain groups have higher frequencies of the disorder than others. Recessive mutation from the normal dominant condition may occur in any ethnic or breeding group. Indeed, a mutation is a fairly rare event. It may not be detected for several generations until two of the mutant alleles occur together in a child. Homozygotes for that disorder would be unlikely in another group unless the same mutations occurred. Even when harmful alleles enter other populations they are rare and less likely to be found in both parents.

Late-Occurring Disorders

Not all hereditary disorders are apparent at birth. Some only appear at a later time, perhaps a month or two after birth. Other disorders may appear as late as 30 or 40 years of age. Some of these genetic disorders include cystic fibrosis, muscular dystrophy, gout, and diabetes mellitus.

The time at which symptoms for a serious hereditary disease begins can be very important. Many severe problems occur early. They may prevent the individual from reproducing. This is one way that their occurrence in the population is kept at a low level. Some disorders occur after a person has already had children. They will already have passed their genes on to the next generation. In dominant disorders, each of the children will have a 50% probability of being affected. In recessive disorders, all of the children will at least be carriers.

QUESTIONS FOR SECTION 1

1. What are congenital defects, high-risk groups, and late-occurring disorders?
2. Compare and contrast the natures of contagious and hereditary diseases.
3. Why may recessive mutations take several generations to appear?
4. What factors restrict the flow of alleles between ethnic groups?
5. What factors cause serious dominant disorders to be late-occurring?

(See page 218 for answers.)

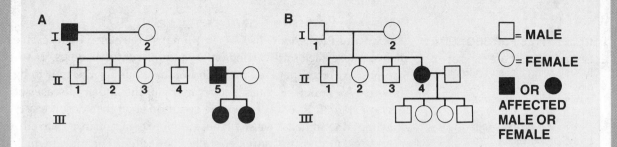

A
I 1 □■ 2 ○
II 1 □ 2 □ 3 ○ 4 □ 5 ■
III ● ●

B
I 1 □ 2 ○
II 1 □ 2 ○ 3 □ 4 ●
III □ ○ ○ □

□ = MALE
○ = FEMALE
■ OR ● AFFECTED MALE OR FEMALE

CHAPTER INVESTIGATION

There are several ways that human genetic traits can be inherited. The above pedigrees are examples of two of these modes. Example A pedigree shows a dominant mode of inheritance. Example B shows a recessive mode of inheritance. The photos below show a variety of traits. The dominant characteristic is shown in the top photo, the recessive below.

A. In pedigree A, which parent is affected? How many of their offspring are affected? How many total people are affected in the entire pedigree?

B. In the second pedigree, B, which could be an example of either phenylketonuria or sickle-cell anemia? Explain how the parents had an affected daughter when they were both normal. After marriage, the affected daughter had all normal children. Explain why none were affected.

C. Survey the class for the characteristics shown in the photos. Set up your results in chart form. Can any conclusion be drawn from your results about dominant and recessive characteristics?

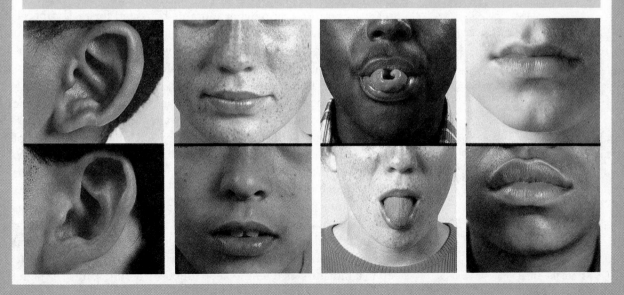

2 DISORDERS IN HUMANS

Autosomal Recessive Disorders

Most of the genetic diseases in humans are caused by recessive alleles. These alleles are carried on the non-sex chromosomes, or autosomes. Afflicted persons must be homozygous for the trait to be shown. We cannot, of course, cover many of the known diseases of this type here. But some of them are common enough to deserve specific mention. Some, as we shall see, are more common in certain ethnic groups. Others are more generally distributed. The rate at which various genes mutate varies considerably. Some mutations have been in existence longer than others. In any event, these and probably a number of other factors contribute to such differences in distribution.

PHENYLKETONURIA Phenylketonuria (fen əl kēt ən *yōōr* ē ə), or PKU, as this disease is usually called, occurs most often among people of northern European descent. Present estimates indicate that about one in 25,000 births in the U.S. is a PKU baby. Afflicted persons are characterized by mental retardation and a light skin complexion. They also often have postural problems and give off a somewhat-musty body odor.

Persons with PKU are unable to transform a certain amino acid, phenylalanine (fen əl *al* ə nēn), into another, tyrosine (*ti* rə sēn). A necessary chain of chemical events in the cells fails to occur. The build-up of phenylalanine acts as a poison to rapidly forming brain tissue. It is also responsible for the unusual body odor.

PKU can be detected at birth by a rather simple laboratory blood test. Most cases can be successfully treated if found in time. Nearly all states now require that newborn infants be tested for PKU. Special diets can be provided for afflicted children that prevent the build-up of the unwanted chemical. Treatment prevents significant brain damage, but does not cure the disease. The child is able to lead a fairly normal life as a result of proper treatment.

CYSTIC FIBROSIS Cystic fibrosis (CF) is a fairly common genetic disease among white Americans. On the average, one in every 1,500 babies in the U.S. is afflicted with this disease. Until recently, most of these children died before reaching adulthood. Today, however, with improved methods of treatment, three out of four have a fair chance of reaching maturity.

CF victims produce very salty tears and sweat. In addition, abnormal amounts of mucus are produced in the lungs and pancreas. This mucus tends to clog breathing passages and hamper the removal of foreign material from the lungs. Many CF victims are required to sleep in a moisture-rich tent to keep mucus in a fluid state. The signs and symptoms of CF have been mistaken for pneumonia, bronchitis, and malnutrition. The genetic character of the disorder is now known. However, how it produces the problem is still unknown. Present research is extensive and is aimed at finding carriers and yet-to-be born babies.

TAY SACHS DISEASE   Like PKU, Tay Sachs disease is an inborn error of metabolism. This means it is a disease in which certain chemical processes do not proceed normally. In many cases, these errors are simply the failure of the body to produce a required enzyme. Victims of Tay Sachs disease are mostly of Jewish descent whose ancestry may be traced back to central and eastern Europe. Perhaps 85% of the Jewish people of the United States are included in this group. Of these, one in 30 to 40 people are thought to be carriers of the defective allele.

Babies that inherit a defective allele from each parent fail to produce a specific blood enzyme known as Hex A. This enzyme is used in a series of reactions that metabolize certain fats. Without Hex A, a victim accumulates these fats, especially in the cells of the brain. The cells swell, rupture, and die. Affected children appear normal for the first few months of life. By the age of four to six months, the signs and symptoms of the disease become evident. The child begins to lose coordination and becomes unable to sit up, roll over, or even respond at all. Blindness and deafness develop and mental progress is lost. Death is inevitable and usually occurs around the age of two years or so.

There is no known treatment for this dreaded disease. Carriers can be identified, however, and counseled. If both parents are found to be carriers of the defective allele, there are still three chances in four that they can have normal children. Two of these, of course, will be carriers. But they themselves will not be affected. To summarize, 25% of the children of parents who are both carriers for an autosomal recessive disorder will be homozygous for the normal condition. Fifty percent will be "carriers" and 25% will exhibit the disorder.

SICKLE-CELL ANEMIA   Mention of this blood disorder has already been made in Chapter 11. It bears mention here because of its connection with people from malarial areas of the world. It affects about one in every 400 black Americans. In spite of its inclusion here, it is not truly a recessive disorder. The defective allele is actually codominant with the normal allele. Under certain conditions, a heterozygous person does produce varying numbers of sickled cells. Such persons are said to have the sickle-cell *trait.* They should avoid activities such as SCUBA diving, high altitude flying in unpressurized planes, and hiking at high altitudes. Otherwise, heterozygotes may lead a fairly normal life. The homozygote, however, suffers from sickle-cell

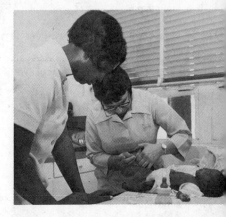

12-3. *Most states require that newborn babies be tested for PKU.*

Answers to Questions for Section 2.
E. 1. **Autosomal recessive:** (1) PKU, a metabolic disorder (the inability to transform phenylalanine into tyrosine); mental retardation, light skin; postural problems; and musty odor. (2) CF, a metabolic disorder (production of very salty tears and sweat, and abnormal amounts of mucus); excessive mucus in pancreas as well as lungs. (3) Tay Sachs: Fats accumulate in brain; lack of coordination, and vision: death before 2. **Autosomal dominant:** (1) Achondroplasia: dwarfism; abnormally short arms and legs; and premature death. (2) Polydactyly: extra fingers or toes. (3) HD: after age 30; progressive motor and mental deterioration; fatal. **Sex-linked:** (1) Hemophilia: failure of blood to clot. (2) Red-green color-blindness. (3) Muscular dystrophy. **Chromosomal.** (1) Down syndrome: extra chromosome in 21st pair; Mental retardation, protruding tongue and lower lip, and unique fold on eyes. (2) Kleinefelter's Syndrome: XXY makeup, male, mentally sub-normal, sterile. (3) Turner's Syndrome. XO make-up; female: short, with webbed neck: sterile.

TABLE 12-1.

Incidence of the Rh factor in humans.	
Ethnic Group	**% Rh negative**
Basques (Spain)	34
American Whites	15
Japanese, Chinese, American Blacks	9
American Indians, African Blacks, Eskimos	<1

anemia. Medical treatment has enabled victims of sickle-cell to lead a somewhat normal life. Like other genetic disorders, however, it cannot be cured.

Rh DISEASE   *Erythroblastosis fetalis* (i rith rə blas *tō* səs fēt *al* əs) is a disease of the newborn that is more commonly called Rh disease. It is due to a mismatch of a blood component between parents. This component is an *antigen* called the *Rh factor*. A person is said to be Rh-positive if the factor is present, and negative if it is absent. The incidence of the Rh factor varies widely in different ethnic groups. (See Table 12-1.) Over all, nearly one marriage in eight is a potentially dangerous mismatch with respect to the Rh factor. However, only about one marriage in 160 actually produces an "Rh baby."

The Rh factor is produced by a dominant allele. Those without the factor are homozygous recessive. Problems arise only when the mother is Rh-negative and the unborn child is positive. If the father

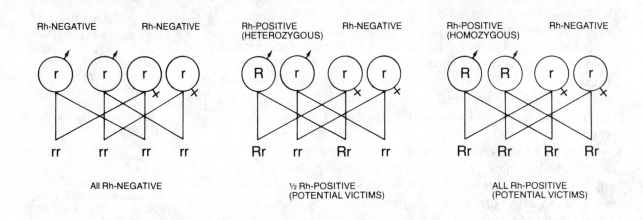

12-4. Diagram of the possible inheritance of Rh blood type.

donates a dominant allele, the baby will be positive. (See Fig. 12-4.) Antigens from a positive baby may sometimes pass into the blood of the mother. If this happens, the mother's body reacts to the foreign antigens by producing *antibodies*. This immune system works in much the same way that the body defends itself against invading disease.

Normally, there are not enough antibodies produced in the mother's blood by the time of birth to affect the first infant. But antibodies may still be present when another Rh-positive child is conceived. If this happens, antibodies may enter the baby's blood and begin to destroy its blood cells. Rh disease results in as many as 5,000 stillbirths annually in the United States. Another 20,000 babies are affected with anemia, heart failure, and/or mental retardation.

Some babies are successfully treated with complete blood transfusions. This can be done at birth or even while the baby is still in the womb. More recently, however, a new technique has been developed for preventing Rh problems. Rh-negative mothers are treated with a protein substance within 72 hours after the birth of the first Rh-positive child. This treatment prevents the production of the antibodies by the mother that cause the problem. Such techniques should significantly reduce the number of Rh babies.

Autosomal Dominant Disorders

Genetic diseases that result from the inheritance of a dominant allele produce a characteristic pedigree. (See Fig. 12-5.) *A pedigree diagram is a picture that shows the pattern of inheritance for an hereditary disorder in a family.* Unless the disorder is a new mutation, every affected child will have at least one affected parent. The preva-

Answers to Questions for Section 2.
  2. Autosomal recessive, autosomal dominant, sex-linked, and chromosomal.
  *3. Non-disjunction during meiosis leads to XXY, XO, or XYY in the sex chromosomes; or to trisomy of the 21st pair in autosomes.
F. *4. An antigen is a substance that stimulates the production by the body of antibodies, formed in reaction to the antigen.
G. 5. Diagram as in Fig. 12-4.
  6. There are not enough antibodies produced in mother's blood by time of the first baby's birth.
  7. By blood transfusion, and treatment with protein that prevents antibody production.

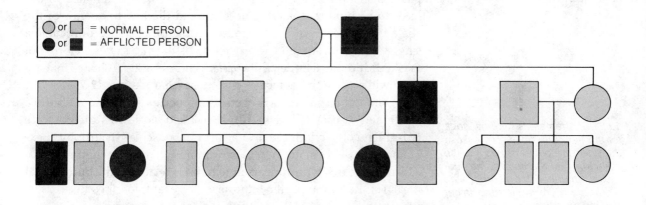

= NORMAL PERSON
= AFFLICTED PERSON

lence of these dominant disorders remains fairly low, just as in those of recessive origin. This is due to the selective pressures that tend to reduce their transmission to the next generation.

One form of dwarfism, *achondroplasia* (ā kon drə *pl*ā zhē ə), appears as a dominant disorder. Affected persons have unusually short arms and legs. Although a few victims reach maturity, most do not. Over 80% of the known cases arise as new mutations. (See Fig. 12-6 on page 222.)

Polydactyly, the appearance of extra fingers or toes, is also a disorder of dominant inheritance. It is one of the few dominant disorders that appears in various ethnic groups with variable frequency. The extra digit is usually removed by surgery to make life easier for the affected individual.

12-5. Victims of a dominant disorder have at least one affected parent unless the disorder is a new mutation.

Answers to Questions for Section 2.
  *8. The disease is not transmitted through genes or chromosomes.
H. *9. See Teacher's Guide Section for Chapter 11 for answer.
  *10. They must receive the defective genes from their fathers who must not be so disabled by the disorder that they do not produce children.

12-6. Anchondroplasia is a form of dwarfism inherited by a dominant allele.

12-7. The female is heterozygous for the trait. She does not possess the disorder, but transmits it to the male on the X-chromosome. Females may inherit the disorder if the mother is a carrier and the father has the disorder.

Dominant disorders of a very serious nature often occur late in life. Transmission to the next generation occurs because symptoms do not show up in the parent until after having children.

Among the dominant disorders that do not appear until later in life is *Huntington's Disease* (HD), also known as Huntington's chorea. The first symptoms do not usually appear until the age of 30 or later. HD is a progressive disorder that affects the nervous system. Victims exhibit uncoordinated movements and progressive mental decline, ending in death. Death comes slowly, sometimes taking ten to twenty years. Treatment is not very satisfactory, and victims cannot be recognized until the onset of symptoms. Research is now being done to find both a means of treatment and perhaps a means of finding victims early.

Sex-Linked Disorders

Recessive alleles carried on the X chromosome may result in sex-linked disorders. The frequency of such alleles is fairly low. Thus, the problem is normally found only in males. Affected females would have to be homozygous for the trait, and the low frequency of the allele usually prevents this. Males, on the other hand, only have a single X chromosome. The existence of the recessive allele is not masked, and the disorder will appear. There is a 50-50 chance that the male will receive the defective chromosome. (See Fig. 12-7.)

Hemophilia has already been mentioned as a classic example of a sex-linked disease (Chapter 10). Also included in this category are red-green color-blindness and a form of muscular dystrophy. Sex-linked disorders are not necessarily limited to males. Whether or not a disorder of this type appears in females is related to the burden that it carries. Red-green color-blindness, for example, does not carry a very great burden. Males with this disorder outnumber females by

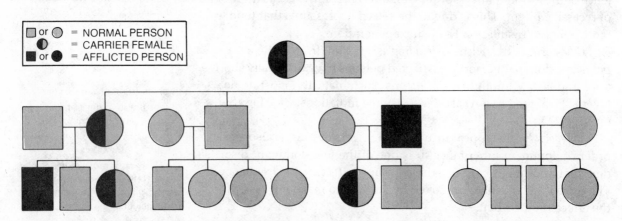

□ or ◯ = NORMAL PERSON
◑ = CARRIER FEMALE
■ or ● = AFFLICTED PERSON

only sixteen to one. At the other extreme, hemophilia is almost unknown in females (although it does occur). Male victims of muscular dystrophy are 100 times more common than females.

Chromosomal Disorders

Chromosomal abnormalities involve whole chromosomes, or at least whole segments of them. They are not genetic in that they are not a result of specific gene action. But they are hereditary for the most part. Chromosome disorders may be caused by translocations, deletions, duplications, or nondisjunction (Chapter 10).

Certain types of disorders occur more often than others. These are shown by well-known signs and symptoms. The term **syndrome** *is often given to a group of defects that routinely occur together as a result of a single, underlying problem.* Many genes appear on a given chromosome. Thus, a large-scale effect can be expected if a chromosome is missing or duplicated. Hence, problems that result from chromosome errors are often referred to as syndromes. These disorders often carry the name of the person that first described them officially.

Most chromosome defects are so severe that a miscarriage occurs during the early months of the pregnancy. However, some babies with major problems do survive to full term. Many of the defects are so severe, however, that the child lives only a few months. Others may live ten to thirty years or more.

DOWN SYNDROME   Down Syndrome, in most cases, is a result of an extra chromosome. The karyotype shows 47 chromosomes and is also known as Trisomy-21 due to the appearance of the third chromosome in the 21st pair. (See Fig. 12-8.) Persons with Down Syndrome are mentally retarded. They also have a protruding tongue and lower lip and possess a unique fold in the inner corners of the eyes. People diagnosed as having Down Syndrome are often, though not always, sterile. Thus, afflicted children nearly always come from normal parents. The breakdown of the meiotic process has been related to the age of the parents. Above the age of 35 parents seem to run an increasing risk that non-disjunction will occur. (See Fig. 12-9.) Until recently the breakdown of meiosis was thought to occur only in the female parent. Evidence is now beginning to show that the father may also bear some responsibility in this regard.

KLINEFELTER'S and TURNER'S SYNDROMES   Klinefelter's and Turner's Syndromes are due to non-disjunction involving the sex chromosomes. In the first case, the affected person has an *XXY* chromosome make-up. Its occurrence has been associated with increased parental age as in Down Syndrome. Hence, the affected person is a male with 47 chromosomes. Klinefelter males are typically long-limbed,

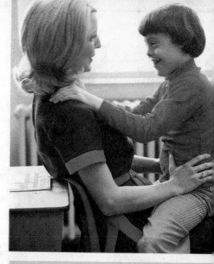

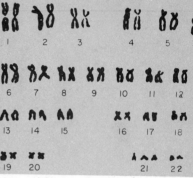

12-8. *Down Syndrome is caused by a trisomy in the 21st chromosome pair.*

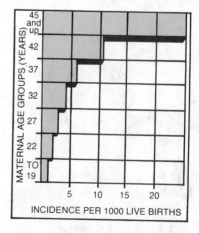

12-9. *Many chromosomal disorders, such as Down Syndrome, have been associated with parental age.*

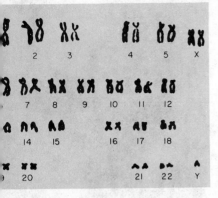

12-10. *Karyotype for Klinefelter's Syndrome.*

mentally sub-normal, and possess underdeveloped male features. Nearly all are sterile. (See Fig. 12-10 on page 224.)

Turner's Syndrome occurs when an offspring possesses an X chromosome without a second sex chromosome. These females (*XO*) are characterized by a short stature, a peculiar webbing of the neck, and sometimes a lower than normal intelligence. Those with Turner's Syndrome may go unrecognized until adolescence when they fail to reach maturity. Although sexual characteristics can be developed with hormone treatment, these persons remain sterile. (See Fig. 12-11.)

Some mention should probably be made of the *XYY* chromosome condition. It may occur as often as one in every 300 male births. Because of the extra Y chromosome, this condition has unofficially been called the "supermale syndrome." An early study showed that *XYY* males tended to be taller than average, aggressive, emotionally unstable, of low intelligence, and often given to violence. More data has tended to dispute these early conclusions, however. The large majority of males with an *XYY* make-up do not fit the common criminal picture. Male children of *XYY* fathers usually have a normal *XY* complement.

Other chromosomal disorders are less common. An extra chromosome in several pairs are known and are somewhat similar to Down Syndrome. The cat-cry syndrome is caused by a deletion in one arm of the 5th chromosome. Victims are mentally retarded, have many physical defects, and produce a peculiar cry much like that of a kitten. While some of these are associated with parental age, not all are so related. Much research remains to be done to understand the causes of chromosomal problems.

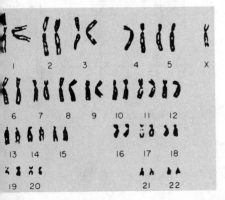

12-11. *Karyotype for Turner's Syndrome.*

QUESTIONS FOR SECTION 2

1. List and describe at least three examples of the following types of hereditary disorders: autosomal recessive, autosomal dominant, sex-linked, and chromosomal.
2. List four general categories of hereditary disorders.
3. How are chromosomal disorders related to the meiotic process?
4. Define and differentiate between the terms antigen and antibody.
5. Make a series of charts to show the possible inheritance patterns for the Rh blood factor.
6. Explain why the first Rh-positive child of an Rh-negative mother is not usually affected by Rh disease.
7. How is modern medicine helping to reduce the incidence of Rh disease?
8. Explain why Rh disease is not really an hereditary disease although it is related to inheritance.
9. Make a chart to show how a female might inherit a sex-linked disorder.
10. Explain why females are more likely to inherit a sex-linked disorder if its burden is not great.

(See pages 219 and 221 for answers.)

3 TREATMENT AND PREVENTION OF BIRTH DEFECTS

Approach

It is difficult to prevent the occurrence of birth defects. We will always be subjected to mutations, spontaneous chromosomal damage or other unknown factors. We can, however, go a long way toward reducing the impact of congenital problems.

There are essentially six ways that the problems of prevention and treatment can be approached. This can be done by: (1) finding high-risk pregnancies or potential pregnancies; (2) screening populations for carriers of harmful disorders; (3) screening newborn infants for identifiable defects; (4) using special methods for finding affected babies while still in the womb; (5) providing genetic counseling to parents about the patterns and risks for genetic disease; and (6) giving therapy to relieve affected persons of signs or symptoms of defects.

Special Procedures

During the 1950's genetic research took a giant leap forward. It suddenly became possible to identify some congenital disorders prior to the birth of the baby. Today, nearly one hundred heritable disorders can be found in this manner. The technique involves the removal of a small amount of fluid from the sac surrounding the yet unborn child, or fetus. This process is called *amniocentesis* (am nē ō sen *tē* səs). The fluid contains cells from the baby's body. These cells are carefully cultured and later studied in a variety of ways. (See Fig. 12-12 on page 226.)

Amniocentesis and testing procedures are most effective if performed soon after the 14th week of pregnancy. By this time fetal development is far enough along to allow detection of many defects.

Other tests have also been developed that help to find disorders in the unborn. High frequency sound (*ultra-sound*) waves can be used to get an image of the child in the womb. Blood samples can be taken if necessary. Even X rays can be used as a last resort to diagnose problems. Photographs of the fetus using special light fibers can be taken in certain instances. Constant research helps to expand the means to identify problems as early as possible.

Counseling and High-Risk Groups

Genetic counseling is one of the fastest growing areas in the health sciences. The knowledge explosion in this field in the last thirty years has been amazing. Today, genetic counselors have a critical role in the treatment and prevention of birth disorders.

OBJECTIVES FOR SECTION 3

I. Distinguish between curing and treating heritable disorders. List six means by which such problems can be treated or prevented.

J. Describe the process of amniocentesis. Explain how it might be used to prevent heritable disorders.

K. Describe various aspects of the role of a genetic counselor.

L. Identify the issue surrounding the use of recombinant DNA. Criticize the various points of view.

A number of pamphlets, brochures, filmstrips and films on the treatment and prevention of birth defects are available from the March of Dimes. Most of these are free.

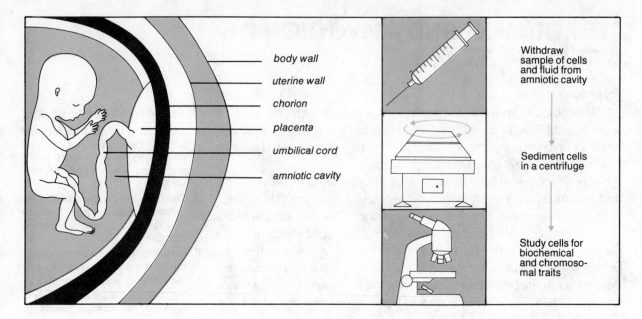

- body wall
- uterine wall
- chorion
- placenta
- umbilical cord
- amniotic cavity

Withdraw sample of cells and fluid from amniotic cavity

Sediment cells in a centrifuge

Study cells for biochemical and chromosomal traits

12-12. Amniocentesis is becoming a very powerful aid in diagnosing genetic conditions in the fetus.

Statistics indicate that an affected fetus is found in less than 10% of all amniocenteses. Thus, the procedure is clearly of value in allaying fears in 90% of the couples where potential problems exist. Even where an affected fetus is found, couples can, with the aid of a genetic counselor, come to grips with the problem in advance and make proper preparations.

One of the counselor's duties is to study the inheritance pattern of hereditary disorders. (See Fig. 12-13.) Many counselors also direct testing (screening) programs to detect carriers of the harmful alleles. The search for these alleles is aided by a knowledge of which groups are at highest risk for the disorder.

Rh-negative mothers whose husbands are positive for the Rh factor is one example of a high-risk group. Parents with family histories of heritable disorders represent another group with significant risk. The search for certain recessive alleles may be confined to specific ethnic groups. Sickle-cell anemia and Tay Sachs disease are examples in this category that have already been mentioned. In these diseases, carriers may be found before they have children. Even where the counselor cannot identify carriers in a population, he or

12-13. Genetic counselor studies the inheritance pattern of various disorders.

she may still play a major role. Many times, early treatment, as in the case of PKU, can help prevent many of the problems.

Not all heritable disorders can be found in the carrier as yet. In some late-occurring disorders, such as HD, affected persons cannot be identified prior to the onset of symptoms. Much research is needed at this time to find safe, reliable and low-cost screening techniques for more of these disorders.

Therapy for Heritable Disorders

There are essentially three methods by which congenital defects can be treated. Note that none of these really cure the problem. The hope is that the affected person will be made able to lead a more normal life. These methods include (1) chemical regulation, (2) surgery, and (3) rehabilitation.

Some disorders, such as PKU and diabetes, are the result of metabolic imbalances. Often, they result from a single defective allele. Sometimes, the missing chemical can be added to the body as in the case of using insulin to treat diabetes. Other imbalances may be treated by placing the patient on special diets that avoid certain foods. Treatment of PKU and Wilson's disease (an inability to metabolize copper) fall into this category.

Corrective surgery may be used for certain structural problems. Clubfoot, cleft lip and some heart malformations may be treated in this manner. For many of these disorders, the actual cause may not be known. (See Fig. 12-14.)

Genetic Surgery

The only way to cure a genetic disease is to alter the gene itself. The prospect of changing improper DNA segments is a highly controversial subject. There are three types of possible genetic surgery. The first type, *transformation*, involves taking DNA from one organism

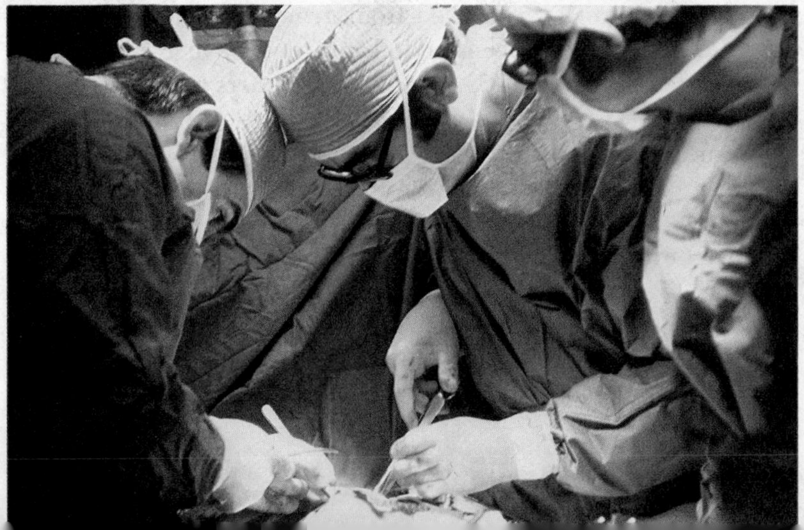

Ask students why these therapeutic measures do not *cure* a congenital disorder.

12-14. Surgery can benefit many victims of congenital disorders.

*7. Biochemical test for certain
suspected substances. Chromosomal
studies, such as the development
of a karyotype.

K. 8. To study the inheritance pattern
of heritable disorders, direct screening programs for carriers, identify
defects in time for early, preventive
treatment.

*9. Treatment cannot change the
genes that will be passed on to the
offspring of the affected person
or carrier.

10. DNA segments exchanged between organisms of different
speicies.

11. A proper DNA segment from a
donor might be combined with the
DNA in a bacterium, which is then
used to "infect" the patient who
has a defective DNA sequence,
replacing the defective genes with
normal ones.

*12. Answers will vary. Discussion
should bring out that one point
in favor of the research is the
possibility of curing genetic diseases. A point against the research
is the hazard posed by accidental
infection from recombinants used
in the research.

L. *13. Answers will vary, and depend
upon current information from
student research.

*14. Genetic counseling may be
needed by persons unaware of or
unsure of being carriers of defective
genes. The hazards as well as
possible benefits of recombinant
DNA research must be considered
whenever public opinion (through
legislation or otherwise) affects
scientific research.

Students often enjoy debating a
topic of such controversial nature.
Will modern medical practices lead
or contribute to the extinction of
the human species?

and combining it with the DNA of another organism. A second type, *transduction*, involves the transfer of DNA by viral particles. The patient would then be "infected" with the carrying agent. The intent would be to have the bacterium or virus transfer the proper segment to the patient's cells. If this worked, the patient could then produce the desired gene product for his or her body. In each of the above cases, however, there is present difficulty in obtaining the desired defective sequence of DNA from the donor.

A third type of surgery uses certain chemicals that act on only certain sections of DNA. It is hoped that the specific nucleotides will then be changed in a desirable direction.

The new DNA segment can actually become part of the cells in the defective organ or tissue. In this case, the patient would be cured. However, the reproductive cells must receive the correct DNA sequence. If not, the disorder could still be transmitted to their children.

The DNA segments exchanged between organisms of different species is known as **recombinant DNA.** Research involving recombinant DNA poses a serious potential hazard that has not been overlooked. Recombinants used in research might accidentally enter the environment. Death-dealing epidemics with no known cures could result. Scientists have acted to set strict guidelines on the use of these organisms to help guard against such potential dangers. In spite of the problems, research in this area holds a promise for the future. Many genetic disorders and even cancer may be able to be treated with recombinant DNA.

Genetic Load

We have benefited greatly from the medical advances of the last 50 years, or even the last century. We enjoy greater longevity, reduced infant mortality, and lives generally free from the threat of many serious diseases. But medical advances have also helped to increase the supply of harmful alleles in the human population. Many who might normally have died from genetic disorders have been saved. Some of these have lived full and productive lives. But many affected with diabetes, PKU, and other disorders have married and produced children with the same defective alleles. Without medical help, most hereditary diseases would reach a balance in the gene pool. Technology, then, has contributed to the genetic load among humans.

Presently, many so-called harmful alleles have little or no effect upon the lives of their owners. Some debate might even be made that some of these could even be an advantage under certain future conditions. For example, the sickle-cell alleles confers a resistance to malaria when in the heterozygous state.

QUESTIONS FOR SECTION 3

1. Distinguish between curing and treating heritable disorders.
2. How does treatment of heritable disorders tend to increase the genetic load on a population?
3. List six means by which hereditary disorders can be treated and/or prevented.
4. Describe the process of amniocentesis.
5. How can amniocentesis contribute to the prevention of heritable disorders?
6. What is the purpose of amniocentesis?
7. What kinds of tests can be performed on cells in amniocentesis to identify genetic disorders?
8. Describe the variety of duties performed by a genetic counselor.
9. Explain how treatment and/or counseling in the event of a heritable disorder does not prevent its transmission to the next generation.
10. What is recombinant DNA?
11. How might recombinant DNA be used to cure a genetic disorder?
12. Discuss and criticize the various points of view regarding DNA research.
13. Research the question of recombinant DNA to discover what safeguards are being implemented to prevent the escape of potential harmful bacteria and viruses.
14. Why is it important that laypersons be aware of topics such as genetic counseling and recombinant DNA research?

Answers to Questions for Section 3.

I. 1. The disorders are not really curable, but may be treated to help person lead more normal life.

2. Many who might have died before having children are now saved, and they pass their harmful alleles on to the next generation.

3. Finding high-risk pregnancies; screening populations for carriers; screening newborn infants; finding affected babies while in the womb; genetic counseling: therapy of affected persons.

J. 4. Fluid is removed from sac around fetus; cells of baby from fluid are cultured and studied.

*5. In certain cases, treatment for heritable disorders can begin before birth.

6. The detection of heritable disorders prior to the birth of the baby.

(See more answers on page 228.)

CHAPTER REVIEW

In the past, the application of genetic knowledge to humans has been difficult. Many reasons may be cited for this. In recent years, we have begun to be aware of the tremendous impact that hereditary disorders have upon our lives. *So great is this impact that continuity from one generation to the next may be disturbed.* To control such disturbances we must know how they occur.

Basic concepts in genetic studies of many plants and animals are useful in studying humans. We have learned about the kinds of patterns that we can also expect to find in humans. *This unity of pattern emphasizes the concept of unity and diversity in the living world.* It enables us to predict patterns in humans and thereby exert some control over their occurrence.

The unity of pattern has its roots in the hereditary material itself. This fact may help us to eventually be able to cure, rather than simply treat or prevent, genetic disorders.

Unanswered Question

1. Considering the nature of the *XYY* syndrome, what approach should be taken by society towards these individuals?

Career Question

2. What kind of training is required to become a genetic counselor?

VOCABULARY REVIEW

1 congenital defect
high-risk group
2 pedigree

antigen
antibody

syndrome
3 amniocentesis

CHAPTER 12 TEST

Copy the number of each test item and place your answer to the right.

PART 1 Multiple Choice: Select the letter of the phrase that best completes each of the following.

c 1. For an autosomal dominant disorder, the probability of an affected child being born to a family (in which one parent showed the trait) would be about **a.** 0 **b.** 25% **c.** 50% **d.** 75%.

b 2. Some ethnic groups have unusually high frequencies of certain genetic disorders. This means that **a.** no other groups possess that trait **b.** other groups also have the disorder but the frequency is less **c.** many members of that ethnic group carry a defective allele for the trait **d.** some groups are more prone to genetic disorders.

d 3. One promising area of research for curing genetic disorders lies in **a.** developing specialized diets for affected people **b.** more specialized counseling **c.** special surgical procedures **d.** recombinant DNA.

d 4. In genetic disorders treated by restricting the individual to a specific diet, the diet **a.** alters the gene for the defect to the normal form **b.** renders the gene inactive **c.** destroys the poisons that cause the problem **d.** prevents the build-up of harmful chemicals.

c 5. Down Syndrome may be identified through the use of **a.** ultrasound therapy **b.** blood tests **c.** karyotypes **d.** throat cultures.

d 6. If the mother is color-blind and the father is normal, what is the probability that the children will be color-blind? **a.** 0% **b.** 50% of the boys **c.** 50% of the girls **d.** 100% of the boys.

a 7. An autosomal recessive disorder of humans that results in an inborn error of metabolism is **a.** PKU **b.** polydactyly **c.** Huntington's Disease **d.** hemophilia

a 8. Non-disjunction may be seen at one time or another in **a.** sex chromosomes only **b.** autosomes only **c.** both sex chromosomes and autosomes **d.** neither sex chromosomes nor autosomes.

d 9. A late-occurring genetic disorder may present a special problem because it **a.** is usually recessive **b.** is usually sex-linked **c.** will be inherited by all of the children **d.** may have already been passed on to the children by the time the affected person learns he or she has it.

d 10. Genetic disorders in humans are **a.** extremely rare **b.** unpredictable **c.** usually associated with the sex chromosomes **d.** not respecters of race, creed, sex, or age.

PART 2 Matching: Match the letter of the term in Column I with its description in Column II.

COLUMN I

a. amniocentesis **f.** developmental disorder
b. autosomal dominant **g.** sex-linked disorder
c. autosomal recessive **h.** high risk group
d. chromosomal disorder **i.** late-occurring disorder
e. congenital defect **j.** pedigree

COLUMN II

e 11. Disorders present at birth

j 12. Diagram showing the pattern of inheritance in a family

a 13. Procedure to remove fluid from the fetal sac to test for various types of disorders

b 14. Inherited disorder that appears in all individuals having even a single allele for it

f 15. Type of defect caused by an environmental factor during pregnancy

d 16. Disorder resulting from non-disjunction

c 17. Inherited disorder requiring presence of two alleles for it to appear in offspring

g 18. Inheritable disorder carried by (but not usually affecting) females

h 19. Population in which the expected rate for a disorder is higher than normal

i 20. Disorders that do not appear immediately at birth and may even be delayed many years

PART 3 Completion: Complete the following.

21. Hemophilia is a disease caused by an allele which is ____. sex-linked recessive

22. If one person in 50 is a carrier of an allele for an autosomal recessive disorder, then the number of affected persons in the population would be about ____. 10,000

23. Carriers of certain hereditary disorders in a population may be identified by ____. screening

24. Chromosomal disorders are probably results of improper division of cells during ____. meiosis

25. Hereditary disorders have impact on our lives because ____. Continuity from one generation to the next may be disturbed.

HISTORY OF LIFE

The variety of living things on Earth is truly astounding. How did such variety come about? This unit will explore some of the possible answers to this question. That organisms do change is a conclusion based on extensive studies of the fossil record as well as existing plants and animals. This conclusion, however, is not shared by all scientists. We will look first at the development of the modern theory of evolution to understand what it is and what it is not. We will then examine the evidence for this concept. It is important to keep in mind that such explanations are theories, not facts. Many but not all scientists feel that these conclusions answer the question of *how* in a satisfactory manner.

Having studied a model for change, we will then consider the fossil record as an outgrowth of that model. Finally, the idea of relatedness among life forms sets up a basis for developing a classification system. Such a system provides us with some degree of order in a highly diverse world of organisms.

EARLY ROCK PAINTINGS

CHAPTER 13

THEORIES OF CHANGE

"A living group is but a link between a dead ancestry and an unborn progeny." This perceptive comment by Sir Arthur Keith underscores the continuity of life theme. In the last unit, we emphasized this continuity. To be sure, cats do come only from other cats. We have seen, however, that these cats are not exactly like their parents. The mechanisms that produce variety among organisms are constantly at work. This brings up two important questions. Can changes occur in the basic characteristics of organisms through these mechanisms? Do new kinds of organisms result from these changes? The answer to both of these questions is usually yes. But this only raises a new and highly significant question: HOW? It is to this question that we now turn our attention.

The continuity of life is an important concept in this chapter as it was in the last unit. That organisms *change through time* is the second and most important concept in this chapter. A third concept, the *interaction of organism and environment*, also begins to take on new meaning. This is the biologist's way of saying that an organism is adapted to its environment. An understanding of how these concepts fit together is important. Without this, it is difficult to give an orderly account of living things.

When you were young, you may have read stories about how the leopard got his spots. Others may have read about how the elephant got his long nose. Today, you recognize these stories for what they are — fantasies. Even so, you may wonder how such things might really have come about. On the practical side, you might be interested in answering such questions as:

- Can we observe significant changes today?
- How do organisms adapt to their environments?

POLAR BEARS IN THE SNOW

◻ DEVELOPMENT OF AN IDEA

Early Views

Most humans are concerned with learning about their environment in some way. As they do so, they are constantly classifying and cataloging their knowledge about things. Perhaps this very trait has enabled us to understand our surroundings. Too, we can transmit this understanding to later generations in a non-genetic way. Even members of primitive societies can identify and classify hundreds of plants and animals. Are such activities dictated solely by a need to survive? Psychologists tell us that we also have a basic need for orderliness and structure in our environment. This need may help us to cope with what otherwise would be chaos.

Early Greek philosophers were concerned about the similarities and differences between living things. As early as the sixth century B.C., they had begun to identify and classify the elements of the natural world. Later, Aristotle (384-322 B.C.) established a system for classifying organisms. This system was used for many centuries. Plants were grouped on a functional basis. For example they were regarded as being trees, shrubs, or herbs. Animals were viewed on the basis of their respective habitats. These living spaces were either the air, water, or land. There were difficulties with such a system, however, as Aristotle recognized. He knew that the whale is structurally more like a mammal than a fish. Thus it seemed to be more closely related to land animals. This concept of relatedness gives us some clues that certain organisms may share a common ancestor.

At the end of the 18th Century, some people began to be more tolerant of the idea of change. Prior to this time, most people believed that all kinds of plants and animals had been placed on the earth at its beginning. Moreover, none had ever become extinct. This idea was known as the "fixity of species." However, it was gradually challenged. The discovery and study of fossils, for example, suggested that species had indeed changed. Some naturalists even suggested that a gradual change in living creatures might have occurred. Such views, however, were not popular.

Inheritance of Acquired Characteristics

In the early 19th Century, Jean Baptiste Lamarck further developed the idea of change through time. He attempted to account for changes observed in the fossil record. His theory rested on two main assumptions. He assumed that parts of the body that were used became more developed than those that were not used. For example, muscles that were used would become larger and more developed. The reverse would also hold. Parts that were not used would become

It is important to note that the observations of natural philosophers such as Aristotle, and their rational approach to the study of nature had great impact upon modern science even though their conclusions were often erroneous.

Answers to Questions for Section 1.

A. 1. Aristotle: established a system for classifying organisms, and recognized relatedness between different species. Lamarck: developed idea of change through time.

B. 2. Parts of the body that were used would become more developed and those not used, less developed. Example: Giraffe that stretched its neck to reach food developed a longer neck.

3. Organisms can pass on traits they gain over a lifetime. Example: the giraffe would pass on to its offspring its longer neck.

4. Body structures changed by environmental influences do not alter the genes, which are all that can be passed to the next generation.

Broken down, Lamarck's theory about how organisms changed had three parts: a need or at least a specific cause, use and disuse of various parts, and the inheritance of acquired features.

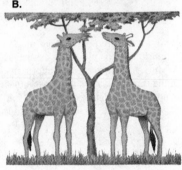

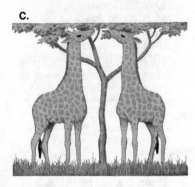

13-1. Lamarck's hypothesis. A. Short-necked ancestors. B. Offspring with longer necks. C. Modern giraffes with very long necks.

smaller. This would occur even to the point of complete disappearance. This first assumption is known today as Lamarck's "Law of Use and Disuse."

The second assumption pointed out that organisms could pass on the traits they had gained over a lifetime. This second point was known as the "Law of Inheritance of Acquired Characteristics." This produced the major flaw in Lamarck's reasoning. In practice, such happenings would cause athletes to be able to pass on acquired physical development to their children. We can use Lamarck's example of the giraffe to illustrate these two "laws" in action. (See Fig. 13-1.)

Lamarck assumed that giraffes evolved from short-necked ancestors. These ancestors, for some reason, had a need to reach the leaves that were in trees nearly out of reach. A lifetime of stretching to reach food caused their necks to become longer. The offspring of these giraffes would inherit the slightly longer neck of their parents. According to the theory, over many generations these animals became the long-necked giraffes we know today.

A number of experiments have been done to show the impossibility of change in a Lamarckian sense. One classic experiment involved the removal of the tails of successive generations of mice. Twenty generations later, there had still been no change in the lengths of the tails of the adult mice. Traits are passed from parents to offspring by way of genes. Body structures changed by environmental influences do not alter the genes. In fact, we know from the last unit that just the reverse is true. Only changes in gene structure, that is, mutations, can alter traits in the offspring. This may result in change through time.

QUESTIONS FOR SECTION 1

1. Identify one contribution with respect to the theory of evolution for each of the following: Aristotle, Lamarck.
2. State and give one example of Lamarck's Law of Use and Disuse.
3. State and give an example of Lamarck's Law of Inheritance of Acquired Characteristics.
4. What was the critical flaw in Lamarck's reasoning?

(See page 233 for answers to questions.)

CHAPTER INVESTIGATION

A. Match the head of the bird shown with the type of feet it most likely possesses.

B. For each picture explain why there are examples of adaptation to the environment that illustrate the concept of complementarity of structure and function.

C. Research to find examples of adaptation of the following animals to their environment: deer, badger, bullfrog, shark, lizard, praying mantis.

 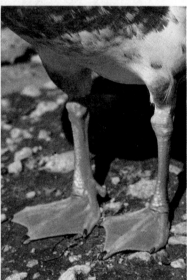 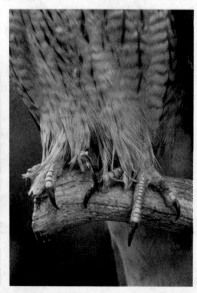

2 NATURAL SELECTION

Charles Darwin and His Voyage

Larmarck's views as to why species had changed did not cause much of a stir among the biologists of the day. However, only a short time later, Charles Darwin was to propose another theory. This theory would excite the imagination of the scientific world.

In 1831, Darwin managed to secure a position on the H.M.S. *Beagle* as the ship's unpaid naturalist. He traveled along the coast of South America. (See Fig. 13-2.) Quite often he went ashore to explore the new land. Darwin was deeply impressed by the observations he made during the five-year voyage. His observations convinced him that species did, in fact, change. Three of these observations were particularly important.

First, he had found giant fossil animals that closely resembled modern armadillos. **Fossils** *are any evidences of organisms that lived in the past.* In this case, Darwin had found the bones of animals that were now apparently *extinct*. This is to say, that at least all known examples had passed out of existence. However, there did seem to be some relationship between the fossils and existing forms. (See Fig. 13-4.)

The young naturalist was equally impressed with his second observation. As the voyage proceeded southward, he noticed that some species were gradually replaced by closely related ones. Gradual

13-2. The voyage of the Beagle brought Darwin into contact with a wide variety of plants and animals in a wide variety of environments.

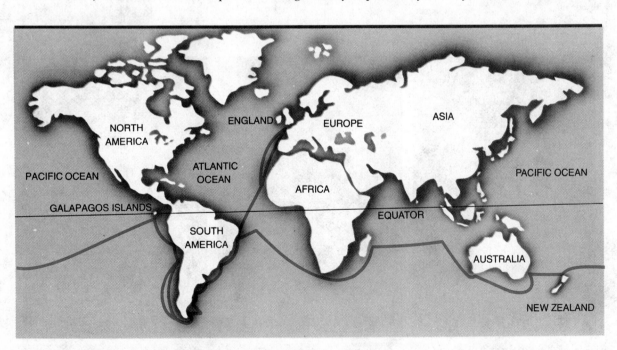

changes in latitude seemed to be related to changes in the environments. The life forms in these environments changed accordingly. Similar niches seemed to be filled by similar kinds of organisms. Moreover, these organisms often appeared to be closely related.

Darwin's third important observation was that of the unique character of life on the Galapagos Islands. These islands are located off the west coast of South America. The giant tortoises differed slightly from island to island. (See Fig. 13-5.) However, they were of the same species. The finches were all quite similar. But they differed sharply in the shapes of their beaks. The similar-yet-different character of life on the Galapagos Islands made a lasting impression on Darwin.

Natural Selection

Darwin was convinced species did change over time. How they did so, however, still required an explanation. For several years after returning from his voyage, Darwin studied his data on other subjects.

In 1842 Darwin finally turned his full attention to the question of how living things change through time. For the first time, he prepared a short paper. In it, he outlined the basic mechanisms that he thought were involved. He worried that his evidence was not yet convincing. Hence, he did not publish his ideas. Sixteen years later he received a momentous letter. It was from Alfred Russell Wallace who was then in southeast Asia. Wallace, like Darwin, had noticed

13-3.   Charles Darwin.

13-4.   Darwin was impressed by the relationships between extinct and modern animals. He found giant fossils of the glyptodon, an ancestor of the modern armadillo.

EXTINCT GROUND SLOTH

EXTINCT GIANT GLYPTODON

SLOTH (PRESENT DAY)

ARMADILLO (PRESENT DAY)

13-5. *Two tortoises from different Galapagos Islands.*

the apparent struggle for existence among all forms of life. The struggle for space, food, and shelter was ever-present.

Both men had also read a paper by Thomas Malthus, "An Essay on Population." The paper pointed out that populations tend to increase faster than their food supply. The final results may be overcrowding, poverty, war, famine, and disease. Not all of the individuals of a population survive.

Darwin and Wallace, working independently of each other, had arrived at the same conclusion. In 1858, they jointly announced their new theory of how change through time took place. A year later, Darwin published his now-famous book, *On the Origin of Species*. The book was a detailed account of how species changed over time.

The Darwin-Wallace Theory

The theory of evolution, as proposed by Darwin and Wallace, had come about by a process of natural selection. **Natural selection** *is the process that results in the survival of those organisms best suited for their environment.* Perhaps even more important, those least suited are less likely to survive. Those best adapted would also leave more offspring than those less suited. These offspring, in turn, tend to be well adapted.

Both Darwin and Wallace were convinced that populations of plants and animals changed. This occurred over long periods of time. Detailed fossil studies had contributed to the evidence in three ways. First, they had shown that many organisms now living on the earth had not been present when early rock sediments were laid down. Second, species preserved as fossils no longer existed in many instances. Finally, some of the new species were quite similar to the ones seen as fossils. Thus, the idea that species were fixed and unchanging was challenged with facts. These facts came from direct observation. The theory of natural selection, however, was unique in one simple way. It proposed a means by which evolution could have occurred. It explained the observations.

The Darwin-Wallace theory of evolution by natural selection can be summed up by following their line of reasoning in six steps.

1. As Malthus had proposed, *populations tended to increase at a geometric rate.*
2. However, *in reality, natural populations remain remarkably constant in number from one generation to the next.*
3. Since the first two observations can be seen as opposing forces, *there must therefore be a struggle for existence.*
4. *All organisms of the same species slightly differ from each other.*
5. Thus, it is likely that *some traits are more favorable for survival than*

others. These favorable traits allow certain individuals to live longer. In the process, they will leave more offspring than those without these traits.

6. *The favorable traits are passed on to the offspring*. This increases the frequency of those traits in the population. After many generations, most of the members of the population have the selected trait.

Because of competition, those with unfavorable traits will have fewer offspring. Hence, in time, unfavorable traits may even disappear.

TABLE 13-1. THE THEORIES OF LAMARCK AND DARWIN COMPARED.

	Lamarck	Darwin
Speed of evolution	gradually, over long periods of time	gradually, over long periods of time
"Fixity of species"	not at all	not at all
Role of the environment	causes change	selects favorable variations
Role of the organism	attempts to change	none

The Role of the Environment

The environment plays a crucial role in natural selection. This role contrasts sharply with that proposed by Lamarck. (See Table 13-1.) Rather than *cause* variations in offspring, the environment acts as a *selector* on existing variety. For example, the snowshoe hare did not develop a white coat in response to the coming of winter. Nor did it develop one because of the need to be camouflaged. Instead, winter changes in coat color enabled some hares to blend with their backgrounds. Those without such variations were more likely to be caught by predators. Thus, organisms may change or evolve in response to their environments. Changes in the environment may create a need for change in an organism. The need for change, however, is not sufficient to produce a "desired" change. A genetic potential must exist. It is the genetic potential of a population that produces variety. The environment can select from that variety.

Let us again use the example of the giraffe. This will point out

Answers to Questions for Section 2.

C. 1. Darwin: collected data on fossils and variations within species. Malthus: pointed out that populations tend to increase faster than their food supply. Wallace: formed conclusions similar to Darwin's.

2. Overcrowding, poverty, war, famine, and disease were also predicted by Malthus.

D. 3. Extinct animals, which closely resembled modern, smaller ones, were somehow related to them.

*4. Changes in the environments seemed related to gradual changes in latitude. Similar niches seemed to be filled by similar, related life forms.

5. Giant tortoises, which differed slightly from island to island, were all of the same species. Finches of the same species, differed sharply in the shapes of their beaks.

E. *6. (a) That organisms of the same species differ. (b) That there must be a struggle for existence. (c) Traits favorable to survival are passed on the offspring.

7. Only the genetic potential of a population can produce variety; the environment acts as selector on existing variety, but does not cause the variety.

*8. It is the "unfit", or those poorly adapted to the environment, that do not survive.

F. *9. Answers will vary.

*10. For Lamarck, giraffes have long necks due to the inheritance of an acquired characteristic. For Darwin, the long necks would be due to environmental selection of a favored chance variation.

G. 11. See page 238-239.

Note the similarities between the Darwin-Wallace theory and that of Lamarck. Point out these as well as the differences.

Be sure that students understand the role of the environment as a *selector* as opposed to a *causer* in a direct sense.

A.

B.

C.

13-5. Darwin's hypothesis. A. Ancestors with necks of varying lengths. B. Longer-necked offspring survive (through natural selection). C. Modern giraffes all have long necks.

how the Darwin-Wallace theory contrasts with that of Lamarck's. We will again begin with the short-necked ancestors. (See Fig. 13-6.) Among these, however, some might have had longer necks than others. This is an example of population variability. Competition from other animals forced these giraffes to seek food from tree branches. Those with longer necks would be favored in such an environment. In turn, they would survive longer. Also, they would produce more offspring than those with shorter necks. Offspring tend to be like their parents. Hence, they would also have somewhat longer necks than average. Over many generations, there would be constant selective pressure by the environment. This would result in the longer necks of the giraffes that we know today.

QUESTIONS FOR SECTION 2

1. Identify one contribution each of the following people made in understanding change through time: Charles Darwin, Malthus, Wallace.
2. What problems might arise if Malthus's prediction regarding the geometric growth of a population actually took place?
3. Of what importance are the giant fossils in South America?
4. Why was Darwin impressed with the related changes of latitude and life forms?
5. What was the importance of the differences observed between the life forms on different islands of the Galapagos?
6. For each of the following observations, draw one conclusion that Darwin might have made: (a) All organisms of the same species differ from each other, even if only slightly. (b) Populations tend to increase at a geometric rate, but they actually remain remarkably constant in number from generation to generation. (c) The offspring of a population possesses the traits of their parents.
7. Distinguish between the ideas of the environment as a *cause* of change and the environment as a *selector.*
8. The phrase "survival of the fittest" has sometimes been used to refer to Darwin's theory of natural selection. Why might the phrase "elimination of the unfit" be more appropriate?
9. How is natural selection important to biology in general?
10. Compare and contrast the concepts of Lamarck and Darwin in regard to the mechanism of change.
11. List the six steps of the Darwin-Wallace theory.

(See page 239 for answers to questions.)

3 EVOLUTION TODAY

New Dimensions in Evolution

Much has been learned since Darwin's time about the mechanisms of evolution. The work of Gregor Mendel (Chapter 9) provided a genetic basis for inheritance. Knowledge of genes and mutations (Chapter 10) has answered questions about the sources of variation. The Hardy-Weinberg Principle (Chapter 11) in effect points out those factors that control allele frequencies. Changes in allelic frequencies result in various changes. They include changes in the genotypes and phenotypes of populations, and hence, change through time.

One usually thinks of the theory of evolution as a fairly slow process. This is not necessarily the case. The changes in the peppered moth of England is a classic case in point. Prior to 1850, most, if not all of the peppered moths were light colored with black speckles. (See Fig. 13-7.) A dark colored mutant of the species was first reported in 1849. Slowly, the dark variation began to increase in number.

With the coming of the Industrial Revolution, tons of soot were deposited in the English countryside. The changed environment directly affected the survival of the peppered moth. Its light color had enabled it to blend with its background as it rested on trees and rocks. The advantage of the moths' protective coloration was lost when soot began to darken these surfaces. The dark mutation had a selective advantage, however, in such an environment. By 1950, nearly all of the moths in these industrial areas were dark colored. A complete reversal in the color form of the peppered moth had occurred. Such reversal is known today as *industrial melanism.* Similar instances of this process have been shown to have occurred in several other species.

The change in the peppered moth is an excellent example of natural selection in action. In unpolluted forests, the light form has a selective advantage over the dark forms. Where pollution is heavy, the reverse is true. H.B.D. Kettlewell, an English biologist, documented the case of the peppered moth during the 1950's. He was able to show that birds fed upon the more obvious moths. This occurred more often than on those that were less obvious. He conducted his experiments in both polluted and unpolluted forests. His findings supported Darwin's notion that the environment acted as the selector.

An interesting side note should be mentioned here. Since Kettlewell's experiments, there has been an effort to reduce pollution. Changing from coal to gas furnaces has reduced the amount of soot being deposited in the countryside. What effect do you think that this might have upon the proportion of light and dark peppered moths?

OBJECTIVES FOR SECTION 3

H. Define the following terms in your own words: *domestication, adaptation, artificial selection, positive mutation, industrial melanism.*

I. Describe the essential elements of the famous peppered moth experiment.

J. Cite several examples that illustrate the role of humans in the change of other species.

K. Give an example of how complementarity of organism and environment provides a key to the Darwin-Wallace theory.

13-7. In each photograph, both forms of the peppered moth are present. In each case, which moth is favored to survive? Why?

13-8. *Domesticated plants and animals are all products of artificial selection.*

Answers to Questions for Section 3.

H. **1.** See glossary.

I. **2.** Before 1849, when the first dark mutant appeared, the moths were all peppered. There followed a slow increase in the dark form until soot covered the moths' background. Now the dark had selective advantage over the peppered, and by 1950, nearly all were dark.

Mutations and Evolution

The theory of evolution may at least in part be the result of changes in the structure of genes, or mutations. Forces that cause mutations operate by chance. Such changes occur regardless of whether the organism is helped or hurt by them. *A positive mutation is one that allows the individual to be better adapted to its environment.* Most changes due to mutations are harmful to the organism. This is because organisms are already adapted to their environments. Any change would most likely work against this adaptation.

Evolutionary changes normally take place over long periods of time. They are the result of a number of minor mutations. Evolutionary change may depend on the diversity shown in the gene pool of a population. As the environment changes, certain alleles become favored. Others may be rejected through natural selection. A population with a wide variety of genetic traits will show little change as alterations occur in the environment.

Artificial Selection

The principles of natural selection had been in use long before Darwin's time. Early humans had no doubt used them to tame or domesticate certain animals. The same principles were used in the development of domestic crops such as wheat and rice. *Using the principles of natural selection to domesticate wild organisms has been called* artificial selection. Organisms that had useful traits were selected by our ancestors, and thus favored. Continued selection eventually produced a wide range of useful plants and animals.

We continue to use these principles today. (See Fig. 13-8.) Horticulture, agriculture, and animal husbandry are applied sciences. They constantly use selection to "improve" many kinds of plants and animals. This "improvement," of course, is dictated by human needs and desires, and thus, artificial. Humans decide what is useful or not. This decision is based on what is desirable at the time. There are many products of artificial selection. Many could not survive in the natural world without human protection. On the other hand, humans are products of their environments as well. Are changes in the environment by humans as natural as those by a beaver?

The many varieties of dogs are all products of artificial selection. (See Fig. 13-9.) Once domesticated, variations in the species allowed selection for hunting, racing, herding, and many other uses. Different kinds of cattle are selected for their ability to withstand extreme weather conditions or to put on weight quickly. Plants may be selected for productivity, resistance to pests, or beauty. The list is endless. Without selection, we would be forced to lead a far different existence.

*3. Answers will vary.

4. In the example of the resistant bacteria, the use of antibiotics

created an environment favorable to the mutants. So the very agent intended to destroy the infection-

The fact that artificial selection works, indicates that there is genetic variation in populations. This exists for almost every characteristic of the organism. The amount of variation in natural populations is much greater than that predicted by Darwin's ideas on survival.

Role of Sexual Reproduction

New mutations may occur in each generation. These are not the only sources of diversity. Because of sexual reproduction, chromosomes are constantly being shuffled into new combinations. Such mixing results in new genotypes and phenotypes. These then can be acted upon by the environment.

Sexual reproduction involves the union of male and female cells. Each reproductive cell contains one set of chromosomes. As these cells unite, the chromosomes are mixed. This recombination of genetic traits may produce new phenotypes. Such random assortment also results in new combinations of chromosomes in the reproductive cells. Recombination and random assortment accounts for the mixing of alleles in a population. They do not, in themselves, cause evolution. The mixing results in new combinations of alleles. These alleles then can be exposed to selection at each generation.

Genetic shuffling allows a population to expose its hidden or recessive traits. This exposure occurs without the need for genetic input by mutation. Large numbers of alleles are available in the heterozygous condition. These alleles result in genotypes and phenotypes that may have selective value. If favorable, they will occur more and more often. Also, they will begin to outnumber less favorable ones. A great genetic variety in natural populations will provide many opportunities for change to occur.

13-9. *Further selection of domesticated organisms can produce a variety of kinds for different purposes.*

Accidental Selection

Humans have also been responsible for accidental changes in the genetic character of many organisms. The case of DDT has already been described in Unit I. Another example is the evolution of bacteria that are resistant to antibiotics. These drugs have been widely used since their discovery during World War II. They have tended to create an environment that favors resistant forms of bacteria. Outbreaks of resistant *Staphylococcus* bacteria have been reported in a number of hospitals across the country. Antibiotics normally used to control infection were not effective. Several patients died of secondary infections following surgery.

The existence of resistant bacterial strains can be demonstrated quite simply. A number of paper discs can be soaked in antibiotics. Next, these discs are placed in a culture of bacteria: This creates an antibiotic environment in the surrounding growth medium. (See Fig.

6. By using antibiotics, insecticides, etc. to destroy susceptible organisms, so that resistant mutants of those same species are favored in an environment created by those substances.

K. *7. Answers will vary.

causing bacteria ultimately caused them to thrive.

J. 5. They select organisms with desirable traits and breed them; continued selection eventually produces great modifications.

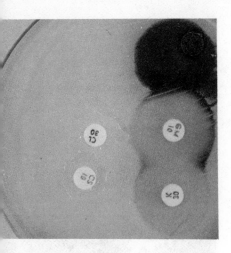

13-10.) The growth of bacteria will be normal in the absence of the antibiotic. Near the discs, no bacteria should appear. Sometimes, however, a colony appears in the clear area around the disc. Such colonies are resistant to the effects of the antibiotic. They stem from a single bacterial cell that had a genetic resistance to the drug.

Even in these now-familiar examples, you should be aware that the altered environment only *selects*. It does not *cause* the appropriate variation to occur. Random mutations may render an organism more fit for certain environments — even if they do not yet exist. If the genetic potential for change is not present, adaptation cannot occur.

13-10. Bacteria resistant to antibiotic discs will be favored in an antibiotic environment. Bacteria are more resistant to the antibiotic discs on the right than those on the left.

Answers to Questions for Section 3. (See pages 242 and 243 for answers.)

QUESTIONS FOR SECTION 3

1. Define each of the following in your own words: adaptation, domestication, artificial selection.
2. Describe the selection of the dark form of the peppered moth in England following the Industrial Revolution.
3. How are changes in peppered moth populations different from those that
4. occurred in DDT-resistant insects or antibiotic-resistant bacteria?
   How may unwitting selection by human "progress" backfire?
5. Describe the role of humans in artificial selection.
6. How have humans been responsible for accidental selection?
7. Does the interaction of an organism with its environment support the Darwin-Wallace theory?

CHAPTER REVIEW

Organisms that share a common ancestor also share a number of similar features. These similarities, indicate a degree of relatedness. They also illustrate the *continuity of life concept*. Since descendants are similar but not identical, we can see that kinds of organisms *change through time*. These concepts were not new with Darwin. In fact, they had been used as the basis of schemes to classify plants and animals.

The Darwin-Wallace theory presents an idea of how change through time could occur. The key to this means is a third basic concept of biology, *interaction of an organism and environment*. Successful adaptation depends upon how well an organism can live with its environment. This ability depends upon the genetic potential of the population.

Using the Concepts

1. Light-colored animals have become adapted to their surroundings in the White Sands National Monument. White insects, lizards, and mammals are fairly common. First explain this phenomenon as Lamarck might have, and then explain it as Darwin might have.
2. The evolution of parasites and their hosts are sometimes cited as examples of "one-upmanship" in the biological world. Explain how one-upmanship is actually natural selection in action.
3. Read about "Darwin's Finches" in the April 1953 issue of *Scientific American*. What factors favored the evolution of so many kinds of finches on the Galapagos Islands?

VOCABULARY REVIEW

1 acquired characteristics	fossil
2 natural selection	extinct

3 adaptation	artificial selection
domestication	

CHAPTER 13 TEST

Copy the number of each test item and place your answer to the right.

PART 1 Multiple Choice: Select the letter of the phrase that best completes each of the following.

b **1.** The fate of organisms that do not have the genetic potential to adapt to a changing environment is **a.** change through time **b.** extinction **c.** mutation **d.** adaptation.

d **2.** Part of Lamarck's theory of evolution involved **a.** isolation **b.** natural selection **c.** struggle for existence **d.** use and disuse of body parts.

c **3.** Variation in a population is usually the result of **a.** use and disuse of body parts **b.** isolation **c.** mutation **d.** adaptation.

b **4.** All of the following offered explanations for how evolution occurred except **a.** Charles Darwin **b.** Aristotle **c.** Lamarck **d.** Erasmus Darwin.

a **5.** A species' ability to adapt to its environment is related to its ability to **a.** reproduce sexually **b.** hide from predators **c.** assess its needs **d.** understand its environment.

c **6.** According to the Darwin-Wallace theory for the evolutionary mechanism, the giraffe has a long neck because **a.** its ancestors all had long necks **b.** the neck is needed for the giraffe to obtain sufficient food **c.** the environment favored giraffes with longer necks **d.** the environment caused the necks of giraffes to become longer.

b **7.** All of the following are parts of the Darwin-Wallace theory except **a.** struggle for existence **b.** metamorphosis **c.** survival of the most fit **d.** natural selection.

Questions 8-10 refer to the following choices:
a. it fits the Darwin-Wallace theory, but not Lamarck's
b. it fits the Lamarck theory, but not the Darwin-Wallace theory
c. it fits both theories
d. it applies to neither theory

c **8.** Adaptations evolved slowly and gradually over long periods of time.

a **9.** Species have remained largely unchanged since the original appearance of life on earth.

b **10.** Fossils are evidences of organisms that lived in the past.

Chapter 13 Test Answers
22. positive mutation
23. pollution or soot-covered trees
24. have a common ancestor
25. fossil

PART 2 Matching: Match the letter of the term in Column I with its description in Column II.

COLUMN I
a. acquired characteristic
b. adaptation
c. artificial selection
d. competition
e. evolutionary theory
f. extinction
g. fixity of species
h. industrial melanism
i. mutation
j. natural selection

COLUMN II
i **11.** Inheritable change in a population
g **12.** Idea that organisms are unchanged since their origin
j **13.** Favoring of the best suited and the elimination of the unfit
b **14.** Modification of an organism in response to its environment
e **15.** Change through time
c **16.** Process by which humans domesticate wild plants and animals
h **17.** Reversal in color pattern from light to dark in response to pollution
d **18.** One environmental factor that helps to create a struggle for existence
f **19.** Dying out of a group of organisms
a **20.** Feature of an organism developed during its lifetime

PART 3 Completion: Complete the following.
21. The role of the environment, according to the Darwin-Wallace theory, is that of a _____. selector
22. A mutation that allows an individual to be better adapted to its environment is referred to as a _____.
23. The environmental change that resulted in industrial melanism was _____.
24. To say that organisms display a certain degree of relatedness means that they _____.
25. Any evidence of a past life form is called a _____.

CHAPTER 14

EVIDENCE OF CHANGE

Much has already been said about changes in organisms. The role of selection in causing these changes has been detailed. We have described some of the evidence that leads us to conclude that changes do occur over a long term. There is more to the story, however. To stop it here would be like omitting the last chapter of a who-done-it mystery.

To complete the story, we must first consider how new species might arise. We can then review the evidence to see if it is consistent with our ideas about change. If we find that it is, we can look at the fossil record (Chapter 15) to further our understanding of earlier discussions of relatedness.

The mechanisms of change discussed in this chapter serve to underscore the concept of *change through time.* The process of change in living organisms has two important features. First, change is certain, that is, we know change has occurred in the past. Also, we can assume it will occur in the future. Second, the patterns of change are regular. We cannot predict what variety will arise. But we do know that they will be changes of existing designs. We will examine the evidence that supports these conclusions. In this chapter, you will also see examples of several other basic concepts of biology. These include the *complementarity of structure and function in organisms, and the interrelationship of organism and environment.*

As you progress through the chapter, direct your attention to the following questions:

- Why are all dogs, in spite of their great variety, considered to be members of the same species?
- How do new species arise?
- How do we know how old fossils are?
- Why does medical research depend on test animals for the development of human medicine?

MOLLUSC FOSSILS

1 MECHANISMS OF CHANGE

The Species Concept

A **species** *is a group of organisms that have the ability to inter-breed.* They are isolated from other such groups in a reproductive sense. This means that the members of a group recognized as a species may breed among themselves. However, they cannot breed outside that group. Furthermore, it means that the members of a species share a common gene pool. For example, all dogs are members of the same species (*Canis familiaris*). To be sure, there is great variety in size, color, and other features. Even so, two quite different dogs can still contribute to a future generation.

Biologists may recognize a number of different kinds of hawks as different species. There are Cooper's hawks, red-tailed hawks, Swainson's hawks, and many more. Many of these look more alike than many dogs. (See Fig. 14-1.) Why should these be given different species names? The reason is that breeding does not normally occur between the recognized groups. Thus, we see that a group can have a lot of obvious variety and still be a single species. Likewise, we see that several different species can be very similar.

There are problems, however, with this definition for a species. In the first place, it may happen that interbreeding sometimes does take place between recognized species. This is taken as evidence of a high degree of relatedness between the two groups. Sometimes, closely related groups may interbreed. If so, the offspring dies or is sterile. The line separating the two species in this case remains intact. At times, an offspring is normal and it survives to reproduce. In this case the line separating the two species becomes blurred.

OBJECTIVES FOR SECTION 1

A. Define the following terms in your own words: *species, isolating mechanism, preadaptation, divergence, speciation.*

B. Discuss the reasons why the term species is such a problem to biologists.

C. Compare and contrast the three types of selection.

D. Describe the various isolating mechanisms.

Ask students how the many varieties of dogs have come about. Use this to illustrate preadaptations. New traits were selected by humans for their usefulness just as the environment selects existing traits for their survival value.

14-1. (left) red-tailed hawk; (right) Cooper's Hawk.

Ask students for examples of species that have changed. They may cite such examples as the peppered moths, DDT-resistant flies and mosquitoes, the Galapagos finches, etc. Ask students if these changes result in new species. Point out that new species arise if and when interbreeding becomes impossible.

Answers to Questions for Section 1.

C. 6. Directional selection: involves changes that take place when a population shows a steady trend through time. Example: hoofed animals developed from 5-toed ancestors. Stabilizing selection: occurs when organisms that represent extreme departures from the normal are removed from the population. Example: an animal's coat color may change, so it is easily preyed upon or cannot find a mate. Those that survive in the population tend to become more alike. Disruptive selection: caused by abnormal features that have high survival value. Example: separation, into two species, as poorly adapted intermediate forms are removed.

D. 7. Premating factors, and post-mating factors.

8. Geographic barriers, in which populations of a species are separated by mountains, etc. prevent gene flow between populations. Habitat preference: isolates such populations as the deer mouse and white-footed mouse. Behavioral differences: courtship displays. Differences in mating seasons, or differences in body size or structure may prevent mating.

9. For example, the Kaibab squirrel and the Abert squirrel are two species that were probably once a single species, that became isolated by the development of the Grand Canyon.

Another problem with the species concept is that groups we call species are constantly changing. We have seen that selection and genetic drift (Chapter 13) are always at work in natural populations. In addition, some organisms breed more abundantly than others. These factors increase the frequencies of some alleles. At the same time these factors decrease others. The term species is useful for us to recognize groups of similar organisms. Even so, we must remember that its use does have certain limits.

Preadaptations

Organisms that are not adapted to their environments are replaced by ones that are. You might ask how this adaptation comes about. If changes take place in the environment, how can an organism survive? Where do the features that help an organism survive come from in the first place? As you might suspect, the answers to these questions lie in diversity. We have already seen how selection acts on diversity in a species. It results in change.

Adaptive traits that exist in an organism before they are of value are called **preadaptations.** In Chapter 13 we saw diversity in the peppered moths. With the environment altered by pollution, the dark form of the moth had a selective advantage over the light forms. The dark mutation was thus a preadaptation. The mutation existed before it had a value for survival. The resistance of some insects to the effects of DDT is another example of preadaptation. Those that had a mutation survived when treated with the insecticide. Can you think of any other examples of preadaptations?

Note that preadaptations are not caused by the changed factor in the environment. They were already in existence as a part of diversity in the species.

Kinds of Selection

Selection may be expressed in three main ways.

DIRECTIONAL SELECTION **Directional selection** *involves changes that take place when a population shows a steady trend through time.* This trend may be the development of a trait. For example, the horse increased in size over millions of years. (See Fig. 14-2.) It may also be reflected in the disappearance of a trait. Examples of this may be seen in the hoofed animals of the world. The "typical" mammal has five toes on each foot. However, hoofed animals have only one or two functional toes. In both kinds of trends, selective pressures have favored certain forms in a fairly consistent manner.

STABILIZING SELECTION **Stabilizing selection** *occurs when organisms that represent extreme departures from the "normal" are removed from the population.* This tends to make the members of the

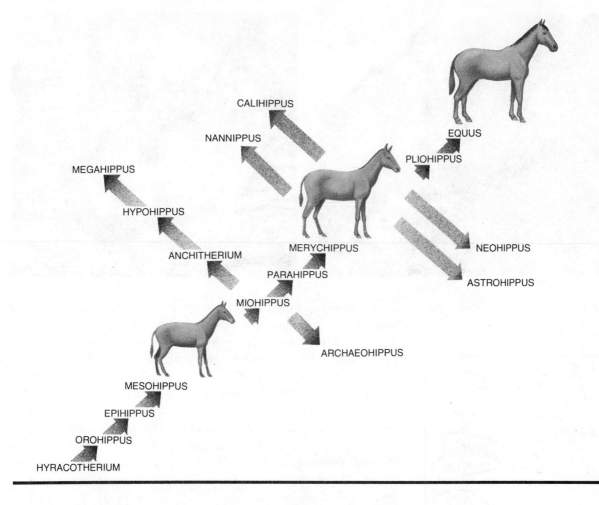

CALIHIPPUS

NANNIPPUS

EQUUS

MEGAHIPPUS

PLIOHIPPUS

HYPOHIPPUS

ANCHITHERIUM

MERYCHIPPUS

NEOHIPPUS

PARAHIPPUS

ASTROHIPPUS

MIOHIPPUS

ARCHAEOHIPPUS

MESOHIPPUS

EPIHIPPUS

OROHIPPUS

HYRACOTHERIUM

population more alike. For example, changes in an animal's coat color might make it more likely to be caught by a predator. It may also make it less able to compete for a mate. A bird's song or behavior may depart from the normal in ways that make it unable to attract a mate. Such changes reduce the chances for that animal to pass its genes to the next generation. Thus, the "abnormal" feature tends to be weeded out of the gene pool. Future generations will tend to become more alike.

DISRUPTIVE SELECTION   The opposite situation may also occur. *"Abnormal" features that have a high survival value cause* **disruptive selection.** In this case, it is the intermediate types that are selected against. An example of this type of selection occurs in two closely related species of mice. The deer mouse and the white-footed mouse are thought to have once been a single species. *The separation of a single species into two is known as* **divergence.** Divergence of these

14-2. The evolution of the horse is an example of directional selection.

14-3. (left) Deer mice prefer the open meadow. (right) White-footed mice prefer the woods.

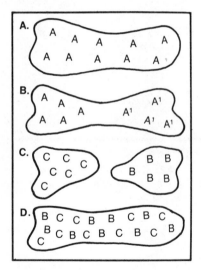

14-4. A. Inland population with uniform gene flow. B. Changing ocean level reduces gene flow, particularly isolating two sub-populations. C. Further change in ocean level shuts off gene flow, completing isolation. Over time, both populations change, resulting in two species. D. Islands may unite again, but the species do not interbreed.

two populations may have come about as they explored different habitats. The deer mouse makes its home today in open meadows. The white-footed mouse may live in nearby wooded areas. Over time, selection favored those forms that were best suited to each of the new habitats. (See Fig. 14-3.) As divergence occurred, the intermediate types would have been at a disadvantage. In either habitat, they could not compete with the better-adapted forms. Thus, over time, they would have been removed from the populations. Breeding encounters between the two adapted forms would have become less frequent. Two species might then be recognized, replacing a single species. *The process by which a new species arises from pre-existing forms is called* **speciation**.

Reproductive Isolation

Members of one population may be prevented from mating with those from another population by factors called **isolating mechanisms.** Isolating mechanisms fall into two main categories. Premating factors tend to prevent mating from taking place at all. Postmating factors operate to reduce the chances for survival of offspring once mating has taken place.

PREMATING FACTORS Populations of a single species may be isolated from each other by mountains, rivers, canyons, or other geographic barriers. While these populations are separated, changes in their respective gene pools can and do occur. The barrier prevents gene flow between the populations. Thus, they become less and less alike. (See Fig. 14-4.) If isolation is long enough, speciation may occur. For example, there are two species of squirrels that live on oppo-

site rims of the Grand Canyon in Arizona. The canyon prevents any contact between the Kaibab squirrel on the north rim and the Abert squirrel on the south rim. (See Fig. 14-5.) Most biologists think that they were once a single species. As the canyon developed, the one species separated into two populations.

In some cases, a barrier may be removed and populations may become reunited. If the differences between them do not serve to prevent gene flow, speciation is not complete. The populations may only show increased diversity of a single species. Speciation will only be complete if the populations remain reproductively isolated from each other.

There are a number of other premating isolating factors. Simple *habitat preference* may serve to isolate populations from each other as we saw in the case of the deer mouse and the white-footed mouse. *Behavioral differences* may be a third isolating factor, especially in the vertebrates (animals with backbones). Elaborate mating displays by the male prairie chicken, for example, must be performed in a fairly precise manner. This display enables him to attract a mate. Examples of such behavioral displays are well known in fish, amphibians, birds, and mammals. Even certain kinds of invertebrates are known to have courtship displays.

A fourth premating isolating factor exists when there are differences in *mating seasons* between populations. The breeding season for grass frogs in Texas may be two to three months earlier than for more northern varieties. Thus, mating could not take place between these populations. Finally, differences in *body size or structure* may act to prevent mating.

14-5. The Grand Canyon may have posed a geographic barrier that isolated two populations of a species of squirrel. Today, the Kaibab squirrel lives on the North rim of the Grand Canyon. The Abert squirrel lives on the South rim.

14-6. *The mule (right) is a sterile hybrid of a horse and a donkey.*

Answers to Questions for Section 1.

A. 1. See glossary.

   *2. See glossary.

   *3. Divergence may occur because of a variety of factors. Selection favored certain forms of a population that were best suited to its new habitat. Over a period of time, the better-adapted forms survived. Breeding encounters would have become less frequent. Finally, two separate species might be recognized.

   4. Dogs (*Canis familiaris*) are all members of the same species, despite differences. Cooper's hawk, Red-tailed hawk, and Swainson's hawk are all different species despite similarities.

B. 5. (1) Interbreeding sometimes does occur between different species. (2) Groups called species are constantly changing, due, e.g., to selection and genetic drift.

(See page 248 for answers 6-8.)

POSTMATING FACTORS Perhaps the best known example of a postmating factor in action is that of the mule. (See Fig. 14-6.) The mule is the offspring of a female horse and a male donkey. Mules are sterile. They cannot reproduce. The horse and the donkey remain reproductively isolated from each other. A "blended" species cannot be produced. In this case, sterility occurs because the chromosomes received from each parent are not homologous. Thus, meiosis cannot take place and the mule cannot reproduce. Other postmating isolating factors may cause the death of the young offspring or the fertilized ovum during development.

QUESTIONS FOR SECTION 1

1. Define and give examples of the following terms: species, isolating mechanism, preadaptation, divergence, speciation.
2. Distinguish between divergence and adaptation.
3. Describe how divergence can lead to speciation.
4. Give an example of a single species with a high degree of diversity. Give an example of several species that are very similar, without many obvious differences.
5. Describe two reasons that the term species is such a problem to biologists.
6. Distinguish between the three types of selection using examples. Under what kinds of conditions would each operate?
7. What are the two main types of isolating mechanisms?
8. What are the differences between the four kinds of premating factors that serve to isolate populations from each other.
9. Describe how isolating mechanisms can lead to reproductive isolation and divergence.

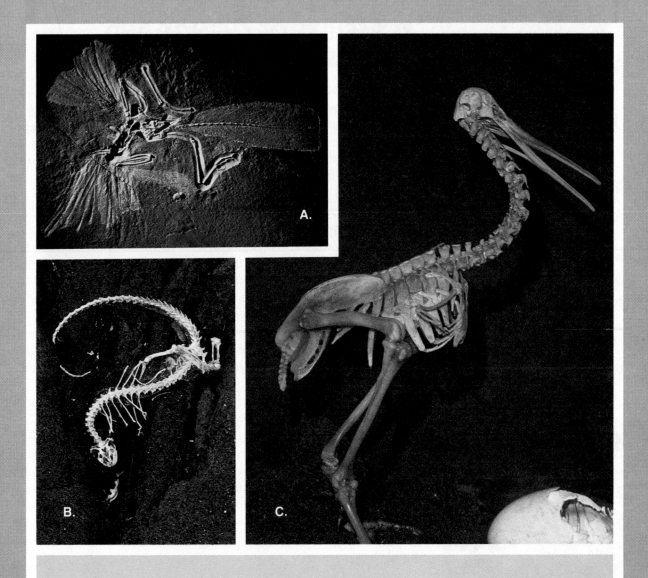

A.

B.

C.

CHAPTER INVESTIGATION

A. How is the fossil of Archaeopteryx (A) *similar* to the skeletons of the lizard (B) and the bird (C)? In what ways is it *different* from each?

B. Evaluate your answers in A and make a conclusion regarding how Archaeopteryx should be classified. Explain your conclusion.

C. Research other "transition" organisms (e.g., fossils known as therapsids) and describe their relationships to organisms past and present.

2 RESULTS OF CHANGE AND THE FOSSIL RECORD

Adaptive Radiation

The adjustment that a population makes to its environment over a period of time is called **adaptation.** Note that individuals do not adapt. It is the gene pool of the population that responds to selective pressures. In the face of a changing environment, those members of a population with the alleles that help them best will survive. Those without them, will not.

When members of a single population undergo evolutionary divergence, **adaptive radiation** *takes place.* Divergence of populations is helped by various isolating factors. As populations are exposed to different selection pressures, they will become less and less alike. In time they may become recognized as separate species. As selection continues, the intermediate forms may drop out. Hence, in time, the degree of relatedness may become less obvious.

Harsh selection pressures on a population might cause it to become extinct. This may happen before adaptation could occur. The speed with which a population can reproduce is also important. Large numbers of offspring increase the chance that an adaptive mutation will occur. Large numbers also increase the chance for the occurrence of the right gene combinations for the environment. (See Fig. 14-7.) The success of insects over the last 400 million years is due, at least in part, to their rapid reproductive rate.

Finally, adaptive radiation is more likely to occur if there is a short interval between generations. Again, insects provide a perfect example. Most can hatch, mature, and reproduce in a single season. Some can even produce two or more generations in one season. This is a definite advantage if the environment is undergoing a very rapid change.

Convergence

If populations can undergo divergence, we might ask if the reverse is also possible. The answer is yes. **Convergence** *is two or more groups developing in such a way that they become more alike in structure or other features.*

Let us look, for example, at two unrelated animals. These animals live in similar habitats. They also occupy similar niches in different parts of the world. The Tasmanian wolf (from Australia) and the timber wolf (from North America) are both predators. However, the Tasmanian wolf is a "pouched mammal." That is, its young are born prematurely. After birth they are carried in a pouch like the kangaroo.

OBJECTIVES FOR SECTION 2

E. Define the following terms in your own words: *adaptation, adaptive radiation, convergence, ecologic equivalent, half life.*

F. Describe the means by which adaptive radiation takes place.

G. Explain why two unrelated organisms may come to resemble each other.

H. Give four reasons why the fossil record is difficult to interpret.

I. Describe the means by which rock strata can be "dated."

14-7. How is a large number of offspring a form of adaptation?

Thus, the Tasmanian wolf is more closely related to the kangaroo and other pouched mammals than to the timber wolf. How might have these two unrelated animals come to resemble each other so closely? The selective pressures on the ancestors of both wolves may have been similar. Thus, the same kinds of traits would be favored in both populations. Over time, selection tended to remove some traits while favoring others. Today, there is a striking resemblance between these two animals. This similarity occurs even though they are not closely related in a genetic sense.

There are a number of other parallels between the pouched mammals of Australia and the more modern mammals. (See Fig. 14-8.) Australia's separation from Asia occurred before the dawn of the modern form of mammals. The primitive egg-laying and pouched mammals were replaced by the placental mammals in most of the world. A placental mammal carries its young to full term within the body of the mother. The placenta serves as the source of nourishment for the developing offspring. Australia became isolated before placental mammals developed. The large expanse of water kept these modern forms from spreading to Australia. Thus, pouched mammals were freed from competition with the more efficient placental forms. Today, the opossum is the only surviving pouched mammal outside of Australia.

14-8. Convergence may be seen between marsupials (left) and placental mammals (right).

You may want to review the concept of continental drift as it applies to biogeography and the distribution of plants and animals. Ask students why they think a marsupial bat did not arise in Australia.

14-9. *Fossils are formed in many ways. (top) fern frond impression; (middle) petrified wood; (bottom) fly in amber.*

Although they are unrelated, pouched and placental mammals have come to fill similar ecologic niches. *Unrelated organisms that fill similar niches are called* ecologic equivalents. Ecologic equivalents are common among both plants and animals. Can you think of any others?

Using the Fossil Record

We are able to see the results of change through the fossil record. **Fossils** *are any evidences of organisms found from the geologic past.* They may be formed in a number of ways. (See Fig. 14-9.) The simplest fossils are merely imprints of an organism or its tracks in a rock. Often, the organism is buried by sediments that prevent it from decaying quickly. In time, minerals may replace many of the tissues. Finally, parts of the organism are turned to stone. Sometimes, whole specimens become imbedded in various substances, including ice.

IMPORTANT FUNCTIONS OF FOSSILS   Fossil remains serve two important functions. First, they provide us with clues. These clues allow us to examine ancestral forms of modern day plants and animals. Second, they help us understand the general order of appearance of various life forms during the course of the earth's history.

IMPERFECTIONS OF THE FOSSIL RECORD   The fossil record is useful as a means of viewing the past. However, it poses some serious drawbacks. The record itself is imperfect. Only a small fraction of the organisms that ever existed have become fossilized. Many species that once thrived on earth came and went without leaving a trace of their existence. About 1.5 million species of living organisms are known today. However, only some 130,000 fossil species have been described. Usually, dead organisms are decayed by the decomposer elements of the ecosystem. This decay occurs before they can become fossilized.

A second reason that the fossil record is imperfect is that organisms are almost never preserved as whole specimens. Even in organisms that become fossils, generally only their hard parts are preserved. This is only a minor problem in following the history of organisms with bones or shells. Tracing the history of plants and animals without hard parts is a major problem.

The time and place that organisms live is of importance in fossil formation. Organisms that live in the shallow seas, rivers, and swamps are more likely to be fossilized than land-dwelling ones. Dead organisms in these places are more likely to be buried by sand and mud deposits. Organisms that live on the dry land are not often preserved as fossils. In these areas the rock is being eroded away, not deposited. Furthermore, it seems that conditions in some periods of geologic history favored the formation of fossils more than during other periods. The surface of the earth has undergone constant change throughout geologic history.

There is a final reason why the fossil record is imperfect. Studies of existing organisms show that the greatest variety of form exists in populations that live in upland or mountainous habitats. In these places, there is also a greater variety of environments. Thus, it is not surprising that most early forms of new groups should appear in these upland areas. Yet, it is just these organisms that are least likely to become fossilized! In the more stable lowlands organisms display less diversity. It is here that plants and animals are more likely to become fossils.

Thus, fossils are valuable records of the past. But it must be kept in mind that there are gaps in the record. Where the gaps are small, the dangers of guesswork are less. Where they are large, the chances for error are greater.

Dating the Record

As we have seen, fossils are found in deposits of sedimentary rocks. These rocks are usually found in layers called *strata*. The sedimentary deposits that underlie most of the central United States were laid down between 600 and 200 million years ago. During that time, shallow seas came and went over much of what is now North America. In any series of strata, the lowest layers were deposited before the ones that lie above them. Thus, they will contain the fossils of organisms that lived earliest. (See Fig. 14-10.) Fossils laid down in each higher strata give us a picture of organisms from the more recent past.

Before the 20th Century, ideas about the ages of sedimentary rocks and their fossils were little more than crude guesses. Most estimates were based on the rates at which sediments are laid down. But such methods pose serious problems. For example, some sediments might be eroded away. This erosion may occur before more sediments are deposited. The time during which erosion took place would leave no record in the form of sedimentary rock strata. About all we could say would be that one layer was older or younger than another. But how much older or younger? No estimate in terms of years was possible.

RADIOACTIVITY The discovery of radioactivity suddenly gave the scientist an instrument for measuring geologic time. **Radioactivity** *is a property of certain forms of some elements called isotopes that causes them to change into other elements. An* **isotope** *is one form of an element that differs from its other forms in the number of neutrons*

14-10. *Much of the earth's crust is made up of sedimentary deposits that later became folded and faulted.*

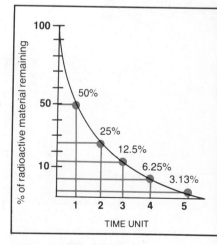

14-11. *The half-life principle. Each time unit corresponds to the half-life of the radioactive material used.*

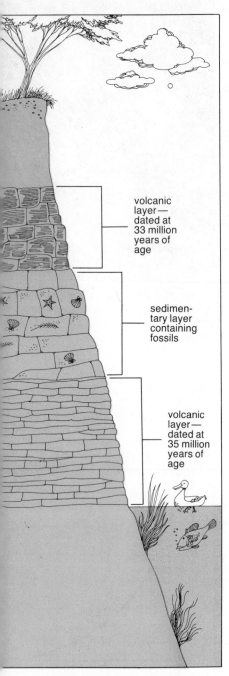

volcanic layer—dated at 33 million years of age

sedimentary layer containing fossils

volcanic layer—dated at 35 million years of age

14-12. The layers of volcanic origin were dated with radioactivity clocks as shown. What is the approximate age of the fossils in the sedimentary layer between the volcanic layers?

within the nucleus. This change, or radioactive decay, takes place at a predictable rate. It is similar to the hands of a clock moving at a steady, predictable rate. Some of these elements require enormous amounts of time for significant decay. Others take a much shorter time. *The time it takes for one-half of the radioactive substance to decay is called its* **half-life.** (See Fig. 14-11 on page 257.)

RADIOACTIVE CLOCKS   One "radioactive clock" that is often used is uranium-238 (U-238). Its half-life is 4.5 billion years. This is also the estimated age of the earth. This means that of the U-238 originally in the rocks when the earth was formed 4.5 billion years ago, one-half remains today. The rest of the U-238 atoms have decayed into lead-206 (Pb-206). Measuring the relative amounts of U-238 and Pb-206 will give us a rather accurate estimate of the rock's age.

There are other radioactivity clocks that are also used to measure rock strata. The potassium-argon clock is useful because it is able to date materials ranging in age from billions of years down to only a few thousand years. The relative amounts of rubidium and strontium is also a useful "clock." Perhaps you have heard of carbon-14. The use of this clock is confined to dating the ages of organic materials. Its use, however, is limited to a maximum of 60 thousand years.

What have these clocks got to do with change through time? Suppose that we find a series of strata that contain fossils. Among these sediments are layers of volcanic rock. In most situations, the radioactivity clocks are not able to tell the ages of sedimentary rocks. They can be used to date rocks of volcanic origin, however. How might a radioactivity clock be used to date the sedimentary stratum in Figure 14-12?

Ages of rocks all over the world can be used to put together the story of the development of life on earth. The dates show that there were times when certain organisms developed very rapidly. The dates also confirm that organisms that live in very stable environments developed only very slowly.

QUESTIONS FOR SECTION 2
1. What are the differences between adaptation and adaptive radiation.
2. Describe how convergence can result in ecologic equivalents.
3. Describe the factors that contribute to adaptive radiation.
4. Describe the factors that contribute to convergence.
5. Give four reasons why the fossil record is often difficult to interpret. Explain.
6. Describe the principle of using the half-life of radioactive elements to date rock strata.
7. Explain why radioactivity clocks are not useful for sedimentary strata. How can these clocks sometimes be used to give approximate ages for sedimentary deposits?

(See page 259 for Answers to Section 2.)

3 INDIRECT EVIDENCE

Comparative Anatomy

The existence of fossils provides us with a direct link to the past. Comparing fossils to living forms presents us with some evidence that change has occurred. However, the evidence for change does not stop with studies of the fossil record. There are at least three important kinds of indirect evidence. The first of these is **comparative anatomy,** *a science that compares and contrasts body structures of plants and animals*.

HOMOLOGOUS STRUCTURES   The forelimbs of vertebrates function in a number of different ways. Note that the forelimbs pictured in Figure 14-13, for example, all have different functions in spite of their structural sameness. *Organs that are similar in structure but not always similar in function are said to be* **homologous.** This sameness provides a strong argument that these forelimbs arose from slight changes in a common ancestral pattern.

Bones are not the only structures studied in comparative anatomy. In animals, attention has been focused on nervous, circulatory, excretory, and reproductive systems as well as others. Plants have been studied with respect to flower structure, leaf structure, and circulatory patterns.

The concept of unity and diversity is illustrated by comparing anatomic structure. The skeletal systems of fish, amphibians, reptiles, and mammals are all quite similar. Each, however, shows varying degrees of specialization. A pattern of increasing complexity is seen from fish to amphibian, to reptiles, and to mammals. Similar patterns may be seen in other systems as well.

Embryology

An **embryo** *is an organism in the early stages of development. The study of the development of an embryo is called* **embryology.** Studies of embryonic development in a number of animals is a second source of indirect evidence for change through time. In Unit 2 you studied mitosis. This is the process by which cells divide and increase in number. All multicellular plants and animals begin life as a single cell and then undergo a series of cell divisions as they develop. The basic pattern of cell division is the same in all of these organisms.

As the organism grows, certain cells begin to specialize. Eventually, a variety of tissues make up the new organism. During early stages of their embryonic development, different types of animals look almost the same. It would be hard to tell a fish embryo from that of a bird, amphibian, or mammal. The basic pattern of development is

OBJECTIVES FOR SECTION 3

J. Define the following terms in your own words: *homologous structures, embryo.*

K. List and describe three kinds of indirect evidence for change through time.

L. Explain how the concept of *change through time* relates to the definition of species.

Using the diagrams on page 261, have students point out similarities and differences between the embryos of different animals.

Answers to Questions for Section 2.

E. 1. See glossary.

   2. Two unrelated species, such as the timber wolf and the Tasmanian wolf may have had ancestors with similar selective pressures. Over time, selection removed some traits and favored others, today the two species resemble one another more than they do their close genetic relatives.

F. 3. Various isolating factors; large numbers of offspring, with increased chances of adaptive mutations; and a short interval between generations.

G. 4. Similar selection pressures on genetically dissimilar populations and geographical isolation.

H. 5. (1) Only a very small fraction of dead organisms become fossilized. (2) Those that are fossilized are almost never preserved as whole specimens. (3) Shallow sea, river, swamp environments favor fossilization, as do certain times in geologic history. So remains of forms living in these places and times are disproportionately represented in the fossil record. (4) Upland and mountain habitats are where early forms of new groups appear, but organisms in these environments are least likely to be preserved.

(See page 260 for answers 6-7.)

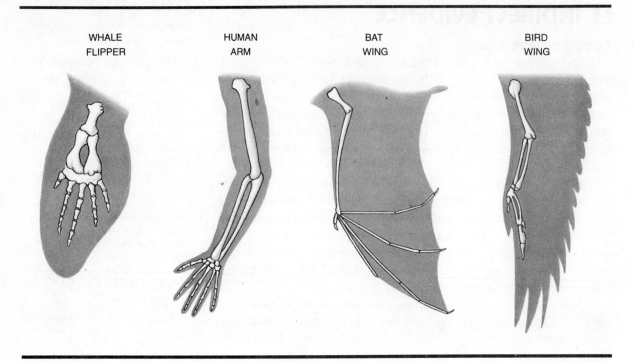

| WHALE FLIPPER | HUMAN ARM | BAT WING | BIRD WING |

14-13. The bone stuctures of all these limbs are homologous.

similar for related organisms. (See Fig. 14-14.) The alterations in structure are derived from a basic pattern. They represent increasing specialization as adaptations to a particular way of life.

Unity at Cellular and Molecular Levels

In Unit 2 you studied the structure and function of cells. You became aware of a great many kinds of cells. All of these cells operate in much the same fashion. Mitochondria, ribosomes, chloroplasts (when present), and other organelles in nearly all cells are similar in both structure and function. Moreover, at the molecular level, the same kind of unity among organisms continues to exist. This fact has been demonstrated by experiments. These studies used transfer RNA from bacterial cells and messenger RNA from rabbit cells. The t-RNA strands with their coded amino acids became attached to the m-RNA from the rabbit. Upon analysis, rabbit protein had been formed! Thus, the basic chemistry of life appears to be much the same in all living things.

Comparative studies of DNA, RNA, and proteins have demonstrated a basic unity of life. These studies help us to understand change through time by showing the degrees of relatedness between organisms. At the same time, they provide us with a third source of indirect evidence for evolution.

Answers to Questions for Section 2.

I. 6. The decay of radioactive isotopes of certain elements into other elements proceeds at a steady, predictable rate. U-238, for example, decays into Pb-206. Measuring the relative amounts of U-238 and Pb-206 in a rock gives an estimate of the rock's age.

*7. Sedimentary rocks are formed from previously-existing rock materials that have eroded, formed sediments, and been consolidated into new rocks. Radioactive dating of the sedimentary strata would yield ages for the original rocks they come from, not the sediments. However, volcanic rocks strata next to the sedimentary ones can be dated.

The degree of relatedness among organisms can be measured. This is usually done by studying similarities in DNA, RNA, and proteins. One hypothesis is that the more closely related that organisms are, the more alike their DNA will be. Another hypothesis involves the fact that DNA dictates the kinds of proteins made. Hence, the same relatedness as seen in DNA should appear in proteins as well.

To test this idea, scientists performed the following experiment. Samples of DNA and proteins were taken from organisms thought to be closely related. Other samples were taken from more distant relatives. The DNA was broken down. It was then analyzed for the proportions of the four nucleotides present. The proteins were analyzed for the proportions or sequences of amino acids. The results support both hypotheses. That is, both the DNA and the proteins are more alike in closely related organisms. More distantly related organisms have greater differences in their DNA and proteins.

At the molecular level, change through time is the substitution of one nucleotide for another. The number of differences in the proper sequence of each species gives evidence of their common ancestry. Molecular similarities confirm the relationships reported from the fossil record, studies in comparative anatomy, embryology, and other areas.

Answers to Questions for Section 3.

*3. The evidence is indirect because it comes from observations made in the present and there is no direct link with the past, as there is in fossil evidence.

4. Species are described as they exist today. However, they are constantly undergoing change and must be defined in terms of their ability to interbreed and produce fertile offspring.

The field of comparative biochemistry is relatively new and challenging. Students may be particularly interested in doing further library research in this area.

14-14. *There is considerable similarity in the development pattern of these embryos.*

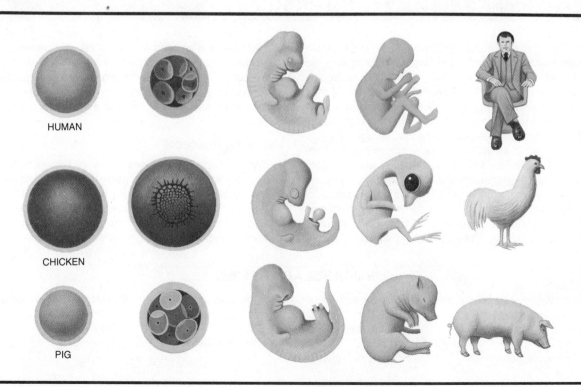

HUMAN

CHICKEN

PIG

J. 1. See glossary.

K. 2. Comparative anatomy: homologous structures provide an argument that they arose from changes in an ancestral pattern. Embryology: the similarity among the early embryos of different animals, and the specializations derived from a basic pattern suggests change through time. Unity at Cellular and Molecular Levels: the many kinds of cells in living things all operate in much the same fashion, with similar organelles. The basic chemistry of life is similar for all living things, and at the molecular level, change through time is the substitution of one nucleotide for another.

(See page 261 for answers 3-4.)

The study of change through time on the molecular level has two advantages. First, the information can be readily gathered and studied. For example, it is easy to detect the differences in the sequence of amino acids in certain kinds of protein from many different organisms. Second, a great variety of organisms can be studied and compared — from a fungus, to a shrub, to a frog. Therefore, this method will make many contributions to our understanding of evolutionary relationships.

QUESTIONS FOR SECTION 3

1. Define the following terms and give examples of each: homologous structures, embryo.

2. List and explain how each kind of indirect evidence contributes to the concept of change through time.

3. Explain why the kinds of evidence listed for question (2) are described as being indirect as opposed to direct.

4. How is the concept of *change through time* related to the definition of species?

CHAPTER REVIEW

The concept of *change through time* is especially evident when defining species. We describe species as they exist today. But they are constantly undergoing change. Hence, they must be defined in terms of their ability to interbreed and produce fertile offspring.

Speciation, adaptive radiation and convergence are brought about by selective processes acting on whole populations. The result is change in organisms where environments change. Also, there is stability among organisms where environments are stable. As organisms are matched with their surroundings by selection, *complementarity of organism and environment* becomes evident. Alterations in generalized body plans result in more specialization. The relationship between *structure and function* is also seen as specialization increases.

Direct evidence of change through time is seen in the fossil record. Indirect evidence is gathered from studies in comparative anatomy and embryology. Cellular and molecular similarities give indirect evidence of change.

Using the Concepts

1. The concept of *complementarity of organism and environment* has been one of the main points of focus throughout this book. Relating this chapter to Unit 1, research the topics of mimicry, protective coloration, and/or camouflage. Report on your findings, and explain how these relate to evolutionary mechanisms.

VOCABULARY REVIEW

1 species
preadaptations
directional selection
stabilizing selection
disruptive selection

divergence
speciation
isolating mechanisms
2 adaptation
adaptive radiation

convergence
ecologic equivalents
fossils
radioactivity
half-life

3 comparative anatomy
homologous
embryo
embryology

CHAPTER 14 TEST

Copy the number of each test item and place your answer to the right.

PART 1 Multiple Choice: Select the letter of the phrase that best completes each of the following.

a 1. Which one of the following pairs of organisms best illustrates the concept of adaptive radiation?
 a. *Lepus americanus* and *Lepus californicus*
 b. timber wolf and Tasmanian wolf   **c.** horse and donkey   **d.** deer and kangaroo.

c 2. Which one of the following pairs of organisms best illustrates the principle of convergence?
 a. spiders and insects   **b.** dogs and bears
 c. kangaroo and deer   **d.** snakes and lizards.

a 3. The evolution of the horse would be an example of
 a. directional selection   **b.** disruptive selection
 c. stabilizing selection   **d.** artificial selection.

c 4. The one barrier that separates species and cannot be overcome is   **a.** geographic   **b.** seasonal
 c. reproductive   **d.** behavioral.

d 5. Which isolating factor would be considered to be a post-mating factor?   **a.** structure or size of organism   **b.** behavioral   **c.** ecologic
 d. hybrid stability

a 6. Indirect evidence for the evolutionary process is gained from all but which one of the following?
 a. fossil record   **b.** cellular and molecular studies
 c. comparative anatomy   **d.** embryology.

d 7. The fossil record is often difficult to interpret because   **a.** there are often large gaps with no intermediate forms   **b.** few organisms are actually preserved as whole specimens   **c.** there is bias in the record because of the particular habitat in which some organisms lived   **d.** all of these.

c 8. Generally, the lower rock strata   **a.** exhibit more complex fossil forms   **b.** have the youngest fossils   **c.** yield fossils with less variability
 d. are thicker.

b 9. The most reliable method for dating the earth's age is through the study of   **a.** fossils   **b.** uranium-lead deposits   **c.** existing volcanoes
 d. earthquakes.

c 10. It is difficult to distinguish between rabbit and chicken embryos. This suggests that   **a.** most embryos breathe by gills before they are born
 b. birds and mammals descended directly from fish   **c.** vertebrates have a common ancestry
 d. mutations occur during the embryonic stage.

PART 2 Matching: Match the letter of the term in Column I with its description in Column II.

COLUMN I

a. adaptive radiation
b. convergence
c. divergence
d. ecological equivalent
e. embryo
f. half life
g. homologous structures
h. isolating mechanisms
i. preadaptations
j. species

COLUMN II

d 11. Organisms that fill the same niche in different parts of the world

i 12. Traits that exist before they are of survival value

c 13. Separation of one species into two or more species

a 14. Divergence of the members of a population in response to selective pressures

j 15. An interbreeding group of organisms

f 16. Time it takes for 50% of a radioactive substance to decay

h 17. Factors that restrict or prevent interbreeding

g 18. Parts of different organisms that are structurally similar but may function differently

e 19. An organism in the early stages of development

b 20. Development through time of some resemblances in two unrelated organisms in response to similar selective pressures

PART 3 Completion: Complete the following.

21. Islands would probably be good places for biologists to study the effects of ____ between populations.   *isolation*

22. The process by which new species arise from pre-existing forms is called ____   *speciation*

23. The adjustment that a population makes to its environment over a period of time is called ____   *adaptation*

24. Evidences of organisms from the geologic past are ____   *fossils*

25. The fact that dates can be established with some accuracy for various rock strata is due to the use of ____   *radioactivity*

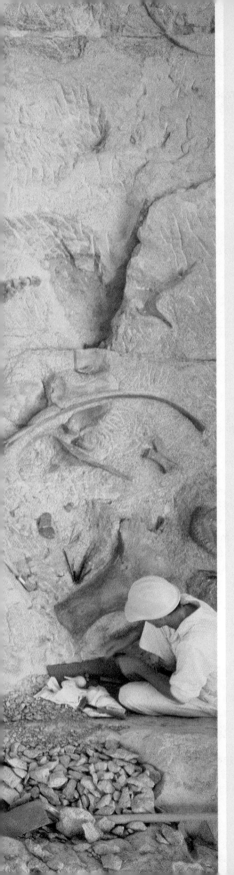

CHAPTER 15

LIFE IN THE PAST

A discussion of the theory of evolution sooner or later leads to the question of the origin of life on the earth. Life on earth began many years ago. However, we cannot be sure how or when it began. Several theories have been suggested. But none of them have been proved. Darwin was not directly concerned with the question of the origin of life. His ideas of natural selection dealt only with the change of species from earlier forms. No one thought about whether natural selection was related to life's origins at first. In this chapter we shall examine this relationship.

By now, you should be well aware of the *concept of change through time* and how it relates to the concept of *unity and diversity.* In tracing the history of life from its onset, we shall be using these concepts again. Change through time is a concept that applies to ideas as well as species. In this unit, we have been following the evolution of an idea as well as studying the evolution of organisms. In this chapter, we will add some more to the story.

As you begin this chapter, there are some basic questions that you might ask. These will help you to focus on the major points of the chapter.

- If living organisms developed from other forms, where did the first life come from?
- How did new kinds of plants and animals appear?

WORKER AT DINOSAUR NATIONAL MONUMENT

1 ORIGINS

Spontaneous Generation

Until the 19th Century, it was widely believed that many life forms arose suddenly from non-living things. This idea is called **abio-genesis** (ā bī ō *jen* ə səs) *which means beginning without life.* The secret of life was thought to be a mystical *substance* or a *vital force.* Those who held such beliefs were called *Vitalists.* The vital force was thought to be a part of all living things. If present in large enough amounts, it was believed that it could give life to non-living things. Examples of such spontaneous generation may be seen in Figure 15-1. The vital force was accepted as a fact by most people until the middle of the 19th Century. (Notice that what is accepted as a fact at one time may be refuted later.)

A small group of scientists opposed this view. They argued that there was no vital force or active principle. They pointed out that its existence was an assumption, not a fact. These scientists were convinced that events seeming to be spontaneous were caused by specific, if unknown, factors. All such events had a cause that could be discovered. Thus, they argued that life came only from life. This idea they called **biogenesis** (bī ō *jen* ə səs), *meaning life from life.* Their belief in cause and effect relationships caused them to be known as *Mechanists.*

Many "experiments" were done by both sides, but the results did not seem to prove anything. In setting up an experiment, scientists must first be sure that only one aspect, or *variable,* is free to change. Second, they must be sure that all factors except the one being tested are the same in all parts of the experiment. Thus, in a *controlled experiment* only one variable is free to change.

OBJECTIVES FOR SECTION 1

A. Define the following terms: *abiogenesis, biogenesis, variable, controlled experiment, sterile.*

B. Differentiate between theories that explain the origin of life.

C. State reasons both for and against the autotroph and heterotroph hypotheses.

D. Describe the experiments of Stanley Miller and Sidney Fox.

E. Summarize the essential events of the heterotroph hypothesis.

This is a good place to review the aspects of a controlled experiment.

15-1. Vitalists could cite many examples of spontaneous generation.

dirty shirt and wheat produce mice

mud produces frogs

OPEN JAR

meat

maggots on
rotting meat

SEALED JAR

meat with
no maggots

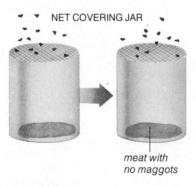

NET COVERING JAR

meat with
no maggots

15-2. Redi's experiment to disprove spontaneous generation.

Many early scientists were often not aware of all of the variables in their tests. For example, in 1668, Francesco Redi, an Italian physician, performed a controlled experiment. He did studies to test the idea of spontaneous generation. Redi first made an hypothesis. He claimed that the maggots that showed up in "dead bodies and decayed plants" came from the eggs of flies. He was sure that they were not produced by the dead material. Redi used a control in his work. He set up flasks with different types of meat and left them open to the air. For his control, he set up more flasks in the same way, but sealed them. (See Fig. 15-2.) Maggots appeared in the open flasks, but not in the sealed ones. Therefore, his hypothesis that maggots came from the eggs of flies was supported.

Those that believed in the vital force did not accept his work. They argued that sealed containers did not allow a free flow of air in the flasks. They claimed that air was necessary for the vital force to work. How might Redi have satisfied his critics on this score? He placed some meat into a flask and covered it with a fine net. This would allow air but not flies to enter the flask. Maggots never appeared in the meat.

Spontaneous generation was also believed to be the cause of the rotting of many types of broth. Some studies showed that heating the broths in sealed containers stopped rotting. It was argued that such heat destroyed the vital force at that time. It was not known that rotting was the work of unseen microorganisms. The use of improved microscopes brought the world of these microbes into view. Also, it set off another wave of experiments. It was not until 1864, however, that the experiments of Louis Pasteur proved that life came only from life.

The Swan-Necked Flasks

Pasteur's experiment was elegant in its simplicity. To set up the experiment, he used a series of flasks whose necks were drawn out into long S-curves. (See Fig. 15-3.) The ends of each curve were open to the air. Each flask was filled with a meat broth and boiled to kill microorganisms that might be in it. They were then left to cool. No microorganisms appeared in any of the flasks. Removing the neck from some of the flasks allowed air-borne material to enter the flask. The result was that rotting occurred. The undisturbed flasks remained without life, *sterile.*

The argument of those who supported the idea of a vital force had been met and answered. The flasks remained open to the air through the long tube. Heat could not have destroyed the "active principle" in the broth. Life did form if the tops were removed.

The question of abiogenesis was now solved — at least as far as complex life forms were concerned. But the question of life's origins were still unanswered. Experiments are going on today in an attempt to answer this question of origins.

Alternative Ideas

Most ideas about the origin of life on the earth do not really answer the questions. Scientists have developed several theories to help explain the origin of life. However, keep in mind that these theories are not facts. For example, one theory suggests that life came to earth from other parts of the Universe. Early life forms might have been able to survive space travel on specks of dust or meteorites. Finding their way to planets with the right conditions, these might have been able to evolve to life as we know it.

While it is possible that life exists elsewhere in the Universe, this idea has two major flaws. First, it still does not answer the question of how life originated. It only moves the origin to some other location. Second, it is highly unlikely that unprotected living things could survive the rigors of space travel. Intense ultraviolet (UV) and cosmic radiation and extreme temperatures would pose severe problems to unprotected microbes. Scientists have studied fragments from space quite closely. No organisms have yet been found in these, but they do contain organic molecules. Thus, it could well be that life exists elsewhere. However, the hazards of space travel reduce the likelihood of outer space being a source of life on the earth.

Living things need a constant input of energy to survive. Consumers are dependent upon the producer elements of the ecosystem. Thus, it might at first seem logical to expect that the first life forms were producers. These would have been able to trap and use light energy. Autotrophs could then give rise to heterotrophs later. This idea has been called the *Autotroph Hypothesis.*

Again a major flaw appears with this idea. The concept of unity and diversity has shown us a basic unity in the make-up of all life forms. Both producers and consumers give off stored chemical energy in much the same way — respiration. But producers also possess the complex chemical make-up for photosynthesis. It seems unlikely that a more complex system of life would have evolved in the first life forms.

The Heterotroph Hypothesis

Theories on how life began on the earth may be related to ideas about the origin of the earth. Whether the earth began as a hot or cold mass has a great deal to do with the kinds of chemical reactions that

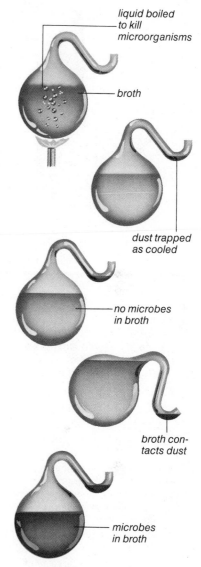

liquid boiled to kill microorganisms

broth

dust trapped as cooled

no microbes in broth

broth contacts dust

microbes in broth

15-3. *Pasteur's experiment to disprove spontaneous generation.*

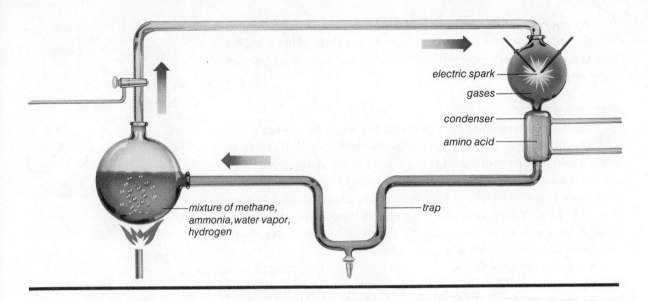

electric spark
gases
condenser
amino acid

mixture of methane,
ammonia, water vapor,
hydrogen

trap

15-4. *Miller circulated hydrogen, ammonia, methane, and water past an electric spark. After a week, he recovered amino acids from the condensed liquid in the trap. How does this support Oparin's hypothesis?*

As improbable as a series of events as described by the Heterotroph Hypothesis sounds, improbable events do occur. Students may like to research the occurrence of "impossible" events in a book of world records.

Point out that the simple account of the experiments that tend to support the Heterotroph Hypothesis tends to lead one to think that the creation of life in the lab is a soon-to-be-expected event. Such a conclusion is not at all warranted.

could produce the chemicals of life. The *Heterotroph Hypothesis,* first outlined in 1936 by A.I. Oparin, a Russian biochemist, assumes that the first organisms were consumers.

Oparin's hypothesis begins by assuming that the early atmosphere of the earth was made up of simple gases. These gases were methane (CH_4), ammonia (NH_3), hydrogen (H_2), and water vapor (H_2O). If enough energy were present, from lightning, for example, these gases would react together. Many different organic molecules might be produced by such activity. In time, continued reactions and changing conditions on the earth would result in the development of the first early life forms. At this stage, chemical change would give way to organic change, another phrase for the development of living organisms.

What evidence is there to support Oparin's hypothesis? First, we know that the earth's crust is constantly changing. Also, the gases that constantly leak from inside the earth support Oparin's theory of what the early atmosphere might have been like. Not all scientists today agree on the exact nature of that atmosphere, however.

In 1953, Stanley Miller was a graduate student at the University of Chicago. He studied under Dr. Harold Urey, a Nobel Prize winner, and tested Oparin's ideas. He set up a complex apparatus to reproduce the early atmosphere of the earth. (See Fig. 15-4.) After a week, a red fluid was withdrawn and tested. It was found to contain several amino acids, the building blocks of proteins! Repeated experiments have confirmed Miller's findings. These experiments added many other kinds of molecules to those first produced.

Certainly the production of amino acids is not the production of life. Nor does it prove Oparin's hypothesis. But it does make us consider the idea as a possible one. Based on these early experiments, many scientists tested other combinations and energy sources. The results were similar.

The next step was taken by Dr. Sidney Fox. He showed that amino acids could be combined into peptide chains by using gentle heat. In addition, by treating these chains with hot water and cooling them, many microscopic droplets were formed. When the acidity of such a system is adjusted, many of these droplets will clump together. Such clumps are called coacervates (kō *as* ər vāts). When viewed under the microscope, they look much like certain microorganisms. (See Fig. 15-5.) Later experiments have shown that these coacervate droplets have some properties of living cells. Some, for example, have shown osmotic and enzyme activity.

Such chemical clumps, occurring in nature, would be subject to natural selection. This would be similar to the selection of living plants and animals. Unstable clumps would break up and be destroyed. Stable combinations would remain. These combinations might even attract other molecules and cause them to be brought into the clump.

Evolution of Autotrophs

The rest of Oparin's hypothesis relates to the evolution of early life forms. Natural selection would have favored certain of these pre-cells. Also, it would have selected against others. Survivors of the selection process would have been able to use energy to maintain themselves. Organic molecules taken from the environment would have been able to supply the necessary energy for such metabolism. Selection would have favored stable systems. Moreover, these systems would have begun to be more and more cell-like. At what point life could be said to have begun is open to discussion.

The early consumers would have been doomed for extinction. This would have occurred as they increased in number and their energy sources became used up. Again, selection would have favored those that could make use of other energy sources. Stability in living systems is achieved through the direction of the cell's DNA. Since enzymes control what materials can be used for an energy source, changes in the DNA are required for new enzymes to be present. The shift from one source to another in early life forms might have occurred many times as each became exhausted. With each shift, a new mutation would be required to provide new chemical possibilities.

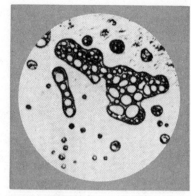

15-5. Microscopic droplets of proteins and carbohydrates will clump and form coacervates. These resemble certain microorganisms.

Answers to Questions for Section 1.

E. 11. The early atmosphere contained ammonia, methane, hydrogen, and water vapor. Lightning would cause these to react together, producing a variety of organic molecules. Continued reactions would lead to first life forms, and then chemical changes would give way to organic change.

12. Natural selection would favor the pre-cells that could use energy-rich organic molecules to maintain themselves. A series of mutations in these first consumers would result in the first photosynthetic organisms, which would have selective advantage over the heterotrophs, whose supply of energy-rich organic molecules by now has greatly diminished. The first hererotrophs would thus become extinct as the first autotrophs become established.

13. The atmosphere contained ammonia, methane, hydrogen, and water vapor, but no oxygen. It was permeated by ultraviolet radiation from the sun, in addition to the sun's light. Energy in the form of lightning was prevalent.

14. The chemical substances used, the random mixing of the substances, and the use of an electric spark to simulate lightning.

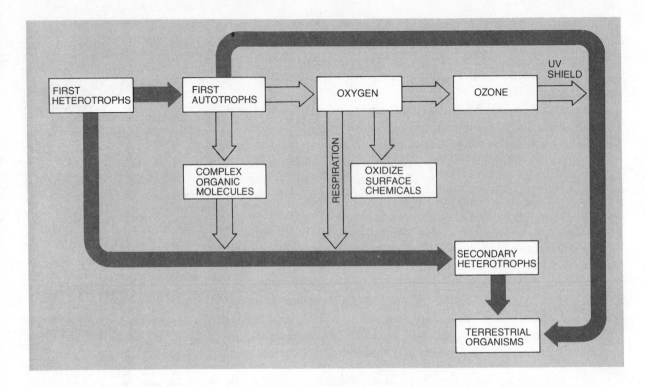

FIRST HETEROTROPHS → FIRST AUTOTROPHS → OXYGEN → OZONE → UV SHIELD

FIRST AUTOTROPHS → COMPLEX ORGANIC MOLECULES

OXYGEN → RESPIRATION

OXYGEN → OXIDIZE SURFACE CHEMICALS

SECONDARY HETEROTROPHS → TERRESTRIAL ORGANISMS

15-6. *The development of autotrophs had a dramatic impact on the living and non-living world.*

Mutations are thought of as fairly rare events. The environment of the early earth, however, may well have been the cause of a higher mutation rate. Even over a fairly short time, the number of mutations may have been quite high. The end result would have been the development of a special sequence of chemical reactions. This would be one that could build complex molecules by using the sun's energy. These organisms would have been the first to carry on photosynthesis. Organisms with such pathways would not need energy-rich molecules from their surroundings. They would be able to use energy supplied by the sun. These unique organisms would be the first autotrophs.

Other Effects of Photosynthesis

The evolution of photosynthesis would have directly affected earth's life forms in two other ways. First, the consumers still living would have been able to use the autotrophs as food sources. Second, the production of oxygen by autotrophs would have changed the atmosphere in a major way.

Some texts refer to the oxygen produced in photosynthesis as a by-product. Its presence is as important to life on earth as is a constant energy source. Thus, it is not simply a by-product. (See Fig. 15-6.)

By changing the selective factors in the environment, new avenues for change in living things are opened up. One such direction is the formation of new chemical pathways for the release of energy from organic molecules. Release of energy in the early life forms was most likely not too efficient. Without oxygen, much of the stored energy would stay trapped in the molecules. The release of this energy within a cell by using oxygen and the proper enzymes is called *respiration*. The evolution of respiration was essential for more complex organisms to evolve.

A second direction for evolution led to life on land. Until oxygen became plentiful, life was confined to the water. The presence of oxygen allowed for the development of an ozone layer. Ozone, a form of oxygen, absorbs UV radiation. Intense UV radiation on the primitive earth would have made life on land impossible. Simple organisms were unprotected and would have died quickly. UV actually is used in hospitals and other places to kill microorganisms. Less UV radiation reaches the earth because of the ozone layer. Therefore, conditions for life on land would have become more tolerable. New potentials for life would be at hand. But many other new problems would make survival on land hard. Can you think of reasons why this might be so?

QUESTIONS FOR SECTION 1

1. Define the following terms: abiogenesis, biogenesis, variable, controlled experiment, sterile, respiration.
2. How did Redi attempt to control his experiment? What was lacking in his control?
3. Explain how each of the Vitalists' criticisms for earlier experiments were answered in Pasteur's "swan-necked flask experiment."
4. Differentiate between theories that explain the fossil record and those that explain the origin of life.
5. How does the heterotroph hypothesis resemble the idea of spontaneous generation? How does it differ?
6. What is the autotroph hypothesis?
7. State reasons both for and against the autotroph hypothesis and heterotroph hypothesis.
8. What is the major weakness of the autotroph hypothesis?
9. Describe the experiments of Stanley Miller and Sidney Fox.
10. What assumptions did Miller and Fox make in designing their experiments?
11. Summarize the essential events of the heterotroph hypothesis.
12. Describe the sequence of events that might have led to the development of autotrophs from heterotrophs.
13. Describe the conditions that are thought to have existed in the atmosphere of the primitive earth.
14. What factors in the experiments of Miller and Fox attempt to create the conditions of the primitive earth?

Living on land would also present problems of conserving moisture, supporting the body, and reproducing.

Answers to Questions for Section 1.

A. 1. See glossary.

   2. He set up flasks with meat in them but sealed the flasks. The sealed flasks did not allow a free flow of air.

   *3. The curved necks of the flasks allowed air to enter but kept out air-borne material. Nothing grew in the sterile broth in the flasks until after the necks were broken, allowing other material than air to enter. This showed that the air alone did not generate life.

B. *4. Theories that explain the fossil record explain how life forms have changed through the ages, and those that explain the origin of life deal with whether life on earth began from forms that came from outer space, or from non-living materials on earth.

   *5. They both state that living things originate in non-living material. The heterotroph hypothesis does not assume a vital force, as did the idea of spontaneous generation.

   6. That the first life forms were producers, able to trap and use light energy.

C. 7. Autotroph hypothesis. For: Since consumers depend upon producers, it seems logical that producers would have come first. Against: The evolution of such a complex process as phtosynthesis in the first forms of life seems unlikely. Hetereotroph hypothesis. For: It is supported by experimental evidence, and theories of the earth's early atmosphere. Against: Disagreement among theorists as to early conditions on earth, and incompleteness of the experimental evidence.

   8. It seems unlikely that such a complex process as photosynthesis would have evolved in the first life forms.

(See page 270 for answers 9-10.)

CHAPTER INVESTIGATION

A. What are the primary differences between the two scenes?

B. Assuming both pictures are "typical" of two different ages of the earth's history, interpret the differences between the two scenes. How might change through time be used to interpret these differences?

C. What factors might have contributed to the replacement of dinosaurs by mammals?

2 MAJOR RADIATIONS

Geologic History

The earth has been going through constant change since its formation. Mountains, oceans, and continents have come and gone time and again. Continents have broken and moved apart. Along with these physical changes, climates have also changed. By studying the rocks and the fossils they contain, scientists have been able to put together a fairly complete history of the earth. A summary of this history is shown in Table 15-1 on page 274.

Little is known about the earliest life forms. We have assumed that life had its origin in the ancient seas. Certainly, life forms that lived on land are not known prior to the Silurian (si *loor* ē ən) Period. Within the last fifteen years, microorganism-like fossils have been found in Precambrian (prē *kam* brē ən) sediments from South Africa. These have been dated to between three and four billion years of age! These findings may prove to be valid. If so, our estimates of two billion years for the origin of life will need to be changed.

There have also been findings of fossils of jellyfish and other animals without backbones *(invertebrates)* in Precambrian deposits. This tells us that invertebrates were already in existence more than 600 million years ago. The fossil record is scanty, however, until the Cambrian Period. (See Fig. 15-7 on page 275.)

The Paleozoic (pā lē ə *zō* ik) Era was an important time for many reasons. Thousands of new forms of organisms appeared during this time. The first known animals with backbones *(vertebrates)* show up in sediments from the Cambrian Period. The vertebrate radiation was at first limited to fishes. But the vacant niches of the seas were quickly filled by the rapidly-evolving vertebrates.

Land plants appeared during the Silurian Period. This development was perhaps one of the most striking events in the history of life. These new organisms greatly changed the hostile land environment. With a more receptive environment, insects and their relatives soon followed. Within 100 million years, great forests thrived in many parts of the world. Today, remains of these forests lie beneath the earth's surface as vast coal and oil deposits.

Vertebrate Radiation

Once plants were rooted on land new potentials for the vertebrates were created. Besides insects and their relatives, vertebrates make up the only other major animal group that lives on land. We don't know what factors might have favored the development of land-dwelling vertebrates. Our knowledge of natural selection, however, allows us to make an educated hypothesis.

OBJECTIVES FOR SECTION 2
F. Define the following terms: *invertebrates, vertebrates, mammals.*
G. Describe how the environment might have been responsible for the first vertebrates to venture onto land.
H. List the Geologic eras and the major events that occurred during their existence.
I. Make a diagram that summarizes the vertebrate radiation through the reptiles.

Emphasize the enormous amount of time that is represented by the fossil record. Challenge some students to develop analogies for the time scale in terms of a 24-hour day, a week, a year, or a set of encyclopedias.

TABLE 15.1   A SUMMARY OF THE GEOLOGIC AND BIOLOGIC HISTORY OF THE EARTH.

		Epoch	Years Ago (millions)	Conditions and Characteristics	Plant Life	Animal Life
CENOZOIC	Quaternary	Recent	.015	moderating climate; glaciers receding	modern	modern man and other animals
		Pleistocene	1 to 2	periodic glaciers; cold climates	decline of woody plants; rise of herbs	appearance of man
	Tertiary	Pliocene	10	cold; snow building	forest recede	appearance of the hominid line
		Miocene	25	temperate climates		
		Oligocene	35	warm climates		modernization of mammals mammalian radiation
		Eocene	55	very warm climates		
		Paleocene	70	very warm climates		
MESOZOIC	Cretaceous		120	warm climates; swamps dry out; Rocky mountains rise	rise of the flowering plants to dominance	rise of primitive mammals; first modern birds; dinosaurs become extinct
	Jurassic		150	warm; extensive lowlands and continental seas	first flowering plants; conifers dominant	first birds; first mammals; dinosaurs abundant; flying reptiles
	Triassic		180	warm, dry climates; extensive deserts	conifers dominant; seed ferns disappear	first dinosaurs
PALEOZOIC	Permian		240	climate variable; increased dryness; mountains rising	decline of club mosses/horsetails	mammal-like reptiles; rise of modern insects
	Carboniferous		325	climate warm/humid; shallow inland seas; swamps	coal forests; club mosses/horsetails	first reptiles; insects common
	Devonian		400	land rises; shallow seas and marshes; deserts	land plants common; first conifers	first amphibians; sharks abundant
	Silurian		450	mild climate; great inland seas	algae abundant; evidence of land plants	first air-breathing animals; first insects
	Ordovician		475	mild climate; warm in Arctic; most land under water	first land plants; marine algae abundant	first fishes
	Cambrian		600	mild climate; extensive lowlands and inland seas	marine algae	invertebrates abundant; trilobites
PRE-CAMBRIAN (PROTEROZOIC)			2,700	conditions uncertain; first glaciers; first life forms	blue-green algae	marine invertebrates; protozoans
ARCHAEOZOIC (AZOIC)			4,600	conditions uncertain	no direct evidence of any life	

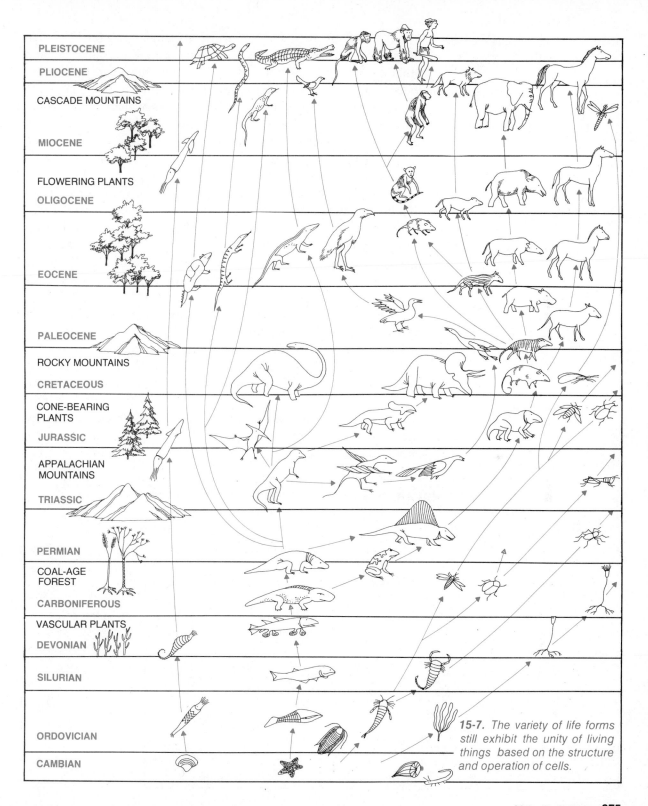

PLEISTOCENE

PLIOCENE

CASCADE MOUNTAINS

MIOCENE

FLOWERING PLANTS

OLIGOCENE

EOCENE

PALEOCENE

ROCKY MOUNTAINS

CRETACEOUS

CONE-BEARING PLANTS

JURASSIC

APPALACHIAN MOUNTAINS

TRIASSIC

PERMIAN

COAL-AGE FOREST

CARBONIFEROUS

VASCULAR PLANTS

DEVONIAN

SILURIAN

ORDOVICIAN

CAMBIAN

15-7. The variety of life forms still exhibit the unity of living things based on the structure and operation of cells.

Major Radiations 275

Many students are especially interested in prehistoric environments and like to build dioramas of these. Field trips to museums of natural history are always helpful in "setting the scene."

We do know that land masses were rising during the Devonian (də *vō* nē ən) Era. Shallow pools were drying out. Many fish and other aquatic forms no doubt died off. Some, however, had fleshy, lobed fins and primitive lungs. These structures had helped them to live in stagnant pools where little oxygen was available. They could exist for short periods out of water in search of better homes. Such preadaptations may have been useful in the evolution of amphibians. Amphibians are vertebrates that start life in the water. However, they are able to live on land as adults.

The first ventures onto land by such animals were not attempts to look for new places to live. On the contrary, such behavior was simply an attempt to survive. Only those that had modified air bladders that served as simple lungs could survive. Old habitats were being taken away. Many forms were doomed to extinction. In many areas of the world, natural selection favored a trend toward life on land.

The transition of animals to the new existence on land could not be thought of as complete until the appearance of a shell-covered egg. Before that time all animals laid their eggs in water. Even those that lived on land returned to the water to lay eggs. This came about during the latter part of the Carboniferous (kär bə *nif* ər əs) Period. The reptiles were the first vertebrates to make the complete transition. These early reptiles were probably very amphibian-like in appearance. The fossil record suggests that adaptive radiation came about quickly.

15-8 THE MAJOR BRANCHES OF THE REPTILIAN RADIATION

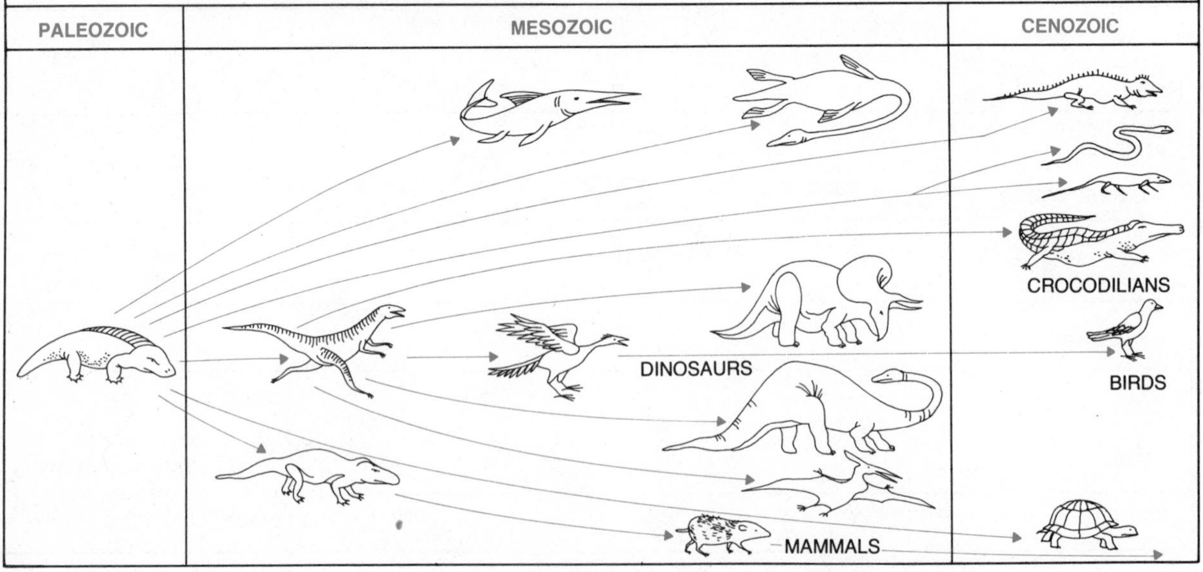
PALEOZOIC
MESOZOIC
CENOZOIC
CROCODILIANS
DINOSAURS
BIRDS
MAMMALS

Perhaps as many as six major lines of early reptiles arose. (See Fig. 15-8.) One of these, in turn, also went through a large-scale radiation that resulted in dinosaurs, flying reptiles, and crocodiles. Reptiles of various kinds dominated the earth for nearly 200 million years. This period, known as the Mesozoic (mes ə zō ik) Era, has also been called the Age of Reptiles.

Two lines of the reptilian radiation are of special interest. These gave rise to two new kinds of animals, birds and mammals. Although the birds have also reached great diversity, the mammals came to replace the reptiles as the dominant land animal.

Toward the end of the Mesozoic Era, the dinosaurs went through mass extinctions. The cause for the Great Dying of dinosaurs and other animals is not known. Changing climates or the rise of mammals might have played major roles in their disappearance.

The Rise of Mammals

Mammals are vertebrates with fur. Most bear their young alive and nurse them with special milk-producing glands called *mammary glands*. The first mammals appeared sometime during the middle of the Mesozoic Era. They increased in variety and in numbers until they gained dominance over the reptiles. The Cenozoic (sē nə zō ik) Era became known as the Age of Mammals.

At least two dozen lines of radiation can be seen among the mammals. (See Fig. 15-9.) Some have become extinct, but most exist today. The first mammals were probably egg-laying, as was typical of

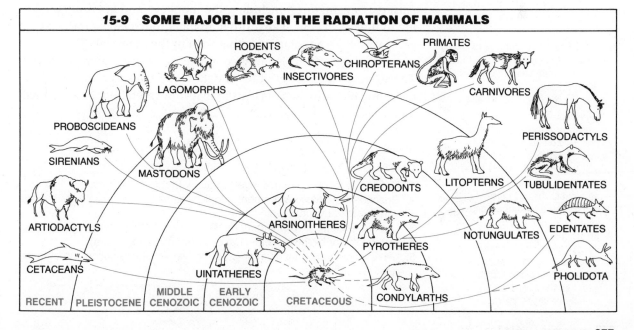

15-9 SOME MAJOR LINES IN THE RADIATION OF MAMMALS

RODENTS
LAGOMORPHS
INSECTIVORES
CHIROPTERANS
PRIMATES
CARNIVORES
PROBOSCIDEANS
PERISSODACTYLS
SIRENIANS
MASTODONS
LITOPTERNS
TUBULIDENTATES
CREODONTS
ARTIODACTYLS
ARSINOITHERES
PYROTHERES
NOTUNGULATES
EDENTATES
CETACEANS
UINTATHERES
CONDYLARTHS
PHOLIDOTA
RECENT | PLEISTOCENE | MIDDLE CENOZOIC | EARLY CENOZOIC | CRETACEOUS

reptiles. Today, only the duck-billed platypus and the echidna (i *kid* nə) exist to suggest such early origins. Both live only on the Australian continent. It appears that changes occurred in mammals on other continents that offered great competition to the egg-laying mammals.

For their first 100 million years, mammals stayed fairly small, unseen, or even rare. Compared to the rapid radiation of amphibians and reptiles, the mammalian radiation was slow. Most of the niches were filled. Competition was no doubt severe.

Changes in the reproductive process gave rise to the marsupial, or pouched mammals. Offspring of marsupials are born prematurely and must complete their development in a small pouch outside the mother. Here they are protected and nourished until they are old enough to begin exploring on their own. Marsupials went through a large-scale radiation. This occurred during the early part of the Cenozoic Era. In time they were replaced by the more efficient placental mammals. In placental mammals, the young develop inside the mother's body, in the uterus. They are nourished by the placenta until they are born. Gradual drifting of the continents isolated Australia from Asia. The Australian marsupials were thus set apart from the emerging placentals. So far this has effectively saved them from severe competition and possible extinction.

Placental mammals have also gone through a large-scale radiation in the past 70 million years or so. Some, such as whales, have adapted to a life in water. Bats, on the other hand, took to the air. Burrowing evolved in many forms, including the kangaroo rat, as underground niches were explored. Most, however, remained on the surface. Several lines, including the monkeys and apes, adapted to life in the trees. Few, if any, other animal groups have produced the great variety of adaptation as that seen in the mammals.

The fossil record is fairly complete for many mammal groups. There is a great amount of fossil data that relates to humans. However, much controversy has arisen in its interpretation. Next, we will look closely at this evidence.

QUESTIONS FOR SECTION 2

1. Define the following terms: invertebrate, vertebrate, mammal.
2. Describe how the environment might have been responsible for the first vertebrates to venture onto land.
3. List the geologic eras and periods beginning with the Cambrian.
4. List the major biologic events that occurred during each era.
5. Make a diagram that summarizes the vertebrate radiation through the reptiles.

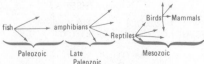

3 HUMAN HISTORY

Primate Relations

Primates are characterized by well developed grasping hands (and often feet). This means that the thumb is able to touch each of the other fingers. They also usually have nails on their fingers and toes instead of claws. Primates have a well-developed collar bone, or *clavicle* (*klav* i kəl) that many other mammals do not have. Their eyes are directed forward rather than to the side. Both eyes can be focused on the same field of vision. Each eye views the field from a slightly different angle. This allows them to see in three dimensions, something that few other animals can do.

The fossil record suggests that the primate line arose from tree-living, or *arboreal* (är *bôr* ē əl) shrew-like animals. It is thought that early in the Cenozoic Era, this line split into two major groups. Today, one of these proposed groups is represented by the *prosimians* (prō *sim* ē əns). These are small, fairly active, often nocturnal primates found only in Africa and Madagascar. They include lemurs, bush babies, and pottos.

It is also thought that the other major primate line gave rise to four smaller groups that exist today. They are all referred to as *anthropoids* (*an* thrə poids). Two of the anthropoid groups are monkeys. The New World Monkeys are found in Central and South America. Many are characterized by having *prehensile* (prē *hen* səl), or grasping tails that they use to survive in the trees. The Old World Monkeys are found in Africa, Asia, and the Middle East. None of these have a prehensile tail. Some spend most of their life on the ground.

The third and fourth anthropoid groups existed as a single, diverse group. This continued until perhaps ten or fifteen million years ago. The Miocene (*mi* ə sēn) Epoch saw a great reduction in the forests of the world. This was perhaps the selective factor that separated the groups into two distinct lines of descent. There is no full agreement among anthropologists. However, there is a general consensus that one group remained at least partly arboreal. These are thought to be the ancestors of the apes. Today, this group includes gibbons, chimpanzees, orangutans and gorillas. The other group is believed to have become the *hominids* (*hom* ə nids).

Hominid Evolution

The piecing together of the long history of humanity has not been an easy task. Fossil remains are commonly incomplete. There are many ways to interpret the evidence. Much remains to be learned about human history.

OBJECTIVES FOR SECTION 3

J. Define the following terms: *primate, arboreal, anthropoid, prehensile, bipedal, hominid, race.*
K. List some of the skeletal features of hominids that apparently underwent change as *Homo sapiens* developed.
L. Describe the concept of race as based upon allele frequencies.

Point out that many people thought that Darwin had suggested that humans evolved from apes. This is not what he meant at all. He pointed out that humans, like other mammals, had arisen from some very early common ancestor.

There may have been population pressures in the reduced forests of the late Miocene Era. This may have forced certain groups of anthropoids onto the ground in search of new homes. Such pressures directly affected the development of certain traits. A two-legged (*bipedal*) form of movement and an erect posture would likely provide greater security in detecting and escaping dangers. This change had an effect on the possible development of other traits as well. For example, bipedal movement frees the hands. This, in turn, favors the development of a precision grasping type of hand. Foot structure, spinal shape, size, and position are other features that would be affected. The result of the adaptations is a true hominid.

According to the theory of evolution, the hominids include modern humans and their ancestors, dating back to their Miocene origin. When tools are found with the skeletal remains, they are taken as evidence of culture during the life of the fossil forms. *Homo sapiens* (hō mō *sā* pē ənz) refers only to the species of human living today. Geologically, *Homo sapiens* is a newcomer, having arrived only some 100,000 years ago.

The Humans

There are few fossils to trace the first ten million years of hominid development. Until 1924, the oldest fossils could only represent part of the last half-million years or so. It was then that Raymond Dart, an anatomy professor at a South African medical school, unearthed a skull. It was that of a five or six year old child. The deposits from which the skull had been taken were estimated to be a million years old. He named his "find" *Australopithecus africanus* (o strā lō *pith* ə kəs af ri *kən* əs).

The names given to new "finds" of fossil hominids suggested that many different species had roamed the African plain. As more fossils were found in various parts of Africa, however, it began to appear that they came from only two or three species. The two most widely accepted species are *A. africanus* and *A. robustus* (rō *bəs* təs). A third species, *A. boisei* (*bwä* zē) is accepted by some scientists.

Australopithecines, as these primitive hominids are known, were bipedal and erect. They had small teeth, and a flattened face. Also, they lacked heavy skull ridges and crests. However, the size of their brain was less than half that of modern humans.

The late L.S.B. Leakey, a prominent anthropologist, had felt that the tools found with the Australopiths were made by another, more advanced hominid. (See Fig. 15-10.) In the late 1950's, Leakey presented his evidence for this position. It was in the form of a fossil he called *Homo habilis* (hə bil əs). By 1972, his son, Richard Leakey, had

15-10. *Louis Leakey with 600,000 year old skull.*

unearthed several fossil fragments. They have been dated at 2.8 million years. Evidence provided by the son's work supports the father's theory.

In the last decade of the 19th Century, Eugene Dubois found what came to be called the Java form. This find, along with a host of others throughout Africa, Asia, and the Middle East are now grouped together as a single species, *Homo erectus* (i *rekt* əs). On the basis of dating evidence, they are thought to have lived between 500,000 and 300,000 years ago. Compared to fossils that lived earlier, they had an enlarged brain case. In addition, they had a more rounded skull, and typical human teeth. (See Fig. 15-11.) In 1975, Richard Leakey uncovered a skull of *H. erectus* at Lake Turkana. This find, dated at 1.5 million years, seems to indicate that *H. erectus* was present before the Australopiths.

15-11. *Skull of H. erectus.*

Homo Sapiens

There is a wealth of fossil material to document the existence of modern humans, *Homo sapiens,* in the last 100,000 years. There is little evidence, however, that tells much about the period between 100,000 and 500,000 years ago.

Perhaps the best known fossils of *H. sapiens* are those of the Neanderthal (nē *an* dər thôl) form, first found in the Neander Valley in Germany. The Neanderthals had a highly formed culture as seen in their cave paintings and burial sites. (See Fig. 15-12.)

The Neanderthals seem to have been replaced by a fully modern, more intelligent form we call Cro-Magnon (krō *mag* non). Recent studies show that Neanderthal and Cro-Magnon populations lived together. Thus, both the Neanderthals and the Cro-Magnons may be thought of as *H. sapiens.* Such a view is not universal, however. Some scientists regard the Neanderthals as an evolutionary dead end. We can never know for certain, but more data may be helpful in understanding the development of the history of the early human races.

15-12. *Neanderthal tools.*

Races

Today, humans are spread throughout the world. They exhibit a wide variety of types and forms. Skin color varies from very light to very dark. Hair may be straight, wavy, or tightly coiled. Variety is seen also in stature, blood type, eye and hair color, and a great many other features. These traits are often characteristic of certain populations. We may refer to these populations loosely as races. However, it is important to realize that a biological definition of this term is based on allele frequency, not on appearance. Thus, a **race** *is an interbreeding population with characteristic allele frequencies different*

15-13. *Selection, drift, and isolation were important factors that produced differences between early populations of humans.*

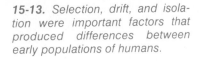

The study of humans, their origins, development, cultures and adaptations is called anthropology.

from those of other such groups. Such differences may be the product of selection and genetic drift. Furthermore, these are magnified by isolation. Note that these are the same factors that result in speciation.

As humans explored new environments, they took with them certain alleles. (See Fig. 15-13.) Certain environments favored certain alleles. Other environments selected different combinations. Over time, populations came to look different from each other. In many cases, however, each population continued to have at least a few of the alleles present in other populations. Differences in how often various alleles appeared, however, was responsible for differences in appearance.

The concept of race has become increasingly blurred in the last few thousands of years. Isolating mechanisms that normally affect plants and animals have had little meaning for humans. Technology has enabled humans to overcome geographical isolation. Mixing of populations of humans has always occurred. Today, it does so with increasing regularity. Thus, races become blurred as differences between populations decrease.

Some biologists try to classify humans into three broad races. Others have suggested five, eight, or some other number. Based on allele frequencies, we see that such systems fail to hold any real meaning.

QUESTIONS FOR SECTION 3

1. Define the following terms: primate, arboreal, anthropoid, prehensile, bipedal, hominid, race.
2. What selection pressures would favor a larger brain in a terrestrial biped?
3. What evidence suggests that Australopithecines were not in the direct line of human evolution?
4. Describe the progressive changes in the skeletal features of hominids from the Miocene to the present.
5. Explain why a biological definition of "race" is based on allele frequency, not on appearance.

Answers to Questions for Section 3.

J. 1. See glossary.

   *2. The need to make tools and use intelligence to hunt food, find places to live, and escape enemies.

K. *3. The size of the brain was less than half that of modern humans, although they were bipedal and erect.

   *4. Decreased brow ridge, larger cranium and brain capacity, larger chin, reduction in the skull ridges.

(See page 282 for answer 5.)

CHAPTER REVIEW

Change through time as a concept, applies to ideas as well as organisms. The Vitalist idea of abiogenesis was not disspelled for many centuries. Controlled experiments aided the Mechanists to show that life came only from life. This settled the question of abiogenesis. However, it did not settle the question of life's origin on earth.

The steps of the heterotroph hypothesis also emphasizes the concept of *change through time* as chemical change leads to organic change. The same factors that guide the development of plants and animals, also influence the development of chemical compounds. Nowhere is the concept illustrated better than in the fossil record. The history of life on earth is one of constant change. This occurs as environments select, favor, and eliminate. The concept of *unity and diversity* is reflected in the history of life on the earth. There is unity seen in the processes that produced diversity. Moreover, there is a basic unity in life itself. This occurs in spite of the diverse forms in which it appears.

Of the many mammalian lines, it is theorized that one of the arboreal groups gave rise to the primates. The modern prosimians are the most like the earliest primates. The other primate line includes, monkeys, apes, and hominids. The latest data seem to indicate the existence of *Homo habilis* and various Australopithecines at the same time. This occurred perhaps as early as three million years ago. The Australopiths represent a divergent line and became extinct. Meanwhile, *H. habilis* appears to have given rise to *H. erectus*. It is from this line *H. sapiens* theoretically arose, perhaps 300,000 years ago.

Using the Concepts

1. Why is a consideration of the ancient atmosphere probably an important aspect of the Heterotroph Hypothesis?
2. Support or reject the Heterotroph Hypothesis as a possible sequence of events that might have led to the first peptide chains.

VOCABULARY REVIEW

1 abiogenesis
  biogenesis
  sterile

2 mammal
3 primate
  arboreal

  anthropoid
  hominid
  race

CHAPTER 15 TEST

Copy the number of each test item and place your answer to the right.

PART 1   Multiple Choice: Select the letter of the phrase that best completes each of the following.

b   1. The Paleozoic Era was a very important time in the history of life in which all but which of the following first appeared?   **a.** land plants   **b.** mammals   **c.** vertebrates   **d.** insects

a   2. Which one of the following is not a fossil?   **a.** an ancient rock   **b.** a leaf imprint in a rock   **c.** the track of an animal in a rock   **d.** a bone.

b   3. The emergence of oxygen in the atmosphere was most likely a result of   **a.** volcanic activity   **b.** development of photosynthesis   **c.** fermentation in heterotrophs   **d.** respiration in heterotrophs.

d   4. Electrical discharges within mixtures of gases considered part of the earth's ancient atmosphere have made possible the formation of   **a.** water   **b.** proteins   **c.** DNA   **d.** amino acids.

d   5. The emergence of the first land animals would have been aided by   **a.** a lack of competition   **b.** availability of niches   **c.** changes in existing aquatic habitats   **d.** all of these.

d   6. In the course of the Mesozoic radiation of reptiles some lines   **a.** became extinct   **b.** exhibited aquatic adaptations   **c.** exhibited flying adaptations   **d.** all of these.

c   7. Which feature would least likely tend to prevent the development of a land form from an aquatic one?   **a.** lack of support   **b.** changes in temperature on land   **c.** lack of oxygen on land   **d.** lack of acceptable food supplies on land.

a   8. Which of the following is considered to be a prosimian?   **a.** lemur   **b.** gibbon   **c.** gorilla   **d.** achidna.

d   9. Which factors were important in the formation of human races?   **a.** isolation of populations   **b.** selection of adaptive features   **c.** genetic drift   **d.** all of these.

c 10. The Heterotroph Hypothesis is based on the assumption that   **a.** organic compounds were formed before inorganic ones   **b.** respiration evolved before fermentation   **c.** organic compounds served as energy sources for the first organisms (cells)   **d.** heterotrophs relied directly on the sun's energy.

PART 2   Matching: Match the letter of the term in Column I with its description in Column II.

COLUMN I

a. abiogenesis   **e.** marsupial   **i.** Pasteur
b. Cenozoic   **f.** Mesozoic   **j.** race
c. fossil   **g.** Miller
d. hominid   **h.** Oparin

COLUMN II

c 11. Evidence of past life forms

f 12. Age of Reptiles

e 13. Pouched mammal

d 14. Member of the human line of descent

i 15. Swan-necked flask experiment

j 16. Interbreeding group within a species having unique allele frequencies

b 17. Age of Mammals

g 18. Experiment to reproduce early earth's proposed atmosphere

h 19. Heterotroph hypothesis

a 20. Spontaneous generation

PART 3   Completion: Complete the following.

21. The four gases thought to have made up the earth's primitive atmosphere were _____.

22. The radiation of reptiles is thought to have given rise to two new kinds of vertebrates, the _____ and the _____.

23. Three characteristics unique to mammals are _____.

24. The idea that life arises from life is _____.   biogenesis

25. Neanderthal, Cro-Magnon, and modern humans are collectively referred to as belonging to the species _____.   Homo Sapiens

Chapter 15 Test Answers

21. water, carbon dioxide, hydrogen, methane
22. birds and mammals
23. fur, bear live young, nurse young from mammary glands

CHAPTER 16

THE CLASSIFICATION OF LIVING THINGS

The different fossils in various layers of Earth's crust suggest long-term changes in the kinds of organisms that have lived on this planet. Adaptive radiation has resulted in a huge number and a great variety of species. Studies in genetics show that changes continue to take place.

As we consider classifying over a million kinds of organisms two basic concepts should be kept in mind. Biologists try to organize all species in a way that makes sense. Those who classify organisms assume some *continuity from one generation to the next.* Yet they must recognize that changes take place through time. So, as they arrange organisms, they must decide whether it is the structure or the function of an organism's parts that is most important. Finally, *in spite of the great diversity there are patterns of unity that all organisms share.* Keep these basic ideas in mind as you consider the classification of living things.

We will be dealing with several questions:

- What are the purposes of classifying organisms?
- On what basis are organisms classified?
- Why do biologists often use scientific names for organisms?
- What classification schemes are used in other countries?
- How can you identify some organism that you find in your house or yard?

SNAIL SHELLS CLASSIFIED

🔢 PATTERNS OF CLASSIFICATION

OBJECTIVES FOR SECTION 1

A. Define *taxonomy*, *taxonomist*, *binomial system*, *species name*, *scientific name*.

B. Give the original and modern purposes of classifying organisms.

C. Name and distinguish among the three parts of a scientific name.

D. List the main levels of classification in order from species to kingdom.

You remember the species concept from an earlier chapter. The species is a group of natural populations able to interbreed but unable to breed with other such groups. Because the concept of species is based on reproductive behavior, it is a natural unit. But any grouping of species is the product of the human mind.

Grouping Species

An estimated half million plant species and well over a million animal species have been classified. This is about 15% of the estimated 10 million living species thought to exist. It may be that a half billion other species have lived in the past and are now extinct.

How does one organize such a multitude of diverse species? Perhaps one should first ask whether we really need to organize them.

The original purpose of classification was probably to arrange organisms for convenient reference. The human mind seems to want to create order out of chaos. So, how one classifies depends on the purpose of classification. In a telephone directory names can be arranged alphabetically for those who know the names of the people they want to call. Or, names can be arranged according to profession or type of business for those who need a certain product or service. Both arrangements fulfill their purpose.

The classification of organisms is **taxonomy.** The persons doing the classifying are taxonomists. One early attempt at taxonomy was made by John Ray. In 1693 he began classifying animals on the basis of numbers of hoofs or claws. Ray also classified several thousand kinds of flowering plants according to certain features in their seeds.

The Binomial System

One generation after Ray another naturalist did an extraordinary amount of work on classification. He was Carolus Linnaeus (li *nē* əs), a Swedish botanist. His work was so thorough that the main features of his pattern are still used today. Linnaeus considered species to be fixed and unchanging. Thus, his system was based on observable features of form and anatomy.

In 1753, Linnaeus published *Species Plantarum*. In this two-volume set he listed the known plants with a short Latin description of each. If species were very similar their descriptions were placed near each other and began with the same word. This beginning term was called the *genus* (*jē* nəs) (plural, genera). The descriptive phrases were considered the official names of the plants. But Linnaeus placed in the margin a single word which when combined with the genus name formed a convenient abbreviation for the species name. The genus name for mint plants was *Mentha*. The word in the margin for spearmint was *spicata*. That for peppermint was *piperita*. Eventually the abbreviated names became official. Thus spearmint became *Mentha spicata*. Peppermint became *Mentha piperita*.

In 1758 Linnaeus published his classification of animals in *Systema Naturae*. Here too he attempted to group very similar species into the same genus. ***The two-name system of naming organisms is known as the* binomial** (bī *nō* mē əl) **system.** *A species name is composed of the genus name plus the specific name.* An organism's species name is also known as its scientific name. The scientific name often includes the abbreviation of the name of the authority who first applied the name to the organism. Linnaeus named so many organisms that his name is abbreviated as simply "L."

A common plant in the American Midwest has the species name, *Solanum rostratum* Dunal. It is assigned to the genus *Solanum*. Its specific name is *rostratum*. The authority who described this species was Michel Felix Dunal (1789-1856), a French botanist.

When the scientific name is used the genus is always capitalized. The specific name should not be capitalized. Both terms should be underlined when handwritten or typed. When printed they should appear in *italics* or **boldface**. The authority is always capitalized but never underlined.

New information may cause taxonomists to transfer a species to another genus. The original authority is then named within parentheses followed by the name of the person who made the change. Example: *Erigeron canadensis* L. was changed by Arthur John Cronquist to *Conyza canadensis* (L.) Cronquist.

Grouping Genera

The categories for the complete classification of an organism are: Species, Genus, Family, Order, Class, Phylum, and Kingdom. Each category from species to kingdom is less specific. Each group includes a greater number of organisms than the previous category.

A telephone directory lists the various Andersons: Anderson, Kathy; Anderson, Sharon; Anderson, Tom; Anderson, William. Anderson is like the genus. Anderson, William is like a species name. In a similar way a taxonomist groups similar species of cats into the genus Felis: *Felis domesticus* (house cat), *Felis leo* (lion), *Felis tigris* (tiger), *Felis pardus* (leopard). These cats are grouped with Genus Lynx and other related genera to form the Family Felidae. Families with similar characteristics are grouped into a larger category called an order. In our example, Families Felidae, Canidae (dogs and wolves), Ursidae (bears), and others form Order Carnivora, the meat eaters. Then, considering even more general characteristics, the orders are grouped into classes. The orders that contain meat eaters, hoofed animals, whales, bats, rodents, and rabbits form Class Mammalia. All of the animals in this class have hair, breathe by means of

TABLE 16-1

The classification at various levels is shown for several species. The genus combined with the specific name make up the species name, or scientific name. Which are the most closely related organisms in the table? Which are the next most closely related? How does the table indicate this information?

Level	Cat	Bobcat	Human	Lady Beetle	Wheat	Paramecium
Kingdom	Animalia	Animalia	Animalia	Animalia	Plantae	Protista
Phylum	Chordata	Chordata	Chordata	Arthropoda	Tracheophyta	Ciliophora
Class	Mammalia	Mammalia	Mammalia	Insecta	Angiospermae	Ciliata
Order	Carnivora	Carnivora	Primates	Coleoptera	Poales	Holotricha
Family	Felidae	Felidae	Hominidae	Coccinellidae	Poaceae	Parameciidae
Genus	*Felis*	*Lynx*	*Homo*	*Hippodamia*	*Triticum*	*Paramecium*
Specific name	*domesticus*	*rufus*	*sapiens*	*convergens*	*aestivum*	*caudatum*

lungs, bear their young alive, provide milk for the young, and are warm-blooded. Other classes which share still more general characteristics are grouped into a Phylum. Some of these characteristics are the presence of a notochord, a dorsal nerve cord, and a ventral heart. Mammals along with birds, reptiles, amphibians, and fish belong to the Phylum Chordata. This is one of many phyla (plural of phylum) in the animal kingdom. Table 16-1 illustrates the classification at various levels for several species. Many biologists use the term "division" instead of "phylum" when referring to plants.

A New Purpose

Early writers often labelled whales as fish. Aristotle, the Greek philosopher of the fourth century B.C., observed porpoises and dolphins, relatives of the whale. He was convinced that the physiology

16-1. Porpoises.

and reproductive procedure of these sea creatures was more important for classification than their habitat or shape. (See Fig. 16-1.)
So he classified whales with what we call mammals rather than
with fishes.

It turns out that Linnaeus agreed with Aristotle. He based his
classification scheme on homologous organs. This was a fortunate choice. The front limbs of bats, whales, and humans have different functions. But they have the same basic structure and the
same embryonic development. Thus bats are considered more likely
to have the same ancestors as whales and humans rather than birds
and insects.

Arranging organisms in a way that expresses evidence of ancestral relationship has become an important means of modern classification. This evidence may be structural. Indeed it must be for fossil
organisms. In some organisms reproductive organs are considered to
be reliable indicators of ancestral relationships. It is for this reason
that life cycles are emphasized in classifying plants. But the evidences
for possible ancestral relationships are increasingly coming from
studies in physiology, biochemistry, genetics, and behavior.

Because new evidence about relationships is being learned each
year, taxonomists are continually reviewing classification schemes.
Not all agree on the importance of certain evidence. For these reasons
different taxonomists favor different patterns of classification.

QUESTIONS FOR SECTION 1

1. Define taxonomy, taxonomist, binomial system, species name, scientific name.
2. Why is the definition of "species" inadequate for all organisms?
3. Give the original purpose of classifying organisms.
4. Explain the purpose of modern biological classification and list the kinds of evidence used to achieve that purpose.
5. Name and explain the three parts of the scientific name of the coyote, *Canis latrans* Say.
6. Explain why the species is the only natural unit of classification.
7. List the main levels of classification of the lady beetle from species to kingdom.
8. Which of the main levels of classification include the largest number of species?

Answers to Questions for Section 1.

A. 1. Taxonomy: the classification of organisms. Taxonomist: person doing the classifying. Binomial system: two-name system of nam- ing organisms. Species name: the genus name plus the specific name. Scientific name: species name (plus the name of the authority who first applied the name to the organism.)

*2. Some organisms capable of interbreeding have much greater dissimilarities than others that may be unable to interbreed yet resemble each other greatly.

B. 3. To arrange organisms for con- venient reference.

4. To express structural and other forms of evidence for ancestral relationship.

C. *5. *Canis*: the genus, or group of related species; *latrans*: species, or group of individuals that are most closely related; Say: name of the authority who first applied the species name to the organism.

6. It is based upon reproductive behavior.

D. 7. *convergens, Hippodamia,* Coccinellidae Coleoptera, Insecta, Arthropoda, Animalia.

8. The Kingdoms: Animalia, Plantae, Protista, Fungi and Monera.

Octipedal optistalk of shallow estuaries

Sprawlis radiatis
of sandy sea bottoms

Hoverall aqueous of the open sea

Biquadripedal terrestris
of the shore

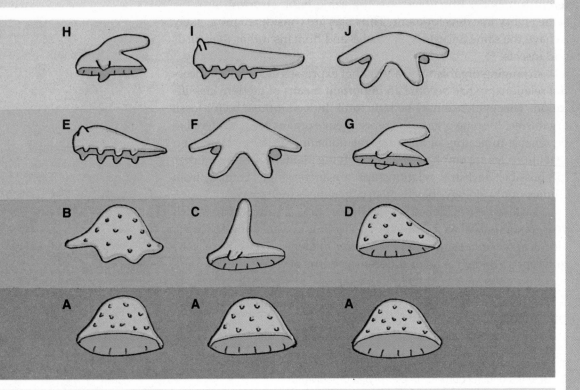

H   I   J

E   F   G

B   C   D

A   A   A

CHAPTER INVESTIGATION

Classification is often based on structural features. But biologists try to arrange organisms in a way that agrees with possible ancestral relationships. In this investigation, assume that four layers of fossils were discovered in an exposed stream bank. The nearby sea or its shore provide homes for four modern imaginary species.

A. The four modern creatures have been classified into three orders. Which two would you place into the same order? Why?

B. Explain how natural selection might have resulted in the production of each of the four modern species.

C. Using only external appearance of the fossils and the arrangement of rock layers, construct an ancestral tree of the modern creatures. Also, construct a key to their identity.

2 MODERN CLASSIFICATION

Five Kingdoms

Scientific names may seem difficult for beginning students. Perhaps their five advantages need to be pointed out.

1. *There is one scientific name for each species. Solanum rostratum* Dunal has many common names: buffalo-bur, sticker bush, prickly nightshade, watermelon sticker, sheepweed, and others. (See Fig. 16-2.)

2. *There is only one species for each scientific name.* One common name may refer to several different species. The term "sandbur" may refer to a member of the grass family or to a very different plant that also produces burs. The term "rat" refers to dozens of species of rodents.

3. *The single scientific name is used throughout the world.* Characters of our alphabet are used for scientific names even in paragraphs otherwise written in another language. A European lily has 245 common names: 15 English, 44 French, 81 Dutch, and 105 German.

4. *Changes in the meanings of scientific names are avoided by the use of Latin.* The scholars of Linnaeus' day usually wrote in Latin. Since Latin is not usually used for ordinary conversation today the meanings of its words do not change. Today scientific names can come from any language, but are written with Latin endings.

5. *Scientific names are part of a system based on fundamental ancestral relationships.* The common name "sycamore" originally referred to the wild fig of Palestine. In European religious drama a maple was used to represent the Palestinian sycamore. It became known as a sycamore maple, and then just sycamore. Europeans migrating to America, seeing the plane tree, observed its similarity to the European sycamore maple. The American plane tree was called sycamore because it resembled the maple that resembled the sycamore. This common name is based only on leaf shape. Leaf shape does not always indicate kinship.

For many years the categories of animal and plant seemed adequate to include all known species of organisms. With the invention of the microscope many organisms were discovered that did not fit neatly into these categories. A classification system that is gaining favor among biologists is one based on five categories or *kingdoms*. (See Fig. 16-3 on pages 292-293.) This five-kingdom system partially corrects the unnatural division of all organisms into plant and animal kingdoms. It also reflects increased knowledge of possible ancestral relationships. See Figures 16-4 — 16-8 for more detailed descriptions of each kingdom.

Kingdom Monera is made up of procaryotes. These are organisms whose cells lack membrane-bound organelles. This group includes the bacteria and blue-green algae. The eucaryotes, organisms

OBJECTIVES FOR SECTION 2
E. Give five advantages of the present system of scientific naming of organisms.
F. Explain the advantages of the five kingdom system of classifying organisms.
G. Name and describe the kingdoms of the five-kingdom system of classifying organisms.

16-2. Solanum rostatum Dunal.

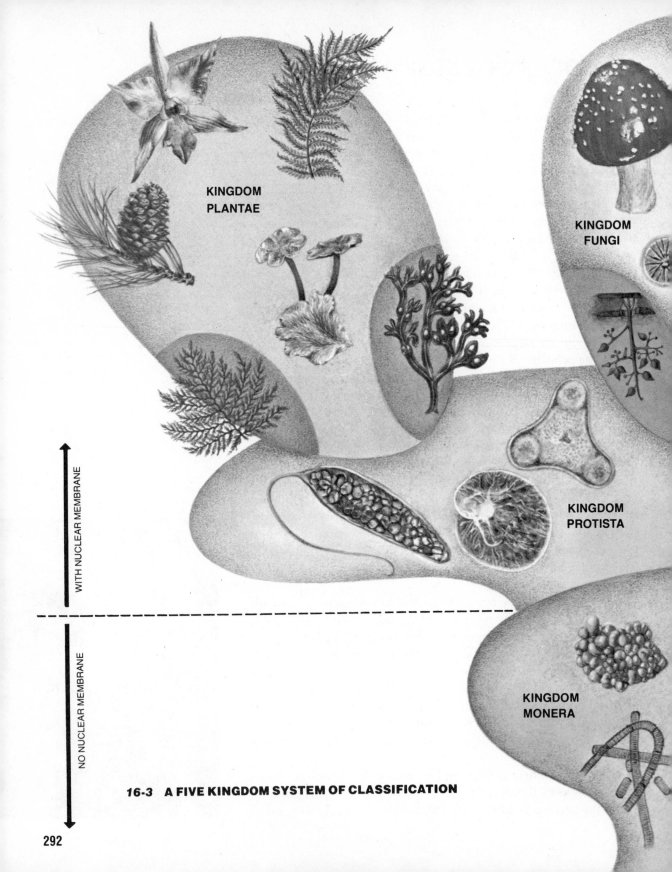

KINGDOM
PLANTAE

KINGDOM
FUNGI

KINGDOM
PROTISTA

KINGDOM
MONERA

WITH NUCLEAR MEMBRANE

NO NUCLEAR MEMBRANE

16-3   A FIVE KINGDOM SYSTEM OF CLASSIFICATION

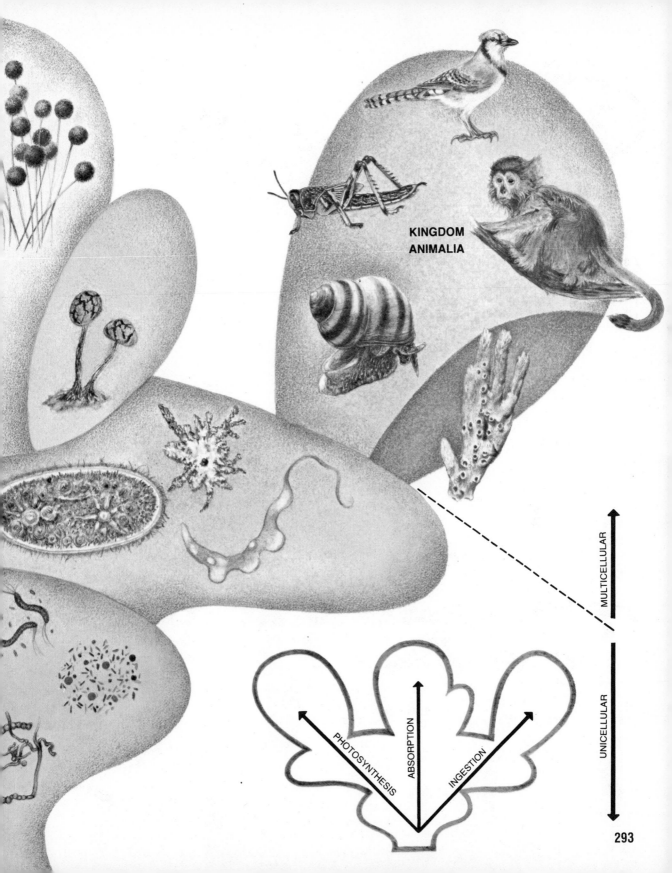

**KINGDOM
ANIMALIA**

MULTICELLULAR

UNICELLULAR

PHOTOSYNTHESIS

ABSORPTION

INGESTION

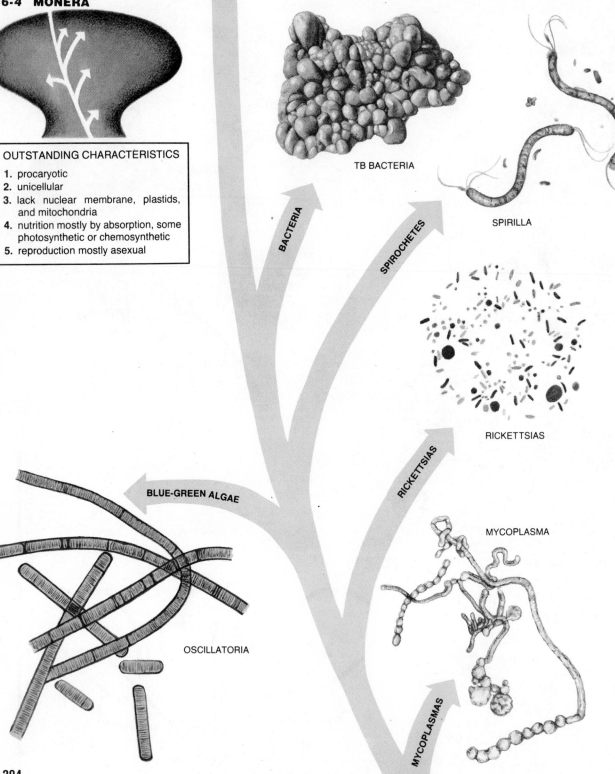

16-4 MONERA

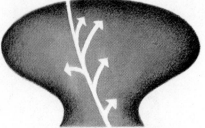

OUTSTANDING CHARACTERISTICS

1. procaryotic
2. unicellular
3. lack nuclear membrane, plastids, and mitochondria
4. nutrition mostly by absorption, some photosynthetic or chemosynthetic
5. reproduction mostly asexual

TB BACTERIA

SPIRILLA

BACTERIA

SPIROCHETES

RICKETTSIAS

RICKETTSIAS

MYCOPLASMA

BLUE-GREEN ALGAE

OSCILLATORIA

MYCOPLASMAS

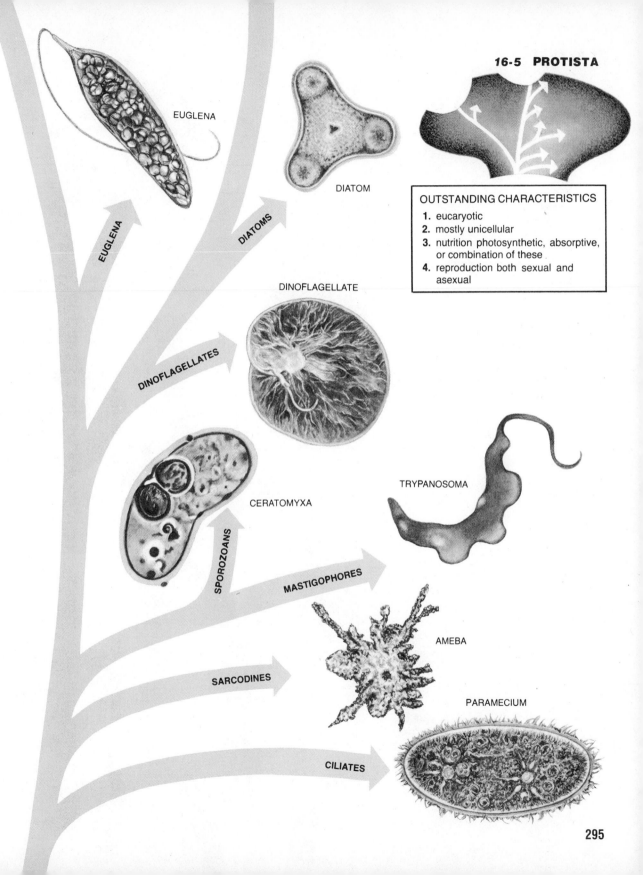

EUGLENA

DIATOM

16-5 PROTISTA

OUTSTANDING CHARACTERISTICS
1. eucaryotic
2. mostly unicellular
3. nutrition photosynthetic, absorptive, or combination of these
4. reproduction both sexual and asexual

EUGLENA

DIATOMS

DINOFLAGELLATE

DINOFLAGELLATES

CERATOMYXA

TRYPANOSOMA

SPOROZOANS

MASTIGOPHORES

AMEBA

SARCODINES

PARAMECIUM

CILIATES

OUTSTANDING CHARACTERISTICS
1. eucaryotic
2. many nuclei distributed in cytoplasm with occasional dividing membrane
3. plastids and photosynthetic pigment lacking
4. nutrition mostly absorptive
5. reproductive cycle usually includes both sexual and asexual stages

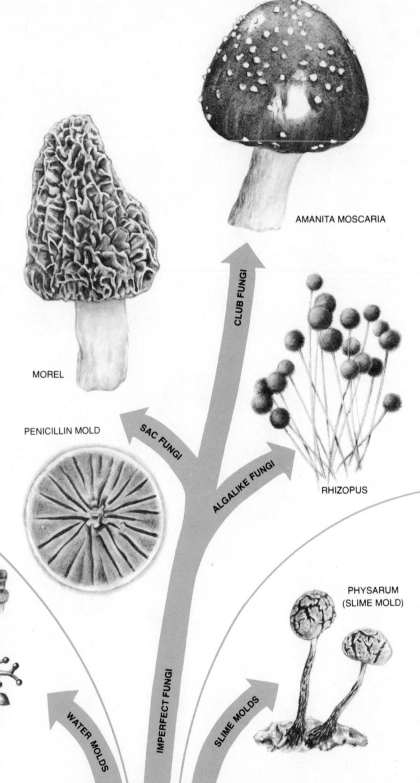

AMANITA MOSCARIA

MOREL

PENICILLIN MOLD

CLUB FUNGI

SAC FUNGI

ALGALIKE FUNGI

RHIZOPUS

POTATO BLIGHT FUNGUS

PHYSARUM
(SLIME MOLD)

WATER MOLDS

IMPERFECT FUNGI

SLIME MOLDS

16-7 PLANTAE

FERN

PINE

ORCHID

FERNS

GYMNOSPERMS

ANGIOSPERMS

CLUB MOSS

CLUB MOSSES

HAIR-CUP MOSS

HORSETAILS

HORSETAILS

OUTSTANDING CHARACTERISTICS
1. eucaryotic
2. multicellular
3. cells with walls, vacuoles, and pigment plastids
4. nutrition mostly photosynthetic, some absorptive
5. many specialized tissues and organs
6. reproductive cycle of alternate haploid and diploid generations

HORNWORT

HORNWORTS

MOSSES

PSILOPSIDS

WHISK FERN

LIVERWORTS

BRYOPHYTA

LIVERWORT

ULVA

BROWN ALGA

GREEN ALGAE

RED ALGA

RED ALGAE

BROWN ALGAE

297

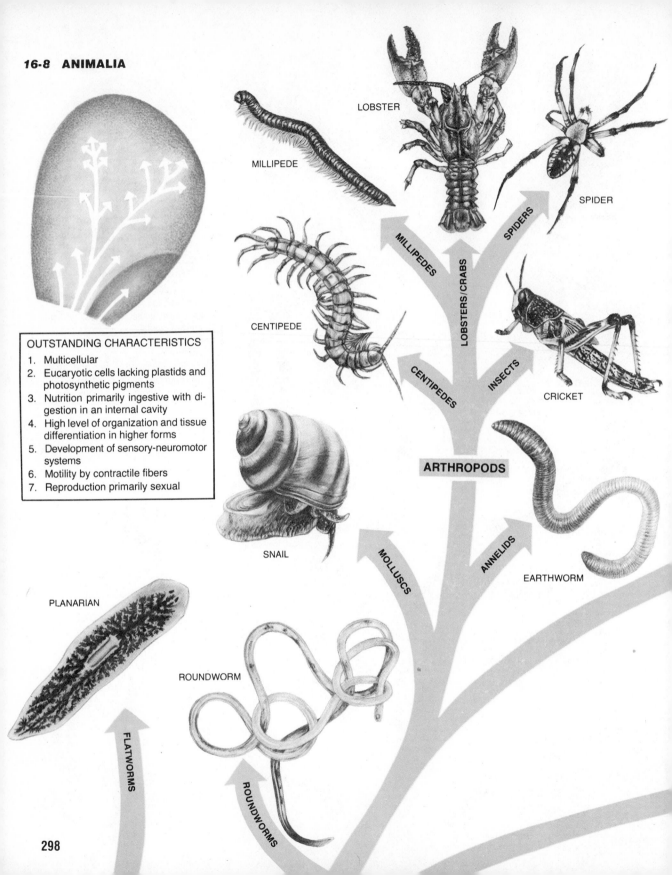

LOBSTER

MILLIPEDE

SPIDER

CENTIPEDE

MILLIPEDES

SPIDERS

LOBSTERS/CRABS

CENTIPEDES

INSECTS

CRICKET

OUTSTANDING CHARACTERISTICS

1. Multicellular
2. Eucaryotic cells lacking plastids and photosynthetic pigments
3. Nutrition primarily ingestive with digestion in an internal cavity
4. High level of organization and tissue differentiation in higher forms
5. Development of sensory-neuromotor systems
6. Motility by contractile fibers
7. Reproduction primarily sexual

ARTHROPODS

SNAIL

MOLLUSCS

ANNELIDS

EARTHWORM

PLANARIAN

ROUNDWORM

FLATWORMS

ROUNDWORMS

FROG

TURTLE

SEAGULL

AMPHIBIANS

REPTILES

BIRDS

FISH

MAMMALS

FISH

MONKEY

VERTEBRATES

CHORDATES

ECHINODERMS

STARFISH

ANEMONE

CNIDARIANS

SPONGES

SPONGE

that contain membrane-lined organelles, are divided into four kingdoms. Kingdom Protista includes the single-celled eucaryotes. The remaining three kingdoms are multicellular. These are grouped largely on the basis of their nutrition. Most members of Kingdom Plantae are photosynthetic. Most members of Kingdom Animalia ingest their food. That is, they swallow their food and digest it internally. In Kingdom Fungi nutrition is absorptive. They absorb food in solution through their exterior cell membranes.

The Identification of Organisms

Identifying organisms can be difficult. After all, there are about one and a half million living species that have been classified. No taxonomist knows them all or even a large fraction of them. A taxonomist will probably know the general traits of the major groups of organisms. Such information could narrow down the possible identity of unknown organisms to a smaller number. A guide to the wildflowers, fishes, algae, or other organisms of your specific area might help, especially if it is well illustrated. Some schools and colleges have collections of certain groups of organisms, especially seed plants and insects, which are helpful in making identifications. The Systematic Entomology Laboratory of the U.S. Department of Agriculture identifies about 350,000 insects sent from around the world each year.

The Dichotomous Key

One method of identifying organisms that is useful to taxonomists and amateur biologists alike is the dichotomous (dī *kot* ə məs) key. *A dichotomous key is a means of identifying objects or organisms through a series of paired statements only one of which applies to the organism. It directs the user to the next pair of statements.*

QUESTIONS FOR SECTION 2

1. Give five advantages of scientific names that are linked to a classification scheme.
2. Explain a disadvantage of the two-kingdom system of classifying organisms.
3. Name and describe each kingdom of the five-kingdom system of classifying organisms.
4. List three methods of identifying an unknown organism.

CHAPTER REVIEW

The human mind searches for regularities in its surroundings. Thus it seems natural that through the years people have tried to classify living things. In spite of the *changes over time* that have occurred in living things, *continuity* was evident. So it seemed possible to find patterns of *unity in the evident diversity*. Fortunately, Linnaeus chose to arrange organisms according to basic structures, homology, rather than function regardless of structure or embryonic origin.

While the species is a unit based on natural reproductive behavior, any grouping of species is human activity. Various kinds of evidence are used in the attempt to arrange species in ways that reflect ancestral relationships. These rely heavily on physical structure. Evidence for understanding relationship between organisms is coming more and more from studies in physiology, biochemistry, genetics, and behavior.

While taxonomists disagree on many details, the general pattern of classification follows a series of levels each including a larger group than the one before. Similar species form a genus. Similar genera form a family. Related families form an order. Similar orders form a phylum. Related phyla form a kingdom. The species name, composed of genus and specific name, is the single, official, universally recognized name for each organism.

Using the Concepts

1. Using the ideas of convergent evolution and radiant evolution explain how certain similarities among species may *not* suggest close kinship.
2. Take a common plant or animal from your area and ask a number of people its name. How many different names did you get for the organism? How many people didn't know its name?
3. Give several reasons why taxonomists will continue to have work for a long time to come.

Unanswered Question

4. Will we ever be able to prove without doubt the superiority of any one of the ways that phyla are grouped into kingdoms?

Career Activities

5. How would taxonomists or a knowledge of taxonomy be useful to each of the following: farmers, stockmen, gardeners, orchard keepers, foresters, physicians, immigration inspectors, outdoor educators, curators of natural history museums, state biological survey personnel, pest control technicians, taxidermists, fishermen?

VOCABULARY REVIEW

1 bionomial system
species name

scientific name
taxonomy

taxonomist
2 dichotomous key

CHAPTER 16 TEST

Copy the number of each test item and place your answer to the right.

PART 1 Multiple Choice: Select the letter of the phrase that best completes each of the following.

a 1. The wild onion, *Allium canadense* L., is in the genus **a.** *Allium,* **b.** *canadense* **c.** L., **d.** Linneaus.

b 2. In the name of the wild onion, *Allium canadense* L., *canadense* is **a.** the scientific name **b.** the specific name **c.** the home of the author **d.** the author's name.

b 3. The use of two names to refer to a kind of organism is called **a.** a dichotomous key **b.** a binomial system **c.** taxonomy **d.** specific name.

c 4. The science of classifying organisms is **a.** dichotomy **b.** binominal system **c.** taxonomy **d.** embryology.

c 5. The Swedish botanist whose system of classification we use today was **a.** Aristotle **b.** John Ray **c.** Carolus Linnaeus **d.** Felix Dunal

c 6. An advantage of a scientific name is that it **a.** differs from place to place **b.** doesn't depend on kinship **c.** refers to a single species **d.** is only one of many scientific names that refer to the same species.

d 7. An advantage of a common name for a species is that **a.** it is the only name for that species **b.** there is only one species that it refers to **c.** it is used throughout the world **d.** it may be familiar to people of a community.

a 8. Linnaeus based his classification on **a.** homologous organs **b.** analogous organs **c.** evolutionary change **d.** biochemistry.

b 9. Evidences of kinship or ancestral relationship are *not* based on comparison of organs with similar **a.** origin **b.** function **c.** embryonic development **d.** biochemistry.

d 10. The group that includes the others listed is the **a.** order **b.** class **c.** genus **d.** phylum.

PART 2 Matching: Match the letter of the term in Column I with its description in Column II.

COLUMN I

a. Family
b. Genus
c. Kingdom
d. Phylum
e. Species
f. Animalia
g. Fungi
h. Monera
i. Plantae
j. Protista

COLUMN II

e 11. Usually includes the greatest number of species
c 12. The most natural unit of classification
b 13. A group of most closely related species
d 14. The largest division of a Kingdom
a 15. A group of most closely related genera
h 16. Procaryotes
j 17. Single-celled eucaryotes
i 18. Multicellular, photosynthetic eucaryotes
g 19. Multicellular, absorptive eucaryotes
f 20. Multicellular, ingestive eucaryotes

PART 3 Completion: Complete the following.

21. According to this chapter, of the 10 million organisms thought to exist, only _15_ percent have been classified.

22. The single, officially recognized name for an organism is its _species name or scientific name_

23. The original purpose of classifying organisms was probably to arrange them for _convenient reference_

24. The modern purpose of classifying organisms is to arrange them in a way that shows possible _ancestral relationship_

25. A device used to identify organisms through a series of paired statements only one of which applies to one organism is the _dichotomous key_

VIRUSES, MONERANS, PROTISTS, AND FUNGI

The grouping of organisms into five kingdoms is a convenient way of recognizing the basic features that are unique to whole groups of organisms. Even this system is not entirely satisfactory, however. It does not consider the position of several so-called borderline forms of life. We will begin this unit by taking a brief look at these borderline "organisms." We will progress from there to a survey of the three most primitive kingdoms of the living world: Monera, Protista, and Fungi.

You should be aware of several trends as you study this unit. There is a trend toward increasing complexity. This, in turn, increases diversity—not only in structure, but in function as well. As these trends develop, you should note the relationship that exists between structure and function. We have tried to stress the interrelatedness of all forms of life. Finally, we review the characteristics of each group and compare them.

BRACKET FUNGUS

CHAPTER 17

VIRUSES

Those forms of life that are too small to be seen clearly without the aid of a microscope are called *microbes*. In this book, we have included them in the Kingdoms Monera and Protista. As noted in Chapter 16, no classification is entirely satisfactory. Any attempt to classify organisms usually gives us too simple a view of a highly diverse group. The members of these kingdoms seem to be less alike in some ways than are plants and animals. The important thing is that whatever system we use, we must remember that it was made by people. The question is not what these organisms are, but only what we decide to call them.

In this chapter, we shall deal mainly with viruses. Whether or not they should be considered living is debatable. How they should be classified is even more so. They do show some of the features common to life, but lack others. They display *diversity and continuity*. They do show *relationships between structure and function*. The same, however, might even be said about automobiles. On the other hand, they do not exhibit a number of life's basic properties. They do not respire. They do not respond to stimuli. They do not grow. And they reproduce only within living cells.

In this chapter you will discover why viruses are such a puzzle to scientists. In addition, you should be able to answer some of the following questions:

- What effect do viruses have on human populations?
- How do viruses cause disease?
- How do scientists develop a vaccine that will protect us against diseases of viral origin?
- Why do we need to be protected against some viral diseases only once and against others each year or so?

TOBACCO MOSAIC VIRUS

1 DIVERSITY AND CONTINUITY

General Characteristics of Microbes

The development of the microscope opened a whole new world to scientists. Until then, life forms could be easily divided into two major groups, plants and animals. When finally seen, the world of microbes presented problems in classification.

Some clearly appeared to be animals. They were heterotrophs and they moved around. Others had chlorophyll and appeared to be more like plants. Most were single-celled, although some lived in colonies or groups of cells. As new techniques in the use of the microscope evolved, scientists learned much about the structure and function of microbes.

The Monerans appear to be very primitive. Their cells lack many parts that we think of as typical of all cells. (See Fig. 17-1.) They contain no membrane-bound organelles such as nuclei and mitochondria. Cells that lack such features are said to be *procaryotic*. Bacteria and the blue-green algae are examples of this primitive group.

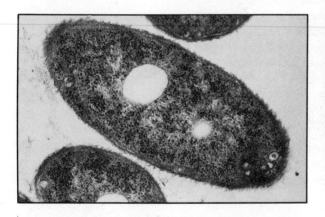
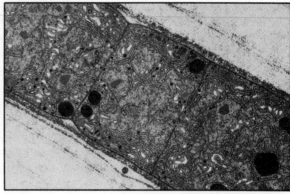

The cells of the Protists are more typical of living organisms. They are still a diverse group, however. Although they vary widely in shape, they share a basic similarity in metabolism. These more modern organisms, having cellular organelles, are termed *eucaryotic*. (See Fig. 17-2.) Protist cells have a membrane-bound nucleus with chromosomes. They also have other organelles common to most cells. These include mitochondria, ribosomes, Golgi apparatus, and possibly others such as vacuoles and lysosomes. Some even have special adaptations for movement. Short bristles called *cilia* may cover the surface of the cell and help to propel it through its watery habitat. Others have a single flagellum for this purpose. Still others have no means of locomotion at all.

17-1. (left) A bacterial cell and (right) a blue-green alga, are examples of procaryotes, whose cells lack membrane-bound organelles.

17-2. *Eucaryote protists are a highly diverse and numerous group. (upper left) Ameba; (upper right) Radiolaria; (lower left) Euglena; (lower right) Paramecium.*

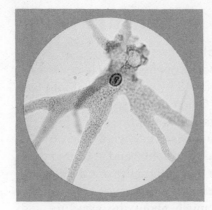
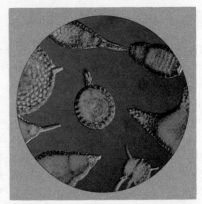
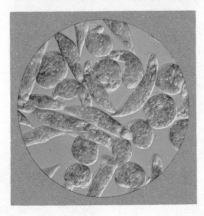
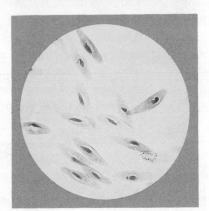

Answers to Questions for Section 1.

6. Non-cellular, do not grow, do not arise from pre-existing similar forms; do not respire; do not respond to stimuli.

7. They can be passed through filters that no cells would pass through.

D. 8. (1) Non-cellular ancestors of cells. (2) Cellular ancestors that became parasitic and lost cellular characteristics. Fragments of other cells.

TABLE 17-1
CHARACTERISTICS OF VIRUSES

1. Non-cellular
2. Do not respire
3. Do not respond to stimuli
4. Do not grow
5. Reproduce only within living cells, but not directly from a pre-existing form like itself
6. Do contain DNA or RNA
7. Do have a protein wrap
8. Do contain small amounts of enzyme material

In Chapter 18, we will take a close look at the procaryote Monerans and their relevance to us. We will study Protists in Chapter 19. In this chapter we will take up the viruses. Their inclusion in a catalogue of life is important for two reasons. They do exhibit some characteristics of living things. Moreover, they directly affect other living things in a way that inorganic things do not.

Characteristics of Viruses

Viruses take many shapes. (See Fig. 17-3.) **Viruses *are structures made of segments of a nucleic acid wrapped in a protein coat.*** Some of the characteristics of viruses were listed in the introduction to this chapter. Table 17-1 summarizes these and other features of viruses. Unlike other life forms (if viruses are indeed alive), they are not cells. Also, they do not arise directly from a previously existing similar structure as cells do.

There are many ideas about where viruses came from. One idea is that viruses represent a link in the origin of life. Perhaps they are the non-cellular ancestors of cells. On the other hand, some scientists feel that viruses had cellular ancestors who became adapted to a para-

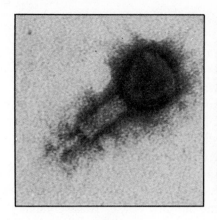

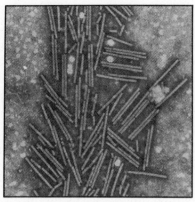

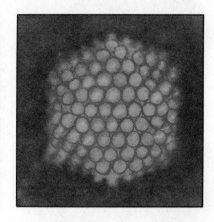

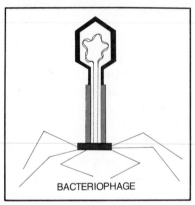
BACTERIOPHAGE

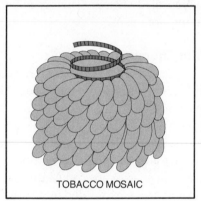
TOBACCO MOSAIC

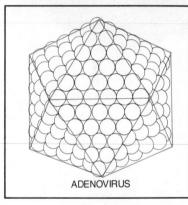
ADENOVIRUS

sitic way of life. Selection would have favored the loss of many of the characteristics of cells. Viruses as we know them today would be the result. Another view is that viruses are simply fragments of other cells.

Viruses also come in many sizes. Most are too small to be seen with an ordinary light microscope. Their existence was only suspected before the electron microscope was available.

Edward Jenner was the first to vaccinate a person against a viral disease, smallpox. In 1796, he used an extract from sores of cowpox in an attempt to give protection against smallpox. He had noticed that milkmaids and others who worked closely with cattle often were infected with cowpox. These same people did not seem to ever contract smallpox. His efforts were successful, but the nature of the disease was still unknown. Nearly a century later, Louis Pasteur developed a vaccine against rabies, another disease of viral origin. It was not until well into the twentieth century that the real culprit of these diseases was isolated.

During the last decade of the 19th Century, Dimitri Iwanowski discovered an important property of viruses. He was studying a plant disease known as tobacco mosaic. It causes a mottled yellow and

17-3. The three main shapes of viruses: (left) Bacteriophage; (middle) Tobacco Mosaic virus; (right) Adeno virus.

Answers to Questions for Section 1.

A. 1. Monerans are procaryotic and lack membrane-bound organelles. Protists are eucaryotic, and have membrane-bound organelles including a nucleus, with chromosomes.

*2. They are not clearly either plants or animals; and they are such a diverse group.

B. 3. Procaryotes lack the specialization of eucaryotes. Both consist of cells.

4. Procaryote: bacteria and blue-green algae. Eucaryote: Paramecium and euglena.

C. 5. They contain DNA or RNA; have a protein wrap; contain enzyme material; reproduce.

(See page 306 for more answers.)

green pattern in tobacco leaves. (See Fig. 17-4.) Iwanowski discovered that fluid extracted from infected leaves would produce the disease in healthy plants. More important, he found that the disease would appear even when the fluid had passed through a special filter. Examination of the fluid revealed that no cells had passed through the filter. The agent that caused the disease was then known to be very small. It was at first thought that a poison produced by these cells had passed through the filter into the fluid. Others were in disagreement. The existence of the virus was postulated, but it was not conclusively shown to exist until 1935. Dr. Wendell Stanley managed to isolate a number of small crystals from the fluid. Put back into solution, these crystals produced the mosaic disease. These crystals were called viruses. They seemed to be more like a chemical than a living organism.

17-4. *(top) Healthy tobacco leaf; (bottom) tobacco leaf infected with mosaic virus.*

The Chemistry of Viruses

Careful analysis of the virus crystals showed them to be made of two kinds of organic molecules. They were at least part protein and part nucleic acid. Thus, the virus did not appear to be a single chemical. Moreover, later studies showed that the nucleic acid in some viruses was DNA. In others, it was RNA. Now, we know that the nucleic acid fragments vary from one kind of virus to another. As the electron microscope came into use, viruses were seen to have a core of nucleic acid surrounded by a protein coat. (See Fig. 17-5.) The overall shape of the virus varied widely, however.

The presence of a nucleic acid supports the idea that viruses are living. No other substances contain DNA or RNA. On the other hand, living organisms cannot be crystallized and stored indefinitely in a bottle. The question as to whether or not viruses should be called living organisms remains unanswered.

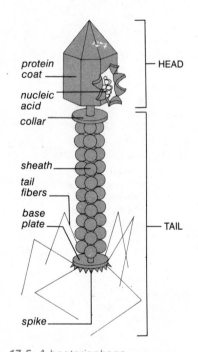

17-5. *A bacteriophage.*

protein coat

nucleic acid

collar

sheath

tail fibers

base plate

spike

HEAD

TAIL

QUESTIONS FOR SECTION 1

1. What are the general characteristics of monerans? Of protists?
2. Why do scientists disagree on the question of classifying protists?
3. How are procaryotes and eucaryotes different? Similar?
4. Give at least two examples each of procaryote and eucaryote cells.
5. What characteristics of viruses might cause them to be considered as living organisms?
6. What characteristics of viruses might exclude them from being considered alive?
7. Explain why viruses are said to be filterable.
8. Give three different ideas about the possible origins of viruses.

(See pages 306 and 307 for Answers

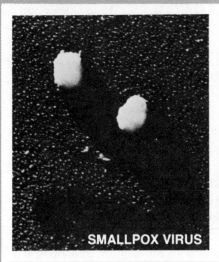

SMALLPOX VIRUS

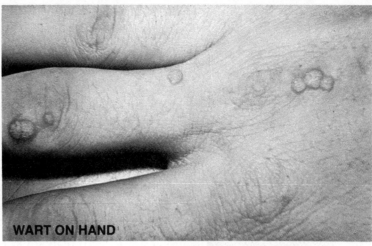

WART ON HAND

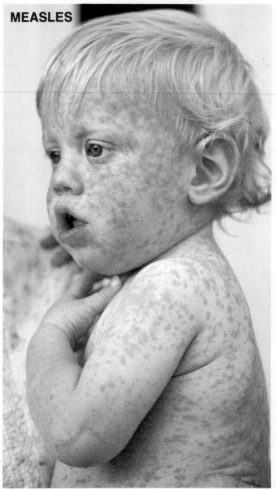

MEASLES

CHAPTER INVESTIGATION

A. Describe the shape of the virus or the viral diseases pictured.

B. Why don't people get some viral diseases again once they have had them?

C. Why are antibiotics that are useful against bacterial infections not useful for virus infections?

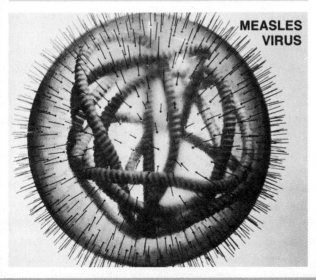

MEASLES VIRUS

☑ ACTIVITIES OF VIRUSES

Types of Viruses

Viruses are able to reproduce only within living cells. They can be spread from infected cells to healthy cells by direct contact. They may also be spread indirectly through air, water, food, or fecal matter. Each kind of virus attaches to a specific cell. Not all cells are attacked by all viruses. In general, three kinds of viruses are recognized by the kind of organisms they attack. *Animal viruses* attack animal cells, including humans. *Plant viruses* invade cells of plants. *Bacterial viruses* attack bacteria. **Bacteria *are unicellular procaryotes.***

Even within these broad groups, viral activity is quite specific. Viruses may invade specific tissues of specific plants or animals. For example, the tobacco mosaic virus, described above, attacks the leaf tissues of tobacco plants. Other viruses are equally specific in their activity. Some, however, are more general than others. We will consider various examples later in this chapter.

The "Life Cycle" of a Virus

A virus that attacks a bacterial cell is known as a **bacteriophage, *or simply* phage.** Several kinds of phages are known. They are useful research tools because they are fairly safe for use around humans. Also, they are convenient to use. Studies of phages have been the main source of what we know about viruses and how they operate. They were first discovered in 1917 when *spots of dead bacteria, or* **plaques,** *appeared in bacterial cultures.* (See Fig. 17-6.) These spots spread rapidly and destroyed the entire culture. Without the electron microscope, the actual agent that destroyed these bacteria went undiscovered for nearly two decades. In the meantime, however, much was learned about its properties.

The electron microscope enabled us to see viruses. Scientists have now been able to photograph phage attacks on host bacterial cells. (See Fig. 17-7.) The steps in a phage attack are called the *lytic cycle.* (See Fig. 17-8.) Lytic refers to the breaking apart of a cell. In the lytic cycle the host cells are broken apart. This term, rather than life cycle, may satisfy those who prefer not to include viruses among the living. *Viruses that produce a lytic cycle are said to be* **virulent.**

The lytic cycle begins as a phage, tail down, attaches to the bacterial cell wall. (Refer to Fig. 17-8.) The wall is opened as a hole is dissolved in it by a phage enzyme. The phage tail then contracts, forcing the DNA core into the cell. The protein coat does not enter the cell itself. During the next stage, the phage DNA breaks up the DNA of the bacterial host. The DNA fragments are then reassembled as phage DNA. The protein coat is produced as the cell fills with phage.

E. Define the following terms in your own words: *bacteriophage, plaque, lytic cycle, virulent.*

F. Explain what is meant by virus specificity.

G. Describe the characteristic lytic cycle of a phage.

H. Explain how the electron microscope has helped us to understand the lytic cycle of a virus.

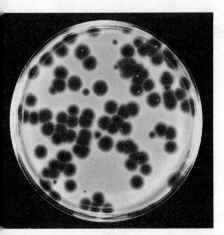

17-6. Phages were first seen as spots or plaques in a plate culture of bacteria.

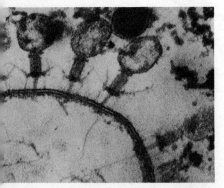

17-7. A bacterial cell under a phage attack. Nucleic acid is being injected into the cell in an early stage of the lytic cycle.

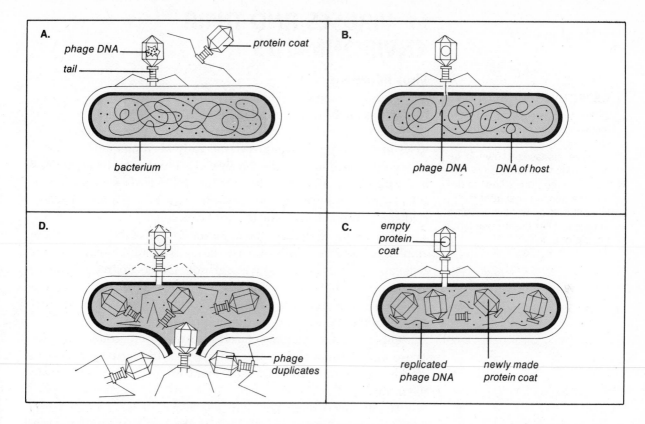

A. phage DNA — tail — protein coat — bacterium

B. phage DNA — DNA of host

D. phage duplicates

C. empty protein coat — replicated phage DNA — newly made protein coat

Finally, the cell ruptures, releasing as many as 300 phages. These attack other cells in the area. The lytic cycle is similar in plant and animal cells. Animal cells, however, have no protective cell walls. In these cells, the phage may be wholly taken into the cell by phagocytosis. Under ideal conditions, the lytic cycle may take 30-45 minutes. It is little wonder that viral infections spread so rapidly.

QUESTIONS FOR SECTION 2

1. Define the following terms in your own words: bacteriophage, plaque, lytic cycle, virulent.
2. What is viral specificity?
3. How is viral specificity related to the idea that viruses came from existing DNA fragments?
4. What are the steps in the lytic cycle of a phage?
5. How does the lytic cycle help to explain why a bacterial colony can be destroyed so rapidly by phages?
6. How has the electron microscope helped us to understand the lytic cycle of a virus?

*5. Under ideal conditions, the phage cycle can be completed in 30 to 45 minutes, with as many as 300 phages produced each time, each having the ability to destroy one bacterium. A rapid geometric progession is thus set in motion.

H. 6. By making it possible to photograph phage attacks. Such tiny objects are not visible with light microscopes.

17-8. Lytic cycle of a virus.

Answers to Questions for Section 2.

E. 1. Bateriophage: virus that attacks a bacterial cell. Plaque: spot of dead bacteria in a bacterial culture. Lytic cycle: A virus' attack and breaking down of host cells, ending in production of more viruses. Virulent: any virus that has a lytic cycle.

F. 2. The attack only of specific kinds of cells by specific viruses.

*3. The virus breaks up the host's DNA, and reassembles it as viral DNA. This suggests that the origin of the virus was in the original breakdown of the host DNA, that contains same segments of nucleotides as the virus that is specific for it.

G. 4. See figure 17-8 .

3 VIRUSES AND THEIR ENVIRONMENTS

Virus Infections

Viruses are important to us for many reasons. They are responsible for a number of diseases, not only in humans, but also in our crops, stock animals, and pets. Most of you are aware of several diseases of viral origin. Smallpox has already been mentioned. Fortunately this dread disease has been nearly, if not entirely, eliminated in the past ten years. Other diseases caused by viruses include polio, chicken pox, mumps, rabies, influenza, warts, hepatitis, measles, cold sores, and at least some forms of cancer.

Many of these viruses attack specific tissues of the body. For example, polio viruses invade nerve tissue. Hepatitis occurs in liver cells, and mumps attacks salivary glands. Others are more general, attacking cells that cover or line various organs of the body. Research has been successful in making vaccines that protect humans from several of the more serious of these diseases.

Other diseases may also affect humans in an economic sense. These include hoof and mouth disease of cattle, or parrot fever in chickens and other birds. Diseases of viral origin can be very costly to the farmer.

The discovery of phages, at first, gave a hope for controlling certain diseases of bacterial origin. It was thought that some diseases could be treated by injecting phages that were specific for the bacterium that caused a certain disease. Such hopes, however, appear to be unfounded. Apparently, blood factors or other natural body defenses can render such phages unable to affect the target host.

Defense Against Infection

The body has several natural defenses to viral and other infections. An invading virus must successfully penetrate each line of defense for an infection to occur. The first of these are the *phagocytic* cells in the blood. These cells are able to engulf and destroy potential infecting agents, including viruses. This occurs before they can affect the target tissues.

The body can also ward off infection through an immune response. The presence of foreign proteins stimulate the production of *antibodies.* Specific antibodies can recognize specific invaders and deactivate them.

For some diseases, the antibodies are produced in other organisms. The antibodies are then collected and injected into the person to be protected. Protection against serious diseases such as mumps and measles can be obtained in this way.

Immunity may not be permanent. After a period of time, the number of antibodies begins to fall off. Follow-up injections called booster shots may be necessary for continued protection against some diseases. In other cases, slight mutations in the virus enable it to not be recognized by antibodies. This is why different strains of influenza require different antibodies for the body to be properly protected. In recent years a number of "flu" strains have been identified by their place of origin. We have seen the "Asian flu," the "Hong Kong flu," the "Russian flu," and others.

For some diseases, such as chicken pox, the body must provide its own antibodies. This occurs when the person has the disease itself. In other diseases, a vaccine can be used. *A **vaccine** is a substance that causes the body to produce antibodies without causing the illness.* The vaccines against polio, measles, and mumps are familiar examples.

The third line of defense lies in the production of a special protein called *interferon* (IF). This substance was discovered in 1957 by virologists Alick Isaacs and Jean Lindenmann. Unlike antibodies, interferon is not specific. It is active against a great many viruses and other infecting agents. IF can be produced in response to an active virus or one that has been deactivated by heat. At least three types of interferon have been discovered. One type is produced by the white blood cells. A second type is produced by cells that form connective tissue in skin and other organs. The third type is produced by part of the body's immune system. There is some evidence to suggest that people differ in their genetic abilities to produce interferon.

The importance of interferon in resisting infection is shown in an experiment with mice infected with viral influenza. The infection stimulates some cells to produce IF. It seems to pass through the cell membrane and warn the surrounding cells of the invading virus. These healthy cells then produce antiviral proteins. Within three days, the level of interferon had reached its peak. Because of this, the viruses are not able to replicate within the new cell. If they do manage to reproduce, the action of the interferon prevents them from leaving the cell. The first antibodies were not detected in the infected mice until a week after infection. The antibodies provide a more lasting immunity. But interferon may be more important in the initial stages of infection.

Interferon has been used successfully to treat some cases of chicken pox. In addition, it has been shown to be effective against some viral diseases that affect newborn babies and kidney transplant patients. IF has also been used in combination with other drugs to treat certain cases of hepatitis. Researchers are hopeful that interferon will be effective against many other viral diseases.

Students may wish to research the topic of cancer and its relationship to possible viral origins.

Students may wish to research the topic of interferon—its production and use.

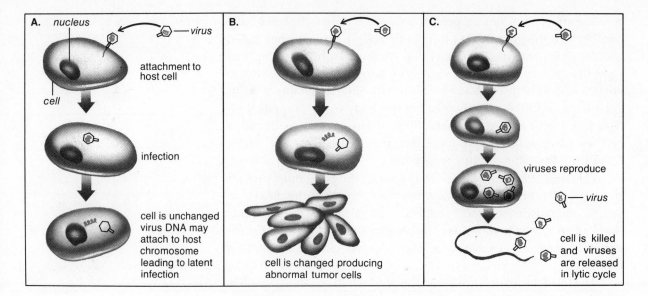

A. nucleus — virus

attachment to host cell

cell

infection

cell is unchanged virus DNA may attach to host chromosome leading to latent infection

B.

cell is changed producing abnormal tumor cells

C.

viruses reproduce

— virus

cell is killed and viruses are released in lytic cycle

17-9. Three different ways viruses can work.

General good health helps all of the body's defenses to operate more efficiently. Proper diet and adequate rest are important. When the body is weakened by one disease it is more susceptible to other diseases.

Kinds of Viral Infections

So far, we have considered only one kind of viral infection — ones that infect and kill the host in a lytic cycle. There are two other kinds that we should consider. Much less is known about these, however.

In one type, the virus may infect a cell but not produce a lytic cycle. *A virus that exists in a cell but remains inactive is said to be latent.* Scientists think that the DNA of such viruses may become attached to a chromosome like an extra gene. (See Fig. 17-9.) As cells divide, the daughter cells receive the viral DNA as well. At any time, the latent "gene" may become activated. This may happen because of a mutation that suddenly causes it to become virulent. It may also be that the host cell loses its resistance for some reason. The lytic cycle then follows. The common cold sore is an example of a latent infection.

The other kind of viral infection may produce masses of abnormal cells (tumors) rather than simply destroying them. Warts are common examples of relatively harmless, or *benign,* tumors. *Malignant* tumors, on the other hand, are capable of being spread throughout the body. These types are the most dangerous. No human cancer virus has yet been definitely identified. However, several kinds of malignant tumors, or cancers, are thought to be caused by viruses.

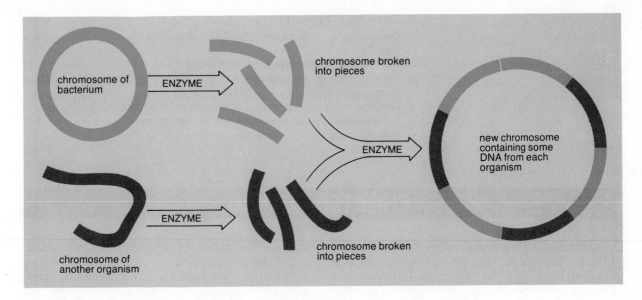

The diagram labels:

- chromosome of bacterium
- ENZYME
- chromosome broken into pieces
- ENZYME
- new chromosome containing some DNA from each organism
- ENZYME
- chromosome broken into pieces
- chromosome of another organism

Included in these are certain leukemias and breast cancer. Also, certain viruses (herpes type II) seem to be related to the development of cervical cancer in women. Furthermore, scientists are examining evidence that may link viruses to certain types of bone cancer. Why some people seem to be more prone to cancer than others remains a mystery.

17-10. The formation of recombinant DNA.

Recombinant DNA

One area of research involves the use of recombinant DNA. Biologists can remove a gene from the DNA of one organism. This gene may contain the code to produce a certain protein. The gene with its code is then spliced into the DNA of a bacterium. This organism now is programmed to genetically produce something new. At least on a theoretical basis it should be possible to infect a person with a virus-carried segment of DNA capable of replacing a defective gene. The patient would then be able to produce the gene product required by the body. (See Fig. 17-10.) For example, some DNA that would direct the making of a protein like insulin might be combined with the DNA of another organism. This organism may be put into the body of a person who has diabetes and needs insulin. The disease might be cured. There are, of course, a number of potential hazards. What, for example, other information might be carried on a viral DNA segment that might prove to be harmful? Recombinant DNA is also being eyed for possible use in the treatment of cancer. For example, the use of re-engineered bacteria to produce interferon is one avenue of current research. Interferon alters cancer cells so that they can no longer rapidly multiply. Much research still needs to be done in these areas.

Recombinant DNA and the controversy surrounding its use may also be a challenging topic for some students to do some outside research.

QUESTIONS FOR SECTION 3

1. Define and give an example of each of the following terms: phagocyte, vaccine.
2. List five diseases known to be of viral origin.
3. How do each of the following act as a defense against a virus infection: phagocytes, antibodies, interferon?
4. Describe three ways a virus can alter the normal functioning of a cell.
5. Differentiate between malignant and benign tumors
6. How does the lytic cycle maintain continuity of viruses?

CHAPTER REVIEW

Microbes are organisms smaller than can be seen without a microscope. They are a highly diverse group. They represent two or more kingdoms. This depends on one's system of classification. The monerans are primitive and lack membrane-bound organelles. The protists have a more complex organization.

Viruses have some properties of living things and lack others. They consist of a nucleic acid core and a protein coat. Variations of these chemicals produce many types of viruses. This demonstrates the concept of *diversity*. Their structure suggests that they represent a link between the living and non-living worlds.

The lytic cycle of viruses has been studied in bacteriophages. The action of the virus within this cycle illustrates the *relationship between structure and function*. It also shows a means of *continuity* of the viruses. Not all viruses go through a lytic cycle. Some may remain latent after becoming part of the host's chromosome. Virulence may occur later. Others may be responsible for producing tumors and cancers in specific tissues. Protection from some viral infections may be had through the action of phagocytes, antibodies, or the production of interferon.

Unanswered Question

1. How would our ideas about the origin of viruses be affected if a virus was discovered to reproduce outside of living cells?

VOCABULARY REVIEW

1 microbe
virus

2 bacteriophage
plaque

lytic cycle
virulent

3 interferon
vaccine

Answers to Questions for Section 3.

I. 1. Phagocyte: cells in the blood able to engulf and destroy infecting agents. Interferon: protein produced in response to a virus, and which acts against many infecting agents. Vaccine: substance that causes the body to produce antibodies against a specific disease without causing the illness.

J. 2. Polio, hepatitis, mumps, measles, influenza, colds, and some forms of cancer, etc.

K. 3. Phagocytes: engulf and destroy virus particle before it can reach target cell. Antibodies: recognize specific invaders and deactivate them. Interferon: produced by infection in first cells, passes to nearby cells and stimulates them to produce antiviral proteins.

L. 4. By infecting and killing host cells in a lytic cycle; by becoming attached to a chromosome like an extra gene, becoming latent, and capable of activation at a later time; by producing masses of abnormal cells, or tumors: some benign, some malignant.

5. A benign tumor is relatively harmless, while a malignant tumor is capable of being spread through-

out the body and is very dangerous.
6. By enabling the virus to produce more of itself, in great numbers.

CHAPTER 17 TEST

Copy the number of each test item and place your answer to the right.

PART 1   Multiple Choice: Select the letter of the phrase that best completes each of the following.

c **1.** Viruses multiply in cells because   **a.** the cell DNA directs the production of new viruses   **b.** the mitochondria become new viruses   **c.** viral DNA takes over the operation of the cell   **d.** DNA does not code for protein.

a **2.** Viruses must be considered to be   **a.** parasitic   **b.** free-living   **c.** both parasitic and free-living   **d.** eucaryotic.

d **3.** The outer protective coat of a virus is mainly   **a.** RNA   **b.** DNA   **c.** cellulose   **d.** protein.

b **4.** When a phage attacks a cell   **a.** it enters the cell   **b.** only the DNA enters the cell   **c.** the outer coat enters the cell   **d.** it injects poisons into the cell.

c **5.** Which of the following features of a virus would support the idea that they are not living?   **a.** they possess a nucleic acid   **b.** they can exhibit change through time   **c.** they can be crystallized   **d.** they illustrate the concept of the relatedness between structure and function.

c **6.** Reproduction in viruses differs from cells in that   **a.** it is asexual   **b.** it is sexual   **c.** new viruses do not arise directly from a pre-existing similar structure   **d.** it does not involve nucleic acids.

a **7.** Viruses   **a.** can pass through a biological filter   **b.** respire   **c.** produce poisons that affect the host cells   **d.** all of these.

d **8.** Body defenses against virus infection include all but which one of the following?   **a.** production of antibodies   **b.** action of phagocytic cells   **c.** production of interferon   **d.** the release of anti-viruses.

a **9.** Malignant tumors   **a.** are known generally as cancers   **b.** are relatively harmless to adults   **c.** are easily controlled   **d.** are due to latent viruses.

a **10.** Various types of viral flu illustrate the concept of   **a.** change through time   **b.** the relationship between structure and function   **c.** continuity   **d.** homeostasis.

PART 2   Matching: Match the letter of the term in Column I with its description in Column II.

COLUMN I

a. vaccine   **e.** lytic cycle
b. bacteriophage   **f.** microbes   **i.** tumor
c. cilia   **g.** phagocytes   **j.** virulent
d. interferon   **h.** procaryotic

COLUMN II

h **11.** Primitive cells that lack membrane-bound organelles

j **12.** Highly infective, disease-producing organism

c **13.** Small bristle-like projections of a cell

a **14.** Causes the body to produce antibodies without causing the illness

g **15.** Body cells that engulf invading foreign cells

b **16.** Type of virus that attacks bacteria

i **17.** Abnormal mass of cells

f **18.** Life forms too small to be seen without the aid of a microscope

e **19.** Stages in the activity of a phage

d **20.** Body chemical produced in response to an infecting virus

PART 3   Completion: Complete the following.

21. The presence of a phage in a bacterial culture is evidenced by the presence of ___plaques___.

22. The first viral disease for which a vaccination was used to protect humans was ___smallpox___.

23. Interferon may be more important in the ___initial___ stages of infection.

24. "Made to order" viral nucleic acids to replace defective genes is known as ___recombinant DNA___.

25. Some people may be more prone to cancers because of differences in abilities to produce ___interferon___.

CHAPTER 18

BACTERIA AND BLUE-GREEN ALGAE

In this chapter, we move into a world that must be considered alive. The monerans are the simplest of living things. They include bacteria and the blue-green algae. Some biologists consider them to be direct descendants of the earth's first life forms. Monerans show great variety.

The bacteria and blue-green algae affect our lives in very direct ways. They cause disease and produce certain foods. Monerans also help to digest food in our intestines. In fact, they are the most common form of life in the world. Without special techniques to exclude them, monerans are found everywhere that life can possibly exist. Bacteria are found in air, water, food, and soil. They also exist on and in our bodies.

Typical of life forms, the monerans exhibit all of the properties of life. In doing so, they illustrate all of the major concepts of biology. There are certain features of monerans that give them a distinct *unity*. At the same time, they are a highly *diverse* group. Some have adapted to conditions that no other life forms can survive. As conditions change, they also have been able to change. This exemplifies a second major theme, *change through time*. Although considered primitive, they have specific *structures* that are *related to specific functions*. Finally, they manage to maintain *homeostasis*.

As we consider the monerans, you will discover their importance to us. Without a knowledge of bacteria and their relatives, the health sciences would indeed be in a primitive state. The contributions of monerans to an ecologic balance are also of prime importance to us. On a more immediate level, you should be able to answer some of the following questions:

- What human diseases are caused by monerans?
- How can these diseases be controlled?
- How can we protect ourselves from these diseases?
- In what specific ways are monerans beneficial to us?

ESCHERICHIA COLI

1 DIVERSITY AND CONTINUITY

General Characteristics of Monerans

The monerans are all procaryotic. (See Table 18-1.) That is, their cells do not have membrane-bound organelles. Most are unicellular. They consist of a single cell. Some do live in colonies, however. The monerans include all of the bacteria and blue-green algae. (See Table 18-2.) Even among these primitive organisms, there is great variety.

Monerans also vary greatly in their ability to move about. Some cannot move or are not motile at all. Others are able to move about through the action of *flagella.* These long whip-like strands extend from the cell. Flagella may occur singly, in tufts, or in great numbers over the surface of the cell. (See Fig. 18-1.) The presence or absence of flagella and their arrangement on the cell serves as one means for classifying the monerans.

Monerans also vary in size and shape. The smallest are just visible with the best light microscopes. Others may be seen with the unaided eye as long thin threads. Monerans may be spherical, rod-like, or spiraled in shape. (See Fig. 18-2.) In fact, shape is another factor often used in classifying them. They often produce large, easily visible colonies of cells. The shape of these colonies is also characteristic of specific monerans.

Finally, there is great variety in the way monerans live. Some are free living. They are able to live quite independent of other living or-

OBJECTIVES FOR SECTION 1

A. Define each of the following terms in your own words: *procaryote, flagellum, pathogen, binary fission, conjugation, endospore.*

B. Describe the characteristics that define the Kingdom Monera.

C. List five moneran groups and give the unifying features of each.

D. List the roles of Monerans that affect humans.

TABLE 18-1

Feature	Procaryotes	Eucaryotes
Nuclear membrane	none	present
Chromosomes	composed of nucleic acid only	composed of nucleic acid and protein
Photosynthetic pigment (when present)	various pigments, including chlorophyll but not in chloroplasts	chlorophyll, when present, contained in chloroplasts
Membrane-bound organelles	absent	present
Flagella, cilia	lack 9 + 2 arrangement	9 + 2 structure
Cytoplasmic streaming	does not occur	may occur
Cell wall	contains amino sugars and muramic acid	when present, does not contain amino sugars and muramic acid

18-1. *Numerous flagella extend from these bacterial cells. They enable the cells to move about.*

TABLE 18-2   MAJOR GROUPS OF MONERANS

	Mycoplasma	Rickettsiae	Spirochetes	Bacteria	Blue-Green Algae
Examples	PPLO	Rickettsia	Spirocheta, Treponema, Leptospira	Escherichia coli, Streptococcus, Staphylococcus, Mycobacterium tuberculosis	Anabaena
Form	smallest free-living cells, no cell walls	extremely small (0.3 X 0.5 micrometers)	extremely long, helical	rod-shaped (bacillus), spherical (coccus), spirillum (many curves), vibrio (one curve)	single cells; filamentous, branched
Motility	none	none	twisting (axial filament)	gliding, flagella	gliding, none
Mode of Nutrition	heterotrophs (many parasites)	heterotrophs (parasites)	heterotrophs	chemoautotrophs, photosynthetic autotrophs, heterotrophs	autotrophs
Distribution	intracellular parasites, soil	lice, ticks, mites	aquatic (polluted water) parasites	soil, water, parasites	stagnant water
Ecological Role	pathogens	pathogens	symbionts (in mollusks), pathogens, decomposers	decomposers, symbionts, pathogens	nitrogen fixation
Diseases	mycoplasma pneumonia	typhus, trench fever	syphilis, infectious jaundice, relapsing fever	lockjaw, diptheria, tuberculosis	none

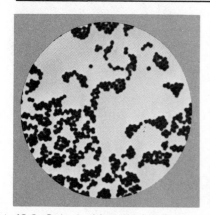

18-2. Spherical bacterial cells are called cocci.

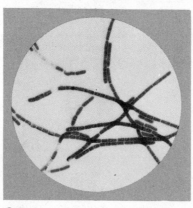

Cylindrical, or rod shaped bacterial cells are called bacilli.

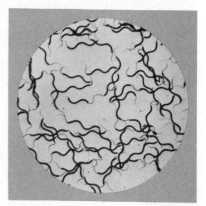

Spiral shaped bacteria, or spirillum occur as unattached single cells.

ganisms. Some of these are autotrophs. These organisms produce their own food. Others are heterotrophic. They may be saprophytes or parasites. Saprophytes obtain their energy from the dead remains of plants and animals. These forms make up an important part of the decomposer elements in an ecosystem. The parasitic forms depend entirely upon living plants and animals. Of these, many are the *disease-causing bacteria referred to as* **pathogens.**

Thus far, we have considered the variety among the monerans. Aside from the fact that they are all procaryotic, we might ask what features do they share? For one, they are cellular and are bounded by cell walls. In fact, they are unicellular. However, some live in colonies of various sizes and shapes. Most are heterotrophic with the exceptions noted earlier. Finally, all reproduce asexually.

The Mycoplasmas

The mycoplasmas (mī kō *plaz* məs) are tiny procaryotic cells. They are often known as pleuropneumonia-like organisms, or *PPLO* for short. More recent information indicates that not all of the mycoplasmas are actually PPLO. Mycoplasmas range in size from 125 to 250 μ. Thus, some forms can pass through a biological filter. In this way, they are similar to viruses. Unlike viruses, however, several forms may be grown in cell-free cultures. The absence of cell walls causes them to take a variety of shapes as seen in Figure 18-3. Mycoplasmas are involved in several human diseases including one form of pneumonia. They have even been implicated in some forms of leukemia. Not very much is known about the mycoplasmas. Even their mode of reproduction is mostly unknown.

The Rickettsias

Another biological puzzle are the rickettsias (rik *et* sē əs). Rickettsias seem to fit somewhere between viruses and bacteria in a classification scheme. They are definitely cellular. The largest are barely the size of the smallest bacteria. At least one species is filterable, as are the viruses. Some are spherical. Others are rod-like. (See Fig. 18-4.) With one exception, they reproduce and grow only within living cells, again like the viruses.

Rickettsias are important to us as pathogens. They are responsible for a number of diseases. Such diseases include trench fever, typhus fever, Rocky Mountain spotted fever, and Q fever. These pathogens, for the most part, must be transmitted to humans through vector organisms. Vectors are lice, fleas, ticks, and mites. Although death may occur in some cases, most people recover with proper treatment. People may, however, run a risk of reoccurrence of the disease if their resistance is allowed to run down.

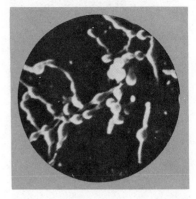

18-3. Tiny microplasmas can take a variety of shapes since they do not have a rigid cell wall.

Answers to Questions for Section 1.
A. 1. See glossary for definitions.
   2. Fission: reproduction involving DNA replication and then splitting in half of a single cell. Conjugation: reproduction in which DNA from one cell passes into another, the donor dies, and the recipient then divides.
B. 3. Unifying features: all are cells that have no membrane-bound organelles; all reproduce asexually. Subdividing features: presence or absence of flagella shape, of both individuals and colonies; some are autotrophic; some are heterotrophic, and may be either saprophytes or parasites.

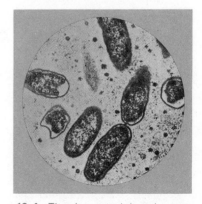

18-4. The largest rickettsias are hardly the size of the smallest bacteria.

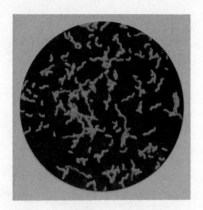

18-5. *Spirochetes occur as unattached individual cells.*

The Spirochetes

Spirochetes (*spī rə kēts*) are very long monerans. Some are as short as five microns. Others may be as long as 500 μ. (See Fig. 18-5.) The body of the cell is wrapped around a filament and thus takes the shape of a double helix, or corkscrew. Some are free-living. Others are parasites of humans and other animals. Perhaps the best known of the spirochete diseases is syphilis. Spirochetes move by a vibrating action that causes them to whirl.

Bacteria

The great majority of monerans belong to a group we generally refer to as bacteria. Many scientists think that some kinds of bacteria may have been the first forms of life on the earth. Fossils of these primitive organisms have been found in the most ancient rock layers known. In fact, the evidence suggests that they were present long before the green plants and the process of photosynthesis.

In spite of some exceptions, most bacteria are heterotrophs. Their simple, procaryotic structure does not allow them to be very complex. They may live singly or in simple colonies. This variety may

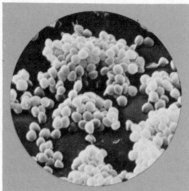
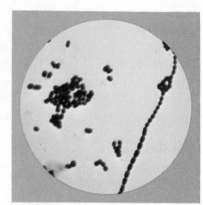
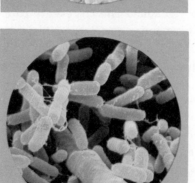
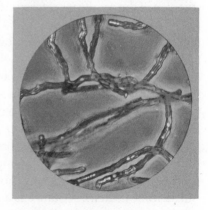

18-6. *Bacteria may be classified according to their arrangement. (upper left) micrococcus, cocci as single units; (upper right) streptococcus, cocci as chains; (lower left) bacillus, bacilli as single units; (lower right) streptobacillus, bacilli as chains.*

serve as one of the bases for classifying them. The phylum names can be observed by reviewing Figure 16-4 on page 294. There are thousands of different species of bacteria. However, three basic shapes are seen in bacterial cells: *coccus* (spherical), *bacillus* (rod-shaped), and *spirillum* (bent rods or spirals). Some species tend to remain attached after their cells divide. This attachment may form pairs, chains, or clusters. (See Fig. 18-6.) These features may be used in lab tests to help identify the cause of an infection. Usually, biochemical or other tests are also required.

Blue-Green Algae

Being procaryotes, blue-green algae are similar to bacteria. In other respects, however, they are more like plants. In fact, some classification schemes include them in the plant kingdom. The electron microscope reveals a more complex cell structure than seen in bacteria. Moreover, the presence of chlorophyll *a* allows for a plant-like form of photosynthesis. The bluish pigment, *phycocyanin* (fī kō sī an ən) gives this group of monerans its characteristic color. Other pigments may also be present. These may cause the color of the blue-green algae to vary from red to purple or even nearly black. A periodic abundance of these red-pigmented algae are responsible for giving the Red Sea its name.

Like bacteria, blue-green algae manage to survive many harsh conditions. Some are found in the hot springs of Yellowstone National Park where temperatures may exceed 80°C. (See Fig. 18-7.) Some are indicators of polluted water. Their presence in swimming pools and drinking water is a danger sign to health officials. Still others are found on wet rocks, in the soil, and in stagnant ponds. Often, large numbers of individuals grow clustered within a gelatinous sheath. This sheath gives a characteristic slimy mass. Blue-green algae are found on rocks and swimming pool walls making them very slick.

Continuity in Monerans

Many monerans can reproduce very rapidly. So why do they not simply take over the earth? The same factors that govern populations in other organisms also control bacterial populations. The optimum temperature range for most bacteria is between 25°C and 38°C. Some operate best in more extreme temperatures, but they are exceptions. Bacteria also require sufficient nutrients. Moreover, some are limited in what foods they can use. Other limitations may include such things as lack of moisture or the build-up of waste products. Harmful environmental conditions may also inhibit growth. These include ultraviolet light or toxic substances.

18-7. *Blue-green algae can survive in the most rigorous of conditions. Here they grow in Emerald Pool, Yellowstone Park.*

18-8. *Fission in a bacterial cell.*

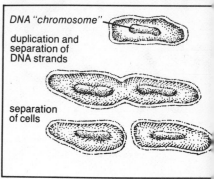

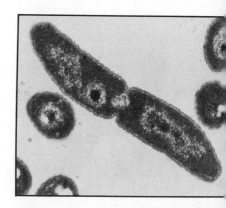

DNA "chromosome"

duplication and separation of DNA strands

separation of cells

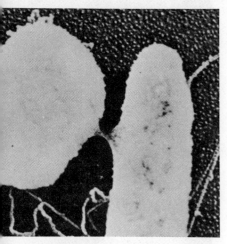

18-9. *Photomicrograph of conjugation in bacteria.*

The failure of bacteria to show up in the swan-necked flasks indicates that spore-forming bacteria were not present.

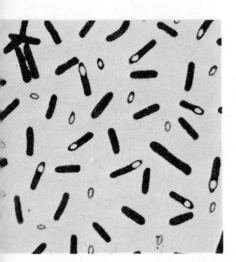

18-10. *Some bacteria will form endospores that will help them survive severe conditions.*

FISSION   Monerans reproduce by an asexual process called *fission*. Their DNA consists of one long, single-stranded "chromosome." During fission, this molecule duplicates and the cell splits in half. Figure 18-8 is an electron micrograph showing a bacterium that is undergoing fission. Under ideal conditions, fission takes only 20 to 30 minutes.

CONJUGATION   Occasionally, a primitive form of sexual reproduction may take place in bacteria. Two cells may come to lie side by side. Their adjacent walls break down and the DNA from one cell passes into the other cell. (See Fig. 18-9.) The donor cell then dies. The recipient cell undergoes division. This process is called *conjugation*. While not truly a sexual process, some mixing of genetic information does take place in the recipient cell. Thus, the new cell is not identical to either of the cells that contributed the DNA material.

ENDOSPORES   Certain bacillus forms have a unique way for surviving harsh conditions. Within the cell, an *endospore* develops that contains the necessary protoplasm for survival. The outer coat of the endospore is able to withstand boiling water and other conditions that would kill the unprotected cell itself. When conditions are again suitable, the endospore becomes active and grows into a normal cell. This is not strictly a form of reproduction, of course. A single cell can produce only one endospore. In turn, an endospore can only produce a single cell. Thus, survival is achieved. Continuity of the species is maintained.

The survival ability of endospores is truly amazing. They can lie dormant for many years before becoming active. At times, this potential for infection becomes a serious medical problem. If endospores are present, sterilization by boiling is insufficient. Only a properly operated sterilizer, called an autoclave, can destroy these hardy forms. (See Fig. 18-10.) How does the knowledge of endospores shed new light on Pasteur's "swan-necked flask" experiment discussed in Unit 4?

QUESTIONS FOR SECTION 1

1. Define each of the following terms in your own words: procaryote, flagellum, pathogen, endospore.
2. Differentiate between fission and conjugation as a means of reproduction. What long term value does each of these processes have to the organism?
3. What are the unifying features of monerans? What features enable them to be subdivided?
4. Describe the unifying features of each of the five moneran phyla described in this chapter.
5. Point out the many kinds of affects that monerans have on humans.
   (See pages 321-322 for answers)

CHAPTER INVESTIGATION

A. Both pictures are of the same area, taken at different times. How are the two scenes different?

B. What is the cause of this phenomenon called a Red Tide?

C. See if you can create an artificial Red Tide in the laboratory using the appropriate algae and various combinations of nutrients.

2 HOMEOSTASIS

Obtaining Energy

OBJECTIVES FOR SECTION 2

E. Define each of the following terms in your own words: *chemosynthesis*, *aerobe*, *anaerobe*, *growth medium*.

F. Differentiate between chemosynthesis and photosynthesis.

G. Differentiate between obligate and facultative anaerobes. Give examples.

H. Differentiate between fermentation and respiration as means of releasing energy in monerans.

I. Explain why a knowledge of how bacterial cells release energy is important to humans.

Monerans obtain energy to carry on the processes of life in a number of ways. Further, it has been suggested that bacteria were present long before green plants were around. Where would such early organisms find a continuous supply of energy to power their life processes? Some modern forms of bacteria may help to answer this question. These cells are able to use energy from inorganic compounds in their environment. With this energy, they are able to build organic compounds. These bacteria are said to be *chemosynthetic*. The process of chemosynthesis is much like that of photosynthesis. (See Fig. 18-11.) However, the reactions are not powered directly by the sun. Rather, the energy comes from inorganic molecules that contain sulfur, iron, and nitrogen. Chemosynthetic bacteria do not represent a very large group today.

Certain purple bacteria rely on the sun as an energy source. Unlike green plants, however, they do not release oxygen as one of the products. Instead, sulfur is produced. Because of this, the purple bacteria have provided an important clue to the nature of photosynthesis. Nearly fifty years ago, C.B. Van Niel noted the similarity between photosynthesis in the purple bacteria and green plants. Both use carbon dioxide. Unlike the green plants, however, water does not take part in the bacterial process. Van Niel reasoned that the oxygen released by green plants must come from the water molecules in the re-

18-11. A comparison between photosynthesis and chemosynthesis.

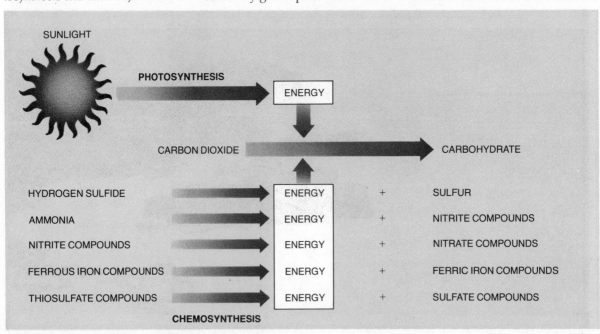

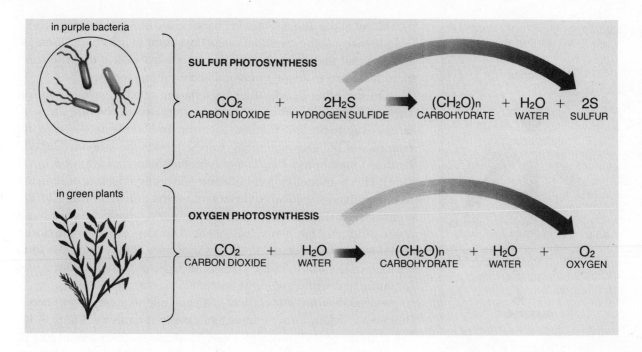

in purple bacteria

SULFUR PHOTOSYNTHESIS

$$CO_2 + 2H_2S \rightarrow (CH_2O)n + H_2O + 2S$$
CARBON DIOXIDE · HYDROGEN SULFIDE · CARBOHYDRATE · WATER · SULFUR

in green plants

OXYGEN PHOTOSYNTHESIS

$$CO_2 + H_2O \rightarrow (CH_2O)n + H_2O + O_2$$
CARBON DIOXIDE · WATER · CARBOHYDRATE · WATER · OXYGEN

action and not from the carbon dioxide. (See Fig. 18-12.) Today, radioactive tracers can be used to "follow" elements through many organic reactions, including photosynthesis. This helps us to understand these processes better. Moreover, it has revealed a unity that is not easily observed.

Mention has already been made of the photosynthetic blue-green algae. Rather than sulfur, as in the purple bacteria, oxygen is released as a product. This is due to the presence of chlorophyll *a*. This organic molecule is not present in bacteria. This fact in part accounts for their inclusion as plants by some scientists.

18-12. A comparison of photosynthesis in the purple bacteria with photosynthesis in green plants.

Energy Release

AEROBES AND ANAEROBES   Both unity and diversity are again apparent in the ways that monerans release energy from organic compounds. *Monerans that use oxygen in the process of respiration are called* **aerobes**. *Monerans that do not use oxygen are* **anaerobes**. Anaerobes rely on the less efficient fermentation processes to provide energy from organic nutrients. Fermentation, you recall from Unit 2, does not use oxygen. Anaerobes are considered to be more primitive forms of life than aerobes.

Even among these two basic forms of energy release, there is variety. *Aerobes that cannot survive in the absence of oxygen are said to be* **obligate aerobes**. *Aerobes that can use fermentation, when oxygen is not present are called* **facultative anaerobes**. (See Fig. 18-13.)

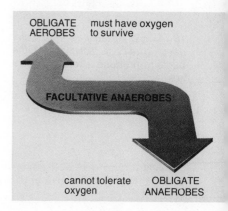

OBLIGATE AEROBES   must have oxygen to survive

FACULTATIVE ANAEROBES

cannot tolerate oxygen

OBLIGATE ANAEROBES

18-13. Nutrition in the Monerans can be viewed as a continuum. Between the extremes, some Monerans can make use of oxygen when it is present or use fermentation when oxygen is not present.

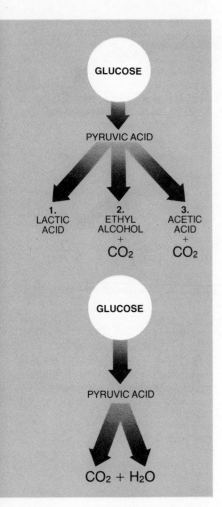

18-14. *Higher animals and some bacteria release lactic acid. Other bacteria produce alcohol or acetic acid.*

Point out that bacteria have modes of nutrition seen in a variety of other organisms.

Many of the disease-causing bacteria are obligate aerobes. These include many of the ones that cause the common infectious diseases. The fact that they grow best in the air is what makes them so common. It is hard to create unfavorable conditions for them.

On the other hand, other bacteria are much easier to control. These **obligate anaerobes** *are bacteria that cannot tolerate the presence of oxygen.* Bacteria that cause tetanus and botulism poisoning are examples of obligate anaerobes. Canned foods that are not properly sterilized may house *Clostridium botulinum* (klä *strid* ē em bäch ə lī nəm). This pathogen causes botulism poisoning. The lack of air in the container makes an ideal environment for the growth of these deadly organisms. Inside the can or jar they grow and release the poison as a waste product. They also release a gas. This gas collects in the closed container. As the pressure of the gas increases, it may cause the jar to explode or the can to bulge. This is an indication that the food was contaminated with dangerous bacteria.

RESPIRATION OR FERMENTATION?   As you might guess, respiration is the most efficient form of energy release in organisms. Many times the number of ATP molecules can be obtained from a molecule of glucose by respiration than can be had by fermentation. The end products of respiration are carbon dioxide and water.

Anaerobes, on the other hand, may produce a number of end products. All of these retain energy that respiratory pathways would have released. Which end product is released depends on which enzymes a particular species has. Figure 18-14 summarizes three possible fermentive pathways and compares them to respiration. By selecting the right organism, great quantities of desired products may be produced on a commercial basis. Without bacteria, cheeses, yogurts, vinegar and alcohol would be unknown. Farmers may use silage to supplement the diet of their cattle. Silage has a high lactic acid content due to certain anaerobic bacteria. Lactic acid helps to stimulate milk production. In the future, by using recombinant DNA, scientists may be able to produce other valuable products from "new" bacteria. Insulin, a valuable hormone lacking in diabetics, is able to be produced using recombinant DNA.

Nutrition

SAPROPHYTE BACTERIA   Enzymes produced by bacteria are used to digest foods inside and outside of the cell. Once broken down to smaller units, these foods can be absorbed through the cell membrane. Each enzyme acts on a certain kind of molecule. The saprophytic bacteria have a wide range of enzymes. These enzymes are used to digest materials in their environment. Thus, they are able to use an equally wide range of foods for energy.

TABLE 18-3. NUTRITIONAL REQUIREMENTS OF SOME HETEROTROPHIC BACTERIA.

Bacteria	inorganic salts	organic carbon	Nitrogen inorganic	Nitrogen one amino acid	Nitrogen two or more amino acids	Vitamins one	Vitamins two or more
Escherichia coli	X	X	X				
Salmonella typhosa	X	X	X	X			
Proteus vulgaris	X	X	X	X		X	
Staphylococcus aureus	X	X	X		X	X	
Lactobacillus acidophilus	X	X	X		X		X

PARASITIC BACTERIA   The parasitic bacteria, on the other hand, are often limited in what foods can be used. They often lack the range of enzymes that other bacteria have. This is one reason that they must remain in close contact with specific host cells. These cells are able to supply the required foods in sufficient amounts. This keeps the bacterial cells alive and reproducing.

Many of the parasitic bacteria cause disease in their hosts. More often than not, these diseases do not usually cause the death of the host. Destruction of the host would act against the parasite. Thus, selection has tended to favor less harmful forms of bacteria. Selection in the host has tended to increase defense against the invader. To be sure, some pathogens result in death for the host. Often, these are the less resistant hosts. Here again, selection is seen to operate.

TYPES OF CARBON REQUIREMENTS   Knowledge about bacterial nutrition has come from a number of interesting studies. These studies have shown that bacteria vary in the kinds of nutrients and other materials required for growth. (See Table 18-3.) They all require a source of carbon, of course. However, they differ as to the form in which the carbon can be made available for use. For example, the autotrophic forms can use carbon dioxide directly. First, photosynthesis must "fix" carbon dioxide into an organic molecule. From this molecule, all of the complex carbon compounds required for life can be made. At the other end of the spectrum are the parasites. These bacteria must get carbon from the complex organic compounds of their hosts. Between these extremes are other forms that can use fairly simple carbon sources. These forms have enzyme pathways to make the more complex compounds for themselves. Others need a great variety of compounds to satisfy their carbon requirement. They apparently have a much simpler chemical make-up.

Answers to Questions for Section 2.

F. 2. Energy is produced in both. In chemosynthesis, the energy comes from inorganic molecules rather than directly from the sun.

G. 3. An obligate anaerobe cannot survive in the presence of oxygen, while a facultative anaerobe can use fermentation when oxygen is not present.

*4. Selection has operated to remove from populations of pathogens their ability to survive outside the host organism.

H. 5. Respiration yields a greater number of ATP molecules than fermentation.

I. 6. Without anaerobic energy release, we would not have many products, such as cheese, alcohol, lactic acid, vinegar, yogurt, or silage.

Examples of non-pathogenic bacteria with special nutritional requirements may be obtained from biological supply houses and grown on special media. This makes a good demonstration for illustrating differences between specialized and generalized forms.

OTHER CHEMICAL REQUIREMENTS Similar variety exists in the way that bacteria get and use nitrogen, sulfur, and vitamins. Some can use nitrogen from the atmosphere. Others require the presence of nitrates or even amino acids. Certain bacteria can use pure sulfur. Other bacteria require nutrients that contain sulfates. There are bacteria that can make their own vitamins. However, others require ready-made vitamins.

GROWTH MEDIUM The studies that showed these great variations in bacterial needs were fairly simple in principle. Many different kinds of bacteria were grown in special culture dishes. These dishes contained *agar* (ăg′ är). *Nutrients mixed with agar form a* **growth medium** for the bacteria. (See Fig. 18-15.) Scientists are able to control the nutrients in the medium. By doing so, they can find out what requirements each species of bacteria has for life. As we have seen, some forms require very little in the way of nutrients. Others require very special and complex media to grow. Once the special requirements for growth are known, unknown bacteria can be identified.

Other Functions

The small size of the monerans makes a complex circulatory system unnecessary. Materials from the environment can be absorbed into the cell by diffusion. These materials are then moved about within the cell by normal cellular processes. Waste materials also diffuse out of the cell as they are formed. The cell wall serves to protect the cell from unfavorable conditions, such as osmotic imbalance.

Monerans also display some limited responses to their environments. Photosynthetic forms tend to move toward the light. At least some bacteria are able to move toward a food source when placed near it. Others have been observed to move away from certain harmful chemicals such as acids. Such responses do not appear to be obvious. However, they are still responses and characteristic of life forms.

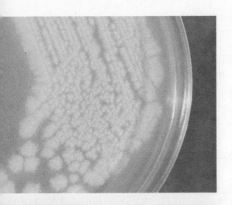
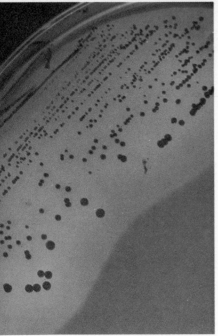

18-15. Many different media are used to grow bacteria that have special nutritional requirements. (top) egg yolk agar; (bottom) blood agar.

Answers to Questions for Section 2.

E. 1. Aerobe: moneran that uses oxygen in the process of respiration. Example: most disease bacteria. Anaerobe: moneran that does not use oxygen in respiration. Example: tetanus bacterium. Growth medium: nutrients mixed with agar, for growing bacteria. Example: blood agar.

(See page 329 for more answers.)

QUESTIONS FOR SECTION 2

1. Define each of the following terms in your own words and give an appropriate example of each: aerobe, anaerobe, growth medium.
2. Differentiate between chemosynthesis and photosynthesis. What is the end result in each case?
3. What are the differences between obligate and facultative anaerobes?
4. Explain why a pathogen would be considered to be an obligate parasite.
5. Why are aerobes considered to be more efficient than anaerobes?
6. Explain why a knowledge of anaerobic energy release in microbes is important to humans.

3 MONERANS AND THEIR ENVIRONMENT

Useful Bacteria

Not all bacteria are harmful to other organisms. In fact, many are quite useful. Some forms, for example, reside in the digestive tract of animals, including humans. The human digestive tract contains *E. coli* bacteria. They help to break down foods that could not otherwise be digested. Intestinal bacteria are also at least in part responsible for synthesizing certain amino acids. They also play a role in producing various vitamins, including vitamin K. Many of these bacteria pass out of the body with the feces. Their presence in water and soil can be easily determined. Thus, tests for contamination by human waste include tests for *Escherichia coli*.

Free-living bacteria are important as decomposers in all ecosystems. They live off the bodies of dead plants and animals. Hence, they are included in the category of *saprophytes*. As such, they are decay organisms. They help to recycle the nutrients otherwise locked in the bodies of dead organisms. Some mention of the importance of a variety of bacteria in the nitrogen cycle has already been made in Unit 1. Bacteria are also used as decomposers in many waste disposal plants. (See Fig. 18-16.)

Disease-Causing Bacteria

Pathogenic bacteria may exert their effects on their hosts in either one of two main ways. First, they may cause damage to cells and tissues directly. For example, bacteria that cause typhoid fever attack cells in the wall of the intestine. A number of different bacteria attack red blood cells. One kind of pneumonia is caused by bacteria that attack cells in the lungs. Some forms of meningitis are caused by bacteria that infect tissues covering the brain and spinal cord.

OBJECTIVES FOR SECTION 3

J. Define each of the following terms in your own words: *saprophyte, venereal disease, antitoxin, toxin, chemotherapy.*

K. Differentiate between the two main venereal diseases.

L. Describe a variety of ways that we can protect ourselves from bacterial action.

M. Describe two main ways that we can treat a bacterial infection in our bodies.

N. Explain how the use of antibiotics can encourage the growth of microbes resistant to treatment.

O. Explain how *continuity* is maintained in some monerans.

18-16. Bacteria are used in many waste disposal plants to break down organic matter.

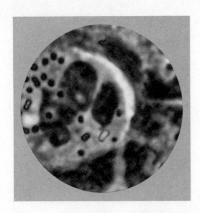

18-17. Gonococcus bacteria that cause gonorrhea.

Point out the value of various mucous membranes, tears, and other fluids secreted by the body that protect against infection.

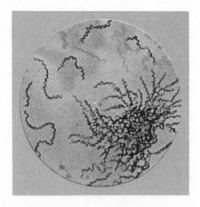

18-18. Syphilis, another common venereal disease, is caused by this spirochete.

The second way that bacteria can affect their host is by producing poisons, or toxins. These toxins then destroy the host's tissues. Included in this group are bacteria that cause diptheria, scarlet fever, and tetanus. Various kinds of food poisoning are due to the action of such bacteria. *Streptococcus* infections are fairly common and usually respond to antibiotics. However, a "strep" infection that is ignored could result in rheumatic fever. Joints and heart valves are the target tissues of toxins produced by these "strep" bacteria.

Venereal Disease

Two important anaerobes deserve special mention because of their increased prevalence in recent years. These are the agents of two venereal diseases, gonorrhea and syphilis. Venereal disease (VD) is intimately associated with sexual activity. The rise of VD to near epidemic levels has been observed among people in the 15-25 year old age bracket. Unlike chicken pox, measles, or many other infectious diseases, venereal diseases do not impart an immunity against future infection. In fact, it is not uncommon for reinfection to occur several times after treatment. Venereal diseases do not limit suffering to those who have contracted them directly. Innocent people may also become victims, including babies born to syphilitic parents.

GONORRHEA   Gonorrhea has been called the "great preventor" because of its ability to cause sterility. It is caused by a coccus-type bacterium. (See Fig. 18-17.) The target organs are the oviducts (in the female) and the sperm ducts (in the male). Scar tissue prevents the movement of eggs or sperm through these tubes. This is the cause of the sterility. Gonorrhea is the most common form of VD. Estimates suggest that as many as 60 million cases occur annually around the world! Infants can contract gonorrhea as they pass through the birth canal. For this reason, most states require that special drugs are placed in the eyes of new babies. Infection is likely to start here.

SYPHILIS   A spirochete is the agent in syphilis. (See Fig. 18-18.) Infection progresses through three stages if not treated. In the first stage, a *chancre* (*shang* kəer), or sore, erupts at the point of infection. This sore disappears in a few weeks even if untreated. A latent stage of a few weeks or months may then follow. The secondary stage appears as a rash that may cover the entire body. Hair may also be lost in patches. Grayish-white blotches may appear on the mucous membranes of the body.

The third stage of syphilis lasts until the death of the victim. During this phase, the victim may suffer from tumors throughout the body. These are finally accompanied by insanity and eventually death. Syphilis has been called the "great destroyer" or the "great imitator." It often goes undiagnosed because of its resemblance to other diseases. Its presence can only be proved by a laboratory examination. Venereal diseases may be successfully treated by antibiotics if diagnosed soon enough. However, they are often spread to others before treatment occurs.

Protection Against Bacterial Action

METHODS OF PROTECTION   Foods can be treated in a number of ways to reduce the risk of spoilage. Some foods can be sterilized by heating before being sealed in an airtight container. Canned foods can be preserved in this way almost indefinitely. Fruits, vegetables, jellies, and meats are examples of foods that can be canned.

In some cases, canning cannot be used because the food tends to lose its taste. It is not desirable if it is precooked. Foods of this type may be frozen, dehydrated, or salt-cured. These methods retard bacterial action while retaining the quality of the food. Another protective measure is the use of a chemical preservative. Preservatives retard the growth of bacteria. Many people object to the use of chemicals to preserve food. They fear the possible long term effects these chemicals may cause.

THE BODY'S LINES OF PROTECTION   Our bodies have several built-in ways to protect us from pathogens. The skin serves as the first line of defense against infection. Sweat produced by the skin also helps protect the body from infecting agents. The mucous membranes that line the nose, mouth, digestive tract, eyes, and genital tracts complete the envelope that encloses our bodies. The fluids on these membranes contain chemicals. These chemicals help to destroy invading bacteria.

In spite of these defenses, pathogens can and do gain entrance to the body. Pores in the skin or cuts may serve as entry points for pathogens. Bacteria usually enter our bodies through our food or the air we breathe. Other bacteria can be injected by the bites of insects, ticks, and other vectors.

Mention has already been made in Chapter 17 of other body defenses. These include the action of phagocytes and the development of antibodies. These are useful against bacteria as well as viruses. The body may also produce antitoxins. **Antitoxins** *deactivate poisons produced by toxin-producing bacteria* such as diptheria. Antitoxins, as well as antibodies, can also be injected into the body. These provide a passive immunity to some diseases. In some cases, the body can be stimulated to produce its own antitoxin. This is accomplished by injecting toxoids into the body. **Toxoids** *are toxins that have already been deactivated.* Protection against tetanus and diptheria is normally gained in this way.

Answers to Questions for Section 3

K. **3.** Gonorrhea and syphilis. Gonorrhea is caused by a coccus-type bacterium that attacks the oviducts in the female and the sperm ducts in the male, causing sterility by blocking these tubes with scar tissue. It can also be transmitted to newborn babies as they pass through the birth canal. Syphilis is caused by a spirochete that produces, in the first stage, a sore at the point of infection. If untreated, a latent stage may follow, lasting a few weeks or months, and then a rash and other symptoms appear. Still untreated, multiple tumors, insanity, and death will follow.

4. Gonorrhea is the "great preventor" because it causes sterility, and syphilis is the "great destroyer" because it effects are so terrible, if it runs its full course.

L. **5.** Treat food in a variety of ways to prevent spoilage; use antitoxins and antibodies to produce passive immunity to diseases; use vaccines and toxoids to produce active immunity to diseases.

*6. Food treatments (sterilization, freezing, salting, adding chemical preservatives) kill bacteria or retard their growth. Antitoxins deactivate toxins produced by bacteria and antibodies deactivate the pathogenic organisms themselves. Vaccines and toxoids stimulate the body to produce its own antibodies against pathogens.

M. **7.** Chemotherapy: the use of synthetic drugs to combat infection. Sulfa drugs are an example. Antibiotics: organic compounds produced by living organisms to treat infection. Penicillin, streptomycin, and aureomycin are examples.

N. **8.** By creating a highly selective environment that favors the growth of microbes resistant to antibiotics.

O. **9.** By enabling them to remain inactive, protected by a tough wall, through periods when the environment is not favorable.

Another body reaction to infection is **fever,** *or increased body temperature.* This tends to stop or at least slow down the growth of the pathogen. However, the cells of the host may also be sensitive to fever if it lasts too long or is too high. Drugs or special baths may be used to keep the fever down.

Other Means of Defense

A number of drugs are routinely used by doctors to combat infection. These do not provide a lasting immunity. But they do destroy pathogens in a fairly selective manner. There is little harm to the host. Perhaps the most famous of these are the sulfa drugs. These "miracle drugs" were first used on a broad scale during World War II. Today, **chemotherapy,** *as the use of synthetic drugs to combat infection* is called, is a widely used means of treatment. (See Fig. 18-19.)

Unlike drugs used in chemotherapy, **antibiotics** *are organic compounds produced by living organisms to treat infections.* Penicillin was the first, and is perhaps the best known of the antibiotics. It is produced by certain forms of fruit mold. Penicillin acts by interfering with the production of the cell wall by bacteria. It also has other effects on the bacterial cell. It damages the cell membrane, upsets protein synthesis, and retards the metabolism of nucleic acids. Penicillin came into general use by the military during the latter stages of World War II. Since that time, a number of other antibiotics have been developed and are commonly used today. These include streptomycin, aureomycin, and others.

18-19. Chemotherapy agents may be prepared in chemical laboratories. These substances are used to treat a variety of diseases.

18-20. Constant research is needed to find new ways of treating resistant strains of bacteria.

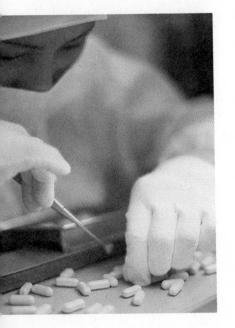

Resistant Bacterial Strains

The widespread use of antibiotics has had several effects upon humans. They have helped us to control a number of bacterial diseases and infections, to be sure. But they have also created highly selective environments. Such environments tend to favor the growth of microbes that are resistant to antibiotics. Researchers must constantly find new drugs and antibiotics to combat the spread of resistant bacteria and viruses. (See Fig. 18-20.) Recent epidemics of staphylococcus infections in hospitals make this point quite dramatically. Also, new strains of gonorrhea have appeared. These strains are resistant to the conventional antibiotics used for treatment. For these strains, treatment is not quite as simple.

Liberal use of antibiotics can also retard the normal presence of intestinal bacteria. These are necessary for proper nutrition, as we have already pointed out. Constant use of such drugs and antibiotics, then, can actually make us less healthy in the long run.

1. Differentiate between parasite and saprophyte.
2. Define the following terms in your own words: venereal disease, antitoxin, toxin, chemotherapy.
3. What are the two most common venereal diseases? Describe their causes, signs and symptoms of infections, and effects on the infected person.
4. Explain why the nicknames "great preventor" and "great destroyer" are appropriate for gonorrhea and syphilis.
5. How can we protect ourselves from bacterial action?
6. How does each type of protection given in question 5 help to prevent bacterial activity?
7. Describe two principal ways that we can treat a bacterial infection.
8. How do antibiotics encourage the growth of resistant strains of bacteria?
9. How do endospores maintain continuity in some monerans?

Answers to Questions for Section 3.

J. *1. Parasites live off the bodies of their living hosts, while saprophytes live off the bodies of dead organisms.

2. Venereal diseases are those associated with sexual activity. An antitoxin deactivates poisons produced by bacteria. A toxin is a poison produced by certain pathogens. Chemotherapy is the use of synthetic drugs to combat infections.

(See page 333 for more answers.)

CHAPTER REVIEW

The monerans include the bacteria and the blue-green algae. They show *unity* in being procaryotic and unicellular. Yet, they show *diversity* in their modes of nutrition, reproduction, motility, size, and shape. Although most are heterotrophs, some can produce their own food. This occurs either by photosynthesis or by chemosynthesis. Bacteria are most notorious as pathogens. But many are also useful to humans.

Monerans reproduce asexually by fission. Bacteria may undergo conjugation. Conjugation is considered by some to be a primitive form of sexual reproduction. Some bacillus bacteria form endospores. This process allows them to survive extremely harsh conditions, and thus maintain *continuity*.

The heterotrophs release energy for life's activities by respiration or fermentation. These activities help maintain a *homeostatic* balance. Cell walls, flagella, and endospores illustrate the concept of *structure and function*.

Bacteria are useful to humans as decomposers. They are also important digesters of foods in the intestinal tract, and producers of some foods. Some are pathogens. They may produce their effects by releasing toxins. Some attack specific cells and tissues. Body defenses against infection include the skin, mucous membranes, phagocytes, the production of antibodies, and fever. Passive immunity to some diseases can be created. Treatment of disease may also include chemotherapy and antibiotics.

There is liberal use of antibiotics and other drugs to combat infection and disease. This has allowed us to observe *change through time* in monerans. Resistant strains of bacteria are favored in environments where selective pressures are strong.

Using the Concepts

1. Why are antibiotics generally effective against bacterial infections, but ineffective against virus infections?
2. Why are hospitals a dangerous place for staphlococcal infections?
3. Why is it unusual for venereal diseases to be spread by means other than sexual contact?

VOCABULARY REVIEW

1️⃣ flagella
pathogens
mycoplasmas
rickettsias
coccus
bacillus

spirillus
fission
conjugation
endospore
2️⃣ chemosynthetic
aerobes

anaerobes
obligate aerobes
facultative anaerobes
obligate anaerobes
growth medium
3️⃣ gonorrhea

syphilis
antitoxins
toxoids
fever
chemotherapy
antibiotics

CHAPTER 18 TEST

Copy the number of each test item and place your answer to the right.

PART 1   Multiple Choice: Select the letter of the phrase that best completes each of the following.

b 1. Monerans include all but which of the following forms?   **a.** spirochetes   **b.** viruses
c. rickettsias   **d.** bacteria.

d 2. Bacteria may be identified by   **a.** their structure   **b.** the foods they use   **c.** the color and shape of their colonies   **d.** all of these.

d 3. Monerans are   **a.** saprophytes   **b.** parasites   **c.** free-living   **d.** all of these.

b 4. Chemosynthetic bacteria are   **a.** parasitic   **b.** autotrophic   **c.** saprophytic   **d.** heterotrophic.

d 5. Monerans are characterized by   **a.** being multicellular   **b.** having flagella   **c.** using sexual processes for reproduction   **d.** lacking an organized or distinct nucleus.

a 6. Bacteria that can live either with or without oxygen are referred to as   **a.** facultative anaerobes   **b.** obligate anaerobes   **c.** obligate aerobes   **d.** autotrophic aerobes.

b 7. The use of inorganic molecules to make complex organic molecules for life is known as   **a.** photosynthesis   **b.** chemosynthesis   **c.** protein synthesis   **d.** biosynthesis.

b 8. The most limited monerans with respect to what foods can be used are   **a.** saprophytic bacteria   **b.** parasitic bacteria   **c.** blue-green algae   **d.** purple bacteria.

d 9. Monerans are useful to humans in that various forms   **a.** synthesize vitamins   **b.** produce foods and other substances   **c.** recycle environmental materials   **d.** do all of these activities.

c 10. Venereal diseases   **a.** cannot be cured   **b.** provide a permanent immunity against infection   **c.** can cause insanity   **d.** can be prevented by vaccination.

PART 2   Matching: Match the letter of the term in Column I with its description in Column II.

COLUMN I
a. aerobes
b. anaerobes
c. bacillus
d. chemotherapy
e. conjugation
f. endospore
g. fission
h. flagella
i. pathogen
j. toxoid

COLUMN II
i 11. A disease- or infection-causing agent
e 12. Passage of genetic material from one cell to another
f 13. Highly resistant stage of some bacteria
a 14. Organisms that use oxygen
j 15. Weakened poison used to develop immunity
d 16. Treatment of infection with drugs
b 17. Organisms that cannot survive in air
c 18. Rod-shaped bacteria
h 19. Cellular whip-like structure used for moving about
g 20. Form of asexual reproduction in unicellular organisms

PART 3   Completion: Complete the following.
21. Anaerobes release energy from organic compounds by the process of fermentation
22. Aerobes release energy from organic compounds by the process of respiration
23. Tests for various pathogenic bacteria rely on controlling certain nutrients in the growth medium
24. Protection against osmotic imbalance in most monerans is achieved by the cell wall
25. Pathogenic bacteria may exert their effect on their hosts by attacking cells and tissues directly or by producing toxins

CHAPTER 19

THE PROTISTS

Having considered the simplest life forms, let us now turn to the next level of complexity. The protists, like the monerans, are unicellular. Unlike the monerans, however, all are eucaryotes. The cells of eucaryotes possess definite nuclei, mitochondria, plastids, and other organelles. Although considered "modern," the fossil record tells us that protists have been around for some 1.5 billion years. Thus, the term modern is a relative term that compares eucaryotes to the more primitive procaryote cells.

Protists make up a highly *diverse* group. In spite of this, they exhibit a basic *unity* in their activities. They also illustrate some of the other basic concepts of biology. These include *homeostasis, change through time, link between structure and function,* and the *interaction of organism and environment.* Protists are so small that you might not have even noticed them before. Even so, they play vital roles in the balance of nature. Included in their ranks are producers, consumers, and decomposers.

As you progress through this chapter, you should find answers to the following questions:

- What features of protists are animal-like?
- What features of protists are plant-like?
- How are protists important to humans?

DIATOMS

1 DIVERSITY AND CONTINUITY

Diversity Among the Protists

OBJECTIVES FOR SECTION 1

A. Describe the general characteristics of the four major groups of the Kingdom Protista.

B. Define the following terms in your own words: *phytoplankton, zooplankton, bioluminescence, phototropic.*

C. Draw an Ameba and a Paramecium and identify their respective parts.

D. Describe and contrast sexual and asexual reproduction in Ameba and Paramecium.

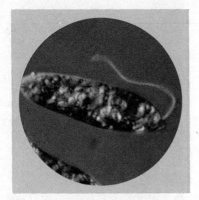

19-1. The Euglena has both plant and animal characteristics.

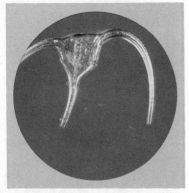

19-2. Dinoflagellates have a rigid cell wall.

As in all living groups, there is great diversity of form and activity among the protists. This diversity is the basis for dividing the Kingdom Protista into some ten phyla. We will consider only four of the major ones briefly. Then we will turn to two specific examples. In general, there appear to be two basic kinds of protists. *Plant-like protists produce their own food and are called* **phytoplankton.** *The* **zooplankton** (zō ə *plangk* tən) *are the animal-like protists that must capture their food.*

EUGLENOIDS   These tiny aquatic organisms are members of the Phylum Euglenophyta (ū glə *näf* əd ə). They are seen to have both plant and animal features. (See Fig. 19-1.) Like plants, they have chlorophyll. Hence, they can make their own food. On the other hand, like animals, they move about freely with the aid of a flagellum. This structure pulls them through the water. Euglenoids are *attracted to light and are thus* **positively phototropic.** Most members of this group live in freshwater. But some grow in damp soil. Although there are some 300 species of euglenoids, *Euglena* is the best known example.

DINOFLAGELLATES   Dinoflagellates belong to the Phylum Pyrrophyta (pə *räf* əd ə). They are mostly marine organisms. Their rigid body is surrounded by a heavy cell wall. The cell wall is separated into plates by two grooves. (See Fig. 19-2.) Most examples of this group have chlorophyll. Thus, like the euglenoids, they are also producers. Dinoflagellates are an important food source in an ocean ecosystem. Although not all are dinoflagellates, as many as 12 million phytoplankton have been found in a cubic foot of sea water.

Some species seem to glow in the dark. This is an example of **bioluminescence,** *a phenomenon in which living things give off light.* When large numbers of these organisms are present, the ocean can appear to glow.

Other species of dinoflagellates contain a red pigment. Many of these produce toxins that can kill fish and other sea animals. Their numbers are normally kept at a low level in a balanced ecosystem. Under certain conditions, however, they may reproduce quite rapidly. The water may turn red as large numbers accumulate. Such a ''bloom'' is referred to as a ''red tide.'' The cause of a red tide is not fully understood. It appears to be related to blooms of other phytoplankton and possibly organic pollution.

DIATOMS   The diatoms and other golden algae are members of the Phylum Chrysophyta (krə *säf* əd ə). They are characterized by having a kind of skeletal system. These ''shells'' remain after the

19-3. *Thick deposits of the remains of diatoms now exposed are responsible for the White Cliffs of Dover.*

death of the organism. They may collect in thick layers on the bottom of the ocean. The White Cliffs of Dover are made largely of diatom deposits that have since been uplifted and exposed by erosion. (See Fig. 19-3.) These deposits are also used in swimming pool filters, silver polish, and toothpaste. The diatom "skeleton" is made of two halves. Each half fits together much like the parts of a pill box. These shells may be quite elaborate, as shown in Figure 19-4. Diatoms are also producers in the ocean biome. As such, they are positively phototropic. Hence, diatoms are found near the surface of the water. Nearly 6000 species of this phylum are known.

PROTOZOANS Protozoans are grouped together in the Phylum Protozoa. Protozoans cannot produce their own food. They may be free-living or parasitic. They are classified by the different ways they move from place to place. (See Fig. 19-5.) Some move by extending a piece of cytoplasm in a flowing motion. Thus, they change shape as they change direction. Included in this class are Amebas and Radiolarians.

Other forms have cilia that move them from place to place. Cilia may also help to sweep food into mouthlike structures. The common ciliates include Paramecia, Stentor, and Vorticella (vort ə *sel* ə).

Flagella are used to propel the members of a third group of protozoans. Many members of this group are parasitic or live in a mutualistic relationship with other organisms. They may have one or more flagella. Examples of this class include Trypanosoma, a blood parasite that causes African sleeping sickness. Other forms are symbionts in the intestines of animals, including humans. These protozoans aid in the digestive process. Without the presence of flagellates in their intestines, termites would starve to death. These tiny protozoans can digest cellulose from the walls of plant cells. The products are then made available to the termite.

Next to bacteria, diatoms are the most abundant forms of life with more than 16,000 recognized species.

19-4. *Diatoms store food in the form of oil. It has been suggested that diatoms might be a potential source of oil for fuel. The fine tracings in diatom shells are passageways connecting the protoplasm within the cell to the exterior surface.*

Although only two representatives of protists are described in detail, you may wish to have cultures of several different types available for comparison and disscussion. Prepared slides can also be quite useful.

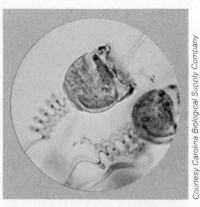

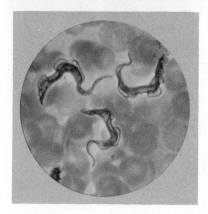

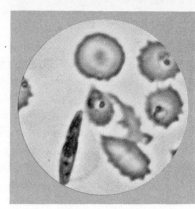

Courtesy Carolina Biological Supply Company

19-5. The protozoans are all heterotrophic. They are further classified on the basis of their means of locomotion: (upper left) Ameba; (upper right) Vorticella; (lower left) Tripanosoma; (lower right) Plasmodium.

Answers to Questions for Section 1.

*3. They have the ability to carry on photosynthesis.

*4. They have the ability to move about from place to place.

*5. Light is needed for photosynthesis, so turning toward the light helps assure an adequate exposure.

6. Living things give off light; some species of dinoflagellates do it.

D. 7. Both reproduce asexually, by binary fission. Ameba can form cysts to get through periods of unfavorable conditions, but Paramecium cannot. Paramecium may also reproduce sexually, by conjugation.

*8. Paramecium has more specialization, can move much faster to escape enemies, and through sexual reproduction has the advantage of genetic reshuffling that is associated with increased chances for survival.

The members of the fourth major class of protozoans have no means of locomotion. All are obligate parasites. The malarial parasite, Plasmodium, is an important member of this group. Most have a complex life cycle that enables them to be transferred from host to host.

The Body Plan of the Ameba

The term Ameba is often used to refer to a group of protozoans that have no specific shape. Under the microscope, an Ameba might appear at first glance to be a dirty spot on your slide. It is surrounded by a thin cell membrane. *Extensions from the main cell mass of the Ameba are called* **pseudopodia** (soo de pō dē ə), *or "false feet."* (See Fig. 19-6.) Within the cell membrane, the cytoplasm appears to be separated into two types. *An* **ectoplasm** *is seen to be represented by a thin, clear area of cytoplasm just inside the cell membrane. Most of the inner body of cytoplasm appears granular and is called the* **endoplasm.** A definite nucleus is usually visible near the central part of the cell.

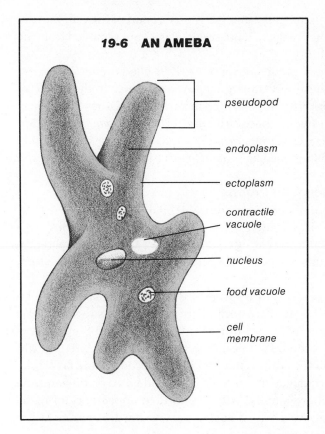

19-6 AN AMEBA

pseudopod

endoplasm

ectoplasm

contractile
vacuole

nucleus

food vacuole

cell
membrane

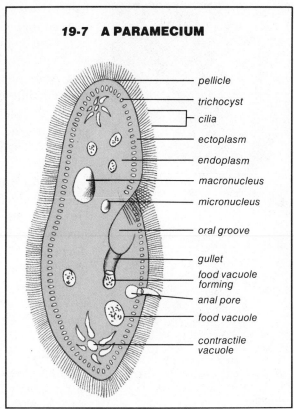

19-7 A PARAMECIUM

pellicle

trichocyst

cilia

ectoplasm

endoplasm

macronucleus

micronucleus

oral groove

gullet

food vacuole
forming

anal pore

food vacuole

contractile
vacuole

The cytoplasm also contains several other organelles. Some of these are fairly easy to see. Others are not able to be seen without the aid of special stains. One or more food vacuoles may be present in the cytoplasm. These may contain pieces of food being digested.

Body Plan of the Paramecium

Unlike the Ameba, the Paramecium has a specific shape. (See Fig. 19-7.) Even so, it is able to bend as it encounters obstacles in its path. It then returns to its slipperlike shape. This shape is maintained by the tough outer pellicle. The pellicle lies just outside the cell membrane.

Surrounding the entire Paramecium cell are cytoplasmic threads called **cilia.** The electron microscope shows that the cilia have a ring of nine inner strands surrounding two central ones. (See Fig. 19-8.) Such an arrangement is typical of cilia, flagella, and other fibers associated with eucaryotic cells. The moneran flagella lack this so-called 9 + 2 arrangement. Cilia propel the Paramecium through the water. They also direct food into a groove on one side called the *gullet.* About

The 11 fibrils found in cilia and flagella of eucaryotic cells have a chemical composition similar to that of actinomyosin found in muscle cells.

19-6. The Ameba moves by extending a pseudopod in a flowing motion.

19-7. The Paramecium moves by means of cilia.

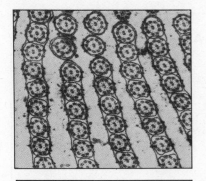

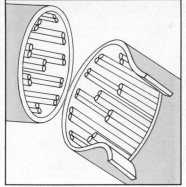

19-8. *The cilia and flagella of protozoans have the typical 9 + 2 arrangement.*

19-9. *Fission in a Paramecium.*

half way between the gullet and the posterior end of the cell, the *anal pore* can sometimes be seen. Undigested wastes are removed from the cell at this point.

Within the cytoplasm, one or more fluid-filled *contractile vacuoles* may be seen. These serve to regulate water balance in the cell. Two nuclei of different sizes are also seen in Paramecia. Other ciliates may have more than two of these structures. The small *micronucleus* appears near the larger *macronucleus.* The micronucleus controls other normal cell activities such as protein synthesis and respiration.

Continuity Among the Protists

Reproduction among the protists is mainly by asexual means. However, there is a limited opportunity for mixing of genes. This mixing of genes may be considered a primitive form of sexual reproduction. While this helps to ensure continuity, it is not strictly a form of reproduction.

Asexual reproduction in protists is by *binary fission.* (See Fig. 19-9.) Both Ameba and Paramecium are typical in this regard. Some protists withdraw into a *cyst* during unfavorable conditions such as dryness or lack of food. Paramecium cannot form cysts, but most ciliates as well as Ameba can. When conditions become more favorable, cysts become activated. If you have ever made a hay infusion from dry grasses you are familiar with the sudden appearance of many protists. Forming cysts helped them to survive the dry conditions until they could be active again.

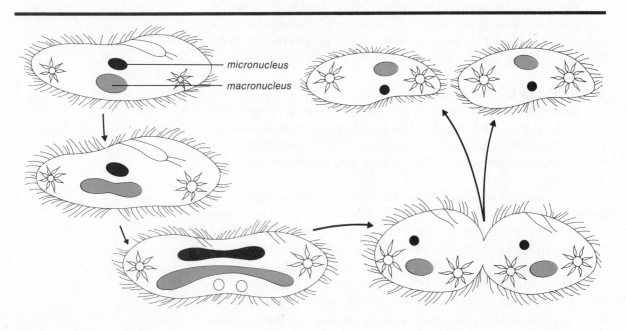

micronucleus

macronucleus

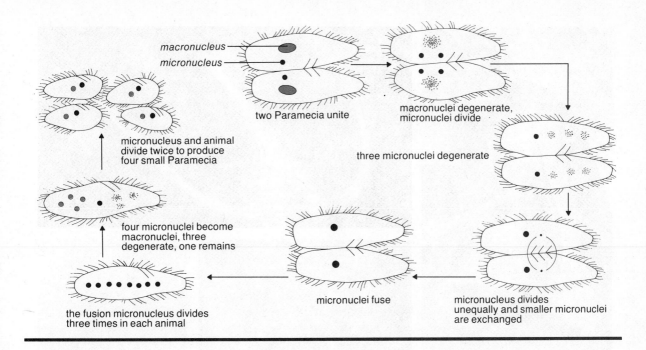

macronucleus
micronucleus

two Paramecia unite

macronuclei degenerate, micronuclei divide

three micronuclei degenerate

micronucleus and animal divide twice to produce four small Paramecia

four micronuclei become macronuclei, three degenerate, one remains

the fusion micronucleus divides three times in each animal

micronuclei fuse

micronucleus divides unequally and smaller micronuclei are exchanged

Reproduction in Paramecium may also be sexual. This occurs by the process of *conjugation*. During conjugation, two cells attach to each other. The micronucleus of each cell then undergoes meiosis. One haploid micronucleus from each cell is exchanged. This is followed by a complex series of nuclear divisions. Finally, the two cells separate, and each divides. This division produces four daughter cells. The final four cells each have one micronucleus and one macronucleus. The whole process is complex, but is summarized in Figure 19-10. Through conjugation, genetic shuffling occurs. The chances for survival are increased as genetic diversity is achieved.

19-10. *Conjugation in Paramecium.*

QUESTIONS FOR SECTION 1

1. Describe the general characteristics of euglenoids, dinoflagellates, diatoms, and protozoans.
2. Distinguish between phytoplankton and zooplankton.
3. Explain why phytoplankton are sometimes considered as plants in some classification schemes.
4. Why are zooplankton sometimes considered as animals in some classification schemes.
5. Explain why positive phototropism is an advantage to autotrophic phytoplankton.
6. Define bioluminescence. What kinds of organisms exhibit this phenomenon?
7. Compare and contrast reproduction in Ameba and Paramecium.
8. Why might the Paramecium be better adapted to its environment than Ameba over the long run?

Answers to Questions for Section 1.

A. 1. Euglenoids: have chlorophyll and make own food; they move about; are positively phototrophic, and live in freshwater or damp soil. Dinoflagellates: rigid body with heavy cell wall separated into plates by two grooves; most have chlorophyll and live in the sea; some are bioluminescent, others have red pigment. Diatoms: have a kind of skeletal system, with two halves that fit together like pill box; have chlorophyll and are positively phototrophic; live in ocean. Protozoans: are consumers; movement by pseudopodia, or cilia, or flagella; obligate parasites do not move; many of the flagellated forms are parasitic, mutualistic or symbiotic.

B. 2. Phytoplankton: plant-like protists that produce own food. Zooplankton: animal-like protists that must capture their food. (See page 340 for more answers.)

Diversity And Continuity **343**

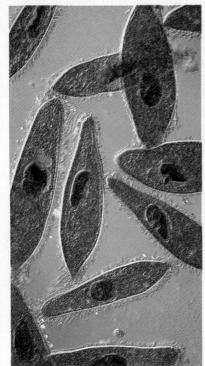

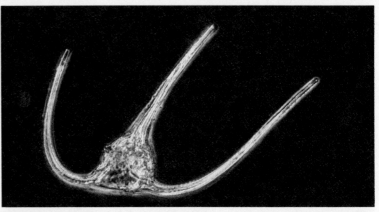

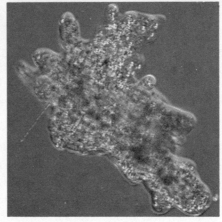

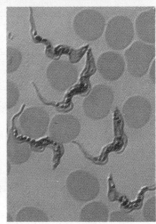

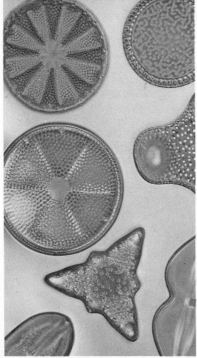

CHAPTER INVESTIGATION

A. How are these protists similar? How are they different?

B. What adaptations do these protists possess that enable them to be successful in their respective niches?

C. How do each of these protists affect humans?

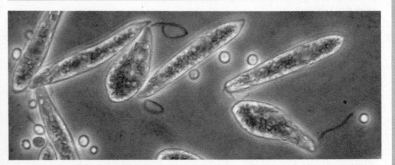

G. *5. For 1 cm cube, surface area = 6 sq cm, and volume = 1 cu cm; Ratio 6:1. For 2 cm cube, surface area = 24 sq cm; volume = 8 cu cm; Ratio 3:1.

*6. Answers will vary, may include if a protist doubled its volume, it would end up with just half the surface/volume ratio.

② HOMEOSTASIS

Obtaining Energy

Among the protists there are both autotrophic and heterotrophic forms. As we have already seen, the autotrophic phytoplankton make up a large share of the producer trophic level in the ocean biome. Furthermore, their role in the world's oxygen supply must not be overlooked. Photosynthesis is used to trap the sun's energy in organic molecules. The chemical pathway for this activity is the same as that used by the green plants. For this reason, phytoplankton are classified in the plant kingdom by some scientists.

The zooplankton, on the other hand, are heterotrophs. Most are free-living. But some do have a symbiotic relationship with other organisms. These relationships may be mutualistic, as we have already seen. There are also parasitic forms. These parasites are seen in some of the disease-causing sporozoans and others. In any case, they obtain their nutrients with the help of other organisms. They cannot produce their own food or obtain it directly as free-living forms do.

The remaining heterotrophic protozoans are either predators or scavengers. The predators prey on other protists. Some predators are able to engulf whole cells. Figure 19-11 shows one protist "swallowing" another. In this case, *Paramecium* is the prey. Scavengers do not engulf whole organisms. Rather, they take in bits and pieces of organic debris found in their surroundings. *Paramecium* is one example of a scavenger.

Energy Release

Most protists are strict aerobes. Some, however, can live without oxygen, at least for short periods. Thus, energy release from organic compounds normally occurs by respiration. This feature reminds us of the basic unity that all eucaryotes share.

Internal Systems of the Ameba

Being a heterotroph, the Ameba cannot make its own food. It must search out its food, mainly other protists, from its surroundings. As it moves, it changes shape continuously. The cytoplasm flows against the cell membrane forming the pseudopodia. The pseudopod enlarges as the cytoplasm flows into it. Other pseudopodia may appear and disappear. This change occurs as the Ameba moves along and changes direction.

The Ameba has no mouth. Food may be taken in at any point on the cell membrane. As the Ameba comes into contact with another protist, it extends pseudopodia. In doing so, the Ameba surrounds the prey. A food vacuole forms around the prey within the cell. (See

OBJECTIVES FOR SECTION 2

E. Describe the external and internal characteristics of both Ameba and Paramecium.

F. In terms of Ameba and Paramecium, explain how species survival is dependent upon the link between structure and function.

G. Explain the relationship between the ratio of surface area to volume in terms of protists' ability to undergo periodic fission.

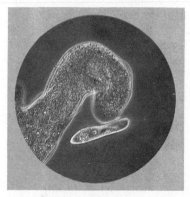

19-11. *Predator forms of protists can engulf whole bodies of other protists. Here an Ameba is shown about to swallow a Paramecium.*

Answers to Questions for Section 2.
  2. Movement by cilia. Prey swept into oral groove, a food vacuole forms and then breaks off and moves through the cytoplasm. It obtains oxygen, and releases carbon dioxide, by diffusion. Canals carry water and wastes into the contractile vacuoles, from which they are released.

F.*3. Answers will vary. May include the contractile vacuoles which maintain optimal water balance.

4. As the area of an ameba grows, the surface area become insufficient. When the cell divides, the optimal ratio of size and surface area is restored.

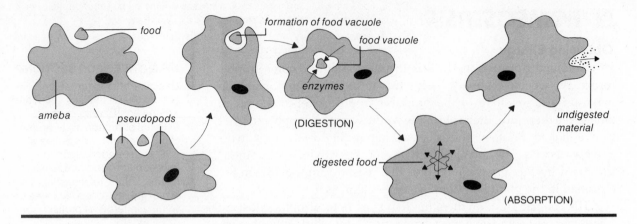

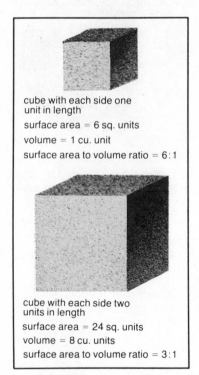

19-12. *Feeding and digestion in the Ameba.*

19-13. *Small unicellular organisms have a large cell surface for exchanging materials with their environment. Larger cells have a proportionately smaller surface area. When the surface area to volume ratio becomes reduced, the cell must divide.*

Fig. 19-12.) Enzymes are then secreted into the vacuole. The food is digested and absorbed into the cytoplasm. Here it can be used for the activities of life. Undigested particles are released from the cell and the vacuole is gone. An Ameba may have several vacuoles at one time. Each vacuole may contain food in various stages of digestion.

As the Ameba moves, the organelles within the cytoplasm are seen to flow and change positions. This movement of the cytoplasm serves to move materials throughout the cell. No complex structures are present to accomplish this function. Gas exchange with the environment is equally simple. Oxygen and carbon dioxide diffuse readily into and out of the cell.

Proper water balance could be a problem for the Ameba. Living in an environment of fresh water, the cell tends to accumulate water by osmosis. The Ameba gets rid of excess water through the contractile vacuoles. Waste materials also go into these vacuoles. The name for these structures describes their operation. The vacuoles may be seen to expand as water collects in them. When they reach a certain size, they suddenly contract. The contents are ejected through a break in the cell membrane. The membrane is quickly repaired. Soon, collection of excess water begins again.

The ability of protists to survive without complex systems found in higher organisms is related to their small size. (See Fig. 19-13.) The surface area of an Ameba is great enough for the exchange of sufficient materials between the cell and its environment. These materials include gases, nutrients, and wastes. As the Ameba grows, however, the ratio of surface area to volume is reduced. The activities of life would be affected if a proper ratio could not be restored. There would simply not be enough surface available to take in enough food to provide for the increased volume. Oxygen diffusion into the cell would also be less. Disposal of excess water and metabolic wastes would present still greater problems. When the cell reaches a critical size, it divides by binary fission. Each daughter cell then has a favorable surface to volume ratio. Under ideal conditions, an Ameba may reproduce every few hours.

Internal Systems of the Paramecium

The Paramecium is also a heterotroph and must seek its own food. Unlike the Ameba, however, it is mainly a scavenger. It moves through the water by wave-like motions of the cilia. These cilia cover its surface. The action of the cilia cause the cell to move forward or backward in a spiraling motion. Under the microscope, a Paramecium may appear to move very quickly as it darts across the field of view. Remember that not only its size, but its rate of movement is greatly magnified. As it changes direction, the cell may bend. However, the slipper shape that is typical of the cell is quickly restored. Thus, unlike the Ameba, the Paramecium has a definite but flexible shape.

As a Paramecium encounters food, the cilia sweep the particle into an oral groove on one side of the cell. At the lower end of the groove, a vacuole forms around the food. This vacuole is then circulated through the cell's cytoplasm. This occurs by a process known as *cyclosis*. (See Fig. 19-14.) Several food vacuoles and other cytoplasmic materials can be seen to move through the cell. These move in a specific pattern. The exchange of respiratory gases between the cell and the environment is by diffusion.

Like the Ameba, Paramecia live in fresh water. Contractile vacuoles are used to rid the cell of excess water. These vacuoles also remove some wastes. Tiny canals empty water into the vacuole from the cytoplasm. When it reaches a certain size, the vacuole empties through the cell membrane. Not all wastes are removed from the cell in this way. Some, like carbon dioxide, diffuse readily through the cell membrane and surrounding pellicle.

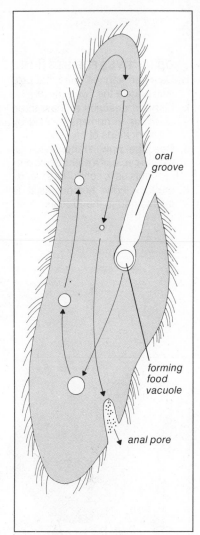

oral groove

forming food vacuole

anal pore

19-14. The path of a food vacuole in a Paramecium is quite characteristic.

QUESTIONS FOR SECTION 2

1. Describe how the Ameba moves, obtains food, releases energy, maintains a proper water balance, and responds to its environment.
2. Describe how the Paramecium moves, obtains food, releases energy, maintains a proper water balance, and responds to its environment.
3. In terms of the Ameba and Paramecium, support the statement, "Species survival is dependent upon the link between structure and function."
4. Describe the advantage of cell division in terms of the cell's ability to obtain nutrients and get rid of wastes.
5. Determine the ratio of surface area to volume in a 1 cm cube and a 2 cm cube.
6. Explain your answer in (5) in terms of protists' adaptation to undergo periodic fission.

Answers to Questions for Section 2.

E. 1. Movement by pseudopodia. These surround prey and form a food vacuole where food is digested. The vacuole disappears as undigested bits are released. Oxygen diffuses into the cell through the cell membrane, and CO_2 diffuses out. Water and wastes collect in the contractile vacuoles, and are released through the cell membrane.

(See page 345 for more answers.)

3 BEHAVIOR AND ENVIRONMENT

OBJECTIVES FOR SECTION 3

H. Describe various roles that protists play in the "web of life."

I. List and describe at least three diseases in humans caused by different kinds of protists.

J. Describe how a knowledge of the life cycle of a pathogenic protist helps us to control its spread.

K. Explain how homeostasis is maintained in the Protists.

Response to Stimuli

Typical of living systems, both Ameba and Paramecium respond to their environments. *Movement in response to a stimulus is called a tropism.* Tropisms can be either positive or negative. Both organisms respond positively to food and certain chemicals. In the presence of food, they move directly toward it. On the other hand, the Ameba and Paramecium are negatively phototropic. This means that they move away from lighted areas. Some protists, such as Euglena, are positively phototropic. Protists also move away from certain harmful chemicals. They also respond negatively to areas of low oxygen levels, extreme temperatures, and objects other than food. Such *negative tropisms are called* avoidance responses. They are typical of most organisms. (See Fig. 19-15.) Avoidance responses are one way that organisms are adapted to their environment.

Many ciliates, including Paramecium, have a special response to certain stimuli. Tiny threadlike "harpoons" called *trichocysts* are associated with the cilia. The trichocysts may be fired at a prey to immobilize it. Certain chemicals or predators may also cause the discharge of the trichocysts as seen in Figure 19-16. Thus, the trichocysts may be discharged during food-getting or as a defense mechanism.

The Role of Protists

Protists may be producers, consumers, or decomposers. Most are free-living. Some, however, live symbiotically with other organisms. Such relationships may include parasitism, mutualism, or commensalism.

Nearly all protists serve as food for other animals. In both marine and fresh water, they are vital links in the food webs. Here they feed and in turn are fed upon. Many have hard shells that form on the sea floors over long periods of time. Today, these sediments are mined and used in filters. They are also used as building materials, chalk, cement, or even special tooth cleaners.

Many protists are important to us because of their negative roles. These are the pathogenic forms. Some are parasitic in our livestock and pets. The ones we are most concerned about, however, are those that cause diseases in humans. Most of the well known diseases are not very common in the United States. High standards for sanitation and disease control have wiped out many of the common protist-caused diseases of humans in this country. This includes malaria. In spite of this, some of these diseases are important to us for two reasons. First, many Americans travel to other parts of the world. In these areas, health standards may not be as high as those in the

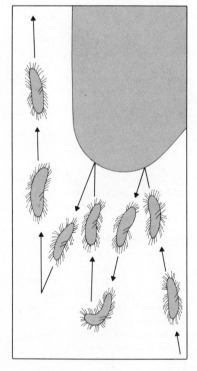

19-15. A Paramecium responds to an obstacle in a trial and error fashion.

United States. Travelers run the risk of infection from various diseases. However, understanding the importance of taking proper precautions may help to prevent infection. The second reason is not so simple. It involves the need to understand the life cycles of protist pathogens. Such scientific knowledge helps us to know and understand how diseases are spread. Using this knowledge, we can learn how to control them. Two protozoan disorders of humans illustrate this idea.

MALARIA   Perhaps the best known disease of humans and other warm-blooded animals that is caused by a protist is malaria. The culprit is a non-motile sporozoan called *Plasmodium*. This parasite has two parts to its life cycle. It is transmitted from one animal to another by the female *Anopheles* (ə *nof* ə lēz) mosquito. An infected animal may be bitten by the mosquito. When this occurs some *Plasmodium* cells are transferred to the stomach of the mosquito. There they grow and reproduce in a sexual phase of their life cycle. They soon enter the mosquito's salivary glands. Later the mosquito may bite an animal. In doing so, it injects saliva that serves to prevent clotting of the blood. In this way *Plasmodium* cells enter the victim's blood. (See Fig. 19-17.)

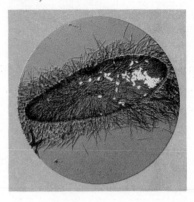

19-16. *The Paramecium may discharge trichocysts in response to a variety of stimuli.*

19-17. *The life cycle of plasmodium, the malarial parasite.*

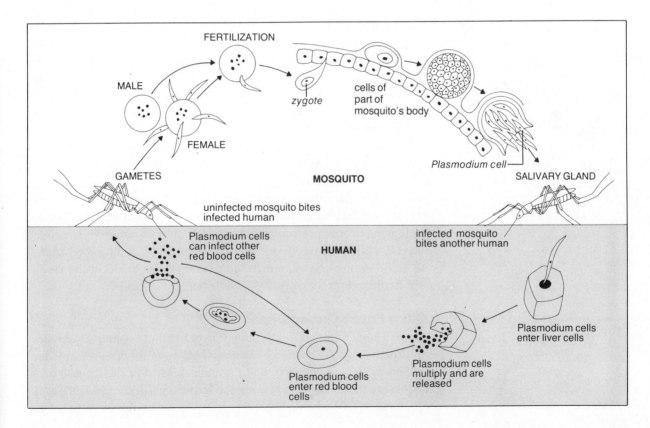

FERTILIZATION

MALE

zygote

FEMALE

cells of part of mosquito's body

GAMETES

Plasmodium cell

MOSQUITO

SALIVARY GLAND

uninfected mosquito bites infected human

Plasmodium cells can infect other red blood cells

HUMAN

infected mosquito bites another human

Plasmodium cells enter liver cells

Plasmodium cells enter red blood cells

Plasmodium cells multiply and are released

The spindle-shaped parasite cells reach the liver. Here they invade the victim's cells and reproduce asexually for about two weeks. Finally, they leave these cells and enter many red blood cells of the new host. At regular intervals, the red cells burst. This action releases many new *Plasmodium* cells. Large numbers of red cells are destroyed. This destruction, along with the release of toxins, cause both chills and fever in the infected person. The new *Plasmodium* cells attack healthy red cells. Thus, the cycle of chills and fever is repeated. Without proper treatment, malaria can severely debilitate a person. Malaria may even cause death. Many people live in malaria zones today. They routinely take certain drugs to prevent them from serving as hosts to the *Plasmodium* parasite.

Knowledge of the life cycle of *Plasmodium* has helped us to control a dangerous parasite in many parts of the world. Malaria is now virtually non-existent in this country. Control of malaria was focused on control of the insect vector. This was the weakest link in the chain of events required for the spread of the disease. A number of other diseases have also been controlled by controlling the vector. This was accomplished by first understanding the life cycles of the agents involved.

AMEBIC DYSENTERY   Certain species of the ameba group of protozoans can also cause serious disease in humans. Some such parasites may simply rob the host of its digested nutrients. Dysentery is caused by an amebic parasite. This parasite attacks the cells of the intestine and also red blood cells. The most common agent is *Entameba histolytica* (ent ə *mē* bə his tə *li* tik ə). The disease is spread by a lack of proper sanitary measures. Cysts of the infecting ameba may leave the body of an infected person in the feces. In certain areas, sewage is allowed to enter the drinking water or is used as fertilizer. In these cases, the cysts may become active when entering another person. The cycle is then complete.

Amebic dysentery is most common in those parts of the world that do not have adequate water or sewage treatment facilities. In such areas proper precautions should be taken to obtain pure drinking water and prepared food. The disease causes bleeding sores in the wall of the intestine of an infected person. Pain, blood in the feces, and malnutrition may rapidly develop in severe cases.

Other Protist-Caused Diseases

We have outlined briefly only two of the more common diseases of humans that are caused by protists. Many other diseases are also caused by this diverse group of organisms. Most of the disease producers are protozoans and are similar to the ones described since they are caused by closely related species. Another common disease is toxoplasmosis. Although less well known, it is one of the most common protist-caused diseases in the world. As much as 30 to 50 percent of the human population is infected with this sporozoan.

Flagellates are responsible for two other fairly famous diseases, Chapas' disease and African sleeping sickness. Both of these are caused by members of the genus *Trypanosoma*. Insect vectors transfer the parasite from host to host. Both of these infect other animals as well as humans. This makes control very difficult.

Protozoans of one type or another are parasitic upon every phylum of animal — and even other protozoans. It is little wonder that they are so important to us.

QUESTIONS FOR SECTION 3

1. Describe and give an example of various roles played by protists.
2. List at least three diseases in humans caused by protists. For each, describe the symptoms, causative agent, and means of infection.
3. Describe how a knowledge of the life cycle of a pathogenic protist helps us to control its spread.
4. How does homeostasis contribute to maintaining water balance in the Protists?

Answers to Questions for Section 3.

H. 1. Producer: makes own food. Example: euglena. Consumer: feeds off other organisms. Example: Ameba. Decomposer: feed upon dead remains of other plants and animals. Example: Paramecium.

I. 2. Malaria: chills and fever, in cycles; caused by *Plasmodium*, carried by *Anopheles* mosquito, which injects the parasite through saliva into its victim. Amebic dysentery: pain, blood in feces, and malnutrition; caused by *Entameba histolytica*, which is spread through sewage drinking water, carrying cysts from infected persons that become active upon entering another person.

J. *3. We can control it by destroying it at its most vulnerable point.

K. *4. Excessive water in the contractile vacuoles contract to reduce water to an optimal level.

CHAPTER REVIEW

As in all other forms of life, there is great unity among the *Protists*. This *unity* is seen in their unicellular, eucaryotic body plan. Their basic life processes also show the same *unity* that exists throughout the living world. Protists also display great *diversity* of shape, means of locomotion, and way of life. Some are marine. Others live in fresh water or in the soil. Some are autotrophic, while others are heterotrophic. Some are free-living. Others live as parasites or as mutualistic partners with other organisms.

Protists maintain a *continuity* through sexual or asexual means. Sexual reproduction helps increase variety. This increase enhances the chances for change in response to altered environments. *Change through time* is particularly important to parasites. Their survival is dependent upon adapting to changes in their host.

Homeostasis is maintained by cellular structures that help regulate water balance and other cellular activities. These *structures and their functions illustrate complementarity*. The protists play important roles by *interacting with their environments*. Many serve as food to higher trophic levels. Others help to regulate the size of these trophic levels by their activities as parasites. Still others are decomposers.

Using the Concepts

1. Research the mechanisms by which bioluminescence is produced. Write a report on your findings. How might such information be useful to humans?
2. Research the factors that help a cell "know" when to divide. For what kinds of applications might such information be useful?

VOCABULARY REVIEW

1 phytoplankton
zooplankton
bioluminescence

phototropic
Euglenoids
Dinoflagellates

Diatoms
Protozoans
3 tropism

avoidance responses
Malaria
Amebic Dysentery

CHAPTER 19 TEST

Copy the number of each test item and place your answer to the right.

PART 1 Multiple Choice: Select the letter of the phrase that best completes each of the following.

d 1. An Ameba moves by means of   **a.** cilia
b. arthropodia   **c.** flagella   **d.** pseudopodia.

a 2. A Paramecium swimming away from a harmful chemical is an example of   **a.** an avoidance response   **b.** a conditioned response   **c.** a habit   **d.** a learned response.

c 3. For each of the two cells involved in conjugation, how many daughter cells result?   **a.** none   **b.** 2   **c.** 4   **d.** 8.

b 4. The "red tide" is due to a "bloom" of   **a.** diatoms   **b.** dinoflagellates   **c.** protozoans   **d.** euglenoids.

d 5. Nearly all of the parasitic protists are   **a.** dinoflagellates   **b.** diatoms   **c.** euglenoids   **d.** protozoans.

a 6. Malaria is caused by   **a.** *Plasmodium*   **b.** *Trypanosoma*   **c.** *Entameba*   **d.** *Paramecium.*

c 7. Circulation of materials within a cell is known as   **a.** osmosis   **b.** pinocytosis   **c.** cyclosis   **d.** phagocytosis.

c 8. Which structure in protists performs a function similar to that of a digestive system in multicellular animals?   **a.** nucleus   **b.** contractile vacuole   **c.** food vacuole   **d.** ribosome.

b 9. Which of the following terms includes all of the others?   **a.** sporozoan   **b.** protozoan   **c.** ciliate   **d.** flagellate.

c 10. Amebic dysentery is spread by   **a.** bleeding sores   **b.** malnutrition   **c.** lack of proper sanitary measures   **d.** dense population.

PART 2 Matching: Match the letter of the term in Column I with its description in Column II.

COLUMN I

a. binary fission
b. bioluminescence
c. conjugation
d. contractile vacuole
e. eucaryotes
f. phytoplankton
g. pseudopod
h. tropism
i. trychocyst
j. zooplankton

COLUMN II

h 11. Movement in response to a stimulus
i 12. Tiny threadlike "harpoons" of ciliates
c 13. Primitive form of sexual reproduction
j 14. Animal-like protists
g 15. "False foot" of ameboid protists
e 16. "Modern" cells with membrane-bound organelles
d 17. Structure specialized for maintaining water balance in protists
b 18. Release of light energy by life forms
a 19. Form of asexual reproduction
f 20. Plant-like protists

PART 3 Completion: Complete the following.

21. A positive tropism means that the organism moved toward the stimulus.

22. Gas exchange in protists occurs between the cell and its environment by diffusion

23. As a protist cell grows, its surface area to volume ratio decreases

24. In terms of their means of releasing energy, protists are said to be aerobes

25. Protists play important roles in the environment as _____ and parasites and decomposers

CHAPTER 20

THE FUNGI

In our survey of living things, we looked first at the monerans which lack nuclear membranes and other membrane-bound organelles. Then we considered the protists. These are also unicellular, but their cells are eucaryotic. We turn now to a group of multicellular, heterotrophic organisms. These obtain food mainly by absorbing it from their environment. They are the fungi.

As we survey this group, look for evidence of these basic concepts: *unity within diversity*, the *continuity of life, homeostasis,* the *link between structure and function,* and *interaction with the environment.*

Aside from the strictly biological aspects of fungi, you should be able to discover answers to some questions you may have already asked at some time or another. For example:

- What is wheat rust?
- Is it safe to eat mushrooms?

MUSHROOM

1 DIVERSITY AND CONTINUITY

General Characteristics of the Fungi

In some ways the fungi are plant-like. They are nonmotile; that is, they cannot move about. They have an external wall that resembles the cell wall of plants. Unlike plants, however, the fungi cannot make their own food. Many of them secrete enzymes that digest food outside their bodies before they can absorb it. Therefore, they are heterotrophic.

The fungi generally have a life cycle that is divided into two phases. One phase is asexual; the other, sexual. The asexual part of the cycle is characterized by the formation of spores. *A spore is a tiny cell that spreads the fungus to new habitats.* Great numbers of spores are released into the air or water. This increases the chance that at least a few of them will land in places where they can grow. When this happens, the spore absorbs water and food from the environment. As it grows, it typically forms *a threadlike extension called a* **hypha.** The hypha grows and develops many branches. *The body of a fungus is composed of a tangled mass of hyphae called a* **mycelium.** (See Fig. 20-1.) Pigments in the mycelium may give it a characteristic color. Many fungi are bright red, orange, yellow, blue, or green. (See Fig. 20-2.) Many mycelia, however, are colorless.

The sexual phase of the life cycle of a fungus is often very short. It may even go unnoticed. A type of conjugation occurs between hyphae. This produces a short-lived 2N zygote. After a short dormant period, meiosis occurs. Hyphae begin to grow, producing the asexual stage of development.

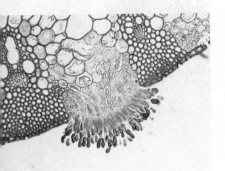

20-1. Mycelium of fungi come in a variety of colors.

20-2. Mushrooms: (left) Bolitus mushrooms; (middle) Cantharellus cinnabarinus; (right) Leucoagaricus naucina.

In some fungi, the hyphae are not divided into cells. Instead, each hypha contains many nuclei within the same body of cytoplasm. In other fungi, the hyphae are divided into sections by cross walls. Each section is a cell with one or more nuclei. Even here, however, the cross walls have holes through which cytoplasm and nuclei are free to flow.

The rigid cell walls of most fungi are made of cellulose, other complex carbohydrates, and chitin (*kī* tin). Cellulose is a chemical combination of many glucose molecules. Chitin is a flexible, horny, protein-carbohydrate substance. Chitin is found in the external skeletons of insects and other invertebrates.

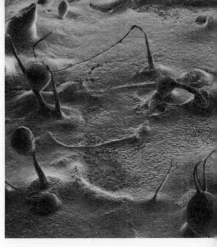

20-3. A slime mold colony in various stages of development.

Diversity Among the Fungi

The classification scheme used in this book considers the fungi as a kingdom. Kingdom Fungi is further divided into at least eight phyla. These groups are generally recognized on the basis of differences in their spore-producing organs. We will consider five of the more common phyla in this chapter.

SLIME MOLDS   The slime molds earn their name because of the stage in their life cycle in which they appear as a spreading slimy mass. The Phylum Myxomycetes (mik sō mī *sēt* ēz) includes slime molds of two types: cellular and acellular, that is, without cells. An acellular slime mold consists of a slimy mass of cytoplasm. Within this cytoplasm are thousands of nuclei. The mass is not divided into cells. Such a mass is known as a *plasmodium.* (See Fig. 20-3.)

The plasmodium lives in moist environments. It moves like an ameba over rotting logs, dead leaves, or forest soil. As it flows, the plasmodium engulfs bits of organic matter. Digestion occurs in vacuoles located in the cytoplasm. The cellular slime molds form by the joining of thousands of ameba-like cells.

Under conditions of stress, the plasmodium may develop several clusters of spore cases, or *sporangia* (spə *ran* jē ə). These so-called "fruiting bodies" rise above the plasmodium to produce and release large numbers of spores. This activity completes the life cycle.

ALGALIKE FUNGI   Some fungi bear spores in a ball-shaped sporangium. These are assigned to the Phylum Phycomycetes (fī kō mī *sēt* ēz), the algalike fungi. They have no cross walls in their hyphae. This group includes bread mold and the water molds that parasitize potatoes and fish. An example of a member of this group is shown in Figure 20-4.

SAC FUNGI   Phylum Ascomycetes (as kō mī *sēt* ēz) includes those whose spores are borne in a sac. The sac usually bears eight spores and is known as an *ascus.* (See Fig. 20-5.) The hypha of the multicellular forms are divided by cross walls. Holes in these walls allow

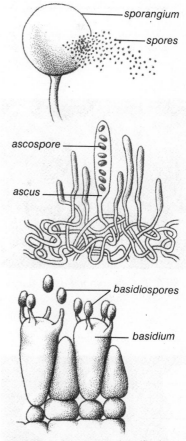

20-4. The fungi are classified according to their spore-producing organs. The phycomycetes produce sporangia. The ascomycetes produce asci. The basidiomycetes produce basidia.

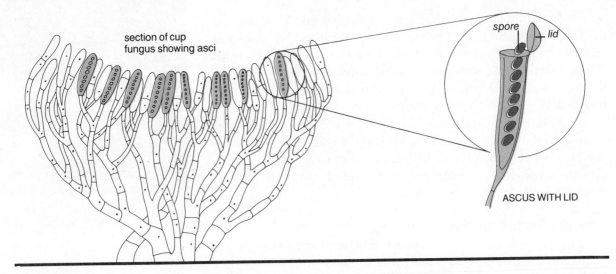

section of cup
fungus showing asci

spore — lid

ASCUS WITH LID

20-5. *The fruiting body of an Asco-mycete bears a number of asci, each of which bear eight spores.*

20-6. *The sac fungi. Peziza Aurantia, a cup fungus.*

20-7. *A club fungus.*

organelles to move from one cell to the next. Many of the sac fungi are familiar to you. Some of the more common types of sac fungi are pictured in Figure 20-6. Molds of the genus *Penicillium* are often seen as velvety blue-green growths on oranges or lemons. *Aspergillus* (as pər jil əs) molds form yellow or black rings on many foods. Yeasts, used in baking, are also examples of this group. The ''cup fungi'' form white, orange, or red cups on leaves or the wood of decaying trees. The morel or sponge ''mushroom'' is a non-poisonous fungus often eaten for its flavor. Sac fungi are parasites on plants. They cause Dutch elm disease, chestnut blight, apple scab, and the ergot disease of rye.

CLUB FUNGI   A fourth group of fungi bear their spores in club-shaped structures called *basidia*. These are grouped into the Phylum Basidiomycetes (bə sid ē ō mī *sēt* ēz). (See Fig. 20-7.) These ''club fungi'' include the mushrooms, shelf fungi, puffballs, rusts, and smuts. The familiar toadstool is a club fungus also. You see only one part of the fungus body, however. While some mushrooms are edible, others are very poisonous. Shelf fungi are commonly seen on rotting trees and stumps. Rust fungi are parasites of wheat, apple, white pine, and other plants. Smuts form large masses of hyphae on corn and other grains.

IMPERFECT FUNGI   The fifth group of fungi is a fairly diverse group. They are referred to as the imperfect fungi because they have not been observed to exhibit any sexual reproductive phase. The Phylum Deuteromycetes (doo tə rō mī *sēt* ēz) includes fungi that cause ringworm and athlete's foot. Sometimes, detailed studies of certain imperfect fungi reveal the sexual aspect of their cycles. Such fungi are then able to be reclassified into one of the other phyla.

LICHENS   Before we leave the topic of diversity among the fungi, something must be said about a unique type of "organism." These are the lichens. A lichen consists of cells of a green alga imbedded in a fungus mycelium. The fungus member is usually an ascomycete, or sac fungus. Occasionally, it is a club fungus. Although the alga is usually a single-celled green alga, some are blue-green. Lichens have been classified as pairs of organisms and given scientific names. For ease in identification, they are classified according to their growth form. They are either leaf-like, crust-like, or shrub-like. Examples of each of these forms may be seen in Figure 20-8.

Some of the algae in lichens also grow independently in nature. Almost all of the fungi are found only in the lichen partnership, however. Most fungi exist on or in organic matter. A lichen is able to survive on exposed rock, on bare soil, on tree trunks, and in the arctic tundra. Radioactive tracer studies show that the sugars made by the

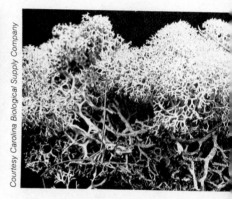

alga are translocated to the fungus. If the algal partner is a blue-green type, fixed nitrogen is donated to the fungus as well. Some biologists think that the fungus protects the alga from intense light and excessive dryness. Others are not sure that the fungus contributes anything to the relationship. Lichens probably reproduce by wind-borne fragments. These fragments contain both members of the pair.

20-8. Three general forms of lichens.

QUESTIONS FOR SECTION 1

1. Define the terms spore, hypha, mycelium, plasmodium, sporangia, basidia.
2. Describe the general characteristics of the Kingdom Fungi.
3. Explain the difference between fungi and plants as a basis for the five-kingdom approach.
4. Some classification schemes classify fungi as plants. What would be the rationale for such a system?
5. Describe and show the difference between each of five fungal groups.
6. Describe the symbiotic relationship present in a lichen.

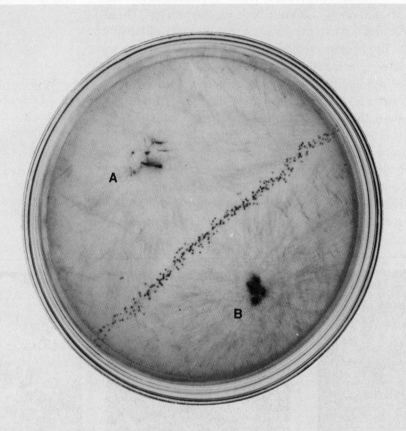

CHAPTER INVESTIGATION

The agar plate shows points A and B where the plate was inoculated with the fungus, *Phycomyces blakesleeanus*. The smaller dark spots show the line of zygospores from which ordinary spores develop.

A. Where do the zygospores form relative to the points of inoculate?

B. What are some possible explanations for the zygospores being formed there rather than someplace else?

C. Biological supply houses can supply various strains of *Phycomyces* and *Rhizopus stolonifer (nigricans)* for culturing in cornmeal agar. How could you test the hypothesis you formed in Number 2 above?

2 HOMEOSTASIS

Nutrition in the Fungi

The fungi are heterotrophic. Most of them live imbedded in their food supply. For many, that food supply consists mostly of nonliving organic matter. This may be the dead bodies of plants and animals, food products, or organic wastes. Bread mold is a good example of such a fungus. Bread is produced from grains of the wheat plant. It supplies all of the nutritional needs of the mold. Starch molecules in the bread are too large to pass through the mold's cell membrane, however. To obtain the nutrient material from the bread, the mold produces an enzyme. This enzyme, amylase, digests the starch. That is, it breaks the starch molecule into smaller chemical units that can be absorbed by the mold.

The fungi are generally regarded as decomposers. They help to break down the dead bodies and waste materials of organisms that would otherwise accumulate in the environment. Not all fungi, however, play this role. Some are parasites. They live by extracting nutrients directly from another living organism. To do this, specialized hyphae called *haustoria* invade the body of the host. The rusts, smuts, and powdery mildews are common examples of parasitic fungi with hyphae of this type. (See Fig. 20-9.)

Energy Release

The fungi are aerobic. This is to say that they release energy from nutrients by respiration. Oxygen is used to help complete the breakdown of foods to carbon dioxide and water. The energy released by these activities is used in reproduction, growth, and various other activities.

Yeasts are also capable of releasing energy from foods by fermentation. In the absence of oxygen, this process also releases alcohol as a waste product. Yeasts are thus important to the industrial production of alcoholic beverages.

Chemical Responses of Fungi

Two responses to chemicals have been observed in the fungi. A hypha secretes certain substances that cause other hyphae to avoid it. This serves to reduce competition from other hyphae. Such chemicals also play an important role in preventing the growth of other forms in the same vicinity of the hypha. In fact, our knowledge of antibiotics stems from a chance discovery following the bacterial contamination of a mold culture. It was noticed that bacteria were growing on the food source. But growth only occurred in places that were not close to the fungal hyphae. Later analysis of the food showed the presence of

OBJECTIVES FOR SECTION 2

D. Define the following terms: *gametophyte generation, sporophyte generation, alternation of generations, budding, ascospore, gill, stipe, basidiospore, haustoria.*

E. Explain how the natural antibiotic produced by a fungus is of adaptive value to its success.

F. Describe a "typical" life cycle of a fungus.

G. Interpret the presence of a "fairy ring" in terms of the growth pattern of a mushroom.

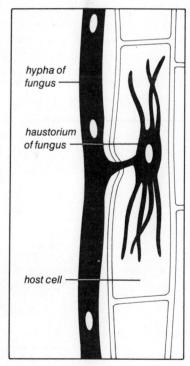

hypha of fungus

haustorium of fungus

host cell

20-9. Specialized hyphae of parasite fungi penetrating the host's cells.

20-10. *Various species of Penicillin mold are responsible for the spoilage of citrus fruits.*

a chemical that prevented bacterial growth. Other similar chemicals were found in other molds. Today, we know these chemicals as antibiotics. They create conditions that do not favor the growth of bacteria. The first chemical of this type came from the mold *Penicillium*. (See Fig. 20-10.) Therefore, the first purified extract became known as penicillin. It is widely used today. However, much of its early effectiveness has been lost. Recently, many strains of bacteria have developed a resistance to its effects.

Attractive responses occur in fungi. Sexual reproduction can occur between different hyphae of the same mycelium. One or both of the mating hyphae may secrete hormones. The hyphae are attracted toward the area of highest concentration of the hormone until they come into contact. This aspect of the life cycle will be discussed in the next section.

Reproduction in Fungi

20-11. *Bread mold reproduces sexually and asexually.*

Continuity from one generation to the next is maintained by a two phase reproductive cycle. The two phases are known as the *gametophyte* and *sporophyte generations.* Such a cycle is often called an *alternation of generations.* The details of the reproductive cycle vary from one species to the next. The basic plan, however, reveals a fundamental unity among the fungi.

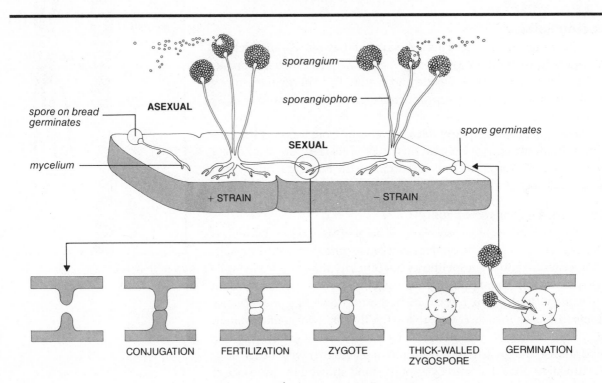

The most conspicuous part of the fungal life cycle is the gametophyte phase. Nuclei in the mycelium of the gametophyte are haploid (N). Asexual reproduction occurs by the production and release of a large number of haploid spores. The manner in which the spores are produced is the basis for the classification scheme for the fungi, as we have seen.

Under certain conditions, sexual reproduction takes place. This allows for the combining and redistribution of chromosomes. Hyphae cannot be identified as being male or female, however. Instead, they are simply referred to as being plus (+) or minus (−) strains. During sexual reproduction, the hyphae form short side branches. (See Fig. 20-11.) These branches may secrete special attracting hormones. These hormones enable hyphae of opposite strains to find each other. When the tips of + and − strains meet, a cross wall forms behind each tip. The two haploid cells fuse, forming a diploid (2N) zygote. This is the sporophyte phase of the life cycle. The zygote then develops a thick outer wall. It becomes dormant for a short period. When conditions are again right for growth, the zygote nucleus undergoes meiosis. The resulting spores, now haploid, then germinate into new hyphae. With the reappearance of the gametophyte generation, the cycle is complete.

BUDDING Yeasts are one-celled fungi that illustrate another form of asexual reproduction, *budding*. Under normal growing conditions, a yeast cell develops a small bulge. As the bud develops, the parent nucleus divides. One nucleus remains with the parent cell. The other moves into the bud. The bud may become detached and produce new buds itself. In some cases, the bud remains attached. If so, it produces a branched chain as new buds develop. (See Fig. 20-12.)

ASCOSPORES Under adverse conditions, a parent nucleus may undergo two successive divisions. This results in four nuclei. These nuclei, along with the surrounding cytoplasm and cell wall are called an *ascospore*. The ascospore can survive long periods of dryness and extremes of temperature. When you purchase active yeast in the grocery store, this is what you are buying. When you provide the right conditions, the ascospores again become active and undergo rapid reproduction.

Mushrooms — "Typical" Fungi

Most fungi are fairly small. They often go unnoticed unless you happen to pick up a piece of moldy food. Nearly everyone, however, is familiar with mushrooms. Mushrooms appear on the damp forest floor. They even appear in yards after a moist spell. What you see above the ground, however, is only part of the fungus organism. Below the surface of the ground is a mycelium. The mycelium is com-

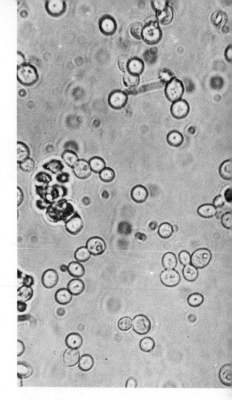

20-12. *The single celled fungus, yeast, reproduces asexually by budding.*
Yeast from the grocery store that has been incubated in a 10% sugar solution for a few hours will enable students to observe budding under the microscope and observe the formation of CO_2 bubbles.

Answers to Questions for Section 2.

E. **2.** The hyphae of the fungus secrete a substance that repels other hyphae, thus reducing competition.

F. **3.** See Fig. 20-11 on page 360.

*4. One of the alternating generations is a dormant form that can survive a period of adverse conditions. Also, the mixing of genetic material in the sexual phase provides the adaptive advantage of greater genetic variety.

*5. See Fig. 20-13 on page 362.

G. **6.** When mold mycelia grow at a fairly steady rate in all directions from a center point, the spore-producing fruiting bodies may form a circle known as a fairy ring.

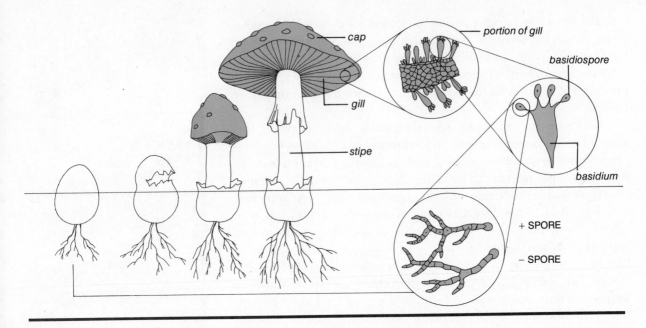

cap

portion of gill

basidiospore

gill

stipe

basidium

+ SPORE

− SPORE

20-13. *The life cycle of a typical mushroom.*

posed of numerous hyphae. The mushroom that you see is a special mass of compressed hyphae that pushes out from the soil. These hyphae form the spore-producing organ. An umbrella shaped cap develops on top of the stalk, or *stipe*. In most mushrooms, the underside of the cap contains a number of paper-thin membranes called *gills*. These gills radiate out from the stipe. The gills contain thousands of tiny structures called *basidia*. Each basidium produces four spores called *basidiospores*. (See Fig. 20-13.) The billions of spores produced by one mushroom are distributed by air currents. Mold mycelia may grow at a fairly steady rate in all directions from a center point. If this occurs, the spore-producing fruiting bodies may form a circle of mushrooms. This circle is called a *fairy ring*. (See Fig. 20-14.)

20-14. *Mushrooms may exhibit a growth pattern known as a fairy ring as they move outward from a food source.*

Answers to Questions for Section 2.

D. 1. See Glossary. Also, Ascospore: dominant cell that has undergone two divisions and has 4 nuclei surrounded by cytoplasm and a tough wall resistant to adverse conditions. Gill: membrane in the underside of a mushroom's cap, that contains spore-producing basidia. Haustoria: specilized hyphae of parasitic fungi, that invade body of the host.

QUESTIONS FOR SECTION 2

1. Define the terms: gametophyte generation, sporophyte generation, alternation of generations, budding, ascospore, gill, stipe, basidiospore, haustoria.
2. Explain how the natural antibiotic produced by a fungus is of adaptive value to its success.
3. Describe a "typical" life cycle of a fungus.
4. Explain how the alternation of generations is an adaptive advantage to the organism.
5. Describe the growth pattern of a mushroom.
6. Explain how the growth pattern of a mushroom is related to the appearance of a fairy ring.

(See page 361 for answers.)

3 FUNGI AND THE ENVIRONMENT

Fungi as Decomposers

Reference has already been made to the decomposer role that fungi play in the environment. They are involved in the natural recycling of dead plant and animal bodies and wastes. Of course, a number of other organisms also act as decomposers. The fungi, however, along with bacteria are the most important. Even these organisms occupy different niches. Certain fungi are active in concentrations of salts, sugars, and acids that would kill most bacteria. Pickles and jams are safe from bacterial attack, but may be decomposed by fungi. The acidic needles of cone-bearing trees are decayed largely by fungi rather than bacteria. The club fungi are especially active in the decay of woody tissue.

Fungi as Symbionts and Parasites

Many of the sac and club fungi form close relationships with plant roots. They may exist on the root surface with some hyphae penetrating the root. Sometimes, they may actually live within the cells of the root. *The complex association of root and fungus is known as a* **mycorrhiza** (mī kə *rī* zə). Many species of plants have them. When pine trees are introduced to new areas, they grow poorly until supplied with the appropriate mycorrhizal fungi. There is experimental evidence that fungi digest organic matter in the soil. Thus, they make nitrogen, sugars, and minerals available to the roots of plants. The plants, in turn, seem to supply growth-promoting substances and food to the fungi.

Most plant diseases are caused by parasitic fungi. The ergot disease of grains transforms the grain into large purple bodies filled with hyphae. These hyphae produce drugs that produce severe effects on the human central nervous system.

Fungi may also be important as parasites on animals. Some water molds are parasitic on fish. Fungal infections are a constant threat to fish hatcheries and hobbyists who raise tropical fish. If you have an aquarium in your classroom or at home, you may be very familiar with the fungal disease "ich." Spores are eaten by the fish. Once in the intestine, the spores germinate. The resulting hyphae penetrate the intestinal wall. They then enter the blood vessels. From here, they may be spread to all parts of the body. (See Fig. 20-15.)

Fungi as Food

Morels (sac fungi) and certain mushrooms (club fungi) have been prized as human food for centuries. (See Fig. 20-16.) Some mushrooms that look and taste like edible species are poisonous, however.

OBJECTIVES FOR SECTION 3

H. Define the following term: *mycorrhiza.*

I. Describe at least three roles of fungi in the natural environment.

J. Point out several uses of fungi as food sources for humans.

20-15. *Ich is a fungus that commonly infects aquarium fish, such as this angelfish.*

Emphasize that students should be very careful when collecting mushrooms for eating.

20-16. *The morel is a prized food for humans.*

Certain fermented foods are more easily preserved than the raw foods from which they were prepared. This is one reason for producing wine, cheeses, sauerkraut, and yogurt. Fermentation may also make such foods more flavorful, digestible, and possibly more nutritious. Many cheeses get their special flavors from sac fungi. These fungi are mixed with the cheeses during the manufacturing process. The most tasty soy sauce is made by fermenting boiled soybeans and wheat with a certain sac fungus for about a year.

Fungi as a Source of Antibiotics

The widely-used antibiotic, penicillin, is produced by the blue-green ascomycete mold, *Penicillium*. Penicillin is effective in controlling bacteria that cause a variety of diseases in humans and other animals. These include pneumonia, gonorrhea, syphilis, *Streptococcus*, and *Staphylococcus* infections. Still other fungi are used to produce vitamins, amino acids, and enzymes. Fungi also produce various alcohols and acids that are everyday products used by humans.

Other Uses of Fungi

Several of the fungi are used as experimental organisms in basic biological research. The mold *Neurospora* was used to study the link between heredity and the formation of enzymes. Water molds are used to study the hormonal control of sex. Plasmodial slime molds provide an opportunity to study mitotic rhythms, and differentiation. These slime molds are also used to study DNA synthesis, inheritance, and other cellular processes.

Lichens as Pioneers

Lichens are often the first plants to colonize bare rocks. They have already been noted in Unit I as being pioneer "species" in a chain of ecologic succession. Their metabolic activities slowly break rocks into particles and add them to humus in the production of soil. Lichens are also a primary food source for a number of grazing animals of the tundra biome. They are responsible for the colors in the tundra.

Answers to Questions for Section 3.

H. **1.** The fungi may live in the roots of plants where they digest organic matter from the soil, making nutrients available to the plants.

I. **2.** Fish with "ich" have a parasitic fungal infection.

J. **3.** Mushrooms, cheeses containing sac fungi, soy sauce from fermented soybeans, bread from yeast.

*4. Yeast undergoes fermentation, producing carbon dioxide and alcohol, both of which escape as gases through the bread dough, causing the bread to rise.

QUESTIONS FOR SECTION 3

1. How can the presence of certain fungi aid the growth of certain plants?
2. Cite an example in which a fungus can act as a parasite.
3. Point out several uses of fungi as food sources for humans.
4. Why are yeasts important in the production of bread?

Emphasize the importance of sexual reproduction as a source of variety in organisms as opposed to asexual means. The development and dependence on sexual means of reproducing is related to complexity. Where asexual means are the principal method of reproducing, success is dependent on enormous numbers of offspring in a short time.

4 COMPARISONS AMONG MONERANS, PROTISTS, AND FUNGI

Diversity and Continuity

The first three kingdoms of the living world that we have considered include the monerans, protists, and the fungi. These groups are separated on the basis of their cellular structures. Monerans are procaryotes. Protists and fungi are eucaryotes. Protists are unicellular. They may or may not have cell walls. Fungi are mostly multicellular and all have cell walls. In these ways, they are like plants. Unlike plants, however, fungi are heterotrophs. Both monerans and protists have autotrophic members, but many are heterotrophs. Table 20-1 summarizes the comparisons among these groups of organisms.

In spite of the differences among these groups, there is still a basic unity. The chemical pathways that release energy for the activities of life are quite similar. To be sure, there are certain modifications of these pathways in each group. The unity and diversity found among these organisms is a basic feature of all life forms.

Not included in any of these kingdoms are the viruses. They are non-cellular. Viruses do not carry on the metabolic activities that are distinctive of living things. They do, however, have features that show some of the basic concepts of life. They do show change through time, unity and diversity, and a complementarity of structure and function.

Unity and diversity are also seen in the members of these kingdoms in other ways. For example, continuity is maintained by asexual as well as sexual means. Moneran cells reproduce asexually by binary fission. This form of reproduction increases unity from one generation to the next. However, binary fission tends to reduce variety that might be necessary for the species to adapt to a changing environment. This is offset by the ability to reproduce quickly. This rapid rate of reproduction increases the chances for mutations. Some monerans display a primitive form of sexual reproduction in which genetic material is shuffled.

Protists also reproduce asexually by fission. Some forms, however, engage in conjugation. This is a sexual process that is more complex than that found in the monerans. Fungi have both asexual and sexual parts to their life cycles. These may be seen as adaptations to survival under different conditions that they may encounter.

Viruses depend directly on living cells to multiply. Unlike living organisms, viruses reproduce indirectly by using the nucleic acids found in the cells of their hosts. Thus, their mode of reproduction is neither asexual nor sexual.

OBJECTIVES FOR SECTION 4

K. Describe differences among monerans, protists, and fungi.

TABLE 20-1   A COMPARISON OF VIRUSES, MONERA, PROTISTA AND FUNGI

Kingdom	Viruses	Monera	
REPRE-SENT-ATIVES	Bacteriophage	Bacteria	Blue-green algae
LEVEL OF ORGANI-ZATION	non-cellular; protein "coat" with DNA or RNA	procaryotic; unicellular; may be colonial	
REPRO-DUCTION	rearrangement of host DNA	asexual by binary fission; "sexual" in some forms by conjugation	
GROWTH	none	limited by ratio of surface area to volume	cell division by fission; unlimited body growth
OBTAIN-ING FOOD	obligate parasite	parasitic; mutualistic; free-living; some chemo- or photosynthetic	
TRANS-PORT OF MATERI-ALS	none	direct contact with environment	
ENERGY RELEASE	none	respiration; fermentation	
METABOLIC PRODUCTS	none	aerobic: CO_2, H_2O, some toxins; anaerobic: CO_2, some toxins	
GAS EX-CHANGE	none	direct exchange with environment	
WATER BAL-ANCE	none	water pressure within cell wall	
TYPICAL HABITAT	everywhere	everywhere	polluted water
RESPONSE TO ENVI-RONMENT	none	some positive phototropism; may have positive or negative chemotaxis	

TABLE 20-1   A COMPARISON OF VIRUSES, MONERA, PROTISTA AND FUNGI *(continued)*

Kingdom	Protista			Fungi	
REPRESENTATIVES	Ameba	Paramecium	Euglena	Yeasts	Bread mold
LEVEL OF ORGANIZATION	eucaryotic; unicellular; some forms with cell walls			eucaryotic; mostly multicellular; all with cell walls	
REPRODUCTION	asexual by binary fission	asexual by transvers binary fission; sexual by conjugation	asexual by longitudinal binary fission	asexual by budding	asexual by spores in a cycle; sexual by conjugation
GROWTH	limited by ratio of surface area to volume			limited by ratio of surface area to volume	mitotic cell division: unlimited body growth
OBTAINING FOOD	predator; scavenger		photosynthesis	parasitic or free-living decomposer	
TRANSPORT OF MATERIALS	direct contact with environment			direct contact with environment and transport between adjacent cells	
ENERGY RELEASE	respiration			respiration and fermentation	
METABOLIC PRODUCTS	aerobic: CO_2 and H_2O			aerobic: CO_2, H_2O, antibiotics (some); anaerobic: CO_2, alcohol, vinegar	
GAS EXCHANGE	direct exchange with environment				
WATER BALANCE	contractile vacuoles; water pressure in cell walls (some forms)			water pressure within cells	
TYPICAL HABITAT	clean fresh-water	polluted water		surface of fruits	moldy bread
RESPONSE TO ENVIRONMENT	negatively phototropic; avoidance response	avoidance response; negatively phototrophic; trychocysts	positively phototropic; negative chemotaxis; thermotaxis	some forms have sexual response to opposite strains	

Homeostasis

Point out that homeostasis is a requirement for all life forms and that organisms differ only in how this is accomplished.

Great variety is found in the way the members of these first three kingdoms obtain nutrients. Some monerans are chemosynthetic; no protists are. Some monerans are photosynthetic; so also are some protists. Fungi are neither chemosynthetic nor photosynthetic. Some monerans are free-living. The same can be said for both protists and fungi. Parasitic and mutualistic forms are present in all three kingdoms. Viruses might also be classified as being parasitic.

The release of energy from nutrients is used to maintain homeostasis in all living organisms. The manner in which this energy release occurs, however, may vary from group to group. Monerans may be aerobic or anaerobic, or both. Protists and fungi are basically aerobic. Some fungi, however, are facultative anaerobes. They can obtain the necessary energy without oxygen when conditions warrant. Great variety exists among the members of these groups with regard to the kinds of nutrients that can be used.

Water balance is important in forms that do not have cell walls. The cell wall protects the organism against excessive intake of water that would burst the cell. Protists without cell walls have special contractile vacuoles. These vacuoles rid the cell of excess water.

Being unicellular, the monerans, protists, and some fungi can obtain materials directly from their environments. This occurs by diffusion. Similarly, they can secrete wastes directly into their surroundings. Multicellular fungi, on the other hand, must transport nutrients to body cells that cannot take in food directly. Wastes and other products of metabolism from these cells must also be transported through the body of the fungus.

Monerans, protists, and fungi respond to their environments in different ways. Some monerans and protists are positively phototropic; others react negatively to light. Motile forms may respond to the presence of food by moving toward it. Harmful substances may provoke an avoidance response. Some protists can even respond by releasing tiny trichocysts as a defensive mechanism. These may also be used in capturing prey.

Relationship to Environment

Members of these three kingdoms represent every trophic level found in ecosystems. There are producers, consumers, and decomposers. The roles of these organisms are important to an orderly ecosystem. Also, many members of these kingdoms are important to humans in more direct ways. Monerans, protists, and fungi all have members that are pathogenic to us and our domesticated plants and animals. Regardless of whether or not they are living, viruses also fall into this category. Others are mutualistic partners with higher organisms, including humans.

The metabolic products of various fungi are also useful to humans. The anaerobic activity of yeasts produces alcohol. Antibiotics are produced by other fungi. These substances are useful in fighting infections caused by various microbes. Bacteria and viruses may someday be produced in laboratories. These new strains may carry DNA fragments to cells of humans suffering from genetic disease. Such recombinant DNA might be able to cure a variety of genetic disorders or produce valuable products for human use.

QUESTIONS FOR SECTION 4

1. Support the most important differences among monerans, protists, and fungi.
2. How are monerans, protists, and fungi important to humans?

CHAPTER REVIEW

In this chapter, we see clear evidence of *unity within diversity*. In spite of the great diversity among the fungi, all are heterotrophic. Most have multicellular bodies composed of hyphae. Most fungi also have cell walls composed of cellulose and chitin. They all absorb nutrients from outside their bodies. The use of these nutrients show evidence of *homeostasis*. Fungi are classified on the basis of differences between the type of spore-producing organ they bear.

Continuity of the species in many cases is accomplished by both sexual and asexual means. All sexually reproducing fungi alternate between a haploid gametophyte phase and a diploid sporophyte phase. Sexual reproduction provides for diversity among the offspring. In turn, diversity increases the probability that at least some offspring will survive changing conditions.

The *relationship between structure and function* is seen clearly in the reproductive structures. This relationship is also seen in the hyphae that absorb nutrients from the environment.

The *interaction of an organism with its environment* is illustrated by the decomposer role that fungi play in an ecosystem. They make nutrients available to living organisms. Decomposers do this by recycling matter from dead bodies of plants and animals. Their importance as symbionts in the formation of mycorrhizae also illustrates this concept. As living organisms, the fungi are unique. In spite of this, however, they exhibit all of the fundamental concepts of biology. In so doing, they serve as vital links between humans and their environment.

Using the Concepts

1. Can you think of examples other than the late blight in potatoes in which fungi have played a role in altering the way of life for humans?
2. Louis Pasteur is reported to have said, "Chance favors the prepared mind." Research the discovery of antibiotics and explain this statement in terms of such a discovery.

VOCABULARY REVIEW

1		**2**			**3** mycorrhiza
spore	plasmodium	gametophyte	budding	stipe	
hypha	sporangia	sporophyte	ascospore	basidiospore	
mycelium	basidia	alternation of generations	gill	haustoria	

CHAPTER 20 TEST

Copy the number of each test item and place your answer to the right.

PART 1   Multiple Choice: Select the letter of the phrase that best completes each of the following.

c   1. Fungi are regarded as a kingdom separate from plants because they   **a.** lack cellulose in their cell walls   **b.** are autotrophic   **c.** are unable to make food from inorganic materials   **d.** do not metabolize.

b   2. Which one of the following is not an asexual structure used to spread the fungus organism?
   a. bud   **b.** zygote   **c.** ascospore
   d. basidiospore.

a   3. The appearance of both haploid and diploid forms of an organism during its life cycle is known as
   a. alternation of generations   **b.** mutualism
   c. symbiosis   **d.** parasitism.

a   4. Which one of the following is not a role of fungi?
   a. producer   **b.** decomposer   **c.** symbiont
   d. parasite.

c   5. Spores from a mushroom are produced on the surface of the   **a.** hyphae   **b.** mycelium
   c. gills   **d.** stipe.

c   6. Fruiting bodies of fungi contain mainly   **a.** gametes   **b.** zygospores   **c.** sporangia
   d. hyphae.

a   7. Budding is a form of asexual reproduction found in
   a. yeasts   **b.** mushrooms   **c.** plasmodia
   d. bread mold.

b   8. Fungi are adapted to life on land as evidenced by their   **a.** freely mobile gametes   **b.** wind-blown spores   **c.** generally colorless features
   d. relatively small size.

b   9. The structure we call a mushroom is actually a fruiting body which specializes in   **a.** securing food for the organism   **b.** reproduction   **c.** decomposition of other organisms   **d.** attachment to host organisms.

d 10. The growth form of a mushroom that is sometimes seen as the fungus spreads from a central food source is known as a   **a.** morel   **b.** lichen
   c. michorrhiza   **d.** fairy ring.

PART 2   Matching: Match the letter of the term in Column I with its description in Column II.

COLUMN I
a. ascus
b. basidia
c. gametophyte
d. haustoria
e. lichen
f. mycelium
g. mycorrhiza
h. plasmodium
i. sporangia
j. stipe

COLUMN II
f 11. Body of a fungus
h 12. An acellular mass of fungus
i 13. Clusters of fungal spore cases
b 14. Fruiting bodies of club fungi
d 15. Specialized hyphae of parasitic fungi that invade the host's cells
e 16. Mutualistic association of an alga and a fungus
c 17. Haploid generation of a fungus
a 18. Fruiting body of a sac fungus
j 19. Stalk of a mushroom
g 20. Mutualistic association of a fungus and plant roots

PART 3   Completion: Complete the following.

21. The tiny, asexually produced cell that is adapted for spreading a fungus to new habitats is known as a ___spore___

22. The cell walls of fungi are composed of ___cellulose___ and ___chitin___

23. Fungi are subdivided into phyla on the basis of differences in their ___fruiting bodies___

24. Extracts purified from secretions of hyphae are used medically as ___antibiotics___

25. In lichen, the alga supplies ___nutrition___ while the fungus is thought to provide ___protection from excess light and/or drying out___.

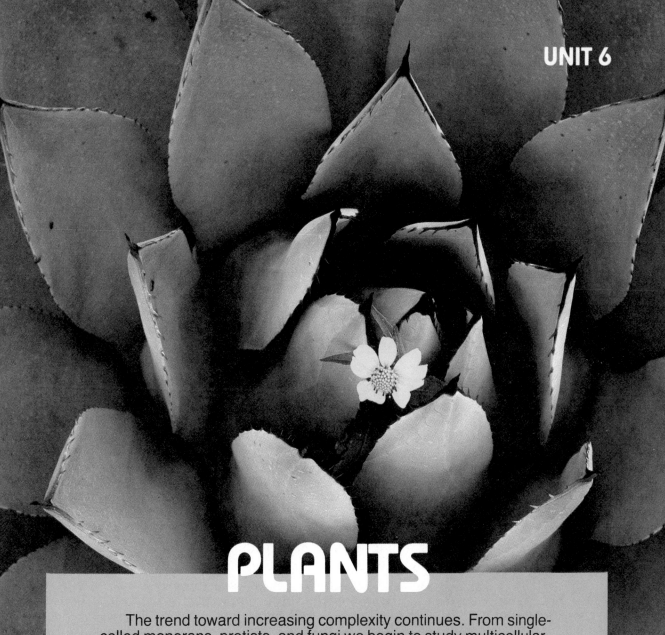

PLANTS

The trend toward increasing complexity continues. From single-celled monerans, protists, and fungi we begin to study multicellular organisms. Their study starts with algae and mosses, through non-flowering plants to flowering plants.

The arrangement of material follows a general pattern to give a complete picture of the organisms. First the external characteristics are studied. Next we examine how the organisms maintain homeostasis. Finally, adaptive responses and other relationships in the environment are described. The last section of the unit reviews these characteristics. In it, comparisons to simpler organisms are made.

AGAVE FLOWER

CHAPTER 21

THE SIMPLEST PLANTS

In our survey of living things we have looked at the single-celled monerans and protists. We have glanced at the more complex heterotrophic fungi that obtain food mainly by absorption. We are now ready to begin our look at the mostly multicellular autotrophic organisms called plants. These plants include the higher algae, mosses and liverworts.

As we survey these simple plants, look for evidence of these basic concepts: *unity within diversity, the continuity of life, homeostasis, the link between structure and function,* and *interactions with the environment.*

Questions we will touch in this chapter include:
- What is the Sargasso Sea?
- Which algae are possible passengers on long-term space flights?
- What roles do mosses play in the ecosystem?
- How do people use algae?
- Why is the vegetation of peat bogs preserved for thousands of years?

SPHAGNUM MOSS

1 RED ALGAE

Most of the multicellular algae and the mosses have cell walls that contain cellulose. They contain chlorophyll inside chloroplasts and carry on photosynthesis. That is, they use water, minerals, and carbon dioxide to make their own food. Therefore they are autotrophs. Multicellular algae, mosses, and higher plants with special conducting tissue make up the Kingdom Plantae.

The term algae is a common name for a number of simple organisms with chlorophyll. Some are single-celled or live as simple colonies of single cells. They are either monerans or protists. Others are multicellular. However, the cells are quite similar with little specialization of function.

Body form was used by Linnaeus to classify algae. But there is a wide range of body forms. This encouraged biologists to use differences in pigments and other substances to classify eucariotic algae. In fact, their group names are based on the main colors of their members. The red algae are members of Phylum Rhodophyta (rō *däf* əd ə), a name which means rose-plant. (See Fig. 21-1.)

Body Form and Habitat of Red Algae

The red algae include small single-celled forms as well as those which may be up to a meter in length. But most are less than 30 cm long. They vary in form from flat ribbons to delicate feathery bodies.

Most red algae are marine species. They are found from above sea level to a depth of 100 meters in clear seas. In fact, they may be the only organisms able to photosynthesize at such depths. Common in tropical coral reefs, the red algae attach themselves to solid structures. These include reefs and rocks.

Diversity and Continuity of Red Algae

DIVERSITY   In addition to a variety of body forms, the red algae vary in color. They range from dull green or brown to rosy red or deep purple.

CONTINUITY   The few unicellular red algae multiply asexually by fission. Multicellular forms produce asexually by spores. They also have relatively complex life cycles that involve sexual exchange of reproductive cells.

Homeostasis of Red Algae

In addition to chlorophyll *a,* the red algae contain chlorophyll *d.* Yellow, orange, red, and blue pigments are also present. The red and blue photosynthetic pigments are *phycoerythrin* (fī kō *er* əth rən) and *phycocyanin,* respectively. These pigments are also found in the blue-

OBJECTIVES FOR SECTION 1
A. List the main features of organisms in the plant kingdom.
B. Describe the characteristics and habitats of the red algae.
C. Tell how red algae meet their basic needs.
D. Describe the interactions between red algae and their natural and human environments.

Another difference in algae is the form in which food is stored: oils, fats, starches, etc. The form of their reproductive cells is also considered in classification.

Answers to Questions for Section 1.
6. They have been used as food, for humans and their livestock; and to make agar, an ingredient of a growth medium for microorganisms.

21-1. Red algae.

Courtesy Carolina Biological Supply Company

green algae. This is one reason that the red algae are believed to have descended from the blue-green algae. These pigments are able to capture wavelengths of light not absorbed by chlorophyll *a*.

The red algae from deeper sea waters are usually a bright rosy red. They are able to absorb blue light. This color penetrates deeper into the water than other colors of light.

RESPIRATION   Carbohydrates not needed in respiration are stored as starch granules in the cytoplasm. As available energy fuel becomes depleted, the starch can be converted into a soluble form for respiration. Thus, a constant supply of energy is supplied to cells.

PHOTOSYNTHESIS   During the process of photosynthesis, water and carbon dioxide are constantly being used up. To replenish this supply, more molecules diffuse into the cells from the sea.

Behavior and Environment of Red Algae

FOOD AND OXYGEN   In coastal waters, red algae are important food producers. During daylight hours they produce more oxygen in photosynthesis than they use in respiration. Thus, they also help oxygenate the sea and the atmosphere.

REEF FORMATION   Red algae contribute to the formation of coral reefs. In tropical oceans, red algae extract calcium carbonate from the sea. They use it to attach themselves to the reef. In the process they add calcium carbonate to the reef. In some areas red algae may contribute more to reef formation than coral animals do. Reef-building corals do not occur deeper than about 70 meters. This may be due in part to the absence of red algae which attract the animals that corals prey upon.

HUMAN USES OF RED ALGAE   One of the most important commercial products of algae is agar. **Agar *is a gelatinous substance produced most abundantly by the red alga, Gelidium.*** It is used in laboratories around the world as a growth medium for bacteria and other organisms. (See Fig. 21-2.) Current research shows promise of a number of substances of medical and agricultural value in the red algae.

21-2. *Bacteria are often grown on agar produced by red algae.*

Answers to Questions for Section 1.

A. **1.** They have cells walls that contain cellulose, and chlorophyll inside chloroplasts that carry on photosynthesis, i.e., are autotrophs.

B. **2.** Some are single-celled and small, others vary in length, up to 1 meter; they vary in form from ribbon-like to feathery; most live in the sea, some to depths of 100 m, many attached to coral reefs or rocks.

C. **3.** The pigment is able to capture wavelengths of light not absorbed by green photosynthetic pigment, thus using a larger portion of the sun's spectrum than plants with only the green pigment.

*4. By diffusion.

D. **5.** Red algae extract calcium carbonate from the sea, and use it to attach themselves to the coral reef, thus helping to build the reef.

(See answers to questions on page 373.)

QUESTIONS FOR SECTION 1

1. What are the main features of organisms in the plant kingdom?
2. Describe the features and habitats of the red algae.
3. Of what advantage is it to the red algae to have red photosynthetic pigment?
4. How do water and carbon dioxide get into the cells of red algae?
5. Describe the relationship between red algae and corals.
6. What are some human uses of red algae?

NORTH   SOUTH

WEST   EAST

CHAPTER INVESTIGATION

Observe the four pictures.

A. On which side of the tree is the moss growing?

B. What environmental differences occur on the different sides of the tree?

C. Which of the environmental differences might be most closely related to the survival of the moss? Design and carry out an experiment that would test your hypothesis. Get other data that would support or nullify your hypothesis.

☑ GREEN ALGAE

The green algae contain chlorophylls *a* and *b* and many other pigments. They store food as starch. Hence, green algae are believed to be closely related to land plants. They make up the Phylum Chlorophyta (klō *rä* fəd ə). The phylum name means green plant.

Body Form and Habitat of Green Algae

Most green algae are small and simple, but vary widely in form. Some are single-celled. Others are thread-like or form hollow balls or broad flat sheets of cells. Some have many nuclei not separated by membranes or cell walls. Most are found in fresh water, but a few grow in the sea. Others inhabit moist rocks, soil, and tree trunks.

Diversity and Continuity of Green Algae

DIVERSITY   A few examples illustrate the variety among the green algae. (See Fig. 21-3.) *Chlamydomonas* is a genus of green algae common in stagnant pools and on damp soil. These single-celled plants have two hairlike flagella which pull them through the water. Surrounding the nucleus is a cap-shaped chloroplast. *Volvox* is a colonial alga. Its cells look much like those of *Chlamydomonas*. They are held together by a gelatinous substance on the surface of a hollow sphere. Some cells of the colony specialize in certain functions. For example, some specialize in reproduction. A colonial form may be the middle step between unicellular and multicellular organisms.

OBJECTIVES FOR SECTION 2

E. List the characteristics and habitats of the green algae.
F. Describe reproduction in *Spirogyra* and *Ulva*.
G. Tell how the green algae maintain homeostasis.
H. Explain the important roles played by the green algae.

21-3. Some green algae.

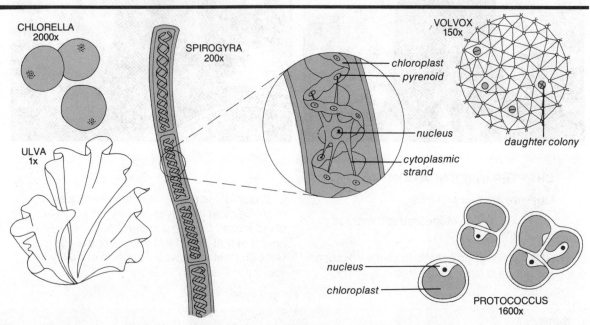

CHLORELLA 2000x

SPIROGYRA 200x

chloroplast
pyrenoid
nucleus
cytoplasmic strand

VOLVOX 150x
daughter colony

ULVA 1x

nucleus
chloroplast
PROTOCOCCUS 1600x

You may have seen *Spirogyra* and *Protococcus*. *Spirogyra* (spī rə jī rə) consist of unbranched filaments. The sheath surrounding the filaments of this pond scum give it its slimy feel. *Protococcus* is a unicellular green alga. Found on tree trunks, it is often called moss.

Chlorella is also unicellular. *Ulva* is often called sea lettuce. Its blades are two cells thick. They are attached to rocks near the tide line.

CONTINUITY   As in many plants, most algae reproduce both sexually and asexually. *Spirogyra* filaments reproduce asexually by the breaking up of existing filaments. By crosswise fission of cells, the pieces of filament increase in length. *Spirogyra* also reproduces sexually. Its filaments may be so close together that they touch each other. The touching cells produce small swellings which extend toward each other and join. The ends of these extensions dissolve and leave an open tube connecting the two cells. The cytoplasm of one cell slips through the tube and unites with the cytoplasm of the other cell. This is an example of conjugation. The contents of all the cells of one filament enter the cell walls of another filament forming zygotes. (See Fig. 21-4.) A thick wall forms around each zygote. This forms a zygospore. The thick walls allow it to survive dry, cold, or hot conditions. When favorable conditions return, the zygospore nucleus undergoes meiosis, producing four haploid spores. Three disintegrate. The fourth grows into a new cell. Eventually a new filament forms.

In *Ulva* diploid blades produce haploid spores. (See Fig. 21-5.) These spores have four flagella with which they swim to a new location. They grow by a series of mitotic divisions to become haploid

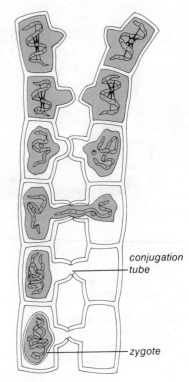

conjugation tube

zygote

21-4. *Conjugation in Spirogyra.*

21-5. *The life cycle of Ulva.*

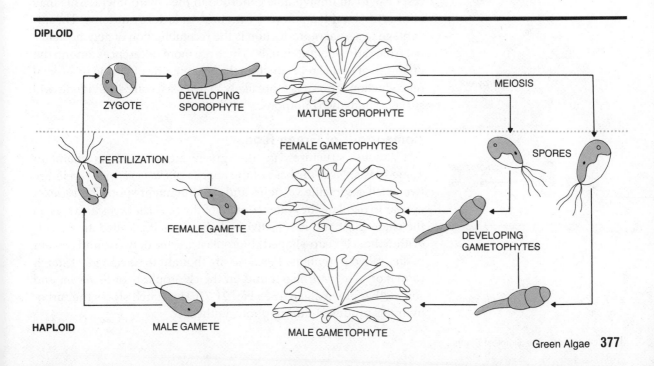

DIPLOID

ZYGOTE

DEVELOPING SPOROPHYTE

MATURE SPOROPHYTE

MEIOSIS

FERTILIZATION

FEMALE GAMETOPHYTES

SPORES

FEMALE GAMETE

DEVELOPING GAMETOPHYTES

MALE GAMETE

MALE GAMETOPHYTE

HAPLOID

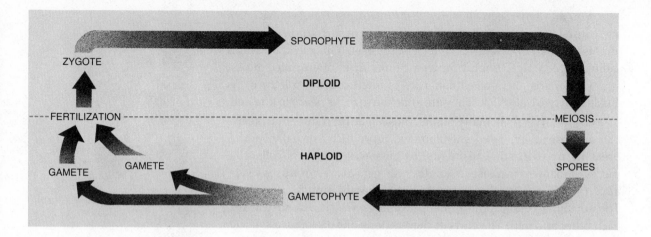

H. 6. They are food producers and oxygenators, helping maintain the supply of oxygen in the atmosphere.
7. The sudden appearance of phosphates or nitrates in water leads to algal bloom and overpopulation. Algae in lower levels are shaded by layers above and die for lack of light. Their decay causes oxygen depletion that kills the fish.

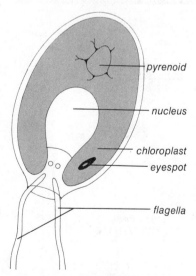

21-7. *The structure of Chlamydomonas.*

blades. These haploid blades then produce gametes. *Because they produce gametes, the haploid blades are called* **gametophytes.** Those producing the smaller cells are male gametophytes. Those producing the larger gametes are female gametophytes. Both male and female gametes have two flagella. When the gametes unite the resulting diploid zygote has four flagella. The zygote develops into the diploid blade. *Since the diploid blade produces spores it is called the* **sporophyte.** The diploid sporophytes differ from the haploid gametophytes only by chromosome number.

All sexually reproducing plants undergo alternation of generations. (See Fig. 21-6.) In many algae sexual reproduction occurs as a response to an unfavorable condition in the environment. This may be shorter days, temperature extremes, or lack of nutrients. The advantage to sexual reproduction is the recombination of genetic material from different individuals. There are more differences among the offspring of sexual reproduction than among the offspring of asexual reproduction. Thus it is more likely that at least some individuals will survive changing conditions.

Homeostasis of Green Algae

Various structures in the green algae serve to maintain homeostasis. Near the base of the flagella of *Chlamydomonas* cells are two small contractile vacuoles and a red pigment spot. The *vacuoles* appear to regulate the water content of the cell. The *pigment spot* is on the chloroplast and is sensitive to light. Thus it is called an *eyespot.* Within the cell's cup-shaped chloroplast are one or two round protein bodies called pyrenoids. *Pyrenoids* are thought to be centers of starch formation. They are also found on the chloroplasts of *Spirogyra* and some other green algae. (See Fig. 21-7.) The starch stores the carbohydrates produced during photosynthesis.

PHOTOSYNTHESIS   A variety of pigments in the green algae are able to trap light energy of colors not absorbed by chlorophyll *a*. They pass the trapped energy on to chlorophyll *a* which uses it in photosynthesis.

MATERIAL EXCHANGES   The flow of needed materials and wastes in the green algae occurs directly between the cells and their environment. Even in the multicellular blades of sea lettuce, each cell is in direct contact with the sea.

Behavior and Environment of Green Algae

The green algae are important food producers both in freshwater environments and in top soil. They also oxygenate freshwater lakes, pools, and the top soil that is exposed to light. In this way they help maintain the oxygen supply of Earth's atmosphere.

Some of the unicellular green algae form mutualistic relationships within the bodies of sponges, hydra, and flatworms. (See Fig. 21-8.)

HUMAN USES   Green algae have not been used widely as human food. One exception is sea lettuce which has been used in some Asian countries. *Chlorella* has been studied as a possible source of food and oxygen in long-range space exploration.

Several green algae are important in basic biological research. *Chlamydomonas* and *Chlorella* have been used in studies of photosynthesis and respiration. *Chlamydomonas* is becoming important in studies involving genetics and the hormonal control of sexual mating.

EFFECT OF HUMAN ACTIVITIES ON GREEN ALGAE   Where phosphates or nitrates are limiting factors in water their sudden appearance may result in an algal bloom. After a period of overpopulation, algae in lower levels are shaded by layers above. The deeper algae die for lack of light. Their decay causes oxygen depletion. This results in the suffocation of fish. Such fish kills may occur in water originating in over-fertilized fields, or sewage without advanced treatment.

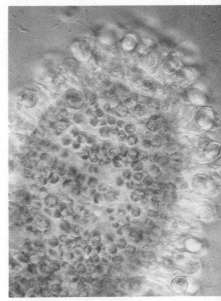

21-8. *Chlorohydra with Zoochlorella lining the digestive tract.*

Answers to Questions for Section 2.

E. *1. Most green algae live in fresh water or on land; have chlorophyll *a* and *b* and lack other pigments. Red algae have chlorophyll *a* and *d*; live in the sea; and have red and blue pigments.

2. In fresh water, and sometimes in the sea; also on moist rocks, in tree trunks, and soil.

F. 3. *Spirogyra*: filaments reproduce asexually by breaking up of existing filaments. Sexual reproduction occurs through conjugation. Cells in adjacent filaments touch, produce swellings that join and make a tube; all the contents of one cell unite with that of the other, making a zygote. A zygospore forms that can survive unfavorable conditions. When reactivated, it undergoes meiosis producing 4 haploid spores. One grows into a new cell forming a new filament.

4. The gametophyte generation produces haploid, male and female gametes, which join to make zygotes. These develop into the diploid sporophyte generation, which produces haploid spores that grow into gametophytes.

QUESTIONS FOR SECTION 2

1. How do the green algae differ from the red algae?
2. Where can you expect to find the green algae?
3. Describe reproduction in either *Spirogyra* or *Ulva*.
4. Distinguish between gametophyte and sporophyte generations in *Ulva*.
5. How do vacuoles, chloroplasts, pyrenoids, and pigments other than chlorophyll *a* help algae to maintain homeostasis?
6. How are the green algae important to ecosystems?
7. Describe the sequence of events that can lead to an algal bloom and the killing of fish.

G.   5. Vacuoles regulate water content of the cell. Chloroplasts are the site of food-making, and of the pyrenoids, which stores a steady supply of food as starch. Other pigments trap wavelengths of light not trapped by chlorophyll *a*, and pass the energy onto *a*, to maintain foodmaking.   (See page 378 for more answers.)

OBJECTIVES FOR SECTION 3

I. List the characteristics and habitats of the brown algae.
J. Describe ways that the brown algae maintain homeostasis.
K. Discuss the importance of the brown algae.

3 BROWN ALGAE

The largest, most complex algae are the brown algae. The name Phylum Phaeophyta (fā *of* ə tə) means "dusky plant." They are brown to olive green in color.

Body Plan and Habitat of Brown Algae

The brown algae range in size from microscopic filaments to giant kelps reaching lengths of 70 meters. There are no single-celled or colonial forms. (See Fig. 21-9.) Most are found attached to rocks in the cool, shallow coastal waters of temperate and near-polar climates. A few live in freshwater.

Diversity and Continuity of Brown Algae

DIVERSITY *Fucus*, or rockweed, the giant kelps, and *Sargassum* are common brown algae. Rockweed forms dense mats on rocks exposed to the changing tides. One end is fastened to rock. The free end is branched. The giant kelps are commonly attached to rocky reefs 10-20 meters below the ocean's surface. A long slender stalk reaches up to form blades which float at the surface.

Sargassum is a brown alga of the Atlantic Ocean. East to northeast of Bermuda an area of more than a million square kilometers is covered largely by masses of free floating *Sargassum*. That part of the Atlantic is known as the Sargasso Sea.

CONTINUITY Asexual reproduction occurs in several species. This is accomplished by the breaking off of fragments that develop into new plants. Most also produce asexual spores. Except for rockweeds, the brown algae have an alternation of free-living gametophyte and sporophyte generations.

21-9. Some brown algae.

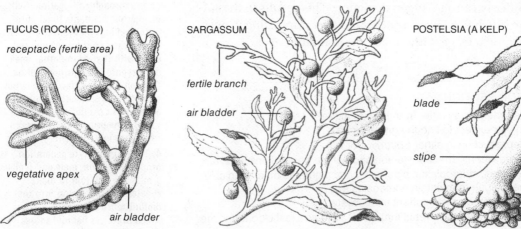

FUCUS (ROCKWEED)
receptacle (fertile area)
vegetative apex
air bladder

SARGASSUM
fertile branch
air bladder

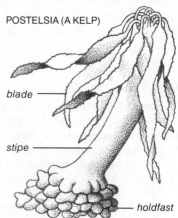

POSTELSIA (A KELP)
blade
stipe
holdfast

Homeostasis of Brown Algae

Homeostasis is maintained by several means in rockweed. When the rocks are covered with water much of the plant floats near the water's surface. Gas-filled air bladders imbedded in tissue buoy up the plants. A gelatinous material covers the plant. This prevents drying when the water level is low and the algae are exposed to air. A dark pigment shields internal tissues from sunlight until high tide returns. Surface cells are tightly packed. They contain most of the chloroplasts. The stalk transports food from the photosynthetic blade to the deeper, shaded parts of the plant. The stalks of some kelps contain cells that resemble the conducting cells in higher plants. These cells are arranged end-to-end, and have holes in their end walls. It is these cells that conduct food.

As in other algae, a number of different photosynthetic pigments are present. A golden-brown pigment masks chlorophylls *a* and *c* along with the orange and yellow pigments.

Behavior and Environment of Brown Algae

Some animals feed directly on the live tissue of brown algae. Others feed on the decaying materials originating from masses of brown algae. Beds of brown algae also serve as protective cover for young fish and small invertebrates. The *Sargassum* of the Sargasso Sea forms large dense beds of algae. This mass of brown algae serves as grazing and breeding areas for marine animals. The larger brown algae are eaten by humans, especially in China and Japan. In some areas this alga is used as fertilizer.

A widely used product of algae is algin. **Algin** *forms a part of the cell wall in several algal groups, especially the kelps.* It is used in human foods as a thickening agent and emulsifier. It is a smoothing agent in lotions. It prevents the formation of ice crystals in foods. Algin serves a wide variety of functions in the food and manufacturing industries.

QUESTIONS FOR SECTION 3

1. What are the main features of the brown algae?
2. Where are the brown algae found?
3. Some algae live attached to solid objects. Others are free-floating. What are the advantages of each arrangement?
4. Where and what is the Sargasso Sea?
5. Explain how air bladders, a gelatinous cover, dark pigment, chloroplasts, and conducting cells help maintain homeostasis in rockweeds.
6. How are the brown algae important to natural and human communities?
7. Write a report on the collection, preparation, and uses of kelp or seaweed.

Answers to Questions for Section 3.

I. 1. Range in size from microscopic filaments to kelps 70 m long; most are marine; may reproduce asexually by spores and have alternation of generations; have golden-brown pigment that masks chlorophyll *a* and *c*, and orange and yellow pigments.

2. Attached to rocks in cool, shallow coastal waters of temperate and near-polar climates.

*3. Attachment assures that the environment — assumed to be favorable — will remain stable. Free-floating would have the advantage of moving to better environment, if other events interfered with favorable conditions.

4. A part of the Atlantic east to northeast of Bermuda covered by masses of free floating *Sargassum*, a brown alga.

J. 5. Air bladders buoy up the plant, so it is exposed to light it depends upon for food-making, so food supply remains constant. Gelatinous cover prevents drying, when water is low, so moisture remains constant. Dark pigment prevents excessive exposure of internal cells to sunlight when tide is low, helping to maintain constant moisture. Chloroplasts are the site of photosynthesis, which maintains constant supply of food. Conducting cells transport food from surface cells where it is made to deeper cells, thus helping maintain constant food supply throughout the plant.

K. 6. Brown algae provide food for many animals, serve as protective cover to small marine animals and as grazing and breeding area for other marine animals, serve as food for humans, and are used as fertilizer. Algin, a product of the algae, is used in manufacturing many products.

*7. Answers will vary, depending on information students obtain in their research.

Phylum Bryophyta (bri *äf* ə d ə) is the first plant phylum that contains primarily land-based organisms. It includes the mosses and liverworts. They are thought to be descendants of haploid algal ancestors. The phylum name means moss plant. Bryophytes are more complex than most algae, but far simpler than most vascular plants.

Body Plan of Mosses and Liverworts

The masses of small velvety green moss plants are the most familiar bryophytes. (See Fig. 21-10.) They have a short main stalk with flat green leaflike structures radiating out from it. These photosynthetic structures are only one or two cells thick. *Root-like organs called* **rhizoids** project from the lower part of the plant into the soil.

Diversity and Continuity of Mosses and Liverworts

DIVERSITY Many liverworts look like the mosses just described. But others possess flattened, lobed bodies. (See Fig. 21-11.) Their resemblance to the animal liver inspired the name liverwort. Wort is old English for plant. While the rhizoids in mosses are multicellular, they are single-celled in liverworts.

CONTINUITY The moss plant is a gametophyte. It may be either male or female, or both. Male gametophytes produce sperm or male gametes. Female gametophytes produce eggs. Following a rain or a heavy dew, the two-flagellated sperm are able to swim to the female gametophyte as shown in Figure 21-12. Sugars, proteins, and acids attract the sperm. A sperm unites with the egg to form a diploid zygote. The zygote becomes the sporophyte plant. As the sporophyte develops, it receives nourishment from the gametophyte tissue. The sporophyte develops an enlarged capsule, or sporangium on top of a long stalk. In some moss species, the sporophyte is photosynthetic.

Inside the capsule, or sporangium, meiosis gives rise to haploid spores. As the tip of the capsule is opened, spores are released. If the spores come to rest on moist surfaces, water diffuses into them and they continue their growth. A spore develops *a body of branching filaments known as a* **protonema** (prōt ə *nē* mə). It looks much like an algal filament. Its cells contain chlorophyll and carry on photosynthesis. After a period of extensive growth, the protonema forms buds. These buds develop into leafy shoots and eventually become able to produce eggs and sperm. Finally, the life cycle has been completed. Alternation of sporophyte and gametophyte generations maintains continuity of life. Also, it provides for genetic variation in the offspring.

21-10. The mosses are multicellular, photosynthetic land plants. They grow mostly in damp places.

Courtesy Carolina Biological Supply Company

21-11. A liverwort, Marchantia.

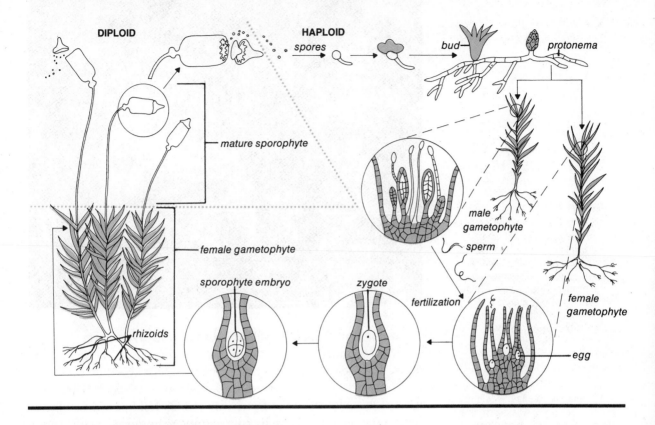

DIPLOID   HAPLOID
                 spores
                 bud   protonema

mature sporophyte

                 male
                 gametophyte
                 sperm

female gametophyte

sporophyte embryo   zygote
                                          female
                       fertilization   gametophyte

rhizoids   egg

Homeostasis of Mosses and Liverworts

To maintain homeostasis the moss plant must have available minerals and water. The rhizoids anchor the plant and absorb minerals. Water diffuses slowly into the rhizoids and on through the plant. Adaptations to this slow movement of water are close crowding and small size. Most mosses are only a few centimeters tall. A waxy cuticle over the outer surface of the plant decreases water loss. Direct sunlight causes rapid evaporation. Therefore, mosses usually survive only in the shade. As in the green algae and the other land plants, mosses contain chlorophyll *a* and *b*.

CONDUCTING CELLS   Some mosses contain a variety of specialized cells. The centers of their stalks contain certain cells that conduct water. Other cells conduct food. But their structures differ from the much more efficient conducting cells of seed plants.

WATER STORAGE   The mosses of the genus *Sphagnum* differ in several ways from other mosses. They are a pale green. This is due to the presence of large nonliving, water-storage cells among the smaller chlorophyllous cells. This moss is also adapted to and produces acidic conditions. Its spores develop if they land upon moist acidic soil.

21-12. The life cycle of a moss.

Sperm are produced in multicellular antheridia (sing. antheridium). Eggs are produced in multicellular archegonia (sing. archegonium).

21-13. *Sphagnum grows in bogs where it forms a thick mat of vegetation.*

Behavior and Environment of Mosses and Liverworts

Mosses and liverworts are important as producers for the tiny organisms in their small habitats. But more important is their role in ecologic succession. They are often found on bare rock. There, like lichens, they slowly convert rock into soil. By holding water they reduce flooding and erosion. By contributing to humus formation, they prepare the soil for a more advanced community of larger plants.

Sphagnum moss is located in glaciated areas of the north central United States. Here, it slowly fills in bogs, ponds, and small lakes and converts them into land habitats. (See Fig. 21-13.) *Sphagnum* increases the acidity of the water. Thus, bacteria of decay are inhibited and organic matter accumulates. *Partially decomposed deposits of such dead mosses are called* **peat.**

HUMAN USES OF MOSSES *Sphagnum* moss and peat are often used by gardeners as soil conditioners. They improve the texture, water-holding capacity, nutrient content, and acidity of the soil. Peat holds up to 90 percent of its own weight in water. *Sphagnum* moss holds up to twice its own dry weight in water. Both peat and undecomposed moss are used to retain moisture in shipping plant nursery stock. People living near peat deposits compress the peat and use it as fuel.

The lower layers of peat bogs may contain materials that are as much as 16,000 years old. Such deposits make possible the study of successively older layers. The kinds of spores and pollen grains located in these layers provide a history of the vegetation of that area. Even the bodies of clothed persons from the Bronze Age have been uncovered in peat excavations in Denmark.

QUESTIONS FOR SECTION 4

(See page 384 for answers.)

1. Describe the bodies of mosses and liverworts.
2. Describe the life cycle of a moss and distinguish between sporophyte and gametophyte generations.
3. Some bryophytes produce separate male and female gametophytes. Others produce both male and female gametes on the same gametophyte. Which type do you think would more likely survive? Explain.
4. What features of a moss plant adapt it for survival on land?
5. How are multicellular algae and mosses able to survive without highly specialized conducting tissue?
6. Explain the importance of mosses in small habitats, ecologic succession, plant nurseries, homes, and the study of past life.
7. What is the advantage of sexual reproduction?

CHAPTER REVIEW

In this chapter we saw clear evidence of *unity within diversity*. All plant groups include mostly multicellular, autotrophic organisms with pigments in plastids. In Kingdom Plantae, the mostly multicellular algae are classified according to the chemistry of their pigment and food storage molecules. The mosses are the first primarily land plants in our survey.

Continuity of the species is accomplished by both sexual and asexual means. All sexually reproducing plants alternate between a haploid gametophyte phase and a diploid sporophyte phase. Sexual reproduction provides for diversity among the offspring. *Diversity* increases the probability that at least some offspring can survive changing conditions.

The different organisms have *specialized structures that allow them to carry out specific functions*. In this way *homeostasis* is maintained.

The plants, as autotrophs, form the first link in the food chain of any ecosystem. Photosynthesis is the link between the sun's energy and the energy path through living systems. The algae have found many uses in human life.

Using the Concepts

1. What changes in the structure and life cycle of marine and freshwater algae would be necessary for them to live permanently on land?
2. Do multicellular sex organs give plants any advantage over other organisms?
3. Devise a demonstration showing the amount of water *Sphagnum* can hold. Compare the mass of the water held with the mass of the dry moss.

Unanswered Question

4. A few green algae lack chlorophyll. They are thought to have been autotrophic at one time and then lost their chlorophyll. Their being heterotrophic is taken as evidence that some fungi originated from algae. Of what advantage might it be for an autotrophic organism to become heterotrophic?

Career Activities

5. What practical importance might there be in the work of a phycologist, one who studies algae?

VOCABULARY REVIEW

1 phycoerythrin	gametophyte	vacuoles	pyrenoids
phycocyanin	sporophyte	pigment spot	**3** algin
agar	alternation of generations	eyespot	**4** protonema
2 conjugation			peat

CHAPTER 21 TEST

Copy the number of each test item and place your answer to the right.

PART 1   Multiple Choice: Select the letter of the phrase that best completes each of the following.

d   1. Most plants have   **a.** cellulose cell walls
   b. many cells   **c.** chloroplasts   **d.** all of these.

a   2. The red, green, and brown algae differ from other algae in being mostly   **a.** multicellular
   b. autotrophic   **c.** heterotrophic   **d.** colonial.

a   3. Blue light penetrates deeper into the water than other colors and is most likely absorbed by
   a. red pigments   **b.** green pigments   **c.** blue pigments   **d.** white pigments.

c   4. The one-million square kilometer bed of brown algae in the Atlantic is known as the   **a.** Bermuda triangle   **b.** doldrums   **c.** Sargasso Sea
   d. Barrier Reef.

d   5. Homeostatic mechanisms not present in rockweed include   **a.** gelatinous covering
   b. shielding pigment   **c.** food-conducting cells
   d. rhizoids.

b   6. During photosynthesis algae produce   **a.** nitrogen   **b.** oxygen   **c.** carbon dioxide
   d. water.

c   7. Among the first plants to begin ecologic succession on bare rock are   **a.** red and brown algae
   b. brown algae and liverworts   **c.** lichens and mosses   **d.** mosses and red algae.

c   8. Spores from sproangium develop a body of branching filaments known as   **a.** pyrenoid
   b. rhizoid   **c.** protonema   **d.** lichen.

d   9. An advantage to sexual reproduction is   **a.** precise conditions for fertilization   **b.** convenience
   c. identical offspring   **d.** variation among offspring.

a   10. Sphagnum moss increases the   **a.** acidity of surrounding water   **b.** rate of decay   **c.** water loss from nursery stock   **d.** growth of bacteria.

PART 2   Matching: Match the letter of the term in Column I with its description in Column II.

COLUMN I

a. Phylum Bryophyta
b. Phylum Chlorophyta
c. Phylum Phaeophyta
d. Phylum Rhodophyta
e. agar
f. algin
g. peat
h. protonema
i. starch-formation
j. sporophyte

COLUMN II

a   **11.** Mosses and liverworts

c   **12.** The most complex algae including kelps, rockweed, Sargassum, and others

d   **13.** Algae with red pigment and which contribute to the formation of reefs

b   **14.** Algae with chlorophylls *a* and *b* and most closely related to land plants

g   **15.** Partially decomposed moss plants

e   **16.** Product of red algae used as a growth medium for bacteria

f   **17.** Product of algae used as a thickening and smoothing agent

j   **18.** Diploid

h   **19.** Haploid

i   **20.** Pyrenoid

PART 3   Completion: Complete the following.

21. Modern biologists classify eucariotic algae by _color_.
22. Two human uses of moss or peat are _soil conditioner, fuel_
23. During respiration algae produce _CO_2_ and H_2O
24. In mosses and some algae the gametophyte stage produces _gametes (sperm and eggs)_
25. The chlorophyll produced by red, green, and brown algae is chlorophyll _a_.

CHAPTER 22

FERNS AND GYMNOSPERMS

We have just studied the multicellular algae and the bryophytes. Algae are classified both within and outside of the plant kingdom. However, mosses are always considered to be plants. Here we continue our study of nonflowering land plants.

As these plants are described we will relate them to familiar basic concepts: *unity within diversity, the continuity of life, homeostasis, the link between structure and function,* and *interaction with the environment.*

Some of the questions we will deal with include:

- How have plants solved the problem of living on dry land?
- What conditions promoted the formation of coal?
- Does the alternation of generations seen in the mosses also occur in ferns and cone-bearing trees?
- What are the largest and the oldest of all living organisms?
- Are pine trees edible?
- What determines the appearance of lumber?
- How does air pollution affect forests?

FERNS

1 THE FERNS

General Characteristics of Vascular Plants

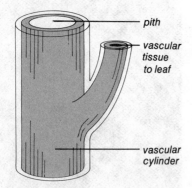

22-1. *The vascular supply to primitive leaves does not affect the shape of the stem's vascular tissue.*

Over a period of time many plants changed from an aquatic environment to a land environment. This change presented several problems. These involved the transport of materials, body support, water loss, and gas exchange. Additional problems included the absorption of nutrients and reproduction. Those plants that had enough of the required characteristics were able to survive on land.

TRANSPORT AND BODY SUPPORT   The problem of transport was solved with hollow cells. These allow liquids to flow through roots, stems, and leaves from one cell to another. Such *cells especially adapted for conducting water and dissolved materials form* **vascular tissues.** Some cells of the vascular tissues had especially rigid walls. They provided physical support for plants that lost the buoyant support of surrounding water.

WATER LOSS AND GAS EXCHANGE   The secretion of *a* **cuticle,** *a fatty, waxy layer on the outer walls of cells* protected leaves and stems against water loss. But such a coating had one drawback. It prevented the gas exchanges used in photosynthesis and respiration. Thus plants with cuticles, that also had pores in the outer surfaces of leaves and stems, were better able to survive.

NUTRIENTS AND REPRODUCTION   An aquatic environment provided a constant water and mineral supply for plants. Plants that developed special absorbing structures that penetrate the soil were able to accomplish the same functions on land.

Wet habitats of aquatic plants and land plants allowed sperm to swim through water to meet the egg. Air currents and insects assisted in the transfer of sperm by land plants. The multicellular sex organs developed an outer layer of cells that protected the tender gametes from drying out.

VASCULAR TISSUE   The combination of traits described made it possible for plants to survive on land. The extensive development of vascular tissue allowed the transport of water and minerals from the soil. It also enabled food to be transported from the leaves to all parts of the plant. The rigid cell walls made possible the support of leaves, exposing them to light and carbon dioxide.

Vascular plants also have a definite alternation of generations. In higher forms the mature sporophyte is dominant and nutritionally independent. In primitive forms the gametophyte is also nutritionally independent. In advanced forms it is dependent on the sporophyte.

In vascular plants, chlorophylls *a* and *b* and other pigments are present in plastids.

Classification of Vascular Plants

For some time, vascular plants have been grouped into the Phylum Tracheophyta (trā kē äf əd ə). The phylum name is Greek for windpipe plant. However, recent fossil records have suggested that the presence of vascular tissue may have been overemphasized in classification. Thus some botanists are dropping Tracheophyta from their classification scheme. This illustrates the continuous modification of classification schemes so that they reflect new information. For now we will continue to use the term Tracheophyta.

Vascular plants may be divided into four subphyla: *Psilopsida, Lycopsida, Sphenopsida,* and *Pteropsida.* The first three of these share several primitive characteristics. They have small leaves which appear to be extensions of outer stem tissue. Each leaf has a single **vein** *which is a bundle of vascular tissue.* (See Fig. 22-1.) Water must be present if sperm are to be transferred to the egg. The sporophyte is larger than the gametophyte. However, both sporophyte and gametophyte are nutritionally independent.

PSILOPSIDA The psilopsids are the simplest of living vascular plants. They have either scale-like leaves or none at all. No true roots are present. They have *underground stems called* **rhizomes** with tiny rhizoids. *Rhizoids* have no vascular tissue but may perform the functions of roots. They anchor the plant and obtain water and dissolved minerals. The stems are simple branching structures with no true leaves. Psilopsids are found mostly in tropical and subtropical areas. (See Fig 22-2.)

LYCOPSIDA The lycopsids, or club mosses, have roots, stems, and leaves. They grow close to the ground in damp areas. However, some are found in deserts and on mountains. Club mosses differ from true mosses in having true vascular tissue throughout their roots, stems, and leaves. Also, they have different life histories. Their sporangia are borne on the upper surface of specialized leaves arranged in the form of a cone. The group includes the ground pine (*Lycopodium*) and club mosses (*Selaginella*). (See Figs. 22-3 and 22-4.)

SPHENOPSIDA Subphylum Sphenopsida is composed of one living genus, *Equisetum.* Its members are usually no taller than one meter though a tropical species reaches five meters. The hollow, jointed stems are rough partly because of their verticle ridges. The stems are gritty because of the silica (sand-like particles) on the inner walls of their epidermal cells. The silica has made the stems useful to settlers and backpackers for scouring pots and pans. Thus they are known as scouring rushes. The appearance of branching forms has inspired the name horsetails. (See Fig. 22-5.) The leaves are tiny and form a ring around the stems. About 300 million years ago some members of the group were tree-like, reaching heights of over 15 meters. Both

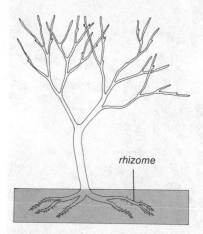

rhizome

22-2. *Psilotum is the simplest living vascular tissue. It is a psilopsid.*

22-3. Lycopodium with spore-bearing cones.

22-4. *Selaginella apoda with spore-bearing cones.*

22-5. *Horsetails today are very similar to those of 300 million years ago.*

22-6. *(below) A typical woodland fern originating from a rhizome covered with forest litter.*

22-7. *Marsilea, a water fern.*

The leaves of ferns are often called fronds.

horsetails and club mosses were common in the ancient swamps of that time. The stagnant, deoxygenated swamps in which they grew did not support decay bacteria. Such conditions were ideal for the formation of coal.

PTEROPSIDA   Subphylum Pteropsida includes ferns, gymnosperms, and flowering plants. Ferns and gymnosperms will be given more detailed attention in this chapter. The next chapter will be devoted to flowering plants.

Diversity and Continuity of Ferns

BODY PLAN   The sporophyte is the larger of the two stages in the fern's life cycle. It is composed of roots, stems, and large leaves. (See Fig. 22-6.) Each leaf appears to be a fused branching system of many veins. The leaves grow from an underground stem called a rhizome. Anchoring the rhizomes to the deeper soil are roots which absorb water and minerals from soil spaces. The other stage in the life cycle of the fern is the gametophyte. The fern gametophyte is a smaller, heart-shaped structure. Both stages are photosynthetic. However, the gametophyte has no vascular tissue or true roots.

DIVERSITY   There are about 11,000 species of ferns. They vary in size from tiny floating plants less than a centimeter in diameter to giant tree ferns, 25 meters tall. The leaves of many species are divided

The fern gametophyte , or prothallus, is only 5-6 mm in diameter.

into a feathery pattern. However, some are undivided and form a variety of designs. Some forms are shown in Figure 22-7 and Figure 22-8.

CONTINUITY   Ferns are autotrophic. The life cycle of typical ferns involves alternation between a diploid sporophyte and haploid gametophyte. The life cycle is illustrated in Figure 22-9. The dominant sporophyte typically develops spores on the underside of its leaves. *The spores are borne in helmet-shaped structures called* sporangia (singular, sporangium). *A cluster of sporangia form a* sorus (plural, sori). When mature, the sori appear as brown patches. These sori look much like disease spots that form on other kinds of plants. After meiosis, haploid spores are discharged. If they land on shady, moist, cool soil, they germinate. Each spore forms a green, heart-shaped gametophyte. It is one cell which is less than 1.5 cm. in diameter thick except toward the middle. Rhizoids are produced on the lower surface in the central area. The male parts of the gametophyte, scattered among the rhizoids, produce up to several hundred sperm cells. Closer to the notch, the female parts of the gametophyte produce haploid eggs. The flagellated sperm swim to and fertilize an egg. The eggs and sperm mature at different times so the eggs of one gametophyte are usually fertilized by sperm from another. Only one zygote develops on a gametophyte.

22-8. *The leaves of two different kinds of ferns.*

22-9   THE LIFE CYCLE OF A FERN

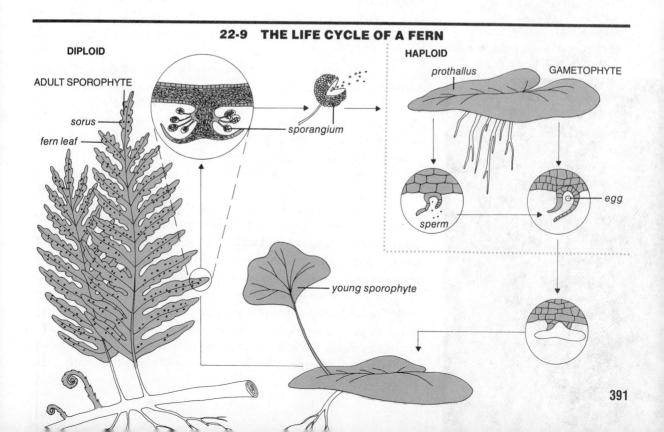

DIPLOID

HAPLOID

ADULT SPOROPHYTE

sorus

fern leaf

sporangium

prothallus

GAMETOPHYTE

sperm

egg

young sporophyte

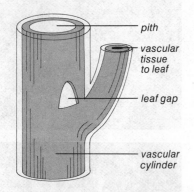

22-10. *A leaf gap appears where a fern's vascular tissue separates out and supplies a leaf.*

Answers to Questions for Section 1.

E. *8. It has an upper and lower epidermis, with mesophyll, composed of a palisade layer and a spongy layer, in between. Pores (stomata) in the lower epidermis allow gases to diffuse into and out of the spaces in the spongy layer. Chlorophyll — and hence, photosynthesis — occurs in the mesophyll, and in the guard cells surrounding the stomata.

(See page 388 for answers 9-10.)

22-11. *Cross-section of a fern leaf showing stomata.*

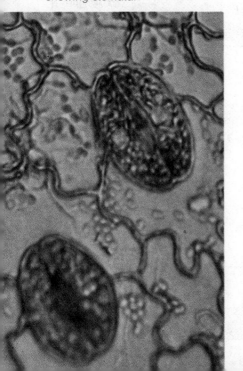

By mitotic divisions the zygote becomes the embryo and develops a root, a stem, and a leaf. The root penetrates the soil. The leaf grows toward the light, turns green, and the sporophyte becomes independent. The gametophyte soon withers. But the sporophyte is *perennial.* Hence, it lives for several years.

Ferns also reproduce asexually by developing leaves from the horizontal, underground rhizome.

Homeostasis of Ferns

Fern plants contain various tissues that make it possible to carry on respiration and photosynthesis.

INTERNAL SYSTEMS   Photosynthesis occurs in the small gametophyte and in the large leaves of the sporophyte. The vascular supply that conducts water to large leaves is quite extensive. *An interruption in the vascular tissue of the stem above the point where it supplies the leaf is known as a* **leaf gap.** At that point the tissue at the center of the stem is continuous with the tissue surrounding the vascular cylinder. (See Fig. 22-10.) Such a gap does not occur in the more primitive subphyla.

The vascular tissues of ferns are xylem and phloem. They form a pipeline system within the plant. **Phloem tissue** *conducts dissolved food from leaves to other parts of the plant body.* Phloem tissue in ferns is composed of *sieve cells* and *albuminous cells.* Mature sieve cells have no nuclei. But their cytoplasm is active in conducting food and extends through pores in the cell wall to the cytoplasm of nearby cells.

Xylem tissue *conducts water and dissolved minerals from roots to leaves.* Most of the cells in xylem are tracheids (trā kē əds). **Tracheids** *are hollow woody cells with pointed ends.* When mature they lose their cytoplasm and nuclei. Tracheid walls have a number of thin places that allow water to pass from the inside of one to the inside of another. The overlapping ends of tracheids allow water to flow through stems, roots, and the veins of leaves. Although these cells are dead, they continue to function as pipelines.

In some ferns, water is conducted through vessels of the xylem. *Vessels* are barrel-shaped cells in which the end walls have holes. Some of these cells lack end walls altogether. Vessels transport water more efficiently than tracheids do. Although they continue to transport water, vessels cells die as they mature.

A fern leaf has an upper and lower epidermis. Both are covered with a cuticle which inhibits water loss. Between the epidermal layers is a layer of cells called the *mesophyll.* The mesophyll is divided into a compact *palisade layer* and a *spongy layer.* The spongy layer has large air spaces among the cells. The lower epidermis has many pores, called *stomata* (singular, stoma). (See Fig. 22-11.) The stomata allow gases to diffuse into and out of the spaces of the mesophyll. ***Each stoma is surrounded by two* guard cells *which regulate its size.*** The leaf stomata of floating water ferns occur only in the upper epidermis.

Chloroplasts occur in the cells of the mesophyll and the guard cells of the epidermis. Water conducted through the xylem tissue and carbon dioxide entering the stomata are the raw materials for photosynthesis. The water and carbon dioxide resulting from respiration in leaf cells are also available for food making.

Seed plants also have leaf gaps.

Behavior and Environment of Ferns

Ferns are not the dominant land plants. But they are important producers in some habitats.

MOSQUITO FERNS   One of the tiny floating water ferns sometimes forms dense floating mats. They are believed to suffocate mosquito larvae. Hence, it is called mosquito fern. The same fern often has blue-green algae living mutualistically in some of its cells. These algae fix nitrogen, converting atmospheric nitrogen into nitrogen compounds usable by green plants. The ferns show improved growth when the algae are present.

HUMAN USES   Ferns make ideal house plants. Many of them grow in little light and are resistant to damage by aphids, mites, and other arthropod attacks. The rhizomes and young leaves of many species have been used as food. The use of ferns in medicine has been widespread. They have been used to treat eye and skin diseases, sore throats, and to expel tapeworms. Native Americans used fern fibers in basket making.

Sieve cells appear to be aided in their functions by nearby albuminous cells which retain their nuclei.

QUESTIONS FOR SECTION 1

1. What special problems do land plants face and what changes made it possible for them to survive?
2. What are the general characteristics and/or a representative of each of the subphyla of vascular plants.
3. What were the conditions that resulted in the formation of coal?
4. Trace the life history of a fern through sporophyte and gametophyte generations.
5. Why are ferns limited to fairly moist conditions?
6. Distinguish between phloem and xylem tissues in terms of structure, kinds of cells, and function.
7. In what ways do the vascular tissues of ferns differ from those of more primitive tracheophytes?
8. Describe the structure of a fern leaf and tell how it relates to photosynthesis.
9. What is the fern's niche in an ecosystem?
10. How have human beings used ferns?

Answers to Questions for Section 1.

A. 1. Special problems were the transport of material, body support, water loss, gas exchange, absorption of nutrients, and reproduction. Changes were: vascular tissue, for transport and support; cuticle, that prevents water loss; pores in leaves and stems for gas exchange; special absorbing structures that penetrate soil for absorption of nutrients; transfer of sperm by wind or insects, and multicellular sex organs that kept gametes moist.

B. 2. *Psilopsida*: have either scale-like leaves or none at all; underground stems called rhizomes with rhizoids. *Lycopsida*: have roots, stems, and leaves; grow close to ground; sporangia on specialized leaves; example: club moss. *Sphenopsida*: usually grow 1 meter tall; gritty, silica lined stems; tiny leaves form ring around stems. Example: horsetails. Pteropsida: Example: ferns.

3. Stagnant, deoxygenated swamps that did not support decay bacteria.

C. 4. See figure 22-9 on page 391.

*5. The sperms and eggs of the gametophytes mature at different times, so cross-fertilization occurs. For the sperm to reach the egg, it needs a moist environment to swim through.

D. 6. Phloem tissue conducts dissolved food from leaves to other parts of the plant body. It is composed of sieve cells and albuminous cells; sieve cells have no nuclei but their cytoplasm functions in transporting food, and extends through pores into nearby cells. Xylem tissue conducts water and dissolved minerals from roots to leaves. Most of its cells are tracheids, which are hollow, with overlapping ends and walls that have thin spaces—both of which allow water to flow from cell to cell.

7. The tissues have more rigid walls, and also has leaf gaps, that do not occur in more primitive plants.

(See page 392 for more answers.)

CHAPTER INVESTIGATION

A. What differences do you notice as you compare the ring pattern in these cross-sections of stems of southern yellow pine?

B. What are the differences in cellular structure between the light and dark rings? How could you explain the sudden change in thickness between the third and fourth ring from the center?

C. Find logs or stumps cut during known seasons and years and relate the growth ring patterns to local weather records, ground water, and other environmental conditions.

2 THE GYMNOSPERMS

Diversity and Continuity of Gymnosperms

BODY PLAN   As in the ferns, the sporophyte is the larger of the two stages in the life cycle of gymnosperms. In fact, most gymnosperm sporophytes are either trees or shrubs containing much woody tissue. The sporophytes have roots, stems, and leaves. All are well supplied with vascular tissue. The leaves are either large or they take the form of needles or scales. Members of this group produce cones with two kinds of spores which develop into gametophytes. The very small gametophytes are dependent on the sporophyte for nutrition. The seed is usually produced on the surface of the scales of a cone. Thus the name gymnosperm, which is Greek for naked seed.

DIVERSITY   We will look at three of the four groups of living gymnosperms. The cycads grow in tropical and subtropical regions. (See Fig. 22-12.) Cycads look much like palms except they have naked seeds produced on large cones. Cycads were abundant 300 million years ago. Dinosaurs may have fed on their leaves and seeds.

Ginkgo is the only surviving species of another once-large group of gymnosperms. It has become a popular tree for street plantings because of its resistance to smog. The pollen-bearing trees are preferred because the female trees produce seeds that have an unpleasant odor.

The conifers are the most common gymnosperms today. Most conifers bear their seeds on cones. They also have needle-like or scale-like leaves with thick cuticles. Pines, spruces, firs, cedars, junipers, and larches are all conifers.

The largest and oldest living organisms are conifers. Some bristlecone pines of California, Nevada, and Utah are more than 4600 years old. (See Fig. 22-13 on page 396.) One coastal redwood of California reaches a height of more than 100 meters. Coniferous forests supply a large part of the lumber used for building and making paper.

CONTINUITY   The pines are typical conifers. The dominant sporophytes produce two kinds of cones. The male cone appears in the spring. Cells in the cone divide by meiosis and produce small spores. Each small spore can become a pollen grain. *A* **pollen grain** *is an immature male gametophyte.* The pollen grains are released into the air as shown in Figure 22-14 on page 396.

In the more familiar female pine cones, larger spores form the female gametophyte. The female gametophyte remains inside the tissue of the parent sporophyte. Water is not necessary for fertilization, because pollen grains are carried by air currents to the female cones. *The transfer of pollen to the female cone is called* **pollination.** When it arrives inside the female cone each pollen grain forms a tiny pollen tube. A pollen grain with its tube is the male gametophyte. The

See Diversity: *Ephedra*, a desert shrub of the southwestern U.S., represents a fourth group of gymnosperms.

OBJECTIVES FOR SECTION 2

G. Describe the body plan of gymnosperms.
H. Name and describe three kinds of gymnosperms.
I. Describe the life cycle of a pine.
J. Describe the ways that the raw materials and products of photosynthesis are conducted through a conifer.
K. Tell what causes a stem to grow in width and describe the changes this growth causes in stem tissues.
L. Tell how a pine needle is adapted to its functions.
M. Describe the formation of compression wood.
N. Distinguish between the activities of the fungus and the conifer's root in a micorrhiza.
O. Describe the role of gymnosperms as sources of food, paper, fuel, and lumber.
P. Describe the effects of various pollutants on forest trees.
Q. List those features that most nonflowering vascular plants have in common.

22-12. Cycads are tropical plants that resemble ferns or palms with seeds borne in cones.

tube grows into the female cone until it reaches an egg. A sperm nucleus from the pollen grain unites with the egg forming the zygote. This fertilization occurs deep within the protective tissues of the parent sporophyte. In pines, about 15 months pass between pollination and fertilization. Figure 22-15 shows three female cones of a pine in different stages of maturity.

The zygote divides many times by mitosis. It becomes an embryonic sporophyte plant. The embryo is surrounded by food storage tissue which is part of the gametophyte. Its food supply, however, comes from the parent sporophyte. Around the embryo and its food supply a protective coat of parent sporophyte tissue develops. (See Fig. 22-16.) *The embryo, stored food, and coat make up a* **seed.** The embryo contains a group of about eight **cotyledons** or *seed leaves.* It also contains the **hypocotyl,** *the portion of the embryo below the cotyledons.* The process of seed development in pines takes place during the year following fertilization.

If the seed is carried to moderately moist soil it absorbs water. At this point it starts to grow. This *renewed growth in a seed is called* **germination.** (See Fig. 22-17 on page 398.) By the time the stored food is used up the young seedling has developed chlorophyll. Thus it can make its own food by photosynthesis.

In junipers, the scales of female cones are fleshy at maturity. They look more like berries than cones.

22-13. *Bristlecone pines may be the oldest living organisms. The living cells of the trees in the background are still "young."*

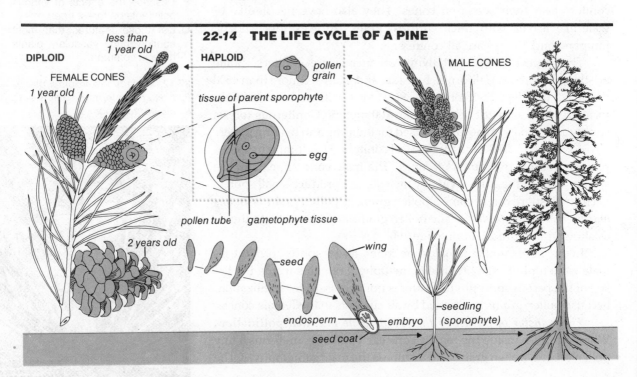

22-14 THE LIFE CYCLE OF A PINE

DIPLOID

HAPLOID

FEMALE CONES

less than 1 year old

pollen grain

MALE CONES

1 year old

tissue of parent sporophyte

egg

pollen tube   gametophyte tissue

2 years old

wing

seed

endosperm — embryo

seed coat

seedling (sporophyte)

Homeostasis of Gymnosperms

INTERNAL SYSTEMS   Like other autotrophs, gymnosperms get their energy through respiration. They also produce food through photosynthesis. These processes can occur only when their raw materials are present. Like ferns, the conifers have vascular tissues. Food made in the leaves is carried to other parts of the plant body through phloem tissue. Sieve cells and albuminous cells form a continuous chain from the leaf vein into the phloem tissue of the stem. (See Fig. 22-18 on page 398.) The dissolved food they carry is used in respiration in all living cells of the plant body.

WOOD   Water and dissolved minerals are conducted from the roots, through the stem, to the leaves. Here they are used in making food. This conduction occurs in xylem tissue which we know as wood. The xylem consists of tracheids but lacks the vessels and fibers present in the woody flowering plants. The absence of tough fibers results in the so-called soft wood of conifers. Scattered among the xylem cells are resin ducts. **Resin ducts** *are lined with cells that secrete resin.* Resin inhibits the growth of fungi and invasion by insects.

TURPENTINE AND ROSIN   When distilled, resin produces *turpentine* and a waxy substance called *rosin.* Turpentine is used as a paint and varnish thinner. It is also used in the manufacture of some medicine. Rosin is used on violin strings and baseballs to minimize slippage.

RAYS   Radiating out from near the center of the xylem are xylem rays. They continue out, becoming phloem rays. The cells of *xylem rays* and *phloem rays* transport food and water radially across the stem. They conduct food to and from storage cells.

CAMBIUM   New xylem and phloem are added to the stems of conifers throughout the life of the tree. This is accomplished by the cambium. *The* **cambium** *is a thin sheet of unspecialized cells between the central xylem of the stem and the phloem of the inner bark.* Cells of the cambium are able to divide by mitosis. Cells produced next to xylem become xylem cells. Those produced next to phloem become phloem cells. The division of cambium cells causes growth in the width of a pine stem. As the xylem expands, the phloem is destroyed. Yearly growth also splits the *cork* which forms the outer bark of the stems. As bark is split it is replaced by *cork cambium.* Other meristematic tissue increases the height of the tree. Cells near the tips of stems can divide by mitosis throughout the life of the tree.

GROWTH RINGS   The tracheids that are formed by cambium during periods of rapid growth are generally large and have thin walls. This usually occurs during late spring and early summer. Smaller thick-walled ones are produced during slower growth later in midsummer. *The differences in the size of these cells produces* **growth rings.** Growth rings can be seen when a stem is cut cross-wise. The

22-15. *Three female cones of a pine. (top) Winter cone following spring pollination; (middle) cone of the following summer; (bottom) mature cone in its second autumn. It is ready to shed its seeds.*

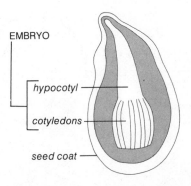

EMBRYO

hypocotyl

cotyledons

seed coat

22-16. *The mature seed of a pine.*

The Gymnosperms   **397**

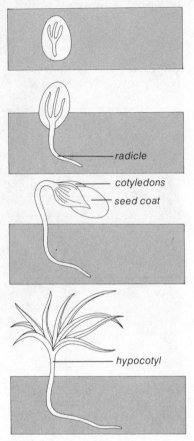

22-17. *The germination of a pine seed.*

- radicle
- cotyledons
- seed coat
- hypocotyl

age of the tree in years can usually be determined by the number of growth rings. The size of growth rings can also tell something about the climate, rainfall pattern, fire damage, and other conditions during the past life of a tree. A thick growth ring indicates a year in which conditions allowed rapid growth. Cutting down the tree or removing a plug of wood with an increment borer can make the growth rings available for study.

As a tree ages, some of the cells in the center of the xylem fill with resins, gums, and pigments. These substances prevent the flow of water. *This older, darker wood at the center of the tree trunk is called* **heartwood.** *The outer, lighter wood which still functions is called* **sapwood.** The heartwood may rot away without affecting the functioning of the tree.

PINE LEAVES Photosynthesis occurs in leaves. The needle-shaped leaves of the pine usually live from 2 to 14 years and are shed gradually throughout the year. Thus the term "evergreen" describes the continuous presence of green leaves. Pines often occur where the topsoil is frozen for part of the year. This makes it difficult for their roots to get water. Therefore, if the leaves were losing water all winter, the tree would dry out by spring. The leaf is adapted for such dry conditions. Each needle is coated with a thick cuticle. (See Fig. 22-19.) The stomata are at the bottom of depressions in the cuticle. This inhibits water loss by evaporation. Leaf veins are surrounded by several layers of protective cells. Like the stems, pine leaves also contain resin ducts or canals.

Other homeostatic relationships are similar to those in flowering plants and will be discussed in the next chapter.

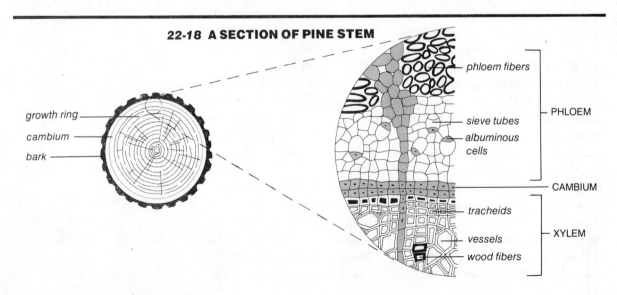

22-18 A SECTION OF PINE STEM

- growth ring
- cambium
- bark

- phloem fibers
- sieve tubes
- albuminous cells — PHLOEM
- CAMBIUM
- tracheids
- vessels
- wood fibers — XYLEM

Behavior and Environment of Gymnosperms

COMPRESSION WOOD   Most conifers maintain a straight central stem throughout their lifetime. If a storm or other force causes a conifer to lean, the underside of the leaning stem develops what is known as compression wood. **Compression wood** *is formed as a reaction to a conifer stem's leaning posture.* It is due to unequal zylem development. There are narrower growth rings on the upper side of a leaning stem and wider rings at the underside. (See Fig. 22-20.) Compression wood results in a slow return of the stem toward a verticle position. Microscopic studies show that the tracheids in compression wood are smaller and more rounded than normal tracheids. Such wood also has more lignin and less cellulose in cell walls than normal wood. Lignin makes cell walls tough and hard. Investigations show that compression wood expands or pushes in the direction required to strengthen the stem.

Interaction With the Environment

MICORRHIZAE   Conifers are common where the topsoil is shallow, infertile, dry, or frozen for part of the year. We have already learned of adaptations that help a leaf survive in dry conditions. The roots of many conifers have a mutualistic relationship with certain soil fungi. This relationship helps the conifers obtain nutrients from the soil. (See Fig. 22-21 on page 400.) Many roots have difficulty absorbing certain elements like phosphorus even when they are abundant in the soil. The fungus increases its absorption rate. The roots in turn supply amino acids to the fungus.

GYMNOSPERMS AS FOOD AND PAPER   Portions of stems of certain cycads and the seeds of ginkgo have provided starch for the human diet. Native Americans have long used parts of conifers for food. The phloem and cambium of the inner bark of pines was used as an emergency food. The needles of eastern white pine are rich in vitamin C. Also, the seeds of nearly all pines are edible and range from 15-30 percent protein.

White spruce are the main source of pulpwood used in the manufacture of many kinds of paper. One midweek issue of a large city newspaper uses the entire year's growth of half a square kilometer of spruce.

WOOD AS FUEL AND LUMBER   Many primitive societies around the world have long used wood as the only available fuel for warmth and cooking. These supplies are fast becoming exhausted. History records several instances of depleted forests. The resulting effect is erosion and loss of fertility of topsoil. Interest in wood as a fuel is increasing as prices of fossil fuels rise in the United States. An advantage to wood fuel is that it is a renewable resource. Fossil fuels are not.

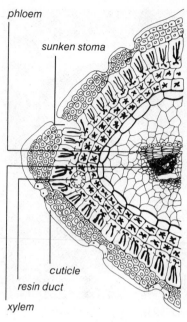

phloem

sunken stoma

cuticle

resin duct

xylem

22-19. *A section of the leaf, or needle, of a pine.*

22-20. *This red spruce was tipped by a wind storm when young. More rapid growth of the underside of the stem formed compression wood. This wood actually pushes in the direction required to straighten the stem.*

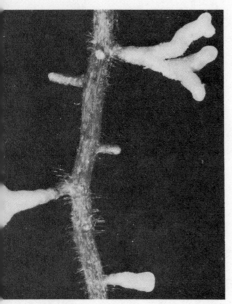

22-21. *Three mycorrhizal short roots of pine.*

22-22. *Douglas fir.*

The use of trees for lumber in the construction of houses and numerous other articles is of great economic importance. The Douglas fir of the Pacific Northwest is probably the most important lumber tree in the world. (See Fig. 22-22.) Most virgin forests of Douglas fir have been harvested. But large numbers of new trees are being grown in managed forests.

THE APPEARANCE OF LUMBER The surface appearance of wood is basically determined by the arrangement, numbers, and shape of xylem cells. But the appearance also depends on the way wood is cut from the tree. Knots are branches embedded within a treetrunk.

The Effects of Human Activities on Forests

Great numbers of coniferous trees are being removed for direct use as lumber, paper, and fuel. In addition, forests are under attack by polluted air. Air pollutants disrupt delicate balances in the forest ecosystem. They also affect coniferous trees directly.

Most air pollution results from the burning of fossil fuels such as gasoline, oil, and coal. Although antipollution devices are in use, pollution continues to increase in many areas. Population growth, industrial expansion, and more vehicles are some of the causes.

Sulfur dioxide is released in the smoke of burning coal and oil. Additional quantities are produced during the refining of the ores of iron, copper, and zinc. Sulfur dioxide enters plants through the stomata. In doing so, it increases the size of stomata which allow the entrance of disease organisms. Loss of water from leaves results from the enlarged stomata. Sulfur dioxide also destroys chloroplasts and eventually kills the mesophyll cells. In lesser quantities it decreases the yield of pine seeds.

The refining of aluminum ores releases *fluorides*. Exposures of pine to even small amounts of fluorides have reduced leaf size and tree height. Fluoride-weakened pines in the Rocky Mountains are being overcome by several species of herbaceous insects.

High temperature combustion and automobile exhausts release harmful substances to the atmosphere. One of these is ozone. (See Fig. 22-23.) As ozone enters leaves, it destroys enzymes, increases respiration, and reduces photosynthesis.

Another substance, *peroxyacetyl nitrate,* commonly called *PAN,* reduces the yield of some plants. PAN reduces enzyme activity, respiration, photosynthesis, and protein synthesis.

Los Angeles smog flowing over the San Bernardino mountains has reduced the resistance of ponderosa pines to invasion by pine beetles. The more resistant sugar pine, white fir, and incense cedar are increasing in numbers. But on exposed ridges all trees are dying

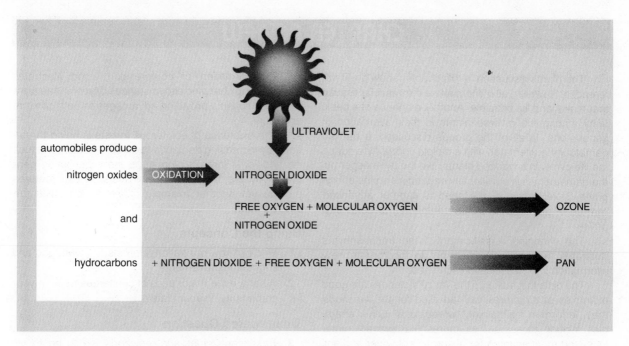

ULTRAVIOLET

automobiles produce

nitrogen oxides →OXIDATION→ NITROGEN DIOXIDE

FREE OXYGEN + MOLECULAR OXYGEN
+
and   NITROGEN OXIDE → OZONE

hydrocarbons + NITROGEN DIOXIDE + FREE OXYGEN + MOLECULAR OXYGEN → PAN

out. Concentrations of air pollutants that have no visible effect on these trees has been shown by tree ring studies to greatly reduce the rate at which wood is produced.

Without controls on pollution and cutting, our forests, once a renewable resource, may no longer exist.

QUESTIONS FOR SECTION 2

1. What distinguishes gymnosperms from the flowering plants?
2. Name and briefly describe three kinds of gymnosperms.
3. Trace the life history of a pine.
4. How are water, minerals, and dissolved food directed to appropriate places in a pine tree?
5. Heartwood lumber is more resistant to decay than sapwood lumber. Yet in a living tree, heartwood may rot away while sapwood remains alive and functioning. Explain the difference.
6. What causes a stem to grow wider and what happens to its outer tissues?
7. Describe conditions in which the number of growth rings might not indicate the age of the tree in years.
8. How is homeostasis maintained in a pine needle?
9. Of what advantage and disadvantage is it to a coniferous tree to keep its leaves through the winter?
10. How and in what situation does compression wood form?
11. Describe the relationship between a conifer's roots and a fungus.
12. Give specific examples of four different human uses of gymnosperms.
13. Give the source and effect on trees of sulfur dioxide, fluorides, ozone, and PAN.
14. What features do the plants of this chapter have in common?

(See page 402 for more answers.)

22-23. Reactions producing smog in some cities. Smog may be 90 percent ozone and 10 percent PAN.

Answers to Questions for Section 2.

G. *1. Most gymnosperms bear naked seeds in cones not enclosed in fruits; have needle-like leaves with thick cuticle, not blade-like leaves; are evergreen not deciduous; have xylem that lack vessels and fibers found in the woody flowering plants.

H. 2. Ginkgo: have male pollen-bearing trees separate from female trees. Conifers: seeds on cones and needle-like leaves. Cycads: look like palms, but have naked seeds on large cones.

I. 3. See figure 21-14 on page 396.

J. 4. Water and minerals move up through xylem tissue, then through xylem rays that become phloem rays which conduct water and food to and from storage cells.

*5. As a tree ages, older cells in the center of the xylem fill with resins, gums, and pigments. These substances prevent the flow of water to the heartwood. The outer sapwood is not affected and should not rot away.

CHAPTER REVIEW

The plants discussed in this chapter show great differences. However, all of them share the vascular tissues that make land life possible. Another evidence of a basic unity among the *diverse* plants is their alternation of generations. In all of the groups discussed, a haploid gametophyte alternates with a diploid sporophyte during the life cycle. In advanced plants, like the gymnosperms, the gametophyte is nutritionally dependent on the sporophyte. Development of the seed is another advanced feature of gymnosperms that contributes to *continuity of life.*

The changing classification of the tracheophytes illustrates the continuous attempt to incorporate new information into classification schemes.

The cells that make up the vascular tissues are good examples of *structures* well adapted for the *functions* they perform in maintaining *homeostasis.* Other examples include those leaf structures that prevent water loss, and roots adapted for absorption of water and soil minerals.

The formation of compression wood illustrates adaptation to changing circumstances. Mycorrhizae are a biotic relationship providing advantages to both conifers and fungi.

The existence of coniferous forests is being threatened by increasing demands for lumber, paper, and fuel. An additional threat to forests is the air pollution generated by the burning of fossil fuels. These features provide yet another example of *interactions with the environment*.

Using the Concepts

1. Find out how our national forests are managed and suggest improvements.
2. What are the major uses of coniferous trees in your community, in your state?

Unanswered Question

3. Bristlecone pines and redwoods live to be thousands of years old. What makes this possible?

VOCABULARY REVIEW

1 vascular tissue
cuticle
vein
rhizome
rhizoids
cone
sporangia
sorus
perennial
leaf gap
phloem tissue
xylem tissue
vessels
mesophyll
palisade layer
spongy layer
stomata
guard cells

2 pollen grain
pollination
seed
cotyledon
germination
resin ducts
xylem rays
phloem rays
cambium
cork
cork cambium
growth ring
heartwood
sapwood

Answers to Questions for Section 2.

K. **6.** The division of cambium produces new xylem and phloem. As the xylem expands, the phloem is destroyed, and yearly cambium growth splits the cork (bark) replacing it by cork cambium.

***7.** Fire damage, extreme conditions in climate, and rainfall pattern.

L. **8.** The needles are leaves adapted for dry conditions by the thick cuticles, stomata at the bottom of depressions, and layers of protection around the leaf veins.

***9.** Advantage: trees can make use of sunlight available for photosynthesis the year round; disadvantage: the use of water in photosynthesis and its loss by transpiration during the winter when it is even more scarce would tend to cause drying.

M. **10.** If a conifer is caused to lean, the underside of the leaning stem develops compression wood, due to unequal xylem development.

N. **11.** In a mutualistic relationship, a fungus helps the roots obtain nutrients from the soil, and the roots in turn supply amino acids to the fungus.

O. **12.** Wood as fuel, as lumber in construction of houses, and to make paper. Leaves, seeds, and parts of stems as food by Native Americans.

P. **13.** Sulfur dioxide: increases size of stomata, causing water loss and disease; also destroys chloroplasts and mesophyll. Fluoride: reduces leaf size and tree height, leads to destruction by insects. Ozone and PAN: destroy enzymes, increase respiration and decrease photosynthesis. PAN: also reduces yield and protein synthesis.

Q. **14.** The vascular tissue that makes land life possible, and their alteration of generations, with a life cycle that alternates a haploid gametophyte with a diploid sporophyte.

CHAPTER 22 TEST

Copy the number of each test item and place your answer to the right.

PART 1 Multiple Choice: Select the letter of the phrase that best completes each of the following.

d **1.** Ferns, gymnosperms, and flowering plants make up Subphylum **a.** Sphenopsida **b.** Psilopsida **c.** Lycopsida **d.** Pteropsida.

a **2.** The largest and oldest living organisms are **a.** conifers **b.** horsetails **c.** cycads **d.** ferns.

d **3.** Hollow woody xylem cells with pointed ends and thin places in their walls are called **a.** albuminous cells **b.** sieve cells **c.** vessels **d.** tracheids.

a **4.** As one progresses from mosses and ferns to gymnosperms, the gametophyte generation **a.** is reduced **b.** enlarges **c.** replaces the sporophyte **d.** beomes more independent.

a **5.** The gametophyte generation is **a.** haploid **b.** diploid **c.** polyploid **d.** pyrenoid.

c **6.** In pines, an embryonic sporophyte and stored food wrapped in covering tissue is a **a.** cone **b.** pollen grain **c.** seed **d.** spore.

c **7.** In ferns the sperm swim to the egg. In pines, the sperm gets to the egg through **a.** water **b.** air **c.** a tube **d.** the stem.

b **8.** A pine seed reaches development **a.** in a fruit **b.** on a scale **c.** in a pollen grain **d.** in a flower.

d **9.** Growth rings in pine trees may be affected by **a.** rainfall pattern **b.** fire damage **c.** air pollution **d.** all of these.

d **10.** Ozone and PAN can affect plants' processes including **a.** enzyme activity **b.** respiration **c.** photosynthesis **d.** all of these.

PART 2 Matching: Match the letter of the term in Column I with its description in Column II.

COLUMN I

a. cuticle   **d.** roots and   **f.** stomata
b. air-borne   rhizomes with   **g.** cambium
    pollen grain   xylem tissue   **h.** mesophyll
c. body of rigid   **e.** stems and roots   **i.** phloem
    cell walls   with phloem tissue   **j.** xylem

COLUMN II

d **11.** Receive water and minerals

e **12.** Transport food by cell-to-cell diffusion

c **13.** Provides support

a **14.** Prevents loss of water

f **15.** A pore through which carbon dioxide, oxygen, and water pass freely

b **16.** Carried by air currents or insects to the female pine cones

j **17.** Conducts water and dissolved minerals from soil to leaves

h **18.** Manufactures food by photosynthesis

i **19.** Conducts food from leaves to other plant tissues

g **20.** Increases diameter of stems and roots

PART 3 Completion: Complete the following.

21. Horsetails and club mosses are believed to have been common in swamps of 300 million years ago because of their remains as huge deposits of __coal__

22. The brown patches appearing on the underside of fern leaves produce __spores__

23. A leaning pine tree produces unequal xylem development with wider growth rings on the __under__side.

24. Branches embedded in the wood of a tree result in lumber with __knots__

25. The sulfur dioxide that destroys chloroplasts is produced by __burning coal and oil__

CHAPTER 23

FLOWERING PLANTS

The last chapter introduced you to plants adapted for life on dry land. The change from a water environment to a land environment required the solution of many problems. These problems included the transport of materials, body support, water loss, and gas exchange. Other problems included the absorption of nutrients, and reproduction. The vascular tissue, rigid xylem tissue, a porous cuticle, roots, and a protective jacket for gametes made survival on land possible for ferns and gymnosperms. The flowering plants display additional features that make them even more successful. All of these features equip plants to use the advantages of life on land — more sunlight, more carbon dioxide, and more oxygen.

Our study of flowering plants will involve familiar basic concepts: *unity within diversity, the continuity of life, homeostasis, the link between structure and function,* and *interaction with the environment.* We will also compare flowering plants with other plants and with fungi, protists, and monerans.

Questions we will discuss include:

- What features make flowering plants so successful?
- What causes leaves to turn different colors in the fall?
- How do trees transport water and minerals to their upper leaves?
- How can you tell the age of a twig?
- Why is a white potato considered a stem, but a sweet potato is considered a root?
- How have human beings learned to take advantage of plant growth regulators?

POPPIES

1 THE ANGIOSPERMS

General Characteristics of Flowering Plants

The general features enabling flowering plants to survive on land are shared with the gymnosperms. These features were described in Chapter 22. The production of flowers and fruits is the unique feature of the flowering plants. (See Fig. 23-1.) The cone-bearing gymnosperms produce naked seeds, often on the surface of scales. The flowering plants enclose their seeds in an additional mass of tissue, the fruit. The fruit protects the seed and its embryo. (See Fig. 23-2 on page 406.) In addition, the fruit often aids in the distribution of the mature seed.

Additional features are found in flowering plants. Their xylem has not only tracheids, but also many larger vessel cells. These features allow for more efficient transfer of water and minerals up the

OBJECTIVES FOR SECTION 1

A. Review the features that make plant life possible on land and the unique advantages of flowering plants.

B. Explain how the classification scheme shows the relationship of *monocots*, *dicots*, *gymnosperms*, and *ferns*.

C. Describe the functional relationship among angiosperm leaves, roots, and stems.

23-1. Orange tree. Flowers and fruits are unique features of angiosperms.

stem. Pollination is by insects as well as by wind. The embryo and food storage tissue of the seed are fertilized separately. This combination of features has enabled the flowering plants to invade nearly every available habitat.

Classification of Flowering Plants

Along with other vascular plants, the flowering plants are classified in Phylum Tracheophyta. With ferns and gymnosperms, they form Subphylum Pteropsida. Their class name is *Angiospermae* (an jē ə spər mē) which literally means capsule-seed, referring to the characteristic enclosed seed. The division of angiosperms into two sub-

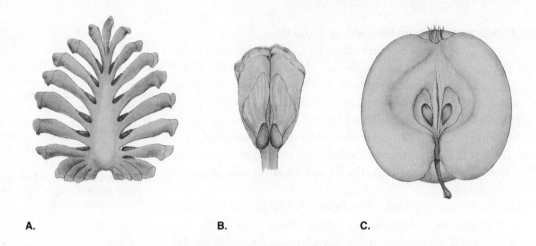

A.   B.   C.

23-2. *A., B.* *A cone and individual scale bearing seeds of a pine tree.* ***C.*** *The enclosed seeds of an apple, a flowering plant.*

classes is based on the number of cotyledons or seed leaves in their seeds. **Dicotyledonous plants *(dicots) have two cotyledons.* Monocotyledonous plants *(monocots) have only one cotyledon.*** Other features that distinguish the two groups will be mentioned later. Monocots are believed to have descended from primitive dicots.

Body Plan of the Angiosperms

The body of the angiosperm sporophyte is made up of three main organs: leaves, stems, and roots. (See Fig. 23-3.) Leaves are the main site of photosynthesis. They may also store food and minerals temporarily. Roots anchor the plant in the soil. It is through the roots that minerals are absorbed and the water diffuses into the plant. Some roots also store food.

Stems produce leaves and display them in such a way that they are exposed to the sun. Stems may also store or even manufacture food. Some stems produce flowers. Stems connect leaves and roots. Water and minerals are conducted from the roots through stems to the leaves. There the water and minerals are used to make food. Food is conducted from the leaves through the stem to the roots and other parts of the plant. In these areas, food is either used by the plant or stored.

Stems may be herbaceous or woody. *Herbaceous stems* are usually soft and green with little or no woody tissue. *Most herbaceous stems live for one season, that is, they are* **annual stems.** *A* **perennial structure** *lives for several years.* An annual stem may have a perennial root. The stem dies back each year and a new stem is produced the next growing season.

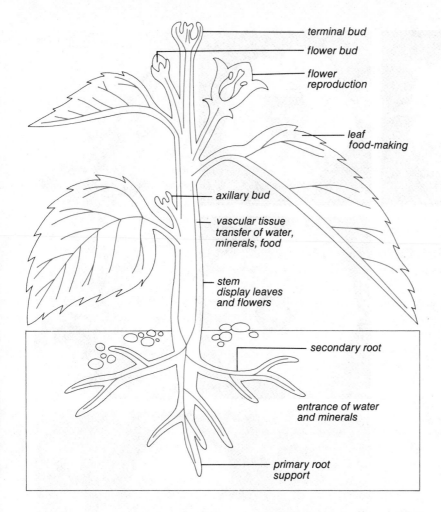

terminal bud

flower bud

flower
reproduction

leaf
food-making

axillary bud

vascular tissue
transfer of water,
minerals, food

stem
display leaves
and flowers

secondary root

entrance of water
and minerals

primary root
support

Answers to Questions for Section 1.

A. **1.** Vascular tissue, rigid xylem tissue, a porous cuticle, roots, and a protective jacket for gametes.

2. In addition to features shared with gymnosperms (see question 1): flowers, and fruits that enclose the seeds and aid in their distribution.

B. ***3.** Subphylum *Pteropsida*: vascular plants. Class *Felicineae* (Ferns): true leaves, but have rhizoids and underground stems. Class *Gymnospermae* (Gymnosperms): bear seeds in cones, true roots, stems, and leaves. Class *Angiospermae*: flowers, and seeds in fruits. Subclass *Monocotyledoneae*: one seed-leaf (cotyledon). Subclass *Dicotyledoneae*: two seed-leaves (cotyledons).

C. **4.** Leaves: carry out photosynthesis that provides food for whole plant. Roots: anchor plant and absorb water and minerals for photosynthesis and whole plant's nutrition. Stem: produces and supports leaves, and carries materials between them and the roots.

23-3. The main parts of a flowering plant.

Woody stems are hard, thick, and long-lived. *If a woody stem branches only at some distance above the ground, the plant forms a* **tree**. *If several stems of similar size occur at or near ground level the plant forms a* **shrub**.

QUESTIONS FOR SECTION 1

1. What features in non-flowering plants make life possible on land?
2. What are the parts of flowering plants and what advantage does each offer?
3. Using information from this and the previous chapters outline Subphylum Pteropsida with the distinguishing feature of each unit.
4. What are the general functions of leaves, roots, and stems? How do they relate to each other?
5. Define and distinguish between herbaceous and woody stems, annual and perennial plants, and trees and shrubs.

5. Herbaceous stems are soft and green, with little woody tissue, and are usually annuals. Woody stems are hard, thick, and long-lived. Annual plants: live one year. Perennial plants: live several years. Trees have woody stems that branch only at some distance from the ground. Shrubs have several stems of similar size at or near ground level.

CHAPTER INVESTIGATION

There are six species of plants shown here.

A. What characteristics do these six species have in common?

B. What observable features would you use to organize or classify these species into several groups?

C. How many main groups would you make of the six species if you were trying to classify them according to ancestral relationships?

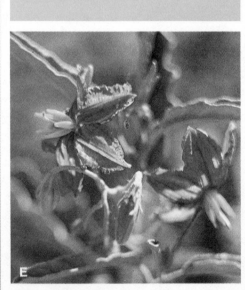

2 FLOWERS

Floral Parts

The unique feature of the angiosperms is the flower. *The flower is a highly modified stem whose leaves are specialized for sexual reproduction.* Parts of the flower become the fruits and seeds that continue the species. Flowers, and especially fruits and seeds, form an important food supply for the many animals that eat them.

While flowers of different plant species vary widely, all share certain basic features. *The enlarged portion of flower stalk to which all floral parts are attached is the* **receptacle.** The outer protective parts of the flower bud are the *sepals* (sē pəls). They are often green and leaf-like. *The entire whorl of sepals is called the* **calyx** (kā liks). (See Fig. 23-4.) As a flower bud opens, its colored petals are exposed. Some insects are attracted to petals by their color nectar glands at their bases. *The entire whorl of petals is called the* **corolla.** In some plants, like tulips, sepals and petals have the same color.

The next innermost whorl consists of **stamens,** *the male parts of a flower.* Each stamen has a slender *filament,* which supports an anther. The *anther* produces pollen grains. The female parts are contained in the pistil. *The* **pistil** *lies in the center of the flower and is composed of an ovary, a style, and a stigma.* The enlarged ovary is attached to the receptacle. Inside the ovary is the *ovule* which later de-

OBJECTIVES FOR SECTION 2

D. Describe the parts of a complete flower and give the functions of each.
E. Give the advantages of separate *staminate* and *pistillate* flowers.
F. List the factors that initiate flowering.
G. Describe the steps in development from blossoming of a flower to the germination and growth of the seedling.

Sepals protect the inner parts of the flower bud.

23-4. *The parts of a complete flower.*

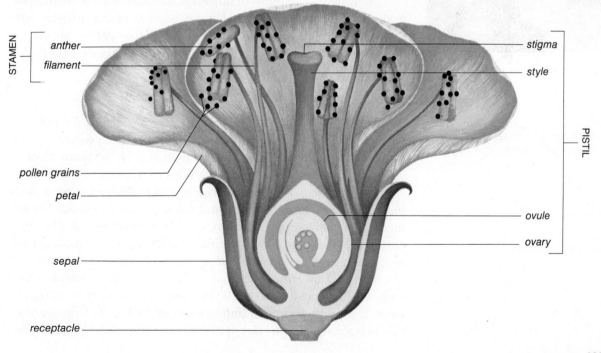

23-5. *(top) azalea, a dicot; (bottom) trillum, a monocot.*

Regular flowers are radially symmetrical. Irregular flowers are bilaterally symmetrical.

velops into a seed. The ovary becomes a fruit. Extending from the ovary is the *style* which supports the sticky stigma. The *stigma* receives the pollen grains produced by the stamens.

Diversity in Flowering Plants

A flower with sepals, petals, stamens, and a pistil is a **complete flower.** Some flowers are *incomplete,* that is, they lack some of these parts. The flowers of wheat and many other grasses lack petals. But these flowers have stamens and a pistil in the same flower. Some incomplete flowers, such as those of oak trees and corn, lack either stamens or pistils. The tassel flowers of corn have stamens but no pistils. The flowers in the corn ear have pistils but no stamens. *Plants with separate staminate and pistillate flowers on the same plant are said to be* **monoecious** (mə nē shəs). *Plants which have staminate and pistillate flowers on separate plants are* **dioecious** (dī ē shəs). Willows and cottonwoods are dioecious. Of course, dioecious plants must be cross-pollinated for fertilization to take place.

Other variations occur. The petals of some flowers are separate. In others, such as the bluebell, they join to form a tube. The shapes of some flowers, like those of buffalobur, are regular. Others, like those of snapdragons and beans, are irregular. Plants differ in how flowers are grouped. Sunflowers and daisies group flowers in heads. They even have two kinds of flowers in each head: disk flowers and ray flowers.

Many of the variations in flowers and fruits are used in the classification of flowering plants. Dicotyledonous plants usually have flower parts in fours and fives or multiples of four or five. Monocotyledonous plants usually have flower parts in threes or multiples of three. (See Fig. 23-5.)

Initiation of Flowering

What causes a plant to stop producing leaf buds and start producing flower buds? In some species it seems to depend on the stage of the plant's maturity. In others, it may be the quantity of reserve food. In many species the stimulus for flowering is external.

TEMPERATURE Temperature is involved in the flowering of many biennial plants. Beets, carrots, and cabbages are biennials. The following are characteristics of biennials. They develop a short stem, a cluster of leaves, and a food-storing root during the first growing season. The tops die in winter. During the next season flowers are produced. But flowering does not occur during the second season without the exposure to cold winter weather between growing seasons. If only the terminal bud is exposed to 1-10°C temperatures, flowering can occur. In fact, if a cold-treated biennial is grafted to a non-cold-treated one, they both flower. This suggests the involvement of a flower-promoting substance, florigen, that travels in the stem.

LIGHT   Another factor that affects flowering is the change in daily periods of light and darkness. *The dependence of flowering on length of day or night is called* **photoperiodism** (fōt ō *pir* ē əd iz əm). Many flowering plants can be classified according to night length requirements. Long night (short day) plants include chrysanthemums, poinsettias, asters, ragweeds, and soybeans. They usually wait for the longer nights of late summer to bloom. Other long night plants, such as tulips and daffodils, produce flowers in the early spring.

Short night (long day) plants include the iris and such vegetables as radishes, lettuce, and potatoes. These plants usually flower in the late spring and early summer.

While night length determines flowering in many plants, they are often described as if day length is the determining factor.

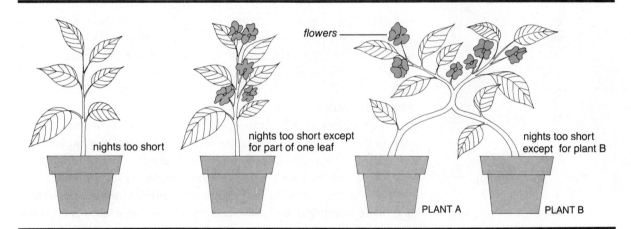

flowers

nights too short

nights too short except for part of one leaf

nights too short except for plant B

PLANT A   PLANT B

Indian grass and forsythia will not flower if nights are too long or too short. Some plants flower under any night length. They include garden beans, carnations, cotton, roses, sunflowers, tomatoes, and dandelions.

Commercial florists make use of photoperiods. With artificial light they manipulate flowering times of certain plant species.

Photoperiodism is believed to be controlled by a pigment, phytochrome. Phytochrome responds to red and infrared light by stimulating the production of florigen which stimulates flowering. (See Fig. 23-6.)

23-6. If just one part of a leaf of a long night plant is subjected to a long night, the entire plant flowers. If a long night plant exposed to a long night is grafted to the same type plant which was exposed to a short night, both plants flower. This suggests that flowering is started by a substance produced in leaves and conducted to the flower buds.

Flower Reproduction

All of the structures of a flower are parts of the sporophyte. Some of the floral parts contribute to the formation of gametophytes. As you know, gametophytes produce gametes which unite, producing

Knowledge of the details of flower reproduction depended on the use of the microscope.

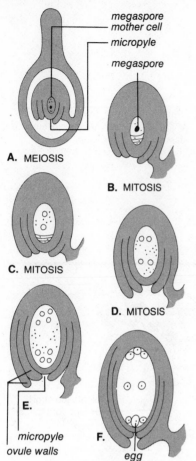

A. MEIOSIS

B. MITOSIS

C. MITOSIS

D. MITOSIS

E.

micropyle
ovule walls

F.

egg

megaspore
mother cell

micropyle

megaspore

23-7. *The development of a flower before fertilization.*

the zygote. The zygote is the next generation sporophyte. Thus, alternation of generations occurs in flowering plants. The male gametophyte is hardly visible. The female gametophyte is imbedded within the flower.

Ovule Formation

Various changes occur within the ovary at the base of the pistil. One or more ovules are produced in each ovary. Each ovule is attached inside the ovary wall and receives nourishment from it. Two layers of protective tissue form outside the ovule. Only a pore, the *micropyle,* remains as an opening in the two layers. Inside the ovule a large diploid *megaspore mother cell* undergoes meiosis. Figure 23-7 illustrates the process. Four haploid *megaspores* form, three of which die. The remaining megaspore divides by mitosis to form eight haploid nuclei within the enlarged megaspore. Three of these nuclei move toward the micropyle. Another three migrate to the opposite end of the megaspore. Two remain near the center. Thus, the female gametophyte consists of several cells within the ovule. One of the cells at the micropylar end is the egg, or female gamete. The remaining cells die after fertilization occurs.

Pollen Formation

Each anther contains *microspore mother cells.* As the anther grows, each of these cells divides by meiosis and produces four haploid *microspores.* (See Fig. 23-8.) Each microspore divides by mitosis, but no walls separate the two nuclei. The smaller one is the *generative nucleus.* The larger one is the *tube nucleus.* **The entire structure consisting of generative nucleus and tube nucleus is a pollen grain.** The pollen grain is an immature male gametophyte.

23-8 THE DEVELOPMENT OF A POLLEN GRAIN

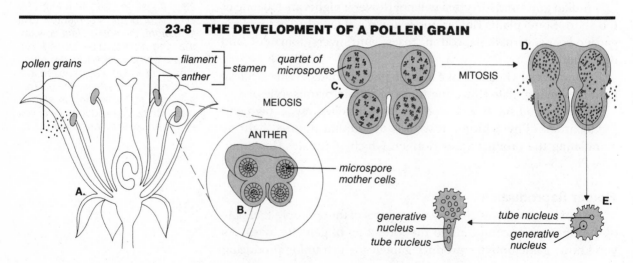

pollen grains

filament

anther

stamen

quartet of microspores

MEIOSIS

C.

MITOSIS

D.

ANTHER

microspore mother cells

A.

B.

generative nucleus

tube nucleus

tube nucleus

generative nucleus

E.

When the pollen grains have formed, the anther splits open and releases them. The generative nucleus eventually divides to form two sperm nuclei.

The female gametophyte containing the eight cells is often called the embryo sac. See Fig. 23-7.

Pollination and the Pollen Tube

The transfer of pollen from an anther to a stigma is **pollination**. *Pollen may be transferred to the stigma within the same flower or to the stigma of any other flower* on the same plant by the process of **self-pollination**. *If pollen is transferred to a stigma on a different plant it is* **cross-pollination**. Cross-pollination results in greater variation in the offspring. It is also required for high production in some species. Cross-pollination requires transfer by wind, water, insects, or birds. Some flowers are adapted for pollen transfer by insects.

The stigma of a pistil is often covered with a sticky substance. This substance holds pollen grains that are transferred to it. Substances in the stigma stimulate growth of a tube from the pollen grain. (See Fig. 23-9.) This pollen tube pushes through the stigma and style into the ovary. Finally it reaches the micropyle of the ovule. As the pollen tube grows it receives nourishment from tissues of the pistil. The generative nucleus moves into the pollen tube. As it does so, it divides by mitosis. This division produces two sperm nuclei. The pollen grain with its tube and two sperm nuclei are the mature male gametophyte.

Fertilization

Once the pollen tube penetrates the female gametophyte, it ruptures and discharges the sperm. One of the sperm fertilizes the egg. The resulting diploid zygote divides many times by mitosis and becomes a multicellular embryo. The other sperm unites with the two

23-9 FERTILIZATION AND DEVELOPMENT OF FRUIT, SEED, AND SEEDLING

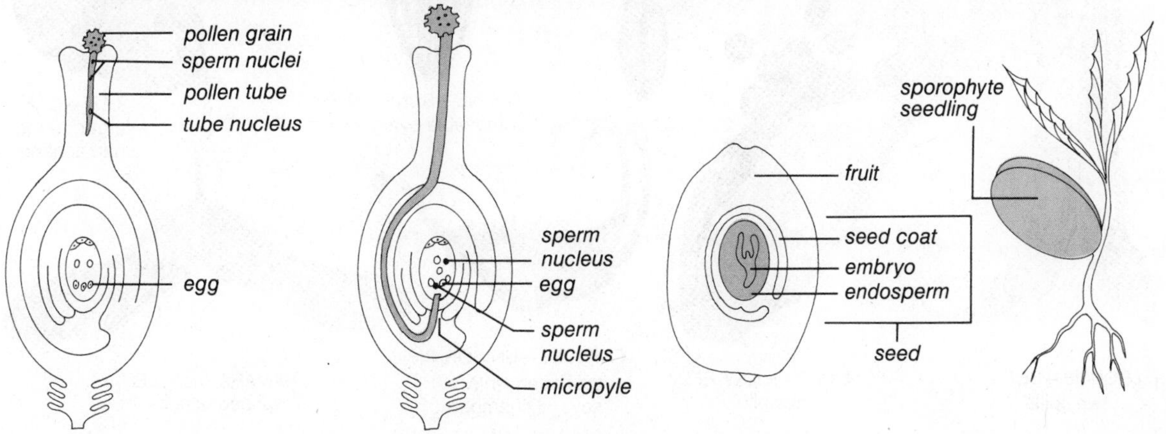

pollen grain
sperm nuclei
pollen tube
tube nucleus
egg

sperm nucleus
egg
sperm nucleus
micropyle

fruit
sporophyte seedling
seed coat
embryo
endosperm
seed

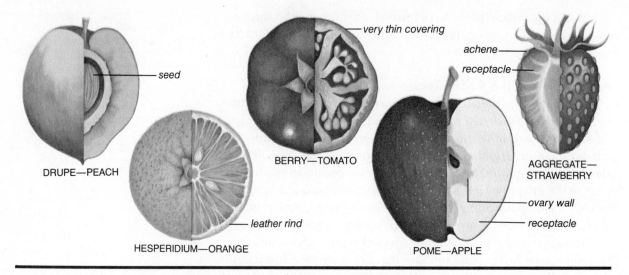

DRUPE—PEACH
seed

HESPERIDIUM—ORANGE
leather rind

BERRY—TOMATO
very thin covering

POME—APPLE
ovary wall
receptacle

AGGREGATE—STRAWBERRY
achene
receptacle

23-10. *Some types of fleshy fruits.*

23-11. *Some types of dry fruits.*

nuclei at the center of the female gametophyte. This triploid nucleus undergoes repeated mitotic division and forms the **endosperm,** *the embryo's food supply. The two fertilizations that form the zygote and the endosperm are called* **double fertilization.** Double fertilization occurs only in the flowering plants.

From Flower to Fruit

After double fertilization is complete, sepals, petals, and stamens quickly wither. The ovary swells and the ovule grows. As the ovary ripens it is known as a fruit. *A* **fruit** *is a mature ovary.* See Figures 23-10 and 11 for variations in fruits. The fruit contains one or more seeds. **Seeds** *are mature ovules.* Various kinds of fruits are use-

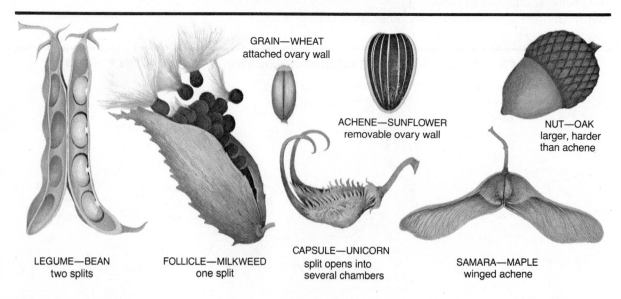

LEGUME—BEAN
two splits

FOLLICLE—MILKWEED
one split

GRAIN—WHEAT
attached ovary wall

ACHENE—SUNFLOWER
removable ovary wall

CAPSULE—UNICORN
split opens into several chambers

NUT—OAK
larger, harder than achene

SAMARA—MAPLE
winged achene

ful in spreading or dispersing the seeds. Seed dispersal reduces the intense competition that occurs if all the seeds grow in the same area. Figure 23-12 shows the structure of a typical dicot seed, the bean. All structures inside the seed coat make up the embryo sporophyte. Removal of the seed coat and separation of the two cotyledons exposes the tiny leaves and tip bud which form the *epicotyl*. On the other side of the cotyledon scar is the fingerlike *hypocotyl*, the embryo stem. At the tip of the hypocotyl is the radicle, the embryo root. In most dicots the endosperm has been used by the time the seed matures. The cotyledons provide food for the developing embryo until it is able to photosynthesize. The cotyledons are part of the embryo; the endospore is not.

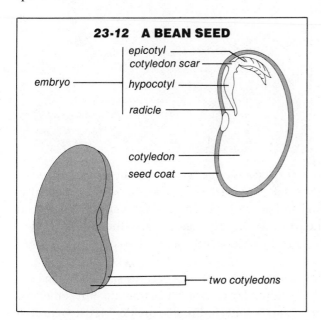

23-12   A BEAN SEED

embryo
epicotyl
cotyledon scar
hypocotyl
radicle
cotyledon
seed coat
two cotyledons

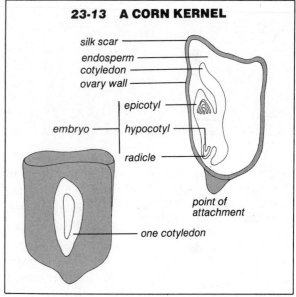

23-13   A CORN KERNEL

silk scar
endosperm
cotyledon
ovary wall
epicotyl
embryo
hypocotyl
radicle
point of attachment
one cotyledon

Figure 23-13 shows the structure of a kernel of corn, a monocot. Here the bulk of the food storage tissue is endosperm. The single cotyledon digests the food stored in the endosperm. This process makes the food available to the developing embryo.

Growth and Differentiation

After a period of dormancy, the seed may be stimulated to germinate. Dormancy may last from a few weeks to many years. When it germinates, the seed absorbs water. The foods stored in the seed are digested. The resulting nutrients are used to make new cells in the embryo. The radicle grows down into the soil. Here, it develops into the root system. In some plants, such as the garden bean, the hypocotyl lengthens and lifts the cotyledons above the soil's surface. (See

23-14 A GERMINATING BEAN SEED

the cotyledons are raised into the air

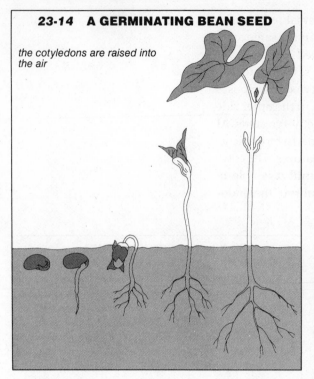

23-15 A GERMINATING CORN KERNEL

the single cotyledon remains in the ground

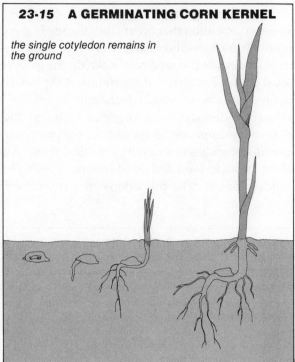

Fig. 23-14.) The two cotyledons of pea seeds and the single cotyledon of corn remain in the soil. (See Fig. 23-15.) The hypocotyl and epicotyl push above the soil and develop stem and leaf structures. Water and minerals enter the roots. When exposed to light, the leaves develop chlorophyll and begin to photosynthesize. The cotyledons wither and die.

As the seedling grows, different cells become specialized in performing different functions. That is, they differentiate. But some cells always remain meristematic and continue to divide. Meristematic tissue is found at the growing tips of roots and stems. Vascular cambium of some stems and some roots also contains meristematic tissue, so does the base of grass leaves.

QUESTIONS FOR SECTION 2

1. List the parts of a complete flower and tell how the structure of each part helps carry out its function.
2. Of what advantage is it to a plant species to be dioecious? monoecious?
3. Explain how temperature and night length affect flowering.
4. Describe each stage in the development of a bean plant from the opening of the flower to the development of the seedling.
5. What are the differences between a bean seed and a corn kernel?

Answers to Questions for Section 2.

D. 1. Sepals: outer protective parts. Petals: color attracts insects needed for pollination. Stamens: support the anther, which bears pollen grains. Pistil: supported by style, receives pollen; ovary at base contains ovule, after fertilization, ovary becomes fruit and ovule, seed.

E. *2. A dioecious species, must be cross-pollinated, that insures likelihood of variety, which is better for survival of species. A monoecious species may be cross-pollinated, or there may be self-pollination, giving more certain transport of sperm to eggs.

F. 3. A biennial will not flower in its second season unless exposed to a cold winter between growing seasons. Short night (long day) plants flower in late spring and early summer, while long night (short day) plants bloom in late summer.

G. *4. Ovary contains ovules made of several cells, one of which is egg cell. Fertilization by sperm from pollen produce both the zygote and the embryo's food supply, the endosperm. The ovary ripens to bean pod and ovules into seeds. Dispersion of seeds may produce germination.

5. Compare Figure 23-12 with 23-13.

⬛ 3 LEAVES

Growth and Functioning of Leaves

As cells of the shoot tip divide, some cells become part of the stem. Other cells become leaf tissues. A leaf begins as a slender rod of dividing cells. The leaf shape is determined by the rate of cell division and the growth of cells. Differentiation produces an upper and lower epidermis, and the mesophyll layer between them as shown in Figure 23-16. The mesophyll includes one or more layers of long palisade cells, and some spongy mesophyll. The palisade and mesophyll cells contain chloroplasts. Within the chloroplasts, photosynthesis occurs. Air spaces among cells of the spongy layer are in contact with the atmosphere through the stomata. Running through the mesophyll are bundles of vascular tissue called veins. The veins are connected to the vascular tissue of the stem. The xylem of veins brings water to the leaves from the roots. The phloem of the veins carries the products of photosynthesis from leaves to stems, roots, flowers, or fruits. The fibers in veins provide some support to the leaves. This exposes them to the rays of the sun and the gases of the atmosphere. Most support is provided by the turgidity of leaf cells. **Turgor** *is the firmness in cells due to water held in them by osmotic pressure.*

OBJECTIVES FOR SECTION 3

H. Describe the different tissues in a leaf and give the function of each.
I. Explain how stomata help maintain homeostasis in leaves.
J. Describe various types, venation, and arrangements of leaves.
K. Describe the falling and changes in color of leaves.

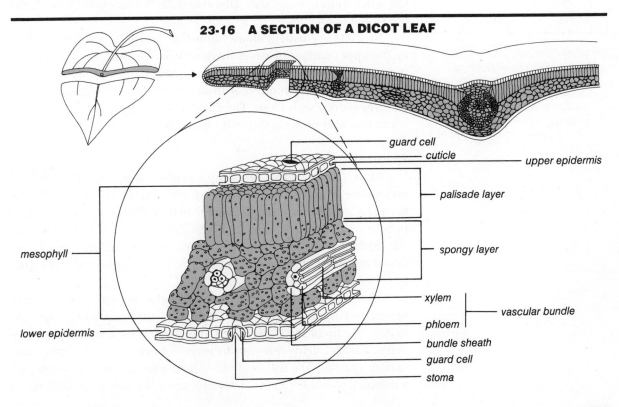

23-16 A SECTION OF A DICOT LEAF

- guard cell
- cuticle
- upper epidermis
- palisade layer
- spongy layer
- mesophyll
- xylem
- vascular bundle
- phloem
- lower epidermis
- bundle sheath
- guard cell
- stoma

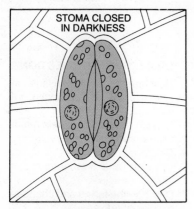

STOMA CLOSED
IN DARKNESS

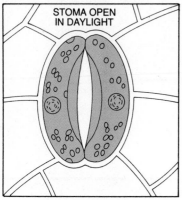

STOMA OPEN
IN DAYLIGHT

23-17. In darkness, carbon dioxide builds up in the guard cells. When daylight returns, photosynthesis uses that carbon dioxide. Also, potassium ions enter the guard cells. As a result, water also enters the cells. The cells separate, and the stoma opens.

Gas Exchange

Plants carry on both photosynthesis and respiration. Thus gas exchange in leaves includes the intake of both carbon dioxide and oxygen and the release of excesses of both gases. Most live plant cells are close to the plant's surface. (The inner cells of large plant parts are not alive.) The loose packing of parenchyma cells allows them to be in direct contact with the air. Furthermore, plant cells respire at rates much lower than those of animals. Thus simple diffusion supplies adequate gas exchange and maintains homeostasis.

Stomata

Stomata in the leaf epidermis allow gas exchange between leaf air spaces and the atmosphere. They are usually open in daylight and closed in darkness. The size of each stoma is controlled by turgor changes in the surrounding guard cells. In darkness, carbon dioxide accumulates in guard cells. Unlike other epidermal cells, guard cells contain chloroplasts. In daylight, photosynthesis decreases the carbon dioxide concentration in guard cells. The concentration of carbon dioxide affects the movement of potassium ions into and out of the cells. This in turn affects their osmotic pressure. Movement of water from neighboring cells into guard cells increases turgor and causes the outer walls to bulge out. This also pulls the inner walls apart and the stoma opens. (See Fig. 23-17.)

Stomata are usually more numerous on the lower surface than on the upper surface of leaves. In desert plants, stomata are often few in number or sunken into the surface. Dead hairs on the leaf surface around the stomata interfere with air currents and reflect heat. These features reduce water loss. The cuticle coating the epidermis retards water loss and protects the cells against invasion by pathogens.

Diversity in Leaves

Many leaves consist of a simple blade and petiole. *The **blade** is the usually broad, flat part of the leaf.* (See Fig. 23-18.) *The stalk connecting the blade with the stem is the **petiole.*** When the blade lacks a petiole and is attached directly to the stem, the leaf is said to be sessile. Some leaves have small leaf-like outgrowths called *stipules* (stip ūlz) at the base of the petiole. Stipules may be thorns as in black locust or spines as in cactus.

The network of veins may be arranged in several ways. In most monocots parallel veins of about equal size run straight from the base to near the tip of the blade. The parallel veins are connected by tiny veins. Parallel veins are seen in leaves of onions, lilies, irises, and various grasses. The leaves of dicots have a few prominent veins and a network of smaller veins. They are said to be net-veined. (Refer to

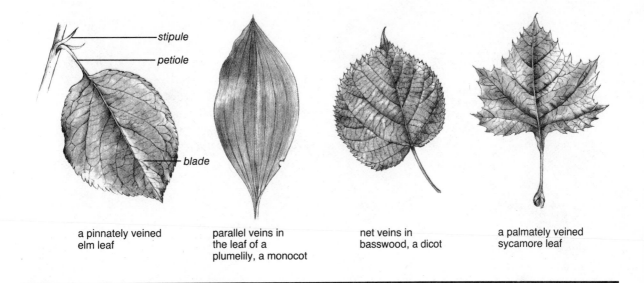

a pinnately veined
elm leaf

parallel veins in
the leaf of a
plumelily, a monocot

net veins in
basswood, a dicot

a palmately veined
sycamore leaf

stipule
petiole
blade

Fig. 23-18.) When small veins branch from one main vein the veins are pinnate. Examples are elm and apple trees. (Refer to Fig. 23-18.) If the veins spread like fingers from a hand the veins are palmate. Examples are maple and sycamore trees. (Refer to Fig. 23-18.)

SIMPLE AND COMPOUND LEAVES   A *simple leaf* has a single blade. A leaf whose blade is divided into several separate flat portions is a *compound leaf.* Each portion appears to be a separate blade. To distinguish between compound and simple leaves one examines the base of the leaf. Buds appear only at the base of a leaf, never at the base of leaflets. A *leaflet* is a separated portion of a leaf blade. Like veins, leaflets can also be arranged pinnately or palmately. (See Fig. 23-19.)

LEAF MODIFICATIONS   Leaves are modified in various ways. The petioles of celery and rhubarb leaves are adapted to store food. Some leaves are modified to coil around a supporting object and are called tendrils. **Tendrils *are elongated petioles, veins, stipules, or stems.*** The tendrils of cucumbers and garden peas are modified leaves. The leaves of Venus's flytrap are able to trap and digest insects. The leaves of poinsettia are modified to form non-green structures around the flowers.

LEAF ARRANGEMENT   Leaves are usually arranged on a stem with either one, two, or three leaves at a node. *A* **node** *is a portion of stem that produces leaves or branch stems. The space from one node to the next is an* **internode.** With one leaf at each node the leaves are arranged alternately. With two leaves per node leaves are arranged oppositely. With three or more leaves per node leaves are arranged in a whorl. (See Fig. 23-20 on page 420.)

23-18. *Diversity in simple leaves.*

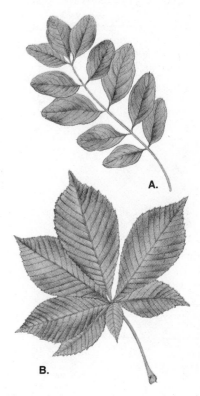

A.

B.

23-19. A. *Pinnately compound leaf.*
B. *Palmately compound leaf.*

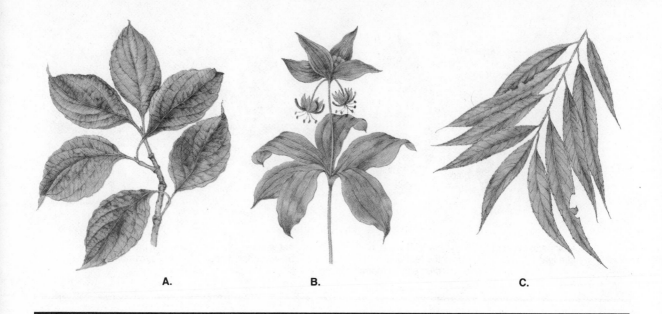

A.   B.   C.

23-20. **A.** *Opposite arrangement of leaves of a dogwood.* **B.** *Whorled arrangement of leaves in an Indian cucumber root.* **C.** *Alternate arrangement of leaves in a willow branch.*

Leaves are usually arranged with little overlapping. Thus there is little shading from their neighbors.

Falling Leaves

In many flowering plants the leaves and fruits fall off the plant. They separate from the plant at the base of the leaf petiole or fruit stalk in a region called the *abscission zone.* (See Fig. 23-21.) In this zone the substance holding the cells together is dissolved by enzymes. Wind and rain complete the separation of the leaf from the stem. A protective layer of cells containing suberin forms on the stem side of the abscission zone. Suberin keeps the plant from drying out.

23-21. *The abscission zone of a leaf is near its attachment to the stem.*

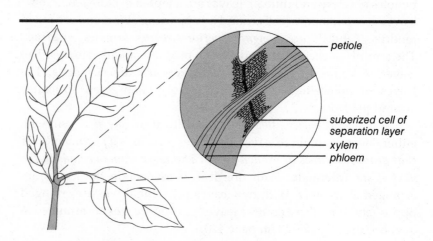

petiole

suberized cell of
separation layer

xylem

phloem

23-22. The brilliant display of colors are exposed in fall when chloro-phyll disappears.

Autumn Colors

The splendor of autumn colors begins with chemical changes in leaves. (See Fig. 23-22.) The days grow shorter, the nights get cooler, and the leaves get older. Chemical changes result in chlorophyll be-ing decomposed faster than it is made. Now the yellow and yellow-orange pigments appear. They have been present all summer but were hidden by the green of the chlorophyll. With the chlorophyll gone they become visible. If fall days are sunny and the nights cool, sugar may accumulate in the leaf. There it reacts with various miner-als to produce the red and purple pigments. The brown color is due to the death of tissues and the production of tannins inside the leaf.

QUESTIONS FOR SECTION 3

1. Explain how each internal tissue of leaves contributes to homeostasis.
2. Describe causes of opening and closing of stomata and explain how they help maintain homeostasis.
3. Describe and give examples of different shapes, venation, and arrangement of leaves.
4. What are the events involved in the falling of leaves?
5. What are the factors that lead to the varieties of colors in autumn leaves?

4 ROOTS

Growth of Roots

OBJECTIVES FOR SECTION 4

L. Describe the development of primary and secondary root tissues.
M. Explain how water and minerals enter roots from the soil.
N. Give the advantages of different types of root systems.

Water and minerals enter a plant through its roots. In the meristem near the tip of the root new cells are continuously produced by mitosis. Follow Figure 23-23 as you read this description. *The cells produced toward the tip of the root become part of the* **root cap.** The root cap protects the inner cells from damage. Above the meristematic region cells grow in length, pushing the root tip through the soil. As it is pushed between soil particles, the outer cells of the cap are rubbed off. These smashed cells leave a slimy coating on soil particles. This coating lubricates the soil for easier penetration by the root. Also, root tip cells give off carbon dioxide during cellular metabolism. This substance reacts with water in the soil. The resulting product is carbonic acid. This weak acid dissolves minerals in the soil. This makes it easier for the root tip to move forward.

When the cells have reached full size they differentiate. Outer cells become the epidermis which forms a protective layer one cell thick. The epidermis also absorbs water and minerals. Some of the epidermal cells form extensions that grow out among soil particles. These *epidermal extensions, called* **root hairs,** *increase the surface area through which water and minerals enter the plant.* Other cells become the cortex, endodermis, pericycle, and vascular tissue. (See Fig. 23-24.)

The cells of the cortex are fitted for food storage. These cells are round and loosely packed. Cells of the endodermis are thick and waxy. They control the movement of materials between the cortex and the center of the root. Cells of the pericycle form secondary roots and some other tissues. Such secondary roots push through the endodermis, cortex, and epidermis out into the soil. The center of the root is composed of xylem. Xylem conducts water and dissolved minerals through the stem to the leaves. Near the xylem are patches of phloem. Phloem conducts food from the leaves and stem to the living cells of the root.

Secondary Growth of Roots

The tissues just described are primary tissues. *Primary tissue is composed of cells produced by meristem at the tips of roots and stems. Secondary tissues originate from the vascular cambium or cork cambium.* The shape of the vascular cambium in roots is shown in Figure 23-24. It is located between the arms of primary xylem and each patch of primary phloem. Parts of the pericycle connect the arcs to form a continuous ring of vascular cambium. In time the cambium takes on a circular form.

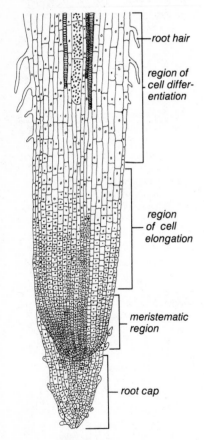

root hair

region of cell differentiation

region of cell elongation

meristematic region

root cap

23-23. *The regions of a root tip.*

ADVENTITIOUS ROOTS   Roots may also originate in meristems of stems or leaves. A mature corn plant produces many roots from the base of the stem. Some climbing plants produce roots on the sides of stems. These roots attach to brick walls or the stems of supporting plants. Many plants produce roots if the stems are placed in damp soil or water. *Roots that are formed by meristems in the stems or leaves of plants are called* **adventitious** (ad ven *tish* əs) **roots.** (See Fig. 23-25.) In some plants, roots form buds which develop adventitious shoots.

Transport of Minerals

Both water and minerals are generally transported in the xylem. Some minerals enter the root with water that diffuses into root hairs. Minerals can enter even when their concentration is greater in root cells than in soil water. Thus active transport must be involved requiring both oxygen and energy.

All the elements used by plants are taken up in inorganic form. The essential ions are nitrate, ammonium, dihydrogen phosphate, potassium, and calcium.

Plants conserve minerals. Prior to the loss of a leaf, some of its minerals enter the phloem tissue. Here they are transported to younger leaves or to the tips of the stem, root, or fruit.

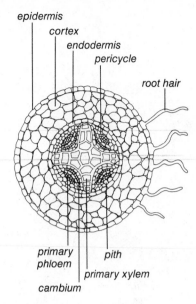

23-24. *A cross-section of root in the region of differentiation.*

23-25. *Adventitious roots.* **A.** *Poison ivy.* **B.** *English ivy.* **C.** *Corn.*

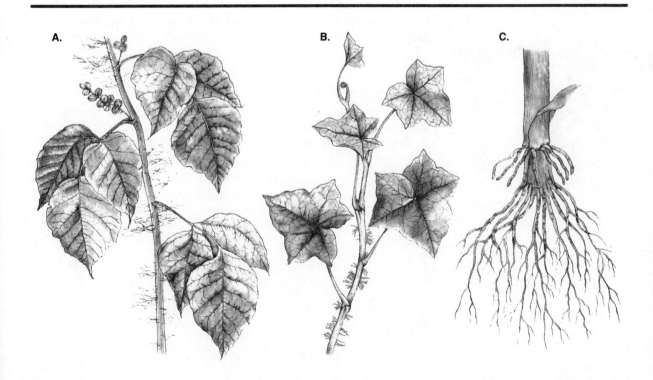

A.

B.

C.

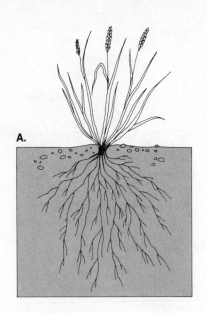

A.

Diversity in Roots

Roots are a continuation of the stem of a plant but differ from them in several ways. Roots do not have nodes and internodes. The tips of young roots develop root hairs. Roots differ from stems also in the arrangement of internal tissues.

Root systems develop as one of two general types: fibrous and tap-root. (See Fig. 23-26.) *The **fibrous root system** is composed of many slender main roots which undergo much branching.*

Fibrous root systems have tremendous numbers of roots and root hairs. A single rye plant is estimated to have over 13 billion roots and about 15 billion root hairs. It is mainly through the surface of root hairs that water and minerals enter a plant. Thus this surface is vital to maintaining homeostasis in the plant. The fibrous root systems of grasses help prevent the erosion of soil by wind or water.

*In **tap root systems** smaller roots branch out from the primary root.* Tap roots often become fleshy and store food. Water and minerals enter the plant through small branching roots connected to the tap root. Examples of plants with tap roots are beets, dandelions, and carrots.

MYCORRHIZAE   Like conifers, many flowering plants have soil fungi associated with their roots. These mycorrhizae are of mutual advantage to both organisms as explained in Chapter 22.

THE NITROGEN CYCLE   The role of legumes and other plants in the nitrogen cycle has been described in Chapter 2. You may wish to review that section now.

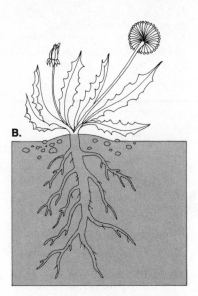

B.

23-26. *A. The fibrous root system of a barley. B. The taproot system of a dandelion.*

QUESTIONS FOR SECTION 4

1. Describe the development of primary and secondary root tissues.
2. Contrast the entrance of water and minerals into roots.
3. Describe different types of root systems and give advantages of each.

Answers to Questions for Section 4.

L. **1.** Primary root tissues are produced by the meristem near the tip. Cells produced toward the tip become part of the protective root cap, and outer cells become epidermis, some of which have extensions or root hairs, adapted for absorbing water and minerals from the soil. Secondary root tissues originate from vascular cambium or cork cambium.

M. **2.** Water enters roots by diffusion, but for minerals, active transport is involved.

N. **3.** A fibrous root system is made up of many slender main roots that undergo much branching. It has the advantage of tremendous surface area for absorption of water and minerals. A tap root system is made up of a primary root from which smaller roots branch out. Their advantage is that they may become fleshy and store food, while water and minerals still can enter through the branches.

5 STEMS

Primary Growth of the Stem

After a plant develops a root system its shoot system begins to grow. A plant's shoot consists of stems, leaves, and reproductive structures. The stem connects the leaves and the roots.

The meristem at the tip of the shoot produces new cells. These cells lengthen and differentiate into epidermis, cortex, and vascular tissues. Epidermal cells fit tightly together and inhibit water loss and invasion by fungi and insects. The waxy cuticle secreted by the epidermis also protects against drying and infection.

Inside the epidermis is the cortex. It strengthens the stem and stores food. The pith at the center of the stem also stores food.

The primary vascular tissues in an herbaceous dicot stem occur as a ring of vascular bundles. (See Fig. 23-27.) Each bundle contains both xylem and phloem. The xylem occupies the part of the bundle toward the center of the stem. The phloem lies toward the epidermis. Each bundle also contains some fiber cells which provide support.

The monocot stem consists of an outer rind filled with pith. (Refer to Fig. 23-27.) The rind provides support for the stem. Scattered throughout the pith are vascular bundles. Each bundle is surrounded by thick-walled cells that provide support. The phloem is nearer the outside of the bundle. Companion cells are positioned near sieve tubes. Xylem tracheids and four vessel cells make up the inside of the bundle. One or more of these vessels may be crushed and leave an air

OBJECTIVES FOR SECTION 5

O. Describe the primary and secondary growths of stems.

P. Define *bud* and describe its development.

Q. Explain how water and food are transferred and gases exchanged in stems and stem tissues.

R. Describe various types of vegetative reproduction in stems and their advantages.

23-27. *A. The cross-section of a corn stem. Vascular bundles in monocots are scattered through out the pith of the stem. B. The cross-section of a sunflower stem. Vascular bundles in herbaceous dicots are arranged in a circle in the stem.*

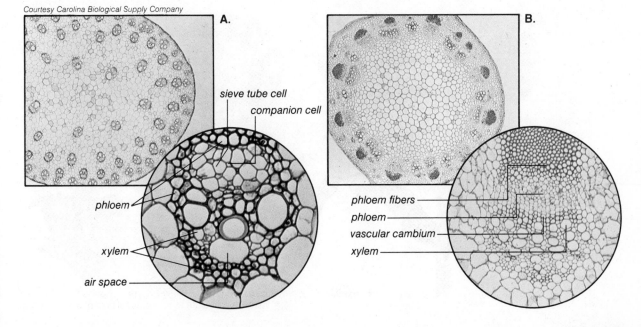

A.

sieve tube cell

companion cell

phloem

xylem

air space

B.

phloem fibers

phloem

vascular cambium

xylem

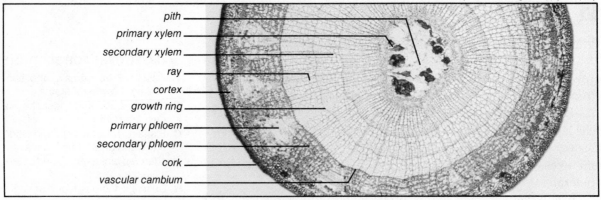

23-28. *Cross-section of a woody dicot stem.*

23-29. *A comparison of dicots and monocots.*

space. Monocot stems do not have a vascular cambium. Therefore, their growth in diameter is limited. The stem becomes long and thin.

Secondary Growth of Stems

The secondary tissues of woody dicots result from cell division in the vascular cambium. As occurs in lower plants, this cell division increases stem diameter by producing new xylem and phloem. Some cortex cells join the cambium and form a continuous ring of dividing cells. Xylem and pith are inside the ring. Phloem, cortex, and epidermis are on the outside. New cells forming on the inside of the ring differentiate into secondary xylem. They are thick-walled and form the wood of the stem. As the mass of xylem increases in diameter, the

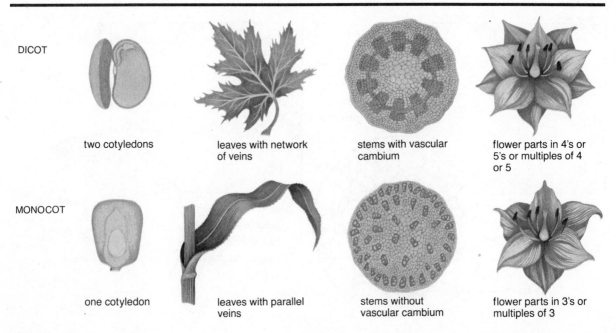

DICOT

two cotyledons

leaves with network of veins

stems with vascular cambium

flower parts in 4's or 5's or multiples of 4 or 5

MONOCOT

one cotyledon

leaves with parallel veins

stems without vascular cambium

flower parts in 3's or multiples of 3

ring of vascular cambium enlarges. It does so by adding more cells to increase its own circumference. Thus, the cambium continues to completely surround the ring of secondary xylem. (See Fig. 23-28.)

Meanwhile, the woody center of the stem expands. As it does so, it breaks the tissues outside the cambium. The destroyed tissue is replaced when the cells produced outside the cambium differentiate as secondary phloem. As the xylem and cambium continue to expand, the secondary phloem is destroyed. More secondary phloem is added to the outside of the cambium. In time, the cortex and epidermis are also stretched and destroyed. But the internal tissues of the stem are not left without protection. Before the cortex is destroyed, some of its cells form cork cambium. *Cork cambium* divides and produces a protective layer of cork or outer bark.

Most monocots are herbaceous annuals or perennials in which shoots die back each year. The perennials produce new primary tissue each growing season. Monocots lack secondary tissue and lateral meristems. A summary comparison of dicot and monocot characteristics appears in Figure 23-29.

Buds and Branches

The small outer branches of a woody plant bear leaves, flowers, and fruits. In the angle between the stem and the petiole of a leaf is a small group of cells that keeps the ability to divide. This patch of meristem produces an axillary or lateral bud. *A bud is a very much shortened, immature section of stem.* This stem has immature leaves or flowers with very short internodes. (See Fig. 23-30.) Where a season of dormancy occurs, the bud is formed one year and resumes growth the next. The tender, miniature stem is covered with tough modified leaves called *bud scales.* When the bud resumes growth, the bud scales are shed. Leaves or flowers enlarge, and the internodes increase in length.

Axillary buds often remain dormant for a while. Their growth is repressed by chemical regulators called *hormones*. These hormones are produced in the meristem at the tip of the stem. If all buds were to develop, the plant would have more branches than it could support. It would also have more leaves than could be exposed to the sun.

Figure 23-31 illustrates a typical woody dicot stem during the winter. Each leaf scar shows where a leaf grew from the stem during the previous growing season. Spots within a leaf scar are the broken ends of vascular bundles. These bundles once connected the vascular system of leaf and stem. Each ring of bud scale scars indicates the position of a terminal bud of some previous year. The amount of twig growth during the last year is that portion from the last ring of bud scale scars to the present terminal bud.

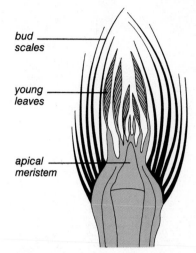

23-30. *A longitudinal section through a terminal bud.*

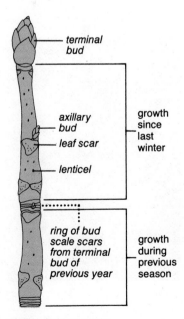

23-31. *A winter twig.*

Water Transport

More than 99 percent of the water entering a plant's root system moves through the stem into the leaves and evaporates into the atmosphere. *The evaporation of water from the leaves is called* **transpiration.** A mature corn plant transpires about 30 liters of water per week. This volume of water passes through vessels and tracheids of the xylem. If a human being used water at this rate, an adult would need to drink over 38 liters per day.

Volumes of water travel from three to six meters below the ground to the upper leaves of trees 90 meters tall. This process has concerned botanists for several hundred years. An early explanation involved the pumping action by the cells surrounding the xylem's vessels and tracheids. But it was observed that water rises even in dead stems. Another explanation suggested that capillary action moved the water. (See Fig. 23-32.) **Capillary action** *is the upward movement of a liquid through a tube with a narrow diameter.* But in xylem cells, capillary action can raise water only a meter or two. Others have mentioned root pressure as the cause of rising water. **Root pressure** *is the force resulting from differences in osmotic pressure between cells from a root hair into the xylem at the center of the root.* In root systems the endodermal layer surrounds the vascular tissues in the older portions of the root. This layer prevents the water from flowing out of the root back into the soil. When the stems of some plants are cut, water is forced out of the cut end by root pressure. Some short plants force water from the tips of their leaves by root pressure. *The forcing of liquid water from the tips of a plant's leaves is called* **guttation.** (See Fig. 23-33.) Some plants, however, demonstrate very little root pressure. In gymnosperms no root pressure at all has been found. Furthermore, root pressures seem to drop in the summer. It is at this time when the movement of water is greatest. Even the greatest root pressures are not enough to push water more than about 60 cm up the xylem.

TRANSPIRATION   In 1727 Stephen Hales, an English clergyman, observed that leafy twigs drew more water out of a container than did twigs stripped of their leaves. This demonstrated what is known as transpiration pull. **Transpiration pull** *is the pulling up of a column of water as it moves into a leaf to replace the water lost by transpiration, or used by photosynthesis.*

This "pulling" of a column of water is based on *the attraction of water molecules for each other, known as* **cohesion.** Cohesion holds water molecules together to form a water drop. The role of cohesion in transpiration was pointed out by botanists Henry Dixon and John Joly near the end of the 19th Century.

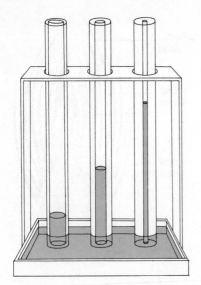

23-32. *Capillarity in narrow tubes. The smaller the tube's diameter, the higher the liquid rises.*

23-33. *Guttation water being forced out of a strawberry leaf.*

TRANSPIRATION-COHESION THEORY The most favored theory of the rise of water in plants involves a combination of transpiration, cohesion, and, where present, root pressure. When water transpires from the mesophyll cells of a leaf these cells become limp. Water diffuses into them from nearby cells. This diffusion chain extends from cell to cell back to the xylem cells of tiny leaf veins. Here the water movement from xylem cells to mesophyll cells is transmitted by cohesion to the water column in the xylem cells. This column of water extends all the way down into the root system. Here cohesion and osmotic pressure combine to continue the chain reaction. This reaction extends through root hairs to the film of water on soil particles. This combination of ideas is known as the *transpiration-cohesion theory*. (See Fig. 23-34.)

23-34. The flow of water according to the transpiration-cohesion theory. Water that evaporates from leaf cells is replaced by diffusion from nearby cells. This movement pulls water through the xylem of stems and roots. Water in the root xylem is replaced by diffusion from cortex cells and root hairs.

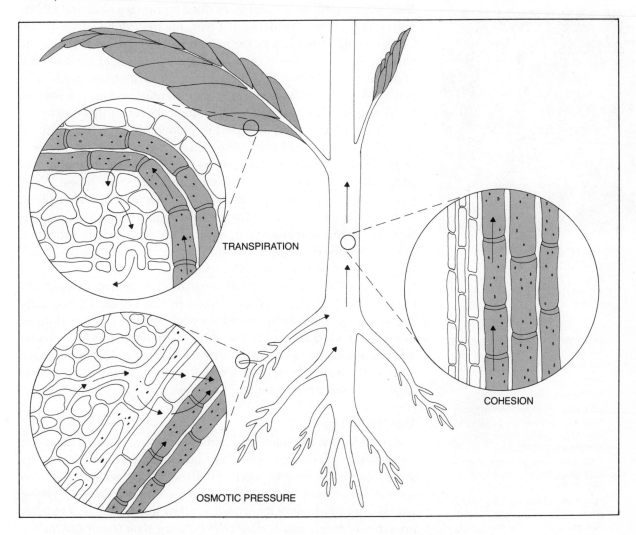

TRANSPIRATION

COHESION

OSMOTIC PRESSURE

3. The amount of twig growth during the last year is that portion from the last ring of bud scale scars to the present terminal bud.

Q. 4. The transpiration-cohesion theory: water transpires from mesophyll leaf cells, water diffuses into them from nearby cells. A diffusion chain extends from cell to cell back to the xylem of leaf veins, where cohesion to another column of water provides water from xylem cells to mesophyll cells. This column extends down into the roots, where cohesion and osmotic pressure continue the chain reaction to soil water.

23-35. *Girdling is the removal of a strip of phloem and all outer tissues from around a tree. Food accumulating above the strip may result in swelling.*

5. It removes the phloem, needed by the tree to transport food from the leaves to the roots, so they starve.

6. The cytoplasm of sieve tube cells extends through pores in the tubes, providing a pathway for flow of materials. Active transport moves carbohydrates into the sieve tubes, and unloaded at other sites where food is being used or stored. The removal of materials at one end of tube and their entry at other causes a pressure difference that results in a flow of materials.

If the transpiration-cohesion theory is a good explanation, the upward pull should stretch the water columns and narrow the diameter of a tree trunk. During daylight hours when water flow is greatest, such a narrowing has been observed.

Transport of Food

It is easy to demonstrate that water is transported mainly through the xylem. The xylem of a tree can be severed, with little damage to the phloem and other non-xylem tissue. This action causes the leaves to soon wilt. If the phloem and all other tissues outside of the xylem are removed, water continues to ascend. But in time, the roots starve and the tree dies. *Removing a strip of outer and inner bark (which includes phloem) from a tree is called* **girdling.** (See Fig. 23-35.) Such girdling is sometimes done by hungry mice and rabbits during the winter. The death of a tree due to girdling suggests that foods formed in the leaves are moved to other tissues through the phloem tissue. Phloem is composed of sieve tubes laid end to end. The side walls of sieve tubes have pores. Through these pores cytoplasm extends from one cell to another. In mature cells, the nucleus has disappeared. The nearby companion cells retain their nuclei.

One theory of food transport in phloem tissue is presently favored by plant physiologists. The concentration of carbohydrates is higher in sieve tubes than in other leaf cells. Active transport moves additional newly made carbohydrates into the sieve tubes. Water passes into the sieve tubes by osmosis. At other locations in the plant, food is being used or stored. There, carbohydrates are unloaded, perhaps by active transport. Again, water follows by osmosis. Since materials enter one end of the phloem column and leave at the other end, the pressure difference results in a flow of materials.

During the summer or fall some food is moved through the phloem and vascular rays and stored in the xylem. During early spring some of the food moves upward in the xylem or diffuses through the vascular rays to the phloem. In maple trees the greater amount of food moves up the xylem. By boring a hole into the xylem sapwood of a sugar maple, dilute sugar water can be collected. It is converted into syrup by boiling off excess water.

Gas Exchange

As in leaves, the stomata of herbaceous stems allow exchange of the gases involved in respiration and photosynthesis. In woody stems, the epidermis is replaced with bark. Its cork cells are dead and contain waterproof and airproof suberin. But the bark of young woody stems has many lenticles that allow gas exchange. **Lenticles** *are areas of loose, unsuberized cells between stem tissue and the at-*

mosphere. Scattered among the cells of the cortex are many air spaces. Air spaces also occur in the xylem of monocot stems. Air spaces form as the result of the destruction of some cells as others grow in size. Thus the gases used or produced by stem cells are supplied or removed by diffusion.

Diversity in Stems

Figure 23-36 illustrates the types of specialized stems among the flowering plants. Some may seem root-like, but differ from roots in having nodes and internodes.

Metabolic wastes are less serious in plants than in most animals. Plant metabolism is slower so wastes accumulate more slowly. Plant structure and metabolism are based on carbohydrates rather than proteins, so plant wastes are often less damaging to tissue.

7. Lenticels allow gas exchange between stem tissue and the atmosphere. Air spaces in the xylem of monocot stems, aid by diffusion of gases.

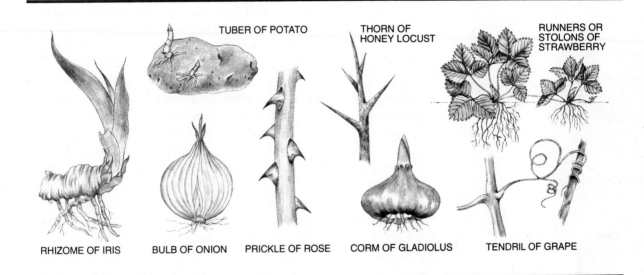

TUBER OF POTATO THORN OF HONEY LOCUST RUNNERS OR STOLONS OF STRAWBERRY

RHIZOME OF IRIS   BULB OF ONION   PRICKLE OF ROSE   CORM OF GLADIOLUS   TENDRIL OF GRAPE

23-36. Specialized stems.

A runner, or stolon, is a long narrow stem growing horizontally along the surface of the ground. Strawberries and Bermuda grass reproduce asexually by stolons. *A **rhizome** is a horizontal underground stem* which may be fleshy as in irises, or slender as in some perennial grasses. *A **tuber** is the bulky, short terminal part of an underground stem* such as the edible portion of the white potato. The "eyes" of a potato are lateral buds which can develop into a new plant when placed underground. *A **bulb** is a very compressed stem bearing fleshy leaves* such as in the onion. *A **corm** is a short, bulky, vertical stem containing stored food.* Examples are found in gladioli and crocuses. *Some **thorns** are modified stems that discourage browsing.* Examples of such thorns are found on honey locust and crabapple. The prickles of roses and raspberries are merely outgrowths of a stem's epidermis and cortex. The long thin coiling tendrils of grapes and Boston ivy are modified stems.

*8. A white potato is a tuber, or underground stem's bulky, short terminal part.

R. 9. Cuttings of roots, stems, or leaves may grow whole new identical plants, in one form of vegetative, asexual reporduction. Grafting is another method, in which a scion, or short piece of stem or bud, is placed into another stem with a root system, called the stock. Keeps the same genetic heritage as that cf the scion, unlike sexual reproduction.

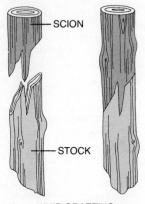

WHIP GRAFTING

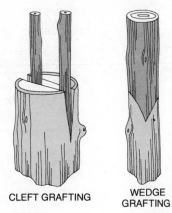

CLEFT GRAFTING   WEDGE
                 GRAFTING

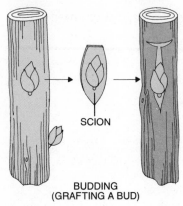

BUDDING
(GRAFTING A BUD)

23-37. Grafting is a kind of asexual reproduction. It is important that the cambium layer of the twig to be grafted touches the cambium layer of the stem to which it is being grafted.

Vegetative Reproduction

In addition to sexual reproduction, flowering plants may produce new plants from their roots, stems, or leaves. Such asexual reproduction is also known as *vegetative reproduction.* This includes the rooting of willow twigs placed in damp soil. Strawberries spread by stolons which take root. Potatoes are commonly planted by placing a piece of tuber underground. Geranium stems or violet leaves are cut and placed in water or damp sand to "multiply" the plants.

All organisms derived from the same individual by vegetative reproduction belong to the same **clone.** Whenever you multiply a plant with cuttings you are cloning that plant.

Another common method of cloning is grafting. *In grafting one inserts a short piece of dormant stem or a bud into another stem with a root system.* The rooted stem is called the *stock.* The stem cutting is the *scion.* (See Fig. 23-37.) The cambia of stock and scion must be in tight contact. The graft wound is covered with wax and wrapped with elastic tape. This prevents water loss and fungus infections. Most successful grafts are between members of the same species. But some grafting joins plants of different genera within the same family.

One advantage to vegetative reproduction is that one keeps the same genetic heritage. All McIntosh apple trees are clones of a tree in Ontario, Canada. A piece of stem from a McIntosh apple tree is grafted to the rooted stem of a different variety of apple tree. All parts beyond the graft have the same genetic make-up as the original tree. Reproducing by seed would require two parents. The pollen could come from other apple trees in the area. The offspring would not be a McIntosh.

QUESTIONS FOR SECTION 5

1. Distinguish between primary and secondary growths of a stem and describe each.
2. Define the term bud and describe its growth.
3. How can you determine the age of a section of twig?
4. Explain the theory of water transport that is most favored by botanists today.
5. Why does girdling kill a tree?
6. Explain how sieve tubes transport food in a stem.
7. Tell how stem tissues exchange gases.
8. Why do we say that the edible portion of a white potato is a stem while that of a sweet potato is a root?
9. Describe the various types of vegetative reproduction and the main advantage of each.

Answers to Questions for Section 5.

0. 1. Primary growth is the production of new cells (epidermis, cortex, and vascular) at tip of shoot. This lengthens stem. Secondary growth occurs in vascular cambium producing increase in stem diameter.

P. 2. A bud is a very much shortened, immature section of stem. It grows from a patch of meristem in the angle between the stem and petiole of a leaf. A bud formed one year resumes growth the next, shedding the bud scales that formed the first year.

(See pages 430-31 for more answers.)

6 BEHAVIOR AND ENVIRONMENT

Plants respond to changes in their external environment in several ways. These responses include chlorophyll production, dormancy, growth movements, turgor movements, and flowering.

Chlorophyll Production

You have probably seen plants that have germinated in dark places. Such plants didn't turn green until exposed to light for a time. This shows that light is necessary for forming chlorophyll. Without chlorophyll photosynthesis cannot occur and the plant will starve.

Plants grown in the dark also grow long, weak stems with widely spaced leaves. (See Fig. 23-38.) If the rapid growth results in reaching light, chlorophyll is formed and food manufacture begins.

The Temperature Effect

Most plants function best between 10° and 38°C. Temperature extremes beyond that range affect the rates of their life processes. These include respiration, photosynthesis, food movement, and transpiration. Temperature influences germination and flowering in some plants. Sugar beets and winter wheat do not flower until after a period of cold weather.

Growth Regulators

Plants respond to the external environment. Many of these responses are movements due either to growth or turgor changes. The chemical regulators that produce the growth effects are called hormones. Plant hormones are usually produced by tissues that are also responsible for other functions.

The plant hormones presently known may be divided into five groups. Auxins, gibberellins, and cytokinins stimulate cell division. Abscisic acid and ethylene usually stimulate dormancy or aging.

AUXINS   Auxins were the first plant hormones, or growth regulators, to be discovered. Charles Darwin had shown by 1880 that seedlings bent toward light if only the tips were exposed. He also demonstrated that the bending resulted from greater growth on the shaded side of the stalk.

Many auxin studies use the **coleoptile,** *the sheath that covers the first leaves of the grass seedling.* The leaves usually push on through the coleoptile. But if the tip is removed, growth stops.

Further experiments have been done. The freshly cut coleoptile tip can be placed back on the cut end, but a bit off center. The side of the shoot supporting the tip grows faster. So the tip leans away from that side even in darkness. (See Fig. 23-39 on page 434.)

OBJECTIVES FOR SECTION 6
S. Tell how plants respond to darkness, temperature, various growth regulators, and turgor changes.
T. List human uses of flowering plants.
U. Tell how air pollution has affected deciduous forests.

Courtesy Carolina Biological Supply Company

23-38. *Light sensitive lettuce seeds. (top) exposed to light; (bottom) left in darkness.*

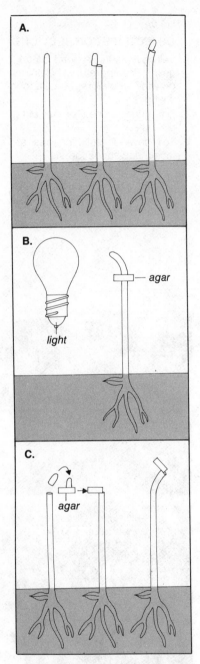

23-39. A. Agar placed between the shoot and its tip does not stop the tip's response to light. **B.** If the coleoptile tip is cut and placed off center, the supporting side of the shoot continues growth. **C.** Auxin may be absorbed by the agar and transmitted to the shoot.

A piece of gelatin or agar may be placed between the stump and the coleoptile tip. The tip still responds by bending toward the light. (Refer to Fig. 23-39.) This suggests that the auxin diffused through the gelatin toward the stump. Coleoptile tips may be cut and placed on agar blocks, for a time. The agar blocks alone cause curvature if placed off center on the stump. Plain agar produces no response. (Refer to Fig. 23-39.)

The experiments illustrate that unequal growth occurs when auxins are unevenly distributed. Further experiments have confirmed the belief that some tropisms are related to auxin distribution. *The bending toward light is called* **phototropism.** The stems of many plants bend toward light. Many botanists believe that auxins tend to move to the shady side of the stem. This action causes those cells to grow faster. **Chemotropism** *is the response to chemicals.* It is seen in the growth of the pollen tube through the pistil.

Much remains to be learned about auxins. Why do they respond to light? How do they move in the plant body? Botanists do agree that the main natural auxin is indoleacetic acid, or IAA. The main centers of auxin production seem to be the tip meristems, buds, young leaves, and young flowers.

SYNTHETIC AUXINS Synthetic auxins have been used as herbicides. These include 2,4-D, and 2,4,5-T. Grasses are less sensitive to low concentrations of auxins than are other herbs. Most lawn weeds are especially sensitive to some synthetic auxins.

GIBBERELLINS Another plant growth regulator was first discovered as a product of a fungus, *Gibberella.* The fungus causes the "foolish seedling" disease in rice. Diseased seedlings grow especially fast. But they are spindly and unhealthy and seldom bear fruit. In 1926, a Japanese scientist discovered that an extract of the fungus produced the same growth stimulation as the fungus disease. By 1935, the substance was purified and named gibberellin or gibberellic acid. More than 50 gibberellins have now been isolated from vascular plants and brown and green algae as well as fungi.

Gibberellins stimulate stems to grow longer. Many dwarf varieties of plants are mutants that do not produce sufficient gibberellins. Gibberellins cause them to grow to the size of normal varieties. Gibberellins have little effect on the growth of stems of normal sized plants. However, they do affect flowering, leaf growth, root formation, and seed dormancy. In germinating grains, gibberellins are produced by the embryo. These gibberellins activate the genes that increase the production of the enzymes that digest the endosperm.

CYTOKININS Cytokinins are another group of plant growth regulators. They promote cell division. They also cause cells to enlarge and differentiate. Cytokinins contribute to the development of chloroplasts, cotyledon growth, and the delay of aging in leaves. Cytokinins are produced in roots. They are then transported through the xylem to the leaves and shoot meristems.

ABSCISIC ACID   Abscisic (ab *siz* ik) acid was discovered in aging tissue. It is produced in mature leaves. Abscisic acid counteracts the effects of auxin when applied to auxin-treated coleoptiles. When applied to growing twigs or germinating seeds abscisic acid returns them to dormancy. There is increasing evidence that it may be a factor in a root's **geotropism,** *the response to gravity.* The acid is produced within the root cap and moved throughout the root system. In horizontal roots it is concentrated on the lower side. Thus the cells of the upper side grow faster and the root turns downward. (See Fig. 23-40.)

Droughts stimulate leaves to produce more abscisic acid. This causes closing of stomata. Thus the plant's water content is maintained. Biochemical studies suggest that abscisic acid functions by halting protein and RNA synthesis.

ETHYLENE   The effects of ethylene on the ripening of fruit was observed in the early 1900's. This gas, emitted by incense burners or kerosene stoves, improved the color and flavor of citrus fruits. It is now known that ethylene is produced by ripening fruits, flowers, seeds, leaves, and roots. Surges of ethylene production occur when fruits are bruised or cut. It is also produced by pea seedlings when they have difficulty penetrating the soil.

The presence of the ethylene stimulates the fruit to produce more of it. This encourages the ripening of the whole fruit at once. It also stimulates the ripening of nearby fruits. Over-ripening can result. Shipments of bananas, pineapples, and citrus fruits, are picked while green to avoid loss by over-ripening. Ripening is stimulated by applying ethylene after they reach their destination.

Ethylene affects the permeability of the cell membrane. This allows a chlorophyll-destroying enzyme to enter the chloroplasts. With the loss of chlorophyll, other pigments are unmasked. This action provides the fruit with its ripened color.

Interactions Among Growth Regulators

There seems to be much interaction among the growth regulators just described. An example is found in apical dominance. **Apical dominance** *is the influence of a terminal (end) bud in inhibiting the growth of lateral buds.* If one removes the terminal bud, a lateral bud grows. Auxin from the terminal bud inhibits the lateral buds. But cytokinin applications can remove that inhibition. Gibberellins stimulate the growth of lateral buds in some plants. But they strengthen apical dominance in others. It appears that bud growth or lack of

Answers to Questions for Section 6.

*3. Loss of turgor during dry periods allows leaves to fold up and decrease water loss through exposure.

T. 4. Cereals, important to human diet; fabrics made from cotton, flax, and hemp, and synthetics from cellulose; alcohol, tars, oils, dyes, etc., used in industry; drugs, such as quinine, morphine, digitalis, etc.; tea, coffee, cocoa, perfumes.

U. *5. There might be decrease in the efficiency of gas exchange, decreasing photosynthesis and respiration, and other functions.

23-40. *A plant one day and four days after being placed on its side. Abscisic acid accumulates on the lower side of horizontal roots. The acid stops growth so the upper side of the root grows faster, turning the root downward.*

growth depends on a balance among various growth regulators.

Abscisic acid prevents seed germination. However, gibberellins, cytokinins, and ethylene can break seed dormancy and produce germination.

Auxins inhibit the separation of abscission layers in the stalks of leaves, flowers, and fruits. When auxin production in a leaf is reduced, abscission occurs. But an old leaf also produces more ethylene which speeds up abscission. Gibberellins and cytokinins also promote abscission. Auxin sprays are used to delay early dropping of fruits, especially apples. However, application of excess auxin can stimulate ethylene synthesis which induces abscission.

Fruit Development

The conversion of an ovary into a fruit usually occurs due to an auxin produced by a pollen grain. The auxin may also be produced by the ovary or its ovules when stimulated by a pollen grain. Some flowers if treated with auxin sprays, develop fruits. This occurs even in the absence of fertilization. Examples are seedless tomatoes and watermelons. However, not all seedless fruits develop in this way.

Turgor Movements

The movements of plants discussed so far are growth movements. They result from varying growth rates. These movements also require several hours to be noticed. They are not reversible. By contrast, some turgor movements take place in a fraction of a second up to 45 minutes. (See Fig. 23-41.) They result from changes in internal water pressure of cells in the cortex. They may also occur at the base of a leaf or leaflet in a special swelling called a *pulvinus.* The pulvinus is part of the petiole. Contact movements observed in the Venus's flytrap, the bladderworts, and sensitive plants are due to turgor changes in cells of the pulvinus. So are the sleep movements in many legumes and other plants. These plants exhibit a regular folding and unfolding of leaves or petals about every 24 hours. *Such daily cycles of activity in organisms are known as* **circadian** (sər kād ē ən) **rhythms.** Folding or drooping of leaves usually occurs at dusk. Unfolding occurs in the morning.

Many grasses have special thin-walled cells which form longitudinal rows in their leaves. During periods of dryness, these cells lose turgor and the leaf rolls. Such rolling has reduced transpiration to less than 10 percent of normal in some prairie grasses.

Effects of Human Action

ECONOMICS   The human use of flowering plants is a topic that requires a separate book. The human diet depends heavily upon the ce-

23-41. (top) Mimosa before being touched; (bottom) Mimosa after being touched.

reals. Rice is used by more people than any other food. Fibers from cotton, flax, and hemp are useful in fabrics. While many synthetic fibers are now produced, most of them use cellulose as a base. Plants produce alcohol, acetone, acetic acid, tars, resins, tannins, oils, gums, and dyes—all used in industry. Rubber and cork are produced by trees. Flowering plants produce quinine, morphine, strychnine, digitalis, and other drugs. Tea, coffee, and cocoa are plant products. And the beauty of flowering plants has long made life more pleasant for Earth's human inhabitants.

SHELTERBELTS   Since 1935, many shelterbelts were established in the midwestern United States to reduce wind erosion. **Shelterbelts *are rows of trees arranged to control wind flow.*** (See Fig. 23-42.) They form a protective screen against the hot south winds of summer and the cold north winds of winter. By interrupting air currents, they trap snow in the fields. Windbreaks, planted around farmsteads, reduce heating fuel use in winter. They provide sources of food and cover for song birds, game birds, mammals, and other animals. Many of these shelterbelts are now being removed to clear the fields for large circular irrigation systems.

THE EFFECTS OF HUMAN ACTIVITY ON DECIDUOUS FORESTS   Chapter 22 describes the various air pollutants on coniferous forests. They also have their effects on deciduous forests. In the early 1900's, in the heart of the Appalachian mountains, copper smelters released 40 tons of sulfur dioxide into the air each day. About 28km^2 of vegetation was destroyed. Another 69km^2 was reduced to grass. But without the protective cover of trees, the grasses washed away with the topsoil. This loss of topsoil left a desert where a lush forest had been. The desert remains.

Less dramatic effects also occur. Leaves from trees in the polluted industrial areas of Montreal, Quebec have one tenth as many stomata per unit area as leaves from an unpolluted area. In other regions, maple leaves from polluted areas had more epidermal hairs than leaves from unpolluted areas. Will these flowering plants become adapted to our way of life?

Also of economic importance are weeds. Weeds are species that spontaneously populate especially disturbed areas. Because they are so adaptable they are fierce competitors of cultivated crops.

23-42. *Shelterbelts control wind flow and snow drifting. They provide food and shelter for wildlife.*

Answers to Questions for Section 6.

S. 1. Darkness: fail to turn green, grow long, weak stems with widely spaced leaves. Temperature: beyond 10° – 38° C range, slow down or speed up life processes. Growth regulators: affect cell division or dormancy or aging. Turgor: rapid reversible movements.

2. Auxins: unequal distribution causes unequal growth. Synthetic auxins: kill weeds. Gibberellins: stimulate stems to grow longer; affect flowering, leaf growth, root formation, and seed dormancy. Cytokinins: promote cell division, enlargement, and differentiation. Abscisic acid: induces dormancy. Ethylene: ripens fruit.

QUESTIONS FOR SECTION 6

1. Describe plant responses to darkness, temperature, various growth regulators, and turgor changes.
2. What are the separate basic effects of auxins, synthetic auxins, gibberellins, cytokinins, abscisic acid, and ethylene?
3. How do various turgor movements help plants maintain homeostasis?
4. How do human beings use plants?
5. How might a reduction in the number of stomata affect the life of a tree?

(See pages 435 for more answers.)

7 COMPARING FLOWERING PLANTS TO OTHER PLANTS, FUNGI, PROTISTS, AND MONERANS

OBJECTIVES FOR SECTION 7

V. Review the main features that distinguish plants from fungi, protists, monerans, and viruses in terms of structure, nutrition, and reproduction.

W. Give an example of how flowering plants illustrate unity within diversity, homeostasis, the relationship between structure and function, and interaction with the environment.

Diversity Among Plants, Fungi, Protists, and Monerans

Flowering plants are distinguished by the production of seeds in specialized structures called flowers. Flowering plants share with other vascular plants a dominant sporophyte generation with roots, stems, and leaves. In flowering plants, the leaves are relatively large. The vascular tissue is especially efficient. The presence of vessel cells in the xylem is common. Vessels are found rarely in gymnosperms and ferns. This combination of traits contributed to the success of flowering plants on land. (See Table 23-1.) Large chlorophyll-bearing leaves provide surface area for obtaining light. Sturdy stems allow exposure of leaves to light with little shading from their neighbors. The efficient vascular system allows a steady water supply from roots through stems to leaves. With carbon dioxide generated by respiration, water from the soil, and energy from the sun, land plants manufacture carbohydrates.

In conifers, leaves are smaller than in flowering plants. The xylem tissue is composed of tracheids. There are no flowers. Seeds are borne on the surface of scales arranged to form a cone.

TABLE 23-1 ADAPTIONS THAT AIDED PLANTS IN CHANGING FROM WATER TO LAND HABITATS

Factor	In Water	On Land	Adaption to Land Habitat
Water	surrounding each cell	mostly underground evaporates quickly in air	rhizoids or roots xylem cuticle to reduce water loss
Minerals	surrounding each cell	in soil	xylem
Gases	dissolved, diluted	plentiful in air	stomata
Light	lowers intensity and removes some wavelengths	plentiful	leaves
Temperature	changes small and slow	changes extreme and rigid	hormones to coordinate responses to change
Support	buoyant support	little support in air	xylem
Reproduction	swimming gametes	water usually not available for swimming gametes	airborne pollen which project tube into female gametophyte
Dispersal	waterborne offspring	water seldom available for dispersal	airborne spores and seeds edible fruits

The leaves of vascular plants develop a cuticle which prevents heavy water loss. Stomata in the leaf surface allow the exchange of gases. These gases are involved in photosynthesis and respiration.

The bryophytes have no highly specialized conducting tissues. Consequently they are only a few centimeters tall. They are successful only in damp environments.

As a group, most algae exist in marine or freshwater habitats. Multicellular forms have little cell specialization. The buoyant support provided by surrounding water avoids the need for strong supporting tissue. Like vascular plants, the green algae contain chlorophylls *a* and *b*. The brown algae possess chlorophylls *a* and *c*. The red algae have chlorophylls *a* and *d*.

The organisms mentioned thus far are photosynthetic. They manufacture food from the carbon dioxide and water that diffuses in from their surroundings. By contrast, the fungi contain no chlorophyll. Fungi cannot manufacture their own food. Instead they get energy from organic food absorbed from their surroundings. The fungi have cell walls that resemble those of plants. Many of the fungi are composed of hyphae that penetrate a living or once-living food source. The hyphae may or may not have cross-walls separating one cell from another. They have no vascular tissue.

Most plants and fungi are multicellular. By contrast the protists are mostly unicellular. They share with plants and fungi their eucaryotic cells. That is, they all possess nuclear membranes, mitochondria, and plastids. The protists have a variety of nutritional processes. Various species are photosynthetic, absorptive, or ingestive.

The monerans are procaryotic single-celled creatures. They are the blue-green algae and the bacteria. The monerans differ from other living things in the absence of nuclear membranes. Monerans also lack plastids, mitochondria, and other organelles with membranes. Monerans derive nourishment mainly by absorption. Some are photosynthetic or chemosynthetic. (See Table 23-2 on page 440.)

All of the organisms reviewed so far are clearly living. While there is disagreement about the classification of viruses, they do have some characteristics of living things. They are essentially a protein coat containing a nucleic acid. DNA and RNA are found in no other nonliving things. But unlike living cells, viruses are noncellular and are able to exist indefinitely as inactive chemicals.

The organisms that you studied have a diversity in body form. They also display diversity in their specific ways of obtaining energy to carry on metabolism, and in their means of maintaining homeostasis. But they all grow, reproduce, and direct life activities through their DNA and RNA.

TABLE 23-2   SUMMARY OF MONERANS, PROTISTS, FUNGI, AND PLANTS

Phylum		Monerans	Protists	Fungi	Plants
BODY PLAN	Com-plexity	unicellular	unicellular	multicellular	multicellular
	Organ-elles	procaryotic	eucaryotic	eucaryotic	eucaryotic
REPRO-DUCTION		asexual	asexual	vegetative spores sexual spores	vegetative sexual
NUTRITION		absorption photosynthesis chemosynthesis	absorption photosynthesis chemosynthesis	absorption	photosynthesis
TRANS-PORTATION		diffusion	diffusion	diffusion active transport	xylem phloem

23-43. *Sexual reproduction in plants involves alternation between halploid gametophyte and diploid sporophyte generations.*

Continuity Among Plants, Fungi, Protists, and Monerans

Continuity in plants may be maintained asexually. However, their reproduction is usually sexual with alternating haploid and diploid generations. (See Fig. 23-43.) The haploid gametophyte pro-

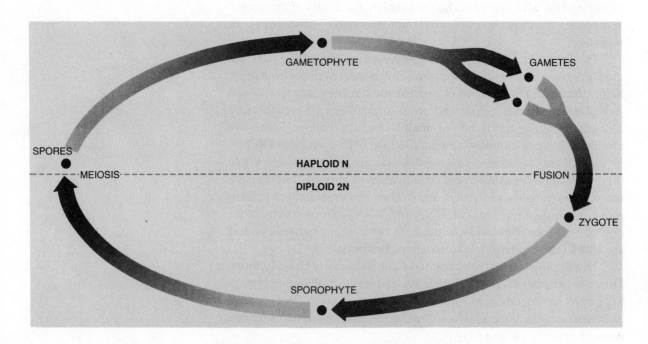

duces the gametes: eggs and sperm. These unite, forming the diploid sporophyte generation. The sporophyte yields spores which produce gametophytes. In mosses, the gametophyte is the dominant form. Proceeding from ferns through gymnosperms to angiosperms, the gametophyte becomes progressively reduced. (See Fig. 23-44.) In gymnosperms and angiosperms, the gametophyte develops within sporophyte tissue. The gametophyte depends on the sporophyte for nourishment and protection.

Gymnosperms and angiosperms do not need free water for fertilization. Carriers, such as insects and wind, transfer immature male gametophytes (pollen grains) to the female cone or to the flower's pistil.

The fungi reproduce vegetatively, by asexual spores, or by sexual spores. Protists also exhibit a variety of reproduction patterns. Most of them include asexual division and a fusion of gametes.

23-44. *Trends in size and complexity of the sporophyte and gametophyte land plants.*

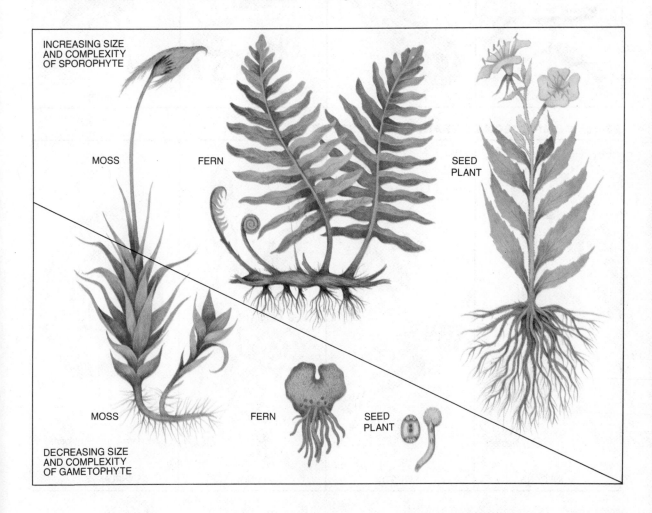

INCREASING SIZE
AND COMPLEXITY
OF SPOROPHYTE

MOSS   FERN   SEED
PLANT

MOSS   FERN   SEED
PLANT

DECREASING SIZE
AND COMPLEXITY
OF GAMETOPHYTE

23-45 COMPARISON OF BODY PLANS

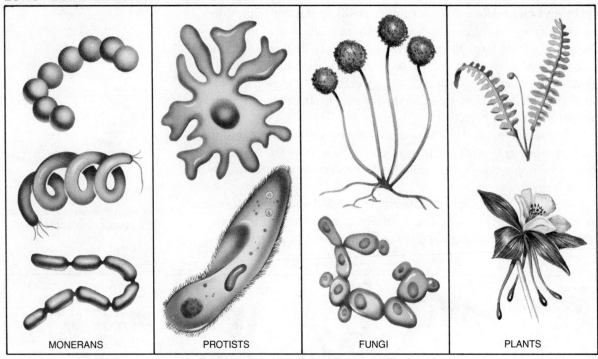

MONERANS

PROTISTS

FUNGI

PLANTS

23-46 COMPARISON OF TRANSPORT SYSTEMS

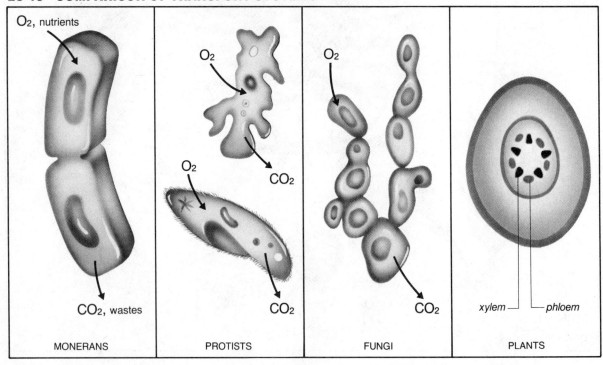

O_2, nutrients

O_2

O_2

O_2

CO_2, wastes

CO_2

CO_2

xylem — phloem

MONERANS

PROTISTS

FUNGI

PLANTS

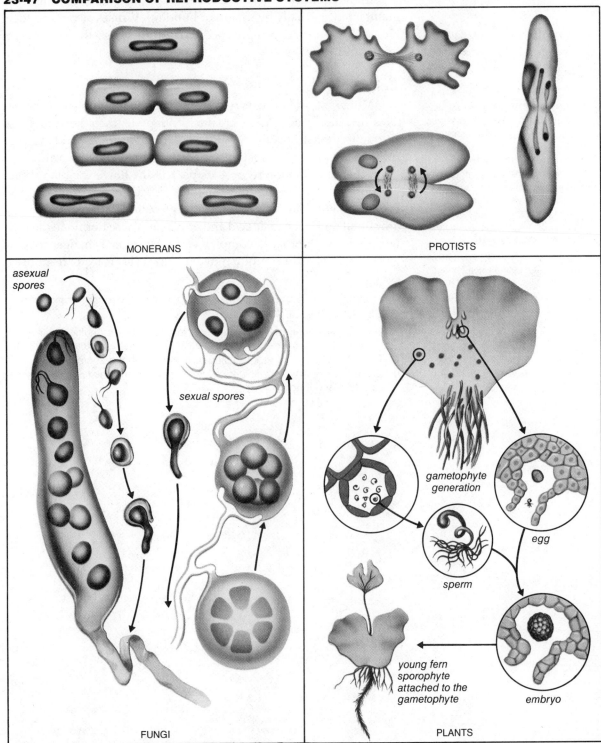

MONERANS

PROTISTS

asexual
spores

sexual spores

FUNGI

gametophyte
generation

egg

sperm

embryo

young fern
sporophyte
attached to the
gametophyte

PLANTS

V. 1. See tables 23-1 and 23-2 and comparison art on pages 442 and 443.

2. Viruses: reproduce through the contents of living cells; monerans: fission or budding; protists: asexual division and fusion of gametes; fungi: asexual or sexual spores; simplest plants (mosses): gametophyte dominant in form; ferns and gymnosperms: gametophyte reduced and begins to develop within sporophyte tissue; angiosperms: sexual, alternating haploid and diploid generations.

W. *3. Sepals: outermost part of flower—protects flower bud when young; petals: various colors attract insects; stamens (anther and filament): produce pollen and are exposed for dispersal of pollen grains; pistil (ovary, style, stigma); sticky surface on stigma to ensure receipt of pollen. Also, ovary structure as receptacle for sperm and as area of development.

In the monerans, sexual-like reproduction is rare. Continuity is maintained asexually by fission or budding. Viruses also reproduce. However, in order to reproduce viruses must use the contents of living cells.

Behavior

Monerans and protists respond to changes in their environment as individual cells. These creatures adapt to their surroundings through simple tropisms. A multicellular organism responds as a co-ordinated whole. Such responses may be complex. In the plant kingdom, this coordination reaches its peak in the flowering plants with hormones and turgor movements. Auxins, gibberellins, and cytokinins stimulate cell division and growth. Dormancy and aging are stimulated by abscisic acid and ethylene. These hormones also interact with each other in complex ways. Hormonal changes involve growth and take time. Turgor movements also bring faster responses.

QUESTIONS FOR SECTION 7

1. Contrast flowering plants, gymnosperms, bryophytes, multicellular algae, fungi, protists, monerans, and viruses in terms of structure and nutrition.
2. Trace the patterns of reproduction from viruses to the angiosperms.
3. Explain how parts of a flowering plant illustrate the relationship between structure and function.

CHAPTER REVIEW

The angiosperms are basically land plants that maintain *continuity* with flowers. As flowers develop, their seeds are enclosed in a fruit. The flowering plants also share with each other many *structure-function relationships* and methods of maintaining *homeostasis*. Many *interactions with the environment* are due to turgor changes and chemical growth regulators. Within this *unity* there is great *diversity* of form in leaves, roots, stems, and flowers.

Using the Concepts

1. It takes only one pollen grain to begin the development of an ovule into a seed. Yet a single flower may produce thousands of pollen grains. What do you think is the value of such high numbers of pollen grains?

2. The public often confines the term fruit to relatively sweet or dessert food. The fruits of tomatoes, beans, cucumbers, and squashes are often called vegetables. These are usually served with the main course of a meal. Which definition of fruit do you favor — the public's or the biologists? Why?

Career Activities

3. With references from your library, find the requirements, occupational activities, and opportunities for people in the fields of agriculture, agronomy, botany, forestry, forest products technology, horticulture, range ecology, soil conservation, and truck gardening.

VOCABULARY REVIEW

1 dicotyledonous plants
monocotyledonous plants
herbaceous stems
annual stems
perennial plant
woody stem
2 receptacle
sepals
calyx
corolla
stamen
filament
anther
pistil
ovary
ovule
style
stigma
complete flower

incomplete flower
monoecious plant
dioecious plant
photoperiodism
micropyle
megaspore mother cell
megaspores
microspore mother cell
generative nucleus
tube nucleus
self-pollination
cross-pollination
endosperm
double fertilization
fruit
epicotyl
hypocotyl
radicle
3 tendrils

node
internode
abscission zone
4 root cap
root hairs
cortex
primary tissue
secondary tissue
fibrous root system
tap root system
5 bud scales
root pressure
guttation
transpiration pull
transpiration-cohesion theory
girdling
lenticel
stolon
tuber

bulb
corm
vegetative reproduction
grafting
stock
scion
6 auxins
coleoptile
phototropism
chemotropism
gibberellins
cytokinins
abscisic acid
ethylene
apical dominance
pulvinus
circadian rhythm
shelterbelt

CHAPTER 23 TEST

Copy the number of each test item and place your answer to the right.

PART 1   Multiple Choice: Select the letter of the phrase that best completes each of the following.

d **1.** The sac with eight haploid nuclei within the ovule make up the   **a.** megaspore mother cell   **b.** seed   **c.** micropyle   **d.** female gametophyte.

c **2.** The male gametophyte is the   **a.** stamen   **b.** anther   **c.** pollen grain   **d.** generative nucleus.

b **3.** Double fertilization results in the development of the   **a.** generative nucleus and embryo   **b.** zygote and endosperm   **c.** endosperm and tube nucleus   **d.** tube and generative nuclei.

c **4.** When the CO_2 concentration in a leaf drops, potassium ions enter guard cells and the stomata   **a.** die   **b.** close   **c.** open   **d.** dissolve.

b **5.** The most commonly eaten portion of the white potato is the   **a.** root   **b.** stem   **c.** leaf   **d.** fruit.

d **6.** Water rises in a stem because of   **a.** root pressure   **b.** transpiration   **c.** cohesion   **d.** a combination of these.

c **7.** Food is transported in sieve tubes because of   **a.** osmosis   **b.** active transport   **c.** both of these   **d.** none of these.

b **8.** Cells produced by the vascular or cork cambia form   **a.** meristem tissues   **b.** secondary tissues   **c.** primary tissues   **d.** herbaceous tissues.

b **9.** Water and minerals enter a root through an epidermal extension called a/an   **a.** branch root   **b.** root hair   **c.** endodermis   **d.** root cap.

d **10.** The place a terminal bud grew during some previous year is shown by   **a.** sepals   **b.** stamens   **c.** cork cambium   **d.** bud scale scars.

PART 2   Matching: Match the letter of the term in Column I with its description in Column II.

COLUMN I

a. flowering plants
b. dicotyledonous plants
c. dioecious plants
d. herbaceous plants
e. monocotyledonous plants
f. perennial plants
g. weed plants
h. fungi
i. monerans
j. protists

COLUMN II

e **11.** Plants whose flower parts are in three's and with vascular bundles scattered in the stem

a **12.** Plants whose seeds are enclosed in a fruit

c **13.** Plants with staminate and pistillate flowers on separate plants

d **14.** "Non-woody"

f **15.** Plants that live for several years.

b **16.** Plants with net-veined leaves

g **17.** Plant species that spontaneously populate especially disturbed areas

i **18.** Procaryotic organisms

j **19.** Unicellular eucaryotic organisms

h **20.** Absorptive, heterotrophic, eucaryotic organisms

PART 3   Completion: Complete the following.

21. Vegetative reproduction such as grafting and stem or leaf cuttings has the advantage of keeping ___the same___ heredity

22. A very much shortened, immature section of stem covered with scales is a ___bird___.

23. Rapid plant movements are due to cellular changes in ___turgor___

24. A gas which stimulates the ripening of fruit is ___ethylene___.

25. Plant hormones that usually stimulate cell division or cell growth are ____, ____, and ____.
_____auxins, gibberellins, and cytokinin_____

INVERTEBRATES

This unit continues our survey of living things. It is the first of two units on animals. The animal kingdom is usually divided into 20 to 30 phyla. Animals without backbones are known as invertebrates. These are the subject of this unit.

A general pattern is followed. The unity and diversity of these organisms will be examined. Relationships between structure and function are stressed. From these concepts, we see how each organism reproduces itself and maintains homeostasis. Once the organism itself has been completely studied, we consider its relationship with the environment. Finally, in the last section of this unit these characteristics are reviewed. Comparisons are then made with simpler organisms to help to give an overall picture of living things.

CRAB

CHAPTER 24

SPONGES, CNIDARIANS, AND UNSEGMENTED WORMS

It was easy to move from the study of unicellular algae to that of plants like the mosses. It should be as easy to move from the study of protists to that of the simple animals like sponges. From here, the move to more complex organisms like worms and insects is just as effortless. The basic needs of these organisms are the same. However, they have different structures with which to perform their functions.

We will be studying the simplest animals. We will look at the general body plan of each and relate it to familiar basic concepts: *the relationship between structure and function, diversity, continuity of life, homeostasis,* and *interaction with the environment.*

Questions this chapter answer will include:

- Of what advantage is it for an animal to be divided into cells?
- Can memory last more than one generation?
- How are coral reefs built?
- How does an animal's shape affect its ability to survive?
- Can jellyfish stings be dangerous to human swimmers?

GREY TUBE SPONGES AND BROWN SPONGE

1 SPONGES

General Characteristics of Animals

The organisms in the animal kingdom are heterotrophic and multicellular. They produce eggs and sperm in multicellular structures.

Being divided into cells became an advantage when organisms became larger. A selective advantage for larger heterotrophs was their ability to eat a greater size range of organisms. In turn, it was also an advantage to be eaten by fewer organisms. But as you discovered in Chapter 19, there is a limit to the volume of cytoplasm that a nucleus can control. Dividing cytoplasm into smaller units increases the surface area. It is this area through which food, oxygen, and waste materials must diffuse. Small units of cytoplasm also reduce the distance these materials must travel by diffusion. Finally, division into cells makes specialization possible. In unicellular organisms parts of the cell are specialized. However, the cell as a whole must fulfill all functions. In multicellular groups, cells can specialize. They become especially efficient in protection, mechanical support, secretion, or reproduction. Of course, as they specialize, some cells become more dependent on other cells. The survival of the organism depends on each type of cell performing its functions.

General Body Plan of Invertebrates

The body structure of most animals is similar to that of a hollow tube. The inside of the tube is specialized for digesting and absorbing food. In some animals the tube is closed at one end. Food enters and wastes leave through the same opening. In other animals the tube is open at both ends. As food enters one end, it is processed on its way through. Wastes are eliminated through the other end.

The outer part of the body becomes specialized to meet the outside world. To do so it develops various protective structures and sense organs. In more complex animals the wall of the tube originates as two layers. The space between inner and outer layers becomes packed with muscles, circulatory structures, and various other organs and glands. (Refer to Fig. 24-14 on page 458.)

Animal Shapes

The shape of an animal affects its interaction with the environment. It affects its approach to prey organisms and its ability to escape from predators. Shape relates to the term symmetry. **Symmetry** *is the similarity of form or arrangement around a point, around a line, or on either side of a flat plane.* An organism that moves slowly and has few special sense receptors may have no symmetry at all. They are

OBJECTIVES FOR SECTION 1

A. Give the advantages for a large organism to be divided into cells.
B. Distinguish among different kinds of symmetry and relate them to activity and to awareness of surroundings.
C. Describe the general body plan of the sponges.
D. Describe how the combined internal systems contribute to homeostasis in the sponges.
E. Describe the various kinds of environmental relationships found in sponges.

Answers to Questions for Section 1.

C. 4. Incurrent pores, ectoderm, endoderm, mesoglea, spicules, spongin. Terms defined in glossary.

D. 5. The flagella of the collar cells produce a current that brings food organisms into the central cavity; the cells capture food and pass it on to other cells. Water surrounding and entering the sponge brings in dissolved oxygen and takes away carbon dioxide and nitrogenous wastes.

E. 6. Pollutants bury sponges or clog their pores. Sponges are protected due to their taste and smell. Some crabs camouflage themselves within sponges.

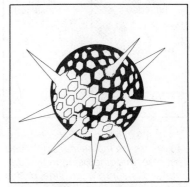

24-1. *Spherical symmetry in a radiolarian.*

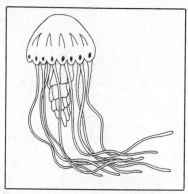

24-2. *Radial symmetry in a jellyfish.*

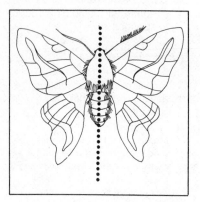

24-3. *Bilateral symmetry in a moth.*

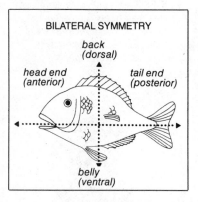

BILATERAL SYMMETRY

back
(dorsal)

head end
(anterior)

tail end
(posterior)

belly
(ventral)

24-4. *A fish has bilateral symmetry. To determine the animal's right and left side, imagine being in that animal's position. Which side of this fish are you viewing?*

said to be *asymmetric*. An ameba is such an organism. **Spherical symmetry** *is that in which all cone-shaped sections around a point are similar.* A golf ball is an example. Radiolarians and Volvox are protists with spherical symmetry. (See Fig. 24-1.) They face their surroundings in all directions at once. They either have poor means of locomotion or are moved about by water currents.

Radial symmetry *is that in which all wedge-shaped sections around a vertical line are similar.* Barrels, wheels, starfish, and jellyfish are examples. (See Fig. 24-2.) Some of these organisms move about sluggishly. Others with radial symmetry spend their lives anchored to one spot. Their sense organs are distributed in a circle.

The most rapidly moving organisms possess bilateral (two-sided) symmetry. **Bilateral symmetry** *is that in which there is only one plane that can divide the body into equivalent parts.* Airplanes, canoes, flatworms, roundworms, and many higher animals have bilateral symmetry. (See Fig. 24-3.) The two sides are mirror images of each other. Bilateral symmetry makes rapid movement possible. Such an organism constantly investigates its environment and remains ready to meet or avoid danger. This can be done most efficiently if one part of the body takes the lead. Sense organs and prey-capturing devices are often concentrated in or near that body part. Bodies with bilateral symmetry are often streamlined. Animals with bilateral symmetry have a *head end* (**anterior**), and a *tail end* (**posterior**). They have right and left sides, and *back* (**dorsal**) and *belly* (**ventral**) sides. (See Fig. 24-4.)

Diversity and Continuity in Sponges

The sponges are the simplest animals and make up Phylum Porifera. Porifera is a Latin term meaning pore-bearer.

BODY PLAN Sponges may look like flat crusts or radially-symmetrical vases. They may also resemble irregularly-shaped masses, or branched plants. (See Fig. 24-5.) A dye added to water near a sponge reveals that water constantly enters the body through hundreds of invisible holes or pores. *The pores through which water enters a sponge are called* **incurrent pores.** The water is expelled from the sponge's central cavity through a larger opening, the *osculum* (os kyə ləm). The body of a simple sponge is generally shaped like a vase. (See Fig. 24-6.) The body wall is composed of two layers of cells. *The outer layer made of flat cells is the* **ectoderm.** *The inner layer of cells is the* **endoderm.** It is composed of *collar cells.* Each collar cell has a fringe collar surrounding a long flagellum. *Separating the two layers of cells is a layer of nonliving jelly-like material called* **mesoglea** (mez ə *glē* ə). It is produced by living cells. The mesoglea contains some ameboid cells which carry food from the collar cells to the ectoderm. They also secrete spicules. **Spicules** *are branched needles of either calcium carbonate or silica which support the bodies of some sponges.* Other sponges are supported by an imbedded network of *spongin,* a tough elastic material. These sponges may also contain spicules. Sponges containing spongin were used in household cleaning tasks before artificial substitutes replaced them.

DIVERSITY   Sponges are classified according to kinds of spicules and the complexity of incurrent canals. These canals may be simple outpouchings of the body wall. Or they may be an elaborate system of canals connecting several chambers lined with collar cells. Sponges appear in almost every color. They exist both individually and in clusters. (See Fig. 24-7.)

Most sponges are marine. They live in shallow water along the coastline. Some live in deep water. A few small ones live in freshwater.

CONTINUITY   Sponges reproduce both sexually and asexually. In sexual reproduction some of the cells in the jelly-like layer become eggs. Others divide to form sperm cells. Sperm cells are brought to the female sponge by water currents. Each fertilized egg becomes a flagellated larva. **A** larva *is an immature form which looks different from the adult.* The larvae (plural) swim to a new location and become attached. Competition with their parents is thus avoided. Many sponges also reproduce asexually through capsules. These are able to survive drying and freezing. When conditions are again favorable, the sponge cells emerge and form a new sponge. The mass of a sponge may increase by budding and branching. Some of these buds or branches may break off and form new individuals.

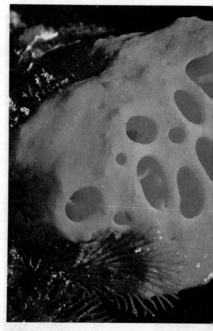

24-5. *Sponges have skeletons of spongin. Sponges have long been used for bathing, scrubbing, or padding.*

24-6. *Part of a colony of a simple sponge.*

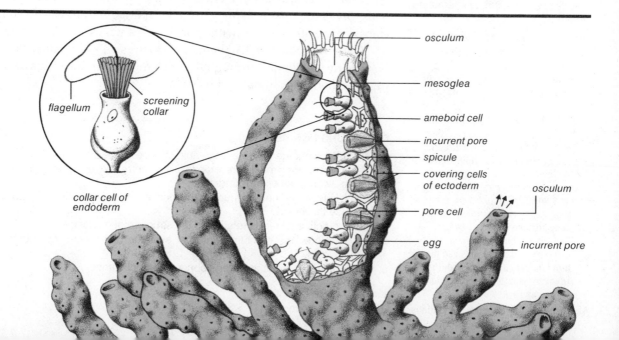

flagellum

screening collar

collar cell of endoderm

osculum

mesoglea

ameboid cell

incurrent pore

spicule

covering cells of ectoderm

pore cell

egg

osculum

incurrent pore

Homeostasis of Sponges

Homeostasis is maintained in sponges through the interaction of their internal systems with surrounding water.

INTERNAL SYSTEMS   A sponge's central cavity acts as its combined *digestive, circulatory, respiratory,* and *excretory* systems. (Refer to Fig. 24-6.) The flagella of the collar cells produce a current by their waving motion. The incoming current brings with it diatoms, bacteria, and other protists. As water current passes through, the collar cells capture and ingest the organisms. Food particles are then enclosed in vacuoles at the base of the collar cell. This food then is passed along to other cells.

The water entering the central cavity as well as that surrounding the sponge, also contains dissolved oxygen. Simple diffusion supplies the cells with this gas. The carbon dioxide and nitrogenous wastes excreted by the cells diffuse into passing water currents.

The sponge has no sense cells or nerve cells. All of its cells are irritable and can be stimulated directly or by nearby cells. However, the sponge does not respond in a coordinated way.

Behavior and Environment of Sponges

Sponges are well adapted to their environment. They have lived their simple way of life for millions of years.

CLEAR WATER   Of the animal groups studied in this chapter the sponges are especially sensitive to water pollution. They can live only in clear water. Pollutants would either bury them or clog their incurrent canals.

RELATIONSHIPS WITH OTHER ANIMALS   Sponges appear to have a disagreeable taste and smell. Hence, they are not attacked by most animals. Small organisms living within the sponge are protected. Some crabs decorate themselves with sponges. This serves as a camouflage.

Certain sponges attach themselves to the shells of shellfish. They bore many small holes through the shell into the animal. This action destroys both the animal and its shell.

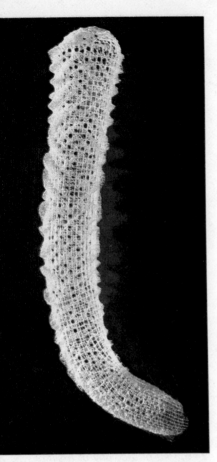

24-7. Venus' flower basket is a glass sponge with a skeleton of silica. Its spicules form an interlacing network.

Answers to Questions for Section 1.

A. **1.** The increased surface area increases diffusion of materials, reduces the distance the materials must travel, and allows cells to become specialized.

B. **2.** See Glossary for definition of terms. Spherical symmetry—the organism faces out in all directions, and has poor locomotion. Radial symmetry—sense organs are distributed in a circle; hardly moves, or is anchored in one spot. Bilateral symmetry—sense organs often concentrated near the head.

*3. Bilateral; because animal is often streamlined and so can move more quickly and has the ability to investigate surroundings constantly and efficiently.

QUESTIONS FOR SECTION 1

1. Of what advantage is it to a large animal to be divided into cells?
2. Distinguish among the different kinds of symmetry and relate them to activity and to awareness of surroundings.
3. Which kind of symmetry is found in the most advanced animals? Why do you suppose this is so?
4. List and define all terms relating to the structure of a sponge.
5. Describe how the combined internal systems of sponges contribute to homeostasis.
6. Describe interactions between sponges and pollutants.

(See page 449 for answers 4-6.)

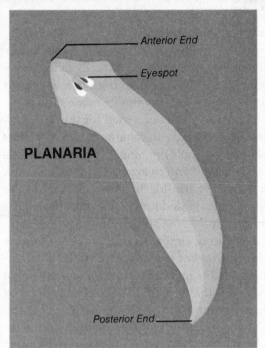

PLANARIA

Anterior End

Eyespot

Posterior End

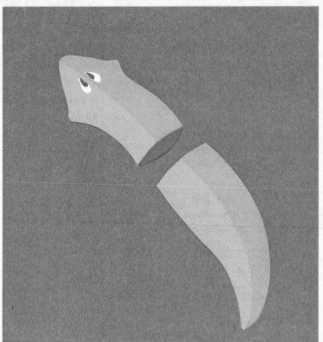

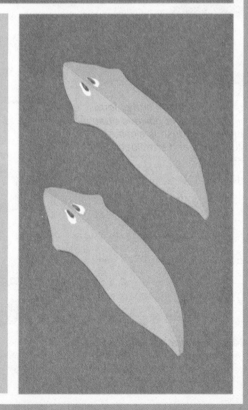

CHAPTER INVESTIGATION

Sponges and Cnidarians are able to regenerate missing parts. So are planaria, the free-living flatworms. The worm can be anesthetized ("put to sleep") with a few crystals of Epsom salts.

A. When the anterior and posterior ends are separated in the middle, can each end regenerate its missing end and form a complete worm?

B. Can a section cut out of the middle of the worm regenerate both head and tail ends?

C. One theory states that a piece of a planarian develops a new head at the end with the highest rate of metabolism. That has been found to be the anterior end. If small enough pieces are cut from near the anterior, middle, and posterior ends, metabolic rates may differ only slightly. Would they also produce new head and tail ends? Try it. Keep pieces in separate dishes and make daily drawings of each piece. Remember to supply fresh water daily. Do your data support the metabolic gradient theory?

☑ CNIDARIANS

Diversity and Continuity of Cnidarians

OBJECTIVES FOR SECTION 2

F. Describe the general body plan of cnidarians.
G. Explain how each internal system contributes to homeostasis in the cnidarians.
H. Describe the various kinds of behavior and environmental relationships found in cnidarians.

Phylum Cnidaria consists of jellyfishes, hydras, sea anemones, and coral. The feature that these animals share are cells called *cnidoblasts* (nīd ə blasts). Cnidoblasts contain threads used to trap or sting prey. It is the cnidoblasts that give the phylum its name. The name Coelenterata (hollow intestine) has also been used for this group.

BODY PLAN   The cnidarians also have in common the body plan of a radially symmetrical bag with a single opening. (See Fig. 24-8.) The opening serves both to take in food and to expel indigestible matter. Surrounding the mouth is a ring of arm-like tentacles. Separating the outer ectoderm from the inner endoderm is the mesoglea. The mesoglea is stiff enough to supply some support to the body.

The body has two alternate but similar forms. *The polyp form is not free to move about, being attached at its base.* Its mouth and tentacles are at the upper free end. *The medusa form is an inverted polyp that is free floating.* Its shape is that of a bell. The clapper is the tube which leads from the mouth opening into the body cavity. The tentacles of both polyps and medusae contain cnidoblasts. Each cnidoblast contains a spirally coiled, hollow thread called a *nematocyst* (ni mat ə sist). When the trigger is touched the nematocyst is thrust into the prey organism, paralyzing or trapping it. Such stinging capsules of large jellyfish or the Portuguese man-of-war can inflict human swimmers with fatal injuries.

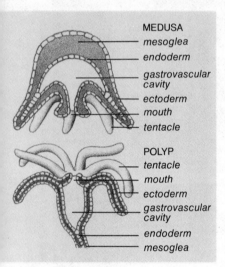

MEDUSA
- mesoglea
- endoderm
- gastrovascular cavity
- ectoderm
- mouth
- tentacle

POLYP
- tentacle
- mouth
- ectoderm
- gastrovascular cavity
- endoderm
- mesoglea

24-8. The two body forms of cnidarians. The polyp is attached, and the medusa is similar but upside down and free-floating.

The medusa form swims by forcing water out of its mouth.

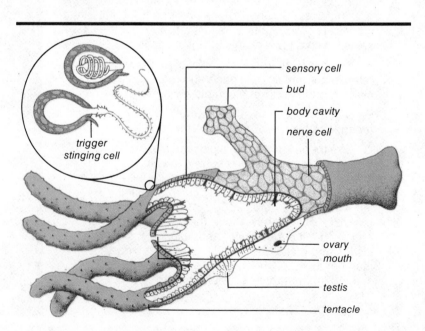

- sensory cell
- bud
- body cavity
- nerve cell
- trigger
- stinging cell
- ovary
- mouth
- testis
- tentacle

24-9. A hydra partially cut away. See expanded view of stinging cell. How does this body differ from that of a simple sponge?

DIVERSITY The Cnidaria are divided into three classes. *Class Hydrozoa* includes the freshwater hydras. (See Fig. 24-9.) These organisms exist as single individuals and only in polyp form. Most other hydrozoans are colonial marine forms which alternate between polyp and medusa stages. These include Obelia and the Portuguese man-of-war.

Class Scyphozoa includes the jellyfishes in which the medusa is the main body form.

Class Anthozoa contains the sea anemones and the corals. (See Fig. 24-10.) They produce the polyp form only.

CONTINUITY The jellyfish and hydra provide examples of continuity in cnidarians. In the adult jellyfish, the medusae swim around and reproduce sexually. They develop either testes or ovaries. **Testes** *are organs that produce* **sperm,** *the male sex cells.* **Ovaries** *are organs that produce* **ova (eggs),** *the female sex cells.* The males discharge sperm into the sea. The sperm are carried by currents and enter a female's body cavity. The fertilized eggs leave through the mouth. Finally, they lodge in folds around the mouth. After developing into ciliated larvae, each attaches to an object and grows into a polyp. The polyp reproduces asexually by budding. **Budding** *is the production of a new organism from a swelling on the side of an adult.* Each swims away as a medusa which will develop into an adult. (See Fig. 24-11.)

Hydras reproduce asexually by budding. The new individual pinches off and lives independently from the parent. Hydras also regenerate missing parts. Even if cut into many pieces, most parts grow

The Portuguese man-of-war consists of a floating gas filled bag from which chains of polyps dangle.

24-10. *Coral tree. Corals are colonial cnidarians that secrete limestone skeletons forming coral reefs.*

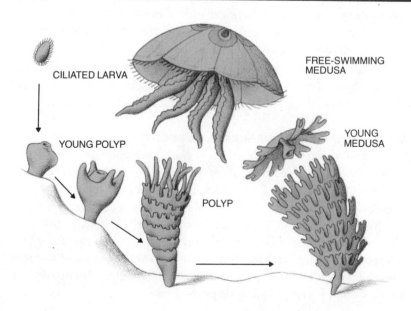

CILIATED LARVA

FREE-SWIMMING MEDUSA

YOUNG POLYP

YOUNG MEDUSA

POLYP

24-11. *Life history of the jellyfish Aurelia.*

missing portions to complete the animal. Hydras reproduce sexually in fall or winter. Unspecialized cells in the ectoderm develop testes or ovaries. A fertilized egg grows by cell division. Finally, it becomes surrounded with a protective covering. This shell may lie dormant for a time. Later, it will hatch when conditions are appropriate.

Homeostasis of Cnidarians

Homeostasis in cnidarians is maintained by the cooperative interaction among various internal systems.

DIGESTION   Cnidarians begin digestion of foods within the central body cavity before they are taken into the cells. Gland cells secrete enzymes that digest the prey organisms. The resulting pieces can then be taken in by other body cells. Indigestible materials left in the central cavity are eliminated through the mouth.

CIRCULATION   The partially digested food particles are circulated throughout the body cavity. This is accomplished through currents generated by body movements. The waving flagella on the endoderm cells also assist in this process. Thus the cavity serves in digestion and circulation alike. *A body cavity that functions in both digestion and circulation is called a* **gastrovascular cavity.**

RESPIRATION AND EXCRETION   Respiration and excretion take place by diffusion. Both ectoderm and endoderm are in direct contact with water.

NERVOUS SYSTEM   Cnidarians display coordinated behavior which suggests nerve tissue. Their tentacles work together to capture prey and push it into the gastrovascular cavity. This coordination is possible because of certain sensory and nerve cells. Cnidarian nerve cells are interconnected. These cells form a network throughout the body. They are most concentrated around the mouth. Sensory cells are especially sensitive to touch or chemical substances in the water.

MUSCULAR SYSTEM   Body movements of cnidarians are constant and rhythmic. They are made possible by muscle cells. By way of the nerve network, these muscle fibers contract when stimulated.

Behavior and Environment of Cnidarians

ADAPTIVE BEHAVIOR   *Responses that increase an organism's chance of survival are examples of* **adaptive behavior.** Some cnidarian behavior is modified by internal conditions. After feeding, the nematocysts no longer discharge. This is an energy-saving response.

Repeated stimulation of a cnidarian causes the body to contract. This eventually results in its relaxation. Such behavior might be considered habituation. **Habituation** *is the tendency to eventually ignore repeated stimulus that produces harmful effects.* Habituation is another energy-conservation response.

Answers to Questions for Section 2.
H. 4. Habituation occurs when a repeated stimulus produces harmful effects, and the organism eventually ignores the stimulus. An advantage in that it conserves energy.

5. Corals extract calcium from sea water and secrete skeletons of calcium carbonate which build up a reef, or forms a ring or atoll around an island that meanwhile has sunk below the surface.

*6. At one time, the water was much shallower at that place; the same forces that cause the land to sink where coral reefs form, deepen the channel.

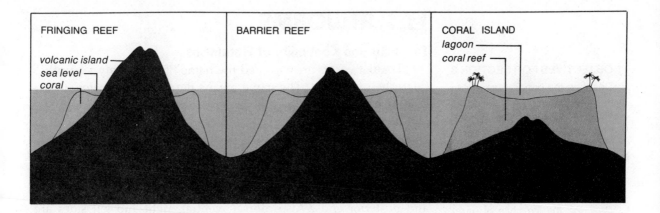

FRINGING REEF	BARRIER REEF	CORAL ISLAND

FRINGING REEF

volcanic island
sea level
coral

BARRIER REEF

CORAL ISLAND

lagoon
coral reef

24-12. The development of a coral atoll.

REEFS AND ATOLLS   Of importance to the shipping industry and to numerous organisms of the tropical seas are the marine corals. Corals extract calcium from sea water. They then secrete partially-enclosing skeletons of calcium carbonate. Generations of these creatures build on top of older skeletons. Reefs and atolls are developed in this manner. Such activity is responsible for the Great Barrier Reef. This band of coral stretches about 2000 kilometers along the east coast of Australia.

Three types of reefs are shown in Figure 24-12. Marginal, or fringing reefs border a coast. These reefs are separated from it only by a narrow, shallow channel. A barrier reef parallels the coastline. A sea channel deep enough for ship travel separates this reef from the coastline. An atoll is a ring-shaped coral island surrounding a shallow central pool. Presumably the central island has sunk since the reef building began. Charles Darwin believed that coral reefs develop where land is slowly sinking. The reefs grow at about the same rate. Their peaks remain just above the surface of the water. The Darwin theory is still widely accepted today. Tropical coral reefs with their rich diversity of creatures are among the most productive ecosystems in the biosphere.

QUESTIONS FOR SECTION 2

1. Describe the general body plan of cnidarians.
2. List and define the terms referring to the major structures found in cnidarians.
3. Describe how each internal system in cnidarians contributes to homeostasis.
4. Of what advantage to an organism is habituation?
5. How are reefs and atolls formed?
6. Corals generally live less than 65 m down in the sea. How do you account for coral reefs that are deeper than 1400 m?

Answers to Questions for Section 2.
F. 1. A radially symmetrical bag with a single opening, surrounded by tentacles, which takes in food and expels wastes.

2. Ectoderm: outer layer. Endoderm: inner layer. Meosglea: somewhat stiff material separating ectoderm and endoderm. Tentacles: arm-like structures around mouth. Cnidoblast: stinging capsule containing nematocyst. Testes: organs that produce sperm. Ovaries: organs that produce eggs. Gastrovascular cavity: serves both digestion and circulation.

G. 3. Digestion: enzymes digest food in gastrovascular cavity; digested pieces move into body cells, and indigestible parts leave through the mouth. Circulation: body movement and waving flagella circulate food particles. Respiration and excretion: take place by diffusion. Nervous system: nerve cells form network throughout body, so tentacles capture prey and push it into the gastrovascular cavity. Muscular system: muscle cells contract so body moves constantly and rhythmically.

3 FLATWORMS

Diversity and Continuity of Flatworms

OBJECTIVES FOR SECTION 3

I. Describe the general body plan of flatworms.

J. Describe how each internal system contributes to homeostasis in the flatworm.

K. Describe experiments with learned behavior in planarians. Give a possible explanation of memory.

L. Describe the life style of parasites and the life history of the sheep liver fluke.

The flatworms are assigned the name Phylum Platyhelminthes (plat i hel *minth ēz*). The name means flat worm and refers to the dorsal-ventral flattening of their bodies.

Body Plan

Flatworms are the most primitive animals to display bilateral symmetry. In addition, cephalization (sef ə lə *zā* shən) and organ systems are first seen in these organisms. They have definite anterior and posterior ends. Also, dorsal, ventral, right and left sides are present. (See Fig. 24-13.) **Cephalization** *refers to the concentration of sensory organs and nervous tissue at the anterior, or head-end of the body.*

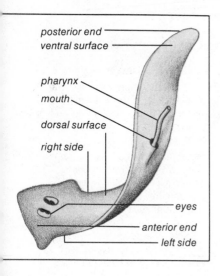

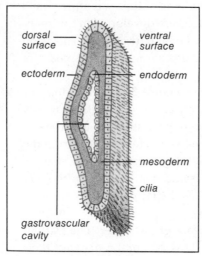

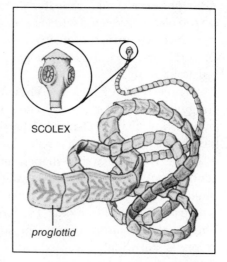

24-13. Body plan of a flatworm, a planarian. (left)

24-14. A cross section of a planarian. (middle)

24-15. Tapeworm attached to the intestinal wall of vertebrates with hooks and suckers of the scolex. The proglottids are full of reproductive structures. (right)

The flatworms also have *a well-developed cell layer between the ectoderm and endoderm, the* **mesoderm.** (See Fig. 24-14.) The mesoderm contains the reproductive, excretory, and muscular organs. Flatworms retain the primitive features of a single opening into the gastrovascular cavity. They lack a separate circulatory system.

DIVERSITY Phylum Platyhelminthes includes three classes. *Class Turbellaria* consists of free-living flatworms. Most are marine living organisms. However, some, such as the planarian, live in freshwater. A few are terrestrial.

Class Trematoda is composed of the parasitic flukes. Some flukes live as external parasites on skin or the gills of a fish. Others are internal parasites living in tissue or internal cavities of animals.

Class Cestoda is made up of the parasitic tapeworms. (See Fig. 24-15.) Tapeworms are long ribbon-like worms that live in the intestines of vertebrates. They have suckers and often hooks borne on a knob-shaped *scolex*.

CONTINUITY   The free-living planarians reproduce asexually by fission. An animal pulls itself into anterior and posterior portions. Each portion regenerates the missing part. Finally, it becomes a whole worm. One can cut a planarian into several parts. In doing so, the same regeneration of parts occurs. (See Fig. 24-16.) Planarians also reproduce sexually. They are **hermaphrodites,** *that is, each contains male and female organs.* They do cross-fertilize, however. Each contributes sperm to and receives sperm from another worm.

Most of a fluke's interior is occupied by reproductive organs. Like planarians, most flukes are hermaphroditic. Many flukes have complex life histories that involve several host species.

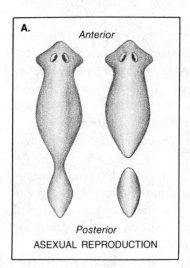

A.

Anterior

Posterior
ASEXUAL REPRODUCTION

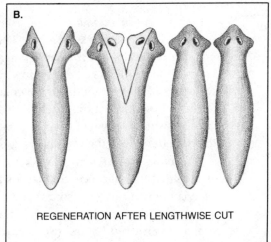

B.

REGENERATION AFTER LENGTHWISE CUT

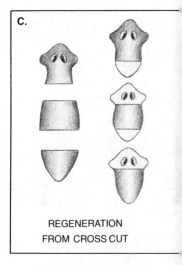

C.

REGENERATION
FROM CROSS CUT

The scolex of a tapeworm is constantly producing body sections called *proglottids* (prō glăt ədz). Each proglottid is filled with a complex set of reproductive organs of both sexes. Fertilization occurs within these structures. Proglottids nearest the scolex are the youngest. Those farther back are progressively more mature and full of fertilized eggs. The mature proglottids detach and pass out of the intestine with the host's wastes. Some tapeworms have two or three different species of hosts in their life histories.

Homeostasis of Flatworms

The internal systems of flatworms maintain constant internal environment. The systems are interrelated.

24-16. A. *Planarian can regenerate missing parts.* **B.** *It can be divided into lengthwise sections. Each section can form a new Planarian.* **C.** *Planarian cut into cross sections. Each section can form a new Planarian.*

Fertilization can occur within a proglottid, across proglottids of the same worm, or across proglottids of different tapeworms in the same host.

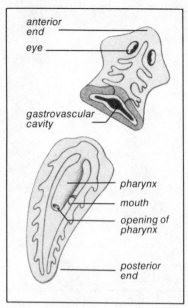

anterior
end

eye

gastrovascular
cavity

pharynx

mouth

opening of
pharynx

posterior
end

24-17. *Digestive system of a Planarian.*

DIGESTION IN PLANARIA   Planarians feed on small animals and on the dead bodies of larger animals. Live animals are often caught in the mucus trails left behind them as they crawl. The mouth is located near the middle of the ventral body surface. Within the mouth cavity is the pharynx (*far* ingks). *The* **pharynx** *is a muscular tube connected by its anterior end to the gastrovascular cavity.* (See Fig. 24-17.) The pharynx can be greatly lengthened and extended through the mouth for feeding. At this point enzymes soften the prey tissues. This allows food to be brought into the pharynx by its sucking motion. Digestion is nearly completed here. However, some digestion occurs in the gastrovascular cavity.

CIRCULATION AND RESPIRATION IN PLANARIA   The much branched gastrovascular cavity serves circulatory and respiratory functions. From this cavity digested food diffuses throughout the body's tissues. The much branched cavity and flat shape serve a specific purpose. They insure that no tissue is very far from its food and oxygen supply.

EXCRETION IN PLANARIA   The excretory system of a planarian consists of two networks of tubes. These run the length of the body. *The fine tubes connect to many enlarged ends known as* **flame cells.** Each flame cell looks like a hollow flask. Within this structure are waving cilia that extend from the enlarged end. Their motion causes fluids to flow toward the external openings. This system only regulates the water content of tissues. Wastes are excreted largely through the endoderm and the mouth.

NERVOUS SYSTEM OF THE PLANARIA   Flatworms are the most primitive animals to have a central nervous system. In planaria, it consists of a pair of ventral nerve cords. These structures extend the length of the body and connect to a pair of ganglia in the head. *A* **ganglion** *is a group of nerve cell bodies.* (See Fig. 24-18.) The two nerve cords are connected by many cross strands. The paired ganglia of primitive organisms may be referred to as a brain. The brain appears to relay sensory impulses from sense organs to the rest of the body.

Sensory cells are most concentrated in the head. Furthermore, light-sensitive cells are found in the eyes. On each side of the head are pits with sensory cells that respond to chemical stimuli. The pointed lobes on each side of the head are sensitive to touch.

MUSCULAR SYSTEM OF THE PLANARIA   Muscles in flatworms exist in several layers just beneath the ectoderm. The outer layer of muscles are circular and constrict the worm when they contract. The inner muscles are longitudinal and shorten the worm. The body moves by means of these contractions by gliding over mucus trails it secretes. The worms use cilia on their ventral surface to do this.

DIGESTION IN FLUKES   Flukes are parasitic. They have at least one sucker by which they attach to their host. The muscular pharynx directs the host's tissue and body fluids into the fluke's gastrovascular cavity.

CIRCULATION AND RESPIRATION IN FLUKES   Flukes use their gastrovascular cavities for circulatory and respiratory functions. They live in tissue that is well supplied with oxygen by the host's blood.

EXCRETION IN FLUKES   Flukes have an excretory system of flame cells and canals.

NERVOUS SYSTEM OF FLUKES   For flatworms, flukes have a well-developed nervous system. However, they lack special sense organs.

MUSCULAR SYSTEM OF THE FLUKES   Muscle layers in flukes are like those of planaria. There are no cilia.

DIGESTION IN TAPEWORMS   Tapeworms have no mouth and no digestive system. They attach themselves to the lining of the host's intestines by suckers and hooks. The worm feeds by absorbing food that was digested by the host. An external thick coat keeps the tapeworm from being digested while in the host's body.

CIRCULATION AND RESPIRATION   Tapeworms may receive dissolved oxygen from the blood vessels in the host's intestinal wall. When dissolved oxygen is not available, they survive without it. Tapeworms obtain the small amount of energy they need by anaerobic respiration.

EXCRETORY, NERVOUS, AND MUSCULAR SYSTEMS OF THE TAPEWORM   The tapeworm's excretory, nervous, and muscular systems are similar to those of planaria. However, the nervous system of tapeworms is less well developed.

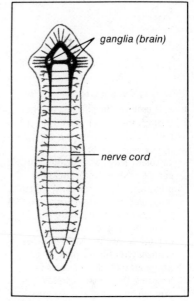

24-18. *Nervous system of a Planarian.*

Behavior and Environment of Flatworms

INNATE BEHAVIOR   Behavior in planarians is largely innate, that is, involuntary. Planarians respond to light, water currents, and chemicals. Having a concentration of nerve tissue at the head end does not insure complicated behavior. But the increased development of sense organs allows greater accuracy and speed in detecting stimuli. Planarians avoid light. Also, they tend to keep their ventral surface pressed against other objects. They respond quickly to the presence of food in the water. Juices from liver or raw meat placed in the well-oxygenated waters of a stream lure planaria from nearby rocks. Furthermore, the lobes at the sides of the head are especially sensitive to water currents. Some species respond to currents by swimming into them. These are examples of taxes (*tak* sēz). **Taxes** *are the automatic movements of an organism in a direction determined by the stimulus.*

LEARNED BEHAVIOR **Learned behavior** *is behavior that has changed because of experience.* There are indications that planarians are capable of associative learning. In one experiment worms were exposed to a light followed two seconds later by an electric shock. This shock caused the worms to shorten quickly. After 150 trials, the worms contracted in response to the light alone. It appears that they had learned a conditioned response. *A* **conditioned response** *is a response to a substitute stimulus which an organism has learned to associate with the original stimulus.* In another experiment, the trained worms were cut in two and allowed to regenerate. Both the head and tail ends "remembered" what they had learned. Even after a second cutting, regenerated worms retained the conditioned response. Some biologists, however, have had difficulty reproducing these results.

In additional experiments, the regenerating pieces of trained worms were placed in water containing an RNA-digesting enzyme. In this case, only the trained head kept its memory. This supports the theory of some biologists that memory can be stored by RNA in the brain.

PARASITISM   The effect of a parasite on its host is usually not severe enough to kill the host. If so, the parasite will be without nourishment. A parasite can damage its host however.

External parasites, such as flukes that attach to the skin of fish, differ little from their free-living relatives. They are adapted for attachment to their host. But internal parasites have generally become very different from their free-living relatives. Natural selection has resulted in the degeneration of nervous, muscular, and digestive systems. The loss of organs that are no longer needed increases the parasites' efficiency. Reproductive systems, however, become very highly developed. There are hazards of transferring eggs from one host to another. Hence, selection has favored the production of a large number of eggs. This helps to insure the survival of the species. Also, many parasite forms of these simple worms have developed complicated life cycles. Some of them require several different hosts and specific sets of environmental circumstances. The life history of a common parasitic flatworm will show this relationship.

The *sheep liver fluke* lives its adult life in the liver. Egg production is almost continuous. Each adult produces up to a half million eggs. The eggs pass from the liver to the intestine. From here, they are eliminated with the sheep's wastes. (See Fig. 24-19.) If the eggs fall in water they hatch into larvae. Later, these larvae will burrow into a certain species of snail. Within the snail the larvae go through several stages. Finally, these larvae burrow out of the snail and swim to the grass at the water's edge. At this point, they form cysts on the leaves

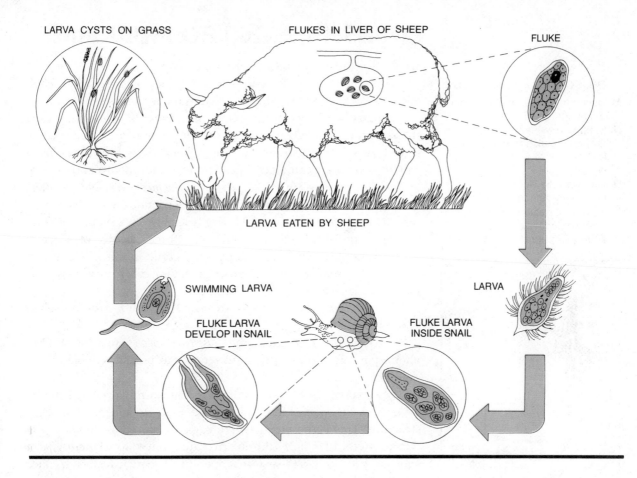

LARVA CYSTS ON GRASS

FLUKES IN LIVER OF SHEEP

FLUKE

LARVA EATEN BY SHEEP

SWIMMING LARVA

FLUKE LARVA DEVELOP IN SNAIL

FLUKE LARVA INSIDE SNAIL

LARVA

of the grass. Cysts may be eaten by sheep or cattle. With their shell removed by digestion, larvae burrow through the intestinal wall. When they reach the liver their life cycle is completed. Completion of the life cycle depends on pastures with marshy areas and the right kind of snails. Liver flukes may cause severe, even fatal damage. Human infestation can occur from the eating of infested sheep or cow livers that are not cooked properly.

24-19. *Life cycle of the sheep liver fluke.*

QUESTIONS FOR SECTION 3
1. Describe the general body plan of flatworms.
2. Describe how each internal system contributes to homeostasis in the flatworms.
3. Describe experiments with learned behavior in planarians and a possible explanation of memory.
4. Describe three adaptations necessary to a parasitic way of life.
5. How can knowing the life history of the liver fluke help one avoid being infested by flukes?

Answers to Questions for Section 3.

I. 1. Bilaterally symmetrical, with cephalization: sensory organs and nervous tissues are concentrated at head end; have ectoderm, endoderm, and mesoderm—containing reproductive, excretory, and muscular systems; have single opening to gastrovascular cavity.

4 UNSEGMENTED ROUNDWORMS

Diversity and Continuity of Roundworms

OBJECTIVES FOR SECTION 4

M. Describe the general body plan of unsegmented roundworms.

N. Explain how each internal system contributes to homeostasis in the unsegmented roundworms.

O. Describe the life histories of the hookworm and the trichina.

P. Tell what makes reproduction possible in animals that are stationary or parasitic.

Unsegmented roundworms are assigned to Phylum Aschelminthes (ask hel *min* thēz). The phylum name means sac worm.

BODY PLAN The unsegmented roundworms are cylindrically shaped and bilaterally symmetrical. The bodies are composed of three layers. The ectoderm produces *a tough outer covering called a cuticle.* There is a complete digestive tract with mouth and anus at opposite ends. (See Fig. 24-20.) *Between the mesoderm and the internal organs is a fluid-filled space called a* **pseudocoelom** (süd ə *sēl* əm). This space has no special lining. (See Fig. 25-1 on page 469.)

DIVERSITY We will mention only three classes of Phylum Aschelminthes. *Class Rotifera* is the only group in this phylum with cilia. The resemblance of their crown of waving cilia to turning wheels gives the class its name. (See Fig. 24-2.)

Class Nematomorpha (nem ə tō *mōr* fə) includes the horsehair worms.

Most roundworms are in the *Class Nematoda* (nem ə *tōd* ə). They abound in soil, marine or fresh water, and as parasites in plants and animals. (See Fig. 24-22.)

CONTINUITY Sexes are separate in the roundworms. In the female, each of a pair of long thin ovaries leads to a somewhat larger structure. This is the *uterus* where eggs are stored as they are produced. (Refer to Fig. 24-20.) The two uteri join to form the *vagina*, a short tube leading to the external opening. The male testis is a coiled tube in which sperm develop. The sperm cells then pass through a sperm duct which opens posteriorly.

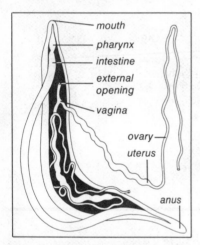

mouth
pharynx
intestine
external opening
vagina
ovary
uterus
anus

24-20. *Body plan of a nonsegmented roundworm, Ascaris. This is a female cut along the mid-dorsal line.*

Homeostasis of Roundworms

Maintaining a constant internal environment is the main function of various internal systems.

DIGESTIVE SYSTEM The worms of Phylum Aschelminthes have a one-way digestive system with a mouth and anus. This arrangement eliminates the mixing of incoming food with outgoing wastes. As food is pushed through the digestive tract it is digested and absorbed in an orderly fashion. The undigested remains continue on through the digestive tract. From here the waste material is eliminated through the anus.

CIRCULATION, RESPIRATION, AND EXCRETION There are no circulatory and respiratory systems in unsegmented roundworms. The fluid in the pseudocoelom distributes digested foods and dissolved oxygen. Nitrogenous wastes are removed from the body through an *excretory* pore.

24-21. *Rotifer. Notice the crown of waving cilia.*

NERVOUS SYSTEM   The nervous system of nematodes consists of a ring of nervous tissue around the pharynx. From this ring, nerves run posteriorly along the body.

MUSCULAR SYSTEM   Roundworms have only longitudinal muscles. Because of this, they can bend only dorsally and ventrally.

Behavior and Environment of Roundworms

PARASITISM   Roundworms are found as parasites of all kinds of animals and plants. Humans are hosts of some 50 species of roundworms. Some are fairly harmless, such as the common intestinal nematode, *Ascaris*. Those that may cause serious damage include the *guinea worms*. These worms form ulcerating blisters in human skin. Another, the filaria worms, block lymph vessels. This causes the immense swelling of the disease elephantiasis. Let us examine in detail two further examples of parasites in humans, hookworms and trichina.

The tiny *hookworm* is a great threat to human health. Larvae invade human hosts by burrowing through the skin of bare feet into blood vessels. From here they burrow into the air passages of the lungs. As they travel to the throat they are swallowed. Finally they return to the intestine where they mature. The eggs pass out with the solid waste. These develop into larvae in warm soil. Since adult hookworms feed on blood, the host may feel weak and tired. Hookworms were once common. However, sanitary toilets and the wearing of shoes have helped control hookworm infestations.

Another dreaded roundworm parasite is the *trichina worm*, *Trichinella*. It is introduced into mammals when they eat uncooked or improperly cooked meat, mainly pork, containing trichina cysts. (See Fig. 24-23.) The larvae within the cysts are released by digestive juices

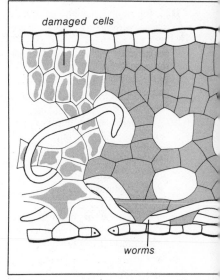

24-22. *Nematodes in a plant leaf. As larvae, they enter the stoma and absorb leaf juices. This may cause withering of leaves.*

24-23. *Life history of the trichina worm.*

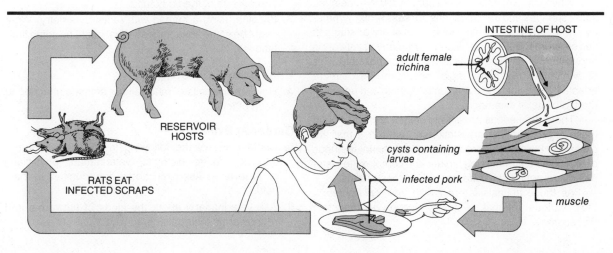

Answers to Questions for Section 4.

M. 1. Bilaterally symmetrical, cylinder shape, with three cell layers; digestive tract with mouth and anus, and pseudocoelom between mesoderm and internal organs.

N. 2. Digestion: food does not mix with wastes. Circulation, respiration, and excretion: fluid in pseudocoelom distributes oxygen and food; wastes go out by excretory pore. Nervous system: a ring of nerve tissue connected to posterior nerves. Muscular system: muscles allow bending dorsally and ventrally.

O. 3. Hookworm: use of sanitary toilets and shoes. Trichina: cook meat (pork) properly.

P. 4. Large numbers of gametes, asexual reproduction, swimming larvae, and complex life histories.

in the intestine. Here the worms mature. After mating, the worms can produce up to 1500 microscopic larvae. The larvae burrow into blood vessels and finally into muscles. There they form cysts. The cysts die unless eaten by a suitable host. It is during the larval migration that the symptoms of trichinosis occur. They include severe pains, muscular weakness, and anemia. Death sometimes results.

Knowledge of life histories of parasitic worms can help you devise ways of avoiding the danger and discomfort of infestation.

QUESTIONS FOR SECTION 4

1. Describe the general body plan of unsegmented roundworms.
2. Describe how each internal system in unsegmented roundworms contributes to homeostasis.
3. What are specific ways one could avoid infestation by hookworms and by trichina worms?
4. What makes reproduction possible in animals that are stationary or parasitic?

CHAPTER REVIEW

In a large organism, there is too much living matter to be serviced by one nucleus. These problems are solved by being divided into cells, each with its own nucleus. Cells are able to specialize. They do this in ways that increase the efficiency of the organism. *Structuring* living matter into cells, tissues, organs, and whole organ-systems makes possible more efficient *functioning* of an organism's body.

While some protozoans are spherically symmetrical, some sponges and the cnidarians possess radial symmetry. This body plan is sufficient for stationary or sluggish sea creatures. But it is the bilateral symmetry of flatworms and roundworms that makes cephalization possible. This body plan allows more rapid movement. Also, more adaptive behavior, and even some learning can be attributed to bilateral symmetry.

There are serious hazards to sexual reproduction in those organisms that are stationary and those that are parasites. Large numbers of gametes, asexual methods of reproduction, swimming larvae, and complex life histories made *continuity of life* possible in these forms.

As these animals *interact with their environment,* their various internal systems function to *maintain homeostasis.*

In spite of the *diversity* within each phylum, certain structural features suggest *similar* genetic origin of those within each phylum.

Using the Concepts

1. What distinguishes animals from plants, protists, fungi, and monerans?
2. Discuss the division of functions between the inside and outside of the body tube.
3. Imagine being a human with radial symmetry. What might be some advantages? What might be some limitations?

Unanswered Question

4. How are the cells of multicellular animals attached to each other?

Career Activities

5. Contact any of the following in your area: parasitologist, marine biologist, veterinarian, physician, coral jeweler. Ask each about opportunities in their field.
6. Ask veterinarians about the kinds of flatworms and roundworms their patients have.

22. large number of gametes, asexual methods, motile larvae, complex life history.

VOCABULARY REVIEW

1 symmetry
 spherical symmetry
 radial symmetry
 bilateral symmetry
 anterior
 posterior
 dorsal
 ventral
 ectoderm

 endoderm
2 medusa
 cnidoblast
 nematocyst
 budding
 gastrovascular cavity
 adaptive behavior
 habituation
 marginal reef

 barrier reef
 atoll
3 cephalization
 mesoderm
 scolex
 hermaphrodite
 proglottid
 pharynx
 innate behavior

 taxes
 learned behavior
 conditioned response
4 cuticle
 uterus
 vagina
 excretory pore

CHAPTER 24 TEST

Copy the number of each test item and place your answer to the right.

PART 1   Multiple Choice: Select the letter of the phrase that best completes each of the following.

a **1.** Dividing cytoplasm into cells decreases the
 a. diffusion distance   **b.** surface area
 c. possibility of specialization   **d.** dependency on other cells.

d **2.** The kind of symmetry in the fastest animals is
 a. asymmetry   **b.** spherical   **c.** radial
 d. bilateral.

c **3.** The animal that best illustrates radial symmetry is
 the   **a.** bath sponge   **b.** planaria   **c.** jelly-fish   **d.** hookworm.

c **4.** The outer layer of cells making up the body wall of many animals is the   **a.** mesoderm
 b. mesoglea   **c.** ectoderm   **d.** endoderm.

d **5.** An animal containing both male and female organs
 is a   **a.** nematocyst   **b.** pseudocoelom
 c. proglottid   **d.** hermaphrodite.

b **6.** A group of nerve cell bodies is a   **a.** cnidoblast
 b. ganglion   **c.** medusa   **d.** collar cell.

c **7.** Experiments with planaria suggest the possibility that memory is stored in the brain's   **a.** ADP
 b. ATP   **c.** RNA   **d.** DNA.

b **8.** Behavior which is involuntary is called   **a.** taxes
 b. innate   **c.** learned   **d.** conditioned.

d **9.** A response to a substitute stimulus is   **a.** habituation   **b.** innate behavior   **c.** cephalization
 d. a conditioned response.

b **10.** The best way to avoid infestation by the dreaded trichina worm is to avoid   **a.** going barefooted
 b. eating improperly cooked meat   **c.** eating improperly cooked liver   **d.** eating snails.

PART 2   Matching: Match the letter of the term in Column I with its description in Column II.

COLUMN I

a. cnidoblast   **e.** proglottid   **i.** platyhelminthes
b. collar cell   **f.** spicule   **j.** porifera
c. flame cell   **g.** aschelminthes
d. polyp   **h.** cnidarians

COLUMN II

e **11.** Tapeworm's body section with ovaries and testes

d **12.** A stationary form of cnidarian with its mouth and tentacles at the upper free end

b **13.** A structure with a waving flagellum that brings in food and oxygen with water currents

c **14.** A structure with interior waving cilia that cause fluids to flow out of excretory pores

f **15.** A needle of calcium carbonate or silica that supports the body of a sponge

a **16.** A cell that contains a stinging or trapping thread

j **17.** Spicules and collar cells

g **18.** Pseudocoelom

i **19.** Flat body and flame cells

h **20.** Nematocysts

PART 3   Completion: Complete the following.

21. A structure that may serve in digestion, circulation, respiration, and excretion is the _gastrovascular cavity_

22. Four ways that make reproduction possible in parasitic or unmoving organisms are ____.

23. The tendency to ignore repeated stimuli that produce no harmful effect is ____.   habituation

24. Many biologists believe that as reef building occurs, the land ____.   sinks

25. Budding is a form of reproduction sometimes occurring in the following two phyla ____.
 Porifera and Cnidaria

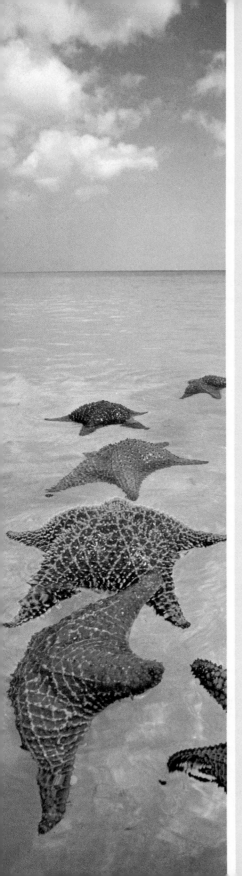

CHAPTER 25

ANNELIDS, MOLLUSCS, AND ECHINODERMS

We have seen an increase in complexity of animals from two to three cell layers. We have followed the change from spherical and radial to bilateral symmetry. Also, we have observed the trend to have a one-way digestive tube. These successful features are retained in the segmented worms, molluscs, and immature echinoderms.

Again we will look at the general body plan of each kind of animal. We will relate each to familiar basic concepts: *The link between structure and function, unity within diversity, the continuity of life, homeostasis,* and *interaction with the environment.*

Questions raised and answered in this chapter include:

- Of what advantages is the space between body wall and food tube?
- What keeps a host's blood from clotting when a leech sucks blood?
- Can an earthworm regenerate missing parts?
- Why do biologists believe that starfish are more closely related to mammals than are earthworms?
- Why is a starfish less able to learn than is an octopus?
- How are pearls formed?

STARFISH

1 ANNELIDS

The Coelom

In the nonsegmented roundworms, a fluid-filled space appears between the mesoderm and the internal organs. In the annelids and molluscs described in this chapter, a split forms within the mesoderm. That split develops into the space that contains various internal organs. *The fluid-filled, mesoderm-lined body cavity is known as a coelom* (sē ləm). (See Fig. 25-1.)

The coelom provides several advantages. It separates the muscles of the body wall from the muscles of the food tube. Thus, movement of food is not affected by general body motion. Likewise body motion is not affected by movement of the food tube. The fluid in the coelom may circulate many substances. These include wastes, food, and dissolved gases in the body. But more importantly, the coelom provides space where a true circulatory system can function. In this instance, there is no interference from other organs. Some biologists consider the development of the coelom to be one of the most important steps in animal change.

Diversity and Continuity of Annelids

The members of Phylum Annelida (an əl *ed* ə) are segmented worms. Their bodies are divided into a series of rings which provide the group their phylum name. Annelida is Latin for ringed.

BODY PLAN   The segmented worms are bilaterally symmetrical. They are composed of three layers, ectoderm, mesoderm, and endoderm. Segmented worms have a complete digestive tract with mouth and anus at opposite ends.

OBJECTIVES FOR SECTION 1

A. Describe the *coelom* and give three advantages it offers.

B. Describe the general body plan of the annelids.

C. Explain how each internal system in earthworms contributes to homeostasis.

D. Summarize learned behavior in earthworms.

E. Describe the relationships between earthworms and DDT, and between earthworms and soil.

*25-1. Body plans of **A.** cnidarian, **B.** flatworm, **C.** roundworm, and **D.** annelid.*

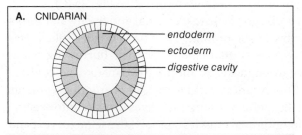

A.   CNIDARIAN
- endoderm
- ectoderm
- digestive cavity

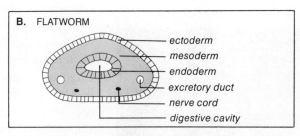

B.   FLATWORM
- ectoderm
- mesoderm
- endoderm
- excretory duct
- nerve cord
- digestive cavity

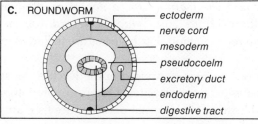

C.   ROUNDWORM
- ectoderm
- nerve cord
- mesoderm
- pseudocoelm
- excretory duct
- endoderm
- digestive tract

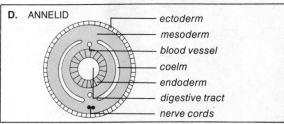

D.   ANNELID
- ectoderm
- mesoderm
- blood vessel
- coelm
- endoderm
- digestive tract
- nerve cords

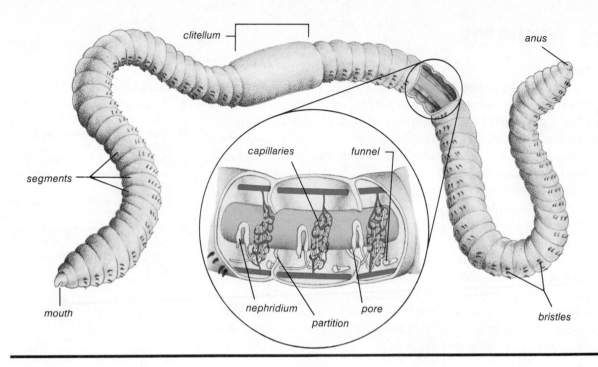

The labels on the figure read:

clitellum

anus

capillaries　funnel

segments

nephridium　pore

mouth　partition　bristles

25-2. *Segmentation in the earthworm. The nephridium, funnel, and pore in each segment are parts of the excretory system.*

25-3. *Shiny bristleworm.*

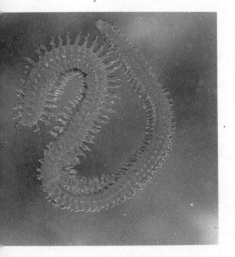

The segmented worms have a coelom. A series of partitions divides the coelom into several repeated sections called segments. (See Fig. 25-2.) Most segments contain duplicate structures of locomotion, excretion, circulation, muscle, and nervous supply. This segmentation is visible on the outside of the worm. It appears as circular grooves that mark the partitions on the inside.

DIVERSITY   The segmented worms are divided into three main classes. *Class Polychaeta* (päl i *kēt* ə) includes mostly marine worms that live in the sand or mud of shallow coastal waters. These include clamworms, bristleworms, and sandworms. (See Fig. 25-3.)

The *oligochaetes* (äl i gō kēts) are terrestrial and freshwater forms which usually burrow in soil or mud. They have bristles called *setae* (*sē* tē) and reduced heads, adaptations for their burrowing habit. Oligochaetes move through soil by alternate expansion and contraction of segments. This occurs as circular muscles of anterior segments are contracted. At this point, the anterior moves forward into existing soil space. When longitudinal muscles contract, the segments expand and enlarge the soil space. *The worms have a dorsal saddle-like swelling, called a* **clitellum** (klī *tel* əm), *which secretes a cocoon.* The cocoon is involved in reproduction. Earthworms are included in this group.

Class Hirudinea (hir *ood* ən ə) is composed of the leeches. Most leeches live in freshwater as external parasites. Others are predators or scavengers. Preferred hosts of the external parasites are fish, am-

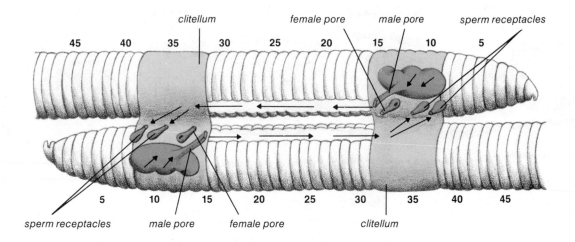

clitellum   female pore   male pore   sperm receptacles

45   40   35   30   25   20   15   10   5

5   10   15   20   25   30   35   40   45

sperm receptacles   male pore   female pore   clitellum

phibians, turtles, water birds, and snails. The leech has a sucker at each end of the body. The anterior one is smaller and contains the mouth. A few species have "teeth." These break through the skin of an animal before sucking its blood. Also, leeches produce an anesthetic which prevents their host from detecting them. Another secretion prevents blood from clotting. Until the present century, doctors used leeches to bleed patients. At that time, bleeding was believed to be therapeutic. The leeches have no setae.

CONTINUITY In polychaetes the sexes are separate. In a few polychaetes the fertilized eggs develop into *free swimming, ciliated larvae called* **trochophores** (*träk ə fōrs*).

Both leeches and earthworms are hermaphroditic. In the earthworms, however, cross-fertilization occurs. (See Fig. 25-4.) Sperm from each worm pass along grooves from the male pores in segment 15 to the *sperm receptacles* of the other worm. The worms separate. When·the eggs are ready for fertilization, cells of the clitellum secrete a slime tube around the worm. Within this tube a cocoon is secreted. This cocoon then glides forward. At this point, ripe eggs released from the female pores in segment 14 are moved past the sperm receptacles. Sperm stored there enter the cocoon and fertilize the eggs. Finally, the worm withdraws from the tube. The cocoon closes into a lemon-shaped case which is left in damp soil. Of the several eggs in the cocoon, only one develops into a worm. Earthworms are also able to regenerate segments removed from the ends of the body.

25-4. *Mating earthworms exchange sperm. The sperm travel from the sperm vesicles of one worm to the sperm receptacles of the other.*

Trochophore larvae occur in several otherwise very different phyla. To many biologists similar larvae suggest ancestral relationship.

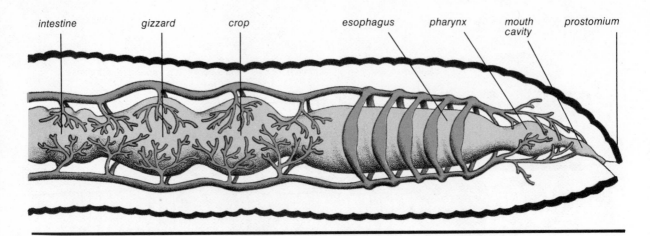

intestine   gizzard   crop   esophagus   pharynx   mouth cavity   prostomium

25-5. Digestive system of an earthworm.

Homeostasis of Annelids

The internal environment of annelids is maintained by the cooperative functioning of various internal systems.

DIGESTION The digestive systems of earthworms are adapted for ingesting leaf fragments, seeds, bodies of small animals and protists, as well as soil. The anterior lobe, the *prostomium* (prō *stō* mē əm), hangs over the *mouth.* It is an extension of segment number 1. Soil and organic matter are sucked into the mouth by the muscular *pharynx.* (See Fig. 25-5.) Muscular action pushes the food through the narrow esophagus into the *crop* for temporary storage. The crop directs food matter into the muscular *gizzard.* The gizzard, with the help of mineral particles, grinds the food into smaller pieces. At this point, the food is pushed into the *intestine.* This organ extends from the gizzard to the anus at the posterior end of the worm. Juices secreted by the gland cells of the intestinal wall contain enzymes. These enzymes digest protein, fats, and carbohydrates, including cellulose. The digested foods are absorbed by the blood passing through vessels in the intestinal wall. Nondigested matter passes out through the anus. This waste material is deposited on the ground in the form of castings.

The muscular action that pushes food and soil through the food tube is called **peristalsis** (per ə *stôl* sis). It results from the alternate contraction and relaxation of certain muscles. This appears as a wave moving along the tube.

CIRCULATORY SYSTEM A closed circulatory system first appears in the annelids. As animals get larger, simple diffusion of food, oxygen, and wastes can no longer meet the needs of all body parts. In annelids, there is a special circulating tissue, called blood. It is directed through a continuous system of muscular tubes called blood vessels. Follow Figure 25-6. In earthworms, the blood flows forward through

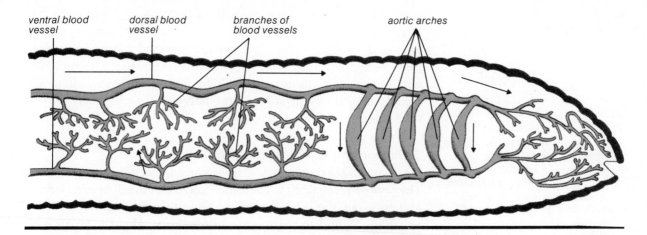

25-6. *Circulatory system of an earthworm.*

25-7. *Nervous system of an earthworm.*

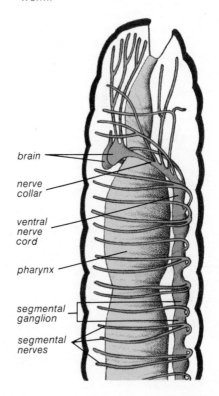

brain

nerve collar

ventral nerve cord

pharynx

segmental ganglion

segmental nerves

the dorsal vessel. From here, five pairs of pulsating (beating) aortic arches direct the flow to the ventral vessel. In each segment branches from the ventral vessel direct blood to the body wall. Others service the intestinal wall where the blood absorbs digested food. In various body tissues, there are tiny blood vessels. These return blood to the dorsal vessel. The small blood vessels that form this network are capillaries. It is through the capillary walls that the blood exchanges materials with its surroundings. Valves in the aortic arches and dorsal vessel prevent the reverse blood flow.

RESPIRATION   Within the capillaries in the body wall of the earthworm, blood exchanges gases with the atmosphere. This occurs by diffusion through the moist surface. The surface is kept moist partly by mucus glands in the epidermis (outer skin). There is a certain substance, dissolved in the blood, that assists in the transport of oxygen. This is hemoglobin, a pigment that attaches loosely to oxygen. This occurs in regions of high oxygen concentration, such as the body wall. Hemoglobin gives the worm's blood its red color.

EXCRETION   The annelid excretory system consists of a pair of nephridia in most segments. *A nephridium consists of a ciliated funnel that directs coelomic fluid through a long coiled tube to the outside.* (Refer back to Fig. 25-2.) Blood in a capillary network surrounding the coiled tube absorbs useful substances. Thus only water and wastes flow out the ventral pore of each nephridium.

NERVOUS SYSTEM   An earthworm's central nervous system consists of several parts as shown in Figure 25-7. A pair of ganglia are located above the pharynx. These are connected to a ganglion below the pharynx by a nerve collar. From the ventral ganglion a nerve cord runs to the posterior end of the worm. An enlargement of the cord in each segment forms the segmental ganglia. From each ganglion three pairs of nerves reach out to all parts of the segment. The ganglia receive impulses from sensory cells in the skin and relay them to muscles. This results in muscle contraction. The coordination of muscles in ordinary creeping is thought to occur by impulses relayed from segment to segment through the ventral nerve cord. The worms react to light, but not red light. They also respond to touch, sound, and chemical substances that stimulate sensory cells in the epidermis.

Behavior and Environment of Annelids

LEARNED BEHAVIOR Associative learning occurs in earthworms. They have been trained to enter the dark, moist chamber of a T-maze, and to avoid the other chamber. The other chamber leads to an irritating solution and causes an electric shock. About 200 trials were required for a worm to respond correctly 90% of the time. The worms remembered what they had learned even if the first five body segments, including the dorsal ganglia, were removed. Untrained worms lacking dorsal ganglia, could also learn. However, their learning was forgotten once the dorsal ganglia regenerated.

EARTHWORMS AND DDT During the early 1960's, DDT was applied to control Dutch elm disease. Enough dripped onto the soil under the trees to cause a 5-10 ppm (parts per million) concentration of DDT. Earthworms ingesting the soil contained 30-160 ppm. During the early spring robins feeding on earthworms under the elms easily received killing doses of the pesticide.

EARTHWORMS AND SOIL Several annelids get most of their energy from leaves that have fallen from trees. Earthworms feed on leaves directly, deriving energy from cellulose. Smaller relatives of the earthworm feed on other organisms. These are the fungi and bacteria which feed on dead leaves.

Answers to Questions for Section 1.

A. **1.** The coelom is the fluid-filled, mesoderm-lined body cavity that develops from a split within the mesoderm. Allows food tube and body wall to function independently. Its fluid circulates substances. It provides space for circulatory system.

*2. Answers will vary, but may include: Each time the worm would draw itself up to inch forward, its food tube would contract the same way.

B. **3.** Bilaterally symmetrical, with three cell layers; complete digestive tract with mouth and anus at opposite ends; coelom divided into segments.

*4. Answers will vary, but may include division of functions, increased surface area for transport across cell boundaries.

C. **5.** Answers vary depending on system selected. Answers should include something about structures of system and how their function contributes to wellbeing of organism.

*6. Material enters mouth, is sucked in by the pharynx, enters the crop — an organ of storage — then the gizzard, which grinds the material, and intestine, where the organic matter is digested and absorbed into the blood; nondigested matter (inorganic part of soil) passes out through the anus.

D. **7.** Worms learned to avoid chamber of T maze that contained irritation solution or electric shock.

E. *8. Yes. Earthworms process large amounts of soil, extracting substances from it and concentrating them.

9. They feed on dead leaves, and derive energy from cellulose.

QUESTIONS FOR SECTION 1

1. Describe the coelom and give three advantages it offers.
2. To illustrate one advantage of a coelom to an earthworm describe its body and food tube motions as if it had no coelom.
3. Describe the general body plan of the annelids.
4. What advantage, if any, do you see in segmentation?
5. Describe how one of the earthworm's systems functions. How does it contribute to homeostasis?
6. Trace a bit of soil and organic matter through the digestive tract of an earthworm naming and giving the function of each organ.
7. Describe evidence of learning in annelids.
8. If the soil contains only small quantities of DDT, can there be any danger to soil organisms? Explain.
9. Describe the role of earthworms as decomposers.

CHAPTER INVESTIGATION

A T-maze is used to study avoiding reactions in earthworms. Arm A is a dark, moist chamber containing humus. Arm B provides light and an electric shock.

A. To which chamber would you expect earthworms to turn most often?

B. Give a reason for your answer to question A and suggest other conditions to be placed at B for similar effects.

C. Some investigators say that earthworms avoid blue light but tolerate red light. Are earthworms able to detect red light? Form an hypothesis and describe the experimental plan that would test it.

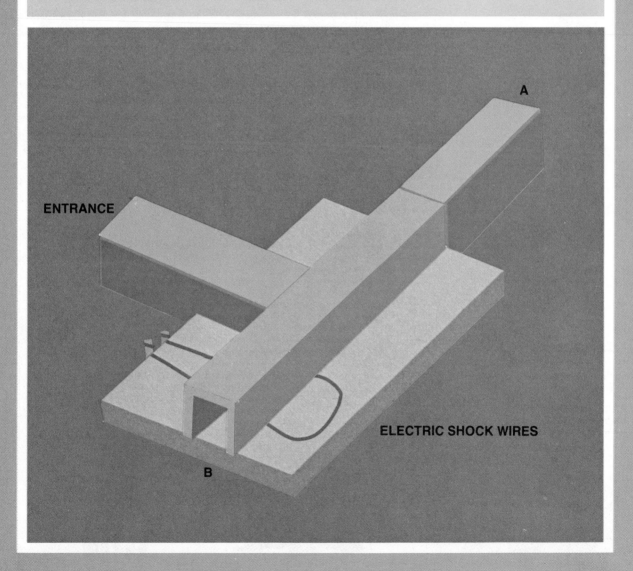

ENTRANCE

A

B

ELECTRIC SHOCK WIRES

2 MOLLUSCS

Diversity and Continuity of Molluscs

The members of Phylum Mollusca have soft bodies that are usually protected by a limy shell. The phylum name comes from the Latin term mollis, which means soft.

BODY PLAN   Despite the differences in outward appearance of snails, clams, octopuses, and chitons, their body plans are basically the same. (See Fig. 25-8.) Their combination of features clearly set them apart from other invertebrates. The soft bodies of molluscs are usually divided into three sections. There is a ventral foot and a dorsal visceral mass. *The visceral mass contains digestive and excretory organs, and the heart.* Covering the visceral mass is a mantle. *The mantle is a fleshy outer layer of the body wall that secretes a limestone shell.* Between the body and the mantle is a space called the *mantle cavity.* In it are gills. **Gills** *are special organs that allow gas exchanges between blood and circulating sea water, fresh water, or air.* The coelom is present though reduced to the cavity around the heart.

DIVERSITY   The over 100,000 species of molluscs may be divided into six classes. They include chitons from the *Class Amphineura* (am fə *nyoor* ə). They live chiefly in intertidal areas of the sea coast.

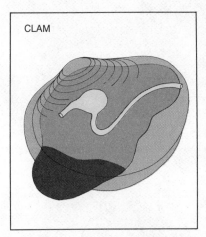

CLAM

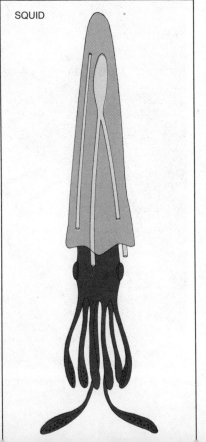

SQUID

25-8. *Body plan of four molluscs. The digestive tract is yellow, the foot is dark brown, and the shell is light brown.*

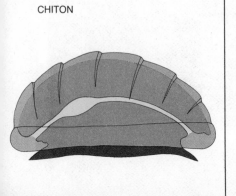

CHITON

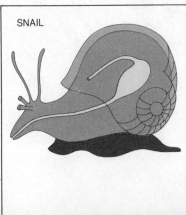

SNAIL

25-9. *A snail is a member of Class Gastropoda.*

25-10. *(left) An octopus. Notice suckers on tentacles.*

Each chiton is attached firmly to rocks by a muscular foot. They graze on algae which they scrape from rocks with *a rasping tongue called a radula* (raj ə lə).

Class Monoplacophora (män ə plə *kof* ə rə) was thought to have been extinct for millions of years. In 1952 *Neopilina,* a member of this class, was discovered off the coast of Central America. This species has all typical molluscan features.

Class Gastropoda (ga *sträp* əd ə) is 33,000 species large. It includes snails, slugs, and whelks. (See Fig. 25-9.) These species have a flat foot. Its shell, if present, is coiled. The head has tentacles and eyes that are often on stalks. Gastropods are slow-moving plant feeders and scavengers. Some marine species are carnivorous.

Members of *Class Pelecypoda* (pə les ə *päd* ə) include clams, mussels, scallops, and oysters. The right and left shells are hinged dorsally. Thus they are often called **bivalves,** *which means two shells.* With head, tentacles, and radula absent, many are adapted to burrow in mud or sand. They feed by filtering food particles from the water passing under the mantle.

Class Cephalopoda (sef ə lə *päd* ə) includes among others the squids, octopuses, and cuttlefish. These are the most highly developed molluscs. (See Fig. 25-10.) Their shells are usually small and internal. The head and eyes are large. The foot is modified into 8-10 grasping tentacles with suckers. The tentacles surround the mouth

Neopilina also has internal segmentation which suggests a relationship between molluscs and annelids.

Slugs have no shells.

There is record of a squid 15 meters long.

which has a horny beak and radula. Gills are in the mantle cavity. Locomotion is achieved by flapping mantles or jets of water forced out of a tube under the mantle. Squids often confuse their predators by squirting an inky substance into the sea. Squids are the largest invertebrates that have ever lived.

CONTINUITY   Many molluscs include a trochophore larva in their early development. Some pass through that stage while still in the egg. In others the larvae are free-swimming. A typical trochophore is shown in Figure 25-11. These are part of the life history of members of several phyla including annelids. These similar larvae support the view that molluscs and annelids are closely related.

Some snails have separate sexes. Others are hermaphrodites. They pass sperm to each other. In other cases, sperm may only be released by one snail.

In clams, sexes are separate. Males shed sperm into outgoing water. They enter the female's mantle cavity with the incoming current. The sperm penetrate the gills where eggs are fertilized. In some species, eggs develop further within the female's body. In others, zygotes develop into larvae within the gills. From here, they are expelled into the water. To survive, the larvae must parasitize the gills or fins of a fish. They remain there until ready for independent existence. The host provides nourishment and dispersal.

In cephalopods, the sexes are separate. Fertilization is internal. Eggs may be free floating or attached to some surfaces in the sea.

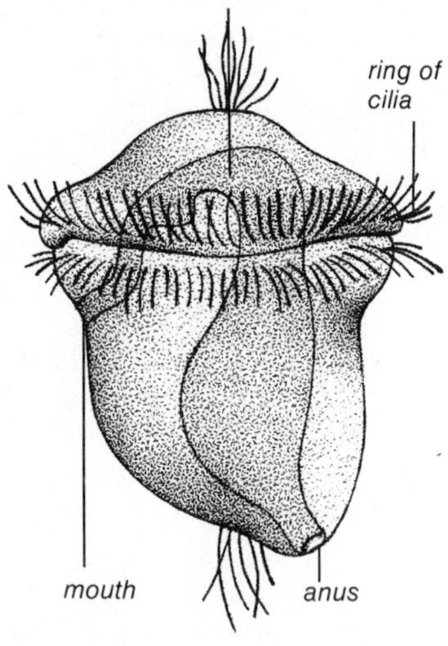

Homeostasis of Molluscs

Homeostasis in molluscs is continued through the functioning of various internal systems. The internal structure of molluscs varies considerably. Here we will describe chiefly the internal systems of the clam.

DIGESTION   The clam screens food particles from the stream of water pumping through the mantle cavity. Food particles attach to the mucus on the gill surface. The mucus is moved by waving cilia forward to the mouth. Waste particles are moved by other cilia down the foot. Finally, the waste material passes between the valves to the outside. Such screening out of small particles is called filter feeding. From the mouth, food passes into the esophagus to the stomach. (See Fig. 25-12.) The stomach is surrounded by a digestive gland. *Ducts* (tubes) direct food particles into the gland. Protein and fat digestion occur within its cells. Carbohydrate digestion occurs in the stomach cavity. From the stomach the intestine runs down into the foot. It extends dorsally through the coelom surrounding the heart. The intestine releases its *feces* (wastes) near the excurrent opening. Finally, wastes are swept away with the current.

25-11. A trochophore larva is bilateral. These larvae are produced by annelids, molluscs, and other animal phyla.

stomach

ring of cilia

mouth   anus

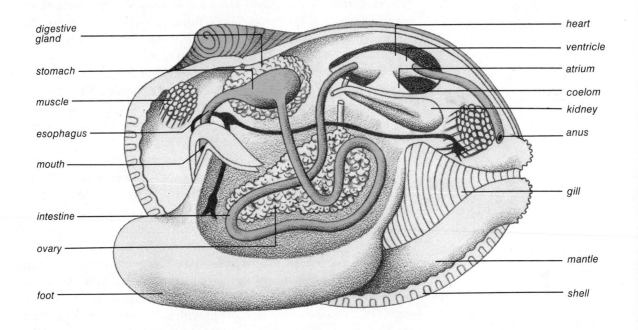

digestive gland

stomach

muscle

esophagus

mouth

intestine

ovary

foot

heart

ventricle

atrium

coelom

kidney

anus

gill

mantle

shell

CIRCULATION   The clam's blood is pumped through tubular vessels by the heart. The heart is located dorsally in the body. **The right and left atria** (singular, atrium) **are the receiving chambers of the heart.** They receive oxygenated blood from the mantle and gills. The atria direct it into the single ventricle (*ven* tri kəl). **The muscular ventricle** *squeezes blood through arteries.* These vessels lead forward into the foot, stomach, intestine, and mantle. Many of the arteries lead into irregular cavities within the tissues. These cavities are called *blood sinuses.* From there blood flows in veins back to the heart. Because the blood is not continuously confined in vessels clams are said to have an open circulatory system. As it flows through various tissues, the blood supplies oxygen and food and picks up wastes.

RESPIRATION   On each side of the clam a pair of gills hangs into the mantle cavity as shown in Figure 25-13. The gills have many pores and are covered with cilia. The beating of the cilia brings water through the incurrent opening. From here, wastes enter into the mantle cavity, and finally into the pores of the gills. Oxygen dissolved in the water diffuses into the blood. At the same time, carbon dioxide dissolved in the blood diffuses out into the water. In a few gastropods and pelecypods, the blood contains red hemoglobin as the oxygen carrier. But most molluscs depend on *an oxygen carrying copper compound dissolved in the blood called* **hemocyanin.** Its bluish color disappears when it gives up its oxygen.

25-12. The internal structure of a clam.

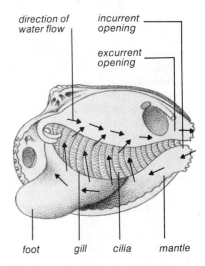

direction of water flow

incurrent opening

excurrent opening

foot   gill   cilia   mantle

25-13. Respiratory system of a clam.

EXCRETION Each of two *kidneys* is U-shaped. They remove organic wastes from the blood and the fluid surrounding the heart. (Refer to Fig. 25-12.) Their collected wastes are stored in a bladder. From here they discharge into a dorsal gill passage.

NERVOUS SYSTEM A clam has a simple nervous system. The mouth, foot, and viscera each have a pair of ganglia. Near the foot ganglia are a pair of balancing organs. On the visceral ganglia are cells thought to be sensitive to chemicals. The mantle appears to be sensitive to touch and light.

In contrast with the nervous system of the clam is the highly developed one of the squid. Its brain is composed of several fused ganglia and lies between the eyes. The two large eyes are able to form images and are constructed quite like human eyes. Many investigations into nerve function are done with squid nerves because they are large.

MUSCULAR SYSTEM Clams have a pair of powerful muscles which pull the valves together. Another pair pull the foot into the shell. When the clam moves, a single muscle helps extend the foot into the sand. While in the sand, the foot fills with blood and forms an anchor. As the muscle of the foot contracts, the body of the clam is pulled forward.

ENDOCRINE SYSTEM *The* **endocrine system** *is composed of glands which have no ducts to direct their secretions directly to the organs they affect.* Instead they rely on the blood to deliver their products. *The products of endocrine glands are* **hormones.**

Connected to the stalks of the octopus brain's optic lobes are optic glands. Experiments suggest that they produce a hormone which stimulates enlargement of the gonad or sex organ.

Behavior and Environment of Molluscs

LEARNED BEHAVIOR Some snails exhibit simple conditioning. They can learn a T-maze. After 60 trials they can retain the learning for about 30 days.

An octopus brain contains about 170 million cells. This fact helps account for its high level of behavior. Cephalopods exhibit complicated fright behavior, mating behavior, territorial behavior, visual and touch learning, and conditioning.

In one experiment with an octopus, a cross and a square were dipped into a tank. When the octopus attacked the square it was given food. When it attacked the cross it was given an electric shock. After 50 trials over a five day period, it usually attacked the square and left the cross alone. In similar experiments, it was learned that the octopus could distinguish between a large card and a small one.

Answers to Questions to Section 2

G. **2.** Reproductive: fertilization occurs in gills; in some species zygotes develop in body, in others, they swim to gills or fins of a fish, where they mature. Digestive: filter feeding occurs in gills, moving from mouth through esophagus into stomach and digestive gland, the intestine releases feces. Circulation: ventricle of heart pumps blood through arteries to foot, stomach, intestine, gills, and mantle; blood flows through veins into right and left atria of heart. Respiration: gas exchange in gills, hemocyanin in blood carries oxygen.

3. They screen food particles from the stream of water that pumps through the mantle cavity.

H. **4.** When an octopus was given electric shocks when it attacked a cross, and food when it attacked a square, it came to prefer the cross to the square.

I. **5.** An increased concentration of *Nannochloris*, an alga, covered the gills of oysters and interfered with feeding and respiration, resulting in the death of the oysters.

EXCHANGING OYSTERS FOR CLAMS A heavily polluted body of water is Great South Bay on the south shore of Long Island, New York. Streams leading into the bay are flushed twice daily by tides. This has made the area ideal for raising ducks. The wastes from these ducks have greatly increased the nitrogen and phosphorus content of bay waters. This has made the bay ideal for a small green alga, *Nannochloris*. Algae covered the gills of oysters. This interfered with their normal feeding and respiration. Starvation or suffocation resulted. Within 20 years the oyster industry was destroyed.

Although duck wastes had destroyed oyster production, clams fared better. Clams can feed on *Nannochloris*. One could imagine switching from oyster collecting to digging clams for human consumption. But these clams absorb certain bacteria common in duck wastes. These bacteria can cause a violent intestinal infection. As a result 40 percent of the clam beds in Great South Bay were closed.

THE FORMATION OF PEARLS Mollusc shells are composed mainly of calcium carbonate and protein. *One of several forms in which calcium carbonate exists is* **nacre** (*nā* kər). Many shells have an inner layer of nacre. A few molluscs have shells that consist almost entirely of nacre. These include the pearly nautilus and the pearl oyster. A sand grain or other irritating particle can get into the mantle cavity. If so, a ball of nacre forms around it as illustrated in Figure 25-14. That ball is a pearl. Nacre is often called mother of pearl.

HUMAN RELATIONSHIPS WITH MOLLUSCS Many clams, oysters, and some snails are used as human food. Cuttlebone, used as a bill-sharpener for caged birds, is furnished by cuttlefish. The nacre of freshwater clams is used to make buttons, pocket knife handles, and beads.

Close relatives of the clams are shipworms. They bore tunnels into wood that is submerged in sea water. These shipworms have damaged many wharves and boats. Terrestrial snails and slugs are responsible for crop destruction. Some marine snails feed on commercially important molluscs. Certain snails serve as intermediate hosts for flukes.

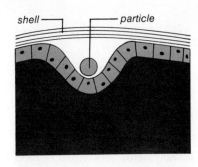

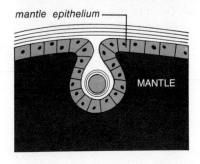

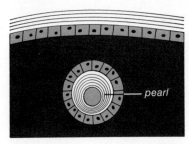

25-14. *A layer of nacre forms around a grain of sand or a parasite to produce a pearl. What function might that layer perform?*

QUESTIONS FOR SECTION 2

1. Describe the general body plan of the molluscs.
2. Describe how the reproductive, digestive, circulatory, and respiratory systems of the clam function.
3. Why are clams called filter feeders?
4. Describe evidence of learning in molluscs.
5. Describe the interactions of molluscs and *Nannochloris*.

Answers to Questions for Section 2.

F. 1. A ventral foot; containing digestive and excretory organs, and heart; a mantle that covers foot and secretes shell; gills that allow gas exchanges between blood, water, or air.

3 ECHINODERMS

Diversity and Continuity of Echinoderms

The animals of Phylum Echinodermata (i kī nə der *mat* ə) have spiny skins, as suggested by their Greek phylum name.

BODY PLAN Phylum Echinodermata includes the starfish, brittle stars, sea cucumbers, sand dollars, sea urchins, and sea lilies. Important features of adults in the group, besides their spiny skins, are radial symmetry and a water vascular system. Their skin is rough because of the limy spines projecting from the *endoskeleton* (inner skeleton) of limy plates imbedded in soft flesh. The water vascular system is a system of canals connected to tube feet. This system of canals helps the echinoderm attach itself to surfaces. In a starfish, the system is composed of a circular canal. From this canal, five canals radiate out into the arms. Each of these bears many pairs of tube feet. Some species have as many as 1200. Each tube foot is similar to a medicine dropper. When the bulb contracts, a valve prevents water from flowing back to the circular canal. Thus the water is forced down into the tube foot. The muscles of the tube foot shorten it. This action forces water back into the bulb. A sucker at the tip of the tube foot has a muscle attached to its center. By raising the center, a vacuum is created. The pressure of sea water outside the tube foot pushes it against a rock or other surface.

The echinoderm body has a coelom. Its coelom originates in a way similar to that in chordates. In doing so, it differs in origin from that of the molluscs and annelids.

DIVERSITY The echinoderms may be divided into five classes. *Class Crinoidea* (krī *noid* ē ə) includes the sea lilies and feather stars. (See Fig. 25-15.) They have many branched arms attached to a stalk. All echinoderms are radially symmetrical. Most are stationary.

Class Asteroidea (as tə *roid* ē ə) includes the familiar starfish. They usually have five bulky arms. Each arm has a double row of tube feet. The central disk contains a ventral mouth.

Class Ophiuroidea (ō fē yər *oid* ē ə) is composed of brittle stars and serpent stars. (See Fig. 25-16.) These animals, usually with five arms, are capable of moving rapidly to catch prey. The tube feet are used mainly as sense organs.

Class Echinoidea (i kī *noid* ē ə) is made up of sea urchins and sand dollars. (See Fig. 25-17.) Their bodies are spherical or disk-shaped and without arms. Spines or colorful hairlike projections cover the body. Their endoskeletons are composed of interlocking plates.

Class Holothuroidea (hō lə thyoor *oid* ē ə) is composed of the sea cucumbers. Their bodies are flattened cylinders without arms or

In molluscs, annelids, and arthropods the coelom develops from slits in the mesoderm. In echinoderms and chordates the coelom forms in the mesodern that originates from outpocketings of the primitive endoderm.

spines. The mouth is at one end surrounded by tentacles. Their skeletons are composed of tiny particles within the leathery epidermis. They usually lie on their sides. They move slowly by tube feet or wiggling motions of the body. Some burrow into the sea bottom, swallowing mud and digesting the organic matter it contains. Others secrete a mucus net which catches small organisms as food.

CONTINUITY   Each arm of the starfish contains either two ovaries or two testes. Eggs and sperm are expelled into the sea where fertilization occurs. The fertilized eggs undergo cell division and structural changes to form free-swimming larvae. These are bilaterally symmetrical. Later they settle to the bottom and take on the radial symmetry of the adult.

The bilateral larvae of echinoderms and their method of coelom formation lead many biologists to believe that they are more closely related to vertebrates than to annelids and molluscs. (See Fig. 25-18 on page 484.) Most echinoderms are able to regenerate missing body parts.

Homeostasis of Echinoderms

The internal systems of echinoderms maintain a relatively constant internal environment.

DIGESTION   Figure 25-19 on page 484 shows the digestive system of the starfish. The tube feet are used in locomotion and in getting food. As the tube feet shorten, the animal moves. A starfish can mount a clam with the hinge away from its ventral mouth. (See Fig. 25-20 on page 485.) The tube feet of several arms pull the shell open slightly. At this point, the starfish extends its inner stomach lining into the opening. Its digestive juices begin digesting the clam's soft tissue. The partly digested food is taken into the digestive glands. Finally, food is absorbed and the stomach is retracted. The wastes pass from the small intestine to the anus at the dorsal surface.

Sea urchins feed on vegetation and have a longer digestive tract. They have five chewing teeth around the mouth.

CIRCULATION   Starfish have no well-organized circulatory system. Their water vascular system and the coelomic fluid help circulate dissolved gases and other materials.

RESPIRATION   Some dissolved gases are exchanged through the thin walls of the tube feet of the water vascular system. But the main gaseous exchange occurs through the skin gills. **Skin gills** *are tiny projections that extend from between the skeletal plates out into the sea water.* They allow coelomic fluid to exchange carbon dioxide for oxygen.

EXCRETION   Metabolic wastes pass to the outside by diffusion.

25-15. *(top) A crinoid on coral.*

25-16. *(middle) A brittle star.*

25-17. *(bottom) A sea urchin.*

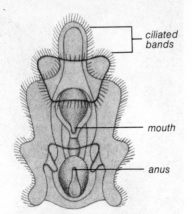

ciliated bands

mouth

anus

25-18. *The bilateral larva of a starfish has bands of cilia for swimming and feeding.*

Ameboid cells in the coelomic fluid engulf nitrogenous wastes and exit through the skin gills.

NERVOUS SYSTEM   Starfish have a simple nervous system. It is composed of a nerve ring around the mouth with a radial nerve extending into each arm. Touch-sensitive cells occur over the entire body surface. At the tip of each arm is a small tentacle thought to be sensitive to touch. Near it is a light-sensitive eyespot.

Behavior and Environment of Echinoderms

INNATE BEHAVIOR   The echinoderms are the most primitive animals described in this chapter. They exhibit limited response, a low level of coordination, and little central control. In starfishes, behavior consists largely of operating their tube feet. Extension and retraction are reflex responses. Moving the entire arm of a starfish requires

25-19 THE DIGESTIVE SYSTEM OF A STARFISH

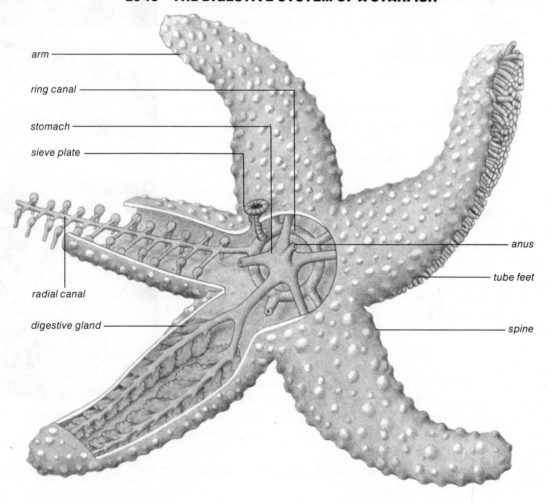

arm

ring canal

stomach

sieve plate

radial canal

digestive gland

anus

tube feet

spine

some coordination of its feet. This coordination occurs through a control center at the base of the arm. Changes of posture or opening a clam require coordination of all arms through the nerve ring. Many starfish and sea urchins exhibit some "caring for" their eggs. Sea urchins show defense reactions. They do this by directing their spines toward the source of danger.

LEARNED BEHAVIOR   Experiments suggest that starfish probably do not learn and cannot profit from experience. Centralization of the nervous system seems to be restricted by radial symmetry.

THE APPETITES OF STARFISH   Coral reefs may appear to be massive and durable. But they are subject to destruction by both physical and biological forces. A population explosion of starfish has occurred since about 1963. The population increase accompanied the destruction of large areas of coral during harbor development. This starfish is a predator of coral. Interestingly enough, the larval stages of the starfish are, in turn, preyed upon by coral polyps. The increasing number of dead corals provided protection for more starfish larvae. This allowed increased numbers of larvae to mature and attack adjoining live coral. One starfish is estimated to kill one square meter of coral per month. By 1970 an estimated 30-40 percent of the Pacific reefs had been destroyed by starfish. Fish leave dead reefs. Therefore, the small coral islands were threatened with the loss of their source of protein food. Even the Great Barrier Reef in Australia is threatened.

The appetite of starfish also affects the production of commercial oysters. A large starfish may consume a half dozen or more oysters per day.

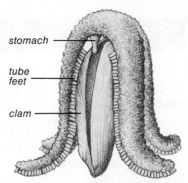

stomach

tube feet

clam

25-20. A starfish opening a clam. The starfish's stomach is inserted into the clam's mantle cavity to digest the clam's soft tissues.

Answers to Questions for Section 3.

J. 1. Spiny epidermis, endoskeleton, radial symmetry, coelom, a water vascular system.

2. A tube foot acts as a medicine dropper. See page 482.

*3. The pieces have the power of regenerating whole starfish.

K. 4. Reproductive: eggs and sperm are expelled into sea where fertilization occurs, and larvae develop. Digestive: the stomach is pushed out and takes the partially digested food into the digestive glands; the small intestine leads to an anus. Circulatory: water vascular system and coelomic fluid circulate materials. Respiratory: skin gills projecting into sea water allow gas exchange between coelomic fluid and sea.

L.*5. Innate: operation of tube feet, extension and retraction reflexes; some caring for eggs. Learned: probably non-existent, due to restriction of centralization of nervous system.

6. Radial symmetry restricts the centralization of the nervous system.

M. 7. Starfish prey upon coral, and one can kill a square meter of coral per month.

*8. Answers will vary, but may include introducing a natural enemy of the starfish that does not attack oysters.

QUESTIONS FOR SECTION 3

1. Describe the general body plan of starfish.
2. Describe how the tube feet in starfish function.
3. Why is it useless for an oyster fisherman to try to eliminate starfish by tearing them apart and tossing pieces into the sea?
4. Describe how the reproductive, digestive, circulatory, respiratory, and excretory systems of the starfish function. Explain how each helps maintain homeostasis.
5. Describe innate and learned behavior in starfish.
6. What physical factor seems to restrict the starfish's ability to learn.
7. Describe how starfish affect coral reefs.
8. Suggest a method of controlling starfish populations near commercial oyster beds.
9. Show how the annelids, molluscs, and echinoderms illustrate unity within diversity.

N. 9. Annelids are all segmented but differ in not having tentacles, suckers, or a reduced head. Molluscs have soft bodies with a shell (usually) but vary widely in structure of the shell(s). Echinoderms have spiny epidermis, radial symmetry, a water vascular system, and bilateral larvae; they vary in shape from star, to disk, to cylinder.

CHAPTER REVIEW

First seen in primitive worms, bilateral symmetry is continued in annelids, molluscs, and larval echinoderms. Also continued are the three embryonic cell layers. A split appears in the mesoderms of all three. This develops into a coelom. It provides space for circulatory organs. The coelom also allows for independent movement of body wall and food tube.

The link between the *structure of an organ and its function* is illustrated by gills, radulas, nephridia, and the heart.

The three phyla illustrate *unity within diversity*. The annelids all display internal and external segmentation. But various annelids have tentacles, suckers, or a reduced head. Most molluscs have unsegmented, soft bodies with a shell. But wide variations exist within the group. The echinoderms share a spiny epidermis, radial symmetry, a water vascular system, and bilateral larvae. Yet their shapes vary from spheres, to stars, disks, and cylinders. These *similarities and differences* are used to classify them according to ancestral relationships.

Many of the forms in these phyla are sluggish. Also, they have methods of reproduction that insure *continuity of the species* even when they are scattered. These methods include hermaphroditism, some care of the fertilized eggs, and the regeneration of lost parts. Dispersal is performed by swimming larvae.

As the animals become larger and leave the sea, the means to maintain *homeostasis* become more complex. Improvements in circulatory and nervous systems make these changes possible. Many of the forms in these phyla *interact with their surroundings* in ways that touch human life.

Using the Concepts

1. Refer to the pollution problems of Great South Bay off the south shore of Long Island, New York. Which industry should have the right to use the bay: duck raisers, clam fishermen, or oyster farmers? How does one decide?
2. The largest vertebrate and the largest invertebrate live in the ocean. Why might this be true?
3. The study of trace elements in ancient clam shells suggested a deficiency of certain elements in the soil. How do you suggest restoring those elements naturally?

Unanswered Question

4. Why does learning ability seem to be so closely related to body symmetry?

Career Activities

5. Find out how cultured pearls are produced.

VOCABULARY REVIEW

1 coelom
clitellum
trochophore larvae
sperm receptacles
pharynx
crop
gizzard

intestine
peristalsis
capillaries
hemoglobin
nephridium
2 visceral mass
mantle

mantle cavity
gills
radula
bivalves
atrium
ventricle
blood sinus

hemocyanin
kidney
nacre
3 endoskeleton
tube feet
skin gills

CHAPTER 25 TEST

Copy the number of each test item and place your answer to the right.

PART 1 Multiple Choice: Select the letter of the phrase that best completes each of the following.

c 1. The walls of small blood vessels through which blood exchanges materials with surrounding fluids are **a.** mesenteries **b.** receptacles **c.** capillaries **d.** blood sinuses.

a 2. The red pigment which increases the ability of an earthworm's blood to carry oxygen is **a.** hemoglobin **b.** hemocyanin **c.** prostmium **d.** nacre.

d 3. Earthworms digest proteins, fats, and carbohydrates using enzymes secreted by the **a.** pharynx **b.** crop **c.** gizzard **d.** intestine.

a 4. The receiving chambers of a clam's heart are the **a.** atria **b.** ventricles **c.** blood sinuses **d.** mantle cavity.

c 5. Of the three phyla studied in this chapter, the one least capable of learning is **a.** Annelids **b.** Molluscs **c.** Echinoderms **d.** Polychaetes.

a 6. The coelom is an important development in animals because it provides space for a true **a.** circulatory system **b.** respiratory system **c.** digestive system **d.** reproductive system.

d 7. An animal that can insert its stomach between the two valves of a clam and digest it is the **a.** sea cucumber **b.** crinoid **c.** sea urchin **d.** starfish.

c 8. The starfish preys on and is preyed upon by **a.** clams **b.** oysters **c.** coral **d.** leeches.

d 9. Earthworms are hermaphroditic but practice **a.** fertilization in water **b.** larval parasitism **c.** larval development in clam gills **d.** cross fertilization.

d 10. Pearls form as a response to **a.** peristalsis **b.** filter feeding **c.** fright **d.** irritation.

PART 2 Matching: Match the letter of the term in Column I with its description in Column II.

COLUMN I

a. clitellum **e.** gizzard **i.** nephridium
b. coelom **f.** hormones **j.** peristalsis
c. endoskeleton **g.** mantle
d. gills **h.** nacre

COLUMN II

b 11. A mesoderm-lined, fluid-filled cavity that allows free motion of body wall and the food tube

a 12. A saddle-like swelling on earthworms that secretes a cocoon

e 13. A muscular ogran that grinds food

j 14. A muscular action that pushes food through the food tube

i 15. A long tube that directs fluid with wastes from the coelom to the outside of an earthworm

d 16. Organs that allow gas exchanges between blood and air or water

f 17. The products of endocrine glands

h 18. Mother of pearl

c 19. The limy plates imbedded in the outer flesh of starfish

g 20. The fleshy outer body wall that secretes the shell in molluscs

PART 3 Completion: Complete the following.

21. A circulatory system in which the blood is continuously confined in muscular tubes is said to be _closed_

22. Irregular cavities within tissues through which the blood of molluscs flows are called _blood sinuses_

23. The near destruction of both oyster and clam industries in Long Island Sound resulted from _green alga_

24. The pair of organs which removes organic wastes from body fluids in clams are _kidneys_

25. Of the phyla described in this chapter, the one with the most highly developed nervous system is Phylum _Mollusca_

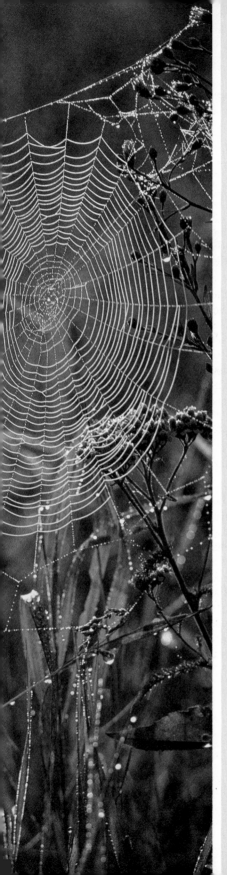

CHAPTER 26

THE ARTHROPODS

In this chapter we will continue the study of the invertebrates, animals without backbones. There are more known species in Phylum Arthropoda than in any other phylum.

We will continue to relate the descriptions of the animals of the phylum to familiar basic concepts: *the link between structure and function, unity and diversity, the continuity of life, homeostasis,* and *interaction with the environment.* At the end of the chapter we will compare invertebrate groups to each other. Also, we will make a comparison of these animals to the plants of the preceding unit.

In this chapter we will answer several important questions:

- Why are land arthropods relatively small?
- How can growth occur in an animal with an outside skeleton?
- How do insects meet the high energy requirements of flight?
- How do bees communicate?
- Are bees intelligent?
- Why do some insecticides lose their effectiveness?

SPIDER WEB

1 ARTHROPODS

Considering numbers of species and variety of habitats, the arthropods (är thrə pods) appear to be Earth's most successful animal group. The nearly one million known species live in freshwater, salt water, and in the soil. Phylum Arthropoda includes insects, spiders, chiggers, centipedes, crabs, and crayfish. The phylum name means jointed feet. More than 75 percent of all animal species are in Phylum Arthropoda. (See Fig. 26-1.)

General Body Plan of Arthropods

The arthropod body displays bilateral symmetry and segmentation. The segments may be combined externally to form three body regions: head, thorax, and abdomen. Internally, segmentation is reduced to the regular branching of circulatory, respiratory, and nervous systems.

An arthropod has a hard *external skeleton called an* **exoskeleton.** Most of the exoskeleton is made up of protein and a flexible substance called *chitin* (*kī* tin). The chitin is coated with a thin waxy layer. This makes the exoskeleton waterproof. The exoskeleton serves as the body's framework. It also prevents the drying out of body tissues. As with human skeletons, the exoskeleton protects body organs from mechanical injury. Also, it provides attachments for muscles.

Arthropods have chitinous jointed appendages. *An* **appendage** *is a moveable extension of the body such as a leg or antenna.* Since the appendages are covered with an exoskeleton, joints are necessary for movement. Arthropod appendages may be modified for food getting, breathing, flying, and other functions.

The coelom of arthropods is usually reduced to cavities of the sex organs. The main body cavity is part of an open circulatory system. In an open circulatory system the blood is not entirely confined within blood vessels. Arteries lead not into capillaries, but into blood spaces. There, various organs are bathed in blood.

The arthropod's dorsal "brain" connects with the ventral nerve cord by nerves surrounding the food tube. Communication exists between the central nervous system and the world outside the exoskeleton. This is maintained by a variety of highly specialized sense organs. These occur over the surface of the skeleton as pits, hairs, and bristles. Some occur on special appendages.

Land arthropods are relatively small animals. An exoskeleton on a large animal would have a crushing weight. Also, it would require huge legs for support. Large crabs measure up to three meters across. But they live in water which supports their weight.

OBJECTIVES FOR SECTION 1

A. Describe the combination of features that distinguish members of Phylum Arthropoda from members of other phyla.

B. Explain the features that distinguish each arthropod class from the others. Name representatives of each.

C. Describe the main parts of a crayfish and give their functions.

D. Describe the life cycle of the crayfish.

E. Explain how each internal system of the crayfish contributes to homeostasis.

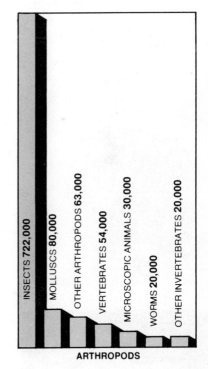

26-1. *The relative numbers of species of various groups in the animal kingdom. Most species of animals are arthropods. What makes this group so successful?*

INSECTS 722,000 — MOLLUSCS 80,000 — OTHER ARTHROPODS 63,000 — VERTEBRATES 54,000 — MICROSCOPIC ANIMALS 30,000 — WORMS 20,000 — OTHER INVERTEBRATES 20,000

ARTHROPODS

26-2. *Peripatus is a member of Class Onychophora. It is a primitive arthropod with several annelid features.*

26-3. *Representatives of Class Crustacea. (upper left) Pillbug; (upper right) Ghost crab; (lower left) Barnacles; (lower right) Cleaner shrimp.*

In addition to limiting body size, an exoskeleton must be periodically shed to make room for growth. This ***shedding of the exoskeleton is called* molting.** When the old skeleton is shed the new one is already formed inside it. At first it is delicate and elastic and stretches to fit the growing body. Then it hardens. Soft shelled crabs are collected before the exoskeleton hardens.

Diversity and Continuity of Arthropods

DIVERSITY Phylum Arthropoda may be divided into six classes. *Class Onychophora* (än i *käf* ə rə) includes the most primitive living arthropods. (See Fig. 26-2.) These worm-like creatures live in the jungles or near the tropics. Their outer coat is thin and flexible.

Class Crustacea (krəs *tā* shē ə) includes crayfish, lobsters, barnacles, crabs, pill bugs, and water fleas. (See Fig. 26-3.) They have head and thorax fused into a *cephalothorax* (sef ə lə *thōr* aks). Except for pill bugs, they are aquatic. Most crustaceans possess gills and two pairs of antennae. Most exchange gases through gills. Their exoskeletons are hardened with lime, except at the joints. Some small forms exchange gases through the body surface. The exoskeleton of those forms is not hardened with lime. Crustaceans are important in the diets of many fish and mammals including whales and humans.

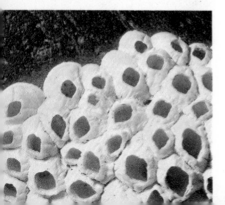

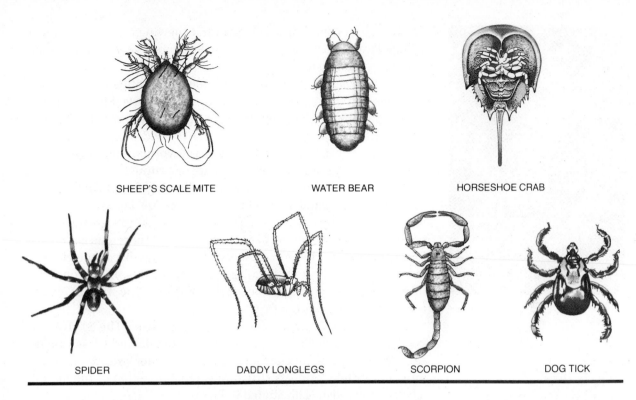

SHEEP'S SCALE MITE   WATER BEAR   HORSESHOE CRAB

SPIDER   DADDY LONGLEGS   SCORPION   DOG TICK

Class Arachnida (ə *rak* nəd ə) includes spiders, scorpions, mites, chiggers, and harvestmen (daddy long legs). (See Fig. 26-4.) Arachnid bodies are divided into a cephalothorax and an abdomen. They have four pairs of walking legs. The Arachnids do not have true jaws. Instead of antennae they have sensory bristles covering the body and its appendages. In front of the mouth is a pair of pincers or *fang-like claws called* **chelicera** (ki *lis* ə rə). In spiders, they serve as poison fangs. Behind the mouth is a pair of pedipalps. **Pedipalps** *are leg-like appendages that in spiders have sensory functions.* In spiders three pairs of *abdominal appendages called* **spinnerets** *secrete silk.* The silk is used for spinning webs, protecting eggs, and snagging prey. Arachnids have one or both of two types of respiratory organs. One kind are air tubes. These branch out from a pair of openings on the ventral surface of the abdomen. They supply air to the tissues. Anterior to the air tube openings are slits that lead to a pair of book lungs. *A* **book lung** *is an air space with wall folds resembling a book.* Each "page" is filled with blood which communicates with the blood sinuses of the abdomen. External respiratory exchanges take place between the air and the blood in the "pages."

Class Diplopoda (dip lə *päd* ə) is composed of the millipedes. They live in moist places and may be found under rocks and logs. They have two pairs of legs on almost every body segment. (See Fig. 26-5.)

26-4. *Representatives of Class Arachnida.*

26-5. *A millipede is a member of Class Diploda.*

The fastest centipede, 22 mm long, runs 42 cm per second.

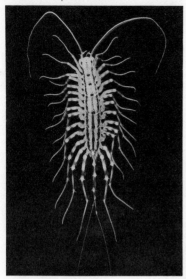

26-6. A centipede is a member of Class Chilopoda.

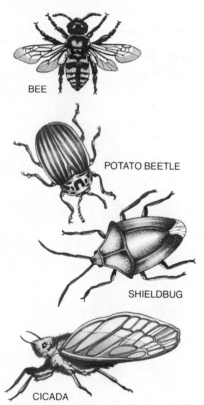

BEE

POTATO BEETLE

SHIELDBUG

CICADA

26-7. Representatives of Class Insecta.

The head bears one pair of antennae and chewing mouth parts. Most millipedes eat decaying plants. Millipedes move very slowly in spite of their numerous legs.

Class Chilopoda (ki *lap* əd ə) includes the centipedes. They also have one pair of antennae and chewing mouth parts. Most segments of their flattened bodies have one pair of legs. (See Fig. 26-6.) The first body segment has a pair of poison claws used in capturing prey. Their prey consists of soft insects, earthworms, and slugs. They have two groups of simple eyes and are fast runners.

Class Insecta is composed of insects. (See Fig. 26-7.) These are the most successful land invertebrates. Insects are about 300 million times as numerous as people. They are humankind's greatest competitors for food. An insect has a distinct head, thorax, and abdomen. Six segments fuse to form the head. Each of the three thoracic segments bears a pair of walking legs. In some insects, the second and third thoracic segments also bear a pair of wings. ***The study of insects is called*** **entomology** (en tə *mol* ə jē).

BODY PLAN OF A TYPICAL CRUSTACEAN, THE CRAYFISH The crayfish is a good representative of both Phylum Arthropoda and Class Crustacea. Various species of crayfish inhabit freshwater streams and lakes in much of the world. Its structure is much like that of the marine lobster. A crayfish is illustrated in Figure 26-8.

The crayfish exoskeleton is hardened with calcium carbonate except at the joints. The head and thorax are fused to form the cephalothorax. ***The rigid dorsal and side portion of skeleton covering the body is the*** **carapace.** Six posterior segments form the jointed abdomen. Except for the first segment, each bears a pair of specialized appendages. Those appendages have a variety of functions.

Antennules appear on the second segment of the head. **Antennules** *are organs of balance and hearing.* The third segment bears the **antennae** *which are organs of touch, taste, and smell.* The next six pairs of appendages are around the mouth. The *mandibles* are biting jaws. They crush food by moving from side to side. The two pairs of *maxillae* (mak *sil* ē) help hold and pass food on to the mouth.

The first three thoracic segments bear the three pairs of *maxillipeds*. Maxillipeds move food forward to the mouth. The fourth thoracic segment bears the large pinching *chelipeds*. Chelipeds are used for capturing and handling prey as well as for defense. There are four pairs of walking legs. These allow the crayfish to move forward, backward, and sideways. The first two pair of walking legs have small pincers which help capture prey.

The first five segments of the abdomen bear swimmerets. **Swimmerets** *aid in swimming and the reproductive process.* The first two pairs differ according to sex. In the male the first swimmerets are tu-

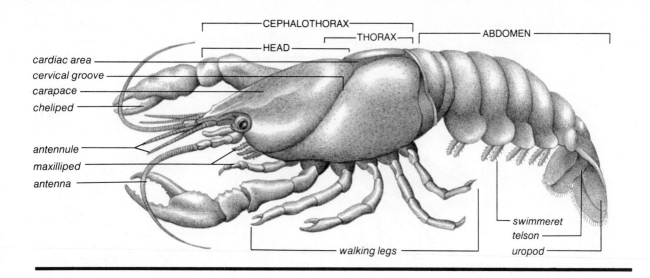

cardiac area
cervical groove
carapace
cheliped

antennule
maxilliped
antenna

CEPHALOTHORAX
HEAD
THORAX
ABDOMEN

walking legs

swimmeret
telson
uropod

bular. They are used for transferring sperm while mating. In females they are reduced or absent. The last three pairs of swimmerets are used for water circulation. Furthermore, in females they are used to carry eggs.

The sixth pair of abdominal segments are the *uropods*. They, with the *telson*, form a paddle. When the abdominal muscles contract, the telson and uropods whip forward. This helps the crayfish move backward through the water.

CONTINUITY Sexes are separate in crayfish. In the male, the two testes are fused and lie under the heart. From each, a coiled tube extends ventrally to open at the base of the last walking leg. In females, the two ovaries lie beneath the heart. Eggs are discharged through an opening near each second walking leg. In the fall males deposit sperm in a cup-like structure under the female's abdomen. In the spring, the eggs are fertilized by the sperm. Eggs then are carried for 5-8 weeks among the female's swimmerets before they hatch. Crayfish molt several times before becoming adults. Even the lining of the stomach and the eye sockets are shed. During adulthood they molt about twice each year. During the molting process, crayfish can replace lost parts, especially appendages and eyes. In this helpless condition, crayfish remain in hiding and avoid danger.

Homeostasis of Arthropods

How arthropods maintain relatively constant internal environments will be illustrated with the crayfish.

DIGESTIVE SYSTEM Crayfish feed on insect larvae, worms, crustaceans, small snails, fish, and tadpoles. They sometimes feed on dead animal matter. After the food is crushed and shredded, it is passed

26-8. External structure of a crayfish.

In early embryos, segments are visible individually and all appendages are similar two-parted structures. As they mature many segments fuse and appendages specialize.

Exactly how fertilization occurs is unknown. Eggs, when discharged, stick to a froth deposited among the swimmerets.

When the old exoskeleton is discarded, the crayfish gorges itself with water, stretching its new skeleton to a larger size before it hardens.

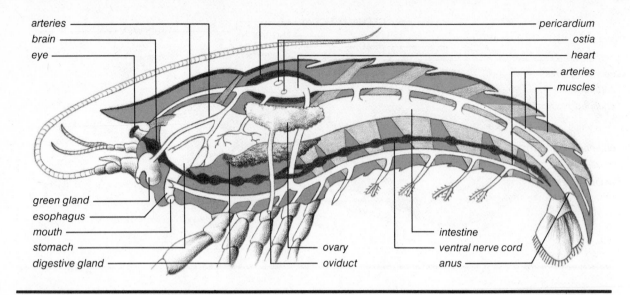

arteries
brain
eye
pericardium
ostia
heart
arteries
muscles
green gland
esophagus
mouth
stomach
digestive gland
ovary
oviduct
intestine
ventral nerve cord
anus

26-9. *Internal structure of a female crayfish.*

*7. They are protected from predators.

*8. The animals need lime to build into their shells.

E. 9. Circulatory system: blood is pumped by heart into sinuses around major organs to the gills, then pericardial sinus, then through the ostia into the heart. Respiratory system: delivery of food and gas exchange occurs as blood bathes organs; in gills, gas exchange with surrounding water occurs. Excretory system: green glands remove organic wastes from blood, and urine flows into bladder and through duct to outside. Nervous system: dorsal brain connected by nerve collar to pair of ventral nerve cords; ganglia send nerves to various body parts; brain connects to sense organs. Muscle system: abdominal muscles extend and flex abdomen and move swimmerets.

into the mouth. From here it passes through the esophagus to the stomach. (See Fig. 26-9.) In the stomach are hard chitinous teeth that further grind the food. A pair of digestive glands secrete enzymes into the mid-gut beyond the stomach. The digested foods are absorbed through the walls of both the mid-gut and digestive glands. This food is distributed to various tissues through the circulatory system. Finally, undigested foods enter the intestine. The intestine empties through the anus under the telson.

CIRCULATORY SYSTEM   The circulatory system of the crayfish is an open system. Blood in the heart is pumped through seven large arteries to various tissue spaces, or *sinuses*. These spaces contain the major organs. The blood eventually collects in the large space in the floor of the thorax. From there blood flows through channels that lead to the gills. From the gills, blood is channeled to the *space surrounding the heart, the* **pericardial sinus.** Three openings, *ostia*, allow blood into the heart. When the heart contracts, valves prevent blood from flowing back out into the pericardial sinus.

The blood of crayfish contains dissolved hemocyanin. This molecule helps carry oxygen from the gills to the other tissues. Some arthropods contain dissolved hemoglobin. Others have no respiratory pigments.

RESPIRATORY SYSTEM   As the blood bathes various tissues and organs, food and dissolved oxygen diffuse from blood into the cells. Carbon dioxide diffuses from cells into the blood. While in the gills, the blood's supply of oxygen is replenished from that dissolved in the water surrounding the crayfish. Likewise carbon dioxide diffuses through gill tissue into the surrounding water.

The gills are attached to the bases of legs. They extend dorsally into the gill chambers which are enclosed by the sides of the carapace. Water passes upward and forward over the gills. It is directed out on either side of the mouth by currents generated by the second maxillae.

EXCRETORY SYSTEM *Organic wastes from the blood are removed by a pair of* **green glands.** They are located in front of the stomach. (Refer to Fig. 26-9.) Each consists of a glandular portion which opens into a bladder. From the bladder, a duct leads urine to an opening at the base of the antenna. As the crayfish swims backwards, it moves away from its wastes.

NERVOUS SYSTEM The brain of the crayfish is located dorsally above the mouth region. It connects by a nerve collar to a pair of ventral nerve cords. Separate ganglia occur in segments 9 to 19. They send nerves to appendages, muscles, and other organs. The brain is connected by nerves to the eyes, antennae, and antennules.

Each eye is at the end of a moveable stalk. Each composed of over 2000 units, the compound eyes are especially efficient at detecting motion. Sensory bristles sensitive to touch are distributed over the body and appendages. Hairs sensitive to taste and smell occur on the antennules, tips of antennae, mouth parts, and the ends of the chilipeds. At the base of the antennules are the **statocysts** *which serve the sense of balance.* The statocysts contain grains of sand perched on top of sensory hairs. Tilting of the body causes the grains to shift position. The crayfish responds by righting itself.

MUSCLE SYSTEM Muscles produce the quick escape motions of the crayfish. Muscles of the abdomen extend and flex the abdomen and move swimmerets. They are attached inside the exoskeleton. It is these abdominal muscles that you eat when you have lobster.

QUESTIONS FOR SECTION 1

1. Describe the combination of features that distinguish members of Phylum Arthropoda from members of other phyla.
2. What are the advantages and disadvantages of an exoskeleton?
3. How does an animal with an exoskeleton grow?
4. Describe the features that distinguish each arthropod class from the others and name representatives of each.
5. What are the main parts of a crayfish? Give their functions.
6. Describe the life cycle of the crayfish.
7. Of what advantage to crayfish eggs is it to be carried by the female after being laid?
8. Of what advantage might it be for a crayfish to live in water originating in areas containing limestone rock?
9. Describe how each internal system of the crayfish contributes to homeostasis.

Answers to Questions for Section 1.

A. 1. Segmented body, exoskeleton, jointed appendages.
   *2. Advantages: provides protection of soft inner parts, plus water-proofing; disadvantages: limits body size.
   3. By growing a new exoskeleton inside the old one, which is then shed, or molted; new one stretches as animals grows, and then hardens.

B. 4. *Onychophora:* worm-like, with thin, flexible outer coat; *Peripatus; Crustacea:* gills; 2 pairs antennae; cephalothorax and abdomen; exoskeletons; crayfish, crabs. *Arachnida:* cephalothorax and abdomen; 4 pairs of legs; bristles; air tubes and books lung; chelicera and pedipalps; spiders, scorpions, mites. *Diplopoda:* 2 pairs of legs on every segment; 1 pair of antennae; chewing mouth parts; millipedes. *Chilopoda:* one pair of legs on most segments; poison claws; 1 pair antennae; chewing mouth parts; centipedes. *Insecta:* head, thorax, abdomen; 3 pairs legs; some have wings; grasshopper, honeybee.

C. 5. Exoskeleton with carapace: protection and attachment for muscles; antennules: organs of balance and hearing; antennae: organs of touch, taste, smell; mandibles: biting jaws; maxillae: hold food and pass it on to mouth; chelipeds: capturing prey and defense; walking legs: locomotion; swimmerets: aid in swimming and reproduction. Uropods and telson: paddles that help animal swim backward.

D. 6. In the fall, males deposit sperm in cup under female's abdomen; in the spring, the sperm fertilize eggs, carried in swimmerettes until they hatch. Molting occurs several times during growth to adulthood, and twice a year afterwards.
(See page 494 for answers 7-9)

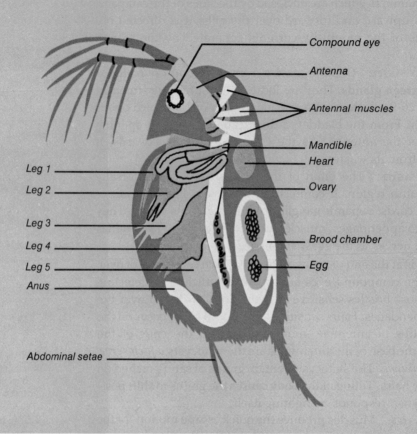

Compound eye

Antenna

Antennal muscles

Mandible

Heart

Ovary

Brood chamber

Egg

Leg 1

Leg 2

Leg 3

Leg 4

Leg 5

Anus

Abdominal setae

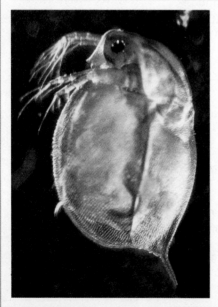

CHAPTER INVESTIGATION

This water flea *(Daphnia similis)* is a freshwater arthropod. The females are about 2.8 mm long. Males reach only 1.8 mm. Their legs serve primarily to circulate water through the valves of the thin shell. This brings oxygen and food particles under the shell. Food particles are carried between the bases of the legs and forward toward the mouth. Gas exchanges occur through the legs and inner walls of the shell.

A. Look at the diagram of *Daphnia* and determine which appendages she uses for locomotion.

B. To which arthropod class does *Daphnia* belong?

C. *Daphnia* are transparent. One can easily observe motions of the intestine and heart. Devise an experiment by which one could determine whether water temperature affects the rate of heart beat in *Daphnia*.

2 COMMON ARTHROPODS — INSECTS

Body Plan of a Typical Insect, The Grasshopper

About three-fourths of all known animal species are insects. But there are many more yet to be discovered. Their success as a group has been credited to their small size, their mobility, and their rate of reproduction. But most of all their success is due to the ability of various insect species to occupy almost every freshwater and terrestrial niche.

The grasshopper is a typical insect. It has an exoskeleton that is not hardened with calcium carbonate. Except in the head, each segment has a dorsal and a ventral plate. The legs are protected with jointed skeletal tubes.

The body of a grasshopper has three regions: head, thorax, and abdomen. (See Fig. 26-10.) The head moves freely and is composed of six segments which fuse during development. It bears the single pair of antennae, three pairs of mouth parts, a pair of compound eyes, and a few simple eyes. The thorax has three segments. The first, the prothorax, bears a pair of segmented walking legs. The second and third segments, the mesothorax and metathorax, each bear a pair of walking legs and a pair of wings. The abdomen has 11 flexible segments.

The grasshopper's antennae serve the senses of touch and smell. The mouth parts are well adapted for chewing leaves. (See Fig. 26-11.) Behind the forward lip, or *labrum,* are the crushing jaws, or

OBJECTIVES FOR SECTION 2

F. Describe the main parts of a grasshopper and give their functions.
G. Distinguish between incomplete and complete metamorphosis.
H. Explain how each internal system of insects contributes to homeostasis.
I. Identify several kinds of learned behavior in insects.
J. Describe the social organization of a honeybee colony.
K. Explain how communication occurs among honeybees.
L. Describe several ways that insects affect humans.
M. Discuss the various methods of insect control giving advantages and disadvantages of each.

26-11. Head and mouth parts of a grasshopper.

26-10 EXTERNAL FEATURES OF A FEMALE GRASSHOPPER

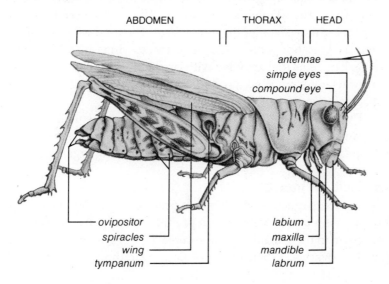

ABDOMEN   THORAX   HEAD

antennae
simple eyes
compound eye

ovipositor
spiracles
wing
tympanum

labium
maxilla
mandible
labrum

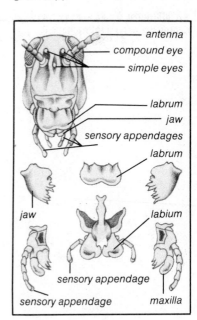

antenna
compound eye
simple eyes

labrum
jaw
sensory appendages
labrum

jaw
labium

sensory appendage
sensory appendage
maxilla

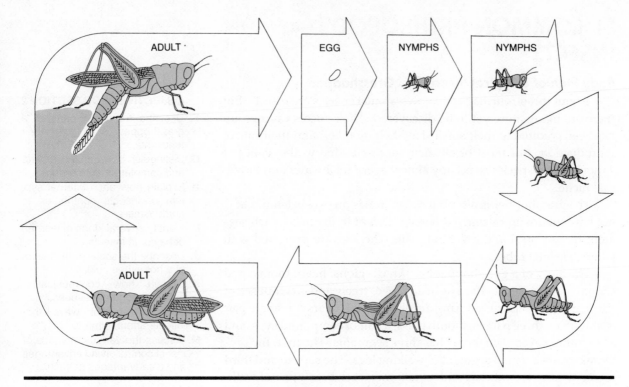

ADULT   EGG   NYMPHS   NYMPHS

ADULT

26-12. *Incomplete metamorphosis of the grasshopper.*

An additional simple eye exists in a depression between the antennae.

mandibles. They move sideways to cut, tear, and chew food. Next is a pair of maxillae, each with a small jaw and a sensory appendage. They help push food into the mouth. Finally, there is the posterior lip, or *labium*. This also has a pair of sensory appendages. The large compound eyes are composed of hundreds of lenses. The simple eyes are just above the base of the antennae.

The last pair of legs is larger and more muscular than the other pairs. They are adapted for jumping. The narrow leathery front wings serve as a cover for the hind wings. The hind wings are folded when the grasshopper is not in flight. Insect wings are stiffened by a network of veins that are filled with circulating blood. The grasshopper's clacking sounds are produced by rubbing the pegs of the hind leg across a wing vein.

The first abdominal segment of grasshoppers contains an oval tympanum on each side. *The **tympanum** is a membrane that responds to sound vibrations.* It covers the hearing organ.

Continuity of Insects

CONTINUITY OF GRASSHOPPERS AND OTHER INSECTS   The male grasshopper has a pair of testes which produce sperm. The male deposits the sperm in the female's sperm receptacle. Eggs are produced in the female's ovaries. When the eggs pass near the sperm receptacle,

26-13. Complete metamorphosis of a butterfly. **A.** Eggs; **B.** Larva; **C.** Pupa; **D.** Adult.

sperm fertilize the eggs. As the eggs pass from the ovaries through the oviduct, a yolk and shell are added.

The posterior segments of female grasshoppers bear two pairs of pointed organs called ovipositors. **Ovipositors** *are used to form a short tunnel in the ground in which eggs are placed during late summer or fall.* These eggs hatch the next spring. The young grasshoppers resemble the adults but have no wings or reproductive organs. The skeletons are shed five or six times during their growth period. After reaching the adult stage, no more molting occurs.

Grasshoppers and several other orders of insects go through moderate body changes as they complete their life cycle. After the egg hatches, the young emerge. They are called nymphs. **Nymphs** *are immature insects which differ little from one stage to the next.* Such *gradual development from egg through nymph to adult is called* **incomplete metamorphosis.** Grasshoppers, dragonflies, lice, bugs, and cicadas have incomplete metamorphosis. (See Fig. 26-12.)

The adults of other insects look entirely different from the larvae. Drastic changes take place at each of four stages: egg, larvae, pupa, adult. The larval caterpillar looks quite unlike the adult butterfly. A grub looks quite unlike the adult beetle. *The* **pupa** *is a nonfeeding stage following the final larval stage.* During the pupal stage, the insect is completely remodeled. (See Fig. 26-13.) *Development in which*

After each molting, the young grasshopper swallows air and increases its volume. The skeleton hardens in its enlarged state.

egg, larvae, pupae and adults are quite different is called **complete metamorphosis.** An advantage to such complete metamorphosis is that the larvae and adults may have different feeding habits. Caterpillars feed on leaves. Adult butterflies suck nectar from flowers. That avoids competition between adults and their offspring. Insects with complete metamorphosis include beetles, butterflies, flies, and bees.

Homeostasis of Insects

How this successful group of animals maintains a relatively constant internal environment is of great interest to biologists.

DIGESTIVE SYSTEM   Food is moistened and lubricated by saliva. The saliva contains an enzyme which digests starch. From the mouth, the food passes through the short esophagus into the enlarged crop. Here, food is stored and partially digested. (See Fig. 26-14.) Next, food is thoroughly chewed by the muscular gizzard which has chitinous teeth. Well chewed food passes through a valve into the stomach. The stomach is the main organ where digestion and absorption

Grasshoppers chew plant fragments with the mandibles and maxillae. Saliva is produced in branched glands that open through the labium.

The thorax of some insects will walk even when severed from the rest of the body. With the brain removed, some insects can walk, jump, or fly.

An exoskeleton has more surface area available for muscle attachment than an inside skeleton of similar size.

PTTH is prothoracicotropic hormone.

26-14   INTERNAL ORGANS OF A GRASSHOPPER

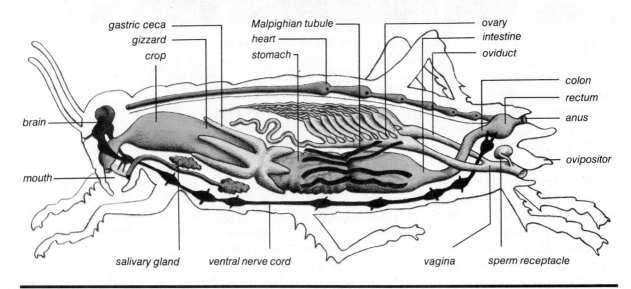

gastric ceca
gizzard
crop
Malpighian tubule
heart
stomach
ovary
intestine
oviduct
colon
rectum
anus
ovipositor
brain
mouth
salivary gland   ventral nerve cord   vagina   sperm receptacle

takes place. At the anterior end of the stomach are six pairs of pouches. These **gastric caeca** *are extensions of the stomach cavity.* Their lining secretes enzymes. From the stomach, undigested materials pass through the intestine and colon to the rectum. Here water and inorganic ions are absorbed from the wastes before they are removed from the body as feces.

An irregularly shaped fat body above the gut stores fats, carbo-hydrates, and proteins. As the blood sugar level goes down, the fat body converts the glucose absorbed from the stomach into a disaccharide.

CIRCULATORY SYSTEM   The grasshopper's circulatory system is an open system. Its only vessel is the dorsal heart which has an anterior extension, the aorta. (Refer to Fig. 26-14.) The heart is almost as long as the abdomen and enlarges in each abdominal segment. Each en-larged chamber has an opening on each side through which blood en-ters. The heart pumps blood forward through the aorta into the head. There blood enters spaces among the tissues. From here, it flows back into the abdomen bathing various organs. With no respiratory pig-ments in the blood the blood of most insects is colorless or greenish. Digested foods are absorbed from the stomach into the blood stream. A grasshopper's blood is about two percent sugar. The sugar content of human blood is usually about 1.0 percent. The grasshopper is adapted to the high energy requirements of flight.

26-15   THE RESPIRATORY SYSTEM OF A GRASSHOPPER

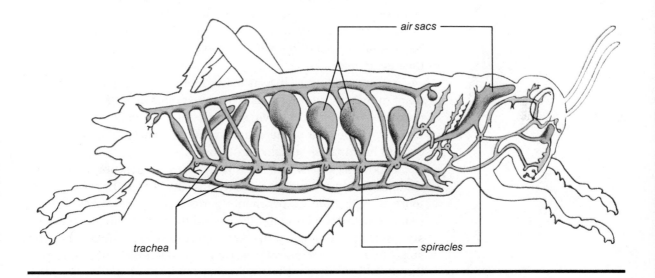

RESPIRATORY SYSTEM   In insects, the circulatory and respiratory systems are separate. Air is distributed directly through *a system of branching air tubes called* **tracheae.** Blood is not involved in the trans-port of oxygen. (See Fig. 26-15.) The tracheae begin as holes in the sides of the thorax and abdomen. These small openings that lead into the respiratory system are called *spiracles* (*spi* rə kəls). The spiracles have valves which control airflow and restrict water loss. Oxygen in the air diffuses through the spiracles and the smallest tracheae to the fluid surrounding the tissues. Carbon dioxide diffuses from tissues in the reverse direction. In some places, the air tubes connect with larger air sacs. During flight, muscular motion helps circulate the air by compressing the air sacs and then allowing them to expand. Insect wing muscles require more oxygen than any other known tissue. When at rest grasshoppers pump air by expanding and contracting the abdomen.

EXCRETORY SYSTEM   At the posterior end of the stomach are a number of threadlike **Malpighian** (mal *pig* ē ən) **tubules** *which take wastes from the blood flowing through the abdomen.* (Refer to Fig. 26-14.) Some of the wastes are removed by active transport and discharged into the intestine. These are eliminated with feces through the anus. Waste nitrogen is excreted as uric acid. The advantage of uric acid as waste is that it can be excreted with little water. This, and the chitinous exoskeleton, allows the grasshopper to live in dry areas.

NERVOUS SYSTEM   The grasshopper's nervous system is composed of a brain connected to the ventral nerve cord by a pair of nerves encircling the esophagus. (Refer to Fig. 26-14.) The brain receives stimuli from sense organs in the head and initiates body movements. The brain does not control all muscular activities. Segmental ganglia of the ventral cord control some of the motion of their segments.

MUSCULAR SYSTEM   Insects have many more separate muscles than humans. Yet each has separate points of attachment. The muscles of both legs and wings nearly fill the thorax. Mitochondria make up 30 percent of the volume of wing muscle cells, which may explain how insects sustain flight power.

ENDOCRINE SYSTEM OF INSECTS WITH COMPLETE METAMORPHOSIS   The changes during complete metamorphosis have been the subject of intense investigation. Experiments performed in the 1920's showed that if a thread is wound tightly around the body of an immature insect, only the front half of the body developed to the next stage. This suggested that metamorphosis was controlled by a hormone produced in the front of the body. Further work revealed a hormone that is now called *ecdysone.*

The secretion of ecdysone is stimulated by a second hormone produced by certain brain cells. This hormone is known as *PTTH.* If the brain of a mature silkworm caterpillar is removed, it does not spin its cocoon. If a few of the appropriate brain cells are then introduced into some part of the body, cocoon spinning proceeds normally.

But why does an insect undergo several molts before it forms a pupa? Further research has shown that a third hormone is produced by a pair of tiny glands behind the brain. This hormone acts as a brake on metamorphosis. It is called *juvenile hormone*, or *JH*. With enough JH present, ecdysone promotes larval growth. When the amount of JH is reduced, ecdysone stimulates the development of the pupa. Absence of JH promotes the development of the adult stage.

Behavior and Environment of Insects

INNATE BEHAVIOR   Arthropods demonstrate a wide variety of reactions to their surroundings. Bees and certain beetles respond to the sun. Several innate behaviors may be combined into complex instinct patterns. For some instincts the brain is not needed. A headless fruit fly can walk and fly. A female silkworm without head or thorax can mate and lay eggs. The brain's function may be to begin, regulate, or prevent those instinctive behaviors.

LEARNED BEHAVIOR   Cockroaches are known to exhibit **habituation,** *that is the ignoring of a continuous, harmless stimulus.* They run when a puff of air is directed at the rear of the abdomen. If the blowing continues, the escape reaction stops. A cockroach seeking food in wind would continually run for cover if it were not for habituation.

When a stimulus and an active response are followed by a reward or punishment, an association may be established. Honeybees have been trained to associate certain background colors with a sugar solution. This is trial and error learning.

Some insects also remember information which may have no immediate function, but which may influence later behavior. The solitary wasp recognizes the arrangement of landmarks. When leaving its nest after a storm the wasp makes a short survey flight over the nest area. This flight provides enough information about new landmarks to locate them on the return flight. Such *learning that occurs without immediate reward and remains useless until a later time is called* **latent learning.**

SOCIAL ORGANIZATION OF THE HONEYBEE   In some arthropod groups systems of innate and learned behavior are combined to form elaborate social organization. These social groups may express cooperation, division of labor, territoriality, leadership, and communication. Social organization is especially well developed among the termites, ants, wasps, and bees.

A colony of domestic honeybees develops from a *single mother, the* **queen.** She lays eggs in chambers, or cells, in the wax honeycomb. Just before the eggs are laid, the queen fertilizes them by releasing sperm from her sperm receptacles. The sperm originally

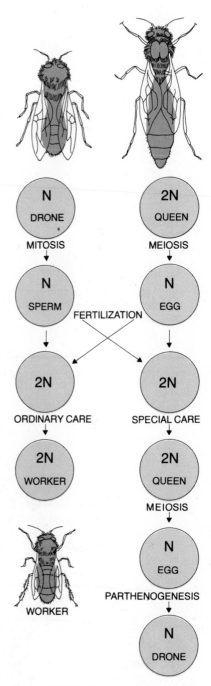

26-16. Variations in honeybees.

came from a male bee during the mating flight. The eggs hatch and the larvae are fed honey and pollen by worker bees. The larvae then enter their pupal stage. Three weeks after the egg is laid, an adult worker bee emerges. *The* **worker** *is a female without functioning sex organs.*

During early spring, the queen lays a fertilized egg in each of several special queen cells. The queen larvae are fed a special "royal jelly" secreted by the workers. One of these may become the future queen of the hive.

The queen also lays *unfertilized eggs. The development of such eggs is called* **parthenogenesis.** They become male bees called **drones.** Their sole function appears to be to mate with the queen. While drones are haploid, queens and workers are diploid because they develop from fertilized eggs. Thus the hive has one queen, a few hundred drones, and up to 70,000 workers. (See Fig. 26-16.)

Before a new queen emerges, the old queen leads many of the workers to a new location where they will establish another colony. After a few days, the new queen mates with one, or more, drone bees and begins laying eggs. (See Fig. 26-17.)

A worker bee spends the first three weeks of her life in or near the hive. She cleans cells, nurses larvae, and secretes beeswax to build honeycomb. The worker also receives nectar which other bees bring

Worker bees appear to be promoted from one task to another in a definite sequence.

26-17 A SECTION OF A HONEYCOMB

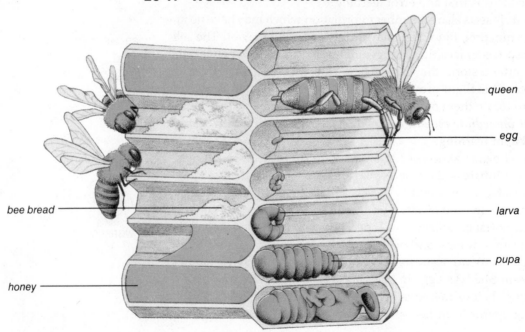

queen

egg

bee bread

larva

pupa

honey

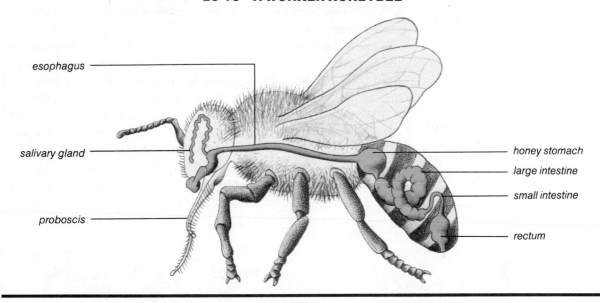

esophagus

salivary gland

proboscis

honey stomach

large intestine

small intestine

rectum

back to the hive. In her stomach, sucrose is digested into glucose and fructose. (See Fig. 26-18.) She deposits this product in the cells and the cell is capped with a layer of wax.

Workers also patrol the front of the hive, stinging any intruders. They can sting another insect and survive. But the sting cannot be easily removed from the elastic skin of vertebrates. It may be pulled from the worker's body, and this may damage her abdominal organs.

After a few days of patrolling, workers collect water, pollen, and nectar for the rest of their lives. Water is brought in and allowed to evaporate. This cools the hive in summer. Muscular activity of the bees warms the hive in winter, keeping it at about 35°C.

Pollen collected by worker bees is moistened with nectar and stored in the hive as another food. **Propolis** (*präp ə ləs*), *gathered from resinous buds, is used as varnish, glue, and a filler of cracks within the hive.* Workers hatched in spring may work themselves to death in three or four weeks. Beekeepers usually leave at least 15 kilograms of honey in the hive, as a winter food supply. This honey is used by the bees.

Bee activity results in the accidental transfer of pollen from one flower to the next. At least 50 seed and fruit crops increase their yields when honeybees are present as a result of cross pollination. The clovers, most varieties of apples, sweet cherries, and plums would not bear fruit without insect pollinators. Honeybees are more important as pollinators than as honey producers.

Removal of a honeybee's sting, or stinger, from human skin may be illustrated with a medicine dropper inserted between two adjacent fingers of a hand. Ask students to explain why it is better to scrape or lift the stinger out with a knife than to pull it out with two fingers. It avoids forcing more of the venom, mostly formic acid, into the wound.

COMMUNICATION AMONG HONEYBEES Most worker bees do not leave the hive until food has been discovered by scout bees. After the scouts return, workers leave and fly directly to their food supply. How scout bees communicate with other workers was discovered by the German zoologist Karl von Frisch. He learned that the scouts deposit their load of nectar or pollen in the hive. Then, they perform a little dance on the vertical surface of the honeycomb. When the food is more than 100 meters from the hive, they perform a tail-wagging dance. The speed of the dance is related to the distance of the food from the hive. The direction of the tailwagging part of the dance varies with the direction of the food from the hive. It also varies with the time of day. When the food source is in a direction toward the

When food is less than 100 m from the hive a round dance is performed. A near circle is made, then traced in reverse.

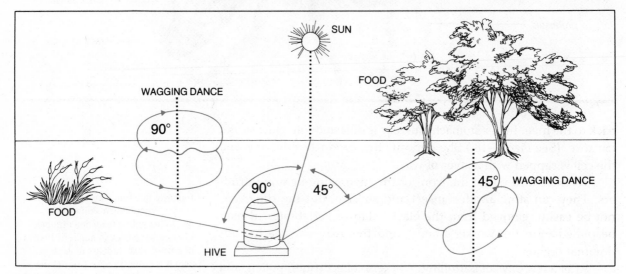

26-19. *The orientation of the honeybee's wagging dance depends on the angle between the direction of the sun and the direction of the food.*

sun, the straight portion of the wagging dance is upward. If the food source is at some angle to the right or left of the sun, that portion of the dance is at the same angle to the right or left of the vertical line. (See Fig. 26-19.) The dance is more vigorous when the food source is more plentiful. If dancing bees are kept in the hive for a long time, they shift the direction of their dance. This compensates for the shifting of the sun's direction. When the sun is invisible, bees orient their dance and their flight according to the pattern of polarized light in the sky. The pattern of polarized light depends on the location of the sun.

A description of life in a beehive or an ant colony may suggest high intelligence. But many experiments indicate that most insect behavior is instinctive and inflexible. Insects often cannot repeat steps in a behavior pattern or perform them in a different order. Still a bee's ability to associate food with a certain location, odor, or time of day is an example of learning. But in general, insects are reflex-bound animals. Additional learning requires a more complex brain than they have.

INSECTS AND OUR ENVIRONMENT   Insects play many roles in maintaining balance in an ecosystem. Bees are essential for the pollination of many flowering plants. Many species of insects play a part in the decay process. Insects are the main food source of many animals. Many carnivorous and parasitic insects feed on other insects that eat crops.

Yet, insects have become important competitors for human food crops. While most are small, insects reproduce rapidly and their total food intake is high. In addition, they may be carriers of disease. The organisms that cause plague, malaria, and encephalitis are spread by fleas and mosquitoes.

INSECT CONTROL   Competition between insect and human populations for available food initiated the systematic spraying of crops with insecticides. But many insecticides cause severe problems. Most of them are toxic to non-target species and kill the natural predators of the target insect. Some insecticides do not disintegrate easily and continue to poison various organisms for a long time. Insecticides in the DDT family become magnified in the food chain. For these and other reasons entomologists have searched for alternatives.

In a previous section you read about juvenile hormone. When *juvenile hormone* is applied at certain times in the life cycle of an insect, abnormal development and death follow. If insect eggs contact JH, their embryonic development is upset. These responses have led to the suggestion that JH might be an effective insecticide. As you are aware, it is a normal substance in their bodies. Therefore, insects would not likely develop a resistance to it. Moreover, JH does not have a toxic effect on other organisms.

Another successful means of controlling insect populations is the *sterile male technique*. It was first applied against the screwworm fly. The female fly lays eggs in the open wounds of livestock. After hatching, the larvae enlarge the wound often resulting in the death of the host. In 1958, laboratory-reared and radiation-sterilized males were released over the affected areas. As the sterile males mated, their mates would lay unfertilized eggs. Thus, each mating resulted in a decrease in total numbers of young flies produced.

Sex attractants have been used as bait to lure insects to their death. They also prevent normal mating by masking the insect's own attractant. Sex attractants belong to the group of substances known as pheromones. **Pheromones** *are substances that organisms release into the environment as a means of communication with other members of the same species.*

Answers to Questions for Section 2.
J. 9. A hive has one queen, a few hundred drones, up to 70,000 workers, and several special queen larvae. A worker prepares cells for the queen's egg-laying, nurses larvae, secretes beeswax, molds cells from the wax, makes honey from nectar, patrols the hive, and collects water, pollen, nectar, and propolis. The queen, after a single mating, may lay as many as a million eggs during her life. The drones' sole function is to mate with the queen.

K. 10. Scout bees locate food supplies outside the hive, return to the hive, and use a tail-wagging dance to communicate the location of the food to the other workers.
   *11. See Figure 26-19 on p. 506.

L. 12. Many insects also compete with humans for food, and carry diseases.

   13. Pollinate flowering plants grown for food, other uses, and aesthetic value; prey on insects that eat our crops; produce honey and beeswax that people use; play role in decay process; serve as food source for many animals.

M. 14. Natural pesticides, biological and integrated control; advantages are low toxicity to most non-target species, rapid decay, and it may not cause resistant populations; disadvantages are slowness, cost and it may not be effective. Inorganic compounds: advantages are low cost and effectiveness; disadvantages are toxicity to non-target species, and long lasting.

   *15. The insecticide kills most members of the insect population. The naturally resistant survive. These reproduce many more of their kind than in a natural situation.

Answers to Questions for Section 2.

F. 1. Exoskeleton: made of chitin, with dorsal and ventral plate except in head; jointed tubes protect legs. Head: moves freely, has pair of antennae serving senses of touch and smell; both compound and simple eyes; and specialized mouth parts: labrum, mandibles, maxillae, labium, and sensory appendages adapted for chewing leaves. Prothorax: bears a pair of walking legs; mesothorax and metathorax: a pair of legs and pair of wings each, the last pair of legs being adapted for jumping. Tympanum: on first abdominal segment, covers the hearing organ.

*2. Small size, mobility, rate of reproduction, and ability of various species to occupy nearly every available niche.

G. 3. Incomplete: grasshopper; eggs; nymphs, and adults. Complete: butterfly; egg, larva, pupa, and adult.

4. Larvae and adults have different feeding habits, avoiding competition.

H. 5. Digestive system: digestion begins in the mouth and continues in the crop and the gizzard; the gastric caeca secrete enzymes, and waste passes through the intestine, colon, and rectum. Circulatory system: the dorsal heart receives blood, which is pumped forward through the aorta into the head, then flows back to bathe abdominal organs. Respiratory system: air is distributed directly through a system of tracheae where gas exchange between air and tissues occurs. Excretory system: Malpighian tubules in abdomen extracts wastes from blood. Some wastes are removed by the intestine. Nervous system: the brain initiates body movements, but segmental ganglia control some body motions. Muscular system: for both leg and wing movement. Endocrine system: the hormones control metamorphosis, and larval growth.

BIOLOGICAL CONTROL In natural ecosystems predators and parasites play an important role in controlling insect populations. In agricultural ecosystems, such controls are often disturbed. This is especially true if insect pests have been introduced from elsewhere. *The use of living organisms to control insects is called* biological control.

If we are to avoid destruction of natural ecosystems pest control must evolve toward integrated control. *Integrated control* uses natural predators and parasites, rotation and increased variety of crops, and the sterilized male technique. Additionally, hormones, pheromones, breeding of resistant crop varieties, and only very limited use of degradable chemical insecticides are involved in this type of control.

QUESTIONS FOR SECTION 2

1. Describe the main parts of a grasshopper and give their functions.
2. List reasons for insects being so successful.
3. Describe the life cycle of an insect with incomplete metamorphosis and another with complete metamorphosis.
4. Of what advantage is it to a species to have complete metamorphosis?
5. Describe how each internal system of grasshoppers and other insects contribute to homeostasis.
6. Give two reasons that insects are able to survive in dry climates.
7. Why is it important to have many mitochondria in an insect's wing muscles?
8. Describe several kinds of learned behavior in insects.
9. Describe the social organization of a honeybee colony.
10. Describe communication among honeybees.
11. Draw the pattern of the honeybee dance when the food is straight south of the hive in the morning.
12. What are several ways that the activities of insects affect humans?
13. Describe five ways in which insects are helpful to humans.
14. What are the various methods of insect control? Give the advantages and disadvantages of each.
15. How do insecticide-resistant varieties of insects develop?

6. Waste nitrogen is excreted as uric acid, a process that requires little water; the chitinous exoskeleton is waterproof, so it prevents drying out of tissues.

*7. They provide energy for cells, and the wings require a large energy supply for flight.

I. 8. Cockroaches have shown habituation learning to ignore a continuous stiumlus of harmless wind. Honeybees have learned by trial and error to associate certain background colors with sugar solution. The solitary wasp exhibits latent learning in remembering new landmarks identified after the environs of its nest have been altered.

(See pages 506-507 for more answers.)

3 A COMPARISON AMONG INVERTEBRATES AND PLANTS

Relationships Among Invertebrates

Invertebrate animals share several features with all animals. They are multicellular. Their cells are eucaryotic and without walls. They lack chlorophyll and are therefore heterotrophic. Nutrition is mostly ingestive. They produce gametes in multicellular structures.

BODY PLAN The more primitive of the invertebrates are radially symmetrical. The echinoderms begin life as bilateral larvae but revert to radial symmetry in adulthood. The rest of the invertebrate phyla we studied exhibit bilateral symmetry. Bilateral symmetry is charactertistic of active animals. Cephalization begins with the flatworms. It continues in all groups except the echinoderms. Segmentation is found in the annelids and arthropods, but not in other groups.

The body wall of sponges and cnidarians have two layers, the ectoderm and endoderm. There is a layer of mesoglea between them. In the other phyla mesoglea is replaced by mesoderm. A pseudocoelom appears in the unsegmented roundworms. A fully-lined coelom develops in the annelids and all groups that follow.

REPRODUCTIVE SYSTEMS Except for the unsegmented roundworms all of these phyla include larvae in their life cycles. Annelids and molluscs have almost identical trocophore larvae. This supports the view that molluscs and annelids are closely related.

CIRCULATORY AND RESPIRATORY SYSTEMS Water plays a crucial role in these systems of the invertebrates. It circulates into and out of the central body cavity of sponges and cnidarians. The water exchanges material directly with both ectoderm and endoderm. In free-living flatworms, every cell is close enough to the surrounding water for diffusion to serve their needs. In unsegmented roundworms, the fluid moving in the pseudocoelom distributes food and oxygen. Annelids have a closed circulatory system of muscular tubes. Through it the blood carries food and oxygen to the cells. Blood carries wastes to the gills where gaseous exchanges occur with the water flowing through them. Some arthropods have gills. Others, such as insects, have a system of branched air tubes. These tubes allow exchanges between air and body cells. In echinoderms, gas exchange with the surrounding water takes places through skin, gills, and tube feet.

Table 26-1 summarizes some of the important similarities and differences among the eight invertebrate phyla discussed in Unit VII. Included are body plans and the main internal systems that maintain homeostasis within the organism. Trace the development of each system across the Table. Figures 26-20, 26-21, 26-22, and 26-23 provide simple comparisons for the more complex systems.

OBJECTIVES FOR SECTION 3

N. Compare body plans of major groups of invertebrates.
O. Describe trends in each of the internal systems of the major invertebrate groups.
P. Compare invertebrate animals with plants.
Q. Show how the appendages of the crayfish illustrate the relationship between structure and function.

TABLE 26-1 *A COMPARISON OF MAJOR INVERTEBRATE PHYLA*

	Phylum	Porifera (Sponges)	Cnidarians (Hydra)	Platyhelminthes (Flatworms)	Aschelminthes (Roundworms)
BODY PLAN	Embryonic layers	two	two	three	three
	Symmetry	none or radial	radial	bilateral	bilateral
	Segmentation	absent	absent	absent	absent
	Body cavity	none	none	none	pseudocoelom
REPRODUCTION		sexual with larvae; asexual buds or capsules; regeneration	sexual medusa alternating with asexual polyp; regeneration	sexual internal fertilization; asexual in some; regeneration	sexual, internal fertilization
DIGESTIVE SYSTEM		collar cells intracellular	gastrovascular cavity with single opening		complete with two openings
CIRCULATORY SYSTEM		canal system	gastrovascular cavity; direct diffusion through body wall		fluid of pseudocoelom
RESPIRATORY SYSTEM					
EXCRETORY SYSTEM				direct diffusion and flame cells	some with flame cells or excretory canals
NERVOUS SYSTEM		none	nerve network	central nervous system of ganglia and cords	nerve ring and several cords
MUSCULAR AND SKELETAL SYSTEMS		spicules	muscle fibers, some with limy cup skeleton	circular and longitudinal muscles	longitudinal muscles
				no skeleton	

TABLE 26-1 *A COMPARISON OF MAJOR INVERTEBRATE PHYLA* (continued)

Phylum		Annelids (Segmented Worm)	Molluscs (Clam)	Arthropods (Grasshopper)	Echinoderms (Starfish)
BODY PLAN	Embryonic Layers	three	three	three	three
	Sym-metry	bilateral	bilateral	bilateral	larvae bilateral; adult radial
	Segmentation	present	absent except in Neoplina	present	absent
	Body Cavity	coelom from slits in mesoderm	much reduced from slits in mesoderm		coelom from outpock-eting of endoderm
REPRO-DUCTION		sexual; trochophore larvae; regeneration	sexual, internal fertili-zation; trochophore larvae; no asexual	sexual, fertilization mostly internal; parthe-nogenesis in some; regeneration	sexual, external fertilization; larvae; regeneration
DIGES-TIVE SYSTEM		complete with two openings			
CIRCULA-TORY SYSTEM		closed	open		poorly developed
RESPIRA-TORY SYSTEM		body wall	gills in mantle cavity	trachae; book lungs; gills	skin, gills, and tube feet
EXCRE-TORY SYSTEM		nephridia	kidneys	green glands; Malpighian tubules	skin, gills, ameboid cells
NERVOUS SYSTEM		ganglia, ventral cord, and segmental nerves	three pairs of ganglia and cross-connections, some highly developed	ganglia, ventral cord, and segmental nerves	nerve ring and radial nerves
MUSCULAR AND SKELETAL SYSTEMS		circular and longitudi-nal muscles	variety of muscles, external or imbedded in shell	variety of muscles inside of chitinous exoskeleton	variety of muscles; endoskeleton of plates
		no skeleton			

26-20 SELECTED DIGESTIVE SYSTEMS OF THE INVERTEBRATES

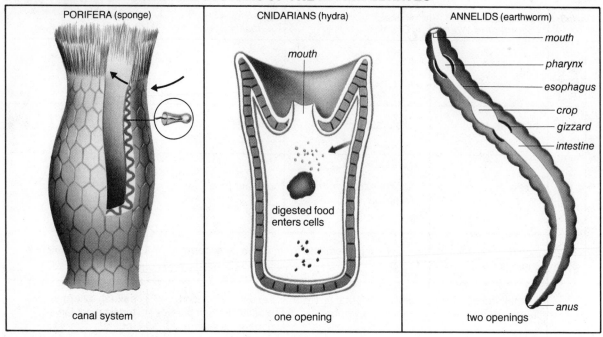

PORIFERA (sponge)

canal system

CNIDARIANS (hydra)

mouth

digested food
enters cells

one opening

ANNELIDS (earthworm)

mouth

pharynx

esophagus

crop

gizzard

intestine

anus

two openings

26-21 SELECTED CIRCULATORY SYSTEMS OF THE INVERTEBRATES

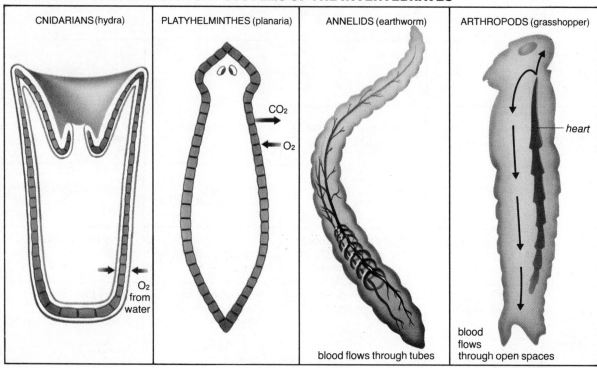

CNIDARIANS (hydra)

O_2
from
water

PLATYHELMINTHES (planaria)

CO_2

O_2

ANNELIDS (earthworm)

blood flows through tubes

ARTHROPODS (grasshopper)

heart

blood
flows
through open spaces

26-22 SELECTED EXCRETORY SYSTEMS OF THE INVERTEBRATES

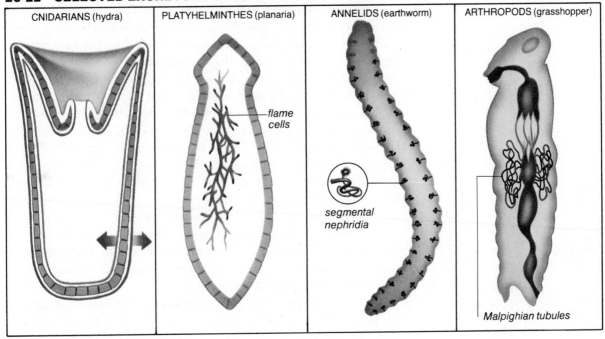

CNIDARIANS (hydra)

PLATYHELMINTHES (planaria)
flame cells

ANNELIDS (earthworm)
segmental nephridia

ARTHROPODS (grasshopper)
Malpighian tubules

26-23 SELECTED NERVOUS SYSTEMS OF THE INVERTEBRATES

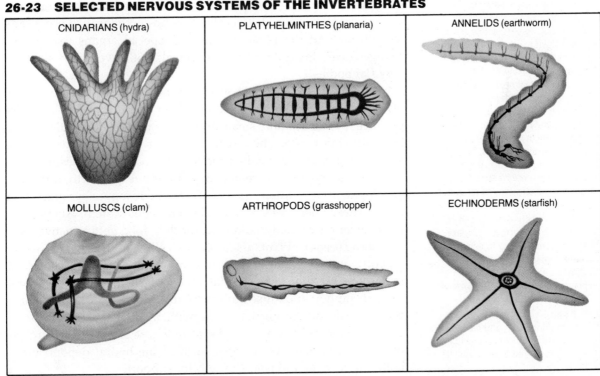

CNIDARIANS (hydra)

PLATYHELMINTHES (planaria)

ANNELIDS (earthworm)

MOLLUSCS (clam)

ARTHROPODS (grasshopper)

ECHINODERMS (starfish)

Comparisons of Invertebrates to Plants

DIGESTION   Green plants are autotrophic. That is, they are able to synthesize large molecules with light energy absorbed by chlorophyll and other pigments. Animals are unable to do this. They are heterotrophic and must get food already manufactured. Some animals strain food from the water flowing through them. Others actively seek food. Most foods need to be digested to make food particles small enough and soluble to be absorbed by cells. Molds and most bacteria secrete enzymes that digest the foods around them. They are then able to absorb them. Except for sponges, the invertebrate animals also digest food outside of cells. Sponges digest food inside of cells. Both internal and external digestion occur in cnidarians, flatworms, molluscs, and arthropods.

CIRCULATION   The transport of water in plants occurs by osmosis and transpiration. Minerals and food are transferred by a combination of active transport and diffusion. In primitive invertebrates, simple diffusion is the only transport system. More active animals have hearts that force liquids to circulate.

RESPIRATION   Most plants have no specialized organs for gas exchange. Each part of the plant takes care of its own gas exchange needs. Plants respire much more slowly than animals do. Even in large plants, each cell is close to the surface. In woody stems, the center is dead. The only live part is near the outside of the stem. Air spaces among loosely packed cells allow gas exchanges to occur rapidly throughout the plant. In animals, special organs for gas exchange occur. Exceptions are sea animals with two body layers or very flat bodies.

EXCRETION   Excretion of wastes is not as great a problem for plants as for animals. They use the water and carbon dioxide they produce. Plants use only small amounts of protein. Thus, they have little nitrogen waste. The larger, more active invertebrates require special organs to remove the products of protein metabolism.

BODY MOVEMENT   Movement in plants is due to growth, turgor, or development. In animals, part or all of the body moves by contracting fibers. These fibers are stimulated by a nervous system. Animals require faster movement than plants for their food getting activities.

BODY SUPPORT   Plants use cellulose cell walls and woody tissue for body support. Many animals use limy compounds of calcium for a supporting skeleton. The skeletal system of the invertebrates serves for both support and muscle attachment. Exoskeletons of the Arthropods provide for protection along with holding the organism together. Sponges have a skeletal system whose skeletons are groups of spicules. Other invertebrates, such as the hydra, depend upon both muscle fiber and layers of cells for support.

culatory system; arthropods have gills; insects have branched air tubes; echinoderms exchange gas with the surrounding water through skin, gills, and tube feet. See Table 26-1 for further information.

P. 3. Food source: plants, autotrophic, animals, heterotrophic; transport of water: plants, osmosis and transpiration, animals, diffusion and circulation; transport of minerals: plants, active transport and diffusion, animals, diffusion and circulation; gaseous exchange: plants, no specialized organs, animals, special organs except sea animals; excretion: plants, little nitrogen wastes, animals, special organs; body movement: plants, growth, tugor, development, animals, contracting fibers, nervous system; body support: plants, cellulose cell walls and woody tissues, animals, limy compounds of calcium.

4. Plants respire slowly, each cell is close to the surface, air spaces allow gas exchanges to occur rapidly; plants use the water and carbon dioxide they produce, plants use only small amounts of proteins.

Q. 5. As an early embryo, appendages are similar two-pointed structures. After maturity, appendages change form and become specialized.

1. For each of the major groups of invertebrates indicate the kind of body symmetry, number of embryonic cell layers, and the presence or absence of cephalization, segmentation, and a coelom.
2. Describe trends in each of the internal structures and systems of the major invertebrate groups.
3. Compare invertebrate animals with plants in terms of food source, transport of water and nutrients, gaseous exchange, excretion, body movement, and body support.
4. How do plants survive without special organs for gas exchange and excretion of wastes?
5. Explain how the appendages of the crayfish illustrate the relationship between structure and function.

Answers to Questions for Section 3.

N. 1. See Table 26-1 on pp. 510-511.

O. 2. Reproduction: all phyla except roundworms include larvae in their life cycles. Annelids and molluscs have trocophore larvae. Circulation and respiration: water circulates through body cavity of sponges and cnidarians; in flatworms there is a diffusion into the surrounding water; in roundworms, fluid in pseudocoelom distributes food and oxygen; annelids have closed cir-

(See page 514 for more answers.)

CHAPTER REVIEW

Phylum Arthropoda offers a special opportunity to study basic biological concepts. The crayfish illustrates clearly the *relationship between structure and function.* As an early embryo, all its appendages are similar two-parted structures. As the crayfish matures, many appendages change form. They become specially fitted for detecting environmental changes, handling food, exchanging gases, walking, swimming, circulating water, or reproduction.

Most arthropods are similar in having jointed exoskeletons. But they differ widely in types of life cycle, method of locomotion, kind of blood pigment, food needs, habitat, and social organization. These diversities are used to classify arthropods into classes, orders, families, genera, and species.

All arthropods continue their species line through sexual reproduction. But some crustaceans and some insects also practice parthenogenesis.

Arthropods have a variety of internal systems which cooperate in maintaining *homeostasis.*

Arthropods exhibit a wide variety of behavior patterns. Innate behavior ranges from simple responses to complex social organization and communication. They also exhibit habituation, trial and error learning, and latent learning.

Insects play many important roles in maintaining balance in ecosystems. However, they compete with humans for food. In response, humans have developed ways to control their numbers. Many of these control methods severely damage ecosystems.

Using the Concepts

1. Devise a plan by which you could determine whether some kinds of insects can distinguish color.
2. Robert Hooke devised a way to determine the frequency of wing beats in insects with a tuning fork. How can this work?
3. Find out from a physician what local insects might carry disease-producing organisms.
4. How could natural selection produce the complex social organization, physical differences, and communication system seen in a honeybee colony?

Career Activities

5. Find out what organizations in your state employ entomologists.
6. Visit the entomology department of nearby colleges and observe their collections of insects. Ask about vocational opportunities in entomology.

VOCABULARY REVIEW

1 exoskeleton	swimmerets	ovipositor	tracheae
chitin	uropods	incomplete metamorphosis	spiracles
molting	telson	complete metamorphosis	Malpighian tubules
entomology	2 tympanum	gastric caeca	parthenogenesis

CHAPTER 26 TEST

Copy the number of each test item and place your answer to the right.

PART 1 Multiple Choice: Select the letter of the phrase that best completes each of the following.

c **1.** The number of known species of arthropods is one **a.** hundred **b.** thousand **c.** million **d.** billion.

d **2.** Most kinds of arthropods are **a.** arachnids **b.** diplopods **c.** crustaceans **d.** insects.

a **3.** A worker bee does her dance to the left of the vertical line early one morning. The other bees head **a.** in the same direction **b.** in the opposite direction **c.** some left, some right **d.** in all directions.

d **4.** A problem with using DDT as an insecticide is **a.** biological magnification **b.** long lasting toxicity **c.** destruction of nontarget species **d.** all of these.

b **5.** Many seed and fruit crops increase their yield greatly because of the work of **a.** beetles **b.** honeybees **c.** grasshoppers **d.** assorted bugs.

b **6.** A digestive tract with a mouth and anus is found in most **a.** jellyfish **b.** snails **c.** flatworms **d.** sponges.

d **7.** Bilateral symmetry is exhibited in most **a.** echinoderms **b.** sponges **c.** cnidarians **d.** molluscs.

d **8.** A true coelom is found in most **a.** nonsegmented roundworms **b.** flatworms **c.** cnidarians **d.** annelids.

c **9.** Trochophore larvae are found in the **a.** annelids **b.** molluscs **c.** both annelids and molluscs **d.** neither annelids nor molluscs.

d **10.** Plants have less nitrogen waste than animals because plants use less **a.** carbohydrate **b.** fat **c.** vitamins **d.** proteins.

PART 2 Matching: Match the letter of the term in Column I with its description in Column II.

COLUMN I

a. Arachnida   **f.** Onychophora
b. Chilopoda   **g.** complete metamorphosis
c. Crustacea   **h.** incomplete metamorphosis
d. Diplopoda   **i.** organs of excretion
e. Insecta   **j.** organs of respiration

COLUMN II

f **11.** The most primitive, wormlike arthropods

c **12.** With cephalothorax, gills, two pairs of antennae, skeleton hardened with lime

a **13.** With cephalothorax, four pairs of walking legs, no true jaws, and no antennae

d **14.** With two pairs of legs per body segment and one pair of antennae

b **15.** With one pair of legs per body segment and one pair of antennae

e **16.** Distinct head, thorax, and abdomen, and three pairs of walking legs

i **17.** Green gland, nephridium, flame cells, Malpigian tubules

j **18.** Gills, book lung, gastrovascular cavity, tracheae

h **19.** Egg, nymph, adult

g **20.** Egg, larva, pupa, adult

PART 3 Completion: Complete the following.

21. The use of living organisms to control insects is called __biological control__

22. Substances that organisms release into the environment to communicate with other members of the same species are called __pheromones__

23. An insect control technique which results in unfertilized eggs is __sterile male technique__

24. Recognizing changes in familiar landscapes is called __latent learning__

25. The most primitive animals have no lined body space called __a coelom__

VERTEBRATES

This unit concludes our survey of living things with a study of the vertebrates. These are animals with backbones. As in earlier units, this unit contains chapters devoted to particular groups of organisms. We will consider fishes and amphibians, reptiles and birds, and mammals.

We will begin our study with the general vertebrate body plan and the characteristics of vertebrates. Then we will see how the major concepts of biology apply to each group of vertebrates. The organisms in each group display organization and maintain continuity of life. They maintain homeostasis and interact with their environments. In the last section of this unit we will compare groups of vertebrates to each other and see how vertebrates differ from invertebrates. Finally we will see how humans are similar to other vertebrates and how they are different.

ANIMALS ON THE PLAINS

CHAPTER 27

FISHES AND AMPHIBIANS

Like all of the invertebrates you have just studied, vertebrates are animals too. They are similar to invertebrates in several ways. Vertebrates move about to get food. Also, they live in a variety of environments. However, the vertebrates are quite different from the invertebrates. Vertebrates all have the same body plan, whereas the different phyla of invertebrates each have a different body plan.

In this chapter, we will study the general body plan of vertebrates. Also, we will see how it is modified in the bony fishes and amphibians. We will use familiar concepts to understand these animals: *unity and diversity, continuity of life, homeostasis,* and *interaction of organism and environment.*

You are a vertebrate. Thus, what you learn about other vertebrates will help you to understand better the Unit on human biology. You will also learn:

- Why you should wet your hands before handling aquarium fish
- How some fish change color
- How tadpoles turn to frogs
- How fish control the depth at which they swim
- How frogs catch insects
- How biologists have sometimes used lower vertebrates for research that has benefitted humans

SCHOOL OF FISH

▌1 BONY FISHES

General Characteristics of Vertebrates

Vertebrates belong to the Phylum Chordata. As members of that phylum, they have three characteristics that separate them from all other animals. They have a dorsal nerve cord, a notochord, and a pharynx that has slits in its walls. The notochord is visible early in the development of vertebrates. It is usually replaced by the vertebral column. The slitted pharynx is modified in different ways in each phylum of vertebrates.

Not all members of the Phylum Chordata are vertebrates. The vertebrates make up the Subphylum Vertebrata. Other subphyla include such animals as amphioxus and the tunicates.

General Body Plan of Vertebrate

Vertebrates get their name from the fact that they all have a *vertebral column* or backbone. Actually, they all have an internal bony framework, the *endoskeleton*. In addition to the vertebral column, the endoskeleton includes a skull, and the bones of the appendages. Some bones attach the appendages to the vertebral column. These structures, and others we will discuss later, are shown in the diagram of the general vertebrate body plan. (See Fig. 27-1.)

The body of a vertebrate consists of a head, neck, trunk, and often a tail. It generally has four appendages, which may be in the form of legs, fins, wings, or arms. Vertebrates are bilaterally symmetrical.

OBJECTIVES FOR SECTION 1

A. List the general characteristics of vertebrates and describe their general body plan.
B. For a typical fish, describe the general body plan, and explain how continuity of life is maintained.
C. Describe the internal structure of a fish and interpret how its internal systems function to maintain homeostasis.
D. Define *pattern of behavior* and *adaptive behavior* and give examples of each.
E. Give examples of ways that human activities affect fishes.

Pharyngeal gill slits are present at some stage of the life of all vertebrates. In humans they appear early in embryological development and disappear long before birth.

27-1. General vertebrate body plan.

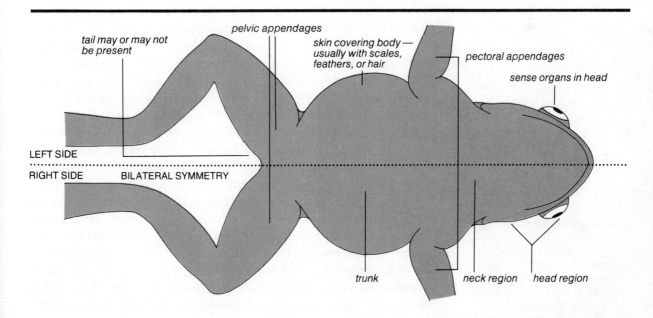

tail may or may not be present

pelvic appendages

skin covering body — usually with scales, feathers, or hair

pectoral appendages

sense organs in head

LEFT SIDE

RIGHT SIDE   BILATERAL SYMMETRY

trunk   neck region   head region

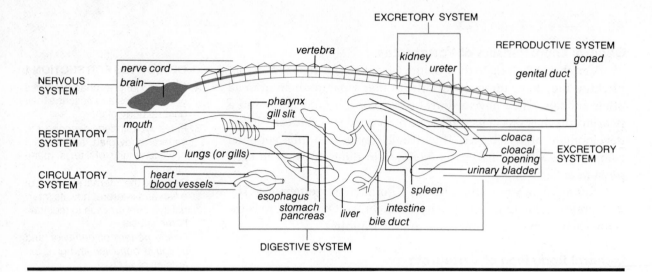

EXCRETORY SYSTEM

REPRODUCTIVE SYSTEM
gonad

vertebra

kidney
ureter

genital duct

NERVOUS SYSTEM
nerve cord
brain

pharynx
gill slit

RESPIRATORY SYSTEM
mouth

cloaca
cloacal opening
urinary bladder

EXCRETORY SYSTEM

lungs (or gills)

CIRCULATORY SYSTEM
heart
blood vessels

spleen

esophagus
stomach
pancreas
liver
intestine
bile duct

DIGESTIVE SYSTEM

27-2. The internal organs of a general vertebrate.

Fish that are live bearers carry eggs within their bodies. This is simply a means of protecting the eggs. All nutrients needed by the embryo are stored in the egg. None are obtained from the mother during development as they are in placental mammals.

VERTEBRATE SYSTEMS The bodies of vertebrates consist of several systems. The *skeletal system* as we have described above, provides support and protection for the animal. The *muscular system* consists of a large number of muscles that are attached to the skeletal system. These systems make it possible for animals to move, get food, and escape predators. Covering the outside of the body is the skin. The skin protects the internal structures and is usually covered with either scales, feathers, or hair.

Some of the systems of the vertebrate body are located inside the body cavity or coelom. (See Fig. 27-2.) The coelom is completely lined with a membrane. It is this membrane that covers and supports the internal organs. Where it attaches and supports organs, it is called the *mesentery* (mes ǝn ter ē). The *digestive system* consists of a long tube that extends from the mouth to the anus. It is modified in some places to form structures such as the stomach. There are several glands associated with the digestive tube. These glands secrete juices that help to digest the food. The *respiratory system* consists of moist membranes. These membranes allow for the exchange of gases between the animal and the environment. The respiratory systems of some vertebrates have gills and others have lungs. Sometimes the skin allows gas exchange to occur. The *circulatory system* consists of a heart and a closed system of blood vessels and blood. The transport of substances to and from all of the cells of the body takes place in these vessels. The *excretory system* removes wastes from the blood. It consists of a pair of kidneys and tubes that carry wastes to the outside of the body.

The *reproductive system* helps to maintain continuity of life. In vertebrates males have testes which produce sperm. Also, tubes are present that carry sperm cells outside the body. Females have

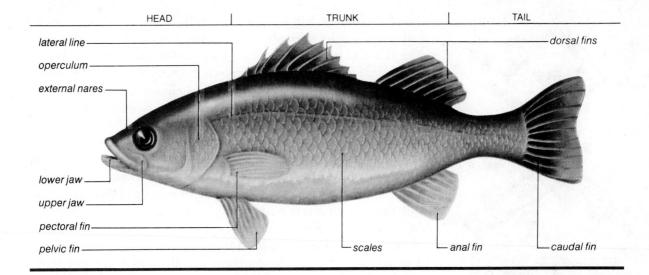

HEAD	TRUNK	TAIL

lateral line

operculum

external nares

dorsal fins

lower jaw

upper jaw

pectoral fin

pelvic fin

scales

anal fin

caudal fin

27-3. The external characteristics of a bony fish.

ovaries which produce eggs. Tubes are present that move the eggs outside the body or to a uterus within the body cavity where embryos develop.

Vertebrates have two control systems, a *nervous system* and an *endocrine system*. The nervous system consists of three main divisions. They are a brain in the head region, a spinal cord protected by the vertebral column, and many nerves that carry messages throughout the body. The *sense organs* are connected directly to the nervous system. Most of the sense organs are located in the head, where they can pick up stimuli from the environment. These include the eyes, ears, and organs for taste and smell. The *endocrine system* consists of several glands that secrete hormones directly into the bloodstream. These control systems regulate the functioning of the vertebrate body. They also allow the animal to detect and respond to stimuli.

Diversity and Continuity in Bony Fishes

BODY PLAN We will use the bony fish as our example of a lower vertebrate. Bony fishes belong to the *Class Osteichthyes* (äs tē *ik* thē ēz). The name describes them well. Osteo means bone and -ichthyos means fish. All bony fishes have jaws, fins, and gills. Their bodies are usually covered with scales. These characteristics distinguish bony fishes from other vertebrates. (See Fig. 27-3.) The presence of jaws separates these fishes from more primitive jawless ones. The pectoral and pelvic fins correspond to the appendages of a general vertebrate. Other fins are modifications of the skin. The gills of a bony fish are located beneath external flaps, the operculum. The posterior edge of the operculum separates the head from the trunk. Fishes do not have a neck region.

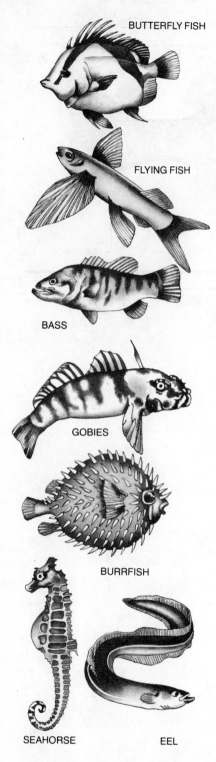

BUTTERFLY FISH

FLYING FISH

BASS

GOBIES

BURRFISH

SEAHORSE

EEL

27-4. Fish show many variations.

The scales of a fish grow from folds in the skin. They form an outer covering for the body. They overlap like the shingles on a roof. The skin also secretes a slimy substance called mucus that lubricates the surface of the body. It also protects the body from invasion by microorganisms. Have you ever picked up a live fish? If so, you know how slippery it is. In managing an aquarium, you should always wet your hands before touching a fish. Otherwise you will remove mucus and increase the chances of your fish getting an infection.

Cells called *chromatophores* are found beneath the outer layer of the skin in some fishes. These cells contain colored granules that can move about in the cell. When the granules are spread throughout the cell, the skin appears to be dark in color. When they are concentrated in a small area in the cell, the skin appears light in color. Changes in the color of the skin are caused by nerve stimulation or hormones. The function of the color change is usually to help the fish blend in with its environment. Sometimes color changes are part of the animal's mating behavior.

DIVERSITY   Though bony fishes generally display the characteristics described here, they also show many variations. Figure 27-4 shows some of the many different kinds of bony fishes.

CONTINUITY   Female fish have ovaries which produce eggs. Male fish produce sperm in their testes. In most bony fish, the female lays eggs in the water. At this point, the male releases sperm into the water over the eggs. This process is called external fertilization. Large numbers of both eggs and sperm are produced. Many of the eggs are fertilized.

In a few species of fish, the eggs are fertilized internally. Then, they are kept inside the female's body until they hatch. Some common aquarium fish, such as guppies and mollies, protect their eggs in this way. They are called live bearers.

Of the large number of eggs that are laid, only some survive to become adults. Many young fish and some adults are eaten by predators. However, the number of adult fish that survive is sufficient to produce eggs and sperm for the next generation. Thus continuity from one generation to the next is maintained.

Homeostasis of Bony Fishes

The internal body systems of fish, like other animals, help to maintain stable internal conditions or homeostasis. These systems are shown in Figure 27-5. Let us see how the structure and function of these systems help to maintain homeostasis.

DIGESTIVE SYSTEM   The digestive system consists of a mouth, pharynx, a short esophagus, stomach, intestine, and anus. Associated with the digestive tract are the liver and the pancreas. Fish have a

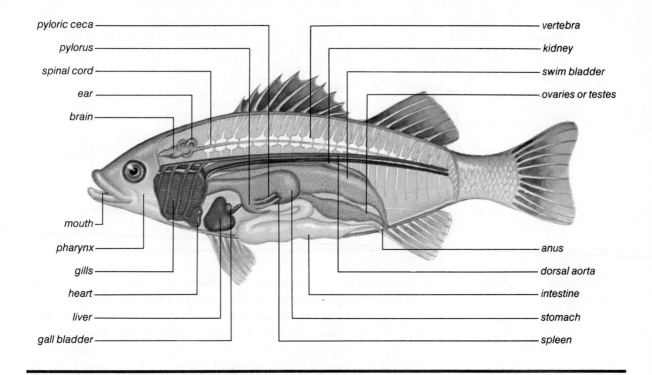

pyloric ceca	vertebra
pylorus	kidney
spinal cord	swim bladder
ear	ovaries or testes
brain	
mouth	
pharynx	anus
gills	dorsal aorta
heart	intestine
liver	stomach
gall bladder	spleen

simple tongue in the floor of their mouths. The tongue is sensitive to touch. As food enters the mouth, it is quickly swallowed and passes to the stomach. Digestion begins in the stomach and continues in the intestine. The fish's intestine is shorter than in most vertebrates. A sac-like *pylorus* (pī lôr əs) and some finger-like *pyloric ceca* (pī lôr ik sē kə) are part of the intestine. These structures increase its surface area. After the food is digested, it is absorbed through the wall of the intestine and enters the blood vessels. The greater the surface area of the intestine, the more efficient is the absorption of molecules of digested food. Thus, the pylorus and the pyloric ceca contribute to homeostasis by making food more easily absorbed. The liver and the pancreas secrete substances that aid in digestion. These organs also contribute to homeostasis by helping to control digestion. After digestion is completed, food particles that have not been digested travel through the intestine. They leave the body as waste material through the anus.

From early life to adulthood, fish vary their diet. The young may eat plankton that includes crustaceans, algae, and water plants. As adults these same fish may be predators consuming insects, worms, crayfish, frogs, and smaller fish. Thus, the digestive tract can adapt to changes in diet as the fish gets older. This is another example of homeostasis.

27-5. *The internal structure of a bony fish.*

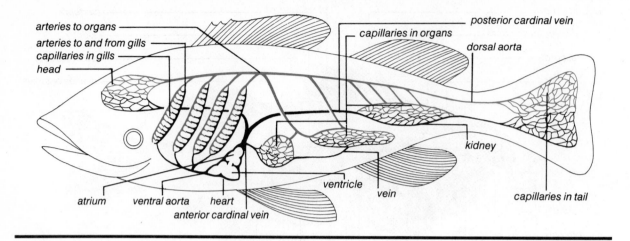

arteries to organs

arteries to and from gills

capillaries in gills

head

posterior cardinal vein

capillaries in organs

dorsal aorta

kidney

ventricle

vein

capillaries in tail

atrium   ventral aorta   heart

anterior cardinal vein

27-6. *The circulatory system of a bony fish.*

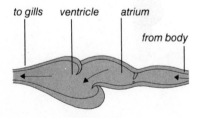

to gills   ventricle   atrium

from body

27-7. *Heart of a fish.*

CIRCULATORY SYSTEM The circulatory system of a bony fish consists of a two-chambered heart and a closed circulatory system. (See Fig. 27-6.) The blood of fishes contains both red and white blood cells. Blood carries substances to and from the cells in three kinds of vessels. Arteries carry blood away from the heart to the gills. Here, blood is oxygenated for use by other organs. As they near organs, the arteries branch many times to form the capillaries. Oxygen, glucose, and other nutrients pass from the capillaries to the cells. Carbon dioxide and other wastes pass from the cells to the capillaries. Capillaries come together to form larger vessels called veins. Veins carry blood back to the heart. The movement of substances between the capillaries and the cells helps to maintain homeostasis. It does so by providing a constant supply of the things cells need. It removes wastes that would damage the cells if they remained.

The heart is divided into an atrium and a ventricle. (See Fig. 27-7.) Blood enters the thin-walled atrium from the body. From here, it is pushed into the thicker-walled ventricle as the atrium contracts. The contraction of the ventricle is much stronger than that of the atrium. When the ventricle contracts, blood is pushed out of the heart with enough force to send it through all of the blood vessels in the body. In a fish, blood leaves the heart by way of the ventral aorta. From there it passes through the capillaries of the gills to the dorsal aorta. Smaller arteries branch off the dorsal aorta. They carry blood to the capillaries of the head, internal organs, and muscles and skin of the trunk and fins. Blood drains from these organs into small veins. Finally, larger veins, the anterior and posterior cardinal veins, return blood to the heart. The pumping action of the heart and the closed system of vessels provides a constant supply of blood to all of the cells of the body. Circulation thus helps to maintain homeostasis.

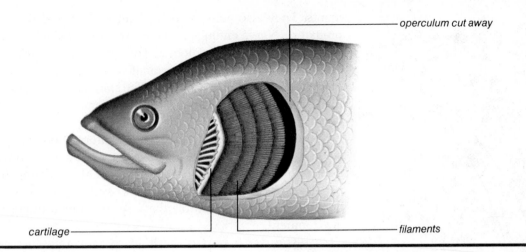

operculum cut away

cartilage

filaments

RESPIRATORY SYSTEM The respiratory system of a bony fish consists of a set of gills located beneath the operculum. There is one set on each side of the body. Each gill is supported by cartilage and contains two thin membranes. Inside the membranes are capillaries. (See Fig. 27-8.) A fish constantly takes in water through its mouth. This water passes over the membranes of the gills and out through the operculum. Blood from the gill artery passes through the membrane capillaries and back into the gill vein. As the blood goes through these capillaries, oxygen from the water enters the blood. In like manner, carbon dioxide from the blood goes into the water. This constant exchange of gases keeps their concentrations in the blood nearly the same all the time.

Also found in the dorsal part of the body cavity of bony fishes is a *swim bladder* (shown in Figure 27-5). The swim bladder is a sac-like structure surrounded by muscles. The fish is able to fill it with gases from the blood or deflate it by returning gases to the blood. When the bladder is full, the fish is more buoyant and floats nearer the surface of the water. By reducing the amount of gas in the bladder the fish becomes less buoyant and floats deeper in the water. The regulation of the amount of gas in the swim bladder is yet another example of homeostasis. A few fish do not have swim bladders. They must swim constantly to keep from sinking to the bottom. In a group of fish called lung fish this bladder provides for gas exchange.

NERVOUS AND SENSORY SYSTEMS The nervous system and sense organs of a fish enable it to detect changes in the environment and make simple responses to them. The nervous system consists of a brain and spinal cord, along with many nerves. These nerves carry messages to and from the brain and spinal cord. The brain of a fish has prominent optic lobes. (See Fig. 27-9.) The optic lobes coordinate eye move-

27-8. *Gills of a fish.*

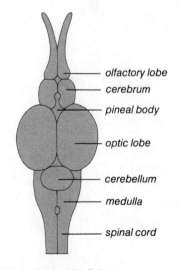

olfactory lobe

cerebrum

pineal body

optic lobe

cerebellum

medulla

spinal cord

27-9. *Brain of a fish.*

Bony Fishes **525**

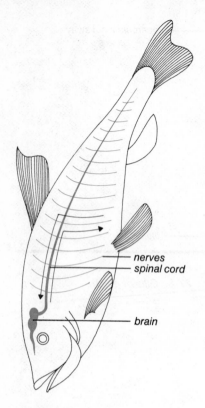

27-10. *Nervous system of a fish.*

nerves
spinal cord

brain

ments. They also help the fish to detect food and the presence of predators. Nerve endings in the nostrils detect smells and relay impulses to the olfactory lobes. The cerebrum controls voluntary activities. The cerebellum coordinates muscular activities while the medulla controls internal organs. The spinal cord is continuous with the brain. It relays messages between the brain and other parts of the body. (See Fig. 27-10.)

The sense organs provide all of the information an organism has about its environment. The nervous system responds to this information by controlling the animal's actions and by regulating many internal processes. Thus, the nervous system helps to maintain homeostasis. It also controls the way the animal interacts with its environment.

OTHER INTERNAL SYSTEMS   Fish, like other vertebrates, have excretory organs called kidneys. The kidneys remove wastes from the blood. In doing so, they help to keep the concentrations of substances in the blood within a narrow range. Fish also have several endocrine glands that produce hormones. These hormones control many different processes. We will delay our consideration of these systems until we reach the higher vertebrates.

Behavior and Environment of Bony Fishes

From your study of invertebrates you may recall that behavior may be innate or learned. The behavior of vertebrates can be much more complex than that of invertebrates. *We speak of a complex set of behaviors as a* **behavior pattern.** Most of these behavior patterns are **adaptive,** *that is, they increase the animal's chances for survival.* The mating behavior of the stickleback fish is an example of an adaptive behavior pattern. (See Fig. 27-11.)

STICKLEBACK FISH   In the spring of the year the lengthening daylight causes chemicals to be produced by the endocrine glands of the stickleback. In response to the chemicals, sticklebacks migrate to their spawning grounds. Here, the male begins to change color. His belly and gill coverings turn bright red. He stakes out a territory and constructs a nest. The male then becomes more aggressive and defends his territory. With the nest completed, the male changes color again. His back becomes bluish-white and his belly remains red. These colors attract a female with eggs. The male lures the female to his nest, where she lays her eggs. After she leaves, the male enters and fertilizes the eggs. Each male usually lures two or three females to his nest.

The male fans the water in order to aerate the eggs until they hatch. Finally, the male's color changes back to the red belly and greenish-black back. He guards the young, catching the strays in his mouth and spitting them back into the nest.

27-11. Mating behavior of stickleback fish. **A.** Stickleback fish. **B.** Male building nest. **C.** Male changes color. **D.** Shape of pregnant female attracts male. **E.** Male nudges female to nest where she lays eggs. **F.** Young fish grow in nest.

27-12. A fish kill.

Answers to Questions for Section 1.

A. 1. Dorsal nerve cord, pharynx with slits in its walls; notochord that is replaced by the vertebral column, early in development.

2. Diagram as in Figure 27-1.

B. 3. Jaws, fins, gills, and usually scales.

4. Eggs laid in water by the female are fertilized when male sprays sperm over them, but a few species have internal fertilization. Large numbers of fertilized eggs help insure survival, as many young are eaten by predators.

C. *5. See Figure 27-4 on page 522.

6. Digestive system: pylorus and pyloric ceca make food more easily absorbed. Circulatory system: the movement of substances between the capillaries and cells provides a constant supply of needed materials and removal of wastes. Respiratory system: by inflating or deflating the swim bladder the fish can maintain a constant level in the water.

This complex behavior pattern is instinctive. The sticklebacks do not learn it. They simply begin to do it when they have reached maturity and the season of the year is appropriate.

GOLDFISH Some learning experiments have been conducted with fish. In one of these experiments, goldfish were trained to swim through a water maze. Some received injections of puromysin at various stages of their training. Puromysin is a chemical that inhibits protein synthesis. Those fish that received the drug during or shortly after training failed to remember what they had learned. If they received the drug more than one or two hours after training, the fish were not affected. The researchers concluded that protein synthesis is needed for an animal to remember what it has learned for a long period of time. This is long-term memory. Short-term memory does not seem to require protein synthesis. You can distinguish between long-term and short-term memory in your own experience. The details of some experience that you remember for only a few minutes or hours is short-term memory. Things you remember for days, weeks, or years represent long-term memory. These may be experiences you have forgotten about and later recall.

EFFECTS OF HUMAN ACTIONS Pollution not only disturbs humans, it also causes problems for other animals. Fish kills are one example of such an effect. (See Fig. 27-12.) Pesticides, particularly chlorinated hydrocarbons, are often responsible for killing fish. Pesticides can also accumulate in the bodies of the fish. These fish are then eaten by others such as birds or humans. The pesticides accumulate in the body of the consumer. Pesticides and other chemicals also reduce the viability of fish eggs which have been deposited in the water. Newly hatched fish are more susceptible to toxic chemicals than are older fish.

QUESTIONS FOR SECTION 1

1. What are the general characteristics of vertebrates?
2. Make a diagram to illustrate the general vertebrate body plan.
3. What are the special characteristics of bony fishes?
4. How do fishes maintain continuity from one generation to the next?
5. Describe some variations in different kinds of bony fishes.
6. Name a way each system of a fish contributes to maintaining homeostasis.
7. What is a behavior pattern?
8. What is an adaptive behavior?
9. How might human activities affect fishes?

Nervous system: responds to information provided by sense organs by controlling actions and regulating many internal processes.

D. 7. A complex set of behaviors, which is usually adaptive.

8. Behavior that increases the animal's chances for survival.

E. 9. Destruction through pollution, especially with pesticides.

CHAPTER INVESTIGATION

A. Describe what you see in the two pictures above.

B. Why do you think the toad refuses to eat the robber fly at left, but eats the dragon fly below?

C. What kind of behavior is illustrated in these pictures? Design an experiment to demonstrate the same kind of behavior that would be safe to do on your friends.

2 AMPHIBIANS

Diversity and Continuity of Amphibians

27-13. *The frog's skin covers the muscles, bones, and other organs.*

BODY PLAN Amphibians belong to the *Class Amphibia*. The word, *amphibia,* means having "two lives." Members of this class spend some of their lives in the water and some on land. They have the general characteristics of vertebrates, but they have some special features of their own. (See Fig. 27-13.) We will use the frog as an example of an amphibian. Frogs have a moist, slimy skin without scales. Their hind legs are adapted for jumping. In addition, they have webbed feet adapted for swimming. The frog's eyes bulge from the top of its head. Each eye can protrude above the surface of the water. In this way a submerged frog can remain hidden as it searches for food or watches for danger. The eardrums of the frog are located on the surface of the head behind the eyes.

DIVERSITY Living amphibians are classified into three orders. *Order Apoda* (ā pō də) consists of a few legless wormlike animals that live in the tropics. *Order Caudata* (ko *dad* ə) includes all of the amphibians that have tails throughout their lives. Salamanders belong in this order. *Order Anura* (ə nyur ə) includes the amphibians·that do not have tails as adults. Frogs and toads belong to this order.

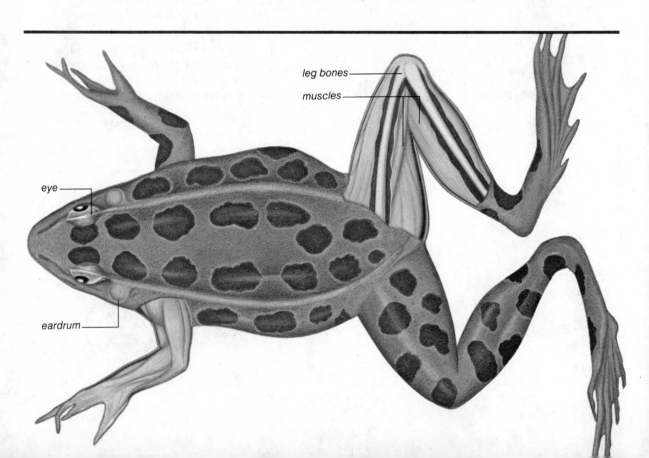

leg bones
muscles
eye
eardrum

You may have wondered how to tell a frog from a toad. The main difference is in the skin and its habitat. Frogs have very moist skin and must live near water. Toads, on the other hand, have somewhat drier skin. They can live in moist soil away from water. They must, however, return to the water to lay their eggs. You may also have heard that handling toads causes warts. This is not true. The idea comes from the appearance of the wart-like glands on the toad's skin. Warts are caused by viruses and are in no way associated with toads, although toads secrete a poisonous fluid.

Some examples of amphibians are shown in Figure 27-14. Can you determine to which order each belongs?

CONTINUITY   The reproductive systems of male and female frogs produce the sperm and eggs. These maintain continuity of life from one generation to the next. (See Fig. 27-15.) In the female frog, eggs develop in the ovaries. As the eggs pass through the long coiled oviducts they are coated with a jelly-like substance. These eggs are then stored in the uterus. When they are released from the uterus, the eggs pass through the cloaca and are shed into water. Here, the jelly swells and protects the eggs from injury and destruction by predators. The jelly also helps to maintain a near constant temperature inside the eggs.

27-14. Three orders of amphibians. Anura: (upper left) frog, (upper right) toad; Apoda: (lower left) Sticky Caecilian ; Caudata: (lower right) salamander.

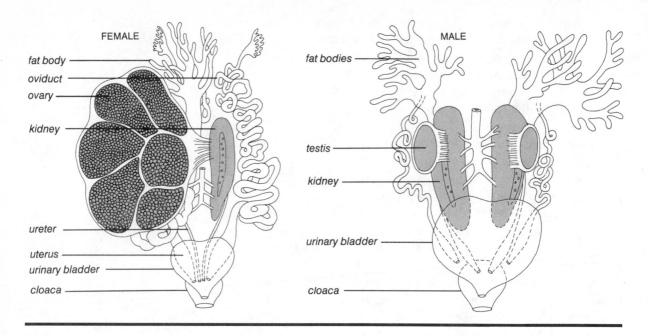

FEMALE

fat body
oviduct
ovary
kidney

ureter

uterus
urinary bladder
cloaca

MALE

fat bodies

testis

kidney

urinary bladder

cloaca

27-15. *Reproductive system of the frog.*

The stages in the development of a frog egg through the gastrula are typical of all vertebrates. The transition from larva to adult in a frog is characteristic of amphibians. Emphasize these changes because they illustrate the different problems an animal encounters in living in water or on land.

27-16. *Amplexus helps to release eggs from the female frog.*

In the male frog, sperm develop in the testes. From here, they pass through tubes into the kidneys. Finally, the sperm are discharged through the ureters into the cloaca.

Many frogs lay their eggs in the spring. A single female may release several hundred eggs. When it's time to lay eggs, the male clasps the female. He presses his front limbs on the female's abdomen. This action, called *amplexus*, helps release the eggs. (See Fig. 27-16.) As the eggs pass from the female, the male releases sperm into the water. There the sperm fertilizes the eggs.

Courtesy Carolina Biological Supply Company

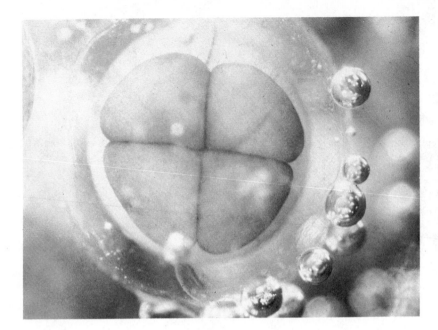

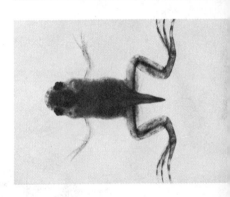

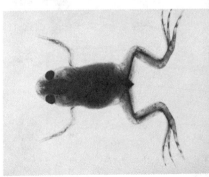

Next, the fertilized egg begins to divide. Eventually, a tadpole or frog larva comes out of the egg. It swims freely and carries on gas exchange through gills. The larva feeds on plant material. As it grows, legs develop and the gills and tail decrease in size. Inside the body lungs are forming. Finally, the legs are strong enough to support the animal on land. Gas exchange is accomplished by lungs and gills. The adult moves out of the water and can live on land. This process of metamorphosis, the changing of a tadpole into a frog, is important in the life cycle of amphibians. (See Fig. 27-17.) It also represents a significant step in the movement of vertebrates from water to land.

Homeostasis of Amphibians

As with fishes, the internal systems of amphibians carry out many functions that help the animal to maintain homeostasis. The internal systems of the frog are shown in Figures 27-18 and 27-19.

DIGESTIVE SYSTEM   The digestive system of the frog includes the mouth, buccal cavity, an elastic gullet, esophagus, and stomach. The small intestine, large intestine, and cloaca make up the rest of this system. The cloaca is a common opening through which all wastes and eggs or sperm leave the body. The organs of the digestive system are suspended inside the body by mesenteries.

Frogs eat mostly insects and worms. They, along with toads, are extremely valuable to farmers. These amphibians help control many kinds of crop-destroying insects.

27-17. *Metamorphosis of a frog.*

27-18   THE DIGESTIVE SYSTEM OF A FROG

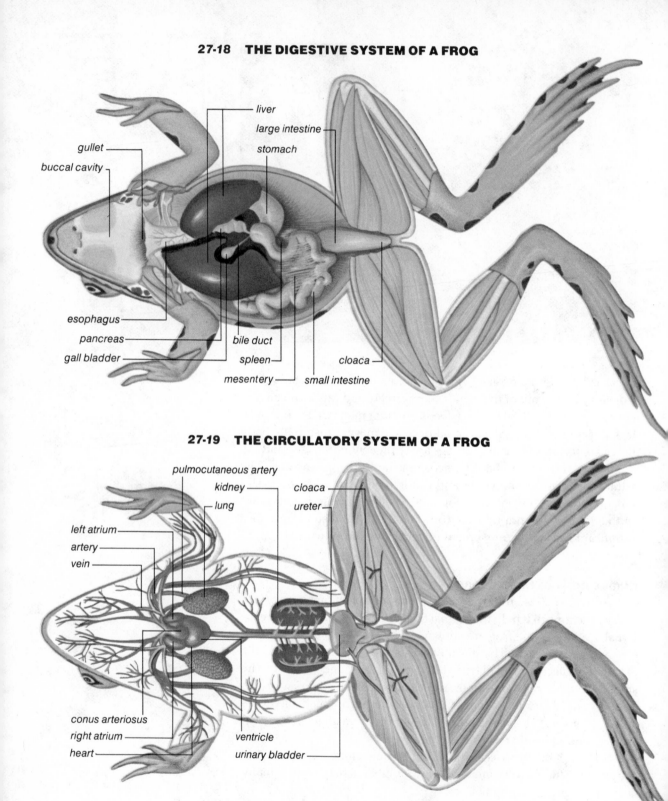

liver

large intestine

stomach

gullet

buccal cavity

esophagus

pancreas

gall bladder

bile duct

spleen

cloaca

mesentery

small intestine

27-19   THE CIRCULATORY SYSTEM OF A FROG

pulmocutaneous artery

kidney

cloaca

lung

ureter

left atrium

artery

vein

conus arteriosus

right atrium

heart

ventricle

urinary bladder

The frog's mouth contains a tongue and several teeth. The tongue is attached at the front of the mouth. It can be quickly extended to catch an insect. (See Fig. 27-20.) A sticky substance on the tongue helps to hold the insect until it can be swallowed. A frog has two *vomerine* teeth in the roof of its mouth. A row of maxillary teeth extend along the border of the upper jaw. (See Fig. 27-21.) These teeth help the frog hold prey in its mouth.

When food enters through the mouth of a frog, it is quickly swallowed and passes into the gullet. Because the gullet is large and stretchy, frogs can eat large quantities of food at one time. The food passes into the tube-like stomach. Digestion begins here. The walls of the stomach have glands that secrete mucus. Other glands secrete digestive juices. Thus, food is partially digested and lubricated in the stomach. The lower end of the stomach is constricted into a valve, the *pyloric valve.* This valve controls the entry of food into the small intestine. The small intestine is divided into the *duodenum* (dōō od ən əm) and the *ileum* (il ē əm). The walls of the small intestine also have some glands similar to those in the stomach. The large intestine carries undigested food from the small intestine to the cloaca.

Two organs, the liver and the pancreas, are associated with the digestive system. The liver occupies most of the upper part of the body cavity. It produces bile which empties into a sac attached to the liver. This sac is called the *gall bladder.* From here, bile is sent through a duct to the small intestine. The bile helps to break down fats so they can be digested. The pancreas lies near the stomach. It releases digestive enzymes through a duct into the small intestine. These enzymes break down all kinds of food.

Through the action of the digestive organs, small molecules are produced. They are absorbed into the blood and transported to all cells. The digestive system helps to maintain homeostasis by making food available in a usable form. Energy for all of the animal's activities comes from digested food.

CIRCULATORY SYSTEM   The circulatory system of the frog is similar to all other vertebrates. It contains a heart, vessels, and blood. Blood leaves the heart through a large artery, the *conus arteriosus* (ko nəs är tir ē ō səs). One branch supplies the head; one, the skin and lungs; and one, the rest of the body. Each of these smaller arteries further divides into capillaries. It is here that blood exchanges materials with the cells. Finally, veins carry blood back to the heart.

The heart of a frog has three chambers. These are the two atria and one ventricle. (See Fig. 27-22 on page 536.) The left atrium receives blood from the lungs. The right atrium receives blood from the rest of the body. Blood from both atria enters the single ventricle. As the ventricle contracts, blood is pumped out of the heart to the body.

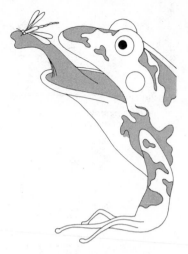

27-20. *The frog's sticky tongue can be extended to catch an insect.*

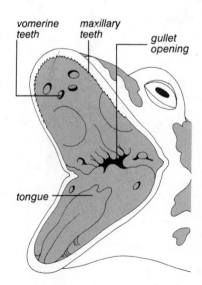

27-21. *Inside of a frog's mouth.*

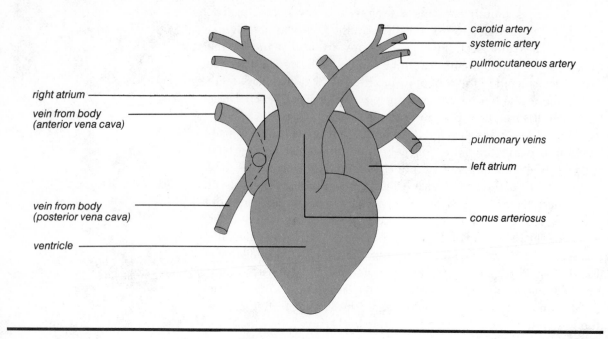

carotid artery
systemic artery
pulmocutaneous artery

right atrium
vein from body
(anterior vena cava)

pulmonary veins
left atrium

vein from body
(posterior vena cava)

conus arteriosus

ventricle

27-22. *Heart of a frog.*

RESPIRATORY SYSTEM   The respiratory system of the frog changes dramatically as the tadpole develops into a frog. The tadpole has gills, similar to those in the fish. As the tadpole changes into a frog, the gills disappear. During this time, thin sac-like lungs grow inside the frog. These lungs are not very efficient. Therefore, the frog's ability to move air in and out of them is limited. Much of the gas exchange in an adult frog takes place through the capillaries in the skin. While oxygen enters, carbon dioxide is removed from the blood. The *pulmocutaneous arteries* carry blood to both the skin and the lungs. The *pulmonary veins* return blood from the lungs to the left atrium. Veins from the skin return blood to the right atrium. Therefore both atria receive blood that has been enriched with oxygen.

That the frog's body adjusts to life on water and life on land is yet another example of homeostasis. In spite of great changes in both the respiratory system and the circulatory system, cells are always supplied with nutrients and oxygen. Carbon dioxide and other wastes are removed. This ability to live first in water and later on land is the reason frogs are classified as amphibians.

EXCRETORY SYSTEM   Excretion of wastes that accumulate in the blood takes place through the kidneys. The kidneys are located in the lower part of the body cavity near the dorsal body wall. Blood goes to the kidneys by way of the renal arteries. After the wastes are removed, blood leaves the kidneys by way of the renal veins. The wastes and some water that were removed from the blood become urine. Urine is carried from the kidneys to the cloaca by the ureters. From the cloaca, urine can be released from the body. However, it can be forced into the urinary bladder and released later. The kidneys regulate the concentration of many substances in the blood. Therefore, they contribute to homeostasis.

NERVOUS AND SENSORY SYSTEMS   The nervous system and sense organs make it possible for the frog to receive and respond to stimuli from the environment. Frogs have large bulging eyes and sharp vision. They do not have external ears. But they do have a membrane on the surface of the head just behind the eyes. This membrane, called the *tympanic* (tim *pan* ik) membrane, is like the eardrum in humans. It transmits sound waves to the inner ear. Nerve impulses are sent from both the eyes and the ears to the brain. Here, they are interpreted and acted upon. The brain and spinal cord receive nerve impulses from all parts of the body. Also, they initiate other nerve impulses that control the actions of the frog. (See Fig. 27-23.) The most anterior part of the brain is divided into the olfactory lobes. These lobes receive impulses from the inside of the nasal cavity and interpret smells for the frog. The cerebrum controls voluntary actions of the frog. A voluntary action is one that an animal can choose to do. For example, when a frog sees an insect, it can act voluntarily to capture it. The optic lobes receive impulses from the eyes and relay them to other parts of the brain. The large size of the frog's optic lobes is related to its sharp vision and its ability to respond quickly to capture prey. The cerebellum serves to coordinate muscular movements. The medulla controls internal organs such as the heart.

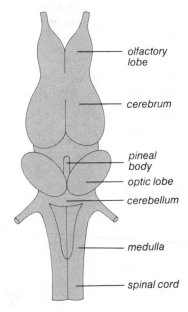

27-23. *Brain of a frog.*

Behavior and Environment of Amphibians

HIBERNATION   Amphibians must cope with changes in temperature and moisture. They do this by hibernating in the winter and estivating in the summer. **Hibernation** *is a period of greatly reduced metabolism during cold weather.* For example, in the fall as the air temperature drops, the frog's body cools until it can no longer remain active. Then it buries itself in mud at the bottom of a pond. Its respiration and circulation slow down. Thus, the frog uses little oxygen. Since it is inactive, it requires little food. This food comes from an organ near the kidneys called the *fat body.* Gradually over the winter the fat body decreases in size. However, it keeps the animal alive until it can become active and begins feeding in the spring.

ESTIVATION   In contrast, **estivation** *is a period of inactivity during hot weather.* During hot weather, a frog's body increases in temperature until it reaches that of the air. It rapidly loses water through its skin and can become dried out very quickly. When water is available in a nearby pond, the frog can cool its body. In doing so, it retains

Answers to Questions for Section 2.

F. 1. Spend some of lives in water, and some on land; undergoes metamorphosis from adaptation from life in water and land on land as part of the life cycle.

2. Ovaries produce eggs and testes produce sperm; fertilization occurs as eggs pass from female's body during amplexus.
The fertilized egg undergoes cleavage. A larva develops (tadpole in the frog). The larva lives in water, swims, and breathes through gills, and gradually undergoes metamorphsis to a land animal.

3. *Apoda*: legless wormlike animals that live in tropics; *Caudata*: have tails all their lives; includes salamanders. *Anura*: tailless as adults; includes frogs and toads.

G. 4. Digestive system: reduces food to small particles that are absorbed by blood and carried to cells, thus making food available in usable form. Circulatory system: heart pumps blood through skin and lungs, where gas exchange occurs, and through rest of body, supplying its needs and removing wastes. Respiratory system: tadpoles are adapted for life in water by gills, and adults for life on land by lungs and skin, where most gas exchange occurs. Excretory system: kidneys remove wastes and some water from blood, regulating the concentration of these substances in blood. Nervous system: makes it possible for the animal to receive and respond to stimuli, so that, for example, it can detect and capture prey.

H. 5. Hibernation is a period of greatly reduced metabolism during cold weather, while estivation is a period of inactivity during hot weather.

6. Reduces rate at which nutrients are used. Decrease in respiratory rate, heart rate, size of fat body, and rate of enzyme reactions. No response to stimuli. Body temperature same as environment.

I. 7. The use of frogs as laboratory animals.
(See page 537 for more answers.)

water. However, many frogs live in an environment where the ponds dry up between rains. This usually occurs during the hottest part of the summer. At this time the frog again buries itself in the mud. Respiration and circulation are reduced, but less so than during hibernation. Estivation lasts for a shorter period of time than hibernation.

EFFECTS OF HUMAN ACTIONS Human actions have caused amphibians and other lower vertebrates to be placed on the endangered species list. (See Table 27-1.) A species is endangered when the total number of members of the species drops to a very small number.

TABLE 27-1 ENDANGERED SPECIES

Group	Number of Endangered Species		
	U.S.	Foreign	Total
mammals	35	251	286
birds	67	145	212
reptiles	11	50	61
amphibians	5	9	14
fishes	29	11	40
snails	2	1	3
clams	23	2	25
crustaceans	1	—	1
insects	6	—	6
plants	49	—	49
Total	228	469	697

When only a few members of the species remain, there is little genetic variation within the population. All breeding is inbreeding and the likelihood of genetically defective offspring increases. An endangered species is threatened with extinction.

QUESTIONS FOR SECTION 2

1. What are the special characteristics of amphibians?
2. How do amphibians maintain continuity from one generation to the next?
3. What are some differences among the three orders of amphibians?
4. Name a way each system of an amphibian contributes to maintaining homeostasis.
5. How does hibernation differ from estivation?
6. Make a list of several effects of hibernation on internal systems and on the behavior of a frog.
7. What kinds of human activities threaten the survival of amphibians?
8. What characteristics are similar in both fish and amphibians?

CHAPTER REVIEW

The bodies of all vertebrates follow the same general vertebrate body plan. They have an endoskeleton and exhibit bilateral symmetry. Usually they have a head, neck, trunk, tail, and four appendages. The structures of internal systems of fish and amphibians show much variation. Yet the functions of these systems are quite similar. Regardless of the *diversity,* the bodies of these animals have the same general *unity.*

Vertebrates *maintain continuity of life* usually by laying eggs that are fertilized externally. Their internal body systems maintain *homeostasis.* These vertebrates display relatively simple behavior in their *interactions with their environment.*

Using the Concepts

1. Why is blood flow slower after the blood passes through capillaries?
2. How would the maintenance of homeostasis in amphibians be changed under the following conditions: (a) lowered availability of oxygen; (b) increased temperature; (c) decreased temperature; (d) decreased moisture?
3. "Every species is endangered." What do you think this means? Do you agree or disagree? Why?
4. It is not always easy to determine what parts of an animal's behavior are innate and what parts are learned. How would you go about studying this problem?
5. Why are most behaviors adaptive?
6. Both fish and frogs are raised commercially for human food. Find out whether there are fish hatcheries or frog farms near where you live. If possible, write or visit one of these places and find out what you would need to do to pursue a career there.
7. Carrying out experiments with vertebrate animals creates some problems. Find some guidelines about the use of vertebrates in experiments. Determine how you and your classmates can follow these guidelines. Discuss whether they are appropriate. Would you make them more restrictive? Less restrictive? Why?
8. Other animals, besides amphibians, are said to hibernate. Use library references to determine in what sense these animals hibernate.

VOCABULARY REVIEW

1
- vertebral column
- endoskeleton
- pectoral
- pelvic
- operculum
- chromatophore
- external fertilization
- dorsal nerve cord
- pylorus

- atrium
- ventricle
- swim bladder
- optic lobes
- olfactory lobe
- cerebrum
- cerebellum
- medulla
- duodenum

- kidneys
- ureter
- adaptive behavior

2
- amplexus
- cleavage
- morula
- blastula
- gastrula
- ileum

- bile
- gall bladder
- conus arteriosus
- pulmonary
- tympanic membrane
- endangered species
- hibernation
- fat body
- estivation

CHAPTER 27 TEST

Copy the number of each test item and place your answer to the right.

PART 1 Multiple Choice: Select the letter of the phrase that best completes each of the following.

c 1. Which of the following is *not* a characteristic of all vertebrates?   **a.** dorsal nerve cord   **b.** notochord   **c.** gills   **d.** pharynx with slits.

d 2. Which vertebrate system(s) provide for movement?   **a.** skeletal   **b.** muscular   **c.** circulatory   **d.** both a and b.

a 3. Bony fishes   **a.** have jaws, fins, and gills   **b.** undergo metamorphosis   **c.** hibernate   **d.** all of the above.

b 4. The pyloric caeca   **a.** are found in amphibians   **b.** increase the surface area of the intestine   **c.** hold hard to digest substances   **d.** function only in early life.

a 5. From the heart blood flows through   **a.** arteries, capillaries, and veins   **b.** arteries, veins, and capillaries   **c.** veins, capillaries, and arteries   **d.** veins, arteries, and capillaries

c 6. The swim bladder   **a.** always acts as a lung   **b.** is found only in primitive fish   **c.** helps fish to control depth at which it swims   **d.** is found only in snail darters.

d 7. Movements of the eyes are coordinated by   **a.** cerebrum   **b.** cerebellum   **c.** medulla   **d.** optic lobes.

d 8. Factors that affect the stickleback mating behavior include   **a.** length of day   **b.** color of male's body   **c.** color of female's body   **d.** both a and b.

b 9. The heart of a frog has   **a.** one atrium and one ventricle   **b.** two atria and one ventricle   **c.** two ventricles and one atrium   **d.** two atria and two ventricles.

b 10. A period of greatly reduced metabolism during cold weather is   **a.** estivation   **b.** hibernation   **c.** metamorphosis   **d.** homeostasis.

PART 2 Matching: Match the letter of the term in Column I with its description in Column II.

COLUMN I
a. circulatory system
b. respiratory system
c. digestive system
d. nervous system
e. sensory system
f. metamorphosis
g. amplexus
h. adaptive behavior
i. cerebellum
j. endangered species

COLUMN II
d 11. Receives and responds to stimuli
a 12. Transports materials throughout the body
e 13. Detects changes in the environment
b 14. Exchanges gases between blood and environment
c 15. Converts food to usable form
h 16. Anything an animal does that helps it survive
j 17. A group of animals that have been reduced in numbers
f 18. A change from life in water to life on land
g 19. Action helping to assure that sperm will reach eggs
i 20. Coordinate muscular movements of a frog

PART 3 Completion: Complete the following.

21. The organization of the body of a vertebrate is called the __vertebrate body plan__

22. External fertilization and development of eggs in water are ways fishes and amphibians maintain __continuity of life__

23. The main overall function of internal systems is to maintain __homeostasis__

24. Patterns of behavior are examples of __environmental interaction__

25. Fish kills and endangered species can be examples of how __humans affect the lower vertebrates__

CHAPTER 28

REPTILES AND BIRDS

In the last chapter we considered the general characteristics of vertebrates. In particular, we examined the characteristics of bony fish and amphibians. In this chapter, we will explore the characteristics of reptiles and birds. We will see how the reptiles and birds are independent of a water environment. Also, we will consider many different kinds of locomotion and behavior in these vertebrates.

In this chapter, we will see how the concepts we have considered in earlier chapters apply to reptiles and birds.

Some things you will learn in this chapter include:

- How do birds find their way south in the fall and north in the spring?
- How does a chicken develop inside a hen's egg?
- How do animals sense time?
- What kinds of social groups are found among animals?

LIZARD

1 REPTILES

Diversity and Continuity of Reptiles

Like the bony fish and the amphibians, the reptiles make up a class of the Phylum Chordata. They belong to *Class Reptilia*. The word reptile means creeping. Actually, many, but not all, reptiles do creep about.

GENERAL BODY PLAN The lizard is representative of the reptiles. (See Fig. 28-1.) It has a dry skin and its body is covered with scales. These structures help to prevent the body from drying out in its land environment. The limbs of a lizard have toes with claws. These help the animal to move about on land. The female's eggs are fertilized inside the body. They are usually buried in soil while they develop. Burying eggs protects them from drying out and protects them from predators. These characteristics allow the reptile to adapt to a land environment.

Internally, the reptile has well-developed lungs. Also, it has a heart with the ventricle partially divided. This allows some separation of oxygenated and unoxygenated blood.

DIVERSITY There are four orders of living reptiles. The turtles, the crocodiles and alligators, and the snakes and lizards make up the three major orders. The fourth order contains the rare and curious *Sphenodon*. (See Fig. 28-2.) *Sphenodons* live today on a few small islands in New Zealand. They represent the last living species of an order of reptiles that flourished about 170 million years ago. The *Sphenodon* has an eye-like structure that is located in the back of its head.

OBJECTIVES FOR SECTION 1

A. For a typical reptile, describe the general body plan. Explain how continuity of life is maintained.
B. Describe the internal structure of a reptile. Interpret how its internal systems function to maintain homeostasis.
C. Summarize ways that reptiles cope with changes in their environments.
D. Interpret the effects of human actions on reptiles.

28-1. The general characteristics of a lizard, a representative reptile.

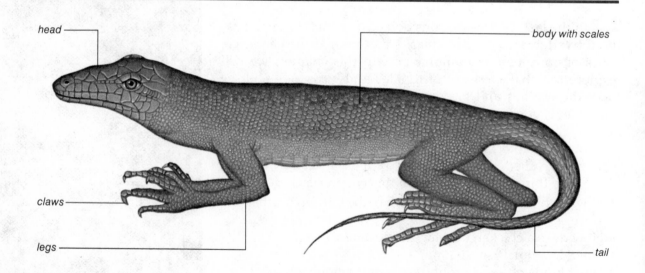

head — body with scales

claws

legs — tail

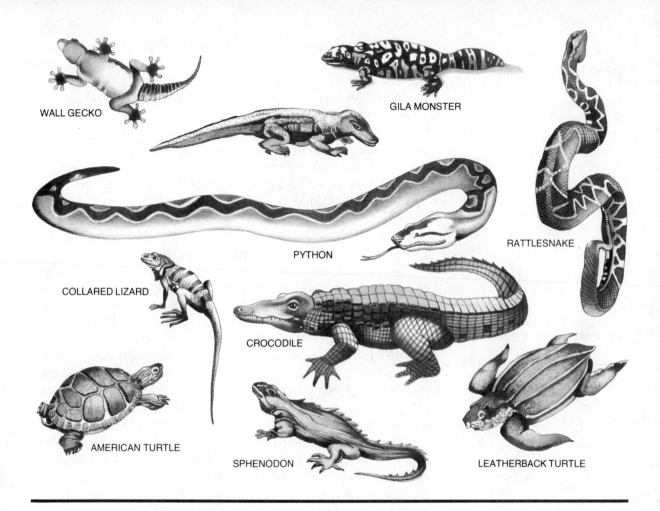

WALL GECKO

GILA MONSTER

PYTHON

RATTLESNAKE

COLLARED LIZARD

CROCODILE

AMERICAN TURTLE

SPHENODON

LEATHERBACK TURTLE

Turtles are reptiles with shells. They include land turtles or *tortoises*, freshwater turtles or *terrapins*, and *true turtles* that live in salt water. The limbs of true turtles are modified to form flippers. Some turtles spend much of their lives in water. However, most come to the surface to breathe. All turtles lay their eggs on land.

Like the *Sphenodon*, turtles have been in existence for over 200 million years. Moreover, their structure is much the same now as it was then. A turtle's shell protects it from predators. The shell also helps it to adapt to its environment. Because the turtle is so well adapted to its environment, it has existed for many generations with little change.

All turtles have a horny beak and lack teeth. They can eat both plants and animals. Their eyes are well-developed. A tympanic membrane lies just behind the angles of their jaws. Most turtles have short legs and five claws on each foot.

28-2. *Each of these animals represents a different order or family of reptiles.*

Water-dwelling turtles usually have webbed feet. They also have nostrils on the top of their heads. By floating near the surface, their nostrils allow the turtle to take air into their lungs.

Crocodiles and *alligators* live in tropical or near tropical climates. They spend much of their time in water. Usually, their nostrils extend out of the water. This way they can breathe air into their lungs and not be noticed by the animals they prey upon.

Crocodiles and alligators are closely related. They can be distinguished from each other by the shapes of their heads and their teeth. The head of a crocodile is triangular in shape. Also, the crocodile's snout is more pointed than that of an alligator. Crocodiles also have a tooth in the lower jaw that fits into a notch in the upper jaw. This tooth arrangement is not present in alligators.

Snakes and *lizards* make up the largest order of living reptiles. Both have elongated bodies covered with scales. Snakes differ from lizards primarily by the absence of limbs. Some snakes have small bones that represent the remains of limb bones. Thus, it appears that snakes have evolved from ancestors that had legs.

All snakes are carnivores. Most feed on insects, fishes, amphibians, and small mammals such as rats and mice. After they capture these animals, many snakes swallow them alive. Many snakes can swallow animals much larger than their own body diameter. Their jaws are attached by flexible joints. These enable the mouth to open very wide. Snakes have teeth that slant inward. Hence, the prey are held and pushed along into the pharynx. Once inside the digestive tract, muscular contractions propel it along. A few large snakes, the *constrictors*, squeeze their prey until the animal stops breathing before swallowing it. Although a few snakes are poisonous, many people are needlessly fearful of all snakes. The benefits of snakes in controlling the numbers of insects and rodents far exceed their harmful effects.

The lizards are an extremely diverse group of reptiles. One kind are the chameleons. These lizards are noted for their ability to change the color of their skin. Like some fish, they too have chromatophores deep in their skin. Another kind are the geckos. Geckos have sticky padded feet. These enable them to climb walls and walk on ceilings. The gila monster and its relatives are a group of poisonous lizards. Toxins released from glands in the lower jaws of these lizards affect the nervous system of the prey. The breathing muscles become paralyzed and the prey dies.

DINOSAURS — A GROUP OF EXTINCT REPTILES Dinosaurs flourished on earth during the period from 70 to 200 million years ago. Scientists still do not know for sure what caused them to become extinct. Changes in the climate are one possible explanation for the disappearance of dinosaurs. Regardless of what caused their extinction,

The absence of limbs in snakes is a good example of a modification of body structure that might prevent taxonomic problems. However, if the early embryos of snakes are studied, it can be seen that they begin to develop legs and subsequently lose them.

they were a successful group of animals over a long period of time. For many years they were believed to be "cold-blooded." Today, there is great debate about what this term really means. Some scientists believe some of the dinosaurs were *endothermic*. Endothermic animals regulate their body temperatures by metabolic activity from within. Today, only birds and mammals are endothermic. Other scientists think that the dinosaurs were *ectothermic*; that is, their body temperature is regulated by the environment. Ectotherms can regulate their body temperatures by certain behavior as they respond to changes in their environment. When it is cool, they position themselves to receive the maximum radiation from the sun. When it is hot, they move out of the sun. Ectothermic dinosaurs may have been "warm-blooded" because they lived in fairly warm regions and had such massive bodies. Night time cooling might not have been great, and daytime cooling mechanisms might have been an advantage that prevented overheating.

Because of many similarities, birds are thought to be the direct descendants of certain dinosaurs. Archaeopteryx had many features of both reptiles and birds. (See Fig. 28-3.) We will study more about birds later in this chapter.

CONTINUITY   Reptiles lay their eggs on land instead of in water as the lower vertebrates do. Their eggs are encased in a tough rubbery shell. This prevents them from drying out. The shell is also porous. Because of this, oxygen enters and carbon dioxide is released as the embryo develops.

The male deposits sperm inside the reproductive tract of the female. There, the sperm fertilize the eggs before the shell is placed around them. The egg contains the developing embryo, a food supply, and four membranes. The eggs are usually buried and left by the female to hatch. The young must then fend for themselves after birth. A few reptiles, however, watch over their eggs. Reptiles generally lay fewer eggs than the lower vertebrates. All the eggs are fertilized, however, and protected during development by the shell. Thus, the species can be maintained from one generation to the next with a relatively small number of eggs. However, in a few reptiles, the eggs are retained inside the female's body until they hatch. The young are born alive.

Homeostasis of Reptiles

The internal systems in reptiles perform the same functions in maintaining homeostasis as those in lower vertebrates. Because most reptiles live all of their lives on land, the problems of maintaining homeostasis are somewhat different. For example, temperatures on the surface of the land vary over a wider range than do water temper-

28-3. How would you classify Archeopteryx?

Emphasize the relationship between internal fertilization and an egg with a hard shell. Also relate these characteristics to the adaption of reptiles to a land environment.

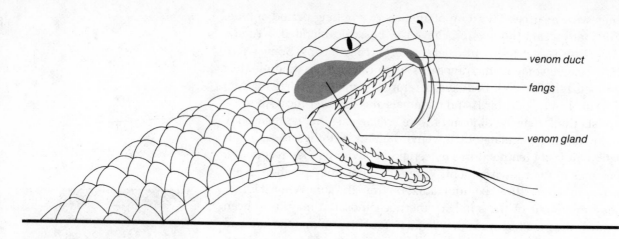

28-4. *Mouth of a poisonous snake.*

28-5. *Three chambered heart of a reptile.*

atures. Being ectotherms, reptiles have special temperature regulating problems. We will discuss the problem of temperature regulation later in the chapter.

DIGESTIVE SYSTEM   The digestive system of a reptile generally follows the vertebrate body plan. However, there are some modifications that are of interest. For example, in poisonous snakes, one pair of salivary glands are modified to produce venom. The venom drains by way of a duct from the gland into the hollow inside of the fangs. (See Fig. 28-4.) All reptiles, except turtles, have teeth. At the time of hatching, reptiles have a single central *egg tooth* on the tip of the upper mandible. This tooth helps the animal to make its way out of the shell. However, it is lost soon after hatching. As you might expect, snakes have an unusually long esophagus, the walls of which are easily stretched as large prey moves through it.

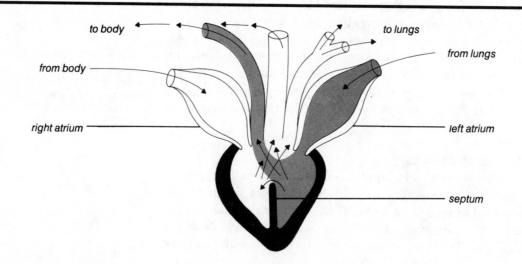

CIRCULATORY AND RESPIRATORY SYSTEMS   The circulatory and respiratory systems are adapted to obtain oxygen from air and transport it to all cells. Even reptiles that live in water, such as sea turtles, had ancestors that lived on land. The heart of all reptiles, except alligators and crocodiles, has three chambers. There are two atria and one ventricle. (See Fig. 28-5.) The single ventricle is partly separated by a septum. However, in alligators and crocodiles, the septum is complete and there are two ventricles. Blood from the body passes through the right atrium to the right side of the ventricle of the heart. From here, it enters the lungs. Blood from the lungs is returned to the left atrium of the heart. It then passes through the left side of the ventricle to all the organs of the body. Even when only a septum divides the ventricle, mixing of blood from the two atria is largely prevented. The lungs are the main respiratory organs of reptiles. They have many capillaries associated with their moist membranes. Thus, blood from *pulmonary circulation* is well supplied with oxygen and contains little carbon dioxide.

The respiratory system of a reptile consists of two openings called *nostrils,* a *nasal passage, pharynx,* and *larynx* or voice box. In addition, a *trachea* (*trā kē ə*), two *bronchi* (*brong kī*), and many smaller *bronchioles* are present. The bronchioles carry air to and from the *respiratory membranes.* Although reptiles have a larynx, only a few can produce sounds. For example, snakes can make a hissing sound and male alligators bellow during the mating season.

The circulatory and respiratory systems work together. Lungs exchange gases between the atmosphere and the blood, and the cells of the body. Cells are constantly supplied with oxygen and carbon dioxide is removed. The flow of blood and the amount of air moving in and out of the lungs are both regulated. Hence, the reptiles' needs are met. These processes help to maintain stable internal conditions or homeostasis.

EXCRETORY SYSTEM   The excretory system of reptiles consists of a pair of kidneys similar to those found in humans. Only lizards and turtles have a *urinary bladder.* Some water-dwelling turtles have a pair of accessory urinary bladders. These serve as respiratory membranes. In doing so, they allow the turtle to stay under water for a longer period than if it had only lungs.

The kidneys filter nitrogen wastes out of the blood. They also regulate the amount of water that stays in the animal's body. At times, there is a special need to conserve water, as in an extremely hot, dry environment. Under such conditions, the quantity of urine will be greatly reduced. Removing wastes and regulating water are two additional ways that stable internal conditions are maintained.

NERVOUS AND SENSORY SYSTEMS   Reptiles see, hear, taste, smell, and maintain balance. They have specialized sense organs to perform

Answers to Questions for Section 1.

6. (a) Enables animal to swallow large prey alive; animal can stun or poison prey through bite of fangs. (b) Makes pulmonary circulation more efficient for oxygenation of blood. (c) Makes excretion more efficient; accessory bladders serve as auxilliary respiratory organs.

C. 7. A part of the hypothalamus acts like a thermostat, "set" for the animal's normal temperature, that sends out nerve impulses whenever surroundings become warmer or colder; animal responds by changing its temperature. The animals may move from the shade into the sun, or vice versa, to raise or lower their temperatures. Many hibernate in winter.

D. 8. Seeking the animals for their skins has made them endangered species.

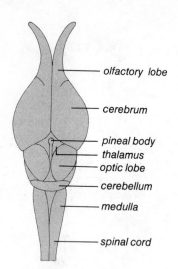

— olfactory lobe

— cerebrum

— pineal body
— thalamus
— optic lobe
— cerebellum
— medulla

— spinal cord

28-6. *Brain of a snake.*

Answers to Questions for Section 1.

A. **1.** Dry skin, covered with scales, toes with claws, internal fertilization, well developed lungs, partial separation of ventricles in heart.

2. After internal fertilization, tough shell forms on the eggs, which are laid on land and buried and usually left. The egg contains food for the developing embryo.

B. **3.** Turtles have shells, and some have modified limbs as flippers; they lack teeth. Crocodiles and alligators vary in the shapes of their heads and teeth. Snakes lack legs. Some lizards can change the color of their skin; others are poisonous, as are a few kinds of snakes.

*4. Answers will vary. They may include: outgrew food supply, were easy prey; changes in climate.

5. (a) In snakes, a long esophagus; and for poisonous ones, a pair of salivary glands that produce venom, which drains into hollow fangs. (b) In alligators and crocodiles, a four-chambered heart. (c) In lizards and turtles, a urinary bladder.

(See page 547 for answers 6-8.)

these functions. When the sense organs receive stimuli from the environment, they relay the stimuli to nerves. Nerves carry impulses to the brain or spinal cord.

The brain of the snake has a larger cerebrum than that of the lower vertebrates. (See Fig. 28-6.) Extending upward from the thalamus is the *pineal body*. This small structure has been a source of much puzzlement. Studies of fossil reptiles have shown that some had a light sensitive area at the site of the pineal body. Literally, they had an eye in the back of the head. Biologists now believe the pineal body is concerned with an organism's ability to respond to changes in the amount of daylight.

The lower part of the thalamus, the *hypothalamus,* is also an important regulatory part of the brain. It contains several different centers. Each is responsible for controlling a particular process. One important process is temperature regulation.

The temperature sensing part of the hypothalamus acts like a thermostat. It seems to be "set" for the animal's normal temperature. When the animal's body becomes warmer or cooler than the setting, the hypothalamus sends out nerve impulses. These impulses cause the animal to respond in some way to change its body temperature.

Behavior and Environment of Reptiles

Reptiles are able to cope with changes in their environment. By moving from one area to another they regulate their body temperature. Snakes and lizards sunning themselves on rocks are raising their body temperatures. Many reptiles hibernate in the same manner as amphibians.

EFFECTS OF HUMAN ACTIONS   Reptiles are frequently sought for their skins. Leather is made from snake, lizard, and alligator skins. By raising these animals on reptile farms, we would assure that more of them do not become endangered species.

QUESTIONS FOR SECTION 1

1. What are the special characteristics of reptiles?
2. How do reptiles maintain continuity of life?
3. What are some variations found among reptiles?
4. Why do you think dinosaurs became extinct?
5. What are some special internal structures in reptiles?
6. How do these structures contribute to the survival of the animals?
7. How do reptiles regulate their body temperature?
8. How have human actions threatened the survival of reptiles?

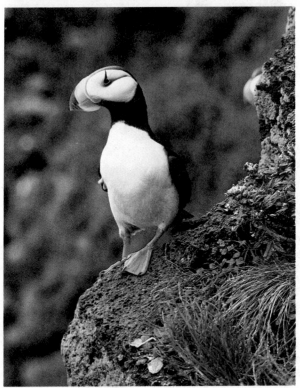

CHAPTER INVESTIGATION

A. List as many similarities and differences between these two animals as you can. Do you think all differences are visible?

B. Did you list the difference between body temperatures? Reptiles have a body temperature near that of their environment. Birds have a nearly constant body temperature around 38-39°C. Do some reading to determine how birds maintain a constant body temperature.

C. What major concept of biology is illustrated by an animal's ability to maintain a nearly constant body temperature? Design an experiment to determine how much the body temperature of a bird and a reptile varies over a 24-hour period. Your experiment must not damage either vertebrate in any way.

② BIRDS

OBJECTIVES FOR SECTION 2

E. For a typical bird, describe the general body plan. Explain how continuity of life is maintained.

F. Describe the internal structure of a bird. Interpret how its internal systems function to maintain homeostasis.

G. Name examples of innate and learned behavior in birds.

H. Identify patterns of behavior and adaptive behaviors in birds.

I. Summarize the ways birds cope with changes in their environment.

J. Interpret the effects of human actions on birds.

28-7. The general characteristics of a bird.

Diversity and Continuity of Birds

Birds belong to the *Class Aves.* Aves is the Latin word for bird.

GENERAL BODY PLAN The pigeon is a good representative of the birds. (See Fig. 28-7.) Like reptiles, birds have scales on the legs and claws on the toes. The eggs of the female are also fertilized internally.

Other characteristics of birds are found only in the Class Aves. These include feathers, light porous bones, and front limbs that are modified as wings. Birds also have a toothless, horny beak. They lay large eggs that are covered with hard shells. Birds are endothermic. Therefore, while the embryo is developing, their eggs must be incubated or kept at a warm temperature.

Most birds have small heads, long flexible necks, and streamlined bodies. The breastbone or sternum is large and has a heavy ventral ridge. The muscles of flight are attached both to the ridge and to the bones of the wings. These powerful muscles, along with the feathers of the wings, allow most birds to fly. Feathers increase the surface area of the wings when they are spread in flight. Such feathers are long and sturdy. They are called quill feathers. Smaller feath-

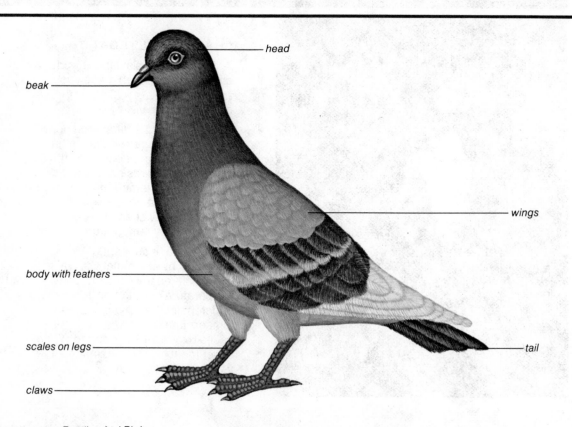

ers, the contour feathers, protect and help to streamline the body. Beneath the contour feathers, especially in water birds, are the down feathers. Down feathers are short and fluffy. They help maintain the bird's constant body temperature. Birds may display feathers of many different colors. Females are usually less brightly colored than males. This helps them to blend into their surroundings. The chance that they will be found by predators during nesting thus decreases. The brighter colors of males are often related to attracting a mate. They may also be used to lure a predator away from a nest.

Birds generally shed their feathers once or more each year in the process of molting. New feathers grow out of the same pits from which the old feathers came. Most birds lose their feathers in the late summer. Then, over a period of several weeks, they get a new set of plumage for winter. Molting is a gradual process. New feathers grow in some areas of the body before all of the old feathers are lost.

DIVERSITY Birds are an extremely diverse group of animals. They are classified in 27 different orders. Biologists use the shape of a bird's feet and beak to determine in what order they belong. These characteristics are also related to what a bird eats and where it lives. For example, birds with short, thick beaks eat seeds. Those with small, sharp beaks eat insects. Long, spear-like beaks may be adapted for catching fish. Likewise, birds with webbed feet are swimmers. Those with short, flexible feet with sharp claws can perch. Birds with short stubby wings are unable to fly. Some birds live on land. Others spend most of their lives in or over water. Still others are shore birds. These birds spend most of their lives near water. They feed on the many sources of food in the water. A few birds such as hawks and owls are predators who usually feed on small mammals. Study the birds in Figure 28-8 and see if you can determine what they eat, where they live, and whether they can fly.

CONTINUITY In birds, eggs are protected by a hard brittle shell. The shell is porous and allows for gas exchange. Inside the shell are four membranes that surround the developing embryo. (See Fig. 28-9 on page 552.) The *chorion* lines the shell. The *amnion* forms a sac around the developing embryo. This sac is filled with fluid and protects the embryo. Another membrane, the *yolk sac,* contains stored food material for the developing embryo. The *allantois* (ə *lant* ə wəs) is a bag that collects wastes from the blood of the embryo. It becomes closely associated with the chorion. Blood vessels in these membranes transport oxygen to the embryo. They also remove carbon dioxide and wastes. After about 21 days of incubation, a young chick hatches from a hen egg. The eggs of other birds hatch between 13 and 50 days. The newly hatched bird has down feathers and looks like a miniature of its parents. The development of a chick embryo is shown in Figure 28-9.

MARSH HAWK

BARN SWALLOW

LOON

KIWI

YELLOW-BELLIED
SAPSUCKER

OSTRICH

28-8. *Some varieties of birds.*

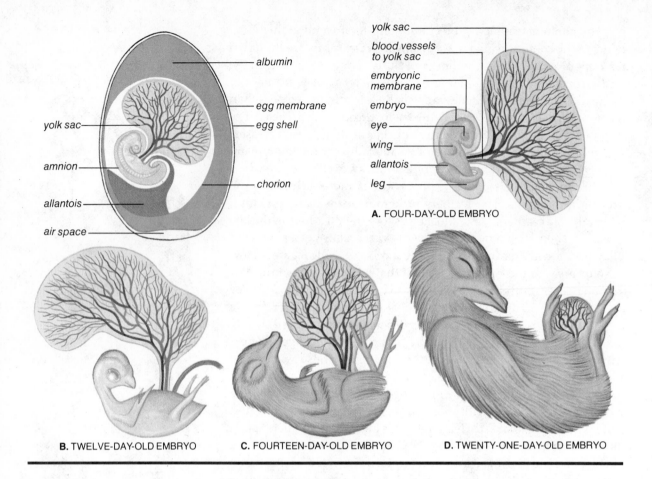

28-9. *Some stages in the develop-ment of a chick embryo.*

Homeostasis of Birds

The internal systems of birds contribute to homeostasis in many of the same ways as the systems of lower vertebrates. The bird is an endotherm and has a constant body temperature. Therefore, temperature regulation is more precise than in lower vertebrates.

DIGESTIVE SYSTEM   The digestive system of birds is highly specialized. (See Fig. 28-10.) Birds maintain a body temperature that is usually higher than the environment. Therefore, they must consume large amounts of food for their size. Food, such as insects or pieces of grain, passes through the mouth. From here, food passes through the esophagus and enters a large sac, the *crop*. Food is stored in the crop until it can be digested. Many birds eat whenever food is available until their crops are filled. This helps to provide a reserve of food. The "wishbone" supports the crop. From the crop food passes to the *proventriculus* (prō ven *trik* yə ləs), the first part of the stomach. Here it is mixed with digestive juices. It then moves on to the *gizzard,* a thick muscular part of the stomach, where it is ground up into smaller

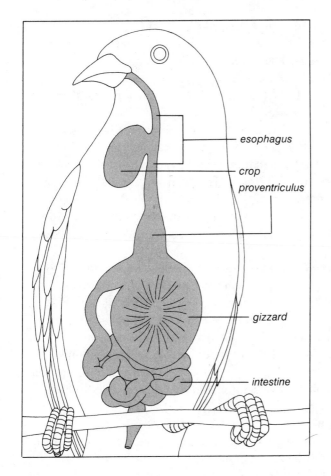

esophagus

crop

proventriculus

gizzard

intestine

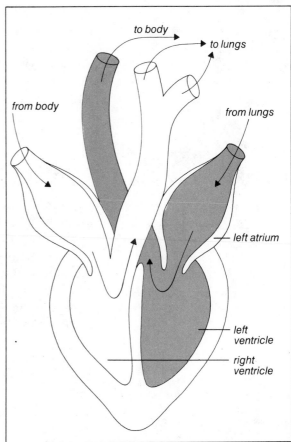

to body

to lungs

from body

from lungs

left atrium

left ventricle

right ventricle

pieces. Some birds swallow small stones that help to grind the food. These special structures in the digestive tract of birds are prominent in grain-eating birds. Since birds have no teeth, the gizzard plays the major role in breaking down food particles. The intestine is a coiled tube, quite like that of other vertebrates.

28-10. *(left) Digestive tract of a bird.*

28-11. *(right) Four chambered heart of a bird.*

CIRCULATORY SYSTEM   The circulatory system of birds includes a four-chambered heart. (See Fig. 28-11.) Large quantities of oxygen are required to maintain the high body temperature of birds. To maintain the high metabolic rate, it is important that the blood carry as much oxygen as possible. The four-chambered heart causes all of the blood to go through the lungs to make one complete circuit of the body. The especially high metabolic rate of birds makes the large constant supply of oxygenated blood very important.

RESPIRATORY SYSTEM   Birds have two important specializations in their respiratory systems. (See Fig. 28-12.) First, they have a *syrinx* (*sir* ingks) at the end of the trachea. Sounds are produced in the syrinx. Second, they have many interconnecting tubes within the lungs.

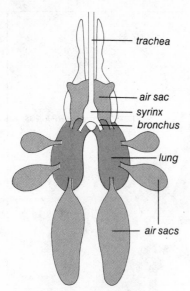

28-12. Respiratory system of a bird.

trachea
air sac
syrinx
bronchus
lung
air sacs

Birds are the first class of vertebrates to maintain nearly constant body temperature. Discuss the significance of this with your students. Ask them to consider how maintaining homeostasis is more complicated in birds (and mammals) than in any other organisms.

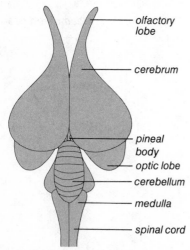

olfactory lobe
cerebrum
pineal body
optic lobe
cerebellum
medulla
spinal cord

28-13. Brain of a pigeon.

This is in contrast to the simple tree-like branching found in the lungs of other vertebrates. The interconnections between the tubes in the lungs of birds allow for a very efficient gas exchange. This exchange helps to maintain the high metabolic rate. Large amounts of oxygen must enter the blood. At the same time, large amounts of carbon dioxide must be removed.

EXCRETORY SYSTEM   The excretory system of birds allows wastes to be removed from the blood with only a small loss of water. One of the reasons birds can fly is that their bodies contain smaller amounts of water than many other animals. They can survive with little water because their kidneys conserve it. Wastes are mostly in the form of uric acid. The small amount of urine is transported from the kidney through the ureters to the cloaca. Among birds, only ostriches have a urinary bladder.

HOW THE SYSTEMS WORK TOGETHER   Homeostasis is maintained by the internal systems working together. The digestive and respiratory systems provide ample food and oxygen. The circulatory system transports these substances to the cells and removes wastes efficiently. The kidney gets rid of wastes and conserves water. These processes are regulated by the nervous and endocrine systems.

NERVOUS AND SENSORY SYSTEMS   The sense organs of birds are well developed. Most birds have color vision and sharp eyesight. Balance and hearing are also very keen. In addition, they have some sense of taste. Birds do not have a well-developed sense of smell.

The nervous system of birds follows the general vertebrate plan. The main parts of the pigeon brain are shown in Figure 28-13. The hypothalamus regulates body temperature within a narrow range of only 1 or 2 degrees. As in other endotherms, the metabolic rate of birds at rest is about five times that of ectotherms. A great amount of heat is produced. Therefore, one of the problems in temperature regulation is to get rid of excess heat. You know from your own experience how difficult it is to keep cool on a hot day. Birds lose heat mostly by increasing their rate of breathing. Water is lost from the respiratory membranes and with it goes some body heat.

The hypothalamus is also closely related to the endocrine system. In fact, some of the hormones released by the *pituitary* (pi tō͞o ə ter ē) *gland* are actually made in the hypothalamus. From here, they are transported to the pituitary.

ENDOCRINE SYSTEM   The pituitary gland is the master gland of the endocrine system. It produces several hormones that are important in regulating other glands of the system. Some of these hormones, called *gonadotrophins* (gō nad ə trō̄ fəns), stimulate the ovaries and testes to produce other hormones. These hormones then stimulate the production of eggs and sperm.

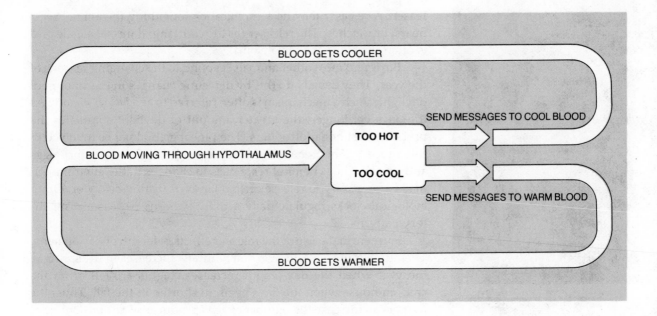

BLOOD GETS COOLER

BLOOD MOVING THROUGH HYPOTHALAMUS

TOO HOT

TOO COOL

SEND MESSAGES TO COOL BLOOD

SEND MESSAGES TO WARM BLOOD

BLOOD GETS WARMER

28-14. The relationship between the nervous and endocrine systems in regulating internal processes.

The pituitary also produces a hormone called *prolactin*. In some birds, this hormone causes the epithelial cells of the crop gland to secrete a "cheesy" substance. This substance, sometimes called pigeon's milk, is produced by both male and female pigeons. Both parents participate in keeping the eggs warm until they hatch. The act of sitting on the eggs stimulates the release of prolactin. This hormone, in turn, causes secretion of the milk given to the young pigeons. This example shows the relationship between the nervous and endocrine systems in regulating internal processes. It also shows how behavior can be related to internal processes. (See Fig. 28-14.)

Behavior and Environment of Birds

The more complex the animal's nervous system, the more complex its behavior can be. Thus, bird behavior is frequently a mixture of innate and learned components that may be difficult to separate. For example, in the laboratory, the Australian zebra finch will incubate the eggs of the Bengalese finch and raise the chicks to maturity. These chicks will display behaviors that are a curious mixture of both species. The mature males will perform the Bengalese finch's courtship dance. They will also make a few simple Bengalese bird calls. However, they will sing the song of the male zebra finch. Thus, in this particular bird, the courtship dance and the simple calls are innate. However, the song is learned.

RELEASER STIMULUS   Regardless of whether a behavior is innate, learned, or some combination of these, it is stimulated to occur in some way. *The stimulus that initiates a given behavior is called a* re-

28-15. *For the herring gull, the larger the egg the better the nesting behavior.*

leaser. A releaser may be a chemical or something the animal sees, hears, or touches. The releaser for the courtship dance of a male bird is often the sight of a female bird.

Birds and most other animals respond to the changing seasons of the year. They usually do this by detecting changes in the amount of daylight. Such a mechanism is often referred to as a *biological clock.* As the days get longer, the greater amount of daylight stimulates the production of gonadotrophins. The pineal gland may be involved in this process. The gonadotrophins cause the birds to produce eggs and sperm. Thus chemical responses to changes in the environment may be necessary to release certain kinds of mating behavior. Other biological clocks regulate daily activity patterns or seasonal migratory patterns.

Farmers make use of the releaser effects of length of day on hens. The number of eggs laid by a hen naturally increases in the spring of the year when the day length increases. Lights are left on in the chicken house when the days begin to shorten in the fall. Thus, the farmer can increase the number of eggs produced. The hen continues to behave as she did during the natural long days by laying more eggs.

Some behaviorists have studied the role of the size, shape, and color of eggs in releasing nesting behavior. The herring gull shows a preference for a large egg marked like her own. (See Fig. 28-15.)

Learned behavior may also be stimulated by a releaser. *Imprinting* is such a learned behavior that is known to occur in many birds. Usually the first object a newly hatched bird sees is its mother. It is said to imprint on the mother and therefore learn to follow her around. The behaviorist Konrad Lorenz arranged for goslings to see him first rather than their mother. He became the releaser for imprinting. Thus, the goslings imprinted on him and followed him wherever he went.

BEHAVIOR PATTERNS AND ADAPTIVE BEHAVIORS Many different behavior patterns have been observed in birds. Here we will consider examples of four behavior patterns and the adaptive value of each. The behavior patterns are locomotion, navigation, territoriality, and social behavior.

LOCOMOTION Locomotion is how an animal gets about. Most birds fly, but a few walk or run. Ostriches, for example, are unable to fly but can run at speeds up to 65 kilometers per hour. Flying birds vary in the way they fly. Some have a very large wing surface and can glide for great distances. Others have smaller wings in proportion to their size. These birds must flap their wings more frequently to remain in the air. Locomotion is adaptive because it helps the bird to obtain food and escape predators.

NAVIGATION How animals find their way has been a puzzling question for many years. Many questions about navigation remain unanswered. However, some experiments with birds have given us clues as to how they find their way.

Homing pigeons have been studied extensively. Normally adult homing pigeons can be released at great distances from their home. Later, they will find their way back. It has been known for some time that these birds make use of the sun to navigate because they sometimes become disoriented on overcast days. The fact that they often do find their way without seeing the sun suggests that they might use some other means of navigating. Experiments have shown that birds have a kind of built-in compass. This may enable them to orient themselves by using the same magnetic field that causes a compass to point north.

In addition to the sun and the earth's natural magnetic field, homing pigeons seem to be able to use a number of clues to find their way home. They can even discount confusing information provided in the experiments. These pigeons find their way home in spite of it.

Many birds migrate great distances. Studies have shown that the decreasing length of daylight in the fall initiates migratory behavior. About two-thirds of the North American song birds migrate south in the fall. Most return to the same territory, within a few square kilometers, the next spring. They often prepare for their flight by consuming large quantities of food. This builds up a store of fat for use as energy. A few, like the blackpoll warbler wait on the New England coast until northwest winds develop. They then depart on an approximately 4000 kilometer flight to the eastern coast of South America. The wind helps them reach their destination.

It is now believed that most migratory birds use a variety of clues in their navigation. The sun and the earth's magnetic field are two. The position of the stars is a third means by which they are able to navigate from one place to another. Various types of navigation are adaptive because they help the bird to find its wintering ground. Likewise, they also help the bird to find its way home. In addition, migration leads to a more ample food supply. Remember that birds maintain a constant body temperature. Adequate energy sources are necessary for this to occur. Rather than hibernating like many other animals do during periods of low food supply, they migrate to a warmer climate.

TERRITORIALITY The song of a bird is an announcement that it has claimed a certain territory. Some birds also use threatening positions to scare away intruders. Establishing a territory during the breeding season is adaptive. This assures that there will be sufficient food for

Ask students to consider why birds do not hibernate. Some homeothermic mammals do, so hibernation is not confined to poikilothermic animals. The more able students may be interested in researching this topic.

28-16. *Courting behavior of Albatross.*

both parents and offspring. Territoriality is always expressed to other members of the same species.

SOCIAL BEHAVIOR   Courtship rituals are common examples of social behavior among birds. The wandering albatross carries out such a ritual. (See Fig. 28-16.) Courtship rituals are adaptive. They help to assure that mating will occur and offspring will be produced. Thus, the behavior is not so much adaptive for the individuals as it is for continuation of the species.

EFFECTS OF HUMAN ACTIONS ON BIRDS   Birds, like fish, have been the victims of pesticides. As birds eat contaminated fish, their bodies, too, accumulate pesticides. Pesticides build up in the tissues of the animal because they are not biodegradable. The bodies of most living organisms have no enzymes that can break down these synthetic molecules. When pesticides accumulate in the tissues of a bird they cause several problems. The birds lay fewer eggs. Furthermore, the eggs may have unusually thin shells. At times, many eggs are broken before the chicks hatch. Thus, the number of offspring is greatly reduced. The American bald eagle and the perigrine falcon are two species out of many that are threatened with extinction. They are threatened because humans have used pesticides without regard for what they might do to other living things.

QUESTIONS FOR SECTION 2

1. What are the special characteristics of birds?
2. What are the extraembryonic membranes of a developing bird embryo and what do they do?
3. Study the birds in Figure 28-8 and make some predictions about their behavior from their beaks, wings, and feet.
4. What are some special internal structures in birds?
5. How do these structures contribute to the survival of the animals?
6. What are the specialized areas of the hypothalamus and what do they do?
7. Describe the function of the hormones that are important in the behavior of birds.
8. Give an example of an innate and a learned behavior in birds.
9. Give examples of each of the following: releaser, biological clock, territoriality.
10. Describe the navigation behavior of a bird and show how it is adaptive.
11. Describe a social behavior of a bird and show how it is adaptive.
12. Name three environmental factors that affect the behavior of birds.
13. How have the actions of humans threatened the survival of birds?

(See page 558 for Answers.)

6. Area that regulates body temperature within narrow range. Area that makes pituitary hormones, such as gonadotropins which stimulate sex glands to produce their own hormones; and prolactin, which stimulates secretion of "pigeon's milk."

G. 7. See above. Also, sitting on eggs stimulates the release of prolactin.

8. Innate: Male Bengalese: courtship dance and simple calls; learned; his singing song of the male zebra finch.

9. Releaser: sight of the female bird is releaser for courtship dance of male. Biological clock: response to change in length of daylight, regulating seasonal migration. Territoriality: bird's use of song to announce claim on territory.

CHAPTER REVIEW

Like other vertebrates, the bodies of reptiles and birds are also organized according to the typical vertebrate body plan. Both reptiles and birds maintain *continuity of life* by laying fertilized eggs enclosed in shells.

Reptiles are ectothermic and birds are endothermic. Yet the internal systems of both groups maintain *homeostasis*. Reptiles, and especially birds, demonstrate a variety of behaviors as they *interact with their environment*.

Using the Concepts

1. Give at least five examples of how birds or reptiles maintain homeostasis.

2. Why do water-dwelling reptiles return to land to lay their eggs?
3. How do birds and reptiles differ in the way they regulate body temperature?
4. Determine whether there are any herpetologists or behaviorists in your area. If so, write a letter to one asking about requirements for entering their profession and about satisfactions and frustrations of their job.
5. What applications of behavior studies on birds can be made to human behavior?
6. Many people want to kill every snake they see. Would you favor or oppose this? Why?

VOCABULARY REVIEW

1 ectothermic
endothermic
egg tooth
larynx
thalamus
pineal body

hypothalamus
2 chorion
amnion
yolk sac
allantois
crop

proventriculus
gizzard
syrinx
trachea
pituitary gland
gonadotrophin

prolactin
releaser
biological clock
imprinting
navigation
territoriality

H. 10. They seem to use the earth's magnetic field, the sun, and position of the stars, to find their way. It is adaptive because winters would be hard without warmth and food needed to maintain high metabolic rate and body temperature.

11. See Figure 28-16 on page 558. This ritual helps to assure mating will occur and offspring produced.

I. *12. Length of daylight, temperature, sight of other birds.

J. 13. Use of pesticides that can cause the egg shells of birds to be too thin, and number of eggs too few, for survival of the species.

CHAPTER 28 TEST

Copy the number of each test item and place your answer to the right.

PART 1 Multiple Choice: Select the letter of the phrase that best completes each of the following.

d 1. Birds can be distinguished from reptiles by
   a. feathers b. body temperature
   c. scales d. both a and b.

c 2. The egg tooth of reptiles and birds is for a. eating eggs b. eating the first food after hatching
   c. breaking out of the shell d. none of the above —it is non-functional.

c 3. Blood passing through the heart of a reptile is
   a. oxygenated b. unoxygenated c. partly oxygenated d. none of the above.

a 4. During development a constant temperature must be kept for the eggs of a. birds b. reptiles
   c. both d. neither.

b 5. The membrane that surrounds the embryo is the
   a. chorion b. amnion c. yolk sac
   d. allantois.

c 6. The lungs of birds differ from those of reptiles by having a. tree-like branching b. simple bag-like structures c. interconnecting tubes
   d. all of the above.

d 7. The excretory system of the bird a. removes nitrogen wastes b. conserves water
   c. excretes uric acid d. all of the above.

d 8. Hormones that affect the behavior of birds include a. gonadotropins b. prolactin
   c. releaser d. both a and b.

c 9. To find their way homing pigeons can use
   a. the sun b. the earth's magnetic field
   c. both d. neither.

d 10. The effects of pesticides on birds include
   a. reduction in number of eggs b. reduction in thickness of shell c. transmitting pesticides to fish d. both a and b.

PART 2 Matching: Match the letter of the term in Column I with its description in Column II.

COLUMN I
a. endothermic   f. releaser
b. ectothermic   g. imprinting
c. molting   h. territoriality
d. biological clock   i. navigation
e. internal fertilization j. courtship

COLUMN II
e 11. A union of egg and sperm inside the body of the female
b 12. Body temperature regulated by the environment
d 13. Mechanism that allows organism to detect length of daylight
c 14. Loss of feathers
a 15. Body temperature regulated by metabolic activity
i 16. How animals find their way
f 17. Stimulus that initiates a given behavior
j 18. Sometimes a ritualistic behavior that leads to mating
g 19. A learned behavior which causes young to follow mother
h 20. Marking off and defending of a breeding space

PART 3 Completion: Complete the following.
21. Turtles have remained unchanged for millions of years because they are ____.
22. The complete separation of oxygenated and unoxygenated blood as it passes through the heart assures that ____.
23. The nervous and sensory systems of both birds and reptiles allow these organisms to ____.
24. The sound producing organ in reptiles is the ____ and in birds is the ____.
25. Four kinds of adaptive behavior patterns are ____.

Chapter 28 Test Answers

21. well adapted to their environment
22. all blood going to the cell is oxygenated
23. detect changes in the environment and respond to them
24. larynx/syrinx
25. locomotion, navigation, territoriality, and social behavior

CHAPTER 29

THE MAMMALS

In this chapter we will complete our survey of living things with a study of the mammals — the group of animals to which we belong. We will see what a diverse group of animals the mammals really are. In addition, we will examine how they manage to survive under many different environmental conditions.

The major concepts in this chapter are similar to those in other chapters that surveyed living things: *unity and diversity, continuity of life, homeostasis,* and *interaction of organism and environment.* We will see how these concepts apply to mammals.

You will find answers to these and other questions in this chapter.

- How do young mammals develop inside the mother's body?
- Why are mammals and especially humans capable of learning more than other animals?
- What are the effects of such substances as alcohol and nicotine on mammals?
- How do humans fit into the world of living things?

DEER

1 MAMMALS

OBJECTIVES FOR SECTION 1

A. Describe the major variations in the vertebrate body plan seen in mammals.
B. Identify examples of diversity among mammals.
C. Interpret the role of the placenta in mammals.

Mammals belong to the *Class Mammalia* and *Subphylum Vertebrata* of the *Phylum Chordata*. Eighteen different orders, including the *Order Primates* (prī *mā* tēz) to which humans belong, are recognized in the Class Mammalia. We will not be able to study each order in any detail. But we will see some of the interesting variations that are found among mammals.

General Body Plan of a Mammal

GENERAL CHARACTERISTICS OF MAMMALS Mammals have hair, and mammary glands. Mammary glands are called breasts in humans. Mammals also have a diaphragm, a muscle that separates the abdominal and thoracic cavities. These characteristics distinguish them from other vertebrates. We will use the fetal pig as an example of a mammal. (See Fig. 29-1.) Fetal pigs are used in many biology classes to illustrate the characteristics of mammals. They demonstrate the

29-1. The general characteristics of the fetal pig, a representative mammal.

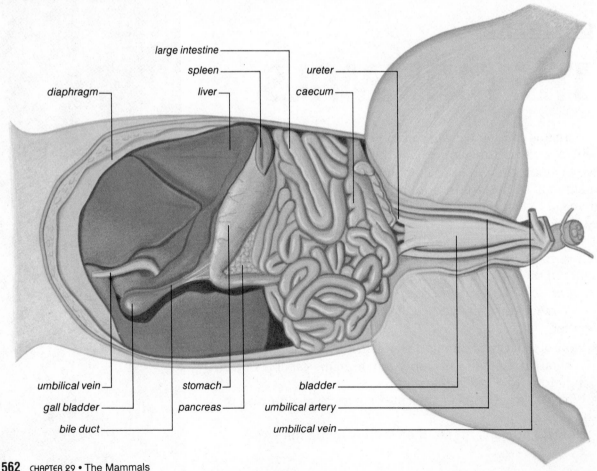

most important structures found in mammals. In addition, fetal pigs allow us to study important things about mammal development.

MAMMALIAN SKIN   The skin of mammals is highly specialized. It contains a number of structures not found in the skin of other vertebrates. Hairs grow from long thin tubes called hair follicles. Living cells at the base of the follicle are able to divide and make new cells. It is here that hair grows. The part of a hair that extends beyond the surface of the skin is dead. Even though hair is dead, it stays shiny and pliable. Next to each hair follicle is an oil gland. This gland secretes an oily substance that lubricates the hair. Can you see why brushing your hair helps to keep it shiny and pliable all the way to the ends? Hair serves as an insulator to help hold heat near the skin. Each hair follicle also has a tiny muscle attached to it. When a mammal gets cold, these muscles contract. This action causes the hairs to stand up from the surface. Thus, the hairs trap more warm air around the skin. You can see this happen on your own skin when you get cold and have "goose flesh." These bumps are the places where the muscle is causing a hair to stand on end.

The skin of mammals also contains sweat glands. These glands excrete a watery fluid, sweat that contains small amounts of wastes from the blood. Sweat is most useful in helping to regulate the body temperature by its cooling action as it evaporates. Not all mammals have enough sweat glands to be effective in cooling them on a hot day. However, humans do.

MAMMARY GLANDS   Mammary glands produce milk in female mammals. They are highly modified sweat glands. Mammary glands are stimulated to produce milk after the birth of the young by the hormone, *prolactin.*

OTHER CHARACTERISTICS OF MAMMALS   The body plan of mammals, like other vertebrates, has a bony skeleton and four appendages. The appendages typically have five toes on each foot. However, you do not see five toes on the feet of the fetal pig. Pigs have two large, well-developed toes on each foot. This is an example of one of the variations on the basic mammalian body plan. No matter what mammal we choose to illustrate the general body plan, we will find some modifications. Let us now look at some other modifications among mammals.

Diversity and Continuity of Mammals

DIVERSITY   Mammals are found in many habitats. Some mammals have wide ranges of tolerance and can be found in almost any climate. Humans, of course, use their technology to help them adapt to some climates. Although some mammals are adapted to live in water, they must surface to breathe. A few can fly.

29-2. *The opossum, a marsupial,
bears its young alive.*

The most primitive mammals, such as the duckbilled platypus,
lay eggs. Another primitive group of mammals are the *marsupials*.
This group includes kangaroos and opossums. (See Fig. 29-2.) Their
young are born in a very immature state. They continue their development in a pouch on the belly of the mother.

Primates have a highly specialized nervous system. They can put
the ends of their thumbs and forefingers together. How many of the
things you do daily depend on that ability? If you want to find out,
tape your thumbs to the sides of your hands for a little while.

Mammals live in many different environments and have a variety of diets. Moles live underground. Manatees live in tropical bays
and porpoises live in the sea. Most mammals live on land. Bats, even
though they live on land, can fly.

Mammals occupy all trophic levels. Some are carnivores, or flesh
eaters. Some are herbivores. Others are omnivores and eat plants as
well as other heterotrophs. Cats, dogs, seals, wolves, and coyotes are
carnivores. Pigs, elephants, rodents, and most primates are herbivores. Bears and humans are examples of omnivores. Among the primates, humans are the only species that normally eat meat.

CONTINUITY   The reproductive systems of mammals follow the
general vertebrate plan. There are a few important exceptions,
however. One of the specializations of mammals is the uterus of females. (See Fig. 29-3.) In most mammals, the uterus is Y-shaped and
several embryos may develop in each arm of the Y. In primates,
which usually have only one offspring at a time, the uterus is a pear-
shaped organ.

Fertilization is internal. Eggs released from the ovaries are fertilized as they pass along the oviducts. The fertilized eggs undergo several cell divisions before they implant in the wall of the uterus. After

the developing embryo implants in the uterus, the placenta forms around it. The placenta contains blood vessels from both the embryo and the mother. No direct connection exists between blood vessels of the mother and the embryo. Food and oxygen diffuse from the blood of the mother to the blood of the embryo. Wastes and carbon dioxide move in the opposite direction.

There is a close connection between the blood of the embryo and the mother. Therefore, anything in the mother's blood can have an effect on the embryo. Many drugs are tested on mammals that have embryos developing in their uteruses. Rats, mice, and sometimes monkeys are used in drug testing experiments. If the drug causes any defects in the embryos, it will not be allowed to be used on humans.

The developing mammalian embryo has the same membranes as other vertebrate embryos. (See Fig. 29-4.) However, the chorion and the blood vessels of the allantois become part of the placenta. Since the embryo gets its food from the blood of the mother, the yolk sac is very small.

Once a mammal is born, the mother breaks the amnion from around the offspring. At times it may be broken during the birth process. She also uses her teeth to cut the umbilical cord that attaches the baby to the placenta. The umbilical blood vessels normally close so that the newborn does not bleed to death. In humans, the amnion usually ruptures a few hours before the birth of the baby. The umbilical cord is tied and carefully cut after the birth of the baby.

During the early life of mammals, the mother spends a lot of time caring for her offspring. The offspring feed by sucking milk from the mammary glands. Mammals have the smallest number of offspring of any animals. However, they have the highest proportion of young surviving to adulthood. Biologists use the term **reproductive efficiency** *to describe the number of survivors among the total eggs produced.* Many of the eggs of mammals survive. This gives mammals a high reproductive efficiency.

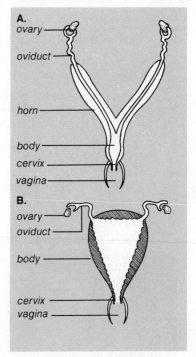

29-3. *Most mammals have: A. Two-horned uterus. B. Primates have a simple pear-shaped uterus.*

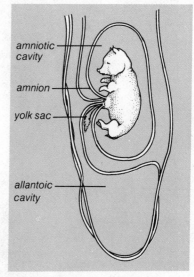

29-4. *Developing embryo of a pig.*

QUESTIONS FOR SECTION 1
1. What are the characteristics that identify mammals?
2. How is the skin of mammals different from other vertebrates?
3. Why is the fetal pig a good animal to use to study mammals?
4. Name three examples of diversity of mammals.
5. Describe an unusual mammal you have seen and tell how you know it is a mammal.
6. What is a placenta?
7. What is reproductive efficiency?
8. How do drugs reach an embryo?

(See answers to questions on page 564.)

A. What differences do you see among the three sets of teeth?

B. What kinds of food would you predict that each kind of animal might eat? Make your predictions first then do some reading to determine whether you were correct in your predictions.

C. What other predictions about these animals can you make from knowing the structure of their teeth?

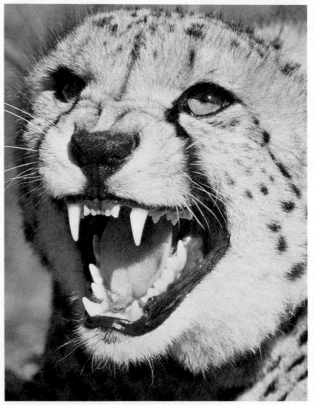

☑ HOMEOSTASIS

Mammals have all of the same internal systems that are found in other vertebrates. In general, their functions are the same. Moreover, they contribute to maintaining homeostasis in the same ways. More is known about the internal processes in mammals than in any other group of organisms. This is probably because they have been used to help us to understand human body functions.

Digestion and Nutrition of Mammals

The digestive systems of mammals are distinguished from other vertebrates by the kinds of teeth they have in their mouths. Furthermore, the kind and number of teeth are used to classify many mammals. There are four basic kinds of teeth. (See Fig. 29-5.) *Incisors* are in the front of the mouth. Rodents have incisors that grow throughout life. They must have something to gnaw on to keep their incisors sharp and from getting too long. On either side of the incisors are the *canines*. Carnivorous mammals have particularly large canines. *Premolars* and *molars* are found farther back in the mouth. They are especially large in mammals that eat large quantities of plant material that must be ground up.

OBJECTIVES FOR SECTION 2
D. Explain how mammals obtain and use nutrients.
E. Describe how circulation, respiration, and excretion occur in mammals.
F. Explain how the nervous system and the endocrine system help maintain homeostasis in mammals.

29-5. The teeth of mammals are specialized to perform different functions.

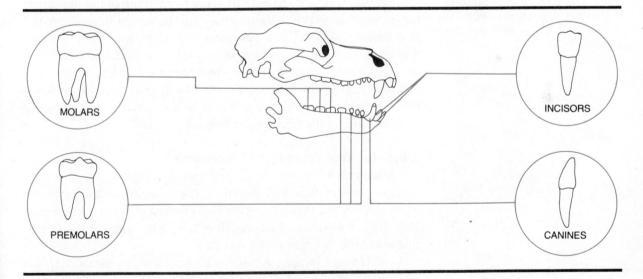

MOLARS

PREMOLARS

INCISORS

CANINES

Another part of the digestive system that varies among different groups of mammals is the stomach. (See Fig. 29-6.) The structure of the stomach is closely related to the diet of the animal. Carnivores, including humans, have a stomach with a single chamber. The lining of the entire stomach contains gastric glands. These glands produce secretions that digest meat.

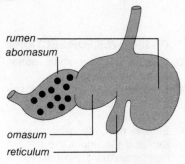

rumen
abomasum

omasum
reticulum

RUMINANT STOMACH

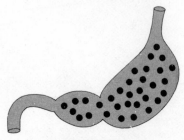

CARNIVORE STOMACH

● gastric gland

29-6. The stomach of a carnivore consists of a single chamber. The stomach of a ruminant has four chambers.

Ruminants *are a group of mammals that chew cud.* They have stomachs with several chambers. Ruminants forage for grain and other plant foods which they swallow quickly. The food enters the rumen of the stomach where it is partially digested by the action of bacteria. It then passes into the reticulum. Here, it is formed into a ball, or cud. It is then regurgitated and chewed by the animal. The food is swallowed again and goes into the omasum. At this point, the action of enzymes from the saliva act on the food. Finally the food goes to the abomasum, the part of the stomach where the gastric glands are located.

Mammals, like all other animals, are heterotrophs. However, which nutrients an organism can make for itself and which it must get from its food is determined by the enzymes an organism has. All mammals require certain essential amino acids in their diet. Their bodies do not have the enzymes to synthesize them. Likewise, most mammals that have been studied require a few essential fatty acids in their diet. Many mammals can make use of cellulose in the food they eat. This occurs in spite of the fact that they do not have an enzyme to break it down. Ruminants, for example, are able to use cellulose as an energy source. Microbes in the first parts of their stomachs digest the cellulose for them.

Mammals usually have fairly large livers. One of the important functions of the liver is to destroy harmful substances that get into the bloodstream. Alcohol is a substance that damages the liver. This damage occurs either directly or through lack of an adequate diet. The cells that contain enzymes that destroy harmful substances no longer function. Finally, the liver becomes filled with fatty deposits and connective tissue. The connective tissue is like scar tissue. It does not carry out any of the functions of normal liver cells.

Other Internal Processes of Mammals

Mammals have well-developed and well-regulated systems for transport, respiration, and excretion. The structure of these systems is very much like those you have just studied in reptiles and birds. Therefore, we will concern ourselves here with some of the factors that affect the function of these systems.

CIRCULATORY SYSTEM   All mammals have a four-chambered heart much like that of a bird. Blood goes from the right side of the heart to the lungs. It is returned to the left side of the heart. From the left side of the heart, blood is pumped to all other parts of the body. The walls of the left ventricle are much thicker than those of the right ventricle.

The amount of blood entering the heart also affects the strength of the contraction of the heart. When the ventricles are very full, they contract more vigorously than when they are only partly full. Exercise causes the heart to beat faster. It also causes the ventricles to fill more completely. Vigorous contractions strengthen the heart muscle. If a mammal has lost a lot of blood, the ventricles will not fill completely. Thus, the contractions will be weak.

Some of the blood vessels are able to change size. The smallest arteries that lead directly to the capillaries can dilate or become larger. They can also constrict or become smaller. If a mammal has lost a lot of blood, many of these tiny arteries become constricted. They allow only a small amount of blood to enter the capillaries. This reduces the volume of blood in the capillaries. More blood enters the ventricles. Thus, they fill more completely.

These tiny arteries also change size as the body temperature changes. When a mammal is too hot, the little arteries in the skin dilate. More blood flows through the capillaries near the surface of the skin. Heat is lost through the skin and the animal is cooled. When a mammal is too cold those same arteries constrict. This prevents cooling of the blood. Alcohol causes these small arteries to dilate. In humans, the skin may be slightly red after the person has drunk alcohol. The blood may be cooled too much and the body temperature will drop. Mammals other than humans do not normally drink alcohol. When they are given it in experiments, they become intoxicated. These mammals suffer the same effects that are seen in humans.

RESPIRATORY SYSTEM   The trachea connect the lungs to the air. At the top of the trachea, mammals have a larynx in which sound is produced. In the chest, the trachea branches into bronchi which, in turn,

29-7. *The respiratory system of a mammal.*

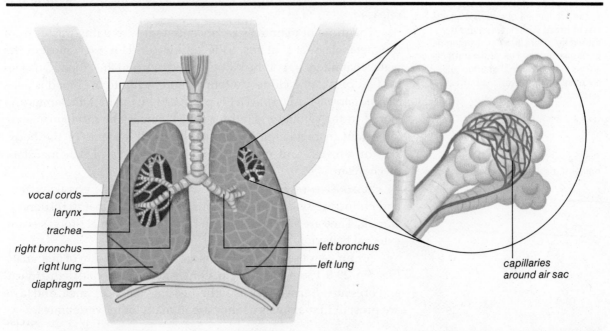

vocal cords
larynx
trachea
right bronchus
right lung
diaphragm

left bronchus
left lung

capillaries around air sac

E. 4. Exercise causes the heart to beat faster. When a mammal becomes too hot, arteries in skin dilate and more blood circulates in the skin.

5. Tars cause cells to undergo changes that may lead to cancer. Carbon monoxide attaches to red blood cells, reducing their oxygen-carrying capacity. Irritant gases lead to smoker's cough and bronchitis.

F. 6. Monitoring, action, and feedback.

7. Paleocortex: processes information from emotional feelings. Neocortex: processes ideas and information from sense organs and other parts; decides on action; stores information in memory.

8. Pain, heat, cold, light, touch, pressure.

Humans sometimes develop a disease called *diabetes insipidus*. This disease should not be confused with diabetes mellitus, although both diseases lead to the production of excessive quantities of urine. Diabetes insipidus is caused by a deficiency of antidiuretic hormone and the lack of the hormone allows large quantities of urine to be excreted. ADH is available to treat such patients.

Emphasize the concept of feedback in homeostatic mechanisms.

branch into smaller and smaller bronchioles. These bronchioles carry air to and from the tiny air sacs called alveoli. These structures are shown in Figure 29-7. The alveoli are surrounded by capillaries. Oxygen diffuses from the alveoli to the capillaries. Carbon dioxide diffuses from the capillaries to the alveoli.

Only mammals have a *diaphragm*. It is a wide band of muscle that separates the body cavity into a thoracic (thô *ras* ik) cavity and an abdominal cavity. The heart and lungs are located in the thoracic cavity. This cavity is completely closed off so that air can enter it only through trachea. The role of the diaphragm in breathing will be discussed in Chapter 31.

Experimental animals are often used to study the effects of substances on the respiratory system. Tobacco has been studied extensively. About 500 chemicals have been found in tobacco smoke. Of these, nicotine, tars, irritant gases, and carbon monoxide have known effects on the respiratory system. Nicotine is a potent poison. Tars cause cells in the lungs to undergo changes. These changes are often cancerous. Irritant gases lead to smoker's cough and bronchitis. Carbon monoxide attaches to red blood cells and reduces the amount of oxygen they can carry. Some chemicals in tobacco smoke destroy the cilia that line the respiratory tract. Normally these cilia prevent dust and other particles from getting into the lungs. When they are destroyed, respiratory infections are more likely to occur.

EXCRETORY SYSTEM   Mammals have a pair of kidneys and tubes through which urine drains. This is similar to both reptiles and birds. All mammals have a urinary bladder. This collects urine until it is released.

The urine of mammals is concentrated. It contains wastes from the metabolism of proteins, salts, and water. However, most of the water that filters out of the kidney goes back into the blood. One factor that causes the kidney to return more water to the blood is *antidiuretic hormone* (ADH). ADH is produced by the hypothalamus and stored in the pituitary gland for use. Homeostatic mechanisms are important in regulating the functions of all systems of the body. The turning on and off of ADH is an example of a homeostatic mechanism.

RESPONSIVENESS AND CONTROL   The sense organs, nervous system, and endocrine system are all important for a mammal to respond to stimuli. They are also important in controlling internal processes and external behavior.

A number of sensory receptors are found in the skin of mammals. (See Fig. 29-8.) Some detect pain. Others detect heat, cold, light, touch, and pressure. Senses such as sight, hearing, balance, smell, and taste are present in mammals as they are in many other vertebrates.

LIGHT TOUCH

COLD

PRESSURE   HEAT

PAIN

It is the brain of mammals that distinguishes their nervous systems from those of other vertebrates. As we have seen in Chapters 27 and 28, the brain has become more complex as we proceeded from fish to birds. This trend continues with mammals. (See Fig. 29-9.)

The unique part of the mammalian brain is the highly developed cerebrum. (Refer to Fig. 29-9.) In the lower vertebrates, the outside of the brain, *cerebral cortex,* is relatively small. It is concerned mainly with sensory perception. Its increased size in mammals is associated with its increased function. Mammals are more versatile in their responses to stimuli because of an expanded cerebral cortex. In humans, the even greater development of the cortex is what makes speech, imagination, and higher learning possible.

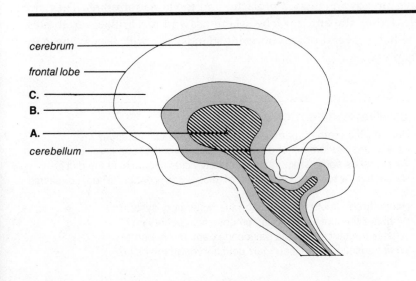

cerebrum

frontal lobe

C.

B.

A.

cerebellum

29-9. The mammalian brain. Area A. is very primitive and governs self-preservation. Area B. processes information from emotional feelings. Area C. processes ideas. This area is well developed in primates.

ENDOCRINE SYSTEM We have already noted that the pituitary gland is the master gland of the endocrine system. We have also noted that there is a close relationship between the nervous and endocrine systems. The main physical connection between the two systems is between the hypothalamus and the pituitary gland. (See Fig. 29-10.) The pituitary gland is divided into the anterior and pos-

29-10   THE PITUITARY GLAND

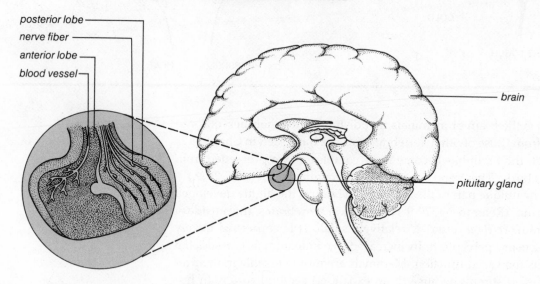

posterior lobe
nerve fiber
anterior lobe
blood vessel

brain

pituitary gland

Answers to Questions for Section 2.

D. 1. Incisors (large in rodents); canines (well developed in carnivores); pre-molars and molars (large in mammals that chew large amounts of plant material).

2. A carnivore's stomach has a single chamber, containing gastric glands. A ruminant's has a rumen, reticulum, omasum, and abomasum — which is the only part that has gastric glands.

3. Bodies of mammals lack enzymes needed to synthesize them, and they are essential for maintenance of cells.

(See page 570 for more answers.)

terior lobes. Each releases several chemicals called hormones. We have already mentioned prolactin and the gonadotropins. They are released by the anterior lobe. Mammals and most other vertebrates also have several other endocrine glands. We will discuss these in Chapter 34.

QUESTIONS FOR SECTION 2

1. How are the teeth of mammals modified for special functions?
2. How does the stomach of a ruminant differ from that of a carnivore?
3. What makes some amino acids and fatty acids essential in the diet?
4. Name two ways the circulation of blood can change when conditions change.
5. Name three effects of tobacco on the respiratory system.
6. What are the three parts of a homeostatic mechanism?
7. What is the function of the paleocortex and the neocortex?
8. What sensations can mammals detect through their skin?

3 BEHAVIOR AND ENVIRONMENT

As we have seen, mammals have more complex brains than other vertebrates. As you might expect, their behavior is much more complex than other vertebrates. Furthermore, a large portion of the behavior of many mammals is learned.

Innate and Learned Behavior

In mammals, only a few simple behaviors are completely innate. The fear of falling seems to be one of them. (See Fig. 29-11.) Many behaviors are partly innate or instinctive. However, as we shall see when we study patterns of behavior, there are learned components in most of these.

TRIAL AND ERROR LEARNING   Several different kinds of learning are recognized. The simplest is trial and error learning. It is not limited to mammals, but can be observed even in some invertebrate animals. As the name suggests, this kind of learning involves trying to do a task over and over again. After some errors, the animal finally learns to do the task correctly. Mazes are often used to study trial and error learning. You use trial and error in learning to put a jig-saw puzzle together. Often, reward and punishment are used to speed up the learning process. For example, if you are teaching your dog a trick, you give it a reward if it does the trick correctly. This reward might be a piece of food. Learning also occurs more rapidly if an animal is motivated. Unless your dog is hungry, it may not be motivated to try to do the trick.

G. Name examples of innate and learned behavior in mammals.
H. Identify patterns of behavior and adaptive behaviors in mammals.
I. Explain how mammals cope with changes in the environment.

29-11. *This kitten is unaware of the sheet of glass covering the drop-off. Its instinctive fear of falling prevents it from stepping onto the glass.*

29-12. The rat in these photos is demonstrating reasoning.

Students should be able to suggest examples of the different kinds of learning from their own experience. Suggest that they provide such examples in a class discussion of learning.

CONDITIONING   There is a second kind of learning, conditioning. This was used by the Russian biologist, Pavlov, in studying animal behavior. Pavlov observed that when dogs smell food, saliva begins to flow from their mouths. This seems to be an innate response. However, Pavlov rang a bell each time he offered his dogs food. After doing this many times, he rang the bell without offering food. The dogs began to produce saliva when they heard the bell, even though no food was present. They had learned to associate the ringing of the bell with food. They had been *conditioned* to expect food when they heard the bell.

IMPRINTING   Imprinting is another simple form of learning. As noted in Chapter 28, it frequently occurs in birds. But it is also thought to occur in some mammals. Some scientists have suggested that human infants may experience imprinting.

REASONING   Reasoning is the most complex form of learning. It involves the invention of concepts or ideas within the brain. It is the kind of learning we use to solve problems. At one time, it was thought that only primates could engage in reasoning. However, experiments have shown that some other mammals are capable of reasoning. The rat in Figure 29-12 is demonstrating reasoning. This rat came from a laboratory colony of rats bred for their learning ability. Not all rats are as smart as this one. But as psychologist Tsai showed, rats do have the ability to reason.

Answers to Questions for Section 3.
I. 5. If the temperature of the environment drops below the level of 5 to 10° C (at which the thermostat has been reset), the animal is aroused and becomes active.

Reasoning involves several kinds of mental operations. One of these is forming concepts or ideas. Humans use words to express concepts and ideas. We can then learn by association. That is, we see relationships among ideas. We can learn to discriminate between things that are quite similar. Finally, we can learn by insight. Insight is the putting together within the mind several different experiences.

Patterns of Behavior and Adaptive Behavior

LOCOMOTION   Locomotion is a kind of behavior. It is adaptive because it allows mammals to obtain food and to escape predators. Although all mammals have four appendages, many have highly specialized limbs. These allow them to run, swim, and even fly. Figure 14-13 on page 260 shows how the structure of these limbs is modified.

Locomotion in the kangaroo is of special interest. (See Fig. 29-13.) At slow speeds up to about 7 kilometers per hour, it uses a pentapedal or five-footed gait. The tail is the fifth "foot." At higher speeds the tail assists in balance but no longer acts as a support. On the two hind legs they can hop at speeds to 50 kilometers per hour.

SOCIAL BEHAVIOR OF LIONS   Social behavior is seen in some mammals. The establishment of territories, pecking orders, and courtship rituals are seen in mammals. The social systems of the lion and the Norway rat have been studied in some detail.

Lions are hunters and are also social animals. They are the only species of cat that is social. They hunt individually and cooperatively. But the females do most of the hunting. This may be because their bodies are lighter and they are not encumbered by a heavy mane. Even so, lions are not especially successful hunters. They can be outrun by most of the species they prey upon.

The social unit of the lion is called a *pride*. A pride usually has from 3 to 12 females of breeding age. In addition, it usually has 2 males of breeding age. The number of males can vary from 1 to 6. It also has a number of cubs of different ages. Each pride occupies a territory, but the boundaries of the territory are not well defined. A few lions live individually as nomads. Female nomads have probably been permanently expelled from the pride into which they were born. Males, on the other hand, leave the pride in groups. They become nomads when they are around three years old. When they reach full maturity they drive out the older males of a pride and take over. They will mate with the females of the pride for a few years, only to be driven out by other young males. The mating of males and females from separate prides allows for genetic diversity in the pride. This prevents it from becoming inbred. Thus, the manner in which males come and go from prides is an adaptive behavior.

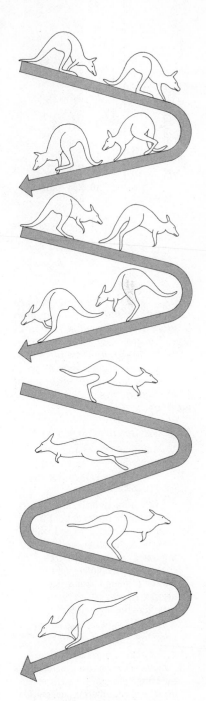

29-13. The kangaroo uses its tail as a kind of fifth foot when it is moving slowly. At higher speeds it uses its tail for balance only.

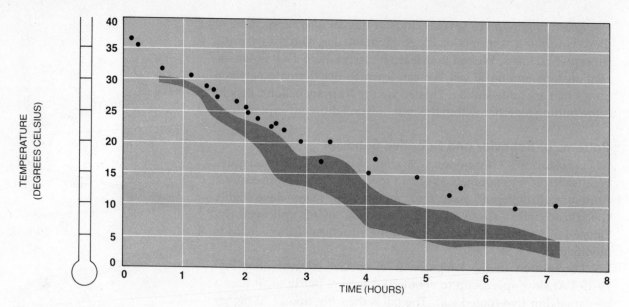

29-14. *External temperatures were reduced as the golden-mouthed ground squirrel entered hibernation. The dots show the temperature of the hypothalamus. The shaded area shows the range of environmental temperatures at which the squirrel's body begins to produce heat.*

Answers to Questions for Section 3.

G. 1. Conditioning is an acquired or learned response to a stimulus. Reasoning is the kind of learning used to solve problems.

H. 2. The mating of males and females from separate prides of lions is adaptive behavior because it allows for genetic diversity. Among rats, the transmission of food preferences within a colony, and from mother to young, is adaptive because it helps rats to avoid extermination by poisons.

 *3. Answers will vary, depending upon the student's choice.

 4. For ectotherms, hibernation involves adapting to a lowering of the temperature of the environment. For endotherms, hibernation involves resetting of the thermostat in the hypothalamus for maintenance at a new, lower level.

(See page 574 for more answers.)

Interactions with the Physical Environment

We have studied hibernation in simple vertebrates. We have seen that it is a method of adapting to a lowering of the temperature of the environment. For some time, biologists thought that when mammals hibernate, they revert back to being ectotherms. It is now known that they continue to behave as endotherms. Going into hibernation requires a "resetting of the thermostat" in the hypothalamus. This maintains the body temperature at a lower level. In experiments with the golden-mantled ground squirrel, the external temperatures were reduced. The temperature at which the animal began to produce heat dropped as the temperature dropped. (See Fig. 29-14.) As can be seen from the figure, going into hibernation requires a series of steps in which the thermostat is gradually lowered. As the animal goes deeper into hibernation, its body produces heat to maintain the body temperature only at lower and lower temperatures. Finally, it maintains a body temperature between 5 and 10°C. If the body temperature drops below this level, the animal arouses and becomes active. This prevents it from freezing to death.

QUESTIONS FOR SECTION 3

1. Define conditioning and reasoning.
2. How are the social behaviors of lions and rats adaptive?
3. Observe an animal (a zoo animal, a pet, a friend), describe a behavior pattern, and determine whether the pattern is adaptive.
4. How is hibernation in endotherms different from that in ectotherms?
5. What keeps hibernating mammals from freezing to death?

4 COMPARISONS AMONG VERTEBRATES AND INVERTEBRATES

Relationships Among Vertebrates

In this, the last section of the last chapter of our survey of living things, we will look for important relationships. (See Table 29-1 on pages 578-579.)

All vertebrates have the same general body plan, but there are many variations on that plan among the different classes of vertebrates. From the simplest vertebrates, the fishes, to the amphibians, reptiles, birds, and mammals there is a trend toward increasing complexity. The transition from water to land dwelling accounts for a number of variations among vertebrates.

EXTERNAL CHARACTERISTICS   The external characteristics of vertebrates, as shown in Table 29-1, illustrate these trends. The skin of reptiles prevents their bodies from drying in the land environments. In contrast, the feathers and hair of birds and mammals are more complex structures than scales. They also serve as insulators. These help homeotherms to maintain a constant body temperature.

REPRODUCTIVE SYSTEM   Reproduction and development is related to the environment of the vertebrate. The type of reproduction and development also depends on the presence or absence of a placenta. The eggs of fishes and amphibians are laid and fertilized in water. These eggs have only a jelly-like substance to protect them. Eggs of reptiles and birds have a heavy shell. The shell requires that fertilization take place internally before the shell develops. The shell protects the egg from drying in a land environment. All of these eggs contain enough food to supply the embryo throughout development. Eggs of mammals have little stored food. They are nourished through the placenta. Reproductive efficiency increases from fishes to mammals. Fish and amphibians lay many eggs, but few survive to become adults. Not all of their eggs are even fertilized. Many of those that hatch may be eaten by predators before they grow to adulthood. In reptiles and birds, more eggs are likely to be fertilized. A smaller proportion of newly hatched reptiles grow to adulthood than newly hatched birds. Reptiles usually do not care for their young. Mammals take the greatest amount of care of their young. (See Fig. 29-15.)

DIGESTIVE SYSTEM   The digestive systems of most vertebrates follow the same general plan. They include the oral cavity, pharynx, esophagus, stomach, and intestine. Variations in this system usually have to do with the kind of food the animal eats. For example, the esophagus is modified to form a food storing crop in birds. Part of the bird's stomach is modified to form a gizzard. Among mammals, the

OBJECTIVES FOR SECTION 4

J. Summarize important relationships among vertebrates.
K. Contrast vertebrates and invertebrates.
L. Compare humans to other vertebrates.
M. Summarize the characteristics of mammals.

Since this is the last section of the last chapter of our survey of living things, emphasis should be placed on trends that parallel the evolution of living things. This will illustrate the concept of change over time. Similarities and differences among organisms will illustrate the concept of unity and diversity. The various ways organisms maintain nearly constant internal conditions regardless of changes in the environment illustrate both the concept of homeostasis and the concept of interaction with the environment.

TABLE 29-1 SUMMARY OF ANIMAL CHARACTERISTICS

SYSTEMS	Invertebrates	General Vertebrates	Bony Fishes	Amphibians
BODY PLAN AND EXTERNAL CHARACTERISTICS	different for each phylum	head, trunk, and tail; four appendages	no neck; fins and protective scales	legs with simple feet, thin moist scale-free skin
REPRODUCTIVE SYSTEM AND DEVELOPMENT	asexual or sexual, some with larvae	sexual, fertilization external or internal; go through cleavage, blastula stages	external fertilization; eggs unattended in water	external fertilization; metamorphosis
DIGESTIVE SYSTEM	none to simple tube	modified tube with accessory glands	pyloric caeca	tongue traps prey in some
CIRCULATORY SYSTEM	none to open or closed system	closed with single heart	heart has two chambers	heart has three chambers
RESPIRATORY SYSTEM	none, gills, or spiracles	moist membrane for gas exchange	blood becomes oxygenated in gills	gas exchange takes place in skin and simple lungs
EXCRETORY SYSTEM	none, flame cells or nephridia	kidneys with tubes to carry urine out of body	simple kidneys	
NERVOUS SYSTEM	none to simple brain	brain, spinal cord, nerves	medulla, optic lobes prominent	some increase in cerebrum
SENSE ORGANS	none to simple	simple to well developed senses	simple senses	hearing better developed
MUSCULAR AND SKELETAL SYSTEMS	no skeleton or exoskeleton; muscle variable	endoskeleton with muscles attached	adapted for swimming	adapted for swimming and moving on land
ENDOCRINE SYSTEM	none to highly specialized in arthropods	isolated cells produce hormones	simple system	metamorphosis controlled by hormones

TABLE 29-1   SUMMARY OF ANIMAL CHARACTERISTICS (Continued)

SYSTEMS	Reptiles	Birds	Mammals	Humans
BODY PLAN AND EXTERNAL CHARACTERISTICS	feet with claws, dry scaly skin	wings, feet with claws, feathers	feet modified in many ways, hair	dexterous hands, some hair
REPRODUCTIVE SYSTEM AND DEVELOPMENT	internal fertilization; eggs on land unattended	internal fertilization; eggs in nest	internal fertilization; placenta	internal fertilization; young cared for over long period of time after birth
DIGESTIVE SYSTEM	some have stretchy pharynx and esophagus	lack teeth, gizzard grinds food	villi and caecae increase surface area in small intestine	typical of mammal
CIRCULATORY SYSTEM	heart has three chambers and septum in ventricle	four chambered heart		
RESPIRATORY SYSTEM	lungs	lungs with connecting tubes	branched alveolar lungs	like mammals; larynx and tongue allow speech
EXCRETORY SYSTEM	more efficient kidneys	kidneys conserve water	kidneys similar to reptiles and birds	
NERVOUS SYSTEM	further increase in cerebrum	increase in cerebrum and cerebellum	further increase in cerebrum	largest cerebrum of any living organism
SENSE ORGANS	see, hear, taste, smell, and maintain balance	eyesight especially good	all senses including skin senses	smell less well developed than most mammals
MUSCULAR AND SKELETAL SYSTEMS	usually adapted for creeping on land	adapted for flying	adapted for running on land	adapted for upright posture
ENDOCRINE SYSTEM		most vertebrate hormones come from specific glands in all higher vertebrates		

ruminants or animals that chew their cud have stomachs with several chambers. Also, animals that eat mostly plant materials have longer intestines than animals that are carnivorous.

CIRCULATORY AND RESPIRATORY SYSTEMS   The circulatory and respiratory systems are closely related. They show many variations that are related to the animal's degree of activity. (See Fig. 29-16) The *fish* has a two-chambered heart. Blood returning from the tissues of the body is pumped directly to the gills where it becomes oxygenated. From the gills, it is sent to the various parts of the body and the circuit is complete. In *amphibians,* the three-chambered heart increases the efficiency of the circulatory system. By returning oxygenated blood to the heart for distribution, the speed with which tissues receive oxygen can be increased. The partially divided ventricle in the three-chambered heart of *reptiles* goes a step further in this efficiency development. Oxygen-poor and oxygen-rich blood is somewhat prevented from mixing. The four-chambered heart of *birds* and *mammals* prevents this mixing and efficiency is enhanced. This adaptation insures that all blood passes through the lungs in each circuit of the body. The results of such efficiency are seen in the increased activity of birds and mammals.

EXCRETORY SYSTEM   The excretory system usually serves two main functions. They are the removal of nitrogen wastes and the regulation of body fluids. Some wastes are removed through the skin, especially in the simpler vertebrates. But the kidney is the major excretory organ. The structure of the kidney is more complex in the higher vertebrates.

NERVOUS SYSTEM   The nervous system increases in complexity from simple to advanced vertebrates. Changes are most apparent in the brain, as shown in Figure 29-17. Increase in the size of the cerebrum is associated with increased intelligence and is most pronounced in humans.

SKELETAL AND MUSCULAR SYSTEMS   With a few exceptions, the skeletal and muscular systems consist of an axial skeleton, a skeleton associated with the four limbs, and muscles that can cause the bones to move. Locomotion is important to all animals. Vertebrates have well-developed and varied kinds of locomotion. The appendages of these animals are modified in a variety of ways as shown in Table 29-1. Exceptions to these general adaptations can be found. For example, snakes that have no appendages use the muscles of their body wall to move in a slithering manner. The appendages of mammals such as bats and whales are adapted to their style of movement. Even so, the inner structure of their limbs shows that they are closely related to other mammals.

ENDOCRINE SYSTEM   The endocrine system is relatively simple in fishes and becomes more complex in the higher vertebrates. However, there are a few cells somewhere in the body of most vertebrates that carry out the function of each of the endocrine glands.

All of the variations on the general vertebrate plan contribute to a particular species being able to adapt to its environment. These variations also allow each species to maintain homeostasis even as the environmental conditions change.

Comparison of Vertebrates to Invertebrates

Both vertebrates and invertebrates are successful in their own ways in solving problems of survival. Yet, vertebrates, the last of the animal phyla to develop, have more complex bodies. Hence, they are capable of more varied activities. The great variety among living things we have studied shows us that change is a part of life. Compare the art on pages 582-583 with that on pages 512-513.

Both vertebrates and invertebrates have specialized structures to carry out the processes that are essential to survival. All are capable of reproducing themselves and maintaining continuity from one generation to the next. All maintain homeostasis. All demonstrate behavior as they respond to the stimuli from their environments. Yet vertebrates and invertebrates have very different kinds of specialized structures.

REPRODUCTION   Reproduction occurs by a variety of means, both asexual and sexual in lower invertebrates. In higher invertebrates and in vertebrates, reproduction is sexual. Sexual reproduction provides for greater diversity in the combinations of genes transmitted from one generation to the next than does asexual reproduction. Reproductive efficiency increases from the lower invertebrates to the higher vertebrates. The eggs and young of invertebrates are usually less likely to survive to adulthood than those of even the simple vertebrates. Generally, all species make up for any low chance of survival of their offspring by producing large numbers of eggs.

DIGESTION   Digestion may occur by the action of single cells as in sponges. It may also occur in a sac-like digestive system with only one opening, or in a tube-like system. The tube may be simple in structure or highly specialized.

CIRCULATION   Transport may be by simple diffusion. Transport also occurs by the circulation of a fluid that carries nutrients and oxygen to cells and removes wastes from them. When a circulatory system is present, a heart pumps fluids either through large spaces or a closed system of vessels. In higher vertebrates the closed system separates oxygenated blood from unoxygenated blood.

29-15 REPRODUCTION IN SELECTED VERTEBRATES

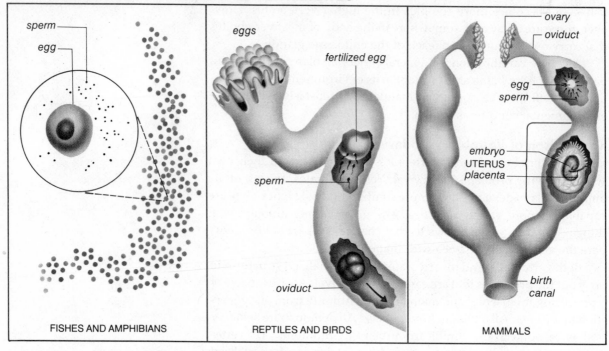

sperm

egg

FISHES AND AMPHIBIANS

eggs

fertilized egg

sperm

oviduct

REPTILES AND BIRDS

ovary

oviduct

egg
sperm

embryo
UTERUS
placenta

birth
canal

MAMMALS

29-17 BRAINS OF SELECTED VERTEBRATES

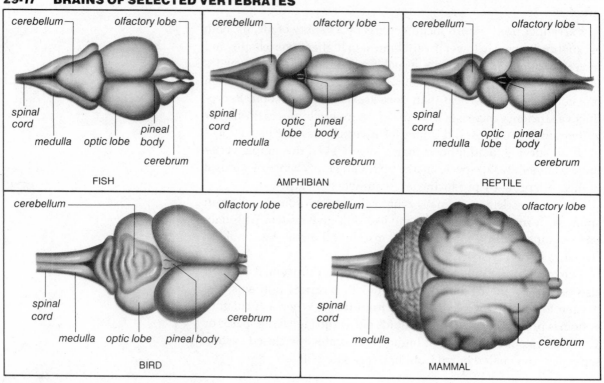

cerebellum

olfactory lobe

spinal
cord

medulla   optic lobe

pineal
body

cerebrum

FISH

cerebellum

olfactory lobe

spinal
cord

medulla

optic
lobe

pineal
body

cerebrum

AMPHIBIAN

cerebellum

olfactory lobe

spinal
cord

medulla

optic
lobe

pineal
body

cerebrum

REPTILE

cerebellum

olfactory lobe

spinal
cord

medulla   optic lobe   pineal body

cerebrum

BIRD

cerebellum

olfactory lobe

spinal
cord

medulla

cerebrum

MAMMAL

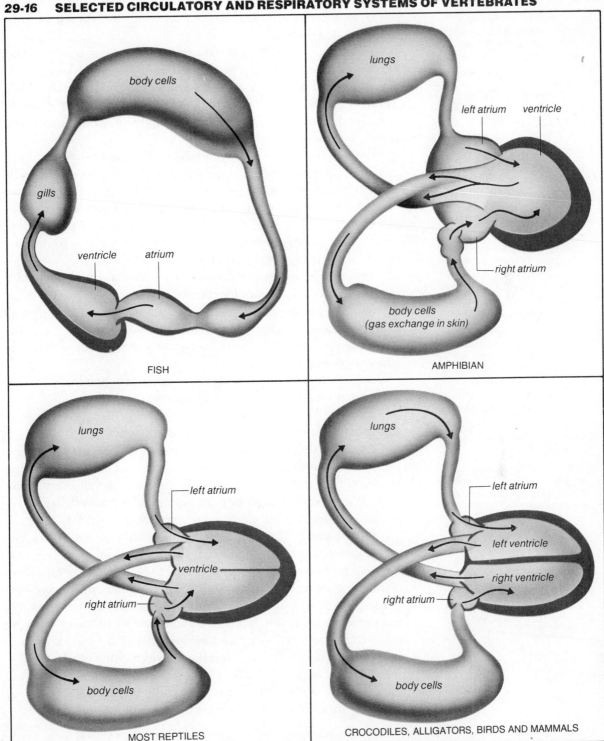

FISH

AMPHIBIAN

MOST REPTILES

CROCODILES, ALLIGATORS, BIRDS AND MAMMALS

Answers to Questions for Section 4.

J. 1. Answers will vary, but might include: digestive systems are similar in that they include the oral cavity, pharynx, esophagus, stomach, and intestine; and different, e.g., in that in birds, the esophagus is modified to form a crop, and the stomach to form a gizzard; among mammals, ruminants have stomachs with several chambers. (See Table 29-1 for other possible answers.)

2. See Table 29-1, external characteristics.

K. 3. Likenesses: specialized structures for functions essential to survival; capacity for reproduction and thus continuity of species; maintain homeostasis; demonstrate behavior in response to the environment. Differences: specialized structures as seen in each of the systems of the body.

*4. Answers will vary. One example may be found in how survival is maintained. Reproductive efficiency increases from the lower invertebrates to the vertebrates. All species make up for any low chance of survival of offspring by producing large number of eggs.

L. *5. See section "Comparison of Humans to other Vertebrates" on page 584.

M. 6. Hair, mammary glands, diaphragm. In addition, mammals have a bony skeleton and four appendages.

RESPIRATION Respiration always occurs across a membrane exposed to the environment. The membrane may consist of gills, spiracles, skin, or lungs.

EXCRETION Excretion also always occurs across a membrane. This membrane may be the body wall or a part of some kind of kidney. Kidneys remove wastes from body fluids and regulate fluids within the body. Organisms with efficient kidneys are better able to maintain homeostasis. This occurs in spite of wide fluctuations within the environment.

NERVES Nervous control may be carried out in a primitive way as in animals that have only a nerve net. Also, nervous control may be very complex as in humans. Coordination of movements in response to stimuli from the environment occurs in most invertebrates and in all vertebrates. However, the complexity of the control mechanisms varies. The capacity to learn new behaviors also increases from lower invertebrates to higher vertebrates.

MOVEMENT AND SUPPORT Locomotion is the main means by which animals obtain food. Except for sponges, other animals usually move about to get food. Invertebrates usually have either a tough body wall or an exoskeleton. Vertebrates have an endoskeleton. All except the lowest invertebrates have muscles attached to the body wall and to whatever skeleton is present.

HORMONES Chemical control by hormones occurs in insects and some other invertebrates and in all vertebrates.

Comparison of Humans to Other Vertebrates

As living things, we too demonstrate the concepts of biology. We have a vertebral column and dorsal nerve cord like all vertebrates. We have hair and mammary glands (breasts) like all other mammals. We are similar to other primates in that we have a large cerebrum and can touch our thumbs and forefingers together.

Our distinctly human characteristics include our ability to speak and to create written language. Our offspring are more likely to survive to adulthood than those of any other species. We are capable of using our own technology to modify our environment. We use eyeglasses. We provide insulin for people with a defective pancreas. We can detect genes that will produce abnormalities in the offspring of prospective parents. Soon, we may be able to cure genetic defects. We are self-conscious — aware of ourselves as individuals. Finally, we can think of past, present, and future events. We also can make ethical judgements. Our genus and species name, *Homo sapiens*, meaning wise human, summarizes these qualities.

Though students will have seen how humans fit into the whole of living things, they should also realize that humans have some unique characteristics. Discuss the responsibility of humans to use their capabilities to maintain rather than destroy the balance of nature.

QUESTIONS FOR SECTION 4

1. Name some similarities and differences among vertebrates.
2. Describe the trends in the development of vertebrates.
3. How are vertebrates alike and different from invertebrates?
4. Give examples of how invertebrates and vertebrates demonstrate the important concepts of biology.
5. How are humans like other vertebrates and how are they different from other vertebrates?
6. What are the main characteristics of mammals?

(See page 584 for answers.)

CHAPTER REVIEW

Mammals have hair and mammary glands. However, their bodies are organized according to the general vertebrate body plan. Most have a placenta that nourishes the young while they develop inside the female body. Thus, *continuity of life* is maintained. There is much variation in the structure of the internal body systems. Even so, these systems function in all mammals to maintain *homeostasis*. Mammals, especially humans, display their complex behavior in their *interactions with their environment*.

Mammals are the most complex of all vertebrates, and are generally more complex than invertebrates. Yet, both vertebrates and invertebrates maintain continuity of life and homeostasis. They all interact with their environment in ways that enhance their chances of survival.

Using the Concepts

1. Design an experiment to demonstrate some kind of learning in a human or other animal. If possible, carry out your experiment and interpret your data.

Career Activity

2. An ethologist studies the natural behavior of all animals. A psychologist studies the behavior of humans. If you had a chance to talk to one of these scientists what questions would you ask?

VOCABULARY REVIEW

1 mammary gland
diaphragm
hair follicle
placenta
sweat gland
reproductive efficiency
prolactin
2 canines

premolars
molars
ruminants
incisors
bronchi
bronchioles
alveoli
thoracic cavity

homeostatic mechanism
3 trial and error learning
conditioning
reasoning
association
pride
Homo sapiens

CHAPTER 29 TEST

Copy the number of each test item and place your answer to the right.

PART 1 Multiple Choice: Select the letter of the phrase that best completes each of the following.

c 1. Which of the following is *not* a characteristic of mammals?   **a.** hair   **b.** mammary glands   **c.** syrinx   **d.** diaphragm.

a 2. The most primitive mammals   **a.** lay eggs   **b.** have pouches   **c.** lack hair   **d.** all of these.

a 3. Materials move between the mother and embryo by   **a.** diffusion   **b.** direct connection between blood vessels   **c.** both a and b   **d.** neither a nor b.

d 4. Reproductive efficiency describes the ratio of number of survivors to   **a.** egg production   **b.** mating behavior   **c.** nesting behavior   **d.** population.

b 5. Amino acids or fatty acids are said to be essential when   **a.** they are used in metabolism   **b.** the body cannot make them   **c.** the body can make them   **d.** they have a certain reactive group.

d 6. The effects of tobacco on the body include   **a.** causing cancerous changes   **b.** irritating membranes   **c.** destroying cilia   **d.** all of the above.

d 7. The components of a homeostatic mechanism are   **a.** monitoring and feedback   **b.** action of some kind   **c.** hypothalamus   **d.** both a and b.

a 8. The part of the brain concerned with imagination is the   **a.** cerebral cortex   **b.** paleocortex   **c.** pituitary gland   **d.** all of the above.

b 9. When mammals hibernate their body temperature is about   **a.** zero degrees   **b.** 5-10°C   **c.** 10-20°C   **d.** below zero.

c 10. Which of the following is *not* an example of social behavior in mammals?   **a.** territoriality   **b.** pecking order   **c.** flying to southern areas in winter   **d.** courtship rituals.

PART 2 Matching: Match the letter of the term in Column I with its description in Column II.

COLUMN I

a. incisor   **f.** trial and error
b. ruminant   **g.** conditioning
c. diuretic   **h.** insight
d. construction   **i.** association
e. dilation   **j.** discrimination

COLUMN II

d 11. Narrowing of a passage
a 12. Tooth shaped for biting
e 13. Widening of a passage
b 14. Animal with a multi-chambered stomach
c 15. Chemical that causes the body to lose water
i 16. Seeing relationships
f 17. Doing things several times and correcting mistakes
j 18. Seeing difference between similar things
g 19. Linking of two stimuli so first causes response to second
h 20. Putting ideas together in the mind

PART 3 Completion: Complete the following.

21. Variations in the digestive system of vertebrates often are associated with ____. the animal's diet

22. From lower to higher vertebrates, the heart is modified from ____. 2 to 4 chambers

23. From lower to higher vertebrates, the part of the brain that shows the greatest increase in size is the ____. cerebrum

24. From lower to higher vertebrates, there is increasing protection of ____.

25. Human characteristics not found in other animals include ____.

Chapter 29 Test Answers

24. embryos and young animals

25. spoken and written language; increased chance of survival of young; use of technology; self-consciousness; ability to think of past present, and future; ability to make ethical judgements.

HUMAN BODY SYSTEMS

You have completed the survey of other living things. Now you are ready to study the human organism. In the next six chapters you will study the different systems of the human body. Keep in mind that each system contributes to the overall function of the whole body. These systems work together to maintain homeostasis.

First, we trace what happens once food enters the body, how it is broken down, transported, and removed. Then we study what happens to information received from the environment. We consider how the body interprets it and acts on it. Finally, we learn how chemicals control body functions, and how reproduction occurs.

VASCULAR SYSTEMS MODEL

CHAPTER 30

DIGESTION AND NUTRITION

The process of digestion begins soon after birth. In order for your cells to grow and reproduce, the food you eat must be broken down into smaller particles. These particles of glucose, amino acids, glycerol, and fatty acids are essential to the very life of the cell. As we explore this chapter, you will discover how digestion occurs in your body. This study of digestion will provide information on the proper nutrients that are needed by the cells of your body.

Like the systems in other living things, the *structures and functions of the human digestive system are closely related.* Through the study of other living things, it became clear that the systems of their bodies usually help in some way to maintain homeostasis. *Likewise, the functions of the human digestive system help to maintain homeostasis in the human body.*

In addition to understanding the structure and functions of the digestive system, you will also discover:

- How to select a nutritious diet and why the body needs all of the substances included in a nutritious diet
- What causes tooth decay, mumps, ulcers, and appendicitis
- The effects of alcohol, junk foods, food additives, and certain medicines and drugs on the body.

WHEAT

1 THE DIGESTIVE SYSTEM AND HOW FOOD MOVES THROUGH IT

The Digestive System

The human digestive system is quite similar to that of many other vertebrates. (See Fig. 30-1.) It resembles a long coiled tube with accessory organs. Its main parts are the *mouth cavity, pharynx, esophagus, stomach, small intestine, large intestine,* and *anus.* Among the accessory organs are the *salivary glands,* the *liver, gall bladder,* and *pancreas* (*pan krē əs*). Although food never enters these organs, their secretions are poured into the digestive tract by means of ducts. Let's trace the pathway of the food we eat through the digestive system.

OBJECTIVES FOR SECTION 1

A. List the organs of the digestive tract from mouth to anus. Tell how the structure and function of each organ are related.

B. Describe the structure and function of the liver, gall bladder, and pancreas. Explain how each is related to the digestive tract.

C. Explain how food is moved through the digestive tract.

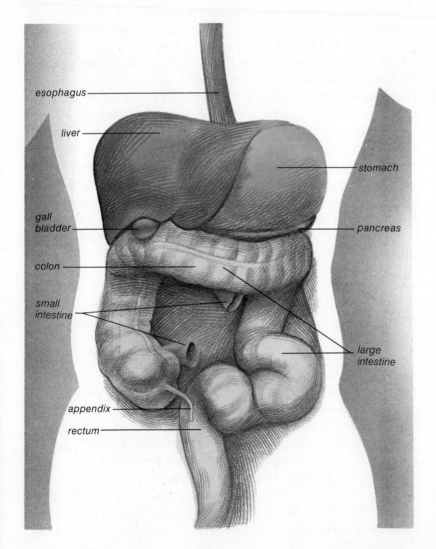

esophagus
liver
stomach
gall bladder
pancreas
colon
small intestine
large intestine
appendix
rectum

30-1. The human digestive system.

Mouth

The first segment of the digestive system is the *mouth cavity*. (See Fig. 30-2.) The mouth cavity is lined by a skin-like mucous membrane. Within this area are found the *tongue* and *teeth*. The roof of the mouth is formed by the *hard palate*. Near the pharynx, or throat, the hard palate extends to the *soft palate*. On the floor of the mouth rests the tongue. The palate separates the mouth cavity from the nasal cavity. Two pairs of salivary glands are located under the tongue and one pair is situated in front of the ears. The disease, *mumps*, is a viral infection that causes the salivary glands located by the ears to swell and become painful. *Saliva* is secreted by the salivary glands and enters the mouth by way of ducts. Saliva moistens and softens food so that it is easier to swallow. It also protects the mouth from drying out. Saliva also contains an enzyme that begins the digestion of starch.

The *tongue* plays an important role in preparing foods for digestion. It helps to mix both food and saliva together in the mouth. The act of swallowing is also initiated by the tongue. On the surface of the tongue are groups of sense organs called taste buds. There are four kinds of taste buds — bitter, salty, sour, and sweet. However, much of what we taste is a combination of both taste and smell.

The breakdown of foods occurs much more rapidly when the meal is finely ground into small particles. The *teeth* are the main agents that grind food. (See Fig. 30-2.) The human adult has 32 teeth. They are arranged in two U-shaped rows of 16 teeth each. One row is located in the upper jaw and one in the lower jaw. Moreover, both the left and right sides of each jaw are identical. The types of teeth on one side of the jaw from the center front backward are two *incisors*, one *canine*, two *premolars*, and three *molars*. The last molar, or "wisdom tooth," usually does not erupt until age 17 or later. In many people the wisdom teeth do not ever erupt. Each kind of tooth serves a particular function. Incisors cut, canines tear, and premolars and molars crush and grind. Together the teeth break food down into smaller particles.

Each tooth has a *crown* above the gum, a *root* below the gum, and a *neck* at the gum line. (See Fig. 30-3.) Inside the tooth is a *pulp cavity* which contains nerves and blood vessels. The pulp cavity is surrounded by *dentine*, a fairly hard, bonelike substance. The outer surface of the root is covered by a harder *cementum* and a fibrous membrane. This membrane attaches the tooth to the jawbone. The outer surface of the crown consists of *enamel*, the hardest substance in the body. Even though enamel is very hard, it can be destroyed by acids produced by bacteria and some yeasts. When this happens, tooth decay results. Regular brushing and flossing of the teeth after meals removes bacteria and acid, thus helping to prevent tooth decay.

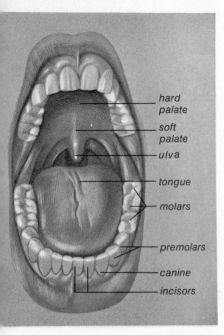

30-2. Structures in the mouth.

- hard palate
- soft palate
- ulva
- tongue
- molars
- premolars
- canine
- incisors

Pharynx and Esophagus

Within the mouth food is broken into smaller pieces and mixed with saliva. This mixture is moved into the *pharynx* by the action of the tongue. The pharynx is a vertical, tubular structure which acts as a common passageway for food and air. As food is swallowed, the larynx (voice box) is pulled forward and upward. It meets the epiglottis, a small flap of cartilage, and thus the air passage is closed. If this passage is not closed properly, food may get into it and cause choking.

Food passes quickly from the pharynx into the *esophagus*. The esophagus is a muscular tube about 25 cm in length extending from the pharynx to the stomach. Food is squeezed along by the contraction of muscles in the wall of the esophagus. These muscles make *waves of contractions* called *peristalsis*. Muscles are also found in the walls of the rest of the digestive tract. They too cause waves of peristalsis.

Stomach

Within seconds, contractions of the muscles of the esophagus force food particles into the *stomach*. The stomach is a J-shaped elastic bag lying in the upper left portion of the abdominal cavity (See Fig. 30-1.) With the addition of food, the stomach walls expand just enough to hold the contents. It then pushes the food toward the small intestine. The opening to the stomach is guarded by a circle of smooth muscle called a *sphincter* (*sfing* tər). When the digestive tract is irritated, the stomach muscles can force food back through the esophagus. From here, the food is expelled from the body through the mouth. This process is called vomiting.

Food may remain in the stomach for several hours, allowing digestion to continue. Some cells in the lining of the stomach produce the enzyme pepsin, while others produce hydrochloric acid. Furthermore, there are cells which secrete mucus. This protects the lining of the stomach from both the enzyme and the acid. *Ulcers* sometimes occur when too much acid is produced or when not enough mucus is present. Contractions of the muscles of the wall of the stomach mix the food with the secretions and also propel it by peristalic waves into the small intestine.

Small Intestine

As the food leaves the stomach, it enters the *small intestine*. The small intestine is a narrow tube about 2.5 cm in diameter and 3 meters long. (See Fig. 30-1.) It is divided into three regions. The *duodenum* (do͞o ə de̅ nəm), nearest the stomach, is where the secretions from the liver and pancreas enter the digestive tract. Much of the digestion of food takes place here. The next region is the *jejunum* (ji jo͞o nəm).

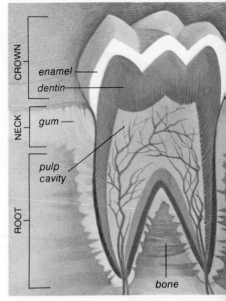

CROWN

NECK

ROOT

enamel

dentin

gum

pulp cavity

bone

30-3. A molar tooth.

Peristalsis occurs throughout the digestive tract. It is controlled by neural reflexes that are triggered by the presence of food in the digestive tract and also be acidity of food entering the small intestine. A layer of circular smooth muscle constricts the diameter of the tube and a layer of longitudinal smooth muscle shortens the tube. Alternating contractions of these two layers propel food through the tract.

In addition to the role of the pancreas in digestion, it also produces the hormones insulin and glucagon. These hormones are discussed in chapter 34.

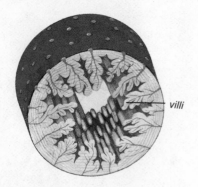
villi

30-4. Villi increase the surface area of the small intestine.

30-5. Ducts carry the secretions of the liver and pancreas into the duodenum.

Finally, the region that leads into the large intestine is the *ileum* (il ē əm). Most of the absorption of molecules of digested food takes place in the jejunum and ileum.

The contents of the small intestine are moved along by peristalsis. The rate at which foods move through the digestive tract depends upon the food eaten. For example, liquids begin to enter the small intestine only 15 minutes after drinking them.

Cells in the lining of the small intestine produce mucus and some digestive juices. The entire lining of the small intestine is covered with very small projections called *villi* (vil ī). The villi greatly increase the surface area of the small intestine. (See Fig. 30-4.) They are important in the absorption of digested food substances.

Liver, Gall Bladder, and Pancreas

The *liver, gall bladder,* and *pancreas* are connected to the digestive tract by ducts. (See Fig. 30-5.) The liver is a large soft organ or gland. Many metabolic reactions take place in it. The liver also produces a green fluid, *bile,* which passes by a system of ducts to the gall bladder. The gall bladder is a small sac on the underside of the right lobe of the liver. It releases bile when fat is present in the duodenum. The gall bladder is a frequent source of trouble in some people. Stones may form in the gall bladder and block the flow of bile. This can become painful and may require surgery. The pancreas lies near the stomach

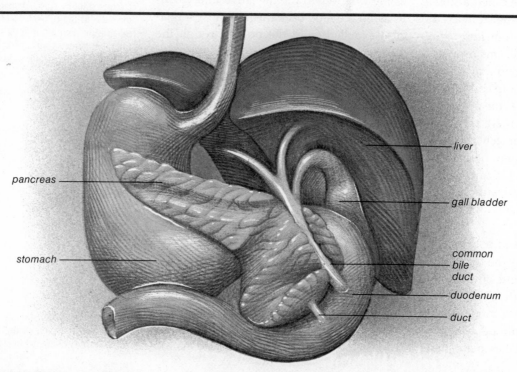
pancreas

stomach

liver

gall bladder

common bile duct

duodenum

duct

and duodenum. It produces several different enzymes and releases them into the duodenum. The pancreas also produces hormones that help to regulate the amount of sugar in the blood. We will have more to say about blood sugar in Chapter 34.

Large Intestine

The *large intestine* is connected directly to the ileum of the small intestine. (See Fig. 30-1.) It is about 6 cm in diameter, and approximately 1½ meters long. Near the point where the large and small intestines join is a small sac called the *cecum* (sē kəm). At the tip of the cecum is a small projection called the *appendix*. The appendix probably helps to fight infections within the body. However, sometimes it becomes infected. Such an infection is called *appendicitis*. The large intestine runs from the appendix to the anus and is divided into the *colon* and the *rectum*. Cells in the lining of the large intestine secrete mucus but not enzymes. Many bacteria are present in the large intestine. Some bacteria synthesize vitamins and other nutrients that are absorbed and used by human cells.

Movement of food residue is slow in the large intestine. Water is absorbed back into the blood stream and the residue becomes semi-solid waste material or *feces* (fē sēz). The discharge of feces through the anus is called *defecation*. It is controlled by a series of nerve impulses. Failing to heed these impulses is a common cause of *constipation*.

QUESTIONS FOR SECTION 1
1. Name the organs of the digestive tract in order as food passes through them.
2. How are the structure and function of each type of tooth related?
3. How are the structure and function of each of the following organs related: (a) tongue, (b) stomach, (c) small intestine?
4. What happens to the salivary glands when a person has mumps?
5. What is appendicitis?
6. Name the functions of the liver, gall bladder, and pancreas.
7. What is peristalsis?
8. Suppose you have just eaten a hamburger on a bun. Describe the mechanical changes that take place as it moves through your digestive tract.

Answers to Questions for Section 1.
A. 1. Mouth, pharynx, esophagus, stomach, small intestine, large intestine, anus.

2. Incisors cut, canines tear, premolars and molars grind.

*3. (a) shape contributes to mashing food against roof of mouth and muscles work to move food toward pharynx; (b) shape suitable for storing food, muscular movements appropriate for mixing; (c) large surface area well suited for absorption.

4. The virus that causes mumps causes the salivary glands to swell and become painful.

5. An inflammation of the appendix.

B. 6. Liver: produces bile and certain other substances. Gall bladder: stores bile and releases it into the intestine. Pancreas: produces digestive juices and hormones that regulate the metabolism of glucose.

C. 7. The wave-like contraction of the muscles of the digestive tract.

*8. Breaking the hamburger and bun into small pieces and mixing with saliva, further mixing with digestive juices in the stomach, absorption of nutrients in small intestine, and movement of residue through large intestine.

CHAPTER INVESTIGATION

A. What are the differences between meal A and meal B?

B. Which meal is more nutritious? Why? What additional kinds of foods should the person who ate meal A eat during the day? What additional kinds of foods should the person who ate meal B eat?

C. Select a series of menus from a popular magazine. Check the menus against the four food groups. Point out good examples of menu planning.

2 WHAT HAPPENS TO FOOD AS IT IS DIGESTED

The Breakdown of Food

Thus far you are familiar with the structures of the digestive system. Now you are ready to discover how the various secretions act on the food you eat. Suppose that for breakfast this morning you had orange juice, one poached egg on buttered toast, and a glass of milk. What has been happening to that food during the day?

Digestion in the Mouth

The smell of good food stimulates glands in your mouth to produce much saliva. As your mouth waters, your body is actually preparing for digestion. **Digestion** *is the chemical breakdown of food into small molecules.* It begins in the mouth cavity. The enzyme in saliva, *salivary amylase* acts on starches. (See Fig. 30-6.) The starch molecules in the toast begin to be broken down into shorter chains of glucose molecules. If you chewed the toast for a long time, you probably noticed it began to taste slightly sweet. The sweet taste is caused by the smaller molecules, maltose, that are present after amylase acts on starch. If you ate very fast, the amylase had little time to act before you swallowed your food.

Digestion in the Stomach

In the stomach the action of amylase is stopped by the acid that is secreted there. Remember that each enzyme has a certain pH at which it works best. Pepsin, unlike amylase, requires a low-pH medium in which to work. Hydrochloric acid (HCl) creates that low pH. This, along with pepsin, breaks down the proteins in the milk and egg you ate into long chains of amino acids called polypeptides. (See Fig. 30-7.) By the time the digested food is ready to leave the stomach it has become a semiliquid mass called *chyme* (kīm). The secretion of digestive juices is controlled by many factors. One of these factors, the hormone gastrin, is released by the cells of the stomach into the blood. Gastrin continues to stimulate the production of gastric juices, HCl and enzymes, until materials begin leaving the stomach.

Have you ever wondered how proteins can be digested in the stomach without the stomach itself being digested? Several things make this possible. First, the lining of the stomach is covered by mucus. Also, the enzyme is secreted in an inactive form called *pepsinogen* (pep *sin* ə jən). It is activated by the hydrochloric acid. Finally, both the acid and the enzymes are quickly mixed with the food. However, if too much acid or too little mucus is produced, the lining of the stom-

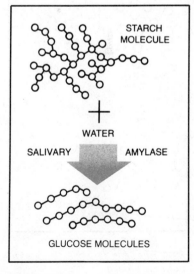

30-6. Salivary amylase breaks starch down to chains of glucose molecules. (Each dot represents a glucose molecule.)

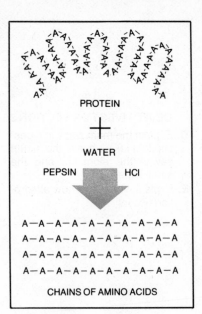

30-7. Pepsin, in the presence of HCl, breaks proteins into chains of amino acids called polypeptides.

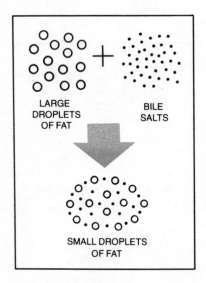

30-8. Bile salts cause fat droplets to become smaller.

ach or small intestine may become damaged. Thus, an ulcer is produced. Ulcers are most common in the lower portion of the stomach. They also frequently occur in the duodenum where the acidic chyme from the stomach enters it. If the ulcer penetrates the wall of the stomach or duodenum, some of the contents of the digestive tract go into the body cavity. Bleeding also occurs. Such perforated ulcers can be fatal unless treated promptly.

Digestion in the Small Intestine

Partially digested food or chyme is created from the breakfast you ate. Chyme contains both undigested and partially digested starch from the toast. It also contains long chains of amino acids from the egg and milk. In addition, chyme contains sugars in the form of fructose from the orange juice and lactose from the milk. The fat portion of chyme originated in the milk and butter on your toast. When chyme enters the small intestine it causes the gall bladder to release some of the stored bile. It also stimulates the pancreas to secrete several substances.

One of the substances from the pancreas is sodium bicarbonate. It neutralizes the acid in the chyme. Three kinds of enzymes are also released from the pancreas. They are *trypsin, pancreatic amylase,* and *lipase.* Trypsin digests long amino acid chains into shorter chains of small polypeptides, dipeptides, and a few amino acids. Trypsin is released in an unactive form called *trypsinogen* (trip *sin* ə jən), and it is activated in the small intestine. Amylase from the pancreas continues the digestion of starch to maltose.

Before lipase can digest the fats in the milk and butter, the fats must be made to mix with the watery part of the chyme. (See Fig. 30-8.) At this point, large droplets of fat are surrounded by chemicals called *bile salts* from the bile. Bile salts cause fat droplets to become smaller and smaller until they finally mix with the water. The same thing happens to grease in dishwater when detergent is added. Once the fat particles are mixed with water, lipase can act more effectively in breaking them down into fatty acids and glycerol.

Some additional enzymes are produced by the cells of the small intestine. One group of enzymes are the *peptidases* (*pep* tə dās əs). In the small intestine they break the small polypeptides and dipeptides down into single amino acids. Other enzymes break down disaccharides into simpler sugars or monosaccharides. The enzyme *maltase* breaks down the disaccharide, maltose, into two molecules of glucose. *Sucrase* breaks down sucrose (table sugar) into glucose and fructose. *Lactase* breaks down lactose, the sugar in milk, into glucose and galactose.

7. The villi are small finger-like projections from the surface of the small intestine that increase the absorptive area.

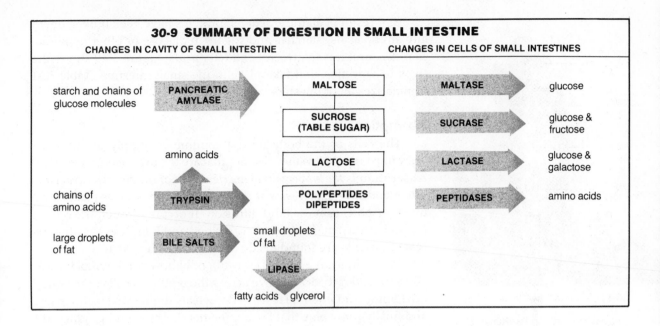

30-9 SUMMARY OF DIGESTION IN SMALL INTESTINE

CHANGES IN CAVITY OF SMALL INTESTINE   **CHANGES IN CELLS OF SMALL INTESTINES**

starch and chains of glucose molecules → **PANCREATIC AMYLASE** → **MALTOSE**

amino acids

chains of amino acids → **TRYPSIN** →

SUCROSE (TABLE SUGAR)

LACTOSE

POLYPEPTIDES DIPEPTIDES

large droplets of fat → **BILE SALTS** → small droplets of fat

LIPASE

fatty acids   glycerol

MALTASE → glucose

SUCRASE → glucose & fructose

LACTASE → glucose & galactose

PEPTIDASES → amino acids

TABLE 30-1. SUMMARY OF HUMAN DIGESTION

Place of Digestion	Source of Enzyme	Enzyme	Substrate	Products
mouth	salivary glands	salivary amylase	starch	chains of glucose
stomach	cells in stomach wall	pepsin	protein	polypeptides
small intestine	pancreas	amylase	chains of glucose	maltose
		trypsin	proteins and polypeptides	small polypeptides, dipeptides, and amino acids
		lipase	fats	glycerol and fatty acids
	cells in intestinal wall	maltase	maltose	glucose
		sucrase	sucrose	glucose and fructose
		lactase	lactose	glucose and galactose
		peptidases	small polypeptides and dipeptides	amino acids

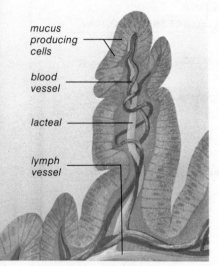

mucus
producing
cells

blood
vessel

lacteal

lymph
vessel

30-10. Structure of a villus.

Answers to Questions for Section 2.

D. 1. Mouth: food broken into small pieces, and digestion of starch begun. Stomach: HCl and pepsin break proteins into polypeptides. Food becomes semi-liquid chyme. Small intestine: digestion of starch completed; digestion of proteins completed; bile salts and lipase digest fats; maltase, sucrase, and lactase digest sugars.

2. Some digestion of starch in the mouth. Some digestion protein in the stomach, mixing of fats with bile salts and rendering them soluble in water in the small intestine, removal of water from the residue in the large intestine.

3. By mucus secretions covering the stomach lining, and by the release of protein-digesting enzymes in inactive forms.

4. Undigested and partially digested starch and long chains of amino acids.

5. Pancreatic amylase: starch → maltose; trypsin: long amino acid chains → short amino acid chains; pancreatic lipase: fats → glycerol and fatty acids; peptidases: short amino acid chains → amino acids; maltase: maltose → 2 glucose; sucrase: sucrose → glucose + fructose; lactase: milk sugar → glucose + galactose. (See pages 596 for more answers.)

As a result of all these actions, proteins have been broken down into amino acids, starches and sugars to glucose or other monosaccharides, and fats to glycerol and fatty acids. Figure 30-9 shows the steps in digestion that take place in the small intestine. Table 30-1 summarizes all of the steps of digestion.

Absorption

The cells of the body need a continuous supply of nutrients. They must receive small molecules that are the products of digestion. **Absorption** *is the movement of nutrients out of the digestive tract and into blood or lymph vessels of the villi.* Absorption takes place by active transport, osmosis, and diffusion. It occurs through the cells of the villi of the small intestine. The blood and lymph vessels that receive nutrients are found inside the villi. (See Fig. 30-10.)

Each villus has a *lacteal* (*lak* tē əl), or blind-ended, lymph vessel. Glycerol and fatty acids move across the epithelial cells of the intestinal lining and enter a lacteal. The lacteals drain into small vessels, and finally into veins that lead to the heart. These end products derived from fat digestion are thus carried to the cells of the body.

Each villus also has a network of blood vessels. Glucose (and other monosaccharides) and amino acids absorbed by the epithelial cells enter directly into the blood vessels. Once the nutrients are inside the blood vessels they are transported to the liver. Some of the glucose is stored in the liver as glycogen and later released as glucose. This way the amount of glucose in the blood stays at about the same concentration all the time.

Although almost all absorption takes place in the small intestine, a few small molecules such as alcohol can be absorbed through the wall of the stomach. This explains in part why the effects of drinking alcoholic beverages can be felt so quickly.

QUESTIONS FOR SECTION 2

1. Briefly outline the steps of digestion in the mouth, stomach, and small intestine.
2. Describe the chemical changes that take place in the hamburger as it moves through your digestive tract.
3. Why does the stomach not digest itself?
4. What products of digestion would you expect to find in chyme?
5. Make a list of the enzymes that act in the small intestine and write a word equation for the action of each.
6. What is absorption and where does it occur?
7. Describe the structure and function of the villi.

3 WHAT IS A NUTRITIOUS DIET?

Nutritional Requirements

Everyone is concerned about what kinds and amounts of food are best for staying in shape. To be fit, it is necessary to understand what makes up a nutritious diet. *A nutritious diet is a meal plan that contains all of the ingredients necessary for maintaining good health.* Such a diet would include *carbohydrates, fats, proteins, water, vitamins,* and *minerals.* Furthermore, each of these kinds of nutrients should be present in the diet in the proper amount.

One way to determine the amount of food needed is to count the calories it contains. *A calorie is a measure of the energy stored in a substance.* Teenage boys need about 3000 calories per day and teenage girls need about 2100 calories per day. Boys need more calories than girls because they are taller and weigh more. Both boys and girls may need more than the average number of calories if they are very active. They may need fewer than the average number of calories if they are very inactive. Our bodies use mostly carbohydrates and fats for energy, but proteins can also be used for energy. The calories of energy provided by some common foods are given in Table 30-2.

OBJECTIVES FOR SECTION 3

F. Explain why you need carbohydrate, fat, and protein in your daily diet.

G. Discuss the body's need for water each day.

H. Define the terms, *vitamin* and *mineral*. Describe why these materials are needed for one's health.

I. Name some vitamin deficiency diseases.

TABLE 30-2.

Calories in Selected Foods, *including grams of protein, and approximate calories from fats and carbohydrates.*						
Food (amount)	Total Calories	Protein (g)	Approximate calories from:			
			saturated fats	unsaturated fats	sugars	complex carbohydrates
Beef (100g)	200	20	45	55	0	0
Butter (15g)	100	0	65	35	0	0
Carrots	40	1	0	0	0	30
Cheese (30g)	100	6	50	25	0	0
Egg (45g)	70	6	15	30	0	0
Frankfurter (50g)	150	6	40	50	0	0
French fries (100g)	210	3	20	70	0	110
Ice Cream (100g)	200	4	65	35	80	0
Margarine (15g)	100	0	20	80	0	0
Milk, skim (240g)	80	8	0	0	15	0
Milk, whole (240g)	160	8	50	25	15	0
Peanut Butter (15g)	80	3	10	50	0	10
Potato (150g)	140	3	0	2	0	130

Carbohydrates

In addition to providing energy, carbohydrates provide roughage. Carbohydrates include sugars, starches, and cellulose. Sugars and starches are digested to glucose and other monosaccharides. Our bodies cannot digest cellulose because we do not have an enzyme that can break it down. Therefore, it is eliminated in the feces. Cellulose provides bulk and stimulates the muscles of the digestive tract to contract. It is found in the walls of plant cells. Therefore, fruits, vegetables, and whole grain cereals should be included in the diet to provide roughage.

Fats

Like carbohydrates, fats are used mostly for energy. Cell membranes and some organelles are made of proteins and lipids (or fats). The body needs a small amount of fat to keep these structures in good repair. Our bodies also store energy in the form of fat. Some fat is deposited under the skin where it helps to maintain our body temperature. Fat is also found around some organs inside the body. If we consume more calories than we use for energy, body maintenance, and growth, our bodies will accumulate fat.

Proteins

Probably the most important food in your diet is protein. Proteins are used to maintain the structure of the cells of the body: They are needed in large quantities while the body is growing to provide the building blocks for new cells. Teenage girls need about 48 grams of protein per day while teenage boys need about 54 grams per day. A 100 gram serving of meat, poultry, or fish provides about 20 grams of protein. A glass of milk provides 8 grams and an egg 6 grams. You may be surprised to learn that dried beans and whole grain cereals also provide about 7 grams of protein per serving. An adequate supply of protein is essential for growth and repair of the body. An excess of protein is of no benefit because it cannot be stored by the body. It does, however, greatly increase the cost of one's food. Amino acids that are not used for growth and repair are *deaminated* (dē *am* ə nāt əd) and used for energy. **Deamination** *is the removal of amine (NH₃)* *groups.* The unused amines are made into *urea* (yōo rē ə) in the liver and excreted in the urine.

Water

Water makes up about two-thirds of the weight of our bodies. Almost all chemical reactions that take place in the body involve the use of water. Nutrients that have been digested are dissolved in water before they are absorbed. Many other substances in the body are dissolved in water. We can live only a few days without water. If we are sweating heavily, we can lose several liters of water in a short period of time. Furthermore, waste materials are dissolved in water and excreted in urine. In these ways our bodies are constantly losing water. This loss of water must be replaced by drinking liquids and by eating foods that contain water. Fruits and vegetables are examples of foods that contain large amounts of water.

Vitamins

A dramatic time in the development of our knowledge of nutrients was the discovery of vitamins. **Vitamins** *are certain kinds of organic chemicals that are needed in small amounts for good health.* They are not used as energy sources. One of the first vitamins to be studied was *thiamine,* or vitamin B_1. In some parts of the world, people eat a diet consisting mostly of polished rice — rice that has had the outer covering of the grains removed. On such a diet people lose weight and fail to digest their food properly. They have little appetite and become tired very easily. Some people also have nervous disorders. In the 1890's, a Dutch scientist named Christiaan Eijkman studied this condition in prisoners in the Dutch East Indies. He discovered that the symptoms could be prevented by providing a diet of unpolished rice. We now know that the outer covering of the rice grains contains the vitamin, thiamine. The disease that is caused by a deficiency of thiamine is called *beriberi* (*ber ē ber ē*).

Many vitamins have been discovered during studies of diseases that did not appear to be caused by bacteria or other infectious agents. Thus, we think of these vitamins as being needed to prevent deficiency diseases. As nutritionists have studied vitamins, they have found that vitamins play a role in certain chemical reactions. It has been established that many vitamins act as coenzymes. As you learned in Chapter 7, a coenzyme is a substance that works with an enzyme to control a biochemical reaction. Table 30-3 on page 602 lists the important characteristics of several vitamins.

In recent years the topic of megavitamins has received much attention. The idea is that very large doses of some vitamins ("mega" means large) will prevent or cure some diseases. The claim that vitamin C will prevent colds is an example. The data from experiments with megavitamins are confusing and more research is needed. It is known that people with certain kinds of diseases, such as some anemias, and some kinds of rickets, need much greater than normal amounts of certain vitamins. However, most of us can obtain the vitamins we need from eating a balanced diet.

TABLE 30-3.   VITAMINS: FOOD SOURCES, FUNCTIONS, AND SYMPTOMS OF DEFICIENCIES.

Vitamin	Food Sources	Functions	Symptoms of Deficiency
A Carotene	egg yolk, green and yellow vegetables, yellow fruits, liver, fish liver oils	growth, healthy skin and eyes	night blindness, retarded growth, susceptibility to infections, dry skin
B_1 Thiamine	milk, meat, seafood, whole grain foods, green vegetables, poultry	growth, helps release energy from food	retarded growth, nerve disorders, loss of appetite, beriberi
B_2 Riboflavin	meat, milk, eggs, poultry, soybeans, green vegetables	growth, health of skin and mouth, helps the body use carbohydrates, fats, proteins to release energy	retarded growth, aging, dim vision, inflamed tongue
Niacin	meat, fish, poultry, peanut butter, whole grain, green leafy vegetables	growth, health of digestive and nervous systems, aids in producing energy from carbohydrates	digestive ailments, nervous disorders, skin eruptions
C Ascorbic acid	citrus fruits, tomatoes, other fruits, green leafy vegetables	growth, healthy blood vessels, gums, and teeth	bleeding gums, ease of bruising
D	liver, eggs, fortified milk, irradiated foods, fish oils	growth, control calcium and phosphorus metabolism, healthy bones and teeth	soft, poorly developed teeth and bones, dental decay, rickets
E Tocopherol	milk, whole wheat, leafy vegetables, butter	probably needed for normal reproduction	not known
K	soybeans, green vegetables, tomatoes	normal clotting of blood	hemorrhage

TABLE 30-4.   MINERALS: FOOD SOURCES AND FUNCTIONS.

Mineral	Food Sources	Functions
Calcium	dairy products, eggs, soybeans, fish	maintain healthy bones and teeth, nerve function, blood clotting
Iodine	iodized salt, fish	part of thyroid hormone
Iron	liver, eggs, beans, raisins, leafy vegetables	part of red blood cells, helps transport oxygen
Magnesium	green and yellow vegetables	maintain normal nerve and muscle function
Phosphorus	dairy products, meat, beans, whole grains	maintain bones and teeth, make ATP and nucleic acids
Potassium	green and yellow vegetables	growth, maintain healthy cells and normal blood

Health food stores often make it seem important to get vitamins from natural food sources. However, a vitamin synthesized by a chemist is identical to the same vitamin synthesized by a plant or animal.

Minerals

With new developments in laboratory technology, it is possible to detect what elements are found in living tissue. Some of these mineral elements are nutrients. **Minerals** *are inorganic substances that are essential for good health.* Like vitamins, minerals often work with an enzyme. Minerals also form part of a body structure. Calcium and phosphorus are needed to form bones and teeth. Another mineral, iron, is needed to make red blood cells that can carry oxygen. Information about some of the more important minerals is given in Table 30-4. Only small amounts of most minerals are needed to maintain good health. These minerals can be obtained from eating a varied diet. This diet should contain plenty of milk, especially while bones and teeth are growing.

QUESTIONS FOR SECTION 3

1. What two food substances are most used for energy?
2. What use does the body make of proteins?
3. What structures in the body contain fats?
4. Why do you need water every day?
5. Why do you need vitamins and minerals daily?
6. What vitamins and minerals are present in the hamburger and bun?
7. Name two vitamin deficiency diseases.

Answers to Questions for Section 3.
F. 1. Carbohydrates and fats.
  2. For growth and repair of cells.
  3. Cell membranes and the membranes of some organelles; fat cells in various places in the body.
G. 4. Water is needed to transport substances and to form a large part of cells, where it serves as a medium for many chemical reactions.
H. 5. Vitamins and minerals are needed to allow many enzymes to function.
  6. B-vitamins, niacin, and phosphorus.
  7. Beriberi, some anemias, rickets.

4 PLANNING YOUR DIET

OBJECTIVES FOR SECTION 4

J. List the basic four food groups. Illustrate how eating food from each of the groups helps to meet your nutritional needs.
K. Contrast the U.S. dietary goals with basic four requirements and determine whether your diet meets these goals.
L. Demonstrate how you can use vegetable proteins to obtain a nutritious diet at a low level on the food chain.
M. Interpret the effects of junk foods, food additives, alcohol, and drugs on nutrition.

What Foods to Eat

By knowing the different nutrients your body needs to stay healthy, you can begin to plan your diet. You may be thinking that this will be a big task because there are so many nutrients to consider. If one had to think about each nutrient it would be, but there is a simpler way. You can use the *basic four food groups*.

The Basic Four Food Groups

Foods are placed into four groups according to the nutrients they contain: (1) the milk group, (2) the meat group, (3) the fruit and vegetable group, and (4) the bread and cereal group. Foods that belong in each group are shown in Figure 30-11. The amounts of foods you should eat from each group and the nutritional needs they satisfy are shown in Table 30-5. Now, you should be able to quickly plan your diet. It should include the proper amounts of foods from each group. If your diet meets these requirements you can be fairly sure that you have gotten all of the vitamins and minerals you need. You will also get enough protein for growth and repair of your body. In addition to this, you will receive enough carbohydrates and fats for your energy needs.

30-11. The basic four food groups.

TABLE 30-5.   THE BASIC FOUR FOOD GROUPS AND THEIR CONTRIBUTIONS TO NUTRITION.

Group	Recommended daily amounts	Nutritional needs satisfied
Milk Group	serving: 240g milk or 20-30g cheese 2 or 3 servings	each serving provides 8 g. protein, 3 g. fat, and about 140 calories. contains vitamins A and riboflavin and provides an especially good supply of calcium, phosphorus, potassium, and magnesium.
Meat Group	serving: 90g lean meat or eggs or 200 g cooked legume, or 60g peanut butter 2 servings	each serving provides 15-25 g. protein, 10-40 g. fat, and 150-400 calories. contains phosphorus, iron, sodium, potassium, riboflavin and other B vitamins. legumes are very low in fat. peanut butter is high in fat but also high in niacin eggs provide some vitamin A
Fruit and Vegetable Group	serving: 100g 4 servings including one good source of vitamin A and one of vitamin C.	foods that provide vitamin A: spinach and other green leafy vegetables, carrots, and other yellow vegetables and fruits. foods that provide vitamin C: citrus fruits and juices. fruits and vegetables also provide some B vitamins and vitamin K, as well as some minerals.
Bread and Cereal Group	serving: 30g of bread or 30g of prepared cereal or 100g cup of cooked cereal, rice, pasta, or noodles. 4 servings	each serving provides energy, some protein, and if made of whole grain, a good supply of B vitamins.

U.S. Dietary Goals

The diet of many Americans now contains large quantities of sugar and animal fats. Sugar provides energy but does not provide any vitamins or minerals. Foods that are high in sugar that have few vitamins and minerals are sometimes said to contain "empty calories." Animal fats contain cholesterol and large amounts of saturated fatty acids. Both cholesterol and saturated fatty acids are thought to contribute to disease of the heart and blood vessels. Because of this, the U.S. Senate became concerned about the effects of such a diet on the health of Americans. A set of dietary goals were prepared to help improve the quality of our diets. These goals recommend reducing the total amount of fat and increasing the total amount of complex carbohydrates. Complex carbohydrates are found in bread, cereal, potatoes, rice, and in fruits and vegetables. The goals also recommend reducing the amount of sugar and saturated fat in the diet. Beef, pork, and dairy products are high in saturated fats. Most fish,

	CURRENT DIET	SAMPLE FOODS	DIETARY GOALS	
42% fat	16% saturated	animal fats	10% saturated	30% fat
	26% unsaturated	vegetable oils oleomargarine	20% unsaturated	
12% protein		meats, eggs, beans, milk	12% protein	
46% carbo-hydrate	22% complex carbohydrate	grains, cereals, fruits	40-45% complex carbohydrates	53% carbo-hydrate
	24% sugar	soda, candy	15% sugar	

30-12. Typical American diet and diet that meets U.S. dietary goals.

poultry, and foods from plants are low in saturated fats. Skim milk, milk that has the fat removed, still has all of the important nutrients. Figure 30-12 shows the difference between a typical American diet and a diet that follows these goals.

You can combine the use of the basic four food groups and the dietary goals to select a nutritious diet. To do this you simply select foods from the milk and meat groups that are low in fat, particularly saturated fat. You should notice that sugar is not included in the basic four groups. Therefore, if you were selecting your food from those groups you would not be getting too much sugar.

Vegetable Protein:
How You Can Eat Lower on the Food Chain

From your study of food chains, you should realize that humans who eat other animals are secondary consumers. By obtaining more of your diet from plant sources you can become a primary consumer at least some of the time. It takes about twenty pounds of plant proteins to make one pound of beef protein. If we eat plant proteins directly, we can help to increase the amount of protein available for other humans. In many parts of the world, many people live almost entirely on plant proteins. In some parts of the world there is a deficiency of protein in the diet. This causes slow growth and mental retardation in young children.

Two other reasons for eating plant proteins are their reduced cost and the fact that they contain fewer pesticides. You probably already know that meat costs a lot more than dried beans, rice, and whole grain cereals. Furthermore, the bodies of animals accumulate some pesticides from the plants they eat. Therefore, when we eat meat, we are likely to take into our bodies larger quantities of stored pesticides. This amount is greater than if we had eaten plants directly.

One problem with eating plant proteins is that any one plant does not contain all of the amino acids our bodies need. However,

TABLE 30-6.

Some sample vegetable protein combinations and some vegetable-dairy protein combinations and their protein content.	
Combination	**Protein content**
30g cheese and 120g whole grain bread or 200g macaroni	15g
150g potato and 35g cheese or 240g milk	12g
170g rice and 75g beans	30g
120g peanut butter and 180g milk	36g

each of the amino acids we need can be found in some plant foods. The way to solve this problem is to combine in the same meal two or more plant foods. For example, rice is deficient in two important amino acids. Moreover, dried beans are deficient in two other amino acids. By combining these foods all amino acids are made available. Some good combinations are given in Table 30-6.

Food Additives and Junk Food

Much of the highly processed food that we find so convenient to eat contain food additives. These additives, which enhance flavor, are usually either dyes or preservatives. Dyes are used to give the food an appealing color. Preservatives are used to prevent bacteria from causing the food to spoil. What do you think preservatives that kill bacteria might do to your cells? Although dyes and preservatives must be approved by the Food and Drug Administration before they can be used, they have no nutritional value.

30-13. Why are these foods considered junk foods?

Answers to Questions for Section 4.

*6. Use table 30-6 to devise a vegetable protein meal.

M. 7. Junk foods crowd out more nutritious foods and also allow additives and other non-nutrient substances to enter the body.

8. Depresses the function of the central nervous system, may deprive the body of more nutritious foods, and damages the liver.

*9. Answers will vary.

30-14. How can these people help you maintain a balanced diet?

Junk foods are foods that are low in nutritional value. Many of them contain large amounts of sugar or fat or both. They contain few vitamins and minerals. Some examples of junk foods are shown in Figure 30-13. One problem with some junk foods is that many of the vitamins and minerals were removed from the natural food as it was processed. However, the manufacturer claims that they are enriched with vitamins and minerals. That is, they are added back, after processing, along with sugar and other substances. Paying for all of this processing is not the most economical way to get your vitamins and minerals.

Alcohol, Drugs, and Medicines

Alcohol has no nutritional value beyond the energy it provides. Alcohol is quickly absorbed from the intestinal tract and carried to the liver. Here it is broken down into a chemical called *acetaldehyde* (as ə tal də hīd). Some scientists think that acetaldehyde causes the symptoms of drunkenness. Alcoholics often suffer from malnutrition and vitamin deficiencies. They are more susceptible to infections. Furthermore, their livers are damaged by the alcohol.

Americans have been called a "pill-taking" society. We seem to think we can find a pill to take for every minor pain. Even aspirin that is usually thought of as a fairly safe medicine can damage the lining of the digestive tract and cause bleeding. We take medicines to neutralize stomach acids, tranquilizers to relax, and many kinds of pills to satisfy a variety of needs. None of these are natural food substances. Most are destroyed by the liver. However, large amounts of them can cause liver damage. People who eat a well-balanced diet often have little need for these substances.

QUESTIONS FOR SECTION 4

1. How are the U.S. dietary goals different from the basic four food groups?
2. How would the quality of your meal be improved if you had lettuce and tomato on your hamburger and a glass of milk with it?
3. Why would a chicken sandwich made with whole wheat bread be more nutritious than a hamburger on a white bun?
4. Why do you need to combine two or more plant foods to get a complete protein?
5. Plan a menu for your family for a day. Determine whether your menu meets the requirements of the basic four food groups and the U.S. dietary goals.
6. Devise a vegetable protein meal that would be as nutritious as the chicken sandwich.
7. What might be some of the effects of eating junk foods or foods with lots of additives?
8. Name some effects of alcohol on the body.
9. What junk foods have you eaten today?

Answers to Questions for Section 4.

J. *1. The U.S. dietary goals encourage reductions in sugars and fats (especially saturated animal fats) and increases in complex carbohydrates.

K. *2. Study tables to see what additional vitamins and minerals are found in milk and in vegetables.

3. Chicken contains less saturated fat and still provides a good source of protein. Whole wheat bread provides more vitamins and minerals than a white bun.

L. 4. Many plant proteins do not contain all of the amino acids needed for human growth and repair.

*5. Answers will vary.

(See page 608 for more answers.)

CHAPTER REVIEW

The digestive system plays an important role in maintaining homeostasis. It is the system that first receives all food substances. It digests the food into molecules small enough to be transported to cells and used by them. The organs of the digestive system each have a certain function in the process of digestion. *The structure and the function of each organ are closely related.*

All of the nutrients used by all of the cells of the body come from the food we eat. Therefore, it is essential that our diet contain all of the nutrients needed. If our diet is lacking in any of the nutrients, the functioning of the cells will be impaired. Homeostasis will not be maintained.

Using the Concepts

1. If your family agrees to it, do the shopping for the menu in Question 5 at the end of Section 4. Determine how much it costs per person to eat a balanced diet.

2. How much could the cost of a balanced diet be reduced by using vegetable proteins?
3. Attitudes about foods have a lot to do with what we eat. Make a list of your ten favorite foods. Put a + by each food that has a high nutritional value. Put a − by each food that has only a small nutritional value. Put an X by each food that has almost no nutritional value—a junk food. Substitute a nutritious food for each food marked X or −. Discuss your list with other class members.
4. Make plans for how you will improve your diet.
5. Hold a class debate on one or more of the following topics: (a) megavitamins, (b) vegetarianism, and (c) the use of food additives in the processing of foods.

Unanswered Question

6. As the world population increases, can we make plans to provide each person with a nutritious diet?

VOCABULARY REVIEW

mouth	peristalsis	colon	carbohydrates
small intestine	esophagus	duodenum	vitamins
liver	anus	bile	beriberi
teeth	pancreas	rectum	fats
epiglottis	stomach	appendix	minerals
pharynx	salivary gland	pepsinogen	proteins
large intestine	tongue	appendicitis	calorie
gall bladder	villi	lacteal	junk food

CHAPTER 30 TEST

Copy the number of each test item and place your answer to the right.

PART 1 Multiple Choice: Select the letter of the phrase that best completes each of the following.

d 1. The part of a tooth that contains nerves and blood vessels is the **a.** crown **b.** root **c.** neck **d.** pulp cavity.

c 2. The waves of muscle contraction that move materials through the digestive tract are called **a.** sphincters **b.** cementum **c.** peristalsis **d.** duodenum.

b 3. The function of the villi of the small intestine is to **a.** secrete enzymes **b.** increase surface area **c.** move food through the tract **d.** prevent absorption

a 4. Protein digesting enzymes do not digest the digestive tract itself because they are **a.** secreted in inactive form **b.** destroyed by acid in the stomach **c.** destroyed by bile **d.** surrounded by starch molecules.

d 5. The number of calories you need in your diet is determined by **a.** your body size **b.** how active you are **c.** the kind of sports you participate in **d.** both a and b.

d 6. You need foods from the milk group for **a.** stronger bones and teeth **b.** growth **c.** roughage **d.** both a and b.

c 7. The fruit and vegetable group of foods provides a good source of **a.** protein **b.** fat **c.** vitamins and minerals **d.** both a and b.

a 8. Many Americans eat **a.** too much sugar and animal fat **b.** too much starch **c.** too little protein **d.** too many fresh fruits and vegetables.

d 9. Junk foods usually contain **a.** too much sugar and fat **b.** dyes and preservatives **c.** few vitamins and minerals **d.** all of the above.

a 10. U.S. Dietary goals recommend **a.** reduce sugar and fat intake **b.** increase fruit and vegetable intake **c.** reduce meat intake **d.** increase milk intake.

PART 2 Matching: Match the letter of the term in Column I with its description in Column II.

COLUMN I

a. salivary amylase
b. pepsin
c. bile
d. sucrase
e. lipase

f. carbohydrates
g. fats
h. proteins
i. vitamins and minerals
j. water

COLUMN II

b 11. Digests protein
e 12. Digests fats
a 13. Digests starch
c 14. Breaks fat into small particles
d 15. Digests sugar
h 16. Growth and repair
i 17. Help enzymes work
f 18. Energy and roughage
j 19. Needed for most chemical reactions
g 20. Energy and healthy cell membranes

PART 3 Completion: Complete the following.

21. The parts of the digestive tract in order as the food passes through them are ____.
22. The basic four food groups are ____.
23. One of the advantages of eating vegetable proteins is ____.
24. Two physical effects of alcoholism are ____.
25. The digestive tract helps to maintain homeostasis by ____.

Chapter 30 Test Answers

21. mouth, pharynx, esophagus, stomach, s. intestine, l. intestine
22. milk, meat, fruits and vegetables, bread and cereals
23. less expensive than meats; lower on food chain
24. malnutrition; vitamin deficiencies
25. providing needed nutrients to cells

CHAPTER 31

TRANSPORT, RESPIRATION, AND EXCRETION

Every living cell uses food and oxygen and gives off carbon dioxide and wastes. Blood carries oxygen from the lungs to the cells in your body. The waste products of metabolism of your cells are carried by the blood to the kidneys and lungs. Here the waste products are eliminated.

The basic concepts in this chapter are as follows: (1) *Structure and function are related.* (2) *The processes of transport, respiration, and excretion help to maintain homeostasis.* These processes provide for the needs of individual cells, the functional units of organisms.

It is now time to explain how each of these processes occurs in your body. You will be able to apply what you learn to answer the following questions:

- What does smoking do to your body?
- Why must deep sea divers come up slowly?
- How does bleeding stop after you cut yourself?
- What is CPR and why should you learn it?
- How does the functioning of your heart and lungs affect your performance in sports?

DIVERS

1 BLOOD

OBJECTIVES FOR SECTION 1

A. Describe the components of blood. Explain the role of each in transport.
B. Distinguish between several different blood types. Explain why different types cannot be mixed.
C. Arrange the steps in the blood clotting mechanism in proper sequence.

From the first time you cut yourself or skinned a knee, you have known that your body contained a fluid, blood. **Blood *is a fluid that transports substances to and from the cells of your body.*** Almost one-tenth of your body weight consists of blood in a total volume of about five liters. Blood helps to control the amount of acids, bases, salts, and water in cells. It is important in regulating body temperature. Furthermore, its clotting mechanism helps prevent loss of this vital fluid. Blood cells play a major role in defending your body against bacteria. In addition to blood, your body contains colorless fluids derived from blood. These fluids are *lymph*, and fluid which surrounds the cells of the body.

What Does Blood Contain?

Blood contains three kinds of formed elements in a fluid called plasma. The three formed elements are red blood cells or *erythrocytes* (i *rith* rə sīts), white blood cells or *leukocytes* (l$\overline{oo}$ kə sīts), and small particles called platelets, or *thrombocytes* (*throm* bə sīts). (See Fig. 31-1.)

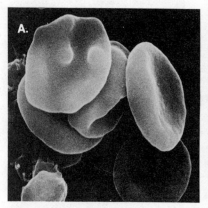
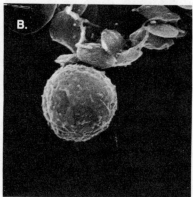
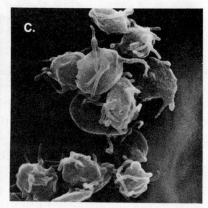

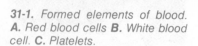

31-1. Formed elements of blood.
A. Red blood cells B. White blood cell. C. Platelets.

ERYTHROCYTES Erythrocytes are red, disc-shaped cells. Both sides are concave. They contain hemoglobin. **Hemoglobin *is a large protein molecule that contains iron.*** Oxygen attaches to the iron in hemoglobin to form the unstable molecule, oxyhemoglobin. This substance is bright red and gives blood its red color. The main function of erythrocytes is to carry oxygen from the lungs to all of the cells of the body.

Your body contains about 25 trillion red blood cells. They are constantly dying and being replaced. It has been estimated that in a normal adult about 20,000,000 red blood cells are destroyed and replaced every minute. Thus the total number of red blood cells in your body remains almost constant. Erythrocytes in humans have no nucleus and as a result cannot reproduce themselves. They circulate in the blood for about 120 days. When red blood cells die, the liver and spleen break them down. Some of the chemical breakdown products are reused to make new erythrocytes. New cells are produced in red bone marrow found inside many of the bones of your body. This marrow consists of a network of connective tissue and thousands of small blood vessels. Cells in the lining of these vessels produce and release new red blood cells. If for some reason the red blood cells are not replaced or do not contain enough hemoglobin, *anemia* results.

ANEMIA   **Anemia** *is a lack of red blood cells or a lack of hemoglobin.* People who have lost a lot of blood from an injury are anemic until their bodies can replace the red blood cells. Anemia also occurs in people who do not get enough iron, proteins, and vitamins in their diets.

LEUKOCYTES   Leukocytes are white blood cells, of which there are several different types. They are much larger than red blood cells. Each has a nucleus but contains no hemoglobin. Your body contains far fewer white blood cells than red blood cells. Only one or two in every thousand blood cells is a white blood cell. Some white blood cells move actively like amebas. They can even move through the walls of tiny blood vessels into the spaces between cells.

The main function of white blood cells is to protect the body against disease-causing organisms or harmful substances. When you have an infection, white blood cells increase in number. They collect in the area of the infection. There they destroy bacteria by surrounding them like amebas surround their food. White cells ingest particles until they are killed by the collection of breakdown products inside them. As white blood cells gather at the site of an infection in great numbers, pus forms. *Pus* is the whitish or yellowish fluid in a healing wound. It is a collection of living and dead white blood cells, dead tissue cells, cell fragments, and the dead bacteria. After all the bacteria have been destroyed, the injured tissue is replaced usually by scar tissue.

LEUKEMIA   Leukemia is the name used for several kinds of cancer in which too many white blood cells are produced. The cells that produce leukocytes release large numbers of them into the blood stream. As their numbers increase, they crowd out the red blood cells. Anemia results. The causes of these leukemias are not well understood. Their effects can sometimes be stopped by certain drugs, however.

PLATELETS   Platelets are small colorless particles that lack nuclei. They are much smaller than red blood cells. By sticking to rough areas or leaks in injured blood vessels, platelets help to seal the leaks. In ad-

It is the introduction of an antigen that is foreign to a person's body that causes a transfusion reaction. This is because the recipient's body can make antibodies in addition to those already present to react with the foreign antigen. Some people think that blood from different races of people should not be mixed. This mixing creates no problem as long as the blood is cross-matched.

dition, platelets also release a blood clotting factor when tissue has been damaged. The main function of platelets is to help in the clotting of blood.

PLASMA **Plasma** *is a straw-colored liquid that surrounds the formed elements of the blood.* It is 90 percent water and contains many different substances. Some of these substances are proteins that help the blood to clot or help the body to fight infections. Plasma also contains glucose, amino acids, and the breakdown products of fats. It transports these nutrients to each of the cells in the body. Carbon dioxide and other waste products, such as urea, are also found in plasma. In addition to these substances, plasma also contains vitamins, minerals, and a group of chemicals called hormones that regulate many different body functions. Finally, the plasma contains antibodies. Antibodies are a type of plasma protein that is formed by special cells in the body.

The contents of blood are summarized in Table 31-1.

TABLE 31-1   THE CONTENTS OF BLOOD

Formed elements	Plasma	
Erythrocytes (R.B.C.)	Water	Vitamins
Leukocytes (W.B.C.)	Proteins	Minerals
Platelets	Glucose	Hormones
	Breakdown products of fats	
	Carbon dioxide	
	Other waste products	

Blood Types and Transfusions

Blood cells have particular kinds of proteins on their surfaces called antigens. As you learned in Chapter 12, antigens are substances that stimulate the body to produce antibodies. There are many different kinds of antigens on red blood cells. However, we will consider only the antigens *A* and *B*. Your blood type is determined by these antigens. Study Table 31-2 and find out which antigens and antibodies are present in each blood type. For example, in blood type *A*, antigen *A* and antibody *B* are present. In blood type *B* antigen *B* and antibody *A* are present. Normally, blood does not contain antibodies that match any of the antigens that are present.

CLUMPING   It was in 1900 that Karl Landsteiner discovered both the antigens on red blood cells and the antibodies in plasma. When matching antigens and antibodies are present, they combine and the

TABLE 31-2

Blood types and the antigens and antibodies they contain.

Blood Type	Antigens	Antibodies
A	A	anti-B
B	B	anti-A
O	none	anti-A, anti-B
AB	A,B	none

red cells clump together. The cells rupture and release hemoglobin. The hemoglobin can block the blood vessels of the kidneys and cause them to stop functioning. This condition can be fatal. However, Landsteiner was able to show that clumping could be prevented. Transfusing blood that contains only the antigens already present in the patient's blood prevents clumping. For example, a person with type *A* blood should not receive a transfusion of type *B* blood. If this does occur, the anti-*B* antibodies in the type *A* blood would react with the antigens in the donor's blood.

CROSS MATCHING Many early attempts at transfusions were unsuccessful. However, today the technician in a laboratory can select blood that is safe for the patient by cross matching. (See Figure 31-2.) In cross matching, a sample of a patient's blood cells is mixed with a sample of a donor's plasma. Also, a sample of the donor's cells is mixed with a sample of the patient's plasma. If clumping does not occur in either case, the blood is said to be cross matched. It is then safe to transfuse the donor blood into the patient.

BLOOD TYPES *O* AND *AB* Sometimes people with type *O* blood are called *universal donors*. Their red blood cells contain neither antigen *A* nor *B*. However, the plasma of type *O* blood does contain both anti-*A* and anti-*B* antibodies. People with type *AB* blood are sometimes called *universal recipients*. Their plasma contains neither anti-*A* nor anti-*B* antibodies. However, both antigens *A* and *B* are present. If either type *O* or type *AB* blood is cross matched with blood of another type, some clumping is likely to occur. Therefore, the terms universal donor and universal recipient are no longer used.

Rh ANTIGENS One other group of antigens that you are familiar with is the Rh group. These antigens may or may not be present on red blood cells in human blood. These antigens are called Rh because they were first found in Rhesus monkeys. The presence of an Rh antigen is independent of the presence of the *A* or *B* antigen. The special problem arising when a mother with Rh negative blood is carrying a baby with Rh positive blood was discussed in Chapter 12.

How Does Blood Clot?

Imagine what would happen if whenever you cut yourself, blood continued to leave your body without stopping. Normally, this does not happen. There are chemical and physical changes that cause blood to clot. Blood clotting is an example of a mechanism that helps the body to maintain homeostasis by preventing excessive blood loss. Blood clotting is not caused by the blood being exposed to air. Nor because it stops flowing, as some people think. Let us see how it does happen.

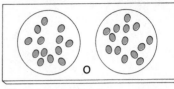

TYPE A BLOOD (contains anti-B antibodies)   TYPE B BLOOD (contains anti-A antibodies)

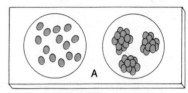

Type O Blood contains no antigens

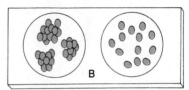

Type A Blood contains A antigens

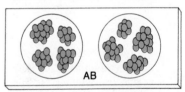

Type B Blood contains B antigens

Type AB Blood contains both A and B antigens

31-2. The effects of cross-matching on red blood cells.

Students may wonder what keeps blood from clotting as it circulates. The major factor that prevents clotting is that the components of the clotting mechanism circulate in their inactive forms. Prothrombin is inactive until it is converted to thrombin. Fibrinogen is inactive until it is converted to fibrin.

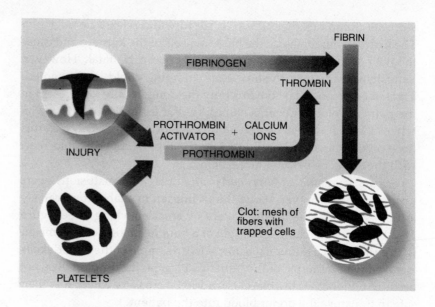

FIBRIN

FIBRINOGEN

THROMBIN

PROTHROMBIN
ACTIVATOR + CALCIUM
IONS

PROTHROMBIN

INJURY

Clot: mesh of
fibers with
trapped cells

PLATELETS

31-3. *The events that lead to blood clotting.*

Circulating in the blood are *prothrombin* (prō *thräm* bən), *calcium ions*, and *fibrinogen* (fī *brin* ə jen). When a blood vessel is cut, the first of the series of changes occurs immediately. Either the injured blood vessel or the platelets release a chemical called prothrombin activator. This activator, along with calcium ions, causes prothrombin to be changed into its active form, thrombin. Thrombin acts as an enzyme and causes fibrinogen to be changed to fibrin. Fibrin is an insoluble fibrous protein that forms a mesh across the cut in a blood vessel. Finally, blood cells become trapped in the mesh of fibers. At this point, the opening in the blood vessels is plugged. Eventually the entire wound is closed. As the fibrin and blood cells dry, they form a scab. The series of steps in blood clotting is summarized in Figure 31-3.

Answers to Questions for Section 1.

A. 1. Leukocytes are larger and fewer in number than erythrocytes. They fight infections while erythrocytes carry oxygen.

2. The fluid portion of the blood. It contains nutrients, wastes, gases, hormones, antibodies and many other substances.

3. Platelets are cell fragments in the blood that are necessary for the clotting of blood.

B. 4. Antigens are proteins that determine the blood type. Antibodies react with the antigens if a person receives blood of the wrong type.

5. Matching antigens and antibodies come together, and red blood cells clump.

C. 6. Blood clotting begins with the activation of prothrombin; prothrombin is converted to thrombin; thrombin causes fibrinogen to be converted to fibrin. Fibrin makes the clot. It stops the loss of blood.

QUESTIONS FOR SECTION 1

1. How do leukocytes differ from erythrocytes?
2. What is plasma and what does it contain?
3. What is the function of platelets?
4. How are antigens and antibodies related to blood types?
5. What happens when different types of blood are mixed?
6. What are the steps in the blood clotting process, and what does clotting accomplish?

CHAPTER INVESTIGATION

A. Describe what you see in the graph. What do the two lines represent? What variable is plotted on the horizontal axis? What variables are plotted on the vertical axis?

B. What can you determine about the effects of exercise from the graph? Can you explain why the line at the top of the graph changes while the one at the bottom of the graph stays about the same?

C. What other changes do you think might occur during exercise? Explain how you would observe these changes.

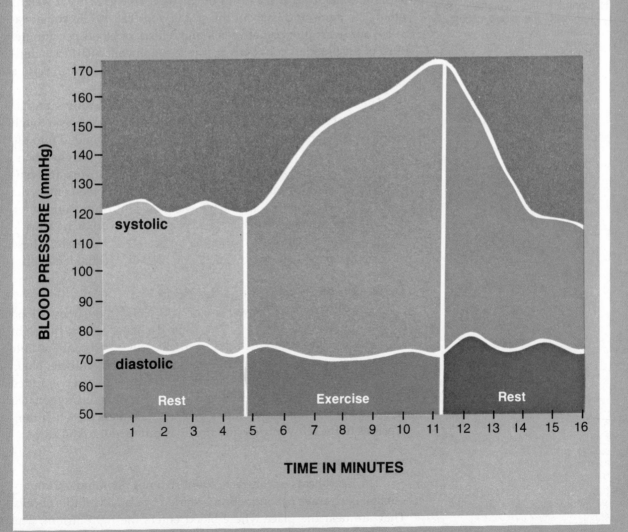

2 CIRCULATION

OBJECTIVES FOR SECTION 2

D. Describe the circulation of blood through the heart. Interpret the roles of *systole*, *diastole*, and the *pacemaker*.

E. Compare the structure and function of *arteries*, *veins*, and *capillaries*.

F. Distinguish among the following circulatory pathways: *pulmonary*, *systemic*, *coronary* and *portal*.

G. Interpret the role of blood pressure in circulation.

H. Contrast the lymphatic system with the blood circulatory system.

Circulation *is the continuous passage of blood through the blood vessels from one region of the body to another.* Together the blood vessels form a closed network of tubes called the circulatory system. The heart is the pump that keeps the blood moving through the circulatory system. In humans, the heart consists of two separate side-by-side pumps. One pump pushes blood through the lungs. The other pushes blood through all of the other organs of the body. The general plan of the circulatory system is shown in Figure 31-4.

The Heart

THE HEART AS A PUMP   The heart is a thick-walled muscular organ with four chambers and a series of valves. (See Fig. 31-5.) It weighs about 300 grams and is about the size of your fist. While you are at rest, your heart pumps between 4 and 5 liters of blood per minute. Most of the blood in your body passes through your heart each minute. The work done by the heart in a lifetime is enough to raise a weight of ten tons to a height of ten miles.

The heart is located between the lungs and beneath the breastbone, almost in the middle of the body. It is surrounded by a tough membrane, the pericardium (per ə *kär* dē əm). It is divided into the left and right sides by a central septum. Each side has two chambers, an upper *atrium* and a lower *ventricle*. Between each atrium and ventricle is a valve. Each valve closes automatically after blood enters the ventricle. Thus, this prevents backflow of blood into the atrium when the ventricle contracts. A valve is also present between each ventricle and the blood vessel that carries blood from the ventricle. These valves prevent blood from flowing back into the heart after it has left.

Circulation of Blood Through the Heart

Let us follow the pathway of a drop of blood in the body. Blood from all of the cells of the body except the lungs enters the right atrium. It then passes to the right ventricle. This blood contains little oxygen. It is said to be deoxygenated. From the right ventricle, blood is pumped into the pulmonary artery. In the lungs, oxygen is added to the blood. The blood is now said to be oxygenated. Oxygenated blood passes through the pulmonary veins, and enters the left atrium. It passes to the left ventricle and finally is pumped into the aorta.

The Heartbeat

The heart beats or contracts about 70 times per minute throughout life. Each wave of contraction is started by a small bundle of cells. They are near the place where blood enters the right atrium. This

Many patients with heart disease have a malfunction of the pacemaker. They suffer from heart arrhythmias. The heart may beat too fast, too slow, or the atria and ventricles may not contract in the proper sequence. The electrocardiogram is useful in determining the nature of the malfunction.

31-4 THE HUMAN CIRCULATORY SYSTEM

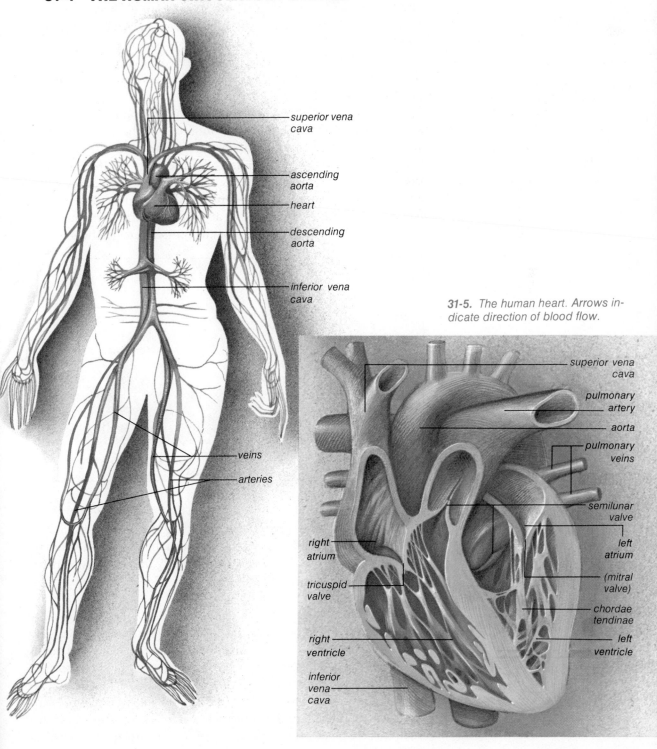

superior vena cava

ascending aorta

heart

descending aorta

inferior vena cava

veins

arteries

31-5. *The human heart. Arrows indicate direction of blood flow.*

superior vena cava

pulmonary artery

aorta

pulmonary veins

semilunar valve

left atrium

(mitral valve)

chordae tendinae

left ventricle

right atrium

tricuspid valve

right ventricle

inferior vena cava

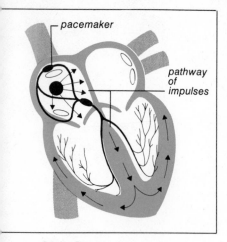

31-6. Pacemaker in the human heart.

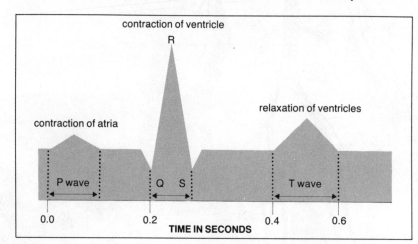

31-7. An electrocardiogram shows how the heart is functioning. Changes in this pattern help diagnose heart disease.

bundle of cells is the pacemaker of the heart. The pacemaker cells stimulate the atria to contract. They also send impulses along the septum toward the ventricles. These impulses cause the ventricles to contract shortly after the atria have contracted. (See Fig. 31-6.) In some kinds of heart disease, the heartbeat is irregular. This condition can be corrected by placing an electronic pacemaker in the patient's body.

By listening to the sounds of the heart through a stethoscope, you can hear a regularly repeated "lubb-dup." The "lubb" is heard when the ventricles contract and the valve between the atria and ventricles close. It marks the beginning of *systole* (sis tə lē). It is the part of the heart cycle in which blood is pumped into the pulmonary artery and into the aorta. You can feel a pulse in your wrist. Also, you can feel a pulse along your temples or at the cartoid artery in your neck. The pulse in these areas is caused by the pressure created by the heart during systole. The "dup" is heard when the valves between the ventricles and the arteries close. It marks the beginning of *diastole* (dī as tə lē). It is the part of the heart cycle in which the heart relaxes and refills. An electronic device can be used to study the heartbeats. Its tracing is called an electrocardiogram or ECG. (See Fig. 31-7.)

Blood Vessels

ARTERIES Blood vessels can be placed in one of three categories. These are based on the structure of the walls of the vessel and on the direction of flow of blood through it. *Arteries* carry blood away from the heart. (See Fig. 31-8.) Their walls contain smooth muscle and are elastic. They are able to stretch as they receive blood under pressure from the contraction of the ventricles. Arteries form many branches as they carry blood toward the many different parts of the body. The

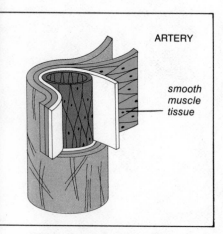

31-8. Structure of an artery.

smaller branches are called *arterioles. These too branch many times within the tissues and finally become capillaries.*

CAPILLARIES   *Capillaries* are very small blood vessels. They are wide enough for blood cells to pass through them only in single file. (See Fig. 31-9.) The walls of the capillaries are only one cell thick. It is through the capillaries that all of the substances transported by the blood are exchanged with the body cells. The capillaries allow nutrients and wastes to enter and leave the cells through the blood vessels. In addition to blood vessels, the human body has a system of lymph vessels. These contain clear fluid called *lymph.* The lymph surrounds and bathes the cells.

VEINS   *Veins* carry blood toward the heart. The walls of veins are slightly thinner and less elastic than the walls of arteries. (See Fig. 31-10.) Blood from the capillaries enters *venules*, or small veins. Venules join together to form larger veins. Veins have valves inside

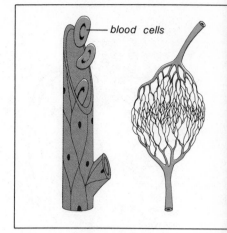

31-9. *Structure of a capillary.*

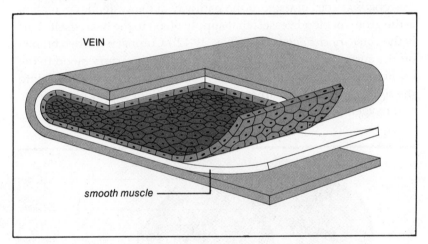
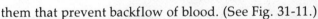

31-10. *Structure of a vein.*

them that prevent backflow of blood. (See Fig. 31-11.)

Blood pressure from the action of the heart is high in the arteries. However, it drops as the blood passes through the arterioles, capillaries, venules, and veins. The return of blood to the heart must be helped by means other than the heartbeat alone. This is especially true for returning blood from the legs while you are standing. The contraction of muscles in the legs during movement helps push blood back toward the heart. The one way action is aided by the valves in the veins that prevent back flow.

Circulation of Blood Through Blood Vessels

PULMONARY CIRCULATION   In review, as blood flows through the right ventricle into the pulmonary artery to the lungs, it picks up oxygen. This oxygenated blood then returns to the left atrium of the

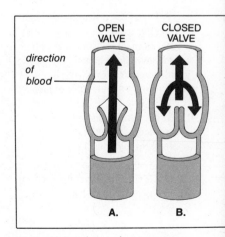

31-11. *Valves in a vein.*

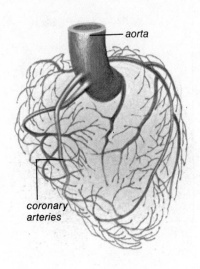

— aorta

coronary
arteries

31-12. Coronary circulation.

In addition to heartbeat and blood pressure, cardiologists (physicians who treat heart disease) are interested in cardiac output. Cardiac output is the amount of blood in milliliters that leaves the heart per minute. It is the product of volume of blood pumped per heartbeat times the number of beats per minute. The normal cardiac output of an adult at rest is about 5000 milliliters, but the cardiac output of an athlete during maximum exertion can be 6 or 7 times this amount.

Answers to Questions for Section 2.

10. The portal system carries blood from the capillaries of the digestive tract to the capillaries of the liver. The blood brain barrier is the special construction of capillaries in the brain that prevents entry of many substances.

G. **11.** The force produced by the contraction of the heart that pushes blood through the blood vessels.

H. *12. Lymph circulation depends on muscle contractions and movements because there is no lymph heart.

31-13. Hepatic portal system.

heart by way of the pulmonary vein. This pathway is called the *pulmonary circulation*. It is through the pulmonary circulation that blood gets rid of carbon dioxide and picks up a new supply of oxygen.

SYSTEMIC CIRCULATION   Oxygenated blood leaving the left ventricle of the heart enters the *systemic circulation*. This pathway supplies blood to all parts of the body except the lungs. The aorta, branching off from the left ventricle, is the main artery of the systemic circulation. Branches from the aorta carry blood through arteries and arterioles. This blood containing oxygen and nutrients is transported to the head, arms, legs, digestive tract, kidneys, and the heart. Deoxygenated blood then returns to the right atrium of the heart through venules and veins.

Cells of the body can store only small amounts of oxygen. Most cells will die quickly if deprived of oxygen for only a short time. Thus, the blood supplies the cells with a continuous supply of oxygen.

CORONARY CIRCULATION   One pathway of the systemic circulation is the group of blood vessels that supply blood to the heart itself. This is the *coronary circulation*. (See Fig. 31-12.) Coronary arteries branch off the aorta very near the heart. In doing so, they carry blood to the capillaries within the muscle of the heart. Veins carry blood back into the right atrium. The heart must have a constant supply of nutrients and oxygen in order to contract.

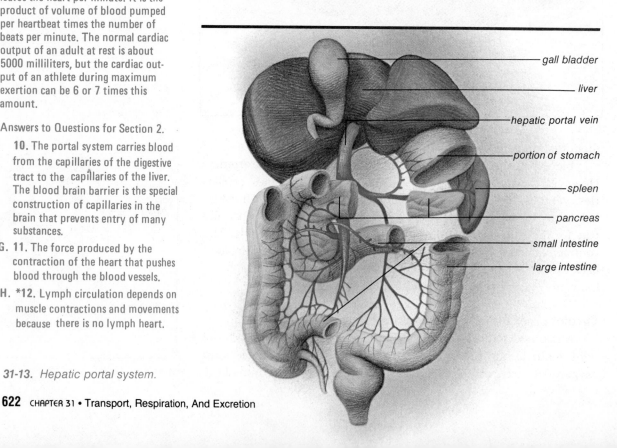

— gall bladder

— liver

— hepatic portal vein

— portion of stomach

— spleen

— pancreas

— small intestine

— large intestine

If a branch of one of the coronary arteries becomes blocked by a blood clot, a heart attack occurs. The heart muscle is temporarily deprived blood and severe pain results. The pain of a heart attack is felt in the left shoulder. The pain may move down the left arm. Sudden death may occur if a large area of the heart is deprived of its blood supply.

Sometimes the artery is not completely blocked. It may be just narrowed by deposits of fats on the inner walls. This hardening of the artery interferes with the proper supply of both oxygen and nourishment to the heart muscle.

HEPATIC PORTAL SYSTEM In most parts of the body, blood passes through only one set of capillaries before it is returned to the heart. However, blood going to the small intestine passes through capillaries and leaves by the *hepatic portal vein.* (See Fig. 31-13.) *A* **portal system** *is a blood vessel that carries blood from one set of capillaries to another.* This vein carries blood to the liver where it passes through another set of capillaries. In this manner, blood entering the liver contains the absorbed foods from the digestive tract. In addition, this blood has a high oxygen level. It is needed for the many metabolic reactions that occur in liver cells. Finally, blood leaves the liver by way of the hepatic vein. It is then carried by the inferior vena cava back to the heart.

31-14a. *Using a sphygmomanometer to measure blood pressure.*

Blood Pressure

HOW TO MEASURE BLOOD PRESSURE **Blood Pressure** *is the amount of "push" that is forcing blood through the blood vessels.* It is measured with a *sphygmomanometer* (sfig mō mə *nom* ə tər). To measure human blood pressure, a cuff containing a rubber bag and an attached rubber bulb is wrapped around the upper arm. (See Fig. 31-14.) The bag is inflated to a pressure of about 200 mm of mercury. This is sufficient pressure to close the arteries inside the arm. Then the pressure in the cuff is gradually released. Blood begins to flow through the arteries when the pressure in the cuff is equal to the pressure in the artery. The sphygmomanometer measures the pressure in the cuff. By using a stethoscope and listening to the blood flowing through the artery, we can determine the blood pressure.

HIGH AND LOW PRESSURE The average pressures for a normal, young adult are expressed as 120 over 80. The 120 is the *systolic pressure*. It is created when the ventricles contract and can support a column of mercury 120 mm tall. The 80 is the *diastolic pressure*. It results from the ventricles relaxing. It will support a column of mercury 80 mm tall. *Hypertension* or high blood pressure is a serious problem for many people. Blood pressure may be increased when the elasticity of the walls of the arteries is reduced. This is often due to deposits of fats

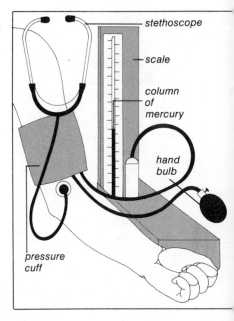

31-14b. *Parts of the sphygmomanometer.*

within the arteries. When the blood pressure is higher than normal it means that the heart is working harder to push the blood through the blood vessels.

Lymphatic System

LYMPH VESSELS   The lymphatic system consists of lymph vessels. (See Fig. 31-15.) They begin as blind-ended, thin-walled vessels called lymph capillaries. These lymph capillaries are located among the cells of all tissues. These capillaries join to form larger lymph vessels. The larger vessels follow the same pathways as the arteries and veins. Finally, the lymph vessels empty into the subclavian veins. (See Fig. 31-15.) The main function of the lymphatic system is to return to the blood stream the fluid that has been filtered out of the blood capillaries. Fluid is moved through these vessels mostly by the contraction of nearby muscles. The larger lymph vessels contain valves similar to those in veins.

LYMPH NODES   At the junctions of lymph vessels are groups of cells called lymph nodes. They produce one kind of white blood cell, the lymphocyte. Lymphocytes filter bacteria and other particles out of the lymph. Thus, the lymph nodes help to prevent infections from reaching the blood stream. Sometimes the lymph nodes become infected by the bacteria they have trapped. You have probably felt the swollen nodes in your neck when you have a sore throat. The lymph nodes in the lungs of heavy smokers are filled with particles of smoke and become dark gray or black. These particles may eventually prevent the lymph nodes from being able to fight infection.

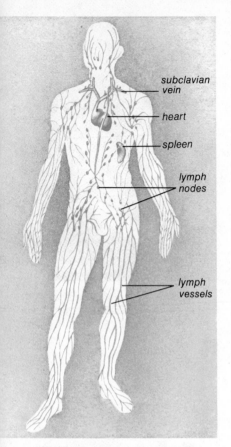

subclavian vein

heart

spleen

lymph nodes

lymph vessels

31-15. *The human lymphatic system.*

Answers to Questions for Section 2.

D. 1. Right atrium, right ventricle, pulmonary circulation, left atrium, left ventricle.

2. To prevent the backflow of blood when the chambers of the heart contract.

3. Initiates the contractions of the heart. Because it does this at a regular rate it maintains a regular heartbeat.

4. Systole is the period during which the chambers of the heart are contracted and diastole is the period during which the chambers are relaxed.

E. 5. Arteries have thicker and more elastic walls and lack valves.

6. They allow for the exchange of materials between the blood and the cells.

QUESTIONS FOR SECTION 2

1. Trace the path of blood through the heart.
2. What is the function of the valves in the heart?
3. What does the pacemaker do?
4. What is the difference between systole and diastole?
5. How do arteries differ from veins?
6. Why might the capillaries be considered the most important blood vessels?
7. Study the back of your hand and find a way to demonstrate that veins have valves in them.
8. What is the function of the systemic circulation? Of pulmonary circulation?
9. What happens to the coronary circulation in a heart attack?
10. Define *portal system*.
11. What is blood pressure?
12. How is the circulation of lymph different from the circulation of blood?

F. 8. The systemic circulation carries blood to the head, trunk, and limbs; the pulmonary circulation carries it to and from the respiratory portion of the lungs.

9. One of the coronary arteries becomes blocked, shutting off the blood supply to part of the heart muscle. (See pages 622 for more answers.)

3 RESPIRATION

The Respiratory System

The study of respiration can be separated into three areas: external respiration, internal respiration, and breathing. We will examine each of these areas in some detail.

The respiratory system includes the lungs and the tubes through which air is moved in and out. (See Fig. 31-16.) Air enters the nostrils and passes through the nasal passages. It is in these passages where hairs trap dust and other debris. When too much mucus is secreted in this area, the nose becomes "stopped up." Then we have the symptoms of a cold. As the air moves along these passages, it is moistened and warmed. It then passes through the pharynx, a common passage for food and air, and enters the trachea. The epiglottis that prevents food from entering the airway allows air to pass through except during swallowing. The upper end of the trachea is enlarged and covered

OBJECTIVES FOR SECTION 3

I. Distinguish among external respiration, internal respiration, and breathing.

J. Describe the pathway of air from the atmosphere to the alveoli.

K. Contrast the exchange of gases in the lungs and in other tissues.

L. Describe what happens during breathing. Explain how it is controlled.

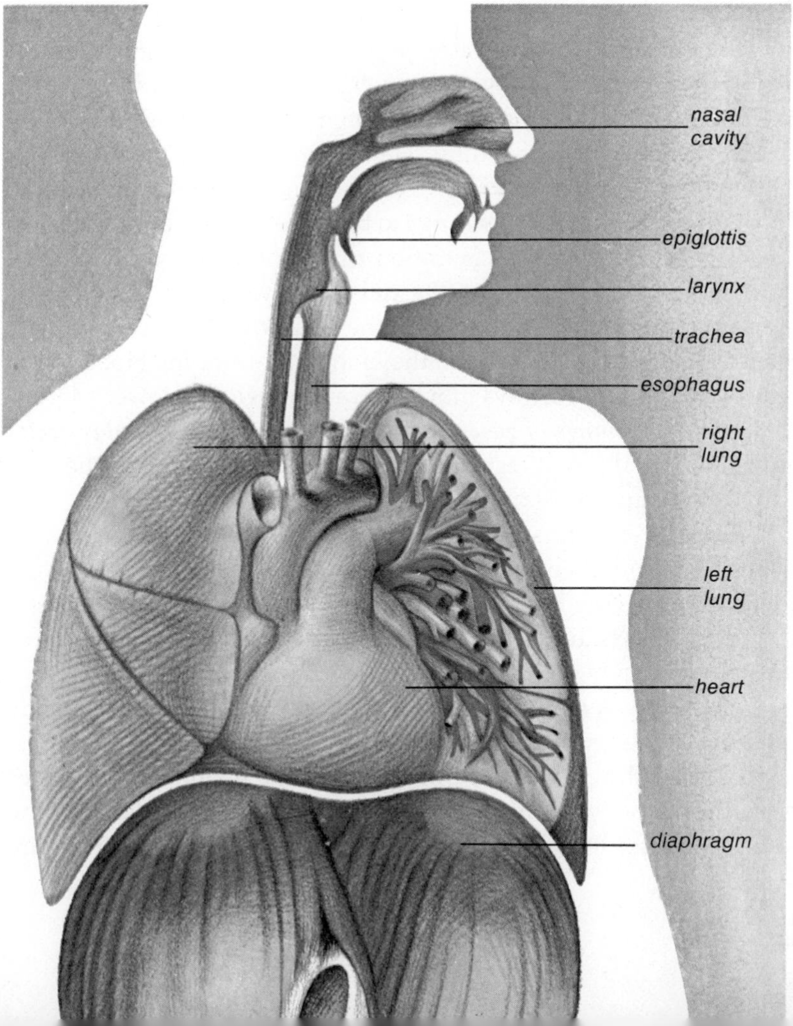

nasal cavity
epiglottis
larynx
trachea
esophagus
right lung
left lung
heart
diaphragm

31-16. The human respiratory system.

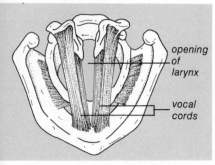

31-17. Cross section of the larynx.

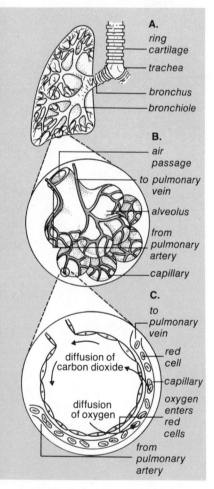

A.
ring cartilage
trachea
bronchus
bronchiole

B.
air passage
to pulmonary vein
alveolus
from pulmonary artery
capillary

C.
to pulmonary vein
red cell
capillary
oxygen enters red cells
from pulmonary artery
diffusion of carbon dioxide
diffusion of oxygen

31-18. A. Structures through which air passes to reach the alveoli. B. Enlarged view of alveoli and blood vessels. C. Cross section of one alveolus.

by plates of cartilage to form the larynx or voice box. It can be evident as the Adam's apple. Thin flaps of tissue, the vocal cords, extend across the larynx. (See Fig. 31-17.) These cords vibrate as air passes over them and sounds are produced. Muscles adjust the tension on the cords to produce different sounds.

TRACHEA   Below the larynx, the trachea has rings of cartilage in its walls. They keep the passageway open. The trachea is lined with cilia, hair-like projections that beat rhythmically. The trachea also has cells that secrete mucus. The cilia continuously move the mucus upward toward the pharynx. Thus, this process helps keep dust and debris from entering the lungs. Smoking causes destruction of the cilia.

WITHIN THE LUNGS   The trachea branches into two tubes called bronchi (brong kē). One bronchus enters each lung and branches many times. The smaller of these branches are called bronchioles. At the ends of the bronchioles are the alveoli (al vē ə lī). Alveoli are small thin-walled sacs that are surrounded by capillaries.

Gas Exchange

The exchange of gases between the air and the blood is **external respiration.** In this process, the alveoli are filled with air from the atmosphere. The blood that flows through the capillaries around the alveoli has been through the systemic circulation. This blood has more carbon dioxide and less oxygen than air in the atmosphere. Throughout the body, from lungs to blood to tissues, oxygen moves from a region of high concentration to one of lower concentration. Oxygen is finally used up in the cells. Likewise, carbon dioxide is present in highest concentration in the cells where it is produced. It moves from the body cells into the blood and from the blood to the lung alveoli. It, too, always moves toward a region of lower concentration. *The exchange of gases between the blood stream and the cells of the body is* **internal respiration.** Gas exchange provides the cells with oxygen and constantly removes carbon dioxide.

These gases diffuse across the moist membranes of the alveoli. They move from their area of high concentration to their area of low concentration. (See Fig. 31-18.) A large quantity of oxygen can enter the blood. This is due to the fact that most of it attaches to the iron in the hemoglobin of the red blood cells.

When the oxygenated blood reaches the capillaries of the body cells, the oxygen concentration in the blood is higher than in the cells. At this point the oxygen separates from the hemoglobin. It diffuses from the blood into the fluid surrounding the cells. Finally, the oxygen diffuses into the body cells. This process is shown in Figure 31-19.

Factors That Affect Gas Exchange

SMOKE AND THE LUNGS   The inhaling of smoke from tobacco or marijuana leaves a deposit of substances inside the bronchioles and alveoli of the lungs. These substances interfere with the exchange of gases across the thin alveolar membranes.

WATER PRESSURE   When SCUBA divers reach depths greater than about 10 meters the pressure of the water exceeds the atmospheric pressure of the air. In such a situation large quantities of oxygen and nitrogen diffuse into the blood. The longer the diver stays in deep water, the more gases diffuse into the tissues. The oxygen is used by the tissues. The nitrogen is not. Instead it accumulates into the blood. As the diver returns to the surface, the pressure decreases. If the return to the surface is too rapid, nitrogen gas expands and forms bubbles in the cells. This may cause serious damage. To prevent this condition, called the "bends", divers must surface slowly. This time should allow for gases to diffuse slowly from the cells.

LACK OF OXYGEN   In drowning, the alveoli of the lungs become filled with water. In the case of pneumonia, they become filled with tissue fluid. When the lungs are filled with fluid, the oxygen cannot reach the surface of the alveoli. Hence, it cannot diffuse into the blood. Another example is carbon monoxide poisoning. In this case, the carbon monoxide unites with the hemoglobin and prevents it from carrying oxygen. Regardless of whether oxygen fails to enter the blood or fails to be transported to the cells, the cells are deprived of oxygen. Death results.

Breathing — How Does It Occur?

So far we have assumed that air from the atmosphere is present in the lungs. But how does it get there? Air enters the lungs when the pressure inside the lungs is less than atmospheric pressure. **Breathing** *is the movements that cause air to pass in and out of the lungs.* The chest cavity is completely closed off from the outside atmosphere and from all other body cavities. It is bounded on the top and sides by the chest wall, where ribs and muscles are located. It is bounded on the bottom by a thick dome-shaped muscle, the diaphragm.

THE ROLE OF THE DIAPHRAGM IN BREATHING   When you inhale or breathe in, the diaphragm contracts and flattens. Also, some muscles of the chest and ribs contract. The contraction of these muscles increases the volume of the chest cavity. (See Fig. 31-20.) As the volume increases, the pressure decreases. Air from the atmosphere flows into the lungs until the pressure is equal inside and outside the lungs. When you exhale or breathe out, the muscles that were contracted relax, and the pressure increases. This causes the volume to decrease and the air is pushed out of the lungs.

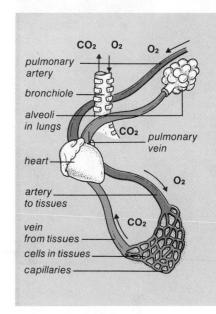

31-19. Gas exchange in the lungs and body tissues.

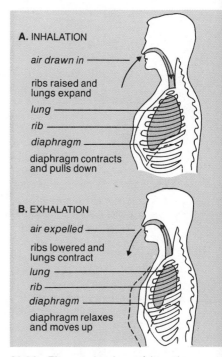

31-20. The mechanism of breathing.

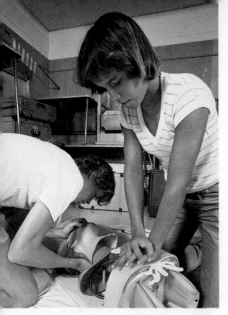

31-21. Find out from your local Red Cross how you can learn to perform CPR.

THE ROLE OF THE BRAIN IN BREATHING   You breathe about 16 to 18 times per minute while at rest. However, when you are active, breathing becomes much more rapid. This process occurs automatically without your having to be aware of it. The breathing rate is under the control of a portion of the brain called the medulla. The medulla can detect changes in the concentration of carbon dioxide in the blood. When the carbon dioxide concentration increases, the brain center sends messages to the breathing muscles, especially the diaphragm. These messages cause the muscles to contract and relax at a faster rate. You can, of course, consciously "hold your breath." It is unlikely that you could ever die from holding your breath. The increasing carbon dioxide concentration will eventually cause unconsciousness. Then the brain center takes over and causes rapid breathing. The carbon dioxide concentration returns to normal. Normal breathing is resumed.

IRRITANTS AND BREATHING   If an irritating gas such as ammonia or acid fumes enter the pharynx and larynx, receptors in these organs are stimulated. The receptors send impulses to the respiratory centers to inhibit breathing. When this happens, you experience the feeling of "catching your breath." This is a temporary and involuntary reaction. Stopping of breathing prevents harmful substances from entering the lungs.

Cardiopulmonary Resuscitation — CPR

Cardiopulmonary resuscitation (kärd ē ō pəl mə ner ē ri sus ə tā shən) is a lifesaving procedure. It keeps the blood circulating and air entering the lungs in a patient whose heartbeat and breathing have stopped. The method involves compressing the chest to force blood out of the heart. This activates the breathing process of the lungs. (See Fig. 31-21.) The technique requires some special training to learn how to do it properly. Many heart attack victims, as well as those affected by other diseases and injuries have been revived by people who know how to perform CPR.

Answers to Questions for Section 3.

I. 1. External respiration occurs in the lungs, internal in the cells; both involve gas exchange.

2. Breathing is the movement that gets air into and out of the lungs; respiration is the exchange of gases.

J. 3. Dust is kept out of the lungs by cilia that beat toward the pharynx and by mucus that traps particles.

4. Oxygen moves from the air in the lungs to the blood. Carbon dioxide moves from the blood to the air in the lungs.

K. 5. In other tissues oxygen moves from the blood to the tissues and carbon dioxide moves from the tissues to the blood.

L. 6. When the diaphragm contracts, a vacuum is produced in the lungs, and new air moves in to fill the vacuum. When the muscle relaxes air flows out of the lungs.

QUESTIONS FOR SECTION 3
1. How is external respiration different from internal respiration?
2. How does breathing differ from respiration?
3. How is dust kept out of the lungs?
4. Describe the movement of oxygen and carbon dioxide in the lungs.
5. How is the movement of oxygen and carbon dioxide different in other tissues?
6. What causes air to enter and leave the lungs?

4 EXCRETION

Excretion *is the process of removing the waste products of metabolism from the body.* We have already considered the removal of materials left over from digestion. These substances never really entered the body. Since they were not absorbed, they only passed through the digestive tract. At this point, we will be concerned with waste products that enter the blood from the cells of the body. One of these wastes, carbon dioxide, is removed from the blood as it passes through the lungs. Other wastes from cellular metabolism include nitrogen wastes and excess water. In addition to these there are excesses of acids, bases, and certain minerals. When cells use proteins, some excess amino groups are released and form urea. Urea is a common nitrogen waste product of the body. Such wastes are toxic if not removed from the cells. Too much acid or base is also harmful to cells. Excessive amounts of these substances must also be removed.

Kidneys

The kidneys are the main organ of excretion. The kidneys and the passages connected to them form the excretory system. (See Fig. 31-22.) The kidneys lie one on each side of the vertebral column in the small of the back. They remove wastes from the blood. The wastes in the form of urine then pass to the ureters and are collected in the urinary bladder. Finally, urine is excreted out of the body through the urethra.

The kidney is a bean-shaped organ about the size of your fist. Inside, it is divided into the cortex and the medulla. The outer cortex consists mostly of nephrons. The medulla consists mostly of collecting ducts. All of the collecting ducts drain into the renal pelvis of the kidney. This funnel-shaped renal pelvis attaches to the ureter.

NEPHRONS — THE FILTERING UNITS OF THE KIDNEYS   Each kidney contains about one million nephrons. (See Fig. 31-23 on page 630.) Each nephron consists of a double-walled hollow sac of cells called Bowman's capsule. This extends into a long coiled tubule. Directly associated with Bowman's capsule is a set of capillaries, the glomerulus (glə mer yə ləs). A second group of capillaries, the peritublar (per ə tōō byə lər) capillaries, surround the tubule of the nephron.

Blood enters the kidney through the renal artery. The artery branches many times to form afferent arterioles. Each of these in turn carries blood to a glomerulus. Then, blood from each glomerulus enters an efferent arteriole. Next it enters the peritubular capillaries. Capillaries from several nephrons join to form venules. These venules finally empty into the renal vein.

OBJECTIVES FOR SECTION 4

M. Describe the structure of the excretory system.
N. Summarize the movement of substances between the blood and the kidney filtrate.
O. Interpret the role of transport, respiration, and excretion in homeostasis.

The human kidney regulates the concentration of many substances in the blood. The tubule of some nephrons has a long u-shaped part, the loop of Henle. Specialized areas of this tube carry out different functions.

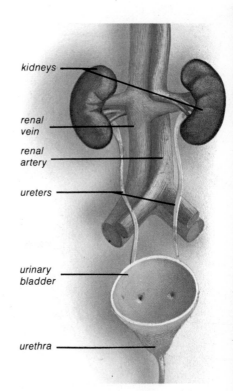

kidneys

renal vein

renal artery

ureters

urinary bladder

urethra

31-22. The human excretory system.

The Filtration Process

Let's see what happens to the blood as it passes through the two sets of capillaries. Many substances are pushed out of the glomerulus into Bowman's capsule. These substances include urea, glucose, amino acids, water, and many other small molecules and ions. This mixture of substances is called the glomerular filtrate. In a normal kidney, blood cells and protein molecules do not leave the capillary. From Bowman's capsule, the filtrate passes into the kidney tubule. Here, glucose, amino acids, and much of the water pass back into the blood. They do this by entering the peritubular capillary. Most of the urea and other wastes along with some water remain in the kidney tubule. These are removed from the body as urine.

FUNCTIONS OF THE KIDNEY The exchange of substances between the glomerular filtrate and the peritubular capillary is a highly selective process. This process regulates the concentration of many substances in the blood. Blood flowing out of the peritubular capillary has been changed three ways: (1) urea and other wastes have been removed, (2) the proper amount of water has been returned to it, and (3) its pH has been adjusted to near neutral. Thus the kidney serves three functions. It removes wastes. It maintains the water balance. It keeps the blood pH within the normal range.

The contents of blood and urine are compared in Table 31-3. The glomerular filtrate is similar to blood plasma except that it does not contain proteins. If all of the substances that enter the filtrate were excreted, excretion would be a wasteful process indeed. However, most useful substances including much of the water in the filtrate are returned to the plasma. Urine contains only those substances the body no longer needs.

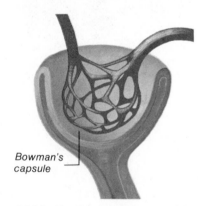

kidney
renal pelvis
renal artery
cortex
medulla
renal vein
ureter

NEPHRON
artery
tubule
peritubular capillaries
vein

Bowman's capsule

31-23. Section from kidney showing a nephron in detail.

TABLE 31-3   *A COMPARISON OF BLOOD AND URINE.*

Substance	Amount in one liter of:	
	Blood	**Urine**
Urea	0.26g	18g
Acids and bases	pH = 7.4	pH = 5.0 to 7.8
Glucose	1.0g	none, except in diseases such as diabetes mellitus
Amino acids	300mg	very small amounts
Proteins	120-160g, many different kinds	none, except when glomeruli are damaged
Blood cells	about 45% of blood volume	none, except when kidney ureter, or bladder is damaged

What Does a Kidney Machine Do?

The kidney machine performs most of the filtering functions for patients whose kidneys are damaged. (See Fig. 31-24.) Blood is removed from an artery and passed through a long thin-walled tube that acts much like a capillary. The tube is immersed in a fluid that contains various substances normally found in the blood. The concentrations of these substances are carefully controlled. Waste materials move out of the blood into the fluid around the tube according to their concentrations. For example, urea diffuses out of the tube because the surrounding fluid contains no urea. However, glucose and amino acids usually do not diffuse out of the tube. They stay in the blood because the fluid contains the same concentrations of these substances as is normally found in blood. Furthermore, excess water, hydrogen ions, and other substances also move out of the blood. Finally, blood is then returned to a vein.

Many patients spend 8 to 12 hours connected to such a machine several times each week. The amount of time required is determined by the seriousness of the patient's kidney disease. The kidney machine does not replace normal kidneys perfectly. Its use does prolong the life of the patient, however.

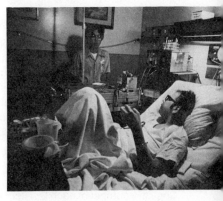

31-24. *The kidney machine filters blood and returns it to the patient's body.*

Answers to Questions for Section 4.

M. **1.** The nephron is the functional unit of the kidney.

N. **2.** The kidney removes wastes, adjusts the concentration of substances in the blood, and maintains acid-base balance.

3. Urine contains no blood cells or protein molecules and should not contain nutrients. It contains all of the chemical substances not needed to maintain the blood concentrations of these substances and also contains nitrogen wastes.

O. ***4.** Answers will vary. Any process that helps to maintain nearly constant internal conditions is acceptable.

QUESTIONS FOR SECTION 4

1. What is a nephron?
2. What are the three functions performed by the kidney?
3. How does urine differ from blood?
4. Make a list of at least ten examples of homeostasis from this chapter.

CHAPTER REVIEW

In this chapter again we have seen that the *structure and function* of organs are closely related. Together, the blood, heart, and blood vessels *transport* materials to and from all of the cells in the body. The organs of the respiratory system provide for the *exchange of gases* between the blood and the atmosphere. The kidney removes wastes and regulates fluid and pH balance.

Respiration, transport, and excretion all contribute to maintaining homeostasis. Breathing is regulated to maintain a constant supply of oxygen and to keep the carbon dioxide level low. The exchange of materials in the kidney keeps the contents of the blood within a normal range. The transport system is regulated to pump blood

faster and in greater volume during exercise. These are only a few examples of how the systems we have studied help to maintain *homeostasis*.

Using the Concepts

1. Suppose you are working in a laboratory and you determine that a patient has an unusually large number of leukocytes. What might be the cause?
2. What are the effects of tobacco and other smoke on the lungs? (Do some reading beyond your text.)
3. What would be the best way to deal with a child that held its breath to get what it wanted? Why?

21. platelets → chromoplastin; prothrombin → thrombin; fibrinogen → fibrin
23. nasal cavity, pharynx, larynx, trachea, **VOCABULARY REVIEW**
    bronchi, bronchioles, alveoli

1 leukocyte   **2** pericardium   pacemaker   **4** cortex
cross matching   systole   arteriole   glomerulus
lymph   pulmonary circulation   systemic circulation   medulla
platelet   diastole   blood pressure   Bowman's capsule
plasma   venule   **3** external respiration   glomerular filtrate
erythrocyte   coronary circulation   internal respiration   urethra
transfusion   lymph vessels

CHAPTER 31 TEST

Copy the number of each test item and place your answer to the right.

PART 1 Multiple Choice: Select the letter of the phrase that best completes each of the following.

a 1. The formed elements of the blood that carry oxygen are **a.** erythrocytes **b.** leukocytes **c.** platelets **d.** plasma.

b 2. The formed elements of blood that fight infections are **a.** erythrocytes **b.** leukocytes **c.** platelets **d.** plasma.

d 3. Nutrients, wastes, gases, hormones, and antibodies are found in **a.** erythrocytes **b.** leukocytes **c.** platelets **d.** plasma.

b 4. A person with type A blood cannot receive a transfusion of type B blood because cell clumping will be caused by **a.** A antigen **b.** B antigen **c.** O antigen **d.** none of the above.

d 5. The heart pacemaker **a.** stimulates atria to contract **b.** sends impulses to ventricles **c.** causes ventricles to contract after atria **d.** all of the above.

c 6. The kind of blood vessel through which materials go to and from the cells is **a.** artery **b.** vein **c.** capillary **d.** all of the above.

c 7. The greater amount of blood pumped during exercise than at rest is called cardiac **a.** input **b.** output **c.** reserve **d.** arrest.

a 8. Returning fluid from around the cells to the blood is the main function of the **a.** lymphatic system **b.** kidneys **c.** capillaries **d.** all of the above.

d 9. Gas exchange in the lungs **a.** provides oxygen **b.** removes carbon dioxide **c.** removes nitrogen wastes **d.** both a and b.

b 10. The process of removing waste products of metabolism is called ___(I)___ and is carried out by ___(II)___ **a.** I-secretion II-kidney **b.** I-excretion II-kidney **c.** I-secretion II-lungs **d.** I-excretion II-lungs.

PART 2 Matching: Match the letter of the term in Column I with its description in Column II.

COLUMN I   Answer
a. pulmonary circulation 22. vena caval → rt. atrium →
b. coronary circulation   rt. ventricle →
c. systemic circulation   pulmonary arteries → lungs →
d. hepatic portal system   pulmonary veins → l. atrium →
e. lymphatic system   l. ventricle → aorta
f. diaphragm
g. CPR
h. systolic pressure
i. nephron
j. urine

COLUMN II
e 11. Returns fluid from cells to blood
a 12. Carries blood through lungs
d 13. Carries nutrients to liver
b 14. Carries blood to heart muscle itself
c 15. Carries blood to head, trunk, and limbs
j 16. Fluid containing metabolic wastes
f 17. Main muscle of breathing
i 18. Functional unit of kidney
h 19. Blood pressure when ventricles contract
g 20. Method of maintaining circulation of oxygenated blood

PART 3 Completion: Complete the following.
21. List the steps in the blood clotting process in order ____.
22. Trace the pathway of blood through the heart ____.
23. To get to the capillaries of the lungs air passes from the nostrils through ____.
24. Before it leaves the body, urine formed in the kidneys passes through _ureters, urinary bladder, urethra_
25. The circulatory system helps to maintain homeostasis by ____. _keeping cells supplied with food and oxygen._

CHAPTER 32

SENSORY PERCEPTION AND NERVOUS CONTROL

In our study of cells we learned that cells can respond to changes in their environment. These changes are called stimuli. Certain cells in the sense organs are particularly able to respond to stimuli. They convert these stimuli to messages called nerve impulses. The nervous system transmits these impulses throughout the body. You are already familiar with some of the basic parts of the brain of vertebrates. Furthermore, you are aware of some of the ways they detect stimuli from their environment. In this chapter we will consider the sense organs and nervous system of humans in some detail.

The structures and functions of the sensory receptors and nervous system are closely related. As these systems receive stimuli, interpret them, and transmit impulses, they enable us to respond to changes in our environment. They help our bodies to maintain homeostasis.

In this chapter you will discover:
- How your body receives, interprets, and reacts to stimuli
- Why you cannot see color at night
- What eyeglasses do
- How loud noises can damage your hearing
- How drugs can affect your nervous system
- What makes you go to sleep and wake up
- How some theories explain learning and memory

HANDS READING BRAILLE

1 HOW OUR SENSE ORGANS TELL US THINGS

Students may have experienced the phenomenon of paradoxical cold. It occurs when one puts a toe in very hot water and experiences the sensation of cold. The sensation is due to the fact that cold receptors are sensitive to extremes of temperature both hot and cold.

Properties of Receptors

Even though different sense organs respond to different kinds of stimuli, they all have some basic properties in common. All sense organs are transducers (trans *dyü* sərs). *A transducer changes a physical or chemical stimulus into another form, in this case, a nerve impulse.* Another property of sense organs is that they respond to a particular kind of stimulus. Furthermore, the sense organs must receive a strong enough stimulus to cause them to respond. They must all create the same kind of nerve impulse. Let's look at these properties in more detail.

SKIN RECEPTORS   Your skin, like that of other mammals, contains many kinds of sensory receptors. If you put your hand in cold water the cold receptors will be stimulated. They transduce the physical stimulus of coldness into a nerve impulse. The other receptors, such as those for pressure and touch, do not usually respond to coldness. However, if you leave your hand in cold water long enough the pain receptors will also be stimulated. If the water is very near the same temperature as your skin, the cold receptors will not receive a strong enough stimulus to respond. The response of any receptor creates a nerve impulse. The nerve impulse is the same regardless of the stimulus. The cold receptor and the pain receptor create the same kind of nerve impulse. But they create it in a different nerve fiber. It is only when the nerve impulse arrives in the brain that you know whether you have experienced cold or pain. The brain recognizes which nerve fiber brought the message. It interprets an impulse in a fiber from a cold receptor as cold. Likewise, the brain interprets an impulse in a fiber from a pain receptor as pain.

PROPRIOCEPTORS   Let's now look at these characteristics in another kind of receptor, a *proprioceptor* (prō prē ō *sep* tər). Proprioceptors are located in the muscles and joints of your body. They are also located at the points where muscles attach to bones by tendons. They transduce the physical stimulus of muscle stretching or joint movement into a nerve impulse. When the nerve impulse arrives in the brain, you become aware of which muscle is being stretched or which joint is being moved. Many such impulses are arriving in your brain all the time. Your brain puts together all of this information. As a result of this action, you are able to know the position of your head, arms, legs, and other body parts. You also know when there is a change in the position of any part of your body. This sense helps you to control your movements. It lets you know how far you have moved and in what direction.

How Our Eyes Work

THE OUTER EYE   The human eye responds to light stimuli. (See Fig. 32-1.) It is protected on the surface by eyelids. If an object or even an air current touches the eyelashes, it causes the eyelids to close. This is the blink reflex. It occurs without your having any control over it. This reflex helps to protect the eye from injury. Furthermore, tears from a tear gland keep the surface of the eye moist. The fluid drains into the nose. That is why your nose runs when you cry. Each eye is held in a bony socket or orbit by six small muscles. These muscles control the movement of the eyes. We can look straight ahead, up, down, or to the side. In addition, these muscles cause both eyes to move together. *Strabismus* (strə *biz* məs), or cross-eye, occurs when one eye does not move with the other in a coordinated way.

THE STRUCTURE OF THE EYEBALL   The structure of the eyeball is shown in Figure 32-2. The front surface of the eye is the *cornea*. Behind the cornea is a fluid-filled chamber, the anterior cavity. The watery fluid it contains is called *aqueous* (ā kwē əs) *humor*. In this chamber is the *iris*, a donut-shaped structure that gives the eye its color. The hole in the center of the iris is the *pupil*. The iris can change shape and cause the pupil to get larger or smaller. This movement regulates the amount of light that enters the eye.

Sometimes a duct that drains the excess aqueous humor from the anterior cavity becomes stopped up. The fluid accumulates in this cavity and exerts pressure on the nerve endings in the eye. This condition is called *glaucoma* (glô *kō* mə). Untreated glaucoma can cause blindness. However, drugs and surgery can be used to treat this disease, so that blindness need not occur.

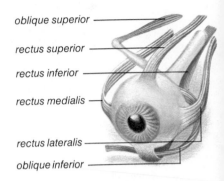

oblique superior
rectus superior
rectus inferior
rectus medialis
rectus lateralis
oblique inferior

32-1. External structures of the human eye.

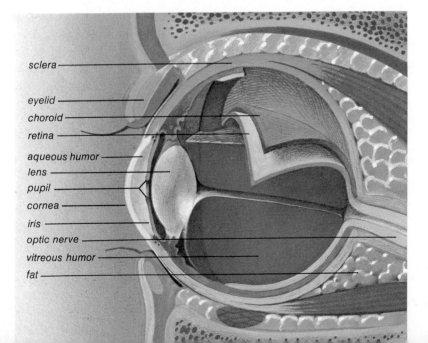

sclera
eyelid
choroid
retina
aqueous humor
lens
pupil
cornea
iris
optic nerve
vitreous humor
fat

32-2. Light passing into the eye is first bent by the cornea and is then focused by the lens so it strikes the fovea.

32-3. *Close your left eye. Focus your right eye on an area about 8 cm to the left of the circle. Start with the page about 12 cm from the eye. Gradually move the page farther away until the circle disappears. At that point the image of the circle falls on your blind spot.*

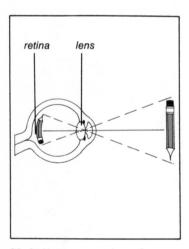

32-4. *How a normal eye focuses.*

The *lens* separates the inside of the eye into two chambers. These are the anterior cavity described above and the posterior cavity. The posterior cavity is filled with a jelly-like substance called the *vitreous* (*vit rē əs*) *humor.* The vitreous humor helps the eyeball to keep its shape. The lens also focuses waves of light on the back of the eyeball. The inner layer of the eyeball, the *retina* (*ret ən ə*), is where the light-sensitive cells are located. Two other layers of tissue surround the retina. They are the *choroid* (*kôr* oid) *coat,* which contains many blood vessels, and the *sclera* (*sklēr ə*), which is made of tough connective tissue. You can see part of the sclera as the "white of your eye."

LIGHT AND THE EYE   Now that we have a general idea of the structure of the eye we can see what happens to light as it passes into it. Light first strikes the curved surface of the transparent cornea. Here it is bent and directed through the pupil. Light then passes through the lens. Its curved surface completes the focusing of the light waves so they strike the *fovea.* This is the area of the retina where vision is best.

Two different kinds of light-sensitive cells are the rods and the cones. They are found in the retina. The *rods* are able to respond to light of very low intensity. They cannot distinguish colors. They send impulses to the brain. These are interpreted in black-and-white. Thus, at night or in dim light you cannot see colors. The *cones* require light of greater intensity than the rods. Different kinds of cones respond to different colors of light. Each cone sends its individual impulse to the brain. Finally, the brain puts together all of the impulses to create a picture in the mind of what is before the eyes. (See Fig. 32-3.)

The nerve fibers of each rod and cone cell come together in the back of the retina. Here they form a bundle of fibers, the *optic nerve.* The optic nerve runs from the eye to the brain. In the area where it leaves the retina, no rod or cone cells are present. Thus, no impulses are created by light striking this area. This specific area is called the *blind spot.* You do not notice a blind spot in your field of vision. This is due to the fact that your brain fills in the spot with details similar to those in the surrounding area. (See Fig. 32-4.)

Malfunctions of the Eye

The lens of the eye can change shape to focus on near or far away objects. As a person gets older the lens loses some of its elasticity. It cannot focus on near objects as well as it once could. This condition is called *presbyopia* (*prez bē ō pē ə*).

Some eyeballs are not perfectly round. They may be longer or shorter than normal. If the eyeball is too short, the lens focuses light behind the retina. In this case, the person can see distant objects better than those close up. People with this condition are said to be *farsighted.* If the eyeball is too long, the lens focuses light in front of the retina. Those people that can see objects close up better than things at a distance are said to be *nearsighted.*

In some eyeballs the surface of the cornea or the surface of the lens is uneven. This irregular shape causes uneven bending of light waves as they pass through the cornea or lens. Such a condition is called *astigmatism* (ə *stig* mə tiz əm).

All of these conditions, presbyopia, farsightedness, nearsightedness, and astigmatism can be corrected with eyeglasses. The lenses of the eyeglasses bend the light waves. This bending causes them to fall directly on the retina.

Colorblindness, another malfunction of the eye, is not correctable with eyeglasses. Colorblindness is due to the genes one inherits. (See Chapter 12.) These genes determine what kind of cone cells will be present and what kind of pigment they will contain. The absence of certain kinds of cone cells or an abnormality in the pigment they contain is thought to be the direct cause of colorblindness.

Students may be surprised to learn that the cornea plays an important role in the focusing of light. The cornea may be likened to the coarse adjustment on the microscope and the lens to the fine adjustment. Cataract involves changes in the lens of the eye so that it becomes opaque to light. All of us are subject to some loss of transparency of the lens as we age. When the lens becomes very opaque, it is removed from the eye during cataract surgery. Contact lenses are often prescribed for cataract patients because a wider angle of vision can be restored than with glasses.

How Our Ears Work

THE STRUCTURE OF THE EAR   The human ear is divided into the *outer ear,* the *middle ear,* and the *inner ear.* (See Fig. 32-5.) It contains two kinds of receptor cells. One kind responds to sound waves. The other responds to movements of the head and helps to maintain balance.

32-5. The structure of the human ear.

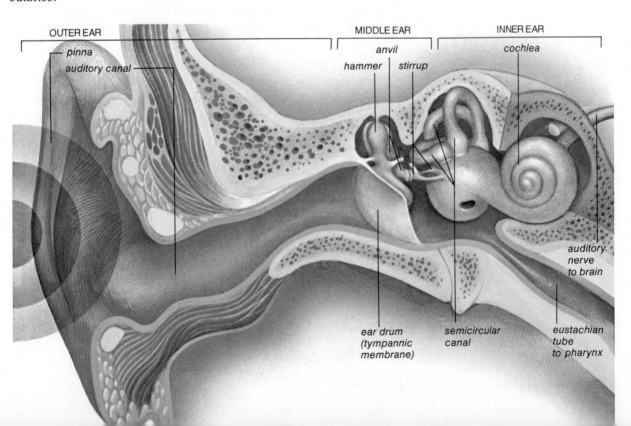

OUTER EAR

pinna
auditory canal

MIDDLE EAR

anvil
hammer   stirrup

INNER EAR

cochlea

auditory nerve to brain

ear drum (tympannic membrane)

semicircular canal

eustachian tube to pharynx

In the atmosphere, sound waves consist of movements or vibrations of molecules in air. These sound waves enter the external ear through the *auditory tube.* The *pinna* helps to collect sound waves and direct them into the ear. When the sound waves strike the *tympanic membrane,* they cause it to vibrate. Those vibrations are transmitted to the three small bones of the middle ear. They are the *hammer,* the *anvil,* and the *stirrup.* The bones transmit vibrations to another membrane, the oval window. Vibrations reaching the oval window are transmitted to fluid inside the *cochlea* (kok lē ə), which is located in the inner ear. The cochlea is a small bony structure that looks like a snail shell. Inside it is a long coiled, fluid-filled tube that contains the sound-sensitive cells. These sensory receptors are called *hair cells* because they have hair-like projections. When the vibrations reach the fluid of the cochlea, they cause waves of pressure in the fluid. These waves shake the sound-sensitive cells. This shaking causes the hair cells of the cochlea to transduce the vibrations into a nerve impulse. The sound receptor cells are lined up along the inside of the tube of fluid much like the strings of a piano. (See Fig. 32-6.) Cells nearest the oval window are sensitive to very high-pitched sounds. Moreover, cells nearest the tip of the cochlea are sensitive to low-pitched sounds. The brain then interprets the various messages sent to it. These may be spoken words, the sound of a siren, or the playing of a symphony orchestra.

FAILURE OF THE EAR   Deafness can be caused by the failure of vibrations to be transmitted to the cochlea. It may also be caused by damage to the receptor cells of the cochlea. Sometimes a bad cold and ear infection prevents the bones of the middle ear from vibrating. In other instances, the bones grow together so they can no longer vibrate. These kinds of deafness are called transmission deafness because the vibrations fail to be transmitted. They can be treated

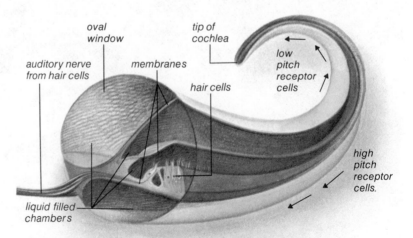

oval
window

tip of
cochlea

auditory nerve
from hair cells

membranes

low
pitch
receptor
cells

hair cells

high
pitch
receptor
cells.

liquid filled
chambers

32-6. *If the cochlea could be unwound and straightened out, the receptor cells would be arranged like the strings of a piano.*

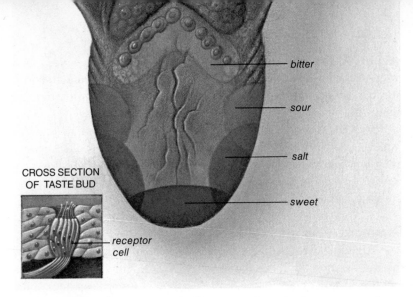

bitter

sour

salt

CROSS SECTION
OF TASTE BUD

sweet

receptor
cell

32-7. Location of different kinds of taste buds on the tongue.

by curing the infection, surgically separating the bones, or using a hearing aid. Some hearing aids transmit vibrations through the bones of the skull to the cochlea. Others amplify vibrations. Deafness due to damage of the delicate receptor cells of the cochlea is called nerve deafness. Exposure to loud noises can damage these cells. Permanent untreatable deafness results.

SENSE OF BALANCE   Also located in the inner ear are the *semicircular canals*. (Refer to Fig. 32-5.) These three fluid-filled canals are arranged in three planes — like the front wall, side wall, and floor of a room. Like the cochlea they also contain sensitive hair cells. These cells are stimulated by the vibration of fluid surrounding them. However, these hair cells also are sensitive to changes in the position of the head. They can detect change in each of the three planes of space.

Many people are affected by motion sickness. It is thought that their semicircular canals are especially sensitive to frequent changes in the position of the head. Even when such a person is sitting still in a moving vehicle, the semicircular canals respond to changes in speed. The canals also respond to movement around curves or up and down hills. At this point impulses are sent to the part of the brain that interprets these movements. In people affected by motion sickness, impulses are sent to the nausea and vomiting center of the brain.

Our Senses Of Taste and Smell

Taste and *smell* are called the chemical senses because both detect chemical substances. The receptors for taste are located in taste buds on the tongue. Each receptor is particularly sensitive to one of the four basic tastes. These tastes are sweet, sour, salty, and bitter. (See Fig. 32-7.) Whatever we think we taste besides these four tastes is really something we smell. Recall how tasteless food seems when you

Answers to Questions for Section 1.

A. 1. See Glossary.

2. Each is receptive to a particular kind of stimulus, of sufficient strength, and converts stimuli to nerve impulses.

*3. Answers will vary.

B. 4. Light waves strike the cornea (are bent) pass through the pupil and strike the lens (are bent). They then pass to the retina where they stimulate the receptor cells.

5. Rods are sensitive to dim light and perceive black, white, and shades of gray; cones are sensitive to bright light and perceive color.

*6. Lenses in the glasses of a far-sighted person are convex. Lenses of a nearsighted person are concave.

C. 7. Through air in the outer ear, bone in the middle ear, and fluid in the cochlea or inner ear. Fluid vibrations stimulate the hair cells of the organ of Corti in the cochlea.

8. They receive stimuli that detect movements of the head.

9. Transmission deafness: part of the ear prevents the transmission of vibrations to the fluid of the cochlea. Deafness due to damage to receptor cells prevents the transmission of impulses even when the vibrations are transmitted to the cochlea.

10. A disturbance of the organs of balance that leads to nausea and vomiting.

D. 11. Both detect chemicals through hair cells; they differ in the kinds of chemicals they detect.

*12. Block the nostrils and attempt to taste foods.

Emphasize that all of the information we get about our environment comes from what our sense organs are able to detect.

have a cold and cannot smell very well. The receptors for smell are located in the lining of the nasal cavity. They are capable of detecting a number of odors based on the shape of the molecules that are being smelled.

Both the receptor cells for taste and for smell have hair-like projections on their surface. To be detected, a chemical in air or water must reach a cell that is sensitive to it. The hair cell is stimulated and sends an impulse to the brain. The brain interprets these stimuli as the various tastes and smells.

Summary — Sensory Perception

Together the various sensory receptor cells provide us with all the information we have about our environment. The receptors detect the stimuli and transduce them into nerve impulses. Our ability to respond to changes in the environment depends on the ability of our sensory receptors to notify us of those changes.

QUESTIONS FOR SECTION 1

1. What is a transducer?
2. What are some other properties of sense organs?
3. What do you think would happen if a sensory receptor received a weak stimulus?
4. Trace the path of light through the eye and tell where the light waves are bent.
5. What is the difference between rods and cones?
6. How do you think the lenses would differ for the glasses of a nearsighted person and a farsighted person?
7. How are vibrations transmitted to the receptor cells in the cochlea?
8. What is the function of the semicircular canals?
9. How does transmission deafness differ from deafness due to damage to the receptor cells?
10. What is motion sickness?
11. How are the senses of taste and smell alike and how are they different?
12. How could you show that much of the flavor of your food is detected as smell?

LIST 1	LIST 2	LIST 3
apple	nucleus	zul
banana	protoplasm	fas
carrot	gene	bix
dewberry	chromosome	moj
eggplant	homeostasis	deg
fig	muscle	chy
ginger	brain	kep

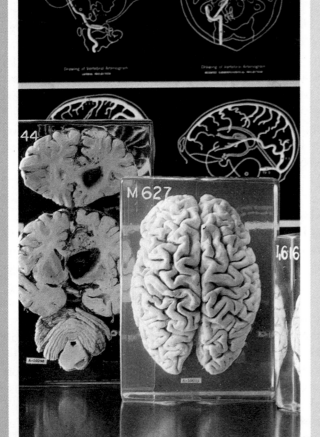

CHAPTER INVESTIGATION

A. Study the words in list 1 for ten seconds. See how many words you can write from memory. Do the same thing for list 2 and for list 3. Which list did you remember the most words from? . . . the least words? Why was one list easier than another?

B. The above activity demonstrates the functioning of short term memory. Some studies have shown that seven bits of information are the maximum that can be stored in short term memory. Why do you think these lists contain seven words?

C. Have some of your friends do the activities in A above. Make a graph of your findings. Add the following words to each list and have some other friends do the activities in A above. How does this change your findings?

Add to list 1: hominy, ice cream, jelly
Add to list 2: bone, mitochondria, intestine
Add to list 3: nar, qui, tov

2 THE NERVOUS SYSTEM

OBJECTIVES FOR SECTION 2

E. Describe the general plan of the nervous system.

F. Explain what happens in a reflex arc.

G. Identify the steps in the transmission of a nerve impulse (a) along a neuron and (b) across a synapse.

H. Summarize the functions of the autonomic nervous system.

How the Nervous System Controls the Body

The nervous system transmits impulses from the sensory receptors. Furthermore, it interprets these impulses. Then it starts new impulses that cause responses to the stimuli. Thus, the nervous system is important in controlling the body.

Plan of the Nervous System

The nervous system is divided into the *central nervous system* and the *peripheral* (pə rif ər əl) *nervous system*. (See Fig. 32-8.) The central nervous system consists of the *brain* and *spinal cord*. The peripheral nervous system consists of the *nerves* that carry impulses to and from the central nervous system. These nerves include the *cranial nerves*, which branch from the brain, and the *spinal nerves*, which branch from the spinal cord. In addition to these, the peripheral nerves include the *autonomic* (ô tə *nom* ik) *nervous system*. This supplies the internal organs of the body.

All of the structures of the nervous system that conduct impulses are composed of a single kind of cell, a *neuron* (nōōr on). (See Fig. 32-9.) A neuron consists of a cell body with a nucleus, an *axon,* and several *dendrites*. Dendrites carry impulses toward the cell body. In contrast to this, axons carry impulses away from the cell body. There are two special types of neurons. *Sensory neurons* carry impulses from a sensory receptor to the central nervous system. At this point, *motor neurons* carry impulses from the central nervous system to a muscle or gland. The combination of these neurons cause a specific response to a stimulus. These stimuli may cause a muscle to contract or a gland to secrete.

What is a Reflex Arc?

A **reflex arc** *is the simplest pathway that includes a stimulus and a response.* If you touch something hot, you automatically jerk your finger away from the object. (See Fig. 32-10.) What causes this reaction? To begin, a pain receptor must first be stimulated. Following this, an impulse is transmitted along a *sensory neuron* to the spinal cord. Here, the impulse is transmitted to an *association neuron* in the spinal cord. Then it goes to a *motor neuron* that goes to the muscles of your finger. The motor impulse causes muscles to contract. At this point, the finger is moved away from the hot object. The pathway of the sensory neuron, the association neuron, and the motor neuron is a reflex arc. It takes only a fraction of a second for the impulse to travel through the reflex arc. Therefore, you move your finger away from a hot object very quickly. Immediately afterwards, you also become

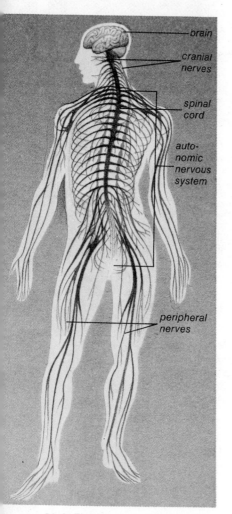

brain

cranial nerves

spinal cord

autonomic nervous system

peripheral nerves

32-8. The human nervous system.

aware of the fact that you have burned yourself. This is due to the fact that the association neuron also transmits an impulse to a neuron in the spinal cord. This impulse travels to the brain. The impulse that travels up the spinal cord and through the brain is *not* part of the reflex arc.

Other examples of reflexes are the eye blink and the knee jerk. Most reflexes are protective. They help to prevent injury. The reflex arc does not carry an impulse to the brain. Therefore, you have no conscious control over a reflex. You are only aware of what has happened after the reflex has occurred.

How Nerves Transmit Impulses

All nerves transmit impulses in the same way. *A nerve is a bundle of nerve fibers composed of the axons or dendrites of many neurons.* The axon of a neuron may be as much as a meter long or it may be very short. *The group of cell bodies of the neurons of a nerve is called a* **ganglion.** Ganglia are usually found at some point along the nerve.

The neurons of most nerves are coated with a fatty substance, *myelin* (mi ə lin). (Refer to Fig. 32-9.) Myelin insulates the neuron and allows the impulse to travel at a rapid rate of speed. In a myelinated neuron, the impulse jumps from one node to the next. Axons that are thick transmit impulses faster than thin axons. Also, in a large nerve, many axons are present. If the nerve is a *mixed nerve,* it carries both sensory and motor impulses. The sensory impulses are going to the central nervous system. The motor impulses are coming from the central nervous system. The way that impulses travel along a large nerve is a little like the way cars travel along a large multilane highway. Although traffic is going in both directions, each car stays in its own lane and travels in only one direction.

Nerve Impulses

An impulse is generated in a neuron by the arrival of a stimulus. (See Fig. 32-11.) Most impulses begin in sensory receptors. We might think of sensory receptors as much like the dendrite of a neuron. When a stimulus such as light waves or vibrations reaches the receptor, it causes changes in the cell membrane.

You have already learned in Chapter 6 that materials move across cell membranes in a variety of ways. The movement of ions, particularly sodium and potassium ions, is important in understanding nerve impulses. In a resting neuron, there is a high concentration of sodium ions in the fluid surrounding the cell. There is also a high concentration of potassium ions inside the cell. Because of other charged particles that are also present, the outside of the membrane of the

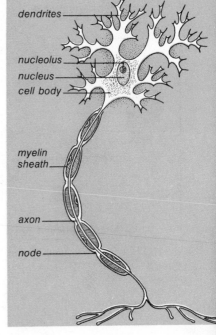

32-9. The structure of a neuron.

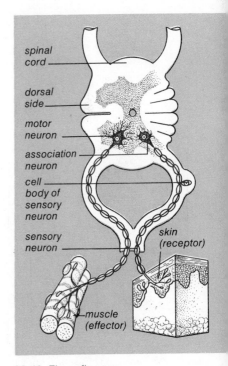

32-10. The reflex arc.

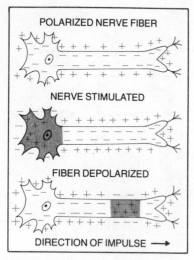

32-11. *How an impulse moves through a nerve fiber.*

neuron is more positive than the inside. We might also say that the inside is more negative than the outside. In this resting condition, the neuron is said to be *polarized*.

When a polarized neuron is stimulated, the sodium ions outside the membrane cross over the membrane and enter the cell. At the same time, potassium ions move out of the cell. This occurs at the point of stimulation. The electrical charge becomes positive on the inside and negative on the outside. The neuron is said to be *depolarized*. The event of depolarization is the beginning of a nerve impulse.

Once the membrane of a neuron becomes depolarized at one point, the depolarization spreads in all directions. This is called a wave of depolarization. Wherever depolarization occurs, the membrane becomes negatively charged on the outside and positively charged on the inside. Thus, the impulse is transmitted along the neuron as a wave of depolarization.

As soon as the impulse has passed by a point on the membrane, the membrane *repolarizes*. During repolarization, the charge on the membrane returns to its original condition. It becomes positive on the outside and negative on the inside. Repolarization requires energy to move the sodium ions out of the cell and the potassium ions back into the cell. This energy comes from ATP. At the end of repolarization, the neuron is ready to receive another impulse.

The wave of depolarization spreads in all directions from the point of stimulus. What then makes an impulse travel in only one direction? To answer that question, we need to know about synapses.

SYNAPSES   When an impulse reaches the end of the axon it must be transmitted to the next neuron in the pathway. Neurons do not touch each other directly. Instead, there is a tiny space between them. However, contact between the two neurons is made chemically. *This functional connection between two neurons is called a* **synapse.** (See Fig. 32-12.) The arrival of an impulse at the end of an axon causes the axon to release a chemical called a *neurotransmitter*. Most nerves release the neurotransmitter, *acetylcholine* (ə sēt əl kō lēn). Acetylcholine diffuses across the space between the neurons. It then attaches to a *receptor site* on the dendrite of the next neuron. The presence of acetylcholine at the receptor site causes the membrane of that neuron to depolarize. With this action the impulse has been transmitted to the next neuron. An enzyme, *cholinesterase* (kō lə nes tə rās), destroys the acetylcholine after it has transmitted the impulse. This prevents the impulse from being transmitted again and again.

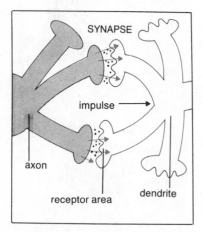

32-12. *Transmission of an impulse across a synapse.*

The Autonomic Nervous System

The autonomic nervous system regulates the functioning of the internal organs. You are not consciously aware of its actions. How-

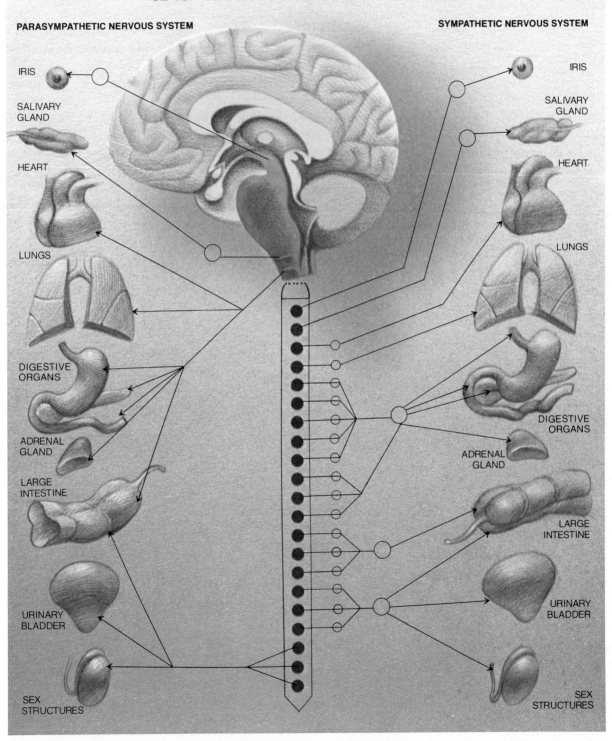

32-13 THE AUTONOMIC NERVOUS SYSTEM

PARASYMPATHETIC NERVOUS SYSTEM

SYMPATHETIC NERVOUS SYSTEM

IRIS

SALIVARY GLAND

HEART

LUNGS

DIGESTIVE ORGANS

ADRENAL GLAND

LARGE INTESTINE

URINARY BLADDER

SEX STRUCTURES

IRIS

SALIVARY GLAND

HEART

LUNGS

DIGESTIVE ORGANS

ADRENAL GLAND

LARGE INTESTINE

URINARY BLADDER

SEX STRUCTURES

Answers to Questions for Section 2.

E. 1. Central nervous system: brain and spinal cord; peripheral nervous system: cranial and spinal nerves (also autonomic nervous system).

2. Sensory nerves carry impulses from receptors to the C.N.S.; motor nerves carry impulses from the C.N.S. to muscles and glands.

F. 3. A sensory neuron, a connector neuron, and a motor neuron.

*4. An impulse going through a reflex arc has caused a response from the impulse traveling along the motor nerve by the time the sensory impulse has arrived in the brain through neurons in the spinal cord.

G. 5. When a membrane is stimulated and becomes depolarized. The wave of depolarization moves along the neuron to the axon end where it reaches a synapse.

6. By a chemical transmitter that is released from the axon and stimulates the dendrite of the next neuron. It is then destroyed by an enzyme.

7. An insulating material secreted by the Schwann cells that cover neurons.

8. A nerve consists of bundles of nerve fibers, sensory and motor. Individual fibers are insulated, so messages on one fiber do not interfere with other messages.

H. 9. The sympathetic nervous system causes the body to respond to stress, parasympathetic nervous system causes the body to return to normal.

10. Stimuli from the parasympathetic part of the A.N.S. cause organs that have been stimulated by the sympathetic system to return to their normal level of function.

ever, this system keeps such processes as digestion, circulation, and respiration going at the proper rate. It is indeed fortunate that we do not have to remember to digest our food, to make our blood circulate, or to breathe. The autonomic nervous system consists of two parts, the *sympathetic nervous system* and the *parasympathetic nervous system*.

The sympathetic nervous system is called into action when we are faced with an emergency or our bodies are under stress. This is sometimes referred to as the "fight or flight" system. It causes our heart rate and breathing to increase. It causes the liver to break down glycogen and release glucose into the blood stream. It stimulates the adrenal glands to secrete epinephrine (ep ə *nef* rən) and norepinephrine (nər ep ə *nef* rən). These chemicals, as we shall see in a later chapter, further stimulate the body to respond to an emergency. The sympathetic system also slows down non-essential functions. It slows down digestion and causes blood to be diverted from the digestive tract to the muscles.

After the emergency is over, the parasympathetic nervous system takes over. These nerves reverse all of the changes that the sympathetic nervous system caused. Heart rate and breathing return to normal and digestion starts again. The nerves of the autonomic nervous system are connected to the brain and spinal cord. (See Fig. 32-13.)

Even when there is no emergency the sympathetic and parasympathetic nerves cause small changes in the rate of many body functions. They operate at all times to help maintain homeostasis.

QUESTIONS FOR SECTION 2

1. Name the parts of the central nervous system and the peripheral nervous system.
2. What is the difference between a sensory nerve and a motor nerve?
3. What is a reflex arc?
4. Why are you not aware of a reflex until after it has happened?
5. How does an impulse pass along a neuron?
6. How is an impulse transmitted across a synapse?
7. What is myelin?
8. How can a nerve carry both sensory and motor impulses?
9. What is the difference between the sympathetic and the parasympathetic nervous system?
10. How does the autonomic nervous system help to bring the body back to normal after an emergency?

3 THE BRAIN IS THE CENTRAL CONTROL UNIT

With the exception of reflexes, most other activities of the nervous system involve the brain. This does not mean that we are consciously aware of each action. Many parts of the brain receive, interpret, and act on stimuli without our being aware of these activities.

Structure and Function of the Brain

The brain is the most complex structure in our body and there is much that we still do not understand about it. Even so, we can get some idea of the major functions of its larger parts. We can see these parts best in a section through the brain that separates it into left and right halves, or hemispheres. (See Fig. 32-14.) The largest single part of the human brain is the *cerebrum* (se rē brəm). It is where conscious decisions are made. Also, the cerebrum is where most memories are stored. We will discuss it in more detail later.

Other parts of the brain occupy far less space. The *corpus callosum* (kôr pəs ka lō səm) is a set of nerve fibers that connect the left and right halves of the cerebrum. Below the corpus callosum is the *thalamus* (thal ə məs). The upper part of the thalamus is the *pineal* (pin ē əl) *gland*. This structure is thought to be involved in maintaining biological rhythms. The thalamus itself is a relay station that sorts out and transmits impulses from sense organs to the cerebrum. The lower part of the thalamus, the *hypothalamus*, contains a number of control

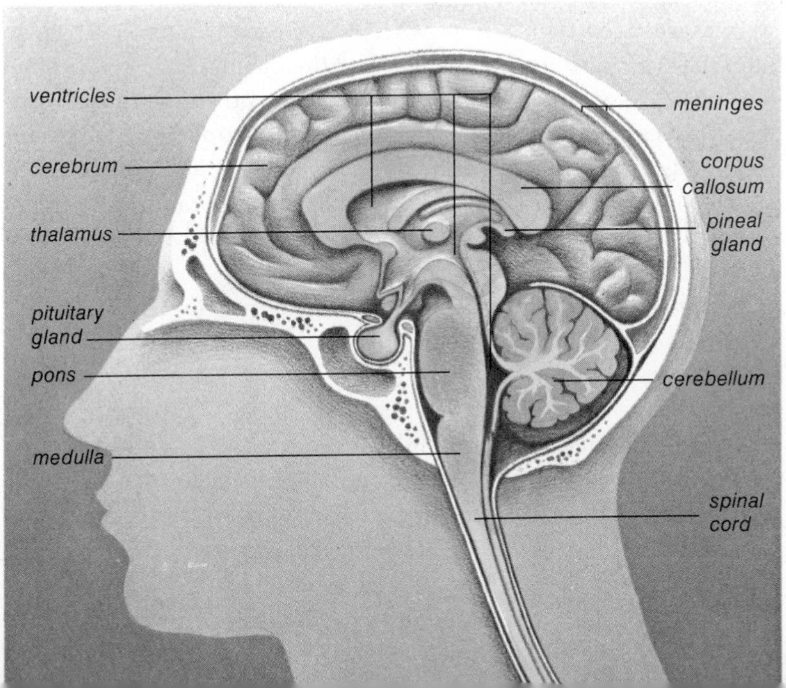

OBJECTIVES FOR SECTION 3
I. List the main structures of the brain and identify their functions.
J. Describe how the brain interprets and responds to stimuli.
K. Summarize the theories about learning and memory.
L. Distinguish between sleep and wakefulness.

ventricles
cerebrum
thalamus
pituitary gland
pons
medulla
meninges
corpus callosum
pineal gland
cerebellum
spinal cord

32-14. Section of the human brain.

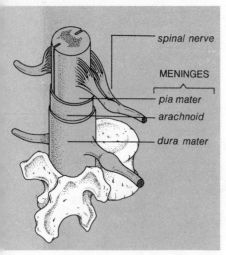

32-15. *The meninges of the spinal cord. These membranes also cover the brain.*

spinal nerve

MENINGES

pia mater

arachnoid

dura mater

centers. It controls body temperature, osmotic pressure in the blood, hunger, thirst, sexual behavior, and even rage and anger.

The *midbrain,* which corresponds to the optic lobes, is much smaller in humans than in other vertebrates. It coordinates eye movements with other movements. The midbrain also relays impulses from other parts of the brain and spinal cord to the cerebrum.

The *cerebellum* (ser ə *bel* əm) is the second largest part of the human brain. Its main function is to coordinate muscular activities. We are not conscious of the activity of the cerebellum. However, such things as walking, writing, and other activities would be uncoordinated without the normal functioning of the cerebellum. The *pons* relays impulses between the two halves of the cerebellum. The pons also acts as a relay system between the cerebellum and the cerebrum.

The *medulla* contains many centers that control the activities of internal organs. Its function is closely integrated with the autonomic nervous system. Some of its centers control vital functions such as heart rate, respiration, and the diameter of blood vessels. Other centers control swallowing, vomiting, sneezing, and coughing. The medulla is connected to the spinal cord.

Surrounding the whole brain and spinal cord are three protective membranes, the *meninges* (mi *nin* jēz). (See Fig. 32-15.) The outer membrane is called the *dura mater* (*door* ə *mā* tər). It is the tough outer covering of the brain. The next layer, the *arachnoid* (ə *rak* noid) *layer,* contains many blood vessels. The innermost layer, the *pia* (*pi* ə) *mater,* lies directly over the surface of the brain and spinal cord.

Inside the brain are a series of connected cavities called *ventricles.* They are connected to the central canal of the spinal cord. All of these cavities are filled with *cerebrospinal fluid.* Some of this fluid is also found between the arachnoid layer and the pia mater. Cerebrospinal fluid serves as a shock absorber for the brain and spinal cord. Sometimes it does not drain into the blood vessels properly and accumulates, causing pressure within the brain. This condition is called *hydrocephalus* (hī drə *sef* ə ləs), or water on the brain. In an infant whose skull bones can be pushed apart, the fluid increases the size of the head. Head enlargement can be prevented by surgically placing a drain from one of the ventricles of the brain to an atrium of the heart.

THE CRANIAL NERVES   Associated with the brain are twelve pairs of *cranial nerves.* Three of these, the *olfactory, optic,* and *auditory* nerves, carry sensory impulses from the nose, eye, and ear. Two nerves carry only motor impulses to the mouth and control speech and swallowing. The other seven nerves carry both sensory and motor fibers. Among other functions, these nerves control movements of the eyeballs and facial sensations.

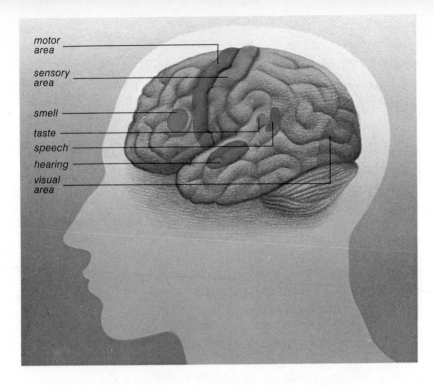

motor
area

sensory
area

smell

taste

speech

hearing

visual
area

32-16. Specialized areas of the cerebrum.

How the Cerebrum Interprets and Responds to Stimuli

The cerebrum is the portion of the brain that receives and interprets conscious sensations from the sense organs. Certain areas of the cerebrum are specialized to do certain things as shown in Figure 32-16. For example, the *somatic sensory area* receives impulses from the skin and the *somatic motor area* sends impulses to the muscles. These areas serve the whole body. In addition, the *visual areas* and *auditory areas* receive impulses from the eyes and ears. Furthermore, the *speech area* starts the formation of words by putting together what is seen, heard, and thought.

TABLE 32–1   *EFFECTS OF DRUGS ON THE CEREBRUM*

Alcohol	*Narcotics*	*Narcotic withdrawal*
diminished self-control	euphoria	irritability
loss of judgment	slurred speech	anxiety
changes in emotions	large dose can cause unconsciousness and death	depression
blurred vision		panic
difficulty in judging distance		confusion
		tremor
slurring of speech		inability to sleep

Effects of Drugs on the Nervous System

Several drugs have effects on the central nervous system and especially on the cerebrum. Alcohol affects the cerebrum by interfering with its normal functions. Table 32-1 lists some of the effects of alcohol on the cerebrum.

Opium and the related drugs, morphine, codeine, and heroin, are all narcotics. Opium comes from the opium poppy. The other drugs are derived from it. Cocaine, another narcotic, comes from the coca plant. Narcotics can lead to physical *addiction* in which the body's physiological processes are dependent on the drug. When an addict tries to stop using the drug, symptoms of withdrawal occur. All of these symptoms indicate effects on the cerebrum.

RECENT RESEARCH   There has been much research on the effects of opiates, opium, and similar drugs. Recent research has shown that brain cells have places on their surfaces into which the molecules of opiates fit. These were termed *opiate receptor sites*. Their discovery puzzled the researchers. They did not expect the brain cells to be prepared to react chemically with such destructive things as opiates. This finding led the scientists to hypothesize that there might be a morphine-like substance normally present in the brain. Such substances have now been found. The first of these substances to be discovered was named *endorphin* (en *dôr* fin). Now several endorphins have been found in the pituitary gland and brain. All of the endorphins studied so far consist of a chain of 31 amino acids. Smaller pieces of the same chain that contain only six amino acids have been named *enkephalins* (en *kef* ə lənz).

Many tests of the effects of these natural opiates have been made in animals. A few tests have also been made in humans. It was found that different pieces of the endorphin chain produce quite different results. One piece produces pain relief and tranquilization. However, another piece produced a greater sensitivity to pain, irritability, and violence. The enkephalins that have been studied produce long-lasting pain relief. One of them has been found that also improves the learning ability of laboratory animals. In humans, some endorphins relieve depression in mental patients. Furthermore, studies of the endorphin level in human blood under different conditions have shown that the level increases when the subject is in pain. Studies are now underway to develop ways to use endorphins and enkephalins to control pain in humans.

Learning and Memory

What might be happening in the brain when learning occurs? One theory states that learning proceeds through the establishment of preferred pathways among the neurons of the brain. Each time the

Encourage interested students to read about and report on recent developments in research on endorphins and enkephalins. Reports on the effects of drugs and other substances on the nervous system would also contribute to interesting class discussions.

pathway is used, the learning becomes more firmly established. This theory would seem to be most useful in explaining the learning of tasks in which one improves with practice. Another theory is that one portion of the thalamus may improve in its performance. This section of the thalamus is one that sorts out stimuli and sends them to the cerebrum. This theory might explain learning by reasoning. However, no theory of learning has yet been correlated with actual brain function.

Theories of memory also lack correlation with brain function. However, two processes have been proposed. One suggests that short-term memory — memory for events that occurred in the last few minutes to hours — is maintained by impulses circling in the association areas of the brain. In contrast, long-term memory seems to involve protein synthesis.

Where memories are stored in the brain remains a mystery. What is certain that there is no one area of the brain that is the memory storage area. In the 1950's, Penfield, a Canadian brain surgeon, was performing surgery on a patient under local anesthesia. (This can be done because the brain itself has no sensory receptors.) He stimulated an area of the brain near the temple. The patient responded by recalling details of childhood experiences including the words of songs not thought of for years. The patient seemed to be reliving these experiences. Other investigators have demonstrated that memories are stored in other areas of the cerebrum. Further research may give us a better understanding of memory.

Sleep and Wakefulness

Have you ever wondered what makes you go to sleep and what makes you wake up? Biologists have found answers to some of these questions in a part of the brain called the *reticular* (ri *tik* yə lər) *formation*. (See Fig. 32-17.) This structure runs from the thalamus back to the medulla and is divided into the *reticular activating system* (RAS) and the sleep centers.

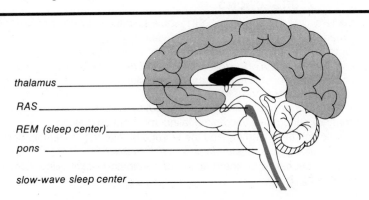

32-17. The reticular formation regulates sleep and wakefulness.

thalamus

RAS

REM (sleep center)

pons

slow-wave sleep center

Answers to Questions for Section 3.

I. 1. See Figure 32-14 on page 647.

 2. See text pages 647-648.

 *3. The human brain has a smaller midbrain (optic lobes) and a much larger cerebrum than most other animals.

J. 4. (a) Receives impulses from skin. (b) Sends impulses to muscles. (c) Center for short term memory. (d) Receives impulses from eyes; receives impulses from ears; initiates formation of words.

 5. They impair the nervous system particularly the thought areas of the cerebrum; some also impair other areas leading to poor coordination.

 6. Chemicals produced in the body that have effects similar to opiates. Research is still being done to find out where they are produced and how they work.

K. 7. One theory suggests that proteins are synthesized in neurons as memories are stored.

L. 8. Sleep is produced when the slow wave sleep center releases serotonin. Wakefulness is maintained by positive feedback — impulses from the reticular activating system excite the cerebrum and impulses from the cerebrum stimulate the RAS.

 9. To cause the body to go into slow-wave deep sleep, but when taken up the reticular activating system can again stimulate wakefulness.

Research has shown that RAS in the thalamus sends messages to the cerebrum. These messages keep the cerebrum active and the person awake. Messages from the cerebrum are also sent to the RAS. They stimulate the RAS to keep sending messages. This is an example of feedback where each organ stimulates the other. Although it is not known for sure how general anesthetics work, some scientists believe that they prevent the RAS from sending impulses to the cerebrum. In an opposite reaction, drugs called amphetamines are stimulants. It is thought that they may act by stimulating the RAS.

Sleep is thought to be regulated by two sleep centers. One is located in the pons and the other in the core of the brainstem. The latter, the slow-wave sleep center, releases a substance called *serotonin* (sir ə tō nən). As the serotonin accumulates, it causes the RAS to stop sending impulses to the cerebrum. Thus, the person falls asleep. It has been noticed that there are periods during sleep when the eyes move beneath the closed eyelids. This is called rapid-eye-movement or REM sleep. The REM sleep center in the pons causes a reduction in the amount of serotonin. This causes the person to be somewhat more active but still asleep. It is thought that many dreams take place during REM sleep. REM sleep seems to occur in cycles throughout the night. When the person has had enough sleep, the REM center causes most of the serotonin to return to the other sleep center. The RAS begins to function again and the person wakes up.

Studies of people who have been deprived of sleep show that memory and thinking are impaired. Also, the attention span is shortened. Some people even have hallucinations. They see or hear things that are not really there. It is thought that a certain chemical accumulates in the brain when a person does not get enough sleep. This chemical probably causes the hallucinations. The cure for the problems of sleep deprivation is sleep. The prevention of such problems is to get enough sleep every night.

QUESTIONS FOR SECTION 3

 1. Make a simple diagram and label it to show the general structure of the brain.
 2. Name a function for each structure in your diagram.
 3. Compare the human brain to the brain of other animals you have studied.
 4. What is the function of the following areas of the cerebrum: (a) somatic sensory area; (b) somatic motor area; (c) association areas; and (d) visual, auditory, and speech areas?
 5. Describe the effects of alcohol and narcotics on the cerebrum.
 6. What are endorphins and enkephalins and what do they do?
 7. How do you think learning and the storage of learning in memory occur?
 8. What makes you go to sleep and wake up again?
 9. What is thought to be the function of serotonin in controlling sleep and wakefulness?

CHAPTER REVIEW

The structures and functions of both the sense organs and the nervous system are closely related. For example, receptor cells in each of the sense organs respond to specific stimuli. The neurons of the nervous system are capable of transmitting impulses. Even though all cells are somewhat responsive to stimuli, receptors and neurons are especially responsive.

The brain is highly specialized to receive impulses and to transmit impulses in response to the information received. *It is the ability of the brain to respond to different stimuli in different ways that allows it to control the rest of the body.* Because nerve impulses travel with great speed, the nervous system responds rapidly. It can exert immediate control. It can cause the body to act on stimuli from the environment. It can cause internal organs to change their rate of functioning. *The nervous system regulates the rate of many different body functions and thus helps to maintain homeostasis.*

Using the Concepts

1. What do you think might happen if you could connect receptors in the eye to the auditory area of the brain?
2. Suppose you arrive in a very scenic area late at night and are surprised the next morning to see how colorful it really is. Explain how this might happen.
3. How might a person become deaf to sounds of a particular pitch, and what might have happened in the cochlea?
4. What would you expect to happen if suddenly your body could not make cholinesterase?
5. What is the difference between depolarization and repolarization of a neuron?
6. Do some additional reading and determine the difference between physiological and psychological addiction.
7. Trace the steps in a reflex arc that occur when a barefoot student steps on a sharp stone.
8. The use of mind-altering drugs is a problem for many people, both users and their friends. How could you try to discourage someone from using such drugs.
9. One of the easiest ways to study learning and memory is to use human subjects. What kind of limits would you place on such research?

Unanswered Question

10. Make some predictions about what will happen in the next ten years in research on (a) endorphins and enkephalins, (b) learning and memory, or (c) sleep and wakefulness.

Career Activities

11. Select one of the research areas mentioned in *Unanswered Question* and find out what kind of work people do on such a research project.
12. Of what value might information in this chapter be to a legislator, a teacher, a parent, or a nurse?

VOCABULARY REVIEW

1		2	
retina	auditory tube	cranial nerves	sympathetic
optic nerve	stirrup	ganglion	parasympathetic
hammer	pupil	receptor site	3 corpus callosum
semicircular canals	fovea	spinal nerves	ventricles
proprioceptor	rods	axon	meninges
cornea	pinna	autonomic	hydrocephalus
choroid coat	oval window	dendrite	arachnoid
blind spot	lens	acetylcholine	olfactory
anvil	cones	brain	dura mater
iris	tympanic membrane	reflex	auditory
sclera	cochlea	synapse	pia mater

CHAPTER 32 TEST

Copy the number of each test item and place your answer to the right.

PART 1 Multiple Choice: Select the letter of the phrase that best completes each of the following.

c 1. A sensory receptor does not **a.** transduce stimuli **b.** respond to a particular kind of stimulus **c.** create many different kinds of nerve impulses **d.** respond only to certain strength of stimulus.

b 2. The receptors that let you know when limbs and joints are moving are **a.** skin receptors **b.** proprioceptors **c.** balance receptors **d.** chemical receptors.

a 3. The parts of the eye that bend light waves are **a.** cornea and lens **b.** pupil and iris **c.** retina and sclera **d.** anterior and posterior cavities.

c 4. The part of the ear that transduces vibrations into nerve impulses is the **a.** tympanic membrane **b.** hammer **c.** cochlea **d.** pinna.

a 5. The part of the brain where decisions are made is the **a.** cerebrum **b.** cerebellum **c.** thalamus **d.** medulla.

a 6. The simplest pathway in the nervous system consists of a **a.** reflex arc **b.** cranial nerve **c.** spinal nerve **d.** autonomic nerve.

d 7. Brain centers that control heart and respiratory rate are located in the **a.** pineal gland **b.** midbrain **c.** hypothalamus **d.** medulla.

c 8. The meninges **a.** carry impulses to the brain **b.** carry blood to the brain **c.** protect the brain and spinal cord **d.** all of these.

d 9. Drugs that can harm the brain include **a.** alcohol **b.** opium **c.** cocaine **d.** all of these.

a 10. Sleep is thought to be produced by **a.** serotonin from the slow wave sleep center **b.** serotonin from the REM center **c.** uptake of serotonin by the RAS **d.** messages from the thalamus to the RAS.

PART 2 Matching: Match the letter of the term in Column I with its description in Column II.

COLUMN I
a. black and white vision
b. color vision
c. taste and smell
d. balance
e. touch
f. sensory nerves
g. motor nerves
h. sympathetic nerves
i. parasympathetic nerves
j. cranial nerves

COLUMN II
b **11.** Cones
d **12.** Semicircular canals
e **13.** Skin receptors
a **14.** Rods
c **15.** Chemical senses
j **16.** Carry impulses directly to and from the brain
f **17.** Carry impulses to the central nervous system
g **18.** Carry impulses from the central nervous system
i **19.** Carry impulses to return body to normal after stress
h **20.** Carry impulses for body to respond to stress

PART 3 Completion: Complete the following.
21. The structures that make up a neuron are ____.
22. The stages from the stimulation of a polarized neuron until it is ready to transmit another impulse are ____.
23. Two important chemicals in the transmission of an impulse are ____.
24. Recent research has shown that the brain contains two natural substances which act as opiates. They are ____.
25. The sense organs and the nervous system help to maintain homeostasis by ____.

Chapter 32 Test Answers

21. dendrite, axon
22. depolarization, wave of depolarization, repolarization
23. sodium, potassium
24. endorphins and enkephalins
25. providing information about changes in the environment and by responding to these changes

CHAPTER 33

PROTECTION AND MOVEMENT

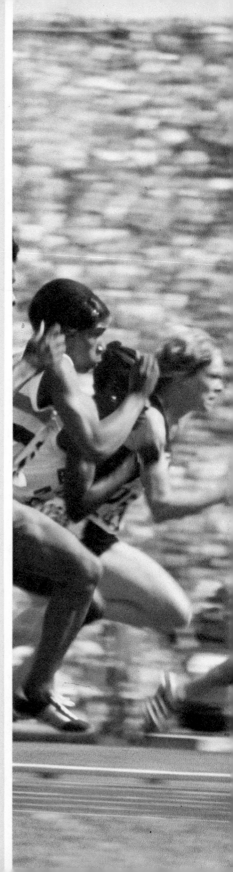

All organisms have some form of protection against the environment. Most animals can move. In the chapter on mammals you became familiar with some things about the skin. Moreover, you also studied different kinds of animal locomotion. In this chapter you will discover more about human skin and about how bones and muscles work together to cause movement.

The basic concepts in this chapter are similar to those in other chapters on the human body. *Structure and function are related. The functioning of the structures that protect the body help to maintain homeostasis. Movement also helps our bodies to maintain homeostasis. The ability to move helps us to respond to stimuli from the environment.*

Many young people are troubled with acne. All of us are bombarded with advertising asking us to buy many different cosmetics and hair care products. In this chapter you will learn:

- What are some of the causes of acne?
- What can cosmetics do for you?
- What happens to your skin when you wash your hands?
- Why do you need exercise?
- Why is good posture important?

RUNNERS

1 SKIN—WHAT'S BETWEEN YOU AND THE WORLD

OBJECTIVES FOR SECTION 1

A. Describe the structure and list the functions of the skin.
B. List some characteristics of hair, nails, oil glands, and sweat glands.

In the discussion of the various parts of the skin, discuss the value or lack thereof of different kinds of cosmetics, hair products, deodorants and anti-perspirants.

Your skin is the largest single organ in your body. It has two main parts, the outer *epidermis* and the inner *dermis*. Besides being a protective covering, the skin has several other functions. It prevents excess loss of fluids. By regulating the amount of sweating, the skin helps to maintain your normal body temperature. Sense organs in your skin help you to receive stimuli from the environment. Your skin even supplies your body with vitamin D. Let's see how your skin carries out these important functions.

Structure of Skin

The epidermis consists of many layers of cells. (See Fig. 33-1.) Only the cells that lie next to the dermis are able to divide. As these cells divide they push the cells above them nearer to the surface. Cells near the surface contain *keratin* (ker ə tin), a substance that makes the skin waterproof. These cells are far away from the blood vessels that lie in the dermis of the skin. Thus, they get few nutrients and eventually die. Because of this, the outer surface of your skin consists of dead cells. Every time you wash your hands some of these cells slough off.

In addition to blood vessels, the dermis contains the sensory receptors, hair follicles, and sweat and oil glands. Beneath the dermis,

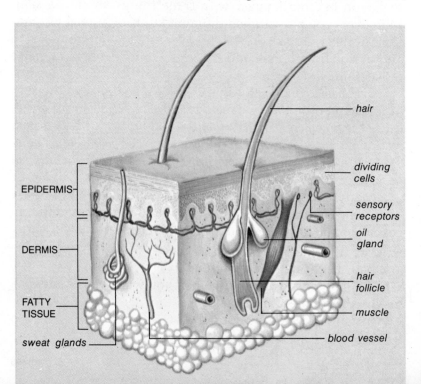

33-1. Section of human skin.

between the skin and the muscles, is a layer of fat. This fat helps to keep you warm in the winter and also serves as a reserve supply of energy.

HAIR The hair, and also the nails and glands, are called skin derivatives. This is because they develop from some of the skin cells. You already know that each hair has an oil gland next to it. This oil gland is nature's way of keeping hair soft and pliable. If you brush your hair frequently this oil spreads over the surface of the hairs. Many people wash their hair so frequently that they remove all of these natural oils. Some cases of dandruff are caused by a thorough removal of natural oils. Because of this, the outer cells of the scalp are lost in large numbers. Shampooing when hair becomes oily and frequent brushing to spread natural oils is a more sensible way to care for one's hair.

Hair color is determined by the amount of pigment in the hair. Each hair consists of a hollow tube in which grains of pigment are deposited. (See Fig. 33-2.) Dark brown hair has large quantities of pigment. In contrast, blond hair has only small quantities of the same pigment. Gray or white hair has no pigment. It appears to be white because light is reflected from the air spaces within the hollow tube.

NAILS Fingernails and toenails are formed from cells of the epidermis. The white moon-shaped area at the base of each nail is the area of growth. This is partly covered by *cuticle,* a fold of skin that grows over the base of the nail. You probably have already noticed that most of your nail looks pink. This is due to blood vessels in the skin beneath the nail.

GLANDS Oil glands are distributed throughout the skin. They secrete an oily substance called *sebum* (sēb əm). During the teen years these glands are stimulated by sex hormones. Excessive amounts of sebum are secreted and *acne* results. Microorganisms present on the skin get into the sebum and cause an infection. Sometimes, the infection causes the duct of the oil gland to rupture and release sebum and pus. This irritates the surrounding skin. Treatment should include frequent cleansing of the skin. Ointments may be applied to the skin to reduce the risk of infection. A new chemical, cis-retinoic (sis rə tə nō ik) acid, seems to work by reducing the amount of sebum produced. In severe cases of acne, its effects were seen to last for several months after treatment.

Sweat glands are also distributed throughout the skin. There are two kinds of sweat glands. One kind produces a watery secretion that helps to cool the body when it is hot. This secretion has little or no odor. The other kind of sweat glands are found under the arms. They produce a milky secretion that contains a number of chemicals. These chemicals give rise to the odor of sweat. Deodorants destroy the odor. Antiperspirants prevent the glands from secreting sweat.

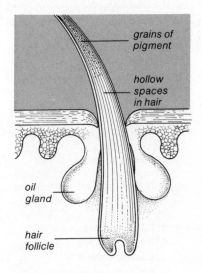

grains of pigment

hollow spaces in hair

oil gland

hair follicle

33-2. *Pigment grains in the hollow core of a hair determine its color.*

How the Skin Protects

We have already mentioned that the skin contains a substance that makes it waterproof. Furthermore, the cells of the skin are packed together tightly. Some layers even fit together like the pieces of a jig-saw puzzle. Because of this feature, the skin prevents bacteria and other substances from entering the body. When the skin is cut, there is danger of infection because the protective barrier has been broken. The skin also contains pigment that protects the body from excessive sunlight. This pigment is the same as the one in the hair. When the skin is exposed to sunlight, some of its cells begin to produce more pigment. This causes the skin to tan. If you get too much sun at one time, a sunburn results. However, with small amounts of sun, the skin will be able to withstand more sun and tan without burning. People with dark skin can naturally spend more time in the sun without burning than those with light skin.

Other Functions of the Skin

We know how the skin helps to regulate body temperature. Furthermore, there is a chemical in the skin that can be made into vitamin D. This occurs when sunlight shines on the skin. Vitamin D is important for the development of strong bones. Some years ago, rickets, the vitamin D deficiency disease, was common among children who lived in cold climates. Today, most milk is supplemented with vitamin D so few children have the disease.

A few substances can be absorbed through the skin. However, they pass through the skin in small quantities. Many cosmetics do many different kinds of things to the skin. Yet, their effects are generally limited to the outermost layers of cells. These are the cells that will slough off the next time you wash.

Some efforts are being made to administer a few medicines through the skin. For example, a small bandage treated with a drug for motion sickness can be stuck to the skin behind the ear. The drug slowly diffuses through the skin and into the bloodstream. Here it travels to the nausea center of the brain and prevents motion sickness. One of the advantages of this way of giving medicines is that they enter the body at a constant rate.

Answers to Questions for Section 1.
A. 1. Epidermis is the outer part of the skin and has cells that can divide to form new sheets of cells; dermis is under the epidermis and consists of connective tissue.

2. Protects, helps to regulate temperature, receives sensory information, and sometimes synthesizes materials.

3. By providing a waterproof covering for the body. The cells are fastened closely together so that substances rarely pass through the cells. Pigment in the skin prevents sun rays from penetrating and burning cells.

B. 4. Oil from sebaceous glands.

5. Oil glands secrete oil and sweat glands secrete sweat.

*6. Cause: the excess secretion of sex hormones. Treatment: keep the skin thoroughly clean and avoid squeezing pimples. Cis-retinoic acid is also used to treat acne.

QUESTIONS FOR SECTION 1

1. What are the differences between epidermis and dermis?
2. What are the functions of the skin?
3. How does the skin prevent things from entering the body?
4. What keeps hair soft?
5. What are the differences between oil glands and sweat glands?
6. What causes acne and how can it be treated?

CHAPTER INVESTIGATION

A. Describe the differences between people who exercise and those who do not.

B. Which group would have the most oxygen delivered to the cells of the body? How do you know?

C. State a hypothesis that would explain each of the above differences. Design an experiment to test one of your hypotheses.

Observations	Average values for people participating in exercise program	Average values for people not participating in exercise program
Resting Pulse	65	70
Pulse After 5 Minutes Of Exercise	110	140
Blood Pumped Per Minute	6000 ml.	4800 ml.

2 BONES AND JOINTS — THE BODY'S FRAMEWORK

OBJECTIVES FOR SECTION 2

C. Distinguish among the axial and appendicular skeleton and list the functions of the skeleton.

D. Describe the structure of a bone and explain how bones develop and how fractures heal.

E. Define *joint* and name three kinds of joints and three kinds of joint injuries.

The human skeleton provides the framework that supports the body. (See Fig. 33-3.) It consists of 206 bones, including the six that are found in the middle ear. The skeleton can be divided into the *axial* (ak sē əl) skeleton and the *appendicular* (ap ən dik yə lər) skeleton. The axial skeleton includes the bones of the skull, the vertebrae, ribs, and sternum (breastbone). It is called axial because it forms the axis, or main supporting structure of the body. The appendicular skeleton includes all the bones of the arms and legs.

In addition to supporting the body, the bones provide places for the muscles to attach. Whenever you move, muscles contract and cause joints between bones to bend. You move your whole body when you run or swim. However, only part of your body moves when you write or talk. In either case, you can move because muscles are pulling on bones.

Bones also protect some of the vital organs of your body. For example, your brain is protected by your skull. In addition, your heart and lungs are protected by the vertebrae, ribs, and sternum.

Finally, you are aware that some bones are able to produce blood cells. This function was described in Chapter 31.

The Structure of a Bone

Bones come in many different shapes and sizes. Let us examine the structure of a long bone, like those in your arms and legs. (See Fig. 33-4.) A long bone consists of a shaft and two ends. The shaft is made of dense bone. Within the shaft is a cavity that contains many blood vessels. Some parts of the cavity contain cells that can divide to make blood cells. Along the surface at each end of the bone is some cartilage. This is the area where one bone touches another bone.

There is an area at each end of the bone that is capable of growing. As new bone cells are formed and minerals are deposited between them, the bone gets longer. The ends are pushed farther and farther apart. By about age 25, bone growth is completed and the growth area disappears.

The whole bone is covered by a tough membrane, the *periosteum* (per ē *os* tē əm). This membrane protects the bone. It also provides bone-forming cells when they are needed to heal a fracture.

As seen through the microscope, bone consists of cells arranged in circles around a central canal. (See Fig. 33-5.) The cells are surrounded by the solid part of the bone. Inside the canal is a blood vessel which carries nutrients to the bone cells. Very tiny passageways

33-3. THE HUMAN SKELETAL SYSTEM.

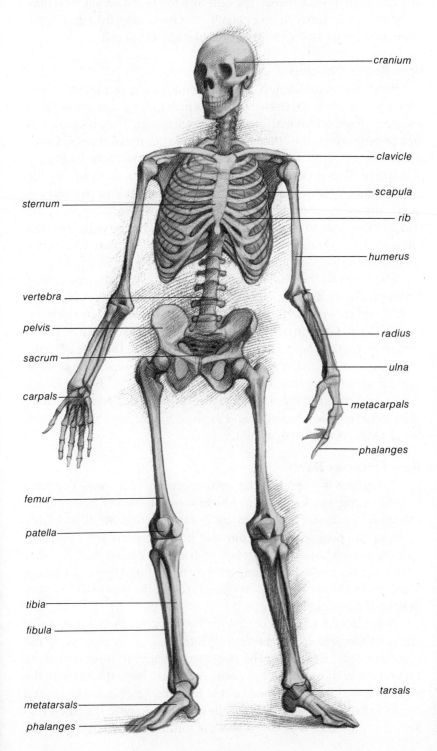

- cranium
- clavicle
- scapula
- rib
- humerus
- radius
- ulna
- metacarpals
- phalanges
- sternum
- vertebra
- pelvis
- sacrum
- carpals
- femur
- patella
- tibia
- fibula
- metatarsals
- phalanges
- tarsals

33-4. *The structure of a long bone.*

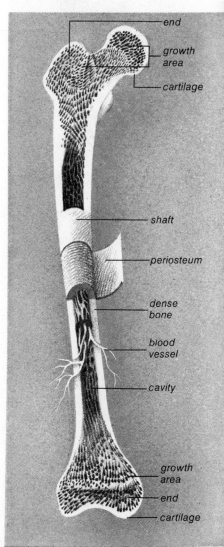

- end
- growth area
- cartilage
- shaft
- periosteum
- dense bone
- blood vessel
- cavity
- growth area
- end
- cartilage

Courtesy Carolina Biological Supply Company

33-5. *Microscopic view of solid bone. Bone forming cells are in dark patches, arranged in concentric patterns. A canal is located in the center of each pattern.*

33-6. *The embryo skeleton consists of fibrous structures shaped like bone. Gradually the process of ossification replaces these structures with bone.*

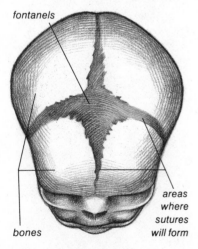

fontanels

areas where sutures will form

bones

33-7. *Human skull at birth.*

connect the cells to the blood vessel. These passageways also allow substances to move between the cells and the blood vessel. You may be surprised to learn that bone cells are metabolically active cells. They use energy and give off wastes like any other cell.

How Bones Develop

Bones begin to develop in human embryos as cartilage models. Cartilage is a semisolid tissue like that which gives shape to your ears and nose. Bone cells move into the cartilage model. They take calcium and phosphorus out of the blood and use it to make the solid substance of bone. The cartilage is removed and the solid bone laid down in its place. This process is called *ossification* (os ə fi kā shən). By the time a human infant is born, most of the bones are at least partially ossified. (See Fig. 33-6.) However, it takes many years for all of the bones of the body to become completely ossified. One of the reasons human infants cannot walk or even sit up at birth is that their bones are not strong enough to support them.

The bones of the skull undergo a somewhat different method of development. Instead of being made by the ossification of cartilage, bone is laid down directly in a tough membrane. Flat plates of bone are produced. Growth occurs around the edges of these plates. In the human infant the plates have not grown together at the time of birth. This leaves areas, called *fontanels* (fänt ən elz), in which the brain is covered only by the tough membrane. (See Fig. 33-7.) By the time a child is two years old these fontanels are replaced by bone. The plates of bone have grown together and *sutures*, the immovable joints between skull bones, have formed.

How Fractures Heal

A fracture is a break in the solid substance of a bone. The bone may be simply cracked or it may be broken into two or more pieces. Fractures are usually detected by X rays. X rays show not only whether the bone is broken, but also how the parts are displaced. (See Fig. 33-8.) Usually the broken ends can be placed back together by moving the bone. If not, surgery may be required to put the pieces together. In either case, a cast is placed around the area of the fracture to keep the bones in place.

Soon after a fracture occurs, healing begins. First a blood clot forms in the area of the fracture. White blood cells clear away the damaged cells. Cells from the periosteum begin to form new bone around the ends of the broken bone. A collar of bone thicker than the original bone forms in the area of the fracture. Fractures take several weeks to heal. At times, there may be severe damage to the blood vessels. If so, the cells will not receive the nutrients they need to divide and healing will be slowed down. Patients with fractures are often encouraged to put weight on the fractured limb as early as possible. This increases the circulation of blood through the limb and speeds the healing process.

Joints and How They Move

A joint *is a place where two bones are held together.* The bones are held together by strong bands of connective tissue called *ligaments.* Most joints are moveable, but a few, like the sutures of the skull, are not moveable. In addition, the joints between the vertebrae are slightly moveable. In contrast, the joints in the limbs are freely moveable.

There are many different types of freely moveable joints. We will study two of them, the ball-and-socket joint and the hinge joint. (See Fig. 33-9.) Ball-and-socket joints are found in the shoulders and the hips. As the name suggests, a ball-shaped end of one bone fits into a hollowed out area formed by another bone. The ball rotates in the socket. This kind of joint provides the maximum amount of movement. For example, you can raise your arms above your head, hold them straight out from the shoulder, or swing them forward and backward. In contrast, a hinge joint moves in one direction only. Your elbows and knees are examples of hinge joints. You can bend your elbow to move your forearm toward your upper arm and you can straighten your arm again. Movement occurs in one plane. Likewise, you can bend and straighten your leg at the knee joint. Movements in any other direction are very limited in hinge joints.

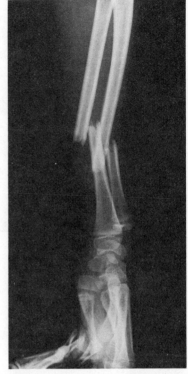

33-8. Breaks, such as this double arm fracture, can be detected by X-rays.

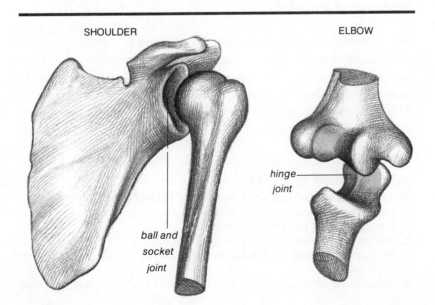

SHOULDER   ELBOW

hinge joint

ball and socket joint

33-9. Two types of joints in the arm.

Injuries to Joints

Dislocations, sprains, and strains are common joint injuries. (See Fig. 33-10.) In a *dislocation,* the surfaces of the bones that should lie next to each other are moved apart. There is swelling, pain, and loss of ability to move the joint. The ligaments that are attached to the bones are usually torn in a dislocation. Such injuries are common in the joints of the thumb, fingers, and shoulder. A *sprain* is a twisting of a joint without dislocating it. Ligaments may be damaged. Likewise, the tendons that hold muscles to bones may be torn. A *strain* is a less severe injury to a joint. Muscles, tendons, and ligaments may be stretched but no serious damage is done to the joint.

33-10. *X ray of a dislocated elbow joint.*

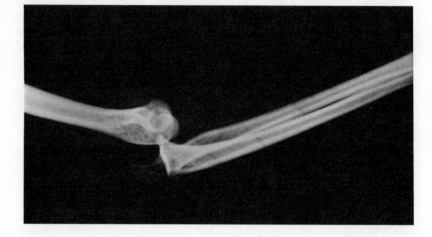

Answers to Questions for Section 2.

C. 1. Axial: includes the bones of the head and trunk; appendicular: consists of the bones of the limbs and girdles.

2. Supports, protects, and provides attachment points for muscles.

D. 3. A diaphysis and two epiphyses are covered with periosteum, and contain a marrow cavity. They grow at the epiphyseal plate.

4. Bone development involves the laying down of hard mineral at the epiphyseal plates and along the surfaces; the healing of a fracture involves growth of fibers and laying down of minerals in the area of the fracture.

E. 5. The ball-and-socket allows movement in three planes, the hinge in only one plane. The sutures are immovable joints in the skull.

*6. Movement can occur in three planes in the hip joint and these movements can be combined to cause rotation. Movement at the knee joint is primarily in one plane only, though slight rotation is possible.

Diseases of the Joint

There are several diseases which directly affect joints. Among these are *arthritis* and *gout.* Arthritis is a painful condition involving inflammation of the joints. It usually occurs between the ages of 40 to 60. However, it may afflict people of any age. Gout is an accumulation of chemicals in the fluid surrounding cells of the affected joint. The most common gout occurs in the joint of the big toe. Gout has a genetic basis and may run in families.

QUESTIONS FOR SECTION 2

1. How does the axial skeleton differ from the appendicular skeleton?

2. What are the functions of the skeleton?

3. Identify the main parts of a long bone.

4. How do bone development and healing of a fracture differ?

5. What are the similarities and differences among ball-and-socket, hinge, and suture joints?

6. Compare the kinds of movement that can occur in your hip and your knee.

3 MUSCLES, MOVEMENT, AND EXERCISE

Kinds of Muscle

Muscle is a tissue that is capable of contracting. Three kinds of muscle are found in the human body. (Their characteristics are summarized in Table 33-1.) *Skeletal muscle* is voluntary. You can voluntarily contract skeletal muscle at will. The *fibers* of skeletal muscle have many nuclei. They also have bands, or striations, that can be seen under the microscope. Skeletal muscles are found attached to the bones of the skeleton. *Smooth muscle* is involuntary. You do not have control

OBJECTIVES FOR SECTION 3

F. Distinguish among the three kinds of muscle tissue.
G. Summarize the processes of (a) excitation of muscles, (b) contraction of muscles, and (c) relaxation of muscles.
H. Explain how whole muscles cause movement and maintain muscle tone.
I. Demonstrate the importance of good posture and exercise.

TABLE 33–1   CHARACTERISTICS OF DIFFERENT KINDS OF MUSCLE

Skeletal muscle	Smooth muscle	Cardiac muscle
voluntary	involuntary	involuntary
fibers multinucleated	fibers have one nucleus	fibers have nuclei separated by intercalated discs.
found attached to bones	found in internal organs	found only in the heart
moves skeleton	regulates function of digestive system, diameter of blood vessels, and other organs	causes heart to beat

over its contraction. Smooth muscle has short fibers that consist of a single cell with one nucleus. It is found in the internal organs of the body. *Cardiac muscle* is also involuntary. Its fibers are similar to skeletal muscle. However, these fibers are branched. In addition, they have divisions, called *intercalated* (in *tur* kə lā təd) *discs,* between some of the nuclei of a fiber. Cardiac muscle is found only in the heart.

How Muscles Contract and Relax

Throughout your waking hours, the muscles of your body are being stimulated to contract and relax. Much of what happens in these processes occurs at the chemical level. Since the contraction process is quite similar in all types of muscle tissue, we will discuss how it occurs in skeletal muscle.

EXCITATION OF MUSCLES   Skeletal muscles are stimulated to contract by nerve impulse. The axon ends of motor neurons lie close to the membrane of muscle cells. The nerve endings of one axon and the

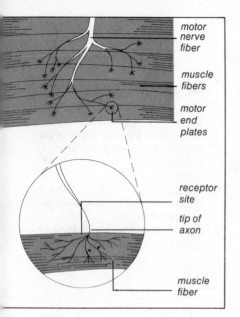

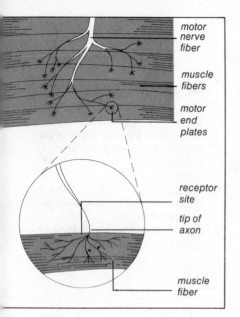

motor
nerve
fiber

muscle
fibers

motor
end
plates

receptor
site

tip of
axon

muscle
fiber

33-11. *The excitation of muscle tissue.*

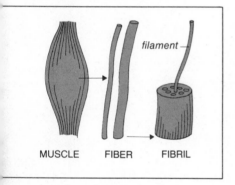

filament

MUSCLE   FIBER   FIBRIL

33-12. *The structure of muscle.*

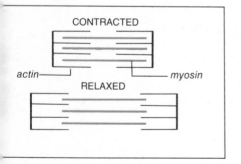

CONTRACTED

actin   myosin

RELAXED

33-13. *The sliding filament theory of muscle contraction.*

muscle fibers they supply is called a *motor unit*. The neurotransmitter, acetylcholine, is released by the axon and diffuses to the motor end plate. Here it attaches to receptor sites and causes the membrane of the muscle cell to depolarize. The transmitter is destroyed by cholinesterase, just as it is at a synapse. This process is shown in Figure 33-11.

The wave of depolarization travels along the membrane of the muscle fiber and passes within the muscle fiber or muscle cell. Each muscle fiber contains many thread-like *fibrils*. Each fibril contains many *filaments*. These filaments are the protein molecules, *actin* and *myosin*. (See Fig. 33-12.) When the membranes within the muscle fiber become depolarized, they release calcium ions. The calcium ions go to the filaments and cause them to contract. Let's see how that happens.

CONTRACTION   The myosin filaments lie next to the thinner actin filaments. When stimulated by calcium, the myosin bind to the actin. Myosin then behaves like an enzyme and causes energy from ATP to be released. This energy causes the myosin to pull the actin filaments closer together. This reaction occurs several times on the same filaments and makes them slide along one another. Thus this theory of how muscles contract is called the *sliding filament theory*. (See Fig. 33-13.) As the filaments slide, the muscle fibril becomes shorter. When many muscle fibrils shorten, this causes the whole muscle to shorten. Hence, the muscle has contracted. Muscle contraction requires energy in the form of ATP. The ATP is produced by cellular metabolism in the muscle cells.

RELAXATION   It may come as a surprise to you to learn that the relaxation of muscles also requires a small amount of energy. As long as the membrane of the muscle fiber is being stimulated by a nerve impulse, it continues to contract. When the stimulation stops, the calcium that was released from the membrane is returned. The return of calcium takes place by active transport. As you will recall from Unit 2, active transport requires energy.

How Whole Muscles Cause Movement

The skeletal muscles of the human body are attached to the bones of the skeleton to form a system of levers. (See Fig. 33-14.) Each muscle is attached to at least two bones. The muscle passes across a joint between those bones. When the muscle contracts it causes movement at the joint. The pull of the muscle causes one of the bones to move in relation to the other. This is what is meant by the lever action.

The muscles that move the elbow joint provide a good example of this lever action. The *biceps* muscle is located on the front surface of

33-14. THE HUMAN MUSCULAR SYSTEM.

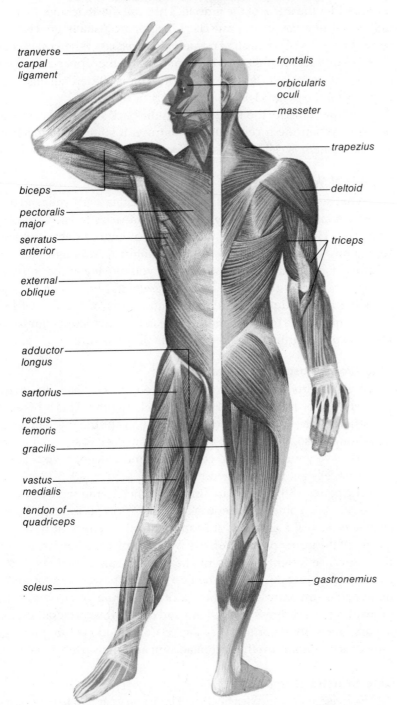

tranverse carpal ligament

frontalis

orbicularis oculi

masseter

trapezius

biceps

deltoid

pectoralis major

serratus anterior

triceps

external oblique

adductor longus

sartorius

rectus femoris

gracilis

vastus medialis

tendon of quadriceps

soleus

gastronemius

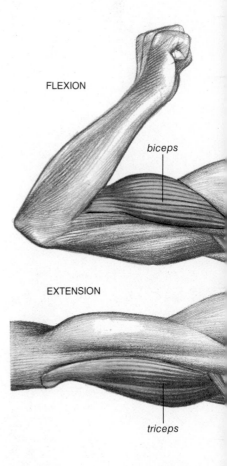

33-15. *Muscles that straighten (extend) and bend (flex) the elbow joint.*

FLEXION

biceps

EXTENSION

triceps

your upper arm. This muscle runs from the bones of the shoulder to the radius, a bone of your forearm. Biologists call the attachment at the shoulder the *origin* of the muscle. They call the attachment on the radius the *insertion* of the muscle. Muscles are usually attached to bones by bands of connective tissue called *tendons*. When the biceps muscle contracts it pulls the forearm toward the upper arm. This movement is called *flexion*. The forearm is flexed against the upper arm. (See Fig. 33-15 on page 667.)

Another muscle, the *triceps,* lies on the back surface of your upper arm. When the triceps muscle contracts it straightens the arm. This movement is called *extension*. The forearm is extended.

What is Muscle Tone?

What keeps you from falling out of your chair while you read this book? You are not consciously contracting muscles to keep yourself sitting up. However, some of the muscles of your vertebral column are slightly contracted while you are sitting up. Although you can voluntarily contract these muscles when you move your back, some of them contract without your being aware of it. Messages go to and from the cerebellum to coordinate contractions of these muscles. These contractions maintain muscle *tone* in the muscles of your back. They keep you sitting up. They maintain your posture.

Why Good Posture is Important

If you sit up straight in your chair, you are less likely to have a backache or become tired after sitting for a long time. This is because less strain is placed on your muscles when you sit straight than when you slump. Also, by sitting up straight, you make it easy for air to enter and leave your lungs. You can breathe more deeply. Your blood and your cells get more oxygen.

The bones of the pelvis are firmly attached to the sacrum, a part of the vertebral column. (Refer back to Fig. 33-3.) This is called the sacroiliac (sak rō *il* ē ak) joint. It is an immovable joint that bears the weight of the upper part of the body. Walking places some stresses on the body. The weight of the trunk, head, and arms is carried by your two legs. Keeping the weight lined up over the pelvis is important in minimizing the stress on this joint. Standing with the belly protruding places stress on this joint and causes the vertebral column to curve more than normal. (See Fig. 33-16.) Good posture prevents unnecessary strains on the sacroiliac joint and the vertebral column.

Why Exercise is Important

Exercise keeps muscles healthy. Have you ever had to have a cast on an arm or leg for a period of time? If so, you know that when the

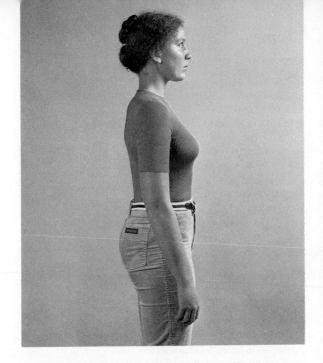
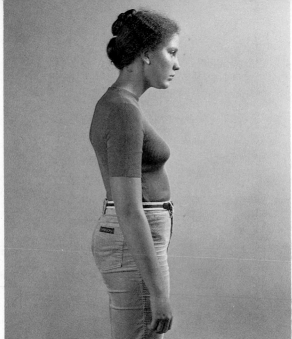

33-16. (left) Person with correct posture. (right) Person with poor posture. Vertebral column is more curved than with good posture.

cast was removed, the limb was smaller than the normal one. The cells of the muscles became smaller during the time they were not being used. This is called *disuse atrophy* (at rə fē). In contrast, exercise causes muscles to get larger. When a muscle gets larger, the number of cells in it does not increase. Instead, the individual cells get larger. They have more filaments in them and can contract more vigorously.

Exercise is beneficial in several ways. When we engage in exercise, our hearts beat faster and our rate of respiration increases. The chambers of the heart fill more completely and more blood is pumped out of the heart with each contraction. Like other muscles, the heart muscle is strengthened by vigorous contractions. The number of actin and myosin filaments increases in heart muscle cells, too.

The increase in the amount of blood being pumped causes the number of capillaries in the tissues to increase. Thus, more blood is carried to the cells and they get more oxygen and nutrients.

In addition to benefitting the muscles and the circulatory system, exercise slows the aging process and helps to regulate the appetite. People who exercise have more energy than those who do not. They are less likely to have stiff joints or become stooped. Many nutritionists believe that exercise is necessary to stimulate the mechanism that regulates appetite. Hunger and satiety centers in the hypothalamus control the amount a person eats. These centers appear to be more effective in maintaining normal body weight if a person exercises.

For many good reasons, you should exercise regularly each day. The teen years are a good time to form habits that delay the aging process.

Regular exercise that causes the heart to beat faster and more forcefully increases the cardiac output. Many physicians believe that such regular exercise strengthens the heart and delays aging.

33-16. (left) Person with correct posture. (right) Person with poor posture. Vertebral column is more curved than with good posture.

Answers to Questions for Section 3

G. 2. (a) An impulse travels along the membranes of the muscle cells; (b) it causes the filaments actin and myosin to overlap; (c) the muscle is no longer stimulated and the filaments move apart.

3. The same chemicals are released and they have the same function.

H. 4. By many filaments contracting; this moves one bone in relation to another bone.

5. The partial contraction of muscles that maintains posture and keeps muscles ready to contract further.

I. 6. Good posture prevents damage to joints and allows for proper functioning of internal organs.

7. Exercise keeps muscles healthy, strengthens the heart, makes the body able to pump more blood to the tissues, helps to regulate the appetite, and slows the aging process.

Answers to Questions for Section 3.

F. **1.** Skeletal muscle is striated and voluntary. Smooth muscle is not striated and involuntary (mostly). Cardiac muscle is found only in the heart and has intercalated discs and anastomoses. Skeletal muscle is attached to the bones and smooth muscle is found in internal organs.

(See page 669 for more answers.)

QUESTIONS FOR SECTION 3

1. What are the main characteristics of each of the three kinds of muscle tissue?
2. Describe what happens when (a) a muscle becomes excited, (b) a muscle contracts, and (c) a muscle relaxes.
3. How is the excitation of the motor end plate like the transmission of an impulse across a synapse?
4. How does a whole muscle cause movement?
5. What is muscle tone?
6. Why should you try to maintain good posture?
7. Why should you exercise?

CHAPTER REVIEW

The skin and the skeleton protect the body. The skeleton and muscles make movement possible. *In both protection and movement, the structures and their functions are closely related.* Glands in the skin secrete oil to lubricate the skin and hair or sweat to help maintain the body temperature. The skeleton protects and provides a place for muscles to attach. Muscles produce movement by contracting. Movement makes it possible to respond to stimuli from the environment and thus to do things that help to maintain homeostasis within the body. The contraction of muscles themselves is regulated by nerve impulses. Energy for contraction is provided by ATP produced by cellular metabolism. Smooth muscles regulate the function of internal organs and the heart keeps the blood circulating. *The contraction of muscles of all kinds helps to maintain homeostasis.*

Using the Concepts

1. Devise an experiment to show how sweating cools your skin.
2. Do some reading on your own on arthritis and gout. What current methods are being used in the treatment of these diseases? What research is being done to find a cure for these problems?
3. Build a model to show how the sliding filament theory explains muscle contraction.
4. Plan how you can maintain better posture and get more exercise. Why should you do these things?
5. Name and explain three examples of homeostasis that involve skin, bones, or muscles.

Unanswered Questions

6. What do you think might be substituted for a plaster cast to immobilize a fracture while it heals?
7. Science fiction stories often describe the replacement of body parts in humans. What limits do you think should be placed on such techniques?

Career Activities

8. How might the following people use the information in this chapter: consumer, physician, physical therapist, engineer, and coach?
9. Find out if your local hospital hires physical therapists. If so, find out what kind of work that person does and what training was required.

VOCABULARY REVIEW

1 epidermis	ossification	arthritis	myosin
dermis	fontanels	gout	sliding filament
cuticle	sutures	**3** motor unit	theory
sebum	ligament	skeletal muscle	origin
acne	joint	smooth muscle	insertion
2 axial	dislocation	cardiac muscle	tendons
appendicular	sprain	intercalated disc	flexion
periostem	strain	actin	extension

CHAPTER 33 TEST

Copy the number of each test item and place your answer to the right.

PART 1   Multiple Choice: Select the letter of the phrase that best completes each of the following.

d   1. The skin   **a.** prevents excess loss of fluids
    b. helps maintain normal body temperature
    c. supplies body with Vitamin D   **d.** all of these.

d   2. Causes of acne include   **a.** excess sebum and secretion of excess hormones   **b.** small amounts of fat and salt in diet   **c.** cleansing and ointments
    d. all of these.

b   3. Ossification of bone is the   **a.** loss of minerals in old age   **b.** laying down of minerals in bone
    c. formation of fontanels   **d.** formation of sutures.

a   4. Bones in a joint are held together by   **a.** liga-ments   **b.** tendons   **c.** hinges   **d.** ball-and-socket fixtures.

c   5. The appendicular skeleton consists of the bones of the   **a.** head   **b.** trunk   **c.** limbs   **d.** all of these.

c   6. The portion of a muscle cell that lies next to an axon is the   **a.** filament   **b.** fibrils   **c.** membrane
    d. synapse.

a   7. The arm muscle which helps flex the arm is
    a. biceps   **b.** triceps   **c.** flexion
    d. extension.

b   8. Good posture is healthful because it   **a.** is attractive   **b.** allows easy breathing   **c.** helps clothes fit well   **d.** helps digestion.

a   9. The muscle fibers that maintain posture   **a.** take turns contracting   **b.** all contract at once
    c. fatigue easily   **d.** never fatigue.

d   10. The failure to use muscles   **a.** leads to disuse atrophy   **b.** allows muscle cells to become smaller   **c.** has no effect on muscles   **d.** both a and b.

PART 2   Matching: Match the letter of the term in Column I with its description in Column II.

COLUMN I
a. keratin
b. cuticle
c. myosin
d. tanning
e. smooth muscle
f. skeletal muscle
g. joint
h. cardiac muscle
i. actin
j. sebum

COLUMN II
b   11. Fold of skin over base of nail
d   12. Pigment formation in the skin
g   13. Place where two bones are held together
j   14. Oily secretion from skin glands
a   15. Waterproofing substance
c   16. Thick filaments of muscle fibers
f   17. Moves limbs
i   18. Thin filaments of muscle fibers
h   19. Found in heart
e   20. Moves parts of internal organs

PART 3   Completion: Complete the following.
21. The healing of a fracture involves three steps ____.
22. The difference between a sprain and a strain is that ____.
23. Some of the benefits of exercise are ____.
24. Some examples of relationships between structure and function are ____.
25. The skin, skeleton, and muscles help maintain homeostasis by ____.

Chapter 33 Test Answers

21. formation of blood clot, white blood cells clear away damaged area, cells from periosteum begin to form new bone around ends of broken bone — a collar of bone thicker than original bone forms.
22. muscle or tendon is damaged in a sprain, but is stretched in a strain
23. benefits muscles and circulatory system, regulates appetite
24. joint structure, muscle structures correlate to functions
25. protection, movement in response to stimuli, movement of heart

CHAPTER 34

INTERNAL REGULATION

From your study of mammals and other animals you are already familiar with some chemicals that help to regulate internal processes. You have discovered that the pituitary gland is closely associated with the hypothalamus of the brain. In this chapter you shall examine the relationship between the endocrine glands of humans and the chemicals or hormones they produce.

In an earlier chapter we discussed antigens and antibodies as they relate to blood groups. Here we will discuss the role of antigens and antibodies in immunity, allergy, and organ transplants. You might think of antibodies as a kind of chemical regulator in that they respond to substances that are foreign to the body. Finally, we will discuss stress and how your body responds to it. Stress provides us with a good example of how both nervous and chemical regulation help the body to maintain homeostasis.

The basic concept in this chapter is that *chemicals play an important role in maintaining homeostasis.* You will see how chemicals influence the functioning of every other system in the body. Also, you will discover how they help to integrate the functioning of the different systems.

In the teen years, your body undergoes many changes. Some of the changes take place in the endocrine glands. In this chapter you will learn:

• How the endocrine glands regulate body functions
• How your body develops immunity to disease
• How the same process that develops immunity could cause your body to reject a transplanted organ
• What happens inside your body when you are under stress?

CYCLERS

1 THE ENDOCRINE SYSTEM

The Glands

The *endocrine* (*en* də krin) *system* consists of several separate glands and groups of cells located throughout the body. (See Fig. 34-1.) Endocrine glands release their secretions into capillaries that pass through them. In contrast, *exocrine* (*ek* sə krin) glands, such as sweat glands and oil glands in the skin, release their secretions through ducts to the outer surface of the body. Some exocrine glands also release their secretions into the digestive tract.

Hormones

Endocrine glands produce one or more chemicals, each with a specific effect in the body. Such chemicals are called *hormones*. Biolo-

34-1. The endocrine glands.

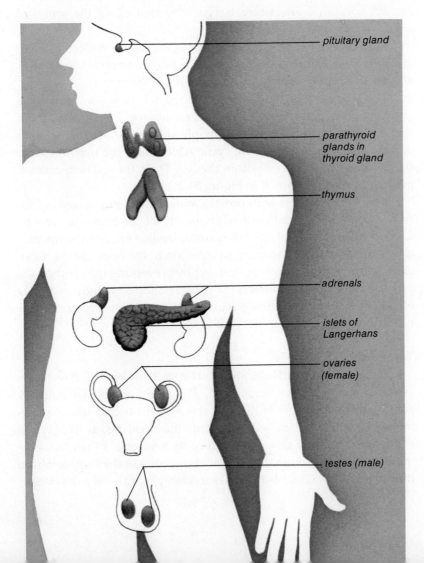

- pituitary gland
- parathyroid glands in thyroid gland
- thymus
- adrenals
- islets of Langerhans
- ovaries (female)
- testes (male)

A.

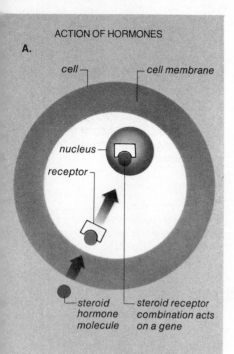

cell — — cell membrane

nucleus —
receptor —

steroid hormone molecule — — steroid receptor combination acts on a gene

B.

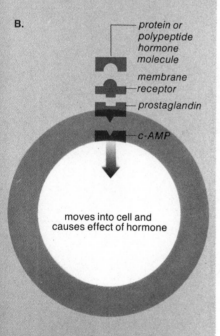

protein or polypeptide hormone molecule

membrane receptor

prostaglandin

c-AMP

moves into cell and causes effect of hormone

*34-2. How hormone molecules move into a cell. **A.** Steroid hormone molecule. **B.** Protein or polypeptide hormone molecule.*

gists study the effects of increases and decreases in the amount of hormone produced by an endocrine gland. Through this research, they have found out what these glands do. For example, *thyroxin* (thī rok sin), is a hormone produced by the *thyroid* gland. Its effect is to regulate the rate of metabolism. Removal of the gland decreases the rate of metabolism. However, the addition of thyroxin increases the rate of metabolism.

HORMONE ACTIONS   Most hormones act on specific parts of the body. The particular organ a hormone acts on is called the *target organ.* How a hormone affects a target organ is due in part to its chemical structure. Hormones can be placed in two groups, *steroids* and proteins or polypeptides, according to their chemical structure.

Steroid molecules are similar to lipids. Also, they are soluble in lipids. Steroids easily pass through the cell membrane of their target organs. Inside the cell the steroid attaches to a receptor molecule. Steroid hormones affect target organs by controlling the action of certain genes.

Protein and polypeptide hormones are larger molecules than steroids. Hence, they cannot enter the cells of their target organs. Instead they attach to receptors on the cell membrane.

The presence of the hormone at the receptor site activates a prostaglandin (präs tə *glan* den) in the membrane. The prostaglandin then activates cyclic adenosine monophosphate (c-AMP) at the inner surface of the membrane. The cyclic AMP relays the message from the hormone to chemicals within the cell. Thus, the cell is stimulated by the hormone as shown in Figure 34-2.

Many experiments with prostaglandins are being carried out today. Scientists expect that a wide variety of medical uses will be found for them. One effect of the prostaglandins seems to be the production of fever when there is an infection in the body. Some biologists believe that aspirin reduces fever by preventing the synthesis of prostaglandins. Other effects of prostaglandins include reducing blood pressure and reducing acid production in the stomach. This reduction of acid helps to prevent ulcers.

The Pituitary Gland

The pituitary gland is located just beneath the brain and is closely associated with the hypothalamus. The secretions of the pituitary gland affect most other endocrine glands. This occurs when a hormone from the pituitary is secreted into the bloodstream. This action stimulates a specific gland to produce its hormone. When this hormone circulates through the pituitary it suppresses the secretion from the pituitary. (See Fig. 34-3.) This is an example of a feedback system.

The pituitary gland has two lobes. The anterior lobe produces six hormones. The posterior lobe stores and releases two hormones that are made in the hypothalamus. In addition, hormones from the hypothalamus stimulate the anterior lobe to secrete its hormones.

HORMONES OF THE ANTERIOR PITUITARY *Growth hormone* is produced by the anterior lobe. It increases the rate of growth in childhood and maintains the adult size in later life. An excess of this hormone during childhood produces a giant. Moreover, a deficiency produces a midget. The growth hormone is the only pituitary secretion that has a general effect on the whole body.

Two other hormones from the anterior pituitary provide examples of feedback effects. *Adreno cortico tropic* (ə *drē* nō kôrt i kō *trō* pik) *hormone*, or ACTH, stimulates the release of hormones from the cortex of the adrenal gland. In turn, *cortisol* (kôr tə sol), an important hormone from the adrenal cortex, suppresses the release of ACTH. *Thyroid-stimulating hormone* (TSH) stimulates the release of thyroxine from the thyroid gland. When the thyroxine concentration in the blood is high enough to maintain a normal metabolic rate, it suppresses the release of TSH.

The final three hormones of the anterior lobe of the pituitary gland regulate reproduction. *Follicle stimulating hormone* (FSH) stimulates the production of estrogen and the development of an ovum within the ovary. In males, FSH stimulates the production of sperm cells. *Luteinizing* (loo ten ī zing) hormone (LH) stimulates the production of progesterone in females. Furthermore, it regulates the production of testosterone in males. Still another hormone, *prolactin* (prō *lak* tin), stimulates milk production after the birth of an infant.

HORMONES OF THE POSTERIOR PITUITARY The hormones that are stored in the posterior lobe of the pituitary gland are *antidiuretic* (ant i dī yoo *ret* ik) *hormone* (ADH) and *oxytocin* (äk si *tōs* ən). ADH causes the kidney to put water back into the blood. It also causes blood vessels to constrict. Moreover, ADH is secreted throughout life as it is needed. A deficiency of ADH causes the disease, *diabetes insipidus* (in *sip* əd əs). This results in the patient eliminating large quantities of urine. ADH can be given to such patients to correct this problem. Oxytocin stimulates contractions of the uterus. It is released only during labor and after childbirth. In fact, oxytocin is sometimes used to start labor. Commercial preparations of this hormone are given to stimulate uterine contraction after delivery of an infant. This lessens the danger of uterine hemorrhage. In addition, the release of milk from the mammary glands after a birth is due to the action of oxytocin.

Table 34-1 on page 676 summarizes the effects of the hormones of the pituitary gland.

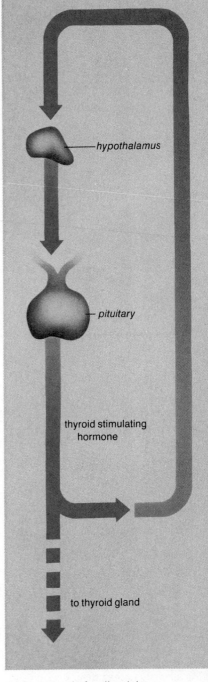

hypothalamus

pituitary

thyroid stimulating hormone

to thyroid gland

34-3. A simple feedback loop.

TABLE 34–1. HORMONES OF THE PITUITARY GLAND.

Hormone	Where Produced	Effect
Growth hormone	anterior	increase rate of growth in childhood, maintain adult size
Thyroid stimulating hormone	anterior	stimulate thyroid gland to secrete thyroid hormones
ACTH	anterior	stimulate adrenal cortex to secrete its hormones
FSH	anterior	development of eggs and sperm
LH	anterior	stimulate ovaries to produce progesterone and testes to produce testosterone
Prolactin	anterior	stimulate milk production after the birth of a child
ADH	hypothalamus, stored in posterior	stimulate kidney to reabsorb water back into blood; cause blood vessels to constrict
Oxytocin	hypothalamus, stored in posterior	stimulate contraction of muscles of the uterus

QUESTIONS FOR SECTION 1

1. Define endocrine gland and target organ.
2. What is the role of prostaglandins and cyclic AMP in the action of hormones?
3. Name the hormones produced by the pituitary gland.
4. What are the functions of each of the pituitary hormones?
5. How does the pituitary gland affect other glands?
6. How do other glands affect the pituitary gland?

Answers to Questions for Section 1.

A. 1. Endocrine gland: releases its secretions into the blood. Target organ: is affected by a particular hormone.

*2. Prostaglandins appear to be present in the membrane of cells and act as messengers between a hormone and the inside of the cell. Cyclic-AMP also acts as a messenger from the prostaglandin to trigger a particular reaction in the cell.

B. 3. Growth hormone, thyroid stimulating hormone, prolactin, follicle stimulating hormone, luteinizing hormone, adrenocorticotropic hormone, oxytocin, antidiuretic hormone.

4. In order as in 3: stimulate and maintain growth, stimulate thyroid gland, stimulate mammary glands, stimulate release of egg from ovary, stimulate preparation of uterus for pregnancy, stimulate adrenal cortex, stimulate uterine contraction, prevent excess fluid loss.

5. The pituitary, often called the master gland, regulates the activity of many other glands.

6. Several glands that are stimulated by hormones from the pituitary produce hormones that cause the pituitary to cease stimulating the glands that produce these hormones.

CHAPTER INVESTIGATION

Two people were each given 50 g of glucose in 200 ml of water at the beginning of this experiment.

A. State in your own words what you can about the blood glucose level of the diabetic individual; the normal individual. Base your statements on the data in the graph.

B. Indicate at what point in each curve insulin became active in the person's body.

C. Make another graph showing what would happen to the blood glucose level in diabetic coma. In insulin shock.

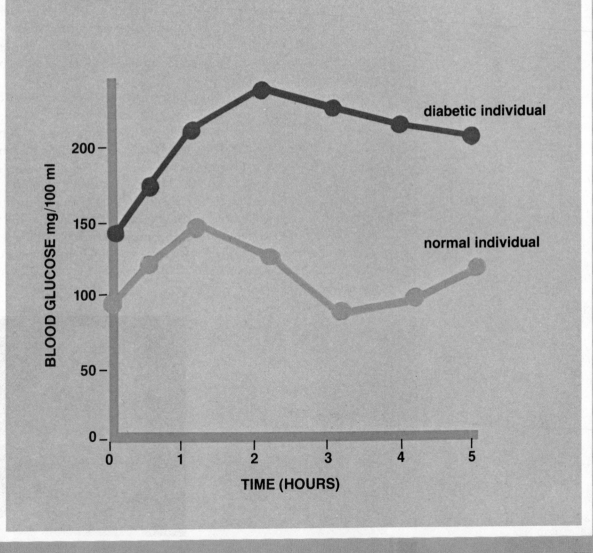

2 OTHER ENDOCRINE GLANDS AND THEIR HORMONES

The Thyroid Gland

The thyroid gland secretes the hormones, thyroxine and triidothyronine. They help to control the rate of metabolism in the cells of the body. Excesses or deficiencies of these hormones are not uncommon in humans. (See Fig. 34-4.)

HYPOTHYROIDISM Hypothyroidism occurs when too little hormones are produced. A patient with this disease will be less mentally alert and less physically active than normal. Another sign of hypothyroidism is a low metabolic rate. Moreover, the person may also become overweight and feel the effects of cold weather more than normal people. Infants born with a thyroid deficiency are called *cretins* (*krē* tins). If not treated, such children will be mentally retarded dwarfs. The thyroid hormones can be supplied in a tablet taken by mouth and the deficiency corrected.

HYPERTHYROIDISM Hyperthyroidism occurs when too much of the thyroid hormones are produced. This disease produces a high metabolic rate in the body. A patient with hyperthyroidism will be nervous, unable to sleep, and may lose weight. Furthermore, the person's eyes may appear to bulge from the head. (See Fig. 34-5.) A drug, *thiouracil* (thī ō *yoor* ə sil), can be used to treat this disease.

GOITER A *goiter* (*goi* tər) is an enlarged thyroid gland. One of the things that can cause goiter is a lack of iodine in the diet. Iodine is needed by the thyroid gland to make its hormones. When there is a shortage of iodine, the gland enlarges in an attempt to make more of the hormone. The simple procedure of adding iodine to table salt provides enough iodine to prevent goiter.

34-4. (left) The thyroid gland is located near the upper end of the trachea.

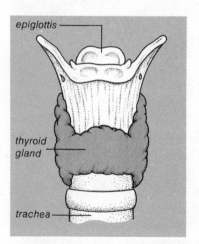

epiglottis

thyroid gland

trachea

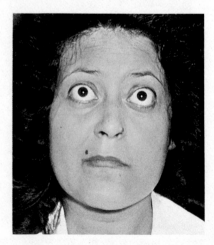

34-5. (right) Person with hyperthyroidism.

The Parathyroid Glands

The *parathyroid glands* are tiny groups of cells imbedded in the back side of the thyroid gland. There are four of these glands, two in each lobe of the thyroid. They secrete parathyroid hormone. Its function is to regulate the amount of calcium and other ions in the blood. Calcium is needed for the maintenance and development of healthy bones. Calcium is also needed for muscle contraction and the transmission of nerve impulses.

The Adrenal Glands

The *adrenal glands* are located above the kidneys. (See Fig. 34-6.) The inner part of the gland, called the *medulla*, produces the hormones, epinephrine and norepinephrine. The outer part of the gland, called the *cortex*, produces several hormones. Let us examine what each part of the gland does.

MEDULLA   The medulla of the adrenal gland is stimulated by the sympathetic nervous system. Hormones from the medulla enter the blood stream and circulate throughout the body. When these hormones stimulate an organ, the effect is the same as that produced by the sympathetic nervous system. However, epinephrine and norepinephrine take longer to reach an organ than an impulse from a nerve. Nevertheless, once these hormones are in the blood stream their effects are longer lasting than those produced by neurons.

CORTEX   The cortex of the adrenal gland secretes several hormones. One hormone of the cortex, *aldosterone* (al *das* tə rōn), controls the amount of salt and water in the blood. Another hormone, *cortisol,* helps to regulate metabolism by converting fats and proteins into glucose. Cortisol and *cortisone* help to prevent redness and swelling around the site of an injury. Both also play a role in the body's response to stress. The cortex of the adrenal gland also secretes small amounts of sex hormones.

The Pancreas

In a previous chapter you discovered that the pancreas produces enzymes that digest food substances in the small intestine. These enzymes travel to the intestine by way of ducts. Thus the enzymes are exocrine secretions of the pancreas. In addition to this, the pancreas also produces endocrine secretions. Small groups of cells scattered through the pancreas, the *islets of Langerhans* (läng ər häns), produce hormones. (See Fig. 34-7 on page 680.) Two of these hormones are *insulin* and *glucagon*. When the concentration of glucose in the blood drops, glucagon is secreted into the bloodstream. It stimulates the release of glucose from the liver. This causes the concentration of glucose in the blood to increase.

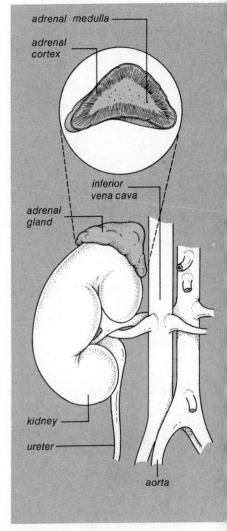

34-6. The adrenal glands are located above the kidneys.

Cortisone is often given to combat inflammations. Poison ivy, rheumatoid arthritis, and a variety of other maladies respond to cortisone therapy. However, the drug has side effects if it is used over long periods of time.

Insulin is secreted when the concentration of glucose gets above the normal level. It stimulates the liver to store glucose in the form of glycogen. Insulin also increases the rate at which glucose enters the cells of the body. In fact, without insulin, so little glucose would enter the cells that they would starve.

The secretion of insulin and glucagon keep a constant level of glucose in the blood. If the level drops too low, the cells of the brain cease to function. These cells will die if the glucose level does not increase within a few minutes. If the level gets too high, much of the excess glucose is excreted in the urine. A lot of water is excreted with the glucose in the urine. This causes the cells to become dried out. A patient with this condition would be very thirsty.

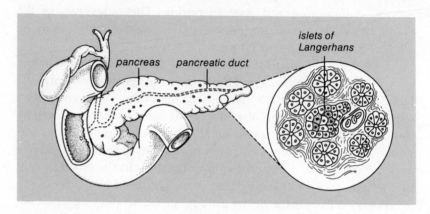

34-7. The islets of Langerhans are located inside the pancreas.

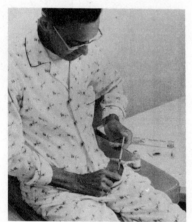

34-8. A person with diabetes giving himself an injection of insulin.

DIABETES MELLITUS The condition, *diabetes mellitus* (mə lī̄ təs), is caused by a deficiency of insulin. Through research, insulin was identified as a protein and eventually was made available to treat human diabetics.

In recent years it has been observed that diabetes tends to run in families. The tendency to develop diabetes seems to be inherited. Other factors that may contribute to diabetes are obesity and eating foods with high sugar content. There also seem to be two different kinds of diabetes mellitus. One begins in childhood or early adulthood. (See Fig. 34-8.) The other begins in middle or old age. The early onset diabetes is more difficult to treat. However, with daily injections of insulin, people can usually live normal lives. The late onset diabetes can often be treated with a carefully planned diet. This should be supplemented with medicines that stimulate the pancreas to produce insulin.

Diabetes patients are subject to becoming unconscious if their blood sugar reaches either a very high or very low level. A high blood sugar level produces *diabetic coma.* Breathing is rapid and deep and the breath may smell of acetone (*as ə tōn*). (Acetone smells like ripe bananas or fingernail polish remover.) A patient in diabetic coma requires emergency medical attention. A very low blood sugar level may occur after a patient has taken too much insulin. In this case unconsciousness is due to insulin shock. However, if the patient is still conscious, sugar can be given by mouth. A glass of orange juice may prevent unconsciousness.

The Ovaries, the Testes, and the Placenta

The *ovaries* in females and the *testes* in males begin to function at the onset of puberty or sexual maturity. These glands have two functions. The first is to produce sex cells. The second is to produce hor-

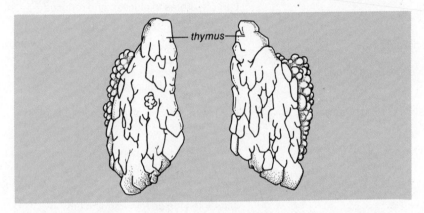

34-9. *The thymus gland is located in the chest cavity.*

mones. The *placenta*, the organ that provides nutrients to the embryo, is also an endocrine gland.

The Thymus Gland

The *thymus gland* is located in the chest cavity. (See Fig. 34-9.) For a long time the function of the thymus was not known. However, through research, it is now established that this endocrine gland produces the hormone, *thymosin* (*thī mə sən*). In the next section we will see how this hormone is associated with immunity.

Other Hormones

Several hormones are produced in the digestive tract. You are already familiar with gastrin. This hormone is made by cells that line the stomach. Another hormone, secretin (*si krət ən*), is secreted into the blood stream by cells in the small intestine. It stimulates the pancreas to secrete digestive juices and the liver to secrete bile.

Table 34-2 on page 682 summarizes the effects of hormones from sources other than the pituitary gland.

Answers to Questions for Section 2.

3. The pancreas produces insulin when the blood sugar rises above the normal level. The insulin causes cells to take up sugar (glucose) from the blood. When the blood sugar level goes below normal, the pancreas produces glucagon. It causes the blood sugar to rise by stimulating the release of glucose from glycogen in the liver.

*4. The adrenal glands consist of a cortex which secretes several steroid hormones and a medulla which secretes epinephrine or norepinephrine.

TABLE 34–2. HORMONES FROM SOURCES OTHER THAN THE PITUITARY.

Hormone	Source	Main Effects of Hormones
Thyroxine and triiodothyronine	thyroid	increase rate of metabolism
Parathyroid hormone	parathyroid	regulate calcium in blood
Epenephrine and norepenephrine	adrenal medulla	stimulates certain organs to allow body to respond to an emergency
Aldosterone	adrenal cortex	stimulates kidney to return sodium ions to blood
Cortisol	adrenal cortex	stimulates change of fats and carbohydrates to glucose and reduces inflammation
Cortisone	adrenal cortex	reduces inflammation
Insulin	islets of Langerhans	stimulates storage of glucose in the liver and the entry of glucose into cells
Glucagon	islets of Langerhans	stimulates release of glucose from supply stored in liver
Estrogen	ovaries	stimulates development of the uterine lining, the mammary glands, and other sexual characteristics
Progesterone	ovaries	stimulates the development of the placenta in pregnancy
Testosterone	testes	stimulates development of male sex organs and secondary sex characteristics
Human chorionic gonadotropin	placenta	stimulates ovaries to produce progesterone
Gastrin	cells of lining of stomach	stimulates secretion of gastric juices
Secretin	cells of lining of small intestine	stimulates secretion of pancreatic juices and bile

Answers to Questions for Section 2.

C. 1. Thyroid: in throat; parathyroids imbedded in thyroid; adrenal glands above kidneys; pancreas between folds of intestine; thymus in chest cavity.

2. See Table 34-2 on page 682.

(See page 681 for answers 3-4)

QUESTIONS FOR SECTION 2

1. Where are each of the five endocrine glands named in this section located?
2. What hormones does each gland produce and what is the function of each hormone?
3. What is the role of the pancreas in regulating blood glucose?
4. What is meant by the statement that the adrenal gland is two glands in one.

3 IMMUNITY

Immunity *is the ability to resist infection and to ward off certain other kinds of injury.* The immune system responds not only to microorganisms but also to certain large molecules that are not normally present in the circulatory system of the body. Immunity is a kind of internal regulation.

You already know that white blood cells surround and engulf foreign substances. This response of the white blood cells provides the body with a kind of general immunity to the effects of invading organisms. The body also has a very specific immune system.

You are already familiar with the chemicals that are involved in the specific immune system. They are antigens and antibodies. (See Fig. 34-10.) This system is able to recognize antigens in a person's own tissues. It does not make antibodies against these antigens. However, the specific immune system is able to recognize and destroy antigens that do not belong in the body. This process is called *specific immunity.* Let us see how the process works.

Specific immunity is the task of certain white blood cells called lymphocytes. Two kinds of lymphocytes, B-cells and T-cells, are found in the bloodstream. B-cells originate in the bone marrow. However, T-cells are produced by the thymus. Furthermore, these cells are activated by the hormone, thymosin.

The Immune Reaction

When a microorganism carrying a specific antigen gets into the bloodstream, a particular B-cell responds to it. This B-cell divides many times and forms a clone of many identical B-cells. *A* **clone** *is a group of identical cells derived from a single cell.* These B-cells produce large quantities of antibodies that react with the antigen carried by the microorganism. Because microorganisms have several molecules of the antigen on their surfaces, several antibodies attach to each microorganism. This reaction causes the organisms to bind together in clumps. The clumps are then engulfed by other white blood cells.

The T-cells perform a different function in the immune reaction. Instead of releasing antibodies, the T-cells retain antibodies attached to their outer cell membrane. They recognize specific antigens just as B-cells do. However, instead of releasing antibodies, the T-cells attach directly to the microorganism. These cells eventually engulf and destroy the foreign substance. Each kind of T-cell will destroy only one kind of microorganism. These processes are shown in Figure 34-11 on page 684.

OBJECTIVES FOR SECTION 3

D. Define: *immunity, antigen, antibody, T-cell,* and *B-cell.*

E. Explain how your body develops immunity to diseases.

F. Interpret the role of the immune system in cancer, allergy, and organ transplantation.

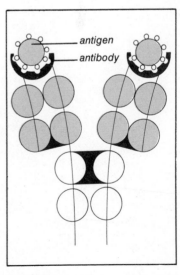

34-10. The specific immune system.

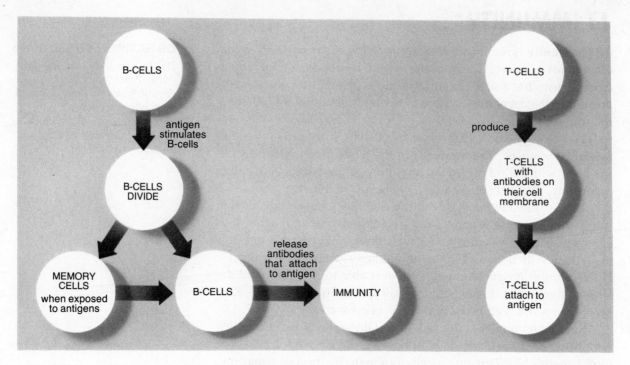

34-11. The immune reaction.

When your body is first exposed to a particular organism, specific B-cells and T-cells respond to it. Even though these cells respond rapidly, it is several days before there are enough antibodies and T-cells to overcome the invading organism. Thus, you may become ill with the disease that the organism causes. However, the second time you are exposed to the organism, it does not make you ill. Your immune system destroys the organism before it can produce any disease symptoms.

How Does the Immune System "Remember?"

How lymphocytes remember and recognize antigens that they have responded to in the past is not well understood. According to one theory, every infant is born with a large number of B-cells. Each B-cell divides many times until it produces a clone of many cells exactly like itself. When an antigen enters the body, the cells of the appropriate clone divide. Some produce antibodies and others become *memory cells.* The memory cells remain in the body ready to begin dividing when the antigen is again encountered. B-cells of clones that are successful in matching with an antigen divide rapidly and are selected to survive. The body selects against other cells, from the same clone, that do not match the antigen. Hence, this theory is called the *clonal selection theory.* This process is summarized in diagram form in Figure 34-12.

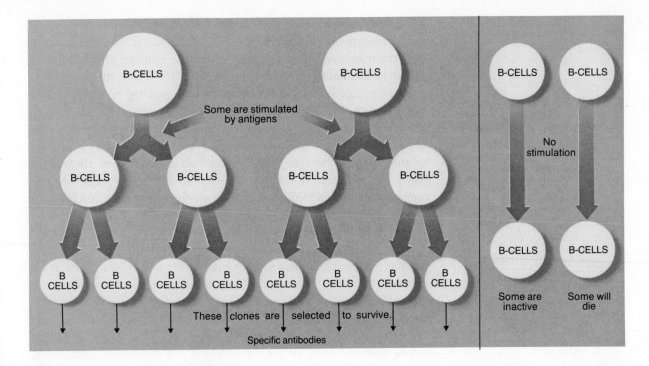

How Does the Immune System Recognize Foreign Substances?

Like the ability to "remember," the ability to recognize foreign substances is also a puzzle to biologists. It is thought that by the time an infant is born, only those B-cells that will respond to foreign substances remain in the body. Others that could respond to the body's own cells were destroyed during the development of the embryo. This process explains how clones that destroy the substance of the body are selected out of existence. Therefore, this fits well with the clonal selection theory.

Kinds of Immunity

Immunity may be innate or acquired. **Innate immunity** *is that which one is born with.* In contrast, **acquired immunity** *is that which an individual develops at any time after birth.*

Acquired immunity can be divided into four categories. It may be *naturally acquired* or *artificially acquired.* Within each of these categories immunity may be *active* or *passive.* Active immunity is relatively permanent. In contrast, passive immunity is temporary. Let's look at some examples of each of these kinds of immunity.

Naturally acquired active immunity is obtained by actually having a disease. The body produces its own antibodies in response to the antigen of the microorganism, toxin, or virus. This type of immunity of-

Encourage students to determine what immunizations they and their younger brothers and sisters have had. Many children have suffered from preventable illness simply because they did not receive immunizations.

fers future protection against similar infections of a given organism. *Naturally acquired passive immunity* is obtained by newborn infants from the transmission of antibodies from the mother. These antibodies can be transmitted through the placenta and by the mother's milk. *Artificially acquired active immunity* is obtained by receiving small doses of a specific antigen. These doses either have been inactivated or are not large enough to cause the disease. However, they are sufficient to cause the immune system to respond. The memory cells are created so that when the person is exposed to the disease, the body is ready to produce antibodies and T-cells to attack the organism. Immunizations of this type are routinely given to small children for a variety of diseases. Some of these diseases are smallpox, polio, measles, and mumps. *Artificially acquired passive immunity* is obtained by injection of antibodies produced actively in other individuals. When a person has been exposed to a serious disease for which he or she has no natural immunity, *gamma globulin* is often given. Gamma globulin is the portion of blood that contains antibodies. It produces a temporary supply of antibodies for the antigen carried by the disease organism. These antibodies do not cause the person's own immune system to create memory cells, so the immunity is not permanent. However, after the disease is over, the person will have developed active immunity against the disease organism. The kinds of immunity are summarized in Table 34-3.

TABLE 34–3. *KINDS OF ACQUIRED IMMUNITY.*

	Active	*Passive*
Acquired naturally	by having the disease	through placenta or mother's milk
Acquired artificially	by receiving vaccine	by receiving gamma globulin

The Immune System and Cancer

Cancer cells are normal body cells that have undergone a change in the genetic make-up of the cells. Furthermore, the antigens on their surface are changed. They therefore become recognizable as cells not normally present in the body. At this point, T-cells combine with these antigen molecules and release chemicals that destroy the cancer cells. It is thought by some biologists that we all have such cancer cells present in our bodies. It is only when the T-cells fail to destroy them that we get cancer.

Allergies

Many people are allergic to various substances found in the environment — dust, pollen, insect bites, certain foods, poison ivy, and penicillin. Their bodies respond to these substances as if they were antigens. Why some systems respond to these substances and others do not is unknown. However, when a person has an *allergy*, the reaction in the body is the same as the immune reaction to a microorganism. What is different about an allergic response from other immune responses is that the antibodies are of a different kind. These antibodies cause inflamed areas on the skin in allergies that produce skin rashes. They also cause the release of a chemical called *histamine* (*his tə mēn*). This chemical produces a secondary response in other cells. For example, histamine causes excess secretion of mucus in such allergies as hay fever. It also constricts the air passageways in the lungs of patients with asthma. One mechanism of allergic reactions is shown in Figure 34-13.

Some allergic reactions cause only annoyance and discomfort. Others can be life threatening. Certain individuals can become sensitized to penicillin, the sting of a particular insect, or some other substance. A second exposure to the substance can cause a violent reaction. Histamine and other substances are released in large amounts. These substances cause the arterioles and veins to dilate. Since the blood vessels are now much larger, the blood pressure may

Answers to Questions for Section 3.

6. From gamma globulin injected into the body or from the mother either through the placenta before birth or through the mother's milk.

7. Through having a disease of through being immunized.

8. Among the B-cells are some that become memory cells. These cells remain in the body after an infection and begin dividing whenever the antigen they recognize enters the body.

F. **9.** It is thought that the body produces antibodies to cancer cells. Such cells are genetically different from normal cells and have different antigens on their surface. Sometimes the body can recognize these cells and destroy them , thus providing immunity to cancer.

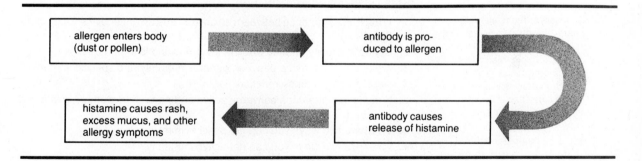

34-13. *The allergic reaction.*

drop to a dangerously low level. At the same time large quantities of fluid tend to leak out of the capillaries. This loss of fluid reduces the total volume of blood. Due to these two conditions very little blood is being returned to the heart. The patient may die within minutes unless emergency medical attention is available.

Autoimmune diseases are a special kind of allergy. In such diseases the body fails to recognize some cells as part of itself. It produces antibodies to these cells. When this happens, some of the body's own cells are destroyed. Rheumatoid arthritis is an autoimmune disease.

Organ Transplants

Today there are many operations in which a kidney, heart, or some other organ is transplanted from one human to another. (See Fig. 34-14.) In some cases, several weeks after a successful operation, the organ ceases to function. Such an event is usually due to rejection of the transplanted organ. *Rejection* of a transplanted organ is caused by an immune response. If too many of the antigens on a transplanted organ are different from those on the recipient's tissues, the organ will be rejected. The recipient's body will produce antibodies to the foreign antigens and the cells of the organ will be destroyed.

Two different methods are used to reduce the risk of an organ being rejected. First, the tissues of the donor and recipient are matched. This is done much in the same way that blood for transfusion is matched. In kidney transplants, the donor is usually a close relative of the recipient. Closely related individuals have many genes in common. Therefore, they have similar antigens on the membranes of their cells. A second method is to treat the recipient with drugs that suppress the body's ability to produce antibodies. This reduces the risk of rejection. However, it also causes the patient to be susceptible to infections. The stress of surgery also lowers the patient's resistance to infection. Transplant patients sometimes die of infections because of their lowered resistance.

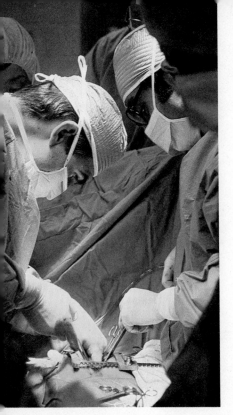

34-14. Transplant operation.

E. 4. The immune reaction occurs in response to the presence of a foreign antigen, as found on microorganisms. B-cells that can respond to it are produced in large quantities of the antibody that reacts with the antigen and causes the organisms to clump together. T-cells also recognize antigens and attach directly to the microorganism and destroy it.

5. Active immunity is produced when the body produces its own antibodies following immunization or having a disease. Passive immunity occurs when antibodies enter the body from another source. Innate immunity: that which one is born with. Acquired immunity: obtained after birth.

(See page 687 for more answers.)

QUESTIONS FOR SECTION 3

1. What is the difference between: an antigen and an antibody? A T-cell and a B-cell?
2. Define immunity and tell why the thymus gland is important in immunity.
3. What is the difference between general immunity and specific immunity?
4. Describe the immune reaction.
5. What is the difference between: active and passive immunity? Innate and acquired immunity?
6. What are two ways you can get passive immunity?
7. What are two ways you can get active immunity?
8. How do cells of the immune system "remember?"
9. What is the role of immunity in cancer?

Answers to Questions for Section 3.

D. *1. An antigen is a protein or polysaccharide that stimulates antibody production. Antibodies are produced in response to the presence of an antigen. T-cells destroy microorganisms and B-cells help body to "remember" and recognize antigens it has been exposed to and react to them.

2. The ability to resist infection and to ward off certain other kinds of injury. The thymus gland is important in immunity because it produces T-cells and thymosin that stimulates their activity.

3. General immunity is the body's general response to any microorganism or foreign substance in the body. The white blood cells destroy these substances. Specific immunity is the body's response to a specific antigen in a way that destroys it and prepares the body to recognize and destroy the same antigen when it enters the body again.

4 STRESS

Any stimulus from the environment causes some kind of response in the body. Much of what we have discussed about how living organisms respond to their environment has emphasized the need for the body to maintain relatively stable internal conditions. Living things are able to maintain homeostasis fairly easily if the changes in the environment are not too great or not too frequent. However, if the changes in the environment are greater than the organism can cope with, stress is produced.

Stress can be produced by injury, infection, prolonged heavy exercise, decreased oxygen supply, or prolonged exposure to pain, fright, cold, or emotional situations. In some ways the response of the body to these different conditions are quite varied. However, in one way, they are all the same. They all cause the adrenal cortex to secrete excessive amounts of cortisol. Thus, **stress** *is defined as a situation in which the body secretes excessive amounts of cortisol.* The activity of the sympathetic nervous system is also increased in stress.

Hans Selye, a Canadian physiologist, was able to recognize three stages in an organism's response to stress. These stages are: (1) the alarm reaction, (2) the stage of resistance, and (3) the stage of exhaustion. In the *alarm reaction* the adrenal medulla secretes an excess of epinephrine or norepinephrine. Also, the sympathetic nervous system becomes more active. In the *stage of resistance* the body has adapted to the stress and the symptoms of alarm disappear. The body has successfully coped with the stress. However, when stress is extremely severe or prolonged, our bodies eventually enter the *stage of exhaustion.* Again the adrenal cortex secretes large amounts of cortisol. This time the amounts are even greater than in the alarm reaction. Resistance to the stress has been lost because the regulating mechanisms have been overwhelmed. Such prolonged stress can lead to death. These stages of stress are summarized in Figure 34-15.

Our bodies vary in their ability to cope with stress. Some of us are more able to resist it than others. A few people even respond to stress by becoming healthier. Others will be made ill by the same level of stress. Furthermore, our ability to resist stress varies at different times in our lives.

Current Ideas About Stress

The body's response to stress provides us with a good example of how the control systems of the body — the endocrine and nervous systems — work together to maintain homeostasis. The overall effects of the actions of these systems are the following. The blood sugar increases making more energy available to the cells. The heart rate and

OBJECTIVES FOR SECTION 4

G. Define *stress* and describe the roles of the endocrine and nervous systems in responding to it.

Encourage interested students to read about and report on recent research on stress.

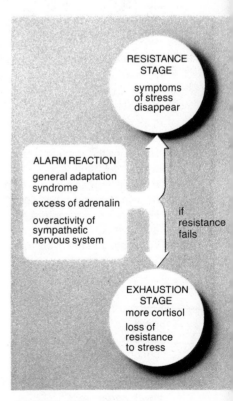

34-15. *The stages of stress.*

blood pressure also increase so the body is prepared for fight or flight. Furthermore, water is retained in the body ready to compensate for losses due to sweating or even blood loss following injury. If these responses are successful, stress is alleviated and the resistance stage is reached. If they are unsuccessful, the exhaustion stage is reached as the body's regulatory mechanisms fail to cope with the stress.

Answers to Questions for Section 4.
G. 1. A situation in which the body secretes excess amounts of cortisol.
2. See 34-15 on page 689.

QUESTIONS FOR SECTION 4
1. What is stress?
2. What are the three stages of stress and what happens in each stage?

CHAPTER REVIEW

In this chapter we have considered the actions of the endocrine system, the immune system, and the effects of stress. In each case we have shown that many different homeostatic mechanisms are involved in internal regulation. We have also shown that the nervous system works with the other regulatory systems to produce homeostasis.

Using the Concepts

1. How do juvenile and adult onset diabetes differ and how is the treatment for them different?
2. Which diseases have you been immunized against? (Did you include immunization by having the disease?)
3. How does the immune system tell the difference between "self" and "non-self?"
4. How is allergy an example of the immune system not helping to maintain homeostasis?
5. How do autoimmune diseases provide another example of the failure to maintain homeostasis?
6. What methods are used to prevent a transplanted organ from being rejected? What problems might the use of these methods create?
7. Give at least three examples of relationships between the endocrine and nervous systems.
8. Why is stress a good example of how control systems function in internal regulation?
9. The drug cortisone is used to treat a variety of ailments. Do some outside reading to determine which ones. Then discuss the advantages and disadvantages of the use of the drug.

Career Activities

10. Suppose you are working in a public health clinic. How would you encourage parents to have their children immunized against various diseases?
11. Suppose an endocrinologist or a physiologist interested in stress were to visit your class. What questions would you ask about their careers?
12. How might the information in this chapter be used by: a parent, physician, patient, politician, teacher, yourself?

VOCABULARY REVIEW

1 endocrine	2 adrenal gland	estrogen	natural immunity
exocrine	medulla	progesterone	acquired immunity
hormone	cortex	testosterone	active immunity
thyroid gland	pancreas	3 T-cells	passive immunity
pituitary gland	islets of Langerhans	B-cells	allergy
growth hormone	insulin	thymus gland	histamine
follicle stimulating hormone	glucagon	memory cells	4 stress

CHAPTER 34 TEST

Copy the number of each test item and place your answer to the right.

PART 1 Multiple Choice: Select the letter of the phrase that best completes each of the following.

d **1.** Endocrine glands **a.** produce hormones **b.** release their secretions into the blood **c.** release their secretions to the outside of the body **d.** both a and b.

a **2.** Steroid hormones affect target organs by **a.** attaching to receptor sites inside the cells **b.** attaching to the cell membrane **c.** activating the prostaglandin hormones **d.** activating cyclic-AMP.

c **3.** Negative feedback regulates by **a.** speeding up a process **b.** slowing down a process **c.** turning off a process that produced the negative feedback substance **d.** none of the above.

b **4.** Which of the following is *not* a malfunction of the thyroid gland? **a.** cretinism **b.** diabetes mellitus **c.** hypothyroidism **d.** hyperthyroidism.

d **5.** The adrenal glands produce **a.** epinephrine **b.** aldosterone **c.** cortisol **d.** all of the above.

d **6.** Immunity is produced by **a.** the manufacture of an antigen **b.** the manufacture of an antibody **c.** the destruction of microorganisms **d.** both a and b.

a **7.** The function of the thymus gland is **a.** to produce T-cells and thymosin **b.** regulate metabolism **c.** regulate other glands **d.** function is unknown.

c **8.** A group of identical cells derived from a single cell is called **a.** T-cells **b.** B-cells **c.** a clone **d.** memory cells.

a **9.** Artificially acquired active immunity is obtained from **a.** a vaccine that causes the production of antibodies **b.** having a disease **c.** mother's milk **d.** gamma-globulin.

b **10.** Stress is a situation in which the body secretes an excessive amount of **a.** epinephrine **b.** cortisol **c.** ACTH **d.** thyroxin.

PART 2 Matching: Match the letter of the term in Column I with its description in Column II.

COLUMN I

a. thyroid gland
b. growth hormone
c. ACTH
d. ADH
e. parathyroid hormone
f. insulin
g. glucagon
h. estrogen
i. progesterone
j. testosterone

COLUMN II

b **11.** Stimulates growth and maintains body size
d **12.** Causes body to retain water
e **13.** Regulates calcium metabolism
a **14.** Regulates rate of metabolism
c **15.** Stimulates adrenal cortex
h **16.** Stimulates development of uterus and mammary glands
j **17.** Stimulates development of male sex characteristics
g **18.** Increases glucose level in blood
f **19.** Decreases glucose level in blood
i **20.** Stimulates development of placenta

PART 3 Completion: Complete the following.

21. Clonal selection offers one explanation for ____.
22. Allergies seem to provide evidence for the immune system's failure to maintain ____.
23. The stages of stress are ____.
24. Hormones help to maintain homeostasis by ____.
25. Immunity contributes to homeostasis by ____.

Chapter 34 Test Answers

21. how lymphocytes remember and recognize antigens
22. homeostasis
23. alarm, resistance, exhaustion
24. regulating the functions of various internal organs
25. minimizing the effect of infections on the body

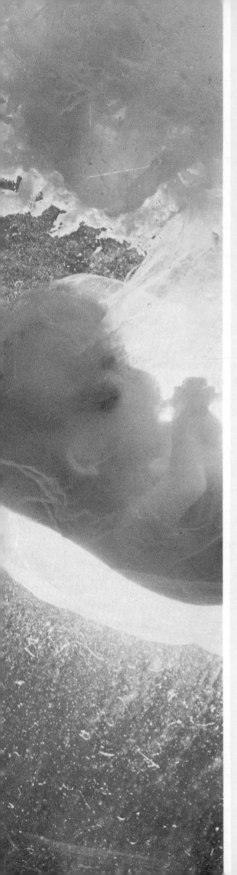

CHAPTER 35

REPRODUCTION AND DEVELOPMENT

A chapter on reproduction and development is a fitting conclusion to our study of the human body. Organisms do not live forever. They must reproduce their kind. The cycle of life is thus complete. Early biologists thought they could see a human form in the head of a sperm. This "seed" only needed to be "planted" for it to grow into a new person. Today, of course, we know that this idea was wrong.

The reproductive system serves to illustrate again several basic life concepts. Careful regulation of the process by hormones helps to maintain a *homeostasis*. Genetic information is passed to the offspring from both parents as gametes unite. Thus, the *continuity of life* as a species is assured. At the same time, sexual reproduction accounts for *diversity*. Genetic shuffling can occur in no other way. The human example also allows us to review the concept of *complementarity of structure and function*. Specific structures have evolved a highly efficient system for assuring that a new generation will be produced.

The study of reproduction is important for more than the sake of knowledge itself. Understanding the processes of reproduction and development have several direct benefits. The reduction of birth defects could be one of these. In this chapter you will learn the pattern of reproduction as it occurs in humans. In addition, you should be able to discover answers to the following questions:

- What is the advantage of sexual reproduction over asexual means?
- Why do some animals maintain a "family" longer than others?
- How do differences between males and females evolve and of what importance are they?

EMBRYO

1 THE BASIS OF SEX

Sexual Reproduction

Sexual reproduction involves the union of two sex cells to form a zygote. The zygote then grows and matures into an adult that resembles its parents. We have already seen that two essential processes are important for sexual reproduction. These are meiosis and fertilization. Meiosis reduces by one-half the chromosome number of diploid cells which divide to form gametes. Fertilization restores the diploid number by joining gametes from separate parents.

Through sexual reproduction, greater diversity is possible within a population. For this reason, sexual reproduction has an important significance beyond simply producing the next generation. Reproduction without this constant shuffling of genes and chromosomes would greatly limit variety and slow the rate of change.

Plants and animals have evolved specific patterns to assure that the two sex cells come together. Regardless of the details of the patterns in each case, the process of sexual reproduction is basically the same.

Sexual Selection

The differences in form between males and females of a species create a condition known as **sexual dimorphism** (dī *môr* fiz əm). Birds and mammals in particular exhibit this condition. They not only differ with respect to their sexual anatomy, but in other ways as well. Sexual dimorphism does more than help members of a species to distinguish one sex from the other. It plays a basic role in the continuation of the species. Sexual differences are the product of natural selection. Features that have helped to attract a sexual partner survive in the offspring. This is the concept of sexual selection and results in sexual dimorphism.

OBJECTIVES FOR SECTION 1

A. Define the following terms in your own words: *sexual dimorphism, puberty, pair-bond.*
B. Describe the role of behavior and selection in the production of sexual dimorphism.

35-1. How do the members of this family resemble one another?

TABLE 35-1.   *SEXUAL DIMORPHISM IN HUMANS.*

Characteristic	Male	Female
Height	average 173 cm	average 162 cm
Weight	average 68 kg	average 52 kg
Skin	less smooth	smooth
Voice	low pitched	high pitched
Body Hair	more	less
Pelvis	narrower	wider
Breasts	undeveloped	pronounced
Bones	heavier	lighter
Skin Fat	less	more

Have students illustrate sexual dimorphism in animals. Ask students how animals that do not have obvious structural differences between the sexes (e.g. dogs) are able to tell the sexes apart. They should be able to suggest differences—behavior, smell.

Humans, of course, are no exception to the phenomenon of sexual dimorphism. Aside from the obvious differences of the reproductive structures, a number of other differences help to distinguish males from females. (See Table 35-1 on page 693.) As in other animals, these differences are no doubt the result of selection. They play an important part, even if we are unaware of it, in the selection of a mate and the production of children.

The triggers that stimulate sexual behavior are not as specific in humans as in other animals. Much variety occurs among the populations of *Homo sapiens* in form and behavior. Different peoples have different standards of beauty and behavior for the opposite sex. The nature of the stimuli, however, is the same for all animals. Visual, tactile (*tak* til) (touching), and olfactory (ol *fak* tər ē) (smelling) senses are used to stimulate members of the opposite sex. The importance of these stimuli increases as children reach sexual maturity, puberty.

Of course, these factors are not the only ones that humans use to select a mate. This is one reason that humans are not limited to the narrow forms and behaviors of other animals. Mate selection in humans is based also upon many subjective factors. Included in these are education level, religion, income, color of hair or eyes, profession, or hobbies and other interests. In any event, all of these, including sex-related characteristics, are used at one time or another to select a mate. Such selection governs which genetic traits will tend to be preserved in the children.

Pair-Bonding

Along with the development of mating patterns in higher animals, two other quite significant developments have taken place. First, there has been a general decrease in the number of offspring with each mating. This means that a larger percentage of the offspring must live to reproduce. The second factor is linked to the first. The offspring are cared for by their parents after they are born. The reproductive act among the higher animals thus ceases to be a relatively casual one-time event. It often results in the creation of a *pairbond. This is a special relationship between the members of a mating pair that persists beyond the act of mating.*

Students may wish to report on pairbonding in a variety of animals and its role in the survival of the species.

Answers to Questions for Section 1.

A. 1. See Glossary. Pair-bond: a special relationship between members of a mating pair that persists beyond act of mating.

*2. Species preservation. The shuffling of genes makes greater diversity possible, and thus greater adaptability within a population.

B. 3. Features that help attract sexual partners survive in the offspring, so that sexual differences are the product of natural selection.

4. Visual, tactile, and olfactory stimuli among others trigger sexual behavior that selects for traits that more sharply differentiate the sexes.

QUESTIONS FOR SECTION 1

1. Define the following terms in your own words: sexual dimorphism, puberty, pair-bond.
2. How is sexual reproduction an advantage over asexual means?
3. Describe the role of sexual selection in the production of sexual dimorphism.
4. Describe the role of behavior in the production of sexual dimorphism.

A

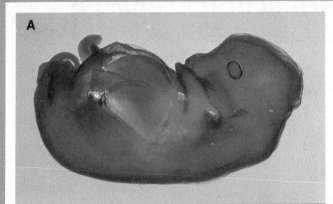

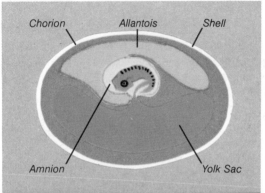

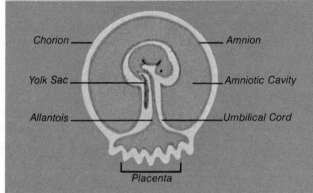

Chorion

Yolk Sac

Allantois

Amnion

Amniotic Cavity

Umbilical Cord

Placenta

Chorion

Amnion

Allantois

Yolk Sac

Shell

B

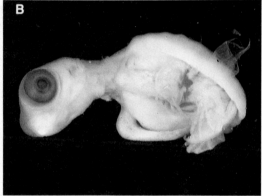

C

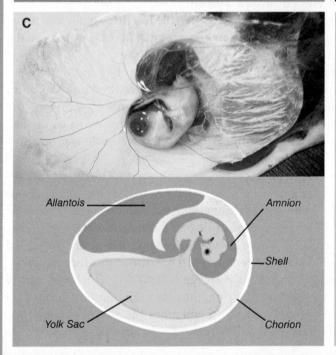

Allantois

Yolk Sac

Amnion

Shell

Chorion

CHAPTER INVESTIGATION

A. Compare and contrast the embryos of the pig (A), the tortoise (B), and bird (C). In what ways are they similar? In what ways are they different?

B. How do mammalian embryos obtain food during development without a yolk as embryos of the tortoise and chick do?

C. The first 72-96 hours of chick development is very similar to the first few weeks of mammalian development. Obtain prepared slides of chick embryos at various stages and write a report on the sequence of events of development. Explain why this particular sequence is of adaptive value in ensuring survival and continuity.

2 REPRODUCTION IN HUMANS

The Male Reproductive System

The use of large charts or models may be particularly helpful in this section.

Essentially, the male reproductive system has two functions. First, it produces sperm and delivers these cells to the reproductive tract of the female. Second, it produces the male sex hormones, called *androgens* (*an* drə jəns). These hormones are responsible for the development of the male's secondary sex characteristics. Spermatozoa, or sperm cells, are produced in the tiny coiled tubules in the two *testes,* or male sex organs. The testes lie outside the body wall in a sac of skin called the *scrotum.*

STRUCTURE OF THE MALE REPRODUCTIVE SYSTEM   Upon leaving the testes, the sperm cells enter the *epididymis.* Here, they complete the process of maturation. From the epididymis, sperm cells are passed along a tube from each testis called the *vas deferens* (vas *def* ə renz), or sperm duct. (See Fig. 35-2.) The vas deferens receives secretions from four sets of glands before emptying into the urethra. These include the *seminal vesicles, prostate, ampulla,* and *bulbourethral glands.* Each gland produces an important secretion which is combined with sperm cells. This makes up the fluid known as *semen.* The urethra then conducts the semen out of the body through the *penis.* Mucous membranes line the urethra.

The Female Reproductive System

The reproductive system of the female has three main functions. First, it produces ova (female gametes or eggs). Second, it secretes the female sex hormones, called *estrogens* (*es* trə jənz) and *progesterones* (prō *jes* tə rōnz). Finally, the female system protects and nourishes the developing individual (*embryo*) from its conception until it is born. The first two functions relate directly to the female sex organs, the *ovaries.* The third function is accomplished by the *uterus* ($\bar{u}$ tər əs). At this point let us study the structure of the female reproductive system.

STRUCTURE OF THE FEMALE REPRODUCTIVE SYSTEM   The ovaries are located in the lower part of the abdominal cavity. (See Fig. 35-3.) These are partially surrounded by funnel-like extensions of the *oviducts* ($\bar{o}$ və dukts) or *Fallopian* (fə lō pē ən) *tubes.* If fertilization occurs, it usually takes place in the upper part of the oviduct. These are connected to the somewhat pear-shaped uterus. It is in the uterus that the development of an embryo occurs if an egg is fertilized. The lower part of the uterus is a thick muscular ring, the *cervix.* The cervix extends partially into the *vagina* (və $j\bar{i}$ nə). Sometimes the vagina is called the birth canal. The vagina is a muscular tube that connects the uterus to the outside.

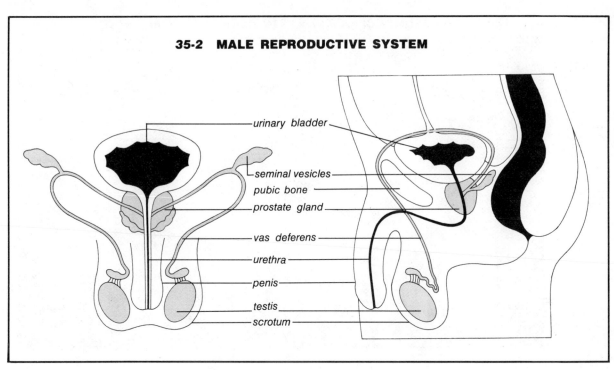

35-2 MALE REPRODUCTIVE SYSTEM

urinary bladder

seminal vesicles

pubic bone

prostate gland

vas deferens

urethra

penis

testis

scrotum

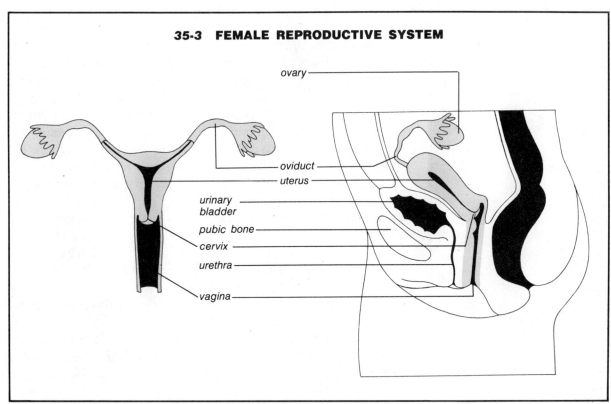

35-3 FEMALE REPRODUCTIVE SYSTEM

ovary

oviduct

uterus

urinary bladder

pubic bone

cervix

urethra

vagina

35-4   THE SEQUENCE OF EVENTS IN THE MENSTRUAL CYCLE

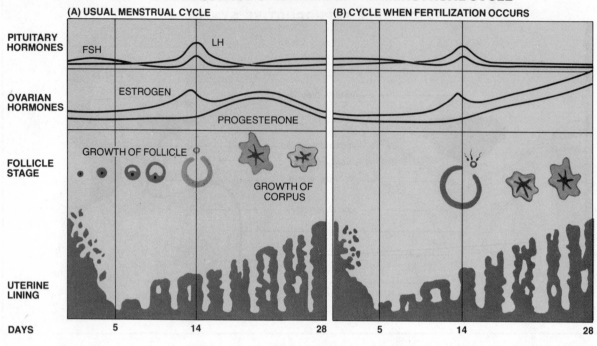

(A) USUAL MENSTRUAL CYCLE

(B) CYCLE WHEN FERTILIZATION OCCURS

PITUITARY HORMONES — FSH — LH

OVARIAN HORMONES — ESTROGEN — PROGESTERONE

FOLLICLE STAGE — GROWTH OF FOLLICLE — GROWTH OF CORPUS

UTERINE LINING

DAYS   5   14   28   5   14   28

The Menstrual Cycle

Human males produce gametes continuously from puberty until some time in old age. Females, on the other hand, do not. Beginning at puberty, eggs are released typically about every twenty-eight days for thirty to thirty-five years. The uterus develops a thick lining where a fertilized egg can implant and grow. If no egg implants, the lining breaks down. This pattern, known as the *menstrual cycle,* is interrupted only during *pregnancy,* when a child has been conceived.

The length of each menstrual cycle may vary somewhat from one person to the next by as much as a week or so. The functioning of the menstrual cycle is first signaled at puberty by the appearance of blood and tissue being discharged through the vagina. This discharge comes from the breakdown of the lining of the uterus. If the egg is fertilized, the menstrual flow does not occur. Instead, the thickened uterine lining is preserved to receive the embryo when it arrives in the uterus a few days later. The cycle does not begin again until sometime after the baby is born. (See Fig. 35-4.)

The principal event of the menstrual cycle is the release of an ovum from the ovary. This event is controlled by hormones produced by the pituitary gland. These hormones also control the release of

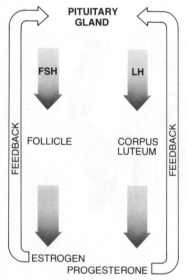

PITUITARY GLAND

FSH — LH

FEEDBACK — FOLLICLE — CORPUS LUTEUM — FEEDBACK

ESTROGEN — PROGESTERONE

35-5. The feedback system that regulates the menstrual cycle.

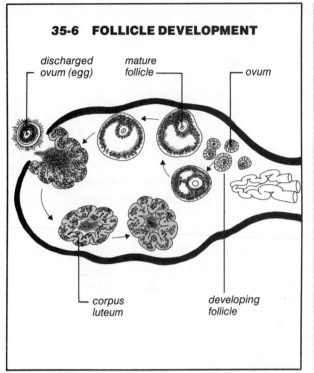

35-6 FOLLICLE DEVELOPMENT

discharged ovum (egg)

mature follicle

ovum

corpus luteum

developing follicle

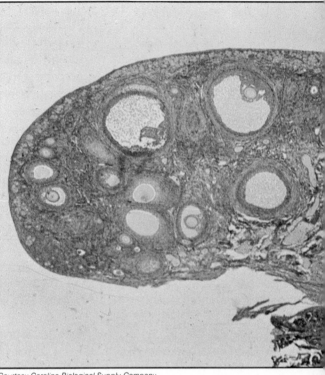

Courtesy Carolina Biological Supply Company

other hormones by the ovary. In turn, the hormones of the ovary regulate those from the pituitary. This is an example of a feedback system. (See Fig. 35-5.)

In the case of the human female, the pituitary secretes *follicle-stimulating hormone.* It is usually called FSH for short. FSH is carried to the ovary by the blood. (See Fig. 35-6.) It causes cells around the egg to develop a fluid-filled sac or *follicle.* (See Fig. 35-7.) At the same time, the follicle cells begin to produce estrogen. FSH also is produced in the male where it stimulates the formation of sperm in the testes.

The estrogen produced by the growing follicle is important for three reasons. In the first place, it causes the development of the female's primary and secondary sex characteristics, including the development of the uterine lining. It also regulates FSH production by the pituitary. As the estrogen level increases, FSH is shut down in a feedback manner.

The third function of estrogen is to stimulate the pituitary to release a second hormone. This hormone, *luteinizing hormone* (LH), together with FSH, causes the follicle to break and release the egg. The release of the egg from the ovary is called *ovulation.*

35-7. *Photomicrograph of a section of the ovary showing follicles and corpus luteum.*

Point out the adaptive value of the female cycle. Only humans and a few other primates have such a cycle. Most other animals have estrus cycles that occur at specific times of the year. Ask students about the adaptive advantages or disadvantages of each form of reproductive cycle.

Estrogen production drops off sharply at ovulation. Stimulated by LH, the remaining cells of the broken follicle develop into a new, temporary gland, the *corpus luteum*. The corpus luteum produces a second female hormone called progesterone. Progesterone further prepares and maintains the lining of the uterus to receive the embryo if the egg is fertilized. It also helps produce the secondary sex features of the female. If fertilization does not take place, the corpus luteum breaks down after ten days or so. This causes a drop in progesterone levels. At this point, the menstrual flow begins as the lining of the uterus breaks down. Thus, LH and progesterone are involved in a second feedback system. Menstruation lasts for about five days. By then, estrogen levels are again high enough to stimulate a rebuilding of the uterine lining.

Let us consider the first day of the menstrual flow as the first day of the cycle. Normally, ovulation would occur near the mid-point of the cycle. The 28th day would be the day just before the onset of the next menstrual flow. (Look back to Fig. 35-3.) It is not unusual for the cycle to vary in length from one month to the next.

The Sex Hormones

The sex hormones develop and maintain the primary sex features of the male and female. In addition, they produce the secondary features. In the male, these include the beard, lower voice, broad shoulders and narrow hips. The secondary characteristics of the female include the wider pelvis, smoother skin, breasts, and a thicker layer of fat under the skin.

QUESTIONS FOR SECTION 2

1. Define and give the functions of each structure and hormone involved in the male and female reproductive systems.
2. State the functions of the male reproductive system.
3. State the functions of the female reproductive system.
4. Describe the path of an egg following ovulation if fertilization does not occur.
5. Describe the path of an egg following ovulation if fertilization does occur.
6. Show how a feedback system operates in the female menstrual cycle.

Answers to Questions for Section 2.

C. 1. Male: androgens — hormones that cause development of secondary sex characteristics; testes produce sperm cells that pass through the vas deferens. Secretions from the seminal vesicles, prostate, ampulla, and bulbourethral glands also enter. Semen, the mixture of sperm cells and the secretions, leaves the body via the urethra through the penis. Female: hormones estrogen and progesterone — development of secondary sex characteristics. Estrogen causes development of the uterine lining, and regulates FSH and LH production by the pituitary. Progesterone prepares and maintains uterine lining. Ovaries produce the ova, which pass through the oviducts into the uterus.

D. 2. To produce sperm and deliver them to female reproductive tract, and to produce hormones (androgens).

3. To produce ova (eggs), and to secrete estrogens and progesterones, to protect and nourish the embryo from conception to birth.

E. 4. Ovary — oviduct — uterus — vagina — to outside the body.

*5. From ovary to oviduct to uterus, where it remains as the embryo develops.

F. 6. Diagram as in Figure 35-5 on page 698.

3 DEVELOPMENT IN HUMANS

Fertilization

Fertilization takes place in the upper one-third end of the oviducts. Sperm cells are deposited in the vagina. They reach the area of fertilization by swimming, helped along by contractions of the uterus and the oviducts. Sperm cells move through the female system fairly quickly. They may enter the oviducts within 15 minutes after sexual activity takes place.

The unfertilized ovum lives only about one day. Sperm cells, however, may survive for two days or so in the oviducts. Thus, ovulation does not have to take place when the sperm cells are deposited to result in fertilization.

At ovulation, the egg has undergone only the first of the two meiotic divisions. The second division takes place when stimulated by the penetration of the sperm cell. The haploid nuclei of the sperm and egg then unite to form the diploid zygote. Fertilization is then complete.

The fertilized egg, or zygote, continues its journey down the oviduct to the uterus. It arrives between the fourth and seventh day of development. (See Fig. 35-8.) The lining of the uterus has been readied to receive the young embryo by the action of hormones secreted by the ovary. Progesterone, from the corpus luteum, prevents the onset of a menstrual period so the embryo can be attached to the uterine lining. When attachment occurs, a new organ, the *placenta*, begins to form. The placenta is composed of tissue from the mother and the embryo. It allows for the exchange of nutrients and wastes

OBJECTIVES FOR SECTION 3

G. Trace the development of a human from fertilization to eight weeks.

H. Describe the process of cleavage and the formation of the three basic cell layers including the structures each will form.

I. Describe a classic series of experiments that demonstrated the phenomenon of embryonic induction.

J. Describe the changes in the fetal circulatory pattern that occurs at birth.

K. Explain how meiosis and fertilization brings about both unity and diversity in humans.

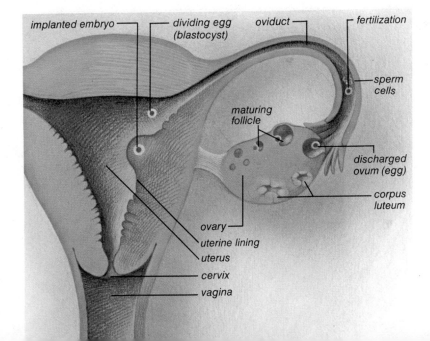

35-8. *Path of a fertilized ovum until it becomes implanted in the lining of the uterus: discharged egg; fertilization; early divisions; blastocyst; implantation.*

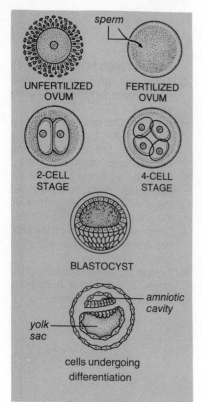

sperm

UNFERTILIZED
OVUM

FERTILIZED
OVUM

2-CELL
STAGE

4-CELL
STAGE

BLASTOCYST

amniotic
cavity

yolk
sac

cells undergoing
differentiation

35-9. *Cleavage stages in the development of the human embryo.*

between the mother and developing baby. The placenta produces estrogen and some other special hormones. One of these hormones, chorionic gonadotropin (HCG), stimulates the ovaries to produce progesterone. This prevents the uterine lining from breaking down during pregnancy. This hormone will appear in the blood and urine of the prospective mother. Thus, HCG is used by doctors as a test for pregnancy.

Early Development

Soon after fertilization, the zygote begins to undergo a series of divisions called *cleavage.* Each of these mitotic divisions takes place at about the same time. Although the number of cells increases during cleavage, the overall size of the embryo does not. (See Fig. 35-9.)

By the age of four days, the embryo consists of some sixteen to thirty-two cells. Divisions no longer occur at the same time. This ball of cells, or *blastula* (*blas* chə lə), arrives in the uterus. It then becomes attached to the uterine lining. A cavity soon forms within the blastula and the cells in the interior are pushed to one side to form the *inner cell mass.* (See Fig. 35-9.) This new structure is known as the *blastocyst.*

The outer layer of cells of the blastocyst become the first of four important membranes to form. Since these membranes are not part of the embryo itself, they are referred to as *extraembryonic* (*ek* strə em brē *on* ik) *membranes.* This first membrane, the *chorion* (*kōr* ē on), develops many small, finger-like extensions called villi. The villi make up the fetal part of the placenta. They penetrate the lining of the uterus as the embryo embeds itself. These tiny fingers absorb nourishment from the mother's body until the time of birth. (See Fig. 35-10.)

35-10 EARLY EMBRYOLOGICAL STAGES OF HUMAN DEVELOPMENT

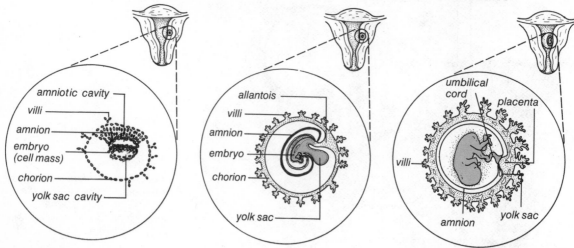

amniotic cavity

villi

amnion

embryo
(cell mass)

chorion

yolk sac cavity

allantois

villi

amnion

embryo

chorion

yolk sac

umbilical
cord

placenta

villi

amnion

yolk sac

The extraembryonic membranes in the mammalian embryo illustrate the relationships of mammals to other vertebrates.

Two new cavities appear in the inner cell mass. Between these, the embryo itself takes shape. The layer of cells that line the two new cavities make up two more of the extraembryonic membranes. The *amnion* (am nē ən) develops above the embryo. It fills with fluid and comes to surround the entire embryo. The amniotic sac thus formed protects the growing embryo from injury. The other cavity is lined by the *yolk sac*. In mammals, although the sac persists for some time, there is no yolk. Nourishment comes directly from the mother through the placenta. A small pouch that extends from the yolk sac near the rear of the embryo is the fourth extraembryonic membrane. This is the *allantois* (ə *lant* ə wəs). This membrane also serves no real function in mammals. In vertebrates that do not have a placenta, the allantois provides for gas exchange and storage of wastes.

As the embryo continues to grow, blood vessels begin to form in the villi. The small vessels in the lining of the uterus break down to form blood cavities around the villi. In this way, food and wastes can be exchanged between the mother and the embryo in an efficient manner. Note, however, that the two circulatory systems are never in real contact with each other. (See Fig. 35-11.)

Organ Formation

With the formation of the amnion and yolk sac, the embryonic cell mass is defined. It is composed of three layers of cells. The top layer, known as the *ectoderm,* is continuous with the cells that line the amniotic cavity. The underside of the cell mass is known as the *endoderm*. These cells form a layer that is continuous with the yolk sac. Between the ectoderm and endoderm is the *mesoderm.*

Answers to Questions for Section 3.

3. After the amnion and yolk sac form, the ectoderm (outer cell layer) forms, continuous with the cells lining the amnionic cavity; the endoderm (inner cell layer) forms, continuous with the yolk sac. The mesoderm lies between the ectoderm and endoderm.

4. Ectoderm: nervous tissue, skin, hair, nails. Mesoderm: circulatory, muscular, reproductive, and excretory systems. Endoderm: lining of digestive tract, lungs, liver, pancreas, and other glands.

5. Spemann removed cells from above the notochord of salamander embryos; no nervous tissue developed. Then he removed a piece of notochord, replacing ectoderm above it. No nervous tissue developed. Into an embryo he planted a piece of notochord from another embryo in place of mesoderm. A second nervous system developed.

(See page 704 for answers 6-8.)

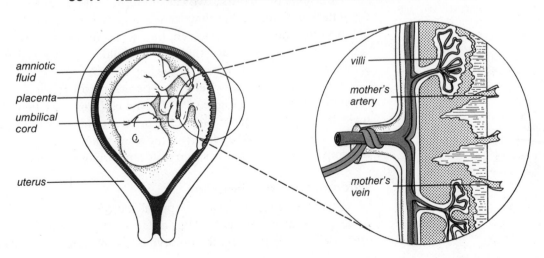

35-11   RELATIONSHIP OF FETAL AND MATERNAL CIRCULATION

amniotic fluid
placenta
umbilical cord
uterus

villi
mother's artery
mother's vein

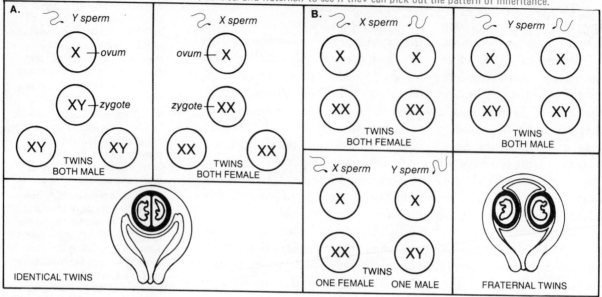

35-12. *(left) Identical twin develops from one egg. (right) Fraternal twins develop from two eggs.*

Each of these cell layers can be followed as they develop into tissues and organs. Ectoderm forms nervous tissue, skin, hair, and nails. The circulatory, muscular, reproductive, and excretory systems come from mesoderm. The endoderm lines the digestive tract and forms the lungs, liver, pancreas, and various other glands.

By the time the embryo is eight weeks old, it is about three centimeters long and weighs about a gram. All of the organ systems have been defined. They need only to grow and mature. The embryo is now referred to as a fetus.

Twinning

Occasionally, the first two cells to form in the cleavage process separate completely rather than remain together. Each contains a full 2N chromosome number. As such, they will continue to develop into separate individuals. Since their genetic make-ups are exactly the same, *identical twins* will result. (See Fig. 35-12A.)

Fraternal twins occur when two separate ova are fertilized by two separate sperm. As in Figure 35-12B, the children may be both female, both male, or one of each sex. They are twins only in the sense that they are conceived and born at the same time. Their genetic relationship is no closer than any two children born of the same parents.

Differentiation and Induction

The fertilized ovum is an unspecialized cell. The potential for a whole person is present. The cells of the blastula are also unspecialized. By the time the embryo is two months old, however, these cells have become muscles, nerves, bones, glands, and other specialized tissues. How does all of this come about? Although much is known about the process, there is a lot to be learned. A number of interesting experiments shed some light on the matter.

Some studies have shown that perhaps the cytoplasm contains activators or preventors that control the cell's gene activity. This may in fact be true. However, the question remains, why are certain genes activated in some cells and not in others?

The generalized cells of the blastula first begin to specialize as the three basic cell layers form. This process is called *differentiation*. During the third week of development, other special structures begin to appear. (See Fig. 35-13.) A dorsal supporting rod called the *notochord* develops from the mesoderm. This structure is a basic feature of all chordates. In vertebrates, the notochord develops into a part of the spinal column. Above the notochord the nervous system takes shape. The heart and circulatory system appear and begin to function at an early age. (See Fig. 35-14.) Along each side of the notochord, several paired masses called *somites* (sō mīts) also appear. These become part of the muscular system.

The differentiation of some cells seems to be caused by chemical signals from nearby cells. For example, notochord cells apparently signal the overlying ectoderm cells to become differentiated into nervous tissue. Studies with salamander embryos some 50 years ago support this conclusion. Hans Spemann showed that neighboring cells induced certain cells to become specialized. Cells from above the notochord were removed and cultured separately. These cells lived, but they failed to develop into nervous tissue.

In another experiment, Spemann carefully removed a piece of notochord. Then he replaced the ectoderm above it. The ectoderm failed to develop into nervous tissue. This showed that notochord cells were involved in the development of the nervous system. A final experiment proved to be convincing. From the belly region of the embryo, Spemann folded back a flap of ectoderm. He then removed a piece of mesoderm. From a second embryo, he removed a piece of notochord. This was put into place on the belly of the first embryo. The ectoderm flap was replaced and development allowed to continue.

Within a short time, the embryo had developed two nervous systems! One appeared in the normal position that was not disturbed. The other appeared in the belly region. The influence of adjacent tissues in differentiation was established. Several other examples of this process, called *embryonic induction*, are now known. The nature of the "organizer chemical" secreted by one tissue to affect another is not known. Much research remains to be done. Knowledge in this area may be helpful in understanding the causes of many birth defects.

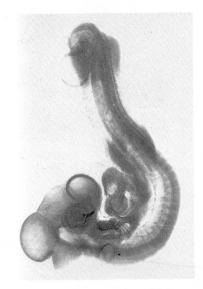

35-13. *Chick embryo at 72 hours shows the development of a notochord.*

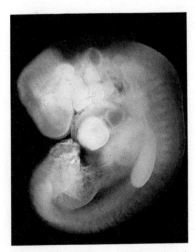

35-14. *The human embryo as it appears at 25 days.*

The appearance of bone cells in the embryo usually occurs during the eighth week and marks the beginning of the fetal stage of development.

Fetal Development

At the age of two months, the fetus has a distinctly human appearance. The remaining seven months of pregnancy allow for the tissues to grow and mature. The picture essay on the following pages shows the fetus as it appears at several stages during its development. (See Fig. 35-15.)

Circulation Changes at Birth

The dependence of the mammalian embryo and fetus on the mother's body is unique. Because of this, some mention should be made of the special features of the fetal circulatory pattern. These features normally disappear at birth. They occasionally persist, and result in disability or death if not corrected by surgery.

The circulatory system of the fetus has three distinctive features. In the heart itself, there is a small oval opening between the left and right sides. A second feature is the short duct between the aorta and the artery leading to the lung. This is called the *ductus arteriosus* (dək təs är tir ē ō səs). Finally, there are two umbilical arteries that lead to the placenta from the fetus, and one umbilical vein that returns blood to the fetus.

Circulatory changes are related to the development of the lungs which are non-functional until after birth.

These features are associated with the fact that the fetus does not breathe. The placenta carries out all of the essential functions of gas exchange. The first two features allow much of the blood to by-pass the lungs as it circulates. Oxygen is obtained from the mother through the placenta. Failure of either the oval opening or the ductus arteriosis to close at birth will result in improper circulation of blood. Blood will not become fully oxygenated. This, in turn, will affect future development. Fortunately, these defects can be detected and treated by surgery. Some new, non-surgical techniques hold a promise for the future.

The umbilical vessels that connect the fetus to the placenta are tied off at birth. The remains of these vessels become converted to connective tissue and do not continue to exist as blood vessels.

Labor and Birth

A full term human pregnancy is about 267 days on the average. This period is called the **gestation** (jes tā shən) **period.** It varies widely in mammals. Gestation for a mouse, for example, takes only some 20 days. An elephant's gestation, on the other hand, is about 660 days, over a year longer than humans. The gestation periods for various mammals is given in Table 35-2.

Short contractions of the uterus are the first signs that the time for birth is near. Over a period of several hours, the contractions become more frequent. *The period of time from initial contraction to*

TABLE 35-2.
GESTATION PERIODS
OF SELECTED ANIMALS.

Animal	Time (days)
Opossum	12-13
Mouse	20
Rabbit	31
Cat, dog	63
Lemur	120-140
Monkeys	139-190
Apes	210-290
Humans	267
Cattle	278
Horse	340
African elephant	660

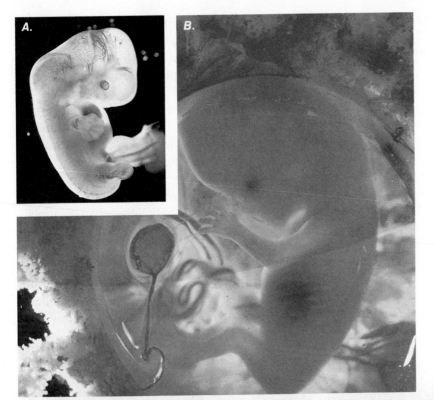

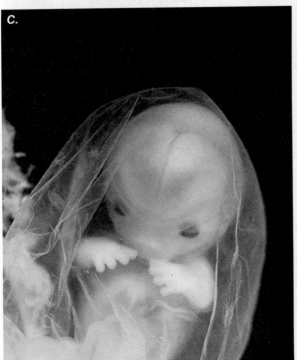

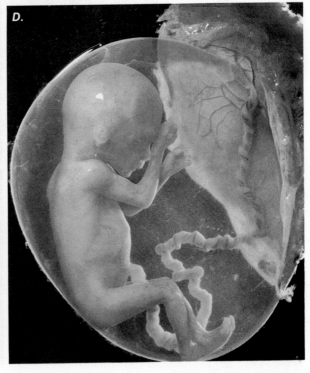

35-15. A. End of the fifth week, the size of the embryo is 11-12mm. The head of the embryo is relatively large and the developing heart is beating. **B.** At the end of the eighth week the embryo is about 4 cm long. It appears human, and sexual characteristics are developing. Organs continue development and bones begin ossification. The head is relatively large because of rapid development of brain. **C.** Into the eleventh week the embryo is about 6 cm long. A definite spinal cord is present, internal structures are on their way to completion. **D.** In the sixteenth week the embryo or fetus may move about in the uterus. Growth of hair may be starting. The head grows more slowly—the body is catching up in growth. The eyes, nose and external ears appear complete.

birth is known as **labor.** The contractions begin slowly. At first, they are weak and far apart. These early contractions serve to position the baby's head against the cervix. As the contractions continue, the cervix is forced to open, or dilate. At some point during this stage, the amnion usually breaks, releasing its fluid. (See Fig. 35-16.)

Sometimes the baby is in the wrong position for a normal birth or it is too large to be born without damage. Doctors are usually able to predict this before the onset of labor. In such cases, the baby must be removed from the uterus by surgery through the abdominal wall. An operation of this nature is called a caesarean (si *zār* ē ən) section. Such operations have saved the lives of many mothers and their babies.

The newborn child will usually begin to breathe when the umbilical cord is severed. This is because the increase of carbon dioxide in its system causes normal reflex actions to stimulate the breathing process. Sometimes a sharp slap on the backside is necessary to make the baby take its first breath. The emergence of the baby into the world is perhaps the greatest shock it will receive in its lifetime. Fluctuating temperatures, alternating hunger periods and other disagreeable factors are suddenly thrust upon the new child.

35-16. Life begins as the uterus contracts to force the baby's head against the cervix. These contractions eventually dilate the cervix and allow the baby to pass through the birth canal.

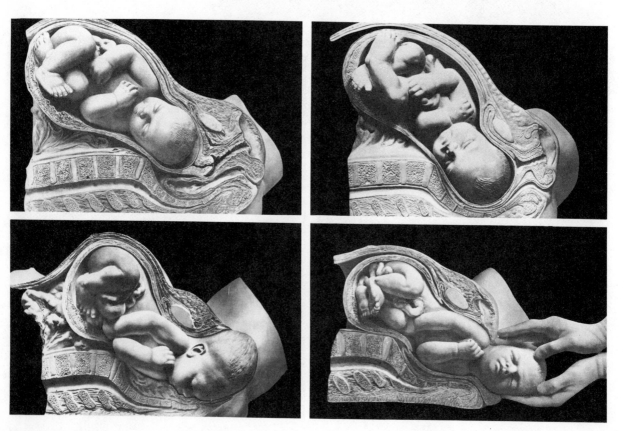

QUESTIONS FOR SECTION 3

1. Briefly trace the development in first eight weeks in the development of a human.
2. Describe the process of cleavage.
3. Describe the formation of the three primary cell layers.
4. List the parts of the body that are derived from each of the three primary cell layers.
5. Describe the classic series of experiments that demonstrated the phenomenon of embryonic induction.
6. Describe the changes in the fetal circulatory pattern that occur at birth.
7. Explain why the changes described in (6) are necessary for life outside the mother.
8. How does meiosis and fertilization result in both the unity and diversity of humans?

H. 2. The fertilized egg cell (zygote) divides by mitosis into two cells, then four, and so on, until it forms a ball of 16 to 32 cells, the blastula. There has been no increase in size from the original zygote. (See page 703 for answers 3-5.)

Answers to Questions for Section 3.

G. 1. After fertilization, cleavage results in the formation of the blastocyst by the beginning of the second week. By the end of the second week, somites are visible. During the third week, heart and blood vessels, the central nervous system, along with both gut and muscles begin to develop. By the fifth week, the developing heart is beating and the development of every major organ system is seen. By eight weeks, a human figure can be seen.

CHAPTER REVIEW

The mammalian reproductive system, as seen in humans, is highly efficient. It helps ensure fertilization and protects the embryo throughout its development. The *continuity of the species* is thus preserved in the new generation.

Meiosis and fertilization are the essential events of sexual reproduction. These cellular events account for both the overall unity of the human condition and its *diversity*. Sexual selection is an important feature of the vertebrates, including humans. This process results in obvious differences between males and females known as sexual dimorphism. This condition is also an important feature that helps to ensure continuity of the species. Different hormones produced by the testes and the ovaries help to account for sexual dimorphism. This creates *homeostasis* in the species.

The step by step development of a fertilized egg further demonstrates these concepts. Induction creates specialized cells for specialized functions. Thus, the unity of the organism is balanced by diversity within its make-up. The placenta provides for a homeostatic balance as well. Food, oxygen, and wastes are exchanged between the fetus and the mother throughout the gestation period. The reproductive system, then, represents the living condition as it illustrates all of the basic concepts of life.

Discussion Points

1. Doctors sometimes have occasion to prescribe estrogen or similar compounds to their female patients. What kinds of disorders do you think might be effectively treated by such prescriptions?
2. How is the success of a pregnancy influenced by the timing of the arrival of the blastula in the uterus?
3. How might further knowledge of the differentiation process be of value to medical science?

VOCABULARY REVIEW

1 sexual dimorphism	uterus	corpus luteum	ductus arteriosus
pair-bonding	Fallopian tubes	**3** blastocyst	labor
2 androgens	vagina	extraembryonic membrane	caesarian section
scrotum	cervix	differentiation	
vas deferens	menstrual cycle	somites	
penis	ovulation	embryonic induction	

CHAPTER 35 TEST

Copy the number of each test item and place your answer to the right.

PART 1   Multiple Choice: Select the letter of the phrase that best completes each of the following.

c **1.** On the average, ovulation in humans occurs **a.** every 5th day   **b.** every 14 days   **c.** every 28 days   **d.** randomly.

c **2.** The function of the uterus is to   **a.** produce eggs **b.** stimulate formation of the corpus luteum **c.** serve as the site of embryo development **d.** produce hormones.

a **3.** In the feedback system operating in the female menstrual cycle, estrogen stimulates the production of a pituitary hormone known as   **a.** LH **b.** FSH   **c.** ICSH   **d.** progesterone.

d **4.** Gametogenesis is accomplished by a unique biological process called   **a.** mitosis   **b.** fertilization   **c.** menstruation   **d.** meiosis.

d **5.** The testes   **a.** produce male gametes **b.** produce androgens   **c.** are homologous to the ovaries of the female   **d.** all of these.

c **6.** In humans, identical twins result from the fertilization of   **a.** two ova by two sperm cells   **b.** two ova by a single sperm cell   **c.** a single ovum by a single sperm cell followed by splitting of the zygote at the 2-cell stage   **d.** a single ovum by two sperm cells.

a **7.** The fact that transplanted notochord cells will produce a second neural plate in the embryo supports the concept of   **a.** induction   **b.** gastrulation **c.** implantation   **d.** cleavage.

b **8.** The developmental period from fertilization until birth is known as the   **a.** menstrual period **b.** gestation period   **c.** placental period **d.** latent period.

d **9.** One of the earliest functioning organ systems in the embryo is the   **a.** skeletal system   **b.** respiratory system   **c.** digestive system   **d.** circulatory system.

b **10.** Changes in the circulatory system at birth are associated with the fact that the fetus does not **a.** digest its own food   **b.** breathe   **c.** respond to stimuli   **d.** produce waste materials.

PART 2   Matching: Match the letter of the term in Column I with its description in Column II.

COLUMN I

a. amnion   **f.** induction
b. cleavage   **g.** menstruation
c. estrogen   **h.** placenta
d. fallopian tube **i.** testis
e. FSH   **j.** vas deferens

COLUMN II

e **11.** Hormone that stimulates follicle growth

d **12.** Site of ovum fertilization

i **13.** Male sex organ

g **14.** Cyclic sloughing of uterine lining

c **15.** Female hormone produced by follicle

j **16.** Duct that carries sperm from testes

b **17.** Early divisions of zygote with no increase in overall size

a **18.** Extraembryonic membrane that serves as mechanical and thermal protector

f **19.** Process by which one group of cells influences differentiation of another

h **20.** Source of nutrients for developing fetus

PART 3   Completion: Complete the following.

21. The germ layer responsible for the production of the digestive system is the _endoderm_

22. The process by which certain cells undergo specialization is known as _differentiation_

23. A chemical system in which one part controls the activity of another part is known as a _feedback system_

24. The process during which the three primary germ layers are formed is known as _gastrulation_

25. External features specifically associated with males or females are known as _secondary sex characteristics_

APPENDIX

THE METRIC SYSTEM AND EQUIVALENTS*

LENGTH

1 kilometer (km)   = 1000 meters (m)   = 0.62 miles
1 m   = 10^{-3} km   =   100 centimeters (cm)   = 39.37 inches = 1.09 yards
1 cm   = 10^{-2} m   =   10 millimeters (mm)   = 0.39 inches
1 mm   = 10^{-3} m   = 1000 microns (μ)   = 0.039 inches
1 μ = 10^{-6} m   = 1000 nanometers (nm)   = 1 micrometer (μm)
1 nm   = 10^{-9} m
1Å   = 10^{-10} m

1 mile = 1.61 km
1 foot = 31 cm
1 inch = 2.54 cm
1 yard = 0.92 m

AREA

1 hectare (ha; square hectometer) = 0.01 km^2 = 10,000 m^2 = 2.47 U.S. acres
1 km^2 = 100 ha = 0.386 square miles (mi^2)
1 m^2 = 10,000 cm^2 = 10.76 square feet (ft^2)

VOLUME

1 liter   = 1000 milliliters (ml)   = 1.06 U.S. quarts
1 ml = 10^{-3}l   = 1 cubic centimeter (cm^3)
1 quart   = 0.94 l
1 pint   = 0.47 l

MASS

1 gram   = mass of 1 ml of water at 4°c
1 metric ton (mt) = 1000 kilograms (kg)   = 2204.6 pounds
1 kg   = 1000 grams (g)   = 2.2 lbs.
1 g = 10^{-3} kg   = 1000 milligrams (mg)
1 mg = 10^{-3} g   = 1000 micrograms (μg)
1 pound (lb.)   = 0.4536 kg   = 454 grams
1 ounce (oz.)   = 28.35 grams (g)

*All Values Are Approximate

TEMPERATURE CONVERSIONS

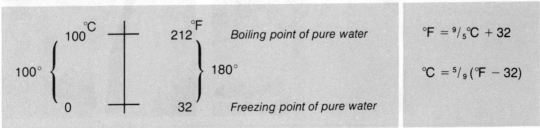

100° $\left\{ \begin{array}{c} \end{array} \right.$ 100 °C — 212 °F $\left. \begin{array}{c} \end{array} \right\}$ 180°   *Boiling point of pure water*

0 — 32   *Freezing point of pure water*

$$°F = \tfrac{9}{5}°C + 32$$

$$°C = \tfrac{5}{9}(°F - 32)$$

CAREERS IN BIOLOGY

These careers give a range of opportunities using biology.

TECHNICAL EDUCATION

A. Laboratory technicians perform lab tests which may be routine.

B. Teacher's aids prepare for experiments and grade papers.

C. Agricultural technicians care for plants and animals. They make observations and keep records.

D. Environmental technicians use a variety of equipment to monitor pollution.

E. Practical nurses help keep records and make patients comfortable.

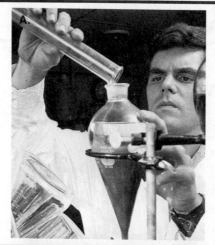

BACHELOR'S DEGREE

A. A researcher performs laboratory experiments that may use extensive equipment.

B. Classroom teachers teach content material, procedural operations, and science skills.

C. Forests are a renewable resource but require care for many years before they mature.

D. All sciences make use of computer technology. This worker is checking telemetric air monitor.

E. Extensive testing of drugs is required before use by humans.

ADVANCED DEGREES

A. A research director may be both an administrator and designer of a research program.

B. College professors can specialize in a narrow subject area.

C. Agricultural researchers study growing conditions.

D. Administrators of environmental groups may handle controversial issues and solutions.

E. Pharmacists require a knowledge of drugs and their effects on humans.

C.

D.

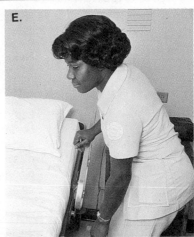

E.

C.

D.

E.

C.

D.

E.

PRONUNCIATION KEY

a   a as in **at, bad**

ā   a as in **ape,** ai as in **pain,** ay as in **day**

ä   a as in **father, car**

e   e as in **end, pet**

ē   e as in **me,** ee as in **feet,** ea as in **meat,** ie as in **piece,** y as in **finally**

i   i as in **it, pig**

ī   i as in **ice, fine,** ie as in **in lie,** y as in **my**

o   o as in **odd, hot**

ō   o as in **old,** oa as in **oat,** ow as in **low,** oe as in **toe**

ô   o as in **coffee, fork,** au as in **author,** aw as in **law,** a as in **all**

oo   oo as in **wood,** u as in **put**

o͞o   oo as in **fool,** ue as in **true**

oi   oi as in **oil,** oy as in **boy**

ou   ou as in **out,** ow as in **cow**

u   u as in **up, mud,** o as in **oven, love**

ū   u as in **use,** ue as in **cue,** ew as in **few,** eu as in **feud**

ur   ur as in **turn,** er as in **term,** ir as in **bird,** or as in **word**

ə   a as in **ago,** e as in **taken,** i as in **pencil,** o as in **lemon,** u as in **helpful**

b   b as in **bat, above, job**

ch   ch as in **chin, such,** tch as in **hatch**

d   d as in **deer, soda, bad**

f   f as in **five, defend, leaf,** ff as in **off**

g   g as in **game, ago, fog**

h   h as in **hit, ahead**

j   j as in **joke, enjoy,** g as in **gem,** dge as in **edge**

k   k as in **kit, baking, seek,** ck as in **tack,** c as in **cat**

l   l as in **lid, sailor, feel,** ll as in **ball, allow**

m   m as in **man, family, dream**

n   n as in **not, final, on**

ng   ng as in **singer, long,** n as in **sink**

p   p as in **pail, repair, soap**

r   r as in **ride, parent, four**

s   s as in **sat, aside, cats,** c as in **cent,** ss as in **pass**

sh   sh as in **shoe, wishing, fish**

t   t as in **tag, pretend, hat**

th   th as in **thin, ether, both**

<u>th</u>   th as in **this, mother, smooth**

v   v as in **very, favor, salve**

w   w as in **wet, reward**

y   y as in **yes**

z   z as in **zoo, gazing,** zz as in **jazz,** s as in **rose, dogs**

zh   s as in **treasure,** z as in **seizure,** ge as in **garage**

N   on as in French **bon;** indicates that the vowel preceding N is nasalized

KH   ch as in **loch,** German **ach** or **ich**

œ   eu as in French **feu,** ö as in German **schön;** similar to oo in **wood**

GLOSSARY OF BIOLOGICAL TERMS

A

abdomen in Arthropods, the body region behind the thorax

abiogenesis beginning without life; spontaneous generation

abscission zone the region at the base of a leaf petiole or fruit stalk where the leaf or fruit separates from the stem. The separation is accomplished by the action of enzymes and with the help of wind and rain.

absorption the movement of nutrients out of the digestive tract and into blood or lymph vessels of the villi

acetylcholine a neurotransmitter, or chemical released by nerves upon the arrival of an impulse

acquired immunity immunity that an individual develops at any time after birth

actin a kind of protein molecule present in muscle fiber

active transport a process requiring energy; movement of material across a cell membrane to an area of greater concentration

adaptations features that help any organism survive in its environment

adaptive increasing an organism's chances of survival

adaptive behavior responses that increase an organism's chances of survival

adaptive radiation the adjustment that a population makes to its environment over a period of time. Adaptive radiation may be said to take place when members of a single population undergo divergence.

adrenal glands glands located above the kidneys

adventitious roots roots that are formed by meristems in the stems or leaves of plants

aerobes organisms that use oxygen in the process of respiration

aerobic respiration the breakdown of pyruvic acid by combination with oxygen

agar a gelatinous substance produced most abundantly by the red alga Gelidium, and used in laboratories as a growth medium for bacteria and other organisms

agriculture the raising and care of plants and animals that are used for food, clothing, and other materials

algal bloom an explosive population increase in algae that occurs when the water suddenly becomes enriched with phosphate and/or nitrate

algin a substance forming a part of the cell wall in several algal groups, especially the kelps, used in a wide variety of functions in the food and manufacturing industries

allantois the membrane in an egg that collects wastes from the blood of the embryo

alleles the two alternative forms of a gene for a Mendelian trait

alternation of generations a reproductive cycle involving the gametophyte and sporophyte generations

alveoli in the respiratory system of mammals, tiny air sacs surrounded by capillaries. Oxygen diffuses from the alveoli to the capillaries, and carbon dioxide from the capillaries to the alveoli.

amino acids the building blocks of protein

amniocentesis the process in which a small amount of fluid from the fetal sac is removed so that fetal cells may be studied prior to birth

amnion the membrane that forms a sac around the developing embryo in an egg

anaerobes organisms that do not use oxygen in the process of respiration

anaerobic respiration cellular respiration occurring without oxygen

anaphase the third of the four stages of mitosis: the stage in which the two molecules of DNA in each chromosome separate

anemia a lack of red blood cells or of hemoglobin

annual stems stems that live for only one season

antennae organs of touch, taste, and smell in some Arthropods

antennules organs of balance and hearing in some Arthropods

anterior the head end of an animal with bilateral symmetry

anther the part of the stamen that produces pollen grains

anthropoids the major primate groups, including the Old World monkeys, the New World monkeys, the apes, and the hominids

antibiotics organic compounds produced by living organisms to treat infections

antibodies chemicals that fight off a virus or other foreign microorganisms

anticodon a group of three exposed nucleotides on the surface of t-RNA that are specific for an amino acid. They pair with particular codons of m-RNA.

antigen a specific protein on the surfaces of red blood cells; any foreign protein

antitoxins substances produced in or injected into a body to deactivate poisons created by toxin-producing bacteria

anus the opening through which undigested materials are eliminated

aorta the main artery of the systemic circulation

apical dominance the influence of a terminal (end) bud in inhibiting the growth of lateral buds

appendage a movable extension of the body, such as a leg or antenna

appendicular skeleton the part of the skeleton that includes all the bones of the arms and legs

aqueous humor the watery fluid contained in the anterior cavity of the eyeball, behind the cornea

arachnoid layer the second protective membrane around the brain

arboreal tree-living

arterioles smaller branches of arteries

artificial selection the use of the principles of natural selection to domesticate wild organisms

atom the basic unit of any element

ATP adenosine triphosphate, a special energy-carrying molecule

atria (singular, *atrium*) the receiving chambers of the heart

auditory nerve the nerve that carries sensory impulses from the ear

auditory tube the passage through which sound waves enter the external ear

autonomic nervous system the nerve system that supplies the internal organs of the body

autosomes the twenty-two pairs of chromosomes other than the sex chromosomes

autotrophic nutrition the production by living things, for use as food, of organic compounds from inorganic substances in the environment

auxins plant hormones that stimulate cell division or cell growth

avoidance responses negative tropisms

axial skeleton the main supporting skeletal structure of the body, including the bones of the skull, vertebrae, ribs, and sternum (breastbone)

axon the part of a neuron that carries impulses away from the cell body

β

bacillus a rod-shaped bacterial cell

bacteria unicellular procaryotes

bacteriophage a virus that attacks a bacterial cell; also, *phage*

balanced polymorphism the maintenance of harmful alleles at higher-than-normal frequencies

basidia club-shaped structures that bear spores of a certain kind of fungi

behavior pattern a complex set of behaviors

bilateral symmetry symmetry in which there is only one plane that can divide the body into equivalent parts

bile a substance produced by the liver to help dissolve fats so they can be digested

binomial system the two-name system of naming organisms

biogenesis generation of life from life

biological control the use of living organisms to control insects

biological magnification the process of concentration of persistent chemicals from one step in the food chain to the next

biological oxidation in aerobic respiration, the process in which hydrogen is combined with oxygen to form water and to release energy in the form of ATP

bioluminescence the phenomenon in which living things give off light

biomes major divisions of the biosphere, consisting of land environments divided according to the major plant communities that are maintained by the climate

biosphere Earth's life-supporting layer of air, soil, and water

biotic community a group of interacting organisms

bipedal two-legged

bivalves molluscs with two shells hinged dorsally

blade the usually broad, flat part of a leaf

blastula the hollow ball of cells in the early development of an embryo

blood a fluid that transports substances to and from the cells of the body

blood pressure the amount of "push" that is forcing blood through the blood vessels

book lung in the respiratory system of Arachnids, an air space with wall folds resembling a book

Bowman's capsule a double-walled hollow sac of cells in each nephron

breathing the movements that cause air to pass into and out of the lungs

bronchi two large tubes branching from the trachea in the lungs

bronchioles tiny branches of the bronchial tubes

bud a shortened, immature section of stem

bud scales tough modified leaves that cover buds during a season of dormancy

budding the production of a new organism from a swelling on the side of an adult

bulb a very compressed stem bearing fleshy leaves

C

calorie the amount of heat energy required to warm one gram of water one Celsius degree; a measure of the energy stored in a substance

calyx the entire whorl of a flower's sepals

cambium a thin sheet of unspecialized cells between the central xylem of the stem and the phloem of the inner bark

cancer uncontrolled cell division

canines in mammals, teeth on either side of the incisors

capillaries small blood vessels

capillary action the upward movement of a liquid through a tube with a narrow diameter

carapace in some Arthropod exoskeletons, the rigid dorsal and side portion of skeleton covering the body

cardiac muscle involuntary muscle that is found only in the heart

carnivore a secondary consumer, or animal that eats mostly other animals

carrying capacity the number of individuals of a species that a particular environment can support indefinitely

catalyst a substance that increases the rate of a reaction without being used up in it

cell the basic unit of structure and function in living things

cell wall the rigid outer boundary of a plant cell, lying outside the cell membrane and composed of porous cellulose layers

cellular respiration the breakdown of foods and the release of energy from them

central nervous system the brain and spinal cord

centrioles in the cytoplasm adjacent to the nucleus in animal cells, two small dark-staining cylindrical bodies that support the spindle fibers between them during mitotic cell division

centromere the specialized region of a chromosome where two molecules of DNA are held together

cephalization the concentration of sensory organs and nervous tissue at the anterior, or head end, of the body

cephalothorax in crustaceans, the head and thorax fused together

cerebellum the second largest part of the human brain. Its main function is to coordinate muscular activities.

cerebrum the largest single part of the human brain, where conscious decisions are made and where most memories are stored

cervix a thick muscular ring at the lower part of the uterus

chelicera fanglike claws, such as those that serve as poison fangs in spiders

chelipeds large pinching appendages on the

fourth thoracic segment of crustaceans, used for capturing and handling prey as well as for defense

chemosynthetic able to use energy from inorganic compounds in the environment to build organic compounds

chemotherapy the use of synthetic drugs to combat infection

chemotropism the response in plants to chemicals

chitin a flexible substance in exoskeletons

chlorophyll a green chemical capable of capturing energy from the sun and other light sources. It is found in plants and is instrumental in photosynthesis.

chloroplast a cellular organelle in autotrophs that contains chlorophyll

chorion the membrane that lines the shell of an egg

choroid coat a layer of tissue containing many blood vessels and surrounding the retina

chromatophores colored cells found beneath the outer layer of the skin in some fishes

chromosome a body consisting of protein and DNA found in the nucleus of a cell

Chromosome Theory of Inheritance a theory explaining that chromosomes are responsible for the inherited characteristics of organisms, acting through their genes

cilia cytoplasmic threads surrounding a Paramecium cell

circadian rhythms daily cycles of activity in organisms

circulation the continuous passage of blood through the blood vessels from one region of the body to another

cleavage a series of simultaneous mitotic divisions in the zygote soon after fertilization

clitellum in segmented worms, a dorsal saddle-like swelling, which secretes a cocoon

clone a group of identical cells derived from a single cell

coccus a sphere-shaped bacterial cell

cochlea a small bony structure in the inner ear that resembles a snail shell. In it is a long, coiled, fluid-filled tube containing sound-sensitive cells.

codominance the expression of two alleles at the same time in one individual without being blended

codon a group of three nucleotides on the messenger RNA, responsible for the placement of one amino acid in the chain making up a protein

coelom the fluid-filled, mesoderm-lined body cavity in annelids and molluscs

coenzyme a molecule that works with enzymes in activating chemical reactions

cohesion the attraction of water molecules for each other

coleoptile the sheath that covers the first leaves of the grass seedling

colloids liquid to semisolid mixtures formed from particles too large to form true solutions and too small to form suspensions

colon part of the large intestine

commensalism a relationship in which one species is benefited but the other is not affected

comparative anatomy the science that compares and contrasts body structures of plants and animals

competition interactions in which two individuals or two species limit one another's supply of food, space, nutrients, water, or light

complete flower a flower with sepals, petals, stamens, and a pistil

complete metamorphosis in insects, development in which eggs, larvae, pupae, and adults are quite different

compound a substance that contains two or more elements combined in definite proportion

compression wood wood formed on the underside of a conifer's leaning stem as a reaction to the stem's leaning posture

concentration in a solution, the amount of dissolved substance (solute) in a certain amount of dissolving medium (solvent)

conditioned response a response to a substitute stimulus that an organism has learned to associate with the original stimulus

cones light-sensitive cells in the retina that require light of greater intensity than the rods and respond to different colors of light

congenital defects disorders that are present at birth

conjugation a primitive form of sexual cell reproduction in which two cells join, the DNA from one cell passes into the other, and the recipient cell undergoes division

connective tissue various animal tissues that serve to connect or support various parts of the body

consumers organisms that eat other living things or their remains

contour farming the use of furrows or trenches across the slope of a hill to conserve soil and water

control treatment a situation in which all the conditions, except the one being tested, are identical to those in the experimental treatment

conus arteriosus in frogs, the large artery through which blood leaves the heart

convergence the development of two or more groups in such a way that they become more alike in structure or other features

cork outer bark of stems

cork cambium deepest layer of outer bark that forms cork

corm a short, bulky vertical stem containing stored food

cornea the front surface of the eye

corolla the entire whorl of a flower's petals

coronary circulation the group of blood vessels that supply blood to the heart

corpus luteum a temporary gland formed at ovulation from the remaining cells of the broken follicle. It produces the female hormone progesterone.

cortex plant tissue that is fitted for food storage

cotyledons seed leaves

covalent bond a chemical union of two atoms that share a pair of electrons

cranial nerves nerves that branch from the brain

crop in earthworms and birds, a chamber where food is temporarily stored

cross-pollination pollination involving the transfer of pollen to a stigma on a different plant

crossing over in meiotic cell division, the process in which chromosome parts are exchanged in order to assort genes into new combinations

cultural energy energy subsidies supplied by humans, their animals, or their machines

cuticle a fold of skin that grows over the base of fingernails and toenails; a tough outer covering of unsegmented roundworms; a fatty, waxy layer on the outer walls of cells, secreted by certain plants to protect leaves and stems against water loss

cytokinesis the division of the cytoplasm

cytokinins plant hormones that promote cell division and cause cells to enlarge and differentiate

cytoplasm the part of a cell, excluding the nucleus, contained within the cell membrane

D

deamination the removal of amine (NH_2) groups during digestion

deciduous trees and shrubs trees and shrubs that lose their leaves in the dry season

decomposers consumers that derive nourishment by decomposing dead organisms and wastes

deductive reasoning the form of reasoning that proceeds from a general statement to a specific case

dendrites the parts of a neuron that carry impulses toward the cell body

density the measure of the mass per unit volume of a substance

density-dependent factors population control factors that have a greater effect as population density increases

density-independent factors population-limiting factors that are not influenced by population density

dermis the inner part of the skin

deserts areas receiving twenty-five centimeters or less of rainfall per year

diaphragm in mammals, a wide band of muscle that separates the body cavity into a thoracic cavity and an abdominal cavity

diastole the part of the heart cycle during which the heart relaxes and refills

dichotomous key a means of identifying objects or organisms through a series of paired statements, only one of which applies to the organism

dicotyledonous plants dicots; plants with two cotyledons

diffusion the movement of ions and small molecules from an area of high concentration to an area of lower concentration, especially through a porous membrane

digestion the chemical breakdown of food into small molecules

dihybrid cross a cross of populations involving two different traits

dioecious having staminate and pistillate flowers on separate plants

diploid number the number of chromosomes in a fertilized cell, twice the number contained in the gametes

directional selection selection involving changes that take place when a population shows a steady trend through time

disruptive selection selection caused by "abnormal" features that have a high survival value

divergence the separation of a single species into two due to genetic drift

diversity the quality of variation among living things

division of labor the taking on of separate functions by different parts of an organism

dominant form the form of the trait that appears in an F_1 generation

dorsal the back of an animal with bilateral symmetry

double bond a covalent bond formed between two atoms that share four electrons

double fertilization the two fertilizations that form the zygote and the endosperm in flowering plants

drones male bees whose sole purpose in the colony is to mate with the queen

ductus arteriosus in the fetus, a short duct between the aorta and the artery leading to the lung

duodenum part of the small intestine

dura mater the tough, outermost protective membrane around the brain

E

ecologic equivalents unrelated organisms that fill similar niches

ecological succession the series of progressive changes in plant and animal communities in an area

ecology the study of how living things relate to each other and to their nonliving environment

ecosystem the combination of a biotic community and the nonliving environment with which it interacts

ectoderm in a simple sponge, the body wall's outer layer, made of flat cells

ectoplasm a thin, clear area of cytoplasm just inside the cell membrane

ectothermic in animals having a body temperature regulated by their environment

efficiency the comparison of the net productivity of one trophic level to that of the preceding trophic level in the food chain

electromagnetic spectrum the display of electromagnetic radiations arranged in order of wave length

embryo an organism in the early stages of development

embryology the study of the development of an embryo

endocrine system a system of glands that have no ducts to direct their secretions to the organs they affect. The hormones they secrete are conveyed by the bloodstream.

endoderm in a simple sponge, the body wall's inner layer, composed of collar cells; in seeds, the embryo's food supply

endoplasm the granular-appearing inner body in a cell's cytoplasm

endoplasmic reticulum a system of interconnected membranes that extends throughout the cell

endoskeleton an inner skeleton

endospore a type of spore formed from a bacterial cell during unfavorable conditions

endothermic in animals, regulating their body temperature

energy the ability to produce motion in an object

energy subsidy the energy supplied in addition to solar radiation in crop production

entomology the study of insects

environment the changeable surroundings of living things

enzyme a protein that serves as a catalyst in speeding chemical reactions in living things

epicotyl the tiny leaves and tip bud inside the typical dicot seed

epidermis the outer part of the skin; sheets of cells that cover and protect the surfaces of leaves, stems, and roots

epithelium animal tissue consisting of cellular layers that cover outer and inner surfaces of the body

erythrocytes red blood cells

esophagus a muscular tube about twenty-five centimeters in length extending from the pharynx to the mouth

estivation a period of inactivity during hot weather

estuary a partly enclosed portion of the sea that is fed by a freshwater stream

excretion the process of removing the waste products of metabolism from the body

exocrine system the system of glands that release their secretions through ducts to the outer surface of the body

exoskeleton a hard external skeleton

experimental treatment a situation in which the condition being tested is different from the corresponding condition in the control treatment: All other conditions are the same in both treatments.

extension muscle contraction that causes a joint to straighten

external respiration the exchange of gases between the blood and the air

extraembryonic membranes four membranes — the chorion, the amnion, the yolk sac, and the allantois — that surround the embryo during its early development

eyespot the light-sensitive pigment spot on the chloroplast of green algae cells

F

F₁ generation in breeding, all of the offspring of original crosses

facultative anaerobes aerobes that can use fermentation when oxygen is not present

Fallopian tubes *See* oviducts.

feedback system in which control over the glands is dependent upon information received from them

fermentation the formation of ethyl alcohol and carbon dioxide from pyruvic acid

fertilization the process of the union of two gametes of the opposite sex

fetus an embryo in the later stages of mammalian development

fever increased body temperature, as a body's reaction to infection

fibrin an insoluble fibrous protein that forms a mesh across a cut in a blood vessel

fibrinogen a substance circulating in the blood that aids in the process of blood clotting

fibrous root system a root system composed of many slender main roots that undergo much branching

filament the slender portion of the stamen that supports the anther

First Law of Probability the law stating that the sum of the probabilities (of frequencies) of occurrence for a chance event is equal to one

fission asexual reproduction of organisms by splitting the cell in half

flagella long whiplike strands that extend from a cell and cause cell movement

flame cells enlarged ends connected to the networks of tubes that comprise the excretory system of a planarian

flexion muscle contraction that causes a joint to bend

flower a highly modified stem whose leaves are specialized for sexual reproduction

food chain the series of steps, from producers through consumers and decomposers, by which energy and matter are transferred through the environment

food web the pattern of interconnected food chains

fossils any evidence of organisms that lived in the past

fovea the area of the retina where vision is best

frequency in genetics, how often an allele occurs in a population compared to how often all alleles for that gene appear

freshwater water running in streams or standing in lakes, ponds, marshes, and swamps

fruit a mature ovary in flowering plants

G

gall bladder a small sac on the underside of the right lobe of the liver. It releases bile when fat is present in the duodenum.

gamete a sex cell

gametophytes haploid blades that produce gametes

ganglion a group of cell bodies of the neurons of a nerve

gastric caeca in insects, extensions of the stomach cavity

gastrovascular cavity a body cavity that functions in both digestion and circulation

gastrula stage of developing embryo following the blastula stage

gene pool the sum of all the genes with their respective alleles possessed by a population at a given time

generative nucleus the smaller of two nuclei that form a pollen grain

genes inheritance factors, as established by Mendel

genetic drift the changing of allelic frequencies in a population due to random mating

genetics the science of inheritance

genotype the particular combination of alleles for a trait

geometric population growth growth in which a population increases by a constant percentage of the existing population in each succeeding year or generation

geotropism the response in plants to gravity

germination renewed growth in a seed

gestation period the full term of a human pregnancy

gibberellins plant hormones that stimulate stems to grow longer and that affect flowering, leaf growth, root formation, and seed dormancy in some plants

gills special organs that allow gas exchanges between blood and circulating sea water, freshwater, or air

girdling removing a strip of outer and inner bark (including phloem) from a tree

gizzard in earthworms and birds, the muscular chamber to which food is directed from the crop or the proventriculus, to be ground into smaller pieces with the help of mineral particles or small stones

glomerulus a set of capillaries associated with the Bowman's capsule in each nephron

glycolysis the process in which pyruvic acid is used to form lactic acid

Golgi apparatus flat membranous sacs stacked one on top of the other in a cell. They are involved in the conversion of proteins into forms the cell can use.

grafting the method of cloning by which one inserts a short piece of dormant stem or a bud into another stem with a root system

green glands in the crayfish excretory system, the pair of glands that serve to remove organic wastes from the blood

"Green Revolution" increased crop production through the use of high-yield plant varieties, fertilizers, irrigation, and pesticides

growth medium nutrients mixed with agar to form a medium for the growth of bacteria

growth rings layer of wood in a tree produced in single period of growth

guard cells the two cells surrounding a stoma and regulating its size

guttation the forcing of water from the tips of a plant's leaves

H

habitat the particular place where an organism lives

habituation the tendency in certain organisms eventually to ignore a repeated stimulus that produces harmful effects

half-life the time required for one-half of a radioactive substance to decay

haploid cell a cell containing one chromosome from each pair and therefore one-half the total number of the original cell

Hardy-Weinberg Principle a principle stating that under certain conditions, the frequencies of alleles in a population will remain constant from generation to generation

heartwood the older, darker wood at the center of a tree trunk

heat the energy of the continuous random motion of molecules

hemocyanin an oxygen-carrying copper compound dissolved in the blood of molluscs

hemoglobin a large protein molecule that contains iron

hepatic portal vein the vein through which blood leaves the small intestine for the liver

herbaceous stems soft, green stems with little or no woody tissue

herbivores primary consumers, or animals that eat only plants

hermaphrodites organisms that contain both male and female organs

heterotrophic nutrition the use by living things, for food, of already-made organic compounds

heterozygous possessing both the dominant and recessive forms of a factor

hibernation a period of greatly reduced metabolism during cold weather

high-risk group a group whose risk for a specific disorder is higher than average

homeostasis the maintenance of constant conditions in an organism through self-regulation

homeostatic mechanisms mechanisms in the body that are important in regulating the functions of all body systems

home range the area to which an individual or a small group of animals confines its activities

hominids modern humans and their ancestors

homologous similar in structure but not always similar in function

homozygous able to pass only one kind of factor to their offspring

hormones chemicals, each with a specific effect in the body, produced by endocrine glands

host See parasite.

humus the partially decomposed remains of plants, animals, and animal wastes

hybrids offspring of crossing populations that differ in one or more traits

hypha a threadlike extension in a spore

hypocotyl the fingerlike embryo stem inside the typical dicot seed; the portion of the embryo below the cotyledons

hypothalamus the lower part of the thalamus. It is responsible for regulating body temperature in reptiles.

hypothesis a temporary explanation

I

ileum part of the small intestine

immunity the ability to resist infection and to ward off certain other kinds of injury

incisors in mammals, teeth found in the front of the mouth

incomplete dominance the condition in which two alleles are both expressed in a heterozygote by being blended

incomplete flower a flower that lacks one or some of the parts that make up a complete flower: sepals, petals, stamens, and a pistil

incomplete metamorphosis in some insects, the gradual development from egg through nymph to adult

incurrent pores the pores through which water enters a sponge

inductive reasoning the development of a general statement based on a collection of observations

innate behavior involuntary behavior

innate immunity immunity that one is born with

insertion the attachment of a muscle at its moving part

interferon a special protein useful in defending against many viruses and other infecting agents

internal respiration the exchange of gases between the bloodstream and the cells of the body

internode the space from one node to the next on a stem

interphase the stage of cell division during which each chromosome begins to replicate

ion a charged particle resulting from the loss or gain of one or more electrons

ionic bond a bond formed by the transfer of electrons from one atom to another

iris a donut-shaped structure in the eyeball's anterior cavity. It gives the eye its color.

islets of Langerhans small groups of cells, scattered through the pancreas, that produce the hormones insulin and glucagon

isolating mechanisms factors that prevent the

mating of members of one population with those from another population

isotope one form of an element that differs from its other forms in the number of neutrons within the nucleus

J K

joint a place were two bones are held together

karyotype an arranged preparation of chromosomes

kidneys the main organs of excretion. They remove wastes from the blood in the form of urine.

kinetic energy the energy of motion

Krebs cycle in aerobic respiration, the process in which acetyl-CoA is broken down into carbon dioxide with the release of electrons and energy; also, *citric acid cycle*

L

labium the posterior lip of an insect

labor the period of time from initial contraction to birth

labrum the forward lip of an insect

lacteal a blind-ended lymph vessel attached to each villus

large intestine the organ connected directly to the ileum of the small intestine, about 6 centimeters in diameter and approximately 1.5 meters long

larva an immature form that looks different from the adult form

larynx the voice box

latent existing in a cell but inactive; said of viruses

latent learning learning that occurs without immediate reward and that remains useless until a later time

leaf gap an interruption in the vascular tissue of a stem above the point where it supplies the leaf

learned behavior behavior that has changed because of experience

lens structure in the eye that focuses light rays on the retina

lenticles areas of loose, unsuberized cells that allow gas exchange between stem tissue and the atmosphere

leukocytes white blood cells

ligaments strong bands of connective tissue that hold bones together

limiting factor a scarce item that limits the survival and productivity of an organism

liver the large, soft organ or gland where bile is produced

lymph a clear fluid that surrounds and bathes the cells

lysosomes small membranous sacs in a cell containing destructive substances that dissolve foreign particles and that also destroy the cell when it dies

lytic cycle the steps in a phage attack on a host bacterial cell

M

malpighian tubules in the excretory system of insects, organs that extract wastes from the blood flowing through the abdomen

mammary glands highly modified sweat glands that produce milk in female mammals

mandibles the biting jaws in crustaceans

mantle in molluscs, the fleshy outer layer of the body wall that secretes a limestone shell

mantle cavity in molluscs, the space, between the body and the mantle, that contains gills

marsupials a primitive group of mammals whose offspring are born in a very immature state and continue their development in a pouch on the belly of the mother

mass a measure of a body's tendency to resist changes in its motion

matter anything that has mass or substance and occupies space

maxillae two pairs of appendages on crustaceans, used to help hold and pass food on to the mouth

maxillipeds three pairs of appendages on crustaceans, used to move food forward to the mouth

medulla the part of the human brain that controls the activities of internal organs

medusa form in cnidarians, the inverted polyp that is free-floating

megaspore mother cell a large diploid cell in a

plant ovary that divides by meiosis to form four haploid megaspores

megaspores four haploid cells, three of which die. The survivor undergoes mitosis and forms a female gametophyte

meiosis the cellular process that reduces the chromosome number of a cell by one-half

Mendelian traits in organisms, traits that exist in either one of only two alternative forms

meninges three protective membranes — the dura mater, the arachnoid layer, and the pia mater — that surround the brain and spinal cord

menstrual cycle monthly series of hormonal changes leading to egg maturation and uterine preparation for a possible pregnancy

meristem plant tissue containing cells that are capable of dividing throughout the life of the plant

mesoderm in flatworms, a well-developed cell layer between the ectoderm and endoderm

mesoglea a layer of nonliving, jellylike material that separates the ectoderm and endoderm of the body wall of a simple sponge

mesophyll a layer of cells between the upper and lower epidermis of a leaf

messenger RNA type of RNA that moves along ribosome and directs making of a protein molecule

metabolism the sum of all the chemical reactions involved in life's activities

metaphase the second of the four stages of mitosis: the stage in which the chromosomes gather in the center of the cell

metastasis the spreading of cancer from one place to many places in the body

microfilaments thin protein strands in a cell that help move the cytoplasm

micropyle a pore that remains as an opening in the protective tissue of an ovule during ovule formation

microspore mother cells cells in the anther that divide by meiosis and produce four haploid microspores

microspores four haploid cells that undergo mitosis to form the generative nucleus and tube nucleus

microtubules threadlike bodies, composed of protein, that form the skeleton of cells and are involved in cell division

midbrain the part of the human brain that coordinates eye and other movements

minerals inorganic substances that are essential for good health

mitochondria small rod-shaped bodies that produce energy for a cell

mitosis in cell division, the duplication of the nucleus in such a way that each new cell receives exactly the same number and kind of chromosomes

molars with premolars, teeth found farther back in the mouths of mammals

molecule the smallest unit of a substance that can exist by itself

molting the shedding of the exoskeleton

monocotyledonous plants monocots; plants with only one cotyledon

monoecious having separate staminate and pistillate flowers on the same plant

monohybrid offspring resulting from a cross of parents with difference in one trait

motor neurons neurons that carry impulses from the central nervous system to a muscle or gland

motor unit the nerve endings of an axon and the muscle fibers they supply

multiple alleles the condition in which there may be three or more alleles for a given gene

muscle a tissue that is capable of contracting

muscle tissue animal tissue that is able to contract

mutagens mutation-causing factors

mutation a change in the hereditary material that may result in a change in the phenotype of the offspring

mutualism a relationship between two species in which both species benefit

mycelium the tangled mass of hyphae that comprises the body of a fungus

mycoplasmas tiny viruslike organisms involved in several human diseases, including one form of pneumonia

mycorrhiza a complex association of root and fungus

myosin a kind of protein molecule present in muscle fiber

N

nacre a form of calcium carbonate that forms the inner layer of some mollusc shells

natural selection the process that results in the survival of those organisms best suited for their environment

nematocyst a spirally coiled, hollow thread contained in the cnidoblasts of Cnidaria and used to paralyze or trap prey

nephridium in the annelid excretory system, a ciliated funnel that directs coelomic fluid through a long coiled tube to the outside

nephrons filtering units of the kidneys

nerve a bundle of nerve fibers composed of the axons of dendrites of many neurons

nervous tissue animal tissue that is able to conduct nerve impulses

net productivity the amount of energy produced by each square meter of land

neuron a nerve cell, consisting of a cell body with a nucleus, an axon, and several dendrites

niche the role that an organism plays in the ecosystem

nitrification the formation of nitrates by bacteria

nitrogen fixation any process that chemically converts nitrogen in the atmosphere to chemical compounds

node a portion of stem that produces leaves or branch stems

non-disjunction the failure of chromosomes to separate during the meiotic process

nucleolus the largest body inside the cell nucleus. It contains a large amount of RNA and is the site of assembly of the ribosomes.

nucleotide the basic unit of both DNA and RNA, consisting of one molecule each of phosphoric acid, a five-carbon sugar, and a nitrogenous base

nucleus the control center of the cell

nutrition the intake and use of organic food by living things for energy, growth, or repair

nutritious diet a meal plan that contains all of the ingredients necessary for maintaining good health

nymphs immature insects that differ little from one stage of their life cycle to the next

O

obligate aerobes aerobes that cannot survive in the absence of oxygen

obligate anaerobes bacteria that cannot tolerate the presence of oxygen

olfactory lobe a structure in the forebrain of fishes and amphibians that interprets odors

olfactory nerve the nerve that carries sensory impulses from the nose

omnivores animals that eat both plant and animal tissue

operculum hard covering of the gill chamber of fishes

optic lobes structure in the brain that registers sight

optic nerve the bundle of nerve fibers at the back of the retina that run from the eye to the brain

organ a group of tissues that work together to carry out a set of functions

organelles little organs; small particles present within cells

organism an independently functioning living thing

origin the attachment of a muscle at its fixed part

osmosis the diffusion of water through a selectively permeable membrane from an area of high concentration to an area of lower concentration

ossification the process by which solid bone replaces cartilage as the skeleton develops

ova female sex cells

ovaries organs that produce ova

oviducts funnel-like extensions, partially surrounding the ovaries, where fertilization usually occurs; also, *Fallopian tubes*

ovipositors pointed organs in the female grasshopper used to form a short tunnel in the ground in which eggs are placed

ovule the part of a plant ovary that develops into a seed during reproduction

P

palisade layer the compact layer of cells in the mesophyll of a fern leaf

pancreas the organ that lies behind the stomach and duodenum. It produces hormones that help regulate the amount of sugar in the blood.

parasite an organism that lives on or in the body of another organism, the host, from which it receives nourishment

parasympathetic nervous system the part of the autonomic nervous system that reverses all of the changes caused by the sympathetic nervous system during an emergency

parenchyma the packing material of the plant, consisting of loosely packed cells inside leaves, stems, and roots

parthenogenesis the development of unfertilized eggs

pathogens disease-causing bacteria

peat partially decomposed deposits of dead mosses

pectoral of or having to do with forelimbs of vertebrates

pedigree diagram a picture that shows the pattern of inheritance for a hereditary disorder in a family

pedipalps in spiders, leglike appendages that have sensory functions

pelvic of or having to do with hindlimbs of vertebrates

peptide a short chain of amino acids held together by peptide bonds

perennial structure a stem that lives for several years

pericardial sinus in crayfish, the space surrounding the heart

pericardium a tough membrane that surrounds the heart

periosteum a tough protective membrane that covers a bone

peripheral nervous system the system of nerves that carry impulses to and from the central nervous system

peristalsis waves of muscle contractions that serve to squeeze food through the esophagus; in earthworms, the muscular action that pushes food and soil through the food tube

petiole the stalk connecting the blade with the stem

phage a virus that attacks a bacterial cell; also, *bacteriophage*

phagocytosis the process by which a cell takes a large particle into itself

pharynx in planarians, a muscular tube on the ventral surface, connected by its anterior end to the gastrovascular cavity; in mammals, a vertical, tubular structure that acts as a common passageway for food and air

phenotype the term used to denote the appearance of an organism with respect to a given trait

pheromones substances that organisms release into the environment as a means of communication with other members of the same species

phloem tissue of the two kinds of vascular tissue in plants, the tissue that conducts dissolved food from leaves to other parts of the plant body

photoperiodism the dependence of flowering on the length of day or night

photosynthesis the process by which green plants combine water and carbon dioxide in the presence of chlorophyll and sunlight to produce carbohydrates and release oxygen

positively phototropic attracted to light

phototropism the bending of plants toward light

phycocyanin the blue photosynthetic pigment in red algae

phycoerythrin the red photosynthetic pigment in red algae

phytoplankton plantlike protists, which produce their own food

pia mater the innermost protective membrane around the brain. It lies directly over the surface of the brain and spinal cord.

pinocytosis engulfing of liquid particles or dissolved food particles by a cell

pistil the center of a flower, composed of an ovary, a style, and a stigma

pituitary gland the master gland of the endocrine system

placenta an organ formed during fertilization that allows for the exchange of nutrients and wastes between the mother and the developing baby

plaques spots of dead bacteria in bacterial cultures

plasma a straw-colored liquid that surrounds the formed elements of the blood

plasmodium a slimy mass of acellular cytoplasm

plastids the parts of plant cells that are involved in the capture and storage of energy from the sun

platelets thrombocytes; small particles in the blood

pollen grain an immature male gametophyte, consisting of a generative nucleus and a tube nucleus

pollination the transfer of pollen from an anther to a stigma, either by self-pollination or by cross-pollination

pollution any substance or energy in such quantity that it degrades the environment

polygenic inheritance the condition in which two or more genes, each with its respective alleles, jointly affect the expression of a given phenotype

polyp form in cnidarians, the body form that is not free to move about, being attached at its base

polyploidy the increase of chromosome number by one or more whole sets of chromosomes

population any group of interacting, interbreeding individuals of one kind of organism

population density the number of a particular kind of organism in a limited area

portal system a system of blood vessels that carries blood from one set of capillaries to another

positive mutation a mutation that allows the individual to be better adapted to its environment

posterior the tail end of an animal with bilateral symmetry

potential energy energy that is inactive or stored in any form .

preadaptations adaptive traits that exist in an organism before they are of value

predator an organism that devours another organism

prehensile grasping

premolars with molars, teeth found farther back in the mouths of mammals

prey organisms that are eaten by predators

primary and secondary tissues tissues that increase the root's diameter. Primary tissue is composed of cells produced by meristem at the tips of roots and stems. Secondary tissues originate from the vascular cambium or cork cambium.

primate a mammal with grasping hands, nails, toes, well-developed collarbones, and eyes that are directed forward

Principle of Dominance one of Mendel's four Principles of Inheritance: the principle that one of the two factors for a trait can mask or overpower the other

Principle of Independent Assortment one of Mendel's four Principles of Inheritance: the principle that pairs of factors separate independently during gamete formation

Principle of Segregation one of Mendel's four Principles of Inheritance: the principle that factors separate during the formation of gametes

Principle of Unit Characters one of Mendel's four Principles of Inheritance: the principle that individuals carry two factors for each trait

producer a living thing, such as a green plant, that makes its own food from inorganic substances in the environment

proglottids sections of a tapeworm

prophase the first of the four stages of mitosis: the stage in which the nuclear envelope disappears and the chromosomes shorten and thicken

propolis a substance gathered from resinous buds, used as a varnish, a glue, and a filler of cracks in a beehive

protonema a body of branching filaments in a spore

proventriculus in birds, the first part of the stomach, where food is mixed with digestive juices

pseudocoelom a fluid-filled space between the mesoderm and the internal organs of an unsegmented roundworm

pseudopodia "false feet," or extensions from the main cell mass of an Ameba

puberty period of becoming sexually mature

pulmonary of the lungs

pulmonary circulation circulation of blood from the heart to the lungs and back to the heart. Through pulmonary circulation blood gets rid of carbon dioxide and picks up a new supply of oxygen.

pupa a nonfeeding stage following the final larval stage

pupil   the hole in the center of the iris. The change in size of the pupil regulates the amount of light that enters the eye.

pure-breeding populations   populations that produce only one form of a trait over many generations

pylorus   a saclike structure in fish that increases the surface area of the intestine

pyramid of energy   characteristic progressive decrease in energy production along a food chain

pyrenoids   round protein bodies in the chloroplast of a green algae cell, thought to be centers of starch formation

Q R

queen   the single mother of a colony of domestic honeybees

race   an interbreeding population with characteristic allele frequencies different from those of other such groups

radial symmetry   symmetry in which all wedge-shaped sections around a vertical line are similar

radioactivity   a property of isotopes that causes them to change into other elements

radula   in Chitons, a rasping tongue ued to scrape algae from rocks

receptacle   the enlarged portion of flower stalk to which all floral parts are attached

receptor site   structure which detects stimuli

recessive form   the hidden form of a trait in an F_1 generation

recombinant DNA   the exchange of DNA segments between organisms of different species

rectum   part of the large intestine

reflex arc   in the nervous system, the simplest pathway that includes a stimulus and a response

releaser   the stimulus that initiates a given behavior

renal artery   the artery through which blood passes into the kidney

renal vein   the vein through which blood passes from the kidney

replicate   to make a duplicate of oneself

replication   the duplication of each chromosome in mitotic cell division

reproductive efficiency   the term used to describe the number of survivors compared to the total number of eggs produced

resin ducts   in the xylem tissue that forms wood, ducts lined with cells that secrete resin, which inhibits the growth of fungi and invasion by insects

respiration   chemical reaction which releases energy from foods and stores as ATP; breathing

retina   the inner layer of the eyeball, where light-sensitive cells are located

rhizoids   rootlike organs in moss plants

rhizome   a horizontal underground stem

ribosomes   the sites at which protein synthesis takes place in a cell

rickettsias   cellular organisms responsible for a number of diseases

rods   light-sensitive cells in the retina that are able to respond to light of very low intensity but are unable to distinguish colors

root cap   the part of a root formed from cells produced toward the root's tip. It serves to protect the inner cells from damage.

root hairs   epidermal extensions on a root, which increase the surface area through which water and minerals enter the plant

root pressure   the force resulting from differences in osmotic pressure between the cells of a root hair and the cells of the xylem at the center of the root

ruminants   a group of mammals that chew cud

runner   a long, narrow stem growing horizontally along the surface of the ground; also, *stolon*

S

saliva   fluid secreted into the mouth by the salivary glands to moisten and soften food so that it is easier to swallow

saprophytes   organisms that secure their food by absorbing it from decaying organic matter

sapwood   the outer, lighter wood that still functions in a tree trunk

saturated fat   a fat in which each carbon atom in the fatty acid chain (except the end carbon atoms) is bonded to two hydrogen atoms

scavengers   animals that feed on dead organisms or the wastes of organisms, and digest them in their intestines

scion in grafting, the stem cutting that is inserted into the stock

sclera a layer of tough connective tissue surrounding the retina and forming the "white" of the eye

scolex a knob-shaped part at the end of a tapeworm that produces proglottids

scrotum a sac of skin outside the male body wall that contains the testes

Second Law of Probability the law stating that the probability that two or more chance events will occur together is equal to the multiplication product of their chances of occurring separately

seed an embryonic plant consisting of the embryo, stored food, and a coat; a mature ovule

self-pollination the process of transferring pollen from an anther to any stigma on the same plant

semicircular canals three fluid-filled canals in the inner ear that are sensitive to changes in the position of the head and so contribute to the sense of balance

sensory neurons neurons that carry impulses from a sensory receptor to the central nervous system

sepals the outer protective parts of a flower

septum muscle which partially divides ventricle of heart in reptiles

sex chromosomes the chromosomes that determine the sex of the offspring

sex-linked traits recessive characteristics that are carried on the X chromosome but usually expressed only in the male

sexual dimorphism a condition created by the differences in form between males and females of a species

shelterbelts rows of trees arranged to control wind flow

shrub a plant consisting of several stems of similar size that occur at or near ground level

skeletal muscle voluntary muscle that is attached to the bones of the skeleton

skin gills in echinoderms, tiny projections that extend from between the skeletal plates out into the sea water

small intestine a narrow tube about 2.5 centimeters in diameter and 3 meters long, into which food passes from the stomach

smooth muscle involuntary muscle that is found in the internal organs of the body

solution a mixture of two or more substances in which the molecules of the substances are evenly distributed

somatic cells all the cells of the body except the reproductive cells

sorus (plural, *sori*) a cluster of sporangia

speciation the process by which a new species arises from pre-existing forms

species a group of organisms that have the ability to interbreed

species name the name for an organism, composed of the genus name plus the specific name

sperm male sex cells

spherical symmetry symmetry in which all cone-shaped sections around a point are similar

spicules branched needles of either calcium carbonate or silica that support the bodies of some sponges

spinal nerves nerves that branch from the spinal cord

spinnerets in spiders, abdominal appendages that secrete silk

spiracles in insects, small openings in the sides of the thorax and abdomen leading into the respiratory system

spirillum bent rod-shaped or spiral bacterial cell

spongy layer in the mesophyll of a fern leaf, the layer that has large air spaces among the cells

sporangia (singular, *sporangium*) helmet-shaped, spore-bearing structures on the underside of ferns' leaves

spore a tiny cell that spreads a fungus to new habitats

sporophyte a diploid blade that produces spores

stabilizing selection selection that occurs when organisms that represent extreme departures from the "normal" are removed from the population

stamens the male parts of a flower, including the filament and the anther

statocysts organs in crayfish that serve the sense of balance

sterile without life

stigma in the pistil of a flower, the sticky structure, supported by the style, that receives the pollen grains produced in the stamens

stipe the stalk of a mushroom

stock in grafting, the rooted stem that supports the scion

stolon a long, narrow stem growing horizontally along the surface of the ground; also, *runner*

stomach a J-shaped elastic bag in the upper left portion of the abdominal cavity

stomata (singular, *stoma*) pores in the lower epidermis of a leaf that allow gases to diffuse into and out of the spaces of the mesophyll

stress a situation in which the body secretes excessive amounts of cortisol

strip cropping a farming technique in which strips of land planted with crops that need cultivation are alternated with strips of crops whose roots hold the soil

style in the pistil of a flower, the structure that extends from the ovary and supports the stigma

suspensions mixtures formed from particles larger than ions or molecules

swimmerets in Arthropods, extensions that aid in swimming and in reproduction

symmetry the similarity of form or arrangement around a point, around a line, or on either side of a plane

sympathetic nervous system the part of the autonomic nervous system that acts during an emergency or when the body is under stress

synapse a functional connection, made chemically, between two neurons

syndrome a group of defects that routinely occur together as a result of a single underlying problem

syrinx in birds, an organ at the end of the trachea where sounds are produced

system a group of organs that work together to carry out a major body function

systemic circulation the pathway of blood to all parts of the body except the lungs

T

tap root systems root systems in which smaller roots branch out from the primary root

taxes the automatic movements of an organism in a direction determined by the stimulus

taxonomy the classification of organisms

telophase the last of the four stages of mitosis: the stage in which the chromosomes have reached opposite poles and a nuclear envelope forms around each daughter nucleus

telson the last abdominal segment of a crustacean. With the uropods, it forms a paddle.

tendons bands of connective tissue that attach muscles to bones

tendrils elongated petioles, veins, stipules, or stems

terraces banks of soil built across the slope of a hill for the purpose of reducing erosion caused by water running rapidly down the hillside

territory an area actively defended by an individual or by a group of animals that inhabits it

test crosses a procedure involving the mating of an unknown genotype with a homozygous recessive phenotype (rr)

testes organs that produce sperm

tetrad in meiotic cell division, a pair of homologous chromosomes that contains four strands

theory a general explanation for a large number of observations

thoracic cavity in mammals, the part of the body cavity that contains the heart and lungs

thorax the middle region of an insect, between the head and abdomen

thorns modified stems that discourage browsing

thrombin the active form of prothrombin, which circulates in the blood. Thrombin acts as an enzyme causing fibrinogen to be changed to fibrin, thus aiding in the blood-clotting process.

thymus gland a gland located in the chest cavity that produces the hormone thymosin

thyroid gland the gland that produces thyroxin, a hormone that affects the rate of metabolism

tissue a group of similarly specialized cells that carry out a particular function

toxoids toxins that have been deactivated

tracheae a system of branching air tubes

tracheids hollow woody cells with pointed ends specialized for water conduction

transducer something that changes a physical or chemical stimulus into another form; in the case of sense organs, a nerve impulse

transduction the conversion of energy from one form to another

transfer RNA type of RNA moves amino acids to correct position of the developing protein as directed by m-RNA

transpiration the evaporation of water from leaves

transpiration pull the pulling up of a column of water as it moves into a leaf to replace the water lost by transpiration or used by photosynthesis

tree a plant whose woody stem branches only at some distance above the ground

trochophore a free-swimming, ciliated larva

trophic level each step in the food chain, by which energy and matter are passed from one organism to another

tropism a movement in response to a stimulus

tube feet hollow structures on the underside of a starfish, used in locomotion and food-getting

tube nucleus the larger of two nuclei that form a pollen grain

tuber the bulky, short terminal part of an underground stem

turgor the firmness in cells due to water held in them by osmotic pressure

tympanic membrane in frogs, a membrane on the surface of the head just behind the eyes, serving as an eardrum; the eardrum

tympanum in grasshoppers, a membrane that responds to sound vibrations

U

unsaturated fat a fat that is not saturated with hydrogen

ureter a tube leading from the kidney to the urinary bladder.

urethra the organ through which urine is passed from the body

urine liquid waste filtered from the blood by the kidneys and passed from the body through the urethra

uropods the sixth pair of abdominal segments. With the telson, they form a paddle.

uterus in female mammals, the organ where an embryo develops; in roundworms, the organ where eggs are stored as they are produced

V

vaccine a substance that causes the body to produce antibodies without causing the illness

vacuoles in plant cells, membrane-surrounded sacs filled with water and salts, involved in water transport and in the support of the cells

vagina the birth canal; a muscular tube that connects the uterus to the outside

variable one aspect of an experiment that is free to change

vascular tissues tissues that form tubes that conduct substances through the body of a plant. They are formed from cells especially adapted for conducting water and dissolved materials.

vas deferens a duct through which sperm passes from the testis

vein a bundle of vascular tissue in vascular plants; a vessel that transports blood to the heart

ventral the belly of an animal with bilateral symmetry

ventricle the part of the heart that squeezes blood through the arteries

venules small veins

vertebral column the backbone

villi (singular, *villus*) structures on the intestinal lining which extend into the hollow of the intestine and increase the surface area for absorption of digested food

virulent producing a lytic cycle; said of viruses

viruses structures made of segments of a nucleic acid wrapped in a protein coat

visceral mass in molluscs, the body part that contains digestive and excretory organs and the heart

vitamins certain kinds of organic chemicals that are needed in small amounts for good health

vitreous humor a jellylike substance in the eyeball's posterior cavity. It helps the eyeball keep its shape.

volume the amount of space a substance occupies

vomerine teeth   teeth in the roof of a frog's mouth

W X

water cycle   the movement of water from ocean to atmosphere, to land, and back to ocean

water table   the level below which the ground is saturated with water

woody stems   hard, thick, long-lived stems

worker   a female honeybee without functioning sex organs

xylem tissue   of the two kinds of vascular tissue in plants, the tissue that conducts water and dissolved minerals from roots to leaves

Y Z

yolk sac   the membrane in an egg that contains stored food material for the developing embryo

zooplankton   animal-like protists, which must capture their food

zygote   a fertilized ovum

INDEX

Page numbers printed in **boldface** include illustrations and those printed in *italic* include definitions.

types of, **551**
wings, 550
birth
circulation changes at, 706
labor and, 706, **708**
birth defects, *see* congenital defects
bison, 12
extinction of, 72
bivalves, 477
blastocyst, 702
blastula, 702, 704
blind spot, 636
blood, *612*
clotting of, 615 – 616, 623
components of, **612** – 614
cross matching of, **615**
plasma in, 612, **614**
transfusing of, 615
urine compared to (table), 630
blood agar, 332
blood cells,
red, **612** – 613
clumping of, 614 – 615
white, **612,** 613, 683
blood pressure, 623 – 624
blood sinuses, 479
blood sugar, 501, 593
and diabetes, 680, 681
blood types, 213, 614 – 615
and heredity, 179
O and AB, 615
blood vessels, human, **620** – 621
blue-green algae, 101, 300, **305,**
318, 320
features of, 323
see also monerans
body, *see* human body
body movement
comparisons of invertebrates to plants, 514
body support
comparisons of invertebrates to plants, 514
bonds, 81 – 83, 91, 94 – 96, 143
covalent, *82,* 94 – 95
double, 82
energy, 121
ionic, *83*
bone(s)
calcium in, 603, 662, 679
development of, 662
fractures of, 662 – 663
of human skull, **662**
structure of, 660, **661,** 662
bony fishes, *see* fish(es)
botulism poisoning, 328
Bowman's capsule, 629, 630
brain, chicken, 554
fish, **525**
frog, **537**
human, *see* human brain
mammalian, **570**
snake, **548**
bread mold, 22, 359, **360**
breathing, process of, **627** – 628
breeding
and food productivity, **61**
test cross used in, **165**
breeding pattern, 205
breeding population(s), 203 – 205
pure-, 159 – **162,** 171 – 173
bronchi, reptilian, 547

and respiration, 626
bronchioles, 547, 626
brown algae, 380 – 381
Bryophyta, *382*
bryophytes, 382 – 385
liverworts, 382, 384
see also moss(es)
bud(s), plant, 419, **427**
bud scales, 427
budding, reproduction by, 361, 455
bulb, *431,* **431**

C

cacti, 2, 12
calcium, 89 – 90
in bone, 603, 662, 679
and diet, 603
calcium ions, 616
caloric energy, 52
calorie(s), *47,* 599
in selected foods (table), 599
calyx, 409
cambium, *397*
Cambrian Period, 273
cancer
air pollution and, 69
cell division and, 146 – 147
immune system and, 686
radioactive fallout and, 69
viruses and, 312, 314 – 315
cancer cells, 116, 147, 686
canine teeth, 567, 590
capillary(ies), 621
peritubular, 629, 630
capillary action, *428,* **428**
carapace, *492*
carbohydrates, 32, 47, 109 – 110, 137
complex, 606
in diet, 600, 606
function and properties of, 91 – 92
carbon, 20, 32
importance to living things, 89
stores of, 33
carbon cycle, 32 – 33
carbon dioxide, 32, 33, 73, 81
carbon-14 dating, 258
carbon monoxide poisoning, 627
Carboniferous Period, 276
cardiac muscle, characteristics of (table),
665
cardiopulmonary resuscitation (CPR), 628
carnivore(s), *21*
stomach of, 567, **568**
carrier molecule, 114
carriers, disease, 216, 219
carrying capacity, population growth and, **30**
cartilage, 662
cat-cry syndrome, 224
catalysts, enzymes as, 119
Caudata, 530
cecum, 593
cell(s), *99* – 103
aging and death of, 147
animal, *see* animal cells
bacterial, *see* bacterial cells
basic types of, 101
blood, 612 – 615
cancer, 116, 147, 686
chromosomes in, *see* chromosome(s)
cork, 148

daughter, **145**
differences in, 156
division of, *see* cell division
egg, **102**
elodea, 102 – **103**
energy used by, 136 – 141
haploid, *167*
in human body, number of, 20
of human cheek, **102**
memory, 684, 686
metabolism and, 118
nerve, **151**
see also neuron(s)
nucleus of, *see* cell nucleus
and nutrition, 20 – 21
organelles of, *see* organelles
osmotic environments and, **113**
plant, *see* plant cells
and protein synthesis, 138 – 141
respiration in, *see* cellular respiration
skin, 656
somatic, *167*
specialization in, 449
sperm, 696, 701
three-dimensional, **102**
yeast, 29, 30
cell division, 143 – 147
and cancer, 146 – 147
importance of, 146
meiosis, 167, **168, 169,** 170, 173
see also mitosis
cell membrane(s), 101 – 103
diffusion through, 112, **112** – 114
functions of, 112 – 116
information and, 115 – 116
movement of substances across, **112** – **115**
permeable, *113*
structure of, **105,** 107
cell metabolism, 137
cell nucleus, 101, 102, **109,** 138
genes in, 143
cell sap, 103
cell theory, development of, 100 – 101
cell vacuoles, 102 – 103, 109, 111
cell wall, 102 – 103, 109, 111
cellular respiration, 123 – 127, **328**
aerobic, 123, *124* – **126,** 127
anaerobic, 123 – 124, **126,** 127
compared to photosynthesis (table), 133
photosynthesis and, 33, 129 – **130,** 132
significance of, 127
cellulose, 92, 141, 355, 373
and diet, 600
Cenozoic Era, 277 – 279
summary of (table), 274
centipede(s), 492
central nervous system, 642
centrioles, 144
centromere, *144, 167*
cephalization, *458*
Cephalopoda, 477 – 478
cephalothorax, 490
cerebellum, 648
cerebrospinal fluid, 648
cerebrum, 647
effects of drugs on, 651
summary of (table), 649
interpretation in, 649
and learning, 650 – 651
and memory, 647, 651

unity among, 360
uses of, 363 – 364
yeasts, 356, 359, 361

G

galactose, 596
Galapagos tortoises, 237, **238**
gall bladder
 of frog, 535
 of human, **592**
gametes, 161, 167, 170, 171, **172,** 173
 diploid, 193
gametophyte(s), *378,* 382, 390, 391,
 411 – 412
 male and female, 412 – 414
 trends in size of, **441**
gametophyte generation, 360
gamma globulin, 686
ganglion, *460,* 643
gastric caeca, 500
gastrin, 595, 681
Gastropoda, 477
gastrovascular cavity, 460
gene(s), 109, *164*
 in cell nucleus, 143
 duplication of, 192
 frequencies among offspring (chart), 200
 mutations in, *see* mutation(s)
 nucleotides in, 143
 unlinking of, 191, **192**
 see also chromosome(s); heredity; Mendelian traits
gene linkage, crossing over and, 191 – **192**
gene pool(s), *178*
 diversity within, 167, 177 – 180
 mutations in, **207**
generative nucleus, 412 – 413
genetic counseling, 225 – 227
genetic diseases, 183, 214 – 216, 218 – 224
 autosomal disorders, 218 – 222
 carriers of, 216, 219
 ethnic groups and, 216, 218 – 220
 high-risk groups and, **216,** 225 – 227
 late-occurring, 216
 surgery for, **227 – 228**
 treatment of, 221, 227 – 228
 vertical nature of, 215
genetic drift, *205,* 206, 248, 282
genetic equilibrium, 203
 disturbing factors to, 204 – 208
genetic load, 209, 229
genetic recombination, 177 – 178
genetic shuffling, 243
genetics, *157*
genotype, *164*
geometric population growth, *29,* 30,
 238
geotropism, *435,* **435**
germination, *396*
 of corn kernel, **416**
 seed, 398, 415 – **416**
gestation period, *706*
 of selected animals (table), 706
gibberellins, 434 – 436
Gila monster, 544
gills
 crustacean, 490
 fish, 521, **525**
 mollusc, 476, 478

mushroom, 362
ginko tree, 395, 399
giraffe, theories about evolution of,
 234, 240
girdling, tree, *430,* **430**
gizzard
 of bird, 553
 earthworm, 472
 grasshopper, 500
glaucoma, 635
glomerulus, 629, 630
glucagon, 679, 680
glucose, 91, 92, 134, 596, 598
 structural formula for, 91
 structure of, **92**
glucose molecules, 123, 125, 127, 128
glycogen, 92, 141, 598
glycolysis, *124* – 125, 127
goiter, 678
goldfish, learning in, **528**
Golgi apparatus, 107, 114, 305
gonadotrophins, 555, 556, 572
gonorrhea, 332, 334, 364
grafting, *432,* **432**
grasshopper(s), 24, 25, 27, 72
 body plan of, **497** – 498
 circulatory system, 501
 digestive system, 500 – 501
 excretory system, 502
 eyes of, 497, 498
 internal organs, **500**
 movement of, 497, 498
 muscular system, 502
 nervous system, 502
 reproduction in, 498 – 500
 respiratory system, **501** – 502
grasslands as biome, **12**
Great Barrier Reef, 457, 485
great crested grebe, courtship behavior
 in, **558**
green algae
 body form of, 376
 diversity among, 376 – 377
 habitat of, 376
 homeostasis in, 378 – 379
 human activities and, 379
 human uses of, 379
 photosynthesis in, 379
 reproduction in, **377** – 378
 types of, **376**
green plants, *see* plants
Green Revolution, 62
greenhouse effect, 73 – 74
growth hormone, 673
growth medium, bacterial, 330
growth regulators, 433 – 435
 interactions among, 435 – 436
growth rings, 397 – 398, **399**
guanine, 96, 143
guard cells, 392, 418
gullet, 341 – 342
 frog, 533, 535
guttation, *428*
gymnosperm cone, angiosperm fruit
 compared to, **406**
gymnosperms, 395 – 400, 401
 body plan of, 395
 diversity among, 395
 flowering plants compared to, 405, **406**

as food, 399
 homeostasis in, 397 – 398
 human uses of, 399
 internal systems, 397
 photosynthesis in, 397
 reproduction in, 395 – 396
gypsy moth(s), 71 – 72

H

habitat(s), *36*
 destruction of, 71
habitat preference, as isolating factor,
 251
habituation, *456*
hair, 657
hair follicles, 563, **656, 657**
Hales, Stephen, and transpiration pull,
 428
half-life, 257, *258*
hard palate, 590
Hardy-Weinberg Principle, population
 genetics, 203 – 209, 241
haustoria, 359
hawks, 24
 kinds of, **247**
hay fever, 687
health revolution, population growth
 and, 58 – 59
heart
 of fish, **524**
 of frog, 535, **536**
 human, and circulatory system,
 618, **619**
 mammalian, 568 – 569
 reptilian, **546,** 547
heart attack, 623
heart transplant, 688
heartbeat, 618, 620
heartwood, 398
hemocyanin, *479*
hemoglobin, 473, 479, *612,* 615
hemophilia, 186 – 188, 208, 222, 223
hepatic portal system, 622, 623
hepatitis, 312, 313
herbivore(s), *21*
heredity
 blood types and, 179
 and disease, *see* genetic diseases
 environment and, 157
 see also inheritance
hermaphroditic, *459*
herring gull, 556
Heterotroph Hypothesis, 267 – 268, **269**
heterotrophic nutrition, *20*
heterotrophs, 305, 321, 322
heterozygotes, 200, 208, 219
 and balanced polymorphism, 210, 211
heterozygous, *162*
hibernation, 11, **537**
 body temperature during, *576*
 in frogs, 537
histamine, 687
home range, *31*
homeostasis, 99, 118, 136, 153
 cell membrane and, 116
 see also under *specific organisms*
homeostatic mechanism, 570
homeothermic, *545*
homing pigeons, 557

Isotonic concentration, *113*
Isotope, *257–258*
Iwanowski, Dimitri, and tobacco mosaic, 307–308

J

jejunum, 591, 592
jellyfish, 8, 273, 454
  life cycle of, **455**
Jenner, Edward, and vaccination, 307
joints, body, *663*, **663**–664
juvenile hormone, 503, 507
junk foods, 608

K

Kaibab squirrel, 251
kangaroo, 254–255, **564**
  locomotion in, **575**
karyotype, *185–186*, **186, 223**
Keith, Arthur, and continuity of life, 232
kelp(s), 8, 380, 381
keratin, 656
Kettlewell, H. B. D., and peppered moth
  experiments, 241
kidney machine, 631
kidney transplant, 688
kidneys
  of frog, 536
  human, 629–630
kilocalorie, 47
kinetic energy, *45*, **45**, 46
Kingdom Animalia, 293, 298–299, 300
Kingdom Fungi, 292, 296, 300, 355
Kingdom Monera, 293, 294, 300, 304
Kingdom Plantae, 292, 297, 300
Kingdom Protista, 292, 295, 300, 304
kitten, innate behavior in, **573**
Klinefelter's syndrome, 223, **224**
knee-jerk reflex, 643
Krebs, Hans, 125
Krebs cycle, 125–126

L

labium, 498
labrum, 497
lactase, 596
lactic acid fermentation, 124, 125, **328**
Lamarck, Jean Baptiste, theory of
  evolution, 233–**234**, 239
Landsteiner, Karl, and blood types,
  614–615
large intestine, 533, 593
larva, *451*
larynx
  human, 591, **626**
  reptilian, 547
latent learning, *503*
latent virus, 314
leaf(ves)
  arrangement of, 419–**420**
  autumn colors, **421**
  compound, **419**
  cross section of, *129*
  dicot, **417**
  diversity in, 418–**419**, 420
  falling, 420
  of flowering plants, 406, **407**
  growth and functioning of, 417
  homeostasis in, 418

modifications of, 419
photosynthesis in, 417, 418
simple, 419
leaf blade, 418
leaf gap, 392
leaf tissues, 417
leaf veins, *389*
  structure of, 418–**419**
leaflets, 419
Leakey, L. S. B., and human fossils, **280**
Leakey, Richard, 280–281
learned behavior, *462*
  in birds, 556
  conditioning and, 574
  in earthworms, 474
  in flatworms, 462
  in goldfish, **528**
  imprinting and, 556, 574
  in insects, 503
  in mammals, 573–575
  in molluscs, 480
  and reasoning, 574–575
leeches, 470–471
legumes, 34
  mutualism and, **28**
lenticles, *430–431*
leucoplasts, 111
leukemia, 315, 321, 611
leukocytes, **612**, 613
levels of organization, 148, 149–152
lichens, 13, 14, 35, **357**
  importance of, 364
  as soil formers, **34**, 35
light
  effect of on plants, **433**
  and flowering, 411
  properties of, 128–129
  as regulator of photosynthesis, 128,
    133
light energy, 21, 45, 46, 118, 128, 129
light microscope, **100**, 105
limiting factor, *48*
Lindemann, Jean, and interferon, 313
Linnaeus, Carolus, classification system
  of, 286–287, 289
lions, social behavior of, 575
lipids, 105, 107, 137, 141
liver, human, **592**
  alcohol and, 568, 608
  and digestion, 535, 592
liverworts, 382, 384
living things
  Earth's advantages and, 3–4
  elements in (table), 79
  elements important to, 89–90
  energy and, 44–46
  minerals in, **89**–90
  water important to, 85–86
  see also organism(s)
lizards, 10, 12, 542, 544, 547
  types of, **544**
Lorenz, Karl, and imprinting, 556
lung book, 491
Lycopodium, 389
Lycopsida, 389
lymph, 621
lymph nodes, 624
lymph vessels, 624
lysosomes, 108

lytic cycle, virus, 310–**311**

M

macronucleus, paramecium, 342
malaria, 211, 229, 349–350
malphigian tubules, 502
Malthus, Thomas, and population trends, 29,
  61, 238
maltose, 92, 596
mammal embryo, 261
Mammalia, 562
mammals, *277*
  Age of, 277
  behavior and environment, **573–576**
  birth process, 565
  body plan of, 562–563
  body temperature control in, 563
  brain of, **570**
  circulatory system, 568–569
  digestive system, 567–568
  diversity among, 563–564
  egg-laying, 277–278
  endocrine system, 572
  excretory system, 570
  general characteristics of, **562**–563
  homeostasis in, 567–572
  hoofed, 248
  marsupial (pouched), 254–**255**, 278, 564
  nervous system, 571
  nutrition in, 558
  orders of, 562
  placental, **255**, 278
  radiation in, 277–278
  reproduction in, 564–565
    see also reproduction
  reproductive efficiency of, 565
  respiratory system, **569**–570
  responsiveness and control in, 570–571
  sense organs, 570, **571**
  skin of, 563, 570, **571**
  stomachs of, 567, **568**
  teeth of, **567**
    see also animals; vertebrates
mammary glands, 277, 562, 563
mandibles
  crayfish, 492
  grasshopper, 498
mantle, mollusc, 476
mantle cavity, mollusc, 478
Marchantia, 382
marsupials, 254–255, 278, 564
mass, *3*
matter, *79*
  building blocks of, 79–83
  composition of, 44, 79
  energy and, 44–45
  path of in food chain, 23–24
  recycling of, 23–24, 32, 66
maxillae
  crayfish, 492
  grasshopper, 498
maxillipeds, crayfish, 492
measles, 312, 313
Mechanists, 265
medulla
  adrenal gland, **679**
  of human brain, 648
meiosis, 167, **168, 169**, 170, 173, 186
  mitosis and, 167, **169**

memory
cerebrum and, 647, 651
immune system and, 684
long-term, 528, 651
RNA and, 462
short-term, 528, 651
memory cells, 684, 686
Mendel, Gregor, 157 – 162, 164 – 166, 171, 173, 176, 178, 241
Mendelian traits, 157 – *158,* **158** – 162, 171 – 173, 198 – 201
dominant, **158,** *160,* 171
inheritance of, 157 – 162
recessive, **158,** *161,* 171
see also inheritance
meninges, 648
menstrual cycle, 698 – 700
meristem tissue, 148, **150,** 397
mesoderm
flatworm, 458
human embryo, 703
mesoglea, *450* – 451
mesophyll, 392, 417
mesothorax, grasshopper, 497
Mesozoic Era, 277
summary of (table), 274
messenger RNA, 138 – 141, 182, 260
metabolism, *51,* 78, 118, 119
cell, 137
enzymes and, 119 – 121
metamorphosis
in amphibians, 533
complete, **499,** *499* – 500
incomplete, **498,** *499*
metastasis, *147*
metathorax, grasshopper, 497
methane molecule, covalent bonds in, **82**
microbes, *304*
general characteristics of, 305 – 306
micronucleus, paramecium, 342
microorganisms, *see* bacteria; virus(es)
micropyle, 412
microscopes, 100 – 101, 105, 305, 310
microspores, 412
microtubules, 108
midbrain, 648
migration
of birds, 5, 557
differential, *204,* **206** – 207
Miller, Stanley, and Heterotroph Hypothesis, 268
millipedes, 10, 22, **491** – 492
minerals
as coenzymes, 120
and diet, 603
food sources and functions of (table), 603
in living things, **89** – 90
Miocene Epoch, 279, 280
mitochondria, 108, 109, **125** – 126
mitosis, *143,* 144, 145, 146
anaphase, 144, **145,** 146
interphase, 143, **145**
meiosis and, 167, **169**
metaphase, 144, **145,** 146
prophase, 144, **145**
telophase, 144, **145,** 146
mixtures, kinds of, 86 – 87
mold(s), 215
Aspergillus, 356
bread, 22, 359, **360**

Neurospora, 364
Penicillium, 27, 356, **360,** 364
slime, **355**
molecules
carrier, 114
DNA, 96, 138, 143, 144, 183
glucose, 123, 125, 127, 128
methane, covalent bonds in, **82**
protein, 107, 112, 119, 138 – 141
RNA, 96, 138
water, 81, **86,** 88, 92, 113
molluscs
behavior in, 480
body plan of, **476**
classes of, 476 – **477,** 478
destructive, 481
gastropods, **477**
homeostasis in, 478 – 480
interaction with environment, 480 – 481
reproduction in, 478
uses of, 481
see also clams
molting, 490
in birds, 551
monarch butterfly, 21 – **22**
monerans, 318 – 336
body plan of, **442**
cells of, 395
characteristics of, 319, 321
summary of (table), 440
classification of, **293, 294,** 300, 304
compared to fungi and protists, 365 – 369
(table), 366 – 367
diffusion in, 330
diseases caused by, 318, 320 – 322
diversity among, 318 – 323
flowering plants compared to, 438 – 441, **442, 443, 444**
homeostasis in, 318, 326 – 330
importance of, 318
major groups of (table), 320
reproduction in, 323 – 324, 441, **443**
and response to environment, 330
shapes of, 319, **320**
transportation in, **442**
unity among, 318
see also bacteria; blue-green algae
monocot(s), *406*
dicots compared to, **427**
flower of, **410**
seeds of, **415, 416**
stem of, **425**
monoculturing, 61 – **62,** 72
monoecious plants, *410*
monohybrid cross, 162
monosaccharides, 92
morel(s), 363 – 364
Morgan, Thomas Hunt, and gene linkage, 191
moss(es), 13, 14, 35, 387
alternation of generations in, 382
body form of, 382
club, 389 – 390
homeostasis in, 383
human uses of, 384
life cycle of, 382, **383**
reproduction in, 382
Sphagnum, 384
motor neurons, 642
motor unit, 665 – 666
mouth, human, **590**

digestion in, 595
mucus, 625, 626
multicellular organisms, 20, 136
mumps, 312, 313
and salivary glands, 590
muscle(s), *665*
arm, 666, **667,** 668
contraction of, **666**
excitation of, 665 – **666**
filaments in, **666**
flexion of, 668
kinds of, 665
characteristics of (table), 665
skeletal, 665, 666, **667,** 668
sliding filament theory and, 666
muscle tissue(s), 150, **151**
muscle tone, 668
muscular dystrophy, 216, 223
muscular systems, comparisons among vertebrates, 580
mushrooms, 354
characteristics of, 361 – 362
life cycle of, **362**
poisonous, 363
mutagens, *183* – *184,* 208 – 209
mutation(s), *183,* **183** – 184
allelic frequencies and, 204, 207
environment and, 270
ethnic groups and, 216
and evolution, 242
in gene pools, **207**
positive, *242*
spontaneous, 208 – 209
mutualism, *27,* **27** – **28**
mycelia, 354
mycoplasma(s), 320, **321**
mycorrhizae, *363,* 399, 424
myelin sheath, 643
myosin, 666

N

nacre, 481
Nannochloris, 481
natural selection, *238,* 269, 273, 276
Darwin's theory of, 237 – 238, 264
Neanderthals, 281
nearsightedness, 637
nematodes, *see* roundworms
nephrons, 630, **631**
nerve cell(s), 151
see also neuron(s)
nerve impulses, 643 – 644
nervous system
comparison among vertebrates, 580, **582,** 578 – 579 (table)
comparison of invertebrates, **513**
comparison of vertebrates to invertebrates, 584
human, **152, 642** – 646
see also specific parts
nervous tissue, 150
net productivity, *48,* 54
neuron(s), 150, 642, 643
polarized, 644
Neurospora, 364
neurotransmitter(s), 115 – 116, 644, 666
neutrons, 80
niche, *36* – 37
nitrification, *34*
nitrogen cycle, 34 – 35

nitrogen fixation, *34*
nodes, 419
 lymph, 624
nondisjunction, chromosome, *193*, 224
norepinephrine, 646, 679
notochord, 705
nuclear envelope, 109
nuclear reactors, 69
nucleic acids, function and properties of, 95–97
 see also DNA; RNA
nucleolus, 102–103, 109
nucleotides, 96, 109, 138–139
 sequence of, 143, 144, 182, 183
nucleus
 atomic, 80, **81**
 cell, 101, 102, **109**, 138
nutrient agar, 330
nutrition, *20*
 autotrophic, *20*
 bacterial, 328–330
 careers in, **608**
 cells and, 20–21
 in fungi, 359
 heterotrophic, *20*
 see also diet
nymphs, 499

O

obligate aerobes, *327*, 328
observations
 making of, 40
 reporting of, 42
octopus, 477
 learned behavior in, 480
oil glands, 656, 657
oil spill, 74
olfactory lobes, frog, 537
olfactory nerve, 648
omnivore(s), 24–25
Oparin, A. I., and Heterotroph Hypothesis, 268, 269
Ophiuroidea, 482, **483**
opossum, 5, 255, **562**
optic nerve, 636, 648
optic lobes, frog, 537
organ, *151*
organ system, *151*
organ transplants, 688
organelles
 of animal cells, 105, **106–109**
 of plant cells, **109–110**, 111
 structure-function relationships in (table), 110
organic compounds, 20
organism(s), *151*
 competition among, 27, 28
 diversity of, *2*
 division of labor among parts of, 151
 genotype and phenotype of, *164*
 interactions among, *see* interactions
 levels of organization in, 148, **149–152**
 multicellular, 20, 136
 symmetry of, **449–450**
 unicellular, 20, 137
 see also living things
osculum, 450
osmosis, *113–114*
osmotic pressure, 113
 and turgor, *417*

ossification, 662
Osteichthyes, 521
ovary(ies), *455*
 of flower, 409
 human, 681, 696, **697**
 follicle development in, **699**
ovipositors, 499
ovulation, *699*
ovules
 flower, 409–410
 plant, formation of, **412**
oxygen, importance of, 270, 271
oxygen atom, 80–81
oxytocin, 675
ozone, 3, 113, 271, 400

P

pacemaker, heart, 620
pair-bonding, 694
Paleozoic Era, 273
 summary of (table), 274
palisade mesophyll, 392, 417
pancreas, human, **592–593**
 and hormone production, 679–680
pancreatic amylase, 596
paramecium, 30, **306**
 body plan of, 341–342
 cyclosis in, **347**
 feeding in, 347
 internal systems, 347
 reproduction in, **342–343**
 response in, 348
 as scavenger, 345, 347
parasite(s), 22
 bacteria as, 329
 fungi as, 363
 see also specific parasites
parasite-host relationship, 22, 28
parasitism, 462–463, 465–466
parasympathetic nervous system, 646
parathyroid glands, 679
parenchyma tissue, 148, 150
passenger pigeon, extinction of, 72
passive immunity, 685
Pasteur, Louis
 and rabies vaccine, 307
 and spontaneous generation, 266–**267**
Pavlovian experiments, 574
pathogens, *321*, 328
pea plants
 crossing of, 160–161
 Mendel's study of, 159–162
 pollination of, **160**
 traits, **158**
pearls, formation of, **481**
peat, 384
peat bog, 384
pectin, 111
pedigree diagram, 221
penicillin, 27, 334
Penicillium, 27, 356, **360**, 364
peppered moth, evolution of, *241*, 248
pepsin, 591, 595
pepsinogen, 595
peptidases, 596
peptide, *95*
peptide bond, 94–**95**, 140
pericardial sinus, *494*
pericardium, 618
peripheral nervous system, 642

peristalsis, *472*, 591, 592
peritubular capillaries, 629, 630
pesticides, 62, 72, 528, 558
petiole, 418
pH scale, 88–89, 95, 96, 115, 119
phages, 307, **310–311**
phagocytes, 312, 333
phagocytosis, **115**, 311
pharynx
 earthworm, 472
 flatworm, 460
 human, 591, 625, 626
 reptilian, 545
phenotype, *164*
phenylketonuria (PKU), 184, 218–219, 227–229
pheromones, *508*
phloem, 148, 150, 392, 397, 426, 430
phosphorus cycle, **16–17**
photoperiodism, *411*, **411**
photosynthesis, *21*, 32–33, 47, *128*–134
 cellular respiration and, 33, 129–**130**, **132**
 chemosynthesis and, **326–327**
 compared to cellular respiration (table), 133
 dark reactions, 130, **132**–133
 effects of, **270**–271
 importance of, 133, 270–271
 light as regulator of, 128, 133
 light reactions, 130, **131**
 oxygen, **327**
 plant parts functioning in, 129
 products of, 130
 role of chlorophyll in, 433
 starting materials of, 130
 sulfur, **327**
 summary reaction for, 129
phototropism, 338, *434*
phycocyanin, 373–374
phycoerythrin, 373–374
phytoplankton, *338*, 345
pine, 395, **396**
 leaves of, 398
 life cycle of, **396**
 stem of, **398**
 see also gymnosperms
pineal gland, 647
pinocytosis, 115
pituitary gland, 554, 555, **572**
 anterior lobe, 675
 endophrins in, 650
 hormones of, *see* hormones
 and hypothalamus, 572, 672, 674–675
 posterior lobe, 675
placenta, 565
 human, 701–702, **703**
placental mammals, **255**, 278
planarians, *see* flatworms
plant cells, 32, 102–**103**
 albuminous, 392, 397
 cambium, 397
 cell plate in, 146
 guard, 392, 418
 organelles of, **109–110**, 111
 osmosis and, 114
 sieve, 392, 397
 in solution, **113**
 tracheids, 392, 397
 see also cell(s)
plant hormones, 433–435
plant productivity, energy and, 47–48

plant stems, *see* stem(s)
plant tissue(s), 148, 150, 388
plant viruses, 307–308, 310
plants
  adaptions from water to land habitats (chart), 438
  classification of, **292, 297,** 300
  and day-night cycle, 5
  endangered, 74
  flowering, *see* flowering plants
  growth regulators, 433–436
  invertebrates compared to, 514
  light, effect on, **433**
  nitrogen cycle and, 34
  polyploidy in, **193**
  protective adaptations in, 21
  temperature, effect on, 433
  turgor movements in, **436**
  vascular, *see* vascular plants
  see also leaf(ves); root(s); stem(s)
plaques, 310
plasma, 612, 614
Plasmodium (malarial parasite), **340,** 349–350
plasmodium (slime mold), 355
plastids, 109, 111
platelets, **612,** 613–615
poikilothermic, *545*
polar regions, as biome, **13**–14
polio, 312, 313
pollen, formation of, 412–413
pollen grain, development of, **412**–413
pollen tube, 413
pollination, *395*
  cross-, **160,** 413
  honeybees and, 505–507
  self-, 413
pollution, *67*
  air, 68–**69, 70,** 400–401, 437
  thermal, **69**
  water, **67**–68, **69, 74**
polychlorinated biphenols (PCBs), 69
polydactyly, 184, 221
polygenic inheritance, *180,* **180**
polyploidy, *193*
  in plants, **193**
polyps, 454, 455
polysaccharides, 92, 141
population(s), *29*
  allelic frequencies in, 200–201, 203–209, *282*
  breeding, 203–205
  carrying capacity and, **30**
  control factors and, 29–30
  genetic load and, 209, *229*
  geometric growth of, *29,* 30, *238*
  human, *see* human population
  probability and, 197–201
  pure-breeding, 159–**162,** 171–173
  trends in, 29
population density, *29*
  control factors, 30
  human, **63**
population genetics, Hardy-Weinberg Principle of, 203–209
Portuguese man-of-war, 8, 454, 455
positive mutation, *242*
posture, importance of, 668, **669**
potassium-argon dating, 258
potential energy, *45,* **45,** 46

pouched mammals, 254–**255,** 278, 564
preadaptations, *248,* 276
Precambrian deposits, 273
predator(s), *21*
  adaptations in, **21–22**
  extermination of, 71
  insects, insecticides, and, 73
predator-prey relationship, **21–22,** 28
  among protists, **345**
pregnancy, 698
  test for, 702
presbyopia, 636
prey, *21*
  adaptations in, **21–22**
primates, characteristics of, 279
probability, and populations, 197–201
  and test cross, 165
procaryotes, 300, 305, 310, 319, 323
  features of (table), 319
producer-consumer relationship, 21, 28
progesterone, 696, 700–702
proglottids, 459
prokaryotes, *see* procaryotes
prolactin, 555, 563, 572, 675
propolis, 505
proprioceptors, 634
prostaglandins, 674
prostate gland, 696
prostomium, 472
protein(s), 32, 137
  in cells, 141
  and diet, 600
  DNA and RNA compared to, 260–261
  function and properties of, 94–95
  temperature and, 3–4, 95
protein molecules, 107, 112, 119, 138–141
protein synthesis, 107, 138–141
  mechanism of, **140**
prothorax, grasshopper, 497
prothrombin, 616
protists, 337–352
  basic kinds of, 338
  body plan, **442**
  cells of, 395
  classification of, **292, 295,** 300, 304
  compared to fungi and monerans, 365–369, (table), 366–367
  disease-causing, 348–351
  diversity in, 337–342
  flowering plants compared to, 438–441, **442, 443,** 444
  homeostasis in, 345–347
  importance of, 348
  predator-prey relationship among, **345**
  reproduction in, **342–343,** 441, **443**
  response to environment, 342
  summary of characteristics (table), 440
  transportation in, **442**
  unity in, 337
  see also ameba; paramecium
protococcus, 377
protonema, 382
protons, atomic, 80
protozoans, characteristics of, 339–**340**
  see also protists
pseudocoelom, 464
pseudopodia, 340, 345
Psilopsida, 389
Pteropsida, 390
PTTH, 502

puberty, 681, 694
pulmocutaneous arteries, 536
pulmonary circulation, human, 621–622
pulmonary veins, 536
pulvinus, *436*
pupa, 499
pure-breeding populations, 159–**162,** 171–173
pyramid of energy, 50, **50**–52
pyrenoids, 378
pyruvic acid, breakdown of, **123**–125

R
rabies, 312
rabies vaccine, 307
races, human, 281–282
radial symmetry, *450,* **450**
radiant energy, 32, 45
radioactive clocks, 258
radioactive fallout, cancer and, 69
radioactive wastes, air pollution and, **69**
radioactivity, 257–258
radiolarian(s), 306, 339
radula, mollusc, 477
rams, mating behavior of, 29
rapid-eye movement (REM) sleep, 652
rat, reasoning in, **574**
Ray, John, classification system of, 286
reasoning, 574–575
  deductive, *41*
  inductive, *40,* 41
receptacle, flower, 409
recessive traits, 158, *161,* 171
reciprocal crosses (pollination), 160
recombinant DNA, *228,* 315, 328
rectum, 593
recycling, natural, of matter, 24, 32, 66
Redi, Francesco, and spontaneous generation experiment, **266**
reflex arc, *642–643*
regeneration
  in flatworms, **459**
  in starfish, 483
releaser stimulus, 556
replication
  chromosome, 182
  DNA, 143–144, 182
reproduction
  in algae, **377**–378
  in ameba, 346–347
  asexual, 324, 342, 361
  in bacteria, 324
  in birds, 551–552
  in clams, 478
  in cnidarians, 455–456
  in crayfish, 493
  in ferns, 391, 393
  in fish, 522
  in flowering plants, 432
  in frogs, 530–**532, 533**
  in fungi, 441, **443**
  in grasshoppers, 498–500
  in humans, 696, **697**–700
  in hydra, 455–456
  in jellyfish, 455
  in mammals, 564–565
  in mosses, 382
  in paramecium, **342–343**
  sexual, 170, 177, 343, 361, 693
  in snakes, 545

structure of, **656 – 657**
skin gills, *483*
sleep, 651 – 652
slime mold(s), 355
small intestine, 533
 absorption in, 598
 digestion in, **596 – 598**
 enzymes in, 596
smallpox, 72, 307, 312
smell, sense of, 639 – 640
smog, 69 – 70, 113, 400
smoking, effects on body, 570, 626, 627
smooth muscle, characteristics of (table), 665
snails, 9, 477, 478
 learned behavior in, 480
snakes, 10 – 12, **23 – 25,** 542
 behavior and environment, 544
 brain of, **548**
 characteristics of, 544
 poisonous, 544, **546**
 reproduction in, 545
 venom, 548
 see also reptiles
sodium chloride, structure of, 83
soft palate, 590
soil(s)
 bacteria in, 34 – 35
 cultivation of, **64 – 65**
 erosion of, 35, 64, 65, 437
 lichens as formers of, **34,** 35
 productivity, of factors in, 64
soil environments, 9 – 10
Solanum rostratum Dunal, 287, **291**
solutions
 concentration of, **87**
 hypotonic, *113*
 isotonic, *113*
 properties of, 86
somatic cells, *167*
somites, 705
sorus, *391*
speciation, *250,* 251, 282
species, 27, *247*
 in classification, 287
 competition within a, 30 – 31
 concept of, 247 – 248, 286
 fixity of, 233
 foreign, introduction into United States, 71 – **72**
 population trends within a, 29 – 30
specific immunity, 683
spectrum, 128
Spemann, Hans, and embryonic induction, 705
sperm, 170, 455
 in sexual reproduction, 696, 698, 701
sperm nuclei, 413
sperm receptacles, 471
Sphagnum moss, 384
Sphenodons, 542
Sphenopsida, 389
spherical symmetry, 449, *450*
sphincter, 591
sphygmomanometer, 623
spicules, sponge, *451*
spinal cord, human, 642
spinal nerves, human, 642
spindle fibers, 144

spiracles, grasshopper, 501 – 502
spirochetes, 320, **322**
Spirogyra, 377, 378
 reproduction in, **377**
sponge(s)
 body plan of, 450 – 451
 diversity in, 451
 homeostasis in, 452
 interaction with environment, 452
 internal systems, **451,** 452
 parts of, **451**
 reproduction in, 451
spongy mesophyll, 392, 417
spontaneous generation, 265 – 267
spontaneous mutation, 208 – 209
sporangia, 355, 382, 391
spore(s), *354*
 diploid, **377**
 haploid, **377,** 382, 391
 reproduction by, 373, 377 – 378, 380, 391
sporophyte generation, 360
sporophytes, 378, 382, 391
stabilizing selection, *248 – 249*
stamens, 409
Stanley, Wendell, and viruses, 308
starch(es), 92
 and saliva, 500, **595**
starfish, 2, 8, 482
 appetite of, 485
 behavior and environment, 484 – 485
 internal systems, 483 – **484**
 reproduction in, 483
 see also echinoderms
statocysts, 495
stem(s) annual, 406
 dicot, **425, 426**
 diversity in, **431**
 of flowering plants, 406 – **407**
 gas exchange in, 430 – 431
 herbaceous, 406
 monocot, **425**
 parts of, **428**
 perennial, 406
 pine, **398**
 primary growth of, 425 – 426
 secondary growth of, 426
 types of, **431**
 vascular tissue in, **425**
 water transport in, 428
 woody, 407, **426,** 430
sticklebacks, mating behavior in, 526 – **527,** 528
stigma, flower, 409 – 410, 413
stimuli, *633*
stipules, 418
stolon, *431*
stomach
 of frog, 533, 535
 human, 591
  digestion in, 595 – **596**
 of mammals, 567, **568**
 of ruminants, **568**
stomata, 392, 398, 417, **418**
 function and work of, 418
strabismus (cross-eye), 635
Streptococcus infections, 332, 364
stress, *689*
 current ideas about, 689 – 690
 stages of, **689**

strip cropping, *65,* **65**
structure-function relationships, 19
 in organelles, 105 – 111
 predator-prey, **21 – 22**
 see also under specific organisms
suberin, 148, 420
sucrose, 92, 596
supermale syndrome, 224
support tissues, plant, 148, **150**
suspensions, properties of, 86 – 87
Sutton, Walter, and cell division, 166
sweat glands, 656, 657
swim bladder, 523, 525
swimmerets, 492 – 493
symbiants, fungi as, 363
symmetry, *449*
 types of, **449 – 450**
sympathetic nervous system, 646
synapse(s) *644,* **644**
syndrome, *223*
syphilis, 322, **332 – 333,** 364
syrinx, 554
systemic circulation, 622
systolic pressure, *623*

T

tadpole, 533
 see also frog(s)
taiga biome, 12 – 13, 35
tap root system, 424
tapeworm(s), 459
 internal systems of, 461
Tasmanian wolf, 254 – 255
taste, sense of, 639, 640
taste buds, 590, 639
taxes, *461*
taxonomy, *286*
 see also classification
Tay-Sachs disease, 226 – 227
teeth
 of frog, **535**
 human, 590, **591**
 mammalian, **567**
 of reptiles, 546
telson, 493
temperature
 effect of on plants, 433
 as environmental factor, 3 – 4
 and flowering, 410 – 411
 and proteins, 3 – 4, 95
tendons, 668
tendrils, *419*
termites, 27 – 28
terraces, *64,* **65**
terrapins, 543
territoriality, birds and, 557 – 558
territory, *31*
test cross, 165
testes, *455*
 of frog, 532
 human. 681. 696
tests: Chapter 1, 18; Chapter 2, 38; Chapter 3, 55; Chapter 4, 76; Chapter 5, 98; Chapter 6, 117; Chapter 7, 135; Chapter 8, 154; Chapter 9, 175; Chapter 10, 195; Chapter 11, 213; Chapter 12, 230; Chapter 13, 245; Chapter 14, 263; Chapter 15, 284; Chapter 16, 302; Chapter 17, 317; Chapter 18, 336; Chapter 19, 352;

vital force, 265, 266
Vitalists, 265, 266
vitamins, 120, 602
    important characteristics of (table),
        601
vitreous humor, 636
vocal cords, **626**
volume, *44*
vomerine teeth, 535
vultures, 22

Ш

wakefulness, 652
Wallace, Alfred Russell, 237 – 238
Wallace-Darwin theory of evolution,
    238 – 239, **240**
warts, 314
water
    density of, **85**
    and diet, 600, 602
    diffusion of, **113** – 114
    importance of, 15, 85 – 86
    increasing demand for, 66
    as a percent of body weight (table), 85

pollution of, **67** – 68, **69, 74**
properties of, 85 – 86
as solvent, 86
transport of in roots, 423
water cycle, 15 – *16,* 65
water molecules, 81, **86,** 88, 92, 113
water table, *65* – 66
whales, 233, 278
    Aristotelian classification
        and, 288 – 289
    blue, 8
White Cliffs of Dover, 339
white-footed mouse, 249, **250**
Wilson's disease, 227
wind erosion, 65
    shelterbelts and, *437,* **437**
wood, 397
    compression, **399**
    heartwood, 398
    human uses of, 399 – 400
    as lumber, 400
    sapwood, 398
woody stems, 407, **426,** 430
    see *also* stems; trees

world population, growth of, **59**
worms, 9, 10, 22
    parasitic, 462 – 463, 465 – 466
    see *also specific types*

X

X chromosomes, 186 – 188, 223
xylem, 148, 150, 392, 397, 426,
    430
xylem rays, 397

Y

Y chromosomes, 186, 188
yeast cells, 29 – 30
yeast colony, 361
yeasts, 356
    budding in, 361
    fermentation by, 359
yolk sac, 551, 565, **702,** 703

Z

zooplankton, *338,* 345
zygospores, 377
zygotes, 377, 382, 411 – 412

CREDITS

Illustrators: Howard Berelson, Eva Celli, Lorraine Epstein, Angela Fernan, Robert Frank, Bob Jackson, Susanna Kelly, George Kelvin, Tina Mercie, John Murphy, Dick Oden, Lynn Udhi.

Photo Credits: © Clara Aich, pp. 43, 78, 84(br), 87, 112, 198, 203, 217, 375, 594, 608(tl), 623, 669; © American Cancer Society, p. 147; American Red Cross Blood Services Laboratory: © Dr. Manley McGill, p. 612; Courtesy American Museum of Natural History, pp. 72, 157, 253(tl), 281, 399; American Shorthorn Association, p. 179; American Society for Microbiology: © Willy Burgdorfer, p. 321; © Dr. Thomas Anderson, Institute for Cancer Research, Philadelphia, p. 324; ANIMALS, ANIMALS: Oxford Scientific Films, p. 527(c, bl, br), © Breck P. Kent, p. 566(bl), © G.B. Ruf, p. 695; © PETER ARNOLD, INC: © Richard Choy, p. 199; © W.H. Hodge, p. 246; © Philip A. Harrington, p. 211, © Manfred Kage, pp. 103, 118, 129, 136, 322(cb, br), 337, 339(br), 344(bl, cr), S.J. Krasemann, pp. 254, 549(bl), © John R. MacGregor, p. 250, © Hans Pfletschinger, p. 19, © David Scharf, p. 319, © Erika Stone, p. 282(tl); A.S.M. SLIDE COLLECTION: © M. Gabridge, p. 321; © Australian Information Service, p. 60(b); © Daniel Benevento, pp. 181, 664; Courtesy of Bausch & Lomb, p. 128; BLACK STAR: © Millard H. Sharp, p. 22(tl); Brown Brothers, p. 100(bl); © H.G. Bungenberg de Jong, p. 269; Center for Disease Control, Atlanta, Georgia, p. 307, © Carey Callaway, Pathology Division, pp. 307, 323 (c), p. 324, 332; © Candace Cochrane, p. 180(bl); BRUCE COLEMAN, INC: © Wolfgang Bayer, p. 155, © Alan Blank, p. 25(tl), © Jane Burton, p. 532, © Phil Degginger, p. 483 (cr), © Jack Dermid, p. 564(tr), © Nicholas Devore III, p. 437, © Robert L. Dunne, p. 490(cl), © Gary R. Jones, p. 21(br), © Jay Lurie, p. 39, © W.E. Ruth, p. 21(bc), © John Shaw, p. 22(cl), © Joseph Van Wormer, p. 5(tl), © Jonathan T. Wright, p. 216(cl, bl); © Daedalus Enterprises, p. 69; © Debbie Dean, p. 353; © Wm. J. Dederick, pp. 150, 496; © Dr. E. R. Degginger, FPSA, pp. 4(br), 5(tr), 10(tl), 64(cr), 253(cl), 256(bl), 306(cr), 354(cb,br), 357(cl), 390(bl,br), 436, 452, 490(cr,br), 499, 531(cl,br),695 (bl); © Phil Degginger, pp. 340(tc), 455; © David M. Dennis: p. 354(bl); © John Hanson, pp. 305, 307; © Mush Emmons, p. 713(cb); Florida Department of Commerce, Division of Tourism, p. 405; © General Biological Supply House, p. 320; © Gernsheim Collection, Humanities Research Center, University of Texas at Austin, p. 237; Courtesy Dr. I.R. Gibbons and Dr. A.V. Grimstone, reproduced by permission of the Editors of the British Medical Journal, p. 342; © C.V. Gooding, p. 308; © The Greater New York Blood Program, pp. 201, 227, 688; © J. Arthur Herrick, Kent State University, p. 428; © Dr. William M. Harlow, p. 394; Courtesy of the Johns Hopkins Institute of the History of Medicine, p. 166; THE IMAGE BANK: © Joe Baker, p. 692, © Nancy Brown, p. 180(br), © Nick Foster, p. 587, © Peter Frank, p. 202, © George Hausman, p. 282(cr), © Margaret W. Peterson, pp. 282(c), 693; © Larry B. Jennings, p. 232; Kansas Biological Survey: © Ralph Brooks, p. 291; © Jane Latta, pp. 26(tl), 156, 252(tr, cl), 282(tr), 391(tr); © L.J. LeBeau, pp. 244, 318, 320, 330; March of Dimes Birth Defects Foundation, pp. 186, 219, 224, 226; Reproduced with permission from the Birth Atlas published and copyright by Maternity Center Association, p. 708; MAGNUM PHOTOS, INC © Paul Fusco, p. 631, © Mark Godfrey, p. 69; © 1970 Medcom, Inc., pp. 309(tr), 678; © David Muench, pp. 371, 404; NASA, pp. 3, 4(bl); National Dairy Council, p. 604; New Jersey Dept. of Agriculture: © J.D. Kegg, p. 72; New York Public Library, p. 101(tr); © Stuart Pankratz, p. 305; © Pepperidge Farm Inc., p. 124; © Willis Peterson, p. 251; © Pfizer, Inc., pp. 334, 713, 309(bl); PHOTO RESEARCHERS, INC: © Michael Abbey, pp. 322(tl), 244(tl), 349(tr), © Edmund Appel, p. 255, © A-Z Collection,p.384, © Dan Bernstein, p. 712(c), © Biology Media, pp. 110, 304, 322(c), © Cosmos Blank, p. 527(tl), © Bjorn Bolstad, p. 252(tl), © John Bova, p. 235(tl), © Carolina Biological, pp. 99, 101(cr), 705(tr), © Richard L. Carolton, p. 390(tl), © Joseph T. Collins, p. 549(t), © Steve Coombs, p. 325(b), © Gerry Cranham, p. 659(c), © Peter Damroth, p. 84(cr), © Treat Davidson/NAS, p. 285, © Kelly Dean, pp. 372, 387, 561, © Mary Ann D'Esopo, p. 356(cl), © Earl Dibble, p. 253(tr), © Robert Dunne, p. 364, © Brian Enting, p. 60(t), © Stephen I. Feldman, p. 712(tc), © Jack Fields, p. 2(l), © Kenneth W. Fink, p. 238 (c), © H.F. Flanders, p. 408 (tr), © Michael Gadomski, pp. 247(r), 410(cl), © J.F. Gemmaro and L.R. Grillone, pp. 100(cr), 142, © Lowell Georgia, pp. 243(b), 309(br), 528, 608(bl), 712(br), © Guy Gillette, p. 641, © Francois Gohier, p. 12(bl), © Robert Goldstein, p. 680, © P.W. Grace, p. 389(cr), © Margot Granitsas, p. 713(c), © Gilbert Grant, p. 6(tl), © Eric Grave, pp. 102(bl), 306(tr), 332(tl), 338, 340, 344(tr, c, br), 345, 464, © Farrell Grehan, p. 408(bl), © Dan Guravich, p. 137, © L. Harlow, p. 400(bl), © Fritz Henle, p. 11(tl), © Robert W. Hernandez, p. 180, © George Holton, p. 205, © Larry B. Jennings, p. 232; © Susan Johns, p. 84(tl), © George E. Jones III, p. 193(r), 243(t), © Jerry Jones, p. 451, © Russ Kinne, pp.6(tr), 26(c), 66, 100(br), 235(tr), 354(cl), 363, 374, 395, 477(tl), 545(cr), 662(cl), 663, 695(tl), 712(cr), © Paolo Koch, p. 339, © S.J. Krasemann/NAS, pp. 20, 408(br), 488, © Dwight Kuhn, p. 527(tr), © Maurice and Sally Landre, p. 238(t), © Leonard Lee Rue III, pp. 21, 26(tr), 566, © George Lower/NAS, p. 9(tr), © Alexander Lowry, p. 243(c), © Laurence Lowry/Rapho Division, p. 303, © Karl and Steve Maslowski, p. 13(br), © Tom McHugh, pp. 6(c), 9(cr, Steinhart Aquarium), 12(cl), 197, 235(bl), 281(tr), 531(bl, Steinhart Aquarium), 272(tr), © Anthony Mercieca, p. 235(tc, br), © Wendell Metzen, pp. 12(tl), 193(l), 322(tr), © Frank J. Miller, p. 356(bl), © Peter Miller, p. 32, © John Moss, p. 1, © Larry Mulvehill, pp. 100(cb), 633, © Joe Munroe, p. 65, © Tom Myers, p. 74, © Hans Namuth, p. 566(tr), © Richard Parker/NAS, p. 408(tl, tc, c), © Roger Tory Peterson, p. 196, © O.S. Pettingill, pp. 247(l), 558, © George Porter, p. 531(cr), © Porterfield-Chickering, pp. 58(r), 216, 541, © Noble Proctor, pp. 27, 360, © Carleton Ray, p. 13(bl), 325(t), © Miriam Reinhart, p. 222, © Earl Roberge, p. 713(tl, tc), © Bruce Roberts/Rapho Division, pp. 58(l), 62, 223, 659(c), © Joe Rychetnik, p. 242, © Kjell B. Sandved, p. 391(cr), 470, © Nancy Sefton, p. 448, © Marshall Sklar, p. 125, © Nancy Simmerman, p. 257, © James Simon, p. 421, © Jeff Smith, p. 517, © Hugh Spencer/NAS, pp. 6(bl), 77, 361, 392, 477, © John Henry Sullivan Jr., p. 588, © M. F. W. Tweedie/NAS, p. 241, © Twomey, p. 13(tr), © Warren Uzzle, p. 713(cl), © Walker, pp. 306(c), 379, © Bernard Pierre Wolff, p. 11(br); © Jeff Rotman, pp. 483(tr, br), 518; © Paul

Schich, p. 322(cr); © Kit Scates, p. 362; © Scientific American, p. 573; © Lee D. Simon, Rutgers University, p. 310; SHOSTAL ASSOCIATES, INC: © Herbert Eisenberg, pp. 214, 215, © David Forbert, p. 608, © Anthony Mercieca, p. 255, © Shostal, p. 231; © Dr. V. Slankis, p. 400; TOM STACK & ASSOCIATES: © Ed Robinson, p. 288, © Gary Stallings, p. 713(tr, br); STOCK, BOSTON, INC: © Erik Anderson, p. 712(cb), © Frederik D. Bodin, pp. 56, 84(bl), © Daniel Brody, p. 67, © Michael Collier, pp. 264, 272(b), © Donald Dietz, p. 712(tr), © Robert L. Dunne, p. 490(cl), © W.B. Finch, p. 9(tl), © Jean-Claude Lejeune, pp. 100(tc), 180(tl), © Oliver Rebbot, p. 468, © John Running, pp. 447, 713 (bl), © Eric Simmons, pp. 22(bl), 382, 490(bl), © Frank Siteman, p. 628; SYGMA: © Ira Wyman, pp. 176(c), 182(c); TIME INC: © Robert W. Kelley/Life Magazine © 1952, p. 574, © Herb Gehr/Life Magazine © 1947, p. 207; TIME-LIFE PICTURE AGENCY: © Thomas McAvoy, p. 556; © M. Tzovaras/United Nations, p. 72; USDA Photos, pp. 28, 34, 51, 61, 256, 410, 491, 492; U.S. Forest Service, USDA, pp. 396, 397, 430; © Wide World Photos, p. 280; © A.M. Winchester, p. 191; WOODFIN CAMP & ASSOCIATES: © Jonathan Blair, p. 611, © Thomas Hopker, p. 655, © Wally McNamee, p. 672, © John Zoiner, p. 62(tl).

Further Acknowledgements

Figure 2-12   from BIOLOGY by Karen Arms and Pamela S. Camp. Copyright © 1979 by Holt, Rinehart and Winston. Reprinted by permission of Holt, Rinehart and Winston.

Table 3-1   from "Food Production and the Energy Crisis," Pimentel, D. et. al., *Science* Vol. 182, pp. 443-449, Illustration, 2 November 1973.

Figure 4-3   is based on "Our Population Predicament: A New Look," *Population Bulletin*, Volume 34, No. 5 (Population Reference Bureau, 1979.)

Figures 10-10, 10-15, and 11-12 are from "An Introduction to Genetics and Evolution" by James L. Mariner, copyrighted and published by The Independent School Press, Inc.

Figure 12-4   Scheme of Inheritance of Rh Disease from HUMAN HEREDITY AND BIRTH DEFECTS by E. Peter Volpe, Copyright © 1971, by the Bobbs-Merrill Co., Inc. Reprinted with the permission of the publisher.

Figure 12-9   is frame #46 from Chromosome Disorders and Parental Age contained in FROM GENERATION TO GENERATION. Permission for reproduction has been granted by The National Foundation-March of Dimes as the copyright holder of the original publication.

Table 27-1   from *Endangered Species Technical Bulletin*

Pronunciation Key on page 714 is reprinted by permission of the publisher from MACMILLAN DICTIONARY, William D. Halsey, Editorial Director. Copyright © 1977, 1973 Macmillan Publishing Co., Inc.

TEACHER'S ANNOTATED EDITION

MACMILLAN
Biology

CREAGER • JANTZEN • MARINER

Table of Contents

INTRODUCTION TO MACMILLAN BIOLOGY

Macmillan Biology is a comprehensive high school biology program designed to provide students with the biological knowledge important for everyday life and to provide a solid foundation for further scientific study. *Macmillan Biology* has been developed with the needs of students and teachers in biology classrooms in mind. Biology is important to students because they are aware of their own physical changes and because they are interested in learning material that will be useful in their daily lives. Teachers must not only accommodate the needs of their students, but also the demands of a rapidly expanding curriculum. At the same time as the body of knowledge in all areas is growing, pressure for achievement is increasing.

To fulfill these needs *Macmillan Biology* has been developed using six basic biological concepts to provide structure to new information. The relationship of new facts to the basic structure will help students remember many new ideas which might quickly be forgotten if no relationship to existing knowledge were provided. The six basic concepts are: *unity and diversity, interaction of living things and the environment, complementarity of structure and function, continuity of life, homeostasis,* and *change through time.* Basic concepts relevant to each chapter are mentioned at the beginning of the chapter and related to new material at the end of the chapter.

To help students relate biology to their everyday lives and to help them realize its usefulness, thought-provoking questions are posed at the beginning of each chapter and answered within it. Throughout the program matters of current biological interest are discussed, such as recombinant DNA, effects of pesticides, and the use of interferon.

To help teachers meet a variety of student needs, *Macmillan Biology* is designed to be flexible and easy to use. The planning charts and suggested teaching strategies in this guide will help the teacher plan various approaches for students of different abilities.

Macmillan Biology Program Components

Student Text

Macmillan Biology is organized in nine units and thirty-five chapters. Each chapter consists of the following:

• A Chapter Introduction, followed by two or more sections each with its own objectives and questions at the end of each section which test the objectives.
• A Chapter Investigation consisting of one or more illustrations and three questions of increasing difficulty requiring observation, interpretation, or experimentation or research.
• A Chapter Review which includes a summary and sections entitled Using the Concepts, Career Activities, or Unanswered Questions.
• A Vocabulary Review which lists important new words by section.
• A Chapter Test with 25 test items designed for easy scoring.

Teacher's Annotated Edition

The Teacher's Annotated Edition for *Macmillan Biology* consists of this guide section and the annotated student edition, which contains answers to the section questions and Chapter Tests in annotated form and some pertinent comments and suggestions.

The guide section includes:
• An overview of the program.
• A description of program components.
• Approaches to teaching the program.
• Provisions for meeting classroom needs including detailed planning charts.
• Chapter materials which provide an introduction to each chapter, answers to both the Chapter Investigations and the Chapter Reviews, suggested Readings and References for teacher and student, classroom demonstrations, and suggestions for individual student investigations.
• A guide to audiovisual materials organized by chapter with separate lists of suppliers and publishers indicated.

Macmillan Biology Laboratory Manual with Study Skills Handbook

The Laboratory Manual includes study skills and laboratory investigations. Study skills, found in the front of the laboratory manual, are organized into three categories—Reading Science (RS), Collecting Data (CD), and Scientific Methods (SM). Many teachers may wish to use the study skills throughout the program, but as a guide each skills is keyed in the planning charts to chapters where it is considered to be particularly useful. The laboratory investigations are correlated to the text chapters and further correlated to chapter sections in the planning charts. They provide students with the opportunity to study firsthand the characteristics of organisms, to investigate the life processes, and to learn procedures of science and laboratory.

Teacher's Annotated Edition for the Laboratory Manual

The Teacher's Annotated Edition provides answers in position on the student pages and a guide section. The guide includes information on preparing solutions, a master list of materials needed for the laboratory investigations, a supplier's list, and further suggestions for using the study skills.

Tests for Macmillan Biology

Easy-to-score tests for each chapter are provided on spirit masters. Each test contains 25 recall questions and optional essay questions and laboratory related questions. This component, in conjunction with the chapter tests in the student text, provides a comprehensive evaluation program.

Teaching Macmillan Biology

The self contained sections in each chapter are designed for easy lesson planning. This feature, together with the strategies and planning charts described below, will help save time in planning lessons and in developing programs suitable for students of different abilities.

Basic Approach

The nine units and thirty-five chapters of *Macmillan Biology* are organized as follows. In Unit 1, the students study their own environment, the use of the microscope, and skills basic to science. In Unit 2 the foundation for biology is established with the introduction of the cell and biochemistry. The principles of genetics and theories of change are developed in Units 3 and 4. In these first four units the fundamental concepts of biology are developed and set the stage for the subsequent units which treat living organisms.

In Units 5 through 8 living organisms are presented from the simple to complex. To give a complete picture of the organism it is studied from the viewpoints of diversity and continuity, homeostasis, and behavior and environment. The final section of each of these units provides an opportunity for students to review the organisms studied, to determine the similarities and differences among them, and to reinforce their learning from a different viewpoint. These comparison sections may also be used to provide a survey of organisms, especially if time is limited.

Unit 9 presents a comprehensive treatment of the systems of the human body.

Alternative Approaches to Teaching Units 5 through 8

Student needs, abilities, and interests, as well as pressures of time may dictate approaches to the teaching of the plant and animal phyla different from the one described above. Table T-1 on page 4T lists pages which emphasize the various approaches described here.

Emphasis on Survey of Living Things—If a broad view of organisms is desired, a basic overview can be provided easily by the study of Chapter 16, *The Classification of Living Things,* and the Diversity and Continuity sections of Chapters 17 through 29. The pages to be assigned and emphasized are listed in Table T-1 under "Survey of Living Things."

Emphasis on Systems of Living Things—Some classes will find a program emphasizing the internal structures and systems of living things useful. A systems approach can be readily set up by emphasizing the Homeostasis sections within Chapters 17 through 29. These pages are listed in Table T-1 under "Systems of Living Things."

TABLE T-1

	Emphasis on Survey of Living Things	Emphasis on Systems of Living Things	Emphasis on Behavior and Environment
Chapter 17 Viruses	304-308	309-311	312-316
Chapter 18 Bacteria and Blue-Green Algae	318-324	325-330	331-335
Chapter 19 The Protists	337-343	344-347	348-351
Chapter 20 The Fungi	353-357	358-362	363-365
Chapter 21 The Simplest Plants	372 375-378 380 382	372-374 378-379 381 383	374 379 381 384-385
Chapter 22 Ferns and Gymnosperms	387-392 394-396	392-393 397-398	393 398-401
Chapter 23 Flowering Plants	404-416 418-423 424-427 431-432	417-418 423 428-431	433-437
Chapter 24 Sponges, Cnidarians, and Unsegmented Worms	448-451 453-456 458-459 464	452 456 459-461 464-465	452 456-457 461-463 465-466
Chapter 25 Annelids, Molluscs, and Echinoderms	468-471 475-478 482-483	472-474 478-480 483-484	474 480-481 484-486
Chapter 26 The Arthropods	488-493 496-500	493-495 500-503	503-508
Chapter 27 Fishes and Amphibians	518-522 529-533	522-526 533-537	526-528 537-539
Chapter 28 Reptiles and Birds	541-545 549-551	545-548 552-555	548 555-559
Chapter 29 The Mammals	561-565	566-572	573-576

Emphasis on Behavior and Environment—a high interest program can be built around the Behavior and Environment sections in Chapters 17 through 29. These pages are listed in Table T-1 under "Behavior and Environment."

Minimum Approach to Living Things—If minimum class time is to be devoted to the study of the phyla, students will gain an appreciation for the complexity of the five kingdoms by studying Chapter 16 and the Comparison sections of Chapters 20, 23, 26, and 29. See Table T-2 for page numbers. Use of selected laboratory investigations 23-7, "Comparing Simple Plants," 26-4, "Comparing Invertebrate Phyla," and 29-2, "How Different Animals Cope with the Problems of Survival" will provide a suitable laboratory program for this approach.

TABLE T-2

	Pages
Chapter 16	285-302
Chapter 20	365-369
Chapter 23	438-445
Chapter 26	509-515
Chapter 29	577-585

Provisions to Meet Classroom Needs

Readability

Many high school students will benefit from a "walk through" of their textbook when they first receive it. Reading the Prologue will be especially helpful in establishing the six basic concepts used to organize *Macmillan Biology* and in discussing special features of the text. Students should become acquainted with the table of contents and glossary. A discussion of how to use the index would also be helpful.

There are several aids to the poor reader in the text. Preteaching the italicized words in the objectives before assigning the section can ease students' reading tasks. Emphasizing how to use the phonetic spellings would also be beneficial. The planning charts indicate questions involving recall, many of which involve definitions of terms and should be stressed with students having difficulty. The type A question in the Chapter Investigations which require observational skills will provide a sense of success for these students. Finally students with reading problems benefit especially from the Reading Science Skills in the *Laboratory Manual*.

Motivation

Students are more interested in a topic if they can see a reason for studying it. *Macmillan Biology* provides a variety of opportunities for motivating students including introductory questions in each chapter, practical problems in Chapter Investigations, and frequent assignment of questions in the Chapter Review. The illustrative material will also be useful to motivate students and to show relevancy. Students will also find that the explicit instructions about collecting and recording data in the Collecting Data Skills will be both useful and interesting.

Independent Study

With students for whom independent study is practical, assignment of the survey course or systems course coupled with the Comparison sections in Chapters 20, 23, 26, and 29 would be appropriate.

Make use of the planning charts which indicate sections in the text considered particularly suitable for above average students. The type C question in the Chapter Investigation should provide a challenge to the student in setting up an hypothesis and testing it, or by the requirement of library research. The Study Skills section in the *Laboratory Manual*, especially "Drawing Inferences from Data" and the Scientific Methods Skills, will be very helpful to students throughout the program.

Structured Overviews

One method of working with the program is the development of stuctured overviews which use the basic concepts relevant to the chapter as a starting point and list new important chapter concepts from the general to the specific. After the concepts are listed, relationships are indicated by drawing lines between them. How detailed an overview is depends on the objective in making it and the background and needs of the user. Also, each individual has a different way of organizing information, so overviews will vary. The overviews may be created by the teacher and presented as a preview or review of the chapter. Or, the teacher may prefer to have students develop their own overviews. Two sample structured overviews are given on page 6T, a specific one for Chapter 2, and a general one for Chapters 17 through 29.

Planning Charts

The following pages contain the Planning Charts for *Macmillan Biology*. There is one chart for each chapter. Sections within each chapter are labeled with suggested ability levels. The charts correlate section objectives with section questions. These questions are separated into recall questions which can be answered directly from material in text, and thought question. Chapter Review questions, Chapter Test questions, and laboratory investigations are correlated to appropriate sections. Appropriate study skills are also suggested.

Structured Overview Chapter 2

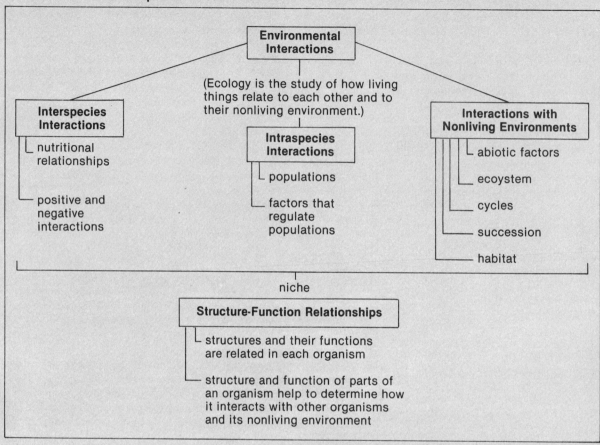

Environmental Interactions

(Ecology is the study of how living things relate to each other and to their nonliving environment.)

Interspecies Interactions
- nutritional relationships
- positive and negative interactions

Intraspecies Interactions
- populations
- factors that regulate populations

Interactions with Nonliving Environments
- abiotic factors
- ecoystem
- cycles
- succession
- habitat

niche

Structure-Function Relationships
- structures and their functions are related in each organism
- structure and function of parts of an organism help to determine how it interacts with other organisms and its nonliving environment

Structured Overview Chapters 17-29

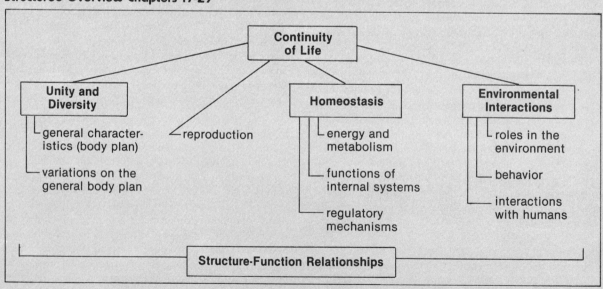

Continuity of Life

Unity and Diversity
- general characteristics (body plan)
- variations on the general body plan

reproduction

Homeostasis
- energy and metabolism
- functions of internal systems
- regulatory mechanisms

Environmental Interactions
- roles in the environment
- behavior
- interactions with humans

Structure-Function Relationships

PLANNING CHARTS

CHAPTER 1
THE ENVIRONMENT

Section 1: Conditions That Make Life Possible (For Basic, Average, Above Average Students)	PAGES	RECALL QUESTIONS	THOUGHT QUESTIONS
Objective A: Describe each of the three advantages that Earth provides for living things.	3-4	1	
Objective B: Demonstrate how the Earth's day-night cycle affects plants and animals.	4-5	2	3

Chapter Review Questions: 1   **Chapter Test Questions:** 1,2,3,4,5,10,18,21,22

Laboratory: 1-1 Introduction to the compound microscope
1-2 Advanced uses of the compound microscope

Section 2: Divisions in the Biosphere (For Basic, Average, Above Average Students)	PAGES	RECALL QUESTIONS	THOUGHT QUESTIONS
Objective C: Define the terms *biosphere, biome, humus, deciduous trees, desert.*	7-12	1	2
Objective D: Distinguish between marine, fresh-water, and estuary environments.	8-9	3,5	4
Objective E: Describe how the climate affects the kinds of plants and animals that exist in various biomes.	10-14	6,7,9	8

Chapter Review Questions: 2   **Chapter Test Questions:** 6,9,11,12,13,15,16,17,19,20,24,25

Laboratory: 1-3 The effect of environmental factors on seed germination.

Section 3: Cycles in Nature (For Basic, Average, Above Average Students)	PAGES	RECALL QUESTIONS	THOUGHT QUESTIONS
Objective F: Organize the various pathways of water into a word diagram illustrating a cycle.	15-16	1	2,3
Objective G: Organize the various pathways of phosphorus into a word diagram illustrating the phosphorus cycle.	16-17	4	5
Objective H: Describe how unity within diversity, interactions in the environment, and the natural cycles are illustrated in this chapter.	1-17	6,7	

Laboratory: 1-4 Succession in pond water

Chapter Test Questions: 7,8,14,28

Suggested Study Skills: RS-1 Making Observations
RS-2 Reading Photographs and Art Work

CHAPTER 2

INTERRELATIONSHIPS IN THE ENVIRONMENT

Section 1: Nutritional Relationships Among Organisms (For Basic, Average, Above Average Students)	PAGES	RECALL QUESTIONS	THOUGHT QUESTIONS
Objective A: Define *nutrition* and the terms that describe nutritional relationships.	20-22	1,2,3	4
Objective B: Give five examples of special adaptations in each predator organism and prey organism.	21-22		5,6,7,8
Objective C: Draw and describe a *food chain* and a *food web.*	23-25	9,10	
Chapter Review Questions: 3,4	**Chapter Test Questions:** 1,2,3,4,5,7,13,15,16,17,18,19,21		

Section 2: Other Interspecies Relationships (For Basic, Average, Above Average Students)	PAGES	RECALL QUESTIONS	THOUGHT QUESTIONS
Objective D: Define and give three examples of *species*, and *biotic community.*	27-28	1	
Objective E: Describe and give examples of two kinds of negative interactions among organisms. Explain the difference between them.	27	2	3,4
Objective F: Describe and give examples of two kinds of positive interactions among organisms. Explain the difference between them.	27-28	5	6
Chapter Review Questions: 3,4	**Chapter Test Questions:** 8,11,20		

Laboratory: 2-1 Population Growth

2-2 Plant Competition   2-3 Growth Inhibitors

Section 3: Relationship Within a Species (For Basic, Average, Above Average Students)	PAGES	RECALL QUESTIONS	THOUGHT QUESTIONS
Objective G: Define each of the following: *population, population density, carrying capacity, home range, territory, geometric population growth.*	29,31	1	2,3
Objective H: Describe ideal conditions for a small new population, and factors that affect growth of a population.	29-30		4
Objective I: List four density-dependent factors and four density-independent factors that determine population growth.	30	5,6	
Objective J: Explain how crowding is prevented among animals of a species and among plants of a species.	30-31	7,8	9
Chapter Review Questions: 2,3,4	**Chapter Test Questions:** 6,14,22,23,24		

Section 4: Biological-Physical Interrelationships *(For Basic, Average, Above Average Students)*	PAGES	RECALL QUESTIONS	THOUGHT QUESTIONS
Objective K: Define *ecosystem, ecologic succession,* and give two examples of each.	32-36	1,2,3	
Objective L: Explain each step in the *carbon cycle* and the *nitrogen cycle.*	32-35	5	4
Objective M: Define and compare the terms *habitat* and *niche.*	36-37	6,7	
Objective N: Summarize relationships among individuals, populations, communities, and ecosystems.	20-37		8,9

Chapter Review Questions: 1,3,4   **Chapter Test Questions:** 9,10,12,25

Suggested Study Skills: RS-3 Learning to Compare and Contrast   CD-1 Determining Frequencies
CD-2 Making a Data Table   CD-3 Making Graphs

CHAPTER 3
ENERGY IN THE ENVIRONMENT

Section 1: Scientific Investigation *(For Basic, Average, Above Average Students)*	PAGES	RECALL QUESTIONS	THOUGHT QUESTIONS
Objective A: Define and give examples of *inductive reasoning, hypothesis, deductive reasoning, control treatment, experimental treatment.*	40-42	1	
Objective B: Design an experiment to test an hypothesis.	40-42		2,3,4

Chapter Test Questions: 11,12,13,14,15,21

Section 2: Energy and Life *(For Basic, Average, Above Average Students)*	PAGES	RECALL QUESTIONS	THOUGHT QUESTIONS
Objective C: Define and give examples of *matter, molecules, energy, transduction, potential energy, kinetic energy, heat.*	44-46	1	
Objective D: Explain why life requires energy.	45	2	
Objective E: State and give an illustration of energy transduction.	46	4	3
Objective F: Explain why energy is not recycled.	46	5	

Laboratory: 3-1 Energy in a Peanut   **Chapter Test Questions:** 1,2,3,19,20,22

Section 3: Storing Energy in Green Plants *(For Average, Above Average Students)*	PAGES	RECALL QUESTIONS	THOUGHT QUESTIONS
Objective G: Define *electromagnetic spectrum, calorie, kilocalorie, net productivity, limiting factor, energy subsidy, cultural energy.*	47-48	1	
Objective H: Determine the net productivity of a vegetated area.	48	3	2
Objective I: Describe the distribution of the sun's energy.	47	4	
Objective J: Explain reasons for the different net productivities of different land biomes and water environments.	48	5	6
Objective K: Compare and explain the difference in energy efficiencies of primitive and modern agriculture.	48-49		7

Chapter Review Questions: 1,2
Laboratory: 3-2 Energy Release in Respiration

Chapter Test Questions: 7,9,10,16,17,18,23,24

Section 4: Energy Flow in the Environment *(For Average, Above Average Students)*	PAGES	RECALL QUESTIONS	THOUGHT QUESTIONS
Objective L: Define *pyramid of energy, metabolism, efficiency.*	50-52	1	
Objective M: Explain the reduced net productivity at each level of the energy pyramid.	52-53	2	
Objective N: Relate the energy pyramid to the problem of world hunger.	53	4	3,5
Objective O: Summarize what happens to energy from the time it leaves the sun until it leaves Earth as heat.	53		6,7

Laboratory: 3-3 The Effect of Light on the Rate of Photosynthesis

Chapter Test Questions: 4,5,6,8,24

Suggested Study Skills: SM-1 Systematic Consideration of Possibilities
SM-2 Control Treatment and Experimental Treatment   SM-3 Formulating Hypothesis I

CHAPTER 4

BALANCES AND IMBALANCES

Section 1: The Human Population Grows in Knowledge and Numbers *(For Basic, Average, Above Average Students)*	PAGES	RECALL QUESTIONS	THOUGHT QUESTIONS
Objective A: Identify features of the lifestyle of the hunter-gatherer society that makes it different from the agricultural society.	57-58	1,3	2

Chapter 4, Section 1 *continued*	PAGES	RECALL QUESTIONS	THOUGHT QUESTIONS
Objective B: Describe early agricultural societies. Explain how they resulted in an increase in the human population.	57-58		4
Objective C: Explain how the scientific-industrial revolution and health revolution encouraged an increase in the human population	58-59	5,6	

Chapter Review Questions: 3,4,5   **Chapter Test Questions:** 1,11

Section 2: The Need for Resources Grows *(For Basic, Average, Above Average Students)*	PAGES	RECALL QUESTIONS	THOUGHT QUESTIONS
Objective D: List three ways that agriculture has increased food productivity. Give five possible solutions to the food shortage.	61-63	1,2	3,4
Objective E: Contrast the effects on soil of high rainfall, and human activity.	64-65	5,6,7	
Objective F: List human uses of water and possible methods of meeting increased demands for it.	65-66	8,9	

Chapter Review Questions: 3,4,5   **Chapter Test Questions:** 2,3,4,12,13,14,15,16,21,24

Section 3: Pollution Accumulates *(For Basic, Average, Above Average Students)*	PAGES	RECALL QUESTIONS	THOUGHT QUESTIONS
Objective G: Describe the problems of wastes from each of the following sources: households, agriculture, pesticides, industry, and radioactivity.	67-70	1,2,3,4,5,6,7, 8,9,10,11	12
Objective H: Suggest solutions for each problem.	67-70	1,2,3,4,5,6, 7,8,9,10,11	

Chapter Review Questions: 3,4,5   **Chapter Test Questions:** 5,8,9,17,18,19,20,25
Laboratory: 4-1 The Effects of Air Pollution on Organisms

Section 4: Natural Ecosystems are Threatened *(For Basic, Average, Above Average Students)*	PAGES	RECALL QUESTIONS	THOUGHT QUESTIONS
Objective I: Describe the roles of habitat destruction, removal of natural predators, introduction of foreign species, and human hunters in threatening the survival of natural populations.	71-72	1,2	
Objective J: Give reasons for using pesticides and their dangers.	72-73	3	4
Objective K: Describe how human activities can affect the oceans, a river-sea system, and separate marine ecosystems.	73-74	5,6,7	

Chapter 4, Section 4 _continued_	PAGES	RECALL QUESTIONS	THOUGHT QUESTIONS
Objective L: Suggest a reason for concern over the increased rate of extinction of plants and animals.	74		8

Chapter Review Questions: 1,2,3,4,5
Laboratory: 4-2 Interrelationships in a Food Web

Chapter Test Questions: 6,7,10,23
Suggested Study Skills: RS-4 Cause and Effect

CHAPTER 5
CHEMISTRY OF LIVING THINGS

Section 1: Building Blocks of Matter and How They Combine _(For Basic, Average, Above Average Students)_	PAGES	RECALL QUESTIONS	THOUGHT QUESTIONS
Objective A: Define the terms, _matter_ and _element,_ and explain how they are related.	79	1	2
Objective B: Describe the structure of an _atom_ in terms of _protons, neutrons,_ and _electrons._	80	3,4	
Objective C: Distinguish between _ionic_ and _covalent_ bonds.	81-83	5,7	6
Objective D: Define the terms, _ion, molecule,_ and _compound._	80-82	8	9

Laboratory: 5-1 Chemical Models

Chapter Test Questions: 1,2,3,4,11,12,14,15,19

Section 2: Simple Chemicals of Life _(For Average, Above Average Students)_	PAGES	RECALL QUESTIONS	THOUGHT QUESTIONS
Objective E: List some properties of water and describe how it is important to living things.	85-86	1,2	
Objective F: List some properties of _solutions, colloids,_ and _suspensions_ and describe how each is important in biology.	86-87	3	4
Objective G: Define the terms, _acid_ and _base._	88	5,6,7	
Objective H: Explain why carbon is important to living things.	89	8	9

Laboratory: 5-2 Mixtures, Acids, and Bases

Chapter Test Questions: 5,6,7,8,21,22

Section 3: Complex Chemicals of Life _(For Average, Above Average Students)_	PAGES	RECALL QUESTIONS	THOUGHT QUESTIONS
Objective I: Describe the properties of _carbohydrates_ and tell how they function.	91-92	1,2	
Objective J: Describe the properties of _fats_ and tell how they function.	93-94	3,4,5	

Chapter 5, Section 3 *continued*	PAGES	RECALL QUESTIONS	THOUGHT QUESTIONS
Objective K: Describe the properties of *proteins* and tell how they function.	94-94	6,7	
Objective L: Describe the properties of *nucleic acids* and tell how they function.	95-96	8,10	9
Objective M: Summarize some ways the chemical structures found in living things are related to their functions.	91-96		

Chapter Review Questions: 1
Laboratory: 5-3 Organic Substances in Foods

Chapter Test Questions: 9,10,13,16,17,18,20,23,24,25
Suggested Study Skills: SM-4 Devise an Experiment I

CHAPTER 6
THE CELL

Section 1: The Cell Theory *(For Basic, Average, Above Average Students)*	PAGES	RECALL QUESTIONS	THOUGHT QUESTIONS
Objective A: State the cell theory and describe some of the major events that led to its development.	100-101	1,2	
Objective B: Describe the structure of a cell as seen with a light microscope.	101-103	3	4
Objective C: Compare an animal cell with a plant cell and list their similarities and differences.	103	5	6

Laboratory: 6-1 Using the Microscope to Study Cells

Chapter Test Questions: 1,3,21,25

Section 2: Organelles—The Little Organs of the Cell *(For Average, Above Average Students)*	PAGES	RECALL QUESTIONS	THOUGHT QUESTIONS
Objective D: Describe the structure of a cell as seen with an electron microscope including the structure of the cell membrane.	105-111	1,2	3
Objective E: Explain how the structure of each cell organelle is well suited to perform its function.	105-111	4	5,6

Chapter Test Questions: 2,4,5,6,7,8,10,11,13,16,17,18

Section 3: The Functions of Cell Membranes *(For Average, Above Average Students)*	PAGES	RECALL QUESTIONS	THOUGHT QUESTIONS
Objective F: Use the following terms to describe how materials cross cell membranes: *diffusion, osmosis, active transport, phagocytosis,* and *pinocytosis.*	112-115	1,2,3	4

Continued

Chapter 6, Section 3 *continued*	PAGES	RECALL QUESTIONS	THOUGHT QUESTIONS
Objective G: Describe how cell membranes receive information.	115-116	5,6	
Objective H: Define homeostatis. Explain how the structure and function of cell membranes contribute to maintaining homeostatis.	116		7,8
Objective I: Summarize the processes that go on in a cell that justify calling it the basic unit of living structure.	100-115		

Chapter Review Questions: 1,2

Laboratory: 6-2 How Materials Enter and Leave Cells

Chapter Test Questions: 9,12,14,15,19,20,22,23,24

Suggested Study Skills: CD-6 Making a Biology Drawing
SM-5 Reporting Results and Drawing Conclusions I

CHAPTER 7
ENERGY RELATIONSHIPS IN THE CELL

Section 1: Enzymes and Metabolism (For Average, Above Average Students)	PAGES	RECALL QUESTIONS	THOUGHT QUESTIONS
Objective A: Define *metabolism, ATP, enzyme,* and *coenzyme.*	119-120	1,2	3
Objective B: Describe the chemical and physical properties of enzymes.	119-121	4,5	6
Objective C: Interpret the role of ATP in metabolism.	120-121	7,8	

Chapter Review Questions: 1,2

Laboratory: 7-1 Properties of Enzymes

Chapter Test Questions: 1,2,3,16,21

Section 2: Cellular Respiration—Getting Energy into Useable Form (For Above Average Students)	PAGES	RECALL QUESTIONS	THOUGHT QUESTIONS
Objective D: Define *cellular respiration, aerobic respiration, anaerobic respiration, fermation,* and *glycolysis.*	123-124	1,2,3	4
Objective E: Interpret the importance of cellular respiration to living things.	123-127	5,6	7

Chapter Review Questions: 4

Laboratory: 7-2 Fermentation

Chapter Test Questions: 4,5,6,11,12,13,17,20,23,24

Section 3: Photosynthesis—Capturing and Storing Energy (For Basic, Average, Above Average Students)	PAGES	RECALL QUESTIONS	THOUGHT QUESTIONS
Objective F: Define *photosynthesis, light reaction,* and *dark reaction.*	128-133	1,2	
Objective G: Interpret the importance of photosynthesis to living things.	133	3	
Objective H: Contrast the roles of cellular respiration and photosynthesis in metabolism. Interpret their importance in homeostatis.	133	4,5	6,7

Chapter Review Questions: 3,5,6

Laboratory: 7-3 Photosynthesis and Respiration

Chapter Test Questions: 7,8,9,10,14,15,18,19,22,25

Suggested Study Skills: RS-5 Building Science Vocabulary

CHAPTER 8
ACTIVITIES OF LIVING CELLS

Section 1: How Do Cells Use Energy? (For Average, Above Average Students)	PAGES	RECALL QUESTIONS	THOUGHT QUESTIONS
Objective A: Explain how cells use energy in response to their environment.	137	1	2
Objective B: Describe how cells make and use proteins.	138-141	3,4	5
Objective C: Name some other substances that cells make and tell how they are used.	141	6	7

Chapter Review Questions: 1

Laboratory: 8-1 Activities of cells

Chapter Test Questions: 1,2,3,8,9

Section 2: Cell Division (For Average, Above Average Students)	PAGES	RECALL QUESTIONS	THOUGHT QUESTIONS
Objective D: Describe the replication of DNA.	143-144	1	
Objective E: Arrange the stages of mitosis in their proper sequence and tell what happens in each stage.	144-146	2	
Objective F: Interpret the importance of cell division in growth and repair of living things.	146-147	3	
Objective G: Define *cancer* and show how it is related to mitosis.	146-147	4	

Continued

Chapter Review Questions: 2	Chapter Test Questions: 4,5,10,11,12,13,14,15,21,25
Laboratory: 8-2 Mitosis	

Section 3: Levels of Organization *(For Basic, Average, Above Average Students)*	PAGES	RECALL QUESTIONS	THOUGHT QUESTIONS
Objective H: Distinguish among the following levels of organization in multicellular organisms: cell, tissue, organ, system, and organism.	148-151	1	2
Objective I: Name the main types of tissue found in seed plants and in vertebrate animals.	148-150	3	4
Objective J: Define the term *division of labor.*	151	5	
Objective K: Interpret how each of the following aids to maintain homeostasis: (a) the ability of an organism to respond to its environment; (b) the synthesis of proteins and other substances; (c) cell division; (d) the division of labor among different parts of an organism.	153		6

Chapter Review Questions: 3

Chapter Test Questions: 6,7,16,17,18,19,20,22,23,24

Suggested Study Skills: RS-2 Reading Photographs and Art Work

CHAPTER 9
PRINCIPLES OF HEREDITY

Section 1: Basic Inheritance *(For Basic, Average, Above Average Students)*	PAGES	RECALL QUESTIONS	THOUGHT QUESTIONS
Objective A: Define the following terms: *dominant, recessive, hybrid, F_1 and F_2 generations, homozygous, heterozygous.*	157-162	1,2,3,4,5,6	
Objective B: State and explain Mendel's *Principles of Unit Characters* and *Dominance.*	161	7,8,9	
Objective C: Trace a Mendelian inheritance for a single trait through two generations using an appropriate diagram.	162		10,11,12

Chapter Review Questions: 1,3

Chapter Test Questions: 2,6,12,14,16,17,19,22

Laboratory: 9-1 Genetics of Leaf Color in Tobacco

Section 2: Application of Mendel's Experiments *(For Basic, Average, Above Average Students)*	PAGES	RECALL QUESTIONS	THOUGHT QUESTIONS
Objective D: Define the following terms: *gene, allele, phenotype, genotype.*	164	1,2	3

Chapter 9, Section 2 *continued*	PAGES	RECALL QUESTIONS	THOUGHT QUESTIONS
Objective E: State the *Chromosome Theory of Inheritance* and relate it to Mendel's principles.	164-166	4,5	
Objective F: Describe a *test cross*.	165	6	7
Objective G: State and explain Mendel's *Principle of Segregation*	166	8,9	
Chapter Review Questions: 3		**Chapter Test Questions:** 3,10,11,20,21,25	

Section 3: Expansion of Mendel's Experiments *(For Average, Above Average Students)*	PAGES	RECALL QUESTIONS	THOUGHT QUESTIONS
Objective H: Define the following terms: *haploid, diploid, gametes, somatic, chromatid, centromere, tetrad, fertilization.*	167-170	1	
Objective I: Describe the process of *meiosis* and be able to explain its application to Mendel's Laws.	167-169	2,3	4
Objective J: Distinguish between somatic cells and gametes with respect to chromosome number.	167-170	5,6	
Chapter Review Questions: 3 **Laboratory:** 9-2 Meiosis: A Model		**Chapter Test Questions:** 1,4,13,15,18	

Section 4: Independent Assortment *(For Average, Above Average Students)*	PAGES	RECALL QUESTIONS	THOUGHT QUESTIONS
Objective K: Define *independent assortment* and *dihybrid*.	171-173	1,2	
Objective L: Explain the results of a *dihybrid cross* including genotypes and phenotypes of the F_1 and F_2 generations.	171-173	3	
Chapter Review Questions: 2,3 **Laboratory:** 9-3 Predicting the Patterns of Inheritance		**Chapter Test Questions:** 5,7,8,9,23,24 **Suggested Study Skills:** CD-4 Drawing Inferences from Data and Determining Ratios CD-5 Drawing Inferences from Data: Chi Square Test	

CHAPTER 10
GENES AND CHROMOSONES

Section 1: Diversity Within the Existing Gene Pool *(For Average, Above Average Students)*	PAGES	RECALL QUESTIONS	THOUGHT QUESTIONS
Objective A: Define the following terms: *gene pool, incomplete dominance, codominance, polygenic inheritance.*	177-180	1,2	
Objective B: Determine how genetic variety can be produced within the limits of the existing gene pool.	177-180	3	

continued

Chapter 10, Section 1 *continued*	PAGES	RECALL QUESTIONS	THOUGHT QUESTIONS
Objective C: Calculate the number of phenotypes and genotypes possible for any number of independently-assorting genes with two alleles.	177		4
Objective D: Explain how multiple alleles for a gene contribute to increased variability. Use the ABO blood type in humans as an example.	179	5	6,7,8

Chapter Review Questions: 1,2   **Chapter Test Questions:** 2,5,7,8,11,12,13

Laboratory: 10-1 Genetic Variety by Incomplete Dominance

Section 2: The Genetic Material *(For Basic, Average, Above Average Students)*	PAGES	RECALL QUESTIONS	THOUGHT QUESTIONS
Objective E: Define the following Terms: *mutation mutagen*.	183-184	1,2	
Objective F: Explain how DNA can dictate the structure of a protein.	182	3	
Objective G: Describe how mutation might occur, including its cause.	183	4	5
Objective H: List four usual characteristics of mutation.	184	6	7

Chapter Review Questions: 2,3   **Chapter Test Questions:** 4,9,14,15

Laboratory: 10-2 Mutations in Bacteria

Section 3: The Role of Chromosomes *(For Basic, Average, Above Average Students)*	PAGES	RECALL QUESTIONS	THOUGHT QUESTIONS
Objective I: Define the following terms: *karyotype, autosome, sex chromosome, sex-linked trait*.	185-186	1,2	
Objective J: Describe the karyotype of a normal male and female.	186	3	
Objective K: Explain how sex is determined in humans.	186	4	
Objective L: Describe the inheritance of a sex-linked trait such as hemophilia or color-blindness.	186-188	5	6
Objective M: Explain why autosomial linkage should produce a 3:1 phenotype ratio in the F_2 generation.	188-189	7	

Chapter Review Questions: 1,2   **Chapter Test Questions:** 6,10,16,17,21,23,24

Laboratory: 10-3 Chromosome Karyotyping

Section 4: Chromosomal Variability (For Average, Above Average Students)	PAGES	RECALL QUESTIONS	THOUGHT QUESTIONS
Objective N: Define the following terms: *inversion, deletion, translocation, duplication, nondisjunction, polyploidy.*	192-193	1,2	
Objective O: Explain why some degree of independent assortment may occur with autosomal linkage.	191-192		3
Objective P: Explain how inversions might tend to increase the chances for crossing over to occur between linked genes.	192-193		4
Objective Q: Describe how an abnormal number of chromosomes might occur in an offspring.	193		5
Objective R: Explain why a polypoid organism would be a different species from its parent.	193	7	6
Chapter Review Questions: 1,2	**Chapter Test Questions:** 1,3,18,19,20,22,25		
	Suggested Study Skills: CD-8 Making a Bacterial Streak Plate CD-9 Making a Bacterial Pour Plate		

CHAPTER 11
GENETICS AND POPULATIONS

Section 1: Probability and Populations (For Above Average Students)	PAGES	RECALL QUESTIONS	THOUGHT QUESTIONS
Objective A: Define the term *frequency* as it relates to population genetics.	198	1	
Objective B: Explain why the reproductive rate of a species is important to its ultimate survival.	198	2,3	4
Objective C: State and give examples of the First and Second Laws of Probability.	199-200	5,6	7,8,9
Objective D: Calculate the frequency of the dominant and recessive alleles of a Mendelian trait from population data.	198-201		10,11
Laboratory: 11-1 The Laws of Probability	**Chapter Test Questions:** 1,11,16,24,25		

Section 2: The Hardy-Weinberg Principle (For Above Average Students)	PAGES	RECALL QUESTIONS	THOUGHT QUESTIONS
Objective E: Define the terms *genetic equilibrium, differential migration, selection, genetic drift, genetic load.*	203-209	1,2	3

continued

Chapter 11, Section 2 *continued*	PAGES	RECALL QUESTIONS	THOUGHT QUESTIONS
Objective F: State the Hardy-Weinberg Principle. Explain how violating each condition would produce changes in the frequencies of alleles in the gene pool.	203-209	4,5,6,7	8
Objective G: Interpret the graph, Figure 11-12, by explaining the relationship between two variables.	208		9
Objective H: Explain how mutagens can increase the genetic load of a population.	207-208	10	

Chapter Review Questions: 3

Chapter Test Questions: 2,4,5,6,7,8,9,12,13,14,17,20,21

Laboratory: 11-2 Genetic Changes in a Population
11-3 The Frequency of an Allele in a Human Population

Section 3: Maintaining Variety *(For Above Average Students)*	PAGES	RECALL QUESTIONS	THOUGHT QUESTIONS
Objective I: Define the terms *balanced polymorphism, hybrid vigor*.	210	1	
Objective J: In terms of allele frequencies, predict the effect of equal selective forces upon the homozygous dominant and on the homozygous recessive individuals in a population.	210	2	
Objective K: Describe an example of balanced polymorphism in humans. Explain how a harmful allele might come to exist in more than token frequencies in such a population.	211	5	3,4,6
Objective L: Explain why selective action of environmental factors upon the human genetic constitution is such a difficult subject for study.	210-211	7,8	
Objective M: Explain the importance of genetic variety to populations living in changing environments.	212		

Chapter Review Questions: 1,2,3

Chapter Test Questions: 3,10,15,18,19,22,23

CHAPTER 12
HUMAN HEREDITY

Section 1: Genetic Disease *(For Basic, Average, Above Average Students)*	PAGES	RECALL QUESTIONS	THOUGHT QUESTIONS
Objective A: Define and give examples of terms *congenital defects, high-risk groups, late-occurring disorders*.	215-217	1	

Chapter 12, Section 1 *continued*	PAGES	RECALL QUESTIONS	THOUGHT QUESTIONS
Objective B: Differentiate between the contagious and hereditary disorders.	215	2	
Objective C: Discuss the factors that result in various high-risk groups exhibiting higher frequencies of certain heritable disorders.	216	3,4	
Objective D: Explain why serious dominant disorders are often late-occurring.	216	5	
	Chapter Test Questions: 9,11,20		

Section 2: Disorders In Humans *(For Average, Above Average Students)*	PAGES	RECALL QUESTIONS	THOUGHT QUESTIONS
Objective E: List and describe examples of the following types of hereditary disorders: *autosomal recessive, autosomal dominant, sex-linked,* and chromosomal.	218-224	1,2	3
Objective F: Define the terms *antigen, antibody, pedigree, syndrome.*	220-224		4
Objective G: Explain why Rh disease is not really an hereditary disorder itself.	220-221	5,6,7	8
Objective H: Make a chart to show how a female might inherit a sex-linked disorder. Explain why this does not usually occur.	222		9,10
Chapter Review Questions: 1 **Laboratory:** 12-1 Family Pedigrees.	**Chapter Test Questions:** 1,2,5,6,7,8,10,12,14,16,17,18, 21,22,24		

Section 3: Treatment of Birth Defects *(For Basic, Average, Above Average Students)*	PAGES	RECALL QUESTIONS	THOUGHT QUESTIONS
Objective I: Distinguish between curing and treating heritable disorders. List six means by which such problems can be treated or prevented.	225-228	1,2,3	
Objective J: Describe the process of amniocentesis. Explain how it might be used to prevent heritable disorders.	225	4,6	5,7
Objective K: Describe various aspects of the role of a genetic counselor.	225-227	8,10,11	9,12
Objective L: Identify the issue surrounding the use of recombinant DNA. Criticize the various points of view.	227-228		13,14
Chapter Review Questions: 2 **Laboratory:** 12-2 Variations in Human Beings	**Chapter Test Questions:** 3,4,13,23,25 **Suggested Study Skills:** CD-7 Preparing a Library Research Paper		

CHAPTER 13
THEORIES OF CHANGE

Section 1: Development of An Idea (For Basic, Average, Above Average Students)	PAGES	RECALL QUESTIONS	THOUGHT QUESTIONS
Objective A: Identify one contribution with respect to the theory of evolution by Aristotle, Lamarck.	233-234	1	
Objective B: State and give an example of Lamarck's two "laws" that he thought governed the process of change through time.	234	2,3,4	
Chapter Review Questions: 1		**Chapter Test Questions:** 2,4,8,9,10,12,14,20,24,25	

Section 2: Natural Selection (For Basic, Average, Above Average Students)	PAGES	RECALL QUESTIONS	THOUGHT QUESTIONS
Objective C: Identify the contributions of the following people made to understanding change through time: Charles Darwin, Thomas Malthus, Alfred Russel Wallace.	236-239	1,2	
Objective D: Explain the importance to Darwin of his three observations.	236-237	3,5	4
Objective E: Given Darwin's three observations, draw three conclusions he might have made.	236-238	7	6,8
Objective F: Give an example of the importance of natural selection to the science of biology.	237-240		9,10
Objective G: Identify the steps of the Darwin-Wallace theory.	238-239	11	
Chapter Review Questions: 1,2,3 **Laboratory:** 13-1 Natural Variations 13-2 Natural Selection		**Chapter Test Questions:** 1,5,6,7,8,13,18,19,21	

Section 3: Evolution Theory (For Average, Above Average Students)	PAGES	RECALL QUESTIONS	THOUGHT QUESTIONS
Objective H: Define the following terms in your own words: *domestication, adaption, artificial selection, positive mutation, industrial melanism.*	241	1	
Objective I: Describe the essential elements of the famous peppered moth experiment.	241-242	2,4	3
Objective J: Cite several examples that illustrate the role of humans in the change of other species.	243-244	5,6	
Objective K: Give an example of how complementarity of organism and environment provides a key to the Darwin-Wallace theory.	241-244		7
		Chapter Test Questions: 3,11,15,17,22,23	

CHAPTER 14
EVIDENCE OF CHANGE

Section 1: Mechanisms of Change (For Average, Above Average Students)	PAGES	RECALL QUESTIONS	THOUGHT QUESTIONS
Objective A: Define the following terms in your own words: *species, isolating mechanism, pre-adaptation, divergence, speculation.*	247-250	1,4	2,3
Objective B: Discuss the reasons why the term species is such a problem to biologiests.	247	5	
Objective C: Compare and contrast the three types of selection.	248-250	6	
Objective D: Describe the various isolating mechanisms.	250-251	7,8,9	
Chapter Review Questions: 1	**Chapter Test Questions:** 3,4,5,12,13,14,15,17,21,22		

Section 2: Results of Change and the Fossil Record (For Average, Above Average Students)	PAGES	RECALL QUESTIONS	THOUGHT QUESTIONS
Objective E: Define the following terms in your own words: *adaption, adaptive radiation, convergence, ecologic equivalent, half life.*	254-258	1,2	
Objective F: Describe the means by which adaptive radiation takes place.	254-256	3	
Objective G: Explain why two unrelated organisms may come to resemble each other.	254-255	4	
Objective H: Give four reasons why the fossil record is difficult to interpret.	256-257	5	
Objective I: Describe the means by which rock strata can be "dated."	257-258	6	7
Chapter Review Questions: 1	**Chapter Test Questions:** 1,2,7,8,9,11,16,20,23,24,25		
Laboratory: 14-1 Fossil History of the Elephant 14-2 The Half-Life Principle			

Section 3: Indirect Evidence (For Average, Above Average Students)	PAGES	RECALL QUESTIONS	THOUGHT QUESTIONS
Objective J: Define the following terms in your own words: *homologous structures, embryo.*	259	1	
Objective K: List and describe three kinds of indirect evidence for change through time.	259-262	2	3
Objective L: Explain how the concept of *change through time* relates to the definition of species.	247-262	4	
Chapter Review Questions: 1	**Chapter Test Questions:** 6,10,18,19		

Continued

23T

CHAPTER 15
LIFE IN THE PAST

Section 1: Origins *(For Basic, Average, Above Average Students)*	PAGES	RECALL QUESTIONS	THOUGHT QUESTIONS
Objective A: Define the following terms: *abiogenesis, biogenesis, variable, controlled experiment, sterile.*	265-267	1,2	3
Objective B: Differentiate between theories that explain the origin of life.	267-269	6	4,5
Objective C: State reasons both for and against the autotroph and heterotroph hypotheses.	267-270	7,8	
Objective D: Describe the experiments of Stanley Miller and Sidney Fox.	267-269	9	10
Objective E: Summarize the essential events of the heterotroph hypothesis.	267-270	11,12,13,14	

Chapter Review Questions: 1,2

Chapter Test Questions: 3,4,10,15,18,19,20,21,24

Laboratory: 15-1 The Formation of Coacervates

Section 2: Major Radiations *(For Basic, Average Above Average Students)*	PAGES	RECALL QUESTIONS	THOUGHT QUESTIONS
Objective F: Define the following terms: *invertebrates, vertebrates, mammals.*	273-277	1	
Objective G: Describe how the environment might have been responsible for the first vertebrates to venture onto land.	273-277	2	
Objective H: List the Geologic eras and the major events that occurred during their existence.	274-275	3	4
Objective I: Make a diagram that summarizes the vertebrate radiation through the reptiles.	275-276		5

Laboratory: 15-2 Evolution of Barbellus

Chapter Test Questions: 1,2,5,6,7,11,12,13,17,22,23

Section 3: Emergence of Humans *(For Basic, Average, Above Average Students)*	PAGES	RECALL QUESTIONS	THOUGHT QUESTIONS
Objective J: Define the following terms: *primate, arboreal, anthropoid, prehensile, bipedal, hominid, race.*	279-282	1	2

Chapter 15, Section 3 *continued*	PAGES	RECALL QUESTIONS	THOUGHT QUESTIONS
Objective K: List some of the skeletal features of hominids that apparently underwent change as *Homo sapiens* developed.	279-280		3,4
Objective L: Describe the concept of race as based upon allele frequencies.	281-282		5
	Chapter Test Questions: 9,14,16,25		

CHAPTER 16
CLASSIFICATION OF LIVING THINGS

Section 1: Patterns of Classification *(For Basic, Average, Above Average Students)*	PAGES	RECALL QUESTIONS	THOUGHT QUESTIONS
Objective A: Define *taxonomy, taxonomist, binomial system, species name, scientific name.*	286-287	1	2
Objective B: Give the original and modern purposes of classifying organisms.	286-289	3,4	
Objective C: Name and distinguish among the three parts of a scientific name.	287	5	6
Objective D: List the main levels of classification in order from species to kingdom.	287-288	7	8
Chapter Review Questions: 1,2,3,5	**Chapter Test Questions:** 1,2,3,4,5,7,8,10,11,12,13,14,15, 21,22,23		

Section 2: Modern Classification *(For Basic, Average, Above Average Students)*	PAGES	RECALL QUESTIONS	THOUGHT QUESTIONS
Objective E: Give five advantages of the present system of scientific naming of organisms.	291	1	
Objective F: Explain the advantages of the five kingdom system of classifying organisms.	291	2	
Objective G: Name and describe the kingdoms of the five-kingdom system of classifying organisms.	292-297	3	4
Chapter Review Questions: 4	**Chapter Test Questions:** 6,9,16,17,18,19,20,24,25		
Laboratory: 16-1 The Dichotomous Key			

CHAPTER 17

VIRUSES

Section 1: Diversity and Continuity *(For Basic, Average, Above Average Students)*	PAGES	RECALL QUESTIONS	THOUGHT QUESTIONS
Objective A: Describe the general characteristics of monerans and protists. Explain why it is difficult to settle upon a single way to classify them.	305-307	1	2
Objective B: Differentiate between procaryote and eucaryote cells.	305	3,4	
Objective C: List the characteristics of viruses. Explain why their inclusion among living things is not universally accepted.	306-307	5,6,7	
Objective D: State three different ideas about the possible origins of viruses.	306-307	8	
Chapter Review Questions: 1	**Chapter Test Questions:** 1,2,3,4,5,6,7,11,13,18,22		

Section 2: Activities of Viruses *(For Average, Above Average Students)*	PAGES	RECALL QUESTIONS	THOUGHT QUESTIONS
Objective E: Define the following terms in your own words: *bacteriophage, plaque, lytic cycle, virulent.*	310-311	1	
Objective F: Explain what is meant by virus specificity.	310	2	3
Objective G: Describe the characteristic lytic cycle of a phage.	310-311	4	5
Objective H: Explain how the electron microscope has helped us to understand the lytic cycle of a virus.	310-311	6	
Chapter Review Questions: 1 **Laboratory:** 17-1 The Effect of TMV on Plants	**Chapter Test Questions:** 4,12,16,19,21		

Section 3: Viruses and their Environment *(For Average, Above Average Students)*	PAGES	RECALL QUESTIONS	THOUGHT QUESTIONS
Objective I: Define and give examples of the following terms: *phagocyte, vaccine.*	312-314	1	
Objective J: List five diseases known to be caused by viruses.	312	2	
Objective K: Describe the body's lines of defense against a viral attack.	312-313	3	
Objective L: Describe three ways in which a virus can alter the normal functioning of a cell.	314-315	4,5,6	
Chapter Review Questions: 1	**Chapter Test Questions:** 8,9,10,14,15,17,20,23,24,25		

BACTERIA AND BLUE-GREEN ALGAE

Section 1: Diversity and Continuity (For Basic, Average, Above Average Students)	PAGES	RECALL QUESTIONS	THOUGHT QUESTIONS
Objective A: Define each of the following terms in your own words: *procaryote, flagellum, pathogen, binary fission, conjugation, endospore.*	319-324	1,2	
Objective B: Describe the characteristics that define the Kindome Monera.	319	3	
Objective C: List five moneran groups and give the unifying features of each.	320		4
Objective D: List the roles of Monerans that affect humans.	319-324		5
Laboratory: 18-1 Representative Monerans	Chapter Test Questions: 1,2,3,5,11,12,13,18,19,20,24		

Section 2: Homeostasis (For Average, Above Average Students)	PAGES	RECALL QUESTIONS	THOUGHT QUESTIONS
Objective E: Define each of the following terms in your own words: *chemosynthesis, aerobe, anaerobe, growth medium.*	326-330	1	
Objective F: Differentiate between chemosynthesis and photosynthesis.	326-327	2	
Objective G: Differentiate between obligate and facultative anaerobes.	327-328	3	4
Objective H: Differentiate between fermentation and respiration as means of releasing energy in monerans.	328	5	
Objective I: Explain why a knowledge of how bacterial cells release energy is important to humans.	326-330	6	
	Chapter Test Questions: 4,6,7,8,14,17,21,22		

Section 3: Monerans and their Environment (For Basic, Average, Above Average Students)	PAGES	RECALL QUESTIONS	THOUGHT QUESTIONS
Objective J: Define each of the following terms in your own words: *saprophyte, venereal disease, antitoxin, toxin, chemotherapy.*	331-334	2	1
Objective K: Differentiate between the two main venereal diseases.	332-333	3,4	
Objective L: Describe a variety of ways that we can protect ourselves from bacterial action.	333-334	5	6
Objective M: Describe two main ways that we can treat a bacterial infection in our bodies.	334	7	

Chapter 18, Section 3 *continued*	PAGES	RECALL QUESTIONS	THOUGHT QUESTIONS
Objective N: Explain how the use of antibiotics can encourage the growth of microbes resistant to treatment.	334	8	
Objective O: Explain how *continuity* is maintained in some monerans.	319-335	9	

Chapter Review Questions: 1,2,3   **Chapter Test Questions:** 9,10,15,16,23,25

Laboratory: 18-2 Distribution of Bacteria

CHAPTER 19
THE PROTISTS

Section 1: Diversity and Continuity *(For Basic, Average, Above Average Students)*	PAGES	RECALL QUESTIONS	THOUGHT QUESTIONS
Objective A: Describe the general characteristics of the four major groups of the Kingdom Protista.	338-339	1	
Objective B: Define the following terms in your own words: *phytoplankton, zooplankton, bioluminescence, phototropic.*	338	2,6	3,4,5
Objective C: Draw an Ameba and a Paramecium and identify their respective parts.	340-342		
Objective D: Describe and contrast sexual and asexual reproduction in Ameba and Paramecium.	342-343	7	8

Chapter Review Questions: 1   **Chapter Test Questions:** 1,3,4,9,13,14,15,16,18,19,20

Laboratory: 19-1 Protists in a Pond

Section 2: Homeostasis *(For Basic, Average, Above Average Students)*	PAGES	RECALL QUESTIONS	THOUGHT QUESTIONS
Objective E: Describe the external and internal characteristics of both Ameba and Paramecium.	345-347	1,2	
Objective F: In terms of Ameba and Paramecium, explain how species survival is dependent upon the link between structure and function.	345-347	4	3
Objective G: Explain the relationship between the ratio of surface area to volume in terms of protists' ability to undergo periodic fission.	346		5,6

Chapter Review Questions: 2   **Chapter Test Questions:** 7,8,17,22,23,24

Section 3: Behavior and Environment *(For Basic, Average, Above Average Students)*	PAGES	RECALL QUESTIONS	THOUGHT QUESTIONS
Objective H: Describe various roles that protists play in the "web of life."	348-349	1	

Chapter 19, Section 3 *continued*	PAGES	RECALL QUESTIONS	THOUGHT QUESTIONS
Objective I: List and describe at least three diseases in humans caused by different kinds of protists.	349-350	2	
Objective J: Describe how a knowledge of the life cycle of a pathogenic protist helps us to control its spread.	349-350		3
Objective K: Explain how homeostasis is maintained in protists.	348-351		4
Laboratory: 19-2 Response in a Paramecium	**Chapter Test Questions:** 2,5,6,10,11,12,21,25 **Suggested Study Skills:** SM-6 Formulating Hypotheses II		

CHAPTER 20
THE FUNGI

Section 1: Diversity and Continuity (For Basic, Average, Above Average Students)	PAGES	RECALL QUESTIONS	THOUGHT QUESTIONS
Objective A: Define the following terms: *spore, hypha, mycelium, plasmodium, sporangia, basidia.*	354-356	1	
Objective B: Describe the general characteristics of fungi. Point out the basis for classifying them as a separate kingdom.	354-355	2,3	4
Objective C: Describe and give an example of each of five major groups of fungi. Explain the basis for such grouping.	355-356	5	6
Chapter Review Questions: 1 **Laboratory:** 20-1 Some Typical Fungi	**Chapter Test Questions:** 1,2,6,8,11,12,13,14,16, 18,21,23,25		

Section 2: Homeostasis (For Basic, Average Above Average Students)	PAGES	RECALL QUESTIONS	THOUGHT QUESTIONS
Objective D: Define the following terms: *gametophyte generation, sporophyte generation, alternation of generations, budding, ascospore, gill, stipe, basidiospore, haustoria.*	359-362	1	
Objective E: Explain how the natural antibiotic produced by a fungus is of adaptive value to its success.	359-360	2	
Objective F: Describe a "typical" life cycle of a fungus.	361-362	3	4,5
Objective G: Interpret the presence of a "fairy ring" in terms of the growth pattern of a mushroom.	362	6	
Chapter Review Questions: 1,2	**Chapter Test Questions:** 3,5,7,9,10,15,17,19,24		

continued

Section 3: Fungi and the Environment (For Basic, Average, Above Average Students)	PAGES	RECALL QUESTIONS	THOUGHT QUESTIONS
Objective H: Define the following term: *mycorrhiza.*	363	1	
Objective I: Describe at least three roles of fungi in the natural environment.	363-364	2	
Objective J: Point out several uses of fungi as food sources for humans.	363-364	3	4

Chapter Review Questions: 1   **Chapter Test Questions:** 4,20

Laboratory: 20-2 Controlling Food Molds

Section 4: Comparisons Among Monerans, Protists, and Fungi (For Average, Above Average Students)	PAGES	RECALL QUESTIONS	THOUGHT QUESTIONS
Objective K: Describe differences among monerans, protists, and fungi.	365-369	1,2	
Chapter Review Questions: 2			

CHAPTER 21
THE SIMPLEST PLANTS

Section 1: Red Algae (For Basic, Average, Above Average Students)	PAGES	RECALL QUESTIONS	THOUGHT QUESTIONS
Objective A: List the main feature of organisms in the plant kingdom.	373	1	
Objective B: Describe the characteristics and habitats of the red algae.	373-374	2	
Objective C: Tell how red algae meet their basic needs.	374	3	4
Objective D: Describe the interactions between red algae and their natural and human environments.	374	5,6	

Chapter Review Questions: 5   **Chapter Test Questions:** 1,2,3,6,13,16,21,23,25

Section 2: Green Algae (For Basic, Average, Above Average Students)	PAGES	RECALL QUESTIONS	THOUGHT QUESTIONS
Objective E: List the characteristics and habitats of the green algae.	376	2	1
Objective F: Describe reproduction in *Spirogyra* and *Ulva.*	377-378	3,4	
Objective G: Tell how the green algae maintain homeostasis.	378-379	5	

Chapter 21, Section 2 *continued*	PAGES	RECALL QUESTIONS	THOUGHT QUESTIONS
Objective H: Explain the important roles played by the green algae.	379	6,7	
Chapter Review Questions: 4,5			
Laboratory: 21-1 Observing Green Algae			

Chapter Review Questions: 4,5 **Chapter Test Questions:** 2,14,18,20,24,25

Laboratory: 21-1 Observing Green Algae

Section 3: Brown Algae *(For Basic, Average, Above Average Students)*	PAGES	RECALL QUESTIONS	THOUGHT QUESTIONS
Objective I: List the characteristics and habitats of the brown algae.	380	1,2,4	3
Objective J: Describe ways that the brown algae maintain homeostasis.	381	5	
Objective K: Discuss the importance of the brown algae.	381	6	7

Chapter Review Questions: 5 **Chapter Test Questions:** 2,4,5,12,17,25

Laboratory: 21-2 Productivity in Algae

Section 4: Mosses and Liverworts *(For Basic, Average, Above Average students)*	PAGES	RECALL QUESTIONS	THOUGHT QUESTIONS
Objective L: Describe the body form of mosses and liverworts.	382	1	
Objective M: Describe the alternating generations in the life cycle of a moss.	382-383	2	3
Objective N: Explain how mosses survive in a land environment.	383	4	5
Objective O: Discuss the importance of mosses.	384	6	
Objective P: Give the advantage of sexual reproduction.	382	7	

Chapter Review Questions: 1,2,3,5 **Chapter Test Questions:** 7,8,9,10,11,15,19,22,24

Laboratory: 21-3 Life Cycle of a Moss

CHAPTER 22
FERNS AND GYMNOSPERMS

Section 1: The Ferns *(For Basic, Average, Above Average Students)*	PAGES	RECALL QUESTIONS	THOUGHT QUESTIONS
Objective A: Describe the adaptations in plants that made possible the change from aquatic to land environments.	388	1	

Continued

Chapter 22, Section 1 *continued*	PAGES	RECALL QUESTIONS	THOUGHT QUESTIONS
Objective B: Give the general characteristics or kinds of plants in each subphylum of the vascular plants.	389-390	2,3	
Objective C: Describe the life cycle of ferns in terms of gametophyte and sporophyte generations.	390-391	4	5
Objective D: Distinguish between phloem and xylem tissues in terms of structure and function.	392	6,7	
Objective E: Describe the organization of leaf tissue in ferns and relate it to the exchange of gases in photosynthesis.	392		8
Objective F: Explain the place of ferns in ecosystems and in human life.	393	9,10	
Laboratory: 22-1 Life Cycle of a Fern	**Chapter Test Questions:** 1,3,5,11,12,13,14,15,17,18, 19,21,22		

Section 2: The Gymnosperms *(For Basic, Average, Above Average Students)*	PAGES	RECALL QUESTIONS	THOUGHT QUESTIONS
Objective G: Describe the body plan of gynosperms.	395		1
Objective H: Name and describe three kinds of gymnosperms.	395	2	
Objective I: Describe the life cycle of a pine.	395-396	3	
Objective J: Describe the ways that the raw materials and products of photosynthesis are conducted through a conifer.	397-398	4	5
Objective K: Tell what causes a stem to grow in width and describe the changes this growth causes in stem tissues.	397-398	6	7
Objective L: Tell how a pine needle is adapted to its functions.	398	8	9
Objective M: Describe the formation of compression wood.	399	10	
Objective N: Distinguish between the activities of the fungus and the conifer's root in a micorrhiza.	399	11	
Objective O: Describe the role of gymnosperms as sources of food, paper, fuel, and lumber.	399-400	12	
Objective P: Describe the effects of various pollutants on forest trees.	400	13	
Objective Q: List those features that most nonflowering vascular plants have in common.	395-401	14	

Chapter Review Questions: 1,2,3	Chapter Test Questions: 2,4,6,7,8,9,10,16,20,23,24,25
Laboratory: 22-2 Study of a Pine Stem	

CHAPTER 23
FLOWERING PLANTS

Section 1: The Angiosperms (For Basic, Average, Above Average Students)	PAGES	RECALL QUESTIONS	THOUGHT QUESTIONS
Objective A: Review the features that make plant life possible on land and the unique advantages of flowering plants.	405-407	1,2	
Objective B: Explain how the classification scheme shows the relationship of *monocots*, *diocots*, *gymnosperms*, and *ferns*.	405-406		3
Objective C: Describe the functional relationship among angiosperm leaves, roots, and stems.	406-407	4, 5	

Chapter Review Questions: 3	Chapter Test Questions: 11, 12, 13, 14. 15

Section 2: Flowers (For Basic, Average, Above Average Students)	PAGES	RECALL QUESTIONS	THOUGHT QUESTIONS
Objective D: Describe the parts of a complete flower and give the functions of each.	409-411	1	
Objective E: Give the advantages of separate *staminate* and *pistillate* flowers.	410		2
Objective F: List the factors that initiate flowering.	410-411	3	
Objective G: Describe the steps in development from blossoming of a flower to the germination and growth of the seedling.	411-416	5	4

Chapter Review Questions: 1, 2	Chapter Test Questions: 1, 2, 3
Laboratory: 23-1 The Flower 23-2 Fruit, Seeds, and Seedlings	

Section 3: Leaves (For Basic, Average, Above Average Students)	PAGES	RECALL QUESTIONS	THOUGHT QUESTIONS
Objective H: Describe the different tissues in a leaf and give the function of each.	417-418	1	
Objective I: Explain how the stomata help maintain homeostasis in leaves.	418	2	
Objective J: Describe various types, venation, and arrangements of leaves.	418-419	3	

continued

Chapter 23, Section 3 *continued*	PAGES	RECALL QUESTIONS	THOUGHT QUESTIONS
Objective K: Describe the falling and changes in color of leaves.	420-421	4,5	

Chapter Review Questions: 3   **Chapter Test Questions:** 4, 16

Laboratory: 23-3 The Leaf and its Pigments

Section 4: Roots *(For Basic, Average, Above Average Students)*	PAGES	RECALL QUESTIONS	THOUGHT QUESTIONS
Objective L: Describe the development of primary and secondary root tissues.	422-423	1	
Objective M: Explain how water and minerals enter roots from the soil.	423	2	
Objective N: Give the advantages of different types of root systems.	424	3	

Chapter Review Questions: 3   **Chapter Test Questions:** 8, 9, 10

Laboratory: 23-4 Roots and Stems

Section 5: Stems *(For Basic, Average, Above Average Students)*	PAGES	RECALL QUESTIONS	THOUGHT QUESTIONS
Objective O: Describe the primary and secondary growth of stems.	425-426	1	
Objective P: Define *bud* and describe its development.	427	2, 3	
Objective Q: Explain how water and food are transferred and gases exchanged in stems and stem tissues.	428-429	4, 5, 6, 7	8
Objective R: Descirbe various types of vegetative reproduction in stems and their advantages.	431-432	9	

Chapter Review Questions: 3   **Chapter Test Questions:** 5, 6, 7, 21, 22

Laboratory: 23-4 Roots and Stems
23-5 Transpiration

Section 6: Behavior and Environment *(For Basic, Average, Above Average Students)*	PAGES	RECALL QUESTIONS	THOUGHT QUESTIONS
Objective S: Tell how plants respond to darkness, temperature, various growth regulators, and turgor changes.	433-436	1, 2	3
Objective T: List human uses of flowering plants.	436-437	4	

Chapter 23, Section 6 *continued*	PAGES	RECALL QUESTIONS	THOUGHT QUESTIONS
Objective U: Tell how air pollution has affected deciduous forests.	437		5
Chapter Review Questions: 3 **Laboratory:** 23-6 Plant Responses	**Chapter Test Questions:** 17, 23, 23, 25		

Section 7: Comparing Flowering Plants to Other Plants, Protists, and Monerans *(For Basic, Average, Above Average Students)*	PAGES	RECALL QUESTIONS	THOUGHT QUESTIONS
Objective V: Review the main features that distinguish plants from fungi, protists, monerans, and viruses in terms of structure, nutrition, and reproduction.	438-444	1, 2	
Objective W: Give an example of how flowering plants illustrate unity within diversity, homeostasis, the relationship between structure and function, and interaction with the environment.	438-444	3	
Laboratory: 23-7 Comparing Simple Plants	**Chapter Test Questions:** 18, 19, 20 **Suggested Study Skills** SM-7 Devising Experiments II SM-8 Reporting Results and Drawing Conclusions II		

CHAPTER 24
SPONGES, CNIDARIANS, AND UNSEGMENTED WORMS

Section 1: Sponges *(For Basic, Average, Above Average Students)*	PAGES	RECALL QUESTIONS	THOUGHT QUESTIONS
Objective A: Give the advantages for a large organism to be divided into cells.	449	1	
Objective B: Distinguish among different kinds of symmetry and relate them to activities and to awareness of surroundings.	449-450	2	3
Objective C: Describe the general body plan of the sponges.	450-451	4	
Objective D: Describe how the combined internal systems contribute to homeostasis in the sponges.	452	5	
Objective E: Describe the various kinds of environmental relationships found in sponges.	452	6	
Chapter Review Questions: 1,2,3,4,5 **Laboratory:** 24-1 A Simple Sponge	**Chapter Test Questions:** 1,2,3,4,5,13,15,17,21,25		

continued

Section 2: Cnidarians *(For Basic, Average, Above Average Students)*	PAGES	RECALL QUESTIONS	THOUGHT QUESTIONS
Objective F: Describe the general body plan of cnidarians.	454	1,2	
Objective G: Explain how each internal system contributes to homeostasis in the cnidarians.	456	3	
Objective H: Describe the various kinds of behavior and environmental relationships found in cnidarians.	456-457	4,5	6

Chapter Review Questions: 5

Laboratory: 24-2 Behavior in Hydra

Chapter Test Questions: 12,16,20,23,24,25

Section 3: Flatworms *(For Basic, Average, Above Average Students)*	PAGES	RECALL QUESTIONS	THOUGHT QUESTIONS
Objective I: Describe the general body plan of flatworms.	458-459	1	
Objective J: Describe how each internal system contributes to homeostasis in the flatworm.	459-461	2	
Objective K: Describe experiments with learned behavior inplanarians. Give a possible explanation of memory.	462	3	
Objective L: Describe the life style of parasites and the life history of the sheep liver fluke.	462-463	4	5

Chapter Review Questions: 5,6

Laboratory: 24-3 Planaria Behavior

Chapter Test Questions: 5,6,7,8,9,11,14,19,22

Section 4: Unsegmented Roundworms *(For Basic, Average Above Average Students)*	PAGES	RECALL QUESTIONS	THOUGHT QUESTIONS
Objective M: Describe the general body plan of unsegmented roundworms.	464	1	
Objective N: Explain how each internal system contributes to homeostasis in the unsegmented roundworm.	464-465	2	
Objective O: Describe the life history of the hookworm and the trichina.	465-466	3	
Objective P: Tell what makes reproduction possible in animals that are stationary or parasitic.	466	4	

Chapter Review Questions: 5,6

Chapter Test Questions: 10,18

ANNELIDS, MOLLUSCS, AND ECHINODERMS

Section 1: Annelids *(For Basic, Average, Above Average Students)*	PAGES	RECALL QUESTIONS	THOUGHT QUESTIONS
Objective A: Describe the *coelom* and give three advantages it offers.	469	1	2
Objective B: Describe the general body plan of the annelids.	469-470	3	4
Objective C: Explain how each internal system in earthworms contributes to homeostasis.	472-474	5	6
Objective D: Summarize learned behavior in earthworms.	474	7	
Objective E: Describe the relationships between earthworms and DDT, and between earthworms and soil.	474	9	8

Chapter Review Questions: 4   **Chapter Test Questions:** 1,2,3,6,9,11,12,13,14,15,21

Laboratory Investigations: 25-1 Earthworm Behavior
25-2 Internal Structure of the Earthworm

Section 2: Molluscs *(For Basic, Average, Above Average Students)*	PAGES	RECALL QUESTIONS	THOUGHT QUESTIONS
Objective F: Describe the general body plan of molluscs.	476	1	
Objective G: Explain how each internal system in clams contributes to homeostasis.	478-480	2,3	
Objective H: Summarize learned behavior in molluscs.	480	4	
Objective I: Describe the interrelationships between various molluscs and human activity.	481	5	

Chapter Review Questions: 1,3,4,5   **Chapter Test Questions:** 4,10,16,17,18,20,22,23,24,25

Section 3: Echinoderms *(For Basic, Average, Above Average Students)*	PAGES	RECALL QUESTIONS	THOUGHT QUESTIONS
Objective J: Describe the general body plan of starfish.	482	1,2	3
Objective K: Explain how each internal system in the starfish contributes to homeostasis.	483-484	4	
Objective L: Summarize innate and learned behavior in starfish.	484-485	5,6	

continued

Chapter 25, Section 3 *continued*	PAGES	RECALL QUESTIONS	THOUGHT QUESTIONS
Objective M: Describe the relationships between starfish and corals.	485	7	8
Objective N: Show how the annelids, molluscs, and echinoderms illustrate unity within diversity.	486	9	
Chapter Review Questions: 4	**Chapter Test Questions:** 5,7,8,19		
Laboratory: 25-3 External and Internal Structures of the Starfish.			

CHAPTER 26
THE ARTHROPODS

Section 1: Arthropods *(For Basic, Average, Above Average Students)*	PAGES	RECALL QUESTIONS	THOUGHT QUESTIONS
Objective A: Describe the combination of features that distinguish members of Phylum Arthropoda from members of other phyla.	489-490	1,2,3	
Objective B: Explain the features that distinguish each arthropod class from the others. Name representatives of each.	490-492	4	
Objective C: Describe the main parts of a crayfish and give their functions.	492-493	5	7,8
Objective D: Describe the life cycle of the crayfish.	493	6	7,8
Objective E: Explain how each internal system of the crayfish contributes to homeostasis.	493-495	9	
Laboratory: 26-1 The Crayfish 26-2 Behavior and Conditioning Pillbugs	**Chapter Test Questions:** 1,2,11,12,13,14,15,16		

Section 2: Common Arthropods—Insects *(For Basic, Average, Above Average Students)*	PAGES	RECALL QUESTIONS	THOUGHT QUESTIONS
Objective F: Describe the main parts of a grasshopper and give their functions.	497-498	1	2
Objective G: Distinguish between incomplete and complete metamorphosis.	499-500	3,4	
Objective H: Explain how each internal system of insects contributes to homeostasis.	500-503	5,6,	7
Objective I: Identify several kinds of learned behavior in insects.	503	8	

Chapter 26, Section 2 *continued*	PAGES	RECALL QUESTIONS	THOUGHT QUESTIONS
Objective J: Describe the social organization of a honeybee colony.	503-506	9	
Objective K: Explain how communication occurs among honeybees.	506-507	10	11
Objective L: Describe several ways that insects affect humans.	507	12,13	
Objective M: Discuss the various methods of insect control giving advantages and disadvantages of each.	507-508	14	15

Chapter Review Questions: 1,2,3,4,5,6   **Chapter Test Questions:** 3,4,5,19,20,21,22,23,24

Laboratory: 26-3 The Grasshopper

Section 3: A Comparison Among Invertebrates and Plants *(For Average, Above Average Students)*	PAGES	RECALL QUESTIONS	THOUGHT QUESTIONS
Objective N: For each of the major groups of invertebrates, indicate the kind of body symmetry, number of embryonic cell layers, and the presence or absence of cephalization, segmentation, and a coelom.	509	1	
Objective O: Describe trends in each of the internal systems of the major invertebrate groups.	509-514	2	
Objective P: Compare invertebrate animals with plants in terms of food source, transport of water and nutrients, gaseous exchange, excretion, body movement, and body support.	514	3,4	
Objective Q: Show how the appendages of the crayfish illustrate the relationship between structure and function.		5	

Laboratory: 26-4 Comparing Invertebrate Phyla   **Chapter Test Questions:** 6,7,8,9,10,17,18,25

CHAPTER 27
FISHES AND AMPHIBIANS

Section 1: Bony Fishes *(For Basic, Average, Above Average Students)*	PAGES	RECALL QUESTIONS	THOUGHT QUESTIONS
Objective A: List the general characteristics of vertebrates and describe their general body plan.	519-521	1,2	

continued

Chapter 27, Section 1 _continued_	PAGES	RECALL QUESTIONS	THOUGHT QUESTIONS
Objective B: For a typical fish, describe the general body plan, and explain how continuity of life is maintained.	521-522	3,4	
Objective C: Describe the internal structure of a fish and interpret how its internal systems function to maintain homeostasis.	522-526	6	5
Objective D: Define _pattern of behavior_ and _adaptive behavior_ and give examples of each.	526-528	7,8	
Objective E: Give examples of ways that human activities affect fishes.	528	9	

Chapter Review Questions: 1,4,5,6

Laboratory: 27-1 Circulation and Respiration in Fish

Chapter Test Questions: 1,2,3,4,5,6,7,8,11,12,13,14 15,16,21,23,24

Section 2: Amphibians _(For Basic, Average, Above Average Students)_	PAGES	RECALL QUESTIONS	THOUGHT QUESTIONS
Objective F: For a typical amphibian, describe the general body plan. Explain how continuity of life is maintained.	530-533	1,2,3	
Objective G: Describe the internal structure of an amphibian. Interpret how its internal systems function to maintain homeostasis.	533-537	4	
Objective H: Explain how amphibians use hibernation and estivation to cope with changes in the environment.	537-538	5,6	
Objective I: Give examples of ways the human activities affect amphibians.	538	7	
Objective J: Summarize the characteristics of both fish and amphibians.	539	8	

Chapter Review Questions: 2,3,4,5,6,7,8

Laboratory: 27-2 The Frog as a Vertebrate and an Amphibian
27-3 The Internal Anatomy of the Frog

Chapter Test Questions: 9,10,17,18,19,20,22,25

REPTILES AND BIRDS

Section 1: Reptiles *(For Basic, Average, Above Average Students)*	PAGES	RECALL QUESTIONS	THOUGHT QUESTIONS
Objective A: For a typical reptile, describe the general body plan. Explain how continuity of life is maintained.	542-545	1,2	.
Objective B: Describe the internal structure of a reptile. Interpret how its internal systems function to maintain homeostasis.	545-548	3,5,6	4
Objective C: Summarize ways that reptiles cope with changes in their environment.	548	7	
Objective D: Interpret the effects of human actions on reptiles.	548	8	
Chapter Review Questions: 1,2,4,6	**Chapter Test Questions:** 2,3,11,12,15,21,23,24		
Laboratory: 28-1 Reptiles			

Section 2: Birds *(For Basic, Average, Above Average Students)*	PAGES	RECALL QUESTIONS	THOUGHT QUESTIONS
Objective E: For a typical bird, describe the general body plan. Explain how continuity of life is maintained.	550-551	1,2	3
Objective F: Describe the internal structure of a bird. Interpret how its internal systems function to maintain homeostasis.	552-555	4,5,6	
Objective G: Name examples of innate and learned behavior in birds.	555-556	7,8,9	
Objective H: Identify patterns of behavior and adaptive behavior in birds.	556-558	10,11	
Objective I: Summarize the ways birds cope with changes in their environment.	555-557		12
Objective J: Interpret the effect of human action on birds.	558	13	
Chapter Review Questions: 1,3,5	**Chapter Test Questions:** 1,4,5,6,7,8,9,10,13,14,16,17 18,19,20,22,23,24,25		

THE MAMMALS

Section 1: Mammals *(For Basic, Average, Above Average Students)*	PAGES	RECALL QUESTIONS	THOUGHT QUESTIONS
Objective A: Describe the major variations in the vertebrate body plan seen in mammals.	562-563	1,2,3	
Objective B: Identify examples of diversity among mammals.	563-564	4	5
Objective C: Interpret the role of the placenta in mammals.	565	6,7	8
Laboratory: 29-1 A Typical Mammal - The Fetal Pig	**Chapter Test Questions:** 1,2,3,4		

Section 2: Homeostasis *(For Basic, Average, Above Average Students)*	PAGES	RECALL QUESTIONS	THOUGHT QUESTIONS
Objective D: Explain how mammals obtain and use nutrients.	567-568	1,2,3	
Objective E: Describe how circulation, respiration, and excretion occur in mammals.	568-570	4,5	
Objective F: Explain how the nervous system and the endocrine system help maintain homeostasis in mammals.	570-572	6,7,8	
	Chapter Test Questions: 5,6,7,8,11,12,13,14,15		

Section 3: Behavior and Environment *(For Basic, Average, Above Average Students)*	PAGES	RECALL QUESTIONS	THOUGHT QUESTIONS
Objective G: Name examples of innate and learned behavior in mammals.	573-575	1	
Objective H: Identify patterns of behavior and adaptive behaviors in mammals.	575-576	2	3
Objective I: Explain how mammals cope with changes in environment.	576	4,5	
Chapter Review Questions: 1,2	**Chapter Test Questions:** 9,10,16,17,18,19,20		

Section 4: Comparisons Among Vertebrates and Invertebrates *(For Basic Average Above Average Students)*	PAGES	RECALL QUESTIONS	THOUGHT QUESTIONS
Objective J: Summarize important relationships among vertebrates.	577-581	1,2	

Chapter 29, Section 4 *continued*	PAGES	RECALL QUESTIONS	THOUGHT QUESTIONS
Objective K: Contrast vertebrates and invertebrates	581-584	3,4,	
Objective L: Compare humans to other vertebrates.	584	5	
Objective M: Summarize the characteristics of mammals.	585	6	
Laboratory: 29-2 How Different Animals Cope with the Problems of Survival	**Chapter Test Questions:** 21,22,23,24,25		

CHAPTER 30
DIGESTION AND NUTRITION

Section 1: The Digestive System and How Food Moves Through It *(For Basic, Average, Above Average Students)*	PAGES	RECALL QUESTIONS	THOUGHT QUESTIONS
Objective A: List the organs of the digestive tract from mouth to anus. Tell how the structure and function of each organ are related.	589-593	1,2,4,5	3
Objective B: Describe the structure and function of the liver, gall bladder, and pancreas. Explain how each is related to the digestive tract.	592	6	
Objective C: Explain how food is moved through the digestive tract.	591-593	7	8
Chapter Test Questions: 1,2,3,21			

Section 2: What Happens To Food As It Is Digested *(For Basic, Average, Above Average Students)*	PAGES	RECALL QUESTIONS	THOUGHT QUESTIONS
Objective D: Explain the main steps in digestion that takes place in the mouth cavity, the stomach, and the small intestine.	595-598	1,2,3,4,5	
Objective E: Explain where and how absorption occurs.	598	6,7	
Chapter Test Questions: 4,11,12,13,14,15			

Section 3: What is a Nutritious Diet? *(For Basic, Average, Above Average Students)*	PAGES	RECALL QUESTIONS	THOUGHT QUESTIONS
Objective F: Explain why you need carbohydrate, fat and protein in your diet.	599-600	1,2,3	

continued

Chapter 30, Section 3 *continued*	PAGES	RECALL QUESTIONS	THOUGHT QUESTIONS
Objective G: Discuss the body's need for water each day.	600-602	4	
Objective H: Define the terms *vitamin* and *mineral*. Describe why these materials are needed for one's health.	602-603	5	6
Objective I: Name some vitamin deficienvy diseases.	602	7	

Chapter Review Questions: 3,4,5   **Chapter Test Questions:** 5,16,17,18,19,20

Laboratory: 30-1 Analysis of Foods
30-2 Vitamins and Minerals

Section 4: **Planning Your Diet** (For Basic, Average, Above Average students)	PAGES	RECALL QUESTIONS	THOUGHT QUESTIONS
Objective J: List the basic four food groups. Illustrate how eating food from each of the groups helps to meet your nutritional needs.	604-605		1
Objective K: Contrast the U.S. dietary goals with basic four requirements and determine whether your diet meets these goals.	605-606	3	2
Objective L: Demonstrate how you can use vegetable proteins to obtain a nutritious diet at a low level on the food chain.	606-607	4	5,6
Objective M: Interpret the effects of junk foods, food additives, alcohol, and drugs on nutrition.	607-608	7,8	9

Chapter Review Questions: 1,2,3,4,5,6   **Chapter Test Questions:** 6,7,8,9,10,22,23,24,25

Laboratory: 30-3 Planning Your Diet

CHAPTER 31

TRANSPORT, RESPIRATION, AND EXCRETION

Section 1: **Blood** (For Basic, Average, Above Average Students)	PAGES	RECALL QUESTIONS	THOUGHT QUESTIONS
Objective A: Describe the components of blood Explain the role of each in transport.	612-614	1,2,3	
Objective B: Distinguish between several different blood types. Explain why different types cannot be mixed.	614-616	4,5	

Chapter 31, Section 1 *continued*	PAGES	RECALL QUESTIONS	THOUGHT QUESTIONS
Objective C: Arrange the steps in the blood clotting mechanism in proper sequence.	615-616	6	

Chapter Review Questions: 1   **Chapter Test Questions:** 1,2,3,4,21

Laboratory: 31-1 Some Components of Blood

Section 2: Circulation *(For Basic, Average, Above Average Students)*	PAGES	RECALL QUESTIONS	THOUGHT QUESTIONS
Objective D: Describe the circulation of blood through the heart. Interpret the roles of *systole, diastole,* and the *pacemaker.*	618-620	1,2,3,4	
Objective E: Compare the structure and function of *arteries, veins,* and *capillaries.*	620-621	5,6	7
Objective F: Distinguish among the following circulatory pathways: *pulmonary, systemic, coronary,* and *portal.*	621-623	8,9,10	
Objective G: Interpret the role of blood pressure in circulation.	623-624	11	
Objective H: Contrast the lymphatic system with the blood circulatory system.	618-624		12

Laboratory: 31-2 Circulation of Blood   **Chapter Test Questions:** 5,6,7,8,11,12,13,14,15,19,22,25

Section 3: Respiration *(For Basic, Average, Above Average Students)*	PAGES	RECALL QUESTIONS	THOUGHT QUESTIONS
Objective I: Distinguish among external respiration, internal respiration, and breathing.	625-627	1,2	
Objective J: Describe the pathway of air from the atmosphere to the alveoli.	625-626	3,4	
Objective K: Contrast the exchange of gases in the lungs and in other tissues.	626	5	
Objective L: Describe what happens during breathing. Explain how it is controlled.	627-628	6	

Chapter Review Questions: 2,3   **Chapter Test Questions:** 9,17,20,23

Laboratory: 31-3 Respiration in Human Beings

continued

Section 4: Excretion (For Average, Above Average Students)	PAGES	RECALL QUESTIONS	THOUGHT QUESTIONS
Objective M: Describe the structure of the excretory system.	629	1	
Objective N: Summarize the movement of substances between the blood and the kidney filtrate.	630	2,3	
Objective O: Interpret the role of transport, respiration, and excretion in homeostasis.	612-631		4
Chapter Test Questions: 10,16,18,24			

CHAPTER 32
SENSORY PERCEPTION AND NERVOUS CONTROL

Section 1: How Our Sense Organs Tell Us Things (For Basic, Average, Above Average Students)	PAGES	RECALL QUESTIONS	THOUGHT QUESTIONS
Objective A: List the general properties of sense organs.	634	1,2	3
Objective B: Explain how the eye functions in seeing black-and-white and colored objects.	636	4,5	6
Objective C: Explain how the ear functions in hearing and balance.	637-639	7,8,9,10	
Objective D: Compare the sense of taste and smell.	639-640	11	12
Chapter Review Questions: 1,2,3,12	**Chapter Test Questions:** 1,2,3,4,11,12,13,14,15		
Laboratory: 32-1 Sensory Perception			

Section 2: The Nervous System (For Average, Above Average Students)	PAGES	RECALL QUESTIONS	THOUGHT QUESTIONS
Objective E: Describe the general plan of the nervous system.	642	1,2	
Objective F: Explain what happens in a reflex arc.	642-643	3	4
Objective G: Identify the steps in the transmission of a nerve impulse (a) along a neuron and (b) across a synapse.	643-644	5,6,7,8	
Objective H: Summarize the functions of the autonomic nervous system.	644-646	9,10	
Chapter Review Questions: 4,5,6,7,8,9,10,11	**Chapter Test Questions:** 6,17,18,19,20,21,22,23		
Laboratory: 32-2 Reflexes and Reaction Time			

Section 3: The Brain is the Central Control Unit (For Average, Above Average Students)	PAGES	RECALL QUESTIONS	THOUGHT QUESTIONS
Objective I: List the main structures of the brain and identify their functions.	647-648	1,2	3
Objective J: Describe how the brain interprets and responds to stimuli.	649	4,5,6	
Objective K: Summarize the theories about learning and memory.	650-651	7	
Objective L: Distinguish between sleep and wakefulness.	651-652	8,9	
	Chapter Test Questions: 5,7,8,9,10,16,24,25		

CHAPTER 33
PROTECTION AND MOVEMENT

Section 1: Skin—What's Between You and the World (For Basic, Average, Above Average Students)	PAGES	RECALL QUESTIONS	THOUGHT QUESTIONS
Objective A: Describe the structure and list the functions of the skin.	656-658	1,2,3	
Objective B: List some characteristics of hair, nails, oil glands, and sweat glands.	657	4,5	6
Chapter Review Questions: 1,5,7,8	**Chapter Test Questions:** 1,2,11,12,14,15		

Section 2: Bones and Joints—The Body's Framework (For Basic, Average, Above Average Students)	PAGES	RECALL QUESTIONS	THOUGHT QUESTIONS
Objective C: Distinguish among the axial and appendicular skeleton and list the functions of the skeleton.	660	1,2	
Objective D: Describe the structure of the bone and explain how bone develop and how fractures heal.	660-663	3,4	
Objective E: Define *joint* and name three kinds of joints and three kinds of joint injuries.	663-664	5	6
Chapter Review Questions: 2,5,6,7,8	**Chapter Test Questions:** 3,4,5,13,21,22		

Section 3: Muscles, Movement, and Exercise (For Basic, Average, Above Average Students)	PAGES	RECALL QUESTIONS	THOUGHT QUESTIONS
Objective F: Distinguish among three kinds of muscle tissue.	665	1	

continued

Chapter 33, Section 3 *continued*	PAGES	RECALL QUESTIONS	THOUGHT QUESTIONS
Objective G: Summarize the processes of (a) excitation of muscles, (b) contraction of muscles, and (c) relaxation of muscles.	665-666	2,3	
Objective H: Explain how whole muscles cause movement and maintain muscle tone.	666-668	4,5	
Objective I: Demonstrate the importance of good posture and exercise.	668-669	6,7	

Chapter Review Questions: 3,4,5,7,8,9

Laboratory: 33-1 Movement

Chapter Test Questions: 6,7,8,9,10,16,17,18,19,20, 23,24,25

Suggested Study Skills: SM-9 Use of Models to Explain Hypotheses I

CHAPTER 34
INTERNAL REGULATION

Section 1: The Endocrine System (For Average, Above Average Students)	PAGES	RECALL QUESTIONS	THOUGHT QUESTIONS
Objective A: Define: *hormone, endocrine gland, target organ, prostaglandin,* and *cyclic AMP.*	673-674	1	2
Objective B: Identify the hormones of the pituitary gland and describe their function.	674-675	3,4,5,6	

Chapter Review Questions: 7,12

Laboratory: 34-1 Circadian Rhythms

Chapter Test Questions: 1,2,3,11,12,15

Section 2: Other Endocrine Glands and Their Hormones (For Average, Above Average Students)	PAGES	RECALL QUESTIONS	THOUGHT QUESTIONS
Objective C: For each of the following glands, give their location, name the hormone(s) they produce, and describe the function of each hormone: (a) thyroid, (b) parathyroid, (c) adrenal, (d) pancreas, and (e) thymus.	678-681	1,2,3	4

Chapter Review Questions: 1,9,12

Chapter Test Questions: 4,5,7,13,14,16,17,18,19,20,24

Section 3: Immunity *(For Average, Above Average Students)*	PAGES	RECALL QUESTIONS	THOUGHT QUESTIONS
Objective D: Define: *Immunity, antigen, antibody, T-cell,* and *B-cell.*	683	2,3	1
Objective E: Explain how your body develops immunity to disease.	683-686	4,5,6,7,8	
Objective F: Interpret the role of the immune system in cancer, allergy, and organ transplatation.	686-688	9	
Chapter Review Questions: 2,3,4,5,6,10,12 **Laboratory:** 34-2 Immunity	**Chapter Test Questions:** 6,8,9,21,22,25		

Section 4: Stress *(For Average, Above Average Students)*	PAGES	RECALL QUESTIONS	THOUGHT QUESTIONS
Objective G: Define *stress* and describe the roles of the endocrine and nervous systems in responding to it.	689	1,2	
Chapter Review Questions: 8,11,12	**Chapter Test Questions:** 10,23 **Suggested Study Skills:** SM-10 Use of Models to Explain Hypotheses II		

CHAPTER 35
REPRODUCTION AND DEVELOPMENT

Section 1: The Basis of Sex *(For Basic, Average, Above Average Students)*	PAGES	RECALL QUESTIONS	THOUGHT QUESTIONS
Objective A: Define the following terms in your own words: *sexual dimorphism, puberty, pair-bond.*	693-694	1	2
Objective B: Describe the role of behavior and selection in the production of sexual dimorphism.	693-694	3,4	
	Chapter Test Questions: 4,25		

Section 2: Reproduction in Humans *(For Basic, Average Above Average Students)*	PAGES	RECALL QUESTIONS	THOUGHT QUESTIONS
Objective C: Define and give the functions of each structure and hormone involved in the male and female reproductive system.	696	1	
Objective D: State the functions of the male and female reproductive systems.	696	2,3	

Chapter 35, Section 2 _continued_	PAGES	RECALL QUESTIONS	THOUGHT QUESTIONS
Objective E: Describe the path of an egg following ovulation (a) in fertilization does not occur, and (b) if fertilization does occur.	698-700	4	5
Objective F: Describe the concept of the feedback system as it operates in the female menstrual cycle.	698-699	6	
Chapter Review Questions: 1		**Chapter Test Questions:** 1,2,3,5,11,13,14,15,16,23	

Section 3: Development in Humans _(For Basic, Average, Above Average students)_	PAGES	RECALL QUESTIONS	THOUGHT QUESTIONS
Objective G: Trace the development of a human from fertilization to eight weeks.	701-706	1	
Objective H: Describe the process of cleavage and the formation of the three basic cell layers including the structures each will form.	702-704	2,3,4	
Objective I: Describe a classic series of experiments that demonstrated the phenomenon of embryonic induction.	704-705	5	
Objective J: Describe the changes in the fetal circulatory pattern that occurs at birth.	706	6	7
Objective K: Explain how meiosis and fertilization brings about both unity and diversity in humans.		8	
Chapter Review Questions: 2,3 **Laboratory:** 35-1 Chick Embryo 35-2 Fetus and Placenta		**Chapter Test Questions:** 6,7,8,9,10,12,17,18,19, 20,21,22,24	

OVERVIEW OF UNITS

OVERVIEW OF UNIT 1
THE WORLD OF LIVING THINGS

Unit 1 approaches the study of living things from surroundings familiar to the student. It gives students an opportunity to ease into the study of biology proceeding from their familiar physical surroundings to the less familiar biological relationships. Interwoven into this unit are the methods used for scientific study. Starting with observations, the student builds skills in listing observations, interpreting photos of living things, using the microscope, collecting, and interpreting data.

Finally, in coordinating these skills the students are asked to propose an hypothesis and devise an experiment to test it in Chapter Investigation 3. For explicit instructions in skills see the *Laboratory Manual* Skills Section. The basic skills for the program start in this unit.

CHAPTER 1   THE ENVIRONMENT

Introduction: As a class, or in small groups, observe a small area that shows some evidence of life. It may be a potted plant, a weed patch, a terrarium, the bank of a stream or pond, an aquarium, or a garden. Invite students to describe the physical conditions that might affect the survival of living creatures in the area. Students may think of air (oxygen), sunlight, moderate temperature, protection from harmful radiations, water, and minerals.

The first laboratory investigation on the use of a microscope is important for all biology students. That skill is necessary to do the yeast population study in Chapter 2.

Answers to Chapter 1 Investigation:

A. Students may notice many differences such as means of locomotion (swimming, crawling, digging, walking), ways of getting food, and body form.

B. Various organisms are suited to their environment by their means of locomotion, water retention, heat, and light tolerance.

C. Water and soil organisms might dry out on the desert surface. Desert and forest creatures might be unable to get enough oxygen or capture prey from the water.

Answers to Chapter 1 Review:

1. Answers may include such facts as proper temperature, proper pressure, and appropriate amount of food, water, and oxygen.

2. Answers will vary but may include the following. Exploitation has already occurred in certain ocean areas and has drastically altered ecosystems and greatly reduced productivity. For example, overfishing and pollution have diminished shellfish supplies close to populated land areas.

References and Readings:

Teacher
Richardson, J.L. 1977. *Dimensions of ecology.* Baltimore, MD: The Williams and Wilkins Co.
Scientific American 1970. *The biosphere.* San Francisco, CA: W.H. Freeman and Co.
Whittaker, R.H. 1975. *Communities and ecosystems,* 2nd ed. New York: Macmillan Publishing Company, Inc.

Student
McGraw-Hill Book Company. *Our living world nature series.* New York. 1967.
Olliver, J., ed. 1977. *The living world.* New York: Warwick Press.

CHAPTER 2   INTERRELATIONSHIPS IN THE ENVIRONMENT

Introduction: One way to begin this topic is to have students observe a small ecosystem, such as an aquarium, park, lawn, weed patch, stream, meadow, or terrarium. Have them list ways in which various components of the ecosystem affect and are affected by other components. Have students organize the relationships in a way that seems meaningful to them.

Answers to Chapter 2 Investigation:

A. The tick is a parasite on the dog. Ticks parasitize all vertebrates except fish.

B. For food, ticks suck bloods from vessels in the dog's skin. They also mate on the host's body surface. The dog receives no known benefit from the relationship.

C. The tick's leathery skin allows stretching as it fills with the blood of its host. Adults may increase their diameter more than four times during a feeding. They are "cold-blooded" and can exist for a long time after becoming engorged with blood. Adult ticks have survived more than two years without food while waiting for a host. The females of some species of ticks secrete a paralyzing toxin. Their saliva may also contain the rickettsia that produce Rocky Mountain spotted fever, the bacteria that cause tularemia, and the bacteria that cause relapsing fever.

Answers to Chapter 2 Review:

1. The following experiment would indicate that nutrient requirement is a factor involved in succession in a pond community.

   Procedure:

   (a) Anchor sponges in a pond with a rock and a string.

   (b) After one week, remove the sponges, squeeze the water from them, and examine samples of the water under a microscope. Record results.

   (c) After two weeks, examine samples. Record results.

   Analysis:

   (a) Algae pioneer the colonization of the sponges because algal spores can float through water, have sticky gelatinous coats, and produce their own food through photosynthesis (producers).

   (b) With increased time the algae do not dominate because they change the nutritional environment allowing other organisms such as protozoans (consumers) to colonize.

2. Answers will vary but may include the following argument. At present, it has been estimated, extinction is proceeding at a far more rapid rate than ever before in evolutionary history, owing partly to human predation but mostly to the wholesale destruction of natural habitats. Conservationists try to indicate the value of these endangered resources, pointing out, for example, that seemingly worthless plants have been proven to contain chemicals with medicinal uses. Most endangered species have no monetary value. Nor has it been proven that the "web of life" will be threatened by their disappearance. It is only known that a species takes a very long time to evolve, and once it is gone, it is gone forever.

3. Answers will vary. Fuel and power companies as well as federal agencies like the Department of Agriculture would probably employ ecologists.

4. Answers will vary. The following example will indicate why a physician would want to know about ecology. Strontium-90 was a radioactive element produced by nuclear testing in the 1950's. It is closely related to calcium and can take its place in many biochemical reactions. In dairy lands, strontium-90 made its way through grasses into dairy cows and into milk; from there it became concentrated in the bones and teeth of children in North America and Europe. Increased amounts of this radioactivity were detected and could possibly account for the increases in leukemia, bone cancers, and reduction of life span in these children.

References and Readings:

Teacher

Brewer, R. 1979. *Principles of ecology.* Philadelphia, PA: W.B. Saunders Co.

Odum, E.P. 1971. *Fundamentals of ecology,* 3rd ed. Philadelphia, PA: W.B. Saunders Co.

Whittaker, R.H. 1975. *Communities and ecosystems,* 2nd ed. New York: Macmillan Publishing Company, Inc.

Student

Alexander, T.R. and G.S. Fichter 1973. *Ecology.* Golden Guide Series. New York: Western Publishing Co.

CHAPTER 3   ENERGY IN THE ENVIRONMENT

Introduction: Methods of scientific study are introduced here so that they can be used during the remainder of the course. You may wish to use additional illustrations even if they do not involve energy.

Early in the section on energy the laboratory investigation, "Energy in a Peanut," may be used to help students understand the concept of the calorie. Without that basic understanding, much of the chapter would have less meaning.

The concepts of energy, productivity, and energy "loss" in each step of the food chain require careful explanation. Once the basic ideas are understood, there are opportunities to include ethical questions, such as the feeding of grain to livestock while millions of people are hungry.

Answers to Chapter 3 Investigation:

A. We know that a peanut seed contains energy because it gives off heat energy and light energy when it burns.

B. The peanut seed obtained its energy from sunlight through photosynthesis.

C. If a food calorimeter is not available, estimates can be made with a homemade calorimeter. A physics teacher might help design the instrument. One simple method may be to remove one end of a soft drink can with a can opener. With a pair of tin snips, cut a hole in the center of the other end of the can. (CAUTION: Watch out for the sharp edges of the can.) With a hammer and nail, punch a series of air holes around the cut out center. Place a heat resistant test tube, containing a measured amount of water, into the hole. Position the open end of the complete apparatus over the object to be burned. A cork with a secured straight pin may be used to hold the piece of food in place. The leaves, stems, and roots should be thoroughly dried in an oven or plant press before burning. A plant other than peanut may be substituted if it has a seed that burns easily.

Answers to Chapter 3 Review:

1. The fraction of cultural energy expended by farmers due to human labor is least in an Illinois corn field of 1970 because such high yield agriculture borrows from the productivity of ecosystems of the past. Energy, and much of

the raw materials for fertilizers and pesticides originate in coal, petroleum, and natural gas. However, in primitive socities, human labor supplies most of the cultural energy.

2. Technology produces convenience and high yields per labor-hour.

References and Readings:

Teacher
Gates, D.M. 1971. The flow of energy in the biosphere. *Scientific American* 225 (3):88.

Kormondy, E.J. 1976. *Concepts of ecology,* 2nd ed. Englewood Cliffs, NJ: Prentice Hall.

Pimentel, D., et al. 1976. Energy in food production. *The American Biology Teacher* 38:402.

Rappaport, R.A. 1971. The flow of energy in an agricultural society. *Scientific American* 225 (3):116.

Woodwell, G.M. 1970. The energy cycle of the biosphere. *Scientific American* 223 (3):69

Student
Baker, J.J.W., and G.E. Allen 1974. *Matter, energy, and life: an introduction for biology students,* 3rd ed. Reading, MA: Addison-Wesley.

Gabriel, M.L., and S. Fogel 1955. *Great experiments in biology.* Englewood Cliffs, NJ: Prentice Hall.

CHAPTER 4   BALANCES AND IMBALANCES

Introduction: With an understanding of basic ecologic interrelationships, students are invited to assess the human impact on this planet. It is easy for any generation to take its standard of living for granted and to believe that technology will solve our environmental problems. At the other extreme, it is possible to be overcome with hopelessness. Such pessimism can be self-defeating. It may now be the teacher's role to suggest a search for alternatives to increasing human populations and to high-consumption, high-pollution lifestyles. Students may want to become active participants in efforts to preserve a natural area, recycle paper and other "wastes," monitor pesticide use, or encourage responsible diets.

Answers to Chapter 4 Investigation:

A. The rabbits are drinking from the pool probably because the plants have been eaten by the many rabbits.

B. The rabbits had no important predators in Australia. So the rabbits' death rate was lower than their birth rate. A female can breed at four months and can average six litters of six young per litter.

C. Control methods attempted unsuccessfully were trapping, shooting, netting, poisoning, fumigation of burrows, and fencing. In 1950, the rabbits were deliberately infected with myxoma virus from Brazil. The resulting epidemic killed as much as 99 percent of the rabbit population. The virus, spread by mosquitoes, affected only rabbits. The virus appears to be controlling the rabbit population at tolerable levels.

Answers to Chapter 4 Review:

1. Answers will vary. The overkilling of whales by humans might be one area of exploration.

2. Answers will vary, but students may mention that scientific experts should be consulted, although the decisions themselves would no doubt have to be made by governments. Informed citizens should be the ultimate decision-makers, since they elect government.

3. Answers will vary, but may include references to individual freedom versus bureaucratic management. Opinions will vary as to whether federal ownership protects or infringes on state, local, or individual rights.

4. Insects live in almost every conceivable type of environment. Their wide distribution is probably a result of their small size and relative indestructibility which enables them to fly, or to be carried by air and water currents. Their extraordinary adaptability enables them to remain in these new habitats. Their resistant eggs may be carried by birds and other animals into new regions.

5. Answers will vary, but may include the following example. A farmer is a person who manages or operates a farm. In today's world of agricultural technology and procedures, a person interested in this vocation most probably would attend a college of agriculture.

References and Readings:

Teacher
Ehrlich, P.R., A.H. Ehrlich and J.P. Holdren 1977. *Ecoscience: population, resources, and environment.* San Francisco, CA: W.H. Freeman.

Foin, T.C. 1976. *Ecological systems and the environment.* Boston, MA: Houghton Mifflin.

Harlan, J.R. 1976. The plants and animals that nourish man. *Scientific American* 235 (3):88 (September).

Jackson, W. 1979. *Man and the environment.* Dubuque, IA: Wm. C. Brown Company.

Schmacher, E.F. 1975. *Small is beautiful: economics as if people mattered.* New York: Harper and Row.

Wagner, R.H. 1978. *Environment and man,* 3rd ed. New York: W.W. Norton and Co.

World population growth and response 1965-1975. Washington, D.C.: Population Reference Bureau, Inc.

Student

Blaustein, E.H. 1977. *Antipollution projects*, rev. ed. New York: Arco Publishing Co.

Commoner, B. 1972. *The closing circle: nature, man, and technology*. New York: Bantam.

Edwards, R.W. 1972. Pollution, *Oxford/Carolina Biology Reader*. Burlington, NC: Carolina Biological Supply Co.

Horwood, R.H. 1973. *Inquiry into environmental pollution*. Toronto, Canada: Macmillan Publishing Co., Inc.

Turk, A., et al. 1978. *Environmental Science*. Philadelphia, PA: W.B. Saunders Co.

van den Bosch, R., and P.S. Mesenger 1973. *Biological Control*. New York: Intext Educational Publishers.

Wilson, E.O., and W.H. Bossert 1971. *A primer of population biology*. Sunderland, MA: Sinauer Associates.

OVERVIEW OF UNIT 2
UNITY OF ALL LIVING THINGS

In this unit we move from a broad view of living things in their environment to a more specialized view of the chemical and cellular levels of life. Students will never have seen atoms, and unless they have had access to a microscope they will not have seen cells. Stress to students that the knowledge of chemistry they will gain in this unit is necessary for understanding processes that go on in all living things.

The building of skills continues in this unit as students learn to devise experiments, report results and draw conclusions, make biology drawings, correctly read photographs and art work, and build their science vocabulary. Students will learn to perform certain chemical tests in the laboratory and will further develop skills in using a microscope.

Specific activities are described in the *Laboratory Manual*.

CHAPTER 5   CHEMISTRY OF LIVING THINGS

Introduction: Many students fear the study of chemistry or complain that chemistry is not relevant to anything else they want to know or do. Try to emphasize that living things are made up of chemicals, and help students to see the need for understanding basic chemistry as a part of understanding living things.

DEMONSTRATION: You may want to perform the following demonstration to illustrate the difference between a chemical mixture and a living system.

Materials: 2 test tubes, water, 2 g glucose, a few grains of dry yeast, an indicator such as phenol red that changes color from neutral to acid.

Time: 5 minutes to set up, standing time—1 hour to 1 day, a few minutes to observe.

Procedure: Fill each of two test tubes half full of water. Add 1 g glucose and 1 drop of indicator to each. To one tube add a few grains of dry yeast. Watch for bubbles in the water and for change in the color of the indicator.

Possible questions: What is different about the two tubes? What caused the bubbles? What caused the color change? What are some differences between a living system and a chemical mixture?

Answers to Chapter 5 Investigation:

A. Part A can be used to stimulate discussion. Obviously, the substance is water, and living things would die without water. Ask students to suggest changes that occur when living things are deprived of water.

B. The properties of water are listed on pages 85-86.

C. If students are designing experiments to demonstrate properties of water, be sure to approve only those experiments that are safe and that involve no harm to animals that can feel pain.

Students might point out that water in (a) is fresh, while water in (b) is salt water. They should be able to apply the concept of osmosis to explain what happens to water moving into or out of the body of an organism. (See Chapter 23 for an explanation of water movement in trees.) Encourage students to question this and other investigations by using library materials. If humans drink salt water, much of the salt will be excreted by the kidneys. If more salt is present than the kidneys can remove, it will accumulate in the spaces between cells and cause the body to accumulate water. Extremely large quantities of salt can lead to dehydration of cells while they are surrounded by salty water. Safe drinking water is more a matter of sanitation than salt content. Checking for the presence of pathogenic organisms and pollutants are two factors in determining whether water is safe to drink.

Answers to Chapter 5 Review:

1. Anwers will vary. Benefits: use of antibiotics to combat infections, of fertilizers to increase crop production, of pesticides to control loss of crops, and tranquilizers to relive anxiety and stress. Harmful effects: antibiotics have paradoxically been known to favor the development of deadly strains of bacteria resistant to the antibiotics, fertilizers and pesticides to damage wildlife and humans through environmental pollution, and tranquilizers to drug addiction.

References and Readings:

Teacher
Baum, S.J., and C.W. Scaife 1975. *Chemistry: a life*

science approach. New York: Macmillan Publishing Co., Inc.

Diener, T.O. 1979. Viroids: structure and function. *Science* 205:859 (August 31).

Student

Arehart-Treichel, J. 1979. Chemical carcinogens: part of the problem. *Science News* 115:411 (June 23).

Kormondy, E.J., et al. 1977. *Biology.* Belmont, CA: Wadsworth Publishing Co.

Ray, K.L. 1979. Flexible proteins. *SciQuest* (formerly *Chemistry*) 52(6):27 (July-August).

Watson, J.D. 1968. *The double helix.* New York: Atheneum.

CHAPTER 6   THE CELL

Introduction: Students will have varying degrees of familiarity with cells, depending on previous experiences. Some may still have difficulty using a microscope; others will be proficient at it. Students who quickly finish laboratory activities might do library research on the function of a particular organelle.

The concept of homeostasis should be emphasized. All of the organelles of a cell and all of the processes by which materials move across cell membranes contribute in some way to homeostasis. What students learn about cells applies to all living things.

DEMONSTRATION: You might want to actually slice a hard-boiled egg as shown in figure 6-3 (p. 102).

Materials: hard-boiled egg, knife

Time: only a few minutes

Procedure: Ask students to imagine that they are looking down on the pointed end of the egg through a large microscope and to tell you what they would expect to see if the microscope were focused on different planes through the egg. Then make a slice through the egg to check their predictions.

Possible questions: How is the demonstration related to looking at a small cell through a microscope? What is meant by focal plane?

Answers to Chapter 6 Investigation:

A. The plants wilted, and water must have been drawn out of the cells.

B. The concentration of salt was greater outside the cells than inside the cells. Water moved out of the cells by osmosis.

C. If the concentration of salt outside a cell is greater than inside the cell, water will move out of the cell by osmosis. Students interested in performing experiments to extend the Chapter Investigation might be encouraged to use slices of potatoes, which they weigh before and after the experiment. Fertilizer might be used in excess instead of

salt, but more time would be required to observe effects. Check all experiments for safety before allowing students to proceed.

Answers to Chapter 6 Review:

1. Answers will vary but may include the following experiment.

Effects of Diffusion—A Cell Membrane Model

Materials: Small plastic bag, rubber bands, 100 ml beaker, test tubes—2, starch solution, iodine solution, graduated cylinder, glass marking pencil (wax).

Procedure:

(a) Fill a plastic lunch bag with 40 ml of starch solution. Seal top of bag by twisting the bag and attaching a rubber band. The plastic bag filled with starch solution represents a cell.

(b) Note and record the exact color of the starch inside the plastic bag cell.

(c) Fill a beaker with 20 ml of water. Add 20 ml of iodine solution to the water. The water and iodine solution represents the environment into which you will place your plastic bag cell.

(d) Pour off 5 ml of the water-iodine solution into a test tube. Label the tube "before."

(e) Place the bag into the beaker of water-iodine solution. Allow the "cell" to stand overnight.

(f) Also stand the test tube inside the beaker.

(g) Label your beaker with the glass marking pencil.

(h) The next day, remove the plastic bag and test tube and put them aside. Pour 5 ml of the liquid in the beaker into a test tube and label this tube "after." Decide which tube, before or after, is the darker and lighter of the two. Record your answer.

(i) Record the color of the starch inside the "cell."

Color Changes

	Before	After *(next day)*
color of starch inside bag (cell)	white	blue
color of iodine outside bag (cell)	dark rust	light rust

Results: These should indicate that iodine diffuses into the bag causing: (a) external solution to become lighter; (b) starch solution to turn blue.

2. Too much fertilization creates a hypertonic environment. In such a situation, water is pulled out of the plant cells. This gives the plants a dried or "burned" look.

References and Readings:

Teacher

Lodish, H.G., and J.E. Rothman 1979. The assembly of cell membranes. *Scientific American* 240 (1):48 (January).

Wolfe, S.L. 1977. *Biology: the foundations.* Belmont, CA: Wadsworth Publishing Co.

Student

Miller, J.A. 1979. New window on biochemistry. *Science News* 115:378 (June 9).

Pines, M. 1978. *Inside the cell.* Washington: Department of Health, Education, and Welfare, The National Institute of General Medical Sciences (DHEW Publication No. NIH 78-1051).

Thomas, L. 1974. *Lives of a cell.* New York: Viking Press.

CHAPTER 7   ENERGY RELATIONSHIPS IN THE CELL

Introduction: As with Chapter 5, Chapter 7 contains a significant amount of chemistry. Students may think they cannot understand it before they have tried to follow the ideas. Though we have omitted many details and emphasized overall results of metabolic reactions, slow students may have difficulty. It may be sufficient for these students to consider photosynthesis and respiration as opposite processes: one captures energy and the other allows cells to use the energy.

DEMONSTRATION: You may want to demonstrate the effects of an enzyme by preparing two cups of gelatin, one with fresh pineapple and the other without. Alternatively, you could add meat tenderizer to a small piece of ground meat in a test tube.

Materials: 1 envelope unflavored gelatin, (2) 500 ml beakers, 50 g fresh pineapple, 400 ml water, refrigerator.

Time: 5 minutes to prepare, several hours for gelatin to set.

Procedure: Dissolve gelatin in 50 ml of cold water. Add dissolved gelatin to 200 ml of hot water and stir. Add 150 ml cold water. Divide gelatin mixture into two containers and add pineapple to one container. Refrigerate both containers for several hours and observe.

Possible questions: How are the two mixtures different? Why did the gelatin with the fresh pineapple not set? (Fresh pineapple contains a proteolytic enzyme that digests gelatin.)

DEMONSTRATION:

Materials: 2 test tubes, 2 g ground meat, water, meat tenderizer.

Time: 5 minutes to prepare, 30 minutes for enzyme to act.

Procedure: Place 1 g ground meat and 5 ml of water in each test tube. Add meat tenderizer (cover surface of water) to one tube and mix thoroughly. Let stand at room temperature for at least 30 minutes and observe.

Possible questions: How do the two mixtures differ? What did the tenderizer do to the meat? (Tenderizer contains a proteolytic enzyme that digests the meat.)

Answers to Chapter 7 Investigation:

A. The flasks with plant material have a blue solution. The flasks without plant material contain a yellow fluid. The plant must do something to change the fluid.

B. The fluid in A and C is acidic. The fluid in B and D is alkaline. (If you wish to have students set up this experiment, the indicator, bromthymol blue, will give the intended results.) The plant uses CO_2 from the fluid and causes the fluid to become alkaline. The animal exhales CO_2 into the solution and it becomes acidic.

C. Photosynthesis and respiration are taking place in flask B. Photosynthesis would stop if the flask were placed in the dark. Respiration would continue and the water would become acidic. In light, more photosynthesis than respiration occurs and so CO_2 does not accumulate. Only respiration is occurring in flask C. In flask D, both the plant and the fish are carrying on respiration; the plant is carrying on photosynthesis. The interaction in flask D is that the plant is using CO_2 from its own respiration and the fish's respiration to carry on photosynthesis. This can be determined by comparing the results in flasks C and D. The plant in either B or D would live longer than the fish in either C or D. The fish in D would live longer than the fish in B because the plant provides oxygen for the fish. If the plant is the only food available to the fish in D, it would die when it has eaten the plant; thus life would be present longest in flask B.

Answers to Chapter 7 Review:

1. The lead in the paint chips permanently deactivates some of the enzymes, especially those containing cysteine, in the child's body.

2. Experiments will vary, but should include mixing saliva in a starchy food and showing that some starch has been broken down. (Iodine or sweet taste could be used as tests.)

3. Plants add oxygen to the atmosphere.

4. Experiments will vary but should show the accumulation of CO_2 gas. A closed container might lead to an explosion due to pressure of the accumulating CO_2 gas.

5. Answers will vary. They may include suggestions of harvesting ocean plant life and feeding it to animals that in

turn would be used for human food, as well as research to find ways to use the plant life directly for human use.

6. Much energy is lost each time it is transferred from one organism, such as the producer plant source, to the next, such as the primary consumer animal in a food chain.

References and Readings:

Teacher
Wilson, E.O., et al. 1978. *Life on earth.* Sunderland, MA: Sinauer Associates, Inc.

Student
Calvin, M. 1979. Fuel from plants. *SciQuest* 52(6):16 (July-August).

Lappe, F.M. 1971. *Diet for a small planet.* New York: Ballantine Books, Inc.

CHAPTER 8   ACTIVITIES OF LIVING CELLS

Introduction: Now that the students are aware of the ways that cells obtain energy, they are ready to look at what cells do with their energy. The slower students may have difficulty with the section on protein synthesis. Our analogy of the master audio tape for making new tapes may be useful in helping them to grasp the main idea.

The topics of cancer, aging, and death are discussed briefly in this chapter. Some students may be interested in investigating one of these topics in more detail. A library research paper would be an appropriate assignment for some of the better students. See study skill CD 7, "Preparing a Library Research Paper," in the *Laboratory Manual.*

DEMONSTRATION: Before beginning the section on cell division, you may want the students to enact the division of the nucleus.

Materials: 12 students and a large circulr area in the middle of the classroom.

Time: about 10 minutes

Procedure: Ask six students to step into the circular area. They represent the six (three pairs) of chromosomes of a particular cell. Each student asks another student to join him or her. This represents the replication of the chromosome. The chromosomes and their replicates join by holding each other's hands in a bridge-like formation. When they are scattered around the cell, they represent prophase. The chromosomes and their replicates now remain together and line up in the middle of the cell where they represent metaphase. Partners back away from each other, slowly breaking hands to represent anaphase. Finally, two separate groups of six students mingle together on each side of the area. This represents telophase.

Possible questions: Ask the students what they represent at each step in the process. Also ask them what part of the process is being acted out. Finally, after the conclusion of the chromosome ballet ask what the significance of the process is.

Answers to Chapter 8 Investigation:

A. The activity many of the cells are carrying out is mitosis. This can be determined by noting the cells whose nuclei are in the process of dividing.

B. The diagram should show prophase, metaphase, anaphase, telophase, and interphase leading back to prophase in a cycle. (See Figure 8-8, p. 145.)

C. (Use of prepared slides is suggested.) One way to estimate the percent of time the cells spend in each of the stages of mitosis is to count 100 cells and classify each according to the stage it is in. A tally something like the following might be a useful way to go about the problem.

Interphase	THL THL THL THL THL THL THL THL //// (44)
Prophase	THL THL (10)
Metaphase	THL THL THL (15)
Anaphase	THL THL //// (14)
Telophase	THL THL THL // (17)

If exactly 100 cells are counted and all the cells in a given area are counted, the number in each stage gives an estimate of the percent of time the cells spend in that stage.

Answers to Chapter 8 Review:

1. This suggests a common origin of all life.

2. Cell division of the unicellular organism.

3. Protein synthesis, mitosis, and DNA replication are sequential processes. Steps have been listed in answers to section questions.

References and Readings:

Teacher
Croce, C.M., and H. Porpowski 1978. The genetics of human cancer. *Scientific American* 238(2):117 (February).

Grobstein, C. 1977. The recombinant-DNA debate. *Scientific American* 237(1):22 (July).

Lazarides, E., and J.P. Revel 1979. The molecular basis of cell movement. *Scientific American* 240(5):100 (May).

Student
Miller, J.A. 1979. Living reagent factories. *SciQuest* 52(6):7 (July-August).

CONTINUITY OF LIFE

This unit is concerned with heredity and how hereditary information is passed from one generation to the next. Chapter 9 begins with the development of the basic Mendelian principles and stresses continuity. Chapter 10 develops the means by which hereditary material can also be responsible for great diversity among organisms. In Chapter 11 students discover how genetic information can characterize a population. They are introduced to some of the factors that cause the genetic character of a population to change over several generations. Finally, in Chapter 12 genetic knowledge is applied to inheritance in humans.

The skills needed in dealing with genetic problems are treated in the study skills section of the *Laboratory Manual*. These skills include determining ratios and analyzing statistical data with the chi square test. The study skills sections may be used to supplement the investigations that accompany each chapter.

CHAPTER 9 PRINCIPLES OF HEREDITY

Introduction: The three exercises associated with this chapter can be used as a basis for developing a solid background for the remaining chapters in Unit 3. Investigation 9-1 needs to be started some ten days before students observe the seedlings. Meanwhile, the necessary skills and background information can be developed. Normal/albino tobacco seeds and the "genetic corn" can be purchased from most biological supply houses.

The concept of meiosis is fundamental to the understanding of genetics. It can be reinforced in a dramatic way with a shoe demonstration. Students are arranged in a circle. Each student contributes both shoes to the cell, represented by the circle. The shoes in turn represent homologous chromosomes. As directed by the teacher, students may act out the steps of meiosis. It's fun and it gets the point across. The laboratory investigation 9-2, "Meiosis: A Model," can also be done with kits containing poppit beads that can be purchased from a biological supply house.

It is important to grasp the significance of the test cross in determining the genotype of an unknown dominant-appearing individual. This will be particularly useful in later chapters.

Answers to Chapter 9 Investigation:

A. 30 normal: 10 vestigial

B. Inferred ratio should be 3:1.

C. i) nn; ii) NN and Nn; iii) Cross an nn fly with a normal-winged fly. If any vestigial-winged (nn) flies appear, the normal-winged fly was heterozygous (Nn).

Answers to Genetic Problems, page 174

1. Brown eyes = B
   Blue eyes = b
   (a) Bb and Bb
   (b) Test cross the unknown genotype with the recessive, bb, for blue eyes.
   (c) Brown and brown or brown and blue.

2. (a) T = tall
   t = short

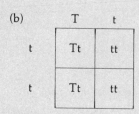

F₁: All heterozygous tall

(b)

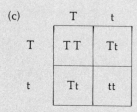

F₁: 2 heterozygous tall: 2 homozygous short

(c)

F₁: 1 homozygous tall: 2 heterozygous tall: 1 homozygous short

	T	t
T	T T	Tt
t	Tt	tt

(d) P₁ AABB × aabb
    F₁ AaBb
    P₂

	AB	Ab	aB	ab
AB	AABB	AABb	AaBB	AaBb
Ab	AABb	AAbb	AaBb	Aabb
aB	AaBB	AaBb	aaBB	aaBb
ab	AaBb	Aabb	aaBb	aabb

F₂

(e) P₁ AAbb × aaBB
    F₁ AaBb
    P₂ and F₂ — same as (d)

Answers to Chapter 9 Review:

3. It can help humans to produce the greatest variety of crops and the hardiest crops.

References and Readings:

Teacher

Burns, G.W. 1976. *The science of genetics*, 3rd ed. New York: Macmillan Publishing Co., Inc.

Feldman, M. 1974. *Basic principles of genetics*. New York: McGraw-Hill.

Sinnot, E.W., L.C. Dunn, and T. Dobshansky 1958. *Principles of genetics*, 5th ed. New York: McGraw-Hill.

Student

Hyde, Margaret O. 1974. *The new genetics*. New York: Franklin Watts.

Parker, G., W. Reynolds, and Rex Reynolds 1977. *Heredity.* Programmed Biology Series. Chicago: Educational Methods.

CHAPTER 10   GENES AND CHROMOSOMES

Introduction: Having introduced classic Mendelian genetics as a means of providing continuity from one generation to the next, we now move into the area of twentieth-century, or neo-Mendelian, inheritance. In the first section of the chapter, we deal with some of the origins of variety-genetic recombination, incomplete dominance, codominance, multiple alleles, and polygenic inheritance. Next, we turn to the structure and function of the genetic material itself, DNA. It is here that the nature of mutations is discussed. Mutations, in general, are rare, random, recessive, and harmful to the bearer in which they occur. In the third section, students are introduced to the basis of sex determination (the sex of an offspring is determined by the chromosome make-up of the sperm cell) and sex-linked traits (females generally do not inherit such traits because they are likely to have a dominant allele on the other X-chromosome). Finally, a variety of chromosomal aberrations and their effects are discussed.

The laboratory exercises have been selected to illustrate the major points of the chapter. Laboratory Investigation 10-1, "Genetic Variety by Incomplete Dominance," illustrates incomplete dominance and reinforces skills developed in Chapter 9. Tobacco seeds for this exercise need to be "planted" at least ten days prior to the time of observation. Care will be needed to be exercised to distinguish the three types of seedlings accurately. Bacterial techniques for Laboratory Investigation 10-2, "Mutations in Bacteria," are provided in the study skills section. Both the streak-plate and pour-plate techniques are given.

The kits for Laboratory Investigation 10-3, "Chromosome Karyotyping," are inexpensive and should be available from your local chapter of the March of Dimes, though they may need some advance notice of your needs. Once obtained, the kits may be reused by storing the chromosome cutouts in film cannisters.

Answers to Chapter 10 Investigation:

A. (Bacterial) growth on the entire surface of the agar plate except in the area surrounding the disk. A few colonies can be seen in the clear area.

B. Drug resistant cultures of bacteria developed due to either mutation or the selection of resistant strains.

C. Answers will vary with research. In a large bacterial population, there may be a few cells that are resistant to a certain drug. If the drug is used over a period of time, the susceptible cells will be destroyed; however, the resistant ones will remain. As these multiply, a popultion of bacterial cells entirely resistant to the drug will be produced. If routine, widespread use of antibiotics continues, an even larger number of disease causing bacteria will be resistant to the treatment now prescribed for them.

Answers to Chapter 10 Review:

1. Student answers may include a reference to the role of the animal breeder in selecting for breeding animals with the desired hereditary traits of good race horses.

2. By studying mutagenic substances in the environment and their effects on hereditary materials.

3. Student answers might include the government's responsibility for public health in regulating industries that release mutagenic substances to the atmosphere and water, or use them as additives for food, etc.

References and Readings:

Teacher

Levine, L. 1973. *Biology of the gene*, 2nd ed. New York: Norton.

Watson, James D. 1969. *The double helix*. New York: New American Library.

——————————. 1976. *Molecular biology of the gene*, 3rd ed. Menlo Park, CA: W.A. Benjamin.

Student

Scientific American Offprints:

Horowitz, N.H. The gene. Jan. 1956. (OP #17)

Crick, F.H.C. Nucleic acids. Sept. 1957. (OP #54)

Benzer, S. The fine structure of the gene. Jan. 1962. (OP #120)

Crick, F.H.C. The genetic code. Oct. 1962. (OP #123)

Nirenberg, M.W. The genetic code II. March 1963. (OP #153)

Sagar, R. Genes outside the chromosomes. Jan. 1965. (OP #1002)

Holley, R.W. The nucleotide sequence of a nucleic acid. Feb. 1966. (OP #1033)

Crick, F.H.C. The genetic code III. Oct. 1966. (OP #1052)

McKusick, V.A. The mapping of human chromosomes. Apr. 1971. (OP #1220)

Crow, J.F. Genes that violate Mendel's rules. Feb. 1979. (OP #1418)

CHAPTER 11   GENETICS AND POPULATIONS

Introduction: The idea of the gene pool is established in this chapter. The first investigation for this chapter is designed to illustrate the role of probability in predicting the random combinations of alleles in offspring. Laboratory Investigation 11-2, "Genetic Changes in a Population" is somewhat more complex. It is a series of three simulations that illustrate what happens in a population (a) when the conditions of the Hardy-Weinberg Principle are met, (b) when one condition—population size—is violated, and (c) when another condition—selection—is violated. The result is change in allele frequencies and hence, changes in the genetic character of a population. If you wish students to make several generations of each model, the number of beans at the beginning of each generation must be adjusted to reflect the genetic character of the offspring.

The students' first introduction to genetics in humans is presented in Laboratory Investigation 11-3. The study skills section on "Determining Frequencies" (CD-1) may be helpful to students here if they find it difficult to understand what is meant by frequency and how to determine the frequency of an event.

Answers to Chapter 11 Investigation:

A. 3 purple to 1 yellow

B. Purple = PP or Pp
   Yellow = pp

C. (i) 0.5
   (ii) answers will vary

Answers to Chapter 11 Review:

1. Answers may include the following explanation. Diversified agriculture is important to populations living in changing environments because it allows them to adapt to the demands of the new conditions.

2. Hybrid wheat and corn mature faster or are more resistant to drought and disease. Also, special hybrid cattle often show high growth rates.

3. Medical advances have helped to increase the supply of harmful alleles in the human population. Many who might normally have died from genetic disorders have been saved.

Some of these have lived full and productive lives. But many afflicted with diabetes, PKU, and other disorders have produced children with the same defective alleles. Without medical help, most hereditary diseases would reach a balance in the gene pool. Technology, then, has contributed to the genetic load among humans.

References and Readings:

Teacher

Cook, L.M. 1976. *Population genetics.* Halsted Press. New York: John Wiley and Sons.

Grant, V. 1963. *The origin of adaptations.* New York: Columbia University Press.

Lewontin, R.C. 1974. *The genetic basis of evolutionary change.* New York: Columbia University Press.

Student

Scientific American Offprints:

Lack, D. Darwin's Finches. April 1953. (OP #22)

Lewontin, R.C. Adaptation. Sept. 1978. (OP #1408)

CHAPTER 12   HUMAN HEREDITY

Introduction: The attempt has been to first present the scope of genetic/chromosomal "disease," (all humans are carriers of at least a few genetic disorders) and the nature of high-risk groups. The second section discusses examples of autosomal disorders. Examples of various ethnic-based disorders are given. Ethnic groups differ only in which of these alleles exist in greater frequency, not in whether or not they exist at all. Space prevented the inclusion of disorders that are apparently caused by the interaction of heredity and environment, which include such things as allergies, ulcers, and a host of others. You may wish to devote some time to a discussion of these as well.

In the third section, the moral and ethical implications of the possibilities for treatment, prevention, and cure of inheritable disorders will be discussed.

Laboratory investigations associated with this chapter are fairly simple. "A Family Pedigree," 12-1, asks students to prepare a family pedigree for an autosomal recessive trait, such as tongue-rolling, PTC tasting, etc. The second investigation points out the bases for differences between humans and human groups and underscores the tremendous human diversity that exists.

Answers to Chapter 12 Investigation:

A.. Male. One. Four.

B. Both parents are heterozygous. The husband did not carry any recessive allele; or chance did not allow for the homozygous condition to appear.

C. Answers will vary.

Traits shown in photographs: (left top) dominant unattached; (left bottom) recessive attached; (middle left) dominant freckles, and recessive clear skin; (middle right) dominant tongue roller, recessive non-roller; (right top) dominant cleft chin; (right bottom) non cleft.

Answers to Chapter 12 Review:

1. Answers will vary. Whether the individuals affected should be treated as dangerous or not is a controversial issue. Each case should be taken individually and perhaps studied by a team made up by a psychologist, sociologist, and genetic counselor.

2. College training in biology, especially genetics, and training in the psychological and sociological foundations of interviewing and counseling. Specialized education beyond these general areas and some medical knowledge would also be desirable.

Answer to question 9 Section 2, page 224

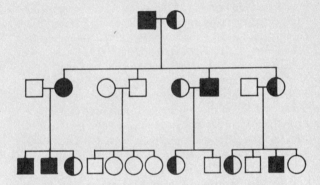

References and Readings:

Teacher
Cavalli-Sforza, L. 1977. *Elements of human genetics*, 2nd ed. Menlo Park, CA: W.A. Benjamin.
King, J.C. 1971. *The biology of race*. New York: Harcourt, Brace, Jovanovich.

Student
Scientific American Offprints
Beadle, G.W. The genes of men and molds. Sept. 1948. (OP #1)
Allison, A.C. Sickle cells and evolution. Aug. 1956. (OP #1065)
Tausig, H. The thalidomide syndrome. Aug. 1962. (OP #1100)
Clark, C.A. The prevention of rhesus babies. Nov. 1968. (OP #1126)
Macalpine, I., and R. Hunter. Porphyria and King George III. July 1969. (OP #1149)
Wills, C. Genetic load. Mar. 1970. (OP #1172))
Friedmann, T. Prenatal diagnosis of genetic disease. Nov. 1971. (OP #1234)
Cerami, A., and C.M. Peterson. Cyanate and sickle-cell disease. Apr. 1975.(OP #1319)

OVERVIEW OF UNIT 4
HISTORY OF LIFE

This unit explores the idea of relatedness among life forms and sets the stage for a taxonomic look at each of the five kingdoms.

The concepts developed within this unit, such as unity and diversity of organisms, complementarity of structure and function of organisms, and interaction of organism and environment and further developed to give them both order and meaning. Change through time is described as natural selection acting on the genetic variations that appear among the members of a population. Explanations of this process are presented as theories, not facts. Many, but not all, scientists feel that these conclusions answer the question of *how* in a satisfactory manner.

With the genetic background presented in the last unit, students should be able to appreciate the evolution of diversity in living things.

CHAPTER 13   THEORIES OF CHANGE

Introduction: There were two keys to Darwin's ideas on evolution. The first lay in the obvious but unrealized diversity that exists in all populations. This diversity is so important to the concept of change through time that the two investigations associated with this chapter both hinge on the differences existing between individuals. The second key involved is the role of the environment as a selecting agent. These points were emphasized in the Darwin-Wallace Theory of Natural Selection. Although Darwin's ideas were soon christened "Survival of the Fittest," they should more appropriately be called "Elimination of the Unfit." In most populations, the members are already fairly well adapted to their respective environments. Populations thus remain relatively stable.

You may find it useful to return briefly to Unit 1 and the topic of ecologic succession. In this instance, the complexion of the community changes as better adapted species replace pioneer forms. The principles involved are similar, although the changes involved in evolution are at the population level rather than the community level and as such, involve genetic changes.

Answers to Chapter 13 Investigations:

A. Upper left with lower middle; upper middle with lower right; upper right with lower left

61T

B. Mallard-an aquatic bird; swims on surface; feet webbed. Hawk- predator, sharp grasping tallons, advantage in catching prey. Ostrich- terrestrial bird, legs adapted for moving quickly over great flat distances.

C. Answers will vary.

Answers to Chapter 13 Review:

1. Lamarck: Dark-colored animals would somehow have acquired the light color of their surroundings, and passed this lighter color on to their descendants, this process continued until the future descendants were completely white. Darwin: Among the individuals in a variously-colored species, some were lighter-colored than others, and these were less likely to be caught and destroyed by enemies before reproducing. Hence, there would be more light ones in the next generation than before. Repeated environmental selection would eventually lead to an all-white population.

2. A parasite that damaged the host too much would cause the host to die. Being deprived of its sustenance, the parasite itself would die and be less likely to leave offspring. Only those somewhat less deadly parasites would, by natural selection, survive. In other words, the "one-upmanship" of the parasite is favorable to its adaptation and to its perpetuation by natural selection.

3. The variety of foods available to the finches enabled those with differently shaped beaks to feed on different diets. They therefore formed populations that were not in direct competition with one another.

References and Readings:

Teacher

Eiseley, L. 1958. Darwin's Century: *Evolution and the man who discovered it*. Garden City, NY: Doubleday.

Mayer, Ernst. 1970. *Populations, species, and evolution*. Cambridge, MA.: Belknap Press.

Student

Darwin, Charles. 1962. *The Voyage of the Beagle*. Leonard Engle, ed. New York: Doubleday.

De Beer, Sir Gavin. 1964. *Charles Darwin*. New York: Doubleday.

Scientific American Offprints:

Lack, D. Darwin's Finches. Apr. 1953. (OP #22)

Eiseley, L. Charles Darwin. Feb. 1956 (OP #108)

Margulis, L. Symbiosis and evolution. Aug. 1971. (OP #1230)

Mayr, E. Evolution, Sept. 1978. (OP #1400)

May, R.M. The Evolution of ecological systems. Sept. 1978. (OP #1404)

Kimura, M. The neutral theory of molecular evolution. Nov. 1979. (OP #1451)

CHAPTER 14   EVIDENCE OF CHANGE

Introduction: Species, up to this point in the book has been rather loosely defined. It is important to be more specific now because the differences between species is often not at all obvious. Moreover, it often happens that organisms appearing superficially different species are in fact not. Thus, reproductive compatibility becomes an important criterion for the definition of species.

Note also that the term change refers to populations. Individuals do not adapt to the environment. They are either adapted by virtue of their genetic make-up or they are not. This emphasizes the importance of pre-adaptations. Small changes due to mutations or particular allele combinations produce features upon which the environment operates. These features, which may or may not be apparent, result in the character of the population. As they change, so also does the character of the species.

Since fossils provide us with direct evidence of life in the past, we have emphasized the use of this record in the laboratory investigations. Of particular interest is the exercise on the half-life principle. You will need to prepare a box for each group as described in the Teacher's Edition of the *Laboratory Manual*. The laboratory investigations on the comparative anatomy of vertebrate skeletons is designed to help the student understand how each type of skeleton is adapted in specific ways for a particular way of life. Indirect evidence from a variety of areas supports the direct evidence of the fossil record. There are other pieces of indirect evidence not mentioned in the text such as vestigal structures: the appendix, the coccyx, muscles for ear movement, body hair, etc.

Answers to Chapter 14 Investigation:

A. (a) similarities: homologous bone structures; similar to lizard in having teeth and claws; similar to bird in having feathers and wings.
(b) differences: lizard does not have feathers or wings; modern birds do not have teeth or claws on wings.

B. Archaeopteryx should be classified as a bird as a result of its feathers which are actually modified scales. This represents a change from the reptilian body plan.

C. Depends on researched organism.

Answers to Chapter 14 Review:

1. Answers will vary but may include the following explanation. Predation is a strong selective force, and many adaptions are related to escaping from or deterring predators. Some animals, insects in particular, have evolved natural defenses that inflict insult or injury on the predator, such as a sting, a revolting smell, or a bad-tasting or poisonous secretion.

The innocuous mimic may fool its predator by resembling a stinging or bad-tasting model that the predator has learned to avoid. Some species of stingless flies, for example, resemble bees or hornets. Mimicry works to the advantage of the mimic by helping it escape predators and encouraging survival of the species.

References and Readings:

Teacher

Eiseley, L. 1958. Darwin's Century: *Evolution and the man who discovered it*. Garden City, N.Y.: Doubleday.

Lightner, J.P., ed. 1977. A compendium of Information on the Theory of Evolution and the Evolution-Creation Controversy. National Association of Biology Teachers.

Mayer, Ernst. 1970. *Population, species, and evolution*. Cambridge, MA.: Belknap Press.

Student

Oxford/Carolina Biology Readers: Burlington, NC: Carolina Biological Supply Co.

De Beer, Sir Gavin, 1971. Homology, An Unsolved Problem. Carolina Biological Supply Co.

_____. 1972. Adaptation. Carolina Biological Supply Co.

_____. 1975. The Evolution of Flying and Flightless Birds. Carolina Biological Supply Co.

Scientific American Offprints:

Wecker, S.C. Habitat selection. Oct. 1964. (OP #195)

Ayala, F.J. The mechanisms of evolution. Sept. 1979. (OP #1408)

CHAPTER 15 LIFE IN THE PAST

Introduction: Any discussion of evolution ultimately brings us to a discussion of orgins. In this context, the historical approach is again relevant. With the advent of experiments that support Oparin's Heterotroph Hypothesis, it is important to see the superficial resemblances to early notions of abiogenesis. The context, of course, is different. The Heterotroph Hypothesis does not suggest that modern life forms might spring full blown from falling leaves or other equally incredible sources. Rather, it is consistent with our notions of natural selection—this time acting at the molecular level: stable molecules survive; unstable, reactive molecules do not.

The second part of the chapter summarizes the history of life on the earth. Since students are understandably interested in their own origins, the attempt has been to focus upon those lines. To this end, the vertebrats receive more attention than plants or lower animals. The third section of the chapter concentrates on the emergence of humans.

DEMONSTRATION: Pasteur's Swan-necked Flasks

Time required: 2-3 weeks; should be set up a few days prior to the time it will be used.

Materials: (5) 250-ml flasks; cotton plugs for 3 flasks; S-shaped glass tube (swan-neck); 425 ml nutrient agar.

Procedure: Prepare the nutrient agar and pour 75 ml into each of the five flasks. Number flasks 1-5 and treat each one as follows: 1) leave open and do not sterilize; 2) leave open after sterilizing it; 3) plug top with a cotton stopper but do not sterilize; 4) seal as in #3 but sterilize it; 5) close top with a cotton plug through which an S-shaped glass tube (the swan-neck) is inserted and sterilize.

Set the five flasks up for observing during and following the discussion of spontaneous generation and Pasteur's contributions to the controversy. Have students record their observations every few days.

Possible questions: What is the source of the microorganisms that appear on the surface of the agar? What parts of the experiment represent controls that earlier investigators had neglected?

Why are microorganisms unable to pass through the "swan-neck?" What practical applications might arise from the knowledge gained by such an experiment?

Answers to Chapter 15 Investigation:

A. Answers will vary with the description of the student. (A) Mesozoic scene. Dinosaurs are present. Area is swampy. (B) Mammals are present. No dinosaurs.

B. Answers will vary. Changes in climate; rising of land masses; drying out of swamps; environment of dinosaurs not condusive for growth of dinosaurs; evolution of new kinds of organisms produced an altered environment—this changed the types of plants and animals present. New organisms created new selective pressures.

C. Climate changes in earth's geography. Mammals were better adapted and more efficient. (This question is difficult to answer. There are many theories and they are difficult to substantiate.)

Answers to Chapter 15 Review:

1. The basic assumption of the Heterotroph Hypothesis is that the first organisms were consumers of environmental organic molecules that supplied the necessary energy for their metabolism.

2. Support: it assumes that the early atmosphere of the earth was composed of such simple gases as methane, ammonia, hydrogen and water vapor. Using lightning as energy, these gases could have produced organic molecules such as amino acids. With gentle heat as a catalyst, these amino acids could easily have combined into peptide chains. Weakness: it rests on the assumption that the earth's early atmosphere was composed of the above mentioned gases. If this assumption is proven incorrect, one would have to reject the Heterotroph Hypothesis.

References and Readings:

Teacher

Colbert, E.H. 1969. *Evolution of the vertebrates.* New York: John Wiley & Sons.

Dillon, J.E. 1973. *Evolution: concepts and consequences.* St. Louis, MO: C.V. Mosby.

Stebbins, G.L. 1966. *Processes of organic evolution.* Englewood Cliffs, NJ: Prentice Hall.

Student

Eiseley, L. 1957. *The immense journey.* New York: Vintage.

Oxford/Carolina Biology Readers: Burlington, NC: Carolina Biological Supply Co.

Bernal, J.D., and A. Synge. 1972. *The origin of life.*

Bone, Q. 1972. *The origin of chordates.*

Day, M.H. 1972. *The fossil history of man.*

De Beer, Sir Gavin. 1975. *The evolution of flying and flightless birds.*

Napier, J.R. 1976. *Primates and their adaptations,* 2nd ed.

Nicols, D. 1975. *The uniqueness of echinoderms.*

Scientific American Offprints:

Wald, G. The origin of life. Aug. 1954 (OP #47)

Napier, J. The evolution of the hand. Dec. 1962. (OP #140)

Dickerson, R.E. Chemical evolution and the origin of life. Sept. 1978. (OP #1401)

Schopf, J.W. The evolution of the earliest cells. Sept. 1978. (OP #1402)

Buffetaut, E. The evolution of the crocodilians. Oct. 1979. (OP #1449)

CHAPTER 16   THE CLASSIFICATION OF LIVING THINGS

Introduction: To introduce students to the great variety of species, you might ask them to list by common name, description, or rough sketch each kind of creature (plant, animal, fungus, etc.) they find on a trip to a creek, or to a park or zoo. Alert students may be surprised at the number of species they find. If time permits you may have students suggest ways to classify their list of organisms. Let them suggest reasons for their classification.

Linneaus' system of classification had only two kingdoms, the plants and the animals. But since Linneaus, discoveries have revealed many creatures that cannot be characterized completely as either plant or animals.

Introduction of the three Kingdom system came with the addition of Kingdom Protista. But some of these unicells differed from others in an important feature. Bacteria and blue-green algae lacked nuclear membranes. Differ-

ences in other organelles were also apparent. Thus, they were grouped together as the separate Kingdom Monera.

The Fungi are often considered to be plants because they are non-motile and have an outside wall that resembles the walls of plant cells. But they cannot photosynthesize. The Fungi, furthermore, are multicellular and they do not ingest food as animals do. So biologist H.R. Whittaker proposed that the Fungi be placed in a kingdom of their own.

Whatever the virtues of any given system, the Whittaker system seems to identify structured and metabolic features that produce the least conflict in providing an order to the problem of taxonomy.

Yet new knowledge, changing interpretations, and continuous evolutionary changes make any system of classification tentative. It is for convenience that we group organisms into conceptual boxes even though the organisms may not fit the boxes perfectly.

Answers to Chapter 16 Investigation:

A. *Octipedal optistalk* and *Biquadripedal terrestris* might be placed into the same order because both appear to have descended from Fossil I.

B. *Octipedal optistalk* has features adapting it to shallow waters. Stalked eyes allow seeing above water without exposing the whole body. Appendages allow walking in shallow water and mud. Spines protect against shore birds and other predators. These features had survival value. *Sprawlis radiatis* may have had a bad taste or spiny skin that discouraged predators and eliminated the advantage of fast locomotion. *Hoverall aqueous'* ability to float under water allow it to wait for prey. Its streamlined form allows fast escape from predators. *Biquadripedal terrestris'* longer legs and its eyes allow faster escape from predators and capture of prey.

C.

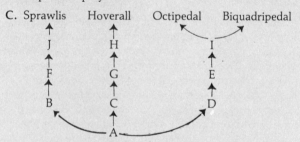

Key: 1a Radial symmetry . . . . *Sprawlis*
1b Bilateral symmetry 2
2a Only appendages are fins and tail . . . . *Hoverall*
2b Cephalic appendages and four pairs
      of legs   3
3a Stalks with eyes . . . . *Octipedal*
3b Stalks without eyes, eyes in front of and
      below stalks . . . . *Biquadripedal*

This is one of many keys that can be made.

Answers to Chapter 16 Review:

1. Organisms that occupy similar environments often come to resemble one another even though they may be only very distantly related phylogentically. The whales, a group that includes the dolphin and porpoise, are similar in many exterior features to sharks and other large fish, but the fins of whales conceal the remnant of a vertebrate hand. Whales are warm-blooded, like their land-dwelling ancestors, and they have lungs rather than gills.

2. The response to this activity will vary.

3. New evidence about the relationships of living organisms is constantly being discovered, as a result, taxonomists must frequently review classification schemes.

4. Proof of superiority of any one way to group phyla into kingdoms is unlikely because living organisms are highly complex and continue to change; and, the systems are all created for human convenience. What seems more convenient for one, might seem less so to another.

5. All people in the stated occupations would need knowledge of taxonomy. Those that breed living organisms such as farmers would need to know which could interbreed, a process based on speciation. Those concerned with diseases, such as physicians, would need to identify correctly causative organisms and their carriers. Those concerned with transport, such as inspectors, would need to identify organisms that could become pests.

References and Readings:

Teacher

Whittaker, R.H. 1969. New concepts of kingdoms of organisms. *Science* 163:150.

Student

Jacques, H.E. 1947. *Living things: how to know them,* rev. ed. Pictured Key Nature Series. Dubuque, IA: William C. Brown Co.

OVERVIEW OF UNIT 5
VIRUSES, MONERA, PROTISTA AND FUNGI

Most students are somewhat familiar with the more conspicuous members of the living world, i.e., plants and animals. Although most students have heard about viruses, bacteria, and fungi, they could not be said to be familiar with them. This book has adopted the five-kingdom approach to the living world because it seems to satisfy most of the critical arguments associated with other approaches. In this unit, we treat the first three and most primitive kingdoms. You will note that all of the units dealing with the taxonomy of organisms follow the same general pattern. Each chapter or chapter section begins with the diversity and continuity of a specific group of organisms. The second part deals with how the members of that group maintain themselves in a homeostatic sense. Finally, the relationship between the members of the group and their respective environments is explored. The concluding chapter in each unit has a fourth section that compares the organisms discussed in that unit or in previous units, where appropriate.

The investigations included in the *Laboratory Manual* for this unit are generally of an observational nature. They involve the use of the microscope to observe the forms and activities of organisms. Note that life cycles are generally played down in favor of the mechanisms for homeostatis and the roles of specific organisms, specifically with reference to humans.

CHAPTER 17   VIRUSES

Introduction: Although this chapter deals with viruses, there is a need for students to understand the spectrum of form in the world of microbes. Thus, the chapter first sets the stage for viruses by describing the world of microbes and contrasting viruses with this view. Included here is a discussion of procaryotic and eucaryotic cells. Perhaps one of the best ways for students to understand what viruses are is to discover what they are not. Differences between primitive (procaryotic) cells and viruses should be stressed. Whether or not they are alive is really a debatable point.

You might find it helpful to project some 2 × 2 transparencies of electron micrographs of viruses and activities of viral cultures.

Answers to Chapter 17 Investigation:

A. Answers will vary. Measles—blotchy red to dark-red rash on face, neck, chest, and part of the trunk. Wart—hard projections arising from the skin. Smallpox virus—cube-like structure resembling bread crumbs or sugar. Measles virus—envelope surrounding a coiled strand of DNA.

B. They are able to develop antibodies that protect them from infection.

C. The antibiotics are chemicals that are directed against specific cellular structures or activities.

Answers to Chapter 17 Review:

1. Answers will vary, but may include argument that this would support the view that viruses are parasitic descendants of independent organisms. Or the other views—that viruses are non-cellular descendants of cells, or the breakdown products of cells—might equally be supported by such a discovery.

References and Readings:

Teacher

Pelczar, M.J., and R.D. Reid. 1972. *Microbiology,* 3rd ed. New York: McGraw-Hill.

Watson, J.D. 1976. *Molecular biology of the gene,* 3rd ed. ed. Menlo Park: CA: W.A. Benjamin, Inc.

Student

de Kruif, P. 1959. *Microbe hunters.* New York: Pocket Books.

Stanley, W.M. 1961. *Viruses and the nature of life.* New York: E.P. Dutton.

Scientific American Offprints:

Isaacs, Alik. Interferon. May 1961. (OP #87)

Jacob, F., and E.L. Wollman. Viruses and genes. June 1961. (OP #89)

Rubin, H. A defective cancer virus. June 1964. (OP #185)

Fraenkel-Conrat, H. The genetic code of a virus. Oct. 1964. (OP #193)

Kellenberger, E. The genetic control of the shape of a virus. Dec. 1966. (OP #1058)

Campbell, A.M. How viruses insert their DNA into the DNA of the host cell. Dec. 1976. (OP #1347)

Burke, D.C. The status of interferon. Mar. 1977. (OP #1356)

Grobstein, C. The recombinant DNA debate. July 1977. (OP #1362)

Oxford/Carolina Biology Reader: Burlington, NC: Carolina Biological Supply Co.

Sanders, F.K. 1975. The growth of viruses.

CHAPTER 18   BACTERIA AND BLUE-GREEN ALGAE

Introduction: As an introduction to the chapter, you may want to point out the borderline forms of monerans and explain why they are usually considered living, although viruses are not. Initial student interest in the monerans probably stems from the disease-causing aspects of bacteria. Students may be surprised at the variety of monerans and to learn that the beneficial forms outnumber the harmful ones. Recall the role of bacteria as decomposers and links in the environmental chemical cycles (Unit 1).

You may also want to point out the metabolic continuum from obligate anaerobe to aerobe. The basis for such differences lies in what enzymes are present and, ultimately, what DNA each form possesses. Students are interested in venereal diseases and how they are spread and controlled. You can do much to dispel myths and get students to understand the need for a responsible approach to venereal disease infection. Finally, emphasize the variety of ways that are used to protect us against bacterial infections. Also point out that widespread, indiscriminate use of antibiotics raises the potential for antibiotic-resistant strains of bacteria, some of which already exist.

The laboratory investigations for this chapter emphasize the types and distribution of bacteria. Laboratory Investigation 18-2, "Distribution of Bacteria," also uses skills in handling bacteria. You will need to have or be able to prepare the special culture media for specific bacteria.

Answers to Chapter 18 Investigation:

A. Water is red, indicating pollution in the upper photograph. The lower photograph shows no sign of the red tide.

B. A red, blue-green alga bloom.

C. The red tide is caused by any one of a number of species of dinoflagellates belong to the genus *Gonylaulax.* Students, in creating the red tide, should first do library research on the conditions responsible for its formation. Laboratory investigation may involve the use of these dinoflagellates with detergents containing phosphates. Pond water enriched with nitrites or phosphorous may also be used. Two variables for testing purposes would be the amount of phosphates and nitrites per unit of water and the amount of light needed to establish the red tide. The serial dilutions, which may be placed in a variety of jars or beakers, can be exposed to either sunlight or artificial light for the experimental period of time.

Answers to Chapter 18 Review:

1. Antibiotics act against various parts of the cell. For example, penicillin damages the cell membrane. A virus, however, is a noncellular particle and is therefore immune to antibiotic effects.

2. Patients are already ill and have a lower resistance to these bacteria. Antibiotics are given as treatment. However, they have created an environment that favors the growth of microbes that are resistant to antibiotics. Researchers must constantly find new antibiotics to combat the spread of resistant staphlococci.

3. Most organisms causing venereal disease are anaerobic. They would not survive outside the body long enough to cause infection. Therefore, it is unusual for venereal disease to be spread by means other than sexual contact.

References and Readings:

Teacher

Pelczar, M.J., and Reid 1972. *Microbiology.* 3rd ed. New York: McGraw-Hill.

Watson, J.D. 1976. *Molecular biology of the gene.* 3rd ed. Menlo Park, CA: W.A. Benjamin, Inc.

Student

de Kruif, P. 1959. *Microbe hunters.* New York: Pocket Books.

Stanley, W.M. 1961. *Viruses and the nature of life.* New York: E.P. Dutton.

Scientific American Offprints

Nossal, G.J.V. How cells make antibodies. Dec. 1964. (OP #199)

Cairns, J. The bacterial chromosome. Jan. 1966 (OP #1030)

CHAPTER 19   THE PROTISTS

Introduction: Protists are indispensible members of food webs and this helps to relate new material to Unit 1. The protists, of course, are separated from the monerans by virtue of their eucaryotic nature. Moreover, they are unicellular, generally separating them from the higher kingdoms. Thus, the protists are a unique group and are recognized as such in the five-kingdom approach used in this text.

Again, the emphasis is couched in terms of the basic concepts of biology: diversity and continuity, homeostatis, and the interaction of organisms and their environments. The latter concept is viewed specifically with respect to humans. The laboratory investigations are designed especially to demonstrate the diversity of protists and their response to environmental conditions.

Answers to Chapter 19 Investigation:

A. Similar: unicellular. Different: Regular shape, irregular shape; presence or absence of flagella; presence or absence of cilia.

B. They move about and search for food (locomotion). They may contain a contractile vacuole for elimination of waste material (excretion). They have a protective cell membrane. Diatoms have a protective shell. Some produce their own food (photosynthesis).

C. Ameba and Trypanosoma: disease causers. Paramecium, euglena, dinoflagellats, and diatoms are important members of the food chain.

Answers to Chapter 19 Review:

1. At the cellular level, bioluminescense is the transduction of chemical energy into light energy in a series of enzyme-controlled reactions. The luciferin (substrate)—luciferas (enzyme) reaction of the firefly can occur only in the presence of oxygen. If luciferin and luciferase are extracted from a firefly and mixed with ATP in a test tube, luminescence occurs. The chemical energy of ATP is converted to light energy in the firefly as follows:

$$\text{luciferin} + O_2 \xrightarrow[\text{ATP \quad AMP}]{\text{luciferase}} \text{luciferin} + CO_2 + \text{light}$$
(reduced)

This area of research provides information on the production of light energy through means other than petroleum products.

2. Cell division is dependent upon the type of cell, temperature, and available nutrients. Cell division occurs when cells reach a certain size. Dividing cells pass through a regular sequence of cell growth and cell division as directed by DNA. Further knowledge of the control mechanisms involved might be of great importance in the control of cancer. Cancer cells differ from normal cells largely in that they keep on dividing at the expense of the host tissues.

References and Readings:

Teacher

Scagel, R.F., et. al. 1966. *An evolutionary survey of the plant kingdom.* Belmont, CA: Wadsworth Publishing Co.

Curtis, H. 1975. *Biology,* 2nd ed. New York: Worth Publishers.

Student

Barnes, R.D. 1963. *Invertebrate zoology.* Philadelphia, PA: W.B. Saunders.

Needham, J.G., and Paul R. Needham 1962. *A guide to the study of fresh water bioogy.* San Francisco, CA: Holden-Day.

Oxford/Carolina Biology Readers: Burlington, NC: Carolina Biological Supply Co.

Leedale, G.F. 1971. The euglenoids.

Smith, D.C. 1973. Symbiosis of algae with invertebrates.

Scientific American Offprint

Allen, R.D. Amoeboid movement. Feb. 1962. (OP #182)

CHAPTER 20   THE FUNGI

Introduction: With the fungi, we take a first look at mostly multicellular, terrestrial organisms. As you progress through this chapter, keep students aware of the adaptations in fungi that enable them to survive.

Again, note that there is little emphasis on specific life cycles of the various fungi. Attention is directed toward the differences in reproductive structures of fungi, but only as a means for classifying them. Most students are no doubt somewhat familiar with some forms of fungi (e.g., bread or fruit mold and athlete's foot). You may want to have students bring in various examples of fungi from lawns, rotting wood, fruit, or bread. Since each of these has a characteristic form, your students might find it interesting to attempt to grow each kind on different substances or under different conditions.

The final section of the chapter is a summary comparison of the first three kingdoms and of the viruses. It is intended to provide a basic review of the essential features in each of the groups of organisms treated thus far.

Answers to Chapter 20 Investigation:

A. Roughly half-way between the two original colonies and along a line where the expansion of the two colonies come in contact with each other.

B. Answers will vary. Zygospores can only form when colonies of opposite strains come in contact with each other.

C. Take three agar plates and innoculate one with two colonies of + strains. In the second plate, place two colonies of − strains. Innoculate the third plate with one + colony and one − colony. Observe where and if growth occurs. A report should be prepared on findings.

Answers to Chapter 20 Review:

1. Answers will vary. Through library research, they might include conditions such as athlete's foot, and wheat rust, a fungus that has the barberry plant as an alternate host.

2. Alexander Fleming discovered penicillin "by chance." He was on the lookout for contamination among his laboratory dishes in which he was culturing bacteria.

References and Readings:

Teacher

Curtis, H. 1975. *Biology*, 2nd ed. New York: Worth Publishers.

Scagel, R.F., et. al. 1966. *An evolutionary survey of the plant kingdom*. Belmont, CA: Wadsworth Publishing Co.

Student

Alexopoulos, C.J., and J. Koevenig 1962. *Slime molds and research*. Boulder, CO: Educational Programs Improvement Corp.

Christensen, C.M. 1975. *The molds and man*, 2nd ed. Minneapolis: University of Minnesota Press.

_____. 1975. *Molds, mushrooms, and mycotoxins*. Minneapolis: University of Minnesota Press.

Kavaler, L. 1965. *Mushrooms, molds, and miracles*. Scranton, PA: John Day Co.

_____. 1964. *The wonders of fungi*. Scranton, PA: John Day Co.

Taber, W.A., and R.A. Taber 1967. *The impact of fungi on man*. Patterns of Life Series. Boulder, CO: Educational Programs Improvement Corp.

Scientific American Offprints

Lamb, I.M. Lichens. Oct. 1959. (OP #111)

Emerson, R. Molds and Men. Jan. 1962. (OP #115)

Oxford/Carolina Biology Readers: Burlington, NC: Carolina Biological Supply Co.

Fincham, J.R.S. 1971. Using fungi to study genetic recombinations.

Smith, D.C. 1973. The lichen symbiosis.

OVERVIEW OF UNIT 6
PLANTS

Unit 6 is a survey of the plant kingdom. As in the surveys of other kingdoms, there is emphasis on the search for unity within diversity, homeostatis, continuity of life, the link between structure and function, and interaction with the environment. You may want to have specimens of a few species in each group that are not well represented in your area. Or you may prefer to stress those the students know, though their acquaintance with even common species is usually superficial.

CHAPTER 21   THE SIMPLEST PLANTS

Introduction: Seeing examples of red, green, and brown algae and doing the laboratory exercises on the green algae and on mosses should help students understand the text.

The wide and varied use of the term "moss" requires the teacher to clarify the quasi-technical use of the term to refer only to certain bryophytes. Reindeer moss (*Cladonia*) is a lichen. Irish moss (*Chrondrus crispus*) is a red marine alga. The "moss" on the side of trees is often a mass of green algae (*Protococcus*). The "moss" floating in fresh waters is often one of several filamentous green algae (*Spriogyra* and others). Club mosses (*Selaginella* and *Lycopodium*) are vascular plants. Spanish moss (*Tillandsia*) is a flowering ephiphyte.

Answers to Chapter 21 Investigation:

A. Moss is growing on the north side of the tree.

B. Most shade and moisture and less heat occur on the north side. The south and west sides have the most light and heat, and the least moisture. The east side has intermediate amounts of heat, light, and moisture. Which side has the most wind depends on the direction of prevailing winds in the area.

C. One might transplant moss plants to controlled environments.

1. light, warm, dry
2. light, warm, wet
3. light, cool, dry
4. light, cool, wet
5. dark, warm, dry
6. dark, warm, wet
7. dark, cool, dry
8. dark, cool, wet

After a given time, determine plant height, number, or productivity, and compare all those in light with those in shade, those in coolness with those in warmth, and those in dry places with those in dampness.

Answers to Chapter 21 Review:

1. Answers will vary. They may include: roots for anchorage and extraction of nutrients; conducting tissue for material transport throughout the plant; waterproof outside layers for moisture conservation; and a system that would not be dependent upon moisture for reproductive cell transport.

2. One reason is protection. The outer cell layers protect the gametes from unfavorable conditions such as dehydration.

3. Student demonstration should include weighing dry *Spaghnum,* adding as much water as it will absorb and then reweighing it.

4. Answers will vary. They may include the following answer. In an environment rich in autotrophs and relatively lacking in heterotrophs, it might be advantageous for an organism to function as a heterotroph.

5. Answers will vary, but may include the following: solving worldwide food and water problems and discovering further practical uses of algae.

References and Readings:

Teacher

Boney, A.D. 1966. *A biology of marine algae.* New York: Hutchinson Educational, Ltd.

Student

Abbot, I.A., and E.Y. Dawson 1978. *How to know the seaweeds.* Pictured Key Nature Series. Dubuque, IA: Wm. C. Brown Co.

Prescott, G.W. 1978. *How to know the freshwater algae,* 3rd ed. Pictured Key Nature Series. Dubuque, IA: Wm. C. Brown Co.

Redfearn, P.L. Jr. and H.S. Conard 1979. *How to know the mosses and liverworts.* Pictured Key Nature Series. Dubuque, IA: Wm. C. Brown Co.

Stern, K.R. 1979. *Introductory plant biology.* Dubuque, IA: Wm. C. Brown Co.

Watson, E.V. 1972. *Mosses.* Oxford/Carolina Biology Reader. Burlington, NC: Carolina Biological Supply Co.

CHAPTER 22   FERNS AND GYMNOSPERMS

Introduction: If you don't have live specimens of primitive vascular plants, try to have a few fern gametophytes *(prothallia)* ready by the time you begin this chapter. Fern culture kits are available from supply houses. A month or more may be required for prothallia to appear from spores. You may find fern prothallia growing near fern sporophytes in greenhouses. It would also be helpful to have a pine life cycle set on display. It may include a male cone, female cones of several ages, seeds, a seedling, and a twig with needles.

Answers to Chapter 22 Investigation:

A. Possible observations in each stem are increasingly larger concentric rings surrounding a center point. Some rings are thicker than others. One stem has many thin rings. The other has thicker rings.

B. Light portions of the ring are composed of larger tracheid cells with thin walls. They are produced when growth is rapid, usually in the spring. Dark parts of the ring are composed of smaller, thicker-walled tracheids formed when growth is slow, usually during the summer. Growth rings are discussed on page 397. A growth ring usually adds more thickness during years of high rainfall than during dry years.

C. If correlations between width of growth rings and rainfall are being studied, the stumps used should be on uplands or near the upper part of slopes so that their water supply is clearly dependent on rainfall amounts. If you have an increment borer, live trees can be used without damage.

Answers to Chapter 22 Review:

1. Answers will vary through research. Forests have supplied lumber for construction, wood for fuel, pulpwood for paper, and seeds for food. Improvements: further education of the population regarding needless forest fires, immediate growth of new trees when harvesting has taken place, and controls on pollution and cutting.

2. Answers will vary. Coniferous trees supply a large part of the lumber used for building and paper making.

3. All woody plants have an inherently limited life span. Growth slows down and the tree becomes more susceptible to attack by natural enemies such as fungi and insects. Ages of 100-200 years or more are common among the conifers. The Sierra redwood, which has very few natural enemies, sometimes reaches an age of 400 years. More recently ring counts have established that some bristlecone pines near timberline in the White Mountains of California are even older, up to 4600 years.

References and Readings:

Teacher

Bold, H.C. 1973. *Morphology of plants,* 3rd ed. New York: Harper and Row.

Harlow, W.M. 1979. *Inside wood: masterpieces of nature.* Washington, D.C.: American Forestry Asociation.

Jensen, W.A. and F.B. Salisbury 1972. *Botany: an ecological approach.* Belmont, CA: Wadsworth.

Student

Cobb, B. 1956. *A field guide to the ferns.* Boston, MA: Hougton Mifflin.

Mickel, J. 1979. *How to know the ferns and fern allies.* Pictures Key Nature Series. Dubuque, IA: Wm. C. Brown Co.

Mirov, N.T. and J. Hasbrouck 1976. *The story of pines.* Bloomington, IN: Indiana University Press.

Stern, K.R. 1979. *Introductory plant biology.* Dubuque, IA: Wm. C. Brown Co.

Symonds, G.W.D. 1958. *The tree identification book: a new method for the practical identification and recognition of trees.* New York: William Morrow and Company, Inc.

CHAPTER 23   FLOWERING PLANTS

Introduction: You will notice the emphasis on the idea that parts of a flower become a fruit with enclosed seed or seeds. Even so, this may need to be stressed by the teacher.

It is easy for the teacher or students to collect a variety of fruits, native and domestic, from you area. The dried ones can be stored and used from year to year. Fleshy fruits can be displayed for a few days and then eaten or recycled in the soil (composted).

Ideas for Individual Student Investigations:

1. Develop a key for the identification of trees in the community or in a specific park.

2. Organize a reference herbarium of pressed plants that are common in the community.

Answers to Chapter 23 Investigation:

A. All six species reproduce by flowers.

B. Students might mention flower color, the number of flower parts, the arrangement and shape of stamens, or a number of other features.

C. (A) Idaho potatoe; (B) Flower-of-an-hour; (C) Crimson-eyed rose mallow; (D) Carolina horsenettle; (E) Purple nightshade; (F) Spiderwort.

Taxonomists group the flowers shown in photographs A, D, E into the same genus. Each has five sepals, a five parted corolla, five stamens, and columnar stamens. Those flowers shown in photographs B and C have five sepals, five petals, and many stamens attached to a tube around the pistil. The flower in photograph F has three sepals, three petals, six stamens, and a three parted pistil.

Answers to Chapter 23 Review:

1. Most flowers are pollinated by such factors in nature as insects, bats, birds, water currents, and wind. Large quantities of pollen must be produced to overcome the tremendous waste inherent in these methods, and assure the occurrence of pollination.

2. Answers will vary from student to student. The ripened ovary, together with any other structures that ripen with it and form a unit with it, is called a fruit. The botanical definition is broader than that of a grocery shopper. Botanically, string beans, tomatoes, corn grains and chestnuts are as much fruits as peaches and strawberries. Vegetable, on the other hand, is a nontechnical term not much used botanically.

3. Students answers will vary according to the library research.

References and Readings:

Teacher

Esau, K. 1976. *Anatomy of seed plants,* 2nd ed. NY: John Wiley and Sons.

Galston, A.W., and P.J. Davies 1970. *Control mechanisms in plant development.* Englewood Cliffs, NJ: Prentice-Hall.

Kingsbury, J.M. 1964. *Poisonous plants of the United States and Canada.* Englewood Cliffs, NJ: Prentice-Hall.

Koch, W.J. 1973. *Plants in the laboratory: a manual and text for studies of the culture, development, reproduction, cytology, genetics, collection, and identification of the major plant groups.* New York: Macmillan Publishing Company, Inc.

Muller, W.H. 1979. *Botany: a functional approach.* New York: Macmillan Publishing Company, Inc.

Stern, K.R. 1979. *Introductory plant biology.* Dubuque, IA: Wm. C. Brown Co.

Weaver, R.J. 1972. *Plant growth substances in agriculture.* San Francisco: W.H. Freeman and Co.

Zimmerman, M.H. 1963. How sap moves in trees. *Scientific American* 208(3)132.

Student

Angier, B. 1974. *Field guide to edible wild plants.* Harrisburg, PA: Stackpole Books.

Bellamy, D. 1979. *Forces of life: the botanic man.* New York: Crown Publishers, Inc.

Leopold, A.C. 1965. *Auxins and plant growth.* Berkeley, CA: University of California Press.

Martin, A.C. 1972. *Weeds.* Golden Guide Series. New York: Western Publishing Co.

Peterson, R.T. and M. McKenny 1968. *A field guide to wildflowers of Northeastern and Northcentral America.* Boston, MA: Houghton Mifflin.

Spencer, P.W. 1973. The turning of leaves. *Natural History* 82(8):56.

Stephens, H.A. 1980. *Poisonous plants of the Central United States.* Lawrence, KS: The Regents Press of Kansas.

Symonds, G.W.D. 1958. *The tree identification book: a new method for the practical identification and recognition of trees.* New York: William Morrow and Company, Inc.

Symonds, G.W.D. 1963. *The shrub identification book: the visual method for the practical identification of shrubs including woody vines and ground covers.* New York: William Morrow and Company, Inc.

Zim, H.S. 1950. *Flowers*. Golden Guide Series. New York: Western Publishing Co.

Zim, H.S., and A. Martin 1956. *Trees*. Golden Guide Series. New York: Western Publishing Co.

Oxford/Carolina Biology Readers: Burlington, NC: Carolina Biological Supply Co.

Black, M. 1972. Control processes in germination and dormancy.

Clowes, F.A.L. 1972. Morphogenesis of the shoot apex.

Heath, O.V.S. 1975. Stomata.

Hillman, W.S. 1979. Photoperiodism in plants and animals.

Northcote, D.H. 1974. Differentiation in higher plants.

Rutter, A.J. 1972. Transpiration.

Woodell, S.R.J. 1973. Xerophytes.

Wooding, F.B.P. 1978. Phloem.

Woolhouse, H.W. 1972. Aging process in higher plants.

OVERVIEW OF UNIT 7
ANIMALS: INVERTEBRATES

It is helpful to have either live or preserved examples of a few species in each animal group studied. A marine aquarium is encouraged, especially in schools far from coastal areas. If your school takes trips to the coast, caution against over-collection. Some coastal areas have been stripped of certain kinds of life for school collections.

The final section of the unit makes comparisons among invertebrates and with plants.

CHAPTER 24 SPONGES, CNIDARIANS, AND UNSEGMENTED WORMS

Introduction: Even if you have no marine aquarium, hydras and planarians can be located in appropriate, freshwater environments. Perhaps you can find freshwater sponges. Laboratory investigations with sponges may begin imediately following the section on Animal Shapes. Microscope slides of trichina cysts, and adult trichina and hookworms are useful.

Answers to Chapter 24 Investigation:

A. Each piece regenerates the missing end.

B. A section from the middle usually regenerates both head and tail if the section is large enough. An exception is mentioned in C.

C. Results vary. In the region just behind the pharynx, where the worm constricts and separates during normal fission, heads do not usually develop. Just behind this zone pieces usually do produce heads. Very short anterior pieces may regenerate a head at both ends. Likewise, short posterior pieces may regenerate a tail at each end.

Answers to Chapter 24 Review:

1. Animals demonstrate the life process, locomotion, or intelligent movement. Such movement may involve the entire organism, or only individual body parts. Even though plants show some movements, these are usually based upon growth or turgor. Protists, fungi and monerans exhibit growth. Some show movement by simple response to stimuli.

2. Inside body tube: digestion and absorption. Outside body tube: protection and sensation.

3. Answers will vary but may include the following. An advantage of human radial symmetry may be that exceptional damage to an organ, such as the heart, would not necessarily result in death because the human being would have many hearts. A limitation may be sluggishness.

4. The cells of multi-cellular animals are attached in a variety of ways. For example, the cells of smooth muscle tissue in humans are connected by means of reticular connective tissue fibers, which act as an intercellular cementing material.

5. Answers will vary.

6. Answers will vary but may include the following. The heartworm, a roundworm living as a parasite in the bloodstream, especially in the heart of dogs, is frequently seen by veterinarians.

References and Readings:

Teacher

Croll, W.A. 1966. *Ecology of parasites*. Cambridge, MA: Harvard University Press.

Fry, W.G. (ed.) 1970. *The biology of the Porifera*. New York: Academic Press.

Rees, W.J. (ed.) 1966. *The Cnidaria and their evolution*. New York: Academic Press.

Schmidt-Nielsen, K. 1972. *How animals work*. New York: Cambridge Book Co.

Student

Buchsbaum, R. 1976. *Animals without backbones*. 2nd ed. rev. Chicago: University of Chicago Press.

CHAPTER 25 ANNELIDS, MOLLUSCS, AND ECHINODERMS

Introduction: While we highlight the earthworm, clam, and starfish, make sure that students are aware of other members of these groups. Many molluscs are interesting as well as involved with human life.

Answers to Chapter 25 Investigation:

A. Earthworms are expected to turn most often to the dark, moist chamber.

B. The conditions in arm A are pleasant and lack light and shock. Rough, cold, hot, dry, or flooded conditions in arm B might produce similar results.

C. One might arrange the T-maze with both arms containing moist humus; one arm should be dark. The other should have red light and an electric shock. Three volts are adequate for a response in earthworms. This can be achieved by two, 1.5 volt dry cells connected in series. The wires can be laid on wet paper toweling. Red cellophane can be used as a filter with a desk lamp or on the front of a flashlight. After the worms have learned to avoid the shock (and the red light if they detect it), the shock is removed, and the red light is moved to the other arm. Observe whether the worms continue to avoid the red light.

Answers to Chapter 25 Review:

1. Answers will vary depending upon students research. Students may suggest that the group which best protects the ecosystem should be favored.

2. Answers will vary but may include the following. The ocean can support the huge weight of the world's largest animals by both buoyancy and food supply. It therefore favors their development.

3. Answers will vary but may include using fertilizers from the sea.

4. Answers will vary. They may include that bilateral symmetry favors the development of a complex centralized nervous system, while radial and spherical symmetry restricts this.

5. The pearl is the result of an injury to the mollusc caused by either an organism or a foreign particle which imbeds itself in the fleshy part of the bivalve and causes an irritation. The irritation stimulates layers of nacre (mother-of-pearl) around the intruding body to form the pearl. When the irritation is intentionally done by man to produce the pearl, the result is commonly known as a cultured pearl.

References and Readings:

Teacher

Edwards, C.A. and J.R. Lofty 1972. *Biology of earthworms*. New York: John Wiley and Sons.

Purchon, R.D. 1968. *The biology of the Mollusca*. Elmsford, NY: Pergamon Press.

Schmidt-Nielsen, K. 1972. *How animals work*. New York: Cambridge Book Co.

Student

Buchsbaum, R. 1976. *Animals without backbones*, 2nd. rev. Chicago: University of Chicago Press.

Morris, P.A. 1973. *A field guide to the Pacific Coast shells including shells of Hawaii and the Gulf of California.* Boston, MA: Houghton Mifflin.

Morris, P.A. 1973. *A field guide to the shells of the Atlantic and Gulf coasts and the West Indies.* Boston, MA: Houghton Mifflin.

Nicholas, D. 1975. *The uniqueness of the Echinoderms.* Oxford/Carolina Biology Readers. Burlington, NC: Carolina Biological Supply Co.

Wickler, W. 1973. *The marine aquarium.* Neputne, NJ: T.F.H. Publications, Inc.

CHAPTER 26   THE ARTHROPODS

Introduction: No matter where you live, there are numerous examples of arthropods that you can observe in their habitat settings. You might begin by displaying some arthropods, and pointing out general phylum and class characteristics. The laboratory study of the crayfish would follow. An alternative is to begin with the laboratory study of the crayfish. Then arthropods of the other classes may be compared to the crayfish.

In the fall, insects can be collected for life-cycle studies or for preservation for later laboratory observation and identification experiences.

Ideas for Individual Student Investigations:

A. A challenging experience for individuals or small groups of students is to culture an arthropod species through its life cycle. Let students, for example, get supplies, or devise suitable habitat. Possible arthropods for such a project include ants, crickets, cockroaches, fruit flies, mealworm beetles, pillbugs, *Daphnia*, cyclops, spiders, or centipedes. Photographing each stage and/or writing a complete report of the project might be part of the experience.

B. A study of the chemical, sound, visual, and other senses of specific arthropod species can be devised.

Answers to Chapter 26 Investigation:

A. The antennae are more prominent, and are used for swimming.

B. *Daphnia* belong to Class Crustacea.

C. One might place depression slides into a small beaker of water containing *Daphnia*. That beaker can be placed inside a larger beaker of water held at 10 to 20 degrees below room temperature with chopped ice. Another small beaker containing depression slides and *Daphnia* can be placed in a warm-water bath held at 10 to 20 degrees above room temperature. A third set can be held at room temperature.

After 10 minutes one *Daphnia* is transferred to the dried depression slide. Excess water is removed with a medicine dropper to reduce motion of the *Daphnia*. With the slide placed under the microscope, heartbeat rate is determined under low power by tapping a soft lead pencil in rhythm with the heartbeat, and counting the dots made in a specific time period. A good *Daphnia* transfer mechanism is a medicine dropper with its bulb transferred to the tip end.

An alternative is to use a Stender dish or other small glass container with a dab of petroleum jelly on the bottom inside. The *Daphnia*'s posterior is embedded in the jelly to retard its motion. Chlorine-free water is added, and the dish placed into a water bath with appropriate temperature, as decribed earlier. Make sure that the whole assembly fits the microscope before proceding with prepration.

Answers to Chapter 26 Review:

1. Answers will vary, but may include conditioned learning as in the following example. Place a red card in front of the insect. Then, give the insect food. Repeat. After a period of time the insect should expect food when the red card apears, and should approach it. See what happens when you use a green card. If the insect hovers around it, like the red one, the evidence might be that it cannot distinguish color.

2. Answers will vary. Tuning forks are calibrated at a certain number of vibrations per second. Compare the sound of the forks with the sound of the beating wings until the same sound is found. Then you would know the wings will have the same vibrations as that fork.

3. Answers will vary depending upon locale.

4. This is easily seen when it is time for a new queen to appear. As the old queen prepares to leave the hive, the new queens are getting ready to emerge. The one with the greatest strength and intelligence will destroy the others, and will pass these traits on.

5. Answers will vary, but may include: museums of natural history, drug companies, and departments of health.

6. Answers will vary.

References and Readings:

Teacher

Borror, D. J., and D. M. De Long. *An introduction to the study of insects*, 3rd ed. New York: Holt, Rinehart, and Winston.

Green, J. 1961. *A biology of crustacea*. New York: Quadrangle Books.

Snow, K. R. 1970. *The arachnids*. New York: Columbia University Press.

Student

Best, R.L. 1978. *Living arthropods in the classroom*. Burlington NC: Carolina Biological Supply Co.

Bland, R. G. 1978. *How to know the insect*, 3rd ed. Dubuque, IA: Wm. C. Brown Publishing Co.

Borror, D. J. and R. E. White 1970. *A field guide to the insects of America north of Mexico*. Boston, MA: Houghton Mifflin.

Buchsbaum, R. 1976. *Animals without backbones*, 2nd ed. rev. Chicago: University of Chicago Press.

Ehrlich, P.R., and A. H. Ehrlich 1961. *How to know the butterflies*. Dubuque, IA: Wm. C. Brown Publishing Co.

Fichter, G. 1966. *Insect pests*. Golden Guide Series. New York: Western Publishing Co.

Levi, H.W., and L.R. Levi 1968. *Spiders and their kin*. Golden Guide Series. New York: Western Publishing Co.

Mitchell, R., and H. Zim 1964. *Butterflies and moths*. Golden Guide series. New York: Western Publishing Co.

Von Frisch, K. 1950. *Bees: their vision, chemical senses, and language*. New York: Cornell University Press.

Zim, H. and C. Cottam 1956. *Insects*. Golden Guide Series. New York: Western Publishing Co.

Oxford/Carolina Biology Readers: Burlington, NC: Carolina Biological Supply Co.

Johnson, C.G. 1976. Insect migration.

Pringle, J.W.S. 1975. Insect flight.

Wigglesworth, V.B. 1974. Insect hormones.

Wigglesworth, V.B. 1972. Insect respiration.

OVERVIEW OF UNIT 8

ANIMALS: VERTEBRATES

In this unit, we will conclude our survey of living things with the vertebrates—the animals with backbones. As with other units in our survey of living things, the last chapter of the unit contains a comparison section. A study of the comparison section will provide students with many of the important generalizations that are developed in these chapters.

The chapter investigations call for designing experiments and making predictions. Specific activities designed to assist students in further development of these skills are found in the *Laboratory Manual*.

The laboratory investigation that accompany this unit will further develop the student's abilities to make careful observations. In some of the activities, students will be making observations of themselves and their classmates. Such activities reinforce the idea that humans are in fact vertebrates.

CHAPTER 27   FISHES AND AMPHIBIANS

Introduction: If you have preserved specimens to illustrate the diversity of fishes and amphibians, set them out for students to observe as an introduction to this chapter. Most of the content of this chapter is descriptive biology, and should not present any particular difficulties. Though none of the laboratory investigations ask the students to experiment on live vertebrates, the issue of when and whether such experiments should be done is worth discussing.

DEMONSTRATION: Frog eggs may be collected from water near the edge of ponds in the early spring. If these are placed in an aquarium in the classroom, students can observe the development of the eggs, their hatching, and the development of the tadpoles.

Materials: aquarium, small rocks and sand, frog eggs (from a biological supply house if not from a pond), aquarium plants, pond water.

Time: about an hour to set up (This could be done during class so that students can observe.)

Procedure: Place rocks and sand in the bottom of a clean aquarium. If tadpoles are to be kept until they have legs, sand and rocks should be arranged so that tadpoles will be able to get out of water at one end of the aquarium. Place aquarium plants in the sand and add pond water. Suspend water plants in the water. Let it settle until the water is clear. Place egg mass in the water so that it is partly camouflaged by the plants. When tadpoles have developed as far as they are to be observed, they can be returned to the pond from which the eggs were obtained. If the eggs were obtained from a biological supply house, release the tadpoles only if they are a species normally found in your area.

Possible questions: How long does it take eggs to hatch? What does the tadpole look like when it first hatches? How does it change over the next several weeks?

Answers to Chapter 27 Investigation:

A. A toad is eating a bumblebee and getting stung. Later, the same toad avoids or ignores a robber fly.

B. One explanation is that the toad learned that eating an animal that looks like a bumblebee results in getting stung. It refuses to eat the robber fly, which resembles the bumblebee, because it has learned not to eat things that sting.

C. The behavior is trial and error learning. The intended kind of experiment that students might do on their friends would involve trial and error, perhaps a paper-and-pencil maze, a list of difficult words to be spelled, or any other experiment that does not risk harm to their friends. Review experimental designs, and have students obtain your approval before they do the experiments.

Answers to Chapter 27 Review:

1. It no longer has the pressure of the heart's contractions directly behind it. Also, moving one cell at a time through capillaries causes it to lose momentum.

2. (a) Rate of respiration and circulation would increase. (b) Rate of respiration and circulation would decrease, and estivation would take place. (c) Rate of respiration and circulation would decrease, and hibernation would take place.
(c) Rate of respiration and circulation would decrease, and hibernation would take place.
(d) Same as (b).

3. Answers will vary. The statement might be interpreted that through natural selection and human activities, species are likely to change in the future. For example, it is possible that every species would be endangered or genetically altered if exposed to radiation produced by unharnessed nuclear activity.

4. Answers will vary. They may include isolation of the young from other individuals, and observation of their developmental behavior.

5. Non-adaptive behavior has been eliminated by selective pressures as part of the evolutionary process.

6. Answers will vary depending upon locale and student interest. A study of ichthyology might be a good preparation for work in a fish hatchery.

7. Answers depend in part upon subjective evaluations. Guidelines set up by organizations for the humane treatment of animals will be felt appropriate by persons who believe that animals should be protected from suffering, and that inflicting such pain is unworthy of civilized human beings.

8. Other animals hibernate in a different sense. Some include chipmunks and ground squirrels, which hibernate in underground nests; and bats which live in caves or buildings.

References and Readings:

Teacher

Gordon, R., and A. G. Jacobson 1978. The shaping of tissues in embryos. *Scientific American* 238(6):106 (June).

Student

Isaacs, J.D., and R.A. Schwartzlose 1975. Active animals of the deep-sea floor. *Scientific American 233(4):85 (October).*

Kent, G.C. 1978. *Comparative anatomy of the verte-brates.* St. Louis: C.V. Mosby Co.

CHAPTER 28 REPTILES AND BIRDS

Introduction: If you have preserved specimens to ilustrate the diversity of reptiles and birds, set them out for students to observe as an introduction to this chapter. A field trip to a zoo might be a good way to interest students. Or students might make observations of pet birds (and if available, pet reptiles). Movements, feeding behaviors, and other kinds of behavior should be observed. A field trip to a museum to study preserved specimens of reptiles and birds, fossils of dinosaurs, dioramas, or any other appropriate exhibits would add interest to this chapter.

DEMONSTRATION: Students might be interested in assembling a complete bird skeleton. This can be done from the bones of baked turkey or chicken.

Materials: One bird carcass with all loose tissue picked from the bones, a large pot, water, ammonia, and detergent.

Time: 4 hours to prepare bones, and variable time for students to assemble skeleton.

Procedure: Place all bones in a large pot of water. Add about 10 ml of detergent and 10 ml of ammonia for each liter of water. Boil until bones are clean. If time permits, lay the bones in a sunny place to bleach. Give the students all of the bones. Allow them to sort the bones, and assemble them in the proper configuration. A wire may be run through the canal in the vertebrae for support. Other wires may be used to support the completed skeleton.

Possible questions: How many vertebrae has a bird skeleton? How do the bones of the forelimbs differ from those of the hindlimbs? How does the weight of the bones of a bird differ from that of the bones of other animals? What was attached to the large breastbone? (muscles) Why do birds have such large muscles running from the breastbone to the forelimbs?

Ideas for Individual Student Investigations:

The topic of behavior in birds—navigation, territoriality, and other social behaviors—is a suitable research topic for the more able students. See the study skills section "Preparing a Library Research Paper," of the *Laboratory Manual,* for information on doing library research, and writing a research paper.

Answers to Chapter 28 Investigation:

A. Similarities between reptiles and birds include the presence of scales somewhere on the body, presence of lungs, laying of eggs (usually on land), internal fertilization, and all other general vertebrate characteristics. (Accept any other correct answers.) Differences between reptiles and birds include a three-chambered heart in reptiles, except for crocodiles and alligators, and a four-chambered heart in birds, ectothermy in reptiles and endothermy in birds, leathery shells on reptile eggs and brittle shells on bird eggs, feathers on birds only, forelimbs usually modified for flight in birds, and far more complex behavior in birds than in reptiles. (Accept any other correct answers.)

B. The high metabolic rate in birds and the insulation provided by feathers are two important ways that birds maintain their high body temperatures.

C. The concept illustrated by the maintenance of nearly constant body temperature is homeostasis. Some possible experiments might include placing a turtle in cool and warm locations, and taking its temperature (skin temperature would do if rectal temperature is not deemed suitable). A clinical thermometer used on humans could be used. A similar experiment might be done with a bird. Be sure the animals are not in any way harmed by the experiment. Students should be encouraged to do library research to find out more about the regulation of body temperature in birds.

Answers to Chapter 28 Review:

1. Answers will vary, but may include: temperature regulation by the thermostat mechanism in the hypothalamus; migration in birds to insure survival of winter; functioning of the three or four-chambered heart to maintain steady levels of oxygen, carbon dioxide, foods, and wastes in the blood and tissues it serves; filter action of kidneys to remove wastes from blood and keep its water content constant; sharp eyesight, and color vision of birds, used to help locate distant food.

2. The eggs are adapted for land survival. This suggests that these animals' ancestors lived on land, and that the water-dwellers are following an innate behavior pattern.

3. The thermostat mechanism of birds is more precise, keeping body temperature within a narrower range than that of reptiles. Also, reptiles often move from shade to sun, or vice versa, to cool or warm their bodies. Birds get rid of excess heat by increasing their rate of breathing.

4. Herpetologists study the science of reptiles. They are frequently employed by museums of natural history.

5. Answers will vary. Probably some students will feel that certain analogies, but no precise predictions or deductions, can be drawn. Another view is that results of studies on birds suggest hypotheses leading to related studies on humans.

6. Answers will vary. Probably most students would suggest that one should learn to identify the few poisonous snakes. Killing snakes should be avoided in general because this process can upset the ecosystem.

References and Readings:

Teacher

Crews, D. 1979. The hormonal control of behavior in a lizard. *Scientific American* 241(2):180 (August).

Student

Anonymous 1979. Animals find their way. *Mosaic*: 25 (May/June)

Bakker, R.T. 1975. Dinosaur renaissance. *Scientific American* 232(4):58 (April).

Emlen, S.T. 1975. The stellar-orientation system of a migratory bird. *Scientific American* 233(2):102 (August).

Heller, H.C., L.I. Crawshaw, and H.T. Hammel 1978. The thermostat of vertebrate animals. *Scientific American* 239(2)102 (August).

Miller, J.A. 1980. A song for a female finch. *Science News* 117:58 (January 26)

Pooley, A.C., and C. Gans 1976. The Nile crocodile. *Scientific American* 234(4):114 (April).

Weis-Fogh, T. 1975. Unusual mechanisms for the generation of lift in flying animals. *Scientific American 233(5):81 (November).*

Williams, T.C. and J.M. Williams 1978. An oceanic mass migration of land birds. *Scientific American* 239(4):166 (October).

CHAPTER 29 MAMMALS

Introduction: If preserved specimens of mammals are available, set them out for students to observe the diversity of mammals. A sequence of preserved specimens might also be used to demonstrate variations among different invertebrate and vertebrate animals. Such a demonstration could be used to introduce the final section of the chapter.

This chapter should be inherently interesting to students, because they themselves are mammals. Most students should be able to read and understand the chapter without great difficulty. The final section of the chapter summarizes much of what has been covered in the last few chapters and emphasizes relationships between mammals and other animals.

Ideas for Individual Student Investigations:

Students might observe the gait of several different kinds of mammals. Students in rural areas might compare the locomotion of horses, cattle, sheep, goats, and pigs. Those students in urban areas might visit a stable, a zoo, or make observations of their own pets. They might observe differences in the structure of the limbs and feet, the speed of the animal, and the sequence in which it steps on each foot when it is walking slowly, and when it is running.

Answers to Chapter 29 Investigation:

A. The teeth in the lower left figure include several large molars with rough surfaces. Those in the lower right figure include very sharp canines and those in the upper right figure are intermediate between the other two set of teeth.

B. The animal whose teeth are shown in the lower left figure would likely eat mostly a plant diet. Here, the large molars are used for grinding the leaves and stems of the plants the herbivore eats. The animal whose teeth are shown in the lower right figure is probably a meat-eater (carnivore). Its sharp canines are well-designed for tearing flesh, and its less prominent molars are suitable for grinding flesh once it is torn into bits by the canines. The girl whose teeth are shown in the upper right figure is an omnivore, who eats both plant and animal foods.

C. Teeth help us to predict other things about the organism. For example, the herbivore most likely has a stomach with several chambers and a long digestive tract. It probably grazes, eats a lot at one time (when predators are not present), and is not a very good runner. The carnivore probably has a stomach with a single chamber and a relatively short digestive tract. It captures its prey by chasing it, and therefore can run fast. It may also eat a lot at one time. The characteristics of humans are less predictable. A digestive tract of intermediate length is present. (Accept all other correct answers.) Students might be encouraged to do some library research on the habits of these organisms after thay have made their predictions.

Answers to Chapter 29 Review:

1. Answers will vary, depending upon the student's choice. Emphasize the importance of the control. (A conditioned response in which a simple action is associated with the sound of a bell, or a ruler tapping on a desk, is easy to demonstrate.)

2. Answers will vary. They may include such questions as the methods used to arrive at the conclusions about learning and other behaviors that are mentioned in the text.

References and Readings:

Teacher

Wilson, E.O. 1979. Interview. *Omni* 1(5):97 (February).

Student

Baker, M.A. 1979. A brain-cooling system in mammals. *Scientific American* 240(5):130 (May).

Bekoff, M., and M.C. Wells 1980. The social ecology of coyotes. *Scientific American* 242(4):130 (April).

Bertram, B.C.R. 1975. The social system of lions. *Scientific American* 232(5):54 (May).

Dawson, T. J. 1977. Kangaroos. *Scientific American* 237(2):78 (August).

Lore, R., and K. Flannelly 1977. Rat societies. *Scientific American* 236(5):106 (May).

MacLean, P.D. 1978. A mind of three minds: evolution of the human brain. *The Science Teacher* 45(4):31 (April).

Raloff, J. 1979. Bloody harvest. *Science News* 115:202 (March 31).

Simons, E.L. 1977. Ramapithecus. *Scientific American* 236(5):28 (May).

Wursig, B. 1979. Dolphins. *Scientific American* 240(3):136 (March).

OVERVIEW OF UNIT 9
HUMAN BODY SYSTEMS

Some passages in chapters of this unit deal with fairly difficult physiological processes. However, most of the information is well within the average student's level of understanding.

Though this unit is at the end of the book, it is by no means last in importance. Rather, one might argue that it contains more information that students will be able to use in the future than any other unit. Thus, we strongly urge that time be taken to study these chapters carefully.

As you begin this unit, ask students to start keeping a record of how many hours of sleep they get during each 24-hour period for the next two weeks. Have them use what they have learned in the study skill CD-3 "Making Graphs," to prepare graphs of the information they have collected. When you discuss sleep in Chapter 32, you can use the students' graphs to study individual variations in sleep requirements.

CHAPTER 30 DIGESTION AND NUTRITION

Introduction: In approaching this chapter, students' inherent interest in the type of food they eat will be useful. A brief review of Chapter 7 will remind students that the food they eat provides the energy and raw materials their body cells need to stay alive.

You might want to begin this chapter by asking students to contribute to a list developed on the chalkboard of most liked foods, least liked foods, most nutritious foods, and least nutritious foods. You might want to copy the list and save it for future use after the students know more about nutrition.

As ideas about nutrition are developed, you might raise the issue of supplying all the people of the world with an adequate, nutritious diet. Lappe's *Diet for a Small Planet* is a useful reference in this context.

Ideas for Individual Student Investigations:

Several topics are discussed briefly in this chapter that could be developed into library research projects and oral reports. Oral reports would allow other members of the class to profit from the information collected by individual students. Suitable topics include: megavitamins, low carbohydrate and other reducing diets, vegetable proteins, food additives and their effects on the body, junk foods, alcohol and how it is metabolized and how it affects the body, various drugs, and "the pill-taking society."

Answers to Chapter 30 Investigation:

A. Meal A includes fruit, vegetables, and milk. In addition to soda pop, meal B also has many starchy and fried foods, and a large quantity of refined sugar in the cake and icing.

B. Meal A is far more nutritious than meal B. Meal A contains both fruit and vegetables that are important sources of vitamins. None of the foods are fried, and none contain large amounts of refined sugars. Milk provides minerals, and the fish and milk both provide protein. Meal B is not very nutritious. The cake, icing, and soda pop provide a large number of calories without many vitamins and minerals. the french fires, bread, and butter provide carbohydrate and fat calories, but few vitamins and minerals. the fried meat provides protein, but an excess of fat, especially saturated fat. To satisfy the needs of a growing person according to the basic four food groups, the person who ate meal A would also need two servings of milk, one serving of meat or other protein, one serving of citrus fruit, and three servings of bread or cereal. The person who ate meal B would need three servings of milk, one serving of protein, four servings of fruits and vegetables including a yellow fruit or vegetable and a citrus fruit, and one serving of bread or cereal.

C. Answers will vary with research.

Answers to Chapter 30 Review:

1. Answers will vary. The variations in answers obtained by different members of the class can be used to stimulate an interesting discussion about nutritional value and food costs.

2. Answers will vary. Compare price of diet using some of the vegetable protein combinations in Table 30-6 with diet containing animal proteins.

3. Answers will vary. Discussion will emphasize the importance of attitudes about foods and good nutrition as well as dietary goals. One of these is reducing the amount of saturated fat in the diet.

4. One problem with eating plant proteins is that any one plant does not contain all of the amino acids our bodies need. Each of the amino acids we need can be found in some plant foods. Therefore, combine in the same meal two or more plant foods for adequate nutrition.

5. Results of class debates will vary. Emphasis would be on use of accurate information in making points in the debate.

6. Answers will vary.

References and Readings:

Teacher

Food and Nutrition Board 1979. *Recommended dietary allowances.* Washington: National Academy of Sciences.

Kappas, A., and A.P. Alvares 1975. How the liver metabolizes foreign substances. *Scientific American* 232(6):22 (June).

Student

Fleck, H.C. 1976. *Introduction to nutrition,* 3rd ed. New York: Macmillan Publishing Company, Inc.

Lappe, F.M. 1971. *Diet for a small planet.* New York: Ballantine Books, Inc.

Mayer, J. 1975. *A diet for living.* New York: David McKay Company, Inc.

Page, L., and B. Friend 1978. The changing United States diet. *BioScience* 28(3):192 (March).

Select Committee on Nutrition and Human Needs, United States Senate 1977. *Dietary goals for the United States.* Washington: U.S. Government Printing Office.

Singer, S., and H.R. Hilgard 1978. *The biology of people.* San Francisco: W.H. Freeman and Co.

Tortora, G.J., and N.P. Anagnostakos 1978. *Principles of anatomy and physiology.* San Francisco: Canfield Press.

CHAPTER 31   TRANSPORT, RESPIRATION, AND EXCRETION

Introduction: Student interest in both sports and in keeping in good physical condition provide the impetus for participation in the various chapter topics. Likewise, students interested in careers related to medicine should respond in a positive manner to this chapter. Slower students may find some of the concepts difficult.

A demonstration of the technique of cardiopulmonary resuscitation (CPR) might be appropriate, particularly if it can be used to encourage students to complete a course and become certified to give CPR. The American Red Cross and the American Heart Association in many locations will provide an instructor for CPR courses, and in some cases will give a free demonstration. (Students should be cautioned that watching one demonstration does not make them experts in the technique.)

DEMONSTRATION: Though we have elected not to include a laboratory activity on urinalysis in the *Laboratory Manual,* the following demonstration might be useful for those who find it suitable for their classes.

Materials: specimen of normal urine; specimens of urine to which glucose, albumin (from an egg), and ketones (acetone) have been added; litmus paper; dipsticks to test for glucose and ketones (available at most pharmacies); concentrated nitric acid; (4) test tubes or small beakers for specimens.

Time: one-half hour to assemble material; only a few minutes for class demonstration.

Procedure: Obtain about 100 ml of normal urine and divide it among four containers. Add glucose to one, albumin to one, and acetone to one. (Amounts are not critical.) The final container is the control. Dip a separate piece of red litmus paper and a separate piece of blue litmus paper into each specimen. Record on the chalkboard whether each specimen is acidic or basic. (Urine is usually slightly acidic.) Follow the instructions on the container and test each specimen for glucose. Record findings on the chalkboard. Repeat for ketones. Add a few drops of nitric acid to each specimen and look for a white to yellowish precipitate. (CAUTION: Nitric acid is harmful to skin and clothing. Rinse with water if spillage occurs.) This indicates that protein is present in the urine. Again, record findings on the chalkboard.

Possible questions: Ask students which of the specimens was normal urine. (the one without glucose, ketones, or protein) What might cause glucose to be present in the urine? (diabetes) What might cause ketones to be present in the urine? (diabetes, fasting, or following a very low carbohydrate diet, such as when the body burns fats, because it has no carbohydrates available or because it cannot metabolize carbohydrates as in diabetes, ketones are produced.) What might cause protein to be present in the urine? (kidney disease in which the glomeruli are damaged and allow large molecules to enter the urine) What might cause the urine to be highly acid or somewhat basic? Foods in the diet are mostly responsible for changes in the pH of urine. A diet high in vegetables may produce alkaline urine; a diet high in acid fruits and meats may produce acidic urine.

Ideas for Individual Student Investigations:

Many clinical conditions related to the circulatory, respiratory, and urinary systems may be of interest to the students. Library research papers and oral reports on topics such as the following are appropriate: atherosclerosis, hypertension, heart disease, cholesterol and heart disease, hyaline membrane disease, sudden infant death syndrome, anemia, leukemia, emphysema, effects of smoking, and nephritis.

Answers to Chapter 31 Investigation:

A. The graph shows blood pressure plotted against time. The upper line on the graph shows the changes that occur in systolic blood pressure during rest and during exercise. Systolic blood pressure is the higher pressure that is created in an artery after the heart contracts. The lower line on the graph shows the changes (or lack of change) in the diastolic pressure during rest and during exercise. Diastolic blood pressure is the lower pressure that exists when the heart is relaxed. The variable on the horizontal axis is time, but periods of rest and exercise are shown. The variable on the vertical axis is blood pressure in millimeters of mercury, but values for both systolic and diastolic pressure are plotted.

B. Exercise causes the systolic blood pressure to increase. The line at the top changes while the one at the bottom stays very near the same because exercise affects only the systolic pressure. Systolic pressure increases during exercise because the heart chambers fill more completely between each contraction and pump a larger volume of blood. The heart also contracts more vigorously. However, the heart relaxes between each contraction, even during exercise, so the diastolic pressure remains nearly constant in a healthy person.

C. Other changes that might occur during exercise are that the pulse rate would increase, the respiratory rate (number of breaths per minute) would increase, and the body temperature would increase slightly. (Students may think of other answers.)

Answers to Chapter 31 Review:

1. Most likely the cause is an infection.

2. Because the smoke destroys the cilia in the respiratory passages, many particles get into the lungs that might have been stopped by cilia. Tars deposit on respiratory membranes. Other information may be presented by students who have done additional readings.

3. Ignore child. One cannot hold one's breath long enough to cause damage. When the level of carbon dioxide gets high enough, the brain causes breathing to resume.

References and Readings:

Teacher

Fardy, R.W. 1979. Hyaline membrane disease: a study in body systems. *The Science Teacher* 46(5):44 (May).

Student

Arehart-Treichel, J. 1979. Microsurgery. *Science News* 115:237 (April 7).

Benditt, E.P. 1977. The origin of atherosclerosis. *Scientific American* 236(2):74 (February).

Marx, J.L. 1976. Atherosclerosis: the cholesterol connection. *Science* 194:711 (November 12).

_____. 1976. Hypertension: a complex disease with complex causes. *Science* 194:821 (November 19).

_____. 1979. The HDL: the good cholesterol carrier. *Science* 205:677 (August 17).

Perutz, M.F. 1978. Hemoglobin structure and respiratory transport. *Scientific American* 239(6):92 (December).

CHAPTER 32   SENSORY PERCEPTION AND NERVOUS CONTROL

Introduction: The sensory section of this chapter will be fairly easy for the students, but they may find the portions on the brain more difficult to comprehend. Illustrate to students the importance of our senses by asking volunteers to function without one of their senses for one class period. One student might be blindfolded, another have ears covered with a pair of headphones, and another might wear gloves. Save time at the end of the period for the volunteers to describe the problems they encountered. If there are sensory impaired students in the class, they might be encouraged to comment on how they have overcome some of their problems.

DEMONSTRATION: When you come to the part of the chapter on sleep and wakefulness, ask students to have ready their graphs of the number of hours they have slept each night for the past two weeks. Each student should calculate the average number of hours slept each night. (Total hours divided by the number of nights. For students who have included naps—most teen-agers don't—use total hours of sleep divided by the number of 24-hour periods.) Next, calculate the range of hours slept per night. This will probably vary from 6 to 10 hours. Using data from everyone, make a bar graph on the chalkboard to show the variation in the mean number of hours of sleep per night. Place hours in one-hour intervals on the horizontal axis (for example, less than 7 hours, 7.00 to 7.99 hours, 8.00 to 8.99, etc.). Place the number of students on the vertical axis. Do another bar graph for the range of hours slept per night.

Possible questions: What is the greatest amount of sleep a student had? What is the least amount of sleep? What was the greatest range of variation? What was the most typical sleep pattern for the class as a whole? What can be said about individual differences in sleep needs?

Ideas for Individual Student Investigations:

Because so much more information is available about the human body than we were able to include in this chapter, we recommend that students pursue topics of interest in more detail through library research projects. Students should share their findings with their classmates.

Some appropriate topics for this chapter are: the use of corrective lenses, colorblindness, transmission deafness, nerve deafness, motion sickness, multiple sclerosis, various mental illnesses, effects of various drugs on the nervous system, endorphins and enkephalins, learning, memory, and how sleep and wakefulness are controlled.

Answers to Chapter 32 Investigation:

A. Students should find List 1 the easiest to remember and List 3 the most difficult. List 1 is easiest because all the items are familiar and they are also presented in alphabetic order. List 2 should be next in difficulty, because even though the words are long, they should be familiar, especially for biology students. List 3 is the most difficult. It makes no sense, is presented in no order, and even uses almost every letter of the alphabet!

B. The lists contain seven words because some research studies show that seven words is the maximum that can be stored in short term memory.

C. It is left to the students to decide what data to graph and how to do it. A common response might be to plot the number of words recalled from each list by each individual—a separate graph for each list. The total number of words recalled should decrease when the list is increased to 10 items. It is likely that the biology oriented students in the class will do better than non-biology oriented students on List 2. The important component of this activity is to encourage students to devise ways of collecting and presenting data. Also of importance is how well students interpret their data and how well their data support their conclusions.

Answers to Chapter 32 Review:

1. Answers will vary. However, it is possible that the organism would neither see nor hear, because its appropriate receptor and appropriate area in the brain are not matched.

2. The rods that are active in dim light do not perceive color. Thus, vivid colors would not be seen under the articifial lights available at night.

3. If a certain part of the cochlea that is sensitive to a particular pitch is damaged, sounds of that pitch will not be detected.

4. Answers will vary. They might include complete paralysis or failure of both sensory and motor impulse transmission.

5. Depolarization is the change in the distribution of sodium and potassium ions across the membrane of a neuron that results in the transmission of an impulse. Repolarization is the change back to the state the ions were in before the neuron was stimulated. A repolarized neuron is ready to receive another stimulus.

6. Answers will vary. Physiological addiction involves changes in the cells of the body so that they require a certain drug for their functioning. Symptoms of withdrawal occur when a physiologically addictive drug is withdrawn. Psychological addiction is a less serious condition that does not have significant physiological effects.

7. A sensory impulse goes to the spinal cord and a motor impulse goes back to the foot causing the foot to be removed from the stone.

8. Answers will vary. They may include citing evidence for damage to the body, danger of addiction, unconsciousness, and death.

9. Answers will vary. Knowledge of what is to be done and consent of the subject are important considerations. Students may think of others.

10. Answers will vary. They may include extensive research to offer a better understanding of memory.

11. Answers will vary. Students may contact research hospitals or any other research facility to find out the procedures involved.

12. Information in this chapter would have value for everyone. As an example, a teacher would want to know that a student is not learning due to lack of sleep, as opposed to lack of ability.

References and Readings:

Teacher

Land, E.H. 1977. The retinex theory of color vision. *Scientific American* 237(6):108 (December).

Student

Greenburg, J. 1979. Psyching out pain. *Science News* 115:332 (May 19).

Johannson, G. 1975. Visual motion perception. *Scientific American* 232(6):76 (June).

Novak, J.D. 1980. Learning theory applied to the biology classroom. *American Biology Teacher* 42(5):280 (May).

Special Issue on the Nervous System 1978. *Science News* 114(22) (November 25).

Special Issue on the Nervous System 1979. *Scientific American* 241(3) (September).

van Heyningen, R. 1975. What happens to the human lens in cataract. *Scientific American* 233(6):70 (December).

Wallace, R.K., and H. Benson 1972. The physiology of meditation. *Scientific American* 226(2):85 (February).

CHAPTER 33 PROTECTION AND MOVEMENT

Introduction: Students interested in exercise, sports and fitness will find this chapter useful. Furthermore, because there are few difficult concepts in the chapter most students will be able to read the chapter and answer the questions without assistance.

Ideas for Individual Student Investigations:

Library research papers and oral reports on the following topics wouls be appropriate: acne, treatment of fractures, treatment of joint injuries, and exercise. Students interested in sports should be interested in finding out more about how to prevent sport injuries.

Answers to Chapter 33 Investigation:

A. According to the data provided, people who participate in exercise programs have a lower resting pulse rate, a lower pulse rate after five minutes of exercise, and more blood being pumped to their cells

B. People who exercise have more oxygen delivered to their cells than those who do not. This occurs because the heart of a person who exercises is capable of more vigorous contraction, and of filling more completely with blood between contractions. Because more blood is pumped through the heart in a given period of time, more oxygen is carried to the cells.

C. Hypotheses might be as follows: Exercise strengthens the heart so that during rest it beats fewer times per minute to supply blood to the cells. The same hypothesis applies to the heart rate after five minutes of exercise. A greater volume of blood is pumped to the cells each minute by the heart of a person who exercises, because the heart contracts more forcefully and fills more completely. Students might design experiments in which they determine resting pulse and pulse after exercise before beginning an exercise program. They might make pulse counts at weekly intervals during their exercise program to determine whether their own pulse rates change. Check the experimental designs before students begin their experiments, and approve only those that are safe to do. Students with heart defects or other handicaps that might be exacerbated by strenuous exercise should not participate in such an experiment.

Answers to Chapter 33 Review:

1. Answers will vary. One way would be to put antiperspirant on an area of the skin and hold under heat lamp or exercise vigorously. Measuring skin temperature where sweating is and is not occurring should demonstrate effect of sweating.

2. Answers will vary. (Student reading.) They may include the use of cortisone in the treatment of arthritis.

3. Answers will vary. Shortening of the unit of structure of the model is the important thing.

4. Answers will vary. The plan should be consistent with information in the text. It may include walking or biking on a regular basis to and from your destinations.

5. Answers will vary, but should include such things as protection, temperature regulation, muscle tone, and ability to move and respond to stimuli so as to keep constant internal body conditions. For example, skin glands secrete sweat to cool the body and maintain body temperature when it is hot outside.

6. Answers will vary. The medial profession has found new workable substitutes.

7. Answers will vary. It is important to consider such questions to help students prepare for a world in which such replacements will be increasingly available.

8. Answers will vary. Any application consistent with information in text is acceptable.

9. Answers will vary depending on locale.

References and Readings:

Teacher

Cohen, C. 1975. The protein switch of muscle contraction. *Scientific American* 223(5):36 (November).

Student

Jenkins, R.R. 1978. Skeletal muscle as a peripheral modifier of behavior. *American Biology Teacher* 40(6):358 (September)

Lester, H. A. 1977. The response to acetylcholine. *Scientific American* 236(2):107 (February).

Maugh, T.H. 1978. Hair: a diagnostic tool to complement blood serum and urine. *Science* 202:1271 (December 22).

Morehouse, L.E., and L. Gross 1975. *Total fitness in 30 minutes a week*. New York: Simon and Schuster.

Sonstegard, D.A., L.S. Matthews, and H. Kaufer 1978. The surgical replacement of the human knee joint. *Scientific American* 238(1):44 (January).

CHAPTER 34 INTERNAL REGULATION

Introduction: Three different topics are considered in this chapter: the endocrine system, immunity, and stress. Each in its own way is related to the maintenance of hemeostasis in the body. The body's ability to develop immunity to infectious agents and to defend itself against foreign substances in another way it maintains homeostasis. Finally, the body's ability to withstand stress is also an example of homeostasis.

If students understand in a general way that hormones, immunity, and response to stress all help to maintain homeostasis, they will have learned what is most significant in this chapter.

Ideas for Individual Student Investigation:

Some of the more able students may be interested in doing library research projects and oral reports on some of the following topics: an excess or a deficiency of any hormone, the laboratory synthesis of hormones, hormones of the intestinal tract, why people do not develop immunity to the common cold, how different vaccines work, immunity and cancer, allergies, organ transplants, and recent research about stress.

Answers to Chapter 34 Investigation:

A. The blood glucose level in a diabetic individual is always higher than that of a normal individual. Students should be able to read data from the graph to show that at any given time (for example, beginning one-half hour, 1 hour, etc.) the blood glucose level of a diabetic is higher than normal. Also, they should note that after being given glucose, the blood glucose level of a diabetic rises more sharply and stays elevated longer than it does in a normal person. Even in normal individuals, the blood glucose level rises for about an hour after they are given glucose.

B. According to the graph, insulin became active after one hour in the normal individual, and slightly active after two hours in the diabetic. The activity of insulin is presumed to take place when the slope of the curve starts to go down.

C. In a diabetic coma, the blood glucose level would continue to rise to as high as 500 mg of glucose per 100 ml of blood. In insulin shock, the blood glucose level would drop below normal to 50 mg/100 ml of blood or lower. Coma is caused by a great excess of glucose, and insulin shock is caused by an extreme deficiency of glucose.

Answers to Chapter 34 Review:

1. Juvenile diabetes: more severe; usually requires injections of insulin. Late onset: relatively mild; can be treated with diet and sometimes medicines that stimulate the pancreas to produce insulin.

2. Anwers will vary. It is important for students to know what diseases they have had and which they have received immunizations for. They may consult their own physicians for this information.

3. One hypothesis is that during embryological development some of the B-cells attach to each of the antigens that are part of the body itself. These are destroyed so that they cannot cause the production of antibodies to antigens normally present in the body.

4. In allergies, antibodies and memory cells are produced when certain substances first enter the body. When the substances again enter the body, an immune reaction to them occurs. The antibodies produced cause histamine to be released and it causes many of the symptoms of allergies. Why some people's bodies respond to such substances as dust, and pollen, while others do not, is unknown. The mechanism that should protect, causes damage instead.

5. Autoimmune diseases involve the failure to recognize some parts of the body as self. They are also destructive, rather than helpful, in maintaining homeostasis.

6. Transplanted organs are prevented from being rejected by using organs from closely related donors, matching the antigens in the donor and recipient tissue, and using drugs called immunosuppressants which reduce the body's ability to produce antibodies and also lower resistance to disease.

7. The role of the hypothalamus in regulating the pituitary gland, the role of the nervous system and the adrenal gland in response to emergencies and stress would be acceptable.

8. The body's reaction to stress shows how the nervous and endocrine systems work together. Their failure to do so results in loss of internal regulation.

9. Cortisone is used to reduce inflammation and promote healing.

10. Answers will vary. Importance of immunization in preventing avoidable infections should be stressed.

11. Answers will vary. Questions should clarify and expand upon information already available in the text. Students might ask questions about work activities, and good and bad aspects of those careers.

12. Answers will vary. All applications of information in the text should be acceptable. For example, with so many pressures made on the family in today's world, a parent would want to know how to reduce stress within the family unit.

References and Readings:

Teacher

Capra, J. D., and A. B. Demunson 1977. The antibody combining site. *Scientific American* 236(1):50 (January)

Cunningham, B. A. 1977. The structure and function of

histo-compatibility antigens. *Scientific American* 237(4):96 (October).

Student

Binkley, S. 1979. A timekeeping enzyme in the pineal gland *Scientific American* 240(4):66 (April)

O'Malley, B. W., and W. T. Schrader 1976. The receptors of steroid hormones. *Scientific American* 234(2):32 (February).

Raff, M. C. 1976. Cell-surface immunology. *Scientific American* 234(5):30 (May).

Wurtman, R. J. 1975. The effects of light on the human body. *Scientific American* 233(1):69 (July).

CHAPTER 35 REPRODUCTION AND DEVELOPMENT

Introduction: The process by which an organism is constructed is remarkable. It begins with the fusion of two single cells, the fertilization of an egg by a sperm. The developing zygote contains genetic information, DNA, from both parents. During cell division, this information directs the differentiation of cells into a complete organism.

The human embryo, in approximately nine months, multiplies from one cell to about ten trillion cells. During this time, the embryo increases in weight from less than a milligram to a minimum of two kilograms. The mother supplies both nutrients and energy necessary for development. The direction of the entire process of development of the embryo originates within the zygote.

In the development section of this chapter, you might point out the circulatory changes that occur in a baby at birth clearly demonstrate the adaption to entirely different ways of life—from complete dependence upon the mother to a relatively independent existence. Students may begin a collage of articles for posting that deal with new developments in the field of human reproduction.

Answers to Chapter 35 Investigation:

A. Similarities: relative positions of limbs; relative degree of development among various parts. Differences: mamalian extra-embryonic membranes; no shell present with pig embryo; placenta and umbilical cord present with pig embryo; egg slightly rounded for turtle compared to chick.

B. Through the placenta, attached to the uterine lining of the mother. The placenta is a mass of spongy tissue through which oxygen, food, and wastes are exchanged between embryo and mother. It is formed from both maternal tissue and the chorion of the fetus, and has a rich blood supply from both. Villi from the chorion extend intothe mother's blood, but the circulatory system of the fetus is not connected to that of the mother's. Therefore, maternal and fetal blood cells do not mix.

C. Research depends upon the actual slides examined by the students. Through fertilization, the zygote acquires new genes. These usually provide the offspring with new, better adapted traits. These traits must be developed during the embryonic stages. These developmental stages provide the means and the necessary time for translating genetic instructions into adaptively improved traits of the adult. This ensures survival and continuity.

Answers to Chapter 35 Review:

1. Discussion should include mention of infertility, disease or surgical removal of the ovaries, failure of development of secondary sexual characteristics, or disorders of menopause.

2. The uterine lining must be prepared with a rich blood supply, which is only available at a certain time during the menstrual cycle.

3. It might help us to understand and prevent some kinds of congenital disorders, in which development does not proceed normally.

References and Readings:

Teacher

Avers, Charlotte, J. 1974. *Biology of sex.* New York: John Wiley & Sons

Pattern, B. M. 1958. *Foundations of embryology.* New York: McGraw-Hill Book Co.

Student

Scientific American Offprints:

Edwards, R.G. Mammalian eggs in the laboratory. Aug. 1966. (OP #1047)

Tietze, C., and S. Lewit. Abortion. Jan. 1969. (OP #1129)

Edwards, R. G., and R. E. Fowler. Human embryos in the laboratory. Dec. 1970. (OP #1206)

Gordon, R., and A. G. Jacobson. The shaping of tissues in embryos. June 1978. (OP #1391)

SUGGESTED AUDIO VISUAL MATERIALS

TITLE	ORDER #/LENGTH/ C OR B&W	SUPPLIER	TITLE	ORDER #/LENGTH/ C OR B&W	SUPPLIER

UNIT 1

CHAPTER 1: THE ENVIRONMENT

Films (16mm)

TITLE	ORDER #/LENGTH/ C OR B&W	SUPPLIER
Cycles, Renewal for Minerals and Fuels	free, N654, 28 min, c	AF
The Physical Environment	2136, 11 min, c	EBE
Spaceship Earth	free, 17 min, c	MD
Plant and Animal Communities: Physical Environment	1455, 10½ min, c	COR

Filmloops

The Biosphere	S25695A, 3-4 min, c	FS
The Physical Environment	S25695, 3-4 min, c	FS
Water Cycle (9)	Unit S-32, 1-4 min, Ave, c	WDNL

Filmstrips

Ecology: Interactions and Environments	S2-3405, 113½ min, 404 frames, c	CB
Ecology: Interdependence II	S25281B, 5 films, c	FS
Introduction to the Carbon Cycle	78W0170, 1 film, c	WNS
Introduction to the Nitrogen Cycle	78W0180, 1 film, c	WNS
Introduction to the Water Cycle	78W0160, 1 film, c	WNS

Transparencies (overhead)

Carbon Cycle	50-1601	CB
Nitrogen Cycle	50-1603	CB
Water Cycle	50-1605	CB
Crossroads: Water	CROSWA, 12, c	SEE

CHAPTER 2: INTERRELATIONSHIPS IN THE ENVIRONMENT

Films (16 mm)

World in a Marsh	22 min, c	MH
Protist Ecology	194x2005, 12 min, c	MH
Protist Ecology	194x2005, 12 min, c	WNS
The Ecosystem: Network of Life	11057, 10¾ min, c	BFA
The Nature of Life: Living Things Interact	3646, 11½ min, c	COR
The Community	1944, 11 min, c	EBE

TITLE	ORDER #/LENGTH/ C OR B&W	SUPPLIER
Plant-Animal Communities: Interrelationships	1456, 12½ min, c	COR
A Desert Place	F2038, 30 min, c	TLF

Filmloops

Diatoms in a Food Web	81-6553, 3-4 min, c	BFA
Ecosystems and Ecology	S25695B, c	FS
Biome	S25695E, c	FS
Communities of Living Things	Unit S-9, 15 loops, 1-4 min. ave.	WDNL

Filmstrips

Introduction to Ecosystems	78W0650, 1 film, c	WNS
Ecology-Interdependence	S25281A, 4 films, c	FS
Environmental Communities	S25283, 6 films, c	FS
Ecology: Interactions and Environments	S24878, 7 films, c	FS
Interdependence of Living Things	S46433, 6 films, c	FS
Living Things and Their Habitats	70W3100, 6 films, 440 frames	WNS

Slides

Food Chains: Producers and Consumers	201059, 20, c	PLP
Nutritional Relationships	201059, 20, c	PLP
Introduction to Interdependence	201056, 20, c	PLP

Transparencies

Ecosystem-Nutrient Cycles	78W8500, 6, c	WNS
Ecology	75W0160, 11, c	WNS

CHAPTER 3: ENERGY IN THE ENVIRONMENT

Films (16 mm)

Energy	11483, 14 min, c	BFA
The Green Machine	F2132, 49 min, c	TLF
Web of Life: Endless Chain	free, 0480, 28 min, c	USDE

Filmloops

Light Requirement for Starch Prod. in Green Plants	S81186, 3-4 min, c	EBE

TITLE	ORDER #/LENGTH/ C OR B&W	SUPPLIER
Filmstrips		
Photosynthesis: End Products	73W1685, 4 min 10 sec, c	WNS(TF)
Energy and Nutrients in Ecology I and II	52-3470, 55 frames, c 52-3471, 56 frames, c	CB
Introduction to the Energy Cycle and Trophic Levels	78W0130, c	WNS
Ecology II	S25281B, 5 films, c	FS
Slides		
Food Chains and Pyramids	20160, 20, c	PLP
Food Webs	201061, c	PLP

CHAPTER 4: BALANCES AND IMBALANCES

Films (16 mm)		
No Turning Back	0461, 27½ min, c	USDE
Endless Chain	0457, 28 min, c	USDE
The Rival World	23 min, c	SFL
Air Pollution— Sweetening the Air	000083, 22 min, c	NAC
Plant-Animal Communities: Changing the Balance of Nature	1287, 10½ min, c	COR
Filmstrips		
Air Pollution	52-3435, 32 min, 150 frames	CB
Endangered Species	(2) SCC4510, c SCR4510, c	PH
Ecological Imbalance: Six Systems	X76, 6 films, c	EG
Doomsday: 21st Century?	52-3455, 25 min, 172 frames	CB
Man in the Biosphere: An Introduction to Human Ecology	70W4100, 6 films, 441 frames	WNS
Environmental Pollution: Our World Crisis	70W3800, 6 films, 414 frames	WNS

UNIT 2

CHAPTER 5: CHEMISTRY OF LIVING THINGS

Films (16 mm)		
Atoms and Molecules	1673, 14 min, b&w	EBE
Chemistry of the Cell I	21 min, c	MH
Chemistry of the Cell II	16 min, c	MH

TITLE	ORDER #/LENGTH/ C OR B&W	SUPPLIER
Molecular Biology	0435, 15 min, c	USDE
Molecules and Life	20 min, c	MH
Filmloops		
Biochemical Tests	SCT 629, 2-4 mins, c	PH(TF)
Filmstrips		
Basic Chemistry for the Biologist (2)	SCC816, c SCR816,	PH
Biology: An Introduction to Life #4 and 5	141, 62-74 frames, c	BP
Introduction to Carbohydrates	78W0090, 1, c	WNS
Introduction to Fats	78W0110, 1, c	WNS
Introduction to Amino Acids	78W0030, 1, c	WNS
Amino Acid Structure and Peptide Links	78W0040, 1, c	WNS
Transparencies		
Basic Biochemistry	S46707, 11, c	FS
Biological Chemistry and Physics	75W0080, 21, c	WNS

CHAPTER 6: THE CELL

Films (16 mm)		
Cell Biology: Life Functions	1478, 11 min, c	COR
Cell Biology: Structure and Composition	1477, 13½ min, c	COR
The Cell: A Functioning Structure, Part I and II	29 min, c 30 min, c	MH MH
Development and Differentiation	20 min, c	MH
Filmloops		
Importance of the Nucleus	S24891B, 3-4 min, c	FS(BSCS)
DNA and Cell Reproduction	S25580, 3-4 min, c	FS(BSCS)
Osmosis: Effective Cell Membranes	S25574, 3-4 min, c	FS
Filmstrips		
Biology, An Introduction to Life	141, Set of 8, 62-74 frames each	BP
Cytology—Cell Studies I	S25268, 3 films, c	FS
The Living Cell	70W3900, 6 films, 222 frames	WNS

TITLE	ORDER #/LENGTH/ C OR B&W	SUPPLIER
Transparencies		
The "Modern" Cell	S46705, 9	FS
Cell Machinery	S24604, 12	FS

CHAPTER 7: ENERGY RELATIONSHIPS IN THE CELL

Films (16 mm)

TITLE	ORDER #/LENGTH/ C OR B&W	SUPPLIER
Photosynthesis: The Biochemical Process	3118, 16½ min, c	COR
Photosynthesis: Chemistry of Food Making	1500, 13½ min, c	COR
Enzymes: The Key to Life	29 min	IU
The Fuel of Life	29 min	IU

Filmloops

TITLE	ORDER #/LENGTH/ C OR B&W	SUPPLIER
Enzyme Action (3) (Catalase, Ptyalin, Pepsin)	SCT600, SCT601, SCT638, 4 min, 30 sec	PH(TF)
Enzyme Action (Effect of Temp.)	SCT603, 4 min, 25 sec	PH
Photosynthesis	73W1685-1689 (8) 4-4½ min ave.	WNS
Respiration: Fermentation	S25569, 4 min	FS
Respiration: Aerobic Respiration	S25571, 4 min	FS
Light Requirement for Starch Production in Green Plants	S81186, 3-4 min	EBE

Filmstrips

TITLE	ORDER #/LENGTH/ C OR B&W	SUPPLIER
Photosynthesis (3)	78W0060, 70, 80	WNS
The Living Cell: Respiration	70W3900, 1 of set	WNS
Cell Respiration	2-4E, c	EG

Transparencies

TITLE	ORDER #/LENGTH/ C OR B&W	SUPPLIER
Energy Release in Living Things	S46707, 10, c	FS

CHAPTER 8: ACTIVITIES OF LIVING THINGS

Films (16 mm)

TITLE	ORDER #/LENGTH/ C OR B&W	SUPPLIER
Mitosis	1900, 24 min, c	EBE
From One Cell	free, 14 min, c	ACS
Learning About Cells	3384, 16 min, c	EBE
The Growth of Plants	1962, 21 min, c	EBE

Filmloops

TITLE	ORDER #/LENGTH/ C OR B&W	SUPPLIER
Cytoplasmic Streaming	4 min, c	BFA
The Dividing Cell	4 min, c	BFA

TITLE	ORDER #/LENGTH/ C OR B&W	SUPPLIER
Mitosis	78W8024, 4 min, c	WNS(BSCS)
Importance of the Nucleus	S24891B, 4 min, c	FS(BSCS)

Filmstrips

TITLE	ORDER #/LENGTH/ C OR B&W	SUPPLIER
Introduction to Mitosis	78W0190, c	WNS
Pumps in the Living Cell	S25271, c	FS
Plant Mitosis	5201642, 50 frames, 7 min	CB
Diffusion and Osmosis	78W0340, c	WNS

Transparencies

TITLE	ORDER #/LENGTH/ C OR B&W	SUPPLIER
Overhead Transparencies for High School Biology	Free	ACS
Animal Mitosis	50-1621, c	CB
Plant Mitosis	50-1641, c	CB

UNIT 3

CHAPTER 9: PRINCIPLES OF HEREDITY

Films (16 mm)

TITLE	ORDER #/LENGTH/ C OR B&W	SUPPLIER
Meiosis: Sex Cell Formation	2020, 16 min, c	EBE
Laws of Heredity	2073, 15 min, c	EBE
Genetics: Mendel's Laws	1312, 13½ min, c	COR
Genetic Investigations	NSC714, 12 min, c	IU
Generation Upon Generation	FS1736, 52 min, c	TLF
Principles of Genetics, No. 6	29 min, c	MH

Filmloops

TITLE	ORDER #/LENGTH/ C OR B&W	SUPPLIER
Chromosome Behavior— Mitosis and Meiosis	14745, 2 min, c	DM

Filmstrips

TITLE	ORDER #/LENGTH/ C OR B&W	SUPPLIER
Heredity	S25274, 6 films, c	FS
Introduction to Genetics	TX236, 6 films, c	EG
Introducing Genetics	70W3400, 6 films, 347 frames, c	WNS
Mendelian Inheritance	78W0220, c	WNS
Introduction to Meiosis	78W0200, c	WNS

Transparencies

TITLE	ORDER #/LENGTH/ C OR B&W	SUPPLIER
Genetics	75W0130, 10, c	WNS
The Laws of Heredity	S24639, 10, c	FS

TITLE	ORDER #/LENGTH/ C OR B&W	SUPPLIER

CHAPTER 10: GENES AND CHROMOSOMES

Films (16 mm)

TITLE	ORDER #/LENGTH/ C OR B&W	SUPPLIER
Gene Action	2138, 17 min, c	EBE
The Living Cell: DNA	3477, 20 min, c	EBE
Genetics: Function of DNA and RNA	1917, 12½ min, c	COR
Riddle of Heredity	30 min, c	MH

Filmloops

TITLE	ORDER #/LENGTH/ C OR B&W	SUPPLIER
DNA Replication	S24999A, 3-4 min, c	FS
RNA Transcription	S24999B, 3-4 min, c	FS
Induction and Repression	S24999C, 3-4 min, c	FS
DNA Composition	SCT617-2, 3-4 min, c	PH

Filmstrips

TITLE	ORDER #/LENGTH/ C OR B&W	SUPPLIER
DNA, RNA and Mutations	X236D, c	EG
DNA and Cell Chemistry	70W3300, 6 films, 388 frames	WNS
Introduction to DNA	78W0250, c	WNS
Introduction to Nucleotides	78W0260, c	WNS

Transparencies

TITLE	ORDER #/LENGTH/ C OR B&W	SUPPLIER
DNA	75W0150, 9, c	WNS
Nucleic Acids	S46708, 8, c	FS
The Biochemical Principles of Heredity	S24641, 5, c	FS
Genotype and the Mechanism of Heredity	S24642, 5, c	FS

CHAPTER 11: GENETICS AND POPULATIONS

Films (16 mm)

TITLE	ORDER #/LENGTH/ C OR B&W	SUPPLIER
Genetics of Mendelian Populations	(Part of Series) 30 min, c	IU(MH)
Genetic Loads in Mendelian Populations	(Part of Series) 30 min, c	IU(MH)
Genetics of Race	(Part of Series) 30 min, c	IU(MH)
Population Ecology	2144, 19 min, c	EBE
Population Patterns in the U.S.	11 min, c	COR

Filmstrips

TITLE	ORDER #/LENGTH/ C OR B&W	SUPPLIER
Introduction to Probability	78W0140, c	WNS
Population Dynamics	78W510, c	WNS
Population Genetics	236F, c	EG

Slides

TITLE	ORDER #/LENGTH/ C OR B&W	SUPPLIER
Hardy-Weinberg Formula	202026, 20, c	PLP
Evolution and the Gene Pool	202024, 20, c	PLP

CHAPTER 12: HUMAN HEREDITY

Films (16 mm)

TITLE	ORDER #/LENGTH/ C OR B&W	SUPPLIER
Genetic Defects: The Broken Code	HSC-982, 87 min, c	IU
Bioengineers	free, 0489, 14 min, c	USDE
The Gene Engineers	F1947, 57 min, c	TLF
Genetics: Human Heredity	1493, 13½ min, c	COR
The Chromosomes of Man	2719, 20 min, b&w	EBE
Blue Print for Life	14 min, c	MD
Letter from Jimmy Lee	15 min, c	MD
Decision	18 min, c	MD
Genetic Counselling I—Heredity and Birth Defects	75-700046, 10 min, c	MIFE
II—Amniocentesis	75-700048, 10 min, c	MIFE

Filmstrips

TITLE	ORDER #/LENGTH/ C OR B&W	SUPPLIER
Genetic Research: Another Genie in a Bottle	352030, 2 films, c	PLP
Mutations and Chromosomal Modifications	78W0270, c	WNS
Hormones and Chromosomes in Man	SCC815, c	PH
Genetics; How Life Remakes Life	264FQ, 3 films, c	SUN

Transparencies

TITLE	ORDER #/LENGTH/ C OR B&W	SUPPLIER
Pedigree of Near Sightedness Hemophilia Colorblindness	S24639, (10) Part of set	(BSCS)FS

Slides

TITLE	ORDER #/LENGTH/ C OR B&W	SUPPLIER
Applications of Human Genetics	S24998, 24, c	FS
Human Genetics: Part I	S24995, 39, c	FS
Part II	S24996, 39, c	FS
Part III	S24997, 22, c	FS

TITLE	ORDER #/LENGTH/ C OR B&W	SUPPLIER

UNIT 4

CHAPTER 13: THEORIES OF CHANGE

Films (16 mm)

TITLE	ORDER #/LENGTH/ C OR B&W	SUPPLIER
Darwin and the Theory of Natural Selection	1737, 13 min, c	COR
Natural Selection	2140, 16 min, c	EBE
Theories of the Evolution of Life	2798, 14 min, c	EBE

Filmloops

The Galapagos: Darwin's Finches	3-4 min, c	BFA
The Galapagos: Geological Evidence	3-4 min, c	BFA

Filmstrips

Evolution	S25299, 6 films, c	FS
Living Things Through the Ages	S46415, 4 films, 48 frames each	FS

Slides

Early Theories	202035, 20, c	PLP
Darwin's Theory of Evolution	202036, 20, c	PLP

CHAPTER 14: EVIDENCE OF CHANGE

Films (16 mm)

The Fossil Story	free, 19 min, c	SFL
Story in the Rocks	free, 18 min, c	SFL
Fossils: Clues to Prehistoric Times	1039, 10½ min, c	COR

Filmloops

Fossil Interpretation	73W8046, c	WNS
Convergence	73W8041, c	WNS
Peppered Moth—A Population Study	73W8042, c	WNS

Filmstrips

Prehistoric Life	7500, set of 6, 55 frames each	EBE
Fossils—Clues to the Past	79W0080, c	WNS
Fossils: What They Are	71W6000, c	WNS
Fossils: How They Are Used	71W6010, c	WNS

Slides

Analogy and Homology	202042, 20, c	PLP
Adaptations: Embryonic Evidence	202043, 20, c	PLP

TITLE	ORDER #/LENGTH/ C OR B&W	SUPPLIER
Galapagos Islands and the Origin of Species	171W0850, 45, c	WNS

Transparencies

Paleontology	S24151K, 15, c	FS
Fossils: Clues to Earth History	18136, 8, c	EBE
Organic Evolution	S24151C, 16, c	FS

CHAPTER 15: LIFE IN THE PAST

Films (16 mm)

Life in the Early Seas	11 min, c	MH
The Beginning and Development of Life	15 min, c	MH
The Origin of Life: Chemical Evolution	2820, 11 min, c	EBE
How Old is Old (NOVA)	FE1358, 30 min, c	TLF

Filmstrips

Life through Geologic Times	79W0170, c	WNS

Transparencies

Order of Cell Material	S24151L, 15, c	FS

CHAPTER 16: CLASSIFICATION OF LIVING THINGS

Films (16 mm)

Characteristics of Plants and Animals	NSC310, 10 min, c	IU
Classifying Plants and Animals	1308, 10½ min, c	COR

Filmstrips

Classification of Plants and Animals	S24873, 7 films, c	FS
Classification of Plants	S45770, 9 films, 50 frames each	FS
Identification and Classification	S25272, 5 films, c	FS
Fundamentals of Biology	S46727, 9 films, c	FS
The Processes of Science: Classifying	3D8000, 5 films, c	BFA

Transparencies

Dyna-Vue Plant and Animal Kingdom Series	75W0400, 85, c	WNS
Zoology Series	S24152, 40, c	FS

TITLE	ORDER #/LENGTH/ C OR B&W	SUPPLIER

UNIT 5

CHAPTER 17: VIRUSES

Films (16 mm)

TITLE	ORDER #/LENGTH/ C OR B&W	SUPPLIER
Viruses: Threshold of Life	14 min	COR
Viruses (2nd Edition)	3817, 13 min	COR

Filmstrips

TITLE	ORDER #/LENGTH/ C OR B&W	SUPPLIER
The Virus—New Discovery (2)	S25279, c	FS

Transparencies

TITLE	ORDER #/LENGTH/ C OR B&W	SUPPLIER
Viruses and Thallophytes	75W0410, 14, c	WNS

CHAPTER 18: BACTERIA AND BLUE GREEN ALGAE

Films (16 mm)

TITLE	ORDER #/LENGTH/ C OR B&W	SUPPLIER
Bacteria	1968, 19 min, c	EBE
Bacteria—Friend or Foe	615, 11 min, c	EBE
Simple Plants: Bacteria	3856, 13½ min, c	COR

Filmstrips

TITLE	ORDER #/LENGTH/ C OR B&W	SUPPLIER
Common Bacterial Types	S81178, 3-4 min, c	EBE
Where Bacteria are Found	S81166, 3-4 min, c	EBe
Effects of Environment on Growth of Different Bacteria	S81175, 3-4 min, c	EBE
A Bacterial Growth Curve	S81182, 3-4 min, c	EBE
Bacterial Reproduction	S80695, 3-4 min, c	EBE

Filmstrips

TITLE	ORDER #/LENGTH/ C OR B&W	SUPPLIER
Concepts of Homeostasis	78W0330, c	WNS
The Protists	S25216A, 4 films, c	FS

Transparencies

TITLE	ORDER #/LENGTH/ C OR B&W	SUPPLIER
Viruses and Thallophytes	75W0410, 14, c	WNS
Bacteria and Other Microorganisms	S24644, 12, c	FS

Slides

TITLE	ORDER #/LENGTH/ C OR B&W	SUPPLIER
Blue-Green Algae Set	48-2850, 10, c	CB

CHAPTER 19: PROTISTS

Films (16 mm)

TITLE	ORDER #/LENGTH/ C OR B&W	SUPPLIER
Protists: Threshold of Life	06190, 12 min, c	NGS
Protozoa: Structures and Life Functions	1092, 16½ min, c	COR
The Single-Celled Animals	1954, 17 min, c	EBE
Protozoa	1495, 11 min, c	EBE
Wee Beasties	194X2000, 12 min, c	WNS
Protist Physiology	194X2010, 13 min, c	WNS

Filmloops

TITLE	ORDER #/LENGTH/ C OR B&W	SUPPLIER
Paramecium (4)		
Ecology	73W1971, 3 min	WNS
Physiology	73W1972, 4 min	WNS
Reproduction	73W1973, 3 min	WNS
Behavior	73W1974, 3 min	WNS
Protist Series	427000, 7 films	BFA
The Paramecium	S80726, 4 min, c	EBE
The Flagellates (Part I)	73W1752, 4 min, 21 sec, c	WNS
Ameba	73W1956, 4 min, 13 sec, c	WNS

Filmstrips

TITLE	ORDER #/LENGTH/ C OR B&W	SUPPLIER
The Protists	70W6400, c	WNS

CHAPTER 20: FUNGI

Films (16 mm)

TITLE	ORDER #/LENGTH/ C OR B&W	SUPPLIER
Fungi	1827, 16 min, c	EBE
Fungi: The One Hundred Thousand	3850, 7 min, c	COR

Filmloops

TITLE	ORDER #/LENGTH/ C OR B&W	SUPPLIER
Growth of Molds	73W0505, 3-4 min, c	WNS
Spore Dispersal in the Fungus Coprinus	168W5116, 3½ min, c	WNS
Different Kinds of Molds	S81180, 3-4 min, c	EBE

Filmstrips

TITLE	ORDER #/LENGTH/ C OR B&W	SUPPLIER
Fungi (Diversity and Ecology)	70W6320, c	WNS
Simple Plants	03754, 13-14 min, c	NGS

UNIT 6

CHAPTER 21: THE SIMPLEST PLANTS

Films (16 mm)

TITLE	ORDER #/LENGTH/ C OR B&W	SUPPLIER
Simple Plants: Algae and Fungi	951, 13½ min, c	COR
Mosses, Liverworts and Ferns	1482, 13½ min, c	COR

TITLE	ORDER #/LENGTH/ C OR B&W	SUPPLIER
Simple Plants: The Algae	1964, 18 min, c	EBE
Origin of Land Plants— Liverworts, Mosses	2017, 14 min, c	EBE

Filmstrips

TITLE	ORDER #/LENGTH/ C OR B&W	SUPPLIER
The Plants	S25216B, 5 films, c	FS
The Development of Plants	S25308, 7 films, c	FS
Classification of Plants	S45770, 9 films, ave. 50 frames ea.	FS
Algae (Diversity and Ecology)	70W6315, c	WNS
Mosses and Liverworts (Life Cycle and Ecology)	70W6325, c	WNS
Introduction to the Algae	52-8200, 52 frames, c	CB
Moss Life Cycle	52-8452, 9½ min, 50 frames	CB

CHAPTER 22: FERNS AND GYMNOSPERMS

Films (16 mm)

Evolution of Vascular Plants—the Ferns	2003, 17 min	EBE
Sexual Reproduction in Ferns	11 min, c or b&w	BFA
Gynosperms	1829, 17 min, c	EBE

Filmstrips

Ferns and Horsetails (Life Cycles and Ecology)	70W6330, Ae. 40-75 frames	WNS
Gymnosperms (Life Cyles and Ecology)	70W6335, Ave. 40-75 frames	WNS

CHAPTER 23: FLOWERING PLANTS

Films (16 mm)

Angiosperms—The Flowering Plants	1932, 21 min, c	EBE
Flowers at work	1433, 11 min, c	EBE
Seed Germination	1837, 15 min, c	EBE
Roots of Plants (2nd Edition)	1510, 11 min, c	EBE
Plant Tropisms and Other Movements	1048, 10½ min, c	COR

Filmloops

Pathways of Water in Woody Plants	168W5114(T), 3½ min	WNS
Pathways of Water in Herbaceous Plants	168W5113(T), 3½ min	WNS
Germination of the Bean	73W0150(T), 3-4 min	WNS

TITLE	ORDER #/LENGTH/ C OR B&W	SUPPLIER
Plant Response	73W0405(T), 3-4 min	WNS
Phototropism	S24890H, 3-4 min	FS
From Flower to Fruit	S46381K, 3-4 min	FS
Pollination and Fertilization of an Angiosperm	14635, 1 min	DM

Filmstrips

Plant Life	S45780, 5 films, Ave. 51 frames ea.	FS
Sexual Reproduction in Flowering Plants	S25303, 8	FS
Plant Structure and Growth	S24872, 8	FS
The Flower	528822	CB
Plant Life	70W0500, 6 films	WNS(EBE)
Flowering Plants: Their Structure and Function	11220, 5 films, Ave. 48 frames ea.	EBE

Transparencies

Higher Plants	75W0430, 21, c	WNS
Botany	S24153, 30, c	FNS
Structure and Function of Flower	S46799, 5 overlays	FNS

UNIT 7

CHAPTER 24: SPONGES, CNIDARIANS, AND UNSEGMENTED WORMS

Films (16 mm)

The First Many-Celled Animals	1946, 17 min, c	EBE
Stinging Celled Animals: Coelenterates	1956, 16 min, c	EBE
Sponges and Coelenterates: Porus and Saclike Animals	1327, 11 min, c	COR
Flatworms	2007, 16 min, c	EBE
Parasitic Flatworms	2065, 16 min, c	EBE

Filmloops

Sponges	73W1901(T), 1 min 28 sec	WNS
Hydra	73W1902(T), 2 min	WNS
Planaria	73W1904(T), 2 min 17 sec	WNS

Filmstrips

Hydra Life Cycle	52-4212, 1, c	CB
The Lower Invertebrates	S25216c, 5 films	FS

TITLE	ORDER #/LENGTH/ C OR B&W	SUPPLIER
The Vocabulary of Biology, The Invertebrate	S46975, 6 films	FS
Classification of Invertebrate Animals	S45820, 11 films 49 frames ea.	FS(EBE)

Transparencies

Invertebrates (Except Arthropods)	75W0310, 19, c	WNS

CHAPTER 25: ANNELIDS, MOLLUSCS, AND ECHINODERMS

Films (16 mm)

Annelids	194X2045, 10 min, c	WNS
Segmentation: The Annelid Worms	1902, 16 min, c	EBE
Earthworm Anatomy	NSC531, 11 min, c	IU
Molluscs	194X2035, 10 min, c	WNS
Adaptive Radition— The Mollusks	1896, 11 min, c	EBE
Echinoderms and Mollusks	1599, 15 min, c	COR
Echinoderms—Sea Stars and their Relatives	1908, 17 min, c	EBE

Filmloops

Nereis	S25464, c	FS
Earthworm	S25467, c	FS
Clam	S25456, c	FS
Characteristics of Mollusks	ES-26, 4 films	WDNL
Starfishes	S25496, c	FS

Filmstrips

Zoology Series—Set II	S46439, 5 films, Ave. 24 frames ea.	FS
Earthworm Anatomy 2: Digestive and Circulatory Systems	52-4364, 1, c	CB
Earthworm Anatomy 3: Excretory, Reproduction and Nervous Systems	52-4365, 1, c	CB

CHAPTER 26: THE ARTHROPODS

Films (16 mm)

The Jointed Legged Animals—Arthropods	1910, 19 min, c	EBE
Insects	11 min, c	EBE
Arthropods	194X2040, 13 min, c	WNS
Arthropods: Insects and their Relatives	1108, 11 min, c	COR

TITLE	ORDER #/LENGTH/ C OR B&W	SUPPLIER
The Grasshopper: A Typical Insect	823, 6 min, c	COR

Filmloops

Characteristics of Arthropods	ES-21, 18 films	WDNL
Crayfish	S25484, c	FS
Orthoptera: Grasshopper	S25692A, c	FS

Filmstrips

About Insects	70W3700, 6 films, total 332 frames	WNS
Orders of Insects	70W0400, 8 films	WNS(EBE)
The Insects	S45850, 4 films, Ave. 50 frames ea.	FS

Transparencies

Arthropods	75W0330, 11, c	WNS

UNIT 8

CHAPTER 27: FISHES AND AMPHIBIANS

Films (16 mm)

What is a Fish?	2033, 22 min, c	EE
Fish Embryo—From Fertilization to Hatching	2045, 12 min, c	EBE
What is an Amphibian?	1952, 11 min, c	EBE
Amphibian Embryo— Frog and Salamander	2128, 16 min, c	EBE

Filmloops

Characteristics of Fish	ES-23	WDNL
Locomotion in Fishes	S25526, c	FS(TF)
Salamanders	S25689B, c	FS(HUB)
Frog Heartbeat I	S25546, c	FS
Frog Anatomy	S25536-S25545, 9 loops	FS

Filmstrips

The Lower Vertebrates	S25216E, 5 films, c	FS
The Vertebrates	S46975G, 6 films, c	FS
Classification of Living Fish	S46428, 4 films, c	FS
Biology of the Sea	S46997-21, 10 films	FS

CHAPTER 28: REPTILES AND BIRDS

Films (16 mm)

Reptiles	06103, 20 min, c	NGS

TITLE	ORDER #/LENGTH/ C OR B&W	SUPPLIER	TITLE	ORDER #/LENGTH/ C OR B&W	SUPPLIER
What is a Reptile?	1858, 18 min, c	EBE	*Human Body: Digestive System*	895, 13 min, c	COR
Reptiles	785, 14 min, c	EBE	*The Digestive System*	2245, 17 min, c	EBE
Reptiles and Their Characteristics	1082, 10½ min, c	COR	*Digestive Systems of Animals*	NSC1262, 15 min, c	IU
What is a Bird?	1948, 17 min, c	EBE	**Filmloops**		
Birds and Their Characteristics	1128, 10 min, c	COR	*Digestion*	S25683A-S25683H, 8 titles	FS(HUB)
Chick Embryo—From Primitive Streak to Hatching	1815, 15 min, c	EBE	*Mechanics of Swallowing*	731006(T), c	WNS
Filmloops			*Enzyme Activity*	S2557-S25562, 6 titles, 3-4 min ea.	FS(TF)
Temperature Activity in Reptiles	73W8033(T), c	WNS(BSCS)	*The Digestive Tract*	S81578, 4 min, c	EBE
Characteristics of Reptiles	ES-27, 15 films	WDNL	*Digestion in the Small Intestine*	S81428, 4 min, c	EBE
Characteristics of Birds	ES-22, 16 films	WDNL	*Villi in the Small Intestine*	S80694, 4 min, c	EBE
Filmstrips			**Filmstrips**		
Classification of Living Birds	S45890, 5 films	FS	*Introduction to Nutrition*	78W0560, c	WNS
			Introduction to Vitamins	78W0570, c	WNS
			Digestive System: Structure and Function	78W0600, c	WNS

CHAPTER 29: MAMMALS

Films (16 mm)

What is a Mammal?	1966, 14 min, c	EBE
Mammals and Their Characteristics	1440, 10½ min, c	COR

Filmloops

Characteristics of Mammals	ES-24, 19 films	WDNL
Marsupials	ES-38, 4 films	WDNL

Filmstrips

What is a Mammal?	S25244A, 4 films, c	FS
Classification of Living Mammals	S46400, 6 films, Ave. 37 frames ea.	FS
Concept of Homeostasis	78W0330, c	WNS
Homeostasis	S25275, 3 films, c	FS

Transparencies

From Vertebrates to Mammals	S24654, 14	FS

UNIT 9

CHAPTER 30: DIGESTION AND NUTRITION

Films (16 mm)

Human Body: Chemistry of Digestion	1653, 15 min, c	COR

Transparencies

The Digestive System	75W4120, 11, c	WNS
Human Digestive System (5)	50-6903, 6905, 6907, 6909, 6911	CB

CHAPTER 31: TRANSPORT, RESPIRATION, EXCRETION

Films (16 mm)

Human Body— Circulatory System	896, 13 min, c	COR
Blood: Composition and Functions	3925, 14½ min, c	COR
Heart, Lungs, Circulation	1204, 10 min, c	COR
The Heart: An Inside Story	3803, 11 min, c	COR
Work of the Heart	2559, 14 min, c	EBE
The Blood	1819, 16 min, c	EBE
Hemo the Magnificent	free, 50 min, c	BTL
Human Body— Respiratory System	1203, 12½ min, c	COR
Respiration in Man	2772, 26 min, c	EBE
The Work of the Kidneys	3163, 20 min, c	EBE
Human Body— Excretory System	1206, 12½ min, c	COR
The Physiology of the Kidneys	SC3075, 6½ min, c	PH

TITLE	ORDER #/LENGTH/ C OR B&W	SUPPLIER
Filmloops		
Heart—Pulmonary Circulation	73W7546(T)	WNS(HUB)
Circulation within the Body	73W7545(T)	WNS(HUB)
The Heart and Circulation	S25681B	FS
Nerves and Heart Beat Rate	S24892B	FS(BSCS)
Respiratory Movement	73W1477(T)	WNS(HUB)
Lung Action and Function	S25681C	FS
Respiration and Waste	S25681E	FS
The Kidney/Homeostasis	S2892A	FS(BSCS)
Liquid Waste and the Kidney	S25681D	FS
Formation of Urine	S25684C	FS(HUB)
Position and Structure of Kidneys	S25684A	FS(HUB)
Reabsorption	S25684B	FS(HUB)
Filmstrips		
Transport: Circulation, Respiration, Excretion	402071	PLP
Circulation (3) Part 1—Blood Part 2—Heart Part 3—Arteries, Veins, Capillaries	30247	PLP
Circulation	SCC633, 3 films	PH
Respiration—External and Internal	SCC632, 2 films	PH
Transparencies		
Human Blood and Vascular System	50-6805, 6807, 6809, 6827, 6831	CB
The Respiratory System	75W4100, 8	WNS
Human Respiration	50-3377	CB
The Excretory System	75W4140, 5	WNS

CHAPTER 32: SENSORY PERCEPTION AND NERVOUS CONTROL

Films (16 mm)		
Nervous System of Man	NSC-1004, 18 min	IU
Human Brain	867, 11 min, b&w	EBE
Fundamentals of the Nervous System	1554, 17 min, c	EBE
The Human Body: The Nervous System	894, 13 min	COR
The Autonomic Nervous System	SC3080, 5½ min	PH

TITLE	ORDER #/LENGTH/ C OR B&W	SUPPLIER
The Nerve Cell	17 min, c	MLS
The Nerve Impulse	3002, 21 min, c	EBE
The Human Body: Sense Organs	1655, 18 min, c	COR
The Human Ear	9 min, c	MLS
Filmloops		
Nerve Action—Reflex Arc	S80101, 4 min	EBE
The Ear: Its Structure and Function	S80099, 1 min 30 sec	EBE
Function of the Inner Ear (2)	73W7490(T), 2 loops	WNS(HUB)
The Eye	73W7500(T), 5 loops	WNS(HUB)
Filmstrips		
The Human Nervous System	S25322, 8 films	FS
Reception: The Five Senses	402075	PLP
The Physiology of Behavior	S25256, 5 films	FS
Transparencies		
Nervous System	75W4040	WNS
Human Eye	50-6951	CB
Human Ear, 1 and 2	50-6961, 6963	CB

CHAPTER 33: PROTECTION AND MOVEMENT

Films (16 mm)		
The Skeleton	669, 13 min, b&w	EBE
Human Body: The Skeleton	625, 9½ min	COR
Human Body: Muscular System	1292, 13½ min	COR
Muscles, Dynamics of Contraction	2836, 22 min, c	EBE
Muscles, Chemistry of Contraction	2838, 15 min, c	EBE
Muscles, Electrical Activity and Contraction	2840, 9 min, c	EBE
Filmloops		
Movement in the Human Skeleton	73W1005(T)	WNS
Spinal Column, Axis of Skeleton	73W7471(T)	WNS(HUB)
The Knee Joint	73W7473(T)	WNS(HUB)
The Shoulder Joint	73W7474(T)	WNS(HUB)

TITLE	ORDER #/LENGTH/ C OR B&W	SUPPLIER
Flexors and Extensors	73W7475(T)	WNS(HUB)
Skeletal and Muscle Action	S25681F	FS
Filmstrips		
Structure: Protection, Support and Movement	402070	PLP
The Human Body: Set 2	S25210B, 5 films	FS
Transparencies		
The Skeletal System	75W4000, 10, c	WNS
The Muscular System	75W4020, 21, c	WNS

CHAPTER 34: INTERNAL REGULATION

TITLE	ORDER #/LENGTH/ C OR B&W	SUPPLIER
Films (16 mm)		
Blueprints in the Bloodstream	F2150, 57 min, c	TLF
What Time is Your Body?	F1926, 23 min, c	TLF
Endocrine Glands	242, 11 min, b&w	EBE
The Principles of Endocrine Activity	NS444, 16 min, c	IU
Filmstrips		
The Human Endocrine System	14048, c	EBE
Regulation and the Ductless and Ducted Glands	402076, c	PLP
Rhythms of Life	SCC642, 5 films, c	PH
Hormones and Chromosomes in Man	SCC815, 2 films, c	PH
Physiology III: Hormones	S25247, 1 of set of 4	FS
Nervous and Endocrine System	70551, 79 frames	DM

TITLE	ORDER #/LENGTH/ C OR B&W	SUPPLIER
Transparencies		
Endocrine System	75W4150, 11, c	WNS

CHAPTER 35: REPRODUCTION AND DEVELOPMENT

TITLE	ORDER #/LENGTH/ C OR B&W	SUPPLIER
Films (16 mm)		
The Beginning of Life	free, 28 min, c	WFL
The First Days of Life	19 min, c	MH
When Life Begins	14 min, c	MH
How Life Begins	46 min (2 parts), c	MH
Human Reproduction (2nd Edition)	20 min, c	MH
Biography of the Unborn	1436, 17 min, b&w	EBE
Filmloops		
Human Reproduction and Birth	89-9914, 6 films, c	BFA
Filmstrips		
Ovaries and Testes: Structure and Function	78W0530, c	WNS
Human Physiology: Embryology	52-3100, 2 films	CB
Reproductive Systems: Structure and Function	78W0640, c	WNS
Human Reproduction	S46785, 6 films, c	FS
Male and Female Reproductive Systems	SCC635, 4 films, c	PH
Reproduction: From Single Cell to Organism	402077, c	PLP
Embryology	302051, 2 films, c	PLP
Human Reproduction Part II, How Reproduction Takes Place	02110/RL, 48 frames	NAC

AUDIO VISUAL SUPPLIERS

ADDRESSES AND ABBREVIATIONS

American Cancer Society   ACS
(Local units in phone directory, if
not listed write to:
American Cancer Society
777 Third Avenue
New York, NY 10017)

Association Films, Inc.   AF
600 Grand Avenue
Ridgefield, NJ 07657

Bell Telephone Laboratories   BTL
(Local Bell System Telephone
Business Office; if not served by
Bell System, write or call Mana-
ger of nearest Bell System office)

Bergwell Productins   BP
839 Stewart Avenue
Garden City, NY 11530

BFA Educational Media   BFA
Division of Columbia
    Broadcasting System, Inc.
2211 Michigan Avenue
Santa Monica, CA 90404

Biological Sciences   BSCS
    Curriculum Study
Sound-Slide Presentation
P.O. Box 390
Boulder, CO 80306

Bray Studios   BRAY
630 Ninth Avenue
New York, NY 10036

Carolina Biological Supply   CB
    Company
Burlington, NC 27215

Coronet   COR
65 East South Water Street
Chicago, IL 60601

Doubleday Multimedia   DM
Box 11607
1371 Reynolds Avenue
Santa Ana, CA 92705

Encyclopedia Britannica   EBE
    Educational Corporation
Sales Promotion Department
425 North Michigan Avenue
Chicago, IL 60611

Eye Gate House, Inc.   EG
146-01 Archer Avenue
Jamaica, NY 11435

Fisher Scientific Company   FS
711 Forbes Avenue
Pittsburgh, PA 15219

Glenn Educational Films, Inc.   GEF
P.O. Box 4257
Sarasota, FL 33578

Harcourt, Brace Jovanovich   HBJ
A/V Subsidiary
757 Third Avenue
New York, NY 10017

Hubbard   HUB
P.O. Box 104
1946 Raymond Drive
Northbrook, IL 60062

Indiana University   IU
Audiovisual Center
Bloomington, IN 47401

Macmillan Library Services   MLS
Division of Macmillan
    Publishing Co.
866 Third Avenue
New York, NY 10022

March of Dimes   MOD
(Nearest local March of
Dimes Chapter

McDonnell Douglas Corporation   MD
St. Louis Library
Department 091
P.O. Box 516
St. Louis, MO 63166

McGraw Hill Book Company   MH
1221 Avenue of the Americas
New York, NY 10020

Milner-Fenwick, Inc.   MIFE
3800 Liberty Heights Avenue
Baltimore, MD 21215

National Audiovisual Center   NAC
Reference Section RL
General Services Administration
Washington, DC 20409

National Geographic Society   NGS
17 and M Streets, NW
Washington, DC 20036

Prentice Hall, Inc.   PH
Englewod Cliffs, NJ 07632

Projected Learning Programs   PLP
P.O. Box 11857
Reno, NV 89510

Selective Educational Equipment   SEE
P.O. Box 98
3 Bridge Street
Newton, MA 02195

Shell Film Library   SFL
1433 Sadlier Circle West Drive
Indianapolis, IN 46239

Sun Burst Communication   SUN
Room 3
39 Washington Avenue
Pleasantville, NY 10570

Thorne Films, Inc.   TF
934 Pearl
Boulder, CO 80302

Time-Life Films   TLF
Multimedia Division
100 Eisenhower Drive
Paramus, NJ 07652

US Department of Energy   USDE
Film Library
P.O. Box 62
Oak Ridge, TN 37830

Walt Disney Nature Library   WDNL
Communications Films
870 Monterey Pass Road
Monterey Park, CA 91754

Ward's Natural Science   WNS
    Establishment, Inc.
P.O. Box 1712
Rochester, NY 14603

Wyeth Film Library   WFL
P.O. Box 8299
Philadelphia, PA 19101

KEY TO PUBLISHERS

ARCO PUBLISHING, INC.
219 Park Avenue South
New York, NY 10003

ATHENEUM PUBLISHERS
Division of the Scribner Book Co.
122 East 42nd Street
New York, NY 10017

BALLENTINE BOOKS, INC.
Division of Random House, Inc.
201 East 50th Street
New York, NY 10022

BANTAM BOOKS, INC.
666 Fifth Avenue
New York, NY 10019

THE BENJAMIN CO., INC.
485 Madison Avenue
New York, NY 10022

WM. C. BROWN COMPANY,
   PUBLISHERS
2460 Kerper Boulevard
Dubuque, IA 52001

CAROLINA BIOLOGICAL SUPPLY
   COMPANY
Burlington, NC 27215

COLUMBIA UNIVERSITY PRESS
562 West 113th Street
New York, NY 10025

DOUBLEDAY & CO., INC.
245 Park Avenue
New York, NY 10017

ELSEVIER-DUTTON PUBLISHING
   CO., INC.
2 Park Avenue
New York, NY 10016

HARCOURT BRACE JOVANOVICH,
   INC.
757 Third Avenue
New York, NY 10017

HARPER AND ROW, PUBLISHERS,
   INC.
10 East 53rd Street
New York, NY 10022

HOUGHTON MIFFLIN COMPANY
1 Beacon Street
Boston, MA 02107

MACMILLAN, INC.
866 Third Avenue
New York, NY 10022

McGRAW-HILL, INC.
1221 Avenue of the Americas
New York, NY 10020

WILLIAM MORROW & CO., INC.
Wholly-Owned Subsidiary of
   Scott, Foresman & Co.
105 Madison Avenue
New York, NY 10016

W.W. NORTON & CO., INC.
500 Fifth Avenue
New York, NY 10036

PRENTICE-HALL, INC.
Englewood Cliffs, NJ 07632

W.B. SAUNDERS COMPANY
Division of CBS, Inc.
West Washington Square
Philadelphia, PA 19105

SIMAUER ASSOCIATES, INC.
Sunderland, MA 01375

THE VIKING PRESS
625 Madison Avenue
New York, NY 10022

WADSWORTH, INC.
Belmont, CA 94002

WESTERN PUBLISHING CO., INC.
Subsidiary of Mattel, Inc.
1220 Mound Avenue
Racine, WI 53404

JOHN WILEY & SONS, INC.
605 Third Avenue
New York, NY 10016